RESEARCH
IN
CLINICAL
ASSESSMENT

RESEARCH IN CLINICAL ASSESSMENT

EDITED BY

Edwin I. Megargee

THE UNIVERSITY OF TEXAS

Harper & Row, Publishers

NEW YORK AND LONDON

TO THE CLINICAL PSYCHOLOGIST—

AWARE OF HIS LIMITATIONS AND THOSE OF HIS INSTRUMENTS,

HE PERSEVERES IN HIS EFFORTS

TO DO THE BEST JOB OF ASSESSMENT

NOW POSSIBLE, WHILE ENGAGING

IN RESEARCH TO IMPROVE

ASSESSMENT TECHNIQUES FOR THE FUTURE.

CONTENTS

PART III

The Integration of Clinical Data in Assessment

PREFACE

CLINICAL ASSESSMENT is a complex, frustrating, and fascinating activity. From small samples of behavior the clinician attempts to come to some understanding of each unique personality with which he deals, and, on the basis of this understanding, attempts to predict how this person is going to behave in the future. The intellectual pleasure this activity affords is tempered with the knowledge that this is not a game and that the decisions made can be vitally important. It is rather melodramatic to talk of "life or death" issues, yet the decision as to whether or not a test protocol indicates a brain tumor, whether a patient is suicidal, or whether a jealous husband is potentially homicidal are in sober fact nothing less than life or death issues. The fact that ultimate responsibility for a final decision may often rest in other hands does not absolve the psychologist from supplying whoever makes this decision with the most accurate data possible.

So it remains incumbent on us to be acutely aware of the strengths and limitations of our assessment techniques and to strive continually to test and improve them. Psychologists have responded to this challenge and have been producing an ever-increasing flood of reports on the validity of clinical assessment.

There is, however, a major problem in the communication of these results. To keep abreast of the current output of studies on the Rorschach it is necessary to read no less than three articles each week. Some seventy books on assessment are published each year. The practicing clinician, beset by service demands and hampered by inadequate library facilities, can quickly lose sight of new developments and issues in the field. The problem should be somewhat less acute for individuals in academic settings, but, despite ample library facilities, the research-oriented clinician all too often becomes an expert on one rather narrow topic and remains relatively ignorant of developments in other areas.

This book is designed to improve communication between researchers and practitioners and between those who specialize in one area and those who focus on another. The book, like Gaul, is divided into three parts. The first contains articles dealing with general issues basic to all research on clinical assessment, such as the criterion problem, the usefulness of the concept of construct validity, the influence of base rates on prediction, and whether or not assessment techniques should be validated in the first place.

The second part focuses on the validity of specific assessment techniques. The first section deals with structured tests and the second with unstructured or projective tests. Three chapters are included on special problems peculiar to both types of instruments, such as response sets, multiple scoring systems, and the like.

Part III deals with the integration of clinical data in assessment. The first chapter presents studies aimed at determining how well clinicians integrate data, the second a debate on whether the clinician or the actuary is the best man for the job.

Throughout the book there is an emphasis on diversity, not only in the techniques and approaches covered, but also in the research designs employed. Yet there is an underlying unity as clinicians of vastly different backgrounds and persuasions grapple with similar problems. The died-in-the-wool Rorschacher who has never extended diplomatic recognition to a paper and pencil test may find with surprise that one of those "dust bowl empiricists" who favor the MMPI has come up with a strategy he is able to apply in his study of projective tests, and the MMPI fancier in turn might be stimulated by work on the TAT.

Not only is there diversity—there is also controversy. The editor feels that there is much to be learned from the head-on clash of differing viewpoints, so whenever possible articles have been selected to present several sides of each issue in an effort to stimulate the reader to think through the problem for himself or to read or experiment further to resolve the matter. Suggestions for further reading are made in the introductions to several chapters.

In selecting the personality tests to be covered, the first criterion was wide use in clinical practice. The MMPI, the Draw-A-Person, the TAT, and the Rorschach were chosen on this basis. Then other less widely used tests were added to provide coverage of important variations in the approach to assessment. Among the other tests covered in some detail are the California Psychological Inventory, the Sixteen Personality Factor Questionnaire, the Myers-Briggs Type Indicator, and the Holtzman Inkblot Technique.

For each test covered, an effort was made to include one study in which the test was used globally and another in which some individual scale or score was validated. Also, an attempt was made to include at least one investigation of the instrument's validity in a clinical setting and another study testing some aspect of the instrument in a laboratory setting.

In choosing among several well-designed studies, the editor would often select the one employing the most novel strategy or the most ingenious criterion measure if other factors were equal. The purpose was to maximize the number of designs employed throughout the book, not only in order to demonstrate the ingenuity of some investigators and the vigor of some instruments, but also, hopefully, to stimulate the use of new approaches by other investigators.

A bias in favor of good writing also guided article selection. All too often psychologists write as if obscurity and dullness were pathognomic of erudition. Whenever possible, papers were chosen which demonstrate that the reader does not have to be anesthetized in order to be informed.

E. I. M.

ACKNOWLEDGMENTS

EDITING a book is similar to managing a baseball team. It is the players who make the team a success, but the manager can make even the best team a failure. So, too, with a book of readings. Whatever merit this book has is a result of the many hours of thought and work put into each individual article by its authors. Without their generous permission and that of the publishers, these articles could not have been reprinted and this book would not have been possible. As a token of gratitude, part of the royalties have been allotted to the authors; as further evidence of their generosity, they have in turn stipulated that these funds should be turned over to the American Psychological Foundation.

While the responsibility for article selection is the editor's, his judgment was improved by the advice of several people. Chief among these was Wayne Holtzman, who was extremely generous with his time and suggestions. The criticism of Harrison Gough was also most helpful. Raymond Cattell and Allen Edwards also took the time to make suggestions which improved the coverage of their work on factor analytic test construction and social desirability, respectively.

When the chapter introductions were being prepared, Joseph Thorpe was kind enough to read them and make suggestions as to how they might be revised.

A major debt of gratitude is owed to the editor's wife, who typed and proofread the entire manuscript while caring for two small children and one medium-sized husband. In justice, she should be listed as co-editor; however, it is cruel enough to ask the reader to pronounce "Megargee" once without making him attempt it twice in succession.

PART I

Problems in

Validating

Clinical Methods

Chapter 1

Problems of Research
in Clinical Assessment

■ This chapter is designed to introduce some of the general problems of research in clinical assessment which will receive more detailed examination in the subsequent chapters. A secondary purpose is to provide the reader with some yardsticks by which he might judge the adequacy and relevance of the specific validation studies to be found in Parts II and III.

Many of the problems in validational research stem from difficulties in specifying the independent and dependent variables. In the typical laboratory experiment the situation is systematically simplified so that stimulus and response are well defined. This approach can also be applied to assessment, but the more the situation is simplified, the less relevance it bears to the clinical situation. At best this approach can only specify that under certain artificial conditions a lawful relationship exists between stimulus X and behavior Y. However, we have no way of knowing whether such a relationship will also be found when this stimulus is part of a complex interpersonal situation and the dependent variable is influenced by myriad other stimuli.

This can be demonstrated by a consideration of what takes place when a client comes to a psychologist's office. The attitude he brings with him will vary greatly depending on whether he is seeking help for himself or for someone else, whether he is attempting to escape anxiety or a jail sentence, whether he is middle class or lower class, and whether he is under tension or sedation. His initial reactions to the psychologist will be influenced not only by these factors, but also by his past learnings derived from contacts with physicians, social workers, school principals, and the like, as well as his perception of the psychologist as young or old, male or female, Jewish or Gentile, warm or cold, accepting or rejecting. When the psychologist opens the interview, asking, "What brings you here?" it is obvious that the client's response to this initial "stimulus" is going to be determined by a host of variables, and each succeeding response as question follows question and test stimulus follows test stimulus is going to be the product not only of the apparent stimulus, such as Card V on the Rorschach, but also of all that has gone before.

When the client leaves, the psychologist is left with his notes, his tests, his books, his biases, his training, his ringing telephone, and his worries about the house payments.[1] His task is to isolate the relevant variables and come to some understanding of the client's personality. Then he typically must communicate this perception to another person in the form of a written report containing descriptive statements and, hopefully, behavioral predictions. His task is then finished; for the researcher who wishes to study clinical assessment the task has just begun.

The researcher must attempt to isolate and define independent and dependent variables from this mass of complex behavior if he is to understand the situation or determine the validity of the instruments used. Typically he will focus on a single set of behavior which is repeated over a number of cases such as a psychological test. Given a psychological test protocol as the independent variable, and temporarily ignoring the fact that many variables other than the client's personality helped produce it, the researcher's next task is to find a criterion or some other independent measure of the same trait against which he can validate his test score. In some cases this is relatively easy. If a test is designed to predict flying success, for instance, a good criterion might be the number of aircraft destroyed by each candidate by the end of the training program. On the other hand, if the test is designed to assess strength of pre-Oedipal fixation the task of criterion selection is going to be more difficult.

Another difficulty is the fact that different cues can be used to derive similar predictions while similar cues, in different contexts, can lead to quite different predictions. The fact that the tests and predictions made are less than perfectly reliable makes the process even more confusing.

In this chapter Edwin Shneidman, Paul Meehl, and Kenneth Hammond discuss various specific problems resulting from the general nature of clinical assessment. Shneidman and Meehl deal with the criterion problem while Hammond focuses primarily on research strategies for coping with the complexity of the assessment process. In addition, Shneidman and Meehl propose standards by which we might judge the results of a study of assessment. Shneidman points out that asking if a test is valid is an overly simple approach. Instead, we should determine under what conditions and for what problems it is more or less valid. Meehl argues that the *minimum* requirement for a test is that it yield clear, accurate statements about a person. He indicates additional criteria which should be fulfilled if a test is to be judged useful as well as valid.

REFERENCE

APPELBAUM, S. A., & SIEGAL, R. S. Half-hidden influences on psychological testing and practice. *Journal of Projective Techniques and Personality Assessment*, 1965, **29**, 128–134.

[1] For an account of how extraneous factors may affect an assessment, see Applebaum and Siegal (1965).

Suggestions for the Delineation of Validational Studies

Edwin S. Shneidman

This symposium on "Current Aspects of the Problem of Validity" is sponsored both by the Division of Clinical Psychology and the Society for Projective Techniques. Our topic relates to one of the most timely issues that might have been selected by either group. It is one that is important to our practice and fundamental to our science. As chairman, my own contribution to this symposium is one that might be called "A Fugue and Variations on a Four-Part Invention by Cron-bach," and is essentially a suggested modification of the types of validity formulated by Cronbach's APA Committee on Test Standards in 1952.

One hardly needs to reiterate that the APA Committee on Test Standards proposed four types of validity, as follows:

1. Predictive validity, which denotes correlation between test measures and *subsequent* criterion measures.

2. "Status validity, which denotes correlation between the test and *concurrent* external criteria.

3. "Content validity, which refers to the case in which the specific type of behavior called for by the test is the goal of teaching or some similar activity, as in an academic achievement test.

4. "Congruent validity, which is established when the investigator demonstrates what psychological attribute a

Paper presented at a symposiom on "Current Aspects of the Problem of Validity" at the American Psychological Association Convention, Washington, D.C., August 30, 1958.

Reprinted by permission of the publisher and the author from the *Journal of Projective Techniques*, 1959, **23**, 259–262.

test measures by showing correspondence between scores on a test and other indications of the state or attribute. This type of validity is used for tests intended to measure a construct arising from some theory; the validation consists of evidence that the scores vary (from person to person or occasion to occasion) as the theory would imply. Essentially, in congruent validity the meaning assigned to test scores is substantiated by demonstrating that scores are consistent with deductions from the theory from which the meaning derived. This validation process is much the same as that involved in evaluating a theory itself."

My own suggested modification is essentially a spelling out of the several dimensions involved in any validational study. I think that I might go so far as to propose that each of these be indicated at the beginnings of any validational study. The headings I suggest are as follows:

1. Validity for *whom,* in which (a) the subjects, (b) the examiners, and (c) the judges would be described. It makes a lot of difference, for example, whether the 700 Rorschachs being reported in a normative matching study were given to Columbia sophomores or Colombian peasants; whether the examiner was an ABEPP grandfather or his comely young granddaughter, and whether the judges were tyros or Tyroleans. This notion is, of course, a sort of tautology in that it begs the question of what are the relevant dimensions in terms of which the subjects, examiners, and judges need to be described.

2. Validity for *when,* in which one (or more) of the three logical temporal

positions would be indicated: past, present, and future. Correlations with future criteria are, of course, called *prediction*, and with past criteria are called *postdiction*. For correlations with more-or-less present criteria (such as "present status") I have suggested the term *paridiction*, from the word "equal."

3. Validity for *which*. Under this rubric one should indicate whether correlations are with essentially *factual* variables or with essentially *conceptual* variables. This category again begs the question because it is precisely in this area that most of our problems concerning validity reside. There are, in clinical psychology, relatively few "facts," if we define a fact as a perception about which several intelligent lay people would instantaneously concur. When we view a body lying in a pool of blood and see a holographic document with suicidal content, it is a "fact" (Alfred Hitchcock aside) that the individual has committed suicide; but in a not-yet-dead individual "being suicidal" is almost entirely conceptual. Most of what we deal with in clinical psychology are not facts but hypothesis-tinged data.

4. Validity for *what*. Under this heading it is suggested that (a) the nature of the stimuli be delineated, and more, that (b) the nature of the continua or dimensions along which the stimuli are believed to be spread be delineated. Dr. Farberow will in his paper expand on this notion and indicate some of the theoretical and practical implications of developing specific psychological testing techniques which focus on the elaboration of stimuli along a single psychological dimension.

5. *How* validity is established. This would be an indication of the basic statistical procedures involved. What I have in mind is the notion that it is not only what the statistics choose to tell, but is also in part which statistical procedures were chosen. Clinically this means that even the statistician must be aware of his own trends toward latent homoscedasticity.

But it is to the notion of congruent validity of tests, and the idea that the validational process is much the same as that involved in evaluating a theory itself, that I wish to return for the remainder of my introductory remarks, and make the to-me-obvious, but I fear in some circles somewhat iconoclastic, comment that our psychological tests or projective techniques are not validatable until the personality theories that give them their intellectual permissiveness themselves gain greater construct validity.

And that is not all. The matter is further complicated inasmuch as the data on the other side of the equation, the so-called criterion measures, are themselves extremely complex and little understood. Let me give two examples, using homicide and schizophrenia—I had promised that I would not dwell upon either suicide or the MAPS test during my presentation. On the first thought it would seem impressive if one were to have not ten, but 200 Rorschach records of individuals who had committed homicide and records of 200 individuals who had not. But a moment's reflection will lead one to the common-sense consideration that individuals kill other individuals in a variety of ways (in a liquor-store hold-up, in the lover's bedroom, on the highway, on the field of battle, etc.)—and that *each* of these occurs with a variety of motives and mixed feelings. Putting all the "homicidal" records together could only yield a kind of psychometric goulash. (Incidentally, suicide is even more complicated.) And now let us, for a few moments, consider schizophrenia—at first blush a perfectly wonderful external criterion for status validity. Whose schizophrenia do we mean? How shall we define schizophrenia?

1. Is schizophrenia, as Kraepelin believed, a mental disease process resulting from an auto-intoxication following

a disorder of metabolism produced by a disordered secretion of the sex glands?

2. Or is it, from Arieti, a primitive form of rationality, based on pathological reasoning in terms of attributes of the predicate?

3. Or, from Alexander, is it a state in which the ego loses its synthetic function of harmonizing the different instinctual demands?

4. Or, from Jung, does the peculiarity of this disease lie in the startling emergence of an archaic psychology accounting for the innumerable points of contact with mythological material, so that what we take for original and individual creations are mostly products which can only be compared with those of antiquity?

Incidentally, Jung states that there are two types of schizophrenia (asthenic and spastic), Beck says there are six, and I had been taught all along that there are really four.

5. Or, is schizophrenia, as Meyer felt, to be thought of as a habit disorganization resulting from a progressive maladaption with increasing use of substitute reaction, instead of effective ones?

6. Or, do we really understand schizophrenic delusions as a projection of repressed passive homosexual desires? I think the formula is as follows: I love him, I do not love him, I hate him, No he hates me. Now I have it, I hate him because he hates me. We hate each other, I don't think that I will invite *him* to my next gay party.

All these are concepts. But there are, happily, three solid facts about schizophrenia. The only three known facts about schizophrenia are:

1. We do not know exactly how to cure it; its remediation is unknown.

2. We do not know exactly what causes it; its etiology is unknown—except when we say that it is cryptogenic.

3. We do not know its nature. We do not know what it is, if it is an it, which it probably ain't.

In 1958, we in clinical psychology (and individuals no less in psychiatry) have to deal primarily with the methodological problems attendant to *construct* validity.

Our task is in some way similar to measuring a floating cloud with a rubber band—in a shifting wind. I used to hear that projective techniques were like taking a plug out of a watermelon. This is a delusion of agronomy.

The science of clinical psychology relates primarily to hypotheses, not to facts. Whether one believes in Freud's, Adler's, Jung's, Murray's, Allport's, Kelly's, or any other individual's personality theory, one still has to subsume his cerebrations under the purview of an essentially untested hypothesis, nothing more. As a clinician, an individual may (in terms of loyalty) be from Vienna, or Topeka, or Baltimore; but as a scientist he must be from Missouri.

Nor do I believe that the physical sciences should be our models. My notion is that we do not do well to attempt to emulate physicists (simply because they have more observable facts interlaced among their hypotheses) but rather I suggest that we look *within* our own field, that we reexamine (with a view toward escaping the tactical and strategic errors of theory-building) the intellectual maneuvers of Wundt, Titchener, Dewey, Watson, MacDougall, etc., not to go back to them, but better to see that they were only trying systematically to explore the implications of *their* hypotheses—all their "facts" followed after. Our task might well be to plan our scientific maneuvers so that even if we adhere more or less rigidly to our current hypotheses, at least learning from *our own* past, we might avoid making some of the methodological errors which beset these earlier movements.

It appears that the kinds of validity discussed by the APA committee and by others are all kinds of "research" or scientific validity, whereas it may be that we may have to deal for a while with faith validity or clinical validity wherein we are not concerned with the veridical value of a hypothesis but rather with its professional sense-appeal within the scope of our contemporary conceptual zeitgeist. But on the other hand, it seems that our notions *ought* to be capable of being metricized so that we can test whether or not the phenomena we think we see occur beyond chance expectation and with statistical significance.

In order to end on a positive note, I want to say that as a meaningful measure of the nature of the unconscious nothing beats our current projective techniques, whatever the unconscious is —if you see what I mean.

Some Ruminations on the Validation of Clinical Procedures

Paul E. Meehl

It is becoming almost a cliché to say that "clinical psychology is in a state of ferment," a remark which is ambiguous as to whether the "ferment" is a healthy or pathological condition. Dr. E. Lowell Kelly finds upon follow-up that about 40 per cent of the young clinicians who were studied in the early days of the Veterans' Administration training programme now state that they would not go into clinical psychology if they had it to do over again (personal communication). In recent textbooks, such as Garfield's, one can detect a note of apology or defensiveness which was not apparent even a decade ago (13, pp. vi, 28, 88, 97, 101, 109, 116, 152, 166, 451, and *passim*). No doubt economic and sociological factors, having little to do with the substance of clinical psychology, contribute in some measure to this state of mind within the profession. But I believe that there are also deeper

Invitational Address to the Canadian Psychological Association's Convention at Edmonton, Alberta, June 12, 1958.

Reprinted by permission of the publishers and the author from the *Canadian Journal of Psychology*, 1959, **13**, 102–128.

reasons, involving the perception by many clinicians of the sad state of the science and art which we are trying to practice (17). The main function of the clinical psychologist is psychodiagnosis; and the statistics indicate that, while the proportion of his time spent in this activity has tended to decrease in favour of therapy, it nevertheless continues to occupy the largest part of his working day. Psychodiagnosis was the original basis upon which the profession became accepted as ancillary to psychiatry, and it is still thought of in most quarters as our distinctive contribution to the handling of a patient. One is therefore disturbed to note the alacrity with which many psychologists move out of psychodiagnosis when it becomes feasible for them to do so. I want to suggest that this is only partly because of the even higher valence of competing activities, and that it springs also from an awareness, often vague and warded off, that our diagnostic instruments are not very powerful. In this paper I want to devote myself entirely to this problem, and specifically to problems of validity in the area broadly labeled "personality assessment."

I have chosen the word "ruminations" in my title. It helps from time to time for us to go back to the beginning and to formulate just what we are trying to do. I shall have to make some points which are perhaps obvious, but in the interest of logical completeness I trust that the reader will bear with me. In speaking about validity and validation, I shall employ the terminology proposed by the APA committee on test standards, making the fourfold distinction between predictive, concurrent, content, and construct validity. (1, see also 6.)

The practical uses of tests can be conveniently divided into three broad functions: *formal diagnosis* (the attachment of a nosological label); *prognosis* (including "spontaneous" recoverability, therapy-stayability, recidivism, response to therapy, indications for one kind of treatment rather than another); and *personality assessment* other than diagnosis or prognosis. This last function may be divided, somewhat arbitrarily, into *phenotypic* and *genotypic* characterization, the former referring to what we would ordinarily call the descriptive or surface features of the patient's behaviour, including his social impact; and the latter covering personality structure and dynamics, and basic parameters of a constitutional sort (for example, anxiety-threshold). Taking this classification of test functions as our framework, let us look at each one, asking the two questions: "Why do we want to know this?" and "How good are we at finding it out?"

Consider first the problem of formal psychiatric diagnosis. This is a matter upon which people often have strong feelings, and I should tell you at the outset that I have some prejudices. I consider that there are such things as disease entities in functional psychiatry, and I do not think that Kraepelin was as mistaken as some of my psychological contemporaries seem to think. It is my belief, for example, that there is a *disease,* schizophrenia, fundamentally of an organic nature, and probably of largely constitutional aetiology. I would explain the viability of the Kraepelinian nomenclature by the hypothesis that there is a considerable amount of truth contained in the system; and that, therefore, the practical implications associated with these labels are still sufficiently great, especially when compared with the predictive power of competing concepts, that even the most anti-nosological clinician finds himself worrying about whether a patient whom he has been treating as an obsessional character "is really a schizophrenic."

The fundamental argument for the utility of formal diagnosis can be put either causally or statistically, but it amounts to the same kind of thing one would say in defending formal diagnosis in organic medicine. One holds that there is a sufficient amount of aetiological and prognostic homogeneity among patients belonging to a given diagnostic group, so that the assignment of a patient to this group has probability implications which it is clinically unsound to ignore.

There are three commonly advanced objections to a nosological orientation in assessment, each of which is based upon an important bit of truth but which, as it appears to me, have been used in a somewhat careless fashion. It is first pointed out that there are studies indicating a low agreement among psychiatrists in the attachment of formal diagnostic labels. I do not find these studies very illuminating (2, 34, 38). If you are accustomed to asserting that "It is well known that formal psychiatric diagnoses are completely unreliable," I urge you to re-read these studies with a critical set as to whether they establish that thesis. The only study of the reliability of formal psychiatric diagnosis which approximates an adequate design is that of Schmidt and Fonda (48); and the results of this study are remarkably encouraging with regard to the reliability of psychiatric diagnosis. As these authors point out, some have inferred unreliability of formal diagnosis from unreliable assessment of other behavioural dimensions. Certainly our knowledge of this question is insufficient and much more research is needed.

I suppose that we are all likely to be more impressed by our personal experience than by what someone else reports when the published reports are not in good agreement and there is insufficient information to indicate precisely why they come to divergent results. For example, it is often said that the concept "psychopathic personality" is a waste-basket category that does not tell us anything about the patient. I know that many clinicians have used the category carelessly, and it is obvious that one who uses this term as an approximate equivalent to saying that the patient gets in trouble with the law is not doing anything very profound or useful by attaching a nosological label. I, on the other hand, consider the asocial psychopath (or, in the revised nomenclature, the sociopath) to be a very special breed of cat, readily recognized, and constituting only a small minority of all individuals who are in trouble because of what is socially defined as delinquent behaviour (in this connection see 31, 50). I consider it practically important to distinguish (a) a person who becomes legally delinquent because he is an "unlucky" sociopath, that is, got caught; (b) one who becomes delinquent because he is an acting-out neurotic; and (c) a psychiatrically normal person who learned the wrong cultural values from his family and neighbourhood environment.

Being interested in the sociopath, I have attempted to develop diagnostic skills in identifying this type of patient, and some years ago I ran a series on myself to check whether I was actually as good at it as I had begun to believe. I attempted to identify cases "at sight," that is, by observing their behaviour in walking down the hall or sitting in the hospital lounge, without conversing with the patient but snatching brief samples of verbal behaviour and expressive movements, sometimes for a matter of a few seconds and never for more than five minutes. In the majority of cases I had no verbal behaviour at all. In the course of a year, I spotted 13 patients as "psychopathic personality, asocial amoral type"; accepting staff diagnosis *or* an MMPI profile of psychopathic configuration as a disjunctive criterion, I was "correct" in 12 of the 13. This does not, of course, tell us anything about my false negative rate; but it does indicate that if I think a patient is a psychopath, there is reason to think I am correct. Now if I were interested in examining the "reliability" of the *concept* of the psychopathic personality, I should want to have clinicians like myself making the judgments.

Imagine, if you will, a psychologist trained to disbelieve in nosological categories and never alerted to those fascinating minor signs (lack of normal social fear, or what I call "animal grace," a certain intense, restless look about the eyes, or a score of other cues); suppose a study shows that such a psychologist tends not to agree with me, or that we both show low agreement with some second-year psychiatric resident whose experience with the concept has been limited to an hour lecture stressing the legal delinquency and "immaturity" (whatever that means) of the psychopath. What importance does such a finding have?

This matter of diagnostic skill involves a question of methodological presuppositions that is of crucial importance in interpreting studies of diagnostic agreement. The psychologist, with his tendency to an operational (20) or "pure intervening variable" type of analysis (32, 47) and from his long tradition of psychometric thinking in which reliability constrains validity, is tempted to infer directly from a finding that people disagree on a diagnostic label that a nosological entity has no objective reality. This is a philosophical mistake, and furthermore, it is one which would not conceivably be made by one trained in medical habits of thinking. When we move from the question of whether a certain sign or symptom should be given a high weight to the quite different question whether a certain disease entity has reality and is worth working hard to identify, disagreement between observers is (quite properly) conceived by physicians as *diagnostic error*. Neurological diagnoses by local physicians in outstate Minnesota are confirmed only approximately 75 per cent of the time by biopsy, exploratory surgery, or autopsy at the University of Minnesota Hospital. The medical man does not infer from this result that the received system of neurological disease entities is unsound; rather he infers that physicians make diagnostic mistakes.

Furthermore, it is not even assumed that all of these mistakes could be eliminated by an improvement in diagnostic skill. One of the most highly skilled internists in Minneapolis (43) published a statistical analysis of his own diagnoses over a period of 28 years based on patients who had come to autopsy. Imposing very stringent conditions upon himself (such as classifying a diagnostic error as eliminable if evidence could have been elicited by sufficient re-examination), he nevertheless found that 29 per cent of his diagnoses were errors which could not in principle have been eliminated because they fell in the category of "no evidence; symptoms or signs not obtained." How is this possible? Because not only are there diseases which are *difficult* to diagnose; there are individual cases which are for all practical purposes *impossible* to diagnose so long as our evidence is confined to the clinical and historical material.

Presumably anyone who takes psychiatric nosology seriously believes that schizophrenia (like paresis, or an early

astrocytoma in a neurologically silent area) is an *inner state*, and that the correct attachment of a diagnostic label involves a probability transition from what we see on the outside to what is objectively present on the inside. The less that is known about the nature of a given disease, or the less emphasis a certain diagnostician gives to the identification of that disease, the more diagnostic errors we can expect will be made. That some psychiatrists are not very clever in spotting pseudoneurotic schizophrenia is no more evidence against the reality of this condition as a clinical entity than the fact that in 1850, long prior to the clinching demonstration of the luetic origin of paresis by Noguchi and Moore, even competent neurologists were commonly diagnosing other conditions, both functional and organic, as "general paralysis of the insane." By 1913 the luetic aetiology was widely accepted, and hence such facts as a history of chancre, secondary stage symptoms, positive spinal Wassermann, and the like were being given a high indicator weight in making the diagnosis (27). Yet the entity could not properly be *defined* by this (probable) aetiology; and those clinicians who remained still unconvinced were assigning no weight to the above-mentioned indicators. This must inevitably have led to diagnostic errors even by very able diagnosticians. It is impossible for diagnostic activity and research thinking to be suspended during the period—frequently long— that syndrome description constitutes our only direct knowledge of the disorder (33).

A second argument advanced against nosology is that it puts people in a pigeon-hole. I have never been able to understand this argument since whenever one uses *any* nomothetic language to characterize a human being one is, to that extent, putting him in a pigeon-hole (or locating him at a point in conceptual space); and, of course, every case of carcinoma of the liver is "unique" too.

That some old-fashioned diagnosticians, untrained in psychodynamics, use diagnostic labels as a substitute for understanding the patient is not an unknown occurrence, but what can one say in response to this except *abusus non tollit usum?* We cannot afford to decide about the merits of a conceptual scheme on the grounds that people use it wrongly.

A derivative of this argument is that diagnostic categories are not dynamics, and do not really tell us anything about what is wrong with the patient. There is some truth in this complaint, but again the same complaint could be advanced with regard to an organic disease concept at any stage in the development of the conception of it prior to the elucidation of its pathology and aetiology.

There is some confusion within our profession about the relation between content or dynamics and taxonomic categories. Many seem to think that when we elucidate the content, drives, and defences with which a patient is deeply involved, we have thereby explained why he is ill. But in what sense is this true? When we learn something about the inner life of a psychiatric patient, we find that he is concerned with aggression, sex, pride, dependence, and the like, that is, the familiar collection of human needs and fears. Schizophrenics are people, and if you are clever enough to find out what is going on inside a schizophrenic's head, you should not be surprised that these goings-on involve his self-image and his human relationships rather than, say, the weather. The demonstration that patients have psychodynamics, that they suffer with them, and that they deal with them ineffectively, does *not* necessarily tell us what is the matter with them, that is, why they are patients.

One is reminded in this connection of what happened when, after several years of clinicians busily over-interpreting "pathological" material in the TAT stories of schizophrenic patients, Dr. Leonard Eron took the pains to make a normative investigation and discovered that most of the features which had been so construed occurred equally or more often in a population of healthy college students (10).

There is no contradiction between classifying a patient as belonging to a certain taxonomic group and attempting concurrently to understand his motivations and his defences. Even if a certain major mental disease were found to be of organic or genetic origin, it would not be necessary to abandon any well-established psychodynamic interpretations. Let me give you an analogy. Suppose that there existed a colour-oriented culture in which a large part of social, economic, and sexual behaviour was dependent upon precise colour-discriminations. In such a culture, a child who makes errors in colour behaviour will be teased by his peer group, will be rejected by an over-anxious parent who cannot tolerate the idea of having produced an inferior or deviant child, and so on. One who was unfortunate enough to inherit the gene for colour blindness might develop a colour neurosis. He might be found as an adult on the couch of a colour therapist, where he would produce a great deal of material which would be historically relevant and which would give us a picture of the particular pattern of his current colour dynamics. But none of this answers the question, "What is fundamentally the matter with these people?," that is, what do all such patients have in common? What they have in common, of course, is that defective gene on the X-chromosome; and this, while it does not provide a *sufficient* condition for a colour neurosis in such a culture, does provide the *necessary* condition. It is in this sense that a nosologist in that culture could legitimately argue that "colour neuroticism" is an inherited disease.

I think that none of these commonly

heard objections is a scientifically valid reason for repudiating formal diagnosis, and that we must consider the value of the present diagnostic categories on their merits, on their relevance to the practical problems of clinical decision-making. One difficulty is that we do not have available for the validation of our instruments an analogue of the pathologist's report. It makes sense in organic medicine to say that the patient was actually suffering from disease X even though there was no evidence for it at the time of the clinical examination, so that the best clinician in the world could not have made a correct diagnosis on the data presented prior to autopsy. We have nothing in clinical psychology which bears close resemblance to the clinico-pathological conference in organic medicine. Our closest analogue to pathology is "structure" and psychodynamics, and our closest analogue to the internist's concept of aetiology is a composite of constitution and learning history. If we had a satisfactory taxonomy of either constitution or learning history, we would be able to define what we meant by saying that a given patient is a schizophrenic. A well-established historical agent would suffice for this purpose, and Freud, for example, made an attempt at this in the early days (before he had realized how much of his patients' anamnesis was fantasy) by identifying the obsessional neurosis with a history of active and pleasurable erotic pre-pubescent activity, and hysteria with a history of passive and largely unpleasurable erotic experience (12).

Since anyone who takes formal diagnosis as a significant part of the psychologist's task must be thinking in terms of construct validity (1, 6), he should have at least a vague sketch of the structure and aetiology of the disorders about which he speaks diagnostically. I do not think that it is appropriate to ask for an operational definition. My own view is that theoretical constructs are defined "implicitly" by the entire network of hypothesized laws concerning them; in the early stages of understanding a taxonomic concept, such as a disease, this network of laws is what we are trying to discover. Of course, when a clinician says, "I think this patient is really a latent schizophrenic," he should be able to give us *some* kind of picture of what he means by this statement. It could, however, be rather vague and still sufficient to justify itself at this stage of our knowledge. He might say:

I mean that the patient has inherited an organic structural anomaly of the proprioceptive integration system of his brain, and also a radical deficiency in the central reinforcement centres (or, to use Rado's language, a deficiency in his "hedonic capacity"). The combination of these proprioceptive and hedonic defects leads in turn to developmental disturbances in the body image and in social identification; the result at the psychological level being a pervasive disturbance in the cognitive functions of the ego. It is this defective ego-organization that is responsible for the primary associative disturbance set forth as the fundamental symptom of schizophrenia by Bleuler. The other symptoms of this disease, which may or may not be present, I would conceive as Bleuler does, and therefore my conception of the disorder is perhaps wider than is modal for American clinicians. By "pseudoneurotic schizophrenia" I would mean a patient with schizophrenia whose failure to demonstrate the accessory symptoms (and whose lower quantitative amount of even the primary symptoms) leads to his being readily misdiagnosed. Pseudoneurotic schizophrenia is just schizophrenia that is likely to go unrecognized.

Such a sketch is, to my mind, sufficient to justify the use of the schizophrenia concept at the present state of our knowledge. It is not very tight, and it is not intellectually satisfying. On the other hand, when combined with the set of indicators provided by Bleuler (3), Hoch and Polatin (21), and others, it is not much worse than the concept of general paresis as understood during most of the nineteenth century following Bayle's description in 1822. In this connection it is sometimes therapeutic for psychologists to familiarize themselves with the logicians' contributions to the methodological problems of so called "open concepts," "open texture," and "vagueness" (18, 19, 23, 41, 49, 57, 60). Even a slight acquaintance with the history of the more advanced sciences gives one a more realistic perspective on the relation of "operational" indicators to theoretical constructs during the early stages of a construct's evolution. (See, for example, 39, 45, 46, 56.)

The formal nosological label makes a claim about an inner structure or state; therefore, the concurrent validity of a test against our psychiatrist as criterion is not an end in itself, but rather is one piece in the pattern of evidence which is relevant to establishing the *construct* validity of *both* the test and the psychiatrist. If I really accept the psychiatric diagnosis as *"the* criterion," what am I doing with my test anyway? If I want to know what the psychiatrist is going to call patient Jones whom he has just finished interviewing, the obvious way to find out is to leave my own little cubicle with its Rorschach and Multiphasic materials and walk down the hall to ask the psychiatrist what he is going to call the patient. This is a ludicrous way of portraying the enterprise, but the only thing which saves it from really being this way is that implicitly we reject concurrent validity with the psychiatrist's diagnosis as criterion, having instead some kind of construct validity in the back of our minds. The phrase "the criterion" is misleading. Because of the whole network of association surrounding the term "criterion," I would myself prefer to abandon it in such contexts, substituting the term "indicator." The impact of a patient upon a psychiatrist (or upon anyone else, for that matter) is one of a *family of indicators of unknown relative weights;* when we carry out a "validation" study on a new test, we are asking whether or not the test belongs to this family.

Note that the uncertainty of the link between nosology and symptom (or test) is a two-way affair. Knowing the formal diagnosis we cannot infer with certainty the presence of a given symptom or the result of a given test; conversely, given the result on a test, or the presence of a certain symptom, we cannot infer with certainty the nosology. (There are rare exceptions to this, such as thought-disorder occurring in the presence of an unclouded sensorium and without agitation, which I would myself consider pathognomonic of schizophrenia.) This uncertainty is found also in organic medicine, where there are very few pathognomonic symptoms and very few diseases which invariably show any given symptom. An extreme (but not unusual) example is the prevalence of those sub-clinical infections which are responsible for immunizing us as adults, but which were *so* "sub"-clinical that they were only manifested by a mild malaise and possibly a little fever, symptoms which, singly or jointly, do not enable us to identify one among literally hundreds of diagnostic possibilities.

One "statistical" advantage contributed by a taxonomy even when it is operating wholly at the descriptive or syndrome level is so obvious that it is easy to miss; I suspect that the viability of the traditional nosological rubrics, which could not be well defended upon aetiological grounds at present, is largely due to this contribution. When the indicators of membership in the class comprise a long list, none of which is either necessary or sufficient for the class membership, the descriptive information which is conveyed by the taxonomic name has a "statistical-disjunctive" character. That is, when we say that a patient belongs to category X, we are at least claiming that he displays indicators *a* or *b* or *c* with probability *p* (and separate probabilities p_a, p_b, and p_c). This may not seem very valuable, but considering how long it would take to convey to a second clinician the entire list of behaviour dispositions whose probability of being present is materially altered by placing a patient in category X, we see that from the standpoint of sheer economy even a moderately good taxonomic system does something for us. More important in the long run is the fact that only a huge clinical team, with a tremendous amount of money to spend on a large number of patients over a long period of time, could hope to discover and confirm all $\frac{N(N-1)}{2}$ of the pair-wise correlations among the family of N indicators that relate to the concept, to say nothing of the higher-order configural effects (22) that will arise in any such material. The research literature can yield cumulative knowledge and improvement of clinical practice in different settings by virtue of the fact that in one hospital an investigator, working with limited means, is able to show that patients diagnosed as schizophrenic tend to perform in a special way on a proverbs test; while another investigator in another hospital is showing that male patients diagnosed as schizophrenic have a high probability of reacting adversely to sexually attractive female therapists. Imagine a set of one hundred indicator variables and one hundred output variables; we would have to deal with ten thousand pair-wise correlations if we were to study these in one grand research project. The advantages in communicative economy and in cumulating research knowledge cannot, of course, be provided by a descriptive taxonomy which lacks intrinsic merit (that is, the syndrome does not objectively exist with even a moderate degree of internal tightness), or which, while intrinsically meritorious, is applied in an unskilful manner.

Let us turn now to our second main use of tests—prognosis. Sometimes the forecasting of future behaviour is valuable even if no special treatment is contemplated, because part of the responsibility of many clinical installations is to advise other agencies or persons, such as a court, as to the probabilities. But the main purpose of predictive statements is the assistance they give us in making decisions about how to treat a patient. Predictive statements of the form "If you treat the patient so-and-so, the odds are 8:2 that such-and-such will happen," will be with us for a long time. As more knowledge about behavioural disorders is accumulated, we can expect a progressive refinement and differentiation of techniques; their differential impact will thereupon become greater, so that the seriousness of a mistake will be correspondingly increased. Furthermore, even if—as I consider highly unlikely but as we know some therapists are betting—it is discovered that for all patients the same kind of treatment is optimal, it is easily demonstrated from the statistics of mental illness, together with the most sanguine predictions as to the training of skilled professional personnel, that there will not be adequate staff to provide even moderately intensive treatment for any but a minority of patients during the professional lifetime of anybody at present alive. So we can say with confidence that the decision to treat or not to treat will be a decision which clinicians are still going to be making when all of us have retired from the scene. As I read the published evidence, our forecasting abilities with current tests are not what you could call distinguished (see, for example, 61).

In connection with this problem of prognosis, let me hark back a moment to our discussion of formal nosology. One repeatedly hears clinicians state that they make prognostic decisions not on the basis of a formal diagnosis but on their assessment of the individual's structure and dynamics. Where is the evidence that we can do this? So far as I am aware there is as much evidence indicating that one can predict the subsequent course of an illness from diagnostic categories (16) (or from crude life-history statistics) as there is that one can predict the course of an illness or the response to therapy from any of the psychological tests available. I should like to offer a challenge to any clinician who thinks that he can cite a consistent body of published evidence to the contrary.

In order to employ dynamic constructs to arrive at predictions, it would be necessary to meet two conditions. In the first place, we must have a sound theory about the determinative variables. Secondly, we must be in possession of an adequate technology for making measurements of those variables. As any undergraduate major in physics or chemistry knows, in order to predict the subsequent course of a physical system, it is necessary both to understand the laws which the system obeys and to have an accurate knowledge of the initial and boundary conditions of the system. Since clinical psychology is nowhere near meeting *either* of these two requirements, it must necessarily be poor at making predictions which are mediated by dynamic constructs. It is a dogma of our profession that we predict what people will do by understanding them individually, and this sounds so plausible and humanitarian that to be critical of it is like criticizing Mother's Day. I can only reiterate that neither theoretical considerations nor the data available in the literature lend strong support to this idea in practice.

Let us turn to the third clinical task which the psychologist attempts to solve by the use of his tests, that of "personality assessment." Phenotypic characterization of a person includes the attribution of the ordinary clinical terms involving a minimal amount of inference, such as "patient hallucinates" or "patient has obsessional trends"; trait

names from common English, such as the adjectives found in the lists published by Cattell (5, p. 219) or Gough (14); and, increasingly important in current research, characterizations in the form of a single sentence or a short paragraph of the type employed by Stephenson (53), the Chicago Counseling Center (44), Block (4), and others. (Example: "The patient characteristically tries to stretch limits and see how much he can get away with.") A logical analysis of the nature of these phenotypic trait attributions is a formidable task although a very fascinating one. I am not entirely satisfied with any account which I have seen, or have been able to devise for myself. Perhaps not too much violence is done to the truth if we say that these are all in the nature of dispositional statements, the evidence for which consists of some kind of sampling, usually not representative, of a large and vaguely specified domain of episodes from the narrative that constitutes a person's life. It is complicated by the fact that even if we attempt to stay away from theoretical inferences, almost any single episode is susceptible of multiple classification under different families of atomic dispositions constituting a descriptive trait. The fact that the evidence for a trait attribution represents only a sample of the concrete episodes that exemplify atomic dispositions introduces an inferential element into such trait attributions, even though the trait name is intended to perform a purely summarizing rather than a theoretical function (6, pp. 292–3).

Phenotypic characterization presents a special problem which differentiates it from the functions of diagnosis and prognosis in the establishment of validity. Since it involves concurrent validity, its pragmatic justification is rather more obscure. Suppose we have a descriptive trait, say, "uncooperative with hospital personnel," an item which is not uncommon in various rating scales and clinical Q-pools in current use in the United States. Why administer an MMPI in order to guess, with imperfect confidence, whether or not the patient is being currently judged as uncooperative by the occupational therapist, the nursing supervisor, and the resident in charge of his case? This is even a more fruitless activity than our earlier example of using a test to guess the diagnosis given by the psychiatrist. From the theoretical point of view, the obvious reply is that the sampling of the domain of the patient's dispositions which is made by these staff members is likely to be deficient, both in regard to its *qualitative* diversity and representativeness as seen within the several contexts in which they interact with the patient, and *quantitatively* (simply from the statistical standpoint of size) during the initial portion of a patient's stay in the hospital. This reply leads to a suggestion concerning the design of studies which are concerned with phenotypic assessment from tests. Such designs should provide a "criterion" which is considerably superior in reliability to that which would routinely be available in the clinic on the basis of the ordinary contacts. If it is concurrent validity in which we are really interested (upon closer examination this often turns out not to be the case), there is little point in administering a time-consuming test and applying the brains of a trained psychologist in order to predict the verbal behaviour of the psychiatric aid or the nurse. If it is our intention to develop and validate an instrument which will order or classify patients as to phenotypic features which are *not* reliably assessed by these persons in their ordinary contacts with the patient, then we need a design which will enable us to show that we have actually achieved this result.

As to the power of our tests in the phenotypic characterization of an individual, the available evidence is not very impressive when we put the practical question in terms of the *increment*

in valid and semantically clear information transmitted. [See, for example, the studies by Kostlan (25), Dailey (8), Winch and More (58), Kelly and Fiske (24), Davenport (9), Sines (51), and Soskin (52).]

The question of concurrent validity in the phenotypic domain can be put at any one of four levels, in order of increasing practical importance. It is surprising to find that research on concurrent validity has been confined almost wholly to the first of these four levels. The weakest form of the validation question is, "How accurate are the semantically clear statements which can be reliably derived from the test?" It is a remarkable social phenomenon that we still do not know the answer to this question with respect to the most widely used clinical instruments. I do not see how anyone who examines his own clinical practice critically and who is acquainted with the research data could fail to make at least the admission that the power of our current techniques is seriously in doubt.

A somewhat more demanding question, which incorporates the preceding, would be: "To what extent does the test enable us to make, reliably, accurate statements which we cannot *concurrently* and *readily* (that is, at low effort and cost) obtain from clinical personnel routinely observing the patient *who will normally be doing so anyway* (that is, whose observations and judgments we will not administratively eliminate by the introduction of the test)?" In the preceding discussion regarding diagnosis and concurrent validity I oversimplified so grossly as to be a bit misleading. "How the staff rates" cannot be equated with "What the staff sees," which cannot in turn be equated with "What the patient does in the clinic"; and that, in turn, is not the equivalent of "What the patient does." If a patient beats his wife and does not tell his therapist about it, and the wife does not tell the social worker, the behaviour domain has been incompletely sampled by those making the ratings; they might *conclude* that he had beaten his wife, and this conclusion, while it is an inference, is still a conclusion regarding the phenotype. We cannot, of course, classify a certain concept as "theoretical" merely on the grounds that we have to make an inference in order to decide about a concrete instance of its application. This is a sampling problem, and therefore mainly (although not wholly) a matter of the time required to accumulate a sufficiently extensive sample. On the other hand, in our sampling of the patient's behavioural dispositions in the usual clinical context, it is not wholly a numerical deficiency in accumulation of episodes, because the sample which we obtain arises from a population of episodes that is in itself systematically biased. That is, the population of episodes which can be expected to come to our attention in the long run is itself a non-representative sub-population of all the behavioural events which constitute the complete narration of the patient's life.

A very stimulating paper is that of Kostlan (25). There are elements of artificiality in his procedure (of which he is fully aware) and these elements will no doubt be stressed by those clinicians who are determined to resist the introduction of adverse evidence. Nevertheless, his procedure was an ingenious compromise between the necessity of maintaining a close semblance to the actual clinical process, and a determination to quantify the incremental validity of tests. What he did, in a word, was to begin with a battery of data such as were routinely available in his own clinical setting and with which his clinicians were thoroughly familiar, consisting of a Rorschach, an MMPI, a sentence completion test, and a social case history. He then systematically varied the information available to his clinicians by eliminating one of these four sources at a time, arguing that the power of a device is probably studied better by showing the effect of its *subtraction* from the total mass of information than by studying it alone. The clinicians were required to make a judgment, from the sets of data presented to them, on each of 283 items which had been culled from a population of 1,000 statements found in the psychological reports written by this staff. The most striking finding was that on the basis of all three of these widely used tests his clinicians could make no more accurate inferences than they could make utilizing the Barnum effect (35, 8, 11, 52, 54, 55) when the all-important social history was deleted from their pool of data. A further fact, not stressed by Kostlan in his published report (but see 25 and 26), is that the absolute magnitude of incremental information, even when the results are statistically significant, is not impressive. For example, clinicians knowing only the age, marital status, occupation, education, and source of referral of a patient (that is, relying essentially upon Barnum effect for their ability to make correct statements) yield an average of about 63 per cent correct statements about the patient. If they have the Rorschach, Multiphasic, and Sentence Completion tests *but are deprived of the social case history*, this combined psychometric battery results in almost exactly the same percentage of correct judgments. On the other hand, if we consider their success in making inferences based on the social history together with the Sentence Completion test and the MMPI (that is, eliminating only the Rorschach, which made no contribution) we find them making 72 per cent correct inferences (my calculations from his Table 3), that is, a mere 9 per cent increment.

A thesis just completed at the University of Minnesota by Dr. Lloyd K. Sines is consistent with Kostlan's findings (51). Taking a Q-sort of the patient's therapist as his criterion, Sines investigated the contribution by a four-page biographical sheet, an MMPI profile, a

Rorschach (administered by the clinician making the test-based judgments), and a diagnostic interview by this clinician. He determined the increment in Q-correlation with the criterion (therapist sort) when each of these four sources of information was inserted at different places in the sequence of progressively added information. The contribution of either of the two psychological tests, or both jointly, was small (and, in fact, knowledge of the Rorschach tended to exert an adverse effect upon the clinician's accuracy). For some patients, the application of a stereotype personality description based upon actuarial experience in this particular clinic provided a more accurate description of the patient than the clinician's judgment based upon any, or all, of the available tests, history, and interview data!

A third level of validation demand, in which we become really tough on ourselves, takes the form: "If there are kinds of clear non-trivial statements which can be reliably derived from the test, which are accurate, and which are not concurrently and readily obtainable by other means routinely available, *how much earlier in time* does the test enable us to make them?" It might be the case that we can make accurate statements from our tests at a time in the assessment sequence when equally trustworthy non-psychometric data have not accumulated sufficiently to make such judgments, but from the practical point of view there is still a need to know just how "advanced" this advance information is. So far as I know, there are no published investigations which deal with this question.

A final and most demanding way of putting the question, which is ultimately the practically significant one by which the contribution of our techniques must be judged, is the following: "If the test enables us to make reliably, clear, differentiating statements which are accurate and which we cannot readily make from

routinely available clinical bases of judgment; and if this additional information is not rapidly picked up from other sources during the course of continued clinical study of the patient; in what way, *and to what extent,* does this incremental advance information help us in treating the patient?" One might have a clear-cut positive answer to the first three questions and be seriously in error if he concluded therefrom that his tests were paying off in practice. On this fourth question, there is also no published empirical evidence.

In the absence of any data I would like to speculate briefly on this one. Suppose that a decision is made to undertake the intensive psychotherapy of a patient. A set of statements, either of a dichotomous variety or involving some kind of intensity dimension or probability-of-correctness, is available to the psychotherapist on the basis of psychological test results. How does the therapist make use of this knowledge? It is well known that competent therapists disagree markedly with regard to this matter, and plausible arguments on both sides have been presented. Presumably the value of such information will depend upon the kind of psychotherapy which is being practised; therapists of the Rogerian persuasion are inclined to believe that this kind of advanced knowledge is of no use; in fact they prefer to avoid exposure to it. Even in a more cognitively oriented or interpretative type of treatment, it may be argued that by the time the therapeutic interaction has brought forth sufficient material for interpretation and working-through to be of benefit to the patient, the amount of evidential support for a construction will be vastly greater than the therapist could reasonably expect to get from a psychological test report. It does not help the patient that there is "truth" regarding him in the therapist's head; since there is going to be a lot of time spent before the patient comes around to seeing it himself, and since this time will have to be spent regardless of what the therapist knows, perhaps there is no advantage in his knowing something by the second interview rather than by the seventh. On the other side, it may be argued that any type of therapy which involves even a moderate amount of selective attention and probing by the therapist does present moment-to-moment decision problems (for example, how hard to press, when to conclude that something is a blind alley, what leads to pick up) so that advance information from psychometrics can set the therapist's switches and decrease the probability of making mistakes or wasting time. It seems to me that the armchair arguments pro and con in this respect are pretty evenly balanced, and we must await the outcome of empirical studies.

One rather disconcerting finding which I have recently come upon is the rapidity with which psychotherapists arrive at a stable perception of the patient which does not undergo much change as a result of subsequent contacts. I was interested in this matter of how early in the game the psychological test results enable us to say what the therapist *will be saying later on*. In our current research at Minnesota we are employing a Q-pool of 183 essentially "phenotypic" items drawn from a variety of sources. We are also using a "genotypic" pool of 113 items which consists of such material as the Murray needs, the major defence mechanisms, and various other kinds of structural-dynamic content. I was hoping to show that as the therapist learns more and more about his patient, his Q-correlation with the Q-description of the patient based upon blind analysis of the MMPI profile would steadily rise; furthermore, it is of interest to know whether there are *sub*-domains of this pool, such as mild and well-concealed paranoid trends, with respect to which the MMPI is highly sensitive early in the game. (From my own therapeutic work, I have the impression that a low

Pa score has almost no value as an exclusion test, but that any patient, however non-psychotic he may be, who has a marked *elevation* on this scale will, sooner or later, present me with dramatic corroborating evidence.) However, I can see already that I have presented the test with an extraordinarily difficult task, because the Q-sorts of these therapists stabilize so rapidly. The therapists Q-described their patients after the first therapeutic hour, again after the second, then after the fourth, eighth, sixteenth, and twenty-fourth contact. If one plots the Q-correlation between each sorting and the sorting after twenty-four hours of treatment (or between each sorting and a pooled sorting; or between each sorting and the next successive sorting), one finds that by the end of the second or fourth hour, the coefficients with subsequent hours are pushing the sort-resort reliabilities. The convergence of the therapist's perception of his patient is somewhat faster in the phenotypic than in the genotypic pool, but even in the latter his conception of the patient's underlying structure, defence mechanisms, need-variable pattern, and so on seems to crystallize very rapidly. Even before examining the MMPI side of my data, I can say with considerable assurance that it will be impossible for the test to "prove" itself by getting ahead, and staying ahead, of the therapist to a significant extent. Of course, we are here accepting the psychotherapist's assessment as one which does converge to the objective truth about the patient in the long run, and this may not be true for all sub-domains of the Q-pool. The extent to which this rapid convergence to a stable perception represents invalid premature "freezing" is unknown (but see 7).

Personality characterization at the genotypic level will undoubtedly prove to be the most difficult test function to evaluate. A genotypic formulation, even when it is relatively inexplicit, seems to provide a kind of background which sets the therapist's switches as he listens to the patient's discourse. What things he will be alert to notice, how he will construe them, what he will say and when, and even the manner in which he says it, are all presumably influenced by this complicated and partly unconscious set of perceptions and expectancies. Process research in psychotherapy is as yet in such a primitive state that one hardly knows even how to begin thinking about experiments which would inform us as to the pragmatic payoff of having advanced information, at various degrees of confidence, regarding specific features of the genotype. Even if it can be demonstrated that the therapist's perception of the patient tends with time to converge to that provided in advance by the test findings, this will never be more than a statistical convergence; therefore, in exchange for correctly raising the probability that one sub-set of statements is true of the patient, we will always be paying the price of expecting confirmation of some other unspecified sub-set which is erroneous.

Let me illustrate the problem by a grossly oversimplified example. Suppose that prior to either testing or interviewing, a dichotomously treated attribute has a base-rate probability of .60 in our particular clinic population. Suppose further that it requires an average of five therapeutic interviews before the therapist can reach a confidence of .80 with regard to the presence of this attribute. Suppose finally that a test battery yields this same confidence at the conclusion of diagnostic study (that is, before the therapy begins). During the five intervening hours, the therapist is presumably fluctuating in his assessment of this attribute between these two probability values, and his interview behaviour (as well as his inner cognitive processes) are being influenced by his knowledge of the test results. Perhaps because of this setting of his switches he is able to achieve a confidence around

the .8 mark by the end of the fourth session, that is, two hours earlier than he would have been able to do without the test. Meanwhile, he has been concurrently proceeding in the same way with respect to a second attribute; but, unknown to him, in the present case the test is giving him misinformation about that attribute (which will happen in one patient out of five on our assumptions). It is impossible to say from our knowledge of the cognitive processes of interpretive psychotherapists, or from what we know of the impact of the therapeutic interaction upon the patient, whether a net gain in the efficacy of treatment will have been achieved thereby. The difficulties in unscrambling these intricate chains of cumulative, divergent (29), and interactive causation are enormous.

I suspect that the present status of process research in psychotherapy does not make this type of investigation feasible. Alternatively, we shift to "outcome" research. Abandoning an effort to understand the fine causal details of the interaction between patient and therapist, we confine ourselves to the crude question, "Are the outcomes of psychotherapy influenced favourably, on the average, by making advance information from a psychometric assessment available to the therapist?" Granting the variability of patients and therapists, and the likely interaction between these two factors and the chosen therapeutic mode, it seems feasible to carry out factorial-design research in which this question might be answered with some degree of assurance. When so much of the clinical psychologist's time is expended in the effort to arrive at a psychodynamic formulation of the patient through the integration of psychological test data, to the point that in some out-patient settings the total number of hours spent on this activity is approximately equal to the median number of hours of subsequent therapeutic contact, I believe that we should undertake research of this kind without delay.

Whatever the future may bring with regard to the pragmatic utility of the genotypic information provided by psychometrics, I am inclined to agree with Jane Loevinger's view that tests should be constructed in a framework of a well-confirmed psychological theory and with attention devoted primarily to construct validity. In her recent monograph (28), Dr. Loevinger has suggested that it is inconsistent to lay stress on construct validity and meanwhile adopt the "blind, empirical, fact-to-fact" orientation I have expressed (35, 36). I do not feel that the cookbook approach is as incompatible with a dedication to long-term research aimed at construct validity as Dr. Loevinger believes. The future use of psychological tests, if they are to become more powerful than they are at present, demands, as Loevinger points out, cross-situational power. It would be economically wasteful to have clinicians in each of the hundreds of private and public clinical facilities deriving equations, actuarial tables, or descriptive cookbooks upon each of the various clinical populations. I would also agree with Loevinger that such cross-situational power is intimately tied to construct validity, and that the construction of a useful cookbook does not, in general, contribute appreciably to the development of a powerful theoretical science of chemistry.

On the other hand, there is room for legitimate disagreement, among those who share this basic construct-validity orientation, on an important interim question. If the development of construct-valid instruments which will perform with a high degree of invariance over different clinical populations hinges upon the elaboration of an adequate psychological theory concerning the domain of behaviour to be measured, then the rate of development of such instruments has a limit set upon it by the rate

of development of our psychodynamic understanding. I personally am not impressed with the state of psychological theory in the personality domain, and I do not expect the edifice of personality constructs to be a very imposing one for a long time yet. Meanwhile, clinical time is being expended in the attempt to characterize patients by methods which make an inefficient use of even that modest amount of valid information with which our present psychometric techniques provide us.

The number of distinct attributes commonly viewed by clinicians as worth assessing is actually rather limited. The total number of distinguishable decision problems with which the psychiatric team is routinely confronted is remarkably small (see, for example, 8). It is not possible to say, upon present evidence, what are the practical limits upon the validity generalization of configural mathematical functions set up on large samples with respect to these decision classes. It is possible that the general *form* of such configural functions, and even the parameters, can be generalized over rather wide families of clinical populations, with each clinical administrator making correction of cutting scores or reassigning probabilities in the light of his local base-rates (37). One could tolerate a considerable amount of shrinkage in validity upon moving to a similar but non-identical clinical population without bringing the efficiency of an empirical cookbook down to the low level of efficiency manifested by clinicians who are attempting to arrive at such decisions on an impressionistic basis from the same body of psychometric and life history evidence. Halbower, for instance, showed that moving from an out-patient to an in-patient veteran population, while it resulted in considerable loss in the descriptive power of a cookbook based upon MMPI profile patterns, nevertheless maintained a statistically significant (and a practically important) edge over the Multiphasic reading powers even of clinicians who were working with the kind of population to which validity was being generalized (15). One of the things we ought to be trying is the joint utilization, in one function or table, of the most predictive kinds of life history data *together with* our tests. Some of the shrinkage in transition to allied but different clinical populations might be taken care of by the inclusion of a few rather simple and objective facts about the patient such as age, education, social class, referral source, percentage of service-connected disability, and the like.

Hence, I agree with Dr. Loevinger's emphasis upon the long-term importance of constructing tests which will be conceptually embedded in the network of psychological theory, and therefore superior in cross-situational power; in the meantime we do not have such tests, and there is some reason to think that in making daily clinical decisions a standard set of decision problems and trait attributions can be constructed. Such empirical research (readily within present limitations of personnel and theory) could result in the near future in cookbook methods which would include approximate stipulations as to those parametric modifications necessary for the main classes of clinical populations and for base rates, whether known or crudely estimated, in any given installation. I do not see anything statistically unfeasible about this, and I shall therefore continue to press for a serious prosecution of this line until somebody presents me with more convincing evidence than I have thus far seen that the clinical judge, or the team meeting, or the whole staff conference, is able somehow to surmount the limitations imposed by the inefficiency of the human mind in combining multiple variables in complex ways.

As for the long-term goal of develop-

ing construct-valid tests, maybe our ideas about the necessary research are insufficiently grandiose. Perhaps the kind of integrated psychometric-and-theory network which is being sought is not likely to be built up by the accumulation of a large number of minor studies. If we were trying to make a structured test scale, for instance, which would assess those aspects of a patient's phenomenology that are indicators of a fundamentally schizadaptive makeup, we would be carrying on an uphill fight against nature if we accepted as our criterion the rating of a second-year psychiatry resident on a seven-step "latent schizophrenia" variable! I would not myself be tempted to undertake the construction of an MMPI key for latent schizophrenic tendency unless I had the assurance that the classification or ordering of the patient population would be based upon a multiple attack taking account of all of the lines of evidence which would bear upon such an assessment in the light of my crude theory of the disease. *The desirability of a "criterion" considerably superior to what is routinely available clinically applies to the development of construct-valid genotypic measures even more than to criterion-oriented contexts.* Between such a hypothetical inner variable or state as "schizophrenic disposition," and almost any namable aspect of overt behaviour, there is interpolated quite a collection of nuisance variables. In order to come to a decision regarding, for example, a certain sub-set of cases which are apparently "test misses" (or which throw sub-sets of items in the wrong direction and hence provide evidence that those items should be modified or eliminated) one has to have a sufficiently good assessment of the relevant nuisance variables to satisfy himself that the apparent test or item miss is a miss in actuality.

This brings me to what I have often thought of as the curse of clinical psychology as a scientific enterprise. There are some kinds of psychological test construction or validation in which it suffices to know a very little bit about each person, provided a large number of persons are involved (for example, in certain types of industrial, educational, or military screening contexts). At the other extreme, one thinks of the work of Freud, in which the most important process was the learning of a very great deal about a small number of individuals. When we come to the construction and validation of tests where, as is likely always to be true in clinical work, higher-order configurations of multi-variable instruments are involved, we need to know a great deal about each individual in order to come to a conclusion about what the test or item should show regarding his genotype. However, in order to get statistical stability for our weights and to establish the reality of complex patterning trends suggested by our data, we need to have a sizable sample of individuals under study. So that where some kinds of psychological work require us to know only a little bit about a large number of persons, and other kinds of work require us to know a very great deal about a few persons, construct validation of tests of the sort that Loevinger is talking about will probably require that we know a great deal, and at a fairly intensive or "dynamic" level, about a large number of persons. You will note that this is not a reflection of some defect of our methods or lack of zeal in their application but arises, so to speak, from the nature of things. I do not myself see any easy solution to this problem.

I am sure that by now you are convinced of the complete appropriateness of my title. I am aware that the over-all tenor of my remarks could be described as somewhat on the discouraged side. But we believe in psychotherapy that one of the phases through which most patients have to pass is the painful one between the working through of patho-genic defences and the reconstitution of the self-image upon a more insightful basis. The clinical psychologist should remind himself that medical diagnostic techniques frequently have only a modest degree of reliability and validity. I have, for instance, recently read a paper written by three nationally known roentgenologists on the descriptive classification of pulmonary shadows, which these authors subtitle "A Revelation of Unreliability in the Roentgenographic Diagnosis of Tuberculosis" (40). I must say that my morale was improved after reading this article.

In an effort to conclude these ruminations on a more encouraging note, let me try to pull together some positive suggestions. Briefly and dogmatically stated, my constructive proposals would include the following:

1. Rather than decrying nosology, we should become clinical masters of it, recognizing that some of our psychiatric colleagues have in recent times become careless and even unskilled in the art of formal diagnosis.

2. The quantitative methods of the psychologist should be applied to the refinement of taxonomy and not confined to data arising from the psychological tests. [I would see the work of Wittenborn (59) and of Lorr and his associates (30) as notable beginnings in this direction.]

3. While its historical development typically begins with syndrome description, the reality of a diagnostic concept lies in its correspondence to an inner state, of which the symptoms or test scores are fallible indicators. Therefore, the validation of tests as diagnostic tools involves the psychiatrist's diagnosis merely as one of an indicator family, not as a "criterion" in the concurrent validity sense. Accumulation of numerous concurrent validity studies with inexplicably variable hit-rates is a waste of research time.

4. Multiple indicators, gathered under optimal conditions and treated by con-

figural methods, must be utilized before one can decide whether to treat inter-observer disagreement as showing the unreality of a taxonomy or merely as diagnostic error.

5. We must free ourselves from the almost universal assumption that when we elucidate the motives and defences of a psychiatric patient, we have thereby explained why he has fallen ill. As training analysts have observed for years, patients and "normals" tend to have pretty much the same things on their minds, conscious and unconscious.

6. The relative power, for prognosis and treatment selection, of formal diagnosis, non-nosological taxonomies based upon trait clusters, objective life-history factors, and dynamic understanding via tests is an empirical question in need of study, rather than a closed issue. We must face honestly the disparity between current clinical practice and what the research evidence shows about the relatively feeble predictive power of present testing methods.

7. There is some reason to believe that quantitative treatment of life-history data may be as predictive as psychometrics in their present state of development. Research along these lines should be vigorously prosecuted.

8. It is also possible that interview-based judgments at a minimally inferential level, if recorded in standard form (for example, Q-sort) and treated statistically, can be made more powerful than such data treated impressionistically as is currently the practice.

9. While maximum generalizability over populations hinges upon high construct validity in which the test's functioning is imbedded in the network of personality theory, there is a pressing interim need for empirically derived rules for making clinical decisions (that is, "clinical cookbooks"). Research is needed to determine the extent to which such cookbooks are tied to specific clinic populations and how the recipes can be adjusted in moving from one population to another.

10. Perhaps there are mathematical models, more suitable than the factor-analytic one and its derivatives, for making genotypic inferences, and especially inferences to nosology. Investigation of such possibilities must be pursued by psychologists who possess a thorough familiarity with the intellectual traditions of medical thinking, a solid grasp of psychodynamics, and enough mathematical skill to take creative steps along these lines.

11. From the viewpoint of both patients' welfare and taxpayers' economics, the most pressing *immediate* clinical research problem is that of determining the incremental information provided by currently used tests, especially those which consume the time of highly skilled personnel. We need not merely validity, but incremental validity; further, the temporal factor, "Does the test tell us something we are not likely to learn fairly early in the course of treatment?" should be investigated; finally, it is well within the capacity of available research methods and clinical facilities to determine what, if any, is the pragmatic advantage of a personality assessment being known in advance by the therapist.

12. In pursuing these investigations we might better avoid too much advertising of the results since neither psychiatrists nor government officials are in the habit of evaluating the efficiency of their own procedures, a fact which puts psychologists at a great propaganda disadvantage while the science is still in a primitive stage of development.

REFERENCES

1. APA COMMITTEE ON TEST STANDARDS. Technical recommendations for psychological tests and diagnostic techniques. *Psychol. Bull. Suppl.*, 1954, **51**, 2, Part 2, 1–38.
2. ASH, P. The reliability of psychiatric diagnosis. *J. abnorm. soc. Psychol.*, 1949, **44**, 272–276.
3. BLEULER, E. *Dementia praecox.* New York: International Univer. Press, 1950.
4. BLOCK, J., & BAILEY, D. *Q-sort item analyses of a number of MMPI scales.* Technical Memorandum OERL-TM-55-7 Officer Education Research Laboratory. Air Force Personnel and Training Research Center, Air Research and Development Command, Maxwell Air Force Base, Alabama, 1955.
5. CATTELL, R. B. *Description and measurement of personality.* New York: World Book Company, 1946.
6. CRONBACH, L. J., & MEEHL, P. E. Construct validity in psychological tests. *Psychol. Bull.*, 1955, **52**, 281–302.
7. DAILEY, C. A. The effect of premature conclusion upon the acquisition of understanding a person. *J. Psychol.*, 1952, **33**, 133–152.
8. DAILEY, C. A. The practical utility of the clinical report. *J. consult. Psychol.*, 1953, **17**, 297–302.
9. DAVENPORT, BEVERLY F. The semantic validity of TAT interpretations. *J. consult. Psychol.*, 1952, **16**, 171–175.
10. ERON, L. D. Frequencies of themes and identifications in the stories of schizophrenic patients and non-hospitalized college students. *J. consult. Psychol.*, 1948, **12**, 387–395.
11. FORER, B. R. The fallacy of personal validation: A classroom demonstration of gullibility. *J. abnorm. soc. Psychol.*, 1949, **44**, 118–123.
12. FREUD, S. Further remarks on the defense neuro-psychoses. *Collected papers*, I, 155–182. London: Hogarth Press, 1948.
13. GARFIELD, S. *Introductory clinical psychology.* New York: Macmillan, 1957.

14. GOUGH, H. G., McKEE, M. G., & YANDELL, R. J. *Adjective check list analyses of a number of selected psychometric and assessment variables.* Institute of Personality Assessment and Research. Berkeley: Univer. California, 1953.
15. HALBOWER, C. C. A comparison of actuarial versus clinical prediction to classes discriminated by MMPI. Unpublished Ph.D. thesis, Univer. Minnesota, 1955.
16. HASTINGS, D. W. Follow-up results in psychiatric illness. *Amer. J. Psychiat.*, 1958, **114**, 1057–1066.
17. HATHAWAY, S. R. A study of human behavior: the clinical psychologist. *Amer. Psychologist*, 1958, **13**, 257–265.
18. HEMPEL, C. G. Problems and changes in the empiricist criterion of meaning. *Revue internat. philosophie*, 1950, **4**, 41–63.
19. HEMPEL, C. G. Fundamentals of concept formation in empirical science. *International encyclopedia of unified science*, II, no. 7. Chicago: Univer. Chicago Press, 1952.
20. HEMPEL, C. G. A logical appraisal of operationism. *Scientific Mon.*, 1954, **79**, 215–220.
21. HOCH, P., & POLATIN. Pseudoneurotic forms of schizophrenia. *Psychiat. Quart.*, 1949, **23**, 248–276.
22. HORST, P. Pattern analysis and configural scoring. *J. clin. Psychol.*, 1954, 10–11.
23. KAPLAN, A. Definition and specification of meaning. *J. Philosoph.*, 1946, **43**, 281–288.
24. KELLY, E. L., & FISKE, D. W. *The prediction of performance in clinical psychology.* Ann Arbor, Mich.: Univer. Michigan Press, 1951.
25. KOSTLAN, A. A method for the empirical study of psychodiagnosis. *J. consult. Psychol.*, 1954, **18**, 83–88.
26. KOSTLAN, A. A reply to Patterson. *J. consult. Psychol.*, 1955, **19**, 486.
27. KRAEPELIN, E. *General paresis* (Trans. J. W. Moore). New York: Nervous and Mental Disease Publishing Co., 1913.

28. LOEVINGER, JANE. Objective tests as instruments of psychological theory. *Psychol. Reports, Monogr. Suppl. 9*, 1957, 3, 635–694.

29. LONDON, I. D. Some consequences for history and psychology of Langmuir's concept of convergence and divergence of phenomena. *Psychol. Rev.*, 1946, 53, 170–188.

30. LORR, M., & RUBINSTEIN, E. A. Factors descriptive of psychiatric outpatients. *J. abnorm. soc. Psychol.*, 1955, 51, 514–522.

31. LYKKEN, D. T. A study of anxiety in the sociopathic personality. *J. abnorm. soc. Psychol.*, 1957, 55, 6–10.

32. MACCORQUODALE, K., & MEEHL, P. E. On a distinction between hypothetical constructs and intervening variables. *Psychol. Rev.*, 1948, 55, 95–107.

33. MAJOR, R. H. *Classic descriptions of disease.* Springfield, Ill.: Charles C Thomas, 1932.

34. MASSERMAN, J. H., & CARMICHAEL, H. T. Diagnosis and prognosis in psychiatry with a follow-up study of the results of short-term general hospital therapy of psychiatric cases. *J. ment. Sci.*, 1939, 84, 893–846.

35. MEEHL, P. E. Wanted—a good cookbook. *Amer. Psychologist*, 1956, 11, 263–272.

36. MEEHL, P. E. When should we use our heads instead of the formula? *J. consult. Psychol.*, 1957, 4, 268–273.

37. MEEHL, P. E., & ROSEN, A. Antecedent probability and the efficiency of psychometric signs, patterns, or cutting scores. *Psychol. Bull.*, 1955, 52, 194–216.

38. MEHLMAN, B. The reliability of psychiatric diagnosis. *J. abnorm. soc. Psychol.*, 1952, 47, 577–578.

39. NASH, L. K. *The atomic-molecular theory.* Cambridge: Harvard Univer. Press, 1950.

40. NEWELL, R. R., CHAMBERLAIN, W. E., & RIGLER, C. Descriptive classification of pulmonary shadows: a revelation of unreliability. *Amer. Rev. Tuberculosis*, 1954, 69, 566–584.

41. PAP, A. Reduction sentences and open concepts. *Methodos*, 1953, 5, 3–30.

42. PATTERSON, C. H. Diagnostic accuracy or diagnostic stereotype? *J. consult. Psychol.*, 1955, 19, 483–485.

43. PEPPARD, T. A. Mistakes in diagnosis. *Minnesota Med.*, 1949, 32, 510–511.

44. ROGERS, C. R., & DYMOND, R. F. *Psychotherapy and personality change.* Chicago: Univer. Chicago Press, 1954.

45. ROLLER, D. E. *The development of the concept of electric charge.* Cambridge: Harvard Univer. Press, 1954.

46. ROLLER, D. E. *The early development of the concepts of temperature and heat.* Cambridge: Harvard Univer. Press, 1950.

47. ROZEBOOM, W. Mediation variables in scientific theory. *Psychol. Rev.*, 1956, 63, 249–264.

48. SCHMIDT, H. O., & FONDA, C. P. Reliability of psychiatric diagnosis: A new look. *J. abnorm. soc. Psychol.*, 1956, 52, 262–267.

49. SCRIVEN, M. Definitions, explanations, and theories. In H. FEIGL, M. SCRIVEN, & G. MAXWELL, *Concepts, theories and the mind-body problem.* Minnesota Studies in the Philosophy of Science, II. Minneapolis: Univer. Minnesota Press, 1958, pp. 99–195.

50. SIMONS, D. J., & DIETHELM, O. Electroencephalographic studies of psychopathic personalities. *Arch. Neurol. & Psychiat.*, 1946, 55, 619–627.

51. SINES, L. K. An experimental investigation of the relative contribution to clinical diagnosis and personality description of various kinds of pertinent data. Unpublished Ph.D. thesis, Univer. Minnesota, 1957.

52. SOSKIN, W. F. Bias in past-diction from projective tests. *J. abnorm. soc. Psychol.*, 1954, 49, 69–74.

53. STEPHENSON, W. The significance of Q-technique for the study of personality. In M. L. REYMERT (ed.), *Feelings and emotions.* New York: McGraw-Hill, 1950.

54. SUNDBERG, N. The acceptability of fake *versus* bona fide personality test interpretations. *J. abnorm. soc. Psychol.*, 1955, 50, 145–147.

55. TALLENT, N. On individualizing the

psychologist's clinical evaluation. *J. clin. Psychol.*, 1958, **14**, 243–244.

56. TAYLOR, L. W. *Physics, the pioneer science.* New York: Houghton Mifflin Co., 1941.

57. WAISMANN, F. Verifiability. *Proc. Aristotelian Soc. Suppl.*, 1945, **19**, 119–150.

58. WINCH, R. F., & MORE, D. M. Does TAT add information to interviews? Statistical analysis of the increment.

J. clin. Psychol., 1956, **12**, 316–321.

59. WITTENBORN, J. R. *Wittenborn Psychiatric Rating Scales.* New York: Psychological Corp., 1955.

60. WITTGENSTEIN, L. *Philosophical investigations.* Oxford: Blackwell, 1953.

61. ZUBIN, J., & WINDLE, C. Psychological prognosis of outcome in the mental disorders. *J. abnorm. soc. Psychol.*, 1954, **49**, 272–281.

Probabilistic Functioning and the Clinical Method

Kenneth R. Hammond

It is probably true that most non-clinicians believe (with considerable justification) that the clinical method does not meet the criteria of science. This belief is ordinarily founded on the following grounds: The process by which the clinician arrives at a decision is private, quasi-rational, and nonrepeatable. Frequently, the clinician cannot report with confidence exactly how he arrives at a decision. He cannot point at the datum, or the configuration of data, which led to his decision. And, if he could, he would be doing nothing more than providing us with an introspective report. When two clinicians are involved, one introspection is left to stand against another. In brief, clinicians' judgments are function of a process they cannot trace.

This paper was part of the Symposium on the Probability Approach in Psychology held at the Berkeley Conference for the Unity of Science, University of California, July, 1953. The author wishes to express his appreciation to Professor Egon Brunswik for suggesting his participation in the symposium.

Reprinted by permission of the American Psychological Association and the author from the *Psychological Bulletin*, 1955, **62**, 255–262.

It is as if we put our empirical data into a computing machine, the processes of which we did not understand and which frequently produced different results depending on which machine we used and when we used it.

These criticisms are difficult to meet; the effort to remove them has centered around the development of clinical tests. The aim of the test is to produce a retraceable process. However, this movement, while vigorous in a numerical sense—there are lots of tests—cannot quite ignore the skeleton in the closet. That is, in the last analysis, in the clinical situation the value of a test depends upon its agreement with *some* clinician's judgment. The objectivity of the test is no defense against the clinician's decision. All the test can do is to become a reasonable facsimile of the clinician. And since the clinician stands alone as the ultimate criterion, tests stand or fall through their agreement with a reduction process which remains a mystery.

Since the clinical decision is the ultimate criterion, the final measuring device against which other techniques are evaluated, and since this decision process is a *private* one, it is hardly surprising that there is some question as to whether knowledge is increasing in clinical psychology and psychiatry. Therefore, this paper proposes a change in point of departure.

The plan of the paper is this: First, two methodological issues are discussed —the partition between the observer and the object, and a distinction between two types of reduction bases. Second, these methodological issues are interpreted to fit with behavioral fact in general and the clinical situation in particular. Third, a method of research congruent with these behavioral facts is discussed. Finally, an example of the utility of this analysis is presented.

Partition Between Subject and Object

Concerning the first of the methodological points, some remarks by Lenzen (6) in connection with physics are quite relevant. Although these remarks may or may not carry significance for psychologists above the level of analogy, they are presented here because they clarify a problem common to psychology and physics; i.e., interaction between observer and object.

According to Lenzen, the partition[1] between the object and observer shifts according to the intent of the observer. For example, "If a physicist is looking at a pointer on a scale, its status de-

[1] Lenzen explicates the meaning of the term "partition" as follows (6, p. 28): "Tactual perception is an interaction between a body and end organs such as those in the tip of a finger. If one touches a desk with a finger, the partition is between them. An observer, however, may be extended by mechanical devices. Bohr has cited the following example: If one firmly grasps a long stick in one's hand and touches it to a body, the body touched is the object of observation, and the stick is an apparatus that may be viewed as part of the observer. It is a psychological fact that one locates the tactual aspect at the end of the stick, so that the partition is between the body and the end of the stick. If, however, the stick is held loosely in the hand, the stick becomes the perceived object, and the partition is between stick and hand."

pends on the purpose of the observation. If he is using the instrument to measure an electric current, the pointer is an extension of the observer; the object is the electric current. If the physicist is calibrating his instrument, the pointer is part of the object of observation; the light by which the pointer is seen is then an instrument which belongs to the observer" (6, p. 29). Thus, the partition shifts according to the purpose of the investigation.

Now the same holds true for the clinical method. If the patient is being studied under usual circumstances, the partition stands between the subject being studied and the observer. Clearly the clinician is the observer, the subject or patient is the object being observed. If the clinician is studying a patient by means of a test, the test is an extension of the clinician just as a meter, say, is an extension of the physicist. If the clinician is studying a test, the scoring categories are the object of observation just as a pointer would be the object for a physicist calibrating a meter. But the clinician almost invariably stands beyond the partition as the observer and in most situations the partition is at the object—the patient.

There is an interesting parallel between difficulties in observation in the clinical situation and in the observation of microphysical entities. Lenzen remarks:

In an observation of a micro-physical quantity there occurs an interaction between object and instrument; the instrument reacts against the object and may produce an unpredictable, finite change in the value of a quantity that is . . . being observed (6, p. 30).

The observations of micro-physics require interpretation in terms of classical concepts but the fundamentally unpredictable, finite effects of the disturbances by the instruments of observation lead to a restriction in the applicability of classical concepts to micro-physical objects. The cognitive partition between object and apparatus is the seat of an indeterminacy which limits theoretical physics to the statistical prediction of the results of classically interpreted experiments (6, p. 31).

The parallel between this situation and the clinical situation is clear. The clinician certainly interacts with the object being observed, and, in principle, "may produce an unpredictable, finite change" in the object. Moreover, the object may produce an "unpredictable, finite change" in the observer.[2]

There are thus two points to be made here. First, in order to understand the interaction between the clinician-observer and patient-object, it is proposed that we shift the partition to a point *beyond* the clinician-observer where our observations can take place in a noninteractive fashion. Second, it is proposed that we consider the "cognitive partition between object and (clinician)" to be an indeterminacy relation in a full theoretical sense, and utilize research procedures congruent with this proposition.

Stated otherwise, it is suggested that we consider the clinician not as a *reader* of instruments, as tradition has it, but as an instrument to be analyzed and understood in terms of a probability model. (An example of research following these propositions will be presented later.) We turn now to problems relating to a reduction base in the study of the clinical method.

Intersubjective Communicability

Consider next the problem of (macro-) physical measurement. The physical scientist begins with events which are *both* intersubjectively observable *and* communicable. That is, observers agree about a given event with a high degree of reliability and can readily communicate the reason for their response. Thus, observers of boiling and freezing points can agree not only as to when the liquid boils or freezes, but can point to, can communicate, the basis for their decision.

Now consider the situation with regard to behavior. Observers of the state of anger may agree that such a state exists (i.e., high reliability may be achieved), *but* they may not be able to communicate the basis for their decision, or they may have decided on different evidence (i.e., intersubjective communicability is not achieved).

The crucial question here is this: Is noncommunicability[3] merely due to technical difficulties sooner or later to be surmounted? Or is noncommunicability a direct reflection of behavior, that is, a starting point for the study of behavior rather than a difficulty to be eliminated if possible? Should it actually be the case that noncommunicability is a direct reflection of behavior, then psychologists should cope with it theoretically rather than treat it merely as a technical difficulty. If, on the other hand, noncommunicability is merely due to poor circumstances of measurement, then we must turn to the laboratory where circumstances can be arranged more neatly. Here it will be hoped that communicability can be arranged via operational definition. If this can be done (and it is likely that most psychologists believe it can), then clinicians will

---

[2] In a sense, the clinician when describing a patient gives a report on the changes which happened to himself. Note Lenzen's remark here: "In such observations (interaction between subject and object) it is not possible to control the action of the measuring instrument upon the object, for the instrument cannot be investigated while serving as a means

of observation" (6). It appears likely that the clinical psychologist has so infrequently been the subject of investigation because he has been serving primarily "as a means of observation."

[3] Perhaps a more nearly correct term here would be "limited intersubjective communicability." In the interests of simplicity the author prefers to risk overstating the case—thus, "noncommunicability."

have to wait for the technical problems of noncommunicability to be overcome in the laboratory.

It is also likely, however, that many psychologists have misgivings about the rapidity with which this goal is being reached. For it does appear that such a position accepts uncritically the hypothesis that noncommunicability is simply a function of inadequate apparatus, i.e., poor techniques. An equally tenable hypothesis would be that the apparatus is not inadequate, but rather that noncommunicability is a phenomenon to be understood rather than one to be eliminated from study. One would then be faced with the problem of developing a behavior theory and a research methodology appropriate to the problem. We now turn to the theoretical problem, that of considering observer-object interaction and noncommunicability jointly in relation to the theoretical concept of vicarious functioning.

Vicarious Functioning

The notion of noncommunicability can be robbed of its metaphysical air by consideration of the behavioral fact of *vicarious functioning*. Almost all students of behavior are in agreement with Tolman (8) and Brunswik (2) that higher organisms may substitute one form of behavior for another in order to achieve a goal. In the biological literature this phenomenon has been termed *equifinality* (2, p. 17). And concerning the perception of the environment, Brunswik and others have shown that cues to distance, say, may substitute for one another (1, p. 48). This phenomenon has been termed *equipotentiality* of cues.[4] Thus, vicarious functioning refers to the *variability* in what might be termed behavioral "output" (equifinality) and "input" (equipotentiality of cues for an organism).

Now the concepts of noncommunica-

[4] This matter is discussed at length by Brunswik (2, pp. 16–25).

bility and observer-object interaction may be set in parallel to the concepts of equifinality and equipotentiality. Consider the clinical situation. The patient is trying, say, to achieve a certain goal. The clinician is attempting to discover the patient's motive. The patient substitutes one form of behavior for another as he attempts to achieve his goal (equifinality). The clinician perceives these behaviors, as they substitute for one another, as cues which also substitute for one another (equipotentiality). Because of vicarious functioning, then, the clinician is hard-pressed to point at, to communicate, the basis for a decision (except in the special case where univocal cues are available). Moreover, the partition between observer and object becomes indistinct for the same reason. *Vicarious functioning, then, lies at the heart of the private, quasi-rational nature of the clinical decision.* [Lenzen's phrase is certainly applicable here: "The cognitive partition between object and apparatus is the seat of an indeterminacy ..." (6, p. 31.)] Thus, assuming vicarious functioning (equifinality and equipotentiality) to occur, noncommunicability and observer-object interaction are not merely regrettable clinical occurrences to turn one's back on, but are starting points for the analysis of the clinical method, provided the appropriate research method is available.

Representative Design

What are the requirements of an appropriate method? An appropriate method must permit vicarious functioning to take place. It must take equipotentiality and equifinality as given, and it must permit inductive generalizations despite them.

Brunswik's development of a methodology which he terms "representative design" (1) seems to meet these criteria. Representative design is in part developed upon the concept of vicarious functioning, and requires that this fact of behavior not be eliminated (1, p. 23 f., 48 f.; 2, sec. 8).

The *uncritical* observance of the criteria of strict classical design (in contrast to representative design) of experiments is, to my mind, a principal stumbling block to the advance of clinical psychology. As long as vicarious functioning is ruled out of the experimental laboratory situation in accord with the tradition of nomothetic behaviorism, and as long as the partition between the clinical observer remains at the object, in accord with the tradition of clinical psychology, so long must clinical psychology and experimental psychology remain isolated disciplines. However, it might be hypothesized that noncommunicability and observer-object interaction are not merely technical difficulties but reflections of vicarious functioning. Accepting this hypothesis, and shifting the traditional place of the partition from between the clinician and object to a point *beyond* the clinician, will then permit clinician-patient interaction to be studied—provided the nomothetic ideal is relinquished and the principles of representative design are invoked.

Before turning to our examples it is worth noting some of Brunswik's remarks (2, p. 9) which will serve to emphasize the importance of the separation of subject and object as well as the ambiguities derived from vicarious functioning:

Crucial turns in the history of ideas . . . are sometimes described as "Copernican revolutions." They define a succession of increasingly threatening blows to the pride of the ego; in psychoanalytic terms, the history of science is one of "retreating narcissism," or disentanglement of the objective from the subjective and wishful. Copernicus himself dethroned man's planet as the center of a faraway universe; Darwin dethroned the human species as the absolute master of the animal kingdom; Freud went still further and dethroned the conscious ego as the true representative of our own motivational dynamics. Kant

and Gestalt psychology complete the picture by showing the subjectivity of the thing-language. Discovery of an ambiguous rather than univocal relationship between distant regions or variables seems to be at the root of most of such revolutions; the new "schools" protest the respective "constancy hypotheses."

This paper, then, protests the "constancy hypothesis" of the clinician, and the nomothetic bias of the laboratory psychologist.

We now turn to two examples of research which ultilize features of representative design and which should serve to clarify the above remarks.

Illustrations

Although our suggestions above indicate that our research should begin with the clinician-patient situation, we have found it simpler to begin with the clinician-test situation. That is, instead of beginning with the clinician "measuring" or interpreting a patient via the interview situation, we found it easier to begin with the situation where the clinician "measures" or interprets the patient via a test. The principle is the same in both cases, however.

Our first example, then, concerns the situation where the clinician interprets the Rorschach test. (Any other interpretive psychological test could have been used, or an example could be taken from clinical medicine.) An investigation carried out by Todd (7) had as its purpose the study of the clinician as he perceives and responds to cues to the subject's intelligence provided by the Rorschach test. Further, Todd's intention was to carry out this study in the same manner as a perception psychologist working within the framework of representative design might study a subject's perception of size, i.e., when multiple cues to distance are available to the subject.

Think of the situation this way. Analogous to the meter stick for measuring the length of a body, we have a standard intelligence test. Analogous to physical cues for judging the length of the body we have Rorschach responses which can be categorized in various ways. The clinician's task is to estimate IQ from the Rorschach responses, or cues, just as the subject's task in the size constancy experiment is to estimate bodily size from physical cues in the environment.

First, we may ask, how well does the psychologist perform? Obviously, the answer depends on the factor of information, i.e., his level of performance

tion of the verbal material in the subject's response help or hinder the clinician? Such addition does help. The correlation increases to +.64.[6]

Note that the first step follows our suggestion to set the subject-object partition which Lenzen speaks of at a point between the clinician and the *experimenter* in order that we may study the clinician. In the above example we discover the overall functional validity of the clinician and Rorschach under two conditions—verbal material present and absent.

Todd next turns to the matter of

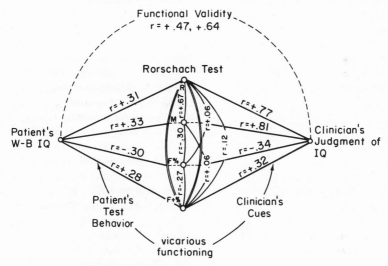

Figure 1. Functional validity and mediating factors in clinicians' judgments of IQ from the Rorschach test.

depends on the kind and amount of information we give him.[5] For ten clinical psychologists judging the records of 78 patients, and provided with categorized responses alone, the median correlation coefficient between Rorschach-estimated IQ and Wechsler-Bellevue IQ was +.47. This is better than chance and fairly impressive. A reasonable question now is, would the addi-

vicarious functioning—the equifinality of responses and equipotentiality of cues. First is the matter of the relationship of various Rorschach factors to IQ. Results concerning this question are presented in the left half of Fig. 1. It is clear that Rorschach responses have a hierarchical probability relationship (in-

[5] The Rorschach test provides two general kinds of material: one consists of the entire protocol which contains the subject's responses verbatim, and the other his categorized responses.

[6] Sophomores in elementary psychology, however, entirely naive with respect to the Rorschach, and estimating IQ on verbal characteristics alone, do practically as well, +.58. Apparently, therefore, training in the use of the Rorschach test adds little to proficiency, at least in this task.

dicated by the less than perfect correlations between Wechsler-Bellevue IQ and the four Rorschach factors) to Wechsler-Bellevue IQ for this population of subjects whose protocols are the stimulus objects for these clinicians.

The right half of Figure 1 illustrates the relationship of certain cues to intelligence for the clinician. Here also we find a hierarchical probability relationship between Rorschach cues and clinicians' judgments of IQ.[7] (Intercue relationships between R and M, etc., are also shown in the figure.)

These data are urged as empirical evidence for the concept of vicarious functioning in the clinical situation. They are also urged as evidence for the difficulties of communication under these circumstances.

It will be recalled that we suggested that the clinician be analyzed and understood in terms of a probability model. We now turn to this question: Will the multiple correlation procedure provide a good model for predicting the responses of the clinician?[8] That is, if a multiple regression formula is developed for each clinician, will it be possible to predict his responses (judgment of IQ) to a new set of Rorschach records? In an attempt to answer this question a multiple regression equation (based on the four factors best for each of the ten clinicians) was developed for each of ten clinicians on a sample of 39 Rorschachs, and predictions made for each clinician for a new sample of 39 Rorschach records. The responses predicted for the clinicians

correlated quite highly with their actual responses. For the ten clinicians the median r was $+.85$, their individual correlations ranging from $+.74$ to $+.92$. Evidently the multiple correlation model which predicts that the clinician combines the data from the Rorschach in a linear, additive fashion is a good one— it predicts quite successfully in comparison with most psychological efforts.[9]

Neither Todd nor the author, however, would urge that the latter data be accepted as more than a surprising bit of evidence for the utility of the multiple correlation procedure as a theoretical model. The point is this: given the shift in locus of the partition between subject and object, applying the concept of vicarious functioning in a representative design framework does make it possible to set up *some* probability model to predict the indeterminacy relation suggested earlier.

Note that the design did not disturb the vicarious functioning of either responses or cues. Todd did not, for example, hold all Rorschach responses constant except one, or disrupt their intersubstitutability by arranging them orthogonally as in a systematic factorial design. It is precisely because representative design requires that vicarious functioning of cues be left undisturbed (and thus "representative") that we can specify the scope and precision of our induction for each clinician—such specification being based upon the nature of the sample of Rorschach protocols and the number of protocols in it. (Obviously inductions to *other clinicians* are

---

[7] Cf. the data concerning perception and "cue-family hierarchies" presented by Brunswik, as well as his discussion of Hull's "habit-family hierarchy" (2).

[8] See Frenkel-Brunswik (3) for the first application of the multiple correlation approach to the analysis of trait-ratings. The reader will recognize the similarity of point of view taken here to that of Kelly and Fiske in reviewing the performance of clinical psychologists in the VA assessment project (5, pp. 200–202).

[9] As an aside, one might ask, as do Kelly and Fiske (5), if the clinicians are as efficient as a multiple correlation procedure? The median correlation between clinicians' judgments of IQ and Wechsler-Bellevue IQ was $+.470$ (see Fig. 1). A multiple R computed on the four most valid Rorschach factors was $+.479$. Evidently the clinicians are as *efficient* as a multiple correlation procedure. Those factors which were most valid also correlated most highly with the clinicians' judgments.

foregone for sampling reasons.)

From a practical standpoint, it should be mentioned that certain variations were found among the ten clinicians in the effective use of various Rorschach factors. Certain clinicians were found to be using invalid cues, others neglecting valid ones. This kind of practical information should lead to higher predictive validities.

A study by Herring (4) illustrates a further application. Herring studied the problem of clinical psychologists' predictions of patients' responses to surgical anesthesia through the use of psychological tests. Because, according to medical authority, variability in response to surgical anesthesia can best be ascertained through medical clinical judgment, Herring utilized the conception of the clinical method outlined above on *both* sides of the experiment, the predictor side and criterion side.

It may be seen from Fig. 1 that Todd worked only with the vicarious functioning of *psychological* variables. His "true" measure, IQ, was a normative one. Herring, on the other hand, dealt with a more common situation—no criterion available other than another expert's judgment. Ordinarily these two measures (judgments) are correlated, with no attention to the integration process involved on either side. Herring was able, however, through the application of the concept of both physiological vicarious functioning and psychological vicarious functioning, to trace through all these (partial) causal(?) chains so that the network of relationships became clear. That is, he was able to make some progress toward understanding the relationships between (and among) the cues to which the medical clinician responded, the cues to which the clinical psychologist responded, and, therefore *the reasons for correspondence and lack of correspondence between the medical and psychological clinicians' judgments,* i.e., the predictor and criterion variables. For example, Herring was able to show that one of three clinical psychologist's predictions did not correlate with the medical clinicians' criterion judgments because the psychologist's judgments were almost totally a function of one test—which happened to be invalid for this purpose.

Summary

The attempt has been made here to scrutinize the clinical method from a systematic, methodological point of view. Lenzen's remarks concerning the partition between the subject and object were introduced in order to suggest that the clinician not be considered a reader of instruments, but an instrument to be understood in terms of a probability model. It was suggested that of two criteria for a reduction base, high reliability and communicability, the latter is difficult to achieve, not because of mere technical difficulties but because of a fundamental fact of behavior described as vicarious functioning. Brunswik's "representative design" is asserted to be the research procedure which is congruent with vicarious functioning; its applicability is demonstrated by Todd, who also demonstrated the feasibility of applying a probability model to the clinical situation.

REFERENCES

1. Brunswik, E. *Systematic and representative design of psychological experiments.* Berkeley: Univer. of California Press, 1947. (Also in J. Neyman (ed.), *Berkeley symposium on mathematical statistics and probability.* Berkeley: Univer. of California Press, 1949. Pp. 143–202.)
2. Brunswik, E. *The conceptual framework of psychology.* Chicago: Uni-

ver. of Chicago Press, 1952. (*Int. Encycl. unified Sci.*, v. 1, no. 10.)

3. FRENKEL-BRUNSWIK, ELSE. Motivation and behavior. *Genet. Psychol. Monogr.*, 1942, **26**, 121–265.

4. HERRING, F. H. A psychological study of patient response during surgery and anesthesia. Unpublished doctor's dissertation, Univer. of Colorado, 1954.

5. KELLY, E. L., & FISKE, D. W. *The prediction of performance in clinical psychology.* Ann Arbor: Univer. of Michigan Press, 1951.

6. LENZEN, V. F. Procedures of empirical science. Chicago: Univer. of Chicago Press, 1938. (*Int. Encycl. Unified Sci.*, v. 1, no. 5.)

7. TODD, F. J. A methodological study of clinical judgment. Unpublished doctor's dissertation, Univer. of Colorado, 1954.

8. TOLMAN, E. C. Cognitive maps in man and rats. *Psychol. Rev.*, 1948, **55**, 189–207.

Chapter 2

Concurrent and Predictive Validation

■ In both concurrent and predictive validation, a test is correlated with some other measure of the same trait or behavior, the difference between them being the time at which the criterion measure is obtained. In the former the criterion is obtained at the same time, while in the latter the criterion data do not become available until a later date.

The problem with both these forms of validation lies in the adequacy of the criterion. If a test of "schizophrenia" does not discriminate between patients diagnosed as schizophrenic and those diagnosed as hysteric, does this mean that the test is invalid, or does it mean that the diagnoses themselves are invalid or unreliable? Shneidman's pointed remarks about the adequacy of the concept "schizophrenia" could well lead us to doubt the "criterion" rather than the test.

One difficulty, as Robert Ebels points out in his article, is that instead of thinking of tests as samples of behavior useful in the prediction of other behavior, we tend to think of underlying traits which both the test and the criterion imperfectly sample. If a number of problems were presented to a child and the results of this sample of behavior were found to be correlated with school grades, we might then have a good test of school performance; its usefulness would lie in the fact that it could be obtained earlier and at less cost than putting a child through a school program and actually observing his performance. However, once we start calling our set of problems an "intelligence test" with the implication that it taps some underlying trait, then we run into difficult criterion problems, for who is to say whether our test is a better or worse measure of "intelligence" than our criterion of school performance?

In the papers in this chapter, C. R. Myers in his 1950 presidential address to the Canadian Psychological Association calls for greater use of predictive studies in clinical psychology. By prediction, Myers does not limit himself to the formal prediction which goes on within a scientific investigation but refers also to informal prediction in routine clinical practice. He points out that the classic method of science is to make explicit predictions, check the results, make revisions in case of error, then to predict and check our results anew. This would perhaps be too obvious to mention if it were not for the fact that it is so rarely done. In many clinical reports, the psychologist writes a description of the patient without ever making any concrete verifiable predictions about his future behavior. Even when such predictions are made,

37

it is unusual for the clinician in the press of new referrals to check back and see how accurate he was on past cases. And in those cases where he does learn of an error in prediction, it is even rarer for him to re-examine the data so as to find the source of error and improve future prediction. Yet such "agonizing reappraisals" are likely to be the most fruitful sources for improvement in assessment.[1] It is in this double and triple checking that the actuary often is able to refine his tools to the point where they are superior to the clinician, as Holt points out in Chapter 13.

One of the most frequently used criterion measures is that of psychiatric diagnosis. As we saw in the last chapter, the adequacy of our nosological system is a matter of some debate. One of the most frequently heard assertions is that psychiatric diagnoses are too unreliable to permit their use as a criterion measure. The article by Schmidt and Fonda examines this assertion empirically and offers data from which the reader may come to his own conclusions about the reliability of psychiatric diagnosis.

The third article in this chapter is a vigorous examination of the criterion problem by Robert Ebels. He asks why we should regard the criterion as a better measure of a construct than the test we have so painfully devised. If it is indeed a better measure, why don't we use it instead of the test? This is similar to Meehl's point about whether or not a test gives us information which would not be routinely available. In a test of ward behavior, a lengthy projective test interpretation might be validated against an aide's reports. In this case, why not use the aide's reports rather than waste a psychologist's time trying to predict the aide's behavior? On the other hand, if we are trying to measure some underlying construct such as "inner alienation," then who is to say that the painstakingly contrived test is "invalid" or worthless if it fails to relate to the aide's perception of the patient's alienation? It is considerations such as these that lead psychologists such as Ebel to question the necessity of concepts such as "validity" when such traits or constructs are being tested. It was these kinds of reservations which led to the notion of construct validation as a partial solution, which shall be explored in the next chapter.

REFERENCE

MEGARGEE, E. I., BOGART, PATRICIA, & ANDERSON, BETTY J. The prediction of leadership in a simulated industrial task. *Journal of Applied Psychology*, 1966, in press.

[1] For an example of a study in which a failure to achieve predictive validity led to increased understanding of a test and the trait being assessed, see Megargee, Bogart, and Anderson (1966). One problem in attempting to predict behavior is that it depends not only on personality but also on the situations encountered, while the clinician can often assess only the latter.

Prediction in Clinical Psychology

C. R. Myers

Introduction

During the past year, I have come to think of the President's Address by its initials: "PA." These initials seem, to me, peculiarly appropriate to the occasion. Perhaps that is because, in the RAF, the symbol "PA" means that the papers so marked are now ready to be "Put Away"—filed, lost, locked up, or otherwise disposed of. And so it is with the President and his Address. The time has come to "PA" them both.

Like many of the tribal customs which characterize both primitive and professional societies, the President's Address is a singularly self-punishing ceremonial. Some few of you know to your cost what it is like to prepare one. The rest of you know, also to your cost, what it is like to listen to one. Consequently, I must join my eminent predecessor in this office, Dean Chant, in wondering audibly why we keep on having the things.

Of course there was a time, in the early days of our North American tribe, when the President's Address had some chance of being more than a hollow gesture. Looking back now from mid-century, through the magnifying haze of forty or fifty years, we can almost hear again the stirring calls to duty, the thundering challenges, the alarums and

Presidential address, delivered at the Annual Meeting of the Canadian Psychological Association, Toronto, May 19, 1950.

Reprinted by permission of the *Canadian Journal of Psychology*, The University of Toronto Press, and the author from the *Canadian Journal of Psychology*, 1950, **4**, 97–108.

excursions of those earlier days. As we listen to the silver tongue of Angell (1906) announcing the Birth of Functionalism, or the brassy boasts of Watson (1915) proclaiming the Behaviourist Manifesto, we get the impression that Presidents in those days really had something to say. Right or wrong, good or bad, it now seems as though it must have been at least worth the price of a meal to have been there.

But now—let us face it—times have changed. No one seems to want to start a large-scale battle in psychology any more. The general common ground on which we all meet seems to be pretty well cleared and settled and quiet. Of course there is always fighting on the frontiers, as there is in any healthy science, but these hot little controversies are mostly private fights between specialists. We no longer understand the problems well enough in any special branch of psychology other than our own to know, really, what all the fighting is about. We must, perforce, leave most of this jungle fighting to the foxhole experts who are specially trained for it.

And so Presidents' Addresses have fallen on evil days. The clarion call to battle has now become merely a "Swan Song," and the Seashore Musical Talent Profile of the average swan is said to be not only low but exceedingly flat as well.

There is, however, one characteristic of the President's Address to which we cling with grim determination. It may or may not be dull. It may or may not be significant. But whatever else happens, it *must* be serious. Since even he who scoffs at tribal ceremonies must still, himself, be buried some day, permit me then, with all due solemnity, to bury myself in my own PA.

Psychology in 1950

The species "Psychologist," as it is found in North America, has undergone profound change within the last decade. In the first half of that decade, the majority of psychologists were more or less abruptly removed from their laboratories and classrooms, and found themselves in the embarrassing position of having to show what they could do to help solve some of the urgent and intensely practical problems of a society at war.

That they acquitted themselves rather well on many strange jobs, in many strange places, is less important for our present purpose than the fact that they, themselves, were changed by the jobs they had to do. Others may have been surprised sometimes to find that a psychologist could be useful, but no one seems to have been more surprised at the effectiveness of his methods than the psychologist himself.[1] Psychologists found, not for the first time to be sure, but on a much larger scale than ever before, that they had a way of studying people which was much more powerful in practical settings than had previously been supposed.

The consequence was that when these same psychologists returned from the temporary digressions of World War II, *they* had changed. They had an appetite for doing things. They had greater confidence in their methods. And they had a heightened sense of their social responsibility. Along with these

"homing" psychologists came large numbers of alert, relatively mature, and very intent veteran students who, for one reason or another, shared this confidence in, and respect for the application of scientific method to human affairs.

It is small wonder then, that the face of psychology in North America has changed. The nature and extent of that change in the United States is too well known to require much elaboration here. There has been a sharp increase in the demand for "applied" psychologists of all kinds. There has emerged a new and vigorous profession of "Clinical Psychology." It is symptomatic of the change that, in June, 1949, one-third of the entire membership of the American Psychological Association named the Division of Abnormal and Clinical Psychology as their "first-choice" among the twenty sub-divisions of that Association.

The fact that parallel changes have taken place in Canada is not so well known. The Canadian Psychological Association is about one-tenth the size of the APA and is, of course, still very young. Yet changes in the occupational distribution of our membership within the decade reflect the same trends to about the same extent.

Comparing our present (May, 1950) membership with that shown in our first published list in 1942, we find that the total membership has risen from 118 to 618, an increase ratio of 1:5. If we classify the names on each list in terms of occupation, we find that this increase has been disproportionately high in the applied, and especially in the clinical areas.

Disregarding "students" and cases in which occupation is insufficiently specified, the remaining names on each list can be classified broadly into "full-time clinical," "part-time clinical," and "non-clinical" occupations.

Whereas in 1942 only 16 of our members were engaged in full-time clinical work in hospitals, clinics, institutions, and agencies, now 138 of our members

---

[1] He discovered, for example, that coefficients of correlation so low that they would have been discarded as worthless in his pre-war laboratory, were in actual practice sometimes capable of being used in such a way as to save vast amounts of time and money.

are so engaged, giving an increase ratio of nearly 1:9.

Classifying as "part-time clinical" those of our members engaged in school teaching, guidance, personnel work, university clinical teaching, and consulting and practising psychologists, we find that in 1942 the number of our members thus engaged was 32. Today the number is 208, and increase ratio of 1:6½.

In 1942, we had 44 "non-clinical" members (mostly university teachers with non-clinical interests). In 1950, the number of these has risen merely to 74, an increase ratio of less than 1:2.

Today, one-third of the CPA membership is engaged in full-time clinical work. Four out of every five of our members are engaged in either full-time or part-time clinical work. Such facts reflect a substantial change in Canadian psychology. Since federal support for clinical training programmes in this country is very recent, this trend toward clinical applications is all the more impressive. Furthermore, there does not seem to be any reason to anticipate an early reduction in this trend.

It must be admitted that any further shift of psychologists in the direction of clinical preoccupations, either here or in the United States, might justify the fear that an over-grown tail is about to wag the psychological dog right off his feet.

Clinical Psychology in 1950

The fact is, however, that the analogy of the "tail-wagging dog" is rather less appropriate than that of the "tail-swallowing snake." For just when so many psychologists are turning clinical, clinical psychology itself, it seems, is turning psychological. One reason for this is that the tremendous demand for increased training facilities in clinical psychology has drawn into that field large numbers of mature and able psychologists from other branches of the discipline. Their effect is now becoming

apparent. They have brought with them the sceptical outlook and the "hard" methodology which they learned in other areas.

The strength of this "scientific" trend in clinical psychology was impressively evident, in August, 1949, at the Boulder Conference on Graduate Instruction in Clinical Psychology. This two-week conference, sponsored by the United States Public Health Service and organized by the American Psychological Association, was attended by representatives of each of the forty-two graduate departments offering recognized Ph. D. programmes of training in clinical psychology. Thanks to the availability of federal support for the training of mental health personnel in Canada, the President of the Canadian Psychological Association was able to accept an invitation to participate.

There is no doubt that the Boulder Conference was held at a very opportune time. Immediately following World War II, there was a heavy demand in the United States for professionally trained clinical psychologists. This large-scale demand came first from a revitalized Veterans' Administration, and later from the United States Public Health Service. It resulted in an almost feverish period of expansion and reorganization in many of the major university departments of psychology. Unlike their colleagues in psychiatry and psychiatric social work, psychologists had no well-established pre-war tradition to follow in developing professional training. Thus, goals and policies had to be formulated; staff and facilities had to be expanded; hordes of high-quality graduate students had to be absorbed; all at top speed.

By 1949, departments of psychology had begun to settle down. The acute emergency had subsided. There was time now to look around, compare notes, and find out how other departments had coped with *their* emergencies. Indeed, it seemed high time that those responsible for training in a new profession should have a proper opportunity to reach agreement on just what sort of a new profession was needed, and what sort of training would best contribute to its future development.

In his address at the opening session of the conference, Dr. Felix, Director of the National Institute of Mental Health (USPHS), stressed the essential dependence of clinical psychology on the research progress of psychology generally. Speaking of the potential contribution of the clinical psychologist in mental health work, he said:

The service which he renders to the community in which he works is dependent upon the contributions to the field made by the social psychologist, the physiological psychologist, the experimental psychologist, working on those basic fundamental problems which may not at first seem to bear directly upon the problem . . . of the mental health worker.

This opening emphasis on the importance of basic research turned out later to be much more than a mere expression of a laudable sentiment. The Boulder group themselves were to decide eventually, though not without much difficulty and debate, that the snake had better swallow his tail, the psychologist had better absorb the clinician.

The final agreement that all clinical psychologists must be trained for research, no less than for service, was a surprising and significant event. Initially, opinions on this question were widely divergent. Throughout the discussions, contrary views were given very full expression. Is this training emphasis on research really desirable? Is it necessary? Is it feasible? The "service" advocates deplored the time-cost involved for future practitioners. The "research" advocates were equally opposed and stressed the alleged rarity of the true "research mind." Yet slowly, and painfully, and reluctantly, by a process not unlike non-directive "clarification," the

group arrived eventually at an astonishing degree of unanimity. All clinical psychologists must be research-oriented and research-trained. They will not all devote themselves primarily to research. But they must all have a high level of competence for they must all be able to stimulate, supervise, and evaluate research. More and better clinical research is the first and basic need of the emerging profession of clinical psychology.

This in one of the many policy questions where analogies to the medical profession can be very misleading. With its long and honourable tradition of service to humanity, the medical profession now has a vast store of dependable knowledge which it can use in daily practice. Thus, a relatively small group of highly trained specialists can be assigned to the task of research. Without such a long tradition of service, and without such a store of well-established knowledge, the clinical psychologist must do "front-line" research. He must have his supporting scientist, not behind him, or even beside him, but *in* him.

It seemed to those at Boulder that the future of clinical psychology is both promising and precarious. It is promising because of the wide current demand for clinical psychologists and the immense unserved needs of our society. It is precarious, however, because clinical psychology has yet to demonstrate its social usefulness. There is now sufficient public and professional faith in its potential usefulness to provide ample opportunity. But what emerged from the discussions was a sober recognition of the fact that, though society may need the services of clinical psychology, what clinical psychology needs most urgently is more dependable knowledge and more valid methods with which to do its job.

A candid examination of the superstructure of clinical practice in the mental health field today forced on the conference reluctant agreement that a much firmer research foundation must be built. Clinical psychologists have a distinctive responsibility for this because of the traditional research orientation of their discipline.

The official report of the Boulder Conference will appear in print shortly. It is a document of some importance since it will be the preliminary blueprint of training policy for an emerging profession. It has, of course, (and it needs) no other authority than the fact that it reports the agreements and disagreements of those responsible for the training of future clinical psychologists.

Let us turn now from the Boulder conclusions and take a brief look at the present situation in clinical research.

Clinical Research

It would appear that the most urgent problem confronting clinical psychology in 1950 is the validation of its own current theories and techniques. Most of our clinical assumptions and methods have not been validated at all. Many of them have simply been borrowed from prestige sources in psychiatry and psychoanalysis. The clinical psychologist will not survive if he is to be no more than a half-baked psychiatrist or an unanalysed analyst. He has a really valuable contribution to make only if he can apply his distinctive scientific training effectively in the clinical area.

The post-war battle of the clinical bulge in psychology is just about over. The excitement is dying down. Now comes the hard grind of scientific validation. The clinical psychologist is going to have to pay his own way in the society that is offering him his present opportunity.

Are the methods of psychologists any more effective than those of common sense? Do they yield any more dependable results than the "intuitions" of experts? Frankly, the evidence in the clinical area is yet to be supplied. In certain other applied areas, such as personnel selection, psychologists have been able to show that their methods are measureably superior to those of common sense or expert opinion. It is my opinion that, in the clinical setting, comparable evidence will only be obtained in essentially the same way, namely by the systematic recording of observations, on the basis of which to make unequivocal predictions which can then be tested for accuracy.

It would be quite incorrect to imply, however, that the application of this familiar method in the clinical setting is going to be as easy as it sounds, or even that it will be no more difficult than it has been in other applied areas. The absence of an impressive research literature in clinical psychology at least suggests that there are some rather special difficulties in its application to this area.

The most obvious, if not the most important, of these difficulties is the clinical atmosphere. By its very nature the clinical setting is strongly biased in favour of immediate service and against long-range research. Our professional colleagues, the psychiatrist and the psychiatric social worker, have been reared in a basically "service" tradition. The welfare of a human being is always at stake and this factor inevitably dominates the value system. Thus, all pressures are in the direction of immediate practical action rather than prolonged, critical thought. Indeed, there is a premium on the confident, rather than the sceptical, outlook.

To state these difficulties is not to object to them. But they do need to be recognized by the clinical psychologist who proposes to try to be scientific. He cannot take his "specimens" off to a quiet laboratory, there to create an atmosphere more congenial to unhurried methodical analysis. For it is precisely *in* the clinical atmosphere that we need more valid methods of examination, appraisal, and therapy. And in that atmosphere the psychologist is not usually free to employ his accustomed experimental weapons.

If, however, we go right back to our own first principles and reexamine conventional scientific method in its most elementary form, we will, I suggest, find that it *is* possible to be scientific within the clinical atmosphere. The old familiar method evolved through the slow centuries from the first harmless astronomers down to their more alarming atomic descendants, goes something like this:

(1) *Hypothesis.* The observer formulates an hypothesis on the basis of his accumulated observations and his background of general knowledge. This is merely his "best guess" in terms of what he has thus far learned.

(2) *Prediction.* He then makes a prediction of a defined type: (*a*) It is sufficiently explicit that he can later tell whether he was right or wrong, and, (*b*) he specifies the grounds upon which the prediction is based.

(3) *Verification.* Then he observes carefully to determine the accuracy of his prediction.

This is the simple pattern, but it does not end there, for the pattern is a spiral. Examining especially his errors in prediction, he revises his hypothesis, and tries again and again and again.

It should be noted that it is precisely in situations where the observer has relatively little control over the events in question, and where an "experiment," in the usual sense, is not possible, that this ancient method is most useful.

Now it is a curious and, I believe, an important fact that the clinical psychologist seldom makes any prediction at all. And when he does predict, he seldom checks to see whether it was right or wrong. And if he does check, he usually discovers, (*a*) that his predic-

tion was too vague for him to be sure whether it was correct or not, and (*b*) that the grounds for the prediction were not very clearly specified anyway.

You may feel that this statement is too severe, and perhaps it is. The point of importance, however, is that unless we satisfy certain of the elementary requirements of the method, we cannot expect it to work. It would seem that, in the clinical setting, we are forever taking the first step—guessing—without being able to (or perhaps without daring to) follow it up with the next two steps—predicting and verifying. Having tried, myself, to use this "prediction-test" method in clinical work, I am not unaware of its difficulties. But I am convinced of the value of the effort and concerned that attempts to use it are not more prevalent in clinical psychology.

Prediction

The *Psychological Abstracts* for 1947, 1948, and 1949, taken together, include a total of 16,810 titles. A search of the subject index in each volume under the entry "Predictions," reveals a "grand" total of 24 titles listed under this heading. While it may be true that prediction studies are, in fact, more frequent than the 1.5 per 1,000 which this suggests, nevertheless it seems fair to conclude that such studies are not prevalent in current psychological literature. (Of these 24 references, incidentally, there were 16 in 1947, 5 in 1948, and only 3 in 1949. It would not appear that they are increasing in frequency either!)

The references themselves are instructive, however. Most of them have to do with the prediction of success at school, or in college, or in marriage, or on parole.

There are two studies (1, 5) on predicting success in pilot training which are relevant here because they are concerned with the use of the "clinical interview" for that purpose. The results indicate that the interview adds nothing to the accuracy of predictions based wholly on objective test methods.[2]

There are two more strictly "clinical" studies which may be mentioned briefly to illustrate the potential value in the use of this method. Tolman (8) reports the outcome, six years after a clinical psychologist had made explicit predictions of success or failure on parole for a group of 193 delinquents. The predictions were confirmed in 70 per cent of the cases. It should be noted that particular importance is attached to the reexamination of the records in cases where the prediction was *not* confirmed by outcome.

Harris and Christiansen (2) report the results of an effort to predict response to brief psychotherapy. Fully recognizing the complexity of the factors involved here and the limitations which must be placed on the interpretation of any single study, it is still of interest to note the crop of stimulating and testable hypotheses which emerge from such an effort at systematic prediction. Is it true that the outcome, in such cases, is *not* related to the patient's level of intelligence? Are there really specific minimal signs of reality distortion which give dependable advance indication of outcome?

My main point here, however, is that prediction is not widely used in psychology generally, nor in clinical psychology in particular. If it is not, we do not have far to search for the reasons.

It is probably a mistake to teach beginners that the prediction of human behaviour is one of the goals of psychology. We end up by believing it ourselves! Making prediction a goal puts it well up on a very high shelf. It becomes one of those laudable but distant and probably unattainable objectives

which no one takes any more seriously than the banner on a political platform.

There are good reasons for thinking of prediction, not as a distant goal, but rather as an important part of our present operating method. As MacLeod (6) points out, "The goal of science as science is not prediction and control but understanding. Prediction is merely the test of understanding and control the practical reward" (p. 209). If then, prediction is really the ultimate test of validity in all scientific endeavour and if validation of current theory and practice is the most urgent need in clinical psychology, it is high time we made more deliberate use of prediction as a means of increasing the precision of our clinical understanding.

There is, however, another and a deeper factor which operates against the use of prediction in clinical work, and that is the lurking suspicion that it is really not possible. This suspicion stems originally from the infamous "man-in-the-street" (including you and me) who likes to think of himself as a free agent and resents the very suggestion that anyone could predict *his* behaviour. Of course, he realizes that his wife's behaviour is highly predictable under specified conditions, and he is often amazed at the uncanny accuracy with which she seems to know what he is going to say or do long before he, himself, has "made up his mind." No, the predictability of human behaviour is not really questionable. On the contrary, it is positively shocking!

And yet it is true that, in psychology, we have had most of our experience (and most of our success) in predicting *group* behaviour. Accordingly, since our familiar statistical devices are group-centred rather than individual-centred, they tend to leave the clinical psychologist stalled with data which have been derived from a single "unique" case. The recent symposium on "Statistics for the Clinician" (9) gives grounds for hoping that many of these technical

---

[2] It appears, from this and other similar studies, that our present confidence in the "clinical interview" is in for a thorough shaking.

problems are on the way to solution.

Of more immediate importance, however, to most of us engaged in clinical work are the ordinary 'practical difficulties of using prediction effectively as a routine procedure for the purpose of improving our own understanding of patients, and thereby our skill in helping them.

Some effort to encourage the prediction habit with students commencing interview training has shown that, although it is difficult, it is also rewarding. Through the use of recordings, it is possible to stop the interview at a predetermined point and ask for an immediate prediction (What is going to happen next? How does the patient feel about this? What will the interviewer say now?) and then move right on to test the prediction against what actually follows. Similarly, predictions from one recorded interview, concerning the subject's subsequent feelings and behaviour, can be checked against the recording of the next interview.

In this process, it becomes apparent quickly that the initial accuracy of predictions is less important than the early opportunity to verify them. It also appears that aptitude for this type of predicting in students is correlated with other (supposed) measures of clinical sensitivity and insight.

One of the by-products of this procedure is both amusing and instructive. Students who have some previous familiarity with the literature on interviewing often find it difficult to believe at first that the recordings of perfectly genuine interviews have not been "staged." They seem to feel that real people should not conform so slavishly to the textbooks! There seems little doubt that the uniformities in human behaviour are impressive enough to permit considerable accuracy in prediction even now.

There is much that we have, or should have, learned from previous experience in personnel selection where prediction is the commonly accepted test of validity. Much of this experience is almost directly applicable to clinical prediction. These lessons and their relevance for the clinical psychologist are admirably summarized in Horst's (4) monograph on *The Prediction of Personal Adjustment.* The general rationale of clinical prediction has been well outlined by Sarbin (7). These carry us well up to the frontier of clinical validation. From there on, it seems to me, we have a great deal of groping to do before we can know how best to apply the prediction method in clinical training, practice, and research.

Meanwhile, there are at least a few elementary pointers which, although obvious enough, are so commonly overlooked in current clinical practice that I venture to enumerate them:

(1) the purpose in developing the habit of making clinical predictions is to improve one's own understanding. Hence the spiral pattern of observe-guess-predict-check-observe-guess-predict-check, and so on, needs to become a routine habit in clinical work, not just a device reserved for self-conscious "research projects."

(2) Clinical predictions which are merely "blind guesses" are of no value. There must be reasons for the prediction and these reasons must be explicitly stated and recorded. "Intuitive" predictions which may prove to be correct, but which cannot be accounted for, add nothing to understanding.

(3) Clinical predictions which are phrased in such vague and qualitative terms that it is later impossible for anyone to know whether they were right or wrong, are worthless. Such predictions may prevent the embarrassment of being wrong, but they also prevent the possibility of learning

(4) Clinical predictions, to be useful, need not be publicized. Indeed, there are usually very good reasons, both professional and scientific, why they should not be communicated to

the patient. They should simply be recorded in a form which will permit subsequent checking.

(5) There is no value at all in making clinical predictions which are *not* subsequently checked against outcome.

(6) Assuming that clinical predictions have been made and checked, the greatest learning value is to be derived from a careful examination of *errors*. Correct predictions may be based on irrelevant reasons. But incorrect predictions not only suggest the need to revise the hypothesis, but can also suggest the sort of revision needed.

(7) Clinical predictions should not be exclusively concerned with long-range outcome. Short-term predictions are not only easier, but generally more profitable. They give much more opportunity for prompt checking and revision.

It may be added that, in attempting clinical predictions, a determinant of major importance is the patient's "idea of himself." Clinically, the most significant predictive clues are likely to come from an attempt to understand his "private" world.

Conclusion

The difficulty of clinical prediction is certainly impressive. It remains only to say that its difficulty is no excuse for our failure to try it. If it is the best test of validity, let us find a way of using it effectively.

Nor have we any real grounds for discouragement. We in psychology are an impatient lot. We seem to think that uniformities in human behaviour should promptly reveal themselves if we but wave our statistical wands and stir our data thoroughly with the latest model of mathematical "Mix-Master."

It appears to have taken the astronomers quite some time to find and formulate the uniformities in the skies which they, and we, now take for granted. According to Hogben (3): ". . . ten or twenty thousand years— perhaps more—may have been occupied in scanning the night skies and watching the sun's shadow throughout the seasons. Mankind was learning the uniformities which signalize the passage of the seasons, becoming aware of an external order . . ." (p. 22).

Mankind has not been looking for uniformities in human behaviour for ten or twenty thousand years. Indeed, it was only yesterday that he found the necessary leisure, and relief from more pressing affairs, to look at himself at all. It could be that we have quite a long way to go.

If we, in the sciences of man, are still "scanning the night skies" of human behaviour in search of uniformities, it is small wonder that the clinical psychologist cannot predict tomorrow's behaviour of John Doe any more accurately than the weatherman can predict tomorrow's weather.

REFERENCES

1. DUNLAP, J. W., and WANTMAN, M. J. *An Investigation of the Interview as a Technique for Selecting Aircraft Pilots.* CAA Airman Developm. Div. Rep. No. 33, 1944; Publ. Bd. No. 50308. (Washington, D.C.: U.S. Department of Commerce, 1947).

2. HARRIS, R. E., and CHRISTIANSEN, C. "Prediction of Response to Brief Psychotherapy" (*Journal of Psychology*, 1946, **21**, 269–84).

3. HOGBEN, L. *Science for the Citizen* (London: George Allen and Unwin, 1938).

4. HORST, P. *The Prediction of Personal Adjustment* (New York: Social Science Research Council, 1941).

5. KELLY, E. L., and EWART, E. *A Preliminary Study of Certain Predictors of Success in Civilian Pilot Training.* CAA Div. Res. Rep. No. 7, 1942; Publ. Bd. No. 50287. (Washington,

D.C.: U.S. Department of Commerce, 1947).

6. MacLeod, R. B. "Phenomenological Approach to Social Psychology" (*Psychological Review*, 1947, **54**, 193–210).

7. Sarbin, T. R. "The Logic of Prediction in Psychology" (*Psychological Re-*

view, 1944, **51**, 210–28).

8. Tolman, R. S. "Six Years After: a Study of Prediction" (*Journal of Consulting Psychology*, 1946, **10**, 154–60).

9. Zubin, J. "Symposium on Statistics for the Clinician" (*Journal of Clinical Psychology*, 1950, **6**, 1–6).

The Reliability of Psychiatric Diagnosis: A New Look

Herman O. Schmidt and Charles P. Fonda

In a recent publication (14, p. 100), we asserted without documentation that "psychiatric diagnosis is too unreliable to permit derivation from our data of substantial conclusions. . . ." At the time that this statement was written, it was the authors' impression that such a proposition was widely accepted and rested securely upon a solid foundation of published evidence. Other writers have made use of this same rationalization for discrediting the use of psychiatrically diagnosed criterion groups (e.g., 7, 13), but during one of our *mea culpa* moods it occurred to us to ask, "Just how unreliable are psychiatric diagnoses anyhow?" The present communication is a report of our odyssey in search of an answer to that question.

Background

Summarizing such documentation as might have been found in the literature,

The authors wish to acknowledge their appreciation to the Superintendent, R. H. Kettle, M.D., whose interest and support made this study possible.

Reprinted by permission of the American Psychological Association and the authors from *The Journal of Abnormal and Social Psychology*, 1956, **52**, 262–267.

we are chagrined to observe that precious little evidence has been published that could have justified our cavalier dismissal of psychiatric diagnosis as "too unreliable." It is true that some disagreements among psychiatrists have been reported, but these have not ordinarily involved the established nosology of their profession. The psychiatrists seem to have been about as successful as the rest of us in their attempts to use unequivocal language to communicate inferences about other people's behavior. That "marked disagreement" (5) and "little consensus" (6) have attended their efforts to appraise character traits and underlying motivations (12), or to recognize such vague entities as "primitive personality" or "nomadic personality" (1), is interesting but probably irrelevant to the problem of determining the reliability of the official diagnostic nomenclature.

Unfortunately, however, it is almost impossible to generalize about reliability from published reports of the studies which did use one of the conventional diagnostic systems. For example, the finding that about 40 per cent of psychiatric diagnoses required "major revision" (8) one year after discharge from a clinic may be due in an unknown degree to actual changes in patient status during the interval. Again, the showing that various psychiatrists use slightly different criteria for deciding between an organic and a psychogenic diagnosis, or between schizophrenia and manic-depressive psychosis (10), proves that these diagnoses must be something less than perfectly reliable, but it doesn't tell us how much less. Finally, the fact that medical students were able to achieve a "moderate" degree of success in arriving at independent agreement with the professor regarding the diagnoses of a half-dozen "classical" cases selected for class demonstration (15) leads only to a conclusion that some diagnoses can be reasonably reliable when applied to certain patients.

From our appraisal of studies in this area, however, it has been possible to generate some specifications for the design (2) of an ideal study of the reliability of psychiatric diagnoses. Five generalizations may be stated as follows: (a) The sample of patients should be representative of the population to whom the diagnoses will be applied. (b) The sample of diagnosticians should be representative of the population of psychiatrists who will do the diagnosing. (c) The diagnostic nomenclature should represent some nosological system in widespread use. (d) The diagnoses should be made independently and concurrently. (e) They should be obtained in a representative sample of clinics and hospitals.

Procedure

Each of 426 patients admitted to the Norwich State Hospital during a six-month period was diagnosed independently by two psychiatrists. The initial diagnosis was made by one of a group of eight psychiatric residents during the patient's first week in the hospital. The second diagnosis was made by one of a group of three chief psychiatrists dur-

ing the patient's third week in the hospital. It might have been instructive to have had every patient diagnosed by each of the eight residents and by each of the three chief psychiatrists, but this cumbersome operation was not attempted. We shall refer hereinafter to the residents' diagnoses as *tentative*. They were communicated privately to one of the staff psychologists,[1] and care was taken to make sure that the tentative diagnoses were not communicated to the chief psychiatrists. The diagnoses made by the latter individuals are designated as *official*. They were made during a formal staff conference and recorded in the patient's chart.

At the time that the tentative diagnoses were made, the residents had the following data at hand: a short statement from the committing physician, the brief report of an admission interview by another physician, and observations during a physical examination and mental status interview. At the staff conference where the official diagnoses were made, the chief psychiatrist had access to reports covering all of the foregoing material, plus additional information from such sources as the social history, the psychological and neurological examinations, a public interview with the patient, and so on. Although the residents were also present at these staff conferences, the chief psychiatrists were never informed of the tentative diagnoses. During the period when data were being collected for the present study, the chiefs had agreed to take special precautions to avoid giving the residents any opportunity to contaminate the official verdicts.

Seven men and one woman constituted the group of residents who participated in this study. All but two were under 30 years of age, and six had received their medical degrees during

[1] Grateful acknowledgment is due to Drs. Margaret B. Scales and Sidney A. Orgel for their gracious cooperation in gathering these data.

the preceding three years. Only three of the eight degrees had been granted by medical schools in the United States. Six members of the group had had no previous psychiatric experience, whereas two had each held one-year psychiatric residencies in other hospitals. The tentative diagnoses were obtained from the residents during their first six months at this hospital, and the group as a whole can be characterized as young, foreign-trained, inexperienced, and psychiatrically naive.

All three of the men (the chief psychiatrists) who made the official diagnoses were certified by the American Board of Psychiatry and Neurology. One was the hospital Assistant Superintendent and two were Clinical Directors. All were mature, American-trained, widely experienced, and psychiatrically well-informed.

All diagnoses employed the nomenclature prescribed in the 1952 revision of the American Psychiatric Association's *Diagnostic and Statistical Manual* (4). This *Manual* lists 91 specific diagnoses available for use at this hospital, of which only 40 were actually used during the period covered by the present study. These classifications will hereinafter be designated as specific *subtype* diagnoses. Representative examples are "schizophrenic reaction, paranoid type" or "obsessive-compulsive reaction."

The subtype diagnoses were grouped for analysis into eleven classes of *disorder*, such as "schizophrenia," "psychoneurosis," "mental deficiency," etc.

As a final step, these eleven disorders were further classified according to their membership in one of three major *categories*: organic, psychotic, or characterological.

Contingency tables were prepared, showing for each resident and for the entire group the degree of concordance between the tentative and the official diagnoses with respect to the major categories. The proportions of official diagnoses for which the tentative diagnosis had correctly anticipated the specific subtype were then computed within each of the eleven disorders. Finally, every resident was assigned a set of "correct anticipation" scores. One set represented the proportions of each of the major categories correctly predicted; the other represented the proportions of subtype diagnoses correctly anticipated within each major category. Each set of scores was submitted separately to an analysis of variance.

Results

Table 1 shows that the tentative and the official diagnoses were in agreement as to the major category in 84 per cent of the 426 cases. A contingency coefficient of .714 computed from these data indicates that a high level of reliable discrimination (3) had been achieved among the three diagnostic categories. (The maximum possible coefficient from a 3 × 3 table is .817; the obtained value is roughly equivalent to

TABLE 1. OVER-ALL AGREEMENT BETWEEN
PSYCHIATRIC RESIDENTS AND CHIEF PSYCHIATRISTS
WITH RESPECT TO MAJOR CATEGORY OF DIAGNOSIS

		Chief Psychiatrists			Total	
		Organic	Psychotic	Character	N	Per Cent
	Character	3	21	51	75	18
Residents	Psychotic	12	128	9	149	35
	Organic	178	12	12	202	47
Total	N	193	161	72	426	
	Per cent	45	38	17		100

a Pearson r of .90 and is highly significant. Chi square is 443.55, and p is well beyond the .001 level.)

What Meehl and Rosen (9) have called "base rates" can be seen along the marginal per cent totals of Table 1. Thus, the organic category is used in about 45 per cent, the psychotic in 38 per cent, and the characterological in 17 per cent of the official diagnoses. That the residents may have acquired a reasonably reliable impressionistic knowledge of these proportions is shown by the fact that they employed the organic category in 47 per cent of cases, psychotic in 35 per cent, and characterological in 18 per cent. The value of the above chi square, however, indicates that mere knowledge of these institutional base rates alone could not have enabled the residents to produce the results obtained.

TABLE 2. TETRACHORIC CORRELATIONS BETWEEN TENTATIVE AND OFFICIAL DIAGNOSES BY MAJOR CATEGORY

| | | r_t | | |
Resident	N	Organic	Psychotic	Characterological
A	31	> .95	> .95	.94
B	58	.93	.95	.95
C	56	.95	.93	.92
D	63	> .95	.88	.90
E	67	.94	.87	.80
F	30	.92	> .95	.80
G	59	.95	.87	.72
H	62	.87	.82	.60
Group	426	> .95	.92	.85

Table 2 shows the relative reliabilities of discrimination achieved for the three major categories by each of the residents. The strength of relationship between tentative and official diagnoses is indicated by tetrachoric coefficients of correlation. These coefficients were computed from fourfold tables giving the numbers of concordant and discordant answers by residents and chief

psychiatrists to the question, "Does this patient have an X diagnosis?" When the question was, "Does this patient have an *organic* diagnosis?," the r_t for the group is above .95, and no individual's r_t is below .87. For the *psychotic* category, the group r_t is .92, and the lowest individual coefficient is .82. The group r_t for the *characterological* is .85 and one individual's coefficient is as low as .60. While all of these coefficients represent statistically significant relationships, and while the differences between the major categories are highly reliable, the differences *between residents* could easily be due to chance. This point will be developed later.

The reliability of the diagnosis of schizophrenia is of particular interest to many investigators (16), especially to those who wish to use diagnosed schizophrenics in criterion groups (7). If we were to consider that pairs of observers had been asked to answer the question, "Is this patient schizophrenic?" regarding all 426 cases, their answers could be tabulated as in Table 3. This table shows that residents and staff were in agreement regarding 386 or 91 per cent of the total number of patients. The tetrachoric r computed from this table is .95, indicating a very substantial degree of reliability. It is widely known, however, that the magnitude of a reliability coefficient is a function of the range of variability represented. If we include in the fourfold table only those patients who had been considered psychotic by a resident, a chief psychiatrist, or both, and tabulate answers to the question, "Is this psychotic patient schizophrenic?" we obtain the tabulation shown in Table 4. Here the percentage of cases in which the resident and staff psychiatrist agree drops to 78 per cent, and the corresponding r_t becomes .73. The lower coefficient reflects the restriction in range produced by the elimination of clear-cut non-psychotics; the effect of such elimination is to increase the difficulty of discriminating between schizophrenics and nonschizophrenics. Nevertheless, the lower value is still significantly better than chance and gives evidence of a minimally adequate degree of reliability. (Chi square is 48.46; p is less than .001.)

tween these two correlated proportions is 6.9 times its standard error and is highly significant. The major category had been correctly anticipated in 92 per cent of the organic, 80 per cent of the psychotic, and 71 per cent of the

TABLE 3.   AGREEMENT BETWEEN RESIDENTS AND CHIEF PSYCHIATRISTS IN THE IDENTIFICATION OF SCHIZOPHRENICS AMONG ALL PATIENTS

| | Chief Psychiatrists | | |
	Schiz.	Non-schiz.	Total
Residents			
Nonschiz.	19	287	306
Schiz.	99	21	120
Total	118	308	426

TABLE 4.   AGREEMENT BETWEEN RESIDENTS AND CHIEF PSYCHIATRISTS IN THE IDENTIFICATION OF SCHIZOPHRENICS AMONG PSYCHOTIC PATIENTS

| | Chief Psychiatrists | | |
	Schiz.	Non-schiz.	Total
Residents			
Nonschiz.	19	43	62
Schiz.	99	21	120
Total	118	64	182

When the data are analyzed in terms of the percentage of official diagnoses correctly anticipated in the residents' tentative diagnoses, as in Table 5, we find 84 per cent correct for the major categories, as against 55 per cent for the specific subtypes. The difference be-

characterological cases. There were 193 official diagnoses in the organic category. Of these, 74 per cent had been correctly predicted as to subtype. The prediction of subtype diagnosis was more efficient for some organic disorders than for others: in the chronic brain syndrome,

TABLE 5.   PROPORTIONS OF OFFICIAL DIAGNOSES CORRECTLY ANTICIPATED IN THE RESIDENTS' TENTATIVE DIAGNOSES

| Classification | Official Diagnoses N | Residents' Diagnoses Agreement as to: | | | |
| | | Major Category | | Specific Subtype | |
		N	p	N	p
Organic	193	178	.92	142	.74
Acute brain syndrome	66			45	.68
Chronic brain syndrome	115			92	.80
Mental deficiency	12			5	.42
Psychotic	161	128	.80	75	.47
Involutional	14			8	.57
Affective	20			7	.35
Schizophrenic	118			60	.51
Unclassified	9			—	—
Characterological	72	51	.71	17	.24
Neurosis	25			4	.16
Personality pattern	12			1	.08
Personality trait	16			1	.06
Sociopathic	19			11	.58
Total	426		357	.84	234	.55

80 per cent of the subtypes had been correctly anticipated, whereas in only 47 per cent of the officially diagnosed cases of mental deficiency were the subtype predictions correct.[2] Of the 128 cases in the psychotic category, the subtypes had been correctly predicted in 47 per cent. When the official diagnosis was schizophrenia, the tentative subtype diagnoses had been correct in 51 per cent. The residents made their poorest showing for the 51 patients in the characterological group, where only 24 per cent of the subtype diagnoses had been accurately predicted.

Carrying the analysis of proportions of correctly anticipated diagnoses one

achievement in the other two. Variability of the scores is such as to preclude a demonstration of consistent differences among the residents with respect to diagnostic acuity. On the other hand, the data do reflect substantial differences in level of achievement between the various categories and thus indicate that official diagnoses are significantly more difficult to predict in some categories than in others.

Discussion and Conclusions

The study reported here is not an ideal one. Although it fully satisfies the requirements that the official nomencla-

TABLE 6. RESIDENTS' ACHIEVEMENT SCORES FOR CORRECT ANTICIPATION OF OFFICIAL DIAGNOSES

		Diagnosis by					
		Major Category*			Specific Subtype†		
Resident	N	Org	Psych	Char	Org	Psych	Char
A	31	92	92	80	85	23	20
B	57	88	85	80	69	50	12
C	56	88	85	83	67	58	0
D	63	96	84	77	76	56	39
E	67	94	73	62	70	38	0
F	30	100	67	70	79	33	50
G	59	94	69	57	78	50	14
H	62	88	73	43	72	43	43

* Between individuals $F = .76$ $p > .05$; between categories $F = 14.94$ $p < .001$.
† Between individuals $F = 1.98$ $p > .05$; between subtypes $F = 27.21$ $p < .001$.

step further, Table 6 gives the correct-anticipation achievement scores of the eight residents for both major category and subtype predictions. Two analyses of variance were performed for between-category differences in the data of Table 6, one for category predictions and the other for subtype predictions. Results of these analyses show that it would be impossible to predict any resident's score in one category from knowledge of his

[2] Mental deficiency has been included with the organic cases for the sake of simplicity although the *Manual* lists this disorder as a separate category.

ture be employed and that the diagnoses be made independently and concurrently, it falls short of being adequately representative of psychiatrists-in-general to the extent that the sample is biased by the presence of inexperienced residents. It can be pointed out, however, that it was impossible to demonstrate consistent individual differences between residents in the ability to anticipate official diagnoses, despite the fact that some had had considerably more training and experience than others. Moreover the "nationally known" psychiatrists in Ash's (1) study had been unable to reach better than 45 per cent agreement as to subtypes (mainly characterological), whereas our residents anticipated 55 per cent of the official subtype diagnoses (mainly organic and psychotic) correctly. The point is that bias undoubtedly exists in our sample of psychiatrists and probably has had the effect of reducing the reliability coefficients somewhat. Our sample of patients is large enough to be fairly representative of state hospital populations, but no attempt was made to evaluate interinstitution diagnostic reliability. Such an evaluation is urgently needed but would have demanded more facilities than our modest resources provide.

When reliability is expressed in terms of a Pearson or a tetrachoric r, the coefficient must approximate .90 in order to insure 80 per cent agreement between two independent measures in a fourfold table. This statement rests upon the assumption that the two variables are continuously and normally distributed and the regression is linear. It is not certain that our data satisfy these assumptions in every detail, but it is clear from our results that a very substantial degree of agreement has been achieved for the two diagnoses which account for more than half of the admissions to this hospital. Thus, when an official diagnosis is either chronic brain syndrome or schizophrenia, the odds are four to one that an independent tentative diagnosis would be in agreement. On the other hand, the situation with respect to the subtype diagnoses in most of the disorders is far from satisfactory, although in another study conducted at this hospital, Orgel (11) found better than 90 per cent agreement among three psychologists who were asked to separate hebephrenic and paranoid schizophrenics from all other patients on the basis of blind diagnoses made solely from the patients' charts. The

psychologists used an experimental set of behavioral criteria somewhat more detailed than those contained in the *Diagnostic Manual* (4). Less than 50 per cent of the cases selected in this way had been similarly classified by the official diagnoses. It also appears that the reliability of psychiatric diagnoses diminishes as the frequency of their incidence decreases. The most unsatisfactory diagnoses from the point of view of reliability are those in the characterological group. Since these are also the furthest removed from possible physiological or medical complications, it is likely that improvement in both the reliability and the usefulness of character diagnoses must await the development of more valid taxonomic methods. It seems reasonable to suppose that psychologists will be able to make substantial contributions to improvement in this area.

Summary

Each of 426 state hospital patients was diagnosed independently by pairs of psychiatrists using the official psychiatric nomenclature. Reliability of the schizophrenic diagnosis was indicated by values of r_t between .73 and .95, depending upon the range of discrimination required. Classification of the diagnoses into three major categories —organic, psychotic, characterological —showed that about four-fifths of such classifications by one psychiatrist were confirmed by another. Agreement with respect to diagnoses of the specific subtype of a disorder occurred in only about half of the cases and was almost absent in cases involving personality pattern-and-trait disorders and the psychoneuroses. It is concluded that satisfactory reliability has been demonstrated for some of the psychiatric diagnoses, but that this carries no implications regarding their semantic validity or usefulness.

REFERENCES

1. ASH, P. The reliability of psychiatric diagnosis. *J. abnorm. soc. Psychol.*, 1949, **44**, 272–276.
2. BRUNSWIK, E. *Systematic and representative design of psychological experiments with results in physical and social perception.* Berkeley, Calif.: Univer. of California Press, 1947.
3. DAVENPORT, BEVERLY F. The semantic validity of TAT interpretations. *J. consult. Psychol.*, 1952, **16**, 171–175.
4. *Diagnostic and statistical manual. Mental disorders.* Washington, D.C.: American Psychiatric Association, 1952.
5. DOERING, C. R., & RAYMOND, A. F. Reliability of observation in psychiatric and related characteristics. *Amer. J. Orthopsychiat.*, 1934, **4**, 249–257.
6. ELKIN, F. Specialists interpret the case of Harry Holzer. *J. abnorm. soc. Psychol.*, 1947, **42**, 99–111.
7. KING, G. F. Research with neuropsychiatric samples. *J. Psychol.*, 1954, **38**, 383–387.
8. MASSERMAN, J. H., & CARMICHAEL, H. T. Diagnosis and prognosis in psychiatry: with a follow-up study of the results of short-term general hospital therapy of psychiatric cases. *J. ment. Sci.*, 1939, **84**, 893–946.
9. MEEHL, P. E., & ROSEN, A. Antecedent probability and the efficiency of psychometric signs, patterns, or cutting scores. *Psychol. Bull.*, 1955, **52**, 194–216.
10. MEHLMAN, B. The reliability of psychiatric diagnosis. *J. abnorm. soc. Psychol.*, 1952, **47**, 577–578.
11. ORGEL, S. A. Clustering of verbal associates in schizophrenia and chronic brain syndrome. Unpublished doctor's dissertation, Univer. of Connecticut, 1956.
12. RAINES, G. N., & ROHRER, J. H. The operational matrix of psychiatric practice. I. Consistency and variability in interview impressions of different psychiatrists. *Amer. J. Psychiat.*, 1955, **110**, 721–733.
13. RUBIN, H. The MMPI as a diagnostic aid in a veterans hospital. *J. consult. Psychol.*, 1948, **12**, 251–254.
14. SCHMIDT, H. O., FONDA, C. P., & LESTER, J. R. Rorschach behavior as an index of color anaesthesia. *J. Psychol.*, 1955, **40**, 95–102.
15. SEEMAN, W. Psychiatric diagnosis. An investigation of interpersonreliability after didactic instruction. *J. nerv. ment. Dis.*, 1953, **118**, 541–544.
16. WOOLLEY, L. F. Experiential factors essential to the development of schizophrenia. In P. H. HOCH, & J. ZUBIN (Eds.), *Current problems in psychiatric diagnosis.* New York: Grune & Stratton, 1953. Ch. 13.

Must All Tests Be Valid?

Robert L. Ebel

Validity has long been one of the major deities in the pantheon of the

Reprinted by permission of the American Psychological Association and the author from the *American Psychologist*, 1961, **16**, 640–647.

psychometrician. It is universally praised, but the good works done in its name are remarkably few. Test validation, in fact, is widely regarded as the least satisfactory aspect of test development. For this the blame is usually placed on the lack of good criterion measures. To assuage their guilt feelings about inadequate test validation, test constructors from time to time urge their colleagues to go to work on the criterion problem.

It is the purpose of this paper to develop an alternative explanation of the problem, and to propose an alternative solution. The basic difficulty in validating many tests arises, we believe, not from inadequate criteria but from logical and operational limitations of the concept of validity itself. We are persuaded that faster progress will be made toward better educational and psychological tests if validity is given a much more specific and restricted definition than is usually the case, and if it is no longer regarded as the supremely important quality of every mental test.

Difficulties with Validity

Definitions of Validity

There are at least four indications that all is not well with the concept of validity as applied to mental tests. The first is that test specialists tend to differ in their definitions of the concept. Gulliksen (1950b) has said: "the validity of a test is the correlation of the test with some criterion" (p. 88). Cureton (1951) writes: "The validity of a test is an estimate of the correlation between the raw test scores and the 'true' (that is perfectly reliable) criterion scores" (p. 625). Lindquist (1942) suggests: "The validity of a test may be defined as the accuracy with which it measures that which it is intended to measure or as the degree to which it approaches infallibility in measuring what it purports to measure" (p. 213). Edgerton (1949) says: "By 'validity' we refer to the extent to which the measuring device is useful for a given purpose" (p. 52). Cronbach (1960b) explains: "The more fully and confidently a test can be interpreted, the greater its validity" (p. 1551).

No exact scientist would accept such diverse statements as operationally useful definition of the same quantitative concept. While there is obviously some conceptual similarity there also are important divergencies. The first specifies correlation with a criterion. The second requires estimation of a corrected correlation coefficient. The third avoids statistical terms, stressing accuracy in relation to the user's intent. The fourth makes validity mean utility. The fifth relates it to interpretability of test scores.

It would be difficult to state in words a core of meaning common to all the various definitions of test validity, of which the foregoing is only a sample. Such a conceptual definition, even if it could be formulated satisfactorily, would probably be too abstract to contribute significantly to more effective validation. What the test developer needs is an operational definition.

Further, the generality of some of these definitions suggests that in the minds of their authors test validity is almost synonymous with test value. But if validity does mean value, then reliability, convenience in use, adequacy of norms, and even the availability of alternate forms become aspects of validity, and we are left without a term for what Gulliksen and Cureton mean by validity. Using the same term for a variety of concepts leads to serious semantic confusions and to procedural pitfalls as well.

Types of Validity

A closely related indication of difficulty with the concept of validity is seen in the diverse forms it must assume to fit different situations. The APA (1954) and the AERA (1955) Technical Recommendations mention four types of validity: content, predictive, concurrent, and construct. Two of these, content and construct, have little in common with the other two, or with each other. Anastasi (1954) discusses face validity, and factorial validity in addition to content validity and various types of empirical validity. Gulliksen (1950a) has discussed intrinsic validity, and Mosier (1947) analyzed face validity into validity by assumption, validity by definition, the appearance of validity and validity by hypothesis.

Again it may be said truly that these types of validity have some common conceptual elements, but the differences are striking. To encompass all the diverse varieties of validity requires an extremely loose and general definition of the basic idea of validity. It is easy to agree with Guilford (1956) that "The question of validity has many facets and it requires clear thinking not to be confused by them." Perhaps one could go farther and suggest that even clear thinking in the frame of reference of the present conceptual structure of validity may not lead to common understanding of a single concept, nor to effective operational use of it. Perhaps what we really need is not clearer thinking about validity, but rather a more concrete and realistic conception of the complex of qualities which make a test good.

Evidence of Validity

A third indication that all is not well with validity is found in this strange paradox. While almost every test specialist agrees that validity is the most important quality of a mental test, almost all of them lament the general inadequacy of test validation. Nearly 30 years ago, in the early years of objective testing, Ruch (1933) made this comment:

There are in use today at least one thousand different educational and mental tests. Convincing critical and statistical data on the validity, reliability, and norms of these measures are available in probably less than 10 per cent of the cases.

One might reasonably expect that the situation would have improved in the intervening years, but this seems not to have happened. In a spaced sample of reviews of 20 tests in the *Fifth Mental Measurements Yearbook* (Buros, 1959) only one was found in which the reviewer judged the evidence of validity to be adequate. Ten tests were criticized for lack of evidence of validity. Nine reviewers made no comment about the validation of the tests they reviewed. This in itself is surprising, if validity is indeed the most important quality of any mental test.

Some years ago, W. J. Cameron in one of his *Ford Sunday Evening Hour* commentaries observed that when someone tries to do a job the wrong way, nature often teaches him his error by refusing to let the job be done. Our failure to demonstrate consistently that our tests possess the quality we value above all others may mean that we have used the wrong approach in trying to gain evidence of it.

Is Validity Essential?

A fourth suggestion that something may be wrong with the mental tester's concept of validity is that corresponding problems of validation seem to be almost nonexistent in the realm of physical measurements. Norman Campbell (1957), P. W. Bridgman (1927), and others have written extensively on the measurement of physical properties, but one searches in vain through their writings for a discussion of the validity of physical measurements. They show much concern for operational definitions of quantitative concepts, for limitations on the measurability of certain properties, and for accuracy of measurement. But the question of the *validity* of a measuring procedure seems to arise only incidentally and indirectly. For some properties, such as the hardness of solids or the viscosity of fluids, different methods of measurement yield inconsistent results. But modern physical scientists seem never to ask which of the methods of measurement is the more valid. One is moved to wonder why this difference between mental and physical measurement. Is it possible that we have fallen into a trap of our own devising when we find it so difficult to validate our mental tests? Have we, in Berkeley's words, "first raised a dust and then complained that we cannot see?"

Refinements in the measurement of distance—by the interferometer—or in the measurement of time—by the atom clock—are not justified on the basis of superior validity, that is, as closer approximations to the measurement of true distance or true time. They are regarded rather as improvements because they permit reproducible measurement to smaller fractions of existing units of measurement, which is to say that they are justified on the basis of superior reliability.

When a shortcut substitute for some more elaborate standard method of measurement is proposed, the question of the validity of the substitute method does arise with logical legitimacy. In such a situation the concept of validity is simple, and the meaning of the term is clear. We will argue for retaining this concept of validity and of restricting the term to this concept. But to ask about the validity of the basic method of measurement, which provides the operational definition of the thing being measured, would seem to most physical scientists as it does to us to be asking a meaningless question.

Why the Difficulties

Scientific Adequacy

These observations suggest that the concept of validity itself may be weak scientifically. Most of the definitions of validity can be shown to be derived from the basic notion that validity is the degree to which a test measures what it is supposed to measure. But how does one know what a test is supposed to

measure? On a superficial level, perhaps, it may be suggested by the test title—academic aptitude, mathematics achievement, or social studies background, for example—but these suggestions are by no means definitive.

Does the criterion tell us what the test is supposed to measure? It might if criteria were given to us. Usually they are not. They have to be *devised*, often after the test itself was constructed. Toops (1944) has said:

Possibly as much time should be spent in devising the criterion as in constructing and perfecting the test. This important part of a research seldom receives half the time or attention it requires or deserves. If the criterion is slighted the time spent on the tests is, by so much, largely wasted.

The ease with which test developers can be induced to accept as criterion measures quantitative data having the slightest appearance of relevance to the trait being measured is one of the scandals of psychometry. To borrow a figure of speech from Thorndike (1922), they will use the loudness of the thunder as a criterion for their measurements of the voltage of the lightning. Even in those rare cases where criterion measures have been painstakingly devised, the validity of the test is not determined unless the validity of the criterion has been established. This requires a criterion for the other criterion, and so on ad infinitum. We can pursue such an infinite regress until we are weary without finding a self-sufficient foundation for a claim that the test is valid. It is an unhappy fact that the general conceptual definition of validity provides no firm basis for operational definitions of validity.

Philosophic Adequacy

The concept of validity is also weak philosophically. It reflects a belief in the existence of quantifiable human characteristics, such as intelligence or skill in arithmetic, independent of any operation used to measure it. Philosophers call this point of view realism but most of them now agree that it is not very realistic. One of Einstein's major contributions was to point out that the concept of time is scientifically meaningless until the clocks used to measure it have been described. As Henry F. Kaiser (1960) said in his review of a measurement book recently:

Chapter 2 repeatedly exhibits the philosophically naive faith that there "exists" an "actual" or "true" scale for a particular phenomenon; the author seems to assume a degree of absolute truth inherent in nature which went out of style in the nineteenth century.

This naive faith in the pre-existence of a quantity to be measured is basic to the general conception of validity.

You may recall the story of the three baseball umpires who were discussing their modes of operation and defending their integrity as umpires. "I call 'em as I see 'em," said the first. The second replied, "I call 'em as they are." The third said, "What I call 'em makes 'em what they are." In philosophical terms, the first was an empiricist; the second, a realist; the third, a positivist. I should like to see test developers be less individualistic in their positivism than baseball umpires are at times, but I think they should be positivists rather than realists. Neither a strike in baseball nor scholastic aptitude in testing is a useful concept until it has been defined in operational terms.

Many of those concerned with mental measurements however, persist in being philosophical realists. They tend to endow abstractions with a real existence. They think of a real trait which "underlies" a test score, and which is meaningfully there even though their best efforts to measure it will never be more than approximations. They think of

intelligence as really existing independent of any operational definition such as those provided by the Binet, the Kuhlman-Anderson, or the Wechsler. They seek to use tests to discover what critical thinking or creativity really are instead of using the tests to define what they mean when they use such terms. They have not yet learned that realistic philosophy is productive mainly of verbal discourse and that it must be shunned if mental measurement is to advance.

So long as what a test is supposed to measure is conceived to be an ideal quantity, unmeasurable directly and hence undefinable operationally, it is small wonder that we have trouble validating our tests. Only if we are willing to accept some actual test, or other actual method of obtaining criterion measures, as a basic (if somewhat arbitrary) operational definition of the thing we wish to measure, and only if we have some other test or measurement procedure that we wish to check against this standard, do we find the concept of test validity useful. Further, if the test we propose to use provides in itself the best available operational definition, the concept of validity does not apply. A basic definition needs to be clearly meaningful, but it does not need to be, and indeed it cannot be validated.

One of the by-products of the realistic philosophy is mistrust of appearances and a reverence for the concealed reality. What a test or test item really measures, we warn ourselves, may be quite different from what it appears to measure. But how a person can possibly determine what it really measures without observing something that it appears to measure is never clearly explained. Those who analyze batteries of tests to determine the "under-lying" factors trust appearances of what a test is measuring very little, but even they fall back on appearances when they must name the factors discovered or provide verbal descriptions of them.

The source of our concern over the deceitfulness of appearances is probably that what a test appears to measure sometimes seems to be different to different observers or when viewed in a different light. If we resolve not to trust any appearances at all the problem vanishes, but so does our confidence in the test (and probably our sanity as well). A better course of action is to seek to understand why the appearances were not consistent, and to find an interpretation which makes them consistent.

Mistrust of appearances, in turn, leads one to seek completely empirical and deductive procedures of test validation. But completely empirical validation is seldom possible. Strictly speaking it is impossible in principle. We cannot escape judgment regarding the choice of a criterion, nor can we escape appearances (i.e., observations) in getting criterion data. To avoid an infinite regress of criterion validations one must stop somewhere and accept or proclaim an arbitrary definition of the thing to be measured. Unfortunately this is seldom done. What happens more often is that we accept highly questionable criteria, obtain discouragingly low correlations, and finally give the whole thing up as a bad job.

Overgeneralization of Validity

A third possible explanation for difficulty with validity is that the concept is too broad. If it is made synonymous with value, or utility, or meaning, if it is made to apply to all mental tests including those used to describe persons or control educational processes as well as those used to predict future achievement, it must obviously have many different meanings. Now the trouble with using the same term to mean a variety of different things is that the meanings tend to get tangled up with each other. When the word is used in one particular sense, connotations appropriate to its use in other senses tend to hover about it and suggest irrelevant procedures.

In the case of the term validity, we tend always to expect evidence in the form of a validity coefficient even though such coefficients are completely appropriate only to tests used as convenient operational substitutes for more tedious, if somewhat more precise, standard measurement procedures. But when tests are used to describe educational achievement, or to assist in the control of the educational process, validity coefficients usually are quite irrelevant. The fact that they are not naturally relevant in these situations may account for some of the difficulty we encounter in trying to obtain data from which to calculate them. The obvious natural criteria we need simply do not exist in the real world, and must be conjured up from the realm of abstract ideals. Perhaps this is why evidence for the validity of educational tests is so often inadequate and unsatisfactory. Perhaps the notion of correlating test scores with criterion scores to obtain a basic index of test quality has been overgeneralized. Perhaps we have often sought to use it in situations where it does not logically apply.

It may even be that some of us, unconsciously perhaps, are glad to honor with our words a procedure of test validation which has limited applicability in practice. By so doing we exhibit our good intentions. If the procedure will not work in the absence of a good criterion, and if a good criterion is unavailable, we are excused from further effort to demonstrate test quality. We also have, in the well recognized shortcomings of available criteria, a convenient scapegoat for the lack of good evidence of test quality. It may often be convenient to sweep the problem of test validation under the rug of inadequate or unavailable criteria, especially when we promise ourselves and others to work to get better criteria when we can find the time.

What Is a Criterion

At this point it may be appropriate to ask what, after all, is the difference between test scores and criterion measures? Is the difference one of substance or only one of function? In the case of predictive validity the distinction is fairly clear. Test scores come first. Criterion measures are obtained later. In the case of concurrent validity the distinction gets blurred. One distinction suggested by frequent practice is that criterion measures should be ratings based on direct observations of behavior under presumably natural conditions. This would serve to distinguish them from test scores, which are almost always based on assessments of output under carefully controlled and hence somewhat artificial conditions. But ratings based on direct observations of behavior have serious and well known psychometric shortcomings. This limits their value as criteria.

Indeed the limitation may be more serious than is commonly realized. Though it has often been done, it makes little sense to judge the accuracy with which a test does the job it is supposed to do by checking the scores it yields against those obtained from a less accurate measuring procedure. If a new method of measurement involves a better (and hence different) definition of the trait to be measured, it obviously makes no sense to judge its quality on the basis of degree of agreement with inferior measures. If the new method does not involve a better definition, but only more precise observations, it does make sense to require that the new agree with the old so far as their respective reliabilities will permit, but in this case it is hard to see the old, inferior measure as a standard or criterion for judging the quality of the new. If the criterion is used as a standard for judg-

ing the accuracy of the scores from the test, it should always exemplify a measurement procedure clearly superior to (i.e., more relevant and precise than) that embodied in the test.

In theory this could provide a useful distinction between test scores and criterion measures. In practice it seldom does. What usually happens is that the test developer pours all the skill, all the energy, and all the time he has into the process of making an outstanding test. He has none left over to spend on obtaining measurements "clearly superior" to those his test will yield, and under the circumstances would have no stomach for the task anyway. Small wonder that many good tests go unvalidated or poorly validated by conventional psychometric standards.

Predictive Validity

Predictive validity has long been recognized as one of the standard types, if not the standard type, of validity. Cronbach (1960a, pp. 17–18), Mosier (1951, pp. 767–768), and others have developed the idea that the purpose of all measurement is prediction. There is a special sense in which this is true, though the surveyor or the analytic chemist might be surprised to find himself in the same occupational class as the weather forecaster. Perhaps the statement "All measurement is for prediction" belongs in the same category as the statement "All education is guidance" or even "All flesh is grass." There is a degree of truth in such statements, but if they are taken too literally they can be seriously misleading. If the predictive function of measurement is regarded as the sole function, it leads to the highly questionable conclusion that the best way to judge the quality of a measurement of something is to determine how accurately it predicts something else.

Why should the quality of a Test X as a measure of Trait X be judged by how well it predicts Trait Y when Y is a function not only of X but also of Z, W, and possibly a host of other factors? Is it reasonable to judge the quality of a barometer solely, or even mainly, by the accuracy of the weather forecasts which are made with its help? Or to consider the matter in another way, is it reasonable to suppose that Test X should by itself be a good measure of Trait Y, when Test X consists of verbal analogies, arithmetic problems, etc., while Trait Y is ultimately measured by grades assigned by a variety of teachers in courses from Art to Zoology?

Scores on Test X may indeed be related to measures of Trait Y, and the size of the correlation may indicate, in part, how useful Test X is for a particular task of selection. But loose logic is involved if that correlation is used as a measure of the validity of Test X as a measure of Trait X. An academic aptitude test does not purport to *measure* academic success. It should not claim to do more than part of the job of *predicting* academic success.

Specificity of Validity

Validity, test theorists agree, is specific—specific to a given group of individuals tested, to the treatment given them, and to a given purpose for testing (or to a given criterion). Anyone who uses a published test is almost certain to give it to a different group than the one on which it was validated. For any user's group the test may be more or less valid than it was for the test author's tryout group. Quite possibly the user may even have a somewhat different purpose for testing than the test author had in mind. His criterion may be different. Again this means that the test may be more or less valid than the author reported. Under these conditions, how can a test author possibly publish fully adequate data on validity? The best he can do is to report validity under certain clearly specified and carefully restricted conditions of use. For the majority of possible uses of a test, validation becomes inevitably a responsibility of the test user. There is thus an element of unfairness in the common complaint that test publishers fail to provide adequate data on validity.

Alternatives

Meaningfulness and Validity

Whether or not you are prepared to agree that validity has serious shortcomings as the primary basis for judging test quality, you may now be interested in what alternatives might be proposed to replace it. What basis for judging test quality would be better than validity? Cronbach's definition, cited earlier, may provide a clue. He said: "The more fully and confidently a test can be interpreted, the greater its validity." The interpretability of a test score depends on its meaningfulness. We would suggest that meaningfulness replace validity in the usual lists of major desirable characteristics of a measuring instrument. Before this suggestion is laughed out of hearing, consider what it implies.

One, but only one, of the kinds of information that help to make test scores meaningful is the relation of those scores to other measures of the same persons. When tests are used to predict, or when they are used as convenient substitutes for more exact but more laborious measurement procedures, validity coefficients expressing the relation between test scores and criterion may be the most essential basis for meaning. Hence we are not proposing that either the term or the concept of validity be abolished but only that they be restricted to situations in which independent criterion measures are feasible and necessary.

Relationships of test scores to other measures can also add meaning to the test scores even when the other measures do not constitute legitimate criteria. When a test is used in a battery, knowledge of intercorrelations among the scores adds to the meaningfulness of the scores from each test. Such intercorrelations show how much the various tests measure in common, and how much independent information they provide. Campbell and Fiske (1959) have suggested a special technique for using this kind of information. From a "multitrait-multimethod matrix" of intercorrelations they secure data on which to base "convergent and discriminant" test validation. Construct validation also depends on relations between measures of various kinds, but thus far it has been of more direct interest and value to the psychological theorist than to the psychometrist.

Unless a measure is related to other measures it is scientifically and operationally sterile. The validity fallacy arises from the assumption that the relation of the measure to one single other measure (the criterion) is all important. The concept of construct validity has helped to break down this unfortunate stereotype.

Operational Definitions. What of the other kinds of information that help make test scores meaningful? Most important of all, scientifically, is a description of the operations used to obtain the scores. Operational definitions have always been basic to the meaning of measurements of length, mass, time, and other physical quantities. Such operational definitions should be basic to mental measurements as well. They would be, I am persuaded, had we not been misled by an overgeneralized concept of predictive validity.

Operational definitions of some kinds of test scores, such as speed scores in typewriting, ability scores in spelling, or vocabulary knowledge scores are not particularly difficult to formulate. For other test scores, the problems seem more formidable. We must acknowledge that the excellence of many current tests has resulted more from the skilled intuitions of the test constructor than from

preconceived excellence of design, recorded in truly controlling test specifications. But there is no apparent reason why an adequate operational definition of the score from any test should be impossible. Such a definition obviously must cover the critical procedures in test construction, in test administration, and in scoring. The development, use, and publication of such operational definitions would, I am persuaded, not only make the test scores more meaningful, but would lead us rapidly to the production of better tests.

Reliability and Norms. There are two other types of information which contribute substantially to the meaningfulness of test scores. These have to do with the reliability of the scores and with the norms of performance for representative groups of examinees. A completely unreliable score is completely meaningless. A perfectly reliable test score is almost certainly meaningful, though it may not be particularly significant or useful.

The importance of norms in making test scores meaningful requires no defense here. In the case of most educational tests they are highly useful. In a few special cases they may be unimportant or even irrelevant.

Importance and Convenience

The stress we have placed on meaningfulness of test scores, subordinating validity, reliability, and norms to it, does not mean that it can be regarded as the sole basis for judging the quality of a mental test. There are two other very important elements. One is the importance (usefulness as a basis for effective or satisfying behavior) of the knowledge or abilities required by the test. The other is the convenience of the test in use. The many factors which contribute to the convenience of a test have been well outlined by numerous authors.

A measurement can be completely

meaningful and still be completely useless. For example, the number of hairs on a person's head is an operationally definable measurement. It can be related to other measurements of a person such as his age or his IQ. We could estimate its reliability and get norms for it. But it would remain, so far as I know, an almost useless measurement, one of little or no importance. Quite properly I think, critics of current educational tests are as much concerned with the importance of what the test is measuring as they are with the meaningfulness of the scores or with the convenience of the test in use.

Conclusions

It may be helpful now to summarize in outline form the characteristics which we regard as determining the quality of a mental test or measurement procedure. They are:

1. The importance of the inferences that can be made from the test scores
2. The meaningfulness of the test scores, based on
   a. An operational definition of the measurement procedure
   b. A knowledge of the relationships of the scores to other measures, from
      i. Validity coefficients, predictive and concurrent
      ii. Other correlation coefficients or measures of relationship
   c. A good estimate of the reliability of the scores
   d. Appropriate norms of examinee performance
3. The convenience of the test in use.

Must all tests be valid? If the term "valid" is not to be made synonymous with the term "good," if validity is a clearly defined concept which can be quantified by finding the correlation between test scores and criterion measures, then the answer is clearly "no" on the basis of the considerations discussed in this paper.

These views may be wrong. If so, and if the current conception of validity is philosophically sound and operationally useful, let us in the name of intellectual honesty, support this claim with some good solid evidence. The time is long past for lame apologies and prolix rationalization of failure to demonstrate that good tests have the quality we have said is more important than any other. Perhaps we should recognize the age-old alternatives so far as validity is concerned. Either put up the evidence or withdraw the claim. It is my view that in general, we have not and will not be able to put up satisfactory evidence. On the other hand, we should not stop being concerned about test quality. What is proposed here is that we stop beating our heads against a stone wall and step back to look for a way over it or around it. There is one, I think, and this article has attempted to elucidate it.

Having followed the argument thus far some will say: "You still want valid tests. All you have done is to propose a different term, meaningfulness, to replace validity." This is surely not what I have been trying to do. I hope that your time has not been wasted in reading one side of a purely lexical debate. I hope that these efforts may contribute to the adoption of a more appropriate and productive procedure than validation has been for determining the quality of a test.

REFERENCES

AMERICAN EDUCATIONAL RESEARCH ASSOCIATION, COMMITTEE ON TEST STANDARDS. *Technical recommendations for* *achievement tests.* Washington, D.C.: AERA, 1955.

AMERICAN PSYCHOLOGICAL ASSOCIATION.

Technical recommendations for psychological tests and diagnostic techniques. Washington, D.C.: APA, 1954.

ANASTASI, ANNE. *Psychological testing.* New York: Macmillian, 1954.

BRIDGMAN, P. W. *The logic of modern physics.* New York: Macmillian, 1927.

BUROS, O. (Ed.) *The fifth mental measurements year-book.* Highland Park, N.J.: Gryphon, 1959.

CAMPBELL, D. T., & FISKE, D. W. Convergent and discriminant validation by the multi-trait multi-method matrix. *Psychol. Bull.*, 1959, **56**, 81–105.

CAMPBELL, N. R. *Foundations of science.* (Originally published as *Physics: The elements.*) New York: Dover, 1957.

CRONBACH, L. J. *Essentials of psychological testing.* (2nd ed.) New York: Harper, 1960. (a)

CRONBACH, L. J. Validity. In C. W. HARRIS (Ed.), *Encyclopedia of educational research.* New York: Macmillan, 1960. (b)

CURETON, E. E. Validity. In E. F. LINDQUIST (Ed.), *Educational measurement.* Washington, D.C.: American Council on Education, 1951, Pp. 621–694.

EDGERTON, H. A. The place of measuring instruments in guidance. In WILMA T. DONAHUE, C. H. COOMBS, & R. M. W. TRAVERS (Eds.), *The measurement of student adjustment and achievement.*

Ann Arbor, Mich.: Univer. Michigan Press, 1949. Pp. 51–58.

GUILFORD, J. P. *Fundamental statistics in psychology and education.* (3rd ed.) New York: McGraw-Hill, 1956.

GULLIKSEN, H. Intrinsic validity. *Amer. Psychologist*, 1950, **5**, 511–517. (a)

GULLIKSEN, H. *Theory of mental tests.* New York: Wiley, 1950. (b)

KAISER, H. F. Review of Virginia L. Senders, *Measurement and statistics. Psychometrika*, 1960, **25**, 411–413.

LINDQUIST, E. F. *A first course in statistics.* (Rev. ed.) Boston: Houghton Mifflin, 1942.

MOSIER, C. I. A critical examination of the concepts of face validity. *Educ. psychol. Measmt.*, 1947, **7**, 191–205.

MOSIER, C. I. Batteries and profiles. In E. F. LINDQUIST (Ed.), *Educational measurement.* Washington, D.C.: American Council on Education, 1951.

RUCH, G. M. Recent developments in statistical procedures. *Rev. educ. Res.*, 1933, 3, 39–40.

THORNDIKE, E. L. Measurement in education. In *Twenty-first yearbook of the National Society for the Study of Education.* Bloomington, Ill.: Public School Publishing Company, 1922.

TOOPS, H. A. The criterion. *Educ. psychol. Measmt.*, 1944, **4**, 271–297.

Chapter 3

Construct Validation

■ As long as tests were designed to predict certain types of observable behavior such as job success, concurrent and predictive validation provided an excellent way of evaluating test validity. With the development of techniques which were aimed at assessing basic personality traits, many of which were felt to be unconscious, it became increasingly obvious that such procedures were inadequate because of the criterion problems which have been pointed out by Shneidman and Ebel in the preceeding chapters.

The problem was thorny. If the traits being assessed did not relate to overt behavior in a simple and direct fashion, obviously the tests designed to assess them could not be validated in any simple fashion. Some test users were inclined to abandon the attempt to validate these instruments and content themselves with "faith validity." Yet the outcome of this could be the abandonment of scientific rigor in favor of unchecked mysticism.

Some investigators clung to predictive validity. If these instruments allowed valid predictions to be made, then they must themselves be valid. The drawback to this approach was that it often merely postponed the task of finding an appropriate criterion. In addition, failure to predict accurately might well be the fault of the clinicians' inability to properly use his data rather than invalidity of the test. Another approach was to use blind analyses or matching in which clinicians independently judged a protocol to see if they could arrive at the same inferences.[1] However, such studies related more to reliability than to validity.

It was in an effort to break through this impasse that the concept of construct validity was proposed in the APA *Technical Recommendations for Psychological Tests* in 1954. This type of validation was proposed for the situation in which ". . . the tester had no definitive criterion measure of the quality with which he is concerned and must use indirect measures to validate the theory" (APA, 1954, p. 214). In this approach, a fundamental distinction is made between behavior relevance and behavior equivalence. If it is impossible to find a criterion measure which is equivalent to the trait, then the investigator can search for other observable behaviors which, while not equivalent to the trait, are nonetheless related to it. For instance, if we have a test of the trait "depression," we might be unable to find a criterion

---

[1] A good example of this approach is the study by Datel and Gengerelli reprinted in Chapter 10.

which is equivalent to this construct; nevertheless we can make a number of predictions about relevant behaviors which are based on our theoretical understanding of what is implied by the term "depression." Such predictions might include the following: those high on the test should show a greater incidence of (1) suicides, (2) sleep disorders, (3) psychiatric hospitalizations, (4) crying, (5) pessimism, etc., than those low on the test. While none of these observable behaviors is in and of itself equivalent to depression, nonetheless the verification of a number of hypotheses such as these would lead us to have increasing confidence in our instrument.[2]

In the first article in this chapter, Cronbach and Meehl spell out in detail what is involved in construct validation, explaining how a "nomological net" of interlocking hypotheses, at least some of which are related to observable behavior, can be formulated and tested. As this body of hypotheses and deductions is formulated and tested the clinician can decide on the basis of something more than just faith whether or not he is empirically justified in placing much confidence in a test.

In the second article, Campbell and Fiske propose a method for helping to establish construct validity, which they term the "multitrait-multimethod matrix." This method requires that a test have "convergent" validity, i.e., that it correlate significantly with an independent effort to measure the same trait. It also requires "discriminant validity," i.e., that a test should not correlate too highly with measures from which it should differ. For instance, a test of "adjustment" should correlate higher with some independent measure of adjustment than it does with a measure of "social desirability."

In the concluding article, Harold Bechtoldt takes issue with the idea of validating tests by means of construct validation. He holds that this is little more than the renaming of the basic process of theory building and that it has the danger not only of introducing undesirable confusion, but more seriously of leading us away from a strict adherance to operational definition which he regards as essential to scientific progress in psychology.

The debate has not ended with Bechtoldt's article, although space prevented including additional material on this topic. Campbell (1960) has published a further analysis of construct validation and a critique of Bechtoldt's position in which he denies that construct validation represents the abandonment of operationalism or encourages the reification of traits.

Other articles which the student of construct validity would do well to read are Loevinger's (1957) paper on tests as instruments of psychological theory and Humphrey's (1960) note on the multitrait-multimethod matrix. For an example of a study in which the multitrait-multimethod matrix is applied, the reader is referred to Dicken's (1963) article on the convergent and discriminant validity of the CPI.

---

[2] For an excellent example of construct validation, the reader is referred to the study by Griffith, Upshaw, and Fowler in Chapter 7.

REFERENCES

AMERICAN PSYCHOLOGICAL ASSOCIATION. Technical recommendations for psychological test and diagnostic techniques. *Psychological Bulletin,* 1954, **51,** 1–38.

CAMPBELL, D. T. Recommendations for APA test standards regarding construct, trait, or discriminant validity. *American Psychologist,* 1960, **15,** 546–553.

DICKEN, C. F. Convergent and discriminant validity of the California Psychological Inventory. *Educational and Psychological Measurement,* 1963, **23,** 449–459.

HUMPHREYS, L. G. Note on the multitrait-multimethod matrix. *Psychological Bulletin,* 1960, **57,** 86–88.

LOEVINGER, JANE. Objective tests as instruments of psychological theory. *Psychological Reports,* 1957, **3,** 635–694.

Construct Validity in Psychological Tests

Lee J. Cronbach and Paul E. Meehl

Validation of psychological tests has not yet been adequately conceptualized, as the APA Committee on Psychological Tests learned when it undertook (1950–54) to specify what qualities should be investigated before a test is published. In order to make coherent recommendations the Committee found it necessary to distinguish four types of validity, established by different types of research and requiring different interpretation. The chief innovation in the Committee's report was the term *construct validity.*[1]

The second author worked on this problem in connection with his appointment to the Minnesota Center for Philosophy of Science. We are indebted to the other members of the Center (Herbert Feigl, Michael Scriven, Wilfrid Sellars), and to D. L. Thistlethwaite of the University of Illinois, for their major contributions to our thinking and their suggestions for improving this paper.

Reprinted by permission of the American Psychological Association and the authors from *Psychological Bulletin,* 1955, **52,** 281–302.

[1] Referred to in a preliminary report (58) as *congruent validity.*

This idea was first formulated by a subcommittee (Meehl and R. C. Challman) studying how proposed recommendations would apply to projective techniques, and later modified and clarified by the entire Committee (Bordin, Challman, Conrad, Humphreys, Super, and the present writers). The statements agreed upon by the Committee (and by committees of two other associations) were published in the *Technical Recommendations* (59). The present interpretation of construct validity is not "official" and deals with some areas where the Committee would probably not be unanimous. The present writers are solely responsible for this attempt to explain the concept and elaborate its implications.

Identification of construct validity was not an isolated development. Writers on validity during the preceding decade had shown a great deal of dissatisfaction with conventional notions of validity, and introduced new terms and ideas, but the resulting aggregation of types of validity seems only to have stirred the muddy waters. Portions of the distinctions we shall discuss are implicit in Jenkins' paper, "Validity for what?" (33), Gulliksen's "Intrinsic validity" (27), Goodenough's distinction between tests as "signs" and "samples" (22), Cronbach's separation of "logical" and "empirical" validity (11), Guilford's "factorial validity" (25), and Mosier's papers on "face validity" and "validity generalization" (49, 50). Helen Peak (52) comes close to an explicit statement of construct validity as we shall present it.

Four Types of Validation

The categories into which the *Recommendations* divide validity studies are: predictive validity, concurrent validity, content validity, and construct validity. The first two of these may be considered together as *criterion-oriented* validation procedures.

The pattern of a criterion-oriented study is familiar. The investigator is primarily interested in some criterion which he wishes to predict. He administers the test, obtains an independent criterion measure on the same subjects, and computes a correlation. If the criterion is obtained some time after the test is given, he is studying *predictive validity*. If the test score and criterion score are determined at essentially the same time, he is studying *concurrent validity*. Concurrent validity is studied when one test is proposed as a substitute for another (for example, when a multiple-choice form of spelling test is substituted for taking dictation), or a test is shown to correlate with some contemporary criterion (e.g., psychiatric diagnosis).

Content validity is established by showing that the test items are a sample of a universe in which the investigator is interested. Content validity is ordinarily to be established deductively, by defining a universe of items and sampling systematically within this universe to establish the test.

Construct validation is involved whenever a test is to be interpreted as a measure of some attribute or quality which is not "operationally defined." The problem faced by the investigator is, "What constructs account for variance in test performance?" Construct validity calls for no new scientific approach. Much current research on tests of personality (9) is construct validation, usually without the benefit of a clear formulation of this process.

Construct validity is not to be identified solely by particular investigative procedures, but by the orientation of the investigator. Criterion-oriented validity, as Bechtoldt emphasizes (3, p. 1245), "involves the *acceptance* of a set of operations as an adequate definition of whatever is to be measured." When an investigator believes that no criterion available to him is fully valid, he perforce becomes interested in construct validity because this is the only way to avoid the "infinite frustration" of relating every criterion to some more ultimate standard (21). In content validation, *acceptance* of the universe of content as defining the variable to be measured is essential. Construct validity must be investigated whenever no criterion or universe of content is accepted as entirely adequate to define the quality to be measured. Determining what psychological constructs account for test performance is desirable for almost any test. Thus, although the MMPI was originally established on the basis of empirical discrimination between patient groups and so-called normals (concurrent validity), continuing research has tried to provide a basis for describing the personality associated with each score pattern. Such interpretations permit the clinician to predict performance with respect to criteria which have not yet been employed in empirical validation studies (cf. 46, pp. 49–50, 110–111).

We can distinguish among the four types of validity by noting that each involves a different emphasis on the criterion. In predictive or concurrent validity, the criterion behavior is of concern to the tester, and he may have no concern whatsoever with the type of behavior exhibited in the test. (An employer does not care if a worker can manipulate blocks, but the score on the block test may predict something he cares about.) Content validity is studied when the tester *is* concerned with the type of behavior involved in the test performance. Indeed, if the test is a work sample, the behavior represented in the test may be an end in itself. Construct validity is ordinarily studied when the tester has no definite criterion measure of the quality with which he is concerned, and must use indirect measures. Here the trait or quality underlying the test is of central importance, rather than either the test behavior or the scores on the criteria (59, p. 14).

Construct validation is important at times for every sort of psychological test: aptitude, achievement, interests, and so on. Thurstone's statement is interesting in this connection:

In the field of intelligence tests, it used to be common to define validity as the correlation between a test score and some outside criterion. We have reached a stage of sophistication where the test-criterion correlation is too coarse. It is obsolete. If we attempted to ascertain the validity of a test for the second space-factor, for example, we would have to get judges [to] make reliable judgments about people as to this factor. Ordinarily their [the available judges'] ratings would be of no value as a criterion. Consequently, validity studies in the cognitive functions now depend on criteria of internal consistency . . . (60, p. 3).

Construct validity would be involved in answering such questions as: To what extent is this test of intelligence culture-free? Does this test of "interpretation of data" measure reading ability, quantitative reasoning, or response sets? How does a person with A in Strong Accountant, and B in Strong CPA, differ from a person who has these scores reversed?

Examples of construct validation procedure. Suppose measure X correlates .50 with Y, the amount of palmar sweating induced when we tell a student that he has failed a Psychology I exam. Predictive validity of X for Y is adequately described by the coefficient, and a statement of the experimental and sampling conditions. If someone were to ask, "Isn't there perhaps another way to interpret this correlation?" or "What other kinds of evidence can you bring to support your interpretation?", we would hardly understand what he was asking because no interpretation has been made. These questions become relevant when the correlation is advanced as evidence that "test X measures anxiety proneness." Alternative interpretations are possible; e.g., perhaps the test measures "academic aspiration," in which case we will expect different results if we induce palmar sweating by economic threat. It is then reasonable to inquire about other *kinds* of evidence.

Add these facts from further studies: Test X correlates .45 with fraternity brothers' ratings on "tenseness." Test X correlates .55 with amount of intellectual inefficiency induced by painful electric shock, and .68 with the Taylor Anxiety scale. Mean X score decreases among four diagnosed groups in this order: anxiety state, reactive depression, "normal," and psychopathic personality. And palmar sweat under threat of failure in Psychology I correlates .60 with threat of failure in mathematics. Negative results eliminate competing explanations of the X score; thus, findings of negligible correlations between X and social class, vocational aim, and value-orientation make it fairly safe to reject the suggestion that X measures "academic aspiration." We can have substantial confidence that X does measure anxiety proneness if the current theory of anxiety can embrace the variates which yield positive correlations, and does not predict correlations where we found none.

Kinds of Constructs

At this point we should indicate summarily what we mean by a construct, recognizing that much of the remainder of the paper deals with this question. A construct is some postulated attribute of people, assumed to be reflected in test performance. In test validation the attribute about which we make statements in interpreting a test is a construct. We expect a person at any time to possess or not possess a qualitative attribute (amnesia) or structure, or to possess some degree of a quantitative attribute (cheerfulness). A construct has certain associated meanings carried in statements of this general character: Persons who possess this attribute will, in situation X, act in manner Y (with a stated probability). The logic of construct validation is invoked whether the construct is highly systematized or loose, used in ramified theory or a few simple propositions, used in absolute propositions or probability statements. We seek to specify how one is to defend a proposed interpretation of a test; *we are not recommending any one type of interpretation.*

The constructs in which tests are to be interpreted are certainly not likely to be physiological. Most often they will be traits such as "latent hostility" or "variable in mood," or descriptions in terms of an educational objective, as "ability to plan experiments." For the benefit of readers who may have been influenced by certain eisegeses of Mac-Corquodale and Meehl (40), let us here emphasize: Whether or not an interpretation of a test's properties or relations involves questions of construct validity is to be decided by examining the entire body of evidence offered, together with what is asserted about the test in the context of this evidence. Proposed identifications of constructs allegedly measured by the test with constructs of other sciences (e.g., genetics, neuroanatomy, biochemistry) make up

only *one* class of construct-validity claims, and a rather minor one at present. Space does not permit full analysis of the relation of the present paper to the MacCorquodale-Meehl distinction between hypothetical constructs and intervening variables. The philosophy of science pertinent to the present paper is set forth later in the section entitled, "The nomological network."

The Relation of Constructs to "Criteria"

Critical View of the Criterion Implied

An unquestionable criterion may be found in a practical operation, or may be established as a consequence of an operational definition. Typically, however, the psychologist is unwilling to use the directly operational approach because he is interested in building theory about a generalized construct. A theorist trying to relate behavior to "hunger" almost certainly invests that term with meanings other than the operation "elapsed-time-since-feeding." If he is concerned with hunger as a tissue need, he will not accept time lapse as *equivalent* to his construct because it fails to consider, among other things, energy expenditure of the animal.

In some situations the criterion is no more valid than the test. Suppose, for example, that we want to know if counting the dots on Bender-Gestalt figure five indicates "compulsive rigidity," and take psychiatric ratings on this trait as a criterion. Even a conventional report on the resulting correlation will say something about the extent and intensity of the psychiatrist's contacts and should describe his qualifications (e.g., diplomate status? analyzed?).

Why report these facts? Because data are needed to indicate whether the criterion is any good. "Compulsive rigidity" is not really intended to mean "social stimulus value to psychiatrists." The implied trait involves a range of behavior-dispositions which may be very imperfectly sampled by the psychiatrist.

Suppose dot-counting does not occur in a particular patient and yet we find that the psychiatrist has rated him as "rigid." When questioned the psychiatrist tells us that the patient was a rather easy, free-wheeling sort; however, the patient *did* lean over to straighten out a skewed desk blotter, and this, viewed against certain other facts, tipped the scale in favor of a "rigid" rating. On the face of it, counting Bender dots may be just as good (or poor) a sample of the compulsive-rigidity domain as straightening desk blotters is.

Suppose, to extend our example, we have four tests on the "predictor" side, over against the psychiatrist's "criterion," and find generally positive correlations among the five variables. Surely it is artificial and arbitrary to impose the "test-should-predict-criterion" pattern on such data. The psychiatrist samples verbal content, expressive pattern, voice, posture, etc. The psychologist samples verbal content, perception, expressive pattern, etc. Our proper conclusion is that, from this evidence, the four tests and the psychiatrist all assess some common factor.

The asymmetry between the "test" and the so-designated "criterion" arises only because the terminology of predictive validity has become a commonplace in test analysis. In this study where a construct is the central concern, any distinction between the merit of the test and criterion variables would be justified only if it had already been shown that the psychiatrist's theory and operations were excellent measures of the attribute.

Inadequacy of Validation in Terms of Specific Criteria

The proposal to validate constructual interpretations of tests runs counter to suggestions of some others. Spiker and McCandless (57) favor an operational approach. Validation is replaced by compiling statements as to how strongly

the test predicts other observed variables of interest. To avoid requiring that each new variable be investigated completely by itself, they allow two variables to collapse into one whenever the properties of the operationally defined measures are the same: "If a new test is demonstrated to predict the scores on an older, well-established test, then an evaluation of the predictive power of the older test may be used for the new one." But accurate inferences are possible only if the two tests correlate so highly that there is negligible reliable variance in either test, independent of the other. Where the correspondence is less close, one must either retain all the separate variables operationally defined or embark on construct validation.

The practical user of tests must rely on constructs of some generality to make predictions about new situations. Test X could be used to predict palmar sweating in the face of failure without invoking any construct, but a counselor is more likely to be asked to forecast behavior in diverse or even unique situations for which the correlation of test X is unknown. Significant predictions rely on knowledge accumulated around the generalized construct of anxiety. The *Technical Recommendations* state:

It is ordinarily necessary to evaluate construct validity by integrating evidence from many different sources. The problem of construct validation becomes especially acute in the clinical field since for many of the constructs dealt with it is not a question of finding an imperfect criterion but of finding any criterion at all. The psychologist interested in construct validity for clinical devices is concerned with making an estimate of a hypothetical internal process, factor, system, structure, or state and cannot expect to find a clear unitary behavioral criterion. An attempt to identify any one criterion measure or any composite as *the* criterion aimed at is, however, usually unwarranted (59, pp. 14–15).

This appears to conflict with arguments for specific criteria prominent at places in the testing literature. Thus Anastasi (2) makes many statements of the latter character: "It is only as a measure of a specifically defined criterion that a test can be objectively validated at all . . . To claim that a test measures anything over and above its criterion is pure speculation" (p. 67). Yet elsewhere this article supports construct validation. Tests can be profitably interpreted if we "know the relationships between the tested behavior . . . and other behavior samples, none of these behavior samples necessarily occupying the preeminent position of a criterion" (p. 75). Factor analysis with several partial criteria might be used to study whether a test measures a postulated "general learning ability." If the data demonstrate specificity of ability instead, such specificity is "useful in its own right in advancing our knowledge of behavior; it should not be construed as a weakness of the tests" (p. 75).

We depart from Anastasi at two points. She writes, "The validity of a psychological test should not be confused with an analysis of the factors which determine the behavior under consideration." We, however, regard such analysis as a most important type of validation. Second, she refers to "the will-o'-the-wisp of psychological processes which are distinct from performance" (2, p. 77). While we agree that psychological processes are elusive, we are sympathetic to attempts to formulate and clarify constructs which are evidenced by performance but distinct from it. Surely an inductive inference based on a pattern of correlations cannot be dismissed as "pure speculation."

Specific Criteria Used Temporarily: The "Bootstraps" Effect

Even when a test is constructed on the basis of a specific criterion, it may ultimately be judged to have greater construct validity than the criterion. We start with a vague concept which we associate with certain observations. We then discover empirically that these observations covary with some other observation which possesses greater reliability or is more intimately correlated with relevant experimental changes than is the original measure, or both. For example, the notion of temperature arises because some objects feel hotter to the touch than others. The expansion of a mercury column does not have face validity as in index of hotness. But it turns out that (*a*) there is a statistical relation between expansion and sensed temperature; (*b*) observers employ the mercury method with good interobserver agreement; (*c*) the regularity of observed relations is increased by using the thermometer (e.g., melting points of samples of the same material vary little on the thermometer; we obtain nearly linear relations between mercury measures and pressure of a gas). Finally, (*d*) a theoretical structure involving unobservable microevents—the kinetic theory—is worked out which explains the relation of mercury expansion to heat. This whole process of conceptual enrichment begins with what in retrospect we see as an extremely fallible "criterion"—the human temperature sense. That original criterion has now been relegated to a peripheral position. We have lifted ourselves by our bootstraps, but in a legitimate and fruitful way.

Similarly, the Binet scale was first valued because children's scores tended to agree with judgments by schoolteachers. If it had not shown this agreement, it would have been discarded along with reaction time and the other measures of ability previously tried. Teacher judgments once constituted the criterion against which the individual intelligence test was validated. But if today a child's IQ is 135 and three of his teachers complain about how stupid he is, we do not conclude that the test has failed. Quite to the contrary, if no error in test procedure can be argued, we treat the test score as a valid statement about an important quality, and define our task as that of finding out what other variables—personality, study skills, etc.—modify achievement or distort teacher judgment.

Experimentation to Investigate Construct Validity

Validation Procedures

We can use many methods in construct validation. Attention should particularly be drawn to Macfarlane's survey of these methods as they apply to projective devices (41).

Group differences. If our understanding of a construct leads us to expect two groups to differ on the test, this expectation may be tested directly. Thus Thurstone and Chave validated the Scale for Measuring Attitude Toward the Church by showing score differences between church members and nonchurchgoers. Churchgoing is not *the* criterion of attitude, for the purpose of the test is to measure something other than the crude sociological fact of church attendance; on the other hand, failure to find a difference would have seriously challenged the test.

Only coarse correspondence between test and group designation is expected. Too great a correspondence between the two would indicate that the test is to some degree invalid, because members of the groups are expected to overlap on the test. Intelligence test items are selected initially on the basis of a correspondence to age, but an item that correlates .95 with age in an elementary school sample would surely be suspect.

Correlation matrices and factor analysis. If two tests are presumed to measure the same construct, a correlation between them is predicted. (An exception is noted where some second attribute has positive loading in the first test and negative loading in the second test; then a low correlation is expected. This is a testable interpretation provided

an external measure of either the first or the second variable exists.) If the obtained correlation departs from the expectation, however, there is no way to know whether the fault lies in test A, test B, or the formulation of the construct. A matrix of intercorrelations often points out profitable ways of dividing the construct into more meaningful parts, factor analysis being a useful computational method in such studies.

Guilford (26) has discussed the place of factor analysis in construct validation. His statements may be extracted as follows:

"The personnel psychologist wishes to know 'why his tests are valid.' He can place tests and practical criteria in a matrix and factor it to identify 'real dimensions of human personality.' A factorial description is exact and stable; it is economical in explanation; it leads to the creation of pure tests which can be combined to predict complex behaviors." It is clear that factors here function as constructs. Eysenck, in his "criterion analysis" (18), goes farther than Guilford, and shows that factoring can be used explicitly to test hypotheses about constructs.

Factors may or may not be weighted with surplus meaning. Certainly when they are regarded as "real dimensions" a great deal of surplus meaning is implied, and the interpreter must shoulder a substantial burden of proof. The alternative view is to regard factors as defining a working reference frame, located in a convenient manner in the "space" defined by all behaviors of a given type. Which set of factors from a given matrix is "most useful" will depend partly on predilections, but in essence the best construct is the one around which we can build the greatest number of inferences, in the most direct fashion.

Studies of internal structure. For many constructs, evidence of homogeneity within the test is relevant in judging validity. If a trait such as *dominance* is hypothesized, and the items inquire about behaviors subsumed under this label, then the hypothesis appears to require that these items be generally intercorrelated. Even low correlations, if consistent, would support the argument that people may be fruitfully described in terms of a generalized tendency to dominate or not dominate. The general quality would have power to predict behavior in a variety of situations represented by the specific items. Item-test correlations and certain reliability formulas describe internal consistency.

It is unwise to list uninterpreted data of this sort under the heading "validity" in test manuals, as some authors have done. High internal consistency may *lower* validity. Only if the underlying theory of the trait being measured calls for high item intercorrelations do the correlations support construct validity. Negative item-test correlations may support construct validity, provided that the items with negative correlations are believed irrelevant to the postulated construct and serve as suppressor variables (31, pp. 431–436; 44).

Study of distinctive subgroups of items within a test may set an upper limit to construct validity by showing that irrelevant elements influence scores. Thus a study of the PMA space tests shows that variance can be partially accounted for by a response set, tendency to mark many figures as similar (12). An internal factor analysis of the PEA Interpretation of Data Test shows that in addition to measuring reasoning skills, the test score is strongly influenced by a tendency to say "probably true" rather than "certainly true," regardless of item content (17). On the other hand, a study of item groupings in the DAT Mechanical Comprehension Test permitted rejection of the hypothesis that knowledge about specific topics such as gears made a substantial contribution to scores (13).

Studies of change over occasions. The stability of test scores ("retest reliability," Cattell's "N-technique") may be relevant to construct validation. Whether a high degree of stability is encouraging or discouraging for the proposed interpretation depends upon the theory defining the construct.

More powerful than the retest after uncontrolled intervening experiences is the retest with experimental intervention. If a transient influence swings test scores over a wide range, there are definite limits on the extent to which a test result can be interpreted as reflecting the typical behavior of the individual. These are examples of experiments which have indicated upper limits to test validity: studies of differences associated with the examiner in projective testing, of change of score under alternative directions ("tell the truth" vs. "make yourself look good to an employer"), and of coachability of mental tests. We may recall Gulliksen's distinction (27): When the coaching is of a sort that improves the pupil's intellectual functioning in school, the test which is affected by the coaching has validity as a measure of intellectual functioning; if the coaching improves test taking but not school performance, the test which responds to the coaching has poor validity as a measure of this construct.

Sometimes, where differences between individuals are difficult to assess by any means other than the test, the experimenter validates by determining whether the test can detect induced intra-individual differences. One might hypothesize that the Zeigarnik effect is a measure of ego involvement, i.e., that with ego involvement there is more recall of incomplete tasks. To support such an interpretation, the investigator will try to induce ego involvement on some task by appropriate directions and compare subjects' recall with their recall for tasks where there was a contrary induction. Sometimes the intervention is drastic. Porteus finds (53) that brain-operated patients show disruption of performance on his maze, but do not show impaired performance on conventional verbal tests and argues therefrom that his test is a better measure of planfulness.

Studies of process. One of the best ways of determining informally what accounts for variability on a test is the observation of the person's process of performance. If it is supposed, for example, that a test measures mathematical competence, and yet observation of students' errors shows that erroneous reading of the question is common, the implications of a low score are altered. Lucas in this way showed that the Navy Relative Movement Test, an aptitude test, actually involved two different abilities: spatial visualization and mathematical reasoning (39).

Mathematical analysis of scoring procedures may provide important negative evidence on construct validity. A recent analysis of "empathy" tests is perhaps worth citing (14). "Empathy" has been operationally defined in many studies by the ability of a judge to predict what responses will be given on some questionnaire by a subject he has observed briefly. A mathematical argument has shown, however, that the scores depend on several attributes of the judge which enter into his perception of *any* individual, and that they therefore cannot be interpreted as evidence of his ability to interpret cues offered by particular others, or his intuition.

The Numerical Estimate of Construct Validity

There is an understandable tendency to seek a "construct validity coefficient." A numerical statement of the degree of construct validity would be a statement of the proportion of the test score variance that is attributable to the construct variable. This numerical estimate can sometimes be arrived at by a factor analysis, but since present methods of factor analysis are based on linear relations, more general methods will ultimately be needed to deal with many quantitative problems of construct validation.

Rarely will it be possible to estimate definite "construct saturations," because no factor corresponding closely to the construct will be available. One can only hope to set upper and lower bounds to the "loading." If "creativity" is defined as something independent of knowledge, then a correlation of .40 between a presumed test of creativity and a test of arithmetic knowledge would indicate that at least 16 per cent of the reliable test variance is irrelevant to creativity as defined. Laboratory performance on problems such as Maier's "hatrack" would scarcely be an ideal measure of creativity, but it would be somewhat relevant. If its correlation with the test is .60, this permits a tentative estimate of 36 per cent as a lower bound. (The estimate is tentative because the test might overlap with the irrelevant portion of the laboratory measure.) The saturation seems to lie between 36 and 84 per cent; a cumulation of studies would provide better limits.

It should be particularly noted that rejecting the null hypothesis does not finish the job of construct validation (35, p. 284). The problem is not to conclude that the test "is valid" for measuring the construct variable. The task is to state as definitely as possible the degree of validity the test is presumed to have.

The Logic of Construct Validation

Construct validation takes place when an investigator believes that his instrument reflects a particular construct, to which are attached certain meanings. The proposed interpretation generates specific testable hypothesis, which are a means of confirming or disconfirming the claim. The philosophy of science which we believe does most justice to actual scientific practice will now be briefly and dogmatically set forth. Readers interested in further study of the philosophical underpinning are referred to the works by Braithwaite (6, especially Chapter III), Carnap (7; 8, pp. 56–69), Pap (51), Sellars (55, 56), Feigl (19, 20), Beck (4), Kneale (37, pp. 92–110), Hempel (29; 30, Sec. 7).

The Nomological Net

The fundamental principles are these:

1. Scientifically speaking, to "make clear what something *is*" means to set forth the laws in which it occurs. We shall refer to the interlocking system of laws which constitute a theory as a *nomological network*.

2. The laws in a nomological network may relate (*a*) observable properties or quantities to each other; or (*b*) theoretical constructs to observables; or (*c*) different theoretical constructs to one another. These "laws" may be statistical or deterministic.

3. A necessary condition for a construct to be scientifically admissible is that it occur in a nomological net, at least *some* of whose laws involve observables. Admissible constructs may be remote from observation, i.e., a long derivation may intervene between the nomologicals which implicitly define the construct, and the (derived) nomologicals of type *a*. These latter propositions permit predictions about events. The construct is not "reduced" to the observations, but only combined with other constructs in the net to make predictions about observables.

4. "Learning more about" a theoretical construct is a matter of elaborating the nomological network in which it occurs, or of increasing the definiteness of the components. At least in the early history of a construct the network will be limited, and the construct will as yet have few connections.

5. An enrichment of the net such as adding a construct or a relation to theory is justified if it generates nomologicals that are confirmed by observation or if it reduces the number of nomologicals required to predict the same observations. When observations will not fit into the network as it stands, the scientist has a certain freedom in selecting where to modify the network. That is, there may be alternative constructs or ways of organizing the net which for the time being are equally defensible.

6. We can say that "operations" which are qualitatively very different "overlap" or "measure the same thing" if their positions in the nomological net tie them to the same construct variable. Our confidence in this identification depends upon the amount of inductive support we have for the regions of the net involved. It is not necessary that a direct observational comparison of the two operations be made—we may be content with an intranetwork proof indicating that the two operations yield estimates of the same network-defined quantity. Thus, physicists are content to speak of the "temperature" of the sun and the "temperature" of a gas at room temperature even though the test operations are nonoverlapping because this identification makes theoretical sense.

With these statements of scientific methodology in mind, we return to the specific problem of construct validity as applied to psychological tests. The preceding guide rules should reassure the "toughminded," who fear that allowing construct validation opens the door to nonconfirmable test claims. *The answer is that unless the network makes contact with observations, and exhibits explicit, public steps of inference, construct validation cannot be claimed.* An admissible psychological construct must be behavior-relevant (59, p. 15). For most tests intended to measure constructs, adequate criteria do not exist. This being the case, many such tests have been left unvalidated, or a finespun network of rationalizations has been offered as if it were validation. Rationalization is not construct validation. One who claims that his test reflects a construct cannot maintain his claim in the face of recurrent negative results because these results show that his construct is too loosely defined to yield verifiable inferences.

A rigorous (though perhaps probabilistic) chain of inference is required to establish a test as a measure of a construct. To validate a claim that a test measures a construct, a nomological net surrounding the concept must exist. When a construct is fairly new, there may be few specifiable associations by which to pin down the concept. As research proceeds, the construct sends out roots in many directions, which attach it to more and more facts or other constructs. Thus the electron has more accepted properties than the neutrino; *numerical ability* has more than the *second space factor*.

"Acceptance," which was critical in criterion-oriented and content validities, has now appeared in construct validity. Unless substantially the same nomological net is accepted by the several users of the construct, public validation is impossible. If A uses *aggressiveness* to mean overt assault on others, and B's usage includes repressed hostile reactions, evidence which convinces B that a test measures *aggressiveness* convinces A that the test does not. Hence, the investigator who proposes to establish a test as a measure of a construct must specify his network or theory sufficiently clearly that others can accept or reject it (cf. 41, p. 406). A consumer of the test who rejects the author's theory cannot accept the author's validation. He must validate the test for himself, if he wishes to show that it represents the construct as *he* defines it.

Two general qualifications are in order with reference to the methodological principles 1–6 set forth at the beginning of this section. Both of them concern the amount of "theory," in any high-level sense of that word, which enters into a construct-defining network of laws or lawlike statements. We do not wish to convey the impression that one always has a very elaborate theoretical network, rich in hypothetical processes or entities.

Constructs as inductive summaries. In the early stages of development of a construct or even at more advanced stages when our orientation is thoroughly practical, little or no theory in the usual sense of the word need be involved. In the extreme case the hypothesized laws are formulated entirely in terms of descriptive (observational) dimensions although not all of the relevant observations have actually been made.

The hypothesized network "goes beyond the data" only in the limited sense that it purports to *characterize* the behavior facets which belong to an observable but as yet only partially sampled cluster; hence, it generates predictions about hitherto unsampled regions of the phenotypic space. Even though no unobservables or high-order theoretical constructs are introduced, an element of inductive extrapolation appears in the claim that a cluster including some elements not-yet-observed has been identified. Since, as in any sorting or abstracting task involving a finite set of complex elements, several nonequivalent bases of categorization are available, the investigator may choose a hypothesis which generates erroneous predictions. The failure of a supposed, hitherto untried, member of the cluster to behave in the manner said to be characteristic of the group, or the finding that a nonmember of the postulated cluster does behave in this manner, may modify greatly our tentative construct.

For example, one might build an intelligence test on the basis of his background notions of "intellect," including vocabulary, arithmetic calculation, general information, similarities, two-point threshold, reaction time, and line bisection as subtests. The first four of these correlate, and he extracts a huge first factor. This becomes a second approximation of the intelligence construct, described by its pattern of loadings on the four tests. The other three tests have negligible loading on any common factor. On this evidence the investigator reinterprets intelligence as "manipulation of words." Subsequently it is discovered that test-stupid people are rated as unable to express their ideas, are easily taken in by fallacious arguments, and misread complex directions. These data support the "linguistic" definition of intelligence and the test's claim of validity *for* that construct. But then a block design test with pantomime instructions is found to be strongly saturated with the first factor. Immediately the purely "linguistic" interpretation of Factor I becomes suspect. This finding, taken together with our initial acceptance of the others as relevant to the background concept of intelligence, forces us to reinterpret the concept once again.

If we simply *list* the tests or traits which have been shown to be saturated with the "factor" or which belong to the cluster, no construct is employed. As soon as we even *summarize the properties* of this group of indicators—we are already making some guesses. Intensional characterization of a domain is hazardous since it selects (abstracts) properties and implies that new tests sharing those properties will behave as do the known tests in the cluster, and that tests not sharing them will not.

The difficulties in merely "characterizing the surface cluster" are strikingly exhibited by the use of certain special and extreme groups for purposes of construct validation. The P_d scale of MMPI was originally derived and cross-validated upon hospitalized patients diagnosed "Psychopathic personality, asocial and amoral type" (42). Further research shows the scale to have a limited degree of predictive and concurrent validity for "delinquency" more broadly defined (5, 28). Several studies show associations between P_d and very special "criterion" groups which it would be

ludicrous to identify as *"the* criterion" in the traditional sense. If one lists these heterogeneous groups and tries to characterize them intensionally, he faces enormous conceptual difficulties. For example, a recent survey of hunting accidents in Minnesota showed that hunters who had "carelessly" shot someone were significantly elevated on P_d when compared with other hunters (48). This is in line with one's theoretical expectations; when you ask MMPI "experts" to predict for such a group they invariably predict P_d or M_a or both. The finding seems therefore to lend some slight support to the construct validity of the P_d scale. But of course it would be nonsense to *define* the P_d component "operationally" in terms of, say, accident proneness. We might try to subsume the original phenotype and the hunting-accident proneness under some broader category, such as "Disposition to violate society's rules, whether legal, moral, or just *sensible.*" But now we have ceased to have a neat operational criterion, and are using instead a rather vague and wide-range class. Besides, there is worse to come. We want the class specification to cover a group trend that (nondelinquent) high school students judged by their peer group as least "responsible" score over a full sigma higher on P_d than those judged most "responsible" (23, p. 75). Most of the behaviors contributing to such sociometric choices fall well within the range of socially permissible action; the proffered criterion specification is still too restrictive. Again, any clinician familiar with MMPI lore would predict an elevated P_d on a sample of (nondelinquent) professional actors. Chyatte's confirmation of this prediction (10) tends to support *both:* (*a*) the theory sketch of "what the P_d factor is, psychologically"; and (*b*) the claim of the P_d scale to construct validity for this hypothetical factor. Let the reader try his hand at writing a brief phenotypic criterion specification that will cover both trigger-happy hunters and Broadway actors! And if he should be ingenious enough to achieve this, does his definition also encompass Hovey's report that high P_d predicts the judgments "not shy" and "unafraid of mental patients" made upon nurses by their supervisors (32, p. 143)? And then we have Gough's report that *low* P_d is associated with ratings as "good-natured" (24, p. 40), and Roessell's data showing that high P_d is predictive of "dropping out of high school" (54). The point is that all seven of these "criterion" dispositions would be readily guessed by any clinician having even superficial familiarity with MMPI interpretation; but to mediate these inferences explicitly requires quite a few hypotheses about dynamics, constituting an admittedly sketchy (but far from vacuous) network defining the genotype *psychopathic deviate*.

Vagueness of present psychological laws. This line of thought leads directly to our second important qualification upon the network schema. The idealized picture is one of a tidy set of postulates which jointly entail the desired theorems; since some of the theorems are coordinated to the observation base, the system constitutes an implicit definition of the theoretical primitives and gives them an indirect empirical meaning. In practice, of course, even the most advanced physical sciences only approximate this ideal. Questions of "categoricalness" and the like, such as logicians raise about pure calculi, are hardly even stable for empirical networks. (What, for example, would be the desiderata of a "well-formed formula" in molar behavior theory?) Psychology works with crude, half-explicit formulations. We do not worry about such advanced formal questions as "whether all molar-behavior statements are decidable by appeal to the postulates" because we know that no existing theoretical network suffices to predict even the *known* descriptive laws. Nevertheless, the sketch of a network is there; if it were not, we would not be saying

anything intelligible about our constructs. We do not have the rigorous implicit definitions of formal calculi (which still, be it noted, usually permit of a multiplicity of interpretations). Yet the vague, avowedly incomplete network still gives the constructs whatever meaning they do have. When the network is very incomplete, having many strands missing entirely and some constructs tied in only by tenuous threads, then the "implicit definition" of these constructs is disturbingly loose; one might say that the meaning of the constructs is underdetermined. *Since the meaning of theoretical constructs is set forth by stating the laws in which they occur, our incomplete knowledge of the laws of nature produces a vagueness in our constructs* (see Hempel, 30; Kaplan, 34; Pap, 51). We will be able to say "what anxiety is" when we know all of the laws involving it; meanwhile, since we are in the process of discovering these laws, we do not yet know precisely what anxiety is.

Conclusions Regarding the Network After Experimentation

The proposition that x per cent of test variance is accounted for by the construct is inserted into the accepted network. The network then generates a testable prediction about the relation of the test scores to certain other variables, and the investigator gathers data. If prediction and result are in harmony, he can retain his belief that the test measures the construct. The construct is at best adopted, never demonstrated to be "correct."

We do not first "prove" the theory, and then validate the test, nor conversely. In any probable inductive type of inference from a pattern of observations, we examine the relation between the total network of theory and observations. The system involves propositions relating test to construct, construct to other constructs, and finally relating some of these constructs to observables. In ongoing research the chain of inference is very complicated. Kelly and Fiske (36, p. 124) give a complex diagram showing the numerous inferences required in validating a prediction from assessment techniques, where theories about the criterion situation are as integral a part of the prediction as are the test data. A predicted empirical relationship permits us to test all the propositions leading to that prediction. Traditionally the proposition claiming to interpret the test has been set apart as the hypothesis being tested, but actually the evidence is significant for all parts of the chain. If the prediction is not confirmed, any link in the chain may be wrong.

A theoretical network can be divided into subtheories used in making particular predictions. All the events successfully predicted through a subtheory are of course evidence in favor of that theory. Such a subtheory may be so well confirmed by voluminous and diverse evidence that we can reasonably view a particular experiment as relevant only to the test's validity. If the theory, combined with a proposed test interpretation, mispredicts in this case, it is the latter which must be abandoned. On the other hand, the accumulated evidence for a test's construct validity may be so strong that an instance of misprediction will force us to modify the subtheory employing the construct rather than deny the claim that the test measures the construct.

Most cases in psychology today lie somewhere between these extremes. Thus, suppose we fail to find a greater incidence of "homosexual signs" in the Rorschach records of paranoid patients. Which is more strongly disconfirmed— the Rorschach signs or the orthodox theory of paranoia? The negative finding shows the bridge between the two to be undependable, but this is all we can say. The bridge cannot be used unless one end is placed on solider ground. The

investigator must decide which end it is best to relocate.

Numerous successful predictions dealing with phenotypically diverse "criteria" give greater weight to the claim of construct validity than do fewer predictions, or predictions involving very similar behaviors. In arriving at diverse predictions, the hypothesis of test validity is connected each time to a subnetwork largely independent of the portion previously used. Success of these derivations testifies to the inductive power of the test-validity statement, and renders it unlikely that an equally effective alternative can be offered.

Implications of Negative Evidence

The investigator whose prediction and data are discordant must make strategic decisions. His result can be interpreted in three ways:

1. The test does not measure the construct variable.

2. The theoretical network which generated the hypothesis is incorrect.

3. The experimental design failed to test the hypothesis properly. (Strictly speaking this may be analyzed as a special case of 2, but in practice the distinction is worth making.)

For further research. If a specific fault of procedure makes the third a reasonable possibility, his proper response is to perform an adequate study, meanwhile making no report. When faced with the other two alternatives, he may decide that his test does not measure the construct adequately. Following that decision, he will perhaps prepare and validate a new test. Any rescoring or new interpretative procedure for the original instrument, like a new test, requires validation *by means of a fresh body of data.*

The investigator may regard interpretation 2 as more likely to lead to eventual advances. It is legitimate for the investigator to call the network defining the construct into question, if he has confidence in the test. Should the investigator decide that some step in the network unsound, he may be able to invent an alternative network. Perhaps he modifies the network by splitting a concept into two or more portions, e.g., by designating types of *anxiety*, or perhaps he specifies added conditions under which a generalization holds. When an investigator modifies the theory in such a manner, he is now required to *gather a fresh body of data* to test the altered hypotheses. This step should normally precede publication of the modified theory. If the new data are consistent with the modified network, he is free from the fear that his nomologicals were gerrymandered to fit the peculiarities of his first sample of observations. He can now trust his test to some extent, because his test results behave as predicted.

The choice among alternatives, like any strategic decision, is a gamble as to which course of action is the best investment of effort. Is it wise to modify the theory? That depends on how well the system is confirmed by prior data, and how well the modifications fit available observations. Is it worth while to modify the test in the hope that it will fit the construct? That depends on how much evidence there is—apart from this abortive experiment—to support the hope, and also on how much it is worth to the investigator's ego to salvage the test. The choice among alternatives is a matter of research planning.

For practical use of the test. The consumer can accept a test as a measure of a construct only when there is a strong positive fit between predictions and subsequent data. When the evidence from a proper investigation of a published test is essentially negative, it should be reported as a stop sign to discourage use of the test pending a reconciliation of test and construct, or final abandonment of the test. If the test has not been published, it should be restricted to research use until some

degree of validity is established (1). The consumer can await the results of the investigator's gamble with confidence that proper application of the scientific method will ultimately tell whether the test has value. Until the evidence is in, he has no justification for employing the test as a basis for terminal decisions. The test may serve, at best, only as a source of suggestions about individuals to be confirmed by other evidence (15, 47).

There are two perspectives in test validation. From the viewpoint of the psychological practitioner, the burden of proof is on the test. A test should not be used to measure a trait until its proponent establishes that predictions made from such measures are consistent with the best available theory of the trait. In the view of the test developer, however, both the test and the theory are under scrutiny. He is free to say *to himself privately*, "If my test disagrees with the theory, so much the worse for the theory." This way lies delusion, unless he continues his research using a better theory.

Reporting of Positive Results

The test developer who finds positive correspondence between his proposed interpretation and data is expected to report the basis for his validity claim. Defending a claim of construct validity is a major task, not to be satisfied by a discourse without data. The *Technical Recommendations* have little to say on reporting of construct validity. Indeed, the only detailed suggestions under that heading refer to correlations of the test with other measures, together with a cross reference to some other sections of the report. The two key principles, however, call for the most comprehensive type of reporting. The manual for any test "should report all available information which will assist the user in determining what psychological attributes account for variance in test scores"

(59, p. 27). And, "The manual for a test which is used primarily to assess postulated attributes of the individual should outline the theory on which the test is based and organize whatever partial validity data there are to show in what way they support the theory" (59, p. 28). It is recognized, by a classification as "very desirable" rather than "essential," that the latter recommendation goes beyond present practice of test authors.

The proper goals in reporting construct validation are to make clear (a) what interpretation is proposed, (b) how adequately the writer believes this interpretation is substantiated, and (c) what evidence and reasoning lead him to this belief. Without a the construct validity of the test is of no use to the consumer. Without b the consumer must carry the entire burden of evaluating the test research. Without c the consumer or reviewer is being asked to take a and b on faith. The test manual cannot always present an exhaustive statement on these points, but it should summarize and indicate where complete statements may be found.

To specify the interpretation, the writer must state what construct he has in mind, and what meaning he gives to that construct. For a construct which has a short history and has built up few connotations, it will be fairly easy to indicate the presumed properties of the construct, i.e., the nomologicals in which it appears. For a construct with a longer history, a summary of properties and references to previous theoretical discussions may be appropriate. It is especially critical to distinguish proposed interpretations from other meanings previously given the same construct. The validator faces no small task; he must somehow communicate a theory to his reader.

To evaluate his evidence calls for a statement like the conclusions from a program of research, noting what is well substantiated and what alternative

interpretations have been considered and rejected. The writer must note what portions of his proposed interpretation are speculations, extrapolations, or conclusions from insufficient data. The author has an ethical responsibility to prevent unsubstantiated interpretations from appearing as truths. A claim is unsubstantiated unless the evidence for the claim is public, so that other scientists may review the evidence, criticize the conclusions, and offer alternative interpretations.

The report of evidence in a test manual must be as complete as any research report, except where adequate public reports can be cited. Reference to something "observed by the writer in many clinical cases" is worthless as evidence. Full case reports, on the other hand, may be a valuable source of evidence so long as these cases are representative and negative instances receive due attention. The report of evidence must be interpreted with reference to the theoretical network in such a manner that the reader sees why the author regards a particular correlation or experiment as confirming (or throwing doubt upon) the proposed interpretation. Evidence collected by others must be taken fairly into account.

Validation of a Complex Test "as a Whole"

Special questions must be considered when we are investigating the validity of a test which is aimed to provide information about several constructs. In one sense, it is naive to inquire "Is this test valid?" One does not validate a test, but only a principle for making inferences. If a test yields many different types of inferences, some of them can be valid and other invalid (cf. Technical Recommendation C2: "The manual should report the validity of each type of inference for which a test is recommended"). From this point of view, every topic sentence in the typical book on Rorschach interpretation presents a hypothesis requiring validation, and one should validate inferences about each aspect of the personality separately and in turn, just as he would want information on the validity (concurrent or predictive) for each scale of MMPI.

There is, however, another defensible point of view. If a test is purely empirical, based strictly on observed connections between response to an item and some criterion, then of course the validity of one scoring key for the test does not make validation for its other scoring keys any less necessary. But a test may be developed on the basis of a theory which in itself provides a linkage between the various keys and the various criteria. Thus, while Strong's Vocational Interest Blank is developed empirically, it also rests on a "theory" that a youth can be expected to be satisfied in an occupation if he has interests common to men now happy in the occupation. When Strong finds that those with high Engineering interest scores in college are preponderantly in engineering careers 19 years later, he has partly validated the proposed use of the Engineer score (predictive validity). Since the evidence is consistent with the theory on which all the test keys were built, this evidence alone increases the presumption that the *other* keys have predictive validity. How strong is this presumption? Not very, from the viewpoint of the traditional skepticism of science. Engineering interests may stabilize early, while interests in art or management or social work are still unstable. A claim cannot be made that the whole Strong approach is valid just because one score shows predictive validity. But if thirty interest scores were investigated longitudinally and all of them showed the type of validity predicted by Strong's theory, we would indeed be caviling to say that this evidence gives no confidence in the long-range validity of the thirty-first score.

Confidence in a theory is increased as more relevant evidence confirms it, but it is always possible that tomorrow's investigation will render the theory obsolete. The Technical Recommendations suggest a rule of reason, and ask for evidence for each *type* of inference for which a test is recommended. It is stated that no test developer can present predictive validities for all possible criteria; similarly, no developer can run all possible experimental tests of his proposed interpretation. But the recommendation is more subtle than advice that a lot of validation is better than a little.

Consider the Rorschach test. It is used for many inferences, made by means of nomological networks at several levels. At a low level are the simple unrationalized correspondences presumed to exist between certain signs and psychiatric diagnoses. Validating such a sign does nothing to substantiate Rorschach theory. For other Rorschach formulas an explicit a priori rationale exists (for instance, high *F%* interpreted as implying rigid control of impulses). Each time such a sign shows correspondence with criteria, its rationale is supported just a little. At a still higher level of abstraction, a considerable body of theory surrounds the general area of *outer control*, interlacing many different constructs. As evidence cumulates, one should be able to decide what specific inference-making chains within this system can be depended upon. One should also be able to conclude—or deny— that so much of the system has stood up under test that one has some confidence in even the untested lines in the network.

In addition to relatively delimited nomological networks surrounding *control* or *aspiration*, the Rorschach interpreter usually has an overriding theory of the test as a whole. This may be a psychoanalytic theory, a theory of perception and set, or a theory stated in terms of learned habit patterns. Whatever the theory of the interpreter, whenever he validates an inference from the system, he obtains some reason for added confidence in his overriding system. His total theory is not tested, however, by experiments dealing with only one limited set of constructs. The test developer must investigate far-separated, independent sections of the network. The more diversified the predictions the system is required to make, the greater confidence we can have that only minor parts of the system will later prove faulty. Here we begin to glimpse a logic to defend the judgment that the test and its whole interpretative system is valid at some level of confidence.

There are enthusiasts who would conclude from the foregoing paragraphs that since there is some evidence of correct, diverse predictions made from the Rorschach, the test as a whole can now be accepted as validated. This conclusion overlooks the negative evidence. Just one finding contrary to expectation, based on sound research, is sufficient to wash a whole theoretical structure away. Perhaps the remains can be salvaged to form a new structure. But this structure now must be exposed to fresh risks, and sound negative evidence will destroy it in turn. There is sufficient negative evidence to prevent acceptance of the Rorschach and its accompanying interpretative structures as a whole. So long as any aspects of the overriding theory stated for the test have been disconfirmed, this structure must be rebuilt.

Talk of areas and structures may seem not to recognize those who would interpret the personality "globally." They may argue that a test is best validated in matching studies. Without going into detailed questions of matching methodology, we can ask whether such a study validates the nomological network "as a whole." The judge does employ some network in arriving at his conception of his subject, integrating specific inferences from specific data. Matching studies, if successful, demonstrate only that each judge's interpretative theory has some validity, that it is not completely a fantasy. Very high consistency between judges is required to show that they are using the same network, and very high success in matching is required to show that the network is dependable.

If inference is less than perfectly dependable, we must know which aspects of the interpretative network are least dependable and which are most dependable. Thus, even if one has considerable confidence in a test "as a whole" because of frequent successful inferences, one still returns as an ultimate aim to the request of the Technical Recommendation for separate evidence on the validity of each type of inference to be made.

Recapitulation

Construct validation was introduced in order to specify types of research required in developing tests for which the conventional views on validation are inappropriate. Personality tests, and some tests of ability, are interpreted in terms of attributes for which there is no adequate criterion. This paper indicates what sorts of evidence can substantiate such an interpretation, and how such evidence is to be interpreted. The following points made in the discussion are particularly significant.

1. A construct is defined implicitly by a network of associations or propositions in which it occurs. Constructs employed at different stages of research vary in definiteness.

2. Construct validation is possible only when some of the statements in the network lead to predicted relations among observables. While some observables may be regarded as "criteria," the construct validity of the criteria themselves is regarded as under investigation.

3. The network defining the con-

struct, and the derivation leading to the predicted observation, must be reasonably explicit so that validating evidence may be properly interpreted.

4. Many types of evidence are relevant to construct validity, including content validity, interitem correlations, interest correlations, test–"criterion" correlations, studies of stability over time, and stability under experimental intervention. High correlations and high stability may consitute either favorable or unfavorable evidence for the proposed interpretation, depending on the theory surrounding the construct.

5. When a predicted relation fails to occur, the fault may lie in the proposed interpretation of the test or in the network. Altering the network so that it can cope with the new observations is, in effect, redefining the construct. Any such new interpretation of the test must be validated by a fresh body of data before being advanced publicly. Great care is required to avoid substituting a posteriori rationalizations for proper validation.

6. Construct validity cannot generally be expressed in the form of a single simple coefficient. The data often permit one to establish upper and lower bounds for the proportion of test variance which can be attributed to the construct. The integration of diverse data into a proper interpretation cannot be an entirely quantitative process.

7. Constructs may vary in nature from those very close to "pure description" (involving little more than extrapolation of relations among observation-variables) to highly theoretical constructs involving hypothesized entities and processes, or making identifications with constructs of other sciences.

8. The investigation of a test's construct validity is not essentially different from the general scientific procedures for developing and confirming theories.

Without in the least *advocating* construct validity as preferable to the other three kinds (concurrent, predictive, content), we do believe it imperative that psychologists make a place for it in their methodological thinking, so that its rationale, its scientific legitimacy, and its dangers may become explicit and familiar. This would be preferable to the widespread current tendency to engage in what actually amounts to construct validation research and use of constructs in practical testing, while talking an "operational" methodology which, if adopted, would force research into a mold it does not fit.

REFERENCES

1. AMERICAN PSYCHOLOGICAL ASSOCIATION. *Ethical standards of psychologists.* Washington, D.C.: American Psychological Association, Inc., 1953.

2. ANASTASI, ANNE. The concept of validity in the interpretation of test scores. *Educ. psychol. Measmt,* 1950, 10, 67–78.

3. BECHTOLDT, H. P. Selection. In S. S. STEVENS (Ed.), *Handbook of experimental psychology.* New York: Wiley, 1951. Pp. 1237–1267.

4. BECK, L. W. Constructions and inferred entities. *Phil. Sci.,* 1950, 17, Reprinted in H. FEIGL and M. BRODBECK (Eds.), *Readings in the*

philosophy of science. New York: Appleton-Century-Crofts, 1953. Pp. 368–381.

5. BLAIR, W. R. N. A comparative study of disciplinary offenders and non-offenders in the Canadian Army. *Canad. J. Psychol.,* 1950, 4, 49–62.

6. BRAITHWAITE, R. B. *Scientific explanation.* Cambridge: Cambridge Univer. Press, 1953.

7. CARNAP, R. Empiricism, semantics, and ontology. *Rév. int. de Phil.,* 1950, II, 20–40. Reprinted in P. P. WIENER (Ed.), *Readings in philosophy of science.* New York: Scribner's, 1953. Pp. 509–521.

8. CARNAP, R. *Foundations of logic and*

mathematics. *International encyclopedia of unified science,* **I**, No. 3. Pp. 56–69 reprinted as "The interpretation of physics" in H. FEIGL and M. BRODBECK (Eds.), *Readings in the philosophy of science.* New York: Appleton-Century-Crofts, 1953. Pp. 309–318.

9. CHILD, I. L. Personality. *Annu. Rev. Psychol.,* 1954, **5**, 149–171.

10. CHYATTE, C. Psychological characteristics of a group of professional actors. *Occupations,* 1949, **27**, 245–250.

11. CRONBACH, L. J. *Essentials of psychological testing.* New York: Harper, 1949.

12. CRONBACH, L. J. Further evidence on response sets and test design. *Educ. psychol. Measmt,* 1950, **10**, 3–31.

13. CRONBACH, L. J. Coefficient alpha and the internal structure of tests. *Psychometrika,* 1951, **16**, 297–335.

14. CRONBACH, L. J. Processes affecting scores on "understanding of others" and "assumed similarity." *Psychol. Bull.,* 1955, **52**, 177–193.

15. CRONBACH, L. J. The counselor's problems from the prespective of communication theory. In VIVIAN H. HEWER (Ed.), *New perspectives in counseling.* Minneapolis: Univer. of Minnesota Press, 1955.

16. CURETON, E. E. Validity. In E. F. LINDQUIST (Ed.), *Educational measurement.* Washington, D. C.: American Council on Education, 1950. Pp. 621–695.

17. DAMRIN, DORA E. A comparative study of information derived from a diagnostic problem-solving test by logical and factorial methods of scoring. Unpublished doctor's dissertation, Univer. of Illinois, 1952.

18. EYSENCK, H. J. Criterion analysis— an application of the hypothetico-deductive method in factor analysis. *Psychol. Rev.,* 1950, **57**, 38–53.

19. FEIGL, H. Existential hypotheses. *Phil. Sci.,* 1950, **17**, 35–62.

20. FEIGL, H. Confirmability and confirmation. *Rev. int. de Phil.,* 1951, **5**, 1–12. Reprinted in P. P. WIENER (Ed.), *Readings in philosophy of science.* New York: Scribner's, 1953, pp. 522–530.

21. GAYLORD, R. H. Conceptual consistency and criterion equivalence: a dual approach to criterion analysis. Unpublished manuscript (PRB Research Note No. 17). Copies obtainable from ASTIA-DSC, AD-21 440.

22. GOODENOUGH, FLORENCE L. *Mental testing.* New York: Rinehart, 1950.

23. GOUGH, H. G., McCLOSKY, H., & MEEHL, P. E. A personality scale for social responsibility. *J. abnorm. soc. Psychol.,* 1952, **47**, 73–80.

24. GOUGH, H. G., McKEE, M. G., & YANDELL, R. J. Adjective check list analyses of a number of selected psychometric and assessment variables. Unpublished manuscript. Berkeley: IPAR, 1953.

25. GUILFORD, J. P. New standards for test evaluation. *Educ. psychol. Measmt,* 1946, **6**, 427–439.

26. GUILFORD, J. P. Factor analysis in a test-development program. *Psychol. Rev.,* 1948, **55**, 79–94.

27. GULLIKSEN, H. Intrinsic validity. *Amer. Psychologist,* 1950, **5**, 511–517.

28. HATHAWAY, S. R., & MONACHESI, E. D. *Analyzing and predicting juvenile delinquency with the MMPI.* Minneapolis: Univer. of Minnesota Press, 1953.

29. HEMPEL, C. G. Problems and changes in the empiricist criterion of meaning. *Rev. int. de Phil.,* 1950, **4**, 41–63. Reprinted in L. LINSKY, *Semantics and the philosophy of language.* Urbana: Univer. of Illinois Press, 1952. Pp. 163–185.

30. HEMPEL, C. G. *Fundamentals of concept formation in empirical science.* Chicago: Univer. of Chicago Press, 1952.

31. HORST, P. The prediction of personal adjustment. *Soc. Sci. Res. Council Bull.,* 1941, No. 48.

32. HOVEY, H. B. MMPI profiles and personality characteristics. *J. consult. Psychol.,* 1953, **17**, 142–146.

33. JENKINS, J. G. Validity for what? *J. consult. Psychol.,* 1946, **10**, 93–98.

34. KAPLAN, A. Definition and specification of meaning. *J. Phil.,* 1946, **43**, 281–288.

35. KELLY, E. L. Theory and techniques of assessment. *Annu. Rev. Psychol.,* 1954, **5**, 281–311.

36. KELLY, E. L., & FISKE, D. W. *The prediction of performance in clinical psychology.* Ann Arbor: Univer. of Michigan Press, 1951.

37. KNEALE, W. *Probability and induction.* Oxford: Clarendon Press, 1949. Pages 92–110 reprinted as "Induction, explanation, and transcendent hypotheses" in H. FEIGL and M. BRODBECK (Eds.), *Readings in the philosophy of science.* New York: Appleton-Century-Crofts, 1953, pp. 353–367.

38. LINDQUIST, E. F. *Educational measurement.* Washington, D. C.: American Council on Education, 1950.

39. LUCAS, C. M. Analysis of the relative movement test by a method of individual interviews. *Bur. Naval Personnel Res. Rep.,* Contract Nonr-694 (00), NR 151-13, Educational Testing Service, March 1953.

40. MACCORQUODALE, K., & MEEHL, P. E. On a distinction between hypothetical constructs and intervening variables. *Psychol. Rev.,* 1948, **55,** 95–107.

41. MACFARLANE, JEAN W. Problems of validation inherent in projective methods. *Amer. J. Orthopsychiat.,* 1942, **12,** 405–410.

42. MCKINLEY, J. C., & HATHAWAY, S. R. The MMPI: V. Hysteria, hypomania, and psychopathic deviate. *J. appl. Psychol.,* 1944, **28,** 153–174.

43. MCKINLEY, J. C., HATHAWAY, S. R., & MEEHL, P. E. The MMPI: VI. The K scale. *J. consult. Psychol.,* 1948, **12,** 20–31.

44. MEEHL, P. E. A simple algebraic development of Horst's suppressor variables. *Amer. J. Psychol.,* 1945, **58,** 550–554.

45. MEEHL, P. E. An investigation of a general normality or control factor in personality testing. *Psychol. Monogr.,* 1945, **59,** No. 4 (Whole No. 274).

46. MEEHL, P. E. *Clinical vs. statistical prediction.* Minneapolis: Univer. of Minnesota Press, 1954.

47. MEEHL, P. E., & ROSEN, A. Antecedent probability and the efficiency of psychometric signs, patterns or cutting scores. *Psychol Bull.,* 1955, **52,** 194–216.

48. *Minnesota Hunter Casualty Study.* St. Paul: Jacob Schmidt Brewing Company, 1954.

49. MOSIER, C. I. A critical examination of the concepts of face validity. *Educ. psychol. Measmt,* 1947, **7,** 191–205.

50. MOSIER, C. I. Problems and designs of cross-validation. *Educ. psychol. Measmt,* 1951, **11,** 5–12.

51. PAP, A. Reduction-sentences and open concepts. *Methodos,* 1953, **5,** 3–30.

52. PEAK, HELEN. Problems of objective observation. In L. FESTINGER and D. KATZ (Eds.), *Research methods in the behavioral sciences.* New York: Dryden Press, 1953. Pp. 243–300.

53. PORTEUS, S. D. *The Porteus maze test and intelligence.* Palo Alto: Pacific Books, 1950.

54. ROESSEL, F. P. MMPI results for high school drop-outs and graduates. Unpublished doctor's dissertation, Univer. of Minnesota, 1954.

55. SELLARS, W. S. Concepts as involving laws and inconceivable without them. *Phil. Sci.,* 1948, **15,** 287–315.

56. SELLARS, W. S. Some reflections on language games. *Phil. Sci.,* 1954, **21,** 204–228.

57. SPIKER, C. C., & MCCANDLESS, B. R. The concept of intelligence and the philosophy of science. *Psychol. Rev.,* 1954, **61,** 255–267.

58. Technical recommendations for psychological tests and diagnostic techniques: preliminary proposal. *Amer. Psychologist,* 1952, **7,** 461–476.

59. Technical recommendations for psychological tests and diagnostic techniques. *Psychol. Bull. Supplement,* 1954, **51,** 2, Part 2, 1–38.

60. THURSTONE, L. L. The criterion problem in personality research. *Psychometric Lab. Rep.,* No. 78. Chicago: Univer. of Chicago, 1952.

Convergent and Discriminant Validation by the Multitrait-Multimethod Matrix

Donald T. Campbell and Donald W. Fiske

In the cumulative experience with measures of individual differences over the past 50 years, tests have been accepted as valid or discarded as invalid by research experiences of many sorts. The criteria suggested in this paper are all to be found in such cumulative evaluations, as well as in the recent discussions of validity. These criteria are clarified and implemented when considered jointly in the context of a multitrait-multimethod matrix. Aspects of the validational process receiving particular emphasis are these:

1. Validation is typically *convergent,* a confirmation by independent measurement procedures. Independence of methods is a common denominator among the major types of validity (excepting content validity) insofar as they are to be distinguished from reliability.

2. For the justification of novel trait measures, for the validation of test in-

The new data analyses reported in this paper were supported by funds from the Graduate School of Northwestern University of Chicago and by the Department of Psychology of the university. We are also indebted to numerous colleagues for their thoughtful criticisms and encouragement of an earlier draft of this paper, especially Benjamin S. Bloom, R. Darrell Bock, Desmond S. Cartwright, Loren J. Chapman, Lee J. Cronbach, Carl P. Duncan, Lyle V. Jones, Joe Kamiya, Wilbur L. Layton, Jane Loevinger, Paul E. Meehl, Marshall H. Segall, Thornton B. Roby, Robert C. Tryon, Michael Wertheimer, and Robert F. Winch.

Reprinted with the permission of the American Psychological Association and the authors from *Psychological Bulletin,* 1959, **56,** 81–105.

terpretation, or for the establishment of construct validity, *discriminant* validation as well as convergent validation is required. Tests can be invalidated by too high correlations with other tests from which they were intended to differ.

3. Each test or task employed for measurement purposes is a *trait-method unit,* a union of a particular trait content with measurement procedures not specific to that content. The systematic variance among test scores can be due to responses to the measurement features as well as responses to the trait content.

4. In order to examine discriminant validity, and in order to estimate the relative contributions of trait and method variance, *more than one trait* as well as *more than one method* must be employed in the validation process. In many instances it will be convenient to achieve this through a multitrait-multimethod matrix. Such a matrix presents all of the intercorrelations resulting when each of several traits is measured by each of several methods.

To illustrate the suggested validational process, a synthetic example is presented in Table 1. This illustration involves three different traits, each measured by three methods, generating nine separate variables. It will be convenient to have labels for various regions of the matrix, and such have been provided in Table 1. The reliabilities will be spoken of in terms of three *reliability diagonals,* one for each method. The reliabilities could also be designated as the monotrait-monomethod values. Adjacent to each reliability diagonal is the *heterotrait-monomethod* triangle. The reliability diagonal and the adjacent heterotrait-monomethod triangle make up a *monomethod block*. A *heteromethod block* is made up of a validity diagonal (which could also be designated as monotrait-heteromethod values) and the two *heterotrait-heteromethod* triangles lying on each side of it. Note that these two heterotrait-heteromethod triangles are not identical.

obtained between that variable and any other variable having neither trait nor method in common. This requirement may seem so minimal and so obvious as to not need stating, yet an inspection of the literature shows that it is frequently not met, and may not be met even when the validity coefficients are of substantial size. In Table 1, all of the validity values meet this requirement. A third common-sense desideratum is that a variable correlate higher

TABLE 1. A SYNTHETIC MULTITRAIT-MULTIMETHOD MATRIX

	Traits	Method 1 A_1	B_1	C_1	Method 2 A_2	B_2	C_2	Method 3 A_3	B_3	C_3
Method 1	A_1	(.89)								
	B_1	.51	(.89)							
	C_1	.38	.37	(.76)						
Method 2	A_2	.57	.22	.09	(.93)					
	B_2	.22	.57	.10	.68	(.94)				
	C_2	.11	.11	.46	.59	.58	(.84)			
Method 3	A_3	.56	.22	.11	.67	.42	.33	(.94)		
	B_3	.23	.58	.12	.43	.66	.34	.67	(.92)	
	C_3	.11	.11	.45	.34	.32	.58	.58	.60	(.85)

Note.—The validity diagonals are the three sets of italicized values. The reliability diagonals are the three sets of values in parentheses. Each heterotrait-monomethod triangle is enclosed by a solid line. Each heterotrait-heteromethod triangle is enclosed by a broken line.

In terms of this diagram, four aspects bear upon the question of validity. In the first place, the entries in the validity diagonal should be significantly different from zero and sufficiently large to encourage further examination of validity. This requirement is evidence of convergent validity. Second, a validity diagonal value should be higher than the values lying in its column and row in the heterotrait-heteromethod triangles. That is, a validity value for a variable should be higher than the correlations

with an independent effort to measure the same trait than with measures designed to get at different traits which happen to employ the same method. For a given variable, this involves comparing its values in the validity diagonals with its values in the heterotrait-monomethod triangles. For variables A_1, B_1, and C_1, this requirement is met to some degree. For the other variables, A_2, A_3 etc., it is not met and this is probably typical of the usual case in individual differences research, as will be discussed in what follows. A fourth desideratum is that the same pattern of trait interrelationship be shown in all of the heterotrait triangles of both the monomethod and heteromethod blocks. The hypothetical data in Table 1 meet this requirement to a very marked degree, in spite of the different general levels of correlation involved in the several heterotrait triangles. The last three criteria provide evidence for discriminant validity.

Before examining the multitrait-multimethod matrices available in the literature, some explication and justification of this complex of requirements seems in order.

Convergence of independent methods: the distinction between reliability and validity. Both reliability and validity concepts require that agreement between measures be demonstrated. A common denominator which most validity concepts share in contradistinction to reliability is that this agreement represents the convergence of independent approaches. The concept of independence is indicated by such phrases as "external variable," "criterion performance," "behavioral criterion" (American Psychological Association, 1954, pp. 13–15) used in connection with concurrent and predictive validity. For construct validity it has been stated thus: "Numerous successful predictions dealing with phenotypically diverse 'criteria' give greater weight to the claim of construct validity than do . . . predictions involving very similar behavior" (Cronbach & Meehl, 1955, p. 295). The importance of independence recurs in most discussions of proof. For example, Ayer, discussing a historian's belief about a past event, says "if these sources are numerous and independent, and if they agree with one another, he will be reasonably confident that their account of the matter is correct" (Ayer, 1954, p. 39). In discussing the manner in which abstract scientific

concepts are tied to operations, Feigl speaks on their being "fixed" by "triangulation in logical space" (Feigl, 1958, p. 401).

Independence is, of course, a matter of degree, and in this sense reliability and validity can be seen as regions on a continuum. (Cf. Thurstone, 1937, pp. 102–103.) Reliability is the agreement between two efforts to measure the same trait through maximally similar methods. Validity is represented in the agreement between two attempts to measure the same trait through maximally different methods. A split-half reliability is a little more like a validity coefficient than is an immediate test-retest reliability, for the items are not quite identical. A correlation between dissimiliar subtests is probably a reliability measure, but is still closer to the region called validity.

Some evaluation of validity can take place even if the two methods are not entirely independent. In Table 1, for example, it is possible that Methods 1 and 2 are not entirely independent. If underlying Traits A and B are entirely independent, then the .10 minimum correlation in the heterotrait-heteromethod triangles may reflect method covariance. What if the overlap of method variance were higher? All correlations in the heteromethod block would then be elevated, including the validity diagonal. The heteromethod block involving Methods 2 and 3 in Table 1 illustrates this. The degree of elevation of the validity diagonal above the heterotrait-heteromethod triangles remains comparable and relative validity can still be evaluated. The interpretation of the validity diagonal in an absolute fashion requires the fortunate coincidence of both an independence of traits and an independence of methods, represented by zero values in the heterotrait-heteromethod triangles. But zero values could also occur through a combination of negative correlation between traits and positive correlation between methods, or the reverse. In practice, perhaps all that can be hoped for is evidence for relative validity, that is, for common variance specific to a trait, above and beyond shared method variance.

Discriminant validation. While the usual reason for the judgment of invalidity is low correlations in the validity diagonal (e.g., the Downey Will-Temperament Tests, Symonds, 1931, p. 337ff.) tests have also been invalidated because of too high correlations with other tests purporting to measure different things. This classic case of the social intelligence tests is a case in point. (See below and also Strang, 1930; R. Thorndike, 1936.) Such invalidation occurs when values in the heterotrait-heteromethod triangles are as high as those in the validity diagonal or even where within a monomethod block, the heterotrait values are as high as the reliabilities. Loevinger, Gleser, and Du-Bois (1953) have emphasized this requirement in the development of maximally discriminating subtests.

When a dimension of personality is hypothesized, when a construct is proposed, the proponent invariably has in mind distinctions between the new dimension and other constructs already in use. One cannot define without implying distinctions, and the verification of these distinctions is an important part of the validational process. In discussions of construct validity, it has been expressed in such terms as "from this point of view, a low correlation with athletic ability may be just as important and encouraging as a high correlation with reading comprehension" (APA, 1954, p. 17).

The test as a trait-method unit. In any given psychological measuring device, there are certain features or stimuli introduced specifically to represent the trait that it is intended to measure. There are other features which are characteristic of the method being employed, features which could also be present in efforts to measure other quite

different traits. The test, or rating scale, or other device, almost inevitably elicits systematic variance in response due to both groups of features. To the extent that irrelevant method variance contributes to the scores obtained, these scores are invalid.

This source of invalidity was first noted in the "halo effects" found in ratings (Thorndike, 1920). Studies of individual differences among laboratory animals resulted in the recognition of "apparatus factors," usually more dominant than psychological process factors (Tryon, 1942). For paper-and-pencil tests, methods variance has been noted under such terms as "test-form factors" (Vernon: 1957, 1958) and "response sets" (Cronbach: 1946, 1950; Lorge, 1937). Cronbach has stated the point particularly clearly: "The assumption is generally made . . . that what the test measures is determined by the content of the items. Yet the final score . . . is a composite of effects resulting from the content of the item and effects resulting from the form of the item used" (Cronbach, 1946, p. 475). "Response sets always lower the logical validity of a test. . . . Response sets interfere with inferences from test data" (p. 484).

While E. L. Thorndike (1920) was willing to allege the presence of halo effects by comparing the high obtained correlations with common sense notions of what they ought to be (e.g., it was unreasonable that a teacher's intelligence and voice quality should correlate .63) and while much of the evidence of response set variance is of the same order, the clear-cut demonstration of the presence of method variance requires both several traits and several methods. Otherwise, high correlations between tests might be explained as due either to basic trait similarity or to shared method variance. In the multitrait-multimethod matrix, the presence of method variance is indicated by the difference in level of correlation between the parallel values of the monomethod block and the heteromethod blocks, assuming comparable reliabilities among all tests. Thus the contribution of method variance in Test A_1 of Table 1 is indicated by the elevation of $r_{A_1B_1}$ above $r_{A_1B_2}$, the difference between .51 and .22, etc.

The distinction between trait and method is of course relative to the test constructor's intent. What is an unwanted response set for one tester may be a trait for another who wishes to measure acquiesence, willingness to take an extreme stand, or tendency to attribute socially desirable attributes to oneself (Cronbach: 1946, 1950; Edwards, 1957; Lorge, 1937).

Multitrait-Multimethod Matrices in the Literature

Multitrait-multimethod matrices are rare in the test and measurement literature. Most frequent are two types of fragment: two methods and one trait (single isolated values from the validity diagonal, perhaps accompanied by a reliability or two), and heterotrait-monomethod triangles. Either type of fragment is apt to disguise the inadequacy of our present measurement efforts, particularly in failing to call attention to the preponderant strength of methods variance. The evidence of test validity to be presented here is probably poorer than most psychologists would have expected.

One of the earliest matrices of this kind was provided by Kelley and Krey in 1934. Peer judgments by students provided one method, scores on a word-association test the other. Table 2 presents the data for the four most valid traits of the eight he employed. The picture is one of strong method factors, particularly among the peer ratings, and almost total invalidity. For only one of the eight measures, School Drive, is the value in the validity diagonal (.16!) higher than all of the heterotrait-heteromethod values. The absence of discriminant validity is further indicated by the tendency of the values in the monomethod triangles to approximate the reliabilities.

An early illustration from the animal literature comes from Anderson's (1937) study of drives. Table 3 presents a sample of his data. Once again, the highest correlations are found among different constructs from the same method, showing the dominance of apparatus or method factors so typical of the whole field of individual differences. The validity diagonal for hunger is higher than the heteroconstruct-heteromethod values. The diagonal value for sex has not been *italicized* as

TABLE 2. PERSONALITY TRAITS OF SCHOOL CHILDREN FROM KELLEY'S STUDY
($N=311$)

		Peer Ratings				Association Test			
		A_1	B_1	C_1	D_1	A_2	B_2	C_2	D_2
Peer Ratings									
Courtesy	A_1	(.82)							
Honesty	B_1	.74	(.80)						
Poise	C_1	.63	.65	(.74)					
School Drive	D_1	.76	.78	.65	(.89)				
Association Test									
Courtesy	A_2	.13	.14	.10	.14	(.28)			
Honesty	B_2	.06	.12	.16	.08	.27	(.38)		
Poise	C_2	.01	.08	.10	.02	.19	.37	(.42)	
School Drive	D_2	.12	.15	.14	.16	.27	.32	.18	(.36)

TABLE 3.   MEASURES OF DRIVES FROM ANDERSON'S DATA ($N=50$)

		Obstruction Box			Activity Wheel		
		A_1	B_1	C_1	A_2	B_2	C_2
Obstruction Box							
Hunger	A_1	(.58)					
Thirst	B_1	.54	( )				
Sex	C_1	.46	.70	( )			
Activity Wheel							
Hunger	A_2	.48	.31	.37	(.83)		
Thirst	B_2	.35	.33	.43	.87	(.92)	
Post Sex	C_2	.31	.37	.44	.69	.78	( )

Note.—Empty parentheses appear in this and subsequent tables where no appropriate reliability estimates are reported in the original paper.

a validity coefficient since the obstruction box measure was pre-sex-opportunity, the activity wheel post-opportunity. Note that the high general level of heterotrait-heteromethod values could be due either to correlation of methods variance between the two methods, or to correlated trait variance. On a priori grounds, however, the methods would seem about as independent as one would be likely to achieve. The predominance of an apparatus factor for the activity wheel is evident from the fact that the correlation between hunger and thirst (.87) is of the same magnitude as their test-retest reliabilities (.83 and .92 respectively).

R. L. Thorndike's study (1936) of the validity of the George Washington Social Intelligence Test is the classic instance of invalidation by high correlation between traits. It involved computing all of the intercorrelations among five sub-scales of the Social Intelligence Test and five sub-scales of the George Washington Mental Alertness Test. The model of the present paper would demand that each of the traits, social intelligence and mental alertness, be measured by at least two methods. While this full symmetry was not intended in the study, it can be so interpreted without too much distortion. For both traits, there were subtests employ-

TABLE 4.   SOCIAL INTELLIGENCE AND MENTAL ALERTNESS SUBTEST
INTERCORRELATIONS FROM THORNDIKE'S DATA ($N=750$)

		Memory		Comprehension		Vocabulary	
		A_1	B_1	A_2	B_2	A_3	B_3
Memory							
Social Intelligence (Memory for Names & Faces)	A_1	( )					
Mental Alertness (Learning Ability)	B_1	.31	( )				
Comprehension							
Social Intelligence (Sense of Humor)	A_2	.30	.31	( )			
Mental Alertness (Comprehension)	B_2	.29	.38	.48	( )		
Vocabulary							
Social Intelligence (Recog. of Mental State)	A_3	.23	.35	.31	.35	( )	
Mental Alertness (Vocabulary)	B_3	.30	.58	.40	.48	.47	( )

ing acquisition of knowledge during the testing period (i.e., learning or memory), tests involving comprehension of prose passages, and tests that involved a definitional activity. Table 4 shows six of Thorndike's 10 variables arranged as a multitrait-multimethod matrix. If the three subtests of the Social Intelligence Test are viewed as three methods of measuring social intelligence, then their intercorrelations (.30, .23, and .31) represent validities that are not only lower than their corresponding monomethod values, but also lower than the heterotrait-heteromethod correlations, providing a picture which totally fails to establish social intelligence as a separate dimension. The Mental Alertness validity diagonals (.38, .58, and .48) equal or exceed the monomethod values in two out of three cases, and exceed all heterotrait-heteromethod control values. These results illustrate the general conclusions reached by Thorndike in his factor analysis of the whole 10 x 10 matrix.

The data of Table 4 could be used to validate specific forms of cognitive functioning, as measured by the different "methods" represented by usual intelligence test content on the one hand and social content on the other. Table 5 rearranges the 15 values for this purpose. The monomethod values and the validity diagonals exchange places, while the heterotrait-heteromethod control coefficients are the same in both tables.

As judged against these latter values, comprehension (.48) and vocabulary (.47), but not memory (.31), show some specific validity. This transmutability of the validation matrix argues for the comparisons within the heteromethod block as the most generally relevant validation data, and illustrates the potential interchangeability of trait and method components.

Some of the correlations in Chi's (1937) prodigious study of halo effect in ratings are appropriate to a multitrait-multimethod matrix in which each rater might be regarded as representing a different method. While the published report does not make these available in detail because it employs averaged values, it is apparent from a comparison of his Tables IV and VIII that the ratings generally failed to meet the requirement that ratings of the same trait by different raters should correlate higher than ratings of different traits by the same rater. Validity is shown to the extent that of the correlations in the heteromethod block, those in the validity diagonal are higher than the average heteromethod-heterotrait values.

A conspicuously unsuccessful multitrait-multimethod matrix is provided by Campbell (1953, 1956) for rating of the leadership behavior of officers by themselves and by their subordinates. Only one of 11 variables (Recognition Behavior) met the requirement of providing a validity diagonal value higher

TABLE 5. MEMORY, COMPREHENSION, AND VOCABULARY MEASURED WITH SOCIAL AND ABSTRACT CONTENT

		Social Content			Abstract Content		
		A_1	B_1	C_1	A_2	B_2	C_2
Social Content							
Memory (Memory for Names and Faces)	A_1	( )					
Comprehension (Sense of Humor)	B_1	.30	( )				
Vocabulary (Recognition of Mental State)	C_1	.23	.31	( )			
Abstract Content							
Memory (Learning Ability)	A_2	.31	.31	.35	( )		
Comprehension	B_2	.29	.48	.35	.38	( )	
Vocabulary	C_2	.30	.40	.47	.58	.48	( )

than any of the heterotrait-heteromethod values, that validity being .29. For none of the variables were the validities higher than heterotrait-monomethod values.

A study of attitudes toward authority and nonauthority figures by Burwen and Campbell (1957) contains a complex multitrait-multimethod matrix, one symmetrical excerpt from which is shown in Table 6. Method variance was strong for most of the procedures in this study. Where validity was found, it was primarily at the level of validity diagonal values higher than heterotrait-heteromethod values. As illustrated in Table 6, attitude toward father showed this kind of validity, as did attitude toward peers to a lesser degree. Attitude

the same method rather than with the same trait measured by a different method. Neither of the traits finds any consistent validation by the requirement that the validity diagonals exceed the heterotrait-heteromethod control values. As a most minimal requirement, it might be asked if the sum of the two values in the validity diagonal exceeds the sum of the two control values, providing a comparison in which differences in reliability or communality are roughly partialled out. This condition is achieved at the purely chance level of three times in the six tetrads. This matrix provides an interesting range of methodological independence. The two "Sociometric by Others" measures, while representing the judgments of the same set of fellow

TABLE 6.   ATTITUDES TOWARD FATHER, BOSS, AND PEER, AS MEASURED BY INTERVIEW AND CHECK-LIST OF DESCRIPTIVE TRAITS

		Interview			Trait Check-List		
		A_1	B_1	C_1	A_2	B_2	C_2
Interview ($N = 57$)							
Father	A_1	( )					
Boss	B_1	.64	( )				
Peer	C_1	.65	.76	( )			
Trait Check-List ($N = 155$)							
Father	A_2	*.40*	.08	.09	(.24)		
Boss	B_2	.19	− .10	− .03	.23	(.34)	
Peer	C_2	.27	.11	*.23*	.21	.45	(.55)

toward boss showed no validity. There was no evidence of a generalized attitude toward authority which would include father and boss, although such values as the .64 correlation between father and boss as measured by interview might have seemed to confirm the hypothesis had they been encountered in isolation.

Borgatta (1954) has provided a complex multimethod study from which can be extracted Table 7, illustrating the assessment of two traits by four different methods. For all measures but one, the highest correlation is the apparatus one, i.e., with the other trait measured by

participants, come from distinct tasks: Popularity is based upon each participant's expression of his own friendship preferences, while Expansiveness is based upon each participant's guesses as to the other participant's choices, from which has been computed each participant's reputation for liking lots of other persons, i.e., being "expansive." In line with this considerable independence, the evidence for a method factor is relatively low in comparison with the observational procedures. Similarly, the two "Sociometric by Self" measures represent quite separate tasks, Popularity coming from his estimates of the choices

TABLE 7.   MULTIPLE MEASUREMENT OF TWO SOCIOMETRIC TRAITS $(N = 125)$

| | | Sociometric | | | | Observation | | | |
| | | by Others | | by Self | | Group Interaction | | Role Playing | |
		A_1	B_1	A_2	B_2	A_3	B_3	A_4	B_4
Sociometric by Others									
Popularity	A_1	( )							
Expansiveness	B_1	.47	( )						
Sociometric by Self									
Popularity	A_2	*.19*	.18	( )					
Expansiveness	B_2	.07	*.08*	.32	( )				
Observation of Group Interaction									
Popularity	A_3	.25	.18	.26	.11	( )			
Expansiveness	B_3	.21	*.12*	.28	*.15*	.84	( )		
Observation of Role Playing									
Popularity	A_4	*.24*	.14	*.18*	.01	.66	.58	( )	
Expansiveness	B_4	.25	*.12*	.26	.05	.66	*.76*	.73	( )

he will receive from others, Expansiveness from the number of expressions of attraction to others which he makes on the sociometric task. In contrast, the measures of Popularity and Expansiveness from the observations of group interaction and the role playing not only involve the same specific observers, but in addition the observers rated the pair of variables as a part of the same rating task in each situation. The apparent degree of method variance within each of the two observational situations, and the apparent sharing of method variance between them, is correspondingly high.

In another paper by Borgatta (1955), 12 interaction process variables were measured by quantitative observation under two conditions, and by a projective test. In this test, the stimuli were pictures of groups, for which the S generated a series of verbal interchanges; these were then scored in Interaction Process Analysis categories. For illustrative purposes, Table 8 presents the five traits which had the highest mean communalities in the over-all factor analysis. Between the two highly

similar observational methods, validation is excellent: trait variance runs higher than method variance; validity diagonals are in general higher than heterotrait values of both the heteromethod and monomethods blocks, most unexceptionally so for Gives Opinion and Gives Orientation. The pattern of correlation among the traits is also in general confirmed.

Of greater interest because of the greater independence of methods are the blocks involving the projective test. Here the validity picture is much poorer. Gives Orientation comes off best, its projective test validity values of .35 and .33 being bested by only three monomethod values and by no heterotrait-heteromethod values within the projective blocks. All of the other validities are exceeding by some heterotrait-heteromethod value.

The projective test specialist may object to the implicit expectations of a one-to-one correspondence between projected action and overt action. Such expectations should not be attributed to Borgatta, and are not necessary to

TABLE 8. INTERACTION PROCESS VARIABLES IN OBSERVED FREE BEHAVIOR, OBSERVED
ROLE PLAYING AND A PROJECTIVE TEST ($N = 125$)

		Free Behavior					Role Playing					Projective Test				
		A_1	B_1	C_1	D_1	E_1	A_2	B_2	C_2	D_2	E_2	A_3	B_3	C_3	D_3	E_3
Free Behavior																
Shows solidarity	A_1	( )														
Gives suggestion	B_1	.25	( )													
Gives opinion	C_1	.13	.24	( )												
Gives orientation	D_1	−.14	.26	.52	( )											
Shows disagreement	E_1	.34	.41	.27	.02	( )										
Role Playing																
Shows solidarity	A_2	.43	.43	.08	.10	.29	( )									
Gives suggestion	B_2	.16	.32	.00	.24	.07	.37	( )								
Gives opinion	C_2	.15	.27	.60	.38	.12	.01	.10	( )							
Gives orientation	D_2	−.12	.24	.44	.74	.08	.04	.18	.40	( )						
Shows disagreement	E_2	.51	.36	.14	−.12	.50	.39	.27	.23	−.11	( )					
Projective Test																
Shows solidarity	A_3	.20	.17	.16	.12	.08	.17	.12	.30	.17	.22	( )				
Gives suggestion	B_3	.05	.21	.05	.08	.13	.10	.19	−.02	.06	.30	.32	( )			
Gives opinion	C_3	.31	.30	.13	−.02	.26	.25	.19	.15	−.04	.53	.31	.63	( )		
Gives orientation	D_3	−.01	.09	.30	.35	−.05	.03	.00	.19	.33	.00	.37	.29	.32	( )	
Shows disagreement	E_3	.13	.18	.10	.14	.19	.22	.28	.02	.04	.23	.27	.51	.47	.30	( )

TABLE 9. MAYO'S INTERCORRELATIONS BETWEEN OBJECTIVE AND
RATING MEASURES OF INTELLIGENCE AND EFFORT $(N=166)$

		Peer Ratings		Objective	
		A_1	B_1	A_2	B_2
Peer Rating					
Intelligence	A_1	(.85)			
Effort	B_1	.66	(.84)		
Objective Measures					
Intelligence	A_2	.46	.29	( )	
Effort	B_2	.46	.40	.10	( )

the method here proposed. For the simple symmetrical model of this paper, it has been assumed that the measures are labeled in correspondence with the correlations expected, i.e., in correspondence with the traits that the tests are alleged to diagnose. Note that in Table 8, Gives Opinion is the best projective test predictor of both free behavior and role playing Shows Disagreement. Were a proper theoretical rationale available, these values might be regarded as validities.

Mayo (1956) has made an analysis of test scores and ratings of effort and intelligence, to estimate the contribution of halo (a kind of methods variance) to ratings. As Table 9 shows, the validity picture is ambiguous. The method factor or halo effect for ratings is considerable although the correlation between the two ratings (.66) is well below their reliabilities (.84 and .85). The objective measures share no appreciable apparatus

overlap because they were independent operations. In spite of Mayo's argument that the ratings have some valid trait variance, the .46 heterotrait-heteromethod value seriously depreciates the otherwise impressive .46 and .40 validity values.

Cronbach (1949, p. 277) and Vernon (1957, 1958) have both discussed the multitrait-multimethod matrix shown in Table 10, based upon data originally presented by H. S. Conrad. Using an approximate technique, Vernon estimates that 61% of the systematic variance is due to a general factor, that 21½% is due to the test-form factors specific to verbal or to pictorial forms of items, and that but 11½% is due to the content factors specific to electrical or to mechanical contents. Note that for the purposes of estimating validity, the interpretation of the general factor, which he estimates from the .49 and .45 heterotrait-heteromethod values, is

TABLE 10. MECHANICAL AND ELECTRICAL FACTS MEASURED BY
VERBAL AND PICTORIAL ITEMS

		Verbal Items		Pictorial Items	
		A_1	B_1	A_2	B_2
Verbal Items					
Mechanical Facts	A_1	(.89)			
Electrical Facts	B_1	.63	(.71)		
Pictorial Items					
Mechanical Facts	A_2	.61	.45	(.82)	
Electrical Facts	B_2	.49	.51	.64	(.67)

equivocal. It could represent desired competence variance, representing components common to both electrical and mechanical skills—perhaps resulting from general industrial shop experience, common ability components, overlapping learning situations, and the like. On the other hand, this general factor could represent overlapping method factors, and be due to the presence in both tests of multiple choice item format, IBM answer sheets, or the heterogeneity of the Ss in conscientiousness, test-taking motivation, and test-taking sophistication. Until methods that are still more different and traits that are still more independent are introduced into the validation matrix, this general factor remains uninterpretable. From this standpoint it can be seen that 21½% is a very minimal estimate of the total test-form variance in the tests, as it represents only test-form components specific to the verbal or the pictorial items, i.e., test-form components which the two forms do *not* share. Similarly, and more hopefully, the 11½% content variance is a very minimal estimate of the total true trait variance of the tests, representing only the true trait variance which electrical and mechanical knowledge do *not* share.

Carroll (1952) has provided data on the Guilford-Martin Inventory of Factors STDCR and related ratings which can be rearranged into the matrix of Table 11. (Variable R has been inverted to reduce the number of negative correlations.) Two of the methods, Self Ratings and Inventory scores, can be seen as sharing method variance, and thus as having an inflated validity diagonal. The more independent heteromethod blocks involving Peer Ratings show some evidence of discriminant and convergent validity, with validity diagonals averaging .33 (Inventory × Peer ratings) and .39 (Self Ratings × Peer Ratings) against heterotrait-heteromethod control values averaging .14 and .16. While not intrinsically impres-

sive, this picture is nonetheless better than most of the validity matrices here assembled. Note that the Self Ratings show slightly higher validity diagonal elevations than do the Inventory scores, in spite of the much greater length and undoubtedly higher reliability of the latter. In addition, a method factor seems almost totally lacking for the Self Ratings, while strongly present for the inventory, so that the Self Ratings come off much the best if true trait variance is expressed as a proportion of total reliable variance (as Vernon [1958] suggests). The method factor in the STDCR Inventory is undoubtedly enhanced by scoring the same item in several scales, thus contributing correlated error variance, which could be reduced without loss of reliability by the simple expedient of adding more equivalent items and scoring each item only in one scale. It should be noted that Carroll makes explicit use of the comparison of the validity diagonal with the heterotrait-heteromethod values as a validity indicator.

Ratings in the Assessment Study of Clinical Psychologists

The illustrations of multitrait-multimethod matrices presented so far give a rather sorry picture of the validity of the measures of individual differences involved. The typical case shows an excessive amount of method variance, which usually exceeds the amount of trait variance. This picture is certainly not as a result of a deliberate effort to select shockingly bad examples: these are ones we have encountered without attempting an exhaustive coverage of the literature. The several unpublished studies of which we are aware show the same picture. If they seem more disappointing than the general run of validity data reported in the journals, this impression may very well be because the portrait of validity provided by isolated values plucked from the

TABLE 11. GUILFORD-MARTIN FACTORS STDCR AND RELATED RATINGS ($N=110$)

	Inventory					Self Ratings					Peer Ratings				
	S	T	D	C	-R	S	T	D	C	-R	S	T	D	C	-R
Inventory															
S	(.92)														
T	.27	(.89)													
D	.62	.57	(.91)												
C	.36	.47	.90	(.91)											
-R	.69	.32	.28	-.06	(.89)										
Self Ratings															
S	.57	.11	.19	-.01	.53	( )									
T	.28	.65	.42	.26	.37	.26	( )								
D	.44	.25	.53	.45	.29	.31	.32	( )							
C	.31	.20	.54	.52	.13	.11	.21	.47	( )						
-R	.15	.30	.12	.04	.34	.10	.12	.04	.06	( )					
Peer Ratings															
S	.37	.08	.10	-.01	.38	.42	.02	.08	.08	.31	(.81)				
T	.23	.32	.15	.04	.40	.20	.39	.40	.21	.31	.37	(.66)			
D	.31	.11	.27	.24	.25	.17	.09	.29	.27	.30	.49	.38	(.73)		
C	.08	.15	.20	.26	-.05	.01	.06	.14	.30	.07	.19	.16	.40	(.75)	
-R	.21	.20	-.03	-.16	.45	.28	.17	.08	.01	.56	.55	.56	.34	-.07	(.76)

validity diagonal is deceptive, and un-interpretable in isolation from the total matrix. Yet it is clear that few of the classic examples of successful meas-urement of individual differences are involved, and that in many of the in-stances, the quality of the data might have been such as to magnify appa-ratus factors, etc. A more nearly ideal set of personality data upon which to illustrate the method was therefore sought in the multiple application of a set of rating scales in the assessment study of clinical psychologists (Kelly & Fiske, 1951).

In that study, "Rating Scale A" con-tained 22 traits referring to "behavior which can be directly observed on the surface." In using this scale the raters were instructed to "disregard any in-ferences about underlying dynamics or causes" p. 207). The Ss, first-year clinical psychology students, rated them-selves and also their three teammates with whom they had participated in the various assessment procedures and with whom they had lived for six days. The median of the three teammates' ratings was used for the Teammate score. The Ss were also rated on these 22 traits by the assessment staff. Our analysis uses the Final Pooled ratings, which were agreed upon by three staff members after discussion and review of the enormous amount of data and the many other ratings on each S. Un-fortunately for our purposes, the staff members saw the ratings by Self and Teammates before making theirs, al-though presumably they were little influenced by these data because they had so much other evidence available to them. (See Kelly & Fiske, 1951, especially p. 64.) The Self and Team-mate ratings represent entirely separate "methods" and can be given the major emphasis in evaluating the data to be presented.

In a previous analysis of these data (Fiske, 1949), each of the three hete-rotrait-monomethod triangles was com-puted and factored. To provide a multi-trait-multimethod matrix, the 1452 heteromethod correlations have been computed especially for this report.[1] The full 66 x 66 matrix with its 2145 coefficients is obviously too large for presentation here, but will be used in analyses that follow. To provide an il-lustrative sample, Table 12 presents the interrelationships among five variables, selecting the one best representing each of the five recurrent factors discovered in Fiske's (1949) previous analysis of the monomethod matrices. (These were chosen without regard to their validity as indicated in the heteromethod blocks. Assertive—No. 3 reflected—was se-lected to represent Recurrent Factor 5 because Talkative had also a high load-ing on the first recurrent factor.)

The picture presented in Table 12 is, we believe, typical of the best valid-ity in personality trait ratings that psy-chology has to offer at the present time. It is comforting to note that the pic-ture is better than most of those previ-ously examined. Note that the validi-ties for Assertive exceed heterotrait values of both the monomethod and heteromethod triangles. Cheerful, Broad Interests, and Serious have valid-ities exceeding the heterotrait-hetero-method values with two exceptions. Only for Unshakable Poise does the evidence of validity seem trivial. The elevation of the reliabilities above the heterotrait-monomethod triangles is further evidence for discriminant valid-ity.

A comparison of Table 12 with the full matrix shows that the procedure of having but one variable to represent

[1] We are indebted to E. Lowell Kelly for furnishing the V.A. Assessment data to us, and to Hugh Lane for producing the matrix of intercorrelations.

In the original report the correlations were based upon 128 men. The present analyses were based on only 124 of these cases because of clerical errors. This reduction in N leads to some very minor discrepancies between these values and those previously reported.

TABLE 12. RATINGS FROM ASSESSMENT STUDY OF CLINICAL PSYCHOLOGISTS $(N = 124)$

		Staff Ratings					Teammate Ratings					Self Ratings			
	A_1	B_1	C_1	D_1	E_1	A_2	B_2	C_2	D_2	E_2	A_3	B_3	C_3	D_3	E_3
Staff Ratings															
Assertive A_1	(.89)														
Cheerful B_1	.37	(.85)													
Serious C_1	-.24	-.14	(.81)												
Unshakable Poise D_1	.25	.46	.08	(.84)											
Broad Interests E_1	.35	.19	.09	.31	(.92)										
Teammate Ratings															
Assertive A_2	.71	.35	-.18	.26	.41	(.82)									
Cheerful B_2	.39	.53	-.15	.38	.29	.37	(.76)								
Serious C_2	-.27	-.31	.43	-.06	.03	-.15	-.19	(.70)							
Unshakable Poise D_2	.03	-.05	.03	.20	.07	.11	.23	.19	(.74)						
Broad Interests E_2	.19	.05	.04	.29	.47	.33	.22	.19	.29	(.76)					
Self Ratings															
Assertive A_3	.48	.31	-.22	.19	.12	.46	.36	-.15	.12	.23	( )				
Cheerful B_3	.17	.42	-.10	.10	-.03	.09	.24	-.25	-.11	-.03	.23	( )			
Serious C_3	-.04	-.13	.22	-.13	-.05	-.04	-.11	.31	.06	.06	-.05	-.12	( )		
Unshakable Poise D_3	.13	.27	-.03	.22	-.04	.10	.15	.00	.14	.06	.16	.26	.11	( )	
Broad Interests E_3	.37	.15	-.22	.09	.26	.27	.12	-.07	.05	.35	.21	.15	.17	.31	( )

each factor has enhanced the appearance of validity, although not necessarily in a misleading fashion. Where several variables are all highly loaded on the same factor, their "true" level of intercorrelation is high. Under these conditions, sampling errors can depress validity diagonal values and enhance others to produce occasional exceptions to the validity picture, both in the heterotrait-monomethod matrix and in the heteromethod-heterotrait triangles. In this instance, with an N of 124, the sampling error is appreciable, and may thus be expected to exaggerate the degree of invalidity.

Within the monomethod sections, errors of measurement will be correlated, raising the general level of values found, while within the heteromethods block, measurement errors are independent, and tend to lower the values both along the validity diagonal and in the heterotrait triangles. These effects, which may also be stated in terms of method factors or shared confounded irrelevancies, operate strongly in these data, as probably in all data involving ratings. In such cases, where several variables represent each factor, none of the variables consistently meets the criterion that validity values exceed the corresponding values in the monomethod triangles, when the full matrix is examined.

To summarize the validation picture with respect to comparisons of validity values with other heteromethod values in each block, Table 13 has been prepared. For each trait and for each of the three heteromethod blocks, it presents the value of the validity diagonal, the highest heterotrait value involving that trait, and the number out of the 42 such heterotrait values which exceed the validity diagonal in magnitude. (The number 42 comes from the grouping of the 21 other column values and the 21 other row values for the column and row intersecting at the given diagonal value.)

On the requirement that the validity diagonal exceed all others in its heteromethod block, none of the traits has a completely perfect record, although some come close. Assertive has only one trivial exception in the Teammate-Self block. Talkative has almost as good a record, as does Imaginative. Serious has but two inconsequential exceptions and Interest in Women three. These traits stand out as highly valid in both self-description and reputation. Note that the actual validity coefficients of these four traits range from but .22 to .82, or, if we concentrate on the Teammate-Self block as most certainly representing independent methods, from but .31 to .46. While these are the best traits, it seems that most of the traits have far above chance validity. All those having 10 or fewer exceptions have a degree of validity significant at the .001 level as crudely estimated by a one-tailed sign test.[2] All but one of the variables meet this level for the Staff-Teammate block, all but four for the Staff-Self block, all but five for the most independent block, Teammate-Self. The exceptions to significant validity are not parallel from column to column, however, and only 13 of 22 variables have .001 significant validity in all three blocks. These are indicated by an asterisk in Table 13.

This highly significant general level of validity must not obscure the meaningful problem created by the occasional exceptions, even for the best variables. The excellent traits of Assertive and Talkative provide a case in point. In terms of Fiske's original anal-

2 If we take the validity value as fixed (ignoring its sampling fluctuations), then we can determine whether the number of values larger than it in its row and column is less than expected on the null hypothesis that half the values would be above it. This procedure requires the assumption that the position (above or below the validity value) of any one of these comparison values is independent of the position of each of the others, a dubious assumption when common methods and trait variance are present.

TABLE 13. VALIDITIES OF TRAITS IN THE ASSESSMENT STUDY OF CLINICAL PSYCHOLOGISTS, AS JUDGED BY THE HETEROMETHOD COMPARISONS

	Staff-Teammate			Staff-Self			Teammate-Self		
	Val.	Highest Het.	No. Higher	Val.	Highest Het.	No. Higher	Val.	Highest Het.	No. Higher
1. Obstructiveness*	.30	.34	2	.16	.27	9	.19	.24	1
2. Unpredictable	.34	.26	0	.18	.24	3	.05	.19	29
3. Assertive*	.71	.65	0	.48	.45	0	.46	.48	1
4. Cheerful*	.53	.60	2	.42	.40	0	.24	.38	5
5. Serious*	.43	.35	0	.22	.27	2	.31	.24	0
6. Cool, Aloof	.49	.48	0	.20	.46	10	.02	.34	36
7. Unshakable Poise	.20	.40	16	.22	.27	4	.14	.19	10
8. Broad Interests*	.47	.46	0	.26	.37	6	.35	.32	0
9. Trustful	.26	.34	5	.08	.25	19	.11	.17	9
10. Self-centered	.30	.34	2	.17	.27	6	- .07	.19	36
11. Talkative*	.82	.65	0	.47	.45	0	.43	.48	1
12. Adventurous	.45	.60	6	.28	.30	2	.16	.36	14
13. Socially Awkward	.45	.37	0	.06	.21	28	.04	.16	30
14. Adaptable*	.44	.40	0	.18	.23	10	.17	.29	8
15. Self-sufficient*	.32	.33	1	.13	.18	5	.18	.15	0
16. Worrying, Anxious*	.41	.37	0	.23	.33	5	.15	.16	1
17. Conscientious	.26	.33	4	.11	.32	19	.21	.23	2
18. Imaginative*	.43	.46	1	.32	.31	0	.36	.32	0
19. Interest in Women*	.42	.43	2	.55	.38	0	.37	.40	1
20. Secretive, Reserved*	.40	.58	5	.38	.40	2	.32	.35	3
21. Independent Minded	.39	.42	2	.08	.25	19	.21	.30	3
22. Emotional Expression*	.62	.63	1	.31	.46	5	.19	.34	10

Note.—Val.=value in validity diagonal; Highest Het.=highest heterotrait value; No. Higher= number of heterotrait values exceeding the validity diagonal.
* Trait names which have validities in all three heteromethod blocks significantly greater than the heterotrait-heteromethod values at the .001 level.

ysis, both have high loadings on the recurrent factor "Confident self-expression" (represented by Assertive in Table 12). Talkative also had high loadings on the recurrent factor of Social Adaptability (represented by Cheerful in Table 12). We would expect, therefore, both high correlation between them and significant discrimination as well. And even at the common sense level, most psychologists would expect fellow psychologists to discriminate validly between assertiveness (nonsubmissiveness) and talkativeness. Yet in the Teammate-Self block, Assertive rated by self correlates .48 with Talkative

by teammates, higher than either of their validities in this block, .43 and .46.

In terms of the average values of the validities and the frequency of exceptions, there is a distinct trend for the Staff-Teammate block to show the greatest agreement. This can be attributed to several factors. Both represent ratings from the external point of view. Both are averaged over three judges, minimizing individual biases and undoubtedly increasing reliabilities. Moreover, the Teammate ratings were available to the Staff in making their ratings. Another effect contributing to the less adequate convergence and discrimination of Self ratings was a response set toward the favorable pole which greatly reduced the range of these measures (Fiske, 1949, p. 342). Inspection of the details of the instances of invalidity summarized in Table 13 shows that in most instances the effect is attributable to the high specificity and low communality for the self-rating trait. In these instances, the column and row intersecting at the low validity diagonal are asymmetrical as far as general level of correlation is concerned, a fact covered over by the condensation provided in Table 13.

The personality psychologist is initially predisposed to reinterpret self-ratings, to treat them as symptoms rather than to interpret them literally. Thus, we were alert to instances in which the self ratings were not literally interpretable, yet nonetheless had a diagnostic significance when properly "translated." By and large, the instances of invalidity of self-descriptions found in this assessment study are not of this type, but rather are to be explained in terms of an absence of communality for one of the variables involved. In general, where these self descriptions are interpretable at all, they are as literally interpretable as are teammate descriptions. Such a finding may, of course, reflect a substantial degree of insight on the part of these Ss.

The general success in discriminant validation coupled with the parallel factor patterns found in Fiske's earlier analysis of the three intramethod matrices seemed to justify an inspection of the factor pattern validity in this instance. One possible procedure would be to do a single analysis of the whole 66 x 66 matrix. Other approaches focused upon separate factoring of heteromethods blocks, matrix by matrix, could also be suggested. Not only would such methods be extremely tedious, but in addition they would leave undetermined the precise comparison of factor-pattern similarity. Correlating factor loadings

over the population of variables was employed for this purpose by Fiske (1949) but while this provided for the identification of recurrent factors, no single over-all index of factor pattern similarity was generated. Since our immediate interest was in confirming a pattern of interrelationships, rather than in describing it, an efficient shortcut was available: namely to test the similarity of the sets of heterotrait values by correlation coefficients in which each entry represented the size values of the given heterotrait coefficients in two different matrices. For the full matrix, such correlations would be based upon the N of the 22 x 21/2 or 231 specific heterotrait combinations. Correlations were computed between the Teammate and Self monomethods matrices, selected as maximally independent. (The values to follow were computed from the original correlation matrix and are somewhat higher than that which would be obtained from a reflected matrix.) The similarity between the two monomethods matrices was .84, corroborating the factor-pattern similarity between these matrices described more fully by Fiske in his parallel factor analyses of them. To carry this mode of analysis into the heteromethod block, this block was treated as though divided into two by the validity diagonal, the above diagonal values and the below diagonal representing the maximally independent validation of the heterotrait correlation pattern. These two correlated .63, a value which, while lower, shows an impressive degree of confirmation. There remains the question as to whether this pattern upon which the two heteromethod-heterotrait triangles agree is the same one found in common between the two monomethod triangles. The intra-Teammate matrix correlated with the two heteromethod triangles .71 and .71. The intra-Self matrix correlated with the two .57 and .63. In general, then, there is evidence for validity of the intertrait relationship pattern.

Discussion

Relation to construct validity. While the validational criteria presented are explicit or implicit in the discussions of construct validity (Cronbach & Meehl, 1955; APA, 1954), this paper is primarily concerned with the adequacy of tests as measures of a construct rather than with the adequacy of a construct as determined by the confirmation of theoretically predicted associations with measures of other constructs. We believe that before one can test the relationships between a specific trait and other traits, one must have some confidence in one's measures of that trait. Such confidence can be supported by evidence of convergent and discriminant validation. Stated in different words, any conceptual formulation of trait will usually include implicitly the proposition that this trait is a response tendency which can be observed under more than one experimental condition and that this trait can be meaningfully differentiated from other traits. The testing of these two propositions must be prior to the testing of other propositions to prevent the acceptance of erroneous conclusions. For example, a conceptual framework might postulate a large correlation between Traits A and B and no correlation between Traits A and C. If the experimenter then measures A and B by one method (e.g., questionnaire) and C by another method (such as the measurement of overt behavior in a situation test), his findings may be consistent with his hypotheses solely as a function of method variance common to his measures of A and B but not to C.

The requirements of this paper are intended to be as appropriate to the relatively atheoretical efforts typical of the tests and measurements field as to more theoretical efforts. This emphasis on validational criteria appropriate· to our present atheoretical level of test construction is not at all incompatible with a recognition of the desirability of increasing the extent to which all aspects of a test and the testing situation are determined by explicit theoretical considerations, as Jessor and Hammond have advocated (Jessor & Hammond, 1957).

Relation to operationalism. Underwood (1957, p. 54) in his effective presentation of the operationalist point of view shows a realistic awareness of the amorphous type of theory with which most psychologists work. He contrasts a psychologist's "literary" conception with the latter's operational definition as represented by his test or other measuring instrument. He recognizes the importance of the literary definition in communicating and generating science. He cautions that the operational definition "may not at all measure the process he wishes to measure; it may measure something quite different" (1957, p. 55). He does not, however, indicate how one would know when one was thus mistaken.

The requirements of the present paper may be seen as an extension of the kind of operationalism Underwood has expressed. The test constructor is asked to generate from his literary conception or private construct not one operational embodiment, but two or more, each as different in research vehicle as possible. Furthermore, he is asked to make explicit the distinction between his new variable and other variables, distinctions which are almost certainly implied in his literary definition. In his very first validational efforts, before he ever rushes into print, he is asked to apply the several methods and several traits jointly. His literary definition, his conception, is now best represented in what his independent measures of the trait hold *distinctively* in common. The multitrait-multimethod matrix is, we believe, an important practical first step in avoiding "the danger . . . that the investigator will fall into the trap of thinking that because he went from an artistic or literary conception . . . to the construction of items for a scale to measure it, he has validated his artistic conception" (Underwood, 1957, p. 55). In contrast with the *single operationalism* now dominant in psychology, we are advocating a *multiple operationalism*, a convergent *operationalism* (Garner, 1954; Garner, Hake, & Eriksen, 1956) a *methodological triangulation* (Campbell, 1953, 1956), an *operational delineation* (Campbell, 1954), a *convergent validation*.

Underwood's presentation and that of this paper as a whole imply moving from concept to operation, a sequence that is frequent in science, and perhaps typical. The same point can be made, however, in inspecting a transition from operation to construct. For any body of data taken from a single operation, there is a subinfinity of interpretations possible; a subinfinity of concepts, or combinations of concepts, that it could represent. Any single operation, as representative of concepts, is equivocal. In an analogous fashion, when we view the Ames distorted room from a fixed point and through a single eye, the data of the retinal pattern are equivocal, in that a subinfinity of hexahedrons could generate the same pattern. The addition of a second viewpoint, as through binocular parallax, greatly reduces this equivocality, greatly limits the constructs that could jointly account for both sets of data. In Garner's (1954) study, the fractionation measures from a single method were equivocal—they could have been a function of the stimulus distance being fractionated, or they could have been a function of the comparison stimuli used in the judgment process. A multiple, convergent operationalism reduced this equivocality, showing the latter conceptualization to be the appropriate one, and revealing a preponderance of methods variance. Similarly for learning studies: in identifying constructs with the response data

from animals in a specific operational setup there is equivocality which can operationally be reduced by introducing transposition tests, different operations so designed as to put to comparison the rival conceptualizations (Campbell, 1954).

Garner's convergent operationalism and our insistence on more than one method for measuring each concept depart from Bridgman's early position that "if we have more than one set of operations, we have more than one concept, and strictly there should be a separate name to correspond to each different set of operations" (Bridgman, 1927, p. 10). At the current stage of psychological progress, the crucial requirement is the demonstration of some convergence, not complete congruence, between two distinct sets of operations. With only one method, one has no way of distinguishing trait variance from unwanted method variance. When psychological measurement and conceptualization become better developed, it may well be appropriate to differentiate conceptually between Trait-Method Unit A_1 and Trait-Method Unit A_2 in which Trait A is measured by different methods. More likely, what we have called method variance will be specified theoretically in terms of a set of constructs. (This has in effect been illustrated in the discussion above in which it was noted that the response set variance might be viewed as trait variance, and in the rearrangement of the social intelligence matrices of Tables 4 and 5.) It will then be recognized that measurement procedures usually involve several theoretical constructs in joint application. Using obtained measurements to estimate values for a single construct under this condition still requires comparison of complex measures varying in their trait composition, in something like a multitrait-multimethod matrix. Mill's joint method of similarities and differences still epitomizes much about the effective experimental clarification of concepts.

The evaluation of a multitrait-multimethod matrix. The evaluation of the correlation matrix formed by intercorrelating several trait-method units must take into consideration the many factors which are known to affect the magnitude of correlations. A value in the validity diagonal must be assessed in the light of the reliabilities of the two measures involved: e.g., a low reliability for Test A_2 might exaggerate the apparent method variance in Test A_1. Again, the whole approach assumes adequate sampling of individuals: the curtailment of the sample with respect to one or more traits will depress the reliability coefficients and intercorrelations involving these traits. While restrictions of range over all traits produces serious difficulties in the interpretation of a multitrait-multimethod matrix and should be avoided whenever possible, the presence of different degrees of restriction on different traits is the more serious hazard to meaningful interpretation.

Various statistical treatments for multitrait-multimethod matrices might be developed. We have considered rough tests for the elevation of a value in the validity diagonal above the comparison values in its row and column. Correlations between the columns for variables measuring the same trait, variance analyses, and factor analyses have been proposed to us. However, the development of such statistical methods is beyond the scope of this paper. We believe that such summary statistics are neither necessary nor appropriate at this time. Psychologists today should be concerned not with evaluating tests as if the tests were fixed and definitive, but rather with developing better tests. We believe that a careful examination of a multitrait-multimethod matrix will indicate to the experimenter what his next steps should be: it will indicate which methods should be discarded or replaced, which concepts need sharper delineation, and which concepts are poorly measured because of excessive or confounding method variance. Validity judgments based on such a matrix must take into account the stage of development of the constructs, the postulated relationships among them, the level of technical refinement of the methods, the relative independence of the methods, and any pertinent characteristics of the sample of Ss. We are proposing that the validational process be viewed as an aspect of an ongoing program for improving measuring procedures and that the "validity coefficients" obtained at any one stage in the process be interpreted in terms of gains over preceding stages and as indicators of where further effort is needed.

The design of a multitrait-multimethod matrix. The several methods and traits included in a validational matrix should be selected with care. The several methods used to measure each trait should be appropriate to the trait as conceptualized. Although this view will reduce the range of suitable methods, it will rarely restrict the measurement to one operational procedure.

Wherever possible, the several methods in one matrix should be completely independent of each other: there should be no prior reason for believing that they share method variance. This requirement is necessary to permit the values in the heteromethod-heterotrait triangles to approach zero. If the nature of the traits rules out such independence of methods, efforts should be made to obtain as much diversity as possible in terms of data-sources and classification processes. Thus, the classes of stimuli *or* the background situations, the experimental contexts, should be different. Again, the persons providing the observations should have different roles *or* the procedures for scoring should be varied.

Plans for a validational matrix should take into account the difference between the interpretations regarding convergence and discrimination. It is sufficient to demonstrate convergence between two clearly distinct methods which show little overlap in the heterotrait-heteromethod triangles. While agreement between several methods is desirable, convergence between two is a satisfactory minimal requirement. Discriminative validation is not so easily achieved. Just as it is impossible to prove the null hypothesis, or that some object does not exist, so one can never establish that a trait, as measured, is differentiated from all other traits. One can only show that this measure of Trait A has little overlap with those measures of B and C, and no dependable generalization beyond B and C can be made. For example, social poise could probably be readily discriminated from aesthetic interests, but it should also be differentiated from leadership.

Insofar as the traits are related and are expected to correlate with each other, the monomethod correlations will be substantial and heteromethod correlations between traits will also be positive. For ease of interpretation, it may be best to include in the matrix at least two traits, and preferably two sets of traits, which are postulated to be independent of each other.

In closing, a word of caution is needed. Many multitrait-multimethod matrices will show no convergent validation: No relationship may be found between two methods of measuring a trait. In this common situation, the experimenter should examine the evidence in favor of several alternative propositions: (a) Neither method is adequate for measuring the trait; (b) One of the two methods does not really measure the trait. (When the evidence indicates that a method does not measure the postulated trait, it may prove to measure some other trait. High correlations in the heterotrait-heteromethod triangles may provide hints to such possibilities.) (c) The trait is not a functional unity, the response tendencies involved being specific to the nontrait attributes of each test. The failure to demonstrate convergence may lead to conceptual developments rather than to the abandonment of a test.

Summary

This paper advocates a validational process utilizing a matrix of intercorrelations among tests representing at least two traits, each measured by at least two methods. Measures of the same trait should correlate higher with each other than they do with measures of different traits involving separate methods. Ideally, these validity values should also be higher than the correlations among different traits measured by the same method.

Illustrations from the literature show that these desirable conditions, as a set, are rarely met. Method or apparatus factors make very large contributions to psychological measurements.

The notions of convergence between independent measures of the same trait and discrimination between measures of different traits are compared with previously published formulations, such as construct validity and convergent operationalism. Problems in the application of this validational process are considered.

REFERENCES

AMERICAN PSYCHOLOGICAL ASSOCIATION. Technical recommendations for psychological tests and diagnostic techniques. *Psychol. Bull., Suppl.*, 1954, **51**, Part 2, 1–38.

ANDERSON, E. E. Interrelationship of drives in the male albino rat, I. Intercorrelations of measures of drives. *J. comp. Psychol.*, 1937, **24**, 73–118.

AYER, A. J. *The problem of knowledge.*

New York: St Martin's Press, 1956.

BORGATTA, E. F. Analysis of social interaction and sociometric perception. *Sociometry*, 1954 **17**, 7–32.

BORGATTA, E. F. Analysis of social interaction: Actual, role-playing, and projective. *J. abnorm. soc. Psychol.*, 1955, **51**, 394–405.

BRIDGMAN, P. W. *The logic of modern physics.* New York: Macmillan, 1927.

BURWEN, L. S., & CAMPBELL, D. T. The generality of attitudes toward authority and nonauthority figures. *J. abnorm. soc. Psychol.*, 1957, **54**, 24–31.

CAMPBELL, D. T. *A study of leadership among submarine officers.* Columbus: Ohio State Univer. Res. Found., 1953.

CAMPBELL, D. T. Operational delineation of "what is learned" via the transposition experiment. *Psychol. Rev.*, 1954, **61**, 167–174.

CAMPBELL, D. T. *Leadership and its effects upon the group.* Monogr. No. 83. Columbus: Ohio State Univer. Bur. Business Res., 1956.

CARROLL, J. B. Ratings on traits measured by a factored personality inventory. *J. abnorm. soc. Psychol.*, 1952, **47**, 626–632.

CHI, P.-L. Statistical analysis of personality rating. *J. exp. Educ.*, 1957, **5**, 229–245.

CRONBACH, L. J. Response sets and test validity. *Educ. psychol. Measmt*, 1946, **6**, 475–494.

CRONBACH, L. J. *Essentials of psychological testing.* New York: Harper, 1949.

CRONBACH, L. J. Further evidence on response sets and test design. *Educ. psychol. Measmt*, 1950, **10**, 3–31.

CRONBACH, L. J., & MEEHL, P. E. Construct validity in psychological tests. *Psychol. Bull.*, 1955, **52**, 281–302.

EDWARDS, A. L. *The social desirability variable in personality assessment and research.* New York: Dryden, 1957.

FEIGL, H. The mental and the physical. In H. FEIGL, M. SCRIVEN, & G. MAXWELL (Eds.), *Minnesota studies in the philosophy of science.* Vol. II. *Concepts, theories and the mind-body problem.* Minneapolis: Univer. Minnesota Press, 1958.

FISKE, D. W. Consistency of the factorial structures of personality ratings from different sources. *J. abnorm. soc. Psy-*

chol., 1949, **44**, 329–344.

GARNER, W. R. Context effects and the validity of loudness scales. *J. exp. Psychol.*, 1954, **48**, 218–224.

GARNER, W. R., HAKE, H. W., & ERIKSEN, C. W. Operationism and the concept of perception. *Psychol. Rev.*, 1956, **63**, 149–159.

JESSOR, R., & HAMMOND, K. R. Construct validity and the Taylor Anxiety Scale. *Psychol. Bull.*, 1957, **54**, 161–170.

KELLEY, T. L., & KREY, A. C. *Tests and measurements in the social sciences.* New York: Scribner, 1934.

KELLY, E. L., & FISKE, D. W. *The prediction of performance in clinical psychology.* Ann Arbor: Univer. of Michigan Press, 1951.

LOEVINGER, J., GLESER, G. C., & DUBOIS, P. H. Maximizing the discriminating power of a multiple-score test. *Psychometrika*, 1953, **18**, 309–317.

LORGE, I. Gen-like: Halo or reality? *Psychol. Bull.*, 1937, **34**, 545–546.

MAYO, G. D. Peer ratings and halo. *Educ. psychol. Measmt*, 1956, **16**, 317–323.

STRANG, R. Relation of social intelligence to certain other factors. *Sch. & Soc.*, 1930, **32**, 268–272.

SYMONDS, P. M. *Diagnosing personality and conduct.* New York: Appleton-Century, 1931.

THORNDIKE, E. L. A constant error in psychological ratings. *J. appl. Psychol.*, 1920, **4**, 25–29.

THORNDIKE, R. L. Factor analysis of social and abstract intelligence. *J. educ. Psychol.*, 1936, **27**, 231–233.

THURSTONE, L. L. *The reliability and validity of tests.* Ann Arbor: Edwards, 1937.

TRYON, R. C. Individual differences. In F. A. Moss (Ed.), *Comparative Psychology.* (2nd ed.) New York: Prentice-Hall, 1942, pp. 330–365.

UNDERWOOD, B. J. *Psychological research.* New York: Appleton-Century-Crofts, 1957.

VERNON, P. E. Educational ability and psychological factors. Address given to the Joint Education-Psychology Colloquim, Univer. of Illinois, March 29, 1957.

VERNON, P. E. *Educational testing and test-form factors.* Princeton: Educational Testing Service, 1958 (Res. Bull. RB-58-3.)

Construct Validity: A Critique

Harold P. Bechtoldt

In order to accomplish more effective communication between test publishers and test users, a series of "essential," "very desirable," and "desirable" characteristics of the content of test manuals was provided in 1954 by the APA Committee on Psychological Tests (APA, 1954). In the following year two members of the Committee, L. J. Cronbach and P. E. Meehl, (1955) prepared an extended statement on the topic of construct validity, a term introduced in the *Technical Recommendations* to refer to one of the several distinctions noted in the use of the term validity. It should be emphasized that these distinctions refer only to ways of talking about tests and test performances and not to empirical questions. However, the conclusions, generalizations, or predictions arising from empirical investigations are involved since such statements influence both the design of subsequent experiments and the development of theoretical formulations. It is, therefore, appropriate to take note of the way psychologists speak about "construct validity."

Methods of protecting test consumers

The encouragement and constructive suggestions of my associates in the Department of Psychology and in the Child Welfare Research Station are gratefully acknowledged. A portion of this paper was presented at the APA Symposium on Views of Construct Validation, Washington, D.C., September, 1958.

Reprinted by permission of the American Psychological Association and the author from the *American Psychologist*, 1959, **14**, 619–629.

from a *laissez-faire* business philosophy are not being considered at the moment. While the *Technical Recommendations* are clearly restricted to commercial nonresearch devices, the concept of construct validity has been presented as of fundamental importance to many psychologists. It has been said that "construct validation is important at times for every sort of psychological test: aptitude, achievement, interest, and so on . . . Much current research on tests of personality is construct validation . . ." (Cronbach & Meehl, 1955, p. 282–283). The article dealing with the elaboration of the notion of construct validity has been termed ". . . one of the most important papers for the differential psychologist appearing during the span of this [1954–1956] review" (Jenkins & Lykken, 1957, p. 81). In further support of this position, we find another writer stating: ". . . Since predictive, and content validities are all essentially *ad hoc*, construct validity is the whole of validity from a scientific point of view" (Loevinger, 1957, p. 636). Still a fourth very favorable comment states: "Construct validity is an important new concept which has immediate implications for both psychometrician and experimentalist" (Jessor & Hammond, 1957, p. 161).

The primary concern of this paper is with the formulation of construct validity as presented in the several articles noted above. A major objective is to consider critically, but necessarily incompletely, the suggestion that psychologists make a place for the notion of construct validity in their methodological thinking. Some of the "dangers" associated with the concept will be discussed as well as the implication that an "operational methodology" is less appropriate for research involving test data, at least in practical testing (Cronbach & Meehl, 1955, p. 300).[1]

Since this is a type of philosophical treatment by a psychologist who is not a philosopher, the philosophical orientation of this analysis must be made clear. The philosophical position taken here is that of one of the branches of logical positivism, sometimes termed logical empiricism, logical behaviorism, or neobehaviorism. Most psychologists are probably familiar with this philosophical point of view as presented by Bergmann (1943, 1951, 1953, 1954, 1955, 1956, 1957), by Bergmann and Spence (1941), and by Brodbeck (1957, 1958a, 1958b), and from articles by psychologists such as Spence (1944, 1948, 1957, 1958) or Spiker and McCandless (1954). It must be also pointed out that this philosophical position differs with respect to several central issues from that taken by Cronbach and Meehl who have used the writings of Beck (1950), Carnap (1953), Feigl (1950, 1951), Hempel (1953), Pap (1953), and Sellars (1948) among others in presenting their formulation of construct validity. The marshaling of references and appeal to authority, however, are of limited value in science and perhaps even in the philosophy of science. The crucial question in science is the matter of empirical laws and the relations among them. The appraisal of a philosophical analysis of science would be in terms of the success achieved in the clarification of the knowledge and methods used by scientists.

Specifically, it is proposed to use the

terms of one branch of logical positivism in analyzing what has been said and done about construct validity in terms of two questions:

1. How are tests and testing used in psychology?
2. What relation, if any does the use of tests and testing have to the notion of construct validity?

Tests and Testing

Although neither the *Technical Recommendations* nor subsequent elaborations specify a definition of the term "test," a statement from representatives of the APA to the Congress of the United States is available (APA, 1958). In a discussion of aptitudes and abilities, it is stated that "Psychological tests are nothing more than careful observations of actual performance under standard conditions." Testing, then, would refer to the process of obtaining these observations. The distinguishing phrase "careful observations of performance under standard conditions" will, therefore, be substituted for the possibly more emotionally toned words "psychological tests."

As given, this definition of tests is a very general one. The definition carries no implication as to the use to be made of the observations as would terms such as aptitude, diagnostic or achievement. The statement further specifies nothing about the classification of content. No restrictions are stated as to method of responding nor of classifying responses as to any of their many conceivable properties such as presence or absence, rate, style or quality, persistence, intensity or amplitude, accuracy or relative probability of occurence. Conceivably, the careful observations could be obtained with complete mechanical control of the stimuli, the time intervals, the feedback or reinforcements, and the recording of responses.

This definition of "psychological tests"

[1] Cronbach and Meehl explicitly state they are not advocating construct validation over other methods (1955, p. 284, 300), but their treatment is somewhat inconsistent on this point. The other papers noted above are definitely favorable toward construct validity as the preferred concept.

states the basic preliminary point of this discussion. "Careful observations of performance under standard conditions" are used by psychologists everywhere: in the laboratory, in the clinic, in the schools, and in industry. There are no fundamental distinctions between "psychological test" observations per se and other equally systematic controlled observations of performance used by psychologists.

The first question can, therefore, be phrased as: "How are careful observations of performance under standard conditions used in psychology?" The work of nearly all psychologists represents two distinctive ways in which observations of performance are used. Stated in the language of the logical behaviorists, these uses are first, in the definition of psychological concepts of varying degree of abstractness and, second, in the statement of laws about concepts and of relations among such laws. The laws, or generalizations, are statements about how the referents of some concepts affect other concepts. Each such law in psychology regularly involves one concept referring to properties of behavior and one or more other concepts which may refer to features, past and/or present, of the organism's physical environment, to physiological states or events within their bodies, or to other concepts defined by experimentally independent observations of behavior (Bergmann, 1951, 1953, 1957; Brodbeck, 1957, 1958a; Spence, 1957).

In the terminology of the philosophy of science being used, sets of these laws or generalizations relating defined concepts, if deductively connected, are called theories with some of the laws called the axioms, logically implying other laws, termed theorems. As a goal for psychology, the development of systems of deductively connected empirical laws is generally accepted and the quantitative comprehensive theories of physics have been held up as prototypes of those for psychology. However,

it is also generally agreed that in psychology we have no comprehensive theories as the term is used in physics, certainly no axiomatized system like that used in atomic physics, nor even a start in the development of the very general laws required for comprehensive theories (Cronbach & Meehl, 1955; Spence, 1957, 1958).

An answer to the first question of how psychological tests are used in psychology has now been indicated. Psychological tests like any other "careful observations of performance" are used in the definition of concepts varying in abstractness; in the development of psychological laws, i.e., those concerned with the prediction of behavior and of changes in behavior, and in the development of limited sets of deductively interrelated empirical laws. It is contended that this formulation of how observations of performance are *currently* used, and will be used for some time, is inclusive, logically sound, experimentally useful, and sufficient.

Construct Validity and Tests

Consider now the second question which deals with the relation between the careful observations of performance obtained by the use of tests on the one hand and the formulation of construct validity on the other. From the viewpoint of logical positivism sketched in outline form above, what can be said about construct validity?

Although no explicit definition of construct validity is offered by any of the writers dealing with this topic, a number of statements are made from which one is to induce the class characteristics:

Construct validation is involved whenever a test is to be interpreted as a measure of some attribute or quality which is not "operationally defined." The problem faced by the investigator is, "what constructs account for variance in test performance?" . . . Construct validity is not to be identified solely by particular investigative procedures, but by the orientation of the investigator (Cronbach & Meehl, 1955, p. 282).

Construct validity is ordinarily studied when the tester has no definite criterion measure of the quality with which he is concerned, and must use indirect measures. Here the trait or quality underlying the test is of central importance, rather than either the test behavior or the scores on the criteria (APA, 1954, p. 14).

An answer to the second question will involve consideration, among others, of the above illustrative statements.

Operational Definitions

Construct validation is introduced by Cronbach and Meehl as being involved whenever a test is to be interpreted as a measure of some attribute or quality which is not operationally defined, with considerable emphasis placed on the rejection of the necessity for operationally defined concepts or constructs. From the view here taken, there either are no cases to which construct validity would apply in an embryonic empirical science, excepting only the simple characters being named by "undefined descriptive terms" (Bergmann, 1957, p. 14); or a different definition of "operationally defined" is used; or the discussion is not germane to an empirical science of psychology.

Can the discrepancy be a matter of the simple notion of an operational definition? An operational definition is simply a verbal statement of the *if-then* type specifying the observable conditions or rules of procedure under which the term is to be applied in the definition of descriptive or empirical concepts or variables (Bergmann, 1957; Brodbeck, 1957). The only contributions made by operational definitions to an empirical science are those of clarity, objectivity, and precision or accuracy of statement; such definitions enable one

to determine, and eventually eliminate, the "ignorance" and "error" represented in any "imperfect" formulation. Terms like hostility, aggression, psychopathic deviate, intelligence, and mechanical ability have some referents and some rules for their use. They are operationally defined in any empirical study, but the specification for their use may change with time. Without specification of rules, or changes therein, for using such defined terms, neither accurate communication nor precise experimentation is possible in any science.

The process of developing definitions for a concept is, in actual practice, neither simple nor unerring. Any creative investigator "breaking ground" will usually have one or more hunches or guesses about the way two or more things in which he is interested might influence one another. As long as the notion remains so personal, so private, and so imprecise that the referents of terms cannot be designated nor the necessary conditions considered as achieved, the guesses are outside the realm of empirical science. When, however, an investigator states explicitly a set of rules or conditions for the application of his terms, the statements are of scientific interest. The explicit statement constitutes an initial definition of the concept; but like any formulation, the initial one may well be useless, somewhat useful, or entirely satisfactory. Those definitions that are of limited usefulness will be re-examined in terms of the available empirical evidence. One common course of action taken in experimental psychology to increase the usefulness of a concept involves redefining the notion by a second, but different, explicit statement (Spence & Ross, 1959). After several experimental studies have resulted in one or more changes of definition, one might say the early concepts were imprecise, incomplete, vague, or of limited usefulness. But, strictly speaking, each change of definition introduces a new concept.

These definitions are *not* alternative definitions of the same concept.

The term "vague" so often applied to "imprecise" concepts requires further comment. Vague may refer to that which has not been defined, to the ambiguous, or to the "private" and "subjective." Or the term may refer to an incomplete explicit definition used in an early statement of a concept. These referents are not identical. Dissatisfaction expressed by investigators with an initial "rough," incomplete definition is a reaction against ignorance and error rather than against a strategy of investigation. To admit ignorance as a temporary state of science is one thing. To raise vagueness or lack of definition to the central status of a methodological principle is another. The "constructs" of construct validity appear to be "vague," open, and "not explicitly defind" as a matter of principle rather than as a matter of ignorance.

The statement that changes in the rules properly imply the use of a new word or a subscript to the old word has met with definite objection when applied to the area of intelligence tests (Jenkins & Lykken, 1957, p. 88). However, the fear that such practice prevents the gradual evolution of ideas is baseless; the logical empiricists recognize the gradual and continuous replacement by scientists of less useful concepts with more useful ones (Bergmann, 1943). At each stage of development of a concept, however, the rules for the current usage of the term are to be stated.

In the *Technical Recommendations* (APA, 1954, p. 15), it is stated with emphasis that *"behavior-relevance* in a construct is not logically the same as *behavior-equivalence"* and that psychological constructs need not be *equivalent* to any direct operational behavior measure. Since concepts and, for the moment, constructs may vary in degree of abstractness or length of the definitional chains, there may indeed be many steps between the undefined basic terms, possibly including direct or immediate observations of behavior, and highly abstract defined concepts.

The distinction between undefined and defined descriptive terms is technically based on the principle of (direct) acquaintance, undefined terms naming characters or properties with which the person is directly acquainted. All other descriptive terms are defined (Bergmann, 1957, p. 14–15). The definition, i.e., the conditional features of the *if-then* statement, is reasonably simple for the case of the "response time" property of the eyelid reflex, of a finger withdrawal, or of some vocalization. The definitional operations are somewhat different, perhaps more complex, but still expressed in terms of manifest behavior, when the W, $F+$ or d responses among others to each Rorschach card are evaluated. Meehl (1956) has reported how Halbower used fairly complex and involved procedures to define a few objective personality descriptions in terms of the observed responses of patients to the MMPI. Other "response defined" and rather "abstract" concepts of interest to psychologists include most of the "psychological qualities" or "attributes" or traits presented in the discussions of construct validity (Cronbach, 1957; Cronbach & Meehl, 1955).

Since nearly all defined psychological concepts require very complicated definitional chains, the concepts are indeed not "behaviorally-equivalent" if we restrict "behavior-equivalence," for example, to speed or accuracy of any one response. The concepts are, however, defined in terms of properties of observable behavior under specified conditions and in accordance with specified procedures. If the APA test committee were restricting the definition of terms to the "immediately, or almost immediately, observable" characters or properties of manifest behavior, its dissatisfaction with "operational definitions" would be understandable. This condition would imply a definition of "operationally defined" which is far more restrictive and limited than that recommended by the logical behaviorists (Bergmann, 1955). However, if the advocates of construct validity are contending that explicit definitions of terms in empirical science are not essential, then the issue is basic; such disagreement is one that has both "philosophical" and scientific overtones.

Characteristics of Constructs

Although the matter of requiring single explicit definitions of concepts or terms may, or may not, be a point of basic disagreement, an issue does seem to arise in connection with the term "construct." That the notion of "construct" is fundamental to the discussion of construct validity seems indicated (APA, 1954; Cronbach & Meehl, 1955; Jenkins & Lykken, 1957; Jessor & Hammond, 1957). A construct is presented by Cronbach and Meehl as involving at least three characteristics. First, it is a *postulated attribute* assumed to be reflected in test performances; second, it has *predictive* properties; and third, the *meaning* of a construct is given by the laws in which it occurs with the result that clarity of knowledge of the constructs is a positive function of the completeness of that set of laws, termed the nomological net.

Meaning. The third of these characteristics uses the term "meaning" which has at least two technical interpretations. On this point, disagreement among philosophers of science again will be found. The logical empiricists have distinguished between two technical usages of the term: one to refer to the operational definition or empirical referent of a concept, i.e., the "meaning" of a concept, and the second usage to refer to the usefulness or "significance" of a concept as indicated by the theoretical or empirical laws into which it enters

(Bergmann, 1951, 1957; Brodbeck, 1957). The logical behaviorists say that a defined concept may be without significance, but significant concepts must be defined. From the logical behaviorists' point of view, the third characteristic above states that concepts vary in usefulness or significance with the greater significance associated with both the number and theoretical or empirical implications of the laws into which they enter.

The development and use of the Taylor Manifest Anxiety Scale (MAS) provides an example of the distinction between meaning and significance. The "meaning" of "manifest anxiety" is given by the procedures for presenting the selected verbal statements or items and for combining the weighted responses of each subject. The resulting score then defines (is the meaning of) the variable "manifest anxiety." Implicit in the defining procedures are such requirements as: to be used with English-speaking adults having an United States cultural background, etc. The usefulness or significance of the MAS score depends on the relations of the MAS with other variables. Two kinds of relations involving the MAS scores have been investigated: one deals with certain drive properties of the MAS variable in experimental studies of simple learning phenomena and the other involves the congruence of two or more response-defined variables both including in the title the word "anxiety." Since both types of relations have been shown to be statistically significant in two or more studies, the MAS can be said to have some degree of usefulness or signficance (Spence, 1958; Taylor, 1951, 1953). If no theoretical or empirical relation could be demonstrated between the MAS and any other variable, the MAS would be said to be well defined or meaningful but without significance.

Significance and Validity. For a number of years one aspect of the "significance" of a variable has been fairly precisely expressed by the notion of "empirical validity." Empirical validity refers to the results of empirical tests of relations between a dependent variable of behavior and one or more independent or predictor measures. There will, of course, be as many indices of validity of a variable as there are dependent variables with which it can be paired (Anastasi, 1950; Bechtoldt, 1951; Cronbach, 1949). A determination of the usefulness or empirical validity of the MAS as a predictor of some other variable also entitled "anxiety" and defined by psychiatric ratings or by responses to other sets of stimuli can be made. But such an appraisal is not an index of the significance of the MAS as a drive variable in Spence's (1958) theory of performance on simple learning situations.

Yet, the "meaning" of the concept of manifest anxiety, according to the formulation of construct validity, is to be given by the laws into which it enters. Which of the many laws, or sets of laws, are to be used? All of them, or only those related by a "theory," a theory some writer may prefer, for example, to the one initially formulated? In construct validity terms the concept may have no "meaning" or some "meaning," the appraisal depending on an arbitrary, or even capricious, selection of a "theory" and of the dependent variables with which the given variable or concept is paired. The logical empiricists would simply say the defined concept is related to some variables but not to others or that the concept enters into some laws but not others. The confusion resulting from the use of the single word "meaning" for both definition and significance seems unnecessary and undesirable.

Constructs and "the criterion." The meaning-significance confusion also occurs in the statements of the relation of constructs to "criteria." It is suggested (APA, 1954, p. 14; Cronbach & Meehl, 1955, p. 282) that construct validity is to be investigated whenever no criterion

or universe of content is accepted as entirely adequate to define the quality to be measured. A failure to separate the defining operations, including content restrictions, from the empirical matter of relations with other variables is evident. In accordance with the construct validity notion, a quality or variable can be defined, when a criterion is available, by the relation of the test to the criterion rather than by the operations of the test itself. But when no criterion is available, the quality is not defined; instead, the construct validity of the test is to be investigated. Three points need to be made with regard to the central position of the "criterion" in this decision making process. First, a criterion measure is a behavioral or response defined variable used as the dependent variable in an investigation. As a behavioral measure, some sequence of operations involving "careful observations of performance" is selected or developed at some (usually earlier) time as the conditional features of the definition. Second, the defining operations are in no way intrinsically different from those used to define any other behavioral variable such as one utilized, for example, as an independent variable. Third, if a variable is *accepted* as the dependent variable, i.e., as the criterion, then indeed a status difference may be created which is reflected in several technical procedures such as the assignment of errors of prediction to the dependent variable and the weighting of the independent variables so as to minimize the errors of prediction. But in no other way is a criterion variable any different from any other test or response defined variable.

Differences among experimenters in the types of predictions they wish to make and the problems of interest to them are reflected in the emphasis placed on the criterion. In situations where the experimenter is task oriented or problem oriented, as is the case in most applied studies and in "practical testing," the dependent variable would be *defined first* and perhaps given status by *naming* it "the criterion," whether intermediate or final. In such admittedly practical problems, the criterion-orientation seems entirely reasonable. The question asked is of the form: "What defined variables of any kind can be used to predict performance on the criterion?" Those variables that show significant relations with the criterion are said to be "valid" (useful) predictors. No claim to theoretical usefulness is involved; the demonstration of one or more stable empirical relations is both necessary and sufficient (Bechtoldt, 1951). In other experimental situations in which the experimenter is interested in a variable per se or as a part of some theoretical formulation, i.e., when he can be said to be variable-oriented, no special status is given to the dependent variable of behavior. In this second case the dependent variable, in fact, is usually selected or developed *after* the independent variable is defined. A "criterion" or behavioral measure will be selected in the second case so that the effect of the independent or experimental variable may be exhibited if the variable enters into the theory or nomological net as hypothesized. The term validity properly could also be applied to such cases in precisely the same sense as in the problem oriented situation. However, the experimental psychologists, who have long used this variable oriented approach and research procedure, have not found the naming of such relations necessary.

Prediction. The second characteristic of a construct appears at first glance to give no occasion for concern. Cronbach and Meehl state (1955, p. 284):

A construct has certain associated meanings carried in statements of this general character: Persons who possess this attribute will, in situation X, act in manner Y (with a stated probability).

The "associated meanings" appear to include the class of "test interpretations," i.e., various predictions, as well as what-

ever "accounts for variance in test performance." The form of the statement is that of the common predictive model. Such statements are laws. The second characteristic asserts that constructs must enter into laws.

Now the notion of explanation in science is often presented, in part, in terms of such a predictive model. If the predictions are logically deduced from other laws and are sustained experimentally, the new observations are said to be "understandable," to be explained by the "axioms" or premises of the set (Bergmann, 1957). However, many predictions in psychology are not deduced from a set of premises but are essentially statements of the reproducibility of previous empirical results. For such "predictions" as well as for "deduced" statements, an empirical test of the accuracy of the prediction regarding behavior Y requires only rules, operations, or procedures for determining, first, whether "manner Y" occurs; second, whether situation X is present; and third, whether the persons with whom we are dealing have the attribute.

For these empirical checks, the concepts must be defined. Every example used by Cronbach and Meehl to elucidate how construct validation can be accomplished requires some definition of the attribute in behavioral terms. The well-known procedures for evaluating changes in a dependent variable as a function of one or more independent variables are exemplified by their illustrations. In fact, the several recommended validation procedures of construct validity are those regularly used by research psychologists investigating hypotheses involving psychological concepts. It is, therefore, considered that, *in practice*, the second characteristic of lawful relations is empirically sound; nothing new nor confusing is involved.

Postulated attributes. The first of the three characteristics of a construct, however, is considered as a serious source of confusion. The statement is that a construct is a postulated attribute assumed to be reflected in test performance. This notion also appears in such statements as: the trait or quality underlying the test is of central importance, rather than either the test behavior or the scores on the criteria (APA, 1954, p. 14); or "the" or the "real" trait is being "indirectly" or "not really" measured by the test performance (Campbell & Fiske, 1959; Loevinger, 1957). The "postulation" and "assumption" features of this characteristic are more accurately labeled hunches, guesses, or working hypotheses about relations among concepts, i.e., about laws or sets of laws termed theories. The third characteristic states that a hypothesis or even a theory about test behavior has been formulated.

As postulated attributes assumed to be reflected in test performance, many possible sets of words or symbols, often referred to as "theories" or "models" (Brodbeck, 1958b) may be generated by an ingenious, talented and persistent writer. As literary or mathematical exercises, they may indeed be accurate, elegant, and internally consistent. The question, however, is the relevance of these formulations to behavior and to experimental investigation of the statements. If the constructs or psychological attributes are response defined, either by a simple or complicated series of *if-then* statements, and if the behaviors involved in these definitions or the performances under consideration, then the statements are not hypotheses about empirical relations but are definitions (Bergmann, 1957). Essentially, such statements apply new names and/or transformations to old things. A "construct," in such cases is a defined concept or variable, values of which are assigned to an individual on the basis of "careful observations of his performance under standard conditions." That "ability" is so defined has been noted by Lord (1952) who states:

Since, in the final analysis, the only observable variables under consideration are the item responses, any operational definition of ability for present purposes must consist of a statement of a relationship between ability and item responses (p. 4).

Nearly all postulated constructs listed in the papers on construct validity are also of the defined type. It is here suggested that a considerable number, if not all, of the so-called theoretical formulations in psychology dealing with postulated attributes simply use complex definitional transformations of a person's performance as a substitute for an empirical theory. Such transformations indeed may prove to be useful in "practical" situations involving communications with clients and employers. The new names and related hunches (surplus meanings) also may reduce (or increase) the generation of false "working hypotheses," but the transformations as such are neither theories nor laws. The transformations provide only definitions of concepts.

The possibility of psychologists confusing tautologies with empirical or theoretical relations was recognized by the APA Test Committee (1954) and by Cronbach and Meehl (1955). In several statements dealing with the nomological net, they insist upon "explicit public steps of inference," upon "contact with observations," and upon "accuracy of prediction" as the final test of a theory. It is also clear that both Cronbach and Meehl favor testing directly or indirectly the hypotheses of the network. However, more than earnest requests for logically correct deductions having some contact with empirical observations is necessary in extending the important but difficult process of building an empirical theory of behavior that will indicate how certain variables may account for variance in test performance. As shown below, the formulation of construct validity can be interpreted as making less of a contribution to the development of such a theory than does an empirically oriented methodology using explicit operational definitions of the variables.

Variables Affecting Behavior

What can be said as to the variables affecting any given behavior, including test performance? It has been demonstrated empirically that behavior is influenced by the amount of formal or informal practice or training on similar materials or methods of response. Strong response tendencies and habits of acquiescence or of avoidance of painful or noxious stimuli would be expected to affect behavior in many given situations. Characteristics of the examiner, of the cultural setting, or of the physiological states of the organism may lead to temporary or persistent behaviors under specified conditions. Surely the formulation of the basic concepts assumed to be reflected in test performance must include reference to such conditions and to other concepts defined by various experimental manipulations or operations. Such empirical concepts are appropriate answers to the question: "What constructs account for variance in test performance?" (Cronbach & Meehl, 1955, p. 282). That response defined variables, such as traits are emphasized in the papers on construct validity as examples of the basic explanatory concepts probably is a reflection of the lack of control and of knowledge of the experiential history of the subjects used in studies involving human behavior. This lack of knowledge and lack of control of the subjects makes the task of developing laws and theories difficult, but probably not impossible.

As practical devices for the prediction of behavior, traits are clearly useful. That they may also be introduced into theoretical formulations of behavior has been shown by Taylor, Spence, and their associates in terms of the Manifest Anxiety Scale (Spence, 1958; Taylor, 1951). That the theoretical use of response defined variables is not widely understood is clear from several discussions dealing with the validity of the A scale (Bechtoldt, 1953b; Jenkins & Lykken, 1957; Jessor & Hammond, 1957; Kausler & Trapp, 1959; Spence, 1958). The confusion attendant upon the notion of construct validity will be obvious to the readers of these papers.

Traits in Psychological Theorizing

The chief difficulty of the trait or response defined variable approach in the development of theoretical formulations is the fact that a given behavior can arise from many different combinations of experimental conditions. These different conditions involve different concepts and different sets of explanatory laws. Any one of dozens of so-called theories or sets of explanatory constructs can be postulated or assumed and be "correct" in terms of the agreement between prediction and observation. Cronbach (1958) has recently added a valuable postscript to this point in a paper dealing with social-perception scores. He says:

To interpret a score as a reflection of subtle interpersonal relations, or of covert attitudes about another person, may be to force complex meanings into a very simple phenomena (p. 353).

And then he adds:

. . . if a behavior which looks like "projection" can arise out of many different processes, there is little point in trying to formulate hypotheses using the concept of "projection" (p. 375).

The point at issue is the development of a theory, or nomological net, using response defined variables which will have explanatory, predictive properties in specified situations. The theory would consist of a set of meaningful concepts and statements about how each given concept enters into specified laws. With such a theory, it is possible to determine whether a given concept, as defined, actually does enter into those laws. To the degree to which the predictions are sustained under the specified boundary conditions of the theory, the concept has significance and, apparently, "construct validity." Extending the hypotheses to include other concepts represents the process of "elaborating the nomological network" (Cronbach & Meehl, 1955, p. 290). Tests of the accuracy of the hypotheses will utilize, among others, the several experimental "validation" procedures of "construct validity." However, as a theory develops and achieves some limited successes, the number of inappropriate and irrelevant "tests" of stated hypotheses can be expected to grow also. Although labeled as "tests of the theory," such studies often represent unwarranted generalizations or improper extensions of the hypotheses or serious misconceptions about the concepts or the structure of the theory itself (Spence, 1958).

It must be emphasized that the private, inductive process involved in the invention of hypotheses, of ideas, or of concepts is not being questioned. There are neither rules nor deductive or inductive principles for the invention of fruitful hypotheses or the definition of significant concepts or the formulation of comprehensive theories. There are no logical reasons why some "theory" of behavior must *a priori* contain defined concepts expressing currently popular "common sense" notions or explanations. Nor are there any reasons to specify some test form or method of test (apparatus) construction as inherently useful or logically necessary in order for the test to be consistent with the procedures of construct validation or with the principles of logical behaviorism (for an opposing view see Jessor & Hammond, 1957, p. 162).

Neither is there any justification for proposing the techniques of empirical, or "classical," validity as the sole methods to be used in selecting test items. The "adequacy" of any technique as a

basis for test construction is a matter of the usefulness of the resulting test for empirical or theoretical purposes (for a contrary view, see Loevinger, 1957, p. 637). However, it is generally recognized that tests developed by utilizing relations with a "criterion" have at least some empirical significance, although they may, or may not, enter into any set of theoretical relations.

What is being questioned is the tendency to consider as a part of a public empirical science hunches involving "vague," ill-defined variables and relations between such variables, these hunches being derived primarily from the observed performance. The extent to which this activity is common in so-called "theorizing" in psychology can perhaps be judged from the frequency with which one encounters "deductions" involving sufficient, but not necessary, conditions such as the following taken from Johnson (1954):

If "Old Dog Tray" was run through a large and powerful sausage-grinder, he is dead; he is dead, therefore, he was sausaged (p. 723).

Amusing? But what about this one?

If a person has an over-compensated inferiority complex, he blusters, is aggressive, domineering and dogmatic; this man blusters, is aggressive, domineering and dogmatic; therefore, he has an inferiority complex.

The weaknesses and dangers of the postulational technique used *without* explicit definitions or empirical referents or "interpretations" for the premises can perhaps be even more clearly seen in the "valid" deduction and "contact with observations" implicit in this old syllogism: "Bread is made of stone, stone is good to eat; therefore, bread is good to eat." The conclusion is "true to fact," but the usual interpretations of the premises are not fulfilled.

Other instances of the postulation of explanatory constructs from behavior in a circular way are often found in discussions of mental abilities and of personality traits. Although frequent reference is made in the literature on construct validity to factor analysis, we find Thurstone quite clear on the point that an ability is *defined* by a specific test procedure and the method of scoring (Thurstone, 1947). Each test defines a separate ability; several tests involving the "same content" but different methods of presenting the stimuli or of responding likewise define different abilities. Thurstone also clearly *names* the "reference or common abilities" as those used to express the scores on the remaining tests in terms of an assumed linear function. The factors, for all experimental purposes, are literally defined as composite scores on specified subsets of tests in such batteries as the Primary Mental Abilities Tests (L. L. Thurstone & T. G. Thurstone, 1950) or the Educational Testing Service Kit of Reference Tests (French, 1954).

It is well to note, in connection with statements about factors, that the "interpretation" of the common source of variance of a "factor" and the "identification" of a "factor" in two different sets of tests as the "same factor" are both statements of hypotheses. Some "empirical generalization" of response tendencies over a variety of stimulus or treatment conditions which can be experimentally varied is implicit in both of these formulations. And, as for any other hypotheses, empirical tests of the predictions are called for. Such tests require unambiguous definitions of the "factors." That the empirical results may not sustain such predictions or "hypotheses" is logically sound and empirically consistent with observations (Bechtoldt, 1953a).

The danger of circularity of a formulation involving the notion of an ability or a "factor" as a concept can easily be eliminated; the "ability" variable can

be defined in advance of an experiment through the use of observations experimentally independent of the behavior and hypothesis to be investigated. This "operational methodology" principle has been extended to some types of factor analysis investigations themselves with a restatement of the factor problem (Bechtoldt, 1958).

Relation of Tests to Construct Validity

An answer to the second question dealing with the relation between the use of tests and the notion of construct validity now can be stated. The relation is simply the linguistic one between any set of empirical observations on the one hand and any philosophy of science formulation on the other, and logically nothing more. The formulation of construct validity as a way of speaking is not restricted to, nor dependent upon, test concepts or performances; rather, the presentation is that of a general methodological viewpoint. For example, recent articles dealing, in part, with construct validity (Campbell & Fiske, 1959; Loevinger, 1957) have mentioned the correspondence between the construct validity formulation and that of "convergent operationalism" advocated for the definition of properties or characteristics of perception (Garner, Hake & Eriksen, 1956). The use of multiple and implicit, rather than single explicit, definitions of terms and the meaning-significance confusion indeed are common to the two notions.

There is, however, a historical accident or coincidence that may account for the identification of construct validity with the area of psychological tests. General dissatisfaction has been expressed from time to time with the usefulness of empirical and statistical concepts of tests and testing; such concepts have been considered inadequate for professional psychological testing activities. Statements of such views tend to create a climate favorable to the acceptance of a new formulation, like construct validity, which emphasizes the language and problems of the practicing counselor or clinician. And the inception and development of the methodological viewpoint of construct validity, in addition, represents a laudable attempt to introduce into clinical and counseling testing activities some integration and understanding of the kind represented by the term theory. That construct validity was the creation of psychologists "interested in and sympathetic to constructs evidenced by performance but distinct from it" is the historical accident.

Conclusions

A major objective of this paper has been to consider critically the suggestion that psychologists make a place for the notion of construct validity in their methodological thinking. This suggestion is rejected for the several reasons given above. The renaming of the process of building a theory of behavior by the new term "construct validity" contributes nothing to the understanding of the process nor to the usefulness of the concepts. The introduction into discussions of psychological theorizing of the aspects of construct validity discussed

in some detail above creates, at best, unnecessary confusion and, at the worst, a nonempirical, nonscientific approach to the study of behavior.

A supplementary objective has been to consider also the relative merits of construct validity and of logical behaviorism plus an operational methodology for the development of psychology as a science. It is suggested here that the terminology of logical behaviorism and the techniques of an "operational methodology" are to be preferred for the formulation and investigation of an empirical, deductive theory of (test) behavior. The statement that an " 'operational methodology' . . . would force research into a mold it does not fit" (Cronbach & Meehl, 1955, p. 300) is rejected as not consistent with published evidence. Considerable space has been devoted to showing how an "operational methodology" can be used in psychological research to improve both the "understanding" and the "prediction" of behavior.

It is, therefore, recommended that the formulation of construct validity, as presented in the several papers noted in this critique, be eliminated from further consideration as a way of speaking about psychological concepts, laws and theories.

REFERENCES

AMERICAN PSYCHOLOGICAL ASSOCIATION, Committee on Psychological Tests. *Technical recommendations for psychological tests and diagnostic techniques.* Washington, D. C.: APA, 1954.

AMERICAN PSYCHOLOGICAL ASSOCIATION. Report of testimony at a congressional hearing. *Amer. Psychologist,* 1958, *13,* 217–223.

ANASTASI, ANNE. The concept of validity in the interpretation of test scores. *Educ. psychol. Measmt,* 1950, *10,* 67–78.

BECHTOLDT, H. P. Selection. In S. S. STEVENS (Ed.), *Handbook of experi-*

mental psychology. New York: Wiley, 1951. Pp. 1237–1267.

BECHTOLDT, H. P. Factor analysis of the Airman Classification Battery with civilian reference tests. *HRRC res. Bull.,* 1953, No. 53–59. (a)

BECHTOLDT, H. P. Response defined anxiety and MMPI variables. *Iowa Acad. Sci.,* 1953, *60,* 495–499. (b)

BECHTOLDT, H. P. Statistical tests of hypotheses in confirmatory factor analysis. *Amer. Psychologist,* 1958, *13,* 380. (Abstract)

BECK, L. W. Constructions and inferred

entities. *Phil. Sci.*, 1950, *17.* (Reprinted: In H. FEIGL & M. BRODBECK (Eds.), *Reading. in the philosophy of science.* New York: Appleton-Century-Crofts, 1953. Pp. 368–381).

BERGMANN, G. Outline of an empiricist philosophy of physics. *Amer. J. Physics,* 1943, *11* (Reprinted: In H. FEIGL & M. BRODBECK (Eds.), *Reading in the philosophy of science.* New York: Appleton-Century-Crofts, 1953. Pp. 262–287).

BERGMANN, G. The logic of psychological concepts. *Phil. Sci.,* 1951, *18,* 93–110.

BERGMANN, G. Theoretical psychology. *Annu. Rev. Psychol.,* 1953, *4,* 435–458.

BERGMANN, G. Sense and nonsense in operationism. *Scient. Mon.,* 1954, *79,* 210–214. (Reprinted: In PH. FRANK (Ed.), *The validation of scientific theories.* Boston: Beacon, 1956. Pp. 41–52.)

BERGMANN, G. Psychoanalysis and the unity of science: Else Frenkel-Brunswik: A review. *J. Phil,* 1955, *52,* 692–695.

BERGMANN, G. The contribution of John B. Watson. *Psychol. Rev.,* 1956, *63,* 265–276.

BERGMANN, G. *Philosophy of Science.* Madison: Univer. Wisconsin Press, 1957.

BERGMANN, G., & SPENCE, K. W. Operationism and theory in psychology. *Psychol Rev.,* 1941, *48,* 1–14.

BRODBECK, M. The philosophy of science and educational research. *Rev. educ. Res.,* 1957, *27,* 427–440.

BRODBECK, M. Methodological individualisms: Definition and reduction. *Phil. Sci.,* 1958, *25,* 1–22. (a)

BRODBECK, M. Models, meaning, and theories. In L. GROSS (Ed.), *Symposium on sociological theory.* Evanston: Row Peterson, 1958. (b)

CAMPBELL, D. T., & FISKE, D. W. Convergent and discriminant validation by the multitrait-multimethod matrix. *Psychol Bull.* 1959, *56,* 81–105.

CARNAP, R. Foundations of logic and mathematics. In *International encyclopedia of unified science.* Vol. I, No. 3. Pp. 56–59. (Reprinted: The interpretation of physics. In H. FEIGL & M. BRODBECK (Eds.), *Readings in the philosophy of science.* New York: Appleton-Century-Crofts, 1953. Pp. 309–318.)

CRONBACH, L. J. *Essentials of psychological testing.* New York: Harper, 1949.

CRONBACH, L. J. The two disciplines of scientific psychology. *Amer. Psychologist,* 1957, *12,* 671–684.

CRONBACH, L. J. Proposals leading to analytic treatment of social perception scores. In R. TAGIURI & L. PETRULLO (Eds.), *Person perception and interpersonal behavior.* Stanford: Stanford Univer. Press, 1958. Pp. 353–379.

CRONBACH, L. J. & MEEHL, P. E. Construct validity in psychological tests. *Psychol. Bull.* 1955, *52,* 281–302.

FEIGL, H. Existential hypotheses. *Phil. Sci.,* 1950, *17,* 35–62.

FEIGL, H. Confirmability and confirmation. *Rev. int. Phil.,* 1951, *5,* 1–12. (Reprinted: In P. P. WIENER (Ed.), *Readings in philosophy of science.* New York: Scribner, 1953, Pp. 522–530.)

FRENCH, J. W. *Manual for kit of selected tests for reference aptitude and achievement factors.* Princeton: Educ. Testing Service, 1954.

GARNER, W. R., HAKE, H. H., & ERIKSEN, C. W. Operationism and the concept of perception. *Psychol. Rev.,* 1956, *63,* 149–159.

HEMPEL, C. G. *Fundamentals of concept formation in empirical science.* Chicago: Univer. Chicago Press, 1952.

JENKINS, J. J., & LYKKEN, D. T. Individual differences. *Annu. Rev. Psychol.,* 1957, *8,* 79–112.

JESSOR, R., & HAMMOND, K. R. Construct validity and the Taylor Anxiety Scale. *Psychol. Bull.,* 1957, *54,* 161–170.

JOHNSON, H. M. On verifying hypotheses by verifying their implicates. *Amer. J. Psychol.* 1954, *67,* 723–727.

KAUSLER, D. J., & TRAPP, E. P. Methodological considerations in the construct validation of drive-oriented scales. *Psychol. Bull.,* 1959, *56,* 152–157.

LOEVINGER, JANE. Objective tests as instruments of psychological theory. *Psychol. Rep.,* 1957, *3,* 635–694.

LORD, F. A. Theory of test scores. *Psychometr. Monogr.,* 1952, No. 7.

MEEHL, P. E. Wanted: A good cookbook. *Amer. Psychologist,* 1956, *11,* 263–272.

PAP, A. Reduction-sentences and open concepts. *Methodos,* 1953, *5,* 3–30.

SELLARS, W. S. Concepts as involving laws and inconceivable without them. *Phil. Sci.,* 1948, *15,* 287–315.

SPENCE, K. W. The nature of theory construction in contemporary psychology. *Psychol. Rev.*, 1944, *51*, 47–68.

SPENCE, K. W. The postulates and methods of behaviorism. *Psychol. Rev.*, 1948, *55*, 67–78.

SPENCE, K. W. The empirical basis and theoretical structure of psychology. *Phil Sci.* 1957, *24*, 97–108.

SPENCE, K. W. A theory of emotionally based drive (*D*) and its relation to performance in simple learning situations. *Amer. Psychologist*, 1958, *13*, 131–141.

SPENCE, K. W., & Ross, L. E. A methodological study of the form and latency of eyelid responses in conditioning. *J. exp. Psychol.*, 1959, *58*, 376–381.

SPIKER, C. C., & McCANDLESS, B. R. The concept of intelligence and the philosophy of science. *Psychol. Rev.*, 1954, *61*, 255–266.

TAYLOR, J. A. The relationship of anxiety to the conditioned eyelid response. *J. exp. Psychol.*, 1951, *41*, 81–92.

TAYLOR, J. A. A personality scale of manifest anxiety. *J. abnorm. soc. Psychol.*, 1953, *48*, 285–290.

THURSTONE, L. L., *Multiple-factor analysis.* Chicago: Univer. Chicago Press, 1947.

THURSTONE, L. L., & THURSTONE, T. G. *Primary mental abilities.* (Manual and tests.) Chicago: Science Research Associates, 1950.

Chapter 4

Population Characteristics
and Clinical Prediction

■ In Parts II and III the reader will find that validation studies often indicate that clinical assessment is not as precise and accurate as most of us would like. This is generally blamed on the instrument, the clinician, the experimenter, or the journal editor's bias, depending on one's outlook. In some cases, however, the fault may lie with none of these scapegoats but instead be a result of the distribution of the trait that is being assessed within a particular population.

In their paper, Meehl and Rosen explore the problems of base rates extensively, demonstrating that the usefulness of a test is often a function of the trait and population that is being studied. This was a point which had been almost totally ignored prior to the publication of this now classic article. Studies were routinely reported in which a test of organicity or delinquency was applied to a sample half of whom were known to have the trait and half not to have it. If the study showed that predictions significantly better than chance were possible with the new test, it was regarded as valid, and, by implication, useful.

However, Meehl and Rosen demonstrate that if the test is applied to a population in which the distribution of the trait differs markedly from this 50–50 division, the use of a moderately valid test may actually result in more diagnostic errors than if the test had not been applied. The test that identifies 90 percent of the delinquents in a sample while misclassifying only 10 percent of the non-delinquents is very impressive in a sample in which the rate of delinquency is 50 percent; such a test would result in correct classification of 90 percent of the testees. If this same instrument were to be applied in a large high school in which the delinquency rate was similar to the national rate of 5 percent, the situation would be quite different. In a school of 1,000 students, 50 would be delinquent and the test would detect 45 of them; however, it should still misclassify 10 percent of the 950 non-delinquents so that 95 would be erroneously called delinquent. This would result in twice as many errors (100) than if the test had not been given and everyone had been termed non-delinquent (50). This dramatically points out the importance of the false positive rate when infrequent traits are being assessed.

It should be pointed out that in certain situations it might be best to administer the test anyway. For instance, in the above example, it might be that the high school assigns one counselor to every 50 students. If three of the school's 20 counselors are especially gifted in working with delinquent or potentially delinquent youngsters, it might be useful to administer the test and assign all the 140 students called "delinquent" to these three counselors. While two-thirds of the students so assigned wouldn't need the services of these particular counselors any more than any other student, such a procedure would maximize the likelihood that the truly delinquent youngsters would be assigned to the men who would work best with them.[1] In effect this procedure would raise the base rate of delinquency among the students counseled by these men from 5 percent to 33 percent. Thus, as Meehl and Rosen point out, the imposition of an externally imposed selection ratio may make tests of infrequent traits worthwhile in some situations.

This same approach of preliminary screening with a moderately valid test to raise the base rate can also be used in what Meehl and Rosen call "successive hurdles" testing in which a second or third test is applied to the group selected on the basis of the first test. Meehl and Rosen state, however, that this approach is best applied only in situations where the decision to be made is of overwhelming importance, as in the case of the identification of operable brain tumors, for even with successive hurdles testing it is often likely that base rate predictions will have a higher success ratio when infrequent events must be predicted.

The reader who wishes to pursue this point would do well to read Rosen's (1954) earlier paper on the prediction of suicide. Since the appearance of the present article, Karson and Sells (1956) have expanded on the point of how supply and demand factors can enter into the consideration of what technique to use. Dawes (1962) has attempted to prove that, contrary to Meehl and Rosen's position, the prediction of infrequent events is a worthwhile activity. The basis for this argument is a reanalysis of Bayes' theorem in terms of conditional probability.

While Meehl and Rosen's primary concern was the large number of false positives that may result when a test is applied to a population in which a trait is quite rare, Jerome Fisher, in the second article in this chapter, addresses himself to the problem of the false negative. He notes that in many studies, such as his investigation of the Rorschach and central nervous system pathology (reprinted in Chapter 11), with a high score one can be fairly confident that the trait is present, but a low score does not necessarily indicate the absence of pathology because of the relatively high false negative rate.[2]

---

[1] A drawback to this procedure would be that a new principal coming into the school, noting the extraordinary amount of delinquency in the students counseled by these three men relative to the other 17 counselors, might fire them on the spot.

[2] It should be pointed out that this applies to samples in which the base rates are closer to a 50–50 split than those with which Meehl and Rosen were concerned. For instance, the base rate for organicity in the Fisher, Gonda, and Little study reprinted in Chapter 11 is 71 percent.

Your editor, growing increasingly restive in the onlooker role, would be inclined to regard this as being, at least in part, a result of the heterogeneity of the criteria which we try to predict. "Organicity," "creativity," "schizophrenia," and many of the other myriad constructs which psychologists attempt to identify are manifested by a number of different non-pathognomic traits which in their totality form the syndrome. The particular test instrument may be sensitive to only one such trait. For instance, one test of schizophrenia may be sensitive to autistic logic, and another to feelings of persecution. On Test A, we might pick up those schizophrenics in whom the primary manifestation is autistic logic; since few normals possess this trait the false positive rate will be low. However, we might miss those schizophrenics who manifest the disorder by feelings of persecution, excessive withdrawal, splitting of associations and so on with the result that the false negative rate is high. Test B, sensitive to feelings of persecution would produce a similar effect. If so, this would be an argument for successive hurdles testing. It would also indicate that if we are searching for an overall test of a construct such as schizophrenia, factorial purity may not be an asset.

REFERENCES

DAWES, R. N. A note on base rates and psychometric efficiency. *Journal of Consulting Psychology,* 1962, **26,** 422–424.

KARSON, S., & SELLS, S. B. Comments on Meehl and Rosen's paper. *Psychological Bulletin,* 1956, **53,** 335–337.

ROSEN, A. Detection of suicidal patients: An example of some limitations in the prediction of infrequent events. *Journal of Consulting Psychology,* 1954, **18,** 397–403.

Antecedent Probability and the Efficiency of Psychometric Signs, Patterns, or Cutting Scores

Paul E. Meehl and Albert Rosen

In clinical practice, psychologists frequently participate in the making of vital decisions concerning the classification, treatment, prognosis, and disposition of individuals. In their attempts to

From the Neuropsychiatric Service, VA Hospital, Minneapolis, Minnesota, and the Divisions of Psychiatry and Clinical Psychology of the University of Minnesota Medical School. The senior author carried on his part of this work in connection with his appointment to the Minnesota Center for the Philosophy of Science.

increase the number of correct classifications and predictions, psychologists have developed and applied many psychometric devices, such as patterns of test responses as well as cutting scores for scales, indices, and sign lists. Since diagnostic and prognostic statements can often be made with a high degree of accuracy purely on the basis of actuarial or experience tables (referred to hereinafter as *base rates*), a psychometric device, to be efficient, must make possible a greater number of correct decisions than could be made in terms of the base rates alone.

The efficiency of the great majority of psychometric devices reported in the clinical psychology literature is difficult or impossible to evaluate for the following reasons:

a. Base rates are virtually never reported. It is, therefore, difficult to determine whether or not a given device results in a greater number of correct decisions than would be possible solely on the basis of the rates from previous experience. When, however, the base rates can be estimated, the reported claims of efficiency of psychometric instruments are often seen to be without foundation.

b. In most reports, the distribution data provided are insufficient for the evaluation of the probable efficiency of the device in other settings where the base rates are markedly different. Moreover, the samples are almost always too small for the determination of optimal cutting lines for various decisions.

c. Most psychometric devices are reported without cross-validation data. If a psychometric instrument is applied solely to the criterion groups from which it was developed, its reported validity and efficiency are likely to be spuriously high, especially if the criterion groups are small.

d. There is often a lack of clarity concerning the type of population in which a psychometric device can be effectively applied.

e. Results are frequently reported only in terms of significance tests for differences between groups rather than in terms of the number of correct decisions for individuals within the groups.

The purposes of this paper are to examine current methodology in studies of predictive and concurrent validity (1), and to present some methods for the evaluation of the efficiency of psychometric devices as well as for the improvement in the interpretations made from such devices. Actual studies reported in the literature will be used for illustration wherever possible. It should be emphasized that these particular illustrative studies of common practices were chosen simply because they contained more complete data than are commonly reported, and were available in fairly recent publications.

Importance of Base Rates

Danielson and Clark (4) have reported on the construction and application of a personality inventory which was devised for use in military induction stations as an aid in detecting those men who would not complete basic training because of psychiatric disability or AWOL recidivism. One serious defect in their article is that it reports cutting lines which have not been cross validated. Danielson and Clark state that inductees were administered the Fort Ord Inventory within two days after induction into the Army, and that all of these men were allowed to undergo basic training regardless of their test scores.

Two samples (among others) of these inductees were selected for the study of predictive validity: (*a*) A group of 415 men who had made a good adjustment (Good Adjustment Group), and (*b*) a group of 89 men who were unable to complete basic training and who were sufficiently disturbed to warrant a recommendation for discharge by a psychiatrist (Poor Adjustment Group). The authors state that "the most important task of a test designed to screen out misfits is the detection of the (latter) group" (4, p. 139). The authors found that their most effective scale for this differentiation picked up, at a given cutting point, 55% of the Poor Adjustment Group (valid positives) and 19% of the Good Adjustment Group (false positives). The overlap between these two groups would undoubtedly have been greater if the cutting line had been cross validated on a random sample from the *entire population* of inductees, but for the purposes of the present discussion, let us assume that the results were obtained from cross-validation groups. There is no mention of the percentage of all inductees who fall into the Poor Adjustment Group, but a rough estimate will be adequate for the present discussion. Suppose that in their population of soldiers, as many as 5% make a poor adjustment and 95% make a good adjustment. The results for 10,-000 cases would be as depicted in Table 1.

TABLE 1. NUMBER OF INDUCTEES IN THE POOR ADJUSTMENT AND GOOD ADJUSTMENT GROUPS DETECTED BY A SCREENING INVENTORY (55% valid positives; 19% false positives)

| Pre-dicted Adjust-ment | Actual Adjustment | | | | Total Pre-dicted |
| | Good | | Poor | | |
	No.	%	No.	%	
Poor	275	55	1,805	19	2,080
Good	225	45	7,695	81	7,920
Total actual	500	100	9,500	100	10,000

Efficiency in detecting poor adjustment cases. The efficiency of the scale can be evaluated in several ways. From the data in Table 1 it can be seen that if the cutting line given by the authors were used at Fort Ord, the scale could not be used directly to "screen out misfits." If all those predicted by the scale

to make a poor adjustment were screened out, the number of false positives would be extremely high. Among the 10,000 potential inductees, 2080 would be predicted to make a poor adjustment. Of these 2080, only 275, or 13%, would actually make a poor adjustment, whereas the decisions for 1805 men, or 87% of those screened out, would be incorrect.

Efficiency in prediction for all cases. If a prediction were made for every man on the basis of the cutting line given for the test, 275 + 7695, or 7970, out of 10,000 decisions would be correct. Without the test, however, every man would be predicted to make a good adjustment, and 9500 of the predictions would be correct. Thus, use of the test has yielded a drop from 95% to 79.7% in the total number of correct decisions.

Efficiency in detecting good adjustment cases. There is one kind of decision in which the Inventory can improve on the base rates, however. If only those men are accepted who are predicted by the Inventory to make a good adjustment, 7920 will be selected, and the outcome of 7695 of the 7920, or 97%, will be predicted correctly. This is a 2% increase in hits among predictions of "success." The decision as to whether or not the scale improves on the base rates sufficiently to warrant its use will depend on the cost of administering the testing program, the administrative feasibility of rejecting 21% of the men who passed the psychiatric screening, the cost to the Army of training the 225 maladaptive recruits, and the intangible human costs involved in psychiatric breakdown.

Populations to which the scale is applied. In the evaluation of the efficiency of any psychometric instrument, careful consideration must be given to the types of populations to which the device is to be applied. Danielson and Clark have stated that "since the final decision as to disposition is made by the psychiatrist, the test should be classified as a screening adjunct" (4, p. 138). This statement needs clarification, however, for the efficiency of the scale can vary markedly according to the different ways in which it might be used as an adjunct.

It will be noted that the test was administered to men who were already in the Army, and not to men being examined for induction. The reported validation data apply, therefore, specifically to the population of *recent inductees.* The results might have been somewhat different if the population tested consisted of *potential inductees.* For the sake of illustration, however, let us assume that there is no difference in the test results of the two populations.

An induction station psychiatrist can use the scale cutting score in one or more of the following ways, i.e., he can apply the scale results to a variety of populations. (*a*) The psychiatrist's final decision to accept or reject a potential inductee may be based on both the test score and his usual interview procedure. The population to which the test scores are applied is, therefore, *potential inductees interviewed by the usual procedures for whom no decision was made.* (*b*) He may evaluate the potential inductee according to his usual procedures, and then consult the test score *only if* the tentative decision is to reject. That is, a decision to accept is final. The population to which the test scores are applied is *potential inductees tentatively rejected by the usual interview procedures.* (*c*) An alternative procedure is for the psychiatrist to consult the test score only if the tentative decision is to accept, the population being *potential inductees tentatively accepted by the usual interview procedures.* The decision to reject is final. (*d*) Probably the commonest proposal for the use of tests as screening adjuncts is that the more skilled and costly psychiatric evaluation should be made only upon the test positives, i.e., inductees classified by the test as good risks are not interviewed,

or are subjected only to a very short and superficial interview. Here the population is *all potential inductees,* the test being used to make either a final decision to "accept" or a decision to "examine."

Among these different procedures, how is the psychiatrist to achieve maximum effectiveness in using the test as an adjunct? There is no answer to this question from the available data, but it can be stated definitely that the data reported by Danielson and Clark apply to the third procedure described above. The test results are based on a selected group of men *accepted* for induction and not on a random sample of potential inductees. If the scale is used in any other way than the third procedure mentioned above, the results may be considerably inferior to those reported, and, thus, to the use of the base rates without the test.[1]

The principles discussed thus far, although illustrated by a single study, can be generalized to any study of predictive or concurrent validity. It can be seen that many considerations are involved in determining the efficiency of a scale at a given cutting score, especially the base rates of the subclasses within the population to which the psychometric device is to be applied. In a subsequent portion of this paper, methods will be presented for determining cutting points for maximizing the efficiency of the different types of decisions which are made with psychometric devices.

Another study will be utilized to illustrate the importance of an explicit statement of the base rates of population subgroups to be tested with a given device. Employing an interesting configural approach, Thiesen (18) discovered five Rorschach patterns, each of which differentiated well between 60

---

[1] Goodman (8) has discussed this same problem with reference to the supplementary use of an index for the prediction of parole violation.

schizophrenic adult patients and a sample of 157 gainfully employed adults. The best differentiator, considering individual patterns or number of patterns, was Pattern A, which was found in 20% of the patients' records and in only .6% of the records of normals. Thiesen concludes that if these patterns stand the test of cross validation, they might have "clinical usefulness" in early detection of a schizophrenic process or as an aid to determining the gravity of an initial psychotic episode (18, p. 369). If by "clinical usefulness" is meant efficiency in a clinic or hospital for the diagnosis of schizophrenia, it is necessary to demonstrate that the patterns differentiate a higher percentage of schizophrenic patients from *other diagnostic groups* than could be correctly classified without any test at all, i.e., solely on the basis of the rates of various diagnoses in any given hospital. If a test is to be used in differential diagnosis among psychiatric patients, evidence of its efficiency for this function cannot be established solely on the basis of discrimination of diagnostic groups from normals. If by "clinical usefulness" Thiesen means that his data indicate that the patterns might be used to detect an early schizophrenic process among nonhospitalized gainfully employed adults, he would do better to discard his patterns and use the base rates, as can be seen from the following data.

Taulbee and Sisson (17) cross validated Thiesen's patterns on schizophrenic patient and normal samples, and found that Pattern A was the best discriminator. Among patients, 8.1% demonstrated this pattern and among normals, none had this pattern. There are approximately 60 million gainfully employed adults in this country, and it has been estimated that the rate of schizophrenia in the general population is approximately .85% (2, p. 558). The results for Pattern A among a population of 10,000 gainfully employed adults would be as shown in Table 2. In order

to detect 7 schizophrenics, it would be necessary to test 10,000 individuals.

TABLE 2. NUMBER OF PERSONS CLASSIFIED AS SCHIZOPHRENIC AND NORMAL BY A TEST PATTERN AMONG A POPULATION OF GAINFULLY EMPLOYED ADULTS (8.1% valid positives; 0.0% false positives)

	Criterion Classification				
Classi-fication by Test	Schizo-phrenia No.	%	Normal No.	%	Total Classi-fied by Test
Schizo-phrenia	7	8.1	0	0	7
Normal	78	91.9	9,915	100	9,993
Total in class	85	100	9,915	100	10,000

In the Neurology service of a hospital a psychometric scale is used which is designed to differentiate between patients with psychogenic and organic low back pain (9). At a given cutting point, this scale was found to classify each group with approximately 70% effectiveness upon cross validation, i.e., 70% of cases with no organic findings scored above an optimal cutting score, and 70% of surgically verified organic cases scored below this line. Assume that 90% of all patients in the Neurology service with a primary complaint of low back pain are in fact "organic." Without any scale at all the psychologist can say every case is organic, and be right 90% of the time. With the scale the results would be as shown in Section A of Table 3. Of 10 psychogenic cases, 7 score above the line; of 90 organic cases, 63 score below the cutting line. If every case above the line is called psychogenic, only 7 of 34 will be classified correctly or about 21%. Nobody wants to be right only one out of five times in this type of situation, so that it is obvious that it would be imprudent to call a patient psychogenic on the basis of this scale. Radically different results occur in prediction for cases below the cutting line. Of 66 cases 63, or 95%, are correctly classified as organic. Now the psychologist has increased his diagnostic hits from 90 to 95% on the condition that he labels only cases falling below the line, and ignores the 34% scoring above the line.

TABLE 3. NUMBER OF PATIENTS CLASSI-FIED AS PSYCHOGENIC AND ORGANIC ON A LOW BACK PAIN SCALE WHICH CLASSIFIES CORRECTLY 70% OF PSYCHOGENIC AND ORGANIC CASES

Classification by Scale	Actual Diagnosis		Total Classified by Scale
	Psycho-genic	Organic	
A. Base Rates in Population Tested: 90% Organic; 10% Psychogenic			
Psychogenic	7	27	34
Organic	3	63	66
Total diagnosed	10	90	100
B. Base Rates in Population Tested: 90% Psychogenic; 10% Organic			
Psychogenic	63	3	66
Organic	27	7	34
Total diagnosed	90	10	100

In actual practice, the psychologist may not, and most likely will not test every low back pain case. Probably those referred for testing will be a select group, i.e., those who the neurologist believes are psychogenic because neurological findings are minimal or absent. This fact changes the population from "all patients in Neurology with a primary complaint of low back pain," to "all patients in Neurology with a primary complaint of low back pain *who are referred for testing.*" Suppose that a study of past diagnoses indicated that of patients with minimal or absent findings, 90% were diagnosed as psychogenic and 10% as organic. Section B of Table 3 gives an entirely different picture of the effectiveness of the low back pain scale, and new limitations on interpretation are necessary. Now the scale correctly classifies 95% of all cases above

the line as psychogenic (63 of 66), and is correct in only 21% of all cases below the line (7 of 34). In this practical situation the psychologist would be wise to refrain from interpreting a low score.

From the above illustrations it can be seen that the psychologist in interpreting a test and in evaluating its effectiveness must be very much aware of the population and its subclasses and the base rates of the behavior or event with which he is dealing at any given time.

It may be objected that no clinician relies on just one scale but would diagnose on the basis of a configuration of impressions from several tests, clinical data and history. We must, therefore, emphasize that the preceding single-scale examples were presented for simplicity only, but that the main point is not dependent upon this "atomism." *Any complex configurational procedure in any number of variables, psychometric or otherwise, eventuates in a decision.* Those decisions have a certain objective success rate in criterion case identification; and for present purposes we simply treat the decision function, whatever its components and complexity may be, as a single variable. It should be remembered that the literature does not present us with cross-validated methods having hit rates much above those we have chosen as examples, regardless of how complex or configural the methods used. So that even if the clinician approximates an extremely complex configural function "in his head" before classifying the patient, for purposes of the present problem this complex function is treated as the scale. In connection with the more general "philosophy" of clinical decision making see Bross (3) and Meehl (12).

Applications of Bayes' Theorem

Many readers will recognize the preceding numerical examples as essentially involving a principle of elementary probability theory, the so-called "Bayes' Theorem." While it has come in for some opprobrium on account of its connection with certain pre-Fisherian fallacies in statistical inference, as an algebraic statement the theorem has, of course, nothing intrinsically wrong with it and it does apply in the present case. One form of it may be stated as follows:

If there are k antecedent conditions under which an event of a given kind may occur, these conditions having the antecedent probabilities $P_1, P_2, \ldots, P_k$ of being realized, and the probability of the event upon each of them is $p_1, p_2, p_3, \ldots, p_k$; then, given that the event is observed to occur, the probability that it arose on the basis of a specified one, say j, of the antecedent conditions is given by

$$P_{j(o)} = \frac{P_j p_j}{\sum\limits_{i=1}^{k} P_i p_i}.$$

The usual illustration is the case of drawing marbles from an urn. Suppose we have two urns, and the urn-selection procedure is such that the probability of our choosing the first urn is 1/10 and the second 9/10. Assume that 70% of the marbles in the first urn are black, and 40% of those in the second urn are black. I now (blindfolded) "choose" an urn and then, from it, I choose a marble. The marble turns out to be black. What is the probability that I drew from the first urn?

$$P_1 = .10 \qquad P_2 = .90$$
$$p_1 = .70 \qquad p_2 = .40$$

Then

$$P_{1(b)} = \frac{(.10)(.70)}{(.10)(.70) + (.90)(.40)} = .163.$$

If I make a practice of inferring under such circumstances that an observed black marble arose from the first urn, I shall be correct in such judgments, in the long run, only 16.3% of the time. Note, however, that the "test item" or "sign" *black marble* is correctly "scored" in favor of Urn No. 1, since there is a 30% difference in black marble rate between it and Urn No. 2. But this considerable disparity in symptom rate is overcome by the very low base rate ("antecedent probability of choosing from the first urn"), so that inference to first-urn origin of black marbles will actually be wrong some 84 times in 100. In the clinical analogue, the urns are identified with the subpopulations of patients to be discriminated (their antecedent probabilities being equated to their base rates in the population to be examined), and the black marbles are test results of a certain ("positive") kind. The proportion of black marbles in one urn is the valid positive rate, and in the other is the false positive rate. Inspection and suitable manipulations of the formula for the common two-category case, viz.,

$$P_{d(o)} = \frac{Pp_1}{Pp_1 + Qp_2}$$

$P_{d(o)}$ = Probability that an individual is diseased, given that his observed test score is positive

P = Base rate of actual positives in the population examined

$P + Q = 1$

p_1 = Proportion of diseased identified by test ("valid positive" rate)

$q_1 = 1 - p_1$

p_2 = Proportion of nondiseased misidentified by test as being diseased ("false positive" rate)

$q_2 = 1 - p_2$

yields several useful statements. Note that in what follows we are operating entirely with exact population parameter values; i.e., sampling errors are not responsible for the dangers and restrictions set forth. See Table 4.

TABLE 4.   DEFINITION OF SYMBOLS

Diagnosis from Test	Actual Diagnosis	
	Positive	Negative
Positive	p_1 Valid positive rate (Proportion of positives called positive)	p_2 False positive rate (Proportion of negatives called positive)
Negative	q_1 False negative rate (Proportion of positives called negative)	q_2 Valid negative rate (Proportion of negatives called negative)
Total with actual diagnosis	$p_1 + q_1 = 1.0$ (Total positives)	$p_2 + q_2 = 1.0$ (Total negatives)

Note.—For simplicity, the term "diagnosis" is used to denote the classification of any kind of pathology, behavior, or event being studied, or to denote "outcome" if a test is used for prediction. Since horizontal addition (e.g., $p_1 + p_2$) is meaningless in ignorance of the base rates, there is no symbol or marginal total for these sums. *All values are parameter values.*

1. In order for a positive diagnostic assertion to be "more likely true than false," the ratio of the positive to the negative base rates in the examined population must exceed the ratio of the false positive rate to the valid positive rate. That is,

$$\frac{P}{Q} > \frac{p_2}{p_1}.$$

If this condition is not met, the attribution of pathology on the basis of the test is more probably in error than correct, *even though the sign being used is valid* (i.e., $p_1 \neq p_2$).

Example: If a certain cutting score identifies 80% of patients with organic brain damage (high scores being indicative of damage) but is also exceeded by 15% of the nondamaged sent for evaluation, in order for the psychometric decision "brain damage present" to be more often true than false, the ratio of actually brain-damaged to nondamaged cases among all seen for testing must be at least one to five (.19).

Piotrowski has recommended that the presence of 5 or more Rorschach signs among 10 "organic" signs is an efficient indicator of brain damage. Dorken and Kral (5), in cross validating Piotrowski's index, found that 63% of organics and 30% of a mixed, nonorganic, psychiatric patient group had Rorschachs with 5 or more signs. Thus, our estimate of $p_2/p_1 = .30/.63 = .48$, and in order for the decision "brain damage present" to be correct more than one-half the time, the proportion of positives (P) in a given population must equal or exceed .33 (i.e., $P/Q > .33/.67$). Since few clinical populations requiring this clinical decision would have such a high rate of brain damage, especially among psychiatric patients, the particular cutting score advocated by Piotrowski will produce an excessive number of false positives, and the positive diagnosis will be more often wrong than right. Inasmuch as the base rates for any given behavior or pathology differ from one clinical setting to another, *an inflexible cutting score should not be advocated for any psychometric device.* This statement applies generally—thus, to indices recommended for such diverse purposes as the classification or detection of deterioration, specific symptoms, "traits," neuroticism, sexual aberration, dissimulation, suicide risk, and the like. When P is small, it may be advisable to explore the possibility of dealing with a restricted population within which the base rate of the attribute being tested is higher. This approach is discussed in an article by Rosen (14) on the detection of suicidal patients in which it is suggested that an attempt might be made to apply an index to subpopulations with higher suicide rates.

2. If the base rates are equal, the probability of a positive diagnosis being

correct is the ratio of valid positive rate to the sum of valid and false positive rates. That is,

$$P_{d(o)} = \frac{p_1}{p_1 + p_2} \quad \text{if } P = Q = \tfrac{1}{2}.$$

Example: If our population is evenly divided between neurotic and psychotic patients the condition for being "probably right" in diagnosing psychosis by a certain method is simply that the psychotics exhibit the pattern in question more frequently than the neurotics. This is the intuitively obvious special case; it is often misgeneralized to justify use of the test in those cases where base-rate asymmetry $(P \neq Q)$ counteracts the $(p_1 - p_2)$ discrepancy, leading to the paradoxical consequence that *deciding on the basis of more information can actually worsen the chances of a correct decision.* The apparent absurdity of such an idea has often misled psychologists into behaving as though the establishment of "validity" or "discrimination," i.e., that $p_1 \neq p_2$, indicates that a procedure should be used in decision making.

Example: A certain test is used to select those who will continue in outpatient psychotherapy (positives). It correctly identifies 75% of these good cases but the same cutting score picks up 40% of the poor risks who subsequently terminate against advice. Suppose that in the past experience of the clinic 50% of the patients terminated therapy prematurely. Correct selection of patients can be made with the given cutting score on the test 65% of the time, since $p_1/(p_1 + p_2) = .75/(.75 + .40) = .65$. It can be seen that the efficiency of the test would be exaggerated if the base rate for continuation in therapy were actually .70, but the efficiency were evaluated solely on the basis of a research study containing equal groups of continuers and noncontinuers, i.e., if it were assumed that $P = .50$.

3. In order for the hits in the entire population which is under consideration to be increased by use of the test, the base rate of the more numerous class (called here positive) must be less than the ratio of the valid negative rate to the sum of valid negative and false negative rates. That is, unless

$$P < \frac{q_2}{q_1 + q_2},$$

the making of decisions on the basis of the test will have an adverse effect. An alternative expression is that $(P/Q) < (q_2/q_1)$ when $P > Q$, i.e., the ratio of the larger to the smaller class must be less than the ratio of the valid negative rate to the false negative rate. When $P < Q$, the conditions for the test to improve upon the base rates are:

$$Q < \frac{p_1}{p_1 + p_2}$$

and

$$\frac{Q}{P} < \frac{p_1}{p_2}.$$

Rotter, Rafferty, and Lotsof (15) have reported the scores on a sentence completion test for a group of 33 "maladjusted" and 33 "adjusted" girls. They report that the use of a specified cutting score (not cross validated) will result in the correct classification of 85% of the maladjusted girls and the incorrect classification of only 15% of the adjusted girls. It is impossible to evaluate adequately the efficiency of the test unless one knows the base rates of maladjustment (P) and adjustment (Q) for the population of high school girls, although there would be general agreement that $Q > P$. Since $p_1/(p_1 + p_2) = .85/(.85 + .15) = .85$, the over-all hits in diagnosis with the test will not improve on classification based solely on the base rates unless the proportion of adjusted girls is less than .85. Because the reported effectiveness of the test is spuriously high, the proportion of adjusted girls would no doubt have to be considerably less than .85. Unless there is good reason to believe that the base rates are similar from one setting to another, it is impossible to determine the efficiency of a test such as Rotter's when the criterion is based on ratings unless one replicates his research, including the criterion ratings, with a representative sample of each new population.

4. In altering a sign, improving a scale, or shifting a cutting score, the increment in valid positives per increment in valid positive *rate* is proportional to the positive base rate; and analogously, the increment in valid negatives per increment in valid negative *rate* is proportional to the negative base rate. That is, if we alter a sign the net improvement in over-all hit rate is

$$H'_T - H_T = \Delta p_1 P + \Delta q_2 Q,$$

where H_T = original proportion of hits (over-all) and H'_T = new proportion of hits (over-all).

5. A corollary of this is that altering a sign or shifting a cut will improve our decision making if, and only if, the ratio of *improvement* Δp_1 in valid positive rate to *worsening* Δp_2 in false negative rate exceeds the ratio of actual negatives to positives in the population.

$$\frac{\Delta p_1}{\Delta p_2} > \frac{Q}{P}.$$

Example: Suppose we improve the intrinsic validity of a certain "schizophrenic index" so that it now detects 20% more schizophrenics than it formerly did, at the expense of only a 5% increase in the false positive rate. This surely looks encouraging. We are, however, working with an outpatient clientele only 1/10th of whom are actually schizophrenic. Then, since

$$\Delta p_1 = .20 \qquad P = .10$$
$$\Delta p_2 = .05 \qquad Q = .90$$

applying the formula we see that

$$\frac{.20}{.05} \not> \frac{.90}{.10}$$

i.e., the required inequality does not hold, and the routine use of this "improved" index will result in an increase in the proportion of erroneous diagnostic decisions.

In the case of any pair of unimodal distributions, this corresponds to the principle that the optimal cut lies at the intersection of the two distribution envelopes (11, pp. 271–272).

Manipulation of Cutting Lines for Different Decisions

For any given psychometric device, no one cutting line is maximally efficient for clinical settings in which the base rates of the criterion groups in the population are different. Furthermore, different cutting lines may be necessary for various decisions within the same population. In this section, methods are presented for manipulating the cutting line of any instrument in order to maximize the efficiency of a device in the making of several kinds of decisions. Reference should be made to the scheme presented in Table 5 for understanding of the discussion which follows. This scheme and the methods for manipulating cutting lines are derived from Duncan, Ohlin, Reiss, and Stanton (6).

A study in the prediction of juvenile delinquency by Glueck and Glueck (7) will be used for illustration. Scores on a prediction index for 451 delinquents and 439 nondelinquents (7, p. 261) are listed in Table 6. If the Gluecks' index is to be used in a population with a given juvenile delinquency rate, cutting lines can be established to maximize the efficiency of the index for several decisions. In the following illustration, a delinquency rate of .20 will be used. From the data in Table 6, optimal cutting lines will be determined for maximizing the proportion of correct predictions, or hits, for all cases (H_T), and for maximizing the proportion of hits (H_P) among those called delinquent (positives) by the index.

TABLE 5.   SYMBOLS TO BE USED IN EVALUATING THE EFFICIENCY OF A PSYCHOMETRIC DEVICE IN CLASSIFICATION OR PREDICTION

Diagnosis from Test	Actual Diagnosis		Total Diagnosed from Test
	Positive	Negative	
Positive	NPp_1 (Number of valid positives)	NQp_2 (Number of false positives)	$NPp_1 + NQp_2$ (Number of test positives)
Negative	NPq_1 (Number of false negatives)	NQq_2 (Number of valid negatives)	$NPq_1 + NQq_2$ (Number of test negatives)
Total with actual diagnosis	NP (Number of actual positives)	NQ (Number of actual negatives)	N (Total number of cases)

Note.—For simplicity, the term "diagnosis" is used to denote the classification of any kind of pathology, behavior, or event studied, or to denote "outcome" if a test is used for prediction. "Number" means *absolute frequency*, not *rate* or probability.

In the first three columns of Table 6, "*f*" denotes the number of delinquents scoring in each class interval, "*cf*" represents the cumulative frequency of delinquents scoring above each class interval (e.g., 265 score above 299), and p_1 represents the proportion of the total group of 451 delinquents scoring above each class interval. Columns 4, 5, and 6 present the same kind of data for the 439 nondelinquents.

Maximizing the number of correct predictions or classifications for all cases. The proportion of correct predictions or classifications (H_T) for any given cutting line is given by the formula, $H_T = Pp_1 + Qq_2$. Thus, in column 11 of Table 6, labelled H_T, it can be seen that the best cutting line for this decision would be between 299 and 300, for 85.9% of all predictions would be correct if those above the line were predicted to become delinquent and all those below the line nondelinquent. Any other cutting line would result in a smaller proportion of correct predictions, and, in fact, any cutting line set lower than this point would make the index inferior to the use of the base rates, for if all cases were predicted to be nondelinquent, the total proportion of hits would be .80.

Maximizing the number of correct predictions or classifications for posi-

tives. The primary use of a prediction device may be for *selection* of (*a*) students who will succeed in a training program, (*b*) applicants who will succeed in a certain job, (*c*) patients who will benefit from a certain type of therapy, etc. In the present illustration, the index would most likely be used for detection of those who are likely to become delinquents. Thus, the aim might be to maximize the number of hits only within the group predicted by the index to become delinquents (predicted positives = $NPp_1 + NQp_2$). The proportion of correct predictions for this group by the use of different cutting lines is given in column 13, labelled H_P. Thus, if a cutting line is set between 399 and 400, one will be correct over 92 times in 100 if predictions are made *only* for persons scoring above the cutting line. The formula for determining the efficiency of the test when only positive predictions are made is $H_P = P_{p1}/(P_{p1} + Q_{p2})$.

One has to pay a price for achieving a very high level of accuracy with the index. Since the problem is to select potential delinquents so that some sort of therapy can be attempted, the proportion of this selected group in the total sample may be considered as a selection ratio. The selection ratio for positives is $R_P = P_{p1} + Q_{p2}$, that is, predictions are

TABLE 6. PREDICTION INDEX SCORES FOR JUVENILE DELINQUENTS AND NONDELINQUENTS AND OTHER STATISTICS FOR DETERMINING OPTIMAL CUTTING LINES FOR CERTAIN DECISIONS IN A POPULATION WITH A DELINQUENCY RATE OF .20[*]

Prediction Score Index	Delinquents			Nondelinquents									
			$\frac{cf}{451}$			$\frac{cf}{439}$	$1-p_2$	$.2p_1$	$.8p_2$	$.8q_2$	Pp_1+Qq_2	Pp_1+Qp_2	$\frac{Pp_1}{R_P}$
	(1) f	(2) cf	(3) p_1	(4) f	(5) cf	(6) p_2	(7) q_3	(8) Pp_1	(9) Qp_2	(10) Qq_2	(11) H_T	(12) R_P	(13) H_P
400 +	51	51	.1131	1	1	.0023	.9977	.0226	.0018	.7982	.821	.024	.926
350–399	73	124	.2749	8	9	.0205	.9795	.0550	.0164	.7836	.839	.071	.770
300–349	141	265	.5876	23	32	.0729	.9271	.1175	.0583	.7417	.859	.176	.668
250–299	122	387	.8581	70	102	.2323	.7677	.1716	.1858	.6142	.786	.357	.480
200–249	40	427	.9468	68	170	.3872	.6128	.1894	.3098	.4902	.680	.499	.379
150–199	19	446	.9889	102	272	.6196	.3804	.1978	.4957	.3043	.502	.694	.285
<150	5	451	1.0000	167	439	1.0000	.0000	.2000	.8000	.0000	.200	1.000	.200

[*] Frequencies in columns 1 and 4 are from Glueck and Glueck (7, p. 261).

made only for those above the cutting line. The selection ratio for each possible cutting line is shown in column 12 of Table 6, labelled R_P. It can be seen that to obtain maximum accuracy in selection of delinquents (92.6%), predictions can be made for only 2.4% of the population. For other cutting lines, the accuracy of selection and the corresponding selection ratios are given in Table 6. The worker applying the index must use his own judgment in deciding upon the level of accuracy and the selection ratio desired.

Maximizing the number of correct predictions or classifications for negatives. In some selection problems, the goal is the selection of negatives rather than positives. Then, the proportion of hits among all predicted negative for any given cutting line is $H_N = Qq_2 / (Qq_2 + Pq_1)$, and the selection ratio for negatives is $R_N = Pq_1 + Qq_2$.

In all of the above manipulations of cutting lines, it is essential that there be a large number of cases. Otherwise, the percentages about any given cutting line would be so unstable that very dissimilar results would be obtained on new samples. For most studies in clinical psychology, therefore, it would be necessary to establish cutting lines according to the decisions and methods discussed above, and then to cross validate a specific cutting line on new samples.

The amount of shrinkage to be expected in the cross validation of cutting lines cannot be determined until a thorough mathematical and statistical study of the subject is made. It may be found that when criterion distributions are approximately normal and large, cutting lines should be established in terms of the normal probability table rather than on the basis of the observed p and q values found in the samples. In a later section dealing with the selection ratio we shall see that it is sometimes the best procedure to select all individuals falling above a certain cutting line and to select the others needed to reach the

selection ratio by choosing at random below the line; or in other cases to establish several different cuts defining *ranges* within which one or the opposite decision should be made.

Decisions based on score intervals rather than cutting lines. The Gluecks' data can be used to illustrate another approach to psychometric classification and prediction when scores for large samples are available with a relatively large number of cases in each score interval. In Table 7 are listed frequencies of delinquents and nondelinquents for prediction index score intervals. The frequencies for delinquents are the same as those in Table 6, whereas those for nondelinquents have been corrected for a base rate of .20 by multiplying each frequency in column 4 of Table 6[2] by

$$4.11 = \frac{(.80)}{(.20)} \frac{(451)}{(439)}.$$

Table 7 indicates the proportion of delinquents and nondelinquents among all juveniles who fall within a given score interval when the base rate of delinquency is .20. It can be predicted that of those scoring 400 or more, 92.7% will become delinquent, of those scoring between 350 and 399, 68.9% will be delinquent, etc. Likewise, of those scoring between 200 and 249, it can be predicted that 87.5% will not become delinquent. Since 80% of predictions will be correct without the index if all cases are called nondelinquent, one would not predict nondelinquency with the index in score intervals over 249. Likewise, it would be best not to predict delinquency for individuals in the intervals under 250 because 20% of pre-

[2] The Gluecks' Tables XX–2, 3, 4, 5, (7, pp. 261–262) and their interpretations therefrom are apt to be misleading because of their exclusive consideration of approximately equal base rates of delinquency and nondelinquency. Reiss (13), in his review of the Gluecks' study, has also discussed their use of an unrepresentative rate of delinquency.

TABLE 7. PERCENTAGE OF DELINQUENTS (D) AND NONDELINQUENTS (ND) IN EACH PREDICTION INDEX SCORE INTERVAL IN A POPULATION IN WHICH THE DELINQUENCY RATE IS .20*

Prediction Index Score Interval	No. of D	No. of ND	Total of D and ND	% of D in Score Interval	% of ND in Score Interval	% of D and ND in Score Interval
400 +	51	4	55	92.7	7.3	100
350–399	73	33	106	68.9	31.1	100
300–349	141	95	236	59.7	40.3	100
250–299	122	288	410	29.8	70.2	100
200–249	40	279	319	12.5	87.5	100
150–199	19	419	438	4.3	95.7	100
<150	5	686	691	.7	99.3	100
Total	451	1804	2255			

* Modification of Table XX-2, p. 261, from Glueck and Glueck (7).

dictions will be correct if the base rate is used.

It should be emphasized that there are different ways of quantifying one's clinical errors, and they will, of course, not all give the same evaluation when applied in a given setting. "Per cent valid positives" ($= p_1$) is rarely if ever meaningful without the correlated "per cent false positives" ($= p_2$), and clinicians are accustomed to the idea that we pay for an increase in the first by an increase in the second, whenever the increase is achieved not by an improvement in the test's intrinsic validity but by a shifting of the cutting score. But the two quantities p_1 and p_2 do not define our over-all hit frequency, which depends also upon the base rates P and Q. The three quantities p_1, p_2, and P do, however, contain all the information needed to evaluate the test with respect to any given sign or cutting score that yields these values. Although p_1, p_2, and P contain the relevant information, other forms of it may be of greater importance. No two of these numbers, for example, answer the obvious question most commonly asked (or vaguely implied) by psychiatrists when an inference is made from a sign, viz., "How sure can you be on the basis of that sign?" The answer to this eminently

practical query involves a probability different from any of the above, namely, the *inverse* probability given by Bayes' formula:

$$H_P = \frac{Pp_1}{Pp_1 + Qp_2}.$$

Even a small improvement in the hit frequency to $H'_T = Pp_1 + Qq_2$ over the $H_T = P$ attainable without the test may be adjudged as worth while when the increment ΔH_T is multiplied by the N examined in the course of one year and is thus seen to involve a dozen lives or a dozen curable schizophrenics. On the other hand, the simple fact that an actual *shrinkage* in total hit rate may occur seems to be unappreciated or tacitly ignored by a good deal of clinical practice. One must keep constantly in mind that numerous diagnostic, prognostic, and dynamic statements can be made about almost all neurotic patients (e.g., "depressed," "inadequate ability to relate," "sexual difficulties") or about very few patients (e.g., "dangerous," "will act out in therapy," "suicidal," "will blow up into a schizophrenia"). A psychologist who uses a test sign that even cross validates at $p_1 = q_2 = 80\%$ to determine whether "depression" is present or absent, working in a clinical population where practically everyone is fairly depressed except a few psychopaths and old-fashioned hysterics, is kidding himself, the psychiatrist, and whoever foots the bill.

"Successive-Hurdles" Approach

Tests having low efficiency, or having moderate efficiency but applied to populations having very unbalanced base rates $(P << Q)$ are sometimes defended by adopting a "crude initial screening" frame of reference, and arguing that certain other procedures (whether tests or not) can be applied to the subset identified by the screener ("successive hurdles"). There is no question that in some circumstances (e.g., military induction, or industrial selection with a large labor market) this is a thoroughly defensible position. However, as a general rule one should examine this type of justification critically, with the preceding considerations in mind. Suppose we have a test which distinguishes brain-tumor from non-brain-tumor patients with 75% accuracy and no differential bias $(p_1 = q_2 = .75)$. Under such circumstances the test hit rate H_T is .75 regardless of the base rate. If we use the test in making our judgments, we are correct in our diagnoses 75 times in 100. But suppose only one patient in 10 actually has a brain tumor, we will drop our over-all "success" from 90% (attainable by diagnosing "No tumor" in all cases) to 75%. We do, however, identify 3 out of 4 of the real brain tumors, and in such a case it seems worth the price. The "price" has two aspects to it: We take time to give the test, and, having given it, we call many "tumorous" who are not. Thus, suppose that in the course of a year we see 1000 patients. Of these, 900 are non-tumor, and we erroneously call 225 of these "tumor." To pick up $(100) (.75) = 75$ of the tumors, *all* 100 of whom would have been called tumor-free

using the base rates alone, we are willing to mislabel 3 times this many as tumorous who are actually not. Putting it another way, whenever we say "tumor" on the basis of the test, the chances are 3 to 1 that we are mistaken. When we "rule out" tumor by the test, we are correct 96% of the time, an improvement of only 6% in the confidence attachable to a negative finding over the confidence yielded by the base rates.[3]

Now, picking up the successive-hurdles argument, suppose a major decision (e.g., exploratory surgery) is allowed to rest upon a second test which is infallible but for practically insuperable reasons of staff, time, etc., cannot be routinely given. We administer Test 2 only to "positives" on (screening) Test 1. By this tactic we eliminate all 225 false positives left by Test 1, and we verify the 75 valid positives screened in by Test 1. The 25 tumors that slipped through as false negatives on Test 1 are, of course, not picked up by Test 2 either, because it is not applied to them. Our total hit frequency is now 97.5%, since the only cases ultimately misclassified out of our 1000 seen are these 25 tumors which escaped through the initial sieve Test 1. We are still running only 7½% above the base rate. We have had to give our short-and-easy test to 1000 individuals and our cumbersome, expensive test to 300 individuals, 225 of whom turn out to be free of tumor. But we have located 75 patients with tumor who would not otherwise have been found.

Such examples suggest that, except

[3] Improvements are expressed throughout this article as *absolute* increments in percentage of hits, because: (*a*) This avoids the complete arbitrariness involved in choosing between original hit rate and miss rate as starting denominator; and (*b*) for the clinician, the person is the most meaningful unit of gain, rather than a proportion *of* a proportion (especially when the reference proportion is very small).

in "life-or-death" matters, the successive-screenings argument merely tends to soften the blow of Bayes' Rule in cases where the base rates are very far from symmetry. Also if Test 2 is not assumed to be infallible but only highly effective, say 90% accurate both ways, results start looking unimpressive again. Our net false positive rate rises from zero to 22 cases miscalled "tumor," and we operate 67 of the actual tumors instead of 75. The total hit frequency drops to 94.5%, only 4½% above that yielded by a blind guessing of the modal class.

The Selection Ratio

Straightforward application of the preceding principles presupposes that the clinical decision maker is free to adopt a policy solely on the basis of maximizing hit frequency. Sometimes there are external constraints such as staff time, administrative policy, or social obligation which further complicate matters. It may then be impossible to make all decisions in accordance with the base rates, and the task given to the test is that of selecting a subset of cases which are decided in the direction opposite to the base rates but will still contain fewer erroneous decisions than would ever be yielded by opposing the base rates without the test. If 80% of patients referred to a Mental Hygiene Clinic are recoverable with intensive psychotherapy, we would do better to treat everybody than to utilize a test yielding 75% correct predictions. But suppose that available staff time is limited so that we *can* treat only half the referrals. The Bayes-type injunction to "follow the base rates when they are better than the test" becomes pragmatically meaningless, for it directs us to make decisions which we cannot implement. The imposition of an *externally* imposed selection ratio, not determined on the basis of any maximizing or minimizing policy but by nonstatis-

TABLE 8. ACTUAL AND TEST-PREDICTED THERAPEUTIC OUTCOME

Test Prediction	Therapeutic Outcome		
	Good	Poor	Total
Good	60	5	65
Poor	20	15	35
Total	80	20	100

tical considerations, renders the test worthwhile.

Prior to imposition of any arbitrary selection ratio, the fourfold table for 100 referrals might be as shown in Table 8. If the aim were simply to minimize total errors, we would predict "good" for each case and be right 80 times in 100. Using the test, we would be right only 75 times in 100. But suppose a selection ratio of .5 is externally imposed. We are then forced to predict "poor" for half the cases, even though this "prediction" is, in any given case, likely to be wrong. (More precisely, we handle this subset *as if* we predicted "poor," by refusing to treat.) So we now select our 50 to-be-treated cases from among those 65 who fall in the "test-good" array, having a frequency of 60/65 = 92.3% hits among those selected. This is better than the 80% we could expect (among those selected) by choosing half the total referrals at random. Of course we pay for this, by making many "false negative" decisions; but these are necessitated, whether we use the test or not, by the fact that the selection ratio was determined without regard for hit maximization but by external considerations. Without the test, our false negative rate q_1 is 50% (i.e., 40 of the 80 "good" cases will be called "poor"); the test reduces the false negative rate to 42.5% (= 34/80), since 15 cases from above the cutting line must be selected at random for inclusion in the not-to-be-treated group below the cutting line [i.e., 20 + (60/65)15 = 34]. Stated in terms of correct decisions, without the test 40 out of 50 selected for therapy will have a good therapeutic outcome; with the test, 46 in 50 will be successes.

Reports of studies in which formulas are developed from psychometrics for the prediction of patients' continuance in psychotherapy have neglected to consider the relationship of the selection ratio to the specific population to which the prediction formula is to be applied. In each study the population has consisted of individuals who were *accepted for therapy* by the usual methods employed at an outpatient clinic, and the prediction formula has been evaluated *only* for such patients. It is implied by these studies that the formula would have the same efficiency if it were used for the *selection* of "continuers" from all those *applying* for therapy. Unless the formula is tested on a random sample of applicants who are allowed to enter therapy without regard to their test scores, its efficiency for selection purposes is unknown. The reported efficiency of the prediction formula in the above studies pertains only to its use in a population of patients who have already been selected for therapy. There is little likelihood that the formula can be used in any practical way for further selection of patients unless the clinic's therapists are carrying a far greater load than they plan to carry in the future.

The use of the term "selection" (as contrasted with "prediction" or "placement") ought not to blind us to the important differences between industrial selection and its clinical analogue. The incidence of false negatives—of potential employees screened out by the test who would actually have made good on the job if hired—is of little concern to management except as it costs money to give tests. Hence the industrial psychologist may choose to express his aim in terms of minimizing the false positives, i.e., of seeing to it that the job success *among those hired* is as large a rate as possible. When we make a clinical decision to treat or not to treat,

we are withholding something from people who have a claim upon us in a sense that is much stronger than the "right to work" gives a job applicant any claim upon a particular company. So, even though we speak of a "selection ratio" in clinical work, it must be remembered that those cases *not selected* are patients about whom a certain kind of important negative decision is being made.

For any *given* selection ratio, maximizing total hits is always equivalent to maximizing the hit rate for either type of decision (or minimizing the errors of either, or both, kinds), since cases shifted from one cell of the table have to be exactly compensated for. If m "good" cases that were correctly classified by one decision method are incorrectly classified by another, maintenance of the selection ratio entails that m cases correctly called "poor" are also miscalled "good" by the new method. Hence an externally imposed selection ratio eliminates the often troublesome value questions about the relative seriousness of the two kinds of errors, since they are unavoidable increased or decreased at exactly the same rate.

If the test yields a score or a continuously varying index of some kind, the values of p_1 and p_2 are not fixed, as they may be with "patterns" or "signs." Changes in the selection ratio, R, will then suggest shifting the cutting scores or regions on the basis of the relations obtaining among R, P, and the p_1, p_2 combinations yielded by various cuts. It is worth special comment that, in the case of continuous distributions, the optimum procedure is *not* always to move the cut until the total area truncated $= NR$, selecting all above that cut and rejecting all those below. Whether this "obvious" rule is wise or not depends upon the distribution characteristics. We have found it easy to construct pairs of distributions such that the test is "discriminating" throughout, in the sense that the associated cumulative frequencies q_1 and q_2 maintain the same direction of their inequality everywhere in the range

$$\left(\text{i.e.,} \frac{1}{N_2} \int_{-\infty}^{x_i} f_2(x)dx > \right.$$

$$\left. \frac{1}{N_1} \int_{-\infty}^{x_i} f_1(x)\,dx \text{ for all } x_i \right);$$

yet in which the hit frequency given by a single cut at R is inferior to that given by first selecting with a cut which yields $N_c < NR$, and then picking up the remaining $(NR - N_c)$ cases at random below the cut. Other more complex situations may arise in which different types of decisions should be made in different regions, actually reversing the policy as we move along the test continuum. Such numerical examples as we have constructed utilize continuous, unimodal distributions, and involve differences in variability, skewness, and kurtosis not greater than those which arise fairly often in clinical practice. Of course the utilization of any very complicated pattern of regions requires more stable distribution frequencies than are obtainable from the sample sizes ordinarily available to clinicians.

It is instructive to contemplate some of the moral and administrative issues involved in the practical application of the preceding ideas. It is our impression that a good deal of clinical research is of the "So what?" variety, not because of defects in experimental design such as inadequate cross validation but because it is hard to see just what are the useful changes in decision making which could reasonably be expected to follow. Suppose, for example, it is shown that "duration of psychotherapy" is 70% predictable from a certain test. Are we prepared to propose that those patients whose test scores fall in a certain range should not receive treatment? If not, then is it of any real advantage therapeutically to "keep in mind" that the patient has 7 out of 10 chances of staying longer than 15 hours, and 3 out of 10 chances of staying less than that? We are not trying to poke fun at research, since presumably almost any lawful relationship stands a chance of being valuable to our total scientific comprehensions some day. But many clinical papers are ostensibly inspired by practical aims, and can be given theoretical interpretation or fitted into any larger framework only with great difficulty if at all. It seems appropriate to urge that such "practical"-oriented investigations should be really *practical*, enabling us to see how our clinical decisions could rationally be modified in the light of the findings. It is doubtful how much of current work could be justified in these terms.

Regardless of whether the test validity is capable of improving on the base rates, there are some prediction problems which have practical import only because of limitations in personnel. What other justification is there for the great emphasis in clinical research on "prognosis," "treatability," or "stayability"? The very formulation of the predictive task as "maximizing the number of hits" already presupposes that we intend *not* to treat some cases; since if we treat all comers, the ascertainment of a bad prognosis score has no practical effect other than to discourage the therapist (and thus hinder therapy?). If intensive psychotherapy could be offered to all veterans who are willing to accept referral to a VA Mental Hygiene Clinic, would it be licit to refuse those who had the poorest outlook? Presumably not. It is interesting to contrast the emphasis on prognosis in clinical psychology with that in, say, cancer surgery, where the treatment *of choice* may still have a very low probability of "success," but is nevertheless carried out on the basis of that low probability. Nor does this attitude seem unreasonable, since no patient would refuse the best available treatment on the ground that even it was only 10% effective. Suppose a therapist, in the course of earning his living, spends 200 hours a year on nonimprovers by following a decision policy that also results in his unexpected success with one 30-year-old "poor bet." If this client thereby gains $16 \times 365 \times 40 = 233,600$ hours averaging 50% less anxiety during the rest of his natural life, it was presumably worth the price.

These considerations suggest that, with the expansion of professional facilities in the behavior field, the prediction problem will be less like that of industrial *selection* and more like that of *placement*. "To treat or not to treat" or "How treatable" or "How long to treat" would be replaced by "What *kind* of treatment?" But as soon as the problem is formulated in this way, the external selection ratio is usually no longer imposed. Only if we are deciding between such alternatives as classical analysis and, say; 50-hour interpretative therapy would such personnel limitations as can be expected in future years impose an arbitrary *R*. But if the decision is between such alternatives as short-term interpretative therapy, Rogerian therapy, Thorne's directive therapy, hypnotic retraining, and the method of tasks (10, 16, 19), we could "follow the base rates" by treating every patient with the method known to have the highest success frequency among patients "similar" to him. The criteria of similarity (class membership) will presumably be multiple, both phenotypic and genotypic, and will have been chosen because of their empirically demonstrated prognostic relevance rather than by guesswork, as is current practice. Such an idealized situation also presupposes that the selection and training of psychotherapists will have become socially realistic so that therapeutic personnel skilled in the various methods will be available in some reasonable proportion to the incidence with which each method is the treatment of choice.

How close are we to the upper limit of the predictive validity of personality tests, such as was reached remarkable early in the development of academic aptitude tests? If the now-familiar ⅔ to ¾ proportions of hits against even-split criterion dichotomies are already approaching that upper limit, we may well discover that for many decision problems the search for tests that will significantly better the base rates is a rather unrewarding enterprise. When the criterion is a more circumscribed trait or symptom ("depressed," "affiliative," "sadistic," and the like), the difficulty of improving upon the base rates is combined with the doubtfulness about how valuable it is to have such information with 75% confidence anyhow. But this involves larger issues beyond the scope of the present paper.

Availability of Information on Base Rates

The obvious difficulty we face in practical utilization of the preceding formulas arises from the fact that actual quantitative knowledge of the base rates is usually lacking. But this difficulty must not lead to a dismissal of our considerations as clinically irrelevant. In the case of many clinical decisions, chiefly those involving such phenotypic criteria as overt symptoms, formal diagnosis, subsequent hospitalization, persistence in therapy, vocational or marital adjustment, and the numerous "surface" personality traits which clinicians try to assess, *the chief reason for our ignorance of the base rates is nothing more subtle than our failure to compute them*. The file data available in most installations having a fairly stable source of clientele would yield values sufficiently accurate to permit minimum and maximum estimates which might be sufficient to decide for or against use of a proposed sign. It is our opinion that this rather mundane taxonomic task is of much greater importance than has been realized, and we hope that the present paper will impel workers to more systematic efforts along these lines.

Even in the case of more subtle, complex, and genotypic inferences, the situation is far from hopeless. Take the case of some such dynamic attribution as "strong latent dependency, which will be anxiety-arousing as therapy proceeds." If this is so difficult to discern *even during intensive therapy* that a therapist's rating on it has too little reliability for use as a criterion, it is hard to see just what is the value of guessing it from psychometrics. If a skilled therapist cannot discriminate the personality characteristic after considerable contact with the patient, it is at least debatable whether the characteristic makes any practical difference. On the other hand, if it can be reliably judged by therapists, the determination of approximate base rates again involves nothing more complex than systematic recording of these judgments and subsequent tabulation. Finally, "clinical experience" and "common sense" must be invoked when there is nothing better to be had. Surely if the q_1/q_2 ratio for a test sign claiming validity for "difficulty in accepting inner drives" shows from the formula that the base rate must not exceed .65 to justify use of the sign, we can be fairly confident in discarding it for use with *any* psychiatric population! Such a "backward" use of the formula to obtain a maximum useful value of P, in conjunction with the most tolerant common-sense estimates of P from daily experience, will often suffice to answer the question. If one is really in complete ignorance of the limits within which P lies, then obviously no rational judgment as to the probable efficiency of the sign can be made.

Estimation Versus Significance

A further implication of the foregoing thinking is that the exactness of certain small sample statistics, or the relative freedom of certain nonparametric methods from distribution assumptions, has to be stated with care lest it mislead clinicians into an unjustified confidence. When an investigator concludes that a sign, item, cutting score, or pattern has "validity" on the basis of small sample methods, he has rendered a certain very broad null hypothesis unplausible. To decide, however, whether this "validity" warrants clinicians in using the test is (as every statistician would insist) a further and more complex question. To answer this question, we require more than knowledge that $p_1 \neq p_2$. We need in addition to know, with respect to each decision for which the sign is being proposed, whether the appropriate inequality involving p_1, p_2 and P is fulfilled. More than this, since we will usually be extrapolating to a somewhat different clinical population, we need to know whether altered base rates P' and Q' will falsify these inequalities. To do this demands *estimates* of the test parameters p_1 and p_2, the setting up of confidence belts for their difference $p_1 - p_2$ rather than the mere proof of their nonidentity. Finally, if the sign is a cutting score, we will want to consider shifting it so as to *maintain* optimal hit frequency with new base rates. The effect upon p_1 and p_2 of a contemplated movement of a critical score or band requires a knowledge of distribution form such as only a large sample can give.

As is true in all practical applications of statistical inference, nonmathematical considerations enter into the use of the numerical patterns that exist among P, p_1, p_2, and R. But "pragmatic" judgments initially require a separation of the several probabilities involved, some of which may be much more important than others in terms of the human values associated with them. In some settings, over-all hit rate is all that we care about.

In others, a redistribution of the hits and misses even without much total improvement may concern us. In still others, the proportions p_1 and q_2 are of primary interest; and, finally, in some instances the confrontation of a certain increment in the absolute frequency (NPp_1) of one group identified will outweigh all other considerations.

Lest our conclusions seem unduly pessimistic, what constructive suggestions can we offer? We have already mentioned the following: (a) Searching for subpopulations with different base rates; (b) successive-hurdles testing; (c) the fact that even a very small *percentage* of improvement may be worth achieving in certain crucial decisions; (d) the need for systematic collection of base-rate data so that our several equations can be applied. To these we may add two further "constructive" comments. First, test research attention should be largely concentrated upon behaviors having base rates nearer a 50–50 split, since it is for these that it is easiest to improve on a base-rate decision policy by use of a test having moderate validity. There are, after all, a large number of clinically important traits which do not occur "almost always" or "very rarely." Test research might be slanted more toward them; the current popularity of Q-sort approaches should facilitate the growth of such an emphasis, by directing attention to items having a reasonable "spread" in the clinical population. Exceptions to such a research policy will arise, in those rare domains where the pragmatic consequences of the alternative decisions justify focusing attention almost wholly on maximizing Pp_1, with relative neglect of Qp_2. Secondly, we think the injunction "quit wasting time on noncontributory psychometrics" is really constructive. When the clinical psychologist sees the near futility of predicting rare or near-universal events and traits from test validities incapable of improv-

ing upon the base rates, his clinical time is freed for more economically defensible activities, such as research which will improve the parameters p_1 and p_2; and for *treating* patients rather than uttering low-confidence prophecies or truisms about them (in this connection see 12, pp. vii, 7, 127–128). It has not been our intention to be dogmatic about "what is worth finding out, how often." We do suggest that the clinical use of patterns, cutting scores, and signs, or research efforts devoted to the discovery of such, should always be evaluated in the light of the simple algebraic fact discovered in 1763 by Mr. Bayes.

Summary

1. The practical value of a psychometric sign, pattern, or cutting score depends jointly upon its intrinsic validity (in the usual sense of its discriminating power) and the distribution of the criterion variable (base rates) in the clinical population. Almost all contemporary research reporting neglects the base-rate factor and hence makes evaluation of test usefulness difficult or impossible.

2. In some circumstances, notably when the base rates of the criterion classification deviate greatly from a 50 per cent split, use of a test sign having slight or moderate validity will result in an *increase* of erroneous clinical decisions.

3. Even if the test's parameters are precisely known, so that ordinary cross-validation shrinkage is not a problem, application of a sign within a population having these same test parameters but a different base rate may result in a marked change in the proportion of correct decisions. For this reason validation studies should present trustworthy information respecting the criterion distribution in addition to such test parameters as false positive and false negative rates.

4. Establishment of "validity" by exact small sample statistics, since it does not yield accurate information about the test parameters (a problem of estimation rather than significance), does not permit trustworthy judgments as to test usefulness in a new population with different or unknown base rates.

5. Formulas are presented for determining limits upon relations among (*a*) the base rates, (*b*) false negative rate, and (*c*) false positive rate which must obtain if use of the test sign is to improve clinical decision making.

6. If, however, external constraints (e.g., available staff time) render it administratively unfeasible to decide all cases in accordance with the base rates, a test sign may be worth applying even if following the base rates *would* maximize the total correct decisions, were such a policy possible.

7. Trustworthy information as to the base rates of various patient characteristics can readily be obtained by file research, and test development should (other things being equal) be concentrated on those characteristics having base rates nearer .50 rather than close to .00 or 1.00

8. The basic rationale is that of Bayes' Theorem concerning the calculation of so-called "inverse probability."

REFERENCES

1. AMERICAN PSYCHOLOGICAL ASSOCIATION, AMERICAN EDUCATIONAL RESEARCH ASSOCIATION, AND NATIONAL COUNCIL ON MEASUREMENTS USED IN EDUCATION, JOINT COMMITTEE. Technical recommendations for psychological tests and diagnostic techniques. *Psychol. Bull.*, 1954, **51**, 201–238.

2. ANASTASI, ANNE, & FOLEY, J. P. *Differential psychology.* (Rev. Ed.) New York: Macmillan, 1949.

3. BROSS, I. D. J. *Design for decision.* New York: Macmillan, 1953.

4. DANIELSON, J. R., & CLARK, J. H. A personality inventory for induction screening. *J. clin. Psychol.*, 1954, **10**, 137–143.

5. DORKEN, H., & KRAL, A. The psychological differentiation of organic brain lesions and their localization by means of the Rorschach test. *Amer. J. Psychiat.*, 1952, **108**, 764–770.

6. DUNCAN, O. D., OHLIN, L. E., REISS, A. J., & STANTON, H. R. Formal devices for making selection decisions. *Amer. J. Sociol.*, 1953, **58**, 573–584.

7. GLUECK, S., & GLUECK, ELEANOR. *Unraveling juvenile delinquency.* Cambridge, Mass.: Harvard Univer. Press, 1950.

8. GOODMAN, L. A. The use and validity of a prediction instrument. I. A reformulation of the use of a prediction instrument. *Amer. J. Sociol.*, 1953, **58**, 503–509.

9. HANVIK, L. J. Some psychological dimensions of low back pain. Unpublished doctor's thesis, Univer. of Minnesota, 1949.

10. HERZBERG, A. *Active psychotherapy.* New York: Grune & Stratton, 1945.

11. HORST, P. (Ed.) The prediction of personal adjustment. *Soc. Sci. Res. Coun. Bull.*, 1941, No. 48, 1–156.

12. MEEHL, P. E. *Clinical versus statistical prediction.* Minneapolis: Univer. of Minnesota Press, 1954.

13. REISS, A. J. Unraveling juvenile delinquency. II. An appraisal of the research methods. *Amer. J. Sociol.*, 1951 **57**, 115–120.

14. ROSEN, A. Detection of suicidal patients: an example of some limitations in the prediction of infrequent events. *J. consult. Psychol.*, 1954, **18**, 397–403.

15. ROTTER, J. B., RAFFERTY, J. E., & LOTSOF, A. B. The validity of the Rotter Incomplete Sentences Blank: high school form. *J. consult. Psychol.*, 1954, **18**, 105–111.

16. SALTER, A. *Conditioned reflex therapy.*

New York: Creative Age Press, 1950.

17. TAULBEE, E. S., & SISSON, B. D. Rorschach pattern analysis in schizophrenia: a cross-validation study. *J. clin. Psychol.*, 1954, **10**, 80–82.

18. THIESEN, J. W. A pattern analysis of structural characteristics of the Rorschach test in schizophrenia. *J. consult. Psychol.*, 1952, **16**, 365–370.

19. WOLPE, J. Objective psychotherapy of the neuroses. *S. African Med. J.*, 1952, **26**, 825–829.

The Twisted Pear and the Prediction of Behavior

Jerome Fisher

"To say that nature should conform to a Gaussian distribution is asking too much. Who is there to tell nature what the statisticians would like?" This statement, made recently by Boring (1957) in an editorial context, seems an appropriate introduction to the question and the point of view presented in this paper. It is by no means a new point of view. Rather, it is a variation on the familiar theme that organisms, whose behaviors are variously studied for purposes of prediction, do not conform to the assumed mathematical conditions which are often assigned to them in statistical manipulations of data.

In substance, the paper raises questions not only about the appropriateness of our statistical assumptions as they concern prediction problems but, also, it ventures the proposition that, because of certain biologic and psychologic variants, organismic behaviors

Based on a paper read at the XV International Congress of Psychology, Brussels, July, 1957.

For many helpful suggestions and for their encouragement the author is especially grateful to Robert C. Tryon and Harrison Gough.

are predictable in only one segment of a predictor-criterion relationship.[1]

Several years ago, in analyzing the results of a cross-validation study (Fisher, Gonda, & Little, 1955) involving the Rorschach, my colleagues and I noted a curious but consistent result. When the Rorschach yielded a score indicating the presence of brain disease, the agreement with independent criterion judgments of brain pathology was extraordinarily good (94%). A low score, however, was *not* accurate in predicting the absence of brain pathology. A Pearson validity coefficient was computed and found to be a respectable, significant, but humble .32.

Next, we subjected several standard neurologic procedures, such as the EEG, the lumbar puncture, etc., to essentially the same validation analysis (Fisher & Gonda, 1955). Except for a few minor variations, five neurologic diagnostic techniques gave the same results: High accuracy in predicting pathology from positive test findings, but like the Rorschach, poor accuracy

[1] Cronbach and Gleser (1957) have recently presented a similar argument to the one advanced in this paper, based on the mathematics and logic of decision theory, for considering the problem of differential validities in psychological testing.

in predicting the absence of pathology from negative diagnostic signs. The over-all validity coefficients ranged from .13 to .32.

When scattergrams were plotted of the relationship between predictor scores and the criterion, a nonlinear heteroscedastic configuration was revealed which looked like a twisted pear; it is approximated in Fig. 1. This finding raised the question: Is the twisted pear unique to these data or is it a general pattern, characteristic of prediction problems?

implicit but functionalistic conception of the corresponding relationships between predictor "good" and "poor" scores and the criterion behavior of organisms. In other words, the predictor becomes *decreasingly* predictive of the criterion as the scores obtained increase from the "poor" to "good" extremes of the predictor. To illustrate this predictor-criterion differential, the findings of studies of intelligence, learning, personality, and pathology will be presented and discussed.

According to Fig. 1, the predictive

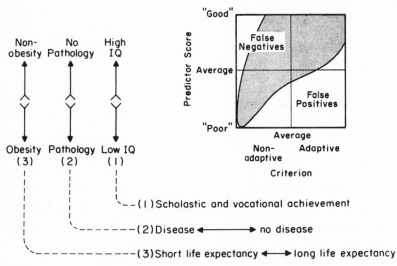

Figure 1. Schematic model of prediction in behavior. Some examples: Predictor vs. Criterion.

The diagram will call to mind many familiar observations and findings. When scattergrams from several sources are examined, where more or less known criteria are plotted against more or less standard predictors, e.g., objective tests, a linear relationship with relatively little array variance will be observable at one end of the plot. The relationship, however, becomes increasingly nonlinear and increasingly variable as it approaches the middle and upper extreme. The terms "adaptive" and "nonadaptive" are used in Fig. 1 to suggest an

efficiency of the IQ at the "poor" extreme should be considerably better than for average and "good" (superior) IQs. Specifically, with IQs below, say 50, it is highly predictable that the individual will require custodial or complete protective care, and that he will not acquire any scholastic skills. With IQs of about 50–70, there appears to be moderately good predictability that the individual will require special training and guidance, particularly at work and at school. With IQs of approximately 70–85, and to a greater degree between

TABLE 1.   COMPARISON OF EDUCATIONAL AND OCCUPATIONAL ACHIEVEMENTS OF GROUPS
OF MEN WHOSE IQS WERE OBTAINED IN CHILDHOOD

Groups	Mean IQ at Time of Test	Mean Age at Time of Test	Follow-Up in Years	Occupational Achievement				Educational Achievement				
				N	Minnesota Occupational Scale[a]			N	8th Grade and Lower	9th–12th	Some College	College Graduation
					VI & V	IV & III	II & I					
Terman's gifted (1940)												
A (N = 96)	155.0			149[b] ⎫				150 ⎫				
B		9.7	18	436 ⎬	10.3%	24.3%	65.3%	481 ⎬	0.0%	14.7%	18.3%	66.9%
C (N = 92)	150.0			139 ⎭				150 ⎭				
Baller's (1935) control	107.8	8–9	21	113 ⎫				124 ⎫				
Fairbank's (1931) control	90.0	12 (?)	17	39 ⎬	43.5	40.6	15.9	25 ⎬	36.0	35.3	15.5	13.1
Baller's (1935) mental defectives	60.5	8–9	21	67 ⎫				113 ⎫				
Fairbank's (1931) mental defectives	68.0	12	17	69 ⎬	77.3	22.7	0.0	43 ⎬	93.5	6.5	0.0	0.0
U. S. Census (1940)[c]					44.7	41.6	13.8		60.4	29.5	5.5	4.6

[a] The Minnesota Occupational Scale was used by Terman for the classification of his gifted men. Because the other follow-up studies cited here were conducted and reported in the same decade (1930–1940), the Minnesota Occupational Scale was adapted and applied to them also. Roe's (1956) more recent two-way classification of occupations gives similar results. Roughly, the classifications I & II refer to professional and managerial; III & IV—skilled labor and agricultural; V & VI—semiskilled and laborer.

[b] The Ns of 149 and 139, respectively, as well as the Ns and percentages of the other studies cited, refer to gainfully employed men only, who were available geographically at the time of the follow-up study.

[c] U.S. census (1951) educational and occupational data for men are included for purposes of general comparison.

85–110, however, vocational and scholastic limitations vs. successes become increasingly difficult to predict.

Table 1 summarizes the results of several longitudinal studies of the vocational and educational achievements of male mental defectives, their controls, and, in addition, the vocational and scholastic attainments of Terman's gifted men (Terman & Oden, 1947). The latter included some 730 subjects whose childhood IQs were 140 or higher and who were classified into two groups by raters on the basis of vocational achievement 18 years later. The A group (mean childhood IQ = 155) was the most successful and the C group (mean IQ = 150) the least successful. The C group of 150 men, therefore, was, by definition and rating procedures, an underachieving group. Table 1 reveals that as a group, Terman's gifted men, 25 years of age and older in 1940, were superior occupationally to the general male population in the U. S. Further analysis of the data (not reported in Table 1), however, discloses that 28% of the C group fell at or below the median occupational level of the employed males in the U. S., as well as of those in California in 1940.[2, 3]

[2] See pp. 361 ff. in Terman and Oden (1947).

[3] The unemployed and incapacitated ($N=16$) in Terman's gifted group were not included in the numbers and percentages given in Table 1; in addition, those who were classified as students were also omitted. A mitigating consideration is the postdepression economy of the period and the relative employment "youthfulness" of the entire gifted group. Many were still in transit occupationally.

The same conditions, however, obtain for the mentally defective and their control groups, because all of the studies cited in Table 1 were based upon the socioeconomic conditions of the decade 1930–1940. In personal communication with the author, Melita H. Oden reported that since 1940, follow-up studies of the gifted group have shown intragroup shifts on the occupational scale; some C men have moved up and others have moved down on the scale; some A men have taken positions in lower (III–VI) occupations.

Terman and Oden (1947) note that:

On the average, those of highest IQ accomplish more and are equally well-adjusted, but one cannot anywhere draw an arbitrary IQ line that will set off potential genius from relative mediocrity. Some of our subjects who have achieved most notably did not, either in childhood or in adult life, rate above the average of the total group in tested intelligence.

With regard to the lower end of the IQ range, Table 1 also gives the occupational achievements of two follow-up studies of mentally defective groups. The data reported are in the form of average percentages for the combined groups. Compared to the gifted and control groups, the findings suggest a stronger, less variable relationship between mental deficiency, as determined mainly by IQ, and occupational achievement. None of the mental defective groups achieve I and II occupational categories; 23% are in III and IV, and 77% in V and VI. For the control samples, whose mean IQs are within the average range, the proportion of cases fall in the several categories as shown. Approximately two-thirds of the gifted group attained superior vocational levels (I and II). The presence of 10 and 24% of the gifted in the lower occupational Categories V and VI, and III and IV, respectively, however, suggests again the greater variability and, hence, the potential predictive "error" associated with "good" IQ scores.

Prediction of scholastic achievement by means of the IQ was studied by review of the same investigations. Table 1 also presents the follow-up findings of the same group of men whose IQs were obtained in childhood. The data are summarized in scatterplot form via averages to make them comparable to Wolfe's (1951) categories of educational achievement.

It appears that the IQ has considerable power in predicting scholastic achievement, particularly in the tails of the distribution of IQs. Compared to the controls and the gifted, however, the lower end of the IQ range (the mental defectives), reveals greater certainty of prediction for the criterion scholastic achievement.

At the upper extreme, the gifted's superiority educationally is self-evident (67% graduated from college). According to Terman and Oden, none of the gifted failed to complete grade school. For the middle and upper range of the predictor, however, the computed percentages, placed in their respective cells, suggest the characteristic variability observed before and again reveal the twisted pear shape.

What about learning, personality, and the "twisted pear" phenomenon? In his genetic research of dull-bright rats and maze-learning ability, Tryon (1940) found that while the poor maze-learning of the dull rats could be predicted very well, the bright rats varied throughout a wide range of learning scores (errors). Table 2 presents a fourfold table which was obtained by plotting around the median value of the total errors of the seventh generation ($N = 153$), the total errors made by their dull and bright offspring of the 15th to 18th generation. The reason for using the seventh generation as the source for the median value comes from Tryon's observation, "There appears to be a law of diminishing returns, for after the F_7 negligible effects of selective breeding are noted." None of the descendants of the dulls fell in the bright category, whereas 30% of the descendants of the bright ancestors performed in the dull category. The results, in short, suggest that the relation between predictor ancestors and criterion descendants, involving the learning of a complex set of highly integrated acts, is that of the twisted pear.

The work of the California-Berkeley group on authoritarianism suggests a similar pattern of differential predictability in personality assessment (Adorno, Frenkel-Brunswik, Levinson, & Sanford,

TABLE 2.   PERCENTAGE OF BRIGHT AND DULL STRAINS 15TH–18TH GENERATIONS, WHO FALL ABOVE AND BELOW THE MEDIAN TOTAL ERRORS OF THE 7TH GENERATION ($N = 153$) (FROM TRYON, 1940)

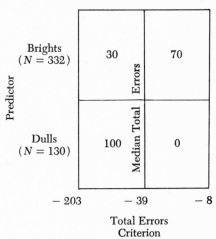

Total Errors
Criterion

1950). While high scorers (authoritarians) and low scorers (nonauthoritarians) "emerge as a result of statistical analysis . . . they consist in accumulations of symptoms frequently found together but they leave plenty of room for variations of specific features. Furthermore, various distinct subtypes are found within each of the two major portions." Analysis of the prejudiced subjects, however, revealed that they are "on the whole more alike as a group than are the unprejudiced. The latter include a great variety of personalities . . ." (pp. 971–972). It seems, therefore, that a high score on the ethnocentrism scale is more predictive of authoritarianism than are low scores of its absence.

Leaving psychology for a moment, an analogue seems to exist in the actuarial determinations of the life insurance field (see Fig. 1). For example, having reviewed their experience tables and having ascertained the extent of their errors of prediction, insurance companies confidently relate obesity to a short span of life and set their premium rates accordingly. As weight approaches nonobesity, however, there appears to be increasing variability in predicting life expectancy. It is, of course, true that no one dies of obesity and the nonobese may die of many other causes; yet as a predictor variable of the probability of life expectancy, insurance companies respect the highly significant relationship found at the "poor"–nonadaptive extreme, i.e., between obesity and short life expectancy.

In their daily practice, my hospital medical colleagues confirm the curvilinear relationship between their tests and their criteria of pathology; at least, they acknowledge implicitly the application of differential predictability. For example, it seems that medical specialists almost always regard a positive test finding ("poor" predictor score) with considerable respect. The reason for this is that their diagnostic techniques are accurate at least 80% of the time when they yield a positive finding, i.e., the false positive rate is low. A negative or even a borderline finding ("good" to average score), however, is invariably disregarded, *if*, in the physician's opinion, this finding is at variance with the patient's history, his presenting complaints, his symptoms and other diagnostic data. With a negative ("good" score) finding, therefore, the physician functions with a clinical relativism and a clinical tolerance of variability and errors of prediction.

When we apply our correlation statistics to measure the magnitude of the relationship between a criterion and a predictor, the coefficient thus obtained gives an average, over-all statement of differential predictions of the test. The result, being a statement of the weighted means of the selection ratios of the predictor classes $Y_1, Y_2, \ldots Y_n$ on the criterion X, is to attenuate the validity coefficient. If the product-moment r is computed without drawing the scatterplot, the plot may or may not be heteroscedastic, and the analyst cannot tell whether there are differential predictions of the various Y classes.

Guilford (1956), among others, has argued for the importance of scattergram inspection. With respect to organismic behavior, therefore, the case of linear association and equal variance obtains and applies partially, but not throughout a predictor-criterion relationship. The case of curvilinear association and unequal variance, however, also applies and, therefore, both cases are relevant and deserve our differential appreciation.

It has been said many times before and in many different ways that the behavior of the adaptive, functioning organism is ordinarily highly complex. I think we mean by this a capacity for variable, substitutive, compensatory behaviors. Under the disruptive conditions of pathology or stress, for example, it is as if special homeostatic mechanisms provide a biologic and/or psychologic *smoke screen* of adaptiveness. These on-going, restorative processes may be largely responsible for the high rate of "normal" responses or false negatives. It is perhaps no accident that many of our most useful diagnostic methods have been devised to assess pathology *in status;* i.e., when the camouflage is no longer impenetrable, or when adaptiveness has been or is curtailed beyond a certain point. I am referring here, in particular, to Binet's original mental test—an extraordinarily fine screening device for mental deficiency.[4] It is precisely in the nonadaptive segment, then, that our predictors seem to prove themselves by virtue of their high rate of predictive accuracy. In this connection, it should be pointed out that they are not entirely without predictive power in the adaptive segment either, albeit

[4] Recently, Jones (1958) advanced the concept of polarity to explain the one-ended conceptual clarity of most psychologic scales. He proposes a method for testing interitem homogeneity at either or both ends of a continuum to determine the degree of scale polarity.

negative errors lessen their accuracy. It seems, therefore, that when predictor measures are extrapolated beyond that "certain point," i.e., from "poor" to "good," the multivariable complexities of behavior multiply and interfere with our predictive accuracy. Hence, it appears that whatever validity a measure may possess for predicting *adaptive* behavior, it is likely to be more accurate in predicting nonadaptive behavior.

Perhaps the hidden determinant in all this is the criterion dimension itself extending from the nonadaptive to the adaptive. It, too, appears to have a partial range of certainty and "truth," probably because more is known about the defining criterion points of nonadaptiveness than about those of adaptive behavior. Our test construction procedures provide us with reasonably good techniques and measures of criterion nonadaptive behavior. If, however, the twisted pear phenomenon possesses the degree of generality suggested by the data reviewed, then, there is reason

to question the assumptions for extrapolating from the nonadaptive to the adaptive extremes of predictor-criterion relationships.

Is it possible that the observed *partial* curvilinearity and differential predictive variance are merely artifacts of sampling (of our tests) or of our criterion determinations? Is the twisted pear solely a "clinical" phenomenon, or is it a more general characteristic of the prediction problem? Perhaps these questions are unanswerable at the present time or perhaps we are dealing with a reality of organismic behavior, one of the existentional dilemmas, to borrow a term from Erich Fromm, for the behavioral sciences. It is as if, on the one hand, there is general acceptance of the dynamic nature of organismic adaptation and change, and the variability thereby induced, while, on the other hand, there is the coexisting pursuit of immutable validity coefficients as an attainable goal in the business of understanding and predicting behavior.

REFERENCES

ADORNO, T. W., FRENKEL-BRUNSWIK, ELSE, LEVINSON, D. J., & SANFORD, R. N. *The authoritarian personality.* New York: Harper, 1950.

BALLER, W. R. A study of the present social status of a group of adults, who, when they were in elementary schools, were classified as mentally deficient. *Genet. psychol. Monogr.*, 1936, 18, 165–244.

BORING, E. G. CP speaks. (Editorial.) *Contemp. Psychol.*, 1957, 2, 261.

CRONBACH, L. J., & GLESER, GOLDINE C. *Psychological tests and personnel decisions.* Urbana: Univer. Illinois Press, 1957.

FAIRBANK, RUTH E. The subnormal child —seventeen years after. *Ment. Hyg., NY*, 1933, 17, 177–208.

FISHER, J., & GONDA, T. A. Neurologic techniques and Rorschach test in detecting brain pathology: A study of comparative validities. *AMA Arch.*

Neurol. Psychiat., 1955, 74, 117–124.

FISHER, J., GONDA, T. A., & LITTLE, K. B. The Rorschach and central nervous system pathology: A cross-validation study. *Amer. J. Psychiat.*, 1955, 3, 487–492.

GUILFORD, J. P. *Fundamental statistics in psychology and education.* New York: McGraw-Hill, 1956.

JONES, M. B. The polarity of psychological tests. *J. consult. Psychol.*, 1958, 22, 25–29.

ROE, ANNE. *The psychology of occupations.* New York: Wiley, 1956.

TERMAN, L. M., & ODEN, MELITA, H. *Genetic studies of genius.* Vol. 4. *The gifted child grows up.* Stanford: Stanford Univer. Press, 1947.

TRYON, R. C. Genetic differences in maze-learning ability in rats. *Yearb. nat. Soc. Stud. Educ.*, 1940, 39, Part I.

WOLFLE, D. Intellectual resources. *Scient. Amer.*, 1951, 185 (3), 42–46.

PART II

Studies of

Specific Techniques

of Assessment

Chapter 5

Special Problems of Structured Tests: Test Construction

■ This chapter initiates Part II which is devoted to an examination of the validity of a number of our more important tests of personality. The first three chapters deal with the validation of structured tests and the next four with the validation of unstructured or projective tests.

The essential difference between the two types of tests is in the freedom of the subject to form his own response or to limit himself to choosing among responses selected by the examiner, usually "true," "false," and "cannot say." Otherwise, the methods are more alike than is generally recognized, for both use more or less ambiguous stimuli and both require a good deal of clinical interpretation before behavioral predictions can be made.

Because of the differences in the range of responses open to the client the process of making inferences from structured and unstructured tests has differed considerably; the structured test literature is largely concerned with scoring and psychometric scale construction while the projective literature is more concerned with the skills of the clinician in utilizing the data. For this reason, each approach has its unique problems. The problems peculiar to structured tests will be dealt with in this chapter and the next while those peculiar to projective tests will be discussed in Chapter 8.

The problems associated with structured tests can be roughly divided into two areas, those concerned with the best method of scale construction, which will be discussed in this chapter, and those concerned with response sets which will be treated in Chapter 6.

The problems associated with structured test construction can in turn be divided into two broad areas. The first is the construction of a pool of items and the second is the combination of these items into a scale. Logically and temporally, item construction precedes scale construction. However, concern for item construction has taken second place to scale construction so that the writing of test items has been much more of an art than a science. In this area, psychological testing has lagged behind opinion polling where the wording of items has been a matter of concern for some time. The reason for this is that the opinion pollers have been much more concerned with the manifest content of the response to an item than have the psychological testers. This in turn is a result of psychological scale construction.

Scale construction is no more than the selection and weighting of certain items for the purpose of measuring some attribute or predicting some criterion. The first method was rational. One or more clinicians would select those items which in their expert opinion would measure a certain trait. At first this was based on manifest content. The Rogers Test of Personality Adjustment, published in 1931, bluntly asked a child, "Do people treat your brother (or sister) better than they treat you?" and the child could check off one of the following responses: never, sometimes, often, almost always, or indicate that he had no brother or sister. The test was scored for such variables as family maladjustment and social maladjustment and in the scoring it was assumed that if the child said his sibling was treated better, then this indicated family maladjustment.

The next step in rational scale construction was for the judge to put himself in the position of the respondent and guess how a person with a given problem would respond to the items. This approach was also evident in the Rogers Test. In response to the question, "Do you have any good friends?" a child was considered to have problems in social adjustment not only if he checked answer (a) "none at all" but also if he checked answer (e) "hundreds of them," since the test constructor apparently felt that a rejected child might well endorse the latter item for defensive reasons. This represents one of the earliest attempts to use suppressor items to improve prediction.

The defects in rational test construction were obvious. The scales were no better than the clinicians' ability to guess the response patterns of various groups and they were relatively open to distortion. The next major step was empirical item selection. In this method well defined criterion groups are compared in their responses to a pool of items, and those items which discriminate between the two groups, regardless of content, are selected to form the scale. This method had been applied successfully to vocational interests by E. K. Strong in 1927 and was adopted by Hathaway and McKinley in the derivation of the MMPI. Since the manifest content did not influence an item on a scale (with the exception of the L scale) the test was termed an "inventory" rather than a "questionnaire."

The unimportance of manifest content in the scoring of the original MMPI scales has been a difficult concept to communicate to the public and as a consequence public objections to the use of the test, based on manifest content, are becoming increasingly frequent as the test is used more and more in schools, industry, and government. Starke Hathaway, in the first article in this chapter, addresses himself to this problem in a thoughtful letter to a citizen concerned about the fact that the MMPI, which is used in selecting police officers in his community, asks questions about a person's religious beliefs. In this letter, Hathaway explains the principle behind empirical item selection, and also points out how difficult it is to alter an item pool once scale construction has begun.[1]

The authors of the MMPI, as well as the architects of other personality scales and inventories, generally focus on the measurement of theoretically determined constructs. Hathaway and McKinley turned to psychiatric nosology for their constructs, Gough to concepts found in the "folk culture," Edwards to Murray's "need system," Myers and Briggs to Jungian psychology and so on. However, there is another group no less determined that items be selected in a scientific manner, which also insists that the very constructs to be measured should also be empirically selected. These are the factor analysts who use multivariate statistical methods to identify what they feel are the important dimensions of personality and then build tests to assess them. Among the most notable spokesmen for this view are Raymond Cattell and Hans Eysenck.

Factor analytic tests have not yet come into widespread clinical use, possibly because the mathematical background of the multivariate statistician and the methods he uses are so alien to the clinician's background and training that the clinician must either accept the factor analytic test constructs superficially and on faith or expend a great deal of effort to understand their derivation and meaning. Since the constructs often lack intuitive appeal for the clinician, he usually resolves the problem by ignoring the factor analysts and their tests in clinical practice, although he may use them occasionally in research.[2]

Because of this lack of communication, the "factor analytic school" is often regarded as being quite monolithic in its methodology and assumptions. While there are indeed broad areas of agreement between such workers as Cattell and Eysenck, there are also points of disagreement as well. In the next article, Cattell presents some of these basic assumptions and defines some of the areas of agreement and disagreement within the factor analytic group.

No matter what method of test construction or item selection is used, however, a test can be no better than the items in the original item pool. While great advances have been made in item selection, item construction still is done in more of an artistic than a scientific manner. Recently, however, there has been renewed interest in improving the items which make up a scale. This has been stimulated in part by disappointingly low test-retest reliability coefficients for both scales and items.

[1] For additional discussion of empirical item selection, the reader is referred to Meehl's (1945) paper which has been reprinted in Welsh and Dahlstrom's (1956) collection of readings on the MMPI as well as to some of the articles describing the derivation of individual MMPI scales contained in that volume.

[2] For an excellent account of factor analytic research in non-technical terms, see Cattell (1965).

Lewis Goldberg in the concluding article in this chapter turns his attention to the problem of unreliable items and concludes ambiguity is a major cause of item instability. A particularly thorny problem has been the fact that interindividual and intraindividual instability go hand in hand; that is, the items which discriminate most between people are also the least reliable and vice versa. One difficulty in correcting this situation and moving toward the goal of obtaining items which maximize discrimination while minimizing instability, has been a lack of adequate ways of measuring item ambiguity. Goldberg derives an index of item ambiguity which paves the way for improved item construction. He also proposes a general model for item ambiguity in an attempt to integrate some of the diverse empirical findings in the area and test some of the implications. Hopefully, this will lead toward improved item technology and improved structured tests.

REFERENCES

CATTELL, R. *The scientific analysis of personality.* Baltimore: Penguin Books, Inc., 1965.

MEEHL, P. E. The dynamics of "structured" personality tests. *Journal of Clinical Psychology,* 1945, **1**, 297–303.

WELSH, G. S., & DALHSTROM, W. G. (Eds.) *Basic readings on the MMPI in psychology and medicine.* Minneapolis: University of Minnesota Press, 1956.

MMPI: Professional Use by Professional People

Starke R. Hathaway

This long letter was prompted by a courteous inquiry that I received. The inquiry referred to the use of the MMPI as an aid in the selection of policemen from among applicants. It was pointed out that there are laws against inquiry about religious affiliation and the specific issue was the presence in the MMPI of items relating to religion.

Reprinted by permission of the American Psychological Association and the author from *American Psychologist*, 1964, **19**, 204–210.

Letter to Mr. R.

First I would like to express my appreciation of your reasonably expressed inquiry about the MMPI as possibly offensive in the statements that relate to religious activities and which might provide personal information on which discriminatory acts might be based. Because of sporadic public antagonism to psychological testing, and in view of our mutual concern for our civil liberties, I am going to answer you at considerable length and with unusual care. I shall send copies of this answer to the Psychological Corporation and to others who may be concerned. Let me assure you at the outset that I believe I am proceeding from a considered position rather than from a defensive attitude that could lead me to irrationally protect the MMPI, other such tests, or psychologists in general. I believe that I would be among the first to criticize some of the uses to which tests are put, and some of those who use them improperly. I must also immediately make it clear that I am antagonistic to ignorant attacks upon tests. Tests are not offensive elements; the offensive elements, if any, come with the misuse of tests. To attack tests is, to a certain extent, comparable to an attack upon knives. Both good and bad use of knives occurs because they are sharp instruments. To eliminate knives would, of course, have a limiting effect upon the occurrence of certain hostile acts, but it would also greatly limit the activities of surgeons. I simply discriminate between the instrument and the objectives and applications of the persons who wield it. I am calling attention to the difference between a switchblade knife, which is good for nothing but attack, and a scalpel knife, good for healing purposes but which can also be used as a weapon. I hope that no one will think that any test was devised in the same spirit that switchblade knives were devised. It is absurd if someone holds the belief that psychologists malignantly developed instruments such as the MMPI for use against the welfare of man, including of course man's personal liberties and rights. But if the MMPI and such tests have origins analogous to the scalpel and are really perversely used to man's disadvantage, we are properly concerned. Let me turn to a history of the MMPI items about which you have inquired.

I should begin with an account of the origin of the MMPI itself. I believe

I am competent to do this, and I hope you will see that its origins were motivated toward virtue as I have suggested above. In about 1937, J. C. McKinley, then head of the Department of Neuropsychiatry of the Medical School at the University of Minnesota, supported me in a venture which grew out of a current problem in our psychopathic hospital. The problem lay in the fact that insulin therapy as a treatment method for certain forms of mental disease had just become a widespread method of treatment. Different clinics were finding highly varied values. Some reported the treatment to be exceedingly effective; others said it was ineffective. The treatment was somewhat dangerous to patients, and it was exceedingly expensive in terms of hospitalization and nursing care. McKinley happened to be one of the neuropsychiatrists of the time who felt that more careful investigation should be undertaken before such treatments were applied, and in particular before we used them on our patients.

It occurred to us that the difficulty in evaluation of insulin treatment lay largely in the fact that there was no good way to be assured that the patients treated by this method in one clinic were like those treated in another clinic. This was due to the fact that the estimations of the nature of a person's mental illness and of its severity were based upon professional judgment, and could vary with the training background of the particular psychiatrist as well as with his personal experiences. Obviously, if the patients treated at one center were not like those treated at another center, the outcome of treatment might be different. At that time there was no psychological test available that would have helped to remove the diagnostic decisions on the patients in two clinics from the personal biases of the local staffs. There was no way that our hospital staff could select a group of patients for the new treatment who would be surely comparable in diagnosis and severity of illness to those from some other setting. It became an obvious possibility that one might devise a personality test which, like intelligence tests, would somewhat stabilize the identification of the illness and provide an estimate of its severity. Toward this problem the MMPI research was initiated.

I have established that decisions about the kind and severity of mental illness depend upon the psychological examinations of the psychiatrists and other professional persons. The items upon which the judgments are based constitute the symptoms of mental maladjustment or illness. Such symptoms have for many, many years been listed in the textbooks of psychiatry and clinical psychology that treat with mental disorder. These symptoms are verbal statements from or about the patient. The simplest and most obvious form of these symptoms are statements that confess feelings of unhappiness, depression, and the like. The statements may also be less personal, as in complaints about one's lot in life and about the inability to find employment or the mistreatment by others.

In summary, the symptoms of mental illness and unhappiness are represented in verbal complaints or statements that relate to personal feelings or personal experiences or reactions to job and home. It should be immediately apparent that unlike most physical illnesses, these verbally presented complaints or symptoms usually do not permit direct observation by others. If a patient reports a painful nodule or abdominal pain, the reported pain can usually be observed by some physical or nonverbal means that lends credence to the complaint. Many symptoms of mental illness are contrastingly difficult to observe by nonverbal means. It is almost impossible to establish that the person presenting the symptom is actually suffering from a distortion of his psycho-

logically healthy mental state by some psychological complex. There is much arbitrariness even in the statement, "I am unhappy." Frequently no physical observation can be brought to bear upon the statement. The complainant may look unhappy and may even add that he is suicidal, yet friends and the examiner can agree that he is, "just asking for sympathy, is no worse off than the average." There is no way of solidly deciding what the words really mean. This point is crucial to what I am writing. If it is not clear at this point, reference books on semantics should be consulted. S. I. Hayakawa would be a good source.

I know of no method which will permit us to absolutely assess unhappiness or mental illness, either as to kind or severity, unless we start from inescapable symptoms that are verbally expressed and subject to the vagaries in the personal connotations of words and phrases. In initiating the research upon what was to produce the MMPI, we collected as many as we could find of the symptomatic statements recognized by authorities as indicative of unhappiness and mental illness. There were hundreds of these statements. We had at one time well over a thousand of them. Every one of these symptomatic statements had already been written into the literature or had been used as a practical bit of clinical evidence in the attempt to understand patients. I repeat this because I want to thoroughly emphasize that every item in the MMPI came from assumed relationships to the assessment of human beings for better diagnosis and treatment of possible mental illness.

Now with all this preamble I am prepared to discuss the particular items that you have highlighted in your letter. It happens that, among the many items collected and finally selected to make up the MMPI, there were at least 19 relating to religion in one way or another:

	Male		Female	
	True	No Answer	True	No Answer
I am very religious (more than most people).	8	9	11	9
Religion gives me no worry.	83	4	70	4
I go to church almost every week.	42	3	52	4
I pray several times every week.	50	3	83	2
I read in the Bible several times a week.	21	5	30	3
I feel sure that there is only one true religion.	49	8	51	11
I have no patience with people who believe there is only one true religion.	56	4	47	10
I believe there is a God.	92	5	96	2
I believe there is a devil and a hell in afterlife.	63	14	67	14
I believe in a life hereafter.	76	12	87	7
I believe in the second coming of Christ.	57	18	68	12
Christ performed miracles such as changing water into wine.	69	16	77	15
The only miracles I know of are simply tricks that people play on one another.	37	10	27	14
A minister can cure disease by praying and putting his hand on your head.	4	10	5	11
Everything is turning out just like the prophets of the Bible said it would.	52	29	54	32
My soul sometimes leaves my body.	8	18	5	12
I am a special agent of God.	14	13	16	21
I have had some very unusual religious experiences	20	5	13	2
I have been inspired to a program of life based on duty which I have since carefully followed.	42	14	50	15

I have listed these items to remind you again of the ones you cited, and I have added others that may further illustrate what I am saying. Now you have asked why we included these statements on religion among the possible symptoms of psychological maladjustment. Why should these items still appear in the MMPI?

In the first instance, the subject matter evidenced in the symptoms of depressed or otherwise mentally disturbed persons often largely centers in religion. There is a well-recognized pattern of psychological distortion to which we apply the term religiosity. When we use the word "religiosity," we indicate a symptomatic pattern wherein the process of an intercurrent psychological maladjustment is evidenced by extremes of religious expression that are out of the usual context for even the deeply religious person. A bishop friend of mine once illustrated the problem he

sometimes had in this connection by his account of a parishioner who had routinely given a tithe as his offering toward support of the church, but who, within a few weeks, had increased the amount he gave until it was necessary for him to embezzle money for his weekly offering. Surely, my friend said, there is more here than ordinary devotion; there is something which should be considered from another frame of reference. In this anecdote there is an element of the symptomatic pattern, religiosity. But, as is true of nearly every other aspect of human personality to which the MMPI refers, no one item will ordinarily establish this distortion of the ordinarily meaningful position of religion. And no one item can be used to detect the problem as it occurs in various persons. Two persons rarely express even their usual religious feelings in identical ways.

It never occurred to us in selecting

these items for the MMPI that we were asking anything relative to the particular religion of our patients. It obviously did not occur to us that there were other than the Christian orientation wherein religiosity might be observed. Because of this oversight on our part, several of our MMPI symptoms that we assumed were indicative of religiosity happen to be obviously related to the Christian religion, although we find that most persons simply translate to their own orientation if it is different. I should hasten to add that although these symptoms were hoped to be specific to persons who suffer from religiosity, they have not all turned out that way. Not every aspect of religion is at times a symptom of mental illness. Certainly it is obvious that there is nothing symptomatic in admitting to one's personal acceptance or rejection of several of the items. The point at which a group of items becomes consistent in suggesting symptoms is subtle to distinguish. As my bishop friend's story illustrated, it is not unusual that one contributes to religious work even though there exists a doubtful extreme. As I will show below, all these items are endorsed or rejected by some ordinary, normal people. If any of the items have value toward clinical assessment, the value comes in combination with other items which probably will not seem to relate to religion.

The MMPI, which started out so small and inconspicuously, has become a world-known and -used instrument. We did not expect this outcome. If I were to select new items, I would again include items that related to religiosity. I would this time, of course, try to avoid the implication that the religiosity occurred only among adherents to the Christian faith. I am obviously unhappy about the limited applicability of these items, but I am, in the same sense, unhappy about other items in the MMPI. A considerable number of the items have been challenged by other groups

from other standpoints. By this I mean only to remind those concerned about these religiosity items that there are frankly stated items on sex, there are items on body functions, there are items on certain occupations; in fact, there are items on most every aspect of psychological life that can be symptomatic of maladjustment and unhappiness. If the psychologist cannot use these personal items to aid in the assessment of people, he suffers as did the Victorian physician who had to examine his female patients by feeling the pulse in the delicate hand thrust from behind a screen. I shall come back to this point later, but it is obvious that if we were making a new MMPI, we would again be faced either with being offensive to subgroupings of people by personal items they object to or, if we did not include personal items and were inoffensive, we would have lost the aim of the instrument.

One may protest that the MMPI is intended for the patient, the mentally ill person, not applicants to schools, high-school children, or to those being considered for jobs. I cannot give a general defense of every such use, but this is a time when preventive health is being emphasized. We urge everyone to get chest X rays and to take immunizing shots. We are now beginning to advocate general surveys with such psychological instruments as the MMPI. The basic justification is the same. We hope to identify potential mental breakdown or delinquency in the school child before he must be dragged before us by desperate parents or by other authority. We hope to hire police, who are given great power over us, with assurance that those we put on the rolls should have good personal qualities for the job. This is not merely to protect us, this also is preventive mental health, since modern job stability can trap unwary workers into placements that leave them increasingly unhappy and otherwise maladjusted. If the personality of an applicant is not appropriate to the job, neither employer nor applicant should go ahead. We have always recognized the employer's use of this principle in his right to personal interview with applicants. Since the items and responses are on record, the MMPI and such devices could be considered to be a more fair method of estimation than the personal interview, and, when they are machine scored, they make possible much greater protection from arbitrary personal judgments and the open ended questions that are standard for personal interviews.

It seems to me that the MMPI examination can be rather comparable to the physical examination for selection of persons. One would not wish to hire a person with a bad heart when the job required behavior that was dangerous to him. I think it would be equally bad to hire a person as a policeman whose psychological traits were inappropriate and then expect him to do dangerous things or shoot to kill as a policeman is expected to do. There is, from physical and psychological examinations, a protection to the person being hired as well as to those hiring him. This is not meant as an argument for the use of the MMPI in every placement that requires special skills or special personality traits. I am arguing a general point.

I would next like to take up MMPI items to bring out a new line of evidence which, I am sorry to say, is not familiar to some psychologists, but which is of importance in giving you an answer to your questions. Turn again to the above items, particularly to the "True" response frequencies. We will look at implications about the people taking the MMPI as we interpret the True frequencies of response for these items.

Before we do so, we should consider the source of the frequency figures. The males and females who provided these standard data, which are the basis for all MMPI standards, were persons who came to the University Hospitals bringing patients or who were around the hospitals at the time when we were collecting data. Only those were tested who were not under a doctor's care and who could be reasonably assumed to be normal in mind and body. These persons, whom we call the normal adult cross-section group, came from all over Minnesota, from every socioeconomic and educational level; there is reason to believe that they are a proper representation of the rank and file people of Minnesota. It is probably well known that, in the main, Minnesota population was drawn from North European stock, is largely Christian in background, and has a rather small number in the several minority groups. Certainly, it can hardly be said that this population is unduly weighted with extremists in the direction of overemphasis upon religion or in atheism or in other belief characteristics. Probably one would expect this population to be rather more religious than the average for all the states. Finally, the majority of the persons who provided these basic norms were married persons and most were parents. Data given in the table can be found in the fundamental book on the MMPI, *An MMPI Handbook* by Dahlstrom and Welsh (1960).

But now consider the items. Let us assume, as is often naively assumed, that when one answers an item one tells the truth about oneself. Of course, there is no requirement that those who take the MMPI should tell the truth, and this is a very important point. Also, I have tried to establish that truth is a very complicated semantic concept. But let us assume for the moment that people do tell the truth as they see it. Take the item, "I go to church almost every week." According to the data given, 42% of the men and 52% of the women go to church almost every week. Now these data are representative of the whole state. I am sure that ministers of the state would be gratified if all these people were reporting accurately. Parenthetically, I suppose that "church" was read as "synagogue" or "temple" without much trouble. But I do not know what percentage of people are actually estimated to go to some church almost every week. At any rate I cannot conceive that 42% of the men of the state of Minnesota are in church nearly every week even if 52% of the women are. I even cannot conceive that half of the men in Minnesota and 83% of the women actually pray several times a week. I might imagine that 21% of the men and 30% of the women would read in the Bible several times a week. This would represent about one-fifth of all the men and about one-third of all the women. My real impression is that people simply do not know that much about the Bible. However, take the next item. Here it says that one feels sure there is only one true religion. To this about half of the men and half of the women answered True. Perhaps these might be considered bigoted, but what of the ones who have obviously answered false? There seems to be a great deal of religious tolerance here; about half of the persons of Minnesota do not even express a belief that there is only one true religion.

It is true that a high percentage say they believe there is a God. This seems to be a noncommittal item, since most people are aware that God has many meanings. The item which follows it, however, which permits denying or accepting a belief in a devil and hell in afterlife, is quite interesting. Twenty-three percent of men and 19% of women reject this belief. By contrast, a life hereafter is denied by 24% of men and by 13% of women. The second coming of Christ is expected by only 57% of men and 68% of women if we accept what these figures seem to say. Again, with reversal, Christ as a miracle worker

is doubted by 31% of men and by 23% of women. Stated more directly, 37% of men and 27% of women come straight out and say that miracles were not performed. The item apparently includes Old and New Testament sources among others. On down in the list, one finds that only 14% of men and 16% of women believe themselves to be special agents of God.

I think I have gone over enough of these items to provide a suggestion of what I am going to next point out. But I would like to add two more MMPI items in sharper illustration of the point. These two additional items have nothing obvious to do with religion. The first of them is, "I almost never dream," and the second is, "I dream frequently." One of the first things we found in the early studies of MMPI items was that the same person frequently answered True to both these items. When asked about the seeming contradiction, such a person would respond, among other possibilities, by saying to the first item that surely he had very few dreams. But, coming to the next item, he changed his viewpoint to say that he dreamed frequently as compared to some of the people he knew. This shift of emphasis led us to recognize that, in addition to the general semantic problem developed above, when people respond to items, they also do not usually respond with the connotations we expect. Apparently even if the people are telling a truth of some kind, one would need an interview with them to know what they really intend to report by answering True or False. I suppose this is similar to the problem of the oath of allegiance over which some people are so concerned. One may state that he is loyal to the United States, for example, yet really mean that he is deeply convinced that its government should be overthrown and that, with great loyalty to his country, he believes revolution to be the only salvation for the country. However much we might object to it, this belief would permit a person to swear to his loyalty in complete honesty. I think most everyone is aware of this problem about oaths, and it is a routine one with MMPI item responses.

In summary of all this, if one wished to persecute those who by their answers to these items seemed inconsistent with some religious or atheistic pattern of beliefs, there would be an embarrassingly large number of ordinary people in Minnesota who would be open to suspicion both ways. In reality, the responses made to these items have many variations in truth and meaning. And it would betray considerable ignorance of the practical psychology of communication if any absolute reliance were placed on responses.

As a final but most significant point relative to these items, I should point out that administration of the MMPI requires that those who are taking the test be clearly informed that they may omit any item they do not wish to answer for whatever purpose. I have never seen any studies that have drawn conclusions from the omission of particular items by a particular person. We found that items among these that are being considered were unusually frequently omitted. You may notice this in the No Answer columns. One-third of all the respondents failed to answer the item relative to the Bible and the prophets, for example. This is a basic fact about the MMPI and such tests, and I cannot see why this freedom will not permit to each person the latitude to preserve his privacy if he is afraid. Still again I would add that, in many settings, possibly nearly every setting, where the MMPI is used in group administration, those who take it are permitted to refuse the whole test. I admit that this might seem prejudicial, and I suspect that if any one chooses to protect himself, he will do it by omitting items rather than by not taking the test at all. Is refusal to take the test any

different from refusing to subject oneself to an employment or admission interview by a skilled interviewer? I think that some people who have been writing about the dangers of testing must have an almost magical belief in tests. Sometimes, when I feel so at a loss in attempting to help someone with a psychological problem, I wish that personality tests were really that subtle and powerful.

Groups of items called scales, formed into patterns called profiles, are the useful product of tests like the MMPI. I note that in your inquiry you show an awareness that the MMPI is usually scored by computers. The scales that are used for most interpretation include 10 "clinical" scales. These are the ones that carry most of the information. Several other scales indicate whether the subject understood and followed the directions. No one of these main scales has less than 30 items in it and most of them have many more than 30. The scores from the machine come back not only anonymously indicating the number of items answered in a way that counts on the scale, but the scores are usually already transformed into what we call T or standard scores. These T scores are still more remote from the particular items that make up a scale. The graphic array of T scores for the scales are finally printed into the profile.

In this connection, there is a very pretty possibility offered by the development of computer scoring. If we wish to take advantage of the presumed advantages of the use of tests, yet be assured that particular item responses shall not be considered, then we only need to be assured that those using the test do not score it, must send it straightway to the computer center, and, in the end, receive back only the profiles which are all that should be used in any case. The original test may be destroyed.

The scales of the profile were not

arbitrarily set up. The MMPI is an experimentally derived instrument. If an item counts on a scale, I want to make it very clear that that item counts, not because some clinician or somebody thought that the item was significant for measuring something about human personality, but it counts because in the final analysis well-diagnosed groups of maladjusted, sometimes mentally ill persons answered the item with an average frequency differing from the average frequency of the normative group that I have used for the above illustrative data. This is an exceedingly significant point and is probably least often understood by those who have not had psychometric training. No one read or composed these items to decide what it meant if one of them were answered True or False. The meanings of the items came from the fact that persons with a certain kind of difficulty answered in an average way different from the "normal" standard. For example, the item "I go to church almost every week" is counted on a scale for estimating the amount of depression. We did not just decide that going to church was related to depression. We had the response frequencies from men who complained that they were depressed. They answered True with a frequency of only 20%. You will note that the normals answered True with a frequency of 42%—22% more often. Now this difference also turned up for women who were depressed. We adopted a False response to this item as a count on the depression scale of the MMPI. We do not even now know why depressed people say they go to church less often. Note that you are not depressed if you say False to this one item. Actually, 55% of the normals answered False. Use of the item for an MMPI scale depended on the fact that even more of the depressed persons answered False and so if you say False you have added one item more in common with depressed people than

with the normals despite the fact that more than half the normals answered as you did.

Even psychologists very familiar with the MMPI cannot tell to which scale or scales an item belongs without looking it up. People often ask for a copy of a test so they can cite their objections to items they think objectionable, and they assume that the meaning of the item is obvious and that they can tell how it is interpreted. I am often asked what specified items mean. I do not know because the scoring of the scales has become so abstracted that I have no contact with items.

One more point along this line. Only 6 of the above 19 items are counted on one of the regular scales that are mostly used for personality evaluation. Four more are used on a measure that is only interpreted in estimation of the ability of the subject to follow directions and to read well enough. In fact, about 200 of the whole set of items did not end up on any one of the regularly used scales. But, of course, many of these 200 other items occur on one or another of the many experimental MMPI scales that have been published.

We cannot change or leave out any items or we lose an invaluable heritage of research in mental health. To change even a comma in an item may change its meaning. I would change the words of some items, omit some, and add new ones if I could. A new test should be devised, but its cost would be on the order of $100,000 and we are not at this time advanced enough so that the new one would be enough better to compensate for the loss of the research and diagnostic value of the present MMPI even in view of its manifest weaknesses.

The subject of professional training brings me to my next line of response. It is appropriate that the public should be aware of the uses of such tests as the MMPI, but I have repeatedly pointed out that it is far more important that the public should be aware of the persons who are using the test and of the uses to which it is put. In this context, the distributor of the MMPI, the Psychological Corporation of New York City, accepts and practices the ethical principles for test distributors that have been promulgated by the American Psychological Association. These rules prohibit the sale of tests to untrained or incompetent persons. Use or possession of the MMPI by others is prohibited but, since this carries no present penalty, the distributor is helpless except for his control of the supply. Tests, as I have said above, are not like switchblade knives, designed to be used against people; they offer potential contributions to happiness. And I cannot believe that a properly accredited clinical psychologist or psychiatrist or physician who may use the MMPI would under any circumstances use it to the disadvantage of the persons being tested. If he does so, he is subject to the intraprofessional ethical-practice controls that are explicit and carry sanctions against those of us who transgress. The MMPI provides data which, like certain medical data, are considered by many to be helpful in guidance and analysis and understanding of people. Of course, in the making of this point, I am aware that there is no absolute meaning to what is ethical. What one group may think should be done about a certain medical-examination disclosure may be considered by another group to be against the patient's interest. I cannot do more than extend this ubiquitous ethical dilemma to the use of the personality test.

The essential point is that such tests should not be used except in professional circles by professional people and that the data it provides should be held confidential and be protected within the lawful practice of ethics. When these requirements are not met, there is reason for complaint. I hope I have made it clear that it is also my conviction that the MMPI will hurt no one, adult or child, in the taking of it. Without defending all uses of it, I surely defend it, and instruments like it, when they are in proper hands and for proper purposes. Monachesi and I have tested 15,000 ninth-grade school children with the MMPI. This took us into public schools all over the state, even into some parochial schools. In all of this testing, we had no difficulties with children, parents, or teachers except for a few courteous inquiries. We are now publishing what we hope will be significant data from this work, data bearing on delinquency and school dropout. We believe that this work demonstrates that properly administered, properly explained, and properly protected tests are acceptable to the public.

At the beginning of this statement I warned that I was going to make it quite long because I felt deeply on the matter. I hope I have not sounded as though I were merely being defensive, protecting us from those who would burn tests and who for good reasons are exceedingly sensitive about psychological testing. I am apologetic if I have sounded too much like the professional scientist and have seemed to talk down to the issue or to be too minutely explicit. I have not meant to insult by being unduly simple, but I have felt that I had to expand adequately on the points. As for psychologists who are those most widely applying such tests, I am aware that the public will look with increasing seriousness upon those who are entrusted with problems of mental health and the assessment of human actions.

I will end with a repetition of my feeling that, while it is desirable for the public to require ethical practices of those using tests, the public may be reassured that the psychologists, physicians, and others who use these new tests will be even more alert to apply the intraprofessional controls that are a requisite to professional responsibility. But I must emphasize that it is not to public advantage to so limit these professional judgments that we fail to

progress in mental-health research and applications from lack of freedom to use the best instruments we have and to develop better ones.

REFERENCE

DAHLSTROM, W. G., & WELSH, G. S. *An MMPI handbook: A guide to use in* *clinical practice and research.* Minneapolis: Univer. Minnesota Press, 1960.

Objective Personality Tests: A Reply to Dr. Eysenck

Raymond B. Cattell

All too often, a review (to transpose the phrase of Gertrude Stein) "is a review, is a review, is just a review." But when it is made by Dr. Eysenck it is something more than a review, and raises matters of fundamental importance for theory and practice. Such was his recent review in this journal of *The Meaning and Measurement of Neuroticism and Anxiety* (1961), by Dr. Scheier and myself.

In this reply I propose to take up his comments and to set out the degree of convergence and the degree of still existing divergence of formulation which exist between what are probably the two most active world research centers in this field of personality structuration and measurement. For critics of the "tough," experimental, factor analytic approach to personality theory are apt to instance, disparagingly, certain apparently wide-open disagreements between the different schools, failing to

Reprinted, by permission of the Editor and the author, from *Occupational Psychology,* 1964, **38,** 69–86, the quarterly journal of the National Institute of Industrial Psychology, 14 Welbeck Street, London, W.1.

recognize either the substantial agreement or the true nature of the matters which are still at issue.

Since the theoretical issues arise in, and return to, the area of practical personality evaluation and clinical diagnosis, let us note in the first place that the Maudsley group and the Illinois University group are far from being in polar opposition in these fields. Indeed, the IPAT extraversion scale and the Maudsley extraversion scale agree better than any two other measures presently available for this dimension. The really dismaying gap, as far as the reputation of practical psychology is concerned, lies rather in that between the numerous intuitive "itemetrists," on the one hand, who manufacture scales, often with great attention to item analysis, but with a purely arbitrary definition of the concepts which they are measuring, and, on the other hand those who use multivariate experimental methods to *locate* natural personality structure, before orienting their scales and batteries to the measurement of such discovered structures (Burt, 1940). Since both Professor Eysenck and the present writer belong in the latter school, the issues are within the family, but, as is often the case, are no less sharp for that reason. Furthermore, these conflicts at the moment suffer from a dearth of good referees. For, if we may explicitly and immodestly come out with what is implicit in the statement above, the fact is that the amount of pioneer work done in the Laboratory of Personality Assessment at the University of Illinois, and in Professor Eysenck's laboratory at the Institute of Psychiatry, the Maudsley Hospital, so far outruns what is being achieved in any systematic way at other research centers that few of the newer issues can yet be referred to third party experiment. Incidentally not only for this reason but for the more pervasive needs of psychology, it is high time that more centers for post graduate training of psychology students be set up covering adequate instruction in multivariate experimental methods. Britain, the birth place of these methods, has become somewhat inactive in comparison with America, and the Continent is far behind Britain. C. P. Snow's "two cultures" are in danger of being paralleled by a similar split in psychology, between personality research pursued by multivariate experimental methods, and personality research still considered to be scientifically pursued but by purely literary, qualitatively clinical and *geiteswissenschaftlich* discussions.

Since this article appears in a journal partly devoted to technology, it may not be inappropriate to point out that the *genuine* advances in a science can often be evaluated, despite the smoke screens of pretentious theorizing, by the amount of actual technical control which ensues. If the clinical and industrial psychologists, in particular, begin more enterprisingly to open their practice to the instruments and concepts now increasingly available from factor analytic research, we shall get answers all the sooner. For the advances in *technical* precision and predictive control which they will gain will quickly offer evidence on *theoretical* soundness, convincing even for those relatively unversed in

the theory. Similarly, some of the theoretical issues discussed in this article are open to the pragmatic proofs of practitioners. If the proof of the pudding is to be gained by the eating, clinical and industrial psychologists should be alertly comparing the results from the objective and factored tests of personality, anxiety, neuroticism, etc., here discussed with those obtainable from older instruments.

With this salute to the importance of the practitioner's ultimate verdict let us return to the (initially) necessarily theoretical analysis of the differences between Dr. Eysenck and ourselves. Perhaps the two major differences in multivariate experimental technique and emphasis which have definitely arisen are: (1) That in determining *uniquely* the nature of a personality structure we have depended more on the general scientific principle of *simple structure rotation*, whereas Eysenck has depended more on the "applied" principle of *criterion rotation*, and, (2) That more of the work at the Maudsley has been upon neurotic and pathological groups, whereas most of ours has been upon normals. Only later, and in the book mentioned above, have we brought our techniques to bear upon abnormals also. Additionally, there arose a third, less fundamental technical difference between the two laboratories in the early stages in that Eysenck took out two or three factors whereas our evidence convinced us that it is necessary to take out from 16 to 21, from essentially similar personality measurement data. Eysneck found, for example, a neuroticism, a dysthymia, and a psychoticism factor, while we found the same factors plus a dozen or so equally substantial traits which were new to existing theory. The fact that the concepts from such different approaches have, nevertheless, in the main, grown together is very significant. But the fact that real differences have been used by onlookers, as suggested above, as a rationalization for avoiding factor analytic disciplines, makes it important to show more precisely how and why they have arisen.

In the first place we would claim that the newer statistical tests of completeness of factor extraction, such as those of Tucker [in Thurstone (1938)], Sokal (1959), Burt (1940), and Lawley (1956) in fact now abundantly justify our early movements towards taking out the larger number of factors. On the other hand, this difference, in practice, does not mean so much as may at first appear. Indeed, as just indicated, the first two or three factors in our series usually agree tolerably well with those in Eysenck's. Nevertheless, for technical reasons which cannot be discussed here, the "fit" in an under-extracted study, even in the first few factors, becomes poorer as one goes beyond the first factor. Indeed, in theory it is never possible exactly to match a factor from an under-extracted analysis with those from a fully-extracted analysis, just as it is an illusion, incidentally, to think that one can line up simple structure 16 Personality Factor Questionnaire (Cattell and Stice, 1949) factors with the orthogonal (and therefore only *approximate* simple structure factors) of the Guilford-Zimmerman Questionnaire (1949).

In the first emergence from the chaos which preceded the various factor incursions into the clinical and personality area, it was gratifying to find as much agreement as in fact arose between the definitions and measurements for anxiety, neuroticism, etc., at Illinois University and at the Maudsley despite the differences of extraction, rotation, and sampling indicated above. But at the finer stage of conceptualization now being entered upon, there has begun to develop a difference of findings, based on these differences of technique, which should be pointed out if theoretical confusions are to be avoided among test users. One practical root of these differences is that the Illinois laboratory

has for some years had the good fortune to use electronic computer programs by Dickman, Wrigley, White, Schönemann, and others, before such programs became available at any other center. The result of these analytical methods of finding simple structure, and the application of Ralph Bargmann's test of significance of simple structure (1955), has been that the factor analytic work has been cross-checked among several researches in a way which until quite recently, was not feasible elsewhere. In one case (Cattell, 1945), with Dr. Eysenck's permission, the present writer re-rotated some of the latter's valuable data, with results which seemed to the present writer to indicate that the rotations prior to the computer application had not reached a maximum level of simple structure resolution.

In answer to criticisms such as these, Dr. Eysenck has pointed out what is approximately correct, namely, that if one does happen to take out just two or three factors, where more exist, and rotates them, he is likely to begin to *approach* what would be obtained as the second order factors, i.e., what one gets when one takes out 16 to 20 primary factors, and again analyzes these at the second order. Unfortunately, like any approximation or half-truth this gets one into difficulties as a higher superstructure of inferences and cross connections is built upon it. For it can be shown that the matching becomes increasingly awry, through an increasing discrepancy (Cattell, 1964) between the true second orders and these rough substitutes, as one goes beyond the first two factors to the third, fourth, and later factors. For example, working with these illegitimates begins to produce very misleading results as soon as one gets to building a superstructure such as the third order factors which Pawlik and the present writer have recently published (1964).

Two issues, in fact, arise here: (1)

Whether it is better to work with primary personality factors such as schizothymia (A), intelligence (B), ego strength (C), surgency (F), etc., as defined by the 16 P.F. (Cattell & Stice, 1949), and IPAT High School Personality Questionnaire (Cattell and Beloff, 1958), etc., or with the fewer, broader, second-order factors derived from them, such as extraversion, general anxiety, etc., as in the IPAT Anxiety and Extraversion scales (Scheier & Cattell, 1960), and the MPI, and, (2) Whether, as just mentioned, the latter can, in any case, be properly defined except on the basis of research having first clearly fixed the primaries.

As to the first, regardless of the psychological field, the general statistical principle holds that *one can get a better prediction in regard to absolutely any criterion from using several primaries* instead of a few secondaries. The user may take a little more time to *record* scores on several primaries, as in the 16 P.F., but the *actual testing time* is generally little greater for the more numerous first order factors than for the fewer second orders. However, even apart from the statistical argument, there is the psychological argument that the primary factors which commonly cohere

in a second order factor, may, *in respect to particular concrete criteria,* even operate in *opposite* directions. For example, in Diagram 1, which shows the 16 P.F. profile obtained for leading researchers in physics and other fields, it will be noticed that the F factor of Surgency-Desurgency and the A factor of Cyclothymia-Schizothymia mark the scientist as an introvert, but the H factor of Parmia-Threctia, or High Autonomic Susceptibility to Threat actually works in the opposite direction. (Extraversion, as a second order, is largely a composite of A, F, H, and Q_2.) In vocational selection one would thus be making a serious blunder by predicting from a single score on the composite defining the second order extraversion-introversion factor.

This same sample will indeed remind us that there are other reasons against using extraversion-introversion as a single concept. For example, the hereditary determination of the A and H factors is quite high (Cattell, Blewett, and Beloff, 1955) whereas that of surgency-desurgency is low, since surgency seems to be largely a consequence of relative permissiveness of early environment. As Jung, the inventor of the extraversion label himself pointed out,

Personality Dimension Label at Lower Pole	Mean Stens	Plotted Mean Sten Scores 3 4 5 6 7 8	Personality Dimension Label at Upper Pole	
A− Reserved, Cool	3.36	avg	Warmhearted, Participating	A+
B− Less intelligent	7.64		More intelligent	B+
C− Emotionally unstable	5.44		Emotionally stable	C+
E− Submissive	6.62		Dominant	E+
F− Serious, Taciturn	3.15		Happy-go-lucky, Enthusiastic	F+
G− Undependable	4.10		Conscientious, Persevering	G+
H− Shy, Diffident	6.01		Venturesome, Socially bold	H+
I− Tough-minded, No-nonsense	7.05		Tender-minded, Sensitive	I+
L− Trusting	5.36		Suspicious	L+
M− Practical, Conventional	5.36		Imaginative, Bohemian	M+
N− Forthright, Natural	5.50		Shrewd, Worldly	N+
O− Placid, Confident	4.38		Worrying	O+
Q_1− Conservative	7.00		Experimenting, Free-thinking	Q_1+
Q_2− Traditional, A "joiner"	7.52		Self-sufficient	Q_2+
Q_3− Casual, Follows own urges	6.44		Controlled, Self-disciplined	Q_3+
Q_4− Relaxed, Tranquil	4.91		Tense, Driven, Frustrated	Q_4+

Diagram 1. Mean 16 Personality Factor Profile of Eminent Researchers (N=140) in Physics, Biology, and Psychology.

at the qualitative level, the extraverts can differ among themselves according to certain qualifying conditions which he names, and which actually have considerable resemblance to the different contributions since recognized to emanate from the different primary factors.

The second issue—namely, that second order patterns can never be reliably tied down until the exploration of the first order has been completed—is pointed up by the recent very accurate survey by Gorsuch (Gorsuch & Cattell, in press): On a sample of over 1,600 cases Gorsuch has rotated 16 P.F. primaries to a definitive simple structure, which gives weights in the secondaries different from those implicit in several existing, "directly approached" and constructed anxiety and extraversion scales. Warburton and Cattell's results (1961) on the HSPQ with children concur.

So far, the differences in the concepts of some major personality factors, i.e., in their description and in the tests validated for them, are comparatively slight. For example, the correlation between the IPAT Extraversion and the MPI Extraversion scales is of the order of 0.70, which, when reliability of response is considered, indicates the possibility of complete identity, though still needing examination in more refined studies. Unfortunately, as we leave these issues of factor extraction and rotation to touch on the remaining issues raised in the review, we encounter something conceptually and practically more serious.

The central issue is that whereas Eysenck speaks of a single neuroticism factor (1959), we find any reliably diagnosed group of neurotics to differ significantly from normals on *several* personality factors (Cattell & Scheier, 1961). This holds regardless of whether analysis is made in the more fine structure of primaries or in the broader organizations which we call secondaries. To understand this point, a brief digres-

sion must be made on the subject of distinctions between questionnaire and objective personality tests and on certain relations which have been found there. By objective tests, as every psychologist knows, we mean miniature situational, projective, and other tests in which the individual does *not evaluate himself*, on a questionnaire item, as in opinionnaires, etc., but reacts in an actual situation and is measured without knowing precisely what aspect of his behaviour is really being measured. The Objective-Analytic or IPAT O–A Battery (Cattell, Hundleby, *et al.*, 1955) contains some fifty such tests which are the survivors from over 500 tried out in twenty years of study by Baggaley, Damarin, Eysenck, Saunders, Hundleby, Pawlik, Warburton, and the present writer. (Hundleby, Pawlik, & Cattell, in press). This outcome in a practical battery—the O–A Battery—contains measures for 18 distinct factors, beginning with U.I. (Universal Index) 16 and proceeding to U.I. 35 (U.I., 1 through 15 are the primary ability factors, put together by French, 1951).

For some time, there was doubt about the relationship of factors found in questionnaires to those found in objective tests, but the clue to the code relating them seems to have been found in a number of studies at the Illinois laboratory. These studies show that second order factors in the questionnaire realm generally correspond to first order factors in the objective test realm. In particular, the objective test dimension which we have called U.I. 24, and labeled anxiety, aligns extremely well with the second order anxiety factor in the 16 P.F. Similarly, the objective test factor which we have called U.I. 32, or extraversion-introversion, aligns with the second largest, second order factor in the 16 P.F. (exvia-invia). An important factor in the O–A series is that which we have called U.I. 23 and which the Maudsley group has called *the* neuroticism factor, because they found it powerfully to distinguish neurotics from normals. Our results fully confirm the important Maudsley discovery that U.I. 23 powerfully distinguishes neurotics from normals, but they also show that neurotics differ from normals, and with an equally high degree of significance, *upon five other factors*, one of which is the general anxiety factor, U.I. 24.

For many years Eysenck has propounded to clinicians a most attractively simple, factor analytic view of clinical diagnosis, centered upon three of four factors. As originally propounded, there was a general intelligence factor, and, orthogonal to it, a neuroticism factor, and orthogonal to both a psychoticism factor. The three major types of institutionalized patients, namely, mental defectives, neurotics and psychotics thus deviated neatly from the general population, each on one factor. A simple trinity of this kind has naturally been eagerly seized upon by textbook writers. What we, as researchers, have regarded from the beginning as a gross oversimplification may perhaps be justified on the grounds that it attracted clinicians to experimental methods. It showed that factor analytic ideas might be very useful to them and that factor analytic test batteries might simplify their diagnostic problems. Unfortunately, perhaps, reality proves to be more complicated than this and the simplifications begin to mislead theory and reduce the potency of practice. Dr. Scheier and the present writer have had to insist in the book cited that the neurotic differs from the normal decidedly *on at least six factors*. Furthermore, we have developed theories in this book as to what the natures of these factors are and why they have contributed to, or developed as a consequence of, the neurotic disorder. These theories integrate a lot of well known observations more effectively, and *in ways more open to checks by measurement,* than does for example, the Freudian theory of neurosis.

Eysenck's reaction to this very significant difference of findings seems to be, in the review cited, that perhaps we do not know what a neurotic is. This denial of the pervasive presence of our foundation of clinical source material reminds one of a small boy who, when told the facts of life, replied to his friend, "Perhaps your parents did something like that, but I'm quite sure mine didn't." Let us freely admit that we ourselves would have anticipated *some* cultural differences in the diagnosis of neurotics in, say, Chicago and London. Regardless of the stated theory of each psychiatrist, the persons picked out as neurotics might be expected to vary with clinic, with the school of psychology, and with the national culture. Theoretical differences in defining a neurotic probably matter less than cultural differences. In view of Fiedler's (1950) findings of how little the theoretical definition adopted by the psychiatrist affects either the choice of the neurotic or the actual therapeutic steps which he takes, there is every reason to solve the question of "What is a neurotic?" by setting aside theory and pointing to the type as defined by those who actually turn up at clinics. Provided that consistency of some degree actually exists from place to place in the type so designated, the real touchstone of definition is found in terms of the profile of the actual minority of our populations set aside in clinical practice as neurotics. In other words, the psychologist accepts the psychiatrist's diagnosis and then applies his measurements to see if there is any consistent pattern or profile in those designated as neurotics.

In our own work we can claim to be less assailable than most researchers on this point, for in order to reduce the danger of bias from particular clinics, schools of thought, or geographical localities, we deliberately took our samples from a wide variety. In the experiments of certain researchers with whom we have disagreed (though this does not apply to Dr. Eysenck's work), the entire neurotic sub-group has been taken from one clinic next door to the investigator's laboratory. In the corresponding researches done at Illinois, we have gone at least 1,000 miles in most compass directions, including samples from Tennessee, from Toronto, and in the case of the 16 Personality Factor Questionnaire data, from countries abroad such as Italy and India, and other countries where the translated 16 P.F. is in use. The upshot is, as Dr. Scheier shows, in the book under discussion and in other publications, that the peculiar personality profile obtained as the mean of the neurotic group in each area is quite remarkably similar and consistent. Though we might have anticipated differences, there was in fact a substantial convergence in the pattern from Canada, California, the American Deep South or the North of England. Either life or the psychiatrist is showing high reliability regarding the neurotic designation.

We therefore feel entitled to stand by our conclusion that we are dealing with neurotics and that these neurotics differ from normals on at least six independent personality factors, whether measurable by objective tests or by questionnaire. In the book itself, we have given extensive consideration to the problem of why the neurotics should differ from non-neurotics on these particular factors, which include anxiety, premsia (I factor), ego strength (C factor), surgency (F factor), super ego strength (U.I. 28), and pathemia (U.I. 22), among others. Under the new and mathematical concept of "adjustment process analysis," presented in this book, we have developed learning theory to include a conception that personality change is to be regarded as a multidimensional change in response to a multidimensional situation. Furthermore, we have developed a matrix multiplication scheme, which could be applied in practical situations, to attempt to understand why certain factors have contributed more in some particular, individual cases than in others. Here begins a new world of technical possibilities of intelligently adjusting the therapeutic process to the particular damages sustained in a given individual development.

In the interests of wise therapy, which properly sorts out the influences of constitutional predisposition from those due to personal history, and evaluates carefully the magnitude of deviation on each dimension which distinguishes a neurotic from a normal, the *full* profile analysis on 16 P.F. or O–A is probably essential to understanding and therapy. But for screening purposes in industrial or military psychology, or for an initial consulting room focussing of the true seriousness of neurosis in a given case, some brief single composite measure of "total degree of neurosis" is often needed. It is here that the difference of the two theoretical positions becomes most acutely evident in practical procedures. For whereas the IPAT Neuroticism Scale Questionnaire (henceforth NSQ) compounds a nine minute, forty item test which carefully weights the several factors which distinguish neurotics, the Eysenck Neuroticism Scale depends upon a single factor which, as we shall show, is essentially the anxiety factor, U.I. 24, only.

If we are correct in our conceptual scheme, according to which neuroticism is a deviation on a complex combination of factors, whereas anxiety is a single second order factor, two quite distinct tests *should* be used for neuroticism and for anxiety. In fact, the IPAT Anxiety questionnaire, consisting of 40 items and requiring nine minutes to administer, i.e., a scale precisely parallel in size and function to the NSQ, or Neuroticism Scale Questionnaire, has recently been validated and constructed for this purpose. Its concept validity ("construct validity" to some) is high —+0.9—as a pure measure of the anxiety factor, i.e., of *the major second order factor in the 16 P.F.* (Gorsuch & Cattell, in press; Warburton, 1961) and the U.I. 24 factor in the objective test battery.

Somewhat less than half the variance in the NSQ score, however, is allocated to anxiety. Let us recognize that this fits not only the statistical findings on the differentiation of psychoneurotics (by discriminant function) but also ordinary clinical experience. Surely, for example, it has long been recognized that conversion hysterics, among neurotic types, show low anxiety, as Janet pointed out in speaking of the "belle indifference" of the hysteric. The low correlation of anxiety and neuroticism scales is equally required, also, by the fact that we should expect to find normal persons sometimes scoring as high on anxiety as neurotics, from occasional situational stresses. Indeed, the anxiety scale does, from time to time, call attention to entirely normal individuals who for temporary situational reasons, are at a very high anxiety level.

Actually, in the NSQ construction, the role of anxiety has deliberately been played down a little. The weighting of anxiety which would produce a type composite *maximally* distinguishing neurotics from normals has here been reduced, on the grounds that when most neurotics are measured, they are in an acute stage of disorder with unduly high anxiety, whereas the object of a neurotic screening test is to pick out those with a *neurotic personality structure*, such as will lead to acute neurotic conflict and anxiety from time to time. The distinct Anxiety Scale exists to supplement the NSQ by evaluating anxiety level at a particular time. The result is that the correlation between the IPAT Anxiety Scale and IPAT NSQ is not that which might follow from 50% of the variance in the latter being anxiety, namely, 0.7, but is down to roughly 0.4. They are intentionally constructed to be different scales for different purposes. If a measure of the former type, i.e., one literally giving maximum discrimination of normals from "neurotics at an acute stage" is actually needed it can readily be obtained from weights[1] on the 16 P.F. factor scores given in the 16 P.F. handbook (1949). Meanwhile the NSQ is properly regarded as a measure of the individual's possession of the neurotic personality, compounded largely of personality factors C−, E−, F−, I+, etc.

The research situation at the present moment is, therefore, that we recognize on the one hand an anxiety factor, U.I. 24 (in objective tests, or as a second order in the 16 P.F. questionnaire primaries), and, on the other, a factor indexed for the last fifteen years as U.I. 23, which Eysenck calls "neuroticism" but which we hypothesize to be "regression"—only one factor in neuroticism. What we believe to be the true, empirical definition of neuroticism is that fixed by a type or sub-group of the population which differs from the rest significantly on U.I. 23, or U.I. 24 and four or more factors beside. For those unfamiliar with the experimental evidence it may be desirable before proceeding to pause and make quite clear that U.I. 23 and U.I. 24 are themselves quite distinct behavioral dimensions. Their independence in simple structure is best shown by Diagram 2. Now although Eysenck's dysthymia factor apparently agrees with this recognition of the distinct natures of U.I. 23 and U.I. 24, his *verbal* measure of neuroticism, which should presumably correlate perfectly (except for error) with his "neuroticism" (or "regression") factor U.I. 23 in *objective* tests, *actually correlates to a degree compatible with identity, with U.I. 24, anxiety.*

[1] National Computer Systems, Minneapolis, has recently set up a program whereby this and other derived scores can be obtained for 16 P.F. users by electronic computer from hundreds of answer sheets at once, and by return mail.

This can be shown either in terms of questionnaires or objective tests. The IPAT Anxiety Scale correlates no more than about 0.4, as it should, with the IPAT Neuroticism Scale, but the Maudsley Neuroticism Scale correlates so highly (0.7) with the IPAT Anxiety Scale that it could be, apart from specifics and error purely a measure of anxiety. A major confusion in interpretation of research findings with these tests is in the offing unless this state of affairs is realized. By the whole fabric of meaning in the clinical and factorial world the MPI Neuroticism scale should be called the Anxiety Scale. Incidentally the anxiety and neuroticism measurement area is likely to be still more seriously confused by some use of the early, unfactored Taylor Anxiety Scale which happens, as subsequent research has shown, to deviate markedly in just the *opposite* direction from that of Eysenck's scale. That is to say, whereas his is called a neuroticism scale, and correlates strongly with anxiety, the Taylor Scale is called anxiety but slopes toward the position

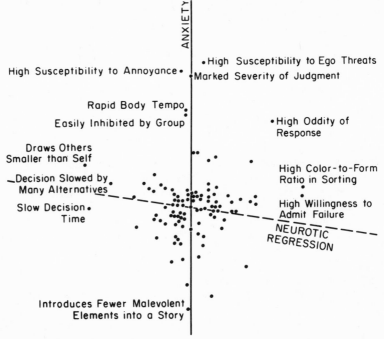

Diagram 2. Independence of the anxiety and regression factors, U.I. 24 and U.I. 23, is shown here in geometric terms. Each dot is the end point of a vector representing a measured variable, its direction and distance from the origin determined by factor-analysis computations. There are as many dimensions in the solid "graph" so produced (from which this is a two-dimensional projection) as there are factors at work on the variables. Test points tend to coagulate in "hyperplanes," or multidimensional galaxies, which indicate the positions in which to place various factors; these factors emerge as axes of the "graph" placed as perpendiculars to the galaxies. Projected in two-dimensional space, a hyperplane should ideally appear as a line, but it is usually (as in this diagram) a lens-shaped swarm of points. A test like "Marked severity of judgment," lying in the hyperplane of neurotic regression, has zero-projection, or "zero-loading," on it; that is, it does not correlate with regression. On the other hand it loads highly on anxiety; it is, in other words, closely associated with anxiety. The greater the angle between two tests or factor axes, the more independent they are of each other. In this case the anxiety and regression axes are nearly perpendicular to each other; they are independent.

With acknowledgments to the *Scientific American*. Reproduced from the March, 1963, issue.

defined by the IPAT Neuroticism axis. This is not surprising, because the items were originally chosen for the Taylor Scale by a curious criterion validation procedure which consisted in accepting as "anxiety" items those MMPI and similar items which maximally distinguish neurotics from normals. If neurotics differ from normals in many things besides anxiety, then the more completely any given item correlates with the neurotic-normal difference, the more it will be contaminated with these factors beyond anxiety. However, all of this shows that the practitioner today has to be very alert when he is choosing his scales. Indeed, the question, "What is in a name?," becomes rather important.

With this degree of definition let us turn to a third issue in our book which Eysenck has expressed his views upon, namely, the relation of *motivation* to neuroticism and anxiety. Here again, we claim that there exist entirely clear and experimentally well replicated findings which he who runs may read. However, let us face the fact that the appreciation of the points involved now involves dealing with technical issues somewhat outside the usual area of training of the clinical psychologist. Like many other "enterprises of great pith and moment" in psychology, this motivation area is a rapidly developing one, but one where concepts and decisions hinge on recondite statistical and mathematical questions. Psychologists with certain backgrounds, usually literary, have sometimes shown no more interest in these mathematical issues than the general public, in watching some space craft approach Venus, shows in understanding the fine calculations that made the movement into space possible. There are others again like the professors of Padua who refused to look through Galileo's telescope, who are less interested in the experimental proofs of ergic and other dynamic structures than in subjective clinical theories or

reference to the clinical equivalents of the authority of Scholasticism and Aristotle.

However, we may perhaps discount those tendencies here because the relation of anxiety to motivation generally is an issue of everyday importance to the practitioner readers of this journal, since so much research in the industrial psychology field turns upon motivation. About five years ago many writers in the general field of personality and learning theory seemed to embrace uncritically the theory of a certain school of learning theory in America to the effect that anxiety is to be considered identical with motivation. Even at a popular level of thought, this identification of motivation with anxiety strikes one as the narrow conclusion of an over-competitive and insecure sub-culture—perhaps especially that of modern psychologists! However, the fact is that when a wide array of well known motivation strength manifestations are factor analyzed, one gets precisely as many factors as there are well known mammalian drives, such as sex, fear, parental protective behavior, etc., and that these, easily recognizable by their content and goal, prove to be quite distinct from the anxiety factor discussed above (Cattell, 1957).

Scheier and the present writer have shown in the book discussed that anxiety, when measured as a uniquely defined factor, correlates significantly, positively, with speed of conditioning, an observation also made (but with contaminated anxiety measures) by those who espouse the theory that anxiety level is identical with motivation level. From Eysenck's comments on our book, it would seem that he has adopted wholesale the view of Spence *et al.* (1956) and some other learning theorists which we have just discussed.

In ignoring the extensive evidence (Cattell and Baggaley, 1956; Cattell, Butcher, and Horn, 1962; Cattell, Radcliffe, and Sweney, 1963) on the structure and manifestations of motivation and dynamic structure, and accepting this narrow concept, he is inconsistent with his own methodology in the clinical field. For whereas he has successfully followed a multivariate concept in defining personality factors and anxiety, he now wishes us to accept a measurement and definition of motivation which hangs on a single variable—a reminiscence effect in a motor task. It is all very well for a psychologist to tell us that some single variable—a memory effect, or a GSR response or a misperceptive ("projective") measurement—defines motivation strength. But such an arbitrary procedure is unlikely to succeed. By contrast, the work of Baggaley, Radcliffe, Horn, Sweney and myself has assumed that the concept of motivation is to be defined by *whatever pervasive factor can be found across dozens of measures which reputable psychologists have theorized at some time to be manifestations of motivation strength*. We have *explored the structure* behind a great many old and newly invented, hypothesized motivation strength manifestations. After fifteen years, by 1962, we had examined more than 90 different alleged motivation manifestations, extending from physiological signs, like the psychogalvanic reflex, through clinical signs, like ego defense mechanisms, to perceptual, reminiscence and learning phenomena, etc. All have been intercorrelated on various groups of subjects and we have found initially seven motivational component factors which reduce to two (or, just possibly, three) at the second order.

This is a very different story from arbitrarily setting up a single thing called "motivation strength." Incidentally, since reminiscence effects load strongly only *one* of these factors, we are compelled to argue that the results which Eysenck obtains on motivation are generalizations which apply to only one part of the totality of motivation

factors. Furthermore, we would argue that Spence, and Eysenck insofar as he adopts the Spencian position that motivation is anxiety, is also likely to be confusing anxiety as a *state* with anxiety as a permanent personality trait characteristic of the individual (psychiatrically his "characterological anxiety level"). *Both* are thus confused with the momentary level which we call the motivation state, and which resolves into distinctly measurable *motivation component factors*. For our work (Cattell and Baggaley, 1956; Cattell, Radcliffe, and Sweney, 1963) shows very clearly that the two major (second order) factors, I, *integrated* motivation, and U, *unintegrated* motivation, are quite distinct from anxiety. Besides, the idea that anxiety is identical with motivation would require that the neurotic be considered a person of really high motivation level, whereas both in our test approach and in the clinical verdict of neurotic indecision and abulia, the neurotic is commonly subnormal in his motivational resources. Our experiments show that one cannot even equate anxiety with the U, or unintegrated motivation component factor, though in this case there is *some* positive correlation.

For the effective practical use of motivation measurement in clinic and industry as well as in the interests of understanding personality structure, it is necessary to know how interests are structured. And if the experimental findings on the main I and U motivation factors are correct the existing evidence on obtained interest structure from merely verbal, consciously-self-evaluative devices (like the Strong or Kuder Tests), on the one hand, or single objective measures like "projection" or "reminiscence," on the other, is distinctly suspect. For these devices account for only about 10% (Correlations of about .33) of the total motivation strength—*as measured by the batteries of well-loaded tests from the ninety-device surveys*—a miserable validity. Incidentally, one of the problems in this field today is to get students to move on from thinking in such categories as "projection" tests (as in the TAT) to the newer concepts of the *motivation factors*, integrated and unintegrated, which transcend such superficial "descriptive" test categories and show that projection is only one— and a poor one at that—among dozens of devices which manifest better correlations with one or another of the meaningful motivation component factors.

When a wide variety of occupational, home and hobby "attitude-interests" are measured by these objective devices and their structure is examined correlationally, the dynamic structures found turn out to be basic drives (*ergs*, as these operational entities are called, to avoid entanglement with "instinct") and acquired sentiments. On the basis of these findings an instrument has recently been constructed, entirely in the objective tests just discussed, called the Motivational Analysis Test (Cattell and Horn, 1964) or MAT. It gives scores on the tension level of five major drive factors (ergs) and five sentiments (to one's job, religion, home, hobby, wife). The reliability of such a one hour test cannot be expected, at this experimental stage, to be high—in the sense of the numerical values we are accustomed to in ability tests. Nor are the *reliabilities* yet as high as for purely verbal tests. But the *validities* are a different story, and surely it is better to have a test which validly and objectively measures important drives and interests, even with only moderate reliability, than one of impeccable, text-book test-retest reliability which is measuring absolutely nothing of importance in motivation!

The issue of what is happening to motivation in the neurotic, or of how motivation level affects experimental findings, as in conditioning, can only be raised with any hope of a meaningful answer if our conceptions of dynamic structure and motivation strength are themselves clear. Such concepts and their measurement must be raised far above that level which consists merely of a vague confusion of motivation strength with anxiety, or which supposes that measures of single variables, like projection or reminiscence are valid and reliable measures of motivation strength. It is now ten years since Wenig showed (Cattell, 1957) that the constantly, negligibly low validity correlations obtained with the TAT and other "simple projection" tests naturally follow from the "misperception" magnitude being a consequence of *several* over-determining and conflicting mechanisms—true projection, naive projection, phantasy, identification, etc. But this demonstration seems neither to have abated the sweeping clinical inferences of some practitioners from tests of this type, nor to have set off more than a small, alert fraction in the new directions of improved practice indicated by the motivation analysis tests.

Nevertheless, the field of effective motivation concepts and their measurement has taken a big step forward in the last decade—as Scheier and I have surveyed in some brief paragraphs in Chapter 14 of the book reviewed. However, it would be no service to research to deny that motivation theory is still beset by complications and by disconcerting gaps in our knowledge. What is relatively certain is: (1) That by batteries combining the most valid of the ninety devices yet tried, as in MAT and the School Motivational Analysis Test (SMAT) (Sweney and Cattell, 1964), we can measure with fair validity the two distinct major motivational component factors, U, unintegrated, and I, integrated. The summed tension level score on these two covers the variance in the main phenomena we call motivation strength, and proves to be distinct from neurotic anxiety (though at times and in complex ways, slightly correlated with it), and (2) That attitude-interests (interests in and responsiveness to courses of action, as defined by attitudes), taken from the total life space, clearly structure themselves into ergs (or drive tensions) of specific kinds, on the one hand, and sentiments, or socially acquired systems of interest, on the other. By measuring an individual's endowment, by MAT or SMAT or other objective, factored and standardized tests, at a given time, on these particular dynamic systems, experimental investigations can be more successfully directed to the many clinical, learning theory, perceptual or physiological relationships to motivation strength which are now under debate and research.

The main obstacle to a rapid gain in real knowledge in the fields discussed above is today a preoccupation of students and their teachers with an artificial scholasticism—and by this I mean something bookish, stereotyped, and verbally easy to discuss, which ranges from psychoanalysis at one extreme to certain Pavlovian conditioning theories at the other. These deal with a few simple ideas—the ego, the superego, the universal reflex model—akin to the oversimplifications of Aristotle's four elements or Galen's four temperaments. Motivation measurement, and the concepts in what has come to be called the *Dynamic Calculus* (Cattell, 1959; Sweney, 1962) are distinct in growth and methodology from either of these hackneyed and over-extended systems. They are complex, in the sense of requiring rather subtle factor analytic reasoning to trace the fractions of the variance in anxiety, motivation U, and motivation I, in this and that criterion behavior, and in requiring attention to the problems of "motivation vehicles," to ipsative scoring statistics, and to concepts of learning going beyond anything so restricted as the penny-in-the-slot reflex. But these concepts fit the facts better than the theories they support, and they lift the whole discussion of human motivation, neuroticism, anxiety and learning out of its present remoteness from experimental checks and its quagmire of inconsistencies.

In summary, my response to Dr. Eysenck's review is not that total, end-on collision of viewpoints which some dramatically minded psychologists seem to expect in this area, but which indeed can come only among totally unrealistic kinds of theories. Rather, I take issue on his not bringing out the points of agreement and disagreement in a way which would be clear both to theoreticians and psychological practitioners. I suspect that in part—especially in motivation—our disagreement arises from Dr. Eysenck's lesser investment in the development of a learning theory not restricted to reflexological formulations, and which, in spite of the almost totalitarian control which this reflexology enjoys in learning circles, I have for over a decade argued to be only one sector of a proper system of learning theory.

The remaining differences are more concrete and particular, namely: (1) My replacement of a three-factor theory of behavioral deviation by one based on six to ten factors (no matter in what medium or order we work) and (2) The resulting difference in the set of concepts developed regarding neuroticism, anxiety and motivation, and in the definition of the resulting instruments to measure these.

The agreements, however, are equally clear and substantial. They begin with a reasoned conviction that the potency of multivariate experimental methods in this "wholistic" behavior analysis is decidedly superior to classical bivariate experiment. They include the belief that a body of clinical theory is now arising *directly* from these experiments which has a greater future than concepts borrowed from the decaying structure of psycho-analysis. They extend to convergence of findings, definitions, and measurements on such factors as regression (or "neuroticism" if the term appeals, but certainly U.I. 23!) and extraversion.

Hopefully we are not in a position where the protagonists will merely reiterate their viewpoints from year to year but where independent researchers will step in and seek independent verdicts. Hitherto, the lag in development here has had the deep-rooted cause that extremely few clinicians can cover both the wide demands of clinical practice and the grasp of a mathematical discipline, such as is ultimately required in all scientific reasearch, simultaneously. (For, since mathematics has properly been named "the queen of sciences" psychologists can no more dispense with it than can any other science.)

Fortunately, the production of actual, finished personality factor measuring instruments in the last few years has made it possible for the applied psychologist to use such concepts and measurements without having to bother himself in the least with the computational complications involved in isolating the structures and in concept-validating the tests. He needs only to know the *logic* of factor analysis, as an objective system of finding functional unities in behaviour and tying them down by unique batteries; and this a part of the logic of scientific method generally. With no more purely mathematical concern than this, however, the practitioner can contribute enormously to *the scientific understanding and psychological interpretation of factors*. So soon as he begins to observe the changes of patients in measures on these particular instruments, aimed at the pure factors of anxiety, extraversion, motivation, etc., in clinical work, or to observe their selective power in industrial personnel work, he becomes a participator in the discussions and a contributor to the basic issues. Through such participation of the practitioner, we are almost certain to see in the next decade an increase in the power of psychological practice itself, and a rapid clarification of the nature of the role of personality factors in personality theory.

BIBLIOGRAPHY

BARGMANN, R. A demonstration study of the effectiveness of factor analytical models. Frankfurt; Hochschule fuer Internationale Paedagogische Forschung, 1955.

BURT, C. *The Factors of the Mind.* London: The University of London Press, 1940.

CATTELL, R. B. The diagnosis and classification of neurotic states: a reinterpretation of Eysenck's factors. *J. Neur. and Ment. Dis.*, 1945, 102, 576–589.

CATTELL, R. B. *Personality and Motivation Structure and Measurements.* New York: Harcourt, Brace and World, 1957.

CATTELL, R. B. The dynamic calculus: concepts and crucial experiments. In M. JONES (Ed.) *Nebraska Symposium on Motivation.* University of Nebraska Press, Lincoln, Nebraska, 1959.

CATTELL, R. B. Higher order factor structures: reticular vs. hierarchical formulae for their interpretation. Chapter in Festschrift for Sir Cyril Burt. Editor C. BANKS. In press.

CATTELL, R. B., and BAGGALEY, A. R. The objective measurement of attitude motivation: development and evaluation of principles and devices. *J. Pers.*, 1956, 24, 401–423.

CATTELL, R. B., and BELOFF, J. R. The High School Personality Questionnaire. Institute for Personality and Ability Testing (IPAT), 1602 Coronado Drive, Champaign, Illinois, 1958.

CATTELL, R. B., BLEWETT, D. B., and BELOFF, J. R. The inheritance of personality. A multiple variance analysis determination of approximate nature-nurture ratios for primary personality factors in Q-data. *Amer. J. Human Genet.*, 7, 122–146, 1955.

CATTELL, R. B., HORN, J. L., and BUTCHER, H. J. The dynamic structure of attitudes in adults: a description of some established factors and of their measurement by the Motivational Analysis Test. *Brit. J. Psychol.*, *53*, 57–69, 1962.

CATTELL, R. B., and HORN, J. L. The Motivation Analysis Test. Institute for Personality and Ability Testing, 1602 Coronado, Champaign, Illinois, 1964.

CATTELL, R. B., HUNDLEBY, et al. The Objective-Analytic Personality Test Battery. IPAT, 1602 Coronado Drive, Champaign, Illinois, U.S.A., 1955.

CATTELL, R. B., RADCLIFFE, J. A., and SWENEY, A. B. The Nature and Measurement of Components of Motivation. *Genet. Psychol. Monogr.*, *68*, 49–211, 1963.

CATTELL, R. B., and SCHEIER, I. H. *The Meaning and Measurement of Neuroticism and Anxiety.* New York: Ronald Press, 1961.

CATTELL, R. B., and STICE, G. F. The Sixteen Personality Factor Questionnaire. National Foundation for Educational Research, Wimpole Street, London, 1949.

CATTELL, R. B., and WARBURTON, FRANK W., A cross-cultural comparison of patterns of extraversion and anxiety. *Brit. J. Psychol.*, *52*, 3–15, 1961.

EYSENCK, H. J. The Dynamics of Anxiety and Hysteria, London: Routledge and Kegan Paul, 1957.

EYSENCK, H. J. Review of Cattell and Scheier's book, *The Meaning and Measurement of Neuroticism and Anxiety,* in *Occupational Psychology*, *35*, 253–256, 1961.

FIEDLER, F. E. A comparison of therapeutic relationships in psychoanalytic, nondirective and Adlerian therapy. *J. Consult. Psychol.*, *14*, 436–445, 1950.

FRENCH, J. The description of aptitude and achievement tests in terms of rotated factors. *Psychol. Monogr.*, No. 5., Chicago: University of Chicago Press, 1951.

GORSUCH, R. L., and CATTELL, R. B. A definitive study of second order personality factors in the questionnaire realm. (In press).

GUILFORD, J. P., and ZIMMERMAN, W. The Guilford-Zimmerman temperament survey: Manual of instructions and interpretation. Sheridan Supply, Beverly Hills, 1949.

HUNDLEBY, J., PAWLIK, K., and CATTELL, R. B. The First Twenty-One Personality Factors in Objective Tests. (In Press, Knapp, San Diego, U.S.A.)

LAWLEY, D. N. Tests of significance for the latent roots of covariance and correlation matrices. *Biom.*, *43*, 128–136, 1956.

PAWLIK, K., and CATTELL, R. B. Third-order factors in objective personality tests. *Brit. J. Psychol.*, *55*, 1–18, 1964.

SCHEIER, I. H., and CATTELL, R. B. The Forty-Item Anxiety Scale, Institute for Personality and Ability Testing, 1602 Coronado Drive, Champaign, Illinois, 1960.

SOKAL, R. R. A comparison of five tests for completeness of factor extraction. *Trans. Kansas Acad. Sci.*, *62*, 141–152, 1959.

SPENCE, K. W., FARBER, I. E., and McFANN, H. H. The relation of anxiety (drive) level to performance in competitional and non-competitional paired-associates learning. *J. Exp. Psychol.*, *52*, 296–305, 1956.

SWENEY, A. B. Human motivation measured by objective tests. *Psychol. Reports*, *10*, 408, 1962.

SWENEY, A. B., and CATTELL, R. B. The School Motivation Analysis Test, Institute for Personality and Ability Testing, 1602 Coronado Drive, Champaign, Illinois, 1964.

THURSTONE, L. L. Primary Mental Abilities. Chicago: University of Chicago Press, 1938.

A Model of Item Ambiguity in Personality Assessment

Lewis R. Goldberg

One of the most common criticisms heard from subjects upon taking almost any popular personality inventory is that "so many of the items seem ambiguous." Further questioning will often elicit statements such as "Many of the items I'd have answered one way today and another way tomorrow" or "The items seemed so ambiguous that I was never sure *how* to respond."

That subjects may become annoyed with the form, content, or response structure of some particular test items would not *in itself* be cause for grave concern, if the instruments which utilized these items yielded highly satisfactory test scores. However, few psychologists would question the need for improving present-day personality tests, and one might well begin by investigating the apparent difficulties encountered by subjects in responding to individual test items.

In any study of item characteristics, one cannot help but be impressed by the marked *inconsistency of response* elicited by most personality test items.

The author gratefully acknowledges the stimulation and help provided by Paul J. Hoffman, Rolfe LaForge, and others at the Oregon Research Institute. This paper has profited from the critical reading of earlier drafts by Hoffman and LaForge as well as by Donald Fiske, Leonard Rorer, Jerry S. Wiggins and Nancy Wiggins. This project has been suported by two grants from the Graduate School of the University of Oregon, and Grant #G-25123 from the National Science Foundation.

Reprinted by permission of the publisher and author from *Educational and Psychological Measurement*, 1963, **23**, 467–492.

Evidence of such response instability has been reported in the psychometric literature since the early 1930's. Table 1 lists some representative figures from this literature showing the percentage of items changed on retest by the average subject for some typical early personality inventories.

Table 2 lists the percentage of items changed by the average subject for six more recently developed personality and "response set" measures (Goldberg, Dufort & Hammersley, in preparation). Approximately 300 college undergraduates were administered a one-hour battery of tests, and 10 random samples from this population were retested over 10 different test-retest intervals. Table 2 lists the average percentage of items changed for each of the six measures for a three-week test-retest interval. Since the amount of item change is obviously related to the number of response options considered (Fiske, 1957), the data are analyzed for different numbers of response categories, thereby permitting the direct comparison across measures utilizing different response formats.

Although the findings presented in Tables 1 and 2 indicate a marked degree of response instability on items from both older and more recent personality inventories, an even more significant indication of intra-individual variability becomes evident when one examines the test-retest reliability coefficients for modern personality *scales*. The majority of these average no more than .70 (for example, Jackson, 1961), indicating that roughly one-third of the

TABLE 1.   PERCENTAGE OF ITEMS CHANGED BY THE AVERAGE SUBJECT UNDER
TEST-RETEST CONDITIONS: SOME REPRESENTATIVE FIGURES FROM THE
PSYCHOMETRIC LITERATURE

Reference	Personality Test	Test-Retest Interval	Number of Response Options Considered	Average % Change
Lentz (1934)	Bernreuter Personality Inventory	1 month	3	20
Neprash (1936)	Thurstone Personality Schedule	2 weeks	2	14
		4 weeks	2	16
		8 weeks	2	16
Benton and Stone (1937)	Landis and Zubin Personal Inquiry Form	immediate	3	11
		1 day	3	11
		3 days	3	16
		4 days	3	19
		5 days	3	19
		7 days	3	19
		8 days	3	20
		21 days	3	19
Farnsworth (1938)	Bernreuter Personality Inventory	1 year	3	29
		2 years	3	35
		3 years	3	35
Eisenberg and Wesman (1941)	Thurstone Neurotic Inventory	23–28 days	3	15
Glaser (1949)	California Test of Personality	1 month	2	16
Chance (1955)	Bell Adjustment Inventory	14 days	3	15
Strong (1962)	Strong Vocational Interest Blank	3 days	3	21

total scale variance is error of measurement, if we make the assumption that the personality trait to be measured is relatively invariant. That is, although psychologists might well expect some changes in responses from one situation to another *different* one, most psychologists concerned with human measurement expect some stability of responses over time when the testing conditions appear to be reasonable constant and the traits to be measured are assumed to be *relatively enduring* ones. In this paper, it is assumed that *some* important personality traits are stable over short periods of time, and the discussion will be limited to the psychometric measurement of such stable traits. One possible way to reduce the error now associated with the measurement of these traits is to construct more stable items to use as initial item pools for later scale development.

Parameters of Item Stability

Common sense considerations, augmented by the reflections of tested subjects, would suggest that a crucial component of item stability is certainly item *ambiguity*. Ambiguity has been traditionally defined as doubtfulness or uncertainty in the meaning of a stimulus; it often denotes a stimulus whose meaning is open to various interpretations. Ambiguity can be measured subjectively by rating methods or objectively as some function of either of two indices: (a) inter-individual variability in the meaning of a stimulus (e.g., Broen, 1960) or (b) intra-individual variability in meaning over repeated administrations of the stimulus (i.e., interpretative instability). It is apparent that indices utilizing either of these two measures will usually be highly correlated, for a stimulus which elicits disparate meanings among a group of persons will typically elicit unstable meanings for an individual over time. The relationship between inter-individual and intra-individual response variability in personality assessment has been documented by Mitra

over repeated administrations of the item than more balanced items (i.e., items to which a population's choices approach a 50–50 split between alternatives). In other words, items at the extremes of any attribute continuum have been shown to elicit less change in responses than those reflecting positions in the middle range of the attribute (Frank, 1936; Hertzman & Gould, 1939; Eisenberg & Wesman, 1941; Mitra & Fiske, 1956; Crockett, Bates, & Caylor, 1958). This finding, of

TABLE 2. PERCENTAGE OF ITEMS CHANGED UPON RETEST BY THE AVERAGE SUBJECT AS A FUNCTION OF THE NUMBER OF RESPONSE CATEGORIES

Scale	Number of Response Options	Percentage Change When Items Are Scored as:		
		Dichotomous	Trichotomous	Absolute % Change
MMPI: Factor A	2	14	—	14
MMPI: Factor R	2	14	—	14
Berg Perceptual Reaction Test	4	30	31	52
Rust and Davies Reported Behavior Inventory	3	9	16	16
Bass Social Acquiescence Scale	3	22	36	36
Couch and Keniston Agreement Response Set Scale	7	24	34	59

and Fiske (1956) and Fiske (1957). The relationship between intra-individual variability and ambiguity has such strong rational appeal that investigators have been led to use intra-individual response variability (item instability) as a *direct* measure of item ambiguity.

However, there is a serious error in such a practice. It has been demonstrated repeatedly that items of extreme endorsement frequencies (for example, items to which 90–100 per cent of a population choose the same alternative) tend to be responded to more consistently (i.e., with a smaller percentage of subjects who change their responses)

the relative stability of extreme items, has occurred in virtually all studies, regardless of the assessment instrument utilized. It seems directly analogous to findings from the area of ability testing, where items at the average difficulty level for a population tend to be less stable over retesting than items of extreme ease or difficulty. Figure 1 is an example of the typical curvilinear relation found between stability and endorsement frequency.[1]

[1] The relationship illustrated in Figure 1 does not result solely from that existing between the standard error of a proportion and the magnitude of the proportion (in this case, the item's endorsement frequency). Changes in endorsement frequency due to sampling

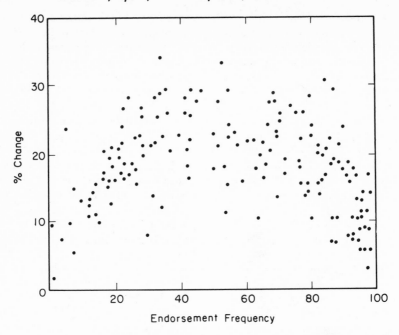

Figure 1. Endorsement frequency vs. percentage of subjects changing responses on second administration of 160 adjectives (*N* = 96 females).

Since items seen by subjects as highly "ambiguous" can dichotomize the attribute continuum at many points, it is desirable to eliminate the effect of differences in endorsement frequency from an index of item ambiguity. That is, the practice of utilizing the percentage of subjects changing their responses to the item as an index of item ambiguity leads one to the position that items dichotomizing an attribute continuum at some extreme point are *all* less ambiguous than items which more evenly dichotomize the

errors provide a lower bound for the degree of instability of any item, but most present-day personality test items are so unstable that this lower bound does not serve as a useful approximation to the item's actual instability; that is, the correlation between the mean shift in endorsement frequency over two administrations of an item and the percentage of subjects changing their responses to the item is virtually zero (for example, *r* = .13 [and .09] for 95 male [and 108 female] college students administered the MMPI and then retested after four weeks).

continuum. An alternative proposal is to formulate an index of item ambiguity which is based upon the percentage of response change but which takes into account the effects of item imbalance.

The Response to a Monotone Item

To more fully understand how such an index might be constructed, let us consider the response of a subject to a test item. It is important to distinguish between two major forms of items, called "monotone" and "nonmonotone" items by Coombs (1952) and Green (1954). The defining characteristic of a "monotone" item is that as the magnitude of the attribute measured by the item increases, the probability of any single response category ("True," "False," "Yes," "No"; etc.) increases monotonically with it. That is, the item dichotomizes the attribute continuum such that there is only one boundary between "Yes" and "No" regions. The item "I am tall" is an example of a monotone item; as height increases in the sample, the probability of a "True" response increases monotonically with it. Now consider a "non-monotone" item—for example, "I am of medium height." In this case, as with all non-monotone items, the probability of a particular response is *not* monotonically related to the underlying attribute continuum. The item divides the continuum into three or more regions; at least two boundaries are required to separate "No" from "Yes" regions.

Although some factual items, as well as well as many attitude items, are non-monotonic, the majority of our present-day personality test items appear to be monotones in form. Take the hypothetical item, "I am a shy person," or—a similar item—the adjective "Shy" administered in an adjective check list. For persons who see themselves as forceful and extraverted, these items are easily checked "False." As progressively more retiring sorts of persons are selected, one begins to find subjects hesitating in responding to the item, as if they were asking themselves, "Just how shy does a person have to be before he considers himself 'shy'?". Eventually one finds subjects responding "True" to this item, and as progressively more shy individuals are selected, one would probably find that the ease with which they answer the item in the "True" direction increases.

Being a bit more precise, for an hypothetically "honest" individual the decision to respond "True" or "False" to a dichotomously-scored monotone item is assumed to be a joint function of: (a) the perceived boundary established by the item on the attribute continuum, and (b) the individual's perceived position on this continuum. If the item is perceived as having a boundary on one side of the individual's own position, one alternative is checked; if the item is seen as having

a boundary on the other side of the individual's position, the other alternative is checked.[2]

Figure 2 is an attempt to graph an hypothetical frequency distribution of subjects on the attribute continuum of "perceived shyness" and to indicate where the item "Shy" in an adjective check list might fall on this underlying continuum. Note that 70 per cent of the population sees this item as establishing a boundary above the point on the attribute continuum where they see themselves and thus respond "False" to the item; the remaining 30 per cent perceives the item as establishing a boundary below the point where they see themselves and thus respond "True." For those individuals who see themselves far from the boundary, B, (i.e., in regions A or C of this distribution), the decision in regard to this item would be an easy one to make, since the item's boundary should be perceived as quite distant from the individual's position. Individual's close to B, however, should face more difficulty since the boundary lies closer to their own position on the attribute continuum.

Those individuals who encounter the most difficulty in making a decision upon the first presentation of an item should be the persons most likely to change their response to the item upon its subsequent presentation. Assuming the usual normal frequency distribution of subjects on most attribute continua, items whose boundaries are seen by the great majority of a population as quite

[2] As Edwards (1957) and his associates have frequently warned, persons may differ in their tendencies to admit socially undesirable aspects of themselves; consequently, an "hypothetically honest" individual may be rare. Social desirability considerations, however, can probably best be conceptualized as influencing a subject's perception of his own position on the attribute continuum (and/or the degree he is willing to *report* an "honest" appraisal of his position) and thus may leave the essential components of this more simple model unchanged.

distant from their own (i.e., extreme items) will be responded to without difficulty for most of the population upon the first presentation of the item and will be changed only by some members of that very small subsection of the population which is itself very extreme on the attribute continuum. On the other hand, items with boundaries falling near the middle of the attribute continuum (i.e., balanced items) will find many individuals having difficulty

an item as the *range of disagreement* in regard to the item's boundary on an attribute continuum. If every individual in the population sees the item's boundary as falling at the same position, the item could be said to have a minimum equivocality band; if some individuals perceive the item's boundary as being extreme in one direction while other individuals perceive it as extreme in the other direction, the item could be said to have a maximum equivocality band.

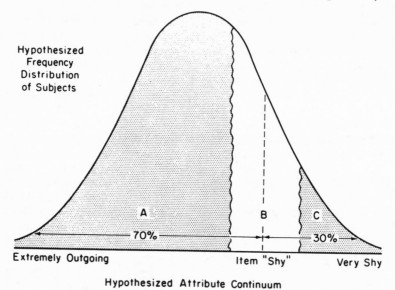

Figure 2. Frequency density and attribute intensity.

in responding to them and many more individuals changing their responses upon retesting.

A Model of Item Ambiguity

Obviously the boundary established by an item is not perceived at the same point on the attribute continuum by everyone in the population. More realistically the boundary of an item can be conceived as occupying a "band" on an attribute continuum corresponding to its perceived position by different members of a population. One could conceptualize the "equivocality-band" of

It is assumed that there is a strong relationship between the degree to which different persons agree in their positioning of the boundary of an item on an attribute continuum (upon the first administration of the item) and the extent to which individuals are consistent in positioning the boundary upon successive presentations of the item. That is, it is assumed that items of broad equivocality bands (as defined by different members of the population on the first administration) will be items of great intra-individual variability in their positioning over repeated administrations of the items and can therefore be considered as having wide "ambiguity bands."

Previously, it has been hypothesized that the closer an individual perceives his position[3] on an attribute continuum to be to the boundary of an item, the more difficulty he will have in respond-

In summary, then, the stability of any item (defined in the traditional way as the percentage of individuals who give a consistent response to the item over repeated administrations) depends upon (a) the narrowness of the ambiguity band of the item (i.e., how

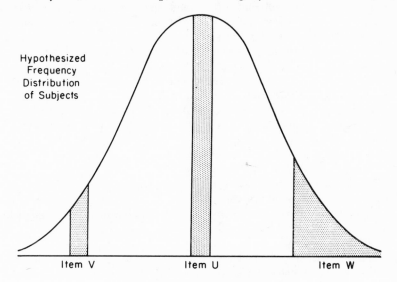

Hypothesized
Frequency
Distribution
of Subjects

Item V   Item U   Item W

Hypothesized Attribute Continuum

Figure 3. Item ambiguity bands and item endorsement frequency.

ing to the item upon its first administration and the more likely will he be to change his response upon its readministration. In addition, it seems reasonable to assume that the wider the ambiguity band of an item (i.e., the greater the intra-individual variability in boundary positioning) the less stable should be the item. Conversely, the narrower the ambiguity band of the item, the more stable it should be.

[3] Obviously, one could hypothesize an "ambiguity band" for an *individual's perceived position* on an attribute continuum, and then response stability could be seen as a joint function of two interacting ambiguity bands. Moreover, items and persons might also be conceptualized as points in multi-dimensional space, rather than as points on a single underlying attribute continuum. The rationales for these more complex models have not yet been completed.

specifically localized is the perceived position of the item's boundary on the attribute continuum over time by the average individual) and (b) the frequency density at the item's boundary point. That is, there should exist *two kinds of "stable"* and *two kinds of "unstable"* items: an item can be stable because it is highly specific and precisely localized (narrow ambiguity band) and/or an item can be stable because it is extreme and few subjects are found near the item's boundary. Conversely, an item may be unstable because it has a broad ambiguity band (i.e., it is perceived as being in many spots on the trait continuum by the average person on different occasions) and/or because it lies in the middle of the attribute continuum (where there are many individuals clustered).

Figure 3 is an attempt to depict these notions graphically for three items, "U," "V," and "W," located on the same attribute continuum. Note that each item is conceived as having an ambiguity band, corresponding to its perceived position on the attribute continuum by the average person on different occasions. Item U is graphed as having a narrow ambiguity band; that is, it is perceived on most occasions as being in about the same position on the attribute continuum. Item W is graphed as having a much broader ambiguity band and as being a more extreme item. Item V is graphed as also being relatively extreme but having an ambiguity band similar to item U. Note that most persons would respond "True" to item V and "False" to item W, and that they could make these choices rather easily.

The shaded areas above each item represent the proportion of individuals who would have difficulty making a decision for the particular item. These are the persons most expected to *change* their responses upon repeated administrations of the item. As can be seen from Figure 3, although item W has a wide ambiguity band, owing to its extreme position on the attribute continuum it elicits about the same percentage change as item U. Item V, with the same width ambiguity band as item U, elicits the least percentage change.

In actual practice, the percentage of individuals who change their responses to a given item can be readily determined by test-retest procedures, as can the item's endorsement frequency. The remaining problem is to ascertain the width of the item's ambiguity band (a distance along the assumed attribute continuum), given these two indices.

Derivation of an Index of Ambiguity

The preceding discussion provides the rationale behind the index of item ambiguity. For every two administrations of any item pool, two indices are immediately available for each item: (a) a measure of *item endorsement frequency* (actually two such measures are available, one for each administration of the item; the average endorsement frequency over both administrations of the item is the index presently utilized[4]), and (b) a measure of *item instability* (defined as the percentage of subjects in the population who change their responses upon a second presentation of the item). The problem is to derive an index of ambiguity, based upon item instability, which corrects for item endorsement frequency. Only the monotonic case will be treated here

Figure 4 graphs the geometric rationale behind this ambiguity index, called, for short, *Ambdex*.

For Figure 4:

E = Endorsement frequency (shaded area above)

A = Ambdex (index of ambiguity; width of ambiguity band)

X_E = Scale value (E^{th} percentile) on the attribute continuum which cuts from the normal curve an area equal to the average endorsement frequency of the item

$f(X_E)$ = Ordinate of the normal curve erected at X_E

$X_1 \epsilon X_2$ = Scale values on the attribute continuum such that $X_2 - X_1 = A$

$\beta = \frac{1}{2}A = X_2 - X_E = X_E - X_1$

I = Average percentage of change (index of instability) taken as equal to the area under the normal curve between $X_E - \beta$ and $X_E + \beta$

The *index of instability (I)* for any item is represented by that portion of the normal curve between $X_E - \beta$ and $X_E + \beta$ and as here defined is equal to the percentage of persons changing their responses to the item upon its second

[4] The geometric mean is being considered as an alternative to the arithmetic mean utilized in the preliminary index.

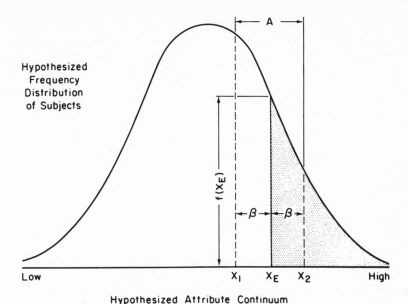

Figure 4. A model for the index of ambiguity (Ambdex).

presentation. X_E and $f(X_E)$ can be readily found from normal curve tables entered for the area cut off the normal curve equal to the item's endorsement frequency, averaged over both administrations of the item. The problem is

to solve for the distance, A, between points X_1 and X_2, each equidistant from X_E.

The solution involves integrating the equation for the normal curve between $-\infty$ and $X_E + \beta$ and subtracting the

TABLE 3.   AMBDEX AS A FUNCTION OF ENDORSEMENT FREQUENCY
AND RESPONSE INSTABILITY

	.00	.01	.02	.03	.04	.05	.06	.07	.08	.09	.10	.15	.20	.25	.30	.35
.50	.00	.02	.05	.08	.10	.12	.15	.18	.20	.23	.25	.38	.50	.63	.75	.88
.45	.00	.03	.05	.08	.10	.13	.15	.18	.20	.23	.25	.38	.51	.63	.76	.88
.40	.00	.03	.05	.08	.10	.13	.16	.18	.21	.23	.25	.39	.52	.65	.78	.91
.35	.00	.03	.05	.08	.11	.14	.16	.19	.22	.24	.27	.41	.54	.68	.81	.95
.30	.00	.03	.06	.09	.12	.14	.17	.20	.23	.26	.29	.43	.58	.72	.87	
.25	.00	.03	.06	.09	.13	.16	.19	.22	.25	.28	.31	.47	.63	.79	.94	
.20	.00	.04	.07	.11	.14	.18	.21	.25	.29	.32	.36	.54	.71	.89		
.15	.00	.04	.09	.13	.17	.22	.26	.30	.34	.39	.43	.64	.86			
.10	.00	.05	.11	.17	.23	.29	.34	.40	.46	.51	.57	.86				
.09	.00	.06	.12	.19	.25	.31	.37	.43	.49	.56	.62	.93				
.08	.00	.07	.14	.20	.27	.34	.41	.47	.54	.61	.68					
.07	.00	.08	.15	.22	.30	.37	.45	.52	.60	.67	.75					
.06	.00	.08	.17	.25	.34	.42	.50	.59	.67	.76	.84					
.05	.00	.10	.19	.29	.39	.49	.58	.68	.78	.87	.97					
.04	.00	.12	.23	.35	.47	.58	.70	.81	.93							
.03	.00	.15	.29	.44	.59	.74	.88									
.02	.00	.21	.42	.63	.83											
.00–.01	.00	.37	.74													

ENDORSEMENT FREQUENCY (row labels)

Percentage of Subjects Changing Response on Second Administration integral between $-\infty$ and $X_E - \beta$, setting this value equal to I and solving for β. Although no formal solution exists, β can be readily found by *interpolation* from the table of values of the unit normal curve.

In practice, a simpler approximation is merely to define the area of the rectangle:

$$I = A \cdot f(X_E)$$

as equivalent to the associated area under the normal curve. Then

$$A = \frac{I}{f(X_E)} \cdot$$

This approximation will slightly underestimate Ambdex when the endorsement frequency is 50 per cent, and it will slightly overestimate Ambdex for extreme endorsement frequencies. It will be most accurate when X_E falls directly under the curve's inflection points.

Table 3 lists some representative values of Ambdex for various item endorsement frequencies and various percentages of subjects changing their responses.

Rust (1961) reported that Ambdex was highly related to an estimate of r-tetrachoric in a population of 169 male undergraduates tested on a 160-item adjective check list at the end of their freshman and senior years at Yale. N. Wiggins (1961) has shown that Ambdex and r-tetrachoric are mathematically related, though not identical, statistics.

Since Ambdex was constructed specifically to provide an index of ambiguity which would be independent of item endorsement frequency, a first test of the proposed statistic was to ascertain its relationship with item endorsement frequency for various subject groups and various item pools. Figure 5 shows one scatterplot illustrative of the lack of relationship between endorsement frequency and Ambdex (eta = .01). The data plotted in Figure 5 come from a double administration of an 160-adjective check list (three week test-retest interval) to 82 University of Oregon male undergraduates from an Introduc-

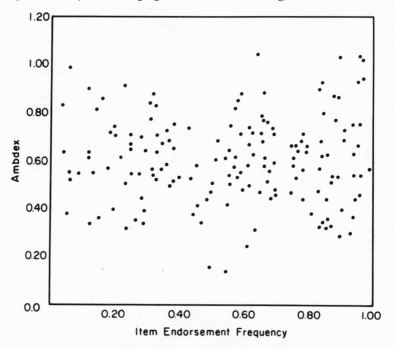

Figure 5. Index of ambiguity vs. item endorsement frequency for 82 males administered 160 adjectives.

tory Psychology course. Note that the attempt to detach ambiguity from item endorsement frequency appears to have been successful for this sample. Rust (1961) found both Ambdex and *r*-tetrachoric unrelated to item endorsement frequency in his sample.

The Use of Ambdex for Item Selection

Personality test development has been marked by diligent interest in the principles of scale construction and marked neglect of the properties of the stimuli from which the scales are normally constructed. It may well be that our most powerful strategies for item grouping are never able to overcome the defects present in the initial item sample. Therefore, our best hope for more valid assessment tools may well lie in the increased understanding of basic *item* properties.

In the history of test development, item construction has typically been considered a relatively inconsequential task. Although the direct investigation of personality test item properties has a long history (e.g., Bain, 1931; Smith, 1933; Lentz, 1934; Benton, 1935; Pintner & Forlano, 1938), early investigators—while spotting some of the more salient problems in item construction and interpretation—soon reached impasses that discouraged further explorations. Meanwhile, test developers were relying far too heavily on rationally constructed items, building face-valid scales and assuming their relevance to the measurement task at hand. The wave of pure empiricism which swept American assessment circles in the decade following World War II was a healthy force in placing the discipline of personality assessment on firmer methodological grounds. During this period there emerged explicit rationales for minimizing the importance of such item properties as item structure and content. One of the earliest of these rationales was presented by Paul Meehl in his influential defense of pure empiricism in inventory construction (Meehl, 1945); a more extreme position with respect to item content has been taken by Irwin Berg (1959).

The rather basic property of *item stability* (response consistency over repeated administrations of the item) seems not to have been exempted from the general neglect of item characteristics, and the reliability of the basic units of personality measurement has not received the systematic attention it deserves. Were one to inquire as to how to insure a *given* degree of reliability in a personality scale (other than simply varying the length of the test), one could not find a complete answer in the literature.

As was pointed out earlier, investigators in the 1930's were interested in improving the stability of their scales through an examination of item properties, but they encountered an apparent enigma—namely, that the most discriminating items (e.g., between neurotics and normals) were the very items which were responded to most inconsistently in the general population. That is, they found that the least stable items were the most useful predictively. In retrospect, the enigma is not difficult to understand. The items which were most useful were balanced items, and the items which were most stable were extreme items. Thus, early investigators (e.g., Bain, 1931; Benton, 1935; Frank, 1936; Hertzman & Gould, 1939; Lentz, 1934) were faced with the choice of having stable scales (composed of extreme items) which were non-differentiating, or scales composed of items with some predictive efficiency but low temporal stability.

This paradox may arise primarily from the strong relationship between inter-individual and intra-individual variability. Isard (1956) has found that the most discriminating forced-choice items in predicting college achievement are those whose alternatives elicit the most inter-individual variability in their preference ratings. Since inter-individual *response* variability is essential for personality assessment, it may be necessary to purchase inter-individual variability in stimulus "meaning" (equivocality) to achieve this end.

In a very significant paper, Broen (1960) specified the conditions under which changes in equivocality should lead to increased item discriminating power. Normally the test constructor seeks to (a) maximize inter-individual response variability (often, as Broen notes, by sanctioning equivocality) and simultaneously (b) minimize intra-individual variability of response (and consequently of stimulus meaning, i.e., ambiguity). However, since items of high equivocality are typically items of high ambiguity, the paradox is complete. To assess stable components of personality, it would appear necessary either to (a) use the average values of repeated measures (an expensive and time-consuming process) or (b) develop an item technology to the point where items can be constructed which elicit both *high inter*-individual variability and *low intra*-individual variability.

The search for both stable and discriminating items leads to another enigma, namely, that typically the more an item reflects some aspect of behavior that is directly observable and easily identifiable the more stable is the item; on the other hand, the more an item reflects some attitude, value, or other "internal" state of mind the more unstable is the item. Consequently, at present, inventory constructors could be faced with the dilemma of choosing stable items reflecting attributes of relatively little personological importance or selecting items of decreased triviality but increased intra-individual variability. For this reason, the investigation of stable biographical inventory questions (e.g., Rust, 1961; Owens, Glennon, & Albright, 1962) for utilization in personality inventories is certainly worth continued effort.

Another approach lies in the general investigation of item properties and the development of objective indices to guide initial item selection (prior to actual scale construction). Ambdex is suggested as a possible index to be used to minimize item ambiguity. It may also be useful to develop an objective index of equivocality (utilizing the dispersions of item boundary placements interindividually) to provide a parallel measure with Ambdex. As Broen (1960) has illustrated, in some prediction situations the test constructor may wish to minimize *both* equivocality and ambiguity, thus loading his initial item pool with low Ambdex *and* low equivocality items. For other situations, however, in which increased equivocality is useful, one might select for an initial item pool those items having high equivocality/Ambdex ratios.

With the exception of Horn (1950), the psychometric literature discloses no opponents to decreasing intra-individual variability, at least until the hypothesized stability of the personality trait itself is attained. Unfortunately, there is less agreement on the *extent* of personality trait variability (e.g., Cattell, 1957; Fiske, 1961; Secord & Backman, 1961). A general review of the literature on variability can be found in Fiske and Rice (1955). Some important empirical findings on the stability of diverse traits over long intervals of time (as measured by early psychometric scales) are reported by Kelly (1956).

Although there is general concordance on the importance of intra-individual response stability in psychometric assessment, the traditional neglect of item properties has turned research attention away from the systematic investigation of item stability. With one very notable exception (Bills, Vance, & McLean, 1951) no major personality inventory has been constructed by explicitly utilizing item stability as a criterion for item selection. There are, however, recent indications of a renewed interest in the stimulus characteristics of items (Owens, Glennon, & Albright, 1962; Hanley, 1962; Edwards & Walsh, 1963) and a trend toward analysis of item parameters associated with specific response patterns. The breadth of explanatory power generated by scaling the single item parameter of social desirability has been repeatedly documented by Edwards (1957). The distinction between content and style (Jackson & Messick, 1958) and the formulation of item properties as mediators of components of strategic, method, and stylistic variance in assessment (Wiggins, 1962) are significant steps forward. These recent theoretical contributions, taken together with the important demonstrations that systematic variation of item properties results in systematic variation in response patterns (Buss & Durkee, 1957; Buss, 1959; Hanley, 1959; Stricker, 1960; Eliott, 1961; Goldfried & McKenzie, 1962; Aiken, 1962), suggest that personality test item construction is progressing from an art to a science. The present paper aims to channel a part of this trend to the area of item stability.

Summary of the Ambiguity Model

The preceding discussion has focused exclusively upon the *practical* uses for an ambiguity index. However, considerations of the role of response variability and stimulus ambiguity in personality assessment also uncover some significant theoretical issues, and the ambiguity model provides the potential opportunity for explaining a large number of relatively diverse empirical findings. Consequently, the model will now be summarized in its present preliminary form, with the hope that it will stimulate independent investigations which in turn may help clarify the ambiguities now present in the ambiguity model. The current model applies solely to monotone items, scored dichotomously; the more general case is being developed.

Brief descriptions of the major postulates and theorems of the model follow.

Postulate 1: The closer the perceived position of a person is to the boundary established by the item on the relevant attribute continuum (as perceived by the person), the more difficult will be his decision for that item. Some manifestations of difficulty include: (a) response in a middle, or "?," category if this is allowed in the response format (or refusal to respond—leaving the item blank—if a middle category is not provided), (b) latency of response (greater latency indicating greater difficulty), and (c) ratings of item difficulty (or, conversely, ratings of low judgmental confidence). Consequently, the following predictions follow from this postulate:

(P:1a) More items whose boundaries are perceived as close to a subject's position than items perceived as further away will be placed in a middle, or "?," category (if this is allowed in the response format) or will be left blank if a middle category is not provided.

(P:1b) The latency of response should be greater for items whose boundaries are perceived as closer to a subject's position than for those perceived as further away.

(P:1c) A person should report more difficulty in responding (and consequently less confidence in his response) to items whose boundaries are perceived as closer to himself than to those perceived as further away.

(P:1d) The three manifestations of difficulty should be interrelated.

Postulate 2: The closer the perceived position of a person is to the boundary established by the item on the relevant attribute continuum (as perceived by the person), the more unstable will be his response.

Theorem 1: Combining Postulates (1) and (2):

The more difficult is a person's response to an item upon its first administration, the more likely is he to change that response upon retesting. Consequently:

(T:1a) Items placed in a "?" category (or left blank) will be relatively unstable.

(T:1b) Items which elicit long response latencies will be relatively unstable.

(T:1c) Items rated difficult (or given low confidence ratings) will be relatively unstable.

Postulate 3: The distribution of subjects on the attribute continuum is specified. In practice, subjects are assumed to be distributed in approximately normal curve frequencies on most psychological attribute continua.

Theorem 2: From Postulate (3):

Fewer persons will see their own positions as falling close to an extreme item's boundary than to a more balanced item.

Theorem 3: Combining Postulate (1) and Theorem (2):

Items of extreme endorsement frequencies, as compared to more balanced items, will be seen by fewer individuals as difficult items. Consequently:

(T:3a) Balanced items will be placed in a "?" category, or will be left blank, by more individuals than will extreme items.

(T:3b) Balanced items will elicit longer response latencies.

(T:3c) Balanced items will be judged more difficult (or given lower confidence ratings).

Theorem 4: Combining Postulate (2) and Theorem (3):

Items of extreme endorsement frequencies, as compared to more balanced items, will be relatively stable.

Postulate 4: The greater the inter-individual variability in the positioning of an item's boundary on a relevant attribute continuum (i.e., the more disagreement among persons as to the position of the boundary of an item on the attribute continuum), the greater will be the intra-individual variability of item positioning over time (i.e., the more likely will individuals be to vary

in their positioning of the item's boundary upon repeated administrations of the item). That is, equivocality is related to ambiguity. Since manifestations of intra-individual variability in boundary positioning should include both subjective ratings of ambiguity as well as an objective index of ambiguity (Ambdex), consequently:

(P:4a) Intra-individual variability in item boundary positioning will be directly related to ratings of item ambiguity.

(P:4b) Intra-individual variability in item boundary positioning will be directly related to Ambdex values.

(P:4c) Ratings of item ambiguity will be related to Ambdex values.

(P:4d) Ratings of item ambiguity will be correlated with item equivocality.

(P:4e) Ambdex values will be correlated with item equivocality.

Postulate 5: The more intra-individual variability in the positioning of an item's boundary, the more unstable will be the response to that item.

(P:5a) Response instability will be correlated with ambiguity ratings.

(P:5b) Response instability will be correlated with Ambdex values.

Theorem 5: Combining Postulate (4) and Postulate (5):

The more inter-individual variability in the positioning of an item's boundary, the more unstable will be the response to that item.

In summary, response stability can be considered as a positive function of (a) self-item distance (for an individual) and (b) item extremeness (for a group), and a negative function of (c) item ambiguity, (d) item difficulty, and (e) item equivocality.

Table 4 summarizes the postulates and theorems of the model and indicates those which have received empirical test.

Evidence for some of these assumptions can be found in a recent study by Hanley (1962). Using 75 MMPI items, Hanley demonstrated that a measure of response latency and a measure of judgmental confidence were both negatively correlated with extremeness of item endorsement frequency (i.e., latency as well as difficulty were inversely related to item balance). Moreover, Hanley showed that item length, which Strong (1962) found to be related to ambiguity in SVIB items, was also highly related to response latency and difficulty.

A very recent study by Edwards and Walsh (1963) provides additional support for the model. When 176 miscellaneous personality statements were administered twice to 110 male and 111 female college students, item stability

TABLE 4.   POSTULATES AND THEOREMS OF THE AMBIGUITY MODEL

Postulate (P) or Theorem (T)	Formula		Empirical Test
	Individual Case	Group Case	
P:1	$D_{ij} = f(d_{ij})$	$D_{.j} = f(d_{.j})$	
P:1a		$O_{.j} = f(d_{.j})$	
P:1b	$L_{ij} = f(d_{ij})$	$L_{.j} = f(d_{.j})$	
P:1c	$R_{ij} = f(d_{ij})$	$R_{.j} = f(d_{.j})$	
P:1d		$O_{.j} = f(L_{.j})$	
	$L_{ij} = f(R_{ij})$	$L_{.j} = f(R_{.j})$	
		$O_{.j} = f(R_{.j})$	
P:2	$I_{i.} = f(d_{i.})$	$I_{..} = f(d_{..})$	
T:1	$I_{i.} = f(D_{i.})$	$I_{..} = f(D_{..})$	
T:1a	$I_{i.} = f(O_{i.})$	$I_{..} = f(O_{..})$	Dodd & Svalastoga (1952); Edwards & Walsh (1963)
T:1b	$I_{i.} = f(L_{i.})$	$I_{..} = f(L_{..})$	Crockett, Bates, & Caylor
T:1c	$I_{i.} = f(R_{i.})$	$I_{..} = f(R_{..})$	(1958)
P:3	Specification of distribution of individuals on underlying attribute continuum (here assumed to be the normal distribution)		
T:2		$d_{.j} = f(\lvert .5 - p \rvert)_{.j}$	
T:3		$D_{.j} = f(\lvert .5 - p \rvert)_{.j}$	
T:3a		$O_{.j} = f(\lvert .5 - p \rvert)_{.j}$	
T:3b		$L_{.j} = f(\lvert .5 - p \rvert)_{.j}$	Hanley (1962)
T:3c		$R_{.j} = f(\lvert .5 - p \rvert)_{.j}$	Hanley (1962)
T:4		$I_{..} = f(\lvert .5 - p \rvert)_{..}$	Edwards & Walsh (1963)
P:4		$\overline{S_{i.}} = f(\overline{S_{.j}})$	Goldberg (present report)
P:4a		$a_{.j} = f(S_{.j})$	
P:4b		$A_{..} = f(\overline{S_{.j}})$	
P:4c		$a_{..} = f(A_{..})$	
P:4d		$a_{..} = f(\overline{Sj_{..}})$	
P:4e		$A_{..} = f(\overline{S_{i.}})$	
P:5		$I_{..} = f(\overline{S_{.j}})$	Edwards & Walsh (1963)
P:5a		$I_{..} = f(a_{..})$	
P:5b		$I_{..} = f(A_{..})$	
T:5		$I_{..} = f(\overline{S_{i.}})$	

Notation: i = individuals ; j = occasions ; k = items (omitted from the notation)
D = item difficulty
d = perceived self-item distance
p = endorsement frequency (proportion) ; $\lvert .5 - p \rvert$ = item balance
I = response instability (proportion of responses changed)
S = dispersion of item boundary positions
L = response latency
O = percentage of individuals omitting item (or placing item in " ? " category)
R = "difficulty" ratings
a = "ambiguity" ratings
A = Ambdex values
[a bar over a symbol indicates a mean value taken over the indicated subscript]

was found to be related to the extremeness of item positioning on the social desirability dimension (as independently assessed by ratings from 47 male and 48 female college students) and item stability was negatively related to the variance of these social desirability ratings. Moreover, this study replicated that of Dodd and Svalastoga (1952) in demonstrating that item stability was

first poll and the percentage of responses changed between poll and re-poll. Another demonstration of the same theorem has been provided in a study in which consistency of response to an 11-item attitude scale was shown to be inversely related to response latency (Crockett, Bates, & Caylor, 1958).

Postulate (4) of the ambiguity model states that inter-individual variation in

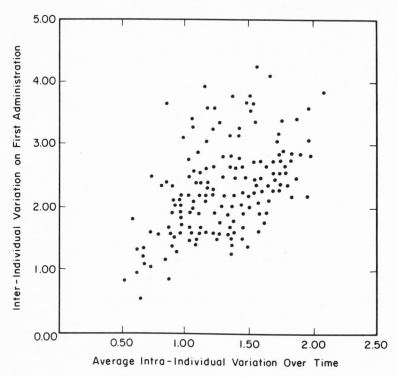

Figure 6. Average inter-individual variation vs. average intra-individual variation for ten subjects positioning 160 adjectives on a social desirability continuum over ten administrations.

inversely related to the percentage of subjects utilizing a middle, or "?," category when this response option is permitted. In Dodd and Svalastoga's study, 271 respondents in a poll on national affairs replied by mail to a second poll in which seven questions from the original poll were embedded. For these seven repeated questions, a correlation of .91 was found between the percentage of "don't know" responses on the

the positioning of an item's boundary should be directly related to the average intra-individual variation of boundary positioning over repeated administrations of the item. Evidence supporting this assumption can be seen in Figure 6.

The data plotted in Figure 6 come from a study in which 160 adjectives were administered on ten occasions (approximately one-week interval between administrations) to ten University of Oregon undergraduates; the task of the subjects was to position each adjective on the underlying attribute continuum of "Social Desirability," defined for them in approximately the same manner as that used by Edwards (1957). The correlation between variation in item positioning inter-individually and variation in item positioning intra-individually (over time) was .52.

Summary

A major stumbling block to improved personality scales may arise from defects in the initial item pool utilized for scale construction. One of the most important defects of both early and recent personality test items may be their ambiguity, here considered as a property of the item which tends to elicit marked intra-individual variability in response over repeated test administrations. Conventional measures of item instability (i.e., the percentage of subjects changing their responses to an item upon its repeated administration) have been shown to be closely related to item endorsement frequency and thus can be shown to have rather severe limitations as indices of ambiguity. This paper attempts to integrate existing knowledge concerning item instability, and a model of item ambiguity and response instability is presented. An item statistic, Ambdex, derived from the model is proposed as a preliminary index of item ambiguity, and its use as an item selection statistic is discussed.

REFERENCES

AIKEN, L. R., JR. "Frequency and Intensity as Psychometric Response Variables." *Psychological Reports,* XI (1962), 535–538.

BAIN, R. "Stability in Questionnaire Response." *American Journal of Sociology,* XXXVII (1931), 445–453.

BENTON, A. L. "The Interpretation of Questionnaire Items in a Personality Schedule." *Archives of Psychology,* XC (1935), #190.

BENTON, A. L., and STONE, I. R. "Consistency of Response to Personality Inventory Items as a Function of Length of Interval between Test and Retest." *Journal of Social Psychology,* VIII (1937), 143–146.

BERG, I. A. "The Unimportance of Test Item Content." In B. M. BASS and I. BERG (Eds.) *Objective Approaches to Personality Assessment.* New York: Van Nostrand, 1959, 83–99.

BILLS, R. E., VANCE, E. L., and McLEAN, O. S. "An Index of Adjustment and Values." *Journal of Consulting Psychology,* XV (1951), 257–261.

BROEN, W. E., JR. "Ambiguity and Discriminating Power in Personality Inventories." *Journal of Consulting Psychology,* XXIV (1960), 174–179.

BUSS, A. H. "The Effect of Item Style on Social Desirability and Frequency of Endorsement." *Journal of Consulting Psychology,* XXIII (1959), 510–513.

BUSS, A. H., and DURKEE, A. "An Inventory for Assessing Different Kinds of Hostility." *Journal of Consulting Psychology,* XXI (1957), 343–349.

CATTELL, R. B. *Personality and Motivation: Structure and Measurement.* New York: World Book Company, 1957, 589–631.

CHANCE, JUNE E. "Prediction of Changes in a Personality Inventory on Retesting." *Psychological Reports,* I (1955), 383–387.

COOMBS, C. H. "A Theory of Psychological Scaling." University of Michigan Bulletin, No. 34, Engineering Research Institute, 1952.

CROCKETT, W. H., BATES, C., JR., and CAYLOR, J. S. "Intra-judge Consistency and Inter-judge Agreement in Responses to Attitude Scale Items." *Educational and Psychological Measurement,* XVIII (1958), 597–605.

DODD, S. C., and SVALASTOGA, K. "On Estimating Latent from Manifest Undecidedness: The 'Don't Know' Percent as a Warning of Instability among the

Knowers." *Educational and Psychological Measurement,* XII (1952), 467–471.

EDWARDS, A. L. *The Social Desirability Variable in Personality Assessment and Research.* New York: Dryden Press, 1957.

EDWARDS, A. L., and WALSH, J. A. "Relationships between Various Psychometric Properties of Personality Items." *Educational and Psychological Measurement,* XXIII (1963), 227–238.

EISENBERG, P., and WESMAN, A. G. "Consistency in Response and Logical Interpretation of Psychoneurotic Inventory Items." *Journal of Educational Psychology,* XXXII (1941), 321–338.

ELLIOTT, L. L. "Effects of Item Construction and Respondent Aptitude on Response Acquiescence." *Educational and Psychological Measurement,* XXII (1961), 405–415.

FARNSWORTH, P. R. "A Genetic Study of the Bernreuter Personality Inventory." *Journal of Genetic Psychology,* LII (1938), 3–13.

FISKE, D. W. "The Constraints on Intra-individual Variability in Test Responses." *Educational and Psychological Measurement,* XVII (1957), 317–337.

FISKE, D. W. "The Inherent Variability of Behavior." In D. W. FISKE and S. R. MADDI (Eds.) *Functions of Varied Experience.* Homewood: Dorsey Press, 1961.

FISKE, D. W., and RICE, L. "Intra-individual Response Variability." *Psychological Bulletin,* LII (1955), 217–250.

FRANK, B. "Stability of Questionnaire Response." *Journal of Abnormal and Social Psychology,* XXX (1936), 320–324.

GLASER, R. "A Methodological Analysis of the Inconsistency of Response to Test Items." *Educational and Psychological Measurement,* XIV (1949), 727–739.

GOLDFRIED, M. R., and McKENZIE, J. D., JR. "Sex Differences in the Effect of Item Style on Social Desirability and Frequency of Endorsement." *Journal of Consulting Psychology,* XXVI (1962), 126–128.

GREEN, B. F. "Attitude Measurement." In G. LINDZEY (Ed.) *Handbook of Social Psychology.* New York: Addison-Wesley, 1954.

HANLEY, C. "Responses to the Wording of Personality Test Items." *Journal of*

Consulting Psychology, XXIII (1959), 261–265.

HANLEY, C. "The 'Difficulty' of a Personality Inventory Item." *Educational and Psychological Measurement,* XXII (1962), 577–584.

HERTZMAN, M., and GOULD, R. "The Functional Significance of Changed Responses in a Psychoneurotic Inventory." *Journal of Abnormal and Social Psychology,* XXXIV (1939), 336–350.

HORN, D. "Intra-individual Variability in the Study of Personality." *Journal of Clinical Psychology,* VI (1950), 43–47.

ISARD, E. S. "The Relationship between Item Ambiguity and Discriminating Power in a Forced-Choice Scale." *Journal of Applied Psychology,* XL (1956), 266–268.

JACKSON, D. N., and MESSICK, S. "Content and Style in Personality Assessment." *Psychological Bulletin,* LV (1958), 243–252.

JACKSON, J. M. "The Stability of Guilford-Zimmerman Personality Measures." *Journal of Applied Psychology,* XLV (1961), 431–434.

KELLY, E. L. "Consistency of the Adult Personality." *American Psychologist,* XI (1956), 659–681.

LENTZ, T. F. "Reliability of the Opinionaire Technique Studied Intensively by the Retest Method." *Journal of Social Psychology,* V (1934), 338–364.

MEEHL, P. E. "The 'Dynamics' of Structured Personality Tests." *Journal of Clinical Psychology,* I (1945), 296–303.

MITRA, S. K., and FISKE, D. W. "Intra-individual Variability as Related to Test Score and Item." *Educational and Psychological Measurement,* XVI (1956), 3–12.

NEPRASH, J. A. "The Reliability of Questions in the Thurstone Personality Schedule." *Journal of Social Psychology,* VII (1936), 239–244.

OWENS, W. A., GLENNON, J. R., and ALBRIGHT, L. E. "Retest Consistency and the Writing of Life History Items: A First Step." *Journal of Applied Psychology,* XLVI (1962), 329–331.

PINTNER, R., and FORLANO, G. "Four Retests of a Personality Inventory." *Journal of Educational Psychology,* XXIX (1938), 93–100.

RUST, R. M. "A Comparison of Statistical Indices of Item Stability and Subject Stability." Paper read at Western Psychological Association meetings, 1961.

SECORD, P. F., and BACKMAN, C. W. "Personality Theory and the Problem of Stability and Change in Individual Behavior: An Interpersonal Approach." *Psychological Review*, LXVIII (1961), 21–32.

SMITH, M. "A Note on Stability in Questionnaire Response." *American Journal of Sociology*, XXXVIII (1933), 713–720.

STRICKER, L. J. "Some Item Characteristics that Evoke Acquiescent and Social Desirability Response Sets on Psychological Scales." Unpublished Ph.D. thesis, New York University, 1960.

STRONG, E. K., JR. "Good and Poor Interest Test Items." *Journal of Applied Psychology*, XLVI (1962), 269–275.

WIGGINS, J. S. "Strategic, Method and Stylistic Variance in the MMPI." *Psychological Bulletin*, LIX (1962), 224–242.

WIGGINS, NANCY. "On the Mathematical Relationship between Ambdex and *r*-Tetrachoric." Unpublished paper, 1961.

Chapter 6

Problems of Structured Tests: Response Sets and Biases

■ The graduate student's frustrations are many and his satisfactions few. One of the few activities which can yield pleasure while not significantly retarding his progress toward a degree or increasing the size of his family is the game of Academic One-upmanship, also known as pseudo-constructive destructive criticism. In recent years a new strategy has been added to the list of this game's classic gambits. This is the "response set ploy." To use the response set ploy, the player waits until his opponent has described some proposed, or, better yet, some recently accomplished research. The player then sighs deeply, shakes his head sadly, and with apparently great reluctance says, "Yes, but couldn't your results be explained just as well in terms of Social Desirability?" The only known defense for this ploy is for the opponent to answer contemptuously, "Of course not," and to continue his presentation. Since there are few situations in which the opponent has the design and/or the coolness to use this defense, the response set ploy is almost always successful and the player is then "One up."[1] What are response sets and what is it about them that makes this ploy so popular and effective?

A response set may be roughly defined as some factor other than the content of items which influences a person's response to a test. This could be the subject's desire to present an overly favorable or unfavorable picture of himself (dissimulation), a tendency to answer in a direction regarded by others as socially desirable or undesirable (SD) or a tendency to agree or disagree with items (Set Acquiescence or Disagreement).

Of these response sets, dissimulation is the most obvious and received the first attention of test constructors and users. The first efforts to control dissimulation focused on the identification of the distorted test protocol. This was done by the construction of validity scales designed to show a significant elevation if the respondent presented an overly favorable or unfavorable picture. Other tactics included using forced choice answers and the construction of suppressor scales.

[1] This applies only if the opponent is of equal or less status. If the student attempts this ploy against a faculty member he is likely to find himself not only "down" but "out."

While these measures have been fairly successful (*vide* Gough, 1950), the interpretability of a dissembled profile is still a matter of doubt. Some hold that it should be discarded altogether; others attempt to interpret it while making allowances for the response set. Canter investigates the effects of the relationships between the ability to present a good picture and the actual adjustment of a person. If such a relation is found, then the ability to "fake good" would in itself be an important diagnostic indicator and not merely a source of error variance.

In recent years, psychologists have become increasingly concerned with the response set of Social Desirability, the conscious or unconscious tendency of some subjects to respond in a socially desirable or undesirable fashion. This variable has been assessed in a variety of ways, but the usual measure has been Allen Edwards' SD scale and the studies from his laboratory have provided the momentum for much of the SD research. In the next article, Edwards summarizes some of his work on SD and the relationship he has found between measures of SD and the MMPI. He indicates that he regards the tendency to respond in a socially desirable or undesirable manner as a basic personality trait, and he feels that it is this trait that many MMPI scales are sensitive to rather than the constructs which they purport to measure. The SD scale has often been regarded as if it were solely a measure of conscious or unconscious dissimulation, although in an early article Edwards (1953) pointed out that it could also be an index of a person's adjustment to the values of his culture. In the next paper Megargee attempts to determine whether the SD scale reflects dissimulation, adjustment, or both.

The final response set which we shall examine is the tendency to endorse items regardless of content. This has been christened "Set Acquiescence," or, more euphoniously, "Yeasaying." Since Jung, it has been difficult for psychologists to posit a trait without also delineating its opposite, so in opposition to "Yeasaying" we naturally have "Naysaying," the tendency to reject items regardless of content. As in the case of SD, the tendency to "Yeasay" or "Naysay" has been hypothesized to be a "central personality syndrome." It has been suggested that this tendency may be determined early in life, as "Yeasayers" and "Naysayers," ". . . tend toward opposite resolutions of the 'anal' problems around control of impulses" (Couch and Keniston, 1960, p. 541).

The reader who is unfamiliar with this literature might wonder how the tendency to say "true" or "false" came to have anal implications. While Cronbach (1946) had pointed out the importance of response sets some time ago, the major impetus for this research came not from the area of psychometrics but instead from personality research. The publication of *The Authoritarian Personality* (Adorno, *et al.*, 1950) stimulated a great deal of research, much of it using the California F Scale which was hypothesized to measure authoritarianism. It was not long before it was noted that a person who tended to acquiesce would score high on the F scale. When the items in the F scale were reversed, it was found that many people agreed both to the original item and to its logical opposite. It therefore seemed that the act of agreeing was more important than the content of the item. While this research was hindered by the difficulty of adequately reversing many items, nevertheless it served to launch the study of agreeing response set as an independent area of research, significant not only for personality but also for psychological measurement.[2]

Whether or not acquiescence is as broad or important a personality trait as was once believed, nevertheless it could still be a major source of variance on verbal psychometric tests. Research has generally taken two directions. The first has been the straightforward investigation of influence of "Yea-" or "Naysaying" in various personality inventories. The second direction was an adroit movement designed to outflank the SD researchers. Since Edwards' SD scale contained a preponderance of items keyed "True" it was possible to regard it, too, as a measure of acquiescence and thereby claim that all the correlations Edwards had obtained were nothing more than a demonstration of the importance of Set Acquiescence in personality testing. Edwards (1961) soon conducted studies designed to disprove this claim. He indicated that social desirability was so much stronger a response set that it was likely that scores on personality scales are, ". . . relatively little influenced by acquiescent tendencies, regardless of whether or not there is an imbalance in the True-False keying of the items" (Edwards, 1961, p. 359).

In the present chapter, Messick and Jackson review several studies of the influence of acquiescence on the MMPI and conclude that ". . . the findings offer clear evidence that acquiescence, as moderated by item desirability, plays a dominant role in personality inventories like the MMPI." On the other hand, Goldberg and Rorer report a study on the basis of which they conclude that "The results indicate that 'acquiescence response style' can be of no more than trivial importance in determining responses to the MMPI."

The issue joined here has been continued in other papers in which Rorer and Goldberg (1964) and Jackson and Messick (1965) have continued to disagree about the importance of acquiescence in structure tests.

If these conflicting interpretations as to the role of the various response sets arouse a modicum of cognitive dissonance in the reader, he can attempt to reduce this by reading some of the studies cited above and also by consulting the papers of Jackson and Messick (1958), Block (1962), and Wiggins

---

[2] The reader who wishes to familiarize himself with some of this work would do well to read the papers by Titus and Hollander; Bass; Christie, Havel, and Seidenberg; and Couch and Keniston which have been reprinted by Mednick and Mednick (1963). More recently, McGee (1962a, 1962b, 1962c) has taken issue with the pervasiveness of "Yeasaying" as a personality variable and, on the basis of studies using both verbal and non-verbal reponse measures, has concluded there is no general trait of response acquiescence.

(1962). If he wants to demonstrate high Need Achievement he can also consult Rorer's (1963) exhaustive review and start working his way through the 461 references from Abrams, E. N. to Zuckerman, M.

Whether responses are caused by dissimulation, SD, or "Yeasaying," there appears to be general agreement among the workers in the response set vineyard that content is of relatively little importance. In an oft-quoted statement, Jackson and Messick (1958, p. 247) trenchantly stated, "In the light of accumulating evidence it seems likely that the *major common factors in personality inventories of the true-false or agree-disagree type,* such as the MMPI and the California Psychological Inventory, *are interpretable primarily in terms of style rather than specific item content.*"[3]

Not all clinicians have been acquiescent in accepting this notion. Block, in a recent award-winning monograph, has vigorously challenged the notion that such response sets as acquiescence and SD play a dominant role in personality inventories and on the basis of several studies which he conducted contends, ". . . (1) acquiescent-response set is *not* a significant component underlying the MMPI and (2) the social desirability interpretation, although seemingly applicable in many MMPI contexts, has achieved its support for fortuitous and epiphenomenal reasons" (Block, 1964, p. 2f).

The reader must evaluate the evidence for himself and reach his own conclusions. But if he should decide that the workers in the response set vineyard who maintain that content is unimportant are correct, what are the implications for the workers in the clinical vineyard? Does it mean that inventories are useless or invalid?

In approaching this question, Campbell's (1960) distinction between practical and trait validity is helpful. Practical validity refers to the ability of a test to predict a criterion, while trait validity is the adequacy of the test as a measure of some construct. The practicing clinician is primarily concerned with the former and the personality researcher with the latter.

To demonstrate, Barron's (1953) Es scale for the MMPI was derived by contrasting groups of patients who responded to psychotherapy with others who did not. It was inferred that the trait which distinguished these two criterion groups was "ego strength" and so the scale was called the "Ego Strength" scale (Dahlstrom and Welsh, 1960). In terms of practical validity, if the clinician can use this scale to predict successful response to therapy, it is irrelevant whether the scale *really* measures ego strength or is instead a measure of SD or Naysaying. The ability to predict the criterion is all that counts. The personality theorist, however, is more concerned with trait validity. If he uses the Es scale as an operational definition of "ego strength" in an experiment, his interpretations of the data are bound to be ambiguous if he should find there is a significant correlation between Es and SD, for the

---

[3] Authors' italics.

212   *Studies of Specific Techniques of Assessment*

theoretical implications of "ego strength" and "social desirability" are considerably different.

Response sets, then, are important in assessing the trait validity of a scale, but may be irrelevant to its practical validity. In the concluding article, Charles Dicken reports the results of a study designed to determine how response sets affect the practical validity of the C.P.I.

REFERENCES

ADORNO, T. W., FENKEL-BRUNSWIK, ELSE, LEVINSON, D. J., & SANFORD, R. N. *The Authoritarian Personality.* New York: Harper & Row, 1950.

BARRON, F. An ego-strength scale which predicts response to psychotherapy. *Journal of Consulting Psychology,* 1953, **17,** 327–333.

BLOCK, J. Some differences between the concepts of social desirability and adjustment. *Journal of Consulting Psychology,* 1962, **26,** 527–530.

BLOCK, J. *The challenge of response sets.* New York: Appleton-Century Crofts, 1965.

CAMPBELL, D. T. Recommendations for APA test standards regarding construct, trait, or discriminant validity. *American Psychologist,* 1960, **15,** 546–553.

COUCH, A., & KENISTON, K. Yeasayers and naysayers: agreeing response set as a personality variable. *Journal of Abnormal and Social Psychology,* 1960, **60,** 151–174. Reprinted in MEDNICK, MARTHA, & MEDNICK, S. *Research in Personality.* New York: Holt, Rinehart and Winston, 1963, 510–542.

CRONBACH, L. J. Response sets and test validity. *Educational and Psychological Measurement,* 1946, **6,** 475–494.

DAHLSTROM, W. J., & WELSH, G. S. *An MMPI Handbook: A Guide to Use in Clinical Practice in Research.* Minneapolis: University of Minnesota Press, 1960.

EDWARDS, A. L. The relationship between the judged desirability of a trait and the probability that the trait will be endorsed. *Journal of Consulting Psychology,* 1953, **37,** 90–93.

EDWARDS, A. L. Social desirability or acquiescence in the MMPI? A case study with the SD scale. *Journal of Abnormal and Social Psychology,* 1961, **63,** 351–359.

GOUGH, H. G. The F minus K dissimulation index for the MMPI. *Journal of Consulting Psychology,* 1950, **14,** 408–413.

JACKSON, D. N., & MESSICK, S. Content and style in personality assessment. *Psychological Bulletin,* 1958, **55,** 243–251.

JACKSON, D. N., & MESSICK, S. Acquiescence: The nonvanishing variance component. *American Psychologist,* 1965, **20,** 498. (Abstract)

MCGEE, R. F. The relationship between response style and personality variables: I. The measurement of response acquiescence. *Journal of Abnormal and Social Psychology,* 1962, **64,** 229–233. (a)

MCGEE, R. K. The relationship between response style and personality variables: II. The prediction of independent conformity behavior. *Journal of Abnormal and Social Psychology,* 1962, **65,** 347–351. (b)

MCGEE, R. K. Response style as a personality variable: By what criterion? *Psychological Bulletin,* 1962, **59,** 284–295. (c)

MEDNICK, MARTHA T., & MEDNICK, S. A. *Research in Personality.* New York: Holt, Rinehart and Winston, 1963.

RORER, L. G. The great response style myth. *Oregon Research Institute, Research Monograph,* 1963, **3,** No. 6, 1–125.

RORER, L. G., & GOLDBERG, L. R. Acquiescence and the vanishing variance component. *Oregon Research Institute Research Bulletin,* 1964, **4,** No. 2, 1–24.

WIGGINS, J. S. Strategic, method, and stylistic variance in the MMPI. *Psychological Bulletin,* 1962, **59,** 224–242.

Simulation on the California Psychological Inventory and the Adjustment of the Simulator

Francis M. Canter

Most studies on the susceptibility of questionaire-type personality tests to deliberate distortion by the subject have used college students or other relatively well-functioning people as subjects. They have usually been asked to take the test under the standard "honest" conditions and then again under instructions to distort the picture in some specified way, with comparison of the score differences as indication of the degree to which the test is vulnerable to "faking." In the *Manual for the California Psychological Inventory* (Gough, 1957) there is evidence that subjects can change their scores on this test to a considerable extent, although this usually resulted in tell-tale changes in the Wb, Gi, or Cm scales. Some tests attempt to correct for these possibilities of "faking" by the addition of validating scales, e.g., the K and L scales of the MMPI, or by forcing a choice between two items of previously determined equal social desirability (Edwards, 1957).

Relatively little attention has been paid to the actual personal adjustment of the subject or his own "natural" inclinations to present himself in the best possible light. In a recent study (Dicken, 1960) a relationship was found between ability to simulate a "good" profile on the California Psychological Inventory (CPI) and the sophistication and techni-

cal knowledge of the subject. Grayson and Olinger (1957), using psychiatric patients as subjects, found that some of their patients under "fake good" instructions could change their MMPI profiles in certain ways and that ability to do this was related to favorability of prognosis for discharge from the hospital. These studies employed the technique of giving instructions to fake good with subjects who presumably had no special motivation to answer other than honestly under the standard instructions. A point of possible theoretical and practical importance is the ability of subjects to present a "good" picture under standard instructions, where there is presumed strong motivation to present such a picture and the relationship of this ability to the subject's actual life adjustment. It is specifically suggested that falsification of test scores and the capacity to do so may be a personality variable of considerable importance in its own right rather than merely an undesirable and incidental factor to be "corrected for."

The present study compared the CPI responses of two groups, each group presumably strongly motivated to present themselves in a favorable light, one group being objectively "well adjusted" and the other "poorly adjusted." Additionally, the performance of the poorly adjusted group under fake good instructions was examined in relationship to rated degree of adjustment and was compared with the well-adjusted group's performance under fake good instructions.

Reprinted by permission of the American Psychological Association and the author from the *Journal of Consulting Psychology*, 1963, **27**, 253–256.

Method

Subjects

The subjects of the study consisted of a group of 50 male alcoholic patients in a state hospital and a group of 50 male applicants for the position of aide at this same hospital. The alcoholic patients (poorly adjusted) were all involuntary admissions who were committed to the hospital for an indefinite period. The applicants, who were accepted for employment and worked for periods of at least 6 months and usually much longer, were rated periodically on their effectiveness and personal adjustment. Only those with a satisfactory rating after at least 6 months were included in the well-adjusted group. In other respects, the groups did not differ significantly from each other. The applicants and the patients came from the same general socioeconomic backgrounds with occupations in the farming, small tradesman, salesman, factory worker, or construction labor areas. Median age for the alcoholic group was 41 and was 43 for the applicant group. Median years of school was, for both groups, 11. Mean Raven Progressive Matrices score was at the sixtieth percentile for the alcoholics and the sixty-third percentile for the applicants.

Procedure

The applicants were examined with the California Psychological Inventory and the Raven Progressive Matrices prior to acceptance for employment. They were given to understand that employment depended in part upon "satisfactory performance" on the psychological tests. It is assumed that these applicants were highly motivated to present a favorable picture on the California Psychological Inventory.

The alcoholic patients were examined within 5 days after admission (their first admission to this hospital) with a battery of psychological tests including the California Psychological Inventory and the Raven Matrices. These patients were involuntary and quite anxious to be discharged from the hospital as soon as possible. They did not regard themselves as "mental patients," felt insulted or put upon by their commitment to a mental hospital, and emphasized, in individual interviews and groups meetings, their basic normality and lack of difference from other people except for their bad habit of drinking too much. The psychological examination was regarded by these patients as an effort to find out whether they were "crazy" or not, particularly since the test battery was prefaced with the Rorschach. In general, it may be said that these patients regarded themselves, at least consciously, as personally "normal" except for the isolated area of drinking (which they were inclined to attribute to their biochemistry) and had ample motivation to convince the hospital staff of their eligibility for discharge at the earliest possible date.

Of this group of 50 patients, 30 who were still available were requested to take the CPI again with instruction to:

imagine you are applying for a job you really want and your employer will judge from this test whether to hire you or not. Answer the test in such a way as to give the best possible impression of yourself.

These 30 patients were then rated for general adjustment and acceptance of their drinking problem according to this scale:

1. Past history: Maximum score of 8 points with 1 point each for items relating to the patient's work stability, maintenance of family relationships, no previous hospitalization for drinking, freedom from legal difficulties, and definite efforts to handle drinking by resort to Antabuse, Alcoholics Anonymous, or psychiatric help

2. Locally devised questionaire: Maximum score of 4 points, based upon 34

items dealing with present acceptance of drinking problem

3. Interview: Maximum score of 4 points, given for acceptance of self as personally maladjusted with drinking as a symptom, 2 points for considering self as "normal" but with a drinking problem, and no points for regarding self as normal and with no drinking problem.

Scores on this rating of relative adjustment ranged from 2 to 16 with a median score of 9.5. The 15 subjects in the upper half were compared with the 15 subjects in the lower half. These two groups did not differ significantly on such variables as age, education, Raven score, or average scores on the standard administration of the CPI.

Seventeen of the applicants who were available were also asked to take the CPI under the fake good instructions. Because of circumstances, these tests were obtained after the applicant had been hired.

Results and Discussion

In Table 1 are presented the individual scale average raw scores of the alcoholics as a group and the applicants as a group under standard instructions. The differences between the two groups are highly significant on all scales except the Cm scale. In Table 2 are presented the individual scale average raw scores of the Applicants, the Better Adjusted Alcoholics, and the Poorer Adjusted Alcoholics (designated as Groups A, B, and C, respectively) under the fake good instructions. All groups are able to improve their scores but the Applicants show more improvement than the Better Adjusted Alcoholics and these, in turn, show more improvement than the Poorer Adjusted Alcoholics. Although, there are fewer statistically significant differences between groups under the faking condition, the general trend of the scores is consistent.

These results suggest that, under standard conditions of administration

TABLE 1. CALIFORNIA PSYCHOLOGICAL INVENTORY RAW SCORES OF ALCOHOLIC AND APPLICANT GROUPS: NORMAL ADMINISTRATION

Scale	Alcoholic (N = 50) M	SD	Applicant (N = 50) M	SD	t
Do	21.9	5.0	32.1	5.9	9.18**
Cs	14.8	4.5	20.8	4.4	6.70**
Sy	20.8	5.3	26.9	3.7	6.57**
Sp	31.0	6.1	35.6	5.8	3.83**
Sa	17.4	3.9	22.3	4.5	5.77**
Wb	34.9	8.4	40.6	4.2	4.22**
Re	26.1	4.1	32.9	4.6	7.76**
So	29.3	6.1	39.2	4.3	8.50**
Sc	26.8	7.9	34.7	6.3	5.48**
To	16.9	4.8	24.6	5.2	7.62**
Gi	14.3	6.0	23.8	6.8	7.31**
Cm	26.4	1.5	26.6	1.7	0.62
Ac	23.3	4.7	31.0	4.8	8.03**
Ai	14.5	3.9	19.5	5.0	5.52**
Ie	32.7	5.3	41.0	5.9	7.36**
Py	8.4	2.6	11.6	2.8	5.86**
Fx	6.7	3.6	8.5	4.8	2.11*
Fe	16.3	5.6	17.2	4.8	0.85

* $p < .05$.
** $p < .01$.

and where there is presumed motivation on the part of subjects to present themselves as normal or well adjusted, there is a positive relationship between the ability to present a good picture on the CPI and the actual life adjustment of the subject. In addition, under fake good instructions, subjects are able to improve their test pictures to a considerable degree but even here there is limitation by actual life adjustment. In this connection, it is noted that the Gi scores of all groups under the faking conditions show the expected and usually found peak, indicating a conscious dissembling. However, Gough (1957) has pointed out that individuals obtaining high Gi scores do, in fact, tend to create a better impression on others and show some realistically better adjustment.

A central issue here is possibly the question of what is meant by dishonesty in answering questionaire items. (Probably, the results of the standard admini-stration are more intrinsically meaning-ful in this study than the faking conditions, because instructions to fake something arouse a number of factors which are difficult to assess, including the subject's interpretation of the pur-pose of the procedure, etc.) As men-tioned above, most of the studies on re-sponse set, social desirability, and con-scious faking have used subjects who by conventional criteria are fairly adequate

behavior). This is not contradictory to the findings of Jackson (1960) who concluded that response set and social desirability factors account for much of the variance in the CPI if the subjects in such investigations are individuals from the same cultural matrix with the same "folk" concepts and hence are able readily and naturally to fit into the way of thinking which is reflected as good adjustment on the CPI. Consistent with this is the finding by Sundberg and

TABLE 2.   CALIFORNIA PSYCHOLOGICAL INVENTORY SCORES OF
AIDES AND PATIENTS UNDER INSTRUCTIONS TO FAKE GOOD

Scale	Group A (N = 17) M	SD	Group B (N = 15) M	SD	Group C (N = 15) M	SD	t A–B	B–C
Do	37.2	4.3	35.7	2.0	31.0	9.3	1.25	0.73
Cs	26.8	3.1	23.6	3.0	20.5	4.9	2.88**	1.31
Sy	33.5	4.1	29.4	3.1	26.8	3.9	3.12**	1.46
Sp	40.5	3.8	35.2	4.2	34.9	3.9	3.60**	0.13
Sa	23.7	3.0	22.9	2.8	21.5	2.3	0.74	1.43
Wb	42.8	2.1	41.7	1.8	37.8	4.4	1.54	2.44*
Re	37.7	3.7	35.7	2.2	28.1	6.3	1.83	2.40*
So	43.5	3.1	42.7	2.7	34.3	7.1	0.75	2.04*
Sc	42.0	4.3	39.1	4.2	29.0	7.7	1.87	1.84
To	28.8	3.2	26.2	2.9	18.8	4.6	2.34*	3.65**
Gi	32.5	5.2	29.9	3.4	23.9	5.2	1.64	2.14*
Cm	26.7	1.4	26.5	1.1	25.9	3.1	0.44	0.38
Ac	32.3	4.0	33.5	1.9	26.5	5.6	1.07	2.80**
Ai	21.2	3.0	18.9	3.0	13.9	3.4	2.09*	3.40**
Ie	43.7	3.7	42.4	3.0	35.3	8.6	1.06	1.20
Py	12.9	2.0	12.3	1.6	9.7	2.2	0.90	4.82**
Fx	7.6	2.4	4.7	2.0	3.1	3.0	3.62**	1.72
Fe	14.7	3.8	15.3	4.1	14.9	3.9	0.41	0.13

* $p < .05$.
** $p < .01$.
Note.—Group A = Psychiatric aides; Group B = Better adjusted alcoholic patients; Group C = Poorer adjusted alcoholic patients.

and "socialized" people who at least have a background of personal sociali-zation and experience to help them to fake good. Gough (1948, 1960a, 1960b) has made a significant and central point of the idea that socialized behavior is rooted in the role-taking experiences of development and the asocial or inade-quate person lacks the set of inter-actional expectancies and reaction pat-terns which permit more socially adequate behavior (including answer-ing questionaire items on the relevant

Bachelis (1956) that their subjects were better able to fake bad than fake good on the California F Scale and the Gough Pr scale. From some recent research, Dicken[1] has indicated that efforts to "correct" for response bias on the scales of the CPI resulted in little improvement or even a reduction in validity, suggest-ing that normal scores, response set and all, are meaningful aspects of the "real" personality, just as the ability to fake

[1] C. Dicken, personal communication, Sep-tember, 1962.

good says something meaningful about the person's present or potential adjustment, given the appropriate situation. Thus, a person who can and naturally does answer items in a more socialized way is drawing upon an actual and potential store of possibility for good adjustment than the person who has to concentrate on answering the items "correctly" and this person in turn has more possibility for good adjustment than the person who naturally does not or cannot answer in a socialized manner, even when asked to bend his conscious attention to it.

Summary

This is a study of the relationship between ability to present a good picture on the California Psychological Inventory and the actual life adjustment of S. A group of 50 alcoholics and 50 applicants for Ward Aide positions both highly motivated to appear "normal" were compared. Additionally, a group of well-functioning Aides, a group of Better Adjusted Alcoholics, and a group of Poorer Adjusted Alcoholics were compared under "fake good" instructions. Results indicate a positive relationship between ability to present a good picture, under standard or faking conditions, and the relative adjustment of S. The results are related to Gough's concepts of socialization and it is concluded that these questionaire responses are meaningful aspects of the personality and not simply sets to be corrected for.

REFERENCES

DICKEN, C. F. Simulated patterns on the California Psychological Inventory. *J. counsel. Psychol.*, 1960, **7**, 24–31.

EDWARDS, A. L. *The social desirability variable in personality assessment and research.* New York: Dryden, 1957.

GOUGH, H. G. A sociological theory of psychopathy. *Amer. J. Sociol.*, 1948, **53**, 359–366.

GOUGH, H. G. *Manual for the California Psychological Inventory.* Palo Alto: Consulting Psychologists Press, 1957.

GOUGH, H. G. Cross-cultural studies of the socialization continuum. *Amer. Psychologist*, 1960, **15**, 410–411. (Abstract) (a)

GOUGH, H. G. Theory and measurement of socialization *J. consult. Psychol.*, 1960, **24**, 23–30. (b)

GRAYSON, N. M., & OLINGER, L. B. Simulation of "normalcy" by psychiatric patients on the MMPI. *J. consult. Psychol.*, 1957, **21**, 73–77.

JACKSON, D. N. Stylistic response determinants in the California Psychological Inventory. *Educ. psychol. Measmt*, 1960, **20**, 339–346.

SUNDBERG, N. D., & BACHELIS, W. D. The fakability of two measures of prejudice: The California F Scale and Gough's *Pr* scale. *J. abnorm. soc. Psychol.*, 1956, **52**, 140–142.

Social Desirability and Performance on the MMPI

Allen L. Edwards

I

Given a set of statements of the kind ordinarily found in personality scales and inventories, it is possible to have judges rate each statement in terms of how socially desirable or undesirable they consider the content of the statement to be. The distributions of ratings assigned to the statements can then be used to find the social desirability scale values of the statements. Once the social desirability scale values of the statements have been obtained, we have a basis for ordering the statements on a psychological continuum of social desirability ranging from highly socially undesirable, through neutral, to highly socially desirable.

There is now considerable evidence to show that when a representative or random set of personality statements is rated for social desirability by different groups of judges, the relative ordering of the statements on the social desirability continuum is much the same from group to group. The product-moment correlations between scale values derived from the judgments of two different but comparable groups of judges are typically .90 or greater [12, 19, 22, 38]. Even when social desirability scale values are derived

Preparation of this paper was supported in part by Research Grant M-4075 from the National Institute of Mental Health, United States Public Health Service.

Reprinted by permission of the publisher and author from *Psychometrika*, 1964, **29**, 295–308.

from the judgments of such diverse groups within our own culture as high school students [33], Nisei [27], psychotic patients [5, 34, 39], sex offenders [6], alcoholics [43], novice nuns [44], and a geriatric sample [3], the correlations between the scale values are generally found to be .85 or higher.

Cross culturally, it has been found that scale values based upon the judgments of Norwegian students correlate .78 with those based upon the judgments of American students [36]. Scale values based upon the judgments of students at the University of Beirut in Lebanon were found to correlate .86 with those based upon the judgments of American college students [35]. Iwawaki and Cowen [30] found that scale values based upon the judgments of students at the Japanese Defense Academy correlated .90 with those based upon the judgments of American college students. Cowen and Frenkel [4] have reported a correlation of .95 between the scale values derived from the judgments of French students and those derived from the judgments of American students. Furthermore, they found that the French scale values correlated .85 with Japanese scale values. It is of some social-psychological significance that cultural norms of what is considered desirable and undesirable in the way of personality traits and characteristics are so similar in such countries as Norway, Japan, Lebanon, France, and the United States, despite other differences which may exist between these nations.

II

If a set of personality statements is administered to a group of subjects with instructions to describe themselves by answering each statement True or False, we can find for this sample the percentage answering each statement True. I refer to this percentage as the probability that an item will be endorsed in self-description under the *standard* instructions ordinarily used in administering personality scales and inventories. If the social desirability scale values of the statements are also known, then it is possible to determine the relationship between probability of endorsement and social desirability scale value.

For a set of 140 personality statements, I found that probability of endorsement was a linear increasing function of social desirability scale value, the product-moment correlation between the two variables being .87 [11]. A correlation of this magnitude might be considered an artifact, either of the particular set of statements investigated or of the particular group of subjects tested, but subsequent research has shown that the relationship holds for all of the sets of statements which have been investigated provided the statements do not have a restricted range of social desirability scale values [7, 8, 12, 13, 14, 28, 32, 39]. The largest population we have studied consists of 2,824 descriptive statements of personality. For a serial sample of 176 statements drawn from this larger population of 2,824 statements, James Walsh and I found a correlation of .92 between probability of endorsement and social desirability scale value [22].

There is evidence to show that the relationship observed between probability of endorsement and social desirability scale value is not uniquely characteristic of American college students, but that it holds true for other diverse groups within our own culture

as well [8, 39]. In fact, there is reason to believe that probability of endorsement should be substantially correlated with social desirability scale value in cultures other than our own [17].

III

If we know the social desirability scale value of a statement, then it is possible to define the concept of a *socially desirable response* to the statement. I originally defined a socially desirable response as a True response to a statement with a socially desirable scale value or as a False response to a statement with a socially undesirable scale value, leaving the concept undefined for statements with precisely neutral scale values of 5.0 on a 9-point social desirability rating scale [12]. I regard the tendency to respond True to statements with socially desirable scale values and False to statements with socially undesirable scale values as a general personality trait.

A scale designed to measure the tendency to give socially desirable responses in self-description under the standard instructions ordinarily employed with personality scales and inventories is called a Social Desirability (SD) scale [12]. In an SD scale all of the items are keyed for socially desirable responses. Since the concept of a socially desirable response is, of necessity, undefined for items with precisely neutral scale values, items of this kind would not be included in an SD scale. In fact, we have found that responses to items falling within the neutral interval, 4.5 to 5.5 on a 9-point scale, are, in general, less consistent than and not highly correlated with responses to items falling outside the neutral interval. The various SD scales we have developed have thus consisted of items with scale values falling to the left of 4.5 or to the right of 5.5 on the 9-point rating scale.

Fig. 1 shows the social desirability

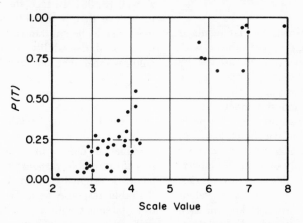

Figure 1. Social desirability scale values and probabilities of endorsement for 39 items in the SD scale.

scale values and probabilities of endorsement for a 39-item *SD* scale, based on items from the Minnesota Multiphasic Personality Inventory (*MMPI*), which I have used in much of my research. The 30 items with scale values falling to the left or socially undesirable end of the continuum are keyed False and the 9 items with scale values on the socially desirable end of the continuum are keyed True. Scores on this 39-item *SD* scale have a test-retest reliability of approximately .87 and the internal consistency of the scale, as measured by the Kuder-Richardson Formula 21 (K-R 21), is approximately .82.

IV

Consider now one of the existing personality scales designed to measure some personality trait such as, for example, hostility, cooperativeness, dominance, rigidity, introversion, neuroticism, or the like. For each of these scales there is a scoring key which indicates whether the trait response to an item is keyed True or False. Presumably, individual responses to the items in these scales are content or trait oriented so that individuals who have a high degree

of the trait are assumed to have a higher probability of giving the trait response to each item than individuals who have a low degree of the trait. Thus, if an individual obtains a high score on one of these scales he has given many trait keyed responses and, in this case, it is assumed that he did so because he has a high degree of the trait which the scale was designed to measure. If he obtains a low score he has given few trait keyed responses, and it is assumed, in this instance, that he did so because he has a low degree of the trait which the scale was designed to measure.

If we obtain social desirability scale values for the items in each of these trait scales, than it is also possible to determine whether the trait response to an item is a socially desirable or a socially undesirable response. If all of the items in a given trait scale are keyed for both trait and socially desirable responses, then, obviously, the trait keying and the social desirability keying of the items in the scale are completely confounded. It may be argued that individuals who obtain high scores on the trait scale are responding to the items in terms of the trait which the scale was designed to measure, but it is equally plausible that they are responding to the items in terms of a trait which the scale was *not* designed to measure, namely, the tendency to give socially desirable responses. If the latter is the case, then scores on the trait scale should be positively correlated with an independently constructed measure of the tendency to give socially desirable responses such as the *SD* scale.

Similar considerations apply to trait scales in which the trait keying is identical with the social undesirability keying. If all of the items in a scale are keyed for both trait and socially undesirable responses, then low scores may be obtained by individuals who have little of the trait which the scale was designed to measure. But, if the tendency to give socially desirable responses is also operating, then low scores on the trait scale should also be characteristic of individuals who have strong tendencies to give socially desirable responses. In this case, scores on the trait scale should be negatively correlated with scores on the *SD* scale.

Consider three examples from the MMPI. First, let us take a scale in which the trait keying is confounded with the social undesirability keying. The Psychasthenia (*Pt*) scale of the MMPI is a good example because it contains 48 items of which 47 are keyed for socially undesirable responses. Thus, individuals with strong tendencies to give socially desirable responses, as indicated by high scores on the *SD* scale, would be expected to obtain low scores on the *Pt* scale and the correlation between the two scales should be negative. It is. For a sample of 150 college males, the correlation between the *Pt* and *SD* scales was found to be −.84.

Second, let us take a scale in which the trait keying is confounded with the social desirability keying. An example is the Leadership (*Lp*) scale of the MMPI. This scale contains 50 items with 44 of the 50 items keyed for socially desirable responses. In this instance, we would expect high scores on the *Lp* scale to be associated with high scores on the *SD* scale and the correlation between the two scales should be positive. It is. The obtained correlation between the two scales for the same sample of college males was found to be .77.

As a third example, let us take a scale in which the number of items keyed for socially desirable responses is approximately the same as the number of items keyed for socially undesirable responses. The Masculinity (*Mf*) scale of the MMPI contains 60 items of which approximately half or 28 are keyed for socially desirable responses, and approximately half or 32 are keyed for socially undesirable responses. Since the trait keying of the items in this scale is fairly well balanced for socially desirable and for socially undesirable responses, the scale should have a fairly low correlation with the *SD* scale. It does. For the sample of college males the correlation was −.16.

The three examples I have cited are not isolated cases. For a set of 43 MMPI scales, I found that the correlation between the MMPI scales and the *SD* scale was directly related to the proportion of items in the MMPI scales keyed for socially desirable responses. The product-moment correlation between the proportion of items keyed for socially desirable responses and the observed correlation of the scale with the *SD* scale was .92 [15].

With a correlation of this magnitude, it is obvious that we could predict quite accurately the correlations of MMPI scales with the *SD* scale from knowledge of the proportion of items keyed for socially desirable responses in the scales. And, similarly, we could predict the proportion of items keyed for socially desirable responses in the scales from knowledge of the correlations of the scales with the *SD* scale.

Does it make sense, in this instance, to regard one of these two variables as the independent variable and the other as the dependent variable? I suggest that it does and that it is the proportion of items keyed for socially desirable responses which should be viewed as the independent variable.

For each scale, for example, the proportion of items keyed for socially desirable responses is fixed and known and is not, therefore, something to be predicted. The correlation of a scale with the SD scale, on the other hand, is unknown, is free to vary, and is subject to sampling error. It thus remains to be predicted. Furthermore, we can experimentally manipulate the proportion of items keyed for socially desirable responses in scales, in much the same way that we can manipulate any other independent variable, and we can observe whether the correlations of the scales with the SD scale vary as a result of this experimental manipulation. At the same time, I do not see how we can experimentally vary the correlations of scales with the SD scale unless, of course, we change the proportion of items keyed for socially desirable responses. But to do this would again make the proportion of items keyed for socially desirable responses the independent variable and the correlation of the scale with the SD scale the dependent variable.

V

I suggested previously that items with scale values falling within the neutral interval of the social desirability continuum are relatively insensitive stimuli for eliciting the tendency to give socially desirable responses. If this is the case, then we would expect scales which contain a large proportion of items with scale values in the neutral interval on the social desirability continuum to have lower correlations with the SD scale than scales which have only a small proportion of items falling within the neutral interval. To test this hypothesis, the proportion of items falling within the neutral interval was obtained for each of 60 True-False personality scales. These proportions were then correlated with the absolute values of the correlations of the 60 scales with the SD scale. The resulting product-moment correlation coefficient was $-.52$ [20]. In this study, the average or mean proportion of neutral items in the 60 scales was .24 and the largest proportion was only .53. I would expect a somewhat higher correlation between the proportion of neutral items in a scale and the absolute value of the correlation of the scale with the SD scale, if there were less restriction in the range of the proportion of neutral items.

The results of this study suggest that we may occasionally find a scale which has either a large or a small proportion of items keyed for socially desirable responses and yet the scale may have a relatively low correlation with the SD scale. If the scale values of the items in a scale deviate only moderately from the neutral point, then we would expect the scale to have a lower correlation with the SD scale than a scale in which the items have more extreme social desirability scale values, despite the fact that both scales may have the same proportion of items keyed for socially desirable responses. This hypothesis has been tested and confirmed in a study which James Walsh and I did on the intensity keying of MMPI scales [23].

VI

Consider a scale in which some of the items are keyed for trait *and* socially desirable responses and other items are keyed for trait *and* socially undesirable responses. To be more specific, take the case of two items, both of which are keyed for trait responses, but such that one of the items is keyed for a socially desirable response and the other is keyed for a socially undesirable response. The joint distribution of responses to these two items can be shown by means of a 2 × 2 table, Fig. 2.

If the trait is the only important determiner of responses to the two items, then we would expect the entries in cells b and c to be large relative to the entries in cells a and d and the trait responses to the two items should be positively correlated. But suppose that the tendency to give socially desirable responses is also operating. In this

desirability keying of the items than for scales in which all of the items are keyed for either socially desirable or for socially undesirable responses, provided subjects are to some degree responding to the items in terms of social desirability tendencies. It is also obvious that if all of the items in a trait scale are keyed either for socially desirable responses or for socially undesirable responses and if the tendency to give socially desirable responses is operating, then this tendency will serve to increase the trait correlations between all possible pairs of items.

Item 2

		SD Non-keyed	SUD Trait keyed
Item I	SD Trait keyed	a	b
	SUD Non-keyed	c	d

Figure 2. Joint distribution of responses to two personality items. For Item 1 the trait response is a socially desirable response, whereas for Item 2 the trait response is a socially undesirable response.

instance, we would expect the entries in cells a and d to be increased and those in cells b and c to be decreased relative to what we would have observed in the absence of any tendency to give socially desirable responses to the items. Obviously, if the tendency to give socially desirable responses is operating, then the increased frequencies in cells a and d will serve to lower the correlation between the trait responses to these two items.

The number of item correlations of the kind shown in Fig. 2 is maximized when a scale contains an equal number of items keyed for socially desirable and for socially undesirable responses, that is, in a scale which has a *balance* in its social desirability keying. Since these correlations contribute to the *average* intercorrelation of the items in a scale, we would expect the average intercorrelation to be lower for scales in which there is a balance in the social

As a somewhat crude test of the prediction that the magnitude of the average intercorrelation of the items in a scale is a function of the imbalance in the social desirability keying of the items in the scale, we obtained K-R 21 values for each of 61 personality scales and correlated the K-R 21 values with the imbalance in the social desirability keying of the items in the scales. The resulting product-moment correlation coefficient was .62 [25]. This finding is consistent with the social desirability prediction that scales which have either a large or a small proportion of items keyed for socially desirable responses will tend to have higher K-R 21 values than scales which are more balanced in their social desirability keying. We also found, consistent with a prediction based upon social desirability considerations, that scales which have a large proportion of neutral items tend to have lower K-R 21 values than scales which contain only a small proportion of neutral items.

VII

I believe that scores on various trait scales are correlated with scores on the *SD* scale to the degree to which the trait scales are measuring the same common factor or personality dimension as that which I believe the *SD* scale to be measuring, namely, the tendency to give socially desirable responses in self-description. A standard technique for determining the degree to which different scales are measuring a common factor is to intercorrelate the scores on the scales and to factor analyze the resulting correlation matrix. To do this, of course, it is necessary to have available scores on a number of personality scales. Furthermore, if we wish to demonstrate that scores on all of these scales are measuring in varying degrees the common or general trait which I describe as the tendency to give socially desirable responses, it would be of value if each scale included in the analysis had been developed to measure some trait which the other scales were not designed to measure.

One source for a variety of personality scales is the MMPI. When the MMPI was first published the authors [29] provided scoring keys for only a limited number of clinical and validity scales. But, over the years, many investigators must have felt that the original scales did not tap the full potentialities of the MMPI item pool. I say this because they proceeded to develop additional MMPI scales which, presumably, they believed would measure some personality trait not already being measured by one of the existing MMPI scales. By 1960 there were, according to Dahlstrom and Welsh [9], scoring keys for a minimum of 212 MMPI scales, and there is no reason to believe that the end is yet in sight.

Factor analyses have been carried out with as few as 11 and with as many as 58 of these MMPI scales. Since there are only 566 items in the MMPI, there is item overlap in the different MMPI scales, even when only the clinical and validity scales are factor analyzed. This is a confounding variable and one to which I shall return later. However, regardless of the number of MMPI scales included in the factor analysis, there is general agreement that there is one dominant bipolar factor which accounts for the major proportion of the total and common variance. This factor, depending on which pole of the factor the investigator has chosen to emphasize, has been variously labeled as anxiety [41], psychoticism [42], general maladjustment [40], ego-strength [31], acquiescence [37], deviance [1], ego-resiliency [2], and last, but not least, social desirability [18, 20, 21, 26].

What basis do we have for choosing among these various interpretations of the first MMPI factor? The choice cannot be made solely on the basis of the names of the scales which have high loadings on the factor. For example, consistent with the social desirability interpretation of the first factor is the fact that the *SD* scale has a high loading on the factor. But, then so also does a scale designed to measure anxiety and so also do a number of other scales which were, presumably, designed to measure still other personality traits. Thus, if I suggest to you that the first MMPI factor is a social desirability factor, I must have more compelling evidence than the mere fact that the *SD* scale has a high loading on the factor. I do. Let me cite to you the results of a study which Carol Diers and I did [18].

We obtained MMPI records from subjects under three sets of instructions: standard instructions, instructions to give socially desirable responses, and instructions to give socially undesirable responses. We intercorrelated and factor analyzed 58 MMPI scales for each set of instructions. The first-factor loadings for all three sets of instructions were highly correlated, the lowest correlation being .97. We also obtained the proportion of items keyed for socially desirable responses in each of the 58 MMPI scales. We then correlated the first factor loadings under standard, socially desirable, and socially undesirable instructions with the proportion of items keyed for socially desirable responses in the scales. These correlations were .89, .92, and .94, respectively.

It is obvious that with correlations of this magnitude the first-factor loadings can be predicted quite accurately from knowledge of the proportion of items in the scales keyed for socially desirable responses. Scales with high loadings at one pole of the factor tend to have a large proportion of items keyed for socially desirable responses and scales with loadings at the opposite pole of the factor tend to have a large proportion of items keyed for socially undesirable responses. Since the loadings of the scales on the first factor vary directly in terms of the proportion of items keyed for socially desirable responses, and since this is precisely what the social desirability interpretation of the first factor would predict, I see no need to resort to such concepts as anxiety, ego-strength, and the like, in describing or interpreting the first factor. In fact, I see no way in which these concepts could be used to predict the loadings of MMPI scales on the first factor.

VIII

It may still be argued that because the 39-item SD scale is based upon items from the MMPI, an instrument that was designed primarily to measure various aspects of psychopathology, scores on the SD scale are reflecting content or trait oriented responses of some sort such as denial of psychopathology or affirmation of psychological health. The argument goes something like this: If one examines the content of the 39

items in the SD scale, it is possible to find a cluster or subset of items such that the items in the cluster will be judged homogeneous in content by a clinical psychologist. If a subject gives the keyed and socially desirable response to these items, he would be described by the same clinical psychologist as free from anxiety, as adjusted, and as a person with a feeling of well-being. If he gives the non-keyed and socially undesirable response to these items, he would be described as chronically tense and anxious. Thus, responses to this subset of items and hence scores on the total SD scale may very well reflect a specific and content oriented trait rather than, as I believe, a general tendency to give socially desirable responses. In addition, the fact that the SD scale has a high loading on the first MMPI factor is regarded as further evidence that the SD scale is measuring the same content oriented trait as the first factor which is, of course, interpreted in terms of anxiety or ego strength or one of the other clinically significant labels which have been used to describe the first MMPI factor. This argument, although plausible, is one which I believe can easily be answered.

SD scales are rational scales and it is possible to build any number of them, provided we have a large pool of items with known social desirability scale values. We have obtained social desirability scale values for the 2,824 personality statements I mentioned previously. These items were developed to describe normal aspects of personality and there are no items in the pool which were specifically designed to relate to mental illness or psychopathology.

From the pool of 2,824 items, I constructed six SD scales by selecting items on the basis of their social desirability scale values and without regard to the content of the items. These six SD scales were included in a factor analysis along with the MMPI SD scale and a number of other experimental scales. In these scales there were no overlapping items. All of the *SD* scales, including the MMPI *SD* scale, had their highest loadings on a common factor, the lowest loading being .85 [16].

In a second study, a number of trait or content oriented scales, including MMPI scales, were factor analyzed together with another set of six *SD* scales and the MMPI *SD* scale. Again there was no item overlap in any of the scales and again the *SD* scales all had their highest loadings on a common factor, the lowest loading being .85 [24].

In view of the nature of the item pool from which the items in these *SD* scales were drawn along with the fact that the items were selected on the basis of their social desirability scale values and without regard to content, it does not seem reasonable to me that the items in these distinct *SD* scales could have a common and homogeneous content. What the scales do have in common is a consistency in their social desirability keying.

The results of these two studies show, I believe, that there is a general trait, the tendency to give socially desirable responses to personality statements

which can be measured by any one of a variety of *SD* scales and which is not dependent on homogeneity of content of the items in the *SD* scales.

IX

I pointed out previously that there is item overlap in MMPI scales. Some of the MMPI scales we have investigated have items in common with the *SD* scale and it is possible that the correlations of these scales with the *SD* scale are, in part, the result of scoring common items. I therefore selected from the pool of 2,824 non-MMPI items a set of 39 items to form a new *SD* scale. Each item in the MMPI *SD* scale was matched with a non-MMPI item in terms of social desirability scale value and probability of endorsement and without regard to item content. This new *SD* scale I shall refer to as a non-MMPI *SD* scale.

Scores on the non-MMPI *SD* scale and 58 MMPI scales were intercorrelated and factor analyzed. Fig. 3 shows the first-factor loadings of the MMPI scales as a function of the zero-order correlations of the scales with

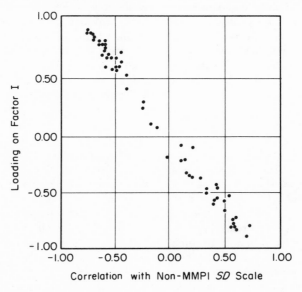

Figure 3. The relationship between first-factor loadings of MMPI scales and the correlations of the MMPI scale with a 39-item non-MMPI *SD* scale.

the non-MMPI SD scale. It is obvious that the first factor loadings are linearly and highly related to the correlations of the MMPI scales with the non-MMPI SD scale. Since the non-MMPI SD scale contains no items in common with any of the MMPI scales, the correlations cannot be attributed to overlapping items, and yet they predict quite accurately the first factor loadings.

I emphasize that the first-factor loadings of the MMPI scales and the correlations of the scales with the non-MMPI SD scale are both linear functions of the proportion of items in the scales keyed for socially desirable responses. In other words, we could predict either the first-factor loadings of the scales or the correlations of the scales with the non-MMPI SD scale in terms of the proportion of items keyed for socially desirable responses in the scales and do so quite accurately.

X

Is it possible to develop True-False scales which will measure psychologically significant traits and such that scores on these scales will be relatively independent of scores on the SD scale? I believe that it is possible and elsewhere I [17] have described some techniques which may prove useful in the process. We know, for example, that if a scale has a balance in its social desirability keying and/or if the items are not too extreme in their social desirability scale values, then either of these two conditions tends to be characteristic of MMPI scales which have low correlations with the SD scale.

We are currently applying these and other principles in an attempt to develop rational scales which are trait and content oriented, which have a high degree of internal consistency, and which are also relatively independent of one another and of the SD scale. Our objective, in other words, is to try to maximize what Philip DuBois [10], in his presidential address to this society, described as redundancy within each scale and, at the same time, to minimize redundancy across or between scales.

Whether our efforts will be successful or not remains to be seen. But I hope that we are going to be able to develop scales which will measure traits other than the tendency to give socially desirable responses in self-description. As I have tried to show we already have, within the MMPI, an ample abundance of scales which are excellent measures of this trait.

REFERENCES

1. BARNES, E. H. Factors, response bias, and the MMPI. *J. consult. Psychol.*, 1956, **20**, 419–421.
2. BLOCK, J. Personal communication.
3. COWEN, E. L., DAVOL, S. H., REIMANIS, G., and STILLER, A. The social desirability of trait descriptive terms: Two geriatric samples. *J. soc. Psychol.*, 1962, **56**, 217–225.
4. COWEN, E. L., and FRANKEL, G. The social desirability of trait descriptive terms: Applications to a French sample. *J. soc. Psychol.*, 1964, **63**, 233–239.
5. COWEN, E. L., STAIMAN, M. G., and WOLITZKY, D. L. The social desirability of trait descriptive terms: Applications to a schizophrenic sample. *J. soc. Psychol.*, 1961, **54**, 37–45.
6. COWEN, E. L., and STRICKER, G. The social desirability of trait descriptive terms: A sample of sexual offenders. *J. soc. Psychol.*, 1963, **59**, 307–315.
7. COWEN, E. L., and TONGAS, P. The social desirability of trait descriptive terms: Applications to a self-concept inventory. *J. consult. Psychol.*, 1959, **23**, 361–365.

8. CRUSE, D. B. Socially desirable responses in relation to grade level. *Child Develpm.*, 1963, **34**, 777–789.

9. DAHLSTROM, W. G., and WELSH, G. S. *An MMPI Handbook.* Minneapolis: Univer. Minnesota Press, 1960.

10. DuBois, P. H. On relationships between numbers and behavior. *Psychometrika*, 1962, **27**, 323–333.

11. EDWARDS, A. L. The relationship between the judged desirability of a trait and the probability that the trait will be endorsed. *J. appl. Psychol.*, 1953, **37**, 90–93.

12. EDWARDS, A. L. *The social desirability variable in personality assessment and research.* New York: Dryden, 1957.

13. EDWARDS, A. L. Social desirability and probability of endorsement of items in the Interpersonal Check List. *J. abnorm. soc. Psychol.*, 1957, **55**, 394–395.

14. EDWARDS, A. L. Social desirability and the description of others. *J. abnorm. soc. Psychol.*, 1959, **59**, 434–436.

15. EDWARDS, A. L. Social desirability or acquiescence in the MMPI? A case study with the SD scale. *J. abnorm. soc. Psychol.*, 1961, **63**, 351–359.

16. EDWARDS, A. L. A factor analysis of experimental social desirability and response set scales. *J. appl. Psychol.*, 1963, **47**, 308–316.

17. EDWARDS, A. L. The objective assessment of human motives. In D. LEVINE (Ed.), *Nebraska symposium on motivation.* Lincoln: Univer. Nebraska Press, 1964.

18. EDWARDS, A. L., and DIERS, CAROL J. Social desirability and the factorial interpretation of the MMPI. *Educ. psychol. Measmt*, 1962, **22**, 501–509.

19. EDWARDS, A. L., and DIERS, CAROL J. Neutral items as a measure of acquiescence. *Educ. psychol. Measmt*, 1963, **23**, 687–698.

20. EDWARDS, A. L., DIERS, CAROL J., and WALKER, J. N. Response sets and factor loadings on sixty-one personality scales. *J. appl. Psychol.*, 1962, **46**, 220–225.

21. EDWARDS, A. L., and HEATHERS, LOUISE B. The first factor of the MMPI: Social desirability or ego strength? *J. consult. Psychol.*, 1962, **26**, 99–100.

22. EDWARDS, A. L., and WALSH, J. A. Relationships between various psychometric properties of personality items. *Educ. psychol. Measmt*, 1963, **23**, 227–238.

23. EDWARDS, A. L., and WALSH, J. A. The relationship between the intensity of the social desirability keying of a scale and the correlation of the scale with Edwards' SD scale and the first factor loading of the scale. *J. clin. Psychol.*, 1963, **19**, 200–203.

24. EDWARDS, A. L., and WALSH, J. A. Response sets in standard and experimental personality scales. *Amer. educ. Res. J.*, 1964, **1**, 52–61.

25. EDWARDS, A. L., WALSH, J. A., and DIERS, CAROL J. The relationship between social desirability and internal consistency of personality scales. *J. appl. Psychol.*, 1963, **47**, 255–259.

26. FORDYCE, W. E. Social desirability in the MMPI. *J. consult. Psychol.*, 1956, **20**, 171–175.

27. FUJITA, B. Applicability of the Edwards Personal Preference Schedule to Nisei. *Psychol. Rep.*, 1957, **3**, 518–519.

28. HANLEY, C. Social desirability and responses to items from three MMPI scales: *D, Sc,* and *K. J. appl. Psychol.*, 1956, **40**, 324–328.

29. HATHAWAY, S. R., and McKINLEY, J. C. *Manual for the Minnesota Multiphasic Personality Inventory.* (Rev. ed.) New York: Psychol. Corp., 1951.

30. IWAWAKI, S., and COWEN, E. L. The social desirability of trait descriptive terms: Applications to a Japanese sample. *J. soc. Psychol.*, 1964, **63**, 199–205.

31. KASSEBAUM, G. G., COUCH, A. S., and SLATER, P. E. The factorial dimensions of the MMPI. *J. consult. Psychol.*, 1959, **23**, 226–236.

32. KENNY, D. T. The influence of social desirability on discrepancy measures between real self and ideal self. *J. consult. Psychol.*, 1956, **20**, 315–318.

33. KLETT, C. J. The stability of the social desirability scale values in the Ed-

wards Personal Preference Schedule. *J. consult. Psychol.*, 1957, **21**, 183–185.

34. KLETT, C. J. The social desirability stereotype in a hospital population. *J. consult. Psychol.*, 1957, **21**, 419–421.

35. KLETT, C. J., and YAUKEY, D. W. A cross-cultural comparison of judgments of social desirability. *J. soc. Psychol.*, 1959, **49**, 19–26.

36. LOVAAS, O. I. Social desirability ratings of personality variables by Norwegian and American college students. *J. abnorm. soc. Psychol.*, 1958, **57**, 124–125.

37. MESSICK, S., and JACKSON, D. N. Acquiescence and the factorial interpretation of the MMPI. *Psychol. Bull.*, 1961, **58**, 299–304.

38. MESSICK, S., and JACKSON, D. N. Desirability scale values and dispersions for MMPI items. *Psychol. Rep.*, 1961, **8**, 409–414.

39. TAYLOR, J. B. Social desirability and MMPI performance: The individual case. *J. consult. Psychol.*, 1959, **23**, 514–517.

40. TYLER, F. T. A factorial analysis of fifteen MMPI scales. *J. consult. Psychol.*, 1951, **15**, 451–456.

41. WELSH, G. S. Factor dimensions A and R. In G. S. WELSH and W. G. DAHLSTROM (Eds.) *Basic readings on the MMPI in psychology and medicine.* Minneapolis: Univer. Minnesota Press, 1956.

42. WHEELER, W. M., LITTLE, K. B., and LEHNER, G. F. J. The internal structure of the MMPI. *J. consult. Psychol.*, 1951, **15**, 134–141.

43. ZAX, M., COWEN, E. L., BUDIN, W., and BIGGS, C. F. The social desirability of trait descriptive terms: Applications to an alcoholic sample. *J. soc. Psychol.*, 1962, **56**, 21–27.

44. ZAX, M., COWEN, E. L., and PETER, SISTER MARY. A comparative study of novice nuns and college females using the response set approach. *J. abnorm. soc. Psychol.*, 1963, **66**, 369–375.

The Edwards SD Scale: A Measure of Adjustment or of Dissimulation?

Edwin I. Megargee

Edwards (1953) has offered three possible explanations for the high correlations between his Social Desirability (SD) Scale and the MMPI. The first is that the behavior patterns which are common in a group may come to be deemed desirable; hence items reflecting such traits would validly be endorsed more frequently. Another is that the subject is attempting to give a good impression of himself, and the third is that both factors are operating. The pur-

Reprinted by permission of the American Psychological Association and the author from the *Journal of Consulting Psychology*, 1966, in press.

pose of the present study was to determine if SD scores are a result of good adjustment, or faking good, or if both factors operate.

Three male groups were selected. Group AF was both well adjusted and motivated to present a good impression. It consisted of 21 Peace Corps trainees who took the MMPI as part of their psychiatric clearance for overseas duty. Group A was well adjusted but not motivated to dissimulate. It consisted of 41 normal college Ss who took the MMPI anonymously for research purposes. Group F was maladjusted but motivated to present a good impression. It consisted of 65 disturbed criminals who were applying for probation so as to avoid prison.

Three hypotheses were formed: H-1: If SD is solely a function of adjustment, then Groups AF and A should be equal and each should exceed F (AF = A; AF > A; A > F); H-2: If SD is solely a result of faking, then Groups AF and F should be equal and each should exceed Group A (AF = F; AF > A; F > A); H-3: If both factors influence SD, then AF should be higher than either A or F, which should be equal (AF > A; AF > F; A = F).

The MMPIs of all three groups were scored on Edwards 39 item SD scale, and the differences tested by t tests. The mean scores in Table 1 show that Group AF had the highest scores, followed by Groups A and F. The t tests indicated that AF was significantly higher than A ($t = 4.17$, $p < .001$) and also significantly higher than Group F [$t = 4.17$, p (corrected for heterogeneity of variance) $< .001$]. There was no significant difference between Groups A and F ($t = 1.21$, N.S.). The results were thus clearly in the direction predicted by H-3, indicating that both dissimulation and good adjustment can elevate SD scores.

TABLE 1.   MEAN SD SCORES OF THE THREE GROUPS

	AF	A	F
$\bar{x}$	35.00	30.83	29.37
s	3.06	4.75	9.74

This is not surprising. The debate over the meaning of the SD scale could hardly continue for over a decade unless there were data available to support both sides. However, the tendency to focus on one variable, such as faking, and control the others has tended to obscure their interaction.

These data do not mean that the concept of social desirability is equivalent to that of adjustment. As others have pointed out, while adjustment does involve social desirability, the converse is not true.

Of course, other variables may also influence SD. One which has been proposed is Set Acquiescence (Acq.). While the present study has no direct relevance to this issue, nevertheless, if it is to be asserted that Acq. is the sole cause of SD variance, then it would have to be demonstrated that it covaries with both adjustment and faking if the present data are to be explained.

REFERENCE

EDWARDS, A. L. The relationship between the judged desirability of a trait and the probability that the trait will be endorsed. *J. consult. Psychol.*, 1953, **37**, 90–93.

Response Styles and the Factorial Structure of the MMPI

Samuel Messick and Douglas N. Jackson

The operation of reliable response sets or stylistic consistencies has been frequently noted on personality and attitude scales with a true-false or agree-disagree format (cf. Cronbach, 1946, 1950; Fricke, 1956; Messick & Jackson, 1958). It has recently been conjectured (Jackson & Messick, 1958) that the major common factors in personality inventories of this type are interpretable primarily in terms of such stylistic consistencies rather than in terms of specific item content. The present paper attempts to annotate the influence of two response styles, the tendency to agree or acquiesce and the tendency to respond in a desirable way, using the Minnesota Multiphasic Personality Inventory (MMPI) as an example of inventories with this general response form. In particular, a high correlation will be noted between factor loadings on the largest factor, as obtained in sev-

This study is part of a larger project on stylistic determinants in clinical personality assessment supported by the National Institute of Mental Health, United States Public Health Service, under Research Grants M-2878 to Educational Testing Service and M-2738 to Pennsylvania State University. The authors wish to thank George S. Welsh for graciously supplying scoring keys for his "pure" MMPI scales and Philip E. Slater for making available his factor analyses of the MMPI.

Reprinted by permission of the American Psychological Association and the authors from the *Psychological Bulletin*, 1961, **58**, 299–304. Originally published under the title "Acquiscence and the Factorial Interpretation of the MMPI." Title altered at authors' request.

eral published factor analyses of the MMPI, and certain indices of acquiescence.

Barnes (1956b), in evaluating the Berg (1955) deviation hypotheses on the MMPI, found that the tendency to answer atypically or deviantly "true" was highly correlated with scores on the psychotic scales, and the tendency to answer atypically "false" was highly correlated with the neurotic triad. This result is consistent with the fact, noted by Cottle and Powell (1951) and others (Barnes, 1956b; Fricke, 1956), that a large proportion of MMPI psychotic items are keyed true and a large proportion of neurotic items keyed false, suggesting that differential tendencies to respond atypically "true" and "false" might have been involved in the discrimination of criterion groups upon which the scoring keys were based. Barnes (1956a) also pointed out a marked similarity between the correlations of MMPI scales with these two deviant response tendencies and factor loadings for the scales on the two major factors reported by Wheeler, Little, and Lehner (1951); he concluded that the number of atypical true answers is a "pure factor test" of the first or "psychotic" factor and that the number of deviant false answers has a high loading on the second or "neurotic" factor. The two major MMPI factors obtained by Welsh (1956) also displayed a similar pattern of loadings, and it is noteworthy that the "pure factor" reference scale A which Welsh developed for his first or "anxiety" factor had 38 out of 39 items keyed true, while the reference scale R for the second or "repression" factor had all 40 of its items keyed false.

In view of the striking similarity between the effects of consistent tendencies to respond "true" and "false" and patterns of factor loadings obtained in two studies of MMPI scales, all factor analyses of the MMPI readily available in the literature were reviewed, in order to evaluate the possible relationship between each scale's factor loading on the major factor and an index of its potential for reflecting acquiescence. The particular index of acquiescence used was the proportion of items keyed true on each scale, which, assuming that the acquiescence-evoking properties of items are uniform over all MMPI scales, can be considered to reflect the extent to which total scores on a scale are influenced by consistent tendencies to respond "true." High scores on a scale with a large proportion of items keyed true would thus be assumed to reflect a general tendency to acquiesce, in addition, of course, to the contribution of other stylistic tendencies and of systematic content responses. Jackson (1960) used this index to evaluate the effects of acquiescence on the California Psychological Inventory, and Voas (1958) used the proportion of items keyed false as a criterion for constructing response bias scales. Voas (1958) also estimated loadings for scales from the MMPI and the Guilford-Zimmerman Temperament Survey on a factor marked by two measures of the tendency to respond "false" and found that these loadings correlated .86 with the proportion of items keyed false on each scale. These findings support the use of the index in the present context.

Factor loadings for MMPI scales were obtained from eight studies by Abrams (1949, summarized by French, 1953), Cook and Wherry (1950), Cottle (1950), Tyler (1951), Wheeler, Little, and Lehner (1951), Welsh (1956), Slater (1958), and Kassebaum, Couch,

and Slater (1959). A fairly uniform finding from these studies is that only two major factors and two or three minor ones are necessary to account for interrelations among the scales. Spearman rank correlations were computed between loadings on the largest factor in each study and the proportion of items keyed true on each scale; the results are summarized in Table 1. In some of the factor analyses, values were not reported for scales with small loadings on the factor, so in computing correlation coefficients these scales were considered to be tied at an appropriate rank below scales with reported positive loadings and above scales with reported negative loadings. Corrections for ties (cf. Siegel, 1956) were computed for two of the studies with the most scales tied at the same rank (Wheeler, Little, & Lehner's normal sample and Tyler's sample), but the coefficients changed only .01.

Of 11 different subject samples represented in these eight studies, significant correlations were obtained for 8 of them, four of the coefficients exceeding .85. These strikingly consistent findings indicate that in most of these studies the largest factor on the MMPI is interpretable in terms of acquiescence. In evaluating the few apparently inconsistent results, it is important to note that for Abrams' (1949) neurotic sample, the correlation with the largest factor was $-.15$, but with the second largest it was .52. Also, in Tyler's (1951) study the correlation with the largest rotated factor was .33, but with the unrotated first centroid it was .52, $p < .05$. These findings suggest that for those studies in which the correspondence between the proportion of items keyed true and the factor loadings was not close, the factor structures could have been rotated to produce a higher correlation. Analytical procedures similar to the computation of B weights in multiple correlation analysis are available (Mosier, 1939) for rotating to maximize the correlation between a factor and a criterion, which in this case would be a vector of proportions of true items. However, an adequate application of this technique requires loadings for all the scales on the factors under consideration, and for those studies providing this information

(e.g., Welsh, 1956) there was usually little need to rotate.

Another consideration which suggests that a rotation of axes might clarify the role of acquiescence on the MMPI is the fact that scales with high loadings

TABLE 1.   SPEARMAN RANK CORRELATION (ρ) BETWEEN FACTOR LOADINGS ON THE LARGEST MMPI FACTOR AND PROPORTION OF ITEMS KEYED "TRUE" ON EACH SCALE

Study	Scales Included	Sample	ρ
Abrams, 1949	11 scales: L, F, Hs, D, Hy, Pd, Mf, Pa, Pt, Sc, Ma	117 normal male veterans	.907**
		201 neurotic male veterans	−.148 (largest factor) .516 (2nd largest)
Cook & Wherry, 1950	11 scales: L, F, Hs, D, Hy, Pd, Mf, Pa, Pt, Sc, Ma	111 male naval submarine candidates	.605*
Cottle, 1950	11 scales: L, F, Hs, D, Hy, Pd, Mf, Pa, Pt, Sc, Ma	400 male veterans	.916**
Tyler, 1951	15 scales: Hs, D, Hy, Pd, Mf, Pa, Pt, Sc, Ma, Si, St, Pr, Ac, Re, Do	107 female graduate students	.328
Wheeler, Little, & Lehner, 1951	12 scales: L, K, F, Hs, D, Hy, Pd, Mf, Pa, Pt, Sc, Ma	112 males college students	.558
		110 male neuropsychiatric patients	.874**
Welsh, 1956	11 pure scales: K', Hs', D', Hy', Pd', Mf', Pa', Pt', Sc', Ma', Si'	150 male VA general hospital patients	.870**
	11 pure scales plus A, Gm, Ja, R	Same 150 males	.897**
Slater, 1958	43 scales: L, F, K, Hs, D, Hy, Pd, Mf, Pa, Pt, Sc, Ma, Si, Nm, Dp, Fm, A, R, Im, Pr, To, C, P, Sp, Rp, Sy, Re, St, Lp, Do, Es, Ie, Ac, Ai, O–I, Lb, Ne, Ca, Pl, Ht, Cht, Z_1, Z_2	102 aged males 109 aged females	.728** .718**
Kassebaum, Couch, & Slater, 1959	32 scales: L, F, K, Hs, D, Hy, Pd, Mf, Pa, Pt, Sc, Ma, Si, Es, Ie, Lp, Ai, Sy, Ac, Re, Do, Pr, St, Im, Sp, Fm, Rp, R, A, Dp, To, OI	160 Harvard College freshmen	.625**

* $p < .05$.
** $p < .01$.

on the second largest MMPI factor usually tend to have a high proportion of false items in their keys. Kassebaum, Couch, and Slater (1959) noticed this in their factor results and suggested that their second factor partly reflected a general tendency to respond "false." Although correlations between the proportion of items keyed true and loadings on the second MMPI factor are usually not nearly as high as correlations with the first factor, some significant coefficients occur; e.g., the correlation between the proportion of items keyed true and loadings on the second factor in the study by Kassebaum, Couch, and Slater (1959) was $-.44$, $p < .05$ with 30 df, and in Welsh's (1956) study it was $-.64$, $p < .05$ with 13 df.

This result is consistent with Barnes' (1956a) finding of a correspondence between atypical true answer and the first MMPI factor and atypical false answers and the second factor. Since these two factors are usually orthogonal, this correspondence might be considered evidence for two relatively independent response biases, one a tendency to agree and the other to disagree. Such a contention is consistent with Barnes' (1956b) finding of a correlation of .11 between deviant responses answered "true" and "false" and with the fact that Welsh's (1956) A and R scales are usually only slightly negatively correlated. Although these results cannot be accounted for by a simple response set of acquiescence, it is not necessary to postulate two independent sets to agree and to disagree. As has been pointed out (Jackson & Messick, 1958) all that is required to account for the findings is the operation of at least one other factor in conjunction with acquiescence. Thus, the A scale can have a high positive loading on an acquiescence factor and the R scale a high negative loading, yet the two scales could be uncorrelated if they both had positive, or negative, loadings on some other dimension. Other factors which could moderate the

operation of acquiescence on the MMPI might be specific content dimensions or some other response style. As previously suggested (Jackson & Messick, 1958), a particularly likely candidate for such a role is the stylistic tendency to respond in a desirable way.

Possible influences on MMPI scores of a set to respond desirably have been widely documented (cf. DeSoto & Kuethe, 1959; Edwards, 1957; Fordyce, 1956; Hanley, 1956, 1957; Jackson & Messick, 1958; Taylor, 1959; Wiggins & Rumrill, 1959). Fordyce (1956) for example, has noted a marked similarity between loadings on the largest MMPI factor from Wheeler, Little, and Lehner's (1951) psychiatric sample and correlations of MMPI scales with a measure of desirability. In fact, the rank correlation between the loadings and the correlation coefficients is approximately $-.75$, and since the proportion of items keyed true on each MMPI scale correlates only about $-.50$ with the desirability coefficients, it seems likely that a combination of desirability and acquiescence would lead to even better prediction of the factor (cf. Messick, 1959). Although this and some other reported relationships are somewhat equivocal because the measures of desirability used were partially confounded with acquiescence, e.g., Edwards' SD scale and Hanley's Ex scale, high correlations have also been reported between MMPI scales and desirability measures having a balanced number of true and false items (Edwards, 1957; Hanley, 1957; Wiggins & Rumrill, 1959).

In an attempt to take these findings into account, it is suggested that the acquiescence-evoking properties of items are not, as assumed above, uniform over all scales, but that acquiescence is elicited differentially as a function, perhaps, of specific item content, of the clarity or ambiguity with which the content is stated, and in particular of the perceived desirability of the statement. In the extreme, it is suggested that the two major factors usually found for the MMPI may be rotated into positions interpretable as two response styles—the tendency to acquiesce and the tendency to respond desirably. The negative poles of these dimensions would be the tendencies to disagree and to respond undesirably, respectively. Response variance on MMPI scales would then be primarily a function of these two stylistic components in various weighted proportions. Studies including independent marker variables for the two styles are of course required to identify the factor positions. Much research is also needed into the precise nature of the set to respond desirably, particularly in view of three complicating results: (a) the finding of consistent individual differences in judgments of desirability (Messick, 1960); (b) the distinction between personal and social desirability (Borislow, 1958; Rosen, 1956); and (c) the differentiation between a tendency to endorse certain desirable items which exhibit large mean shifts under desirability instructions and the tendency to endorse other desirable items which presumably reflect a group norm (Voas, 1958; Wiggins, 1959).

In conclusion, the findings offer clear evidence that acquiescence, as moderated by item desirability, plays a dominant role in personality inventories like the MMPI. Focused empirical investigations are required to develop a refined interpretation of these and other stylistic consistencies in terms of personality organization and psychopathology.

REFERENCES

ABRAMS, E. N. A comparative factor analytic study of normal and neurotic veterans. Unpublished doctoral dissertation, University of Michigan, 1949.

BARNES, E. H. Factors, response bias, and the MMPI. *J. consult. Psychol.*, 1956, **20**, 419–421. (a)

BARNES, E. H. Response bias and the MMPI. *J. consult. Psychol.*, 1956, **20**, 371–374. (b)

BERG, I. A. Response bias and personality: The deviation hypothesis. *J. Psychol.*, 1955, **40**, 61–72.

BORISLOW, B. The Edwards Personal Preference Schedule (EPPS) and fakability. *J. appl. Psychol.*, 1958, **42**, 22–27.

COOK, E. B., & WHERRY, R. J. A factor analysis of MMPI and aptitude test data. *J. appl. Psychol.*, 1950, **34**, 260–266.

COTTLE, W. C. A factorial study of the Multiphasic, Strong, Kuder, and Bell inventories using a population of adult males. *Psychometrika*, 1950, **15**, 25–47.

COTTLE, W. C., & POWELL, J. O. The effect of random answers to the MMPI. *Educ. psychol. Measmt*, 1951, **11**, 224–227.

CRONBACH, L. J. Response sets and test validity. *Educ. psychol. Measmt*, 1946, **6**, 475–494.

CRONBACH, L. J. Further evidence on response sets and test design. *Educ. psychol. Measmt*, 1950, **10**, 3–31.

DE SOTO, C. B., & KUETHE, J. L. The set to claim undesirable symptoms in personality inventories. *J. consult. Psychol.*, 1959, **23**, 496–500.

EDWARDS, A. L. *The social desirability variable in personality assessment and research.* New York: Dryden, 1957.

FORDYCE, W. E. Social desirability in the MMPI. *J. consult. Psychol.*, 1956, **20**, 171–175.

FRENCH, J. W. *The description of personality measurements in terms of rotated factors.* Princeton, N.J.: Educational Testing Service, 1953.

FRICKE, B. G. Response set as a suppressor variable in the OAIS and MMPI. *J. consult. Psychol.*, 1956, **20**, 161–169.

HANLEY, C. Social desirability and responses to items from three MMPI scales: D, Sc, and K. *J. appl. Psychol.*, 1956, **40**, 324–328.

HANLEY, C. Deriving a measure of test-taking defensiveness. *J. consult. Psychol.*, 1957, **21**, 391–397.

JACKSON, D. N. Stylistic response determinants in the California Psychological Inventory. *Educ. psychol. Measmt,* 1960, **20,** 339–346.

JACKSON, D. N., & MESSICK, S. Content and style in personality assessment. *Psychol. Bull.,* 1958, **55,** 243–252.

KASSEBAUM, G. G., COUCH, A. S., & SLATER, P. E. The factorial dimensions of the MMPI. *J. consult. Psychol.,* 1959, **23,** 226–236.

MESSICK, S. Review of Allen Edwards' *The social desirability variable in personality assessment and research. Educ. psychol. Measmt,* 1959, **19,** 451–454.

MESSICK, S. Dimensions of social desirability. *J. consult. Psychol.,* 1960, **24,** 279–287.

MESSICK, S., & JACKSON, D. N. The measurement of authoritarian attitudes. *Educ. psychol. Measmt,* 1958, **18,** 241–253.

MOSIER, C. I. Determining a simple structure when loadings for certain tests are known. *Psychometrika,* 1939, **4,** 149–162.

ROSEN, E. Self-appraisal, personal desirability, and perceived social desirability of personality traits. *J. abnorm. soc. Psychol.,* 1956, **52,** 151–158.

SIEGEL, S. *Nonparametric statistics for the behavioral sciences.* New York: McGraw-Hill, 1956.

SLATER, P. E. Personality structure in old age. Progress Report, 1958, Age Center of New England, Project M-1402, National Institute of Mental Health.

TAYLOR, J. B. Social desirability and MMPI performance: The individual case. *J. consult. Psychol.,* 1959, **23,** 514–517.

TYLER, F. T. A factorial analysis of fifteen MMPI scales. *J. consult. Psychol.,* 1951, **15,** 451–456.

VOAS, R. B. Relationships among three types of response sets. Report No. 15, 1958, Naval School of Aviation Medicine, Pensacola, Project NM 16 0111 Subtask 1.

WELSH, G. S. Factor dimensions A and R. In G. S. WELSH & W. G. DAHLSTROM (Eds.), *Basic readings on the MMPI in psychology and medicine.* Minneapolis: Univer. Minnesota Press, 1956.

WHEELER, W. M., LITTLE, K. B., & LEHNER, G. F. J. The internal structure of the MMPI. *J. consult. Psychol.,* 1951, **15,** 134–141.

WIGGINS, J. S. Interrelationships among MMPI measures of dissimulation under standard and social desirability instructions. *J. consult. Psychol.,* 1959, **23,** 419–427.

WIGGINS, J. S., & RUMRILL, C. Social desirability in the MMPI and Welsh's factor scales A and R. *J. consult. Psychol.,* 1959, **23,** 100–106.

Acquiescence in the MMPI?

Leonard G. Rorer and Lewis R. Goldberg

Responses to personality inventory items have traditionally been thought of as "multiply determined," but only recently have the response determinants which are variously referred to as "sets," "biases," and "styles" been held to be

This article is based on a portion of the first author's doctoral dissertation (Rorer, 1963). This study was supported in part by National Science Foundation Grant G–25123 to Oregon Research Institute under the direction of the second author. The analysis of much of the data was carried out through the facilities of Western Data Processing Center at the University of California at Los Angeles. The authors acknowledge with thanks the assistance of Dr. Paul E. Meehl, who made a number of helpful suggestions for improving an earlier draft of this article.

Reprinted by permission of the publisher and the authors from *Educational and Psychological Measurement,* 1965, **25,** 801–817.

more important than item content in accounting for such responses (e.g., Berg, 1959; Berg, 1961; Christie & Lindauer, 1963; Jackson & Messick, 1958; Loevinger, 1959; McGee, 1962c; Messick & Jackson, 1961). Recently, Rorer (1965) has proposed a conceptual distinction between "sets" and "styles." The term "set" is used to refer to the criteria according to which a respondent evaluates item content when selecting his answer. Sets have been designated by such terms as "dissimulation," "defensiveness," and "social desirability." The term "style" is used to refer to a way or manner of responding, such as a tendency to select some particular response option independently of the item content. Styles have been described by such terms as "yeasaying," "naysaying," and "extreme position response bias." Sets operate in relation to meaningful item content; styles operate in the absence of such content. In the current literature "acquiescence" has been conceptualized as a generalized tendency to be agreeable (a set), but has been operationally defined in terms of a disproportionate tendency to select a certain response category (a style).

On the basis of an extensive review of the literature, Rorer (1965) concluded that, current opinion to the contrary notwithstanding, there is no evidence that acquiescence response style accounts for a significant proportion of the response variance in present personality inventories. Response styles could be established as an important response determinant either (a) by showing that two or more "content-independent" stylistic measures are significantly related, or (b) by showing that inconsistent responses are given to the same content presented in more than one form. Studies in which content-independent measures of style have been intercorrelated have found the measures to be unrelated—a result that holds for instruments which purportedly measure the same style as well as for instruments which purportedly measure different styles (e.g., Bass, 1956; Forehand, 1962; Gray & Crisp, 1961; Husek, 1961; McGee, 1962a; McGee, 1962b; McGee, 1962c; Siller & Chipman, 1962). These uniformly negative results have led to the hypothesis that response styles are "test specific." The establishment of response styles as an important response determinant in personality inventories rests, therefore, on the "reversed-content" design. In this design a respondent is presented with an item and with the reversal (logical contradictory) of that item. To the extent that correlations between responses to the original and the reversed items are high and negative (approaching the reliability of the test), individuals are responding consistently to the content of the items. To the extent that the correlations are high and positive, individuals are responding to a particular response category rather than to the content of the items. Most of the previous studies employing this design have utilized the California F scale. All have obtained intermediate correlations between the original and reversed forms of the test, and all have concluded that content and style are both important response determinants, though there is some difference of opinion as to which is the more important (e.g., Peabody, 1961). Rorer (1965) has criticized these studies on the grounds that the reversals employed were inadequate, and has concluded that they do not provide sufficient evidence to warrant the conclusion that response styles are an important response determinant. However, neither do they offer evidence for rejecting that conclusion. Furthermore, there is in the literature today almost complete unanimity of opinion concerning the importance of response styles. It therefore seems that the weight of presumptive evidence in favor of the importance of response styles has become so strong in the minds of most investigators that it is incumbent upon one who would challenge that position to demonstrate that adequate item reversals can be written so that even test-specific response styles can be shown to be unimportant in determining responses to personality inventories.

Method

Procedure

An experimental group composed of 96 male and 125 female sophomores, juniors and seniors from four psychology classes at the University of Minnesota was given the original MMPI and a reversed form of the MMPI two weeks apart. A control group composed of 95 male and 108 female students from an introductory psychology class at the University of Oregon was given the regular MMPI twice under similar conditions. The experimental and control groups will also be referred to as the reversal and reliability groups, respectively.

Instruments

In view of the previous research in this area, there were two tests which it seemed reasonable to use for this experiment—the California F scale and the Minnesota Multiphasic Personality Inventory. For both instruments, previous researchers had concluded that the proportion of the response variance attributable to styles was greater than that attributable to item content. Because it provided a larger, more diversified item pool, the MMPI was selected.

The development of the reversed items proved to be the most difficult part of the study. Conceptually the task was clear enough. Each of the original MMPI items had to be rewritten so that no matter in what way a respondent would answer the original item (and no matter what his reason for answering it in that way) he would be forced to answer the new item in the opposite way

in order to say the same thing. To put it another way, if a respondent were to be presented with the original and the reversed items simultaneously he would have to answer them in opposite directions if he were to avoid contradicting himself.

Items constructed in this way are reversals of the originals, not opposites. For example, in everyday speech the opposite of "black" is "white," but the reverse of "black" is "white and all shades of grey up to but not including black." The opposite of "loving" is "hating"; the reverse of "loving" is simply "an absence of loving," which may mean "hating," but also may simply mean indifference or no relationship at all. The opposite of "all" is "none"; the reversal is "any number excluding at least one." In other words, the reverse of a statement is that statement's logical contradictory, not its logical contrary or subcontrary. Two statements are contraries if they might both be false, but cannot both be true; two statements are subcontraries if they might both be true, but cannot both be false; two statements are contradictories if one must be true and the other false. A universal affirmative and a particular negative are contradictories, as are a universal negative and a particular affirmative, but a universal affirmative and a universal negative are not contradictories, and neither are a particular affirmative and a particular negative (see Copi, 1954, pp. 66–74).

If item reversal writing could be treated as the simple, logical task that it is conceptually, it would be a trivial exercise in symbolic logic. One could, for example, preface each item with "It is not the case that . . ." or "It is not true that. . . ." Unfortunately, prefixes such as this would also in most cases alter the item style, length, and complexity simultaneously, and so are to be avoided if possible. Except for being reversed, the new items should be as much like the originals as possible. In almost all cases this means that the reversal should be as simple as possible. Unfortunately, the original items are in varying degrees vague, indefinite, ambiguous, and idiomatic, which means that in many cases there are no simple reversals.

The problems that are encountered in item reversal writing are best indicated by example. "I like mechanics magazines" cannot be reversed by "I do not like mechanics magazines," because the latter implies dislike. An individual who has no particular feelings about mechanics magazines one way or the other may consistently reject both items. "I seldom worry about my health" is undoubtedly most often rejected by individuals who have a tendency to worry about their health, but it may also be rejected by some individuals who never worry about their health, on the grounds that the item implies at least some worry. A related problem is encountered with an item such as "At times I feel like smashing things." Some individuals feel that one or two incidents comprise sufficient grounds for endorsement; others feel that "at times" implied a recurring phenomenon which could be inferred only on the basis of a sizable number of such incidents. The item "I cry easily" cannot be reversed by "I do not cry easily," because to most respondents the latter item implies that it is difficult to make them cry. On the other hand, the confusion caused by reversing a negative item such as "I do not tire quickly" by "It is not true that I do not tire quickly" should be readily apparent even for this short item.

Though seven judges[1] provided innumerable suggestions concerning item interpretation and phrasing, the selec-

tion of the items to be included in the reversed form was ultimately based on the first author's notions concerning the relative importance of logical consistency as opposed to stylistic simplicity. Because the former was given more weight than the latter, the reversed items are probably appropriate only for college-level groups.[2] For a more detailed account see Rorer (1963).

If the final results show that respondents given both item forms are as consistent as respondents given the same item twice, then there is no problem with this procedure. The experimentals have had to change their answer in order to be consistent, and they have been as consistent as the controls who were given the same item twice. The experimentals must be responding to the content. However, should the results show lower consistency for the experimentals, then the results might be attributable either to response bias or to inadequate reversals.

Analysis

The results for males and females were analyzed separately. This split results in four groups which will be designated C-M (control males who took the original MMPI twice), C-F (control females who took the original MMPI twice), E-M (experimental males who took the original MMPI and the reversed MMPI), and E-F (experimental females who took the original MMPI and the reversed MMPI). For each of the four groups, the following statistics were calculated for each item on an IBM 7090 computer.

TT—The percentage of subjects responding "true" on both administrations of the item. (For the reversal groups, the subjects have actually marked "false" on the second administration. They are

[1] The authors are indebted to Dr. and Mrs. Philip Gough, Dr. Starke R. Hathaway, Mrs. Denise Hawkins, Dr. and Mrs. James C. Kincannon, and Dr. Gail La Forge, all of whom spent much time evaluating preliminary item reversals. Whatever merit the final item reversals have rests heavily on the combined critical comments of these individuals.

[2] A copy of the reversed MMPI may be obtained from the authors, without charge, or from the American Documentation Institute. Order Document No. 8454.

listed in this way because they have consistently responded to the item content and are to be compared with the reliability group which has consistently responded to the item content by marking "true" both times.)

TF—The percentage of subjects responding "true" on the first administration and "false" on the second administration of the item. (In this case, the reversal groups have actually marked "true" on both administrations of the test. These are the potential "acquiescence" responses.)

TB—The percentage of subjects responding "true" on the first administration and omitting a response on the second administration of the item. (In this case, no adjustment is made for the responses of the reversal groups.)

Qualifications concerning the reversed scoring of the reversal groups will not be continued in the following descriptions, but it is essential to remember that throughout the analyses the answers to the reversed form of the MMPI have also been reversed.

FT—The percentage of subjects responding "false" on the first administration and "true" on the second administration of the item.

FF—The percentage of subjects responding "false" on both administrations of the item.

FB—The percentage of subjects responding "false" on the first administration and omitting a response on the second administration of the item.

BT—The percentage of subjects omitting a response on the first administration and responding "true" on the second administration of the item.

BF—The percentage of subjects omitting a response on the first administration and responding "false" on the second administration of the item.

BB—The percentage of subjects omitting a response on both administrations of the item.

Blank-1—(BT + BF + BB) The percentage of subjects who failed to respond to the item on the first administration.

Blank-2—(TB + FB + BB) The percentage of subjects who failed to respond to the item on the second administration.

End%-1—(TT + TF + TB) The percentage of subjects responding "true" to the item on the first administration.

End%-2—(TT + FT + BT) The percentage of subjects responding "true" to the item on the second administration.

Shift—(End%-2—End%-1) The net shift (increase or decrease) between first and second administrations in the percentage of subjects endorsing the item.

Stable—(TT + FF + BB) The percentage of subjects who are consistent in their responses to the item.

Results

The detailed results of the analyses for each item over all subjects in each group are presented elsewhere (Goldberg & Rorer, 1963; Rorer, 1963). The mean of each of these statistics over all items is presented in Table 1. Because of rounding errors, there are .01 discrepancies in some of the results, but it should be noted that, prior to rounding, the computer performed all calculations to eight-digit accuracy.

In general, the results for the various groups are similar. Inspection of the End%-1, End%-2, and Shift rows of the table shows that there was a 2% difference between the groups in over-all endorsement frequency on the first administration, and that this difference disappears on the second administration. This is due to the endorsement proportion for the controls decreasing slightly

TABLE 1.   MEAN VALUES OF ITEM
STATISTICS OVER ALL SUBJECTS AND
ALL ITEMS

Index	Males C	E	Females C	E
TT	.35	.33	.35	.32
TF	.07	.08	.07	.07
FT	.06	.09	.06	.08
FF	.51	.50	.52	.52
Blank-1	.00	.01	.00	.00
Blank-2	.00	.00	.00	.00
End%-1	.42	.40	.42	.39
End%-2	.42	.42	.41	.41
Shift	− .00	.01	− .00	.01
Stable	.87	.83	.87	.84

Note.—Values for TB, FB, BT, BF, and BB
were all .00.

while the experimentals were increasing. In other words, the groups were
more alike during the second testing
when the experimentals were taking the
reversals than during the first testing
when both groups were taking the same
items.

In order to assess the extent to which
response styles rather than content account for the responses, it is necessary
to compare the consistency of the experimentals with that of the controls.
The values for Stable indicate that for
both the male and female control
groups, 87% of the responses were the
same on both tests.

Because the reversed form of the
MMPI was administered only once, no
comparable test-retest stability values
are available for it. However, for the
16 items which are repeated in the
MMPI, intra-test stability values may be
calculated for both forms. These values
are shown in Table 2. It can be seen
that the greater complexity of the reversed items has resulted in decreased
response stability. If the relationship between inter- and intra-test stability for
the reversed form is assumed proportional to that for the originals (a conservative assumption), then it would
be predicted that 82% of the responses
to the reversed form would be un-

changed from one administration to another. If respondents are influenced entirely by item content, the stability of
their responses when taking both forms
of the test would be expected to fall
somewhere between 82% and 87%.

For the experimental groups in the
present study, 83% of the responses of
the males and 84% of the responses of
the females were consistent; i.e., the
subjects marked either TF or FT, indicating that they were responding to
the item content rather than to the response category. Comparing the controls
and the experimentals, there is a discrepancy of 4% for the males and 3%
for the females, with greater response
stability among the controls.

If the experimental subjects were ac-
quiescing, then this discrepancy should
be accounted for by a disproportionate
percentage of "true" responses on the
second administration by subjects who
answered "true" on the first administration. Inspection of the table shows that
for both the male and the female controls, 7% of the responses were changed
from "true" on the first administration
to "false" on the second administration.
By comparison, for the reversal groups,
8% of the responses by the males and
7% of the responses by the females were
"changed" from "true" to "true." In
other words, using the most stringent
possible criterion, double "trues" can account for only a .01 discrepancy in the
males, and for none of the discrepancy
in the females. What small discrepancy
there is between the groups even on this
criterion can almost all be accounted for

TABLE 2.   WITHIN-TEST STABILITY
VALUES FOR 16 REPEATED ITEMS

Group	Males Admin. 1	Admin. 2	Females Admin. 1	Admin. 2
Controls	.94	.95	.95	.95
Experi- mentals	.96	.90	.95	.90

by inconsistent double false responses by the reversal groups. When the greater instability of the reversed form is taken into account, even this "discrepancy" disappears. These results show quite clearly that acquiescence response style is of negligible importance in accounting for responses to the MMPI.

Figures 1 and 2 show scatter plots of the stability of each item for the experimentals and the controls. Figure 1 is for males and Fig. 2 is for females. In Fig. 1, a 45° line has been drawn to show the point at which items are equally stable for experimentals and controls. In Fig. 2, the best fit regression line has been added. While this line may deviate from 45° because of real differences between the original and reversed items, it also may deviate from 45° because of the unreliability of the stability values. Since the obtained correlations (.64 for males and .61 for females) are as high as could be expected on the basis of existing estimates of the reliability of stability scores, it may be inferred that the stabilities of the original and the reversed items are almost perfectly related.

Figures 1 and 2 show that items differed considerably in their stability, and that the reversals differed in their relative success. It is of interest to examine the least successful reversals in order to see if they possess any common characteristics. Variation about the 45° line was used as a selection criterion. Since there is no reason for the reversed items to be more stable than the originals administered twice, the range on the top side of the 45° line may be taken as an indication of the variation in item response stability that might occur by chance, and the same range was marked off on the bottom side of the 45° line. This will be termed the "outer confidence band." While the term "confidence band" is being used rather loosely, the empirically determined range seems as good as any of the possible alternatives. This value was

14% for the males and 16% for the females, but the smaller value was adopted for both groups. In addition to this outer confidence band, an inner band was drawn between 10% and 11% discrepancy. This procedure is illustrated in Fig. 1.

In order to see if they shared some common characteristic, items were selected which (a) fell beyond the outer confidence band for both males and females, or (b) fell beyond the inner confidence band in both groups. The items selected in this manner are presented in Tables 3 and 4, where they are broken down into three groups: (a) items for which the instability was of the TT type; (b) items for which the instability was of the FF type; (c) items for which the instability was about equally of the TT and FF type.

The items in Tables 3 and 4 are heterogeneous with respect to scale membership, content, and form of reversal. Inspection indicates only one common characteristic: TT items tend to have high initial endorsement frequencies, FF items tend to have low initial endorsement frequencies, and mixed items tend to have medium endorsement frequencies. Inspection of the items indicates that their instability most likely stems from either misunderstanding on the part of the respondents (e.g., 175, 460, 16, and 218) or inadequacies inherent in the reversals (e.g., 2, 17, 83, 205, and 499).

Discussion

The response stabilities obtained for the experimentals and controls in this study may be compared with values previously reported. Schofield (1948) found that a group of normals were consistent in 86% of their responses to 495 MMPI items on two different occasions. Schofield also reported stability percentages of 78% for psychiatric out-patients, 82% for hospitalized neurotics, and 69% for psychotics. Neprash (1936) found

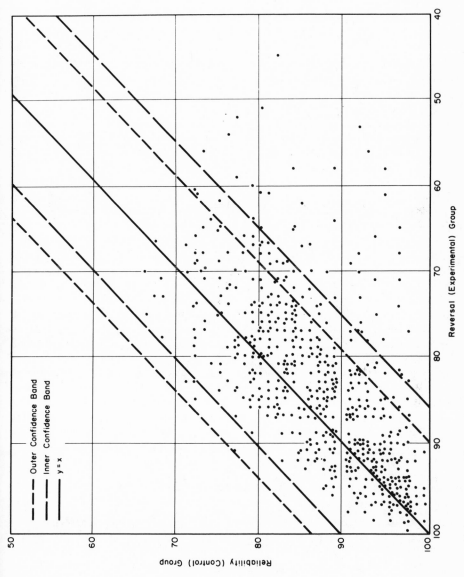

Figure 1. Proportion of stable responses among males for each item. (Each dot represents an item.)

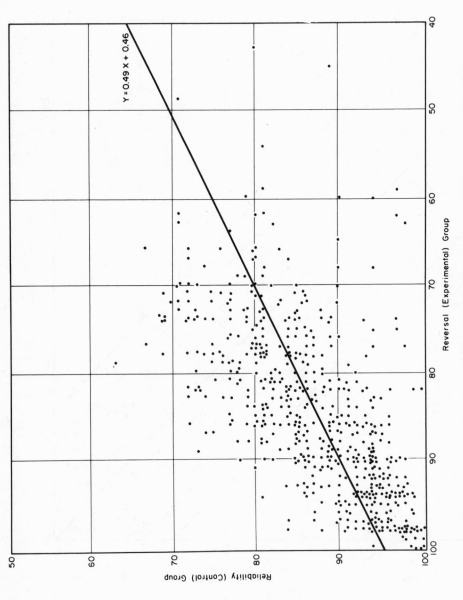

Figure 2. Proportion of stable responses among females for each item. (Each dot represents an item.)

Y = 0.49 x + 0.46

Reliability (Control) Group

Reversal (Experimental) Group

True-True

2. I have a good appetite.

   I do not have a good appetite (or it is about average).

17. My father was a good man.

    My father was not a good man (or he was about average).

83. Any man who is able and willing to work hard has a good chance of succeeding.

    Not every man who is able and willing to work hard has a good chance of succeeding.

127. I know who is responsible for most of my troubles.

     I know of no one who is responsible for most of my troubles.

175. I seldom or never have dizzy spells.

     It is not true that I seldom or never have dizzy spells.

460. I have used alcohol moderately (or not at all).

     I have used alcohol immoderately.

479. I do not mind meeting strangers.

     It is not true that I do not mind meeting strangers.

499. I must admit that I have at times been worried beyond reason over something that really did not matter.

     I have never been worried beyond reason over something that really did not matter.

513. I think Lincoln was greater than Washington.

     I think Lincoln was no greater than Washington.

Both True-True and False-False

254. I like to be with a crowd who play jokes on one another.

     I do not like to be with a crowd who play jokes on one another (or I am indifferent to it).

441. I like tall women.

     I do not like tall women (or I neither like nor dislike them).

False-False

16 (& 315). I am sure I get a raw deal from life.

    I am not sure I get a raw deal from life.

49. It would be better if almost all laws were thrown away.

    It would be no better if almost all laws were thrown away.

104. I don't seem to care what happens to me.

     I do seem to care what happens to me.

205. At times it has been impossible for me to keep from stealing or shoplifting something.

     It has never been impossible for me to keep from stealing or shoplifting something.

218. It does not bother me particularly to see animals suffer.

     It is not true that it does not bother me particularly to see animals suffer.

250. I don't blame anyone for trying to grab everything he can get in this world.

     I do blame some people for trying to grab everything they can get in this world.

265. It is safer to trust nobody.

     It is no safer to trust nobody.

284. I am sure I am being talked about.

     I am not sure I am being talked about.

287. I have very few fears compared to my friends.

     I do not feel that I have very few fears compared to my friends.

375. When I am feeling very happy and active, someone who is blue or low will spoil it all.

     When I am feeling very happy and active, even someone who is blue or low cannot spoil it.

387. The only miracles I know of are simply tricks that people play on another.

     I know of miracles that are more than simply tricks that people play on one another.

461. I find it hard to set aside a task that I have undertaken, even for a short time.

     It is not true that when I have undertaken a task, I find it hard to set it aside for a short time.

TABLE 4.   REVERSALS FOR WHICH THE PERCENTAGE OF STABLE RESPONSES WAS AT
LEAST 10% LOWER FOR THE REVERSAL SAMPLE THAN FOR THE RELIABILITY SAMPLE

True-True

64. I sometimes keep on at a thing until others lose their patience with me.	I do not keep on at a thing until others lose their patience with me.
176. I do not have a great fear of snakes.	I can't honestly say that I do not have a great fear of snakes.
498. It is always a good thing to be frank.	It is not always a good thing to be frank.
563. I like adventure stories better than romantic stories.	I like adventure stories no better than romantic stories.

Both True-True and False-False

58. Everything is turning out just like the prophets of the Bible said it would.	Not everything is turning out just like the prophets of the Bible said it would.
399. I am not easily angered.	It is not true that I am not easily angered.
523. I practically never blush.	It is not true that I practically never blush.

False-False

10. There seems to be a lump in my throat much of the time.	It is not true that there seems to be a lump in my throat much of the time.
14. I have diarrhea once a month or more.	I have diarrhea less than once a month.
39. At times I feel like smashing things.	I never feel like smashing thing.
100. I have met problems so full of possibilities that I have been unable to make up my mind about them.	I have never met problems so full of possibilities that I have been unable to make up my mind about them.
198. I daydream very little.	I daydream more than a very little.
328. I find it hard to keep my mind on a task or job.	Maybe some people find it hard to keep their mind on a task or job, but not me.

that after two weeks' time, 85.9% of his subjects' responses to the Thurstone Personality Schedule were unchanged. Benton and Stone (1937) found that for Landis and Zubin's Personality Inquiry Form, which also has a yes-?-no format, 81% of their subjects' responses were unchanged after five days, 80% after eight days, and 81% after 21 days. In other words, the failure to find acquiescence in this study cannot be attributed to an inconsistent or poorly motivated control group. The controls in this study were more consistent in their responses than any other group to be found in the literature.

When this fact is considered in conjunction with the undoubtedly lower test-retest stability of the reversed form, and the inadequacies of some of the reversals, it seems remarkable that the consistency of the experimentals could be even close to that of the controls,

much less identical to it (as was the case for the TT or "acquiescent" category of responses for the females).

Perhaps the point is best made in reverse. If one wishes to interpret these results in terms of response styles, and if he is willing to give *no* weight to: (a) the possibility of some discrepancies due to sampling error, (b) the extreme consistency of this control group in relation to all other groups reported in the literature, (c) the undoubtedly lower test-retest stability of the reversed MMPI, and (d) the possibility that some of the reversals are not perfect, then it could be said that 1% of all responses made by males are "acquiescent," and 3% of all responses by males and 2% of all responses by females are "critical." Absurd as this line of reasoning is, the amount of response style variance which it manages to salvage is trivially small.

It has become fashionable to interpret the first two orthogonal MMPI factors in terms of acquiescence and social desirability, and to give response style names to scales constructed on the basis of certain item characteristics such as endorsement percentage or direction of keying. This naming and interpretation is necessarily equivocal. Since the scales are composed of verbal items, the respondent may be giving factual answers, no matter how many of them are true or false.

The fact that an individual gives a preponderance of "true" responses to the items on a personality inventory, or even to any subset of items from an inventory, provides no basis on which to conclude that he "acquiesced." For personality, attitude, and interest inventories, unless the items are stated in more than one way, the content and the keying are inevitably confounded, no matter how much statistical legerdemain is performed upon the results. Previous studies concluding that acquiescence response style is an important variable in determining MMPI responses have all done so on the basis of such content-confounded measures.

Such conclusions are no longer tenable. Chapman and Campbell (1959) have previously shown that adequate reversals could be written for the MMPI At scale, and Block (1962) has shown that MMPI scales balanced for "true" and "false" keyings yield the same factor structure as the present unbalanced scales. Factors extracted using balanced scales obviously cannot be interpreted in terms of acquiescence or criticalness response styles. The results of these investigators, taken in conjunction with the results of this experiment, indicate quite clearly that acquiescence and criticalness response styles are of negligible importance in determining MMPI responses for the groups that have been studied. It is conceivable that this would not be the case among other groups. Scales might be discriminative because certain groups, such as college students, lack acquiescence and criticalness set, whereas various clinical groups have one or the other. However, in a study aimed at precisely this question, Jackson and Messick (1962) concluded that the "massive" effects of response styles are almost identical for college students, prison inmates, and hospitalized neurotics. Since their results indicate the same effects for all three groups, this study may be similarly generalized and serves to call all of them into question.

Summary

Reversals (logical contradictories) were written for all MMPI items. Responses of an experimental group given the original MMPI and the reversed MMPI were compared with those of a control group given the original MMPI twice. The results indicate that "acquiescence response style" can be of no more than trivial importance in determining responses to the MMPI.

REFERENCES

BASS, B. M. Development and evaluation of a scale for measuring social acquiescence. *J. abnorm. soc. Psychol.*, 1956, 53, 296–299.

BENTON, A. L., & STONE, I. R. Consistency of response to personality inventory items as a function of interval between test and retest. *J. soc. Psychol.*, 1937, 8, 143–146.

BERG, I. A. The unimportance of test item content. In B. M. BASS & I. A. BERG (Eds.), *Objective approaches to personality assessment.* New York: Van Nostrand, 1959.

BERG, I. A. Measuring deviant behavior by means of deviant response sets. In I. A. BERG & B. M. BASS (Eds.), *Conformity and deviation.* New York: Harper, 1961.

BLOCK, J. *The challenge of response sets.* New York: Appleton-Century-Crofts, 1965.

CHAPMAN, L. J., & CAMPBELL, D. T. Absence of acquiescence response set in the Taylor Manifest Anxiety Scale. *J. consult. Psychol.,* 1959, **23,** 465–466.

COPI, I. M. *Symbolic logic.* New York: Macmillan, 1954.

CHRISTIE, R., & LINDAUER, F. Personality structure. *Annu. Rev. Psychol.,* 1963, **14,** 201–238.

FOREHAND, G. A. Relationships among response sets and cognitive behaviors. *Educ. psychol. Measmt,* 1962, **22,** 287–302.

GOLDBERG, L. R., & RORER, L. G. Test-retest item statistics for original and reversed MMPI items. *Oregon Res. Inst. Res. Monogr.,* 1963, **3,** No. 1.

GRAY, C. W., & CRISP, H. E. The credibility of pure response set. Paper read at the annual meeting of the Southeastern Psychological Association, Gatlinburg, Tennessee, 1961.

HUSEK, T. R. Acquiescence as a response set and as a personality characteristic. *Educ. psychol. Measmt,* 1961, **21,** 295–308.

JACKSON, D. N., & MESSICK, S. Content and style in personality assessment. *Psychol. Bull.,* 1958, **55,** 243–252.

JACKSON, D. N., & MESSICK, S. Response styles on the MMPI: Comparison of clinical and normal samples. *J. abnorm. soc. Psychol.,* 1962, **65,** 285–299.

LOEVINGER, JANE. Theory and techniques of assessment. *Annu. Rev. Psychol.,* 1959, **10,** 287–316.

McGEE, R. K. The relationship between response style and personality variables: I. The measurement of response acquiescence. *J. abnorm. soc. Psychol.,* 1962, **64,** 229–233. (a)

McGEE, R. K. The relationship between response style and personality variables: II. The prediction of independent conformity behavior. *J. abnorm. soc. Psychol.,* 1962, **65,** 347–351. (b)

McGEE, R. K. Response style as a personality variable: By what criterion? *Psychol., Bull.,* 1962, **59,** 284–295. (c)

MESSICK, S., & JACKSON, D. N. Acquiescence and the factorial interpretation of the MMPI. *Psychol. Bull.,* 1961, **58,** 299–305.

NEPRASH, J. A. Reliability of questions in the Thurstone Personality Schedule. *J. soc. Psychol.,* 1936, **7,** 239–244.

PEABODY, D. Attitude content and agreement set in scales of authoritarianism, dogmatism, antisemitism, and economic conservatism. *J. abnorm. soc. Psychol.,* 1961, **63,** 1–11.

RORER, L. G. The function of item content in MMPI responses. Unpublished doctoral dissertation, Univer. of Minnesota, 1963.

RORER, L. G. The great response style myth. *Psychol. Rev.,* 1965, **63,** 129–156.

SCHOFIELD, W. S. MMPI changes with certain therapies. Unpublished doctoral dissertation, Univer. of Minnesota, 1948.

SILLER, J., & CHIPMAN, A. Response set paralysis: Implications for measurement and control. *Amer. Psychologist,* 1962, **17,** 391. (Abstract)

Good Impression, Social Desirability, and Acquiescence as Suppressor Variables

Charles Dicken

This study uses social desirability and acquiescence as suppressor variables for the California Psychological Inventory (CPI) (Gough, 1957).

A suppressor variable is defined as one which is significantly associated with a predictor, but essentially unassociated with the criterion for which the predictor is valid. When these relationships hold, validity can be improved by accounting for a portion of the variance of the predictor which is not associated with the criterion (Lubin, 1957; McNemar, 1945). Lubin expresses this increase in validity in terms of the relationship of r_{vc} to $R_{c.vs}$ where c is the criterion, v a valid predictor, s a suppressor variable, R the multiple correlation coefficient. He shows that when r_{sc} is approximately equal to zero, r_{vs} must exceed .40 for a predictive gain of 10 per cent. In the case of a suppressor variable, the regression weight of s (β_s) is negative. If r_{sc} is positive, the suppression effect tends to be vitiated unless r_{sc} is large enough to merit using s as simply another valid predictor (β_s positive). Intermediate levels of

The author is indebted to Harrison Gough, Donald MacKinnon, and Wallace Hall of the Institute of Personality Assessment and Research, Berkeley, for furnishing the data on which this study was based. Thanks are also due Donald Fiske, Lew Goldberg, Harrison Gough, Ardie Lubin, and Jerry Wiggins, who read a preliminary version of the report and furnished valuable comments and criticism.

Reprinted by permission of the publisher and the author from *Educational and Psychological Measurement*, 1963, **23**, 699–720.

r_{sc} yield no predictive gain. Lubin also distinguishes the "negative suppressor," a variable whose correlation with v is opposite in sign from its validity.

The suppression paradigm prompts search for variables related to criterion-irrelevant, "unwanted" predictor variance. Response sets or styles such as the "fake-good"–"fake-bad" dimension (Meehl & Hathaway, 1946), social desirability (Edwards, 1953, 1957b) and acquiescence (Cronbach, 1946; Fricke, 1956b; Jackson & Messick, 1961) have often been cited as potential contributors of irrelevant variance to personality inventories. Edwards and his associates (Edwards, 1953, 1957b, 1962; Edwards & Walker, 1961) have interpreted positive correlations between item desirability and item endorsement frequency and correlations between personality scores and the scales' or respondents' desirability level as indicating that the social desirability factor is highly significant. Factorial studies of the MMPI (Fordyce, 1956; Jackson & Messick, 1961; Wiggins, 1962) have been interpreted as indicating substantial components of both desirability and acquiescence variance.

Some attention has been given to response sets as personality dimensions in their own right (Berg, 1955; Couch & Kenniston, 1960; Meehl & Hathaway, 1946). Gough (1957) argues that empirical construction of self-report devices minimizes the problem of invalid response set variance since criterion-relevant aspects of response sets tend to be included and criterion-irrelevant components excluded.

Whatever the magnitude and relevance of response set variance, there is little doubt that individual differences in set can be demonstrated and reliably measured. Wiggins (1962) cites 11 measures of desirability responding and seven measures of acquiescence. Social desirability scales have been rationally constructed from item desirability judgments and empirically constructed by constrasting responses under standard and role-playing instructions. Acquiescence scales key all "true" items with heterogeneous or nondiscriminating content or items selected for high "controversiality" (middle-range endorsement frequency). There is also little doubt of the power of measures of the desirability type in detecting records of Ss who deliberately misrepresent themselves (Dicken, 1960; Gough, 1947; Wiggins, 1959).

If response sets contribute substantial amounts of invalid variance to personality scores of typical assessment subjects, then measurement of the set component and nullification of its effect by the suppression technique should increase validity. The suppressor model is implicit in the forced-choice social desirability control proposed by Edwards (1957a). McKinley, Hathaway, and Meehl (1948) reported increases in the concurrent validity of five MMPI clinical scales by using K, an empirically derived favorability bias measure, as a suppressor. However, later studies of MMPI scales with and without the K-correction have shown no differences in corrected and uncorrected scores (Tyler & Michaelis, 1953), insignificant gains in validity (Hunt, Carp, Cass, Winder, & Cantor, 1948; Schmidt, 1948), mixed gains and decrements (Monachesi, 1953), or consistent decrements in validity (Fulkerson, Freud, & Raynor, 1958). Suppressing acquiescence yielded no gain in validity for MMPI Hy (Fricke, 1956a) but did result in significant though small gains for a teacher effectiveness scale (Fricke, 1956b) and an MMPI adjustment key (Fulkerson, 1958).

The CPI is especially suitable for testing the effectiveness of suppression of response set variance. It measures socially favorable traits but lacks explicit control for desirability bias. Imbalance of true-false keying of some of the scales leaves it open to acquiescent bias. There is considerable validity data for the instrument in its present form (Gough, 1957, references revised, 1960).

Development of Response Set Measures

Good Impression (Gi)

Gough (1952) asked high school Ss to respond to 115 specially written items under standard instructions and again under instructions to create "an exceptionally favorable impression on an important person . . . the best picture of yourself." Significant endorsement frequency shifts occurred for 40 items, which were keyed for the Good Impression (Gi) scale in the direction of higher endorsement in the role-playing condition. Later studies (Gough, 1957; Dicken, 1960) indicate Gi is highly effective in identifying CPI protocols consciously biased in a favorable direction. Since more than three-fourths of the items on Gi are keyed false, it is possible that acquiescent tendencies as well as favorability bias are reflected (Jackson, 1960). Fricke (1956b) and Hanley (1956) contend that MMPI K, keyed 29/30 false, reflects acquiescence as well as favorability.

Social Desirability (SD) and Acquiescence (Acq)

A CPI key scorable for independent components of social desirability and acquiescence was derived according to Hanley's (1957) rationale. Hanley reasoned that an ideal desirability scale would consist of items for which endorsement frequency (communality) and item desirability are *negatively* related for "honest" subjects, i.e., items of high desirability which are *not* endorsed by unbiased Ss. Biased Ss would score high, "honest" Ss low on such a key.

Unfortunately, item desirability and item communality tend to be positively correlated for most items and subject groups (Edwards, 1957b). Both "honest" Ss who in fact possess the traits to which desirable items refer, and "biased" Ss who falsely claim the same traits may earn relatively high desirability scores. This expectation is supported by Wiggins' (1962) finding of high average desirability scores and low variability on Edwards (1957b) SD scale, in which item communality and item desirability are highly correlated. Wiggins' desirability key (Sd), composed of items with a low desirability-communality correlation showed greater variability and was more effective in screening desirability role players.

Hanley's procedure for selecting items with a low relationship between communality and desirability was used in the present study. A desirability scale so composed should yield high scores for desirability biased Ss, moderate scores in "honest" Ss, and low scores in "undesirability" biased Ss (malingerers). Hanley suggested that the usual high positive relationship of item desirability and item communality can be lowered by restricting the range of the latter. Items varying in desirability but falling in the middle endorsement frequency range (e.g., 36 per cent–64 per cent) are sought. Such an item pool also has properties suitable for an acquiescence key provided the desirability variable is counterbalanced.

For most normative samples, roughly 25 per cent of the 480 CPI items fall in the 36 per cent–64 per cent communality range (Gough, unpublished data). Communalities for Gough's high-school male ($N = 527$) and high-school female

($N = 510$) normative samples were used to identify 117 items which fall within the (36 per cent–64 per cent) range in both samples and which show no sex differences greater than 15 percentage units. Two clinicians rated these items for the social desirability of a "true" response. An excess of potentially "true-undesirable" items in relation to "true-desirable" items was reduced by random elimination from among the first item type, leaving 91 items. These were submitted to 41 male and 45 female high-school student judges for desirability ratings.[1]

Each item was rated separately by each judge on a 7-step scale from "true" socially undesirable to "true" socially desirable. "Socially desirable" was defined as "what people in general or society believes would be a good thing for a person to say about himself or herself in answering questions like this." Median SD ratings were computed for each item. Sixty-one of the items fell in the "neutral" desirability range (medians 3.0 to 4.99). There were 16 items with medians in the range 1.0 to 2.99 (true-undesirable) and 14 items in the range 5.0–6.99 (true-desirable). Two items with medians between 4.9 and 5.0 were added to the true-desirable group, yielding a 32-item key (SD) with 16 items keyed true and 16 items keyed false for desirability responding. Scale Acq consists of all 32 items keyed "true," half the Acq-keyed responses being "desirable," the other half "undesirable." Six items, all keyed false, are common

[1] High-school student judges were used in view of the large high-school samples available for testing the suppressor keys. The generality of the judgments for other populations is open to question, although high agreement on desirability ratings in diverse rater groups has been demonstrated (Edwards, 1957b; Klett & Yaukey, 1959). The similarity of the relationships of the Gi and SD scales to each other and to the predictor and criterion measures in both the high-school and non-high-school samples in the present study (Tables 2 and 3) also argues for generality of the judgments.

to *SD* and *Gi* and common with inverse keying to *Acq* and *Gi*.[2]

The median desirability values for the 32 CPI items obtained from the high school male judges correlate .50 with endorsement frequencies from Gough's normative high school males and .39 with endorsement frequency among 313 normative college males. Desirability medians from the high school female judges correlate .32 with endorsement frequency in Gough's normative high school females and .60 with endorsement frequency in 375 normative college females. These communality-desirability correlations are considerably lower than those reported for Edward's (1957b) *SD* scale (*r* = .91), indicating at least partial satisfaction of Hanley's rationale.

Reliability estimates for *SD* and *Acq* appear at the lower left of Table 1. Response set keys of the Hanley type would presumably have zero internal consistency in a population composed entirely of Ss not prone to social desirability or acquiescence. Large internal consistencies would be expected in subject groups with wide individual differences in desirability bias or acquiescence. Hanley's MMPI desirability key, *Sx*, which is logically similar to *SD*, has a KR 20 coefficient of .31. His *AT*, logically similar to *Acq*, has a KR 20 of .32. (These coefficients are .44 and .46 if adjusted for length to *SD* and *Acq*.) Low internal consistencies like these are what would be expected in populations with some Ss affected and some unaffected by response sets. *SD* is somewhat more internally consistent than *Sx*, which may reflect a greater communality-desirability association or a higher proportion of biased respondents. The

---

[2] CPI item numbers (published version) for the *SD-Acq* scale and keying direction for desirability are: *True* 52, 95, 97, 108, 135, 140, 152, 168, 242, 246, 276, 347, 354, 380, 389, 473; *False* 7, 44, 67, 70, 81, 101, 194, 219, 231, 233, 270, 298, 331, 335, 375, 462.

reliability estimates for *Acq* approximate those for Hanley's *AT*.

The intercorrelations of *Gi*, *SD*, and *Acq* in six samples are shown in Table 2. Item overlap determines a correlation of +.17 between *Gi* and *SD* correlation of −.17 between *Gi* and *Acq* (common-elements correlation, McNemar, 1949, pp. 117–118). Considering the reliabilities, the two desirability measures correlate enough to indicate that the empirical and rational and construction procedures give functionally similar measures. The *Gi-Acq* correlations suggest a small acquiescence component in the former. Scales *SD* and *Acq* are insignificantly correlated in these samples. The method of keying these scales restricts their potential intercorrelation although it does not require that it be zero. Dr. A. Lubin has pointed out to the author the following relationship. "Let 16 true-item scores = *t*, let 16 false-item scores = *f*. Then $SD = t + f$, $ACQ = t + (16 − f)$. The correlation between *SD* and *ACQ* must be zero if $s_t = s_f$. If $s_t > s_f$, the correlation will be positive; if $s_t < s_f$, the correlation will be negative."

Testing the Suppressor Paradigm

Samples and Criteria

The right-hand half of Table 1 summarizes the behavior rating criteria used in the six samples studied and shows rating reliability estimates from four of the samples. Names, abbreviations, scale lengths, keying proportions, and reliability estimates for CPI scales selected for pertinence to the criteria appear in the left half of the table. Lubin's notation *v* (predictor), *c* (criterion), and *s* (suppressor) is used here and in subsequent tables.

High-school cases. These were drawn from Gough's (1957) CPI cross-validation cases. Four schools are represented. The total samples from these

TABLE 1. IDENTIFICATION AND RELIABILITY ESTIMATES OF CPI, CRITERION, AND SUPPRESSOR VARIABLES

CPI Variables (v)

Scale	Abbr.	No. of Items	Proportion Keyed True	Reliability Estimates[a]
Dominance	Do	46	.52	.80
Sociability	Sy	36	.61	.84
Social presence	Sp	56	.45	.80
Self acceptance	Sa	34	.40	.71
Responsibility	Re	42	.36	.85
Self Control	Sc	50	.12	.86
Intellectual efficiency	Ie	52	.37	.80
Flexibility	Fx	22	.05	.49
Femininity	Fe	38	.45	.73
Suppressor Variables (s)				
Good impression	Gi	40	.23	.81
Social desirability	SD	32	.50	.62, .53, .67
Acquiesence	Acq	32	1.00	.23, .59, .27

Criterion Variables (c)

Rating	Abbr.	Reliability Estimates[b]			
		MED	ENG	SCI	CW
Dominance	Domin	.86	.89	.86	.88
Social participation	Soc Part	—	—	—	—
Social presence	Soc Pres	.84	—	—	—
Self acceptance	Self Acc	—	—	.77	—
Responsibility	Respons	.68	.74	.80	—
Impulsivity	Impuls	.75	.84	.77	.76
Intellectual competence	Int Comp	.76	.88	.82	—
Rigidity	Rigid	.69	.73	.77	.83
Cognitive flexibility	Cog Flex	—	.86	.77	—
Masculinity	Masc	—	.77	.65	—
Femininity	Fem	—	—	—	.91

[a] Retest, 7–21 days, 200 prison males (Gough, 1957) for predictor scales and for *Gi*. Estimates for *SD* and *Acq* are corrected split-half values from 100 college males, 100 college females, and 70 medical applicants, respectively.
[b] Corrected split-half coefficients: 3 raters vs 3 raters, MED sample; 5 raters vs 5 raters, ENG sample (40 cases) and SCI sample; 6 raters vs 6 raters, CW sample.

TABLE 2.   INTERCORRELATIONS OF SUPPRESSOR SCALES IN SIX SAMPLES

Samples	N	r_{Gi-SD}	r_{Gi-Acq}	r_{SD-Acq}
High School Males	120	74	− 27	− 02
High School Females	123	80	− 25	− 01
Medical Applicants	70	78	− 16	14
Student Engineers	66	65	− 36	− 20
Research Scientists	45	65	− 26	10
College Women	51	59	− 42	− 06

schools contain 519 males *(HSM)* and 543 females *(HSF)*. Selecting each third case from the junior-senior students in each school gave samples of 120 males and 123 females on which all r_{vs} (Pearsonian) correlations in the high-school data are based.

The trait criteria for the high-school cases are principals' and assistant principals' nominations of students judged extremely high and extremely low in each characteristic. The proportion of the students nominated at each extreme varies from 8 per cent to 9 per cent, proportions to be nominated having been specified by Gough. Thus from 82 per cent to 84 per cent of the sample falls in the unnominated middle range with respect to each trait. Typically a single rater nominated an S, so no interrater reliabilities are available. Correlations involving the criterion in the high-school samples (r_{vc} and r_{sc}) are biserial, computed by the wide-split formula which accounts for the omission of the middle cases (Peters & Van Voorhis, 1940, p. 385; see also Dicken, 1961). For purposes of the multiple regression analysis to follow, these biserial correlations are treated as estimates of the Pearsonian correlation between the test scores and a continuous criterion.

The analyses for the Dominance, Social Participation, and Impulsivity criteria are based on juniors and seniors only. There were 32 high and 32 low nominees in each sex sample. The Social Presence, Self-acceptance, and Responsibility criteria are based on 45 high and 45 low males for each of the first

two criteria, 44 high and 44 low males for the last, and 44 high and 44 low females for each criterion. The .05 significance levels for *r* cited in Table 3 for the high-school samples are based on Peters and Van Voorhis's error estimate for the widespread biserial with the smallest number of cases. The .05 level for the Pearsonian value based on the 120 and 123 cases used in computing r_{vs} is the same ($r = .17$).

IPAR cases. Male medical applicants (MED), engineering students (ENG), research scientists (SCI), and female college students (CW) assessed at the Institute of Personality Assessment and Research, Berkeley, (IPAR) were also used. Criterion rating scores for the traits are the averages of ratings of independent observers. The subjects' behavior was observed during comprehensive, two-day assessments. Procedures of the IPAR assessment program have been described in detail elsewhere (MacKinnon, Crutchfield, Barron, Block, Gough, & Harris, 1958). The subjects' behavior in group discussions, group problem-solving, laboratory and "stress" assessment procedures, informal social interactions, etc. were observed by the raters, who recorded their judgments at the close of the two-day period. Ten to 15 Ss were assessed during any given session. The MED rating scores are averages from seven independent raters. Ten raters were used for the SCI sample and for 40 of the ENG cases, 15 raters were for the remaining ENG cases, and 12 raters for the CW sample. Ratings for the MED, ENG, and CW cases were made with reference to a five-point, quasi-normal distribution and then averaged for each subject; the SCI cases were ranked in subsamples of 15 and average rating scores derived from the ranks.

The trait definitions used by the IPAR raters appear below.

Dominance. Personal ascendance in relations with others (resolute, self-assured, forceful, not easily intimidated, authoritative).

Responsibility. Willingness to accept the consequences of one's own behavior; dependability, trustworthiness, sense of obligation to the group. (This need not require the person to assume leadership or direction of group activity.)

Impulsivity. Inadequate control of impulse; lacking in self-discipline: self-centered, quick-tempered, and explosive.

Intellectual competence. The capacity to think, to reason, to comprehend, and to know.

Rigidity. Inflexibility of thought and manner. Stubborn, pedantic, unbending, firm.

Masculinity. Characteristically masculine in style and manner of behavior; self-sufficient; not sentimental or romantic; strong.

Cognitive Flexibility. The ability to shift and to adapt, and to deal with the new, the unexpected, and the unforeseen.

Femininity. Not further defined.

The IPAR rating reliabilities (Table 1) indicate substantial inter-judge agreement and relatively high stability for the composite ratings. The majority of the raters were psychologists highly experienced in assessment, and all raters were extensively pretrained with the trait definitions. Ratings of favorable traits share common or halo variance (MacKinnon, *et al.*, 1958). However, some degree of differentiation or discriminant validity of the present ratings is suggested by analyses of the MED, ENG, and SCI samples. The median

inter-trait, intra-sample criterion correlations for five traits in these three samples is $+.37$, a value considerably lower than the rating reliabilities.

CPI Scales

Predictor scales *Do, Sy, Re, S, Ie,* and *Fe* were empirically constructed; *Sp, Sa, Sc,* and *Fx* were constructed by rational item selection and internal consistency analysis. The sign of *Sc* is reversed in all analyses to correspond to the original scale (Impulsivity) and the trait ratings. The signs of *Fx* and *Fe* are reflected in samples MED, ENG, and SCI to correspond to the directionality of the rigidity and masculinity ratings.

Correlation Analysis

All entries *r* in Tables 3 and 4 are Pearsonian correlations with the exception of the high-school r_{vc} and r_{sc} values mentioned. The predictor-criterion relationships are exhaustive, i.e., all logically related CPI-rating criterion dyads available for each sample are included. Three instances of zero predictor-criterion validity are shown but left unanalyzed with respect to the suppressor paradigm. Some instances of very low validities are included for completeness although the potential predictive gains are negligible. Acquiescence was investigated as a suppressor variable (Table 4) in only those instances where the predictor scales' keying proportions substantially deviate from .50.

The multiple correlations for criterion prediction by *v* and *s* combined were computed and contrasted with the original validities by substracting r_{vc}^2 from $R_{c.vs}^2$. The "Gain" column in Tables 3 and 4 shows this difference, the increase in variance accounted for by the predictor variables when they are "corrected" for response set. Gain values marked* and ** indicate $R > r$ at the .05 and .01 significance levels, respec-

TABLE 3. GOOD IMPRESSION (Gi) AND SOCIAL DESIRABILITY (SD) AS SUPPRESSOR VARIABLES (s)

| | | Gi (s) | | | | | | SD (s) | | | | |
| | | | | | Gain | | | | | | Gain | |
v	c	r_{vc}	r_{sc}	r_{vs}	$R_{c.vs}$	$R_2 - r_{vc}^2$	Mode	r_{sc}	r_{vs}	$R_{c.vs}$	$R^2 - r_{vc}^2$	Mode
	HSM Sample (N:[a], r_{0s} = .17[b])											
Do	Domin	32	−02	19	32	00	VS	13	40	32	00	SC
Sy	Soc Part	19	−07	25	22	01	VS	05	47	20	00	SC
Sp	Soc Pres	31	−06	−38	31	00	VS	09	−32	36	03*	NS
Sa	Self Acc	21	03	−18	22	00	VS	11	08	23	01	VS
Re	Respons	45	04	62	54	09**	S	16	22	45	00	VS
−Sc	Impuls	18	−10	−81	19	00	SC	−22	−66	22	02	SC
	HSF Sample (N:[a], r_{0s} = .17[b])											
Do	Domin	36	04	38	37	01	VS	17	56	37	01	SC
Sy	Soc Part	38	18	43	38	00	SC	28	63	39	01	SC
Sp	Soc Pres	18	16	23	21	01	VS	26	39	27	04*	P
Sa	Self Acc	16	07	02	16	00	VC(VS)	04	26	16	00	VC(VS)
Re	Respons	38	22	26	41	02	VS	28	57	39	00	SC
−Sc	Impuls	14	01	−86	28	06**	NS	07	−71	29	06**	NS
	MED Sample (N = 70, r_{0s} = .24)											
Do	Domin	48	32	35	51	03	VS	35	45	50	02	SC
Re	Respons	−02	−05	47	—	—	VC	−02	49	—	—	VC
−Sc	Impuls	22	10	−75	46	16**	NS	11	−57	36	08*	NS
Ie	Int Comp	34	08	25	34	00	VS	19	33	35	01	VS
−Fx	Rigid	12	03	14	12	02	VC(VS)	−04	22	12	01	VC(VS)
Sp	Soc Pres	41	22	00	47	05*	P	24	10	42	00	VS

($N = 66$, $r_{05} = .24$)											
Do	Domin	56	09	16	56	00	VS	26	47	56	00	SC
Re	Respons	-03	09	34	—	—	VC(VS)	24	56	—	—	VC
-Sc	Impuls	-05	09	-75	33	01	VC	08	-59	32	00	VC
Ie	Int Comp	32	16	25	30	05	VC(VS)	13	37	23	01	VS
-Fx	Rigid	21	-23	-05	11	00	VS	-13	23	17	01	VC(VS)
-Fe	Masc	11	00	-29	11	00	VC(VS)	11	-21	17	01	VC(VS)
SCI Sample											
($N = 45$, $r_{05} = .30$)											
Do	Domin	16	-18	16	26	04	VC(VS)	-09	35	23	05	VC(VS)
Re	Respons	38	05	26	38	00	VS	09	27	38	00	VS
-Sc	Impuls	28	-25	-65	29	01	VC(SC)	-24	-41	31	02	VC(SC)
Ie	Int Comp	41	03	28	42	01	VS	02	47	45	03	(S)
-Fx	Rigid	23	-21	-23	28	02	VC(VS)	-07	13	26	01	VC(VS)
-Fe	Masc	43	-11	-08	44	01	VS	-17	10	47	04	VS
CW Sample											
($N = 51$, $r_{05} = .28$)											
Do	Domin	26	-23	05	36	06	VC(VS)	-13	18	31	03	VC(VS)
Fx	Cog Flex	26	-28	00	38	08*	P	-29	00	39	08*	P
Fe	Fem	19	06	-08	21	01	VC(VS)	-06	-17	20	00	VC(VS)

a See text for Ns used in High School Analyses.
b Based on smallest sample size: see text.
* $R > r$, $p < .05$
** $R > r$, $p < .01$

TABLE 4.   ACQUIESCENCE (Acq) AS A SUPPRESSOR(s)

Sample	v	c	r_{vc}	r_{sc}	r_{vs}	$R_{c \cdot vs}$	Gain	Mode
SCI[a]	Re	Respon	38	37	13	49	10*	P
HSM	Sc	Impuls	18	01	36	19	00	VS
HSF	Sc	Impuls	14	04	32	14	00	VC(VS)
MED	Sc	Impuls	22	09	36	22	00	VC(VS)
SCI	Sc	Impuls	28	−02	48	33	03	V.C(S)
MED	Ie	Int Comp	34	00	−07	34	00	VS
ENG	Ie	Int Comp	32	−03	16	33	01	VS
SCI	Ie	Int Comp	41	06	03	41	00	VS
MED	Fx	Rigid	12	−06	29	16	01	VC(VS)
ENG	Fx	Rigid	21	17	20	25	02	VC(VS)
SCI	Fx	Rigid	23	04	49	29	03	VC(S)
CW	Fx	Cog Flex	26	08	−29	31	03	VC(VS)

[a] *Acq* scores for the high school responsibility nominee samples not available.

tively (McNemar, 1949, p. 266). The "Mode" column is a classification of the manner of operation of the suppressor paradigm or the basis of its failure as follows.

S   Significant gain, s functions as a suppressor: high correlation with v, essentially no correlation with c, β_s is negative.

NS   Significant gain, s is a negative suppressor: correlation with v opposite in sign to correlation with c.

P   Significant gain, s is a predictor (β_s positive).

VC   No significant gain, r_{vc} not significantly greater than zero.

VS   No significant gain, r_{vs} too low (less than .40).

SC   No significant gain although r_{vc} significant and $r_{vs} \geq .40$: r_{sc} too large for suppression and too small for s to function as a predictor.[3]

[3] Since R is a function of three continuous variables, any categorization of the "mode" of the suppressor paradigm is arbitrary. Choice of the criterion of statistical significance of r_{vc} or $R > r$ is particularly arbitrary when N's vary. The VC category suffers, for instance, from the possibility of a significant $R > r$ even when r_{vc} fails of significance, and conversely a nonsignificant $R > r$ when r_{vc} is significant. Category VC was adopted to reflect the fact that r_{vc} must be of a certain magnitude before any level of r_{vs} is effective in pro-

Results

Suppression of desirability resulted in significant predictive gain in only 4 of 24 comparisons in the high-school data. In the non-high-school data, only 2 of 36 comparisons show a significant suppression effect, a result attributable to chance. There is no instance in the grand total of 50 comparisons of a large gain in validity by suppressing desirability. In almost half the instances in which R significantly exceeds r_{vc}, s functions as a predictor. The expectation that correcting personality scores for individual differences in desirability responding will increase validity is not fulfilled. There were no instances of significant gain in validity by suppression of acquiescence variance.

ducing a substantial gain. Similarly, the arbitrary level of $r_{vs} = .40$, the point of a 10% gain, was adopted to reflect the need for relatively large values of r_{vs}, even though a significant gain might be possible with a smaller value if the original validity were great enough. In a majority of instances the mode is clearcut: the categories adopted are assigned to all instances to give a general impression of the operation of the suppressor paradigm. Values of $r_{vs} < .40$ have been noted secondarily in instances of category VC, and one instance of satisfaction of the suppressor model which resulted in a nonsignificant gain because of a small r_{vc} noted (S).

Instances of Suppression

The desirability scales are most consistently correlated with the predictor scale Sc. The r_{vs} values invariably exceed .40. Suppression of desirability in Sc accounts for four of the six instances of a suppression effect. The failures are due to suppressor-criterion overlap or invalidity of v. Of the CPI scales studied, Sc is the only one constructed with reference to an "unfavorable" trait (Impulsivity), a similarity to the MMPI clinical scales in which substantial desirability variance has been reported.

Predictor Re might be expected to contain considerable desirability variance because of the highly evaluative nature of the trait. In the HSM sample, Gi functions as a suppressor for Re, but otherwise the desirability scales either fail to account for enough predictor variance or are criterion-related. An interesting paradox arises in the case of Sp, a scale also *a priori* suspect of a substantial desirability component. High desirability-responding high-school males tend to score *low* on Sp, enough so that s functions as a negative suppressor in one instance. High desirability-responding high-school females tend to score *high* on both Sp and the criterion, s functioning as a predictor of the criterion ratings. This suggests that the females are more successful simulators in relation to the raters or that social desirability tendencies are seen as an aspect of social presence in females but of its absence in males.

The Suppressor-Criterion Relationship

Where suppression does not fail because of insufficient suppressor-predictor-association (below), the model tends to be vitiated by low but positive association of the suppressors and the criterion. The average r_{sc} values in Table 5 are all positive except for the CW sample. Suppressor SD, typically more correlated with the predictors than is Gi, also correlates more with the criteria, which nullifies its advantage. Instances of s predicting the criterion have been noted. Association of s with c is not important in the case of the acquiescence scale, with the exception of the one instance where s is a predictor.

Predictor Variance Associated With Response Set

The preponderance of failures in predictive gain stem from an insufficient level of r_{vs}. Low validities play a role, but the typical r_{vs} values allow only negligible *proportional* gains regardless of validity. Table 5 shows the average

TABLE 5.   AVERAGE CORRELATIONS OF DESIRABILITY
MEASURES WITH "DESIRABLE" CRITERIA[a] AND
"DESIRABLE" PREDICTORS[b]

Sample	N_c	Gi		SD	
		r_{sc}	r_{vs}	r_{vc}	r_{vs}
HMS	6	00	22	13	25
HSF	6	11	36	16	52
All HS	12	06	29	14	39
MED	6	07	28	12	29
ENG	6	08	31	13	33
SCI	6	04	28	03	21
CW	3	−15	−01	−16	00
All Non-HS	21	03	25	06	24
Total	33	04	26	09	29

[a] Values of r_{vc} involving Impulse and Rigid reflected.
[b] Values of r_{vs} involving $-Sc$, $-Fc$, $-Fx$ reflected.
[c] N = number of correlations on which average value based.

r_{vs} values for the desirability suppressors in each sample and for the total high-school and non-high-school samples. Signs of predictors *Sc*, *Fe*, and *Fx* which were reflected in Tables 3 and 4 were again reflected before computing the average *r*'s, so that the correlations of "desirable" predictor scales with the desirability measures is represented in all instances.

Somewhat more of the variance of the high-school females' predictor scales is associated with the desirability measures than for the high-school males, and *SD* is somewhat more effective than *Gi* in accounting for predictor variance. Only in the most favorable case (HSF-SD) does the average r_{vs} exceed .40, and it is this case that has the greatest suppressor-criterion relationship. For HSM, all the other samples, and for all samples combined, less than 10% of the predictor's variance is associated, on the average, with the desirability measures.

These low desirability-predictor correlations and the results of an independent study suggest social desirability is less important in the CPI than might have been assumed from previous questionnaire studies, most of which have been based on the MMPI. Fordyce (1956) found an average correlation of .60 between Edwards' *SD* scale and the MMPI clinical scales, but Goldberg, Rust, and Korn (unpublished data, Stanford University Counseling Center, 1960) found average correlations of only .20 (88 college males) and .34 (39 college females) between Wiggins' (1959) MMPI social desirability scale and the 15 CPI personality scales.

To investigate the role of desirability in the CPI further, item desirability values (Messick & Jackson, 1961) based on judgments of 83 males and 88 female collegians, sex samples pooled, were correlated with CPI normative item endorsement frequencies (313 male and 375 female college students, sex samples averaged) for 174 CPI items

taken from the MMPI. While Edwards (1957b) cites the communality-desirability correlation of .87 for personality items, the correlation for these 174 CPI items is .71, indicating about half of the variance of CPI item endorsement frequency is associated with mean item desirability level. The stability afforded both the desirability and communality variables by the large numbers of judges and respondents lends confidence to the obtained correlation as an estimate of the association of the two variables in these 174 items. The correlation is if anything an overestimate of the association of communality and desirability in the full CPI item pool, since CPI items common to the MMPI are likely to vary more in degree of psychopathological content (low desirability-low endorsement) than non-MMPI items.

With respect to acquiescence, even the most imbalanced predictor keys (*Sc* and *Fx*) are not frequently enough associated with the acquiescence scale to indicate that acquiescence variance is a predictive hazard.

Discussion

Like good men, good suppressor variables are hard to find. In addition to the studies indicating ineffectiveness or minimal effectiveness of the MMPI *K* correction and of acquiescence keys, unpublished studies by Harrison Gough (personal communication) and by the Personnel Research Branch, Adjutant General's Office (personal communication from Jack Sawyer) which failed to find means of improving validity by suppression of test-taking attitudes may be cited. Although the response set measures used in suppressor studies have often been quite carefully constructed, are reliable and capable of reflecting a range of individual differences, and are effective in detecting extremes of test-taking attitudes (faking), they do not ordinarily account for enough criterion-irrelevant predictor variance to warrant their use in correcting the scores of typical assessment subjects. Two different rationales were employed in constructing the desirability measures used in the present study; neither is effective. It seems unlikely that further refinements of scaling the desirability variable will be fruitful in this context. Norman (1961) points out that until predictors can be developed that account for more criterion variance than is usually the case, the absolute predictive gain from suppression where r_{vs} is at or about .40 is negligible, and suggests that attention should be given to discovering independent primary predictors rather than suppressor variables.

The criterion is probably the most questionable element in the evidence pointing to the futility of attempting to control response set variance. Criterion measures with more construct validity than ratings or psychiatric or socially defined classifications might be best predicted by personality measures freed from social desirability. While composite behavior ratings such as those obtained at IPAR are probably about as valid as is possible with respect to such factors as rater training, spectrum of behavior observed, reliability, and minimization of rater bias, ratings may not be a suitable basis for evaluating either test validity or the response set problem. The best ratings may show contamination by the social desirability factor that a better criterion would not.

The significance of this for the present data is limited, however, by the fact that low r_{vs} values rather than high r_{sc} values are the most frequent source of difficulty.

Some degree of desirability "bias" on the part of the subject may be a relevant aspect of personality, perceived and (properly) included in the criterion by raters. Above-average self-esteem, or absence of psychopathology may result in above-average social desirability

responding, as may actual possession of more than the average amount of desirable personality traits. The positive relationship of MMPI K to such variables as class status (Dahlstrom & Welsh, 1960), improvement in psychotherapy (Barron & Leary, 1955), and pilot adjustment (Fulkerson *et al.*, 1958) may indicate greater defensiveness in groups with more favorable status but is also interpretable as indicating that moderately elevated K scores reflect good personality integration. Anxiety scales such as Taylor's MAS or Welsh's A (Welsh, 1956) are substantially (negatively) related to social desirability and yet appear to have considerable construct validity. Schultz (1962) contends that factors which best account for variance in groups of items or tests (factors frequently interpreted as social desirability or acquiescence) may reflect a combination of content and response sets. He suggests, "Edwards' SD scale accounts for much of the variance of other MMPI scales since its keying is similar to those scales in terms of Social Desirability, Acquiescence, and content" (Schultz, 1962, p. 34).

The available evidence supports Gough's position that social desirability variance need not and perhaps should not be removed from scales designed to measure personality traits of the type studied here. The kind of interpretation placed on the social desirability variable (Edwards, 1953, 1957b, 1962; Edwards & Walker, 1961) which Wiggins (1962) termed "sinister" does not seem justified. Wiggins (1962, p. 226) notes the logical similarity of the desirability and communality concepts, pointing out that it is not surprising ". . . that the majority of normals will endorse what is considered to be the acceptable response by the majority of normals." A desirability-communality correlation such as observed for CPI items, leaves considerable latitude for deviation of the *group* item endorsement level from that predictable from item desirability. An *individual* has even more latitude for deviating from the desirable response on an appreciable number of items, since individuals would deviate from the communal response even if desirability and communality were perfectly correlated in group data. Even though probability of a desirable response is high (e.g., .81, Edwards, 1962), the number of non-desirable responses which will typically occur (91 in a 480 item inventory) is sufficient to elevate or depress several personality scores quite distinctively. Several studies (Heilbrun & Goodstein, 1961; Rosen & Mink, 1961; Taylor, 1959, 1961) document the willingness of at least some Ss to make self-descriptive responses which run counter to their own desirability judgments. CPI *Re*, is made up of items for which the keyed response is almost invariable "desirable," yet individuals differ in the number of items endorsed and these differences predict non-test behaviors. In the case of "subtle-zero" items (Meehl, 1945) the desirable response is the significant one: deviations from the norm in terms of hyper-desirability or hyper-communality are in this instance diagnostic.

It seems unremarkable that mean personality scale scores can be predicted by considerations of desirability (Edwards, 1962). Mean scores are in fact used to reflect response communalities in establishing norms for gauging an individual's distinctiveness relative to the normative group. The present data do not indicate a high degree of predictability of individuals' scores on the basis of social desirability. The high individual predictability implied by Edwards and Walker's (1961) study

appears equivocal because of differences in the lengths of the scales across which an individual's desirability-personality score correlation was computed.

The present data indicate accounting for individual differences in acquiescence is not worthwhile. This finding is consistent with item reversal studies of the Taylor MAS (Chapman & Campbell, 1959) and the MMPI (DeSoto & Kuethe, 1959; Dicken & Van Pelt, unpublished data) which suggest acquiescence is of relatively little importance in determining endorsement of items which make specific personal references. Factor analyses indicating substantial acquiescence variance in personality scales may be at least in part a result of content differences in items worded in a positive or negative fashion. Schultz (1962) found only a very small acquiescence factor when item content and keying direction were systematically counterbalanced.

Summary

Measures of good impression, social desirability, and acquiescence were used as suppressor variables with nine personality scales of the California Psychological Inventory. Nine corresponding behavior ratings were used as a criteria in one or more of six independent samples. Significant gains in validity by accounting for good impression and desirability were rare. No gain in validity resulted from suppressing acquiescence. Existing methods of correcting for response set variance in personality scales do not appear pragmatic. The importance of social desirability and acquiescence in questionnaire personality assessment may have been overemphasized.

REFERENCES

BARRON, F., and LEARY, T. "Changes in Psychoneurotic Patients with and without Psychotherapy." *Journal of Consulting Psychology*, XIX (1955), 239–245.

BERG, I. "Response Bias and Personality: The Deviation Hypothesis." *Journal of Psychology*, XL (1955), 61–72.

CHAPMAN, L., and CAMPBELL, D. "Absence of Acquiescence Response Set in the Taylor Manifest Anxiety Scale." *Journal of Consulting Psychology*, XXIII (1959), 465–466.

COUCH, A., and KENNISTON, K. "Yeasayers and Naysayers: Agreeing Response Set as a Personality Variable." *Journal of Abnormal and Social Psychology*, LX (1960), 151–174.

CRONBACH, L. "Response Sets and Test Validity." *Educational and Psychological Measurement*, VI (1946), 475–494.

DAHLSTROM, W., and WELSH, G. An *MMPI Handbook*. Minneapolis: University of Minnesota Press, 1960.

DeSOTO, C., and KUETHE, J. "The Set to Claim Undesirable Symptoms in Personality Inventories." *Journal of Consulting Psychology*, XXIII (1959), 496–500.

DICKEN, C. "Simulated Patterns on the California Psychological Inventory." *Journal of Counseling Psychology*, VII (1960), 24–31.

DICKEN, C. "Note on Biserial Correlation and the Validity of the California Psychological Inventory." *Journal of Counseling Psychology*, VIII (1961), 185–186.

EDWARDS, A. "The Relationship Between the Judged Desirability of a Trait and the Probability that the Trait Will Be Endorsed." *Journal of Applied Psychology*, XXXVII (1953), 90–93.

EDWARDS, A. *Manual for the Edwards Personal Preference Schedule*. (Rev.) New York: Psychological Corporation, 1957. (a)

EDWARDS, A. *The Social Desirability Variable in Personality Assessment and Research*. New York: Dryden, 1957. (b)

EDWARDS, A. "Social Desirability and Expected Means on MMPI Scales." *Educational and Psychological Measurement*, XXII (1962), 71–76.

EDWARDS, A., and WALKER, J. "A Short Form of the MMPI: The *SD* Scale." *Psychological Reports*, VIII (1961), 485–486.

FORDYCE, W. "Social Desirability in the MMPI." *Journal of Consulting Psychology*, XX (1956), 171–175.

FRICKE, B. "Conversion Hysterics and the MMPI." *Journal of Clinical Psychology*, XII (1956), 322–326. (a)

FRICKE, B. "Response Set as a Suppressor Variable in the OAIS and the MMPI." *Journal of Consulting Psychology*, XX (1956), 161–169. (b)

FULKERSON, S. "An Acquiescence Key for the MMPI." Report No. 58–71. School of Aviation Medicine USAF, Randolph AFB, Texas, 1958.

FULKERSON, S., FREUD, S., and RAYNOR, G. "The Use of the MMPI in the Psychological Evaluation of Pilots." *Journal of Aviation Medicine*, XXIX (1958), 122–129.

GOUGH, H. "Simulated Patterns on the MMPI." *Journal of Abnormal and Social Psychology*, XLII (1947), 215–225.

GOUGH, H. "On Making a Good Impression." *Journal of Educational Research*, XLVI (1952), 33–42.

GOUGH, H. *Manual for the California Psychological Inventory*. Palo Alto: Consulting Psychologists Press, 1957.

HANLEY, C. "Social Desirability and Responses to Items from Three MMPI Scales: D, Sc, and K." *Journal of Applied Psychology*, XL (1956), 324–328.

HANLEY, C. "Deriving a Measure of Test-Taking Defensiveness." *Journal of Consulting Psychology*, XXI (1957), 391–397.

HEILBRUN, A., and GOODSTEIN, L. "Consistency Between Social Desirability Ratings and Item Endorsement as a Function of Psychopathology." *Psychological Reports*, VIII (1961), 69–70.

HUNT, H., CARP, A., CASS, W., WINDER, C., and KANTOR, R. "A Study of the Differential Diagnostic Efficiency of the MMPI." *Journal of Consulting Psychology*, XII (1948), 331–336.

JACKSON, D. "Stylistic Response Determinants in the California Psychological Inventory." *Educational and Psychologi-*

cal Measurement, XX (1960), 339–346.

JACKSON, D., and MESSICK, S. "Content and Style in Personality Assessment." *Psychological Bulletin*, LV (1958), 243–252.

JACKSON, D., and MESSICK, S. "Acquiescence and Desirability as Response Determinants on the MMPI." *Educational and Psychological Measurement*, XXI (1961), 771–790.

KLETT, C., and YAUKEY, D. "A Cross-Cultural Comparison of Judgements of Social Desirability." *Journal of Social Psychology*, XLIX (1959), 19–26.

LUBIN, A. "Some Formulae for Use With Suppressor Variables." *Educational and Psychological Measurement*, XVII (1957), 286–296.

MACKINNON, D., CRUTCHFIELD, R., BARRON, F., BLOCK, J., GOUGH, H., and HARRIS, R. "An assessment Study of Air Force Officers." Technical Report WADC-TR-58-91. Lackland AFB, Texas, 1958.

MCKINLEY, J., HATHAWAY, S., and MEEHL, P. "The MMPI: VI. 'The K Scale.'" *Journal of Consulting Psychology*, XII (1948) 20–31.

MCNEMAR, Q. "The Mode of Operation of Suppressant Variables." *American Journal of Psychology*, LVIII (1945), 544–555.

MCNEMAR, Q. *Psychological Statistics*. New York: John Wiley & Sons, 1949.

MEEHL, P. "The Dynamics of Structured Personality Tests." *Journal of Clinical Psychology*, I (1945), 296–303.

MEEHL, P., and HATHAWAY, S. "The K Factor as a Suppressor Variable in the MMPI." *Journal of Applied Psychology*, XXX (1946), 525–564.

MESSICK, S., and JACKSON, D. "Desirability Scale Values and Dispersions for MMPI Items." *Psychological Reports*, VIII (1961), 409–414.

MONACHESI, E. "Personality Patterns of Juvenile Delinquents as Indicated by the MMPI." In HATHAWAY, S., and MONACHESI, E. (Eds.) *Analysing and Predicting Juvenile Delinquency with the MMPI*. Minneapolis: University of Minnesota Press, 1953.

NORMAN, W. "Problems of Response Contamination in Personality Assessment." ASD-TN-61-43. Personnel Laboratory, Lackland AFB, Texas, 1961.

PETERS, C., and VAN VOORHIS, W. *Statistical Procedures and Their Mathematical Bases*. New York: McGraw-Hill, 1940.

ROSEN, E., and MINK, SHIRLEY. "Desirability of Personality Traits as Perceived by Prisoners." *Journal of Clinical Psychology*, XVII (1961), 147–151.

SCHMIDT, H. "Notes on the MMPI: The K Factor." *Journal of Consulting Psychology*, XII (1948), 337–342.

SCHULTZ, C. "Response Set Factors Revealed by Factor Analysis of an Unconfounded Item Pool." Mimeographed: ONR Contract 477 (33), University of Washington, Seattle, May, 1962.

TAYLOR, J. B. "Social Desirability and MMPI Performance: The Individual Case." *Journal of Consulting Psychology*, XXIII (1959), 514–517.

TAYLOR, J. B. "What Do Attitude Scales Measure: The Problem of Social Desirability." *Journal of Abnormal and Social Psychology*, LXII (1961), 386–390.

TYLER, F., and MICHAELIS, J. "K-Scores Applied to MMPI Scales for College Women." *Educational and Psychological Measurement*, XII (1953), 459–466.

WELSH, G. "Factor Dimensions A and R." In WELSH, G., and DAHLSTROM, W. (Eds.) *Basic Readings on the MMPI in Psychology and Medicine*. Minneapolis: University of Minnesota Press, 1956.

WIGGINS, J. "Interrelationships Among MMPI Measures of Dissimulation under Standard and Social Desirability Instructions." *Journal of Consulting Psychology*, XXIII (1959), 419–427.

WIGGINS, J. "Strategic, Method, and Stylistic Variance in the MMPI." *Psychological Bulletin*, LIX (1962), 224–242.

Chapter 7

Validation Studies of Structured Tests of Personality

■ Having explored some of the problems peculiar to structured tests of personality, we now turn our attention to studies of the validity of four of the more than 200 objective personality tests now available (Horrocks, 1964). The tests selected represent a broad spectrum of the approaches to structured personality testing currently in use. The first is the Minnesota Multiphasic Personality Inventory, by far the most widely used structured personality test (Sundberg, 1961). As was noted in Chapter 5, the MMPI is used primarily for the assessment of psychological disturbances of various types, although a variety of new scales have been derived since it was first published. The California Psychological Inventory (CPI) is similar in form and in method of construction, but it has as its goal the assessment of "folk culture" variables, constructs which are cultural universals existing among all people at all times and places (Gough, 1960a). "Dominance," "sociability," "responsibility" and so on are examples of these dimensions which Gough feels that people everywhere use in their appraisals of one another and which the CPI seeks to assess. The Sixteen Personality Factor Questionnaire is the best known of a number of factor analytic personality tests which have in common the assumption that it is necessary to define operationally the factorially pure personality constructs to be assessed through the use of multivariate statistical methods (Horrocks, 1964). The Myers-Briggs Type Indicator, on the other hand, derives its constructs directly from Jungian psychology.

The four studies of the MMPI which are included here test its validity not only in the clinic and the laboratory but also use a variety of criteria and study the global use of the test as well as the validity of some individual MMPI scales. In the first study, Little and Shneidman investigate how well clinicians can interpret an MMPI profile using interpretations based on more complete information as the criterion and a Q sort as the dependent variable. Branaca and Podolnick have subjects take the MMPI normally, under instructions to feign anxiety and under hypnotically induced anxiety, and study the effects on the clinical and validity scales. Griffith, Upshaw, and Fowler, in a construct validation study, hypothesize that students high on the Pt scale will show more uncertainty while making psychophysical weight discriminations than will students high on the Ma scale. Megargee and Mendelsohn investigate the validity of 12 measures of hostility and control devised since the MMPI was originally published using criminal assaultiveness as a criterion.

For further material on the MMPI, the reader should consult Welsh and Dahlstrom (1956) and Dahlstrom and Welsh (1960).

As noted above, one of the goals of the CPI is to assess constructs which are culturally universal. Cross-cultural validation studies are especially relevant, therefore, and both of the articles included in this chapter are of this type. The first reports an effort to derive and cross-validate a multiple regression equation to predict high school grades in the United States and Italy, while the second focuses on the Socialization scale, which has been found capable of discriminating socialized from unsocialized groups in the United States, and applies it to the task of differentiating groups varying in socialization in India.

The reader who is interested in the CPI would do well to read the *California Psychological Inventory Manual* (Gough, 1960b). Further material can be located by referring to the indexed bibliography accompanying the *Manual*, which is brought up to date regularly by the publishers.

In the next study, Raymond Cattell describes the validation and improvement of the Sixteen Personality Factor Questionnaire. As might be expected, factor analysis is a major validational technique. While this study has been dated somewhat by the vigorous research program being carried out by Cattell and his associates at the Institute for Personality and Ability Testing (IPAT), it is included since it contains a good basic description of this instrument which is relatively unfamiliar to many clinicians. The reader who wishes to further familiarize himself with factor analytic personality assessment would do well to consult Cattell (1965) and the references in Cattell's article in Chapter 5. Nor should he overlook the earlier series of factor analytic personality inventories published by Guilford culminating in the Guilford-Zimmerman Temperament Survey in 1949.

The last instrument discussed is a relative newcomer to the clinician's armamentarium, the Myers-Briggs Type Indicator. In this monograph, Stricker and Ross report the relation of the test's four major variables with a number of other test measures including the MMPI, the CPI, and the SVIB. Further work on the MBTI can be found by consulting Myers (1962), Stricker and Ross (1964), and by writing the publisher.

REFERENCES

CATTELL, R. B. *The Scientific Analysis of Personality.* Baltimore: Penguin Books, Inc., 1965.

DAHLSTROM, W. G., & WELSH, G. S. *An MMPI Handbook: A Guide to Use in Clinical Practice and Research.* Minneapolis: University of Minnesota Press, 1960.

GOUGH, H. G. Cross-cultural studies of the socialization continuum. *American Psychologist,* 1960, **15**, 410–411. (Abstract) (a)

GOUGH, H. G. *Manual for the California Psychological Inventory.* Palo Alto, California: Consulting Psychologist Press, Inc., 1960 (b)

HORROCKS, J. E. *Assessment of Behavior.* Columbus, Ohio: Charles E. Merrill Books, 1964.

MYERS, ISABEL BRIGGS. *The Myers-Briggs Type Indicator Manual.* Princeton, N.J.: Educational Testing Service, 1962.

STRICKER, L. J., & ROSS, J. An assessment of some structural properties of Jungian personality typology. *Journal of Abnormal and Social Psychology,* 1964, **68,** 62–71.

SUNDBERG, N. D. The practice of psychological testing in clinical services in the United States. *American Psychologist,* 1961, **16,** 79–83.

WELSH, G. S., & DAHLSTROM, W. G. (Eds.) *Basic Readings on the MMPI in Psychology and Medicine.* Minneapolis: University of Minnesota Press, 1956.

THE MINNESOTA MULTIPHASIC PERSONALITY

INVENTORY

The Validity of MMPI Interpretations

Kenneth B. Little and Edwin S. Shneidman

In clinical psychology, diagnostic tests are the most common source of personality descriptions. The descriptions range from short paragraphs, emphasizing a single salient characteristic of the subject, to elaborate many-paged analyses of several aspects of his psychological functioning. Very rarely are the conclusions drawn by the clinician restricted simply to a diagnosis. The

Presented with the approval of the Chief Medical Director of the Veterans Administration. The statements and conclusions published by the authors are a result of their own study and do not necessarily reflect the opinion or policy of the Veterans Administration.

This investigation was supported by a research grant from the National Institute of Mental Health of the National Institutes of Health, Public Health Service, administered by the University of Southern California.

Reprinted by permission of the American Psychological Association and the authors from the *Journal of Consulting Psychology,* 1954, **18,** 425–428.

protocol, whether in the form of the set of scores or a profile from a personality inventory or the verbatim responses to projective materials, leads the interpreter to make a large number of inferences, only one of which is a diagnosis qua diagnosis. These inferences seldom have a direct overt relationship to objective characteristics of the protocol; they are a function of the interpreter's experience, skill, personality, etc., as well as of the test itself.

This situation is taken somewhat for granted with projective tests but is frequently ignored in considering the more objective personality measures such as the MMPI. The pristine beauty of the quantitative scores on this inventory has generally led investigators into testing a single inference, i.e., diagnosis, when judging the test's validity. Yet in practice the MMPI is used quite differently. The clinician inspects the profile, occasionally scores additional scales, perhaps examines the actual responses to individual items, and somehow during the process arrives at a number of conclusions which he embodies in a formal or informal psychological report. The validity, in clinical practice, of the instrument would therefore seem best reflected by some measure of the number of correct inferences arrived at by the clinician. The present paper is the report of a study of the validity, as just defined, of the MMPI.

It is obvious that an index of validity as described above will vary with the clinician who does the interpreting and that no unique figure will be obtained. The authors have suggested in a previous paper [1] that the central tendency of such indices among competent clinicians interpreting a variety of subject protocols might be considered the validity of the instrument itself. In this study, the results for a number of interpreters working with a single protocol are presented. They indicate only what *can* be achieved and not necessarily what might occur with other protocols. In addition, the results were examined to determine the types of inferences made on the basis of the MMPI and the relationship between the resultant types and their accuracy.

Procedure

The general procedure has been described in more detail elsewhere [1] and is presented here in synoptic form.

Eleven psychologists, competent in the use and interpretation of the MMPI and accustomed to writing psychological reports from it, were presented with the MMPI profile of a subject identified to them as male, age 25, and single.[1] On the basis of the information conveyed to them by this profile, each made a Q sort [3] of 150 items of

[1] The test materials and case history data of the subject are presented in *Thematic Test Analysis* [2].

personality description. The continuum was from "Most True" to "Most False" for the subject. The items were a stratified sample from a total item population of 1604 items abstracted from 17 psychological reports written about the subject on the basis of his TAT and MAPS test protocols. The 1600 items covered, so far as could be determined, the usual aspects of psychological functioning presented in psychological reports.

The intercorrelations of the distribution of items for the 11 MMPI judges are presented in Table 1.

TABLE 1.   AMONG THE Q SORTS OF 11
MMPI INTERPRETERS*

Inter-preter	2	3	4	5	6	7	8	9	10	11
1	63	62	50	65	73	56	68	64	56	67
2		68	56	62	66	51	68	72	61	55
3			62	56	50	55	64	68	51	49
4				48	45	52	60	66	47	49
5					68	42	72	51	67	62
6						54	63	61	61	67
7							50	64	43	48
8								60	66	56
9									52	55
10										58

* Decimal points omitted.

The criterion consisted of the consensus of 29 experienced clinical psychologists and psychiatrists who Q sorted the same 150 items, except that their sorting was made on the basis of a complete clinical folder about the subject. The folder contained medical examination reports, laboratory data, course of treatment notes, psychotherapy notes, social history, consultation reports, etc., but excluded the psychological test reports.

A factor analysis of the intercorrelations of the 29 criterion judges [1] indicated that a single general factor would account for 90% of the communality among them. Accordingly, a new Q sort was constructed for the criterion itself, as follows:

1. A multiple-regression equation for estimating the criterion general factor was derived using the criterion judges' general factor loadings as correlations. It was found that with only three variables (judges) a correlation of .925 with the general factor was secured.

2. The Beta coefficients for these three criterion judges were used to weight each of their Q-sort scores for the 150 items. The three weighted scores for each item were summed to form a new composite score for that item.

3. The 150 items were then ordered into the criterion Q sort on the basis of their rank position in the distribution of composite scores.

To determine the validity coefficients, the 11 MMPI judges were correlated with this composite criterion Q sort.

Results

A cluster analysis [4] of the matrix of intercorrelations of the MMPI interpreters (Table 1) yielded three groups of judges. Table 2 gives the estimated correlations of each judge

TABLE 2.   ESTIMATED CORRELATIONS OF EACH MMPI INTERPRETER WITH THE CLUSTER DOMAINS AND THE VALIDITY COEFFICIENT FOR EACH INTERPRETER

Cluster	Judge	Cluster Domain A	B	C	h^2	Validity
A	1	.84	.77	.73	.71	.72
	6	.84	.77	.64	.71	.74
	11	.81	.71	.63	.66	.70
B	5	.78	.84	.64	.71	.71
	8	.75	.83	.76	.69	.73
	10	.70	.81	.62	.66	.58
C	3	.65	.69	.80	.64	.70
	4	.58	.62	.79	.62	.56
	9	.72	.66	.83	.69	.66
	2	.74	.77	.81	.66	.70
	7	.63	.54	.71	.50	.52

Note.—Italicized figures are the correlations of the judges with the domain of which they are a member.

TABLE 3.   ESTIMATED CORRELATIONS AMONG THE CLUSTER DOMAINS

Cluster Domain	A	B	C
A	1.00	.90	.80
B	.90	1.00	.81
C	.80	.81	1.00

with each of the three cluster domains and also their communalities. (The correlation of a judge with the domain of which he is a member is analogous to a factor loading in a factor analysis.) Table 3 gives the correlations among the cluster domains themselves.

To test the hypothesis that the three clusters were sufficient to account for all the common variance among the judges, a table of theoretical correlations was computed on the basis of each judge's correlation with the cluster of which he was a member and the correlations among the domains (Tables 2 and 3). A comparison with the 55 empirical correlations of Table 1 indicated that 44 (76%) of the theoretical correlations were within one standard deviation of the corresponding empirical ones, 54 (98%) were within two standard deviations, and only one theoretical correlation deviated from its empirical counterpart by more than two standard deviations. The mean absolute discrepancy between the two sets of correlations was .024. It appears, therefore, that the three clusters do adequately account for the common variance in the matrix.

To identify the groups of judges, an average Q sort was made for each of the clusters. The 20 Most True items in each average Q sort were examined, and those items that appeared for one and only one cluster were isolated. The same process was also repeated for the 20 Most False items of the three clusters.

The *Most True* items for cluster A were:

He is in the early stages of paranoid schizophrenia.

He has strong latent homosexual feelings.

The psychological threat to him is really of a homosexual nature.

He has an enormous amount of hostility.

He would be threatened by interpretations given early in psychotherapy.

His principal conflict is in the sexual area.

He has at least bright normal intelligence.

The *Most False* items for cluster A were:

He does not have much anxiety.

He should be able to progress satisfactorily in psychotherapy without excessive support.

Masturbation creates no psychological problems for him.

He seems little concerned with his bodily well-being.

His ideation is not paranoid.

The *Most True* items for cluster B were:

He appears to be a solitary person.

An acute break with reality has probably occurred.

The total picture is consistent with a schizophrenic disorder with potential paranoid and hebephrenic coloring.

He aviods social disapproval by engaging in solitary activity.

He has never learned to solve his problems by other than avoidant means.

He has never adequately learned social skills.

The *Most False* items for cluster B were:

He appears to be an outgoing person.

For him, withdrawal is a relatively unimportant mode of reacting to frustration.

He has little guilt feelings concerning his aggressive impulses.

He has the well-preserved mind of a person who is not psychotic.

He is probably not disoriented.

The *Most True* items for cluster C were:

He perceives the world as consistently unloving.

He has marked guilt feelings.

His guilt feelings may overwhelm him.

He feels deprived of the oral gratifications of childhood.

He suffers from feelings of rejection.

In fantasy he longs for kind parents.

The *Most False* items for cluster C were:

He feels generally that he is master of his own fate.

He has little orality.

His superego is relatively mature.

This technique of identification emphasizes differences among the clusters; the actual high degree of agreement is apparent from the correlations among the cluster domains (Table 3). However, inspection of the cluster-identifying items suggests that the judges of cluster A had a slight preference for emphasizing the nature of the conflicts (over sexual impulses) of the subject; the judges of cluster B had a preference for emphasizing the primary defenses (withdrawal) of the subject; and the judges of cluster C had a preference for emphasizing the affective reactions (feelings of rejection) of the subject. All are describing a person who is essentially schizophrenic.

The right-hand column of Table 2 gives the validity figure for each judge in the form of a correlation with the composite Q sort described previously. The mean value of this validity figure for cluster A was .72, for cluster B, .67, and for cluster C, .63, with an over-all value for the 11 judges of .67. An analysis of variance indicated that the differences among the three clusters were not significant.

Discussion

The data presented above indicated that substantial agreement may occur between descriptions of an individual based upon his MMPI profile and those based upon an elaborate clinical history. The degree of agreement can be emphasized by pointing out that the average general factor loading (or correlation with the criterion) of the criterion judges themselves was only .74 [1] as compared to the average of .67 for the test judges with the composite criterion Q sort. Moreover, the former figure is a correlation with a criterion of unit reliability whereas the latter is with an estimate of that criterion only. Correction of the average validity figure of the MMPI judges for the unreliability of the "true" criterion estimate would further decrease the difference between the two figures cited.

Certain cautions need to be kept in mind in evaluating these data, however. The results indicate only what *can* be done by competent clinicians with a specific protocol and not what might occur with different interpreters or with the same interpreters and different protocols. The subject used in this study presented an ambiguous clinical picture at the time of testing but his MMPI profile appears to be anything but equivocal (see Table 4). A strong possibility exists, therefore, that the comparison of the MMPI Q sorts with the criterion Q sorts tested the agreement of two sets of statements about a certain nosological classification rather than inferences about a specific person.[2] One critic was so unkind as to suggest that the data merely demonstrate the existence of a common delusional system among test and criterion judges. However, insofar as the statements made have a descriptive utility, agreement between test interpretations and those made on the basis of exhaustive clinical material seems a desirable form of validity no matter how the statements are derived.

Three clusters of judges could be found among the 11 judges used in this study, but the differences among them do not seem to be related to their

[2] A further study, using a variety of subjects, psychological techniques, and interpreters to increase the representativeness of the results and to test this hypothesis, is currently being conducted.

TABLE 4.   MMPI SCORES OF THE SUBJECT

Scale	Raw Score	Standard Score
?	68	60
L	2	43
F	13	73
K	10	46
Hs	22	90
D	36	95
Hy	35	85
Pd	27	79
Mf	36	80
Pa	21	88
Pt	43	111
Sc	49	120
Ma	25	75

over-all validity. This would follow logically from the discussion set forth above. The variations in description represent different emphases upon certain aspects of the same disorder rather than disagreement as to diagnosis. Thus the average validity of the three clusters is about the same.

A final conclusion from the study is that the Q technique has considerable value in the study of the reliability and validity of clinical techniques. It permits the quantification of results without loss of the idiographic approach, a characteristic ideally suited to clinical research.

Summary

The validity of inferences made from the MMPI was tested using an interpreter population of 11 experts working with the MMPI profile of one subject. The criterion was the consensus, in the form of a general factor, of 29 clinicians who Q sorted 150 items on the basis of a comprehensive clinical record of the same subject. A cluster analysis of the matrix of intercorrelations among the MMPI interpreters yielded three groups of judges. These groups were described in terms of the Most True and Most False Q-sort items peculiar to each cluster. Validity figures for each MMPI judge were computed as correlations with a weighted composite Q sort of the criterion judges. The general results indicated that MMPI interpreters can achieve a level of consensual validity on the basis of the MMPI profile approximating the average general factor loading of the criterion judges. Certain cautions in interpreting the results were presented, especially in the light of the rather unequivocal nature of the MMPI profile used in this case.

REFERENCES

1. LITTLE, K. B., & SHNEIDMAN, E. S. The validity of thematic projective technique interpretations. *J. Pers.*, in press.
2. SHNEIDMAN, E. S. (Ed.) *Thematic test analysis.* New York: Grune & Stratton, 1951.
3. STEPHENSON, W. S. *The study of behavior.* Chicago: Univer. of Chicago Press, 1953.
4. TRYON, R. C. *Cluster analysis.* Ann Arbor, Mich.: Edwards Brothers, 1939.

Normal, Hypnotically Induced, and Feigned Anxiety as Reflected In and Detected By the MMPI

Albert A. Branca and Edward E. Podolnick

The use of hypnosis as a technique for the production of signs of disorder in normal people has been attempted. Luria (1932), and Huston, Shakow, and Erickson (1934) showed that word association techniques together with certain motor responses were successful in revealing the presence of emotion arousing conflicts that had been suggested in hypnosis. Fisher and Marrow (1934) reported significant differences in reaction times obtained in hypnoti-

This research was supported by a University of Delaware Faculty Summer Research Grant.

Reprinted by permission of the American Psychological Association and the authors from *Journal of Consulting Psychology*, 1961, **25**, 165–170.

cally induced "moods" of elation and depression. Sweetland (1948) suggested certain psychiatric syndromes to normal subjects who had been hypnotized. Comparison of MMPI profiles obtained when these syndromes were suggested indicated that it was possible to produce "laboratory neuroses" by hypnosis. Grosz and Levitt (1959) suggested anxiety to 12 hypnotized medical and nursing students. They reported increased scores on the Taylor Manifest Anxiety Scale and diminished scores on the Barron Ego Strength scale. They also reported that scores on the two tests taken during the waking state did not differ from scores obtained during hypnotic states when anxiety was not suggested.

Studies also show that the MMPI validity scales can identify dissemblers. Gough (1947) showed that the MMPI was able to identify "fakers" even when they were psychiatrists, clinical psychologists, and social workers who were familiar with the diagnostic signs of behavior disorders as well as the MMPI. Other investigators (Cofer, Chance, & Judson, 1949; Hunt, 1948) also indicate that the MMPI, through separate or combined use of its validity scores, is capable of differentiating between dissemblers and other groups.

In 1952 Welsh added an Anxiety (A) scale to the MMPI. This development has made it possible to observe the effects of suggesting this simpler and more general symptom of disorder.

The specific hypotheses of this experiment are:

1. There will be a significant increase in the A scale of the MMPI between scores obtained under normal conditions and under conditions of hypnotically induced anxiety.

2. The validity scales of the MMPI will differentiate between profiles obtained under conditions of dissembling and profiles obtained under conditions of both normal and hypnotically induced anxiety.

Method

Subjects

Ten students, of whom eight were female, were used as subjects in this experiment. The normal records were obtained from students who had taken the MMPI as part of a classroom demonstration. At the time the first profiles were obtained, the students were not aware that they might be called upon to participate in an experiment. Students from other freshman and sophomore courses volunteered to participate when they had heard about the study.

Two of these students were used as experimental subjects. These two were given to believe that the MMPI was being used as a screening device and not a part of the experiment proper.

Experimental candidates were selected on the basis of: (a) normal MMPI profiles and anxiety scores; (b) absence of a history of treatment for mental disorder; (c) absence of a history of epilepsy, or convulsions, or neurological disease of any type; (d) a willingness to participate in the experiment. Actual subjects were selected from this larger group on the basis of hypnotizability. The criterion for depth of trance was the elicitation of positive auditory and visual hallucinations. Out of a total of 50 experimental candidates, 10 met this criterion, 2 males and 8 females. This percentage is consistent with others also reporting approximately 20% success in obtaining a deep trance (Dorcus, 1956). A disproportionately large number of females volunteered to participate in the experiment.

Procedure

Each hypnotic session was held in a room with a one-way observation screen and an intercom system. In this way one experimenter was able to observe each session while the other performed the hypnosis. Each candidate was made aware of this observation.

The first phase of the experiment consisted of training sessions wherein the experimental candidates were trained to achieve the trance state. When a depth of trance was reached in which positive auditory and visual hallucinations were produced, the candidate met the criterion for inclusion as an experimental subject and an anxiety state was suggested. The instructions for producing anxiety were obtained from definitions and descriptions of anxiety by various authors

(Conklin, 1936; Heyns, 1958; Lehner & Kube, 1955; May, 1950; Shaffer & Shoben, 1956; Warren, 1934). These instructions were as follows:

You are beginning to feel very uneasy and anxious. You don't know why, but this uneasy feeling is making you nervous, irritable, and frightened. You feel as if something dreadful is about to happen but you don't know what. This feeling of dread is mingled with a curious feeling of hope that is very unpleasant. You are becoming more and more apprehensive. You are in a state of anxious expectation and self-doubt. You feel now as if you are threatened and it frightens you. You feel as if you are about to lose something important to you, or be hurt. This anxiety is becoming stronger and stronger. Now you feel as if something is wrong, as though you had neglected to do something very important, but you can't recall what it is. You feel, though, that whatever it is, it is making you feel on edge and uneasy. It is making you feel blue, melancholy, unhappy, and excited in an unpleasant way. You feel frightened, but you don't know what it is you are frightened about. This is certainly an unpleasant form of excitement. You are now very apprehensive and anxious.

After the anxiety instructions were read, the MMPI was readministered. The subjects took between 70 and 90 minutes to complete the MMPI. In order to maintain the trance state for that period instructions and suggestions reinforcing the trance state were given when the subject had reached the half-way point in the test. At that time the anxiety instructions were also reread to each subject. The subjects were aroused from the trance state after suggestions counteracting the anxiety were made. These instructions, given twice, were as follows:

You are beginning to feel less apprehensive and anxious. The unpleasant form of excitement caused by the fact that you were frightened is leaving you. You are beginning to feel happier, more alert, and relaxed. You no longer feel on edge or

uneasy, and you are experiencing a feeling of well-being. You are now confident and at ease. You feel happy and at peace with the world. You are experiencing a soothing calmness and you feel warm, relaxed, comfortable, and alert. You don't feel nervous, irritable, or frightened any more. You are no longer apprehensive and no longer feel self-doubt. You don't feel as if you are frightened or are about to be hurt. You don't feel as if you're about to lose something but don't know what. You are now very relaxed. You feel as if all of your troubles and problems are leaving you. You feel as if all of your fears are gone and this gives you a feeling of ease and comfort. You are happy and relaxed and normal.

At the hypnotic session, subjects were instructed to remember all events that occurred during the trance state.

In the final phase of the experiment, which took place approximately a week after the first phase, each subject was told that he was to make believe that he was anxious and that he was to "fake" anxiety while taking the MMPI The same description of the anxiety state was read to him again with the statements "make believe that" or "pretend that" prefixing each sentence. He was further instructed to mark the test as though he were trying to create the test profile of a person suffering great anxiety.

In order to provide an additional subjective check of the subjects' emotional states during the experiment, an anxiety rating scale was constructed according to the Likert technique (Edwards, 1957). It consisted of 40 questions about the way the subject felt at the time of responding to the scale. It included items such as: "I am at ease," "I feel tense without any good reason," "My morale is low," "I am restless and irritable now." Each of its 40 items had been shown to discriminate between high anxious and low anxious groups. It has a split-half reliability coefficient of .97. This scale was administered with the MMPI as part of a classroom demonstration. It was also given under conditions of hypnotically induced anxiety.

Results

The data of this experiment consisted of the MMPI profiles obtained under normal conditions (N), conditions of hypnotically induced anxiety (HIA), and conditions of dissembling (D), as well as scores on the anxiety rating questionnaire obtained under the first two conditions. The means and the standard deviations of the T scores for each scale are listed in Table 1. Both the $?$ and F scales are given in raw scores. The scores on $?$ were well enough below the necessary 30 that conversion to T scores would necessitate each raw score having the same T, i.e., a T of 50. The scores on F were so high under conditions of dissembling that conversion to T scores tended to hide differences between this condition and the other two. Because of the small

TABLE 1. MMPI T SCORE MEANS AND STANDARD DEVIATIONS UNDER NORMAL CONDITIONS, UNDER CONDITIONS OF HYPNOTICALLY INDUCED ANXIETY, AND UNDER CONDITIONS OF DISSEMBLING

Scale	N Condition		HIA Condition		D Condition	
	M	SD	M	SD	M	SD
$?$a	1.4	1.84	.3	.68	.2	.42
L	47.9	7.78	46.3	6.62	42.4	4.81
Fa	3.1	2.96	6.0	3.83	25.0	11.87
K	58.1	8.49	51.3	8.79	42.9	8.99
Hs	52.4	7.28	50.3	5.16	70.8	15.61
D	47.8	5.41	56.1	12.50	79.3	17.31
Hy	56.2	7.73	54.9	9.42	71.0	7.09
Pd	53.8	10.90	59.0	13.26	80.5	14.49
Mf	42.2	8.16	45.5	9.16	49.7	10.24
Pa	49.4	6.13	60.4	10.85	87.3	21.49
Pt	54.1	7.95	61.4	12.77	85.4	14.91
Sc	55.2	6.48	65.3	10.87	98.8	19.25
Ma	60.6	10.30	63.7	11.85	71.5	11.44
Si	49.9	8.67	56.5	12.42	72.2	13.12
A	44.3	4.83	54.5	10.70	72.6	9.36
R	47.4	7.07	46.7	5.54	49.0	8.62

Note.—$N = 10$.
a Based on raw scores.

$N(N = 10)$, $N - 1$ was used in computing the standard deviations (Edwards, 1950).

An analysis of variance was performed for each scale under the three conditions. A comparison was then made between the T scores on each scale obtained under N and HIA conditions, N and D conditions, and HIA and D conditions. A t test was employed for this purpose. Because the scores obtained under these three conditions were not random with respect to each other, a t comparing the differences between correlated means was computed using the differences between the scores (McNemar, 1949). The mean differences and the t's for each scale for all combinations of the three conditions are listed in Table 2. Although all values of t were reported they were marked as significant, in the conventional manner, only for those scales where significantly large Fs were obtained.

In comparing the scores between the N and HIA conditions, the F, K, Pa, Sc, Si, and A scales showed significant changes. In comparing the scores between the HIA and D conditions, only the $?$, L, Mf, Ma, and R scales showed insignificant changes. Likewise, the differences between the scores for N and D conditions were insignificant for the L, Ma, $?$, Mf, and R scales, being significant for all others.

A t was also computed for the anxiety rating questionnaire. The scores on this questionnaire, given twice (N and HIA conditions) showed a mean change which is significant at the .01 level.

Discussion

Observation of Subjects

During the HIA session, there were indications of stress on the part of the subjects. When asked how they felt, they made comments such as: "I don't feel good," "I feel like I want to get out

TABLE 2. ANALYSES OF SCORES UNDER NORMAL, HYPNOTICALLY INDUCED ANXIETY, AND DISSEMBLING CONDITIONS

Scale	F^a	N and HIA		HIA and D		N and D	
		MD	t	MD	t	MD	t
P^b	3.31	-1.1	1.88	-.1	1.00	-1.2	2.09
L	1.88	-1.6	1.14	-3.9	2.03	-5.5	2.84
F^b	29.39**	2.9	3.65**	19.0	4.80**	21.9	5.50**
K	7.55**	-6.8	4.37**	-8.4	3.03*	-15.2	6.15**
Hs	11.80**	-2.1	1.60	20.5	4.22**	18.4	3.84**
D	16.48**	8.2	2.21	23.2	3.65**	31.5	5.89**
Hy	12.08**	-1.3	.79	16.1	4.23**	14.8	4.46**
Pd	11.91**	5.2	1.07	21.5	5.55**	26.7	4.20**
Mf	1.66	3.3	2.36	4.2	1.10	7.5	1.99
Pa	16.45**	11.0	2.78*	26.9	6.00**	37.9	6.04**
Pt	17.93**	7.3	2.17	24.0	5.94**	31.3	7.21**
Sc	29.44**	10.1	3.07*	33.5	6.13**	43.6	7.13**
Ma	2.51	3.1	1.45	7.8	1.82	10.9	2.47
Si	9.80**	8.6	4.00**	15.7	3.06*	22.3	4.42**
A	27.34**	10.2	4.31**	18.1	5.44**	28.3	10.90**
R	0.27	-.7	.56	2.3	.72	1.6	.45

Note.—Minus signs indicate that the scores for the second condition listed were lower than those of the first.

^{a} Values of F obtained by analysis of variance for each scale under the three conditions of the experiment.

^{b} Based on raw scores.

* Significant at the .05 level.

** Significant at the .01 level.

of here," "I feel unhappy," and "I feel as if something were wrong." In addition to these comments, the subjects showed signs that the experimenters interpreted as discomfort and distress. These signs were: furrowing of the brow, clenching of hands, frowning, tenseness, biting of lips, sighing deeply. One subject, a female, burst out crying while answering the MMPI items. The experimenter stopped the test and, seeing that she could not continue because of excessive crying, read the alleviating instructions. She stopped crying as the instructions were being read and agreed to complete the test the following day under the same experimental conditions.

In general, the subjects concentrated on the test and appeared to be making an effort to read and answer the items carefully. All subjects appeared relieved when the alleviating instructions were read. This relief was evidenced by smiling, relaxation of facial muscles, restrained laughter, and remarks such as: "I feel good now."

The A Scale

Hypothesis 1 stated that there would be a significant increase in the A scale between scores obtained under normal conditions and under conditions of hypnotically induced anxiety. This hypothesis was supported by the data, the difference in the scores being significant at the .01 level.

The A scale is made up of items which occur on several of the other scales. Cluster and factor analyses indicated that the scale was relatively homogeneous and seemed to be related to anxiety. The scale contains very few "obvious" items that deal directly with the word anxiety and its synonyms. However, the experimenters found seven such items that they considered obvious with respect to the "anxiety" instructions the subjects received: "I feel anxiety about something or some-one almost all of the time," "I must admit that I have at times been worried beyond reason over something that really did not matter," "I worry quite a bit over possible misfortunes," "I brood a great deal," "I wish I could be as happy as others seem to be," "Most of the time I feel blue," "I very seldom have spells of the blues." A count was made of the number of times these seven items were chosen under the three conditions, N, HIA, and D. They were chosen a total of 13 times under N condition, 34 times under HIA condition, and 63 times under D condition. These differences were significant at the .01 level. A t was then computed for the A scale with these seven items omitted to find if significant differences would still be obtained without the obvious items. The removal of these items did not alter the degrees of significance obtained previously with the full scale. This reduces the likelihood that the elevation of the A scale was the simple result of a heightened and conscious intent to comply with the suggestions of the experimenters.

The Validity Scales

Hypothesis 2 stated that the validity scales would differentiate between profiles obtained under conditions of dissembling and profiles obtained under conditions of both normal and hypnotically induced anxiety. This hypothesis was supported. Using the validity scales separately and the F minus K dissimulation index with a cutoff point of plus five (Gough, 1950), all profiles from both the N and HIA conditions were in the normal range indicating valid profiles. In addition, the F scale alone identified all but one of the profiles obtained under conditions of dissembling. The F minus K index also did not identify this one profile, but identified all others.

The significant changes in the F and K scales obtained from Condition N to Condition HIA do indicate that a change in test-taking attitude occurred in the latter state. The K scores were significantly lower in Condition HIA as compared with Condition N, indicating that the subjects became more critical of themselves. In addition, the F scores were significantly higher in the HIA condition, indicating that while in this state, the subjects answered more of these items in the direction away from the direction the normal standardization groups answered them. The experimenters feel, however, that this might be expected in that the HIA state represents a condition removed from the condition under which standardization was obtained.

It is interesting to note that, although not significantly so, L scores were consistently lower in the HIA and D states as compared to N. Perhaps the criticalness of the subjects, as evidenced by their lower K scores in the HIA and D conditions, also made them more "honest."

An hypnotic scale has not been derived from the MMPI item pool. Admittedly such a scale would be of little clinical value, but it would be of considerable experimental interest. A scale capable of differentiating between the waking and the hypnotic state would serve as an objective device for indicating achievement of the trance state. It might also provide the basis for an objective method of appraising depth of trance.

The Diagnostic Scales

All diagnostic scales except *Mf*, *Ma*, and *R* showed significant differences from N to D conditions. All diagnostic scales except *Mf*, *Ma*, and *R* showed significant differences from HIA to D conditions. Since the validity scales identified dissembling profiles in Condition D, but not in Condition HIA, these differences further support these results in indicating a real difference between the two conditions. Profiles obtained under conditions of hypnotically induced anxiety do not resemble those obtained under conditions of dissembling. The differences between profiles obtained in these two conditions suggest that hypnosis is not a state of mere heightened cooperation.

In going from Conditions N to HIA, it might be expected that only the A scale would be increased, since the instructions under hypnosis were directed to this effect. However, the Pa, Sc, and Si scales were also significantly heightened.

The rise in Pa may be considered as a direct result of the anxiety instructions. Looking post priori, it can be seen that suggestions such as "You are beginning to feel very uneasy and anxious," and "You don't known why, but this uneasy feeling is making you nervous, irritable, and frightened," might easily be reflected in the items composing the Pa scale as these items were derived from patient samples "symptomically . . . to have ideas of reference, to feel that they were persecuted by individuals or groups . . ." (Hathaway, 1956, pp. 109–110).

The heightened Sc and Si scales can be considered in the same way. Feelings of apprehension and anxiety, as well as feelings of being blue and melancholy, might be reflected in items dealing with social introversion, and schizophrenic symptoms have been described in much the same way. The D scale, however, was not significantly increased, indicating that the part of the instructions relating to feelings of depression were not alone responsible for these changes.

The changes in scores in the Likert-type anxiety questionnaire from Conditions N to HIA were significant at the .01 level. The questionnaire was not given under Condition D because of its transparency. The change indicates that each subject's subjective evaluation of the way he felt during the HIA session corresponded to the overt behavioral differences observed and to the detection of these differences effected by the A scale. Most of the scores doubled and some increased by as much as 100 out of a possible 160 points. Only 1 subject out of 10 failed to report an increase in anxiety as reflected in the questionnaire.

It is impossible to estimate the effect of the order of the experimental conditions upon test performance. The order used in this design was chosen so as to minimize contamination of experimental conditions by prior experience. Obviously the "normal" administration of the MMPI which served as a control and also as the basis for selecting subjects had to come first. It was felt that the faking conditions should be last in order to prevent the establishment of a faking set which might persist and intrude upon the hypnotically induced anxiety condition.

Summary and Conclusions

Ten college students took the MMPI under three conditions. In the first condition, the test was taken as part of a classroom demonstration. The second administration occurred under conditions of hypnotically induced anxiety. The third administration occurred in the waking state after instructions were given to "fake" anxiety.

Comparisons of the test profiles and the results of the specially constructed anxiety questionnaire permitted the following conclusions to be drawn:

1. Anxiety suggestions, when culled from definitions and descriptions of anxiety from independent sources, cause a significant increase in the Welsh A scale of the MMPI when they are given to hypnotized subjects.

2. Overt behavioral signs indicate that affective changes are experienced when anxiety is suggested to hypnotized subjects.

3. The anxiety questionnaire revealed that the subjects reported a marked increase of feelings of tension, discomfort, unpleasantness, and apprehension following the "anxiety" instructions in the hypnotized state over their reports in the normal waking state.

4. The validity scales of the MMPI successfully identify 9 out of 10 dissemblers and show that, in a state of hypnotically induced anxiety, valid profiles are obtained.

5. Significant differences in the diagnostic and validity scales between conditions of hypnotically induced anxiety and conditions of dissembling indicate that the former is different enough from the latter to strongly suggest that hypnosis is not a state of mere exaggerated cooperation.

REFERENCES

COFER, C. N., CHANCE, J., & JUDSON, A. J. A study of malingering on the Minnesota Multiphasic Personality Inventory. *J. Psychol.*, 1949, 27, 491–499.

CONKLIN, E. *Principles of abnormal psychology.* New York: Holt, 1936.

DORCUS, R. M. (Ed.) *Hypnosis and its therapeutic applications.* New York: McGraw-Hill, 1956.

EDWARDS, A. L. *Experimental design in psychological research.* New York: Rinehart, 1950.

EDWARDS, A. L. *Techniques of attitude scale construction.* New York: Appleton-Century-Crofts, 1957.

FISHER, V. E., & MARROW, A. J. Experimental study of moods. *Charact. Pers.*, 1934, 2, 201–208.

GOUGH, H. G. Simulated patterns on the Minnesota Multiphasic Personality Inventory. *J. abnorm. soc. Psychol.*, 1947, 42, 215–225.

GOUGH, H. G. The *F* minus *K* dissimulation index for the Minnesota Multiphasic Personality Inventory. *J. consult. Psychol.*, 1950, 14, 408–413.

GROSZ, H. J., & LEVITT, E. E. The effects of hypnotically induced anxiety on the Manifest Anxiety Scale and the Barron ego-strength scale. *J. abnorm. soc. Psychol.*, 1959, 59, 281–283.

HATHAWAY, S. R. Scales 5 (masculinity-femininity), 6 (paranoia) and 8 (schizophrenia). In G. S. WELSH & W. G. DAHLSTROM (Eds.), *Basic readings on the MMPI in psychology and medicine.* Minneapolis: Univer. Minnesota Press, 1956.

HEYNS, R. W. *The psychology of personal adjustment.* New York: Dryden, 1958.

HUNT, H. F. The effect of deliberate deception on Minnesota Multiphasic Personality Inventory profiles. *J. consult. Psychol.*, 1948, 12, 396–402.

HUSTON, P. E., SHAKOW, D., & ERICKSON, M. H. A study of hypnotically induced complexes by means of the Luria technique. *J. gen. Psychol.*, 1934, 11, 650–697.

LEHNER, G. F., & KUBE, E. *The dynamics of personal adjustment.* Englewood Cliffs, New Jersey: Prentice-Hall, 1955.

LURIA, A. R. *The nature of human conflict.* New York: Liveright, 1932.

McNEMAR, Q. *Psychological statistics.* New York: Wiley, 1949.

MAY, R. *The meaning of anxiety.* New York: Ronald, 1950.

SHAFFER, L., & SHOBEN, E. *The psychology of adjustment.* (2nd ed.) Boston: Houghton Mifflin, 1956.

SWEETLAND, A. Hypnotic neuroses: Hypochondriasis and depression. *J. gen. Psychol.*, 1948, 39, 91–105.

WARREN, H. C. *Dictionary of psychology.* Boston: Houghton Mifflin, 1934.

WELSH, G. S. An anxiety index and an internalization ratio for the MMPI. *J. consult. Psychol.*, 1952, 16, 65–72.

The Psychasthenic and Hypomanic Scales of the MMPI and Uncertainty in Judgments

Albert V. Griffith, Harry S. Upshaw, and Raymond D. Fowler

Problem

In the validation of the clinical scales of the MMPI, the major criterion was the ". . . prediction of clinical cases against the neuropsychiatric staff diagnosis . . ."[1, p. 6] The psychiatric constructs underlying these clinical scales assume a syndrome of behavioral characteristics; e.g., psychasthenic individuals (identified by MMPI Pt scale) are said to be marked by vacillation, excessive doubt, worry, lack of confidence, and mild depression.[1, p. 20; 6, p. 81] Hypomanic individuals (identified by MMPI Ma Scale) are said to be active, enthusiastic, confident, aggressive, and expansive.[1, p. 21; 6, p. 167] Obviously, these two types of individuals should differ in the degree of confidence with which they make even simple judgments. This is the hypothesis tested in this study.

As a simple, objective measure of confidence in judgments, third-category or "doubtful" judgments in a psychophysical weight discrimination experiment were used. Much evidence has accumulated that the third-category measures confidence more than sensitivity. Woodworth,[7, p. 65] for example, suggests that the frequency of third-category judgments is a measure of the "take a chance" attitude of the subject. If the subject is willing to

take chances and follow the lead of slight impressions he will make a judgment while the more cautious subject will report doubt. Kellogg[2, p. 6] infers from this argument that the frequency of third-category judgments furnishes a better measure of a subject's confidence than it does of his discrimination.

With the measure of confidence defined, the experimental hypotheses may now be stated more exactly: (a) Individuals with a psychasthenic profile on the MMPI will give significantly more doubtful judgments than individuals with a hypomanic profile in a psychophysical weight discrimination experiment; and (b) Individuals with no T-score above 60 or below 30 on any of the MMPI scales (a "dull" profile) will give a number of doubtful judgments intermediate to the psychasthenic and hypomanic groups.

Method

Subjects. The subjects were male students entering the University of Alabama in the Fall semester, 1956, and the Spring semester, 1957. All had been given a battery of tests which included the MMPI. A total of approximately 1,200 MMPI profiles were screened. In selecting subjects for the experiment, none were chosen who had T-scores of 70 or above on any of the validity scales (L, F, or K). Those students who were not excluded by this condition, and who had "7'2" pro-

Reprinted by permission of the American Psychological Association and the authors from *Journal of Clinical Psychology*, 1958, **14**, 385–386.

files (the highest T-score, equal to or greater than 70, on the Pt scale, and the next highest T-score on the D scale) were classified as psychasthenic. Assignment to the hypomanic group was on the basis of "9'4" profile (the highest T-score, equal to or greater than 70, on the Ma scale, and the next highest T-score on the Pd scale). Finally, a control group was selected on the basis that all of their T-scores fell between 30 and 60.

The total number of students selected by the above criteria was 28, 30, and 36 respectively for the psychasthenic, hypomanic, and control groups. Each individual was contacted by a letter from the office of the Dean of Men which requested his cooperation in the study. The result was that 16 subjects classified as psychasthenic, 14 as hypomanic, and 15 as control agreed to be tested.

Experimental task. In the psychophysical aspect of the study, the method used was that of constant stimulus differences. The experimental task was that of weight discrimination. A series of eight weights ranging from 92 to 108 grams with an interval of two grams between stimuli was used. The standard weight was 100 grams. The subject lifted the weights simultaneously, giving a judgment that either the weight in his right hand seemed heavier, the weight in his left hand seemed heavier, or he was doubtful as to which weight was heavier. By a randomizing procedure, the standard weight was placed equally often in the subject's right and left hand. Each subject gave a total of 144 judgments.

Results

The mean number of doubtful judgments for the psychasthenic, hypomanic, and control groups was 41.9, 20.1, and 31.0 respectively. Bartlett's test[5, pp. 206, 207] demonstrated that the variances of the judgments were significantly different ($\sigma^2_{PT} = 1013.8$; $\sigma^2_{MA} = 223.1$; $\sigma^2_{CONTROL} = 604.3$). It has been established that such violations of the parametric assumptions of the analysis of variance lead to too many rejections of the null hypothesis.[3, p. 255] To guard against this error, the Kruskal-Wallis procedure,[4, pp. 184-193] a non-parametric analogue to the analysis of variance, was used to test for differences among the groups. The Kruskal-Wallis procedure employs for this purpose a statistic "H," distributed as Chi-square.

TABLE 1. SUMMARY OF KRUSKAL-WALLIS PROCEDURE FOR THE DATA IN THE PRESENT STUDY

Group	Number of Subjects	Sum of Ranks	"H"
Pt	16	459.0	
Ma	14	232.5	
Control	15	343.5	6.331*

* Sig. at the 5% level.

Table 1 summarizes the Kruskal-Wallis procedure for the data in the present study. As noted in Table 1, the "H" is significant at the 5% level of confidence. It is inferred, therefore, that a significant difference in the frequency of doubtful judgments exists among the groups, thus verifying the first hypothesis. An inspection of the means of the three groups verifies the second hypothesis. This behavioral correlate for the two MMPI scales provides, therefore, an indirect validation of the psychiatric constructs of psychasthenia and hypomania as measured by the MMPI.

Summary

This paper studied the relation of the psychasthenic and hypomanic scales of the MMPI to uncertainty in psychophysical judgment. The following predictions were made: (a) Individuals with a psychasthenic profile on the

MMPI will give significantly more doubtful judgments than individuals with a hypomanic profile in a psychophysical weight discrimination experiment; and (b) individuals having a dull profile on the MMPI will give a number of doubtful judgments intermediate to the psychasthenic and hypomanic groups. Both predictions were verified.

REFERENCES

1. HATHAWAY, S. R., and McKINLEY, J. C. *Minnesota multiphasic personality inventory manual.* New York: Psychol. Corp., 1951.
2. KELLOGG, W. N. An experimental evaluation of equality judgments in psychophysics. *Arch. Psychol.,* 1930, No. 112.
3. McNEMAR, Q. *Psychological statistics.* New York: John Wiley, 1955.
4. SIEGEL, S. *Nonparametric statistics for the behavioral sciences.* New York: McGraw-Hill, 1956.
5. SNEDECOR, G. W. *Statistical methods applied to experiments in agriculture and biology.* Ames, Iowa: Iowa State College Press, 1940.
6. WELSH, G. S., and DAHLSTROM, W. G. (Eds.). *Basic readings on the MMPI in psychology and medicine.* Minneapolis: U. of Minn. Press, 1956.
7. WOODWORTH, R. S. Prof. Cattell's psychophysical contributions. In "The psychological researches of James McKeen Cattell." *Arch. Psychol.,* 1914, 30, 60–74.

A Cross-Validation of Twelve MMPI Indices of Hostility and Control

Edwin I. Megargee and Gerald A. Mendelsohn

Dahlstrom and Welsh's (1960) recently published MMPI handbook contains an appendix listing 213 scales, indices, and scoring procedures for the MMPI. This proliferation of scales has produced nearly one scale for every two MMPI items. Each of these scales is supposed to measure validly some meaningful facet of human personality ranging from "hypochondriasis" to "success in baseball." While the 10 original scales and some of the new ones were derived by careful empirical study, not all authors have been equally thorough in establishing the validity of their instruments. Consequently there is considerable variability in the confidence with which the 213 scales may be used.

The clinician or researcher who wishes to measure some aspect of personality by using one of these scales often has little information about their real meaning or usefulness. A search of

The authors wish to express their appreciation to Lorenzo Buckley, Chief Probation Officer of Alameda County, California, John Clausen of the Institute of Human Development, and their respective staffs for providing the data for this study. In addition, the writers are grateful to Jack Block for his help in analyzing the data of this study and the University of California Computer Center for donating time on the IBM 704.

Reprinted by permission of the American Psychological Association and the authors from the *Journal of Abnormal and Social Psychology*, 1962, **65**, 431–438.

the literature generally reveals little data on which to base a decision, for the amount of cross-validation is too often nonexistent or inadequate. Frequently the only information available is that which Dahlstrom and Welsh (1960) have gleaned from unpublished sources, or the title which the scale-maker has given to his instrument. The question naturally arises as to how valid these scales are and whether their publication represents progress or merely additional noise in the field. The present study, in which an attempt was made to cross-validate the scales and indices relating to a single aspect of behavior, focuses on this question.

The particular aspect of behavior studied, assaultive acting out, was chosen because of the need of the senior author to measure aggressive potential in candidates for probation. Such measurement would be of great value in deciding whether a criminal should be incarcerated or could be safely returned to the community. Since a number of MMPI scales purport to measure such traits as hostility, impulsivity, and control, a study was undertaken to select those best suited to the above purpose. This involved a cross-validation of the relevant scales using groups known to differ, on the basis of their past behavior, in regard to these traits. Criminal assaultiveness was used as an operational definition of hostility and lack of control. The assumption was made that any useful scale of hostility or control should discriminate between criminals convicted of highly aggressive crimes and those criminals whose records showed no history of overt violence.

Procedure

Scales

Ten scales and two scoring indices for the MMPI were selected. In each case either the name or the description of the scale indicated that a trait was measured which may be assumed to be related to the expression or control of hostility. A description of these scales appears in Table 1.

Subjects

The MMPI protocols of three groups of men referred to the Alameda County, California, Probation Department Guidance Clinic during the last 3 years were selected from the clinic files.

Group I, the extremely assaultive group, consisted of 14 men convicted of violation of one or more of the following sections of the California Penal Code (State of California, 1959): 187, Murder, second degree; 192.1, Voluntary manslaughter; 203, Mayhem; and 245, Assault with a deadly weapon. Their ages ranged from 20 to 51 with a mean of 30.

Group II, the moderately assaultive group, consisted of 25 men randomly selected from those referred to the clinic after having been convicted of Section 242, Battery, defined in the Penal Code (State of California, 1959) as ". . . the unlawful use of force or violence on the person of another. . . ." Their ages ranged from 18 to 68 with a mean of 36.

Group III was a control group consisting of 25 men randomly selected from all those who had been referred during the last 3 years after conviction of a nonassaultive crime. In order to ensure that the members of this group would be nonassaultive, anyone convicted at any time of one of the violent crimes mentioned above, as well as men who were convicted of other lesser charges which have an assaultive component, were excluded from consideration. The crimes thus excluded were such offenses as attempted murder, assault, resisting arrest, forcible rape, and disturbing the peace. The control group obtained consisted primarily of thieves and those convicted of nonviolent sex offenses, e.g.,

TABLE 1. DESCRIPTION OF SCALES AND INDICES ASSESSING HOSTILITY AND CONTROL

Symbol	Name	Author	Description
Ap	Adjustment to Prison	Panton, 1958	36 items, empirically derived from protocols of 56 nonadjusted male prisoners versus 72 adjusted inmates. Adjustment is defined as absence of severe infractions such as fighting, assaulting a guard, or refusing to obey orders. Scale thus derived was later validated and refined using two adjusted samples totaling 177 subjects and three nonadjusted samples totaling 204 subjects. Scale held up with $p \leq .01$ on these cross-validations.
Hc	Hostility Control	Schultz, 1954	34 items, empirically derived. One hundred nineteen Veterans Administration therapy patients were rated by their therapists on the adequacy of the methods they used to deal with hostility. The protocols of the top and bottom 25% were used in the item analysis. Obtained items later cross-validated on therapists' ratings in a college sample.
Ho	Hostility	Cook & Medley, 1954	50 items. The MMPI protocols of those teachers in Minnesota who were rated in the top and bottom 8% of the teachers in the state on the basis of the Minnesota Teacher Aptitude Inventory were compared. Fifty of the discriminating items were selected by five judges as measuring hostility. McGee (1954) obtained a significant correlation with hostility as reflected in Szondi sorts.
Hv	Overt Hostility	Schultz, 1954	14 items. Same derivation as Hc except therapists rated the patients' frequency of expression of overt hostility.
Hy-5	Inhibition of Aggression	Harris & Lingoes, 1955	7 items in the *Hy* scale which, on rational examination by the authors, appear to reflect this quality.
Im	Impulsivity	Gough, 1960	21 items. This consists of those items on the CPI "self-control" scale which are common to both tests. People scoring high on Im are ". . . impulsive, shrewd, excitable, irritable, self-centered, and uninhibited. Aggressive and assertive" (Gough, 1960, p. 12). Cross-validations yield positive correlations with ratings of impulsivity in normal samples.
Jh	Judged Manifest Hostility	Siegel, 1956	47 items. One hundred ten items deemed to indicate hostility were submitted to five judges who chose items reflecting manifest hostility as defined by Veterans Administration nomenclature. Items on which there was 80% agreement were used in the scale.

TABLE 1. (*Continued*)

Symbol	Name	Author	Description
Eo	Ego Over-control	Block, 1955	23 items. Empirically derived from samples of 200 males tested at the Institute of Personality Assessment and Research, Berkeley, California, designated Ec-3 by Block, Eo by Dahlstrom and Welsh.
Nu	Neurotic Under-control	Block, 1955	33 items. Dahlstrom and Welsh (1960) quote Block as stating this measures ". . . susceptibility of the personality structure to stress and anxiety in which the anxiety is handled by impulsive acting out, aggression, and erratically directed hyperactivity . . ." (p. 302, source not cited). Block[a] reports this scale is effective only if the subject is both neurotic and undercontrolled.
Bc	Bimodal Control	Block, 1955	48 items. "By bimodal control is meant an inconsistency in controls and expressive modes of behavior. . . . In some behavioral areas he acts in an overcontrolled manner and in other areas in an undercontrolled manner" (Block, 1953, p. 1).
AHI	Active Hostility Index	Welsh & Sullivan, 1952	The sum of T scores on Pd and Ma. Means and SDs of various samples reported in Dahlstrom and Welsh (1960).
FTI	Frustration Tolerance Index	Beall & Panton, 1957	A ratio of the T scores on four clinical scales: $$FTI = \frac{Pd + Ma}{D + Hy}$$

[a] J. Block, personal communication, 1961.

homosexual activities. The ages ranged from 19 to 62 with a mean of 41.

Group IV, consisting of normals, was included as a second control to provide a group so unlike the assaultive (and nonassaultive) criminal groups that it could be ascertained if the scales had the power to measure gross differences in control and hostility. This group of normals consisted of men tested as part of the follow-up in the Oakland Adolescent Growth Study, a longitudinal project being carried out by the Institute of Human Development, Berkeley, California. Entire lower-middle-class high school classes were selected in the 1930s (in the same county in which the criminals reside) and have been studied up to the present (Jones, 1933). The MMPIs were obtained within the last 2 or 3 years when the subjects ranged in age from 36 to 39 with a mean of 37.

All random selection was done by means of a table of random numbers. No subject whose MMPI was incomplete was included, and all the MMPI profiles selected were later judged to be valid in that no indications of random responding were present.

It was felt that these groups should be ideal for the cross-validation of any scales designed to measure the expression and control of hostility. The members of two of the groups (I and II), had clearly demonstrated in their behavior both sufficient hostility and insufficient control to lead them to attack other people with degrees of violence ranging from battery to murder. Group III is a group of criminals who have never been charged with such behavior. Group IV is a group of normal subjects who are not known to have been convicted of any serious crimes and can therefore be presumed to be less hostile and more controlled as a group than any of the criminal samples. Thus it is to be expected that if the experimental scales measure what they claim to measure, some significant differences between these groups should be obtained.

Results

The data for both the clinical and experimental, scales were subjected to a series of *t* tests. Both assaultive groups were compared with the nonviolent criminal group (I versus III and II versus III) and then both assaultive groups combined were compared with the nonviolent criminal control group (I and II versus III). This process was repeated using the normal control group (I versus IV, II versus IV, and I and II versus IV). Then the combined criminal groups were compared to the normal sample (I, II, and III versus IV). Finally all assaultive subjects were combined and tested against all nonviolent subjects (Groups I and II versus III and IV). For the sake of completeness the two criminal groups were compared (I versus II) as well as the two nonviolent groups (III versus IV).

The means and standard deviations for all groups on the experimental as well as the clinical scales are presented in Table 2 and the results of the *t* tests of the above comparisons are presented in Table 3.

Discussion

Representativeness of the Samples

An examination of the results for the standard MMPI scales as presented in Tables 2 and 3 indicates that the criminal samples are representative of the general population of tested criminals. Their profiles are quite close together and are clearly differentiated from that of the normal sample. In addition the patterns of the criminal groups are similar to those reported in the literature. Since many of these men were in jail, Dahlstrom and Welsh's (1960) report of Beall and Panton's (1957) findings is most pertinent. These authors found a mean Welsh code for male prisoners of 4'28 91763–50/. In the present samples Group I has a mean code of 4278236–950/; Group II, 4358–27916 0/; and Group III, 42–86735910/. The coefficient of concordance for these data is .716 ($p = .001$). Thus the four criminal groups are very similar in their overall patterns. Furthermore it should be noted that the code for the normal group (IV) is 59 341726/08, none of the mean scale values exceeding ± 1 SD from a *T* score of 50. Thus the data indicate that the criminal and normal samples are representative of the general populations from which they were drawn.[1]

Clinical Scales

An examination of Table 3 shows that while several of the standard scales discriminate between criminals and non-

---

[1] In passing, it is important to note the finding attributed to Levy, Southcombe, Cramer, and Freeman (Dahlstrom & Welsh, 1960, p. 308) that violent criminals differ from the nonviolent in the amount of elevation of *Pd* is certainly not borne out. (A reading of the Levy *et al.*, 1952, article shows there is no statement to this effect, nor do their data seem to support such a conclusion, since both violent and nonviolent criminals appear to have equal *Pd* scores.)

TABLE 2. MEANS AND STANDARD DEVIATIONS OF ALL GROUPS ON ALL SCALES

Scale	Group I Extremely Assaultive Criminals		Group II Moderately Assaultive Criminals		Group III Nonassaultive Criminals		Group IV Noncriminals	
	$\overline{X}$	SD	$\overline{X}$	SD	$\overline{X}$	SD	$\overline{X}$	SD
L	4.786	3.215	5.800	2.814	4.760	2.905	2.760	1.666
F	5.429	3.502	3.960	3.034	6.080	4.609	3.400	1.936
K	15.429	5.417	17.800	5.492	15.320	5.793	14.680	3.287
Hs	7.429	5.680	4.440	5.628	5.000	5.260	5.040	3.910
Hs + .5K	15.357	5.692	13.600	5.132	12.880	5.011	12.600	4.472
D	21.429	3.857	20.240	5.761	23.240	5.925	17.600	4.103
Hy	21.857	5.573	23.360	6.343	20.120	5.380	19.680	5.942
Pd	20.786	3.378	19.080	4.847	20.480	4.104	14.760	4.549
Pd + .4K	26.929	3.562	26.200	3.948	26.640	4.221	20.560	4.976
Mf	24.571	4.291	25.000	5.173	23.160	5.080	25.120	4.106
Pa	10.857	3.592	9.560	2.873	10.200	3.663	8.640	2.447
Pt	12.857	8.698	9.160	8.764	11.160	7.386	9.920	5.385
Pt + 1K	28.286	5.928	26.960	5.624	26.480	5.205	24.600	5.307
Sc	12.929	9.311	9.680	9.616	11.000	9.828	6.240	3.282
Sc + 1K	28.357	6.570	27.480	7.512	26.320	7.728	20.840	4.327
Ma	16.571	4.637	15.800	4.388	16.120	4.147	17.440	4.565
Ma + .2K	19.571	4.256	19.440	3.852	19.240	3.951	20.280	4.569
Si	28.714	8.081	25.440	8.021	28.840	10.535	24.480	10.481
AHI	125.714	16.406	123.800	15.777	122.920	17.445	112.520	21.028
FTI	1.051	.179	1.041	.170	1.036	.205	1.062	.207
Ap	12.786	2.607	14.640	2.215	13.560	3.513	15.320	2.625
Hc	7.714	4.214	6.800	3.674	8.280	4.306	5.600	2.273
Ho	20.714	8.973	15.440	8.451	19.480	9.592	16.480	5.775
Hv	4.429	1.785	3.800	1.915	4.040	1.946	3.960	1.695
Hy − 5	3.286	1.729	4.160	0.850	3.000	1.500	3.400	1.190
Im	6.643	4.448	5.560	3.465	6.680	3.350	7.200	1.936
Jh	14.786	6.997	10.800	6.351	13.360	7.012	13.120	4.428
Eo	13.000	4.132	13.840	3.091	13.360	2.643	10.520	3.293
Nu	12.571	6.186	10.360	4.923	12.520	5.051	12.120	3.100
Bc	22.357	9.565	21.240	10.829	23.080	8.514	20.320	6.656

TABLE 3. VALUES OF t AND SIGNIFICANCE LEVELS FOR ALL COMPARISONS ON ALL SCALES

Scale	I versus II	I versus III	I versus IV	II versus III	II versus IV	III versus IV	I and II versus III	I and II versus IV	I, II, and III versus IV	I and II versus III and IV
L	1.026	0.026	2.604*	1.286	4.649**	2.986**	0.897	4.111**	3.863**	2.864**
F	1.372	0.459	2.341*	1.921	0.778	2.680**	1.623	1.510	2.098*	0.334
K	1.300	0.057	0.539	1.553	2.437*	0.480	1.130	1.853	1.358	1.803
Hs	1.586	1.344	1.552	0.363	0.438	0.031	0.359	0.360	0.225	0.450
Hs + .5K	0.987	1.411	1.674	0.502	0.735	0.208	1.012	1.269	0.932	1.399
D	0.688	1.026	2.854**	1.815	1.866	3.913**	1.841	2.513*	3.322**	0.209
Hy	0.740	0.955	1.122	1.948	2.117*	0.274	1.818	2.041*	1.495	2.354*
Pd	1.165	0.237	4.324**	1.102	3.250**	4.668**	0.716	4.314**	5.104**	1.999
Pd + .4K	0.572	0.216	4.212**	0.381	4.440**	4.659**	0.176	5.377**	5.967**	2.774**
Mf	0.263	0.878	0.394	1.269	0.091	1.500	1.337	0.235	0.835	0.697
Pa	1.236	0.541	2.289*	0.687	1.219	1.771	0.202	1.859	1.975	0.893
Pt	1.267	0.646	1.306	0.872	0.369	0.678	0.317	0.289	0.466	0.033
Pt + 1K	0.693	0.989	1.995	0.313	1.526	1.265	0.677	1.996	1.920	1.623
Sc	1.023	0.599	3.274**	0.480	1.693	2.297*	0.062	2.327*	2.379*	1.224
Sc + 1K	0.365	0.831	4.309**	0.538	3.830**	3.094**	0.782	4.389**	4.072**	2.846**
Ma	0.516	0.313	0.567	0.265	1.295	1.070	0.039	1.186	1.307	0.749
Ma + .2K	0.098	0.245	0.476	0.181	0.703	0.861	0.244	0.737	0.918	0.310
Si	1.220	0.039	1.307	1.284	0.364	1.467	0.952	0.917	1.340	0.022
AHI	0.358	0.490	2.024	0.187	2.145*	1.903	0.371	2.593*	2.710**	1.742
FTI	0.184	0.236	0.167	0.090	0.404	0.454	0.182	0.374	0.472	0.113
Ap	2.354*	0.720	2.899**	1.300	0.990	2.007	0.552	2.062*	2.251*	0.749
Hc	0.707	0.397	2.045	1.307	1.389	2.752**	1.115	1.793	2.305*	0.235
Ho	1.829	0.394	1.795	1.580	0.508	1.340	0.913	0.425	0.857	0.361
Hv	1.007	0.615	0.813	0.439	0.313	0.155	0.029	0.142	0.165	0.065
Hy − 5	2.125	0.540	0.244	3.364**	2.598**	1.044	2.403*	1.392	0.359	2.280*
Im	0.845	0.029	0.545	1.162	2.066*	0.672	0.782	1.513	1.257	1.428
Jh	1.813	0.610	0.912	1.353	1.498	0.145	0.642	0.580	0.303	0.756
Eo	0.720	0.332	2.058*	0.590	3.675**	3.363**	0.219	3.462**	3.917**	2.222*
Nu	1.227	0.028	0.305	1.531	1.513	0.337	1.008	0.807	0.383	1.148
Bc	0.322	0.243	0.782	0.668	0.362	1.277	0.583	0.570	0.900	0.031

Note.—The significance levels reported take into account heterogeneity of variance when necessary.
* $p \leq .05$.
** $p \leq .01$.

criminals, none is able to discriminate among the criminal groups (I and/or II versus III).[2] Nevertheless the *Hy* (Hysteria) scale is promising in this regard. The two violent groups are significantly higher than the two control groups on this scale. In addition, the comparison of the assaultive criminals with the nonviolent group (I and II versus III) approaches significance ($p < .10$). This is in agreement with Welsh and Sullivan's 1952 findings (Dahlstrom & Welsh, 1960, p. 190) that people with 43 (*Pd-Hy*) profiles while generally inhibited, occasionally lash out and express their chronic hostile feelings directly and intensely.

Experimental Indices

Examination of the experimental indices, Active Hostility Index (AHI) and Frustration Tolerance Index (FTI), shows that the former is capable of significantly discriminating criminals from noncriminals but is unable to differentiate assaultive from nonassaultive criminals. Since AHI is the sum of the *T* scores on *Pd* and *Ma* and the *Pd* scale is a highly significant discriminator, this is not a surprising result. While this index may be a good screening device in the general population (although poorer than *Pd* alone), it does not appear useful in differentiating between an assaultive criminal and his peaceable cellmate.

The FTI makes no significant discriminations. This is partly due to the pattern of scores on *Hy* noted above. It is possible that this index may be a predictor rather than a postdictor, since *D* may rise after apprehension and conviction.

Experimental Scales

The results on the experimental scales are, on the whole, discouraging. Some

[2] It is worth noting that the addition of *K* to *Pd* and *Sc* improves the discriminations

of the scales do not discriminate anything, others separate criminals from noncriminals, but only one is able to separate the assaultive from the nonviolent criminals. No significant discriminations were found on Ho, Hv, Jh, Nu, and Bc. In the case of Ho (Hostility), Hv (Overt Hostility), and Jh (Judged Manifest Hostility) this result certainly calls into question the validity of these scales. For the others it is a moot point.

The Nu (Neurotic Undercontrol) scale is meant to identify only subjects who are both neurotic and undercontrolled (see Table 1). While the criminal subjects appear undercontrolled, it cannot definitely be stated that they are neurotic as well. Therefore the present study cannot be considered a crucial test of this scale. The same reasoning applies to the Bc (Bimodal) scale which is supposed to identify subjects who are sometimes overcontrolled and at other times undercontrolled. While it can be stated that these subjects were undercontrolled at least once, it is not certain that they are often overcontrolled as well. However, since the assaultive groups were higher on *Hy*, Hy-5, Hc, and Eo we suspect that they may in fact be generally overcontrolled and lash out only on occasions. If this is the case, we would expect the Bc scale to make better discriminations.

In the case of Im (Impulsivity) the data indicate that the scale as described by Dahlstrom and Welsh (1960) is of questionable validity. However it should be noted that this scale is a shortened version of Gough's CPI scale (see Table 1). Since there is one barely significant result and a slight trend for the two nonviolent groups to be higher on the Impulsivity scale, it is possible that the longer scale could better discriminate

between criminals and normals despite the fact that it was derived from a much different population.

among the groups. There is a reversal[3] in the results, though, the two non-violent groups scoring higher than the assaultive criminals.

Three other scales, Ap (Adjustment to Prison), Hc (Hostility Control), and Eo (Ego Overcontrol), separate the criminals from the noncriminals but do not separate assaultive criminals from non-assaultive criminals. Thus it is not clear whether these scales are measuring hostility control or whether they are detecting only general maladjustment or criminality. Ap produces significant differences on several comparisons and has the distinction of being the only scale on which normals score in the direction of less hostility or more control than the criminals. Two comparisons on Hc reach significance but each time in the reverse direction. Likewise, in the case of Eo, where the clearest discriminations are obtained, there are reversals, the scale attributing more control to the assaultive groups. It should be noted that the failure of the Eo scale to differentiate assaultive from nonassaultive criminals does not necessarily suggest invalidity, since there is no reason to suppose that one group of criminals has more control in a general sense than another group of criminals. However, it is surprising that the criminals should all be measured as having more control than the normals.

Finally, there is one scale, Hy-5 (Inhibition of Aggression), which apparently differentiates the combined assaultive criminal groups from the non-assaultive criminal group (I and II versus III) and from the combined control groups (I and II versus III and IV). Once again there is a reversal since the mean of the combined assaultive groups (I and II) exceeds that of the nonassaultive groups (III and IV). Moreover if the

means of the groups are examined, we find that their order is Battery > Normals > Extreme Assaultive > Nonviolent criminals. Thus one would conclude that Battery cases inhibit their aggression more than normals, and murderers more than thieves. From a practical standpoint this would have unfortunate results, for not only is individual prediction impossible, but also in a probation setting it could mean releasing the men most likely to attack someone while retaining in prison those who are relatively harmless. This possibility points up the need for careful research and cross-validation before these or any scales are used in clinical or probation practice.

Despite the generally negative findings, there is a consistent trend: on those scales where significant results were obtained, the nonviolent groups appear less controlled or more hostile than the aggressive groups. One possible explanation for the reversals is that the criminal subjects, applicants for probation, are "faking good" in order to avoid prison. This hypothesis receives some support from the facts that the criminals are significantly higher than the normals on the L scale and that their average $F\text{-}K$ indices are in the minus or "fake good" direction. However, the criminals were sufficiently frank in answering to obtain elevated Pd scores as well as elevations on many other scales. In addition, the $F\text{-}K$ indices for the normal control group are just as strongly in the minus direction as those for the criminals. Consequently neither the insignificant findings nor the obtained direction of the significant findings can be attributed solely to faking on the part of the criminals. Further, even if the results, both significant and insignificant, can be attributed to dissimulation, it seems unlikely that such easily faked scales have great utility.

If dissimulation did not produce these reversals on Hy-5, Im, Eo, Hc, and Hy, how else may these data be explained?

[3] The word *reversal* as used in this paper means a pattern of scores which indicates greater impulsivity or hostility or less control for the two nonviolent groups than for the two groups of assaultive criminals.

An alternative hypothesis is that the extremely assaultive person is often a fairly mild-mannered, long suffering individual who buries his resentment under rigid but brittle controls. Under certain circumstances he may lash out and release all his aggression in one, often disastrous, act. Afterwards he reverts to his usual overcontrolled defenses. Thus he may be more of a menace than the verbally aggressive, "chip-on-the-shoulder" type who releases his aggression in small doses. If this is the case it means that the detection of assaultiveness is a difficult diagnostic task since we must separate the overly controlled but potentially aggressive person from the well-controlled non-aggressive person. The possibility that assaultive criminals may at different times be both overcontrolled and undercontrolled presents a particular problem to those who would construct scales on a rational rather than an empirical basis.

The existence of the trend just discussed should not obscure the basic finding that the experimental scales of hostility and control do not produce the expected differences between groups. In the cases of Ap, Im, Hc, Hy-5, and Eo there are some significant although often inconsistent results, but for the other five scales, not one of the 50 comparisons reached the .05 level of confidence. Why is this the case? Perhaps they measure something other than what their names imply. Or the cross-validation may have been insufficient. (In at least two cases apparently no cross-validation was attempted.) Another possibility is that they are so restricted in scope that the general title given to them is a misnomer. For example, the Hv (Overt Hostility) scale may be a fine measure of overt hostility as interpreted by a therapist in a permissive atmosphere, but it does not seem to have much relation to the overt hostility involved in the act of one of our subjects who bit off a man's nose in a fight. Thus Overt Hostility appears to be too general a description of the scale.

A final possibility that cannot be discarded is that these five scales measure nothing at all.

Certainly the data indicate it is difficult if not impossible to identify an assaultive individual with reasonable accuracy using the MMPI scales now available. However there is some hope that the MMPI may have the potential to detect assaultive people since some items seem to be discriminating.

Summary

Ten scales and two scoring indices of the MMPI which purport to measure hostility and control were cross-validated using four groups known on the basis of past behavior to differ on these dimensions. Group I, the most hostile and uncontrolled group consisted of 14 men convicted of Assault with a deadly weapon, Mayhem, Voluntary manslaughter, or Murder. Group II, moderately hostile and uncontrolled, consisted of 25 men convicted of Battery. Group III was a control group of 25 nonviolent criminals and Group IV a control group of 25 normals. Despite the wide variation in subjects, five scales and one index, Ho, Hostility; Hv, Overt Hostility; Jh, Judged Manifest Hostility; Nu, Neurotic Undercontrol; Bc, Bimodal Control; and FTI, Frustration Tolerance Index, showed no significant differences whatsoever in 60 comparisons. Five other scales and one index, Ap, Adjustment to Prison; Hc, Hostility Control; Hy-5, Inhibition of Aggression; Im, Impulsivity; Eo, Ego Overcontrol; and AHI, Active Hostility Index, showed some ability to separate criminals from noncriminals, but were generally unable to discriminate between the assaultive and nonassaultive criminal groups. An unexpected finding was that the great majority of the significant differences on the scales were reversals, the data indicating that assaultive criminals were better controlled and less hostile than the nonviolent criminals or the normals.

REFERENCES

BEALL, H. S., & PANTON, J. H. Development of a prison adjustment scale (PAS) for the MMPI. Unpublished manuscript, Central Prison, Raleigh, North Carolina, 1957. Cited by W. G. DAHLSTROM & G. S. WELSH (Eds.), *An MMPI handbook: A guide to use in clinical research and practice.* Minneapolis: Univer. Minnesota Press, 1960. P. 308.

BLOCK, J. The development of an MMPI based scale to measure ego control. University of California, Berkeley, Department of Psychology, 1955. (Ditto)

COOK, W. W., & MEDLEY, D. M. Proposed hostility and pharasaic virtue scales for the MMPI. *J. appl. Psychol.*, 1954, 38, 414–418.

DAHLSTROM, W. G., & WELSH, G. S. *An MMPI handbook: A guide to use in clinical research and practice.* Minneapolis: Univer. Minnesota Press, 1960.

GOUGH, H. G. *California Psychological Inventory manual.* Palo Alto: Consulting Psychologists Press, 1960.

HARRIS, R. H., & LINGOES, J. C. Subscales for the MMPI: An aid to profile interpretation. San Francisco: University of California School of Medicine, 1955. (Mimeo)

JONES, H. E. Personality study of adolescence. In *Fourth conference on research on child development.* Washington: National Research Council, Division of Anthropology and Psychology, 1933. Appendix I.

LEVY, S., SOUTHCOMBE, R. H., CRAMER, J. R., & FREEMAN, R. A. The outstanding personality factors among the population of a state penitentiary: A preliminary report. *J. clin. exp. Psychopathol.*, 1952, 13, 117–130.

McGEE, SHANNA. Measurement of hostility: A pilot study. *J. clin. Psychol.*, 1954, 10, 280–282.

PANTON, J. H. Predicting prison adjustment with the MMPI. *J. clin. Psychol.*, 1958, 14, 308–312.

SCHULTZ, S. D. A differentiation of several forms of hostility by scales empirically constructed from significant items on the MMPI. *Pa. State U. Abstr. Doct. Dissertations*, 1954, 17, 717–720.

SIEGEL, S. M. The relationship of hostility to authoritarianism. *J. abnorm. soc. Psychol.*, 1956, 52, 368–372.

STATE OF CALIFORNIA. *Penal code of the State of California.* San Francisco: Bancroft-Whitney, Bender-Moss, 1959.

THE CALIFORNIA PSYCHOLOGICAL INVENTORY

Academic Achievement in High School as Predicted from the California Psychological Inventory

Harrison G. Gough

As everyone knows, there is a current wave of pessimism concerning the predictive validity of psychological tests and particularly of personality inventories. For several years the author has been asking qualifying examination candidates to cite a counter instance,

Work on this project was supported by a Ford Foundation grant for basic research in the behavioral sciences, 1957–1962.

Reprinted by permission of the American Psychological Association and the author from the *Journal of Educational Psychology,* 1964, 55, 174–180.

an example where, in reference to a meaningful nontest criterion and in a sample large enough to compel attention, a personality inventory has given rise to a predictive correlation equal to or greater than .40. Seldom if ever is the question answered. Whether from ignorance or from acceptance of the current skepticism about tests, few students can cite such a finding.

One implication of this state of affairs is that more attention should be paid to those instances in which testing has yielded dependable findings. A second implication is that more studies of the predictive value of personality inventories are badly needed. It is the aim of this paper, therefore, to call attention to the predictability of one such criterion, academic achievement in high school, from the California Psychological Inventory (CPI; Gough, 1957), a personality test designed for use in educational settings.

Prior Studies

No attempt will be made to review or comment on all prior work on this problem. During the past 5–10 years more than 100 studies (see Carter, 1959) have appeared which could merit citation; only investigations of direct relevance to the present endeavor will be considered.

A first question to be asked concerns the base line of predictive accuracy provided by tests of ability and aptitude. Three representative coefficients may be taken from Carter's report: in a sample of 116 students the Henmon-Nelson test correlated .66 with grade-point average (GPA); in a sample of 239 students the ACE gave a coeffiecient of .53; and in a third sample of 211 students the correlation between ACE and GPA was .50. Gough (1953) reported correlations between IQ and high school GPA of .62, .80, .76, .63, and .47 in samples of 135, 35, 66, 205, and 234 students. A weighted mean value for these eight

coefficients would be .57

The second question concerns prediction from personality measures.[1] Gill and Spilka (1962) composed matched groups (on Otis IQ) of achieving and under-achieving Mexican-American high school students. The Siegel (1956) Manifest Hostility Scale differentiated at the .01 level of probability for both sexes, as did the Achievement via conformance (Ac) scale of the CPI. In the initial presentation of the scale (Gough, 1953), Ac revealed a cross-validational correlation with GPA of .44 in a sample of 234 students, a coefficient significantly greater than its correlation of .26 with IQ in this same sample.

Keimowitz and Ansbacher (1960) found 13 of the 18 scales of the CPI to differentiate significantly between achievers and underachievers in mathematics, and Lessinger and Martinson (1961) obtained similar results in comparing gifted and average junior high school students. Morrow and Wilson (1961) did not use the CPI, but felt that their results with bright high achieving and underachieving boys clearly substantiated earlier findings with the CPI on the importance of socialization and impulse regulation in differential achievement at the high school level.

A fifth and last study to be mentioned is that of Pierce (1961) who contrasted 27 high and low achieving tenth-grade boys and 25 high and low achieving twelfth graders. Fourteen CPI scales were considered, of which five differentiated significantly in both comparisons: Responsibility (Re), Tolerance (To), Achievement via conformance (Ac), Achievement via independence (Ai), and Intellectual efficiency (Ie). It is worth mentioning that all three scales

---

[1] Our emphasis here is on studies of personality factors, primarily on those studies using the CPI. It should be noted, nonetheless, that Carter (1959) found a median coefficient of .54 between the four scores of his California Study Methods Survey and GPA in three high school classes (total $N=566$).

TABLE 1.   MEANS AND STANDARD DEVIATIONS ON CPI FOR THE ORIGINAL AND
CROSS-VALIDATING SAMPLES

| | Male | | | | Female | | | |
| | Original (N = 571) | | Cross validating (N = 649) | | Original (N = 813) | | Cross validating (N = 722) | |
Scale	M	SD	M	SD	M	SD	M	SD
Do	23.56	6.28	23.83	5.88	23.88	6.38	23.66	6.10
Cs	15.59	4.25	15.70	4.43	16.60	5.16	16.18	4.83
Sy	21.78	5.52	22.08	5.30	22.12	5.94	21.33	5.85
Sp	32.83	5.66	33.61	5.67	31.63	6.19	31.06	5.83
Sa	18.91	4.17	18.95	3.84	19.29	4.41	18.67	4.44
Wb	33.54	5.48	34.16	5.36	34.22	5.70	34.07	5.61
Re	26.82	6.02	26.91	5.50	30.18	5.39	30.04	5.27
So	35.62	6.11	36.19	5.92	39.03	5.38	39.60	5.78
Sc	25.19	8.01	25.45	7.62	27.80	8.87	28.42	8.46
To	17.88	5.33	17.87	5.19	19.32	5.72	18.72	5.41
Gi	14.82	6.16	15.45	5.89	15.79	6.44	16.07	6.38
Cm	24.97	3.03	25.22	2.71	26.09	1.69	26.15	1.75
Ac	22.81	5.57	22.87	5.04	24.47	5.41	24.18	5.53
Ai	14.90	4.21	14.66	4.00	16.05	4.24	15.49	4.27
Ie	34.10	6.40	34.06	6.25	35.54	6.28	34.41	6.48
Py	9.37	2.59	9.32	2.71	8.81	2.61	8.69	2.65
Fx	9.22	3.50	8.94	3.30	9.14	3.36	8.89	3.37
Fe	14.99	3.58	15.09	3.98	23.94	3.61	24.05	3.51

intended to relate to academic achievement (Ac, Ai, and Ie) did in fact function validly in Pierce's study. Pierce also considered McClelland's need: achievement index from the Thematic Apperception Test (McClelland, Atkinson, Clark, & Lowell 1953), but obtained only slight and insignificant differences at each grade level.

These prior efforts at forecasting achievement in specific subjects and in over-all performance in high school from CPI scales have given promising results. However, before putting full confidence in the predictive validity of the CPI as a forecaster of high school academic achievement, data from larger samples and from schools in different regions are needed. Also, combinations of scales and regression equations should be evaluated along with consideration of the scales one at a time.

Procedure

Testing with the CPI was carried out in 14 high schools in 11 states. Two

samples were then defined: an original sample[2] of 571 males and 813 females, and a cross-validating sample[3] of 649 males and 722 females. Summary statistics on the CPI for these samples are presented in Table 1.

The profiles of mean scores on the CPI for the original and cross-validating samples are very similar: out of 36 comparisons only 1 shows a difference

[2] The original sample included students from Butler, Pennsylvania; Franklin, Pennsylvania; Hartsville, South Carolina; Rock Island, Illinois; and Santa Rosa, California. I should like to thank C. O. Austin, D. W. Boggs, F. F. Duey, G. N. Harriger, and R. F. Wilson for directing this testing and furnishing research data.

[3] The cross-validating sample included students from Boone, Iowa; Brownsville, Pennsylvania; Clarksdale, Mississippi; Globe, Arizona; Kingston, Pennsylvania; Lebanon, New Hampshire; Mt. Vernon, Washington; Russell, Kansas; and St. Cloud, Minnesota. I should like to thank J. L. Bennett, Jean E. Donahey, L. E. Gilbreath, Mercedes S. Gleason, C. J. Martindale, C. P. Quimby, M. P. Smith, R. H. Sorenson, and R. W. Taylor for directing the testing and furnishing research data.

of more than 1 point (Ie for females). The samples may therefore be considered comparable with respect to factors assessed by the inventory. If expressed in standard score form, 15 of the 18 scales would be below 50 for males and 14 of 18 for females; this is to be expected, as many CPI scales are age related, particularly those having to do with social poise and self-confidence.

TABLE 2. CORRELATIONS BETWEEN CU-MULATIVE GPA IN HIGH SCHOOL AND THE VARIABLES INDICATED IN THE ORIGINAL SAMPLES

Variable	Males	Females	Total
Do	.31	.31	.31
Cs	.32	.34	.34
Sy	.27	.27	.26
Sp	.17	.10	.12
Sa	.25	.21	.23
Wb	.27	.24	.26
Re	.43	.37	.41
So	.30	.31	.33
Sc	.13	.15	.15
To	.30	.36	.34
Gi	.06	.16	.13
Cm	.25	.11	.19
Ac	.35	.35	.36
Ai	.30	.35	.34
Ie	.41	.38	.40
Py	.24	.23	.22
Fx	−.03	.01	−.01
Fe	.05	.04	.10
IQ	.51	.57	.53

Note.—571 males, 813 females, 1,384 total. All coefficients except those in boldface type are significant at the .01 level.

The personality inventory testing had been done in the spring or fall of the same calendar year. In the spring of the next year cumulative GPAs and IQs were obtained for all students. Because of different grading practices and recording systems and because different tests of ability had been used, some method of equating schools had to be adopted. To achieve this, for each school separately GPAs were converted to standard scores having means of 50 and standard deviations of 10, and intel-

lectual ability measures were converted to standard scores with a mean of 110 and standard deviations of 15. The 18 scales of the CPI and standard scores on IQ were then correlated with GPA in the original sample of 1,384 students from five schools, with results as indicated in Table 2.

The highest correlation with GPA comes, as would be expected, from IQ with a coefficient of .53 for the total sample.[4] At the same time, 17 of the 18 CPI scales reveal statistically significant values, topped by the scales for Re (.41), Ie (.40), and Ac (.36).

The next step in the analysis was the derivation of predictive equations on the CPI, using multiple-regression techniques.[5] Three equations were constituted, one for males (M), one for females (F), and one for the total sample (T). These equations are offered below:

$$Ach\text{-}M = 20.388 + .258Sa + .445Re - .396Gi + .230Ac + .181Ai + .180Ie + .326Py$$
$$Ach\text{-}F = 24.737 + .175Do + .450Cs - .344Sp + .373So - .315Gi + .175Ac + .328Ai + .158Ie$$
$$Ach\text{-}T = 20.116 + .317Re + .192So - .309Gi + .227Ac + .280Ai + 244Ie$$

Because of an additional interest in determining how accurate a prediction might result from conjoint use of the CPI and IQ, a fourth analysis was conducted using both measures; the following equation was developed:

[4] Use of IQs may have led to a slight underestimation of the correlation between GPA and ability; unfortunately, raw scores or mental ages were not available for the samples studied.

[5] These analyses were conducted at the Computer Center of the University of California, Berkeley. The author wishes to thank the Center for time granted for this study, and also Q. Welch, senior statistician at the Institute of Personality Assessment and Research, for his help in conducting the analyses.

$$IQ + CPI = -.786 + .195Re + .244So$$
$$- .130Gi + .190Ac +$$
$$.179Ai + .279IQ$$

The weights given in all four equations are the computing weights using raw scores on the scales of the CPI and IQ with the mean set at 110 and standard deviation set at 15. It is of interest to note that the equation for both sexes incorporates all three achievement-relevant scales of the inventory (Ac, Ai, and Ie), and that when IQ itself is considered it replaces Ie while the other components of the Ach-T equation are retained.

Cross Validation

The CPI, IQ, and four equations were next correlated with GPA in the cross-validating sample of 1,371 students as indicated in Table 3. As before, IQ by itself is the single most powerful predictor with a correlation of .60 for the total sample. Re (.48), Ie (.43), and Ac (.40) were again the three most effective scales of the inventory.

The three equations based wholly on the CPI gave predictive validities of .55, .55, and .56. This similarity in predictive accuracy is paralleled by a high degree of interrelatedness; in this cross-validating sample Ach-M and Ach-F correlated .83 with each other and .94 and .91 with Ach-T. The third equation, Ach-T, is slightly superior to the other two as a predictor, and has another advantage in that it contains only six scales versus seven for Ach-M and eight for Ach-F. Ach-T is therefore the equation recommended for use when a forecast of academic achievement in high school is to be made from the CPI alone. It should also be noted that in this instance the attempt to predict from subgroups (males and females) was less effective than the equation developed for the total sample.

The optimum prediction of achieve-

TABLE 3. CORRELATIONS BETWEEN CUMULATIVE GPA IN HIGH SCHOOL AND THE VARIABLES INDICATED, IN THE CROSS-VALIDATING SAMPLES

Variable	Males	Females	Total
Do	.26	.32	.28
Cs	.28	.36	.33
Sy	.24	.27	.24
Sp	.11	.18	.09
Sa	.19	.28	.23
Wb	.26	.26	.25
Re	.45	.45	.48
So	.33	.30	.35
Sc	.14	.11	.08
To	.32	.40	.37
Gi	**.02**	.11	.08
Cm	.28	.31	.31
Ac	.37	.40	.40
Ai	.33	.42	.39
Ie	.42	.45	.43
Py	.18	.23	.17
Fx	**−.03**	**−.03**	**−.03**
Fe	**.00**	**.00**	.18
Ach-M	.53	.55	.55
Ach-F	.50	.54	.55
Ach-T	.53	.55	.56
IQ	.58	.62	.60
IQ + CPI	.66	.68	.68

Note.—649 males, 722 females, 1,371 total.
All coefficients except those in boldface type are significant at the .01 level.

ment, within the set of predictors considered, is given by the equation incorporating IQ along with five CPI scales. The coefficient for this equation is .68, significantly higher than that for IQ alone (.60) or for Ach-T (.56).

Information on expected values for Ach-T and IQ + CPI equations might be of interest and is therefore offered in Table 4, as derived from the cross-validating samples only.

Cross-Cultural Validation

An explicit theoretical aim of the CPI is to define dimensions having cultural universality, i.e., "folk concepts" of personality; and a practical corollary is to provide measures which are valid in translation.

TABLE 4

Equation	Male		Female		Total	
	M	SD	M	SD	M	SD
Ach-T	48.43	4.82	50.50	4.67	49.52	4.85
IQ + CPI	48.61	5.99	50.97	6.03	49.86	6.12

In a recent study (Gough, 1964) the CPI was applied to the prediction of academic achievement in four Italian *licei* in three cities, using an Italian translation of the personality inventory. The D 48 test (see Cusin, 1959; Ferracuti & Rizzo, 1959) was also employed as a measure of intellectual ability. The best individual predictors in this study were Ai, Ac, and Re scales of the CPI, with values comparable to those observed in the United States. A regression equation of the form

$$Ach = 34.77 + .33Ac + .85Ai - .56Fx$$

gave a correlation of .44 with grades in the total sample of 341 Italian students, whereas the measure of ability (the D 48 test) gave a correlation of .17.

The equations presented in the present report were not available for the earlier study. Ach-T, when computed for the 341 Italian students, yields a mean of 47.50, a standard deviation of 3.49, and a correlation of .39 with GPA. This coefficient is significant well beyond the .01 level of probability, and is not too far below the coefficient of .44 observed for the equation developed directly from the Italian data.

The IQ + CPI equation was also applied to the Italian sample, after first converting D 48 scores to standard scores with a mean of 110 and a standard deviation of 15. For IQ + CPI, after this adjustment, the Italian mean was 48.30, standard deviation of 5.20, and the correlation with grades was .33. In this cross-cultural validation of the two equations the CPI alone fares better than the combination of CPI plus a measure of intellectual ability.

Discussion

The samples reported in this study (1,384 and 1,371) seem large enough to lend confidence to the stability and validity of the equations derived. Furthermore, the demonstration of cross-cultural validity adds further strength to the findings. It would therefore seem justifiable to consider the content of the equations and their implications for the psychology of achievement.

Two CPI measures of internalized value systems appear in both Ach-T and IQ + CPI, Re and So. These two scales have repeatedly been shown to have relevance for achievement and interpersonal effectiveness in settings where self-discipline, adherence to value, and the management of impulse are desirable. By inference, academic achievement in high school calls on this domain of effectiveness.

However, the negative weighting on the Good impression (Gi) scale exercises a tempering influence on these dispositions. It is not just conventionality for convention's sake, or an undifferentiated desire to please and to do what is expected that is emphasized by the equations. The less a student is concerned with social desirability, in fact, the higher will be his score on the two equations.

The Ac and Ai scales introduce a third note—an emphasis on both of the primary forms of the achievement motive (conformance or form manifesting, and independence or form creating).

A fourth component of the achievement equations comes from the Ie scale in one instance or directly from IQ in the other—the presence of intellective and cognitive talent.

We might conclude and restate these contentions in the following way: the personological basis for differential achievement at the high school level which seems indicated by our findings is one in which there is a sensitivity to and acceptance of social values but with retention of individuality, a cathexis of constructive endeavor, and an initial advantage in talent.

Summary

Can valid predictions of meaningful nontest criteria be made from personality inventories? To counter a prevailing skepticism on this issue positive evidence from large samples is needed. A regression equation for high school grade-point average was developed from California Psychological Inventory scores on 1384 students from 5 schools. A cross-validational coefficient of .56 was obtained on 1371 students from 9 schools, and a cross-cultural coefficient of .39 for 341 students in Italy. Addition of an ability measure raised the 1st correlation to .68, but lowered the cross-cultural coefficient to .33. The predictive equation stressed traits of responsibility and social maturity, capacity for both independent and adaptive achievement, and efficiency in the use of personal resources.

REFERENCES

CARTER, H. D. Improving the prediction of school achievement. *Educ. Admin. Super.*, 1959, 45, 255–260.

CUSIN, S. G. Contributo alla taratura italiana del D 48. [A contribution to the Italian norms of the D 48.] *Boll. Psicol. Sociol. appl.*, 1959, No. 31–36, 259–261.

FERRACUTI, F., & RIZZO, G. B. Studio sul test D 48 applicato ad una populazione italiana di livello scolastico superiore. [A study of the D 48 test as applied to an Italian population of higher educational level.] *Boll. Psicol. Sociol. appl.*, 1959, No. 31–36, 77–83.

GILL, LOIS J., & SPILKA, B. Some nonintellectual correlates of academic achievement among Mexican-American secondary school students. *J. educ. Psychol.*, 1962, 53, 144–149.

GOUGH, H. G. What determines the academic achievement of high school students? *J. educ. Res.*, 1953, 46, 321–331.

GOUGH, H. G. *Manual for the California Psychological Inventory.* Palo Alto, Calif.: Consulting Psychologists Press, 1957.

GOUGH, H. G. A cross-cultural study of achievement motivation. *J. appl. Psychol.*, 1964, 48, 191–196.

KEIMOWITZ, R. I., & ANSBACHER, H. L. Personality and achievement in mathematics. *J. indiv. Psychol.*, 1960, 16, 84–87.

LESSINGER, L. M., & MARTINSON, RUTH A. The use of the California Psychological Inventory with gifted pupils. *Pers. Guid. J.*, 1961, 39, 572–575.

MCCLELLAND, D. C., ATKINSON, J. W., CLARK, R. A., & LOWELL, E. L. *The achievement motive.* New York: Appleton-Century-Crofts, 1953.

MORROW, W. R., & WILSON, R. C. The self-reported personal and social adjustment of bright high-achieving and under-achieving high school boys. *J. child Psychol. Psychiat.*, 1961, 2, 203–209.

PIERCE, J. V. Personality and achievement among able high school boys. *J. indiv. Psychol.*, 1961, 17, 102–107.

SIEGEL, S. N. The relation of hostility to authoritarianism. *J. abnorm. soc. Psychol.*, 1956, 52, 368–372.

Validation of the CPI Socialization Scale in India

Harrison G. Gough and Harjit S. Sandhu

The goal of the California Psychological Inventory is to measure those traits of character which arise directly and necessarily from interpersonal life, and which should therefore be relevant to the understanding and prediction of social behavior in any and all situations and in any culture. Specifically, the inventory seeks to assess "folk concepts" which are culturally universal.

One such concept is that referring to "socialization." All cultures and all societies have rules, proscriptions, and stipulated ways of conducting the activities of life. A more socialized person is one who has better understood and internalized these rules, so that his life and behavior are more thoroughly governed in accordance with the structured pattern of controls of the society than are the actions of the less socialized person. It should be mentioned that these regulatory patterns need not always be inhibitory; cultural admonitions favoring independence and self-expression are as omnipresent as those demanding restraint and self-denial.

With respect to the socialization continuum, it has been hypothesized (Gough, 1954, 1960b, 1960c) that a sociological dimension can be identified, ranging from behaviors of greater waywardness and recalcitrance at one end, through an intermediate zone of partial balance and adaptation, to an extreme

Work on this study was supported, in part, by a Ford Foundation basic research grant to the senior author.

Reprinted by permission of the American Psychological Association and the authors from the *Journal of Abnormal and Social Psychology*, 1964, **68**, 544–547.

of archetypal virtue and probity. Given this conception, the task of psychological measurement is to locate persons and groups in their proper positions along this continuum. The validity of a measure of socialization can be judged by the degree to which it succeeds in this positioning. The value of the measure can be judged by the degree to which it betokens a psychological rationale for the classifications and for the behaviors on which they rest.

Socialization Scale

The conceptual basis of the Socialization (So) scale (Gough, 1948, 1960c; Gough & Peterson, 1952) derives from the theory of role taking. The less socialized individual is hypothesized to be less adept at sensing and interpreting the nuances and subtle cues of the interpersonal situation, and hence less able to evolve reliable and trustworthy residual control systems. Items are included in the scale which attempt, both directly (e.g., "Before I do something I try to consider how my friends will react to it" and "I often think about how I look and what impression I am making upon others") and indirectly (e.g., "I find it easy to 'drop' or 'break with' a friend"), to appraise these dispositions.

Although the scale originated in role-taking conceptions, this does not mean that all of its items involve only role-taking content. Other items having diagnostic power (e.g., "I have often gone against my parents' wishes" and "If the pay was right I would like to travel with a circus or carnival") were also used. The warrant for this strategy is found in the scale's primary function, which is to locate an individual in his proper place along the socialization continuum; then, *from this positioning itself,* the aforementioned role-taking implications are hypothesized to follow.

The So scale was first introduced by Gough and Peterson (1952) in a 64-item version. A shortened 54-item version (Gough, 1960c) was included in the California Psychological Inventory (CPI; Gough, 1957). Empirical evidence of the scale's validity may be drawn from the later report (Gough, 1960c). For males, 25 samples involving 10,296 cases were considered, ranging from nominated "best citizens" through work groups, disciplinary problems, and county jail inmates, to institutionalized delinquents and felons. The biserial correlation for the dichotomy or more versus less socialized was + .73. For women, 16 samples totaling 10,560 cases were studied. These samples covered the same range of the continuum—"best citizens," work groups, disciplinary problems, jail inmates, and institutionalized delinquents. The biserial correlation for more versus less socialized was + .78.

A recent study of military personnel (Datel, 1962) involving 1,065 subjects, classified into four categories of "socialization," has confirmed the above findings; Datel reports a biserial correlation of + .77 for his cases.

The theory of the So scale requires differentiation within zones of the socialization continuum as well as the separation of more from less socialized subjects. One study relevant to this requirement is that of Vincent (1961), in which 232 women observed during illegitimate pregnancies were classified as having had no previous pregnancies of this type, one previous, and two or more. The mean scores on the So scale (33.60, 24.39, and 22.23) agreed with this progression, and the biserial cor-

relation comparing those with no prior pregnancies versus those with one or more was + .83.

Other studies have demonstrated the validity of the scale when used with children (Reckless, Dinitz, & Kay, 1957), adolescents (Jaffee & Polansky, 1962), parolees (California Youth Authority, 1956–58), prison inmates (Cohen, 1959), reformatory inmates (Donald, 1955), and juvenile offenders (Peterson & Quay, 1959).

Evidence pertaining to the role-taking hypothesis for the scale, and its implications for a defect of social acuity, is available in a paper by Reed and Cuadra (1957). These authors studied 204 student nurses undergoing training at a Veterans Administration neuropsychiatric hospital. Each subject described herself on the Gough Adjective Check List (Gough, 1960a; Gough & Heilbrun, 1964), and then the other three members of a four-person group to which she was assigned. Finally, each nurse attempted to predict how she would be described by her group. A point was earned for a predicted adjective if two of the three peers had in fact checked the adjective, and a total predictive accuracy score was defined as the sum of such points. The correlation between predictive accuracy on this interpersonal task and the So scale was + .41, a value significant well beyond the .01 level of probability.

The studies cited above are thought to be representative of the many investigations which have made use of the So scale. They appear to agree in confirming the validity of the measure, both as a forecaster of significant social behavior and as an index of the psychological state theorized to underlie such behavior. However, all of the studies cited were conducted in the United States, and hence cannot be said to bear upon the broader aim of the CPI, viz., to delineate "folk concepts" having cross-cultural relevance. It is the purpose of this paper to present data drawn from one such cross-cultural application.

Method

In 1959 the So scale was translated into Hindi and Punjabi by the second author, and administered to 251 subjects in India.[1] Six of the 54 items were found to be more or less untranslatable, so that the version of the scale used in the study contained 48 items. Approximately 160 of the subjects were illiterate, and for these persons the items were read aloud with the respondents entering a tick for "true" and cross (X) for "false" on numbered sheets. To facilitate this testing, 5 introductory items having nothing to do with the So scale were given first so that the examiner could identify any subjects having difficulty or not understanding the task. Little or no difficulty was experienced during the testing, and it is believed that all 251 protocols are reliable.

The correctional system in use in the province where testing was done provides a classification of offenders by severity: hardened habituals and repeaters, habitual offenders, and casual and first offenders. Seven samples were tested, five of which can be classified under these headings:

Hardened and habitual offenders: 22 inmates from the central jail in Ambala, India.

Habitual offenders: 20 inmates from the jail at Delhi, and 23 inmates from the Borstal Institution at Hissar.

[1] A 6-page table presenting the 54 items in the So scale and the Hindi and Punjabi translations of the 48 items used in this study has been deposited with the American Documentation Institute. Order Document No. 7859 from ADI Auxiliary Publications Project, Photoduplication Service, Library of Congress, Washington, D. C. 20540. Remit in advance $1.25 for microfilm or $1.25 for photocopies and make checks payable to: Chief, Photoduplication Service, Library of Congress.

Casual and first offenders: 99 inmates from the jail at Faridkot, and 39 inmates from the Borstal Institution at Hissar.

In addition, 28 males and 20 females from Brijindra College at Faridkot were tested.

In order to render data comparable to those from other studies, scores on the 48-item test were prorated to a 54-item basis. Summary statistics on the So scale for these prorated scores are offered in Table 1.

TABLE 1.   SUMMARY STATISTICS ON THE 54-ITEM SOCIALIZATION SCALE OF THE CALIFORNIA PSYCHOLOGICAL INVENTORY FOR SAMPLES TESTED IN INDIA

Sample	N	M	SD
College students			
Females	20	37.80	5.84
Males	28	35.32	4.53
Casual offenders			
Borstal inmates	39	33.95	2.06
Faridkot jail	99	34.31	4.01
Habitual offenders			
Borstal inmates	23	24.78	6.42
Delhi jail	20	23.15	6.03
Hardened and habitual offenders			
Central jail, Ambala	22	21.55	4.31

Results

The F ratio over the seven samples in Table 1 was 54.34, which, with $df = 6/244$; is significant well beyond the .001 level. It is quite clear, too, that the progression of means on the So scale is in accord with the continuum from more socialized to less socialized. A word should also be added concerning the correspondence of the means in Table 1 to those customarily observed in the United States. For 9,001 nondelinquent males in this country the mean on So was 36.74, compared with a mean of 35.32 for the 28 college males from India. For 9,776 nondelinquent females in the United States the mean was 39.46, compared to a mean of

37.80 for the 20 college females in India.

The Indian casual offenders (means of about 34) score higher than county jail inmates in the United States (mean of 29), whereas both the habitual and hardened habitual offenders (means of 25, 23, and 22) score below values typically observed for institutionalized delinquents and felons in this country (a mean score of 27 is representative). Perhaps a more appropriate American comparison would be the 96 reformatory inmates from Donald's (1955) study whose first commitment occurred at age 15 or before; for these subjects the mean score on So was 24.76.

In order to obtain correlational evidence on the validity of the So scale in India, arbitrary "socialization" scores were assigned to each of the 251 subjects, using this weighting: nondelinquents =4, casual and first offenders =3, habitual offenders =2, and hardened and habitual offenders =1. The product-moment correlation between these scores and the So scale was +.70.

It might be urged that a stricter test of the validity of the scale would be its ability to differentiate among the 203 delinquents. Each delinquent was assigned a socialization score of 3, 2, or 1, using the same coding as described above, and these scores were then correlated with the So scale, yielding a coefficient of +.73. This value, it may be noted, is the same as the biserial coefficient calculated on a sample of 10,296 males in the United States (Gough, 1960c), but below the coefficient of +.77 reported by Datel (1962) for military personnel.

Discussion

To establish the cross-cultural validity of the So scale, and of the psychological theory which it embodies, will require a great deal more work than that summarized in this short study. Studies in other countries, larger samples, and clinical appraisals of high- and low-scoring subjects on the scale are obvious first-order needs. It is hoped that such studies will be initiated and will be forthcoming. One such inquiry has been conducted in Costa Rica (Adis-Castro, 1957), with results very similar to those reported here for India. Studies are also under way in Japan, Puerto Rico, France, Germany, and Italy.

In spite of the admitted need for more evidence, it nonetheless appears that the results of this study in India have been quite promising. It also seems permissible to say that these findings tend clearly to strengthen the presuppositions, both theoretical and practical, of the Socialization scale.

Summary

The California Psychological Inventory (CPI) seeks to assess culturally universal dimensions of personality, i.e., "folk concepts." Validation must therefore include cross-cultural validation. The CPI Socialization (So) scale was translated into Hindi and Punjabi and given to 203 delinquents and 48 college students in India. Behavioral ratings were assigned, 4 to nondelinquents, 3 to casual and 1st offenders, 2 to habitual offenders, and 1 to hardened and habitual offenders. The ratings correlated +.70 with So in the full sample ($N = 251$), and +.73 within the subsample of 203 delinquents. A coefficient of +.73 had also been observed for 10,296 males tested in the USA. Findings are interpreted as supporting the theoretical presuppositions and practical utility of the measure.

REFERENCES

ADIS-CASTRO, G. A. Study of selected personality dimensions by means of the questionnaire method in a Latin American Culture. Unpublished doctoral dissertation, University of California, Berkeley, 1957.

CALIFORNIA YOUTH AUTHORITY AND STATE DEPARTMENT OF CORRECTIONS. *Technical report series.* Tracy, Calif.: Deuel Vocational Institution, Pilot Intensive Counseling Organization, 1956–58.

COHEN, L. M. The relationship between certain personality variables and prior occupational stability of prison inmates. Unpublished doctoral dissertation, Temple University, 1959.

DATEL, W. E. Socialization scale norms on military samples. *Milit. Med.,* 1962, **127,** 740–744.

DONALD, E. P. Personality scale analysis of new admission to a reformatory. Unpublished master's dissertation, Ohio State University, 1955.

GOUGH, H. G. A sociological theory of psychopathy. *Amer J. Sociol.,* 1948, **53,** 359–366.

GOUGH, H. G. Systematic validation of a test for delinquency. *Amer. Psychologist,* 1954, **9,** 381. (Abstract)

GOUGH, H. G. *Manual for the California Psychological Inventory.* Palo Alto, Calif.: Consulting Psychologists Press, 1957.

GOUGH, H. G. The adjective check list as a personality assessment research technique. *Psychol. Rep.,* 1960, **6,** 107–122. (a)

GOUGH, H. G. Cross-cultural studies of the socialization continuum. *Amer. Psychologist,* 1960, **15,** 410–411. (Abstract) (b)

GOUGH, H. G. Theory and measurement of socialization. *J. consult. Psychol.,* 1960, **24,** 23–30. (c)

GOUGH, H. G., & HEILBRUN, A. B., JR. *Manual for the Adjective Check List.* Palo Alto, Calif.: Consulting Psychologists Press, 1964.

GOUGH, H. G., & PETERSON, D. R. The identification and measurement of predispositional factors in crime and delinquency. *J. consult. Psychol.,* 1952, **16,** 207–212.

JAFFEE, L. D., & POLANSKY, N. A. Verbal inaccessibility in young adolescents showing delinquent trends. *J. Hlth. hum. Behav.,* 1962, **3,** 105–111.

PETERSON, D. R., & QUAY, H. C. Extending the construct validity of a socialization scale. *J. consult. Psychol.,* 1959, **23,** 182.

RECKLESS, W. C., DINITZ, S., & KAY, BARBARA. The self-component in potential delinquency and potential non-delinquency. *Amer. sociol. Rev.,* 1957, **22,** 566–570.

REED, C. F., & CUADRA, C. A. The role-taking hypothesis in delinquency. *J. consult. Psychol.,* 1957, **21,** 386–390.

VINCENT, C., *Unmarried mothers.* Glencoe, Ill.: Free Press, 1961.

Validation and Intensification of the Sixteen Personality Factor Questionnaire

Raymond B. Cattell

The Aim of Improving an Instrument

Although the ideal in personality measurement, as in ability measurement, is to deal with functionally unitary traits, there are as yet extremely few personality factor scales available. The clinical, educational or industrial psychologist who is ready for the sophisticated and effective diagnosis and prediction which the use of factors—in the specification equation and in pattern functions of factor profiles—makes possible, finds available only one instrument of objective factor measurement[6] and three or four questionnaires.[12, 17, 28, 39] Compared with the former, the latter have the virtue of brief and simple administration and the defect of distortability, which together permit a widespread usage, but with cooperative subjects only. Accordingly, though objective personality factor tests are on the march, [5, 6, 18] cooperative subjects are common enough to justify considering the pencil and paper questionnaire as a permanent part of the psychologist's equipment, and seeking to perfect it. This paper is an account of the concepts, methods and results in producing a revision of the 16 P. F. Questionnaire.

The Sixteen Personality Factor Questionnaire, which consists of fifteen temperamental or dynamic factors and one general intelligence factor, has been in

Reprinted by permission of the publisher and the author from *The Journal of Clinical Psychology*, 1956, **12**, 205–214.

use seven years.[17] During that time it has been translated for use in eight countries. It has accumulative valuable social validation data in the form of profiles for about thirty occupations [7] and six clinical and delinquency syndromes.[17] Certain important regression weights of factors on criteria have also been determined, notably for predicting certain occupational successes, [21, 14] accident proneness,[36] success in various kinds of leadership,[20] the selection of researchers and creative persons,[14, 22] and the prediction of that part of educational achievement not due to ability.[34, 44]

Although the 1948 factorization on which the construction of the 16 P. F. was based, and which we shall henceforth call "the original factor foundation," availed itself of the most advanced factor techniques then possible, and was based on an exceptionally wide area of items, it was the stated intention of the designers at the time to re-check the factor structure, later, by cross validation on different populations, and by entirely independent rotations. The term *validation* in the present title applies to determining personality factor validity, i.e., internal concept or construct validity, while the term "intensification" is borrowed from photography, as a useful designation in psychometrics for the special, additional process of raising the saturation of items on required factors and reducing irrelevant correlations, i.e., correlations with factors other than the intended one. Thus, validation concerns the confirmation of a factor; while intensification connotes the development of items to express it more strongly and distinctly, as happens in intensifying a photographic negative. The notion of "homogenizing" a scale is not the same as "intensifying" it, for a test may be made more homogeneous without being made more factor-pure, and we have argued elsewhere[10] that there are systematic psychological reasons why this may actually tend to *lower* factor saturations. Our discussion of test construction theory and its illustration by a particular case, though centered on validation and intensification, makes a complete review of necessary principles in factored test construction.

The Original 16 P. F. Foundation in the Full "Personality Sphere"

Emphasis on certain particular standards and requirements in what follows can be understood only if the reader is first given some perspective on the emergence of the 16 P. F. in relation to basic personality research. For this test is only one part of a whole series of test developments which are unique in that the constructors are primarily concerned with basic personality structure and only secondarily with test "gadgets" *per se*. In the first place, the adult 16 P. F. is developed in conjunction with other questionnaire constructions, cross-sectioning personality at different age levels, notably at the level of early adolescence;[15] at seven years; and at four years.[16] It thus implies dependence on research findings and emerging concepts about basic personality development. Secondly, at the level of adult cross-section, the 16 P. F. is an integrated part of a research advance conceived broadly in terms of three possible observation media—life records *in situ*, questionnaires and objective-tests. This attention to breadth of manifestation increases our understanding of the primary personality structures in terms of different media and situational expressions.

The 16 P. F. can thus claim a somewhat more intensive and extensive research basis than the few excellent factored questionnaires otherwise available, notably in (1) the coverage of the personality sphere, which in this case is extended by cross-media factorings,[18, 19] with the wider reference of meaning thus ensured, and (2) a factor loading has been determined for every item, instead of for conglomerate blocks of items, by virtue of the special techniques of factoring invented for handling large numbers of variables. The resulting better selection of items permits measures of higher factor saturation though still with small numbers of items per factor.

The first of these advances can be briefly substantiated and given essential descriptive detail as follows. The original research on verbal responses from which the 16 P. F. emerged was based on a population of questionnaire items derived from:

(1) A complete survey[2] of all well-known questionnaire, opinionnaire, interest and value scales. The evidence[1] thereof indicated that about twenty factors could be discerned as of 1946. Each of these factors was represented in the ensuing research by sufficient markers, and by newly invented items directly designed to measure the concepts better than by any existing tests.

(2) Evidence of entirely new personality factors, from non-questionnaire sources. In particular, new items were added to the pool of variables to cover the fourteen factors found in factoring rated behavior based on the complete

---

[1] These factors resulted largely from the work of Guilford,[27] Ferguson, Humphrey and Strong,[24] Flanagan,[25] Layman,[31] Mosier,[33] Reyburn and Taylor,[35] Thorndike,[38] Thurstone,[40] and Vernon[41] and covered, among many others, the data of such tests as the Bernreuter, Bell, Strong, Allport-Vernon and other tests.

personality sphere,[2] as well as on objective tests. Parenthetically, the interfactor studies [18, 19] and Saunders' projection of questionnaire factors into behavior rating space, have shown that the questionnaire factors can be matched with behavior rating factors much more closely and completely than with the objective test factors, at the present stage of the latter. Only life record factors D, J, and K are missing from the questionnaire factors and only questionnaire factors Q^1, Q^2, Q^3 and Q^4 are, missing from the life record factors. (Hence the unique Q designation for these four factors.)

The outcome of the original factoring was a good confirmation both as to number and kind of factors, agreeing with the hypothesized twenty from the above broad survey of evidence in questionnaire and rating media. Nevertheless it seemed to us appropriate and necessary research strategy at that time to drop the three or four most poorly defined factors in the original factoring and to build the 16 P. F. from intelligence and the clearest fifteen factors. Research should at some time pick up the four discards, but it has seemed sufficiently ambitious a task for our laboratory to concentrate on the definition of the fifteen, and their internal and social validities. And even these sometimes exceed the span of attention of certain applied psychologists!

Now the original structure was based on an 82 x 82 matrix, so the additions necessary for the 187 item A and B forms (giving either 10 or 13 items per factor per scale) were made from items known to correlate with the factors in the survey[2] or picked up by item analyses against the separate factors. The mean coefficient of equivalence for all factors between the two forms was .51, and the mean consistency coefficient .68, which may be considered good for 10 to 13 items, but since the simple structure showed factors oblique up to about 0.3, better consistencies

could be desired. Accordingly a series of re-factorings, with search for more highly loaded items, was planned, as described here, to give the highest possible factor validities for a test of this length.

Canons of Factored Test Construction

An *ideal factor scale* differs from a *Walker-Guttman* scale[29, 42] only in that it yields a measure of a factor instead of a composite of factors. It should meet the conditions that (1) all items have the same factor composition, namely that of a pure, psychologically meaningful, simple structure factor, and (2) items are graded in degree of difficulty according to equal intervals on a normal distribution, since factors can be defined as normally distributed. (In the more general context of personality, which includes ability, "difficulty," which applies only to abilities, is better expressed as "eccentricity of cut.") if the first condition is guaranteed, item comparisons in all possible pairs as in Guttman scaling are unnecessary to ensure the second, since grading can be determined from cutting positions on the distribution. On the other hand, if it is not, application of the Walker-Guttman condition may, according to present experience, prevent anything broader than a scale for a factor of a relatively specific nature being formed.

The aim of a multiple factor questionnaire is to form distinct factor scales, in this case sixteen, with mutual obliquities no greater and no less than those discovered to exist among the simple structure factors themselves. Since perhaps only one item in a thousand initially tried ultimately turns out to be a pure factor measure it is likely to be several years before a sufficiency of items is discovered to make sixteen ideal factor scales. Accordingly at present the aim must be to obtain *scales operating with suppressors*, i.e., obtaining the requisite degree of freedom from factor intercorrelation by using the *principle of summated factor suppression*. This states that *the collection of items used for one factor scale should have the highest mean loading on the required factor consistent with loadings on all other factors summing to zero.* For example, in a two item (a and b) scale for Factor F_1, we should require that if $a = xF_1 + sF_2$ then $b = yF_1 - sF_2$.

In any refined statistical work it is important not to lose sight of basic matters of psychology and common sense. For example a highly loaded and statistically perfect item in the given student sample is no good if it contains words obscure to non-students; contains a reference to an event likely to be unknown a year later; has an eccentricity of cut of 95% to 5%, and takes two minutes to read!

Accordingly the construction of the revised 16 P. F., from start to finish, followed the following canons of procedure.

(1) A very large number of items (in this case 1552) is made up by at least six people (to avoid person-specific factors sometimes demonstrable in tests), in the light of all that is known (in questionnaire, rating and 16 P. F. criterion prediction data) about the number and nature of the primary personality factors.

(2) These are to be submitted to persons of different background, and to word count surveys, to eliminate uncommon words (Flesch word count), items that are too long, ambiguous or tied to matters too specific in place or time.

(3) Two population samples are to be taken, one toward the upper and one the lower half of the range for which the test is intended and correlation matrices are calculated among the items separately for these.

(4) Items with extreme cuts (under 10% in one end category of three), in either sample, are eliminated before the calculation of correlation matrices.

The phi co-efficient or the tetrachoric is used. Phi divided by the maximum possible phi for the given extremity of cut has been used by us before and, like the tetrachoric, has the advantage of getting rid of "difficulty factors,"[43] but since it is prone to yield non-Gramian matrices, and since the alternative tetrachoric involves undue assumptions, the present study used phi.

(5) The two matrices are separately factored and rotated blindly to simple structure. It is very important that the latter be truly and thoroughly done.

(6) Items are picked for each factor having the highest loadings on the required factor and, if possible, suppressing, (*i.e.*, cancelling) loadings on the others. At this point only those items are carried further which show emphatic consistency in their factor patterns in the two studies. For example, no matter how significant the positive loading on one study may be, the item would be rejected if it has insignificant or negative loading on the other.

(7) To get suitable means, variance and grading on each factor scale, the cuts (alternative response frequencies) must be examined. It is possible to predict both mean and variance of the resultant scale, by certain assumptions, [26] from the cuts on the included items. The choice of items by cuts should accordingly give a mean that is central on the scale range and a maximum scatter (near-even cuts) (to an extent compatible with usefulness for extreme samples) as well as equal means and variances for the equivalent A and B forms.

(8) An even balance of "Yes" and "No" answers must be chosen, from the surviving items, to score *positively* on each factor, in order to abolish position or response set effects.

(9) The item should be symmetrically divided between A and B forms, as to factor loading, mean, variance, yes and no answer, etc., as determined above. (Partly to ensure the kind of equivalence

cited in (7) above.) Then they need to be arranged in that form of cyclical order, avoiding several items in sequence for the same factor, most convenient for the scoring key.

(10) The scales must be standardized with the usual attention to stratified sampling, etc.

Procedures Followed in the Two Factorings and Final Construction

The present revision of the 16 P. F. has in principle followed the above ten canons, but economic compromises with the ideal have had to be made in steps 4 and 6 as will be described. Since at almost every step there is loss from a particular selection process, one must start with a far larger number of items than the 374 which in this case are intended to constitute the final A and B forms of the 16 factor scale. There is no obstacle in starting with quite a large number to be submitted to the verdict of the first four canons, and in fact we began with 1552. But owing to the bottle neck created by the limits of size of factorizable matrices, every stage beyond step 5 tends to suffer more or less grievously from a dearth of items necessary to reach the desired standards. Indeed in past test construction, this has proved a well nigh insuperable obstacle to producing multifactor scales with loadings known and confirmed for every item. Although the obstacle has not been completely overcome here, we feel that the device of "parcelled factor analysis," with the use of extension matrices, described here is perhaps the most important technological contribution of this article—apart from the finished instrument itself.

By this device, and the use of the electronic computer, larger initial matrices have here been factored than any hitherto reported, and the bottle neck partly eliminated. Accordingly, taking steps 1 through 4 as understood in current psychological practice we shall concentrate on the two factor analyses which have succeeded the original factor analysis[4] and which we shall henceforth refer to as the second and third checking analyses. The first of these was done in connection with producing a "Basic English" Form C of the 16 P. F. and has been described elsewhere.[8] On 295 men and women undergraduates, it began with 720 items which were reduced by steps 1 and 2 to a set of 450, which we shall call Extension Questionnaire A and which was reduced to exactly 300 by step 4. At this point a further selection down to 126 was made (a 300 x 300 matrix being still unmanageable factorially) by taking only those items showing significant (P = .01) correlations with factors in the existing 16 P. F. or with each other.

"Parcelled factoring" was now carried out for these 126 survivors and the 374 items of the existing 16 P. F. combined as follows. Each 16 P. F. factor was entered as two variables (the minimum for "marking" and recognizing the resultant factors expected). One variable was the score on the 13 items of the given factor on the A form and the other the 13 on the B form. The 126 *new* items were grouped in "parcels" of three (and sometimes two) of a homogeneity guaranteed by original intercorrelations on a 126 x 126 matrix, and a relative factor purity indicated by correlations with the separate 16 P. F. factors. This gave 75 "parcel" variables (30 from the 15 personality factors of the 16 P. F., and 45 parcels of the new 126 items), a number readily factored. The saving in thus factoring a 75 x 75 matrix, despite the two preliminary special correlation jobs, over the 500 x 500 matrix otherwise necessary, is considerable and has been evaluated elsewhere.[8]

The blindly rotated factors agreed well with the original 16 P. F. factoring[4] as to number and nature, except for some confusion of the factors of neuroticism and anxiety, commonly labelled O and C. In view of these relatively modest loadings on the two less clear factors, every factor was accordingly estimated by the most exact method from Thomson[37] and the correlation of each item in the questionnaire determined with the factors (a 15 x 500 matrix). The results were used both to evaluate the existing 16 P. F. items and to construct the C form. It is the first of these which is relevant to the present study. By eliminating deadwood from the original 16 P. F. it enabled us to start out with clearer, unconfused markers of the 15 factors for cross validation in the third factorization, and to guide the pulling in of new items from the second or B Extension Questionnaire, of 252 items described below, while it also supplied factor loadings for every item so that by the final factoring every loading would have a double check.

In the second experiment, with 408 subjects, (227 Air Force men and 181 undergraduates from four Illinois colleges) the markers for the known 16 P. F. factors were made up, not as previously, by taking *all* the factor items from one form to make one parcel, but by putting together only those 9–11 items for each factor shown by the second factoring above to be most highly loaded. Five "parcels" were made up in this case from the above proven items in the existing 16 P. F. to represent each factor. For the aim in this third factoring was to test the 16 P. F. structure more exactly than in the second factoring and to determine the correlations among simple structure factors with a high degree of exactitude. Also it aimed to get such well saturated factor estimates for each factor that they could be used to determine the loadings of new items, from the second extension questionnaire, with a precision comparable to a direct factoring, to permit replacement of any of the 169 existing items by any discovered in the extension having higher loadings.

The new 75 x 75 matrix was centroid-factored and rotated to simple structure with great care. Every hyperplane is above the .01 level of significance by Bargmann's test.[1] It was gratifying to find that most of the cross loadings among the O and C factor (and to some extent the Q_1, Q_2 and Q_4 factor) parcels encountered in the second factoring disappeared in the better parcels of the third factoring. Fifteen factors were significant and were clearly identifiable by their markers.[2] The C = lambda[1] x lambda matrix, giving cosines among the reference vectors when simple structure was reached, is set out in Table 1. It will be seen that the obliquities are moderate. A second order factoring of these inter-factor correlations is in press.[9]

Extension questionnaire B, of 512 items, was reduced by steps 1 to 4 to 252 items, which were then correlated, on 408 subjects, as above, with each of the 15 factors, estimated from the parcel variables and their loadings, by the method indicated before.

Whenever existing items in the original 16 P. F. correlated, on *both* factorings, .20 or less with the factor they represented, they were cut out as "deadwood" and replaced by items found to be more highly loaded from Extension Questionnaire B. Unfortunately at this point more poor items were found in factors M, C, O and Q_2 than there were items to replace them. So a third Extension Questionnaire, C, was made, beginning with 320 and reducing to 200 items deliberately aimed at these factors. Thus, by direct correlation with the factors, on a sample of 200 men and women undergraduates, sufficient items loaded above 0.2 were found to supplant the unsatisfactory items in factors M, C, O and Q_2.

In the following section the resultant

[2] The unrotated, rotated, and transformation matrices for this analysis are deposited with the American Documentation Institute, Library of Congress.

TABLE 1.   COSINE MATRIX OF CORRELATIONS AMONG REFERENCE VECTORS

16 P. F. Test Factors	A	C	E	F	G	H	I	L	M	N	O	Q_1	Q_2	Q_3	Q_4
A	1.00														
C	.13	1.00													
E	.07	.06	1.00												
F	−.01	.05	.00	1.00											
G	.00	.04	−.02	.05	1.00										
H	−.36	−.12	−.18	−.26	.00	1.00									
I	−.29	−.04	−.06	.01	.00	.14	1.00								
L	−.01	−.01	−.06	−.11	−.04	.26	−.04	1.00							
M	.03	.14	.06	.26	−.04	.05	−.14	−.07	1.00						
N	.08	.01	−.11	−.12	.13	−.05	.26	−.05	−.02	1.00					
O	.02	.19	.00	−.04	.02	.13	−.11	−.08	−.06	.04	1.00				
Q_1	−.15	.05	−.31	−.02	.11	−.09	.02	.01	−.19	.00	.01	1.00			
Q_2	.07	−.01	.18	.22	.02	.03	−.11	−.01	−.11	.03	.08	−.14	1.00		
Q_3	.30	−.19	.12	.22	−.19	−.29	−.02	.11	−.04	−.22	.20	.00	.12	1.00	
Q_4	.04	.09	.02	.05	−.05	.01	.15	−.15	−.01	−.07	−.17	.03	.01	.23	1.00

structure of the 16 P. F. is illustrated by two items from each factor, one from the A form and one from the B form. These are neither the highest loaded items in the factorings nor the highest loaded among those which survived the ensuing selections of steps 5 through 10. They are selected instead to illustrate the degree of constancy of loading of particular items on particular factors on two independent factorizations; the range of mean loadings; and the psychological nature of the items expressing each factor.

Confirmation and Degree of Invariance of the Sixteen Factors

Each item below is set out under the factor as usually symbolized by letter and contingent names. To the right are set out (1) the response—left or right for ([a] or [b] or yes or no)— which scores positively on the factors; (2) the loadings in the two factor studies (second and third); and (3) the frequency of the positive scoring, central and negative scoring responses in 408 subjects.

FACTOR A. CYCLOTHYMIA-VS-SCHIZOTHYMIA

Test Form	Item	Positive Response	Loadings	Response Frequencies		
1. A	If the earnings are the same I would rather be (A) a lawyer (B) a freight air pilot	Lt.	.36 .48	105	20	283
2. B	In a factory I would rather be: (A) in charge of mechanical matters (B) engaged in interviewing and hiring people.	Rt.	.57 .65	240	10	158

FACTOR B. GENERAL INTELLIGENCE

(These items were factored apart from the main study.)

Factor C. Ego Strength

Test Form	Item	Positive Response	Loadings		Response Frequencies		
3. A	I occasionally have realistic dreams that disturb my sleep.	Rt.	.48	.46	356	12	40
4. B	I sometimes feel compelled to count things for no particular purpose.	Rt.	.36	.22	255	16	136

Factor E. Dominance

5. A	I occasionally tell strangers about the things I am interested in and good at, without direct questions from them.	Lt.	.20	.21	22	13	373
6. B	I have on occasion torn down a public notice forbidding me what I felt I had a perfect right to do.	Lt.	.24	.21	64	11	233

Factor F. Surgency-vs-Desurgency

7. A	I like a job that offers change, variety and travel, even if it involves some dangers.	Lt.	.30	.31	327	27	51
8. B	I would prefer the life of: (A) a master printer in a modern plant (B) an advertising man and promoter.	Rt.	.38	.47	294	22	92

Factor G. Super Ego Strength

9. A	I think that good manners and respect for law are more important than excessive freedom.	Lt.	.36	.47	324	23	43
10. B	I admire more a person who: (A) is brilliantly intelligent and creative (B) has a strong sense of duty to the things he believes in.	Rt.	.28	.31	308	19	81

Factor H. Immunity (or Adventurous Cyclothymia)

11. A	I have at least as many friends of the opposite sex as of my own sex.	Lt.	.26	.35	212	23	103
12. B	If people in the street, or standing in a store, watch me I feel slightly embarrassed.	Rt.	.39	.49	345	21	42

Factor I. Sensitivity-vs-Toughness

13. A	I would rather spend a free evening: (A) with a good book (B) working on a project with friends.	Lt.	.32	.28	24	25	359
14. B	In art and music we should: (A) give popular demand what it wants, regardless of quality (B) try to raise standards, by giving experts a chance to control taste.	Rt.	.33	.26	57	23	328

Factor L. Paranoid Trend

15. A	If I am quite sure that a person is unjust or behaving selfishly I show him up, even if it takes some trouble.	Lt.	.37	.34	112	34	262
16. B	I suspect the honesty of people who are more friendly than I would naturally expect them to be.	Lt.	.29	.47	160	31	217

FACTOR O. FREE ANXIETY

Test Form	Item	Positive Response	Loadings		Response Frequencies		
17. A	I feel grouchy and just do not want to see people: (A) occasionally (B) rather often.	Rt.	.14	.32	41	23	344
18. B	I am moved almost to tears by something upsetting: (A) never (B) sometimes.	Rt.	.19	.21	54	15	339

FACTOR Q1. RADICALISM-VS-CONSERVATISM

19. A	It would be better if we had more strict observance of Sunday, as a day to go to church.	Rt.	.32	.55	101	32	275
20. B	In my work more troubles arise from men who:— (A) are constantly changing methods that are already O. K. (B) refuse to employ up-to-date methods.	Rt.	.22	.46	197	68	143

FACTOR Q2. SELF SUFFICIENCY

21. A	I like to take an active part in social affairs, committee work, etc.	Rt.	.23	.43	172	47	189
22. B	I get as many ideas from reading a book myself as from discussing its topics with others.	Lt.		.19	201	16	190

FACTOR Q3. WILL CONTROL

23. A	When talking I like:— (A) to say things just as they occur to me. (B) to wait and say them in the most exact style possible.	Rt.	.17	.24	229	39	137
24. B	However difficult and unpleasant the obstacles I always persevere and stick to my original intentions.	Lt.	.58	.54	324	39	45

FACTOR Q4. TENSION (SOMATIC ANXIETY)

25. A	At times of stress or overwork I suffer from indigestion or constipation:— (A) practically never (B) occasionally.	Rt.	.36	.36	99	28	281
26. B	My nerves are sometimes on edge, so that certain sounds, e.g., a screechy hinge, are unbearable and "give me the shivers."	Lt.	.42	.38	112	13	283

Summary

(1) A multiple factor-scale questionnaire, covering fifteen personality factors and the cognate factor of general intelligence, based on an older factor analysis, has had its factor structure re-examined, the factor loading of every item determined, and items of low validity replaced by new items of improved validity. The process is defined as *validation and intensification*, since the conceptual factor validity of each item is determined, and the factor saturation and independence of the sixteen scales is intensified.

(2) Ten canons for multiple factor scale construction are laid down and

exemplified in operations with the Sixteen P. F. Questionnaire.

(3) The principal innovation is the introduction of "parcelled factor analysis" in which a much larger number of items than could usually be handled is first grouped, by clustering and correlation with existing factors, into a smaller number of homogeneous (but factor impure) "parcels" or short, rough scales. The factor structure is determined on this relatively small matrix (75 x 75 in this example) and the parcels are then "undone" and all constituent items correlated directly with the factors estimated in terms of parcels. An "extension questionnaire" of items hypothesized to be highly correlated with the factors is also correlated item by item with this same factor score, whereby weak items in the original questionnaire are replaced. This device gives the factor loading of every item in the original test and in the extension with every substantial factor, and under comparable conditions, at a small fraction of the prohibitive labor for a matrix of order 1000 x 1000. The item loadings could be, but were not, corrected for attenuation by unreliability of factor estimate, since only *relative* goodness of items need be accurate in this procedure.

(4) Two parcelled factorizations, on 400 and 169 items, were carried out on independent population samples and with independent computing and blind rotation. However the process was iterative in that clearer factor definition was achieved in the second through entering with more factor-pure and homogeneous parcels as a result of the findings of the first. Both yielded, by existing tests of completion of factor extraction, 15 factors (i.e., 16 with intelligence) and, through the marker variables, they were confirmed to be the same factors in all three factorings, i.e., to be the same in both experiments here and the same as named in the original study.

It may be asked how far the inclusion of more items that are good measures of the factors found in the first factorization prejudges the structure of a second factoring. The writer would answer (1) the insertion of items high in one factor does not strengthen pre-existing hyperplanes for the other factors (unless factors are orthogonal and the items are factor-pure as well as highly loaded). (2) An infinity of rotation positions are still possible, so if the same is found again it is proof that the structure is inherent and that new items adhere to it for this reason, since they are not made to adhere for any other reason.[1]

(5) A total of 1552 newly constructed items were brought into three extension questionnaires. Extension A began with 720, reduced to 450 before final correlation on a group of 295 men and women undergraduates. These items were relevant only to the initial factor structuring and were actually used for Form C, whereas extensions B and C were used here for intensifying Forms A and B of the 16 P. F. Extension B began with 512 items, reduced by the first steps to 252 and then correlated on a sample of 408 young men and women, half Air Force, half undergraduates. Extension C began with 320, reduced to 200 before correlation on 200 men and women undergraduates. From the 1552 items, 110 eventually strengthened the original 16 P. F. (replacing the weakest 110 of the 374 items in A and B forms).

(6) Further work on the structure, psychological meaning and prediction value of the factors, in clinical and other work, is in progress. As to the re-standardization of the revised test it may be pointed out that one of the advantages of factor scales is that the clinical and occupational profiles, criterion regressions and specification equations found for standard scores on the older test continue to apply (with some attenuation correction) to the new. The meaning of the present factors in terms of second order factors is being determined

from Table 1.[9] It is also an important aspect of the meaning of factors to determine whether they persist in different cultures and for that reason the present confirmation of constancy within a culture is being extended by a similar comparison of factorizations on British, French, Italian, Indian and Chinese versions of the 16 P. F.[11]

BIBLIOGRAPHY

1. BARGMANN, R. Significanzuntersuchungen der einfachen Struktur in der Faktoren-Analyse. *Mitteil. f. Math. Statist.*, Sonderdruck, Physica-Verlag, Wurzburg, 1954.

2. CATTELL, R. B. *The Description and Measurement of Personality*. New York: World Book Company, 1946.

3. CATTELL, R. B. A Guide to Mental Testing. Inst. Pers. & Abil. Test, 1602 Coronado Drive, Champaign, Illinois, 2nd Edition, 1948.

4. CATTELL, R. B. The main personality factors in questionnaire, self-estimate material. *J. Soc. Psychol.*, 1950, 31, 3–38.

5. CATTELL, R. B. The principal replicated factors discovered in objective personality tests. *J. Abnorm. Soc. Psychol.*, 1955, 3, 291–314.

6. CATTELL, R. B. *et al.* The Objective-Analytic Personality Factor Batteries. Adult and Child Forms. I. P. A. T., 1602 Coronado Drive, Champaign, Ill., 1955.

7. CATTELL, R. B. Occupational profiles on the I. P. A. T. 16 Personality Factor Questionnaire. *Occupat. Psychol.*, Feb., 1956, in press.

8. CATTELL, R. B. A shortened "Basic English" version (Form C) of the 16 P. F. Questionnaire, *J. Soc. Psychol.*, 1956, 30, 1–10.

9. CATTELL, R. B. A determination of the second order personality factors among the 16 P. F. questionnaire primaries. *J. consult. Psychol.*, 1956, in press.

10. CATTELL, R. B. *Personality and Motivation Structure and Measurement*. New York: World Book Co., 1956.

11. CATTELL, R. B. Are personality factors constant across cultures? In press.

12. CATTELL, R. B., BELOFF, J., FLINT, D., and GRUEN, W. The Junior Personality Quiz I. P. A. T., 1602 Coronado Drive, Champaign, Illinois. 1954.

13. CATTELL, R. B., DAY, M., and MEELAND, T. La standardisation du questionnaire de personalite en 16 facteurs de l'I.P.A.T. *Rev. de Psychol. Appliquee*, 1953, 3, 67–83.

14. CATTELL, R. B., and DREVDAHL, J. E. A comparison of the personality profile (16 P. F.) of eminent researchers with that of eminent teachers and administrators, and of the general population. *Brit. J. Psychol.*, 1955, 46, 248–261.

15. CATTELL, R. B., and GRUEN, W. G. Primary personality factors in the questionnaire medium for children eleven to fourteen years old. *Educ. Psychol. Measmt*, 1954, 14, 50–76.

16. CATTELL, R. B., and PETERSON, D. R. Personality factor structure in verbal responses of four year olds. In preparation.

17. CATTELL, R. B., SAUNDERS, D. R., and STICE, G. F. The Sixteen Personality Factor Questionnaire, I.P.A.T., 1602 Coronado Drive, Champaign, Ill., 1949.

18. CATTELL, R. B., and SAUNDERS, D. R. Inter-relation and matching of personality factors from behavior rating, questionnaire, and objective test data. *J. Soc. Psychol.*, 1950, 31, 243–260.

19. CATTELL, R. B., and SAUNDERS, D. R. Beitrage zur Faktoren-Analyse der Personlichkeit Z. f. exper. u. angew. *Psychol.*, 1953, 2, 325–356.

20. CATTELL, R. B., and STICE, G. F. Four formulae for selecting leaders on the basis of personality. *Hum. Relat.*, 1954, 7, 493–507.

21. CATTELL, R. B., and SHOTWELL, A. M. Personality profiles of more successful and less successful psychiatric technicians. *Amer. J. Ment. Def.*, 1954, 8, 496–499.

22. DREVDAHL, J. E. Factors of importance for creativity. *J. clin. Psychol.,* 1956, **12,** 21–26.

23. EYSENCK, H. J. *The Scientific Study of Personality.* London: Routledge, 1952.

24. FERGUSON, L. W., HUMPHREY, L. G., and STRONG, E. K. A factorial analysis of interests and values. *J. Educ. Psychol.,* 1939, **30,** 151–156.

25. FLANAGAN, J. C. *Factor Analysis in the study of Personality.* Stanford Univ., Cal.: Stanford University Press, 1935.

26. GUILFORD, J. P. *Psychometric Methods. 2nd Edit.* New York: McGraw-Hill, 1954.

27. GUILFORD, J. P., & GUILFORD, R. B. Personality factors D, R, T and A, *J. Abnorm. Soc. Psychol.,* 1939, **34,** 21–36.

28. GUILFORD, J. P., and MARTIN, H. G. The Guilford-Martin Questionnaire. Sheridan Supply Co., Beverly Hills, Calif.

29. GUTTMAN, L. The Cornell technique for scale and intensity analysis. *Educ. Psychol. Measmt,* 1947, **7,** 247–279.

30. HADLEY, S. T. A study of the predictive value of several variables for student teaching success as measured by student teaching marks. *Res. for the Teaching Profession.* 1953.

31. LAYMAN, E. M. An item analysis of the adjustment questionnaire. *J. Psychol.,* 1940, **10,** 87–106.

32. McCLELLAND, D. C. *Personality.* New York: Sloane, 1951.

33. MOSIER, C. J. A factor analysis of certain neurotic symptoms. *Psychometrika,* 1937, **2,** 263–286.

34. O'HALLORAN, A. An investigation of Personality Factors associated with Under-achievement in Arithmetic and Reading. M. S. Thesis. Purdue Univ. Library, Lafayette, Ind., 1954.

35. REYBURN, H. A., and TAYLOR, J. G. Some factors of temperament: a re-examination. *Psychometrika,* 1943, **8,** 91–104.

36. SUHR, V. W. The Cattell 16 P. F. as a prognosticator of accident susceptibility. *Proc. Iowa Acad. Sci.,* 1953, **60,** 553–561.

37. THOMSON, G. H. On estimating oblique factors. *Brit. J. Psychol. Stat. Sect.,* 1949, **2,** 1–2.

38. THORNDIKE, E. L. The interests of adults: 2, The interrelations of adult interests. *J. Educ. Psychol.,* 1935, **26,** 497–507.

39. THURSTONE, L. L. *The Thurstone Temperament Schedule.* Chicago: Science Research Associates, 1948.

40. THURSTONE, L. L. A multiple factor study of vocational interests. *Person. J.,* 1931, **10,** 198.

41. VERNON, P. E. The Assessment of Psychological Qualities by Verbal Methods. *Indus. Health Res. Council,* Rept. No. 81, London, H.M.S.O., 1938.

42. WALKER, D. A. Answer-pattern and score-scatter in tests and examinations. *Brit. J. Psychol.,* 1931, **22,** 73–86; 1936, **26,** 301–308; 1940, **30,** 248–260.

43. WHERRY, R. J., and GAYLORD, R. H. Factor pattern of test item and tests as a function of the correlation coefficient: content, difficulty and constant error factors. *Psychometrika,* 1944, **9,** 237–244.

44. WRIGHT, S. Some psychological and physiological correlates of certain academic underachievers. Ph.D. Thesis, University of Chicago Library, 1955.

THE MYERS-BRIGGS TYPE INVENTORY

Some Correlates of a Jungian Personality Inventory

Lawrence J. Stricker and John Ross

While Jung's personality typology (Jung, 1923, 1933, 1953) has been widely influential, its main impact on personality measurement has been to promote an abiding interest in just one facet of the typology—extraversion-introversion. The many scales which have been developed through the years to measure this variable attest to the intensity of this interest.

The measurement of the other variables in Jung's typology, however, has not been entirely neglected. Some time ago, the Gray-Wheelwright Psychological Type Questionnaire (Gray, 1947a, 1948, 1949a; Gray & Wheelwright, 1946) was developed to measure all the variables in Jung's typology—the attitudes (extraversion and introversion) as well as the functions (sensation, intuition, thinking, and feeling). More recently, there has been growing interest in a similar inventory, the Myers-Briggs Type Indicator (Myers, 1962b).

In view of the potential value of these inventories in operationally defining Jung's typology, an assessment of their

The following people graciously furnished the raw data which are the basis of the studies reported in this article: Dr. William C. Craig of Stanford University, Mr. David W. Galloway of Golden Gate College, Dr. C. Hess Haagen of Wesleyan University, Dr. Harold A. Korn of Stanford University, and Mrs. Kathryn Pruden of Long Island University.

Reprinted by permission of the publisher and authors from *Psychological Reports*, 1964, 14, 623–643.

construct validity seems appropriate. Studies concerned with one facet of the Indicator's construct validity—the existence of the underlying typological framework—have already been reported elsewhere (Lord, 1958; Myers, 1962a, 1962b; Stricker & Ross, 1964). The studies in the present article, like some others (Howarth, 1962; Myers, 1962b; Ross, 1961, 1963; Saunders, 1960), primarily bear on another facet of the Indicator's construct validity—the correspondence between the scales and the underlying constructs which are integrated by the typological framework. The series of studies reported in this article were undertaken by the present authors to appraise two related issues: (a) whether the Indicator scales appropriately reflect the distinctions embodied in the typology and explicitly described in the conceptual definition of each of the typological variables; and, alternatively, (b) whether the Indicator scales reflect, to a greater or lesser extent, other variables which are not a part of the typology. These studies investigated (a) the scales' correlations with ability, interest, and personality scales and (b) differences on the scales between the sexes, and between high school students in college preparatory and general-vocational programs.

Myers-Briggs Type Indicator

The Indicator is a self-report inventory which consists of four scales: Extraversion-Introversion (E-I), Sensation-

Intuition (S-N),[1] Thinking-Feeling (T-F), and Judging-Perceiving (J-P).

These scales were expressly developed to classify people into type categories (e.g., classification as an extravert, an introvert, or, in those cases where the two tendencies are equal, "indeterminate") which would have real meaning. The cutting (or "zero") points used in making these classifications were so chosen that those people who are on one side of a scale's cutting point, and, hence, in one type category, are presumed to be qualitatively different from those who are on the other side of it, and hence, in the opposite type category. In addition to these categorical classifications, continuous scores for each scale can be derived by arbitrarily considering one end of the scale high (Stricker & Ross, 1963, p. 287).[2]

In the studies described in this article, results are reported for continuous

[1] Note that the abbreviation of Intuition is N; I is used as the abbreviation of Introversion.

[2] After the studies reported in this article were completed, the Indicator's manual appeared, changing the scoring system so as to eliminate indeterminate type categories. This goal was accomplished by combining a scale's indeterminate type category with one of the two other type categories on that scale. The original continuous scores were also linearly transformed. The use of the new scoring would have no appreciable effect on these studies' type category results, in view of the small number of Ss in the indeterminate type categories, and would not alter the t tests and correlations reported for the continuous scores in these present studies, although it does affect the means and standard deviations. Note that in reporting the results of the present studies as well as discussing previous studies, the scoring convention described in the Indicator's manual (Myers, 1962b) has been followed: the I, N, F, and P ends of the scales are high and the E, S, T, and J ends are low. Hence, high scores on the E-I, S-N, T-F, and J-P scales signify, respectively, tendencies toward introversion, intuition, feeling, and perceiving, and low scores on these scales, signify, respectively, tendencies towards extraversion, sensation, thinking, and judging. In two previous articles by the present authors (Stricker & Ross, 1963, 1964) the opposite scoring convention was followed: the E, S, T, and J ends of the scales were high.

scores, and, in some cases, type categories as well.

The conceptual definitions of the four dimensions that the Indicator's scales are presumed to represent (Myers, 1962b) appear below. These definitions seem to differ somewhat from Jung's (Stricker & Ross, 1962).

Extraversion-Introversion

This attitude is defined in the following way.

The introvert's main interests are in the inner world of concepts and ideas, while the extravert's main interests are in the outer world of people and things Therefore, when circumstances permit, the introvert directs both perception and judgment upon ideas, while the extravert likes to direct both upon his outside environment. . . . (Myers, 1962b, p. 57).

Judging-Perceiving

It is argued (a) that a great part of *overt* cognitive activity can be regarded as either judging (coming to a conclusion about something) or perceiving (becoming aware of something),[3] and (b) that there are two ways of judging —thinking and feeling—and two ways of perceiving—sensation and intuition.

There is a fundamental difference between the two attitudes. In the judging attitude, in order to come to a conclusion, perception must be shut off for the time being. The evidence is all in. Anything more is incompetent, irrelevant and immaterial. One now arrives at a verdict and gets things settled. Conversely, in the perceptive attitude one shuts off judgment for the time being. The evidence is not all in. There is much more to it than this. New developments will occur. It is much too soon to do anything irrevocable (Myers, 1962b, p. 58).

[3] No separate and explicit variable reflecting individual differences of this kind is found in Jung's typology, but Jung does classify each of the four functions as either rational and judging or irrational and perceiving.

Thinking-Feeling

The two modes of judgment—thinking and feeling—are described in the following way.

. . . *thinking* . . . is a logical process, aimed at an impersonal finding . . . *feeling* . . . is a process of appreciation . . . bestowing on things a personal, subjective value.

. . . If, when one judges these ideas, he concentrates on whether or not they are true, that is thinking-judgment. If one is conscious first of like or dislike, of whether these concepts are sympathetic or antagonistic to other ideas he prizes, that is feeling-judgment (Myers, 1962b, p. 52).

Sensation-Intuition

The two modes of perception—sensation and intuition—are described in the following way.

There is not only the familiar process of *sensing*, by which we become aware of things directly through our five senses. There is also the process of *intuition*, which is indirect perception by way of the unconscious, accompanied by ideas or associations which the unconscious tacks on to the perceptions coming from outside. These unconscious contributions range from the merest masculine "hunch" or "woman's intuition" to the crowning examples of creative art or scientific discovery.

. . . When people prefer sensing, they find too much of interest in the actuality around them to spend much energy listening for ideas out of nowhere. When people prefer intuition, they are too much interested in all the possibilities that occur to them to give a whole lot of notice to the actualities (Myers, 1962b, pp. 51–52).

Study I. Correlations with Scholastic Aptitude Test, Concept Mastery Test, Ship Destination Test, Survey of Study Habits and Attitudes, and Minnesota Multiphasic Personality Inventory

Method

A large battery of tests, including the Concept Mastery Test (Terman, 1956),

the Ship Destination Test (Christensen & Guilford, 1956), the Survey of Study Habits and Attitudes (SSHA) (Brown & Holtzman, 1956), and the Minnesota Multiphasic Personality Inventory (MMPI) (Hathaway & McKinley, 1951), was administered to an entering freshman class of 254 male students at Wesleyan University. The Scholastic Aptitude Test's (College Entrance Examination Board, 1962; Dyer & King, 1955) verbal (SAT-V) and mathematical (SAT-M) subtest scores were also obtained from school records. The MMPI was scored for the standard clinical and validity scales and three response style scales: Edwards' (1957b) Social Desirability (SD) scale, a balanced SD scale designed to reduce content and acquiescence effects (Stricker, 1963), and an acquiescence scale based on the same items as the balanced SD scale. The results were analyzed for the 225 students for whom complete data were available.

Results

The product-moment correlations between the Indicator's continuous scores and the other scales appear in Table 1.

The E-I and S-N scales had a similar pattern of significant $(p < .01)$ correlations with three ability tests: SAT-V, SAT-M, and the Concept Mastery Test. The E-I scale's correlations ranged from .20 to .29, and the S-N scale's correlation's ranged from .22 to .34. However, neither of these Indicator scales correlated significantly $(p > .05)$ with a fourth ability test, the Ship Destination Test, and none of the other Indicator scales correlated significantly $(p > .05)$ with any of the ability tests.

The T-F and J-P scales correlated significantly $(p < .01)$ with the SSHA $(r = -.20$ for the T-F scale and $r = -.31$ for the J-P scale).

The Indicator had generally low but significant $(p < .05)$ correlations with the MMPI clinical scales (corrected for

TABLE 1. CORRELATIONS BETWEEN INDICATOR AND SCHOLASTIC APTITUDE TEST, CONCEPT MASTERY TEST, SHIP DESTINATION TEST, SURVEY OF STUDY HABITS AND ATTITUDES, AND MINNESOTA MULTIPHASIC PERSONALITY INVENTORY FOR MALE FRESHMEN AT WESLEYAN UNIVERSITY ($N = 225$)

Scale	Indicator Scale			
	E-I	S-N	T-F	J-P
SAT-V	.27**	.34**	−.10	.08
SAT-M	.20**	.22**	−.15*	−.03
Concept Mastery Test	.29**	.28**	−.09	−.04
Ship Destination Test	−.04	−.01	−.04	−.06
Survey of Study Habits and Attitudes	−.07	.12	−.20**	−.31**
MMPI				
?	−.04	.11	.08	−.03
L	−.12	.06	−.17*	−.11
F	.22**	−.05	−.03	.24**
K	−.23**	.06	−.13*	−.18**
Hs	.10	−.05	−.01	.03
D	.39**	−.06	.05	.10
Hy	−.05	.05	.01	.06
Pd	−.08	.11	.12	.23**
Mf	.22**	.33**	.22**	.17*
Pa	.12	.04	.12	.03
Pt	.30**	−.07	.19**	.13*
Sc	.23**	.03	.07	.17*
Ma	−.29**	.09	−.06	.16*
Si	.63**	−.06	.02	.10
Edwards' SD	−.38**	.08	−.19**	−.19**
Balanced SD	−.28**	.03	−.11	−.19**
Balanced Acquiescence	−.19**	.06	.06	.06

* $p = .05$.
** $p = .01$.

K where appropriate). One important exception was the E-I scale's correlation of .63 with an extraversion-introversion scale—Si. The E-I scale also correlated with a neurotic scale—D ($r = .39$), three of the four psychotic scales—Pt ($r = .30$), Ma ($r = −.29$), and Sc ($r = .23$), and a masculinity-femininity scale—Mf ($r = .22$). The S-N scale's only significant correlation was one of .33 with a masculinity-femininity scale —Mf. The T-F scale had two significant correlations—one of .22 with a masculinity-femininity scale—Mf, and the other of .19 with a psychotic scale —Pt. The J-P scale's highest correlation was one of .23 with a psychopathic deviate scale—Pd.

There were also some low but significant ($p < .05$) correlations with the MMPI validity scales. The highest were the E-I scale's correlations of −.23 with

K and .22 with F, and the J-P scale's correlations of .24 with F and −.18 with K.

There were also some significant ($p < .01$) correlations with the MMPI response style scales. The E-I scale correlated −.38 with the Edwards SD scale, −.28 with the balanced SD scale, and −.19 with the acquiescence scale. The T-F scale correlated −.19 with the Edwards SD scale, and the J-P scale correlated −.19 with each of the SD scales.

Study II. Correlations with Gray-Wheelwright Psychological Type Questionnaire

Method

The Indicator and the 14th edition of the Gray-Wheelwright Psychological

Type Questionnaire[4] were administered in counterbalanced order to the 51 students in two undergraduate classes at Golden Gate College. The results for the 47 men were analyzed. They were about evenly distributed between day and evening sessions, and their age range was 19 to 55.

Results

As Table 2 indicates, all the product-moment correlations between the continuous scores for the corresponding scales on the two inventories were significant ($p < .01$). The E-I scales correlated .79, the S-N scales correlated .58, and the T-F scales correlated .60. In addition, the Indicator T-F scale correlated $-.37$ ($p < .01$) with the Gray-Wheelwright E-I scale, and the Indicator J-P scale correlated .41 ($p < .01$) with the Gray-Wheelwright S-N scale and .33 ($p < .05$) with the Gray-Wheelwright T-F scale.

Study III.   Correlations with California Psychological Inventory and Strong Vocational Interest Blank

Method

A battery of tests, including the Indicator, the California Psychological In-

[4] A copy of this version of the inventory may be obtained by writing to Dr. Joseph B. Wheelwright, 2206 Steiner Street, San Francisco, California. Gray and Wheelwright report continuous scores based on the percentage of extravert responses to answered E-I items, the percentage of intuitive responses to answered S-N items, and the percentage of feeling responses to answered T-F items (Gray, 1947b, 1949b; Gray, Personal communication, August 14, 1961; Gray & Wheelwright, 1944). In the present study, so as to be consistent with the direction of the scoring used with the continuous Indicator scores, continuous scores for the Gray-Wheelwright inventory were based on the percentage of introvert responses, the percentage of intuitive responses, and the percentage of feeling responses.

TABLE 2.   CORRELATIONS BETWEEN INDICATOR AND GRAY-WHEELWRIGHT PSYCHOLOGICAL TYPE QUESTIONNAIRE FOR MALE STUDENTS AT GOLDEN GATE COLLEGE ($N = 47$)

Gray-Wheelwright Scale	Indicator Scale			
	E-I	S-N	T-F	J-P
E-I	.79**	.00	$-.37$**	$-.16$
S-N	$-.24$	.58**	.15	.41**
T-F	$-.20$	.17	.60**	.33*

* $p = .05$.
** $p = .01$.

ventory (CPI) (Gough, 1957), and the Strong Vocational Interest Blank (SVIB) (Strong, 1959), was administered to an entering male freshman class at Stanford University, which totaled 889 students. Scores were available for both the Indicator and the CPI for 713 students, and both the Indicator and the SVIB for 727 students.[5]

Results

The product-moment correlations between the Indicator's continuous scores and the CPI scales appear in Table 3. Many significant ($p < .05$) correlations were obtained.

The E-I scale's highest correlations, all of which were negative, were with ascendance and self-assurance scales—*Sy* ($r = -.67$), *Do* ($r = -.53$), *Sa* ($r = -.53$), and *Sp* ($r = -.47$). It had somewhat lower negative correlations with a social status scale—*Cs* ($r = -.35$), two achievement and intellectual potential scales—*Ie* ($r = -.21$) and *Ac* ($r = -.16$), and two of the three response bias scales—*Wb* ($r = -.23$) and *Gi* ($r = -.16$). The S-N scale's highest correlations, all of which were positive, were with a social status scale—*Cs*

[5] In computing the correlations with the SVIB scales, the SVIB standard scores were grouped into 10 intervals, which were derived from the intervals on which the SVIB letter ratings are based.

TABLE 3.   CORRELATIONS BETWEEN INDICATOR AND CALIFORNIA PSYCHOLOGICAL
INVENTORY FOR MALE FRESHMEN AT STANFORD UNIVERSITY $(N = 713)$

CPI Scale	Indicator Scale			
	E-I	S-N	T-F	J-P
Do	−.53**	.07	.00	−.06
Cs	−.35**	.29**	.02	.03
Sy	−.67**	.05	.06	−.01
Sp	−.47**	.15**	.00	.22**
Sa	−.53**	.08*	.04	.09*
Wb	−.23**	.02	−.06	−.17**
Re	−.06	.03	−.01	−.30**
So	−.03	−.12**	−.03	−.32**
Sc	.09*	−.10**	−.06	−.34**
To	−.16**	.16**	.03	−.08*
Gi	−.16**	.02	−.01	−.27**
Cm	−.06	−.17**	−.02	−.24**
Ac	−.16**	−.01	−.05	−.37**
Ai	.10**	.27**	.06	.00
Ie	−.21**	.24**	−.06	−.03
Py	.01	.25**	−.07	.02
Fx	.04	.29**	.09*	.45**
Fe	.13**	−.05	.17**	−.19**

* $p = .05$.
** $p = .01$.

$(r = .29)$, a flexibility scale—Fx $(r = .29)$, two achievement and intellectual potential scales—Ai $(r = .27)$ and Ie $(r = .24)$, and a "psychological mindedness" scale—Py $(r=.25)$. The T-F scale's highest correlation was one of .17 with a masculinity-femininity scale —Fe. The J-P scale's highest positive correlations were with a flexibility scale —Fx $(r = .45)$, and a social presence scale—Sp $(r=.22)$. Its highest negative correlations were with an achievement potential scale—Ac $(r = -.37)$, and maturity, socialization, and responsibility scales— Sc $(r = -.34)$, So $(r = -.32)$, and Re $(r = -.30)$. It also correlated negatively with the three response bias scales—Gi $(r = -.27)$, Cm $(r = -.24)$, and Wb $(r = -.17)$.

The product-moment correlations between the Indicator's continuous scores and the SVIB scales appear in Table 4.

There were many significant $(p < .05)$ correlations with the SVIB occupational scales. The E-I scale's highest positive correlations were with the professional (Group I) and technical-scientific (Group

II) scales; its highest negative correlations were with the social service (Group V) and business contact (Group IX) scales. The S-N scale's highest positive correlations were with the professional (Group I), technical-scientific (Group II), social service (Group V), and verbal (Group X) scales; its highest negative correlations were with the business detail (Group VIII) and business contact (Group IX) scales. The T-F scale's highest positive correlations were with the social service (Group V) scales; it had significant but not appreciable negative correlations with several groups of scales. The J-P scale's highest positive correlations were with the verbal (Group X) scales; its highest negative correlations were with the business detail (Group VIII) scales.

There were some scattered significant $(p < .05)$ but moderate correlations with the non-occupational scales. The E-I and J-P scales were negatively correlated with the Interest Maturity scale $(r = -.20$ for the former, and $r = -.09$ for the latter), and the S-N and T-F

TABLE 4. CORRELATIONS BETWEEN INDICATOR AND STRONG VOCATIONAL
INTEREST BLANK FOR MALE FRESHMEN AT STANFORD UNIVERSITY ($N = 727$)

SVIB Scale	Indicator Scale			
	E-I	S-N	T-F	J-P
Group I				
Artist	.26°°	.37°°	.03	.20°°
Psychologist	.10°°	.55°°	.06	.15°°
Architect	.29°°	.39°°	−.01	.13°°
Physician	.14°°	.44°°	.07	.13°°
Osteopath	−.01	.22°°	.13°°	.08°
Dentist	.24°°	.19°°	−.00	.01
Veterinarian	−.08°	−.18°°	.07	−.01
Group II				
Mathematician	.37°°	.25°°	−.12°°	.00
Physicist	.35°°	.25°°	−.09°	.01
Engineer	.24°°	.12°°	−.18°°	−.05
Chemist	.31°°	.28°°	−.09°	−.01
Group III				
Production Manager	−.11°°	−.15°°	−.20°°	−.14°°
Group IV				
Farmer	.17°°	−.15°°	−.02	.02
Aviator	.06	.04	−.06	.11°°
Carpenter	.11°°	−.10°°	−.04	−.08°
Printer	.17°°	.12°°	.04	.03
Math. Phys. Sci. Teacher	.04	.10°°	.03	−.07
Ind. Arts Teacher	.03	−.03	−.02	−.06
Voc. Agricul. Teacher	−.10°°	−.15°°	.09°	−.02
Policeman	−.17°°	−.13°°	.05	−.07
Forest Service Man	−.05	−.02	.02	.02
Group V				
Y.M.C.A. Phys. Director	−.35°°	.12°°	.20°°	.01
Personnel Director	−.31°°	.14°°	.07	.01
Public Administrator	−.28°°	.21°°	.07	.01
Y.M.C.A. Secretary	−.32°°	.09°	.19°°	−.02
Soc. Sci. H. S. Teacher	−.24°°	.03	.17°°	−.02
City School Sup't.	−.26°°	.19°°	.18°°	−.03
Social Worker	−.25°°	.29°°	.18°°	.07
Minister	−.17°°	.31°°	.21°°	.04
Group VI				
Musician (Performer)	.05	.37°°	.16°°	.17°°
Group VII				
C.P.A.	.03	.05	−.13°°	−.06
Group VIII				
Senior C.P.A.	−.04	−.06	−.10°	−.09°
Accountant	−.04	−.29°°	−.15°°	−.24°°
Office Man	−.13°°	−.30°°	.02	−.18°°
Purchasing Agent	−.11°°	−.49°°	−.22°°	−.22°°
Banker	−.09°	−.51°°	−.09°	−.23°°
Mortician	−.33°°	−.37°°	.09°	−.10°°
Pharmacist	−.17°°	−.18°°	−.01	−.09°
Group IX				
Sales Manager	−.37°°	−.22°°	−.04	−.03
Real Estate Salesman	−.26°°	−.22°°	.02	.08°
Life Insurance Salesman	−.35°°	−.13°°	.14°°	.02

TABLE 4. (*Continued*)

SVIB Scale	Indicator Scale			
	E-I	S-N	T-F	J-P
Group X				
Advertising Man	−.10**	.25**	.11**	.19**
Lawyer	−.03	.15**	.06	.12**
Author-Journalist	.14**	.29**	.05	.19**
Group XI				
President Mfg. Concern	−.06	−.16**	−.17**	−.09*
Interest Maturity	−.20**	.06	.03	−.09*
Occupational Level	.01	.06	−.06	−.04
Masculinity-Femininity	.05	−.17**	−.22**	−.03

* $p = .05$.
** $p = .01$.

scales were negatively correlated with the Masculinity-Femininity scale ($r = −.17$ for the former and $r = −.22$ for the latter). None of the Indicator scales were significantly ($p > .05$) correlated with the Occupational Level scale.

Study IV. Differences Between Sexes and Between High School Programs

Method

The Indicator was administered to (a) the 12th grade classes of eight Massachusetts high schools, consisting of 397 male and 614 female students; and (b) an entering freshman class at Long Island University (LIU), consisting of 300 male and 184 female students. All but a few of the high school students were classifiable, on the basis of the program that they reported on their Indicator answer sheets, into those in the college preparatory program and those in the general-vocational program.

Differences between the sexes and between high school programs were assessed by χ^2 tests of differences in the distributions of Indicator type categories and t tests of mean scores on Indicator scales.

Results

The distributions of type categories appear in Table 5, and the means and standard deviations of the continuous

scores appear in Table 6. The χ^2 tests appear in Table 7 and the t tests in Table 8.

There were significant ($p < .05$) differences between the boys and girls within (a) the college preparatory high school group; (b) the general-vocational high school group; and (c) the LIU class. (a) Within the college preparatory group, a greater proportion of girls than boys were classified as sensing and feeling. These findings are supported by the mean differences of the S-N and T-F scales. (b) Within the general-vocational group, a greater proportion of girls than boys were classified as judging. This finding is supported by the mean difference on the J-P scale. The mean difference on the T-F scale indicated that the girls also tended to more feeling. (c) Among the LIU students, a greater proportion of girls than boys were classified as sensing and feeling. These findings are supported by the mean differences on the S-N and T-F scales. The mean differences on the E-I and J-P scales indicated that the girls also tended to be more extraverted and judging.

There also were significant ($p < .05$) differences between students in the college preparatory and general-vocational high school programs. (a) Among the boys, a greater proportion of those in the college preparatory program than

TABLE 5. PERCENTAGE OF Ss IN EACH TYPE CATEGORY

Group	N	E	X	I	S	X	N	T	X	F	J	X	P
High School Students													
Male Coll. Prep.	146	64.4	6.2	29.5	54.8	3.4	41.8	56.2	.7	43.2	55.5	2.1	42.5
Male Gen'l-Vocat.	230	58.3	1.7	40.0	85.2	4.8	10.0	43.5	4.3	52.2	52.6	1.7	45.7
Female Coll. Prep.	148	67.6	2.7	29.7	68.9	2.7	28.4	31.1	2.0	66.9	49.3	2.7	48.0
Female Gen'l-Vocat.	433	61.0	3.5	35.6	87.3	1.8	10.9	37.6	2.3	60.0	62.1	3.0	34.9
LIU Students													
Male	300	68.0	2.7	29.3	64.3	1.7	34.0	58.0	3.7	38.3	60.7	.7	38.7
Female	184	73.4	1.6	25.0	66.8	5.4	27.7	32.1	2.2	65.8	69.0	.5	30.4

TABLE 6. MEANS AND STANDARD DEVIATIONS OF INDICATOR SCORES

Group	E-I		S-N		T-F		J-P	
	M	SD	M	SD	M	SD	M	SD
High School Students								
Male Coll. Prep.	5.25(E)	11.46	2.04(S)	12.54	1.34(T)	9.24	1.20(J)	12.82
Male Gen'l-Vocat.	2.46(E)	11.77	11.13(S)	9.28	1.12(F)	8.17	1.15(J)	12.05
Female Coll. Prep.	5.20(E)	12.82	4.92(S)	10.95	4.16(F)	9.88	1.64(J)	13.84
Female Gen'l-Vocat.	3.69(E)	12.51	12.02(S)	9.36	3.00(F)	9.65	4.28(J)	12.37
LIU Students								
Male	4.88(E)	11.15	3.80(S)	11.25	2.40(T)	9.84	3.40(J)	14.26
Female	7.10(E)	11.32	6.27(S)	12.17	4.77(F)	9.76	7.15(J)	12.53

Note.—The number of Ss in each group is reported in Table 5.

TABLE 7. χ^2 TESTS OF DIFFERENCES IN TYPE CATEGORIES FOR HIGH SCHOOL AND LIU STUDENT GROUPS

	Difference Between Sexes			Difference Between HS Programs	
Scale	College Prep. Program	Gen'l-Vocat. Program	LIU	Males	Females
E-I	2.11	2.54	1.78	8.38*	2.06
S-N	6.26*	4.69	6.76*	52.02**	27.01**
T-F	19.11**	4.98	34.35**	8.56*	2.20
J-P	1.15	7.77*	3.45	.39	8.06*

Note.—Each χ^2 is based on 2 df.
* $p = .05$.   ** $p = .01$.

TABLE 8. t TESTS OF DIFFERENCES IN MEAN INDICATOR SCORES FOR HIGH SCHOOL AND LIU STUDENT GROUPS

	Difference Between Sexes			Difference Between HS Programs	
Scale	College Prep. Program	Gen'l-Vocat. Program	LIU	Males	Females
E-I	.04	1.24	2.11*	2.26*	1.25
S-N	2.10*	1.16	2.27*	7.55†**	7.06†**
T-F	4.93**	2.64†**	2.58**	2.72**	1.25
J-P	.28	3.13**	3.03†**	.04	2.18*

* $p = .05$.   ** $p = .01$.
† t test based on separate rather than pooled variances because variances were significantly ($p < .05$) different.

those in the other program were classified as extraverts, intuitive, and thinking. These findings are supported by the mean differences on the E-I, S-N, and T-F scales. (b) Among the girls, a greater proportion of those in the college preparatory program than those in the other program were classified as intuitive and perceptive. These findings are supported by the mean differences on the S-N and J-P scales.

Discussion

Extraversion-Introversion Scale

The E-I scale is intended to measure a dimension that is conceptually defined as an interest in things and people versus concepts and ideas. Its items, which resemble those on many extraversion-introversion scales, however, seem to describe interest and facility in social relations, frequently involving talkativeness.[6] An interpretation of this scale's meaning on the basis of this item content may be contrasted with the scale's conceptual definition. The emphasis on social relations found in such an item-content interpretation may be a surface reflection of the underlying interest in things and people that the conceptual definition associates with extraversion, but it seems unrelated to the interest in

[6] This interpretation of the item content of the E-I scale, as well as the item-content interpretations for the other scales, is based on an inspection of the items on each of the scales, as they appear on the standard scoring keys, and the results of unpublished item analyses by the present authors. Reproduction of any of the Indicator items in this article is precluded by the refusal of the Indicator's authors, who hold its copyright, to grant such permission.

concepts and ideas that the conceptual definition ascribes to introversion.

The E-I scale's high correlations in the present studies with the extraversion-introversion scales on the Gray-Wheelwright Psychological Type Questionnaire and the MMPI as well as its previously reported high correlation with the Maudsley Personality Inventory (Eysenck, 1959), MPI Extraversion scale (Howarth, 1962) and its loading on a factor identified as extraversion-introversion (Ross, 1963) make it appear that this scale is, to a large extent, measuring extraversion-introversion as it is commonly defined. None of these relationships necessarily imply, however, that the scale is measuring this variable precisely as it is described by the conceptual definition.

The scale's conceptual definition and the item-content interpretation are both consistent with the scale's positive correlations with the SVIB technical-scientific scales, which involve an interest in concepts and ideas, and a dislike of social relations, and its negative correlations with scales which reflect and the SVIB social service and business contact scales, which involve both an interest in things and people and an interest in social relations. These negative correlations with scales which reflect both an interest in things and people as well as an interest in social relations are consistent with the E-I scale's previously reported positive correlation with a rating of Solitary (Myers, 1962b; Ross, 1961), and its negative correlation with the Personality Research Inventory (PRI) Gregariousness scale (Myers, 1962b).

The conceptual definition, but not the item-content interpretation, seems consistent with the scale's positive correlations with three of the four ability tests, which should, at least, reflect a facility with concepts and ideas, if not an interest in them. In previous studies, the E-I scale was also consistently and positively correlated with ability tests (Myers, 1962b), but it did not load a factor identified as general ability (Ross, 1963).

The conceptual definition, however, is not consistent with the scale's negative correlation with two other scales—the CPI *Ac* and *Ie* scales—which should also reflect either an interest in or a facility with concepts and ideas. Moreover, in previous studies, the scale was not significantly correlated with measures that are similar to these two CPI scales—the PRI Liking to Think scale (Myers, 1962b) and ratings of Poor at Analyzing, and Good Grasp of Abstract and Fundamental (Myers, 1962b; Ross, 1961).

The item-content interpretation is more directly supported than the conceptual definition by the finding that the E-I scale was negatively correlated with the CPI *Do* and *Sp* scales, both of which involve a facility in social relations, but not necessarily an interest in things and people. These results are consistent with the scale's previously reported correlations with other measures which should also involve a facility in social relations but not necessarily an interest in people—a positive correlation with a rating of Not a Potential Leader (Myers, 1962b; Ross, 1961), and negative correlations with the PRI Talkativeness and Social Know-How scales (Myers, 1962b). However, the last correlation, though significant, was slight.

Most of the other relevant findings, however, seem inconsistent with the scale's conceptual definition, but neither confirm nor refute the item-content interpretation. One such finding involves the correlations with five SVIB skilled trades scales—Aviator, Farmer, Carpenter, Printer, and Forest Service Man. All these scales primarily reflect an interest in things, though not an interest in people. Hence, on the basis of the conceptual definition, the E-I scale should be expected to correlate negatively with them. In fact, four of its five correlations with these scales were positive, three of them significantly so.

A second inconsistent finding is that the boys in the college preparatory program (the program that should most reflect an interest in concepts and ideas) tended to be more extraverted than those in the general-vocational program. The meaning of this finding may be limited, however, because no corresponding differences were obtained for the girls.

The additional possibility that the scale may also be measuring adjustment is suggested by its positive correlations with several MMPI scales—D, Pt, and Sc. This finding may be limited, however, since the E-I scale correlated negatively with the CPI Sa scale, and was not consistently correlated with other relevant MPI scales. Still, this scale was consistently correlated with measures of adjustment in previous studies. It correlated positively with the MPI Neuroticism scale (Howarth, 1962), the PRI Free-Floating Anxiety scale (Myers, 1962b), and such ratings as Needs Psychologist's Attention and Low Stamina (Ross, 1961), and it correlated negatively with such ratings as Carefree (Myers, 1962b; Ross, 1961).

This scale's consistent but typically moderate correlations with the CPI response bias scales and the MMPI validity and SD scales also suggest that this scale may be somewhat susceptible to test-taking distortion.

Sensation-Intuition Scale

The S-N scale's items seem to describe an interest in tangible, realistic things versus an interest in abstract ideas. Interest in tangible, realistic things seems congruent with the conceptual definition of sensation, which stresses the focus of sensation on actualities. Interest in abstract ideas, however, seems to be, at best, only one facet of intuition. The latter is described in the conceptual definition as sensory perception modified and combined with unconscious components, and, in effect, characterized by an interest in "possibilities."

Some of the scale's items seem to resemble those on the Thinking Extraversion scale of the Minnesota T-S-E Inventory (Evans & McConnell, 1957) and the Q_1 scale of the 16 P. F. Test (Cattell, Saunders, & Stice, 1957).

Both the conceptual definition and the item-content interpretation are supported by the scale's positive correlations with the SVIB verbal scales, which presumably reflect either intuition or an interest in abstract ideas, and its negative correlations with the SVIB business detail and business contact scales, all of which involve a focus on tangible things or actualities. In addition, a previous study (Myers, 1962b) found that the scale correlated positively with two other scales which also reflect intuition or an interest in abstract ideas—the PRI Tolerance of Complexity and Artistic vs. Practical scales—but did not correlate significantly with the PRI Spiritual vs. Material scale.

Two previous findings, involving measures concerned with the focus on possibilities inherent in the notion of intuition, are relevant to the conceptual definition, but not the item-content interpretation. The conceptual definition is supported by the scale's positive correlation with a rating of Shows Originality (Myers, 1962b; Ross, 1961), but it is not supported by the scale's nonsignificant correlation with the scores on the PRI Foresight scale (see, e.g., Myers, 1962b).

The item-content interpretation is also supported by several findings which are consistent with it but are not easily explained in terms of the conceptual definition. These findings involve relationships with variables that cannot be readily characterized as reflecting either sensation or intuition, but seem to reflect either an interest in abstract thinking (i.e., the positive correlations with the SVIB professional and technical-scientific scales), or at least, a facility with it (i.e., the positive correlations with most of the ability scales, the CPI Ie scale, and the SVIB social service scales, and the finding that the high school students of each sex in the college preparatory program tended to be more intuitive than those in the general-vocational program). These findings are consistent with previous ones. The scale's positive correlations with measures that reflect an interest in abstract thinking are paralleled by its positive correlation with the PRI Liking to Think scale (Myers, 1962b) and its positive loading on an intellectuality factor (Ross, 1963); the scale's positive correlations with ability measures are paralleled by its positive correlations with a number of ability tests (Myers, 1962b) and its positive loading on an ability factor (Ross, 1963).

Some findings are inconsistent with both the conceptual definition and the item-content interpretation. One such finding is that the S-N scale only had significant negative correlations with three of the six SVIB skilled trades scales—Farmer, Aviator, Carpenter, Printer, Policeman, and Forest Service Man—which should primarily involve an interest in either actualities or tangible things.

Other findings are simply inexplicable in terms of either the scale's conceptual definition or the item-content interpretation. One such finding is that girls tended to be more sensing than boys. Paradoxically, this finding, which is inconsistent with the popular notion that intuition is typically a female trait, is not supported by the S-N scale's correlations with the MMPI and SVIB masculinity-femininity scales. Both of these correlations indicate that femininity is associated with intuition rather than sensation. In previous studies (Myers, 1962b), a sex difference was not apparent on the S-N scale in a junior high school sample, but this scale did correlate with the PRI masculinity-femininity scale in the same direction as the masculinity-femininity scales in the present studies.

A second set of inexplicable findings include the scale's positive correlations with the CPI *Cs*, *Ai*, and *Fx* scales. This pattern, when considered with the S-N scale's previously reported negative correlations with the PRI Gregariousness scale (Myers, 1962b) and such ratings as Willing to Take Direction and Cooperative (Myers, 1962b; Ross, 1961), suggests, in part, independence or nonconformity.

Thinking-Feeling Scale

The content of the T-F scale seems to describe a rational versus a sentimental approach to life. A rational approach to life may correspond to thinking, which is described by the conceptual definition as a "logical process" that relies on objective criteria (e.g., true or false) in evaluating phenomena. A sentimental approach to life, however, seems quite unlike feeling, which is conceptually defined as a relatively personal process that uses subjective criteria (e.g., like or dislike) in evaluating phenomena.

Very few of the variables investigated in the present studies or previous ones are relevant to an assessment of either the conceptual definition or the item-content interpretation. It may be partly as a consequence that the results for this variable are not at all clear-cut.

Slight support for both the conceptual definition and the item-content interpretation comes from the finding that the high school boys in the college preparatory program tended to be more thinking than those in the general-vocational program. No corresponding differences, however, were found for the girls.

Neither the conceptual definition nor the item-content interpretation is particularly supported by the scale's scattered and quite moderate negative correlations with the SVIB technical-scientific and business detail scales, which should reflect either thinking or a rational approach. Previous findings involving other measures which should also reflect either thinking or a rational approach offer even less support. The T-F scale had only a slight, though significant, negative correlation with the PRI Liking to Think scale (Myers, 1962b); it did not correlate significantly with a rating of Poor at Analyzing (Myers, 1962b; Ross, 1961); and it did not load an intellectuality factor (Ross, 1963).

The item-content interpretation is supported by (a) the scale's positive correlations with the SVIB social service scales, which should reflect a sentimental approach; and (b) the finding that, in general, the boys in each of the three student groups tended to be more thinking than the girls, which is paralleled by the T-F scale's correlations with MMPI, CPI, and SVIB masculinity-femininity scales. These two findings agree with previously reported results (Myers, 1962b). The T-F scale's positive correlations with measures which reflect sentimentality are consistent with its positive correlation with the PRI Spiritual vs. Material scale, but inconsistent with the T-F scale's nonsignificant correlations with the PRI Altruism and Social Conscience scales. The sex differences on the T-F scale and the scale's correlations with masculinity-femininity scales are consistent with the observed tendency for the boys in a junior high school sample to be more thinking than the girls and the scale's correlation with the PRI masculinity-femininity scale.

Several correlations are inexplicable in terms of the conceptual definition and the item-content interpretation, including the scale's negative correlation with the SSHA. This finding resembles the T-F scale's previously reported negative correlation with the PRI Attitude to Work scale (Myers, 1962b). Other previous findings which are inexplicable include the Indicator scale's positive correlations with the PRI Free-Floating Anxiety scale (Myers, 1962b) and the MPI Neuroticism scale (Howarth, 1962).

Judging-Perceiving Scale

Although judging-perceiving is defined as reaching a conclusion about something versus becoming aware of it, the items on this scale seem to describe planned and organized versus spontaneous activity, time-binding, or even compulsivity. These items appear to be very similar to those on the Orderliness scale of the Edwards Personal Preference Schedule (Edwards, 1957a).

The scale's conceptual definition and the item-content interpretation are both consistent with the scale's positive correlations with the CPI Fx scale, which should reflect either an openness to the environment or a tendency toward spontaneity, and its negative correlations with the SVIB business detail scales, which should reflect either a tendency to reach conclusions or engage in planned and organized activity, etc. These findings, however, are not entirely supported by other studies. The J-P scale's correlation with the CPI Fx scale is supported by the previously reported positive correlation between the Indicator scale and the PRI Tolerance of Complexity scale (Myers, 1962b), but it receives almost no support from the modest, though significant, positive correlation of the Indicator scale with the PRI Artistic vs. Practical scale (Myers, 1962b). The Indicator scale's correlations with the business detail scales are lent little support by its previously reported slight and not always significant positive correlation with a rating of Poor on Details (Myers, 1962b; Ross, 1961).

The conceptual definition, but not the item-content interpretation, is supported by two previous findings, involving measures which should reflect awareness of phenomena—the scale's positive correlation with a rating of Has No Self-Understanding (Ross, 1961), and its slight but significant positive correlation with the PRI Self-Insight scale (Myers, 1962b).

The item-content interpretation is supported by the scale's negative correlations with the CPI *Sc* scale and the SSHA, both of which seem to reflect something like time-binding or compulsivity, rather than readiness to reach conclusions. These results are consistent with the scale's previously reported positive correlations with the PRI Impulsiveness scale (Myers, 1962b) and a rating of Performs Below Capacity (Myers, 1962b; Ross, 1961), and its negative correlations with ratings of Industrious, and Works Steadily and on an Even Keel (Myers, 1962b; Ross, 1961). However, the J-P scale's correlation with the PRI Compulsiveness scale, although significantly negative, was slight (Myers, 1962b).

Several findings seem inexplicable in terms of both the conceptual definition and the item-content interpretation. Some of these findings, including the scale's negative correlations with the CPI *Re, So,* and *Ac* scales, when considered together with the scale's negative correlations with the CPI *Sc* scale and the SSHA, suggest still another interpretation of the J-P scale, namely, that it is measuring something akin to prudence. Such an interpretation is further supported by such previous results as the J-P scale's negative loading on a factor identified as prudence for boys, though not for girls (Ross, 1963); and its negative correlations with the PRI Attitude to Work scale (Myers, 1962b) and such ratings as Responsible (Myers, 1962b; Ross, 1961), Mature (Ross, 1961), and Acts Ethically (Ross, 1961). This interpretation is not consistent, however, with the J-P scale's nonsignificant correlation with a rating of Not Self-disciplined (Ross, 1961).

Other findings point to a sex difference on this scale. With some exceptions, the girls in the various student groups tended to be more judging than the boys. This finding is supported by the scale's correlation with the CPI masculinity-femininity scale but it conflicts with the scale's correlation with the MMPI masculinity-femininity scale. The latter correlation indicates that femininity is associated with perception rather than judgment. Moreover, in other studies (Myers, 1962b) no sex difference was apparent on the J-P scale in a junior high school sample, and the scale was not significantly correlated with the PRI Masculinity-Femininity scale. However, another study (Ross, 1963) did find a sex difference in the factor structure of the scale—it loaded prudence and extraversion-introversion factors for boys, but a general ability factor and an unidentified one for girls.

The interpretation of this scale is further complicated by its consistent but moderate correlations with CPI response bias scales and MMPI validity and SD scales.

Overview

This research bears on the perennial problem that indirect measurement inevitably introduces extraneous sources of variance. The issue is the extent to which the measuring instruments reflect variance attributable to the underlying variables—in the present case, the typological distinctions of the Jungian system —and the extent to which they reflect variance from other, perhaps more superficial, sources. This issue is complicated by the existence of a sequence of questions. First in the sequence is the question of truth or falsity: *Do the underlying variables really exist?* (In the present case, the question takes the form: *Is the Jungian system a set of true assertions about individuals, and, hence, are there basic typological distinctions among human beings?*) If the answer to this first question is negative, the second question becomes unreal, because it is: *Do the measuring instruments validly reflect the underlying variables?* In the present case, for example, since extraversion-introversion is measured by reported talkativeness and other such characteristics, it may be that the E-I scale is more responsive to other determinants of talkativeness than extraversion-introversion, *per se.*

The position advanced in interpreting the results reported in this article was that, in addition to the conceptual definition for each scale, there are one or more equally plausible interpretations of the scale's meaning. These alternative interpretations, which are outside of the Jungian typology, satisfactorily account for many of the properties and correlates of the scale. While many of the findings are also consistent with the conceptual definitions, the empirical support for the alternative interpretations does suggest that the Indicator's scales are strongly subject to influences other than the typological variables. In particular, the E-I and J-P scales seem to reflect something quite different from their postulated dimensions, and the S-N and T-F scales, at best, seem to reflect restricted aspects of them.

Discrepancies of this kind between the empirical meaning of the scales and their conceptual definitions may explain the failure of a series of related studies with the Indicator to find support for the structural properties attributed to the Jungian typology (Stricker & Ross, 1964).

In any event, even if the typology that the Indicator is intended to reflect does exist, it would be premature to assume that the Indicator operationally defines it until (a) on the one hand, the alternative hypotheses about the scales' meaning which are suggested by the findings reported in this article are tested and rejected; and (b) on the other, a body of findings accumulate which explicitly link each scale to its conceptual definition.

Summary

The Myers-Briggs Type Indicator is a self-report inventory which is intended to measure four variables stemming from the Jungian personality typology: extraversion-introversion, sensation-intuition, thinking-feeling, and judging-perceiving. The construct validity of each of its scales was assessed in a series of studies which investigated the scales' correlations with ability, interest, and personality scales and differences on the scales between the sexes and between students in different high school programs. The findings suggest that the Sensation-Intuition and Thinking-Feeling scales may reflect restricted aspects of the dimensions that they are intended to represent, and the Extraversion-Introversion and Judging-Perceiving scales may reflect something quite different from their postulated dimensions.

REFERENCES

BROWN, W. F., & HOLTZMAN, W. H. *Manual, Brown-Holtzman Survey of Study Habits and Attitudes.* (Rev. ed.) New York: Psychological Corp., 1956.

CATTELL, R. B., SAUNDERS, D. R., & STICE, G. *Handbook for the Sixteen Personality Factor Questionnaire, "The 16 P. F. Test;" Forms A, B, and C.* Champaign, Ill.: Institute for Personality and Ability Testing, 1957.

CHRISTENSEN, P. R., & GUILFORD, J. P. *Manual of instructions and interpretations, Ship Destination Test.* Beverly Hills, Calif.: Sheridan Supply Co., 1956.

COLLEGE ENTRANCE EXAMINATION BOARD. *A description of the College Board Scholastic Aptitude Test.* Princeton, N. J.: Author, 1962.

DYER, H. S., & KING, R. G. *College Board scores: their use and interpretation.*

Princeton, N. J.: College Entrance Examination Board, 1955.

EDWARDS, A. L. *Manual, Edwards Personal Preference Schedule.* (Rev. ed.) New York: Psychological Corp., 1957. (a)

EDWARDS, A. L. *The social desirability variable in personality assessment and research.* New York: Dryden, 1957. (b)

EVANS, C., & McCONNELL, T. R. *Manual, Minnesota T-S-E Inventory.* (Rev. ed.) Princeton, N. J.: Educational Testing Service, 1957.

EYSENCK, H. J. *Manual of the Maudsley Personality Inventory.* London: Univer. London Press, 1959.

GOUGH, H. G. *Manual for the California Psychological Inventory.* Palo Alto, Calif.: Consulting Psychologists Press, 1957.

GRAY, H. Jung's psychological types: meaning and consistency of the questionnaire. *J. gen. Psychol.,* 1947, **37,** 177–186. (a)

GRAY, H. Psychological types and changes with age. *J. clin. Psychol.,* 1947, **3,** 273–277. (b)

GRAY, H. Jung's psychological types in men and women. *Stanford med. Bull.,* 1948, **6,** 29–36.

GRAY, H. Jung's psychological types: ambiguous scores and their interpretation. *J. gen. Psychol.,* 1949, **40,** 63–88. (a)

GRAY, H. Psychological types in married people. *J. soc. Psychol.,* 1949, **29,** 189–200. (b)

GRAY, H., & WHEELWRIGHT, J. B. Jung's psychological types and marriage. *Stanford med. Bull.,* 1944, **2,** 37–39.

GRAY, H., & WHEELWRIGHT, J. B. Jung's psychological types, their frequency of occurrence. *J. gen. Psychol.,* 1946, **34,** 3–17.

HATHAWAY, S. R., & McKINLEY, J. C. *Manual, Minnesota Multiphasic Personality Inventory.* (Rev. ed.) New York: Psychological Corp., 1951.

HOWARTH, E. Extroversion and dream symbolism: an empirical study. *Psychol. Rep.,* 1962, **10,** 211–214.

JUNG, C. G. *Psychological types.* London: Routledge & Kegan Paul, 1923.

JUNG, C. G. *Modern man in search of a soul.* New York: Harcourt, Brace, 1933.

JUNG, C. G. *Collected works of* . . . Vol. 7. *Two essays on analytical psychology.* New York: Pantheon, 1953.

LORD, F. M. *Multimodal score distributions on the Myers-Briggs Type Indicator: I.* Princeton, N. J.: Educational Testing Service, 1958. (Res. Memo. 58-8)

MYERS, I. B. Inferences as to the dichotomous nature of Jung's types, from the shape of regressions of dependent variables upon Myers-Briggs Type Indicator scores. *Amer. Psychologist,* 1962, **17,** 364. (Abstract) (a)

MYERS, I. B. *Manual (1962), the Myers-Briggs Type Indicator.* Princeton, N. J.: Educational Testing Service, 1962. (b)

ROSS, J. *Progress report on the College Student Characteristics Study: June, 1961.* Princeton, N. J.: Educational Testing Service, 1961. (Res. Memo. 61-11)

ROSS, J. *The relationship between the Myers-Briggs Type Indicator and ability, personality and information tests.* Princeton, N. J.: Educational Testing Service, 1963. (Res. Bull. 63-8)

SAUNDERS, D. R. Evidence for a rational correspondence between the personality typologies of Spranger and of Jung. *Amer. Psychologist,* 1960, **15,** 459. (Abstract)

STRICKER, L. J. Acquiescence and social desirability response styles, item characteristics, and conformity. *Psychol. Rep.,* 1963, **12,** 319–341. (Monogr. Suppl. 2-V12)

STRICKER, L. J., & ROSS, J. *A description and evaluation of the Myers-Briggs Type Indicator.* Princeton, N. J.: Educational Testing Service, 1962. (Res. Bull. 62-6)

STRICKER, L. J., & ROSS, J. Intercorrelations and reliability of the Myers-Briggs Type Indicator scales. *Psychol. Rep.,* 1963, **12,** 287–293.

STRICKER, L. J., & ROSS, J. An assessment of some structural properties of the Jungian personality typology. *J. abnorm. soc. Psychol.,* 1964, **68,** 62–71.

STRONG, E. K., JR. *Manual for Strong Vocational Interest Blanks for Men and Women.* Palo Alto, Calif.: Consulting Psychologists Press, 1959.

TERMAN, L. M. *Manual, Concept Mastery Test, Form T.* New York: Psychological Corp., 1956.

Chapter 8

Special Problems of Projective Tests

■ As we have seen, in both structured and projective tests, the S is free to define the stimulus as he sees fit, whether it be a statement such as "I loved my mother" on the MMPI or plain white card on the TAT. The essential difference is that in the first case the subject must confine his response to "true," "false," or "cannot say," while in the latter situation he is more or less free to give any response he desires.[1]

This very freedom, which is one of the major strengths of projective tests, is also their major weakness, giving rise to most of the problems peculiar to the validation of such instruments. A number of the specific problems are discussed on the following pages. Briefly they can be reduced to the following:

(1) uncertainty about the determinants of projective responses. This concerns not only the characteristics of the test stimuli but also such nontest determinants as the personality of the examiner and the nature of the setting;

(2) uncertainty about how to best code or classify a response once it has been obtained, especially when competing schools or systems have emerged;

(3) uncertainty about how to interpret a given response. This, as we shall see, is one of the most basic difficulties. Not only is there disagreement how a given response may be interpreted, depending on the context of the total protocol and test situation, but also on the basic issues of whether projective responses bear a direct or inverse relation to overt behavior. The effect of this is to compound the criterion problem which is difficult enough when there is no unreliability in interpretation to worry about.

(4) uncertainty as to what constitutes adequate research in the area of projective test validation, with the result that a great deal of irrelevant and poorly designed research has been published, obscuring the well-designed studies.

The papers in the present chapter review various specific aspects of these general problems. Murstein and Rosenzweig focus on the disagreements as to the determinants and the interpretation of projective responses. Murstein reviews the evidence for a number of assumptions basic to projective test interpretation and finds it quite weak.[2] He suggests a conceptual model based

---

[1] The phrase "more or less" is quite deliberate, for while the instructions of a projective test typically tell the respondent that he is completely free to respond in any fashion, nevertheless he is bound by the implicit constraints fostered by the fact that he is in a social setting interacting with another person whose job it is to make some decisions regarding his character and/or future. In fact, the patient's conformity to these implicit constraints is often one of the most important diagnostic clues that can be obtained from a projective test.

[2] It should be pointed out that Lindzey in his review of the evidence for the basic assumptions of the TAT comes to different conclusions. See Chapter 11.

on adaptation level theory and increased emphasis on the importance of the total setting in determining the response and its proper interpretation. Rosenzweig also focuses on these problems and points out how the nature of the relation between fantasy and overt behavior depends on the level at which a person is responding. He defines three levels of response, dependent upon the circumstances under which the person is responding, and points out how the interpretation of the response will vary drastically from level to level.

Ainsworth ranges over all of the problems mentioned, but in particular points out some of the difficulties which have plagued those who would do research on the validation of projective techniques, such as the global nature of clinical interpretation, the difficulty of formulating studies which are both well designed and relevant to projective hypotheses, the influence of situational variables upon the responses, and so on. In a later essay, Ainsworth (1954) has expanded on these problems as they affect the Rorschach in particular. For other good discussions of the problem of projective test validation, the reader is referred to MacFarlane and Tuddenham (1951) and Meehl (1959).

REFERENCES

AINSWORTH, MARY D. Problems of validation. In KLOPFER, A., AINSWORTH, MARY D., KLOPFER, W. G., & HOLT, R. R. *Developments in the Rorschach Technique.* Vol. 1. New York: Harcourt, Brace & World, 1954.

MACFARLANE, JEAN W., & TUDDENHAM, R. D. Problems in the validation of projective techniques. In ANDERSON, H. H., & ANDERSON, GLADYS L. (Eds.) *An Introduction to Projective Techniques.* Englewood Cliffs, N.J.: Prentice-Hall, 1951.

MEEHL, P. E. Structured and projective tests: Some common problems in validation. *Journal of Projective Techniques,* 1959, **23,** 268–272.

Assumptions, Adaptation Level, and Projective Techniques

Bernard I. Murstein

It has been almost 40 years since the introduction of projective techniques on a formal basis. Ignored at first, attacked later as unscientific, these instruments have currently achieved wide empirical employment if not theoretical acceptance. Perhaps now that the first flush of youth has passed it is time for some "middle-aged" self-reflection. It is the purpose of this paper to examine some

This investigation was supported by a Public Health Grant (M-4698) from the National Institute of Mental Health.

Reprinted by permission of the publisher and author from *Perceptual and Motor Skills,* 1961, **12,** 107–125.

ten more or less popularly held assumptions regarding these techniques, which are believed to be contrary to current research findings, logic, or both. The critique will be followed by a conceptual approach directed toward achieving a better understanding of the meaning of projective responses in the behavior system of the individual being examined.

Assumptions

1. *The more ambiguous the stimulus properties of the projective techniques the more the response reflects the personality of the perceiver.* This assumption at first sight appears incontrovertible and has been seconded by clinicians (Abt, 1950; Shneidman, 1956) and non-clinicians (Bruner, 1948). It is held that if, to use an extreme example, a blank card (Card 16, TAT) is presented to S and he is asked to tell a story, he must of necessity project since there are no stimulus properties to guide his themes. To adhere to this view, however, is to commit the grievous error of assuming that the stimulus presented to S is the stimulus to which he reacts. It is not meant by this statement to enmesh the reader in the morass of the old objective reality-phenomenological reality dichotomy. Rather it is our purpose to state that the cards of themselves are only part of the total stimulus situation. Also to be considered are the environmental variables and those relating to S himself. Hence, the blank card, though it is bare of stimulus imprint, may so structure the testing situation that the response repertoire of S shows less variation than would be the case were he to receive a more structured card. Thus, the *actual stimulus* impinging on S may result in his perceiving himself as being called upon to *reveal something of himself through a story, since there is obviously no objective picture for him to talk about.* In that case we should be dealing with a *response set* of a fairly stereotyped na-

ture having as its purpose the censoring of any material which would cause S to appear in an unflattering light.

Still a further problem is the multiple connotative usage of the term "ambiguity." Sometimes, ambiguity has been used to describe the physical properties of the cards as in the "hazy appearance" of some TAT cards (Weisskopf, 1950b). Bijou and Kenny (1951), however, give the term more of a psychological meaning in defining it as the number of possible interpretations that could be given to a card. The important distinction has not been made between physical structure and ambiguity. It is proposed that the Funk and Wagnall's dictionary provides a basis for distinguishing the two terms. *Structure* is defined as "the arrangement and organic union of parts in a body or object" (Funk & Wagnall's, *New Standard Dictionary of the English Language,* p. 2401). *Ambiguity* is defined by the same dictionary as "the quality of being ambiguous, obscure, or uncertain in meaning, especially where either of two interpretations is possible" (p. 86).

The correlation between lack of structure and ambiguity is not unity. Card 16, for example, as stated earlier, is quite unstructured. It does not possess a high degree of ambiguity, however, since the extreme absence of structure also limits the number of possible interpretations of the card (Eron, 1950; Ullmann, 1957). Accordingly, Ss often claim they cannot give a story, and when pressed give a trifling banality. Despite the variation of meaning in ambiguity the research literature is hardly conducive to the belief that ambiguity is linearly related to projection.

In the field of projective techniques, and specifically the TAT, Weisskopf (1950a) found that photographs of the test given in reduced exposure, thus making them more hazy, did not increase projection. Using time of presentation as a measure of ambiguity, she found that cards exposed for a sufficient length of time so that they were clearly perceived were superior for projective purposes to cards only fleetingly seen. Again (Weisskopf, 1950b), completely traced line drawings were found to be more effective in evoking fantasy than incompletely traced drawings.

Murray himself has described the TAT cards as "divided into two series of ten pictures each, the pictures of the second series (numbers 11 through 20) being purposely more unusual, dramatic and bizarre than those of the first" (Murray, 1943, p. 2).

The question arises as to which of these series is the more ambiguous? By way of answer, Bijou and Kenny (1951) had groups of men and women (college students) rank 21 "male series" TAT cards on the dimension of "ambiguity" (estimated number of different interpretations that might be derived from each card). A t test between the means of both series indicated that the "fairytale" series was more ambiguous at the .05 level. Granted the "fairytale" series is more ambiguous, does it elicit more projection on the part of S? Weisskopf (1950a) found that her sample of college students projected with more fantasy to the "everyday" series.

Can we then assume that the least ambiguous pictures precipitate the greatest amount of projection? While the foregoing data might hint at such an interpretation, two studies specifically aimed at this question indicate that the relationship is curvilinear rather than linear. Kenny and Bijou (1953) divided 15 TAT cards into three piles of low, medium, and high ambiguity. The stories derived from these cards were rated for "personality-revealingness" with the result that cards of medium ambiguity were the most revealing. Murstein (1958c) using Bijou and Kenny's ranking for ambiguity and frequency of theme appearance rankings obtained from Eron's study (1950), correlated the two variables using both product-moment and curvilinear methods. While the linear correlation was non-significant, the curvilinear one proved to be quite significant. The moderately ambiguous cards produced the most themes, while the high and low ambiguous cards were less productive.

In another study Murstein (1958a) had female Ss rank a "female" series of cards for "pleasantness" and for "psychological ambiguity." He correlated these rankings with each other and with Eron's "emotional tone" scores obtained from the TAT stories of a similar female population (1953). "Ambiguity" was found to correlate significantly (*rho*) with "pleasantness," .40; and with "emotional tone," .56.

In sum, it appears that extremely ambiguous TAT cards do not stimulate S's private world so much as they elicit a "response set" resulting in a sparsely themed pleasant type of response. The study of ambiguity has received little attention apart from the TAT and it is to be hoped that the Rorschach and other techniques will stimulate further studies of this type.

2. *The more similar the stimulus to S, the greater the degree of projection.* This question has been discussed at some length elsewhere (Murstein, 1959). The experimental literature was reviewed with regard to the Negro TAT versus white TAT, modification of the central character to resemble S, who might be a student, nun, crippled, or obese person, and the use of animal versus human pictures with children. The results are in general negative to the belief that making the central character in the picture more similar to S increases projection, and to the belief that children project more readily to pictures of animals than they do to humans. Such views do not adequately consider the importance of the "background" factors and S's "personalities."

Also overlooked is the fact that the stimulus is perceived in accordance with *cultural experience*, resulting in perceptions which can not be understood solely on the basis of a description of the physical properties of the picture. Negroes, for example, perceive the TAT figures *not as whites, but as people in general* (Cook, 1953). Such is the adaptation of the Negro to the "white" norms, that being shown a Negro TAT card arouses suspicion because of the novelty of such a test. Accordingly, one is hardly surprised to find that such cards given to Negroes have often been reported as resulting in *less* projection than when the usual TAT cards were used.

In the case of animal versus human pictures, the evidence is largely in favor of the use of humans in preference to animals. CAT versus TAT comparisons offer only indirect evidence, since the quality of response is a function of the *kind of situation depicted* as well as the use of animals or humans. Happily, several studies have used humanized analogues of the CAT pictures, and noted the superiority of the analogues.

In sum, projection is enhanced by the use of the same species as S (*homo sapiens*) but, within species, increased physical similarity to S in terms of physical affliction, occupation, or appearance does not produce more meaningful objective responses.

3. *Since the stimulus is more or less ambiguous, it is of little importance as compared to the value of the response elicited.* The proponents of this view hold that the determinant of the response is hardly so much the immediate stimulus as the basic idiosyncratic perceptions which stem from S's "private world" (Rosenzweig, 1951). Since the stimulus is standard for all Ss, differences in response are said to stem from S's projections. Actually, there has been less variation in response than commonly believed. Eron (1950, 1953) demonstrated that his Ss regardless of their psychiatric classification (schizophrenic, neurotic, normal), tended to tell stories to the TAT that were of sad emotional

tone. Murstein (1958a) found the unpleasantness in the emotional tone of the TAT stories scored by Eron's scale to be positively related to the *lack of ambiguity* of the cards. Several TAT-type cards have been scaled for aggression and sex by the Guttman technique (Auld, Eron, & Laffal, 1955; Lesser, 1958; Murstein, *et al.*, 1959). These results imply that the TAT is not nearly so ambiguous as has been thought.

4. *No response is accidental. Every response is meaningful for the analysis of personality.* Taken literally, the first of these two statements is beyond dispute if one adheres to a concept of psychic determinism. The second statement, however, would seem to run contrary to what general test theory propounds; namely, that a certain portion of the variance accounting for a response may be profitably treated as "error variance." This "error variance" stems from two factors. First, the fluctuation caused by lack of consistency of response. Second, Ss differ not only with regard to personality but in many other ways. One of these ways is in experience. An emphasis on anatomical details in a farmer has different implications from similar perception by a medical student. Ss differ in their verbal fluency and habits (most projective tests may be nominally perceptual) but *it is the verbalizations not the perceptions which are scored.* Intellect is still another factor making for differences in response. Lastly, Ss differ in the cognitive response habits or response sets which they bring to the testing situation. Where these response sets are themselves analyzed there is no problem. Often however, these habits are not discerned by the examiner. A habit, for example, which is very difficult to detect, is the "saw tooth phenomenon" which has been extensively described by Atkinson with reference to the TAT (1950). Using a Latin square design for order of presentation, he showed that there was a significant difference between mean

achievement-motive scores for odd and even serial positions (adjusted to remove systematic differences attributable to the pictures). Further, he found a significant relationship (*rho* = .66) between S's mean achievement scores for the first four positions and the size of the decrease from these scores to the scores based on the last four positions with scores, again equated for systematic differences due to the pictures. A logical explanation of this phenomenon is that the expression of achievement in early stories leads to a relative satiation with regard to the occurrence of this motive in later stories.

The conclusions to be derived are that there is considerable variation in the meaningfulness of a response to a projective technique, depending upon the effects of S's experience, intelligence, verbal ability, and the "response set."

5. *Projective techniques are complementary in tapping the various layers of personality* (Harrison, 1940; Henry, 1947; Sterns & Horinson, 1949). One of the popular views among clinical psychologists is that the Rorschach delves into the "basic personality," while the TAT is said to be more sensitive to situational influences. Thus, Shneidman (1956) depicts the Rorschach as probing the unconscious, while the TAT seems to tap the unconscious, pre-conscious and conscious. There has been some research which seems to indicate that rather than being complementary, two projective techniques may on occasion give contradictory findings.

Shatin (1953, 1955), using a sign approach in his analysis of the Rorschach, obtained a Rorschach Adjustment Inventory (RAI) for a psychiatric patient population. Adjustment on the Rorschach was found to correlate with the following TAT variables: "unpleasant feeling tone" (*p* < .10), "degree of inner conflict" (*p* < .05), and "verbal and emotional aggression" (*p* < .04).

In a study by Murstein and Wheeler (1959) 36 female breast cancer patients at a southwestern hospital received the Rorschach and a Thematic Stories Test (TST) consisting of five TAT cards and five cards from the Caldwell Picture Series[1] a thematic-type test depicting mainly elderly persons. Holding word count on the TST and number of responses on the Rorschach constant, the correlation between the measurement of hostility on the Rorschach and on the TAT was −.41 which was significant at the .01 level for a one-tailed test of significance. A study by Murstein on parents of hospitalized children (1960) resulted in a correlation of .31 (*p* < .05) between the pleasantness of the "emotional tone of stories" as scored on the TAT and the anxiety score on the Taylor Manifest Anxiety Scale. Carr (1956) tested 50 neurotic male patients to whom he administered the TAT, Sentence Completion, and Rorschach tests. Many of the "signs" on one test were contrary to those of the others. Thus, *the perception of less than two females on the Rorschach* was correlated with a *lack of mother-hostility on the TAT and Sentence Completion.*

Two points should be made with regard to these studies. The first is that often the assumption that two quantitative signs taken from two different tests are "qualitatively" equivalent is not sufficiently justified by research evidence. We may thus do serious insult to the data by engaging in "miniature psychoanalysis" utilizing these signs. Hence, one may ask with considerable justification whether the lack of perception of females on the Rorschach is related to hostility toward them for the majority of test-takers. Until research supports this assumption with experimental evidence we might be wiser to avoid the utilization of such "face validity."

Secondly, however, negative correlations have been reported in which the operations used in measuring a trait in

[1] An unpublished test by B. M. Caldwell, Washington Univer. School of Medicine, 1953.

different tests have pretty much the same meaning (e.g., the projection of hostility on the Rorschach and TAT). If one keeps in mind the fact that the techniques are structured to a different degree with regard to their stimulus properties, then a negative correlation may be more easily understood. Accordingly, a "well adjusted" individual might get a high hostility score on the TAT because many of the cards are so structured as to depict violence and aggression (Eron, 1950; Murstein, 1958b). Getting a high hostility score on the TAT would not then indicate a person possessing considerable hostility, but instead, one who manifested a high degree of confidence in perceiving the stimulus properties objectively. Such a person, however, would be expected to manifest little hostility in the more ambiguous Rorschach because there is little need for the release of hostility and because the stimulus properties of the Rorschach are not necessarily structured in a hostile manner. While such a hypothetical "normal" S's behavior would not be *constant* it would be *consistent*. Much more work is needed in which the stimulus properties of the cards, in addition to environmental and personality variables, are utilized in assessing the complementary or contradictory results obtained.

6. *A protocol is a sufficiently extensive sampling of S's personality to warrant formulating judgments about it* (MacFarlane & Tuddenham, 1951, p. 34). It is true that one can learn something from the omission of response to a technique such as the Rorschach or TAT. Webb and Hilden (1953), however, have shown that there is a fairly high correlation between the amount of words used in stories to the TAT and S's intelligence (.40) and verbal fluency (.50). Thus, while absence of an adequate number of responses for interpretation conceivably may be a function of personality disturbance, it also might be a function of intelligence or verbal flu-

ency. The evidence, therefore, seems to indicate that the absence of response is not nearly so meaningful for personality interpretation as the presence of an adequate number of responses. Consequently, one can expect to encounter protocols from time to time which reveal little of S except that his response set is not geared to excessive production. One must therefore conclude that individual protocols vary in the amount of knowledge that may be gained from their analysis.

7. *S is unaware of what he discloses about himself.* The impetus for this assumption may be traced to L. K. Frank's important article in which he suggested that projective techniques were an excellent medium with which to tap the "private world of the individual comprising as it does, the feelings, urges, beliefs, attitudes, and desires of which he may be dimly aware and which he is often reluctant to admit even to himself much less to others" (1948, p. 66).

Murray, in similar vein, also has said that

. . . whatever peculiar virtue the TAT may have, if any, it will be found to reside not as some have assumed, in its power to mirror overt behavior or to communicate what the patient knows and is willing to tell, but rather in its capacity to reveal things that the patient is unwilling to tell because he is unconscious of them (1951, p. 577).

Disagreeing sharply is Allport, who has stated that

. . . Normal subjects . . . tell you by the direct method precisely what they tell you by the projective method. They are all of a piece. You may therefore take their motivational statements at their face value, for even if you probe you will not find anything substantially different (1954, p. 110).

The evidence seems to favor Allport not only insofar as normal Ss are concerned but also for those whose adjustment is considerably less than optimal. Scodel and Lipetz (1957) and Wirt (1956) found that neurotics projected more hostility on the TAT and Rorschach, respectively, than did equally hostile psychotics. Indeed, Rader (1957) posits that projection is closely related to strength of ego-control as well as to general socio-cultural background.

Thus, with poor control one may find a positive correlation between content (which was earlier hypothesized to be an index of underlying drive) and behavior, while with strong control one may find a negative correlation (Rader, 1957, p. 304).

Clark's work (1952) also supported the relationship of projection to ego-control. He found that male Ss expressed *little sexual content on the TAT after seeing nude pictures.* The use of alcoholic beverages to loosen ego control resulted in an increase in sexual fantasy to the cards.

Murstein (1956) gave the Rorschach to fraternity men designated hostile-insightful and hostile-non-insightful on the basis of pooled rankings. The hostile-insightful men projected significantly more hostility on the Rorschach than the hostile-non-insightful men. He concluded that projection on the Rorschach was in part a function of the *willingness* of the individual to disclose data from his "private world."

A curvilinear relationship between overt hostility and hostility measured via the content of the Rorschach was hypothesized and found by Smith and Coleman (1956). Persons with little overt hostility and those with a good deal of overt hostility projected little hostility as compared with those occupying the middle range. Comparing dreams with TAT protocols, Gordon (1953) concluded that the TAT protocols reflected the idealized self (subject to conscious control) compared to the more need-orientated self depicted in dreams. Lindzey and Tejessey (1956) found that aggressive indices derived

from the TAT correlated more highly with self-ratings than with other ratings, including those of clinical observers.

Finally, a study by Davids (1955) seems to bear on the issue very well. He employed the usual rationale in recruiting Ss from a college population in that they were told that they were contributing time to the furthering of science. Several measures of maladjustment were obtained, including the use of two projective techniques, and the intercorrelations were fairly high. When, however, a new group of students were led to believe that, from their protocols, an individual of considerable emotional stability and maturity would be selected for a high paying job, the intercorrelations dropped considerably. It would hardly appear conceivable that these changes occurred independently of the Ss' volition.

The experimental evidence seems to indicate a good deal of awareness on the part of S as to what he "projects" on a projective technique. It has also been shown that a "response set" to an ambiguous picture often results in pleasant but superficial associations (Murstein, 1958a). Synthesizing these two findings, we may adumbrate a schema whereby many Ss quite consciously control their words in an ambiguous situation, issuing more or less pleasant banalities in order to appear in a pleasing light to the examiner. The key to this guarded behavior lies in the ego-involving aspect of being probed psychologically in order to find out whether one is "adjusted or maladjusted."

This interpretation of the projective test situation is consistent with the results of Singer and Young (1941) in an experiment which did not involve projective techniques. The authors presented students with a series of tones, tastes, odors, and odor-taste alternations and had them rate this more or less representative series on "pleasantness" and "unpleasantness." The students also participated in a heterogeneous array of 30 activities which was followed by their being presented with a series of words or phrases to which they associated activities and then evaluated these activities for their attractiveness. In addition, they rated their moods. The ratios of pleasant to unpleasant ratings were as follows: Mood, 4.48; Activity, 1.77; Words, 1.59; Odor, .54; Odor-taste, .53; Taste, .46; Tone, .38.

It is noteworthy that the more personal the category rated, the more pleasant was the rating. Thus, moods reflect the emotional life of the student and, accordingly, they rated their moods of the previous hour as quite pleasant. With regard to activities and word-associations there is no direct reference to emotion and yet, one must favorably impress the examiner that one is a "pleasant sort of chap." Odors, tastes and tones have little ego-involvement and perhaps the tediousness of the tasks results in unpleasant ratings. The important finding is that in situations where *they were personally involved,* the students tended to give pleasant ratings though this "response set" took on a negative cast when sensory discriminations were called for.

In sum then, if one returns to a consideration of projective techniques, one is struck by their relative inefficacy in dealing with sophisticated Ss. The very ambiguity of projective techniques as well as lack of stimulus structure (Lazarus, 1953) alerts S to the possibility that what he says "may be held against him." Accordingly, the resulting protocol is often most consistent with the "public self" which "self" the clinicians are usually not very interested in examining.

8. *The strength of a need is a function of its manifestation directly or symbolically on the projective technique.* The work of Pittluck (1950) has indicated that no simple relationship exists between a need and its manifestation on a projective technique. Assuming that the expression of a need is a function of the need and of the anxiety opposing its expression, she was able to show that Ss who relied heavily on defense mechanisms such as "rejection" or "denial of aggression," putting aggression in a socially approved context or displacing it to non-human characters, were not apt to act out their hostility despite protocols containing many expressions of hostility. Murstein (1956) found that merely taking account of a need without considering the stimulus, self-concept, and environment surrounding an administration of the test would be of little predictive value with regard to overt behavior. He was able to show that two equally hostile groups differed significantly in the projection of hostility on the Rorschach as a function of their self-concepts. That even prolonged semi-starvation does not significantly increase the number of food responses on the Rorschach was reported by Brozek and co-workers (1951). Levine and associates (1942) found that the number of food responses given in response to an ambiguous picture was less after 9 hours than it had been after 3 to 6 hours. Rader (1957), studying prison inmates, found only certain kinds of hostile projection (mutilation) related to overt hostile behavior. In a study by Smith and Coleman (1956) persons with high and low overt hostility (not including prison inmates) were found to project little hostility on the Rorschach as compared to those possessing a moderate amount of hostility.

It appears that the strength of a need is only one of many variables determining the projection of hostility. An accurate prediction of the manifestation of a need in overt behavior must consider the total situation (stimulus properties of cards, examiner, S, environment, and their interactions). More will be said about this point shortly.

9. *There is a parallel between projective technique behavior and behavior in the social environment.* This assumption has been recently supported

(Piotrowski, 1957) but more often than not disavowed (Murray, 1943; Symonds, 1949). It has already been indicated that persons expressing overt hostility may project little hostility on the projective techniques. Does the converse occur so that persons projecting a lot of hostility on the Rorschach manifest little hostility in the outside world? Smith and Coleman (1956) found that their high hostility projection on the Rorschach occupied a medium range in the manifestation of overt hostility. Murstein (1956) however, found that those persons projecting the most hostility on the Rorschach of the four groups which he used, were both hostile and insightful with regard to their hostility as measured by pooled rankings. Rader (1957) has further emphasized the parallel when socio-culture conditions sanction aggressive behavior as well as when ego control breaks down. Moving to the TAT, however, one might expect to find the expression of hostility via the protocols to show either no relationship or a negative one to the manifestation of overt hostility. This reversal from the behavior vis-à-vis the Rorschach should occur because, while the Rorschach is more or less ambiguous, the TAT is negatively structured (Eron, 1950, 1953; Murstein, 1958b). Thus, people who have the confidence to correctly perceive the objectively structured negative stimuli may be those persons who as a correlate of this confidence have little need to manifest anxiety in their behavior. By way of support of this thesis, Murstein found a positive correlation between pleasantness of emotional tone on TAT stories and anxiety on the Manifest Anxiety Scale for a population of parents of hospitalized children (1960).

It seems clear that the various arguments supporting or refuting the parallel between overt and test behavior have not indicated sufficient awareness of differences in the stimulus and background values often encountered in the two situations. Unless the total interaction between person, test, and background is quite similar in stimulus value in both projective and overt situations, we have little reason to expect a correspondence in behavior.

10. *The Rorschach is idiopathic? qualitative? a game of misperception?* Were it not for the serious effects upon graduate students, psychiatrists, and the lay public, the amount of anthropomorphizing and projection orbiting about the Rorschach might be amusing. Some believe it is the answer to the nomothetic monster tests which "swallow up the individual" (Rosenzweig, 1951). Others believe it is a "qualitative oasis" in a vast "quantitative desert" (Murstein, 1958c), or yet, "a game of controlled misperception" (Gibson, 1956). One feels, therefore, as if he possessed a great deal of "gall" in stating that the Rorschach is a series of 10 blots which has served as a *technique* for analysis of what people *verbalize* about their perceptions of these blots. Surely we have heretofore countenanced a serious error in not realizing that the technique has often been *confounded with the interest of the researcher.* Some authors have implied that the Rorschach could not be quantified. Perhaps they should have said that they could not or would not devise quantifiable variables from the Rorschach. During the 1930's and early 40's when clinicians were almost the only psychologists interested in the Rorschach, the technique was viewed as essentially idiopathic. Currently, we are witnessing an increasing number of nomothetic studies as well as theoretical articles on the Rorschach. Shall we now call it an idiopathic-nomothetic-theoretical instrument, or simply an ambi-valent one?

A Conceptual Model for Studying Projective Techniques

My remarks up to this point have been made for the purpose of illustrating that several cherished beliefs have been accepted by some clinical psychologists without the support of sufficient research validation. Several current viewpoints however, are helping to give us a clearer understanding of the projective technique situation. One view holds that the Rorschach, for example, should be analysed through focus on the examiner-S interaction (Sarason, 1954; Schafer, 1954). On the other hand, Piotrowski (1957) has favored an avenue of approach centered on the analysis of the formal characteristics of the blots. Perhaps one of these schools of thought is not necessarily better than the other. Because of the undue emphasis on one aspect of the testing situation, neither of these approaches is sufficiently inclusive to account for the determination of response to projective techniques.

Some 10 years ago a theory was published which appears of considerable help in this problem. Helson's theory of adaptation level (1948) was initially formulated as a means of accounting for the perception of certain visual phenomena. The theory has been successfully extended to the fields of social psychology and personality (Helson, 1955; Rosenbaum & Blake, 1955). The theory briefly stated is:

Operationally, the adaptation-level (AL) is represented by the stimulus to which the organism responds either not at all or in an indifferent or neutral manner. In a large variety of situations the AL proves to be a weighted log mean of three classes of stimuli: the stimulus in the focus of attention; all stimuli in the field forming the context or background; and residuals from past experience. These three classes of stimuli pool or interact to determine the AL and hence the adjustment of the organism. As stimulation of behavior varies, the adaptation-level fluctuates accordingly. A simple formula expresses these facts more clearly and concisely, as follows:

$$\log A = p \log X + q \log B + r \log R$$

where p, q, and r are weighting factors showing the relative importance of X, the stimulus, B, the background, and R, the residual (Helson, 1955, pp. 91–92).

In adapting the theory for use with projective techniques the projective technique may be regarded as the stimulus (e.g., TAT card), the effect of the examiner, his instructions, and the locale of the test serve as "background" factors, and Ss needs, self concept, and goals (e.g., "life space") serve as the residual or perhaps more appropriately termed, organismic factor. A somewhat more detailed account of these variables may be found elsewhere (Murstein, 1959d). Translating Helson's terms into those more meaningful for describing response to a projective technique,

$$PR = S^a B^b O^c,$$

where PR stands for the projective response, S for the stimulus, B for the background characteristics, and O for the organismic variable. a, b, c stand for the weights for each variable.

Both the "stimulus"and "background" may be objectively determined without reference to the individual. For example, a TAT card could be readily scaled for stimulus pull for hostility. The background factors also could be scaled for hostility without too much difficulty. It should be possible, for example, to draw up a continuum of environments varying in permissiveness of the perception of hostility, and, to place the particular projective test situation at some point on the continuum. The most difficut variable to quantify is O. If the individual experiences an elevation of a tension gradient in some trait (hostility) the likelihood of maximum contribution from the O component is a function of the individual's need and his expectancy of satisfaction of the need. Rotter (1954) states that

$$BP = (E \& RV),$$

where BP is the behavior potential, E is the expectancy, and RV, the reinforcement value.

Since the objective characteristics of S and B are considered in addition to O, Rotter's equation has been subsumed under the O component so that

$$O = (E, RV),$$

where E and RV have the same meaning as before.

To allow for interaction between E and RV the components are treated in a multiplicative manner. It should be emphasized, however, that the O component refers to the totality of the individual's experience prior to his being confronted with the testing situation. This allows one to view the projective response as the resultant of the objective stimulus and background conditions, and the individual's needs and expectancies which influence his reaction to these conditions.

The use of a term such as "expectancy" implies a strong volitional component on the part of S with regard to the determination of the response he makes. One must not suppose, however, that S's awareness necessarily results in the prevention of the appearance of highly personal material. Rather, this awareness has the effect of more carefully filtering the material to be manifested so that it is consistent with S's self concept. Thus, if S needs to express his hostility visually via the Rorschach and finds such material not ego-threatening, he may perceive "angry men" or "fierce looking tigers." If however, the individual publicly or privately believes himself to be friendly, he will not permit such perceptions to be exhibited to the examiner. Instead he will substitute contrived but more pleasant associations.

Implicit in the foregoing has been the belief that S is capable of differentiating between responses which are favorable and unfavorable to his self concept. The validity of this belief will vary with the stimulus properties of the projective technique. Previous experience and research (Murstein, 1956, 1958a, 1958d) indicate, however, that the more popular techniques such as the Rorschach and the TAT are the most susceptible to S's control. It is logical to presume that not all Ss are completely capable of sensing the import of their responses. Nevertheless, the average intelligent college student, who makes up a good deal of manpower employed in psychological research, can readily distinguish between the personality-revealing properties of an "azalea" and "an axe buried in the head of an old lady with blood oozing down the handle."

Under what circumstances do uncontrollable responses occur? They may occur when the stimulus is so clearly defined that the need cannot dent the reality context. Likewise, when a need becomes overwhelmingly strong, S may exhibit an inability to censor some particular perception he otherwise might not release. Admittedly, such occasions are rarely encountered when the techniques are administered to normal or only slightly disturbed populations whose ego-control remains fairly strong.

Another approach would be to disguise the techniques so that we could be fairly confident that S was not aware of what an adequate response was as opposed to an inadequate one. This approach has been tried in a recent personality inventory by equating the choice of responses for social desirability (Edwards, 1954). Still another method would be to use a full range of stimuli from non-ambiguous to highly ambiguous for any given personality dimension the researcher is interested in tapping. One might then study the strength of relationship between the degree of ambiguity and the response educed. By thus extending the range of stimuli past the current narrow continuum of a test like the TAT, we widen the appropriate range of response. In this way, a person, who employs a rigid "set" to see "good" regardless of the stimulus properties of the cards, is less likely to mask his perceptual shortcomings. If for example, an ego-defensive S decides to see "good" on every picture, he will see highly ambiguous pictures as "good," as well as pictures which are highly structured in a negative sense. The latter responses, however, will be inadequate in terms of the stimulus properties of the cards.

Let us consider two examples of how previous work might be analyzed from the AL viewpoint. Brozek and co-workers (1951) did a study in which a group of volunteers (conscientious objectors) went on a semi-starvation diet for six months. Ss were given a series of tests before the diet started and after several intervals during the course of their regime, followed by testing during the subsequent rehabilitation period. The results were in general negative, in that despite the fact that Ss talked about food all day long, and day-dreamed of huge feasts, very little material relating to food was obtained on any of the projective test measures. Centering on just one test, the Rorschach, let us examine possible reasons for the lack of projection of the need for food. Are there stimulus limitations to the perception of food on the Rorschach (Eriksen, 1954)? There is no direct experimental evidence on this question, but the possibility should not be overlooked.

McClelland and Atkinson (1948) found that the use of ink blots resulted in fewer perceptions of food objects than did blank cards. In view of the high intensity of the hunger need in Brozek's study, however, we must look further for a more complete explanation.

It may be a temptation to ascribe the lack of perception of food on the Rorschach to the fact that the conscientious objectors wanted to "prove" to the Navy officials (psychological examiners) that they were "as tough as the armed forces personnel." The fact that Ss talked freely about their hunger fantasies and even rated their increasing degree of hunger for these same examiners negates this possibility.

If a need (hunger) is manifest, and the expectancy of satisfaction of the need is not immediate, fantasy may serve as a homeostatic mechanism. The adequacy of the fantasy is dependent on the anticipated reduction of the need. Hence, an exceedingly hungry person driving across country will be able to control his hunger more adequately if he believes that food may be obtained in the next town than if he thinks that he will not encounter a restaurant for several hundred miles. Further, the more the fantasy resembles a real life possibility, the more satisfying it is apt to be. Accordingly, for our driver at least, the thought of getting a club sandwich at a local restaurant will probably have more meaning than fantasies relating to eating *pâté de foie gras* at the Waldorf-Astoria.

This statement is in accordance with the conclusions arrived at by Knapp (1948), who stated that as a need increased in intensity there was a "Drang nach Realität."

That is, as a need gets more intense a person's phantasy and perception begins to concern itself more and more with realistic means of satisfying the need. For example, a relatively satiated person may dream of food, but a hungry person begins to dream of ways of getting food—of walking out of the room for example (Knapp, 1948, p. 219).

In short, where a need is strongly present, the closer the fantasy comes to satisfying the need the more readily it will be employed. In a choice between two kinds of fantasy, the fantasy promising a more realistic solution of the need will be the one apt to be employed by the individual concerned. It follows that the free discussion of the satisfaction of hunger needs with an associate, or with the examiner, allows more fantasy gratification than the perception of food on the Rorschach.

There are after all, few limitations to the *verbalization of fantasy* while the perception of fantasy on the Rorschach is limited due to the limitations attendant upon the components of the examiner–S interaction, and the stimulus properties of the cards. Consequently, one could hardly expect to find anyone perceiving a restaurant with himself as owner, on the Rorschach, although this image was verbalized fully by several Ss in their conversations with each other and with the examiner. In sum, *within the possibilities of tension reduction through the use of fantasy, certain outlets take priority. These are the ones which are most applicable for use in approximating a real life situation.* Thus, we would conclude that within the universe of fantasy gratification, the perception of food did not occur, because there was less expectancy of fantasy gratification via the Rorschach medium than by free verbalization. Had Ss been isolated or not permitted to discuss food, it would be predicted that Ss perceptions would contain a great deal of food imagery.

From the adaptation-level viewpoint, the foregoing can be outlined as follows. The stimulus, the Rorschach, is not very structured toward the perception of food, and the background is not very influential in this study for the organism; (a) need is quite high and intense while (b) expectancy of satisfaction is low for two reasons. First, it was known that the experiment would continue for a period of six months. Second, other means of fantasizing were more satisfactory than that afforded by structural limitations of the blots. Referring to our equation, $PR = S^a B^b O^c$, the weighting of the stimulus and background are quite low. The weighting of O also is low due to the fact that the mode of response (perception of food) provides less alteration of the need than that obtainable by free verbalization.

If one wished to study the effect of manipulation of the stimulus, back-ground, and organismic variables on perception, the following factorial design might be employed. The stimulus would be thematic cards which would differ in stimulus-pull for food, one group being high, the other low. The background might be represented by the examiner's inducing both high and low arousal states for the perception of food. The organismic variable might be the differing expectancy of receiving food by two groups of hungry Ss. Thus, one group would expect to receive food immediately after administration of the cards, while the other would be told several further tasks would need to be completed before they were free to leave the testing situation. This design should provide further insight into some of the determinants of the perception of food on a projective card when a need state is high.

It should be noted that the conceptual model sketched here places considerable emphasis on the importance of the stimulus as a determiner of perception. Heretofore, the stimulus properties of the projective techniques have been given short shrift. It was assumed that R-R theory emphasizing the correlation of responses to projective techniques with responses to other situations was the royal road to the understanding of personality (Rosenzweig, 1951). The stimuli of a given test for any particular group of Ss were assumed to be standard so that differences in response were presumed to be due to differences in personality. The exact degree of stimulus pull exerted by the cards was of little concern. There is no reason, however, why TAT and Rorschach cards could not be scaled for dimensions such as aggression and sex as Auld and co-workers (1955), Lesser (1958), and Murstein and associates (1959) have done. The assignment of a quantitative objective value for each card for different personality dimensions should enable us to learn the significant personality correlates of perceptual adherence to stimulus properties of the cards as opposed to the neglect of those same properties. Under present circumstances, if a person has a high hostility score derived from his TAT stories, we do not know whether it reflects his respect for the obviously negatively structured pictures, or is indicative of a projection of hostility to the relatively unstructured ones.

Considered in conjunction with the manipulation of the background and organismic variables, it should be possible to broaden our understanding of the relationship of projective technique behavior to overt behavior by noting the relative strength of each of the variables in both situations.

Further, we have often mouthed the glib phrase, "The response is a function of the total field." Perhaps it is time we converted this literary phrase to quantitative expression and proceeded to measure the components which comprise the "field."

Summary

Ten assumptions commonly held by users of projective techniques are evaluated in terms of relevant evidence, and a conceptual model for studying projective techniques is outlined. The need for measurement of the total field is emphasized.

REFERENCES

ABT, L. A theory of projective psychology. In L. E. ABT & L. BELLAK (Eds.), *Projective psychology.* New York: Knopf, 1950. Pp. 33–66.

ALLPORT, G. W. The trend in motivational theory. *Amer. J. Orthopsychiat.,* 1953, **23**, 107–119.

ATKINSON, J. W. Studies in projective measurement of achievement motivation. Unpublished doctoral dissertation, Univer. of Michigan, 1950.

AULD, F., ERON, L. D., & LAFFAL, J. Application of Guttman's scaling method to the TAT. *Educ. psychol. Measmt,* 1955, **15**, 422–435.

BIJOU, S. W., & KENNY, D. T. The ambiguity of TAT cards. *J. consult. Psychol.,* 1951, **15**, 203–209.

BROZEK, K., GUETZKOW, H., & BALDWIN, M. V. A quantitative study of perception and association in experimental semi-starvation. *J. Pers.,* 1951, **19**, 245–264.

BRUNER, J. S. Perceptual theory and the Rorschach test. *J. Pers.,* 1948, **17**, 157–168.

CARR, A. C. The relation of certain Rorschach variables to expression of affect in the TAT and SCT. *J. proj. Tech.,* 1956, **20**, 137–142.

CLARK, R. A. The projective measurement of experimentally induced levels of sex-

ual motivation. *J. exp. Psychol.,* 1952, **44**, 391–399.

COOK, R. A. Identification and ego defensiveness in thematic apperception. *J. proj. Tech.,* 1953, **17**, 312–319.

DAVIDS, A. Comparison of three methods of personality assessment: direct, indirect, and projective. *J. Pers.,* 1955, **23**, 423–440.

EDWARDS, A. L. *Edwards Personal Preference Schedule, Manual.* New York: Psychological Corp., 1954.

ERIKSEN, C. W. Needs in perception and projective techniques. *J. proj. Tech.,* 1954, **18**, 435–440.

ERON, L. D. A normative study of the Thematic Apperception Test. *Psychol. Monogr.,* 1950, **64**, No. 9 (Whole No. 315).

ERON, L. D. Responses of women to the Thematic Apperception Test. *J. consult. Psychol.,* 1953, **17**, 269–282.

FRANK, L. K. *Projective methods.* Springfield, Ill.: Thomas, 1948.

Funk & Wagnall's new standard dictionary of the English language. New York: Funk & Wagnall's, 1955.

GIBSON, J. J. The non-projective aspects of the Rorschach experiment: IV. The Rorschach blots considered as pictures. *J. soc. Psychol.,* 1956, **44**, 203–206.

GORDON, H. L. A comparative study of

dreams and responses to the TAT I. A need-press analysis. *J. Pers.*, 1953, **22**, 234–253.

HARRISON, R. Studies in the use and validity of the TAT with mentally disordered patients. II. A quantitative validity study. III. Validity by the method of "blind analysis." *Charac. & Pers.*, 1940, **9**, 122–138.

HELSON, H. Adaptation-level as a basis for a quantitative theory of frames of reference. *Psychol. Rev.*, 1948, **55**, 297–313.

HELSON, H. An experimental approach to personality. *Psychiat. res. Rep.*, 1955, **2**, 89–99.

HELSON, H., BLAKE, R. R., MOUTON, J. S., & OLMSTEAD, J. A. Attitudes as adjustments to stimulus, background and residual factors. *J. abnorm. soc. Psychol.*, 1956, **52**, 314–322.

HENRY, W. E. The TAT in the study of culture-personality relations. *Genet. Psychol. Monogr.*, 1947, **35**, 3–135.

KENNY, D. T. & BIJOU, S. W. Ambiguity of pictures and extent of personality factors in fantasy responses. *J. consult. Psychol.*, 1953, **17**, 283–288.

KNAPP, R. H. Experiments in serial reproduction and related aspects of the psychology of rumor. Unpublished doctoral thesis, Harvard Univer., 1948.

LAZARUS, R. S. Ambiguity and non-ambiguity in projective testing. *J. abnorm. soc. Psychol.*, 1953, **48**, 443–445.

LESSER, G. S. Application of Guttman's scaling method to aggressive fantasy in children. *Educ. psychol. Measmt*, 1958, **18**, 543–550.

LEVINE, R., CHEIN, I., & MURPHY, G. The relation of the intensity of a need to amount of perceptual distortion: a preliminary report. *J. Psychol.*, 1942, **13**, 283–293.

LINDZEY, G., & TEJESSY, C. Thematic Apperception Test: indices of aggression in relation to measures of overt and covert behavior. *Amer. J. Orthopsychiat.*, 1956, **26**, 567–576.

MACFARLANE, J. W., & TUDDENHAM, R. D. Problems in the validation of projective techniques. In H. H. ANDERSON & G. L. ANDERSON (Eds.), *An introduction to projective techniques.* New York: Prentice-Hall, 1951. Pp. 26–54.

MURRAY, H. A. *Thematic Apperception Test Manual.* Cambridge: Harvard Univer. Press, 1943.

MURRAY, H. A. Uses of the TAT. *Amer. J. Psychiat.*, 1951, **107**, 577–581.

MURSTEIN, B. I. The projection of hostility on the Rorschach and as a result of ego threat. *J. proj. Tech.*, 1956, **20**, 418–428.

MURSTEIN, B. I. Nonprojective determinants of perception on the TAT. *J. consult. Psychol.*, 1958, **22**, 195–199. (a)

MURSTEIN, B. I. The relationship of stimulus ambiguity on the TAT to the productivity of themes. *J. consult. Psychol.*, 1958, **22**, 348. (b)

MURSTEIN, B. I. Review of Klopfer, Bruno and others, *Developments in the Rorschach Technique.* Vol. II. *Fields of Application. J. proj. Tech.*, 1958, **22**, 248–250. (c)

MURSTEIN, B. I. Some determinants of the perception of hostility. *J. consult. Psychol.*, 1958, **22**, 65–69. (d)

MURSTEIN, B. I. A conceptual model of projective techniques applied to stimulus variations with thematic techniques. *J. consult. Psychol.*, 1959, **23**, 3–14.

MURSTEIN, B. I., COULTER, W., BOWDISH, C., DAVID, C., FISHER, D., FURTH, H., & HANSEN, I. A study of scaling methods applied to the TAT for the dimension of hostility. Univer. of Portland, 1959 (mimeographed).

MURSTEIN, B. I., & WHEELER, J. I., JR. The projection of hostility on the Rorschach and Thematic Stories Test. *J. clin. Psychol.*, 1959, **15**, 316–319.

MURSTEIN, B. I. The effect of long-term illness of children on the emotional adjustment of parents. *Child Develop.*, 1960, **31**, 157–171.

PIOTROWSKI, Z. A. *Perceptanalysis.* New York: Macmillan, 1957.

PITTLUCK, P. The relation between aggressive fantasy and overt behavior. Unpublished doctoral dissertation, Yale Univer., 1950.

RADER, G. E. The prediction of overt aggressive verbal behavior from Rorschach content. *J. proj. Tech.*, 1957, **21**, 294–306.

ROSENZWEIG, S. Idiodynamics in personality theory with special reference to projective methods. *Psychol. Rev.*, 1951, **58**, 213–223.

ROTTER, J. *Social learning and clinical psychology.* New York: Prentice-Hall, 1954.

SARASON, S. B. *The clinical interaction.* New York: Harper, 1954.

SCHAFER, R. *Psychoanalytic interpretation in Rorschach testing.* New York: Grune & Stratton, 1954.

SCODEL, A., & LIPETZ, M. E. TAT hostility and psychopathology. *J. proj. Tech.,* 1957, 21, 161–165.

SHATIN, L. Rorschach adjustment and the TAT. *J. proj. Tech.,* 1953, 17, 92–101.

SHATIN, L. Relationships between the Rorschach and the TAT. *J. proj. Tech.,* 1955, 19, 317–331.

SHNEIDMAN, E. S. Some relationships between the Rorschach technique and other psychodiagnostic tests. In B. KLOPFER (Ed.), *Developments in the Rorschach technique.* Vol. II. *Fields of application.* New York: World Book, 1956. Pp. 595–642.

SINGER, W. B., & YOUNG, P. T. Studies in affective reaction. I. A new affective rating-scale. *J. gen. Psychol.,* 1941, 24, 281–301.

SMITH, J. R., & COLEMAN, J. C. The relationship between manifestations of hostility in projective tests and overt behavior. *J. proj. Tech.,* 1956, 20, 326–334.

STERN, E., & HORINSON, S. Concordances et divergences du test de Rorschach et du Thematic Apperception de Murray. *Proc. Int. Orthoped. Cong.,* II. Amsterdam, 1949. Pp. 448–455.

SYMONDS, P. M. *Adolescent fantasy: an investigation of the picture-story method of personality study.* New York: Columbia Univer. Press, 1949.

ULLMANN, L. P. Productivity and the clinical use of TAT cards. *J. proj. Tech.,* 1957, 21, 399–403.

WEBB, W. B., & HILDEN, A. H. Verbal and intellectual ability as factors in projective test results. *J. proj. Tech.,* 1953, 17, 102–103.

WEISSKOPF, E. A. An experimental study of the effect of brightness and ambiguity on projection in the TAT. *J. Psychol.,* 1950, 29, 407–416. (a)

WEISSKOPF, E. A. A transcendence index as a proposed measure in the TAT. *J. Psychol.,* 1950, 29, 379–390. (b)

WIRT, R. D. Ideational expression of hostile impulses. *J. consult. Psychol.,* 1956, 20, 185–189.

Levels of Behavior in Psychodiagnosis with Special Reference to the Picture-Frustration Study

Saul Rosenzweig

In both the clinical and experimental analysis of personality the level of behavior represented in a subject's responses is psychologically crucial. The distinction in question is implied whenever the overt behavior of the person is explained away as a facade for something more honest and direct which he

Reprinted by permission of the publisher and author from *The American Journal of Orthopsychiatry,* 1950, **20**, 63–72.

is unwilling to express, or as a cover for deeper things unknown to him. While the problem has received some recognition in the interpretation of dreams and in the projective methods of personality appraisal, it has not as yet had any clear conceptual delineation or concerted empirical study. To formulate and illustrate the general issue is the purpose of the present paper. The accompanying chart depicts the hypothesis of three such levels of behavior with psychodiagnosis as a point of departure.

The relationship of these levels to typical methods of personality assessment may first be indicated. It is possible conveniently to classify these methods as *subjective, objective,* or *projective* (1) according to whether the subject takes himself as a direct object of observation, whether the observer takes the subject as a direct object of observation, or whether the subject in cooperation with the observer "looks the other way" at some ego-neutral object. The subjective methods include the questionnaire or inventory and the autobiography, in both of which the individual expresses from his standpoint opinions or judgments about himself or about other objects and situations.

The objective methods comprise such direct observations of gross behavior as can be made through one-way screens and such more covert measures as become possible by employing physiological indicators, e.g., the psychogalvanometer. The projective methods embrace, among other instruments, the Rorschach technique, the Thematic Apperception Test, word association, play technique, and motor-expressive types of performance like handwriting, gait and voice.

The subjective, objective and projective methods characteristically differ in the superficiality or depth, in the censorship or ingenuousness of their products. It thus becomes possible to depict certain levels of behavior which will here be numerically designated. To be noted at the outset, however, is the fact that these levels are not dependent upon and not exclusively associated with one or another of the psychodiagnostic methods. A preferential, not a definitive relationship, is assumed.

Level I typically involves a certain

CHART I.   LEVELS OF RESPONSE IN TYPICAL METHODS OF PERSONALITY APPRAISAL

Level	Psychodiagnostic Methods	Behavior Elicited in Test Situation	Mode of Prediction
I	*Subjective:* Subject takes self as direct object of observation; e.g., inventory or questionnaire, opinion or attitude poll, autobiography.	*Opinion:* Subject gives self-critical or censored responses in keeping with his concepts of what is right or proper, intelligent or socially acceptable.	*Extrapolation* to other self-consciously critical situations.
II	*Objective:* Examiner takes subject as object of observation; e.g., time-sampling observations, miniature life situations, physiological measures, some rating scales.	*Overt:* Subject functions as he observably would in the corresponding actual situations of everyday life, thus providing a sample of his gross behavior.	*Extrapolation* to similar externally defined situations.
III	*Projective:* Both subject and examiner "look the other way" at some ego-neutral object; e.g., Rorschach, TAT, word association, play technique; expressive movement (handwriting, gait, voice).	*Implicit:* Subject responds impersonally in terms of unconscious or latent attitudes, feelings or thoughts.	*Interpretation* from manifest content to underlying factors.

amount of self-critical scrutiny or censorship which, if neglected in interpretation, gives rise to "opinion errors" (3). Even when dishonesty is not involved—and it may be—self-deception, courtesy or formality affects the responses made. The subject functions, in other words, according to a rather deliberately invoked standard of what he considers to be right or proper, appropriate or otherwise acceptable to himself or others in the particular situation and, if necessary, he may distort his original reaction tendencies to fit these opinions. Sometimes it is actually in an expression of opinion that behavior at this level emerges or is elicited. To characterize both opinion-modified behavior and statements of opinion at Level I the term *opinion behavior* is employed.

Level III, at the other extreme, includes reactions which in their full significance are usually denied expression (sometimes through conscious censorship, more often because of deeper-lying repressive forces) but which achieve some partial or symbolized manifestation under favorable conditions. To evoke such manifestations special techniques that encourage the free play of "imagination" are required—free association as employed by the psychoanalyst and the projective methods used by the psychodiagnostician. Since the responses here elicited become meaningful only when interpreted to represent what underlies the manifest content, *implicit behavior* is said to occur at this level. A subdivision of the third level is indicated according to whether the implicit determinants of the observed behavior refer to *content* or *style*. By *style* is meant the more formal ways or modes of the person's performance while *content* refers to autistic behavior or fantasy closely related to particular goals or drives.

Level II entails behavior which is not, on the one hand, self-consciously censored, and which does not, on the other, represent a free play of imagina-

tion that practically disregards reality. What emerges here is a sample of the subject's usual observable performance under external conditions defined in common-sense terms. As thus understood *overt behavior* is elicited at this level.

It should be noted before proceeding further that though it is possible and desirable for purposes of exposition to delineate the three levels and to separate them from each other with a certain degree of cogency, in the actual behavior of the person, whether in a test situation or in everyday life, the levels are apt to mingle and merge kaleidoscopically to a degree that defies analysis. Moreover, it sometimes happens, as will be illustrated later, that the difference among the levels is not maintained; e.g., Level I may coincide with Level II when the subject characteristically behaves in everyday life with the same self-critical censorship prevalent in the special conditions of observation. The heuristic value of the classification transcends these seeming exceptions.

What are the possibilities of predicting at each level? It may be hypothetically assumed that Level I, however much it may represent self-critical or even deliberate falsification in certain respects, permits insight into the subject's *defenses* as these have developed in *his particular culture*. In other words, to know in detail how and why he censors his responses is to have obtained significant information about him. This statement becomes more meaningful in the light of everyday knowledge that persons even of one culture have individually characteristic concepts of the acceptable and unacceptable. Information about these differences is psychodiagnostically valuable and makes it possible to predict by *extrapolation* what the subject's performance is apt to be in other self-consciously critical situations. In addition, an understanding of the subject at Level I throws light upon the overt behavior of Level II under certain conditions of mixture. Occasionally even Levels I and III may have significant relationships, especially when the standards invoked at I derive in part from unconscious inhibitions at III.

At Level II itself prediction proceeds by *extrapolation* from the specimen in question to similar externally defined situations. It is, in other words, assumed that if a representative sample of the subject's gross behavior is available, it may reasonably be inferred on a statistical basis what he would observably do in other circumstances of the same "objective" variety. An inductive process from the observed to the unobserved is thus involved, on the assumption that what has occurred with sufficient frequency to be representative will occur again at the same level under similar circumstances. Such prediction obviously depends not at all upon the interpretation of motives or other underlying forces that may have been operative to produce the overt behavior; the approach is therefore—in the Lewinian terminology—*phenotypical*.

Finally, the implicit behavior of Level III is signficant predictively not by permitting extrapolation from the observed to the as yet unobserved on the basis of sampling but by reliance upon certain *interpretations* which here play a special role. Level III data are always subjected to a type of translation that is encountered in dream interpretation— from the manifest to the latent content —and in some of the projective techniques. The translation in question follows, of course, assumed transformations of a corresponding sort within the personality and proceeds upon the assumption of what in the Lewinian terminology would be called *genotypical* factors. To a certain extent the interpretations that figure at Level III aim at the prediction of overt behavior; from the manifest or projective content at Level III they invoke intervening variables from which the observable or overt performance at Level II may be inferred. Since these variables are considered to be more

fundamental and stable than the descriptive ones at II, prediction of the interpretive type is regarded by those who practice it as more reliable than the exclusively extrapolative type.

This exposition of the predictive relevance of the levels unmistakably demonstrates again their necessary interweaving in the understanding of individual behavior. Any comprehensive approach to personality must include them all. The essential problem hence becomes that of determining the principles according to which the levels influence each other, now by opposition and now in cooperation. To have distinguished the levels makes it possible to approach their synthesis at a later stage of inquiry.

If an attempt is made to achieve the beginnings of such a synthesis, a first step is to examine the manner in which the three levels, despite the preceding expository exclusiveness, may appear in any one of the typical psychodiagnostic instruments—subjective, objective or projective. Since the point is crucially relevant to the projective methods especially, illustrations will be drawn from that field.

These techniques were, of course, designed to illuminate Level III—to elicit knowledge regarding the unconscious determinants of behavior. It was in such a tradition that Jung adapted the word association technique as a projective tool of psychodiagnosis, Rorschach developed the method that bears his name, and Morgan and Murray constructed the Thematic Apperception Test. In practice, however, the assumption that Level III is exclusively tapped by the projective methods is not substantiated and if taken literally often results in misleading predictions.

An example from the Thematic Apperception Test may first be adduced. Let it be assumed that a subject tells a story in which he has identified with a hero who is involved in some relationship to a mother figure and in which the mother is depicted as a very kind and generous person. In such a production the subject may be functioning at Level I and reporting what he thinks is the socially approved conception of mothers—they are supposed to be kind and generous. In actuality he may be feeling and concealing considerable hostility toward his own mother. Again, he may be functioning at Level II and stating what he experiences consciously and demonstrates observably in relation to his own mother. Finally, if valid at Level III, the story would be revealing tender feelings of attachment, possibly even incestuous, toward a mother whom in real life the subject might reject with considerable conscious hostility. Needless to say, the interpretation that would follow from the mentioned production would vary greatly according to the level which was actually operative.

The status of the Rorschach method in the present formulation is somewhat more involved. Insofar as this technique is assumed to sample the subject's characteristic perceptions of his environment, it must be considered to entail Level II in its formal scoring. The psychological analogy on which, for instance, it is stated that a person who consistently perceives the blots as wholes is apt in everyday life to size up situations in abstract and general terms rather than by primary reference to practical details represents the extrapolation from the observed to the unobserved which has already been assigned to the overt level above described. But it is possible also to construe the Rorschach method as depending essentially upon that subdivision of Level III concerned with the style or manner of behavior (rather than with content). From this point of view the responses scored in formal terms would not be taken as direct samples of the person's everyday behavior but would instead be thought to have some representative value; e.g.,

color would on this basis be held to stand for emotion in a symbolized, rather than a literal, sense. Which of these two views of the Rorschach method is more adequate present knowledge does not indicate. But there is less room for difference of construction regarding other aspects of this technique. There is, for instance, little doubt that Level III figures in the autistic content of many movement responses. Similarly Level I is involved in those associations that are either completely rejected by the subject or emerge in modified form after relatively long delays. The experienced examiner has some cues at his disposal for distinguishing differences in the level of Rorschach responses, e.g., in respect to the superficiality or depth (consciousness or unconsciousness) of anxiety, but the criteria have not been experimentally established and are far from being completely reliable in clinical practice.

If attention is now turned to the Picture-Frustration (P-F) Study (2, 4, 5) it becomes possible to demonstrate perhaps even more clearly than has been done in the preceding examples the relevance of the depicted levels. The social situations pictured in the P-F tend readily to set the stage for either self-conscious and censored responses, or verbal behavior like that which the subject would actually demonstrate in everyday life, or inhibited thoughts and feelings that appear only in the projective guise of the instrument. The Study—to express the characterization otherwise—makes it possible for the subject to identify himself with the represented anonymous person at any one of the three levels even though, it is true, the instructions are intended to favor the third. What the individual does in construing the instructions thus becomes of great importance since the projective nature of the technique makes it necessary to follow where the subject leads instead of imposing upon him any pre-established set that the examiner has designed. Failure to recognize the possibility of differences in identification level can result, as in the case of the Rorschach method and of the Thematic Apperception Test, in erroneous interpretations. To make matters even worse it must be acknowledged that the set assumed by the subject may be kept by him during the examination either consistently or inconsistently.

An example from item 13 in the P-F Study (which depicts one person approaching another to keep an appointment only to learn that the previously made arrangement has been abruptly terminated) may be useful. Some subjects respond with "That's quite all right" and in so doing reflect what they believe would be the polite or otherwise correct behavior in the situation. While such a response could actually represent what the subject would say or do in the circumstances, it may signify only an opinion of what should be said or done. In the former case Level II would be indicated; in the latter, Level I. The very same words can thus have two quite different interpretive meanings. Again, the item may elicit the response "Why didn't you let me know?" or, similarly, "You mean and inconsiderate person." Retorts of this kind may, of course, be made by some individuals in the scene depicted but it would seem more reasonable to suppose that such unrestrained expressions of aggression would be reserved for special and perhaps intimate occasions, remaining inhibited, if experienced at all, in the usual social situation. If the former circumstances apply, Level II would be indicated; if the latter, Level III. Different predictions would obviously be entailed in the two cases.

It should once more be recognized that the distinction among the levels is not always hard and fast. Level I in the subject's test performance may at the same time reflect his self-critical approach in everyday life, Levels I and

II then being coincident. It is likewise possible for Levels II and III to be indistinguishable in the behavior of certain psychopathic personalities or even of unusually free and untrammeled individuals who do not function according to conventional standards. It thus becomes essential for the making of definitive interpretations not only to know at what level the subject has performed but also to have information about the integration of his personality in terms of these very levels.

When one approaches the interpretation of total scores in the Picture-Frustration Study, a similar problem exists. If it be supposed that a subject has obtained an extrapunitive score of 90 per cent—twice the normal mean—it still remains to determine whether this markedly deviant result represents a first, second or third level of reaction. If Level I were involved, this very elevated extrapunitive score would reflect an unusually aggressive person who was, moreover, consciously and with full acceptance by his ego oriented toward society in the overtly hostile fashion disclosed by the Study. If this same score represented Level II, it would be necessary to conclude that the subject would perform likewise in real life though he might not consciously acknowledge or be aware of such behavior when it was occurring. Others would observe his aggressiveness but he might not know that he responded in this fashion. Finally, if the assumption of Level III were made, the 90 per cent extrapunitive score mentioned would mean neither that the person consciously endorsed hostility as a social orientation nor that this degree of aggressiveness was characteristic of his overt performance; instead it would be justifiable to infer from the projected hostility that the subject harbored considerable repressed aggression that could be expected to appear in various unconscious equivalents—symptoms, dreams, etc.

In the same fashion it is necessary

to interpret differently, according to the indications, an elevated impunitive score, say, one that reaches 60 per cent instead of the average normal score of 30 per cent. At Level I such a score would imply that the person had an ego ideal in which consideration of others, tactfulness and courtesy dictated much of his behavior in frustrating circumstances of the kind represented in the P-F; it would not follow that he would in actual practice exemplify this approach. One would have learned only that the subject believed in politeness and kindliness and, moreover, was perhaps attempting to impress the examiner in those terms. The same score at Level II would signify that the subject actually did in everyday life behave with an unusual degree of tact and consideration though it would not be known from this score alone whether residual aggression had or had not been repressed. If the mentioned score represented a third-level orientation, it would be appropriate to conclude that while this individual had highly conciliatory attitudes toward others, his overt behavior could still express considerable hostility, perhaps on some symptomatic basis. The same score would, therefore, have quite different predictive significations depending upon the judgment made as to level.

This discussion of levels in the P-F Study obviously raises serious questions regarding the interpretations which are justified after a subject's record has been scored and summarized. As a working assumption the P-F Study is ordinarily taken to have validity at Level II unless there is specific information to the contrary. The reason for this assumption lies in the facts of clinical experience, such as they are. Any other assumption would be harder to justify. At the same time it must be recognized that there is no guarantee of correctness for this working assumption, and it thus becomes incumbent upon the careful examiner to seek from whatever sources he can all possible supplementary information as to the actual level adopted by the subject in his test performance.

How can such supplementary knowledge regarding level be elicited? It is suggested that to this end the usual inquiry in relation to the scoring of the individual items be extended at the very conclusion of the examination to include several questions on general orientation. One may thus ask, "What was the basis on which you gave your responses as you went through the Study?" If this indefinite prod fails to elicit the desired information as to level, it may be appropriate to ask more directly, "Have you ever been in any of the situations shown in the pictures?" One might sometimes proceed even more pointedly to ask whether the subject was thinking of himself or not as he gave his responses to the various items. A frank admission that the Study was taken at Level I—"I thought you wanted me to put down what I would say"—leaves little room for interpretation at Level III though both I and II are still possible. Naive surprise that the replies were supposed to have any self-reference would reflect an adherence to the instructions favoring interpretation at Levels II or III. Statements to the effect that the responses were framed to exemplify what a person *should* say in the pictured situations would rather definitely imply Level I. The subject's replies to the interrogation itself would, of course, also have to be interpreted since rationalization might figure prominently in the usual case; but it would seem wiser to ask one or two questions for what they may be worth than to forego altogether the limited advantages of an inquiry.

Until experimental investigation of the various possible levels of response in the P-F has been completed—and some such studies are in progress—the working assumption of Level II as supplemented by clinical inquiry will have to suffice. But only on the foundation of such experimental evidence will it be possible to obtain reasonably sound interpretation. In the meantime two cautions should be observed: (1) In the clinical use of the P-F Study reliance upon this instrument alone is hazardous. Included in a battery of instruments and interpreted in connection with interview and case history data it can, as it were, "find its own level" and add its bit to the total picture. (2) Research efforts related to the validity of the P-F Study should take seriously into account not only the range of possible levels at which the individual subject could have responded but also the levels represented in the independent criteria of validity. Negative results in such investigations may otherwise readily represent errors of definition in respect to level just as positive ones may prove to be inconclusive.

As an example of an experimental design for investigating levels, the following outline of a project that would involve the P-F Study may be offered.

1. The P-F Study would be administered in the usual way. A full inquiry would be conducted.

2. To tap Level I a questionnaire comprising a variety of verbally described situations corresponding to the items of the P-F would on another occasion be employed, the same subject now being asked to indicate the responses he would, in his opinion, make if he were reacting according to his ideas of fitness and propriety.

3. To elicit Level II arrangements would be made for directly observing the subject in life situations like those pictured in the P-F. It might be possible to improvise such situations or perhaps to observe the person in his natural environment until these or similar incidents occurred.

4. To approximate Level III one might use one or more of the following devices: free association to various items of the P-F Study or to the responses of the subject on these items; exploration under sodium amytal with the P-F as a basis; hypnosis with discussion of feelings and emotions in frustrating situations like those represented in the P-F. An attempt might even be made to employ subjects who were undergoing psychoanalysis, the analyst serving as collaborator.

Once the data from these various sources had been obtained, it would be possible to determine how and to what degree the responses in the P-F Study agreed with the behavior observed under the conditions for Levels I, II and III.

In conclusion it should be reiterated that it is not alone the P-F Study which is in need of investigation with respect to levels of response. The projective techniques in general require such research if we are to obtain any clear understanding of their scope and limitations. In such work the concept of levels would have both methodological implications, as regards the role of psychodiagnostic instruments and their relationship to each other, and systematic ones, with reference to problems of personality integration.

On the methodological side one obvious value of such investigations lies in the possibility of their disclosing how the projective techniques are related to other devices for the study of personality. Since in the end it is necessary to recognize the psychodiagnostic value of responses at all three levels, and of the subjective, objective and projective instruments that typically exemplify these levels, knowledge regarding the interrelationships of the methods and hence of the levels should go a long way toward overcoming the present artificial lines of separation.

Research on levels also has important systematic implications for an understanding of personality integration. A strongly favored and consistent level of response may very well represent a distinctive personality characteristic. The guardedness of the person who typically adopts Level I, the naivete of the Level II approach, and the uninhibited expressiveness of the Level III orientation may serve as examples. Similarly the relationships among levels of response in the same subject could reasonably be expected to reflect the nature and degree of his particular personality organization.

Summary

In the psychodiagnostic situation subjects may respond at various levels of which three are usefully distinguished and result in behavior characterized as either *opinion, overt* or *implicit*. The relevance of this distinction to the typical methods of appraising personality is readily schematized (subjective, objective, projective) but even more important is the mixture of levels in any one of the typical psychodiagnostic approaches. Because of the crucial importance of these levels in the projective techniques, the basis for determining the level of response in these methods is a chief desideratum of future research. The Picture-Frustration Study readily lends itself for illustrative purposes since a subject may here respond at any of the three levels and the interpretative validity of the test will depend upon the presumed level of response. Investigation of this topic is urgently needed both for validating the projective methods and for gaining systematic knowledge about the intergration of personality.

REFERENCES

1. ROSENZWEIG, S. "Investigating and Appraising Personality." Chap. 18 in *Methods of Psychology* (T. G. ANDREWS, Ed.), Wiley, New York, 1948. See alternatively Available Methods for Studying Personality. *J. Psychol.*, 28: 345–368, 1949.
2. ROSENZWEIG, S. The Picture-Association Method and Its Application in a Study of Reactions to Frustration. *J. Pers.*, 14: 3–23, 1946.
3. ROSENZWEIG, S. A Suggestion for Making Verbal Personality Tests More Valid. *Psychol. Rev.*, 41: 400–401, 1934.
4. ROSENZWEIG, S., E. E. FLEMING, and H. J. CLARKE. Revised Scoring Manual for the Rosenzweig Picture-Frustration Study. *J. Psychol.*, 24: 165–208, 1947.
5. ROSENZWEIG, S., E. E. FLEMING, and L. ROSENZWEIG. The Children's Form of the Rosenzweig Picture-Frustration Study. *Ibid.*, 26: 141–191, 1948.

Some Problems of Validation of Projective Techniques

Mary D. Ainsworth

The process of validation of projective techniques is in many ways more similar

Reprinted by permission of the publisher and author from the *British Journal of Medical Psychology*, 1951, **24,** 151–161.

to the familiar scientific process of validation of hypotheses than to validation of a test. Projective techniques are used as tests of personality, and manifest a number of similarities to tests of cognitive processes, but the differences are sufficiently crucial for it to be better to consider them as another genus among the family of appraisal methods. The chief similarity is that all individuals are observed in a controlled and standardized situation, in which the structural characteristics of the individual are to be considered the independent variable and the resultant performance the dependent variable; but here the resemblance ends. Tests of cognitive processes are essentially quantitative, while projective techniques do not lend themselves easily to quantification. The usual psychological test deals with one variable or one function, and attempts to provide a means of placing all tested individuals on a continuum with respect to that function. The projective technique deals with "n" functions or variables, and attempts to describe the individual in terms of a dynamic pattern of interrelated functions or variables. This multiplicity of variables constitutes the most important difference, presents the greatest problem of validation and therefore should be dealt with more fully.

All projective techniques are based on the fundamental hypothesis that the dynamic structure of the individual, which we call his personality (in interaction with the structure of the field), determines the way the individual perceives his world. To the extent that the individual has learned to communicate with his fellows in terms of some kind of symbol system, the fact that he uses the same symbol that others use with respect to an object, tends to cloak the fact that his perception of that object is distinctively individual, and a product of his own unique experience and development as well as a function of the stimulus provided by the object. Projective techniques attempt to high-light the contribution to perception of the inner dynamic structure of the individual by employing stimulus objects which are sufficiently ambiguous for there to be

no obvious applicable common symbol upon which all are agreed. To observe an individual in such a situation is to obtain a sample of his behaviour from which can be deduced his own individual ways of perceiving the situation. On the assumption that the personal determinants of his perception are something which he carries around with him from situation to situation, certain generalizations are made from this sample concerning the customary ways in which he sees his world, on the basis of which certain predictions may be ventured as to the way he will behave towards it.

With reference to the great multiplicity of projective materials, the comment has often been made that anything can be a projective technique. In the sense that predictions may be made from any sample of behaviour, this seems a justifiable statement. Indeed, the experienced psychologist reporting on an intelligence test performance says much more about the individual than a statement of I.Q. From observing the quality of performance and the test behaviour he makes generalizations and predictions very similar in kind to those made from one of the projective techniques. Any experienced clinician, whether from interview, test or simple observation, makes such generalizations. For the most part the basis upon which these generalizations are made is not communicable; it is something that can be learned only through experience. The unique contribution of projective techniques is that they attempt to provide a basis of generalization from performance in a standardized situation, which translates the intuitive hypotheses of the clinician into the form of communicable hypotheses which can be used and checked by others.

Projective techniques produce an unwieldy mass of qualitative observations which must be transmuted into some manipulable form before it can yield valid information about the individual personality. Hence an important first aspect of the technique is the method of analysis of data. Its basis is classificatory; even if the term "scoring system" is applied, as in the Rorschach technique, this implies classification rather than measurement. The basis of classification has been developed in close relationship to the interpretive hypotheses. However, with classification the problem is not one of validity but reliability. It is important to communicate the principles or rules of classification in a clear-cut way so that others may repeat it, and thus apply the appropriate interpretative hypotheses in a pertinent manner. It may be mentioned in passing that each of the better known sets of projective materials has various methods of analysis, some more widely accepted than others.

The second aspect of a projective technique consists of a body of interpretative hypotheses attached to the various classifications of responses. Different sets of interpretative hypotheses have been presented by different workers with the same type of projective material. With the Rorschach ink-blot material, we associate not only the name of Rorschach (1921) himself, but also Klopfer & Kelly (1942), Beck (1944), Hertz (1942) and others, to mention only those most prominent in America at the present time. Although all have a certain common core of interpretation and that derived chiefly from Rorschach himself, all have modified the basis of interpretation and added hypotheses from their own observation. Similarly, although Murray (1938, 1943) first presented the Thematic Appercep-tion Test materials together with a method of analysis and basis of interpretation, each exponent has modified both to a greater or lesser extent, to name a few: Henry (1947), Tomkins (1947), Wyatt (1947), Bellak (1948). To an even more striking extent variation in interpretative hypotheses is true of the Szondi test (1947), for Deri (1949) who has been instrumental in introducing the

test to the English-speaking world has made very radical departures in interpretation, from Szondi's constitutional typology to one thoroughgoing in its psycho-analytic base. Perhaps it would be better to apply the term technique to the methods of analysis and interpretation than to the materials themselves. Thus there is a variety of Rorschach techniques, of T.A.T. techniques, of techniques for analysis of drawings and paintings, even though there is much overlap among all the techniques and especially among those pertaining to certain materials.

That there should be differences between the hypotheses of various workers inevitably follows from the fact that these hypotheses in the first instance grew up empirically, from clinical observations and experience. That there should be a large common core follows partly as a suggestion of validity of the hypotheses as formulated separately by different workers, and partly because there is a rapidly accumulating literature of both clinical impressions and systematic and controlled scientific observations which has been influential in casting certain of the hypotheses into common mould. But the fact remains that the task of validation pertains to the various sets of interpretative hypotheses rather than to any prototype interpretation originally attached to the test material itself.

Evidence of invalidity of any hypothesis or set of hypotheses cannot be said to apply to the value of the test material as a method of investigating personality. For example, Fisher & Fisher (1950) chose to test a set of hypotheses put forward by Machover (1949) regarding the diagnosis of strong paranoid attitudes and paranoid pathology from drawings of the human figure. "Figure drawings of thirty-two paranoid schizophrenics were evaluated by means of a detailed atomistic analysis and also by means of a total impressionistic analysis for the presence of paranoid trends and it was found that the majority of these drawings did not fall under the category of paranoid in terms of the criteria implicit in each method." They conclude that "the total results suggest that it is precarious to accept most of the current assumptions regarding figure drawing analysis (particularly as expounded by Machover) without the confirmation of further research." They do not conclude that figure-drawing analysis is an invalid approach to personality, which permits of no valid assumptions or hypotheses. They certainly overgeneralize from the investigation of one set of hypotheses by one worker, namely, Machover, but at least they do acknowledge that hypotheses pertain to the person who advances them and are not inherent in the approach to personality evaluation through figure drawing.

With the foregoing as introduction, let us now consider the major problems of validation of projective techniques. These problems may be classified under three main headings: (*a*) those pertaining to appropriate use of the test in validation research, (*b*) those pertaining to reliability, and (*c*) those pertaining to outside criteria against which hypotheses are to be checked.

Problems Relating to the Appropriate Use of the Technique in Research

The first and most basic general problem of the validation of projective techniques is that of framing the research so as to investigate the technique as it is actually used, that is to say, to investigate the interpretative hypothesis so that conclusions may be drawn regarding the validity of the hypothesis as used clinically in appraisal of the individual personality.

As aspects of this problem we have a number of subsidiary problems, some of which will be discussed beginning with the ones which seem simplest.

(1) Projectives are generally used as individual rather than group tests, and interpretation involves an intensive investigation of the personality of the individual which is very time-consuming. Odom (1950) has recently investigated the time required to do a Rorschach examination, for example, and finds that the time required to do an average test, including administration and all steps of analysis and report, is a little more than four hours, although sometimes less than two hours or more than eight hours may be required, depending upon the complexity of the response pattern of the individual. Although presumably beginners may take much longer than this, the experts (and he quotes Beck, Klopfer and Hertz) feel that the figures quoted are a conservative estimate even as applied to themselves. Experience with other projective techniques supports the assumption that similar figures would apply to T.A.T., the Szondi test, to analysis of drawings, and probably to all the other most important methods of appraisal. With this time involvement for a single subject, it is easy to understand why so many investigations are based on a number of subjects falling somewhat short of the ideal for proper sampling and statistical measures of significance.

Some workers attempt to overcome this limitation by using group methods of administration and abbreviated and necessarily mechanical methods of analysis and interpretation. For example, Lazarus (1949) investigated the phenomenon of colour shock in the Rorschach in an otherwise well-designed test-retest experiment in which subjects were asked to respond to both the regular chromatic series of blots and to a special achromatic series. Group administration was used and quantitative findings quoted for each scoring category. The various criteria of colour shock did not appear significantly more frequently with the chromatic than with the achromatic series, which seems to throw doubt on the whole basis of colour shock in Rorschach interpretation. This may be so, but the fact remains that he has not demonstrated this with reference to colour shock as judged from a careful qualitative analysis of the performance of an individual with the materials administered individually as is usually the case. A similar criticism applies to the work of Sappenfield & Buker (1949) on the validity of the Rorschach percentage of responses to the last three colour cards as an index of basic responsiveness to environmental stimulation.

(2) A considerable degree of expertness, based on special training and experience, is necessary before the research worker can assimilate the communicable basis of interpretation of any one of the projective techniques and thus use the technique as it is used in clinical practice. This degree of expertness is unfortunately not common among those who have a good working knowledge of experimental and statistical techniques in the field of psychology, and indeed, one might say, vice versa. Not only do statistical experts such as Cronbach (1949a) shudder at the inadequate statistical techniques used in investigations of projective techniques, but the experts in projectives shudder equally at the fact that many investigations simply are not pertinent to the interpretative hypotheses as used by the expert because of the inadequate understanding of the investigator. This can be true even among the experts themselves, to say nothing of the worker who is almost totally untrained in projectives.

An example of a blunder at the expert level may be quoted from the noteworthy Rorschach investigation of Buhler, Buhler & Lefever (1948), which included protocols from 518 subjects spread over a number of different clinical groupings including three groups of normals. This investigation was intended as basic to standardizing a quantitative Rorschach score. However, in comparing the various clinical groupings, an attempt was made to check the validity of certain interpretative hypotheses put forward by Klopfer (Klopfer & Kelly, 1942), whose method of analysis and interpretation Buhler claimed to follow. On the whole these hypotheses seemed to be interpreted correctly, but with respect to one there seems to be room for criticism. Buhler attributed to Klopfer the hypothesis that a high $F\%$ (a high percentage of responses determined only by the form of the ink-blot and not by colour, shading or movement) indicates a high degree of intellectual or rational control, and hence may be considered a sign of strong superego development. If this hypothesis is true, she argues, clinical groupings characterized by strong superego development, such as obsessive-compulsives and hysterics, ought to show high $F\%$, and those, such as psychopaths who have meagre superego development, should show low $F\%$. Although obsessive-compulsives as a group did indeed support this version of the hypothesis, hysterics were found to have low $F\%$, and, perhaps more serious, psychopaths were found to have high $F\%$. On the face of it this seems to dispose of Klopfer's hypothesis. However, the Klopfer technique does not judge intellectual and rational control on the basis of $F\%$ alone. Indeed, it specifies that this judgment is to be made in the light of a number of other considerations, notably the degree of careful match between the form of the percept named and the form of the blot. The kind of vague, cheap or inaccurate form responses characteristic of feeble-minded subjects, young children, or psychopaths are specifically not indicative of intellectual or rational control, according to his original hypothesis. Thus Buhler did not put Klopfer's hypothesis to the test, since she did not take account of the form-level of the $F\%$. If this error can be made by one of Buhler's stature, it can be imagined how likely it is for the research worker who has had little training or experience with the technique in question, and who can scarcely be expected to formulate an investigation to test the validity of a set of complex and highly interrelated hypotheses.

(3) The personality appraisal which is the end-result of analysis of performance of an individual with a projective material represents the integration of a large number of different interpretative hypotheses, each one of which may influence the applicability of the others. Projective techniques are holistic rather than atomistic. That is not to imply that the interpretation is based on a total, unanalysed impression growing out of clinical experience. On the contrary, a great deal of highly differentiated perception on the worker's part has gone into the analysis. But the final interpretation is in the form of a dynamic sketch of the way the personality functions, which is a highly integrated and articulated whole. This introduces a very serious difficulty when it comes to validation, for in our tried-and-true method of scientific investigation one variable at a time is explored through a range of variation. The beginner, when learning a projective technique, is first presented with a series of discrete hypotheses attached to the various classifications set up in the method of analysis. At first glance, these present themselves as hopeful starting points for validation research. But the beginner soon learns that each discrete hypothesis is applicable only within a certain range of configurations, and modified by the configuration.

To exemplify this problem in perhaps its simplest context, let us consider the question of assessing intelligence from the Rorschach performance, which is a frequent aspect of interpretation by Rorschach workers. Rorschach originally suggested that certain features are indicators of a high level of intelligence, including a large percentage of clearly visualized forms $(F + \%)$, many kinaesthetic influences in perception (M), a large number of responses using the whole blot (W), and a small percentage of animal percepts $(A\%)$. Altus & Thompson (1949) chose to investigate this set of hypotheses, taking each one as a discrete hypothesis with performance on a group intelligence test as the outside criterion. The subjects were American college students. Correlation coefficients of 0.35 and 0.45, respectively, are found for movement responses (M) and whole responses (W). The percentage of animal responses did not correlate significantly, nor did the $F + \%$. Any positive results are somewhat surprising in view of the fact that a group administration of the Rorschach and group intelligence test were used, and a very narrow range of intellectual ability was represented by college students. But, most important, these Rorschach signs of intelligence are never considered singly. The worker comes to an estimate of intelligence from the various factors considered in combination and within the context of the rest of the personality. For example, it is common clinical knowledge that many neurotic but highly intelligent persons show little kinaesthetic influence in their perception, and that many subjects of rather mediocre, or even low, intellectual level have a high proportion of whole responses. Always the maximum form quality shown in the record is given heavy weighting, although this was not included in Rorschach's original list. In other words, Altus & Thompson were not putting to the test the hypotheses connected with estimation of intellectual level as they are actually used. The integrative nature of the process of estimation was left out of consideration entirely.

There have been attempts to test the validity of projective techniques by holistic methods, chief of which involve "matching" methods, such as the classic study of Vernon (1935) on Rorschach and of Harrison (1940) with T.A.T. The method involves a number of judges who are required to match personality sketches drawn from analysis of the projective protocol with personality sketches based on the case history or some other independent criterion. Both Vernon and Harrison and other investigators have established a highly significant relationship between the criterion and appraisals drawn from projectives. However, this holistic approach bears testimony to the uniqueness of the personality organization, and generally indicates that the projective technique "probably has something," rather than providing evidence of the validity of the hypotheses upon which the interpretation is based. Correct matching is conceivable with only a few of the various hypotheses involved being valid, the rest being incorrect or inadequate. We are faced squarely with the problem of finding an approach which does justice to the interrelatedness of the judgements made in interpretation, and which also sorts out the various interpretative hypotheses, so that their relative degree of validity may be ascertained. This is a difficult problem, but one which should not be impossible to surmount.

Problems Relating to Reliability

Let us turn to the problems of validity which pertain to the question of the reliability of the projective technique. In the context of psychometric tests it is commonly stated that although a test may be reliable without being valid, it cannot be valid without being reliable. This statement implies that the function being measured is a stable function, and therefore if repeated measurement brings differing results the instrument of measurement is an unreliable one. The assumption has often been made that the basic personality structure of the individual is a stable function, and therefore to the extent that projective techniques tap the basic personality structure, repeated testing should give essentially the same picture each time.

There are two problems here: whether personality structure is indeed an unchanging function, and whether the projective technique taps basic personality structure alone and is uninfluenced by any other factors, either pertinent dynamic factors or those pertaining to accidents of the test situation. As might be expected, studies with children, such as those reported by Kerr (1934) and Swift (1944), show changes when test and retest are separated by a considerable time interval, as, indeed, they must be if a pseudo-reliability is not to be introduced in terms of a memory factor. On the other hand, Brosin & Fromm (1942) report considerable stability in Rorschach performance in serial retesting through psycho-analytic treatment.

Evidence is also apparently conflicting with respect to the influence of set upon projective performance. Fosberg (1938) administered the Rorschach three times, under standard conditions, then asking the subject to make the best impression and again asking the subject to make the worst impression. He found that the subjects were unable to change their basic psychogram significantly. On the other hand, Hutt and associates (1950) found that when specific instructions were given on Rorschach retest to help the subject see more human movement responses, detailed responses or colour responses combined with good form there were significant differences in the retests with respect to certain of the scoring classifications. The fact that there are limits to the extent to which an experimentally induced set may be effective is shown, however, by common clinical experience in the "testing the limits" part of Rorschach administration where some patients are unable to improve their perception even when given increasingly directive instructions.

A final consideration in reliability is the influence of the personality and manner of the examiner. Traditional psychometric testing emphasizes the necessity of establishing good "rapport" as a condition of reliable test administration. The fact that poor rapport may obtain is not considered to be a fault of the test but either a fault of the examiner or due to the condition of the subject. There have been some very interesting recent explorations of the influence of the examiner on Rorschach performance, the most thorough study being that of Lord (1950), who in a carefully designed test-retest-retest investigation influenced the relative importance of repetition, personality of the examiner and deliberately induced alterations in the emotional climate of the test situation. Although she found that richer records came with a warm testing situation, and less productive, more constricted records with a situation deliberately structured to produce a hostile, critical atmosphere, she found that the greatest differences of all were produced by the three examiners.

Alternative interpretations may be given to the evidence on reliability of projectives, either that the techniques are unreliable and hence invalid, or that the projective technique is a sensitive instrument which validly reflects differences in perceptual and personality function under varying influences. The latter alternative is incompatible with the claim that projective techniques are primarily tests of basic personality structure, for obviously this cannot be considered to change with experimentally altered sets or differences in examiners or conditions of testing. Rather, one must accept the view that the performance of the subject in response to the projective material is a sample of the way he perceives situations, and different samples may reflect somewhat different facets of perceptual and personality function. This position with respect to sensitivity of the instrument involves both disadvantages and advantages pertinent to validation studies. Validation studies are in one sense more difficult if stability of function cannot be assumed,

and yet the variability of function may itself be of advantage if the investigation is designed to exploit the variability and predict the direction and extent of change expected under various circumstances. However, before discussing this possibility more fully, the question of criteria must first be considered.

Problems Relating to Criteria

The third set of problems in the validation of projective techniques involves the choice of satisfactory outside criteria against which to test the validity of the interpretative hypotheses. This is perhaps the most formidable problem of all. Were criteria available for assessing personality characteristics, such criteria themselves being of irreproachable validity, there would be little problem of validation. Despite the facts that such criteria are non-existent, and that to find even moderately satisfactory criteria involves very considerable caution and ingenuity, there has been a very large amount of research which might be said to throw some light upon validity. This research may be classified in three chief groups: (1) *Diagnostic* studies, which use distinctions in nosological classification as criteria against which to check the validity of diagnoses based on the projective technique. (2) "*Single variable*" studies which isolate the various interpretative hypotheses and check them one at a time against some outside criterion presumed to relate to the function or characteristic with which the hypothesis deals. (3) *Prediction* studies which use the interpretative hypotheses as a basis for a prediction which can be checked.

(1) *Diagnostic studies*. These are in turn of two main kinds; those which check the accuracy of a diagnosis based on blind analysis of the protocol, and those which attempt to test the validity of hypotheses relating to diagnostic signs which should distinguish between nosological groups. Of the first type, the

study by Benjamin & Ebaugh (1938) may be cited. This involved completely independent diagnoses on the basis of the Rorschach protocol without even a glimpse of the patient himself, and the diagnosis arrived at by the psychiatric conference on the basis of the usual procedures.

In thirty-nine out of forty-six cases the diagnoses were identical, in the remaining seven there was no serious discrepancy. This represents a higher degree of agreement than one would expect usually to result if different psychiatrists were to arrive independently at a diagnosis. It would indicate that Benjamin & Ebaugh, working within the framework of diagnostic categories used in their particular setting, and backed by a wealth of psychiatric experience, were able to arrive at a diagnosis on the basis of the sample of performance elicited by the Rorschach ink-blots which was nearly always in agreement with a diagnosis based on the more usual samples of performance.

The qualifications voiced above indicate the limitations of this type of approach. Diagnostic classification is a difficult criterion, since the bases of classification differ considerably from one psychiatric setting to another. As Ross (1950) points out, different labels sometimes mean the same thing, while the same label may mean different things as applied by different diagnosticians. Moreover, both Ross and Schafer (1948, 1949) insist that psychiatric diagnosis on the basis of projectives does not imply a direct judgment, but rather an intermediate step. A judgment is first made of the modes of functioning of the personality on the basis of the protocol and then, working from a knowledge of what processes of thinking and acting are characteristic of various diagnostic groupings, a diagnosis is made.

This objection is one which is quite pertinent to the second type of diagnostic study which involves a comparison between diagnostic classifications on the basis of objective features of the protocol, leaving out the intermediate step. The number of studies of this sort are very numerous indeed. One example is a very well-known study by Miale & Harrower-Erickson (1938) in which nine Rorschach signs are listed which distinguish neurotics from normal subjects. Further studies showed both that these signs indeed showed statistically significant differences between neurotic and normal groups, but also that their usefulness is much limited by the fact that similar signs are manifested by patients with organic brain disease, schizophrenia, psychosomatic disorders of various kinds, and indeed by some normal subjects. Even where statistically significant differences between groups can be established, these differences are of relatively little use in diagnosis, at least when used in a mechanical rather than clinical way. Generally, one may sum up the situation as follows: those "signs" which seem exclusive to the given diagnostic group are sufficiently rare with that group for many of the cases to be missed in diagnosis, or they are shown by enough patients in other groupings for errors of commission rather than omission to be made. Thus, "contamination" of responses has held up as a fairly reliable sign of schizophrenic process in thinking, but is often not found in the protocols of schizophrenics. On the other hand, characteristic of nearly all schizophrenics are responses which are generally assigned minus form-level ratings in that the concept involved bears a very inaccurate relationship to the form of the blot used; but these minus form responses are by no means rare with organics, other psychotics, neurotics and are sometimes even found with normal subjects.

In general, diagnostic studies involving both systematic and unsystematic clinical observations have proved very useful as a source of interpretative hypotheses, but involve difficulties as sources of stable and valid outside criteria in validation research. It is not to be wondered that this is so, for there are many individual differences, and important ones, between patients with the same diagnostic label, many overlappings, and much fluidity of boundaries between diagnostic groups. It is perhaps indirect evidence of the validity of projectives that they fail to establish clearcut differentiation between diagnostic groupings while yet showing some undeniable relationship to them.

(2) *"Single variable"* studies characteristically select one interpretative hypotheses at a time and check its relationship with some relevant outside criterion. One example of this approach is the Altus & Thompson study of the relationship of indicators to intellectual capacity with scores on a group intelligence test, mentioned above. Another recent example is an investigation by Holtzman (1950), who tested four Rorschach hypotheses relating to introversive-extratensive balance against ratings of shyness and gregariousness. This involved an intermediate hypothesis that the introversive-extratensive balance expresses itself behaviourally in terms of shyness-gregariousness, an hypothesis which seems unjustified and may well explain the fact that his findings were essentially negative. However, this illustrates very well a major difficulty of finding suitable criteria, in that the interpretative hypotheses of projectives tend to be framed in terms of inner dynamics relating to needs, feelings, emotions, identifications, phantasies and the like, rather than in behavioural terms. To frame a hypothesis in behavioural terms introduces something new, which perhaps is itself very worthwhile and which can be tested, but which provides no definitive check on the underlying dynamic hypothesis if the results prove to be negative.

Benton (1950) quotes an unpublished thesis by Fitzgerald in which he tested the Rorschach hypothesis that a preponderance of good form-colour responses over responses which use colour in a context of vague form indicates socialization of the expression of emotional reactions. The outside criterion was pooled group ratings of social adaptibility. A rank-difference coefficient of 0.5 was found, indicating a moderate but significant relationship. Young & Higginbotham (1942) checked the same hypothesis against ratings of positive social and emotional adjustment from case records, and judged it to be a valid indicator. Baker & Harris (1949) designed an experimental investigation to investigate both hypotheses relating to socialized control ($FC:CF$ balance) and rational control ($F\%$). Working on the assumption that weak control would tend to give way under strain and result in less co-ordinated behaviour, they produced strain by laboratory methods and measured loss of control in terms of loss of co-ordination in speech as indicated by word intelligibility and intensity variations. Correlation coefficients of 0.45 and 0.41 were found with the indices of socialized control and rational control respectively, although the small number of subjects precluded statistical significance. This study therefore is significant chiefly as a promising attempt to apply experimental methods to the problem of validation of projective techniques.

Benton (1950) quotes an unpublished thesis by Eichler, which represents an even more noteworthy attempt to check the validity of Rorschach "anxiety indicators" by comparing two carefully matched groups of subjects, one of which was tested under standard conditions, the other under conditions designed to evoke anxiety. Certain anxiety indicators distinguished significantly between the two groups, others did not. With respect to experimentally produced anxiety or tension the question can be raised, however, as to whether this can be strictly comparable in its effects to sustained or recurrent anxiety in everyday life, perhaps particularly throughout the developmental period. Eichler's experiment tends to lend weight to the claim for validity of certain of the indicators, but provides no definitive evidence regarding the remainder. This is not a counter-indication for experimental studies, however, for validation is of necessity a long process involving many different approaches and the dovetailing of findings from many types of investigations.

(3) *Prediction studies.* This area of research is noteworthy more as a promising field for future research than as one already represented by a body of completed investigations. This type of study would involve prediction as a criterion of validity. It promises certain important advantages. Subjects can be tested individually and interpretation carried out using the full resources of the technique, since numbers of subjects could be kept small where exactness of prediction rather than statistical tendencies are involved. The prediction could be made on the basis of integration of a number of interpretative hypotheses, although the precise basis of the prediction would have to be stated. The design of the experiment could exploit the sensitivity of the instrument to change, by predicting changed behaviour under changed life conditions, or experimentally varying test conditions and predicting the result. The major disadvantage would be that the interpretation would have to be carried one step further than is now the case, namely, to formulate a prediction regarding the behaviour of the subject, so that the subject's own behaviour would form the criterion. This implies translating hypotheses referring to inner dynamic processes to behavioural hypotheses, which involves a major area of research in itself. Moreover, the exact conditions towards which one is predicting would have to be known precisely in terms of their demand on individuals of varying personalities. The failure to have made these two extensions of understanding is a prominent factor in the failure of a recent large-scale attempt reported by Kelly & Fiske (1950) to predict the success in training in clinical psychology of a number of post-graduate students, from a large variety of bases, including projective techniques.

There are a wide variety of possibilities for predictive studies. One would involve the prediction of response to treatment of specific kinds, which would yield practical results as well as evidence of validity. A second possibility is now being explored at the Tavistock Clinic in an attempt to predict the reactions of patients in a variety of interpersonal relationships arising in group therapy sessions. One could also suggest the prediction of changes in performance in the projective situation with controlled change in examiners, for example, with respect to sex, authority, status and so on. In general, to suggest this area as one promising both an improved approach to validation and increased practical usefulness is to underline the fact that the projective technique is not a final, finished instrument to be proved valid or invalid. Rather, increased understanding of the relationship of hypothesized inner dynamics to behaviour, progressive refinement and extension of interpretative hypotheses and validation research are interlocked, concurrent processes.

Summary

An examination of the problems of validation of projective techniques not only involves detection and criticism of the shortcomings of the methods and findings of previous validation studies, but should also stimulate future research. The principles which may be advanced on the basis of the present discussion are as follows:

(1) Interpretative hypotheses should be validated under conditions of administration, scoring and interpretation

similar to those in which they were originally formulated and in which they are customarily used. This implies individual rather than group administration, adequate training of research personnel in administration, scoring and interpretation, and, most important, the application of the interpretative hypothesis in full context rather than in terms of atomistic analysis. Although pattern analysis presents certain difficulties, new techniques such as those suggested by Cronbach (1949b) may prove helpful.

(2) Validation research should go hand in hand with exploration of the influence of variables which influence test performance, such as set, circumstances leading to testing, personality of the examiner. These considerations should not only set certain limits of applicability of interpretative hypotheses but should also be exploited as providing criteria of the validity with which the technique is sensitive to changes in the function being studied.

(3) Diagnostic studies should turn in the direction of improved understanding of the personality functions in terms of which diagnostic groupings are made, with a view to refining of interpretative hypotheses, rather than emphasize the diagnostic grouping itself as an outside criterion of validity.

(4) The search should continue for definitive outside criteria for interpretative hypotheses, with further exploration of the possibilities of laboratory studies, with the two provisions that the hypotheses be tested so as to do justice to their essential integration with the whole interpretative framework, and that caution be employed in generalization from laboratory conditions to everyday life.

(5) The interpretative basis of projective techniques should be widely extended in the direction of translating hypotheses now framed in terms of inner dynamic processes to hypotheses framed in behavioural terms. This would permit of the design of studies in which predicted behaviour would form the criterion of validity.

REFERENCES

ALTUS, W. D., & THOMPSON, GRACE M. (1949). The Rorschach as a measure of intelligence. *J. Consult. Psychol.* 13, 341.

BAKER, L. M., & HARRIS, J. S. (1949). Validation of Rorschach test results on laboratory behaviour. *J. Clin. Psychol.* 5, 161.

BECK, S. J. (1944). *Rorschach's Test*, 2 vols. New York: Grune and Stratton.

BELLAK, L. (1948). *Bellak TAT Blank, Analysis Sheets and Guide to the Interpretation of the TAT.* New York: Psychological Corporation.

BENJAMIN, J. D., & EBAUGH, F. G. (1938). The diagnostic validity of the Rorschach test. *Amer. J. Psychiat.* 94, 1163.

BENTON, A. L. (1950). Experimental validation of the Rorschach test. *Brit. J. Med. Psychol.* 23, 45.

BROSIN, H. W., & FROMM, E. O. (1942). Some principles of Gestalt psychology in the Rorschach experiment. *Rorschach Res. Exch.* 6, 1.

BUHLER, C., BUHLER, K., & LEFEVER, D. W. (1948). *Development of the Basic Rorschach Score with Manual of Directions.* Rorschach Standardization Study, I. Copyright, Mimeographed Edition.

CRONBACH, L. J. (1949a). Statistical methods applied to Rorschach scores: a review. *Psychol. Bull.* 46, 393.

CRONBACH, L. J. (1949b). Pattern tabulation: a statistical method for analysis of limited patterns of scores, with particular reference to the Rorschach Test. *Educ. Psychol. Measmt,* 9, 149.

DERI, S. K. (1949). *Introduction to the Szondi Test: Theory and Practice.* New York: Grune and Stratton.

FISHER, S., & FISHER, R. (1950). A test of certain assumptions regarding figure drawing analysis. *J. Abn. Soc. Psychol.* 45, 727.

FOSBERG, I. A. (1938). Rorschach reactions under varied instructions. *Rorschach Res. Exch.* 9, 12.

HARRISON, R. (1940). Studies in the use and validity of the Thematic Appperception Test with mentally disordered patients. II. A quantitative validity study. *Character & Pers.* **9**, 122.

HENRY, W. E. (1947). The Thematic Appperception Technique in the study of culture-personality relations. *Genet. Psychol. Monogr.* **35**, 135.

HERTZ, M. R. (1942). The scoring of the Rorschach ink-blot method as developed by the Brush Foundation. *Rorschach Res. Exch.* **6**, 16.

HOLTZMAN, W. H. (1950). Validation studies of the Rorschach test: impulsiveness in the normal superior adult. *J. Clin. Psychol.* **6**, 348.

HUTT, M. L., GIBBY, R., MILTON, E. O., & POTTHARST, K. (1950). The effect of varied experimental 'sets' upon Rorschach test performance. *J. Project. Tech.* **14**, 181.

KELLY, E. L., & FISKE, D. W. (1950). The prediction of success in the VA training program in clinical psychology. *Amer. Psychol.* **5**, 395.

KERR, M. (1934). The Rorschach test applied to children. *Brit. J. Psychol.* **25**, 51.

KLOPFER, B., & KELLEY, D. M. (1942). *The Rorschach Technique.* Yonkers-on-Hudson, N.Y.: World Book Company.

LAZARUS, R. S. (1949). Influence of colour on the protocol of the Rorschach test. *J. Abn. Soc. Psychol.* **44**, 506.

LORD, EDITH (1950). Experimentally induced variations in Rorschach performance. *Psychol. Monogr.* **64**, no. 316.

MACHOVER, K. (1949). *Personality Projection in Drawings of the Human Figure,* Springfield, Illinois: Charles C Thomas.

MIALE, F., & HARROWER-ERICKSON, M. R. (1938). Personality structure in the psychoneuroses. *Rorschach Res. Exch.* **2**, 153.

MURRAY, H. A. *et al.* (1938). *Explorations in Personality.* New York: Oxford University Press.

MURRAY, H. A. (1943). *Thematic Apperception Test.* Cambridge: Harvard University Press.

ODOM, C. L. (1950). A study of the time required to do a Rorschach examination. *J. Project. Tech.* **14**, 464.

RORSCHACH, H. (1921). *Psychodiagnostics.* Bern: Verlag Hans Huber.

ROSS, W. D. (1950). The relation between Rorschach interpretation and clinical diagnoses. *J. Project. Tech.* **14**, 5.

SAPPENFIELD, B. R., & BUKER, S. L. (1949). Validity of the Rorschach 8–9–10 per cent. *J. Consult. Psychol.* **13**, 268.

SCHAFER, R. (1948). *The Clinical Application of Psychological Tests.* New York: International Universities Press, Inc.

SCHAFER, R. (1949). Psychological tests in clinical research. *J. Consult. Psychol.* **13**, 328.

SWIFT, J. W. (1944). Reliability of Rorschach scoring categories with preschool children. *Child Developm.* **15**, 207.

SZONDI, L. (1947). *Experimentelle Triebdiagnostik.* Bern: Verlag Hans Huber.

TOMKINS, S. S. (1947). *The Thematic Apperception Test.* New York: Grune and Stratton.

VERNON, P. E. (1935). The significance of the Rorschach test. *Brit. J. Med. Psychol.* **15**, 199.

WYATT, F. (1947). The scoring and analysis of the Thematic Apperception Test. *J. Psychol.* **24**, 319.

YOUNG, R. A., & HIGGINBOTHAM, S. A. (1942). Behaviour checks on Rorschach method. *Amer. J. Orthopsychiat.* **12**, 87.

Chapter 9

Validation of Projective Drawings

■ Man has been expressing himself through drawings since at least the Paleolithic Age if not longer (Herskovits, 1955). While no record of the early history of artistic criticism is available, it is likely that it started a few minutes after the first artist started the first painting on the wall of a cave. Since we know nothing about this first critic, it is impossible to say whether she recognized that in his work the artist expressed aspects of his personality. However, an awareness that artistic productions reveal personality characteristics has long been with us. Therefore it is not surprising that today drawings are our second most widely used assessment device, trailing only the Rorschach in popularity (Sundberg, 1961).

While many clinicians use human figure drawings informally, Machover (1949) has taken the important step of stating a number of interpretive hypotheses in explicit, testable form. Since then a large body of research aimed at validating these hypotheses has grown up.

In the present chapter, Charles Swensen reviews the first eight years of work testing Machover's hypotheses. His findings are discouraging. Research has seldom supported Machover's hypotheses in a consistent or unequivocal manner. In part this is a result of the fact that relatively few studies were designed to test Machover's specific hypotheses. Swensen suggests that future research would do better to test specific hypotheses and patterns rather than randomly testing unrelated hypotheses.

Swensen hypothesizes that the Draw-A-Person's popularity, aside from its ease of administration, is the result of the fact that in a few isolated cases it provides an indication of the nature of a client's problems. If so, the result would be that the clinician is on a random partial reward schedule and hence the habit of administering the DAP would be very resistant to extinction. Since most empirical studies call for clinicians to make judgements about every drawing with which they are confronted, it is impossible to determine if the cases for which valid inferences can be made are masked by the large numbers of ones for which no clear-cut valid interpretation can be offered.

Another difficulty is the relative infrequency of some signs. Holtzman (personal communication, 1964) reports that in one large-scale study of Air Force personnel a particular type of drawing was so reliably associated with the diagnosis that it could be used as a pathognomic or "stop" item in screening. This drawing, consisting of a nude female with twirling propellers on her nipples, was invariably associated with superior adjustment. However, its extreme rarity made it of limited utility and prevented systematic research on this sign. It may well be there are other signs whose rarity prevents any convincing cross-validation.

Simmons (1965), in a review of the recent projective drawing literature, has ventured the opinion that research to date has not adequately tested Machover's basic body image hypothesis since almost all studies interpose an interpreter, judge, or clinician into the design. He calls for research in which the subject describes himself and then describes his projective drawings to determine whether the relationships which Machover hypothesized do indeed exist.

For a critique of Swenson's review the reader is referred to Hammer (1959). For another review of the DAP literature covering roughly the same period, the reader can consult Jones and Thomas (1961).

REFERENCES

HAMMER, E. F. Critique of Swensen's "Empirical evaluations of human figure drawing." *Journal of Projective Techniques,* 1959, **23,** 30–31.

HERSKOVITS, M. F. *Cultural Anthropology.* New York: Alfred A. Knopf, 1955.

JONES, LEMA W., & THOMAS, CAROLINE P. Studies on figure drawings: A review of the literature (1949–1959). *Psychometric Quarterly Supplement,* 1961, **35,** 212–261.

MACHOVER, KAREN. *Personality Projection in the Drawings of the Human Figure.* Springfield, Ill.: Charles C Thomas, 1949.

SIMMONS, A. D. A test of the body image hypothesis in human figure drawings. Unpublished doctoral dissertation, Univer. of Texas, 1966.

SUNDBERG, N. D. The practice of psychological testing in clinical services in the United States. *American Psychologist,* 1961, **16,** 79–83.

Empirical Evaluations of Human Figure Drawings

Clifford H. Swensen, Jr.

Since the publication, in 1949, of Karen Machover's *Personality Projection in the Drawing of the Human Figure* (55) the Draw-A-Person Test (DAP) has become an instrument used routinely by many clinical psychologists.

The author is indebted to Drs. Ernest Furchtgott and E. E. Cureton for many helpful suggestions in the preparation of this paper. He also wishes to express his thanks to Miss Rebecca Mallory, Mrs. Marjorie Truan, and Mrs. Ann Black.

In the eight years that have elapsed since the publication of Machover's monograph many research studies on the DAP have been published. It seems desirable at the present time to examine the hypotheses Machover presented in her monograph in the light of the empirical evidence that has accumulated.

It is the purpose of this paper to attempt to analyze all of the research on the DAP reported in the literature from January, 1949, to December, 1956. Machover's hypotheses will be examined in the light of the evidence produced by these studies.

Reliability

Machover (55, p. 6) states that "structural and formal aspects of drawing, such as size, line, and placement, are less subject to variability than content, such as body details, clothing, and accessories." Machover goes on to state that Ss render consistently such features as the following: size of the figure, placement of the figure on the page, kinds of lines (long, continuous lines versus short, jagged ones), stance of the figure, proportions of the body, observance of symmetry compulsions, tendency to incompletions, presence of erasures, and presence of shading.

Both Bradshaw (13) and Lehner and Gunderson (49) have attempted to determine the reliability of both the structural aspects of figure drawings and the content of figure drawings. Since the aspects of figure drawing that they investigated overlap considerably, these two studies will be considered together.

Bradshaw (13) gave the DAP as a group test to 100 psychology students, both male and female, ranging in age from 19 to 55, with a mean age of 27.57. He used the test-retest method with one week between the two administrations of the test. Bradshaw considered 25 different body areas or parts in his study. He scored for 17 possible different kinds of drawing treatment, and each body area or part was scored for as many of these kinds of drawing treatment as were applicable to it. For example, the hands were scored for whether they were present or not, whether they were clothed or not, presence of erasing, presence of shading, degree of detailing, proportional size, line quality, and shape. Bradshaw determined reliability primarily by percentage of consistency from the first administration of the test to the second administration of the test. If, for example, of 10 drawings, four had shading on the hands of both drawings and five had no shading on the hands of either drawing, and one had shading on one drawing and no shading in the other drawing, there would be 90 per cent consistency for shading in the treatment of the hands. However, he did use in addition the product-moment correlation coefficient in determining the consistency of quantifiable dimensions such as distance from the side of the paper, distance from the top of the paper, and vertical height. These were measured in centimeters.

Lehner and Gunderson (49) gave the DAP to 91 psychology students, ranging in age from 18 to 26, with four months between the two administrations of the test. They also determined reliability by the test-retest method and in addition investigated intrajudge reliabilities and interjudge reliabilities. They scored the drawings on 21 "dimensions," using rating scales for the scoring. The authors report that most of the rating scales had 10 points, but some of the rating scales had as few as 2 points. They do not present the scales used to rate the dimensions. The authors state that "all results are percent of agreement between the sets of ratings, i.e., per cent of cases in which the matched ratings are identical."

Table 1 summarizes the reliabilities reported by Bradshaw and Lehner and Gunderson on the content as indicated earlier. Bradshaw scored each body part

TABLE 1. RELIABILITIES OF DAP CONTENT REPORTED BY TWO STUDIES

DAP Part	Bradshaw Range[a],[b] Per Cent	Bradshaw Mean Per Cent	Lehner & Gunderson
Whole drawing	(100–66)	84	—
Whole head	(100–59)	78	—
Whole trunk	(100–59)	83	—
Legs and feet as whole	(100–62)	75	—
Arms	(99–44)	72	—
Mouth	(94–50)	68	44
Lips	(74–54)	65	—
Chin	(91–57)	74	—
Eyes	(96–55)	76	61
Eyebrows	(90–68)	78	—
Ears	(78–62)	70	—
Hair	(84–35)	68	70
Nose	(97–55)	74	52
Face	(79–73)	76	—
Neck	(95–55)	68	—
Arms	(99–65)	77	—
Hands	(97–55)	76	67
Fingers	(87–54)	70	—
Legs	(98–60)	74	—
Feet	(97–54)	75	56
Shoulders	(96–59)	73	—
Hips, buttocks	(83–45)	65	—
Waistline	(78–60)	66	—
Breasts	(100–50)	71	42
Crotch	(78–44)	68	—

[a] All figures represent percentage of agreement.

[b] All parts were rated for many different characteristics, such as line quality, proportion, shape, etc.

on several different scales. For example, the hands might be scored for presence vs. absence, presence of erasures, presence of shading, etc., so that for each body part several different percentages of agreement were reported. The range of these percentages of agreement is presented in the table, and to the immediate right of the range the mean of the ratings for that particular part is presented. It will be noted that Bradshaw found the lowest percentage of agreement (65%) on the lips and the hips and buttocks. He found the highest percentage of agreement (84%) in rat-

ing the whole drawing. Lehner and Gunderson found the lowest percentage of agreement (42%) on the breasts and the highest percentage of agreement (70%) on the hair.

Table 2 summarizes the reliabilities reported by the two studies on the structural and formal aspects of the DAP, based upon the analysis of the same drawings as reported in Table 1. Bradshaw reports three reliabilities (distance from top of paper, distance from left side of paper, and vertical height) in product-moment rs. All other figures are percentage of agreement. In this table also, Bradshaw had several ratings for each of the aspects of the drawings. For example, presence of shading was rated in regard to several different body parts such as the arms, hands, face, etc. In this table the range of percentage of agreement obtained by Bradshaw is reported, and to the immediate right of it the mean of the percentages of agreement is presented.

Bradshaw reports the lowest percentage of agreement (60%) on the shape of the figure and the highest percentage of agreement (90%) on the presence or absence of the various parts of the body. The three rs Bradshaw reports are all significant at the .01 level of confidence.

Lehner and Gunderson report the lowest percentage of agreement (45%) on the position of the figure on the page, and the highest percentage of agreement (93%) on body type.

It will be recalled that Machover suggested that the structural and formal aspects of the DAP tend to be more reliable than the content. In order to give a comparison of the percentages of agreement obtained by Bradshaw and Lehner and Gunderson, Table 3 was prepared. In Table 3 the number of parts falling at each level of percentage of agreement for the body parts and the structural and formal aspects of the DAP for each study is presented. It will be noted that there is no great difference between the percentages of

TABLE 2. RELIABILITIES OF STRUCTURAL AND FORMAL ASPECTS OF DAP
AS REPORTED BY TWO STUDIES

	Bradshaw		Lehner & Gunder-son
DAP Aspect	Range,[a,b] Per Cent	Mean Per Cent	
Presence of parts	(100–72)	90	—
Presence of clothing	(98–65)	86	—
Presence of erasing	(98–54)	69	56
Presence of shading	(93–62)	76	59
Presence of accessories	—	75	—
Profile vs. full-face	(72–85)	80	65
Direction of profile	(70–89)	83	—
Sex first figure	—	68	—
Distance from left of paper	—	$r = .46$[d]	45[c]
Distance from top of paper	—	$r = .54$[d]	45[c]
Vertical height	—	$r = .61$[d]	—
Degree of detailing	(65–90)	76	79
Proportional size	(52–100)	64	—
Line quality	(50–84)	72	71
Shape	(35–75)	60	—
Stance	(44–96)	72	78
Reinforcement	—	—	64
Body type	—	—	93
Transparency	—	—	77
Position of hands	—	—	46
Extraneous drawing	—	—	75
Symmetry	—	—	60

a All figures percentage of agreement unless otherwise noted.
b Several aspects were rated for presence on several different parts of DAP.
c Reported as "position on page," such as head, legs, breasts, etc.
d Significant at the .01 level.

agreement on the content and the percentages of agreement on the structural aspects of the DAP.

Serious criticism must be leveled against the use of the percentage of agreement as a measure of reliability. The significance of the percentage of agreement on the DAP is entirely dependent upon the base rate of the particular body part or structural aspect of the drawing that is being investigated. The "base rate" refers to the frequency with which a particular sign is ordinarily present in the population of Ss that is being studied. Meehl and Rosen (60) have pointed out the importance of including the base rate in the validation of a clinical instrument. The more frequently a particular sign is found in a particular part of the DAP, the higher the percentage of agreement

must be in order to be significant. If a particular sign is drawn by 90% of the population on the DAP, then a consistency of 82% would not be significant. This is illustrated in Table 4. Table 4 is a purely fictional table designed to illustrate this point. It will be noted in Table 4, on the first administration of the DAP, that of 1,000 subjects 900, or 90%, drew hands and 100, or 10%, omitted the hands. On the second administration of the DAP to this same group 90% drew hands and 10% omitted the hands. So, it may be stated that the base rate for the drawing of hands on the DAP for this particular sample is 90%. Of those who drew hands on the DAP at the first administration 810, or 81% of the total sample, also drew hands on the DAP at the second administration. Of those who omitted the

TABLE 3. PERCENTAGE AGREEMENT OF
DAP CONTENT COMPARED WITH PERCENT-
AGE AGREEMENT OF STRUCTURAL AND
FORMAL ASPECTS OF DAP

	No. of Items Reaching Percentage of Agreement Levels			
	Bradshaw		Lehner & Gunderson	
Percentage of Agreement Level	Content	Structural Aspects	Content	Structural Aspects
90–100	0	1	0	1
80–89	2	3	0	0
70–79	16	5	0	5
60–69	7	4	3	3
50–59	0	0	2	2
40–49	0	0	2	3

hands on the first administration 10 or
1% of the total sample also omitted the
hands on the second administration of
the DAP. Adding the 81% who drew
hands on both administrations to the 1%
who omitted the hands on both administrations, we arrive at a figure of 82%
consistency on the presence or absence
of hands. However, if we calculate the
significance of this relationship by either
chi square or ϕ/ϕ maximum[1] we find
that in both cases we obtain a result
of .00. In other words, we have obtained
82% consistency, but it is not a statistically significant relationship, and the
correct conclusion should be that
the presence or absence of hands on the
DAP has zero reliability.

Since neither Bradshaw nor Lehner
and Gunderson report the base rates of
the various parts and aspects of the
DAP, it is impossible to tell the actual
significance of the percentages of agreement that they report. Therefore, with
the exception of the product-moment rs
reported by Bradshaw, the author would
suggest that these studies do not provide valid estimates of the reliability of
the DAP.

[1] This point was suggested by Dr. E. E.
Cureton.

Wagner and Schubert (79) developed
a scale for rating the "quality" of the
DAP. They constructed this scale by
having judges grade the drawings of
75 college girls into 7 categories ranging from the poorest to best quality. The
closer a drawing came to resembling a
"real life-like person" the higher it was
to be rated in the quality categories.
With this scale they obtained interjudge
reliabilities of approximately .90 for
experienced judges and .85 for inexperienced judges. The reliability of the quality of the same-sex figure for 176 coeds
in a school of education was .86, apparently using the test-retest method
and employing experienced judges for
assessing reliability. The authors did
not report the amount of time between
the two administrations of the DAP.

TABLE 4. HYPOTHETICAL FREQUENCIES
DEMONSTRATING HOW PERCENTAGE OF
AGREEMENT CAN BE HIGH
AND RELIABILITY LOW

DAP Second Administration	DAP First Administration		
	Hands Present	Hands Omitted	Totals
Hands present	810	90	900
Hands absent	90	10	100
Totals	900	100	1,000

$\chi^2 = .00$
ϕ/ϕ maximum $= .00$
% agreement $= 82\%$

Wagner and Schubert's study suggests
that the "quality" of the DAP, when
judged as a whole, is reliable. Bradshaw's data (13) suggest that the placement of the figures on the page and the
size of the figures also appear to be
reliable, but less reliable than judgments
of the quality of the total figure. No
other data are available to determine the
reliability of the other parts or aspects
of the DAP, or to evaluate the validity
of Machover's hypothesis that the structural and formal aspects of the DAP are

more reliable than the content of the DAP.

Research Applying to the "Body-Image" Hypothesis

The basic hypothesis underlying figure drawing interpretation is that when a person responds to the request to draw a picture of a person he draws a picture of himself. This is sometimes called the "body-image" hypothesis. Machover (55, p. 35) states that "the human figure drawn by an individual who is directed to 'draw a person' relates intimately to the impulses, anxieties, conflicts, and compensations characteristic of that individual. In some sense, the figure drawn *is* the person, and the paper corresponds to the environment. This may be a crude formulation, but serves well as a working hypothesis."

Unfortunately, there have been few studies that would appear to bear at all upon the question of whether or not human figure drawings do, in fact, represent the drawer's perception of himself.

Berman and Laffal (10) come the closest to testing the hypothesis. They were interested in determining if Ss, when instructed to draw a picture of a person, tend to draw a figure that represents themselves, or draw an idealized figure, or draw a figure that shows no discernible relationship to themselves. They used as their basic data the human figures drawn by 39 male patients in a VA hospital. Using an inspection technique, they rated the body type of the patient. They used Sheldon's types as the categories into which they placed the Ss. They then rated the body type of the figures drawn by these patients, and correlated the ratings of the patient with the ratings of the drawings. The authors do not describe how they converted their ratings into numerical scores from which a Pearson "*r*" could be computed. They obtained a Pearson *r* of .35, which is significant at the .05 level of confidence. These results suggested to the authors that when an S is asked to draw a figure he tends to draw the type he is most familiar with, i.e., his own. However, inspection of Berman and Laffal's data shows that only 18 of their 39 Ss drew figures that were judged to be of the same body type as the S's body. This suggests the possibility that for some Ss the figure drawn represents the S's own body, but that for the majority of Ss the figure drawn represents something else.

In connection with a series of studies of obese women, Kotkov and Goodman (47) made a careful investigation of the differences between the human figures drawn by obese women and the figures drawn by ideal-weight women. They used as Ss 25 obese and 20 ideal-weight women who were matched as groups for age, educational level, IQ, marital status, and the "career vs. housewife" dichotomy. They compared both the male and female figures drawn by the Ss on 43 items of measurement. They ran 129 chi-square tests of significance and found that 32 of them were significant at the .20 level or better. Of the 32 chi squares that were significant at the .20 level, seven were found to be significant at the .05 level of confidence. In view of the fact that 129 chi squares were computed, this suggests the possibility that the significant statistics were due to chance alone. But examination of the report shows that most of the significant differences were due to the greater area on the page covered by the obese female. Kotkov and Goodman suggest that the female figures drawn by their subjects did represent a projection of the body image.

But the authors feel that certain inconsistencies in their results "lead us to look for the operation of dynamic personality principles in the determination of differences between the groups." In other words, they feel the body-image hypothesis accounts for only part of the differences they obtained.

Lehner and Silver (48) and Giedt and Lehner (30) were interested in determining the ages assigned to the figures drawn by Ss. These studies do not provide data showing a relationship between the physical dimensions of the patient's body and the dimensions of the figure he draws, but they do suggest a relationship between a characteristic of the S and the characteristics he assigns to the figures he draws. In the first study (48) the DAP was given to 229 men (ages 17 to 45) and 192 women (ages 18 to 54). It was found that as the S's chronological age increased he tended to ascribe a higher age to the figure he had drawn. This tendency continued until age 25 when the age of the figure drawn ceased to increase as rapidly as the S's age. This change in rate seems to be more pronounced for female Ss than for men subjects. Both sexes tended to assign older ages to the male drawing than to the female drawing. The authors also noted that the men tended to draw male and female figures that were similar to each other, and that this same tendency was noted in the women Ss. The second study (30) used as Ss 188 male neuropsychiatric patients in a VA hospital and 229 male students in a psychology class. The authors found that the age assigned to the figure drawn tends to increase with an increase in the S's age, but that younger Ss (students under 25 and patients under 35) tend to assign ages to the figures that are older than the subject's own age, and the older Ss (students over 30 years old and patients over 40 years old) tend to assign ages to the figures that are younger than the S's age.

Prater (66) compared the human figure drawings of hemiplegic patients with the drawings of a matched group of normals. He was interested in determining whether or not there was any relationship between hemiplegia and the drawing of heads and limbs. He used as an experimental group of Ss 49 hemiplegics and a control group of 43 normals. He obtained the ratio of the area covered by the head to the area covered by the trunk of the figure drawing, and also measured the length of the limbs of the drawings of both groups. He found no significant differences between the drawings of the normals and the hemiplegics on relative head size. He found that the drawings of the hemiplegics showed no tendency to emphasize the head or the limbs by excessive shading or by any other means. He found no differences between the limbs either on the part of the limbs that were on the same side of the body as the hemiplegics' paralyzed limbs, or those that were on the same side of the body as the hemiplegics' normal limbs. These results suggest that, for hemiplegics at least, abnormalities of the body are not reflected in the drawings.

These few studies suggest that there is slight basis for believing that the figure drawn usually represents the S's own body. The results suggest that for many, or perhaps most, Ss the figure drawn does not represent the S's own body. Goldworth (32), on the basis of a review of the literature that had been published prior to 1948, has suggested that the body-image hypothesis may only be valid for Ss whose perceptions are determined primarily by senses other than the visual. He also points out that for adult Ss the drawings reflect the S's ability to evaluate his own drawing, and thus reflect his capacity for self-criticism. He feels that research into factors affecting an S's ability for self-criticism would also throw some light on the meaning of human figure drawings.

It is apparent from the few studies reviewed above that the most outstanding conclusion that can be drawn is that definitive research on the basic meaning or significance of human figure drawings is lacking.

Content and Structural and Formal Aspects of Drawings

Machover (55, p. 21) stresses that, in interpreting the DAP, the patterns of the traits in the drawings must be considered when they are being interpreted. But she suggests that particular kinds of treatments of particular parts of the body tend to have a particular significance. Therefore, in the section that follows, the hypotheses of Machover which apply to particular parts of the drawings, or which deal with the meaning of a particular kind of treatment of a particular body part (e.g., shading the breasts) will be discussed.

In the following discussion the various parts of the body will be discussed, first presenting Machover's hypothesis concerning the meaning of various kinds of rendering of the part of the body under consideration, followed by the results of the applicable studies. Discussion of those parts of the body for which no research is reported in the literature has been omitted.

In the following discussion any statistic that is referred to as being "significant" is significant at the .05 level or higher. The specific level of significance will not be mentioned unless it is below the .05 level, or unless the level of significance is of particular interest. This is done to eliminate much awkward repetition.

Head

Machover (55, p. 36) feels that "the head is essentially the center for intellectual power, social balance, and the control of body impulses." A disproportionately large or small head suggests that the S is having difficulty in one of these areas of psychic functioning. For the most part, none of the studies get at any of the above factors directly. Perhaps the investigator to come the closest was Cook (21) who found that, in a group of 21 male college students, those who drew the female head larger than the male head attributed the "social function" to the female to a significantly greater degree than to the male. Cook determined "social function" by a 15-item attitude scale.

Goodman and Kotkov (35) found no significant relationship between the size of the head on the DAP and repression or inhibition.

Machover (55, p. 37) also suggests that disproportionate heads will often be drawn by individuals who are suffering from organic brain damage, preoccupied with headaches, or other special head sensitivity, and that this will be because of the weakened intellectual power and control which fixates consciousness on the head as the primary organ in the hierarchy of body values. She, in addition, hypothesizes that "a youngster whose emotional or social adjustments have been dislocated because of a severe reading or other subject disability will frequently draw a large head on his figure," and that "the mentally defective will . . . often give a large head." She also feels that the paranoid, narcissistic, intellectually righteous, and vain individual may draw a large head as an expression of his inflated ego, and that the inadequate male will draw the female figure with a much larger head than the male figure. Several studies bear directly on these points. Fisher and Fisher (28) obtained DAP's from 32 paranoid schizophrenics. They rated these drawings on six signs Machover considers indicative of paranoid schizophrenia (eye emphasis, large grandiose figure, speared fingers, large head, rigid stance, and large ears). They found that only 13 of the 32 drawings had as many as 3 of the signs present. They concluded that their results cast doubt upon the validity of these signs, including the large head, as being indicative of paranoid schizophrenia. Holzberg and Wexler (44) compared 38 schizophrenic female patients with 78 student nurses on 174 scoring items of the DAP, including head size. Eighteen paranoid schizophrenics were included in their group of patients. They found no significant differences between the normals and paranoids in head size. Prater (66) compared the DAP's of 49 male hemiplegics with a matched group of 43 normal males. He found no significant difference between the two groups in head size. Royal (67) found no significant difference between the shape of the head on DAP's rendered by 80 VA Mental Hygiene Clinic patients diagnosed as anxiety neurosis and the DAP's rendered by 100 VA dental patients. De Martino (25) found no significant difference between the head size of the DAP's of mentally retarded homosexuals and mentally retarded normals.

On the other hand, Goldworth (32) found significant differences between the heads drawn by normals, neurotics, psychotics, and brain-damaged patients. He compared the drawings of 50 normals, 50 neurotics, 50 psychotics, and 50 brain-damaged patients on 51 scoring items of the DAP. He scored each of the items with a rating scale. He tested the significance of the differences between the diagnostic groups of Ss with the chi-square technique. In addition to testing for the significance of the differences between the diagnostic groups, he also tested for the significance of the differences between the male and female Ss, using the chi square. He found differences significant at the .05 level or higher on 38 of the 51 scoring items. He found that normal Ss tend to draw heads that are more accurate, better proportioned, and better differentiated than heads drawn by neurotic, psychotic, or brain-damaged subjects. He particularly noted that the brain-damaged subjects tended to draw heads that were either grossly disproportionate or omitted significant details. Rarely, according to Goldworth, does a brain-damaged S draw a head that is reasonably correctly proportioned, with the correct shape, and containing the essential details that are included in a

normal head. His research suggests that the normal tends to draw a "normal head"; neurotics tend to draw heads that are generally fairly accurate, well proportioned, well differentiated, and containing the essential details of a human head, but not quite as good as heads drawn by normals; that schizophrenics tend to draw relatively more frequently distorted heads, inaccurate heads, misproportioned heads, or heads with significant details missing; and brain-damaged generally draw the least well-proportioned heads. His research also suggests that there is a considerable amount of overlap between these groups. Kotkov and Goodman (47) found that obese females tended to draw heads that were significantly larger than females of normal weight. However, since obese females draw figures that cover a larger area of the page than normal females do, it might be considered that the larger head area is a function of the general tendency of the obese female to draw a larger figure.

The Face

According to Machover "the face is the most expressive part of the body" (55, p. 40). Machover feels that the face is the center of communication and that it is the easiest part of the body to draw. She states that Ss who draw the head as the last feature usually show disturbance in interpersonal relationships. Subjects who deliberately omit facial features in their drawings are evasive about the frictional character of their interpersonal relationships. She feels that omitting facial features is a graphic expression of the avoidance of social problems. She states that superficiality, caution, and hostility may characterize the social contacts of an individual who omits drawing the facial features. However, she does feel that occasionally normal Ss will omit them.

Holzberg and Wexler (44) found no significant differences between normal Ss and schizoprenic Ss in the presence or absence of facial features. On the other hand, Margolis (58), in reporting the case of a schizophrenic girl treated by outpatient psychotherapy, noted that at the end of nine months of therapy this girl drew facial features last in sequence on the DAP. Margolis suggests that this indicates the difficulty the girl had in facing the world. However, this girl is reported as having improved her interpersonal relationships while in therapy.

Facial expression. According to Machover (55, p. 42), facial expression is one of the characteristics of drawings which may be judged directly with considerable confidence. Machover feels that regardless of the S's skill he unconsciously sets the tone for the drawing by giving the figures expressions of fear, hate, aggression, meekness, etc. She mentions, for example, that schizoid individuals will frequently draw a facial expression reflecting autistic and narcissistic preoccupation, with "large size and aborted or blocked movement trends to inforce the fantasy quality of the subject's ego concentration."

Fisher and Fisher (28) found that there was low agreement among seven judges judging facial expression on drawings taken from 32 paranoid schizophrenics. The authors mentioned the fact that they repeatedly ran across wide disagreement between one rater and another in the judgment concerning the facial expression. In this study Fisher and Fisher used two psychiatrists, three psychologists, and two stenographers as judges. Only the psychologists had experience in figure-drawing analysis. However, the highest agreement among judges on the facial expression was between the two stenographers who agreed in regard to 13 of the 32 DAP's. On the other hand, Goldworth (32) found significant differences between normals, neurotics, psychotics, and brain-damaged patients on facial expression. He noted that neurotics' drawings show fewer instances of "happy" expressions and more of "unhappy" ex-

pressions than the normal Ss. Schizophrenics show by far the largest incidence of "peculiar" and "doll-like" facial expression. The brain-damaged group resembles the schizophrenic group in the sense that they do not often draw "happy" expressions. The brain-damaged group shows many instances of an "unhappy" expression. "Empty" expression on a figure is drawn almost exclusively by brain-damaged subjects.

The mouth. According to Machover (55, p. 43), "Oral emphasis is marked in the drawings of young children, primitive, regressed, alcoholic, and depressed individuals. Since the mouth is often the source of sensual and erotic satisfaction, it features conspicuously in in the drawings of individuals with sexual difficulties. Overemphasis of the mouth is frequently tied up with food faddism and gastric symptoms, profane language, and temper tantrums." According to Machover, mouth detailing with the teeth showing is considered an index of infantile, oral aggression often seen in simple schizophrenics or hysterical types. The concave or orally receptive mouth is, according to Machover, generally seen in the drawings of infantile, dependent individuals. The mouth that is defined by a heavy line slash is generally an indication of aggression and is found in verbally aggressive, overcritical, and sometimes sadistic subjects. The mouth that is "heavy but brief," that is, one in which an individual starts to draw a heavy line slash but then suddenly withdraws from the page during the drawing, is generally found in individuals who are aggressive but who anticipate rebuff for their aggression and so withdraw cautiously. A single line for a mouth is generally considered by Machover to be an indication that the individual is shutting the mouth against something. This kind of mouth is sometimes seen in individuals who have had active homosexual experience. The wide, grinning mouth, giving the effect of a grinning clown, is interpreted as forced congeniality, an effort to win approval, or even inappropriate affect, depending upon other aspects of the drawing. Machover also states that asthmatics sometimes omit the mouth.

Holzberg and Wexler (44) found that normal women more frequently drew female figures in which the corners of the mouth were turned up and in which the mouth was shaded than schizophrenic women did. They found there were no significant differences between schizophrenic and normal women in the frequency of having the corners of the mouth turned down and having the mouth represented by a single line. They found that normal women more frequently had the mouth turned up than hebephrenic women, but that there was no significant difference between normal women and hebephrenic women in having the corners of the mouth turned down, having an object in the mouth, having the mouth open, or having the mouth represented by a single line. They found that normal women significantly more frequently had shading in the mouth than paranoid women, but there was no significant difference between normal and paranoid schizophrenic women in having the mouth open, having an object in the mouth, having the corners of the mouth turned down, or the corners of the mouth turned up, or in having the mouth represented by a single line. There were no significant differences between normal women and any classification of schizophrenic women in the presence or absence of teeth.

Cramer-Azima (22) found that a man recovering from the effects of exposure to beryllium dust showed changes in his treatment of the mouth that were concomitant with the changes in his behavior. He was originally meek, depressed, and uncooperative. At this time nothing unusual was noted about his mouth by the author. As treatment progressed he became moderately anxious, restless, and angry about certain conditions existing in his home. At this time he showed "aggressive treatment" of the mouth. After three weeks of treatment he was expansive, somewhat grandiose and anxious. At this time the teeth were featured in the mouth as well as other "aggressive" indicators. After discontinuation of treatment when he was feeling physically better and showing no overt signs of anxiety or hostility, it was noted that the drawing of his mouth showed fewer "aggressive" features.

Margolis (58), in noting the changes of the DAP of a 16-year-old schizoid girl during nine months of psychotherapy, noted that at the beginning of treatment the girl was fearful, childish, with no social activities, no friends, and seeking to enter a convent. At this time she drew a mouth which was a "forced, grinning one." After nine months of treatment when the patient was more outgoing and sociable, and more efficient in intellectual functioning, she drew a mouth that was fuller but narrower. However, the author notes that at the termination of therapy the mouth was drawn with a more dissatisfied expression than in the drawings produced earlier in therapy.

Gutman (40), in comparing patients who improved in therapy to patients who did not improve in therapy, found no significant differences between the two groups in representing the mouth with a single line or in drawing the mouth open.

The lips. Lips are difficult to separate from the mouth in treatment as is indicated in some of the discussion which preceded in the case of the mouth. However, Machover states (55, p. 45) that full lips in a male figure generally indicate effeminacy and appear with other features reflecting "foppish and narcissistic interests." She states that individuals who draw lips that resemble a phallus have had homosexual experience. Girls drawing elaborate cupid-bow lips in combination with other heavily cosmetized features are generally sexually precocious. Objects drawn in the mouth, such as a straw or toothpick or, on a more sophisticated level, cigarette or pipe, generally indicate oral erotic trends.

Holzberg and Wexler (44) found that normal women significantly more frequently show line emphasis in the outline of the lips than schizophrenic women do. They found no significant difference between normals and schizophrenic women in shading the lips or drawing an object in the mouth. They found no significance differences between normal women and hebephrenic schizophrenic women in drawing objects in the mouth, shading, or line emphasis in the lips. De Martino (25) found no significant differences between homosexual and nonhomosexual mentally retarded males in their drawing of the lips, or in placing an object in the mouth.

The eyes. According to Machover (55, p. 47), the eye can be regarded as the "window of the soul," revealing the inner life of the individual, ". . . (and) is a basic organ for contact with the outside world." Therefore, she feels that the eye is the chief point of concentration for the feeling of "self" and the vulnerability of "self." Since the eye is the window through which the self is revealed and also the means by which the individual maintains contact with the outside world, it follows that the individual who is most concerned with keeping contact with the outside world, namely the suspicious individual looking for hostility from the outside world, is most apt to emphasize the eye. The paranoid, of course, is the psychopathological category most nearly fitting this description, and therefore we would expect to find that the paranoid most frequently draws overemphasized eyes. People concerned with social functions are more apt to detail the eye, elaborating such things as eyelashes. Since females are more sociable than males, ac-

cording to Machover, women would be expected to have a greater tendency to elaborate the drawing of the eyes. Also effeminate men, such as homosexuals, would be expected to elaborate the eyes and perhaps draw eyelashes on the figure. Machover mentions that homosexuals will sometimes draw eyelashes, and in addition draw a figure with a "well-specified pupil." On the other hand, she states that people with a tendency to shut out the world will tend to draw figures with the eyes closed, or perhaps draw a circle for an eye and omit the pupil. She states that this is most apt to be seen in a patient who is emotionally immature and egocentric.

De Martino (25) noted that his homosexual mentally retarded males drew eyelashes on their figures significantly more often than the nonhomosexuals.

Gutman (40) found that patients who did not improve in therapy had a tendency to draw either piercing eyes or blank eyes. The piercing eyes would be characteristic of a paranoid schizophrenic, and the blank eyes characteristic of the simple schizophrenic or schizoid individual, both types having a poor prognosis for psychotherapy.

On the other hand, De Martino (25) found no significant differences between homosexual mentally retarded males and nonhomosexual males in the way they drew the parts of the eyes other than the eyelashes. Fisher and Fisher (28) were unable to differentiate between normal Ss and paranoid schizophrenic Ss using six DAP signs. One of the six DAP signs they used was eye emphasis.

Holzberg and Wexler (44) found that there was no significant difference between normals and paranoid schizophrenic women in any aspect of the eyes. However, they did find that hebephrenic women had a significantly greater tendency to draw eyes represented by circles, dots, or dashes and curves than normal women. Taking the schizophrenic group as a whole, however, they found that there was no significant difference between normal women and schizophrenic women in dealing with the eyes.

The eyebrow. Machover (55, p. 49) suggests that the eyebrow is probably related to other hair indicators. The trim eyebrow reflects the refined and well-groomed individual, while the bushy brow suggests the primitive, rough, and uninhibited individual. The raised eyebrow suggests disdain, haughtiness, or query.

Holzberg and Wexler (44) found that normals tend to be significantly more careful in detailing the eyebrows than schizophrenics, and normals tend significantly more often to have carefully detailed eyebrows than their paranoid schizophrenic subgroup. They found no significant difference between normals and schizophrenics in the presence or absence of eyebrows. De Martino (25) found no significant difference between homosexual and non-homosexual mentally retarded males in the presence of eyebrows.

The ear. The ears, according to Machover (55, p. 50), are probably of less significance than some of the other parts of the body. However, if the ears are emphasized in a drawing, this suggests that the ears have been particularly sensitized for the individual who is doing the drawing. Particularly the paranoid individual, with his guardedness and suspiciousness, will likely give emphasis to the ears.

Holzberg and Wexler (44) found that schizophrenics draw either no ears, or ears where none should be, significantly more often than normals. However, when Holzberg and Wexler compared the normals with the paranoid and hebephrenic schizophrenics divided into subgroups, neither subgroup alone differed significantly from the normals in the drawing of the ears.

Gutman (40) found that the presence or absence of ears did not differentiate significantly between patients who

improved and patients who did not improve in psychotherapy. Fisher and Fisher (28) used large ears as one of the six signs by which paranoids might be distinguished from normals. In their study these signs did not differentiate the two groups.

The hair. Machover notes (55, p. 51) that hair emphasis, regardless of where it occurs, is generally considered an indication of striving for virility. This emphasis may be manifested by drawing a large amount of hair, with an elaborate coiffure, or with shading the hair. Machover feels that messy hair suggests immorality. A drawing of a hairy woman suggests the woman is viewed as being sexually passionate. She suggests that emphasis on wavy, glamorous, and cascading hair, when combined with other outstanding cosmetic details, is usually seen in the drawings of adolescent girls who are either sexually delinquent or entertain aspirations of an amorous sort.

Holzberg and Wexler (44) found that normals drew the hair inadequately significantly more frequently than their total group of schizophrenics. However, when the paranoid schizophrenic subgroup and the hebephrenic subgroup were independently compared with the control group of normals, no significant differences were found in the treatment of the hair. When Cramer-Azima's (22) beryllium-dust-poisoned man had received ACTH treatment for 21 days he began acting euphoric and exhibited considerable interest in a female patient. At this time he drew a female figure with glamorous and wavy hair.

Royal (67) was unable to find any significant difference between normals and anxiety neurotics in the shading of the hair. Gutman (40) was unable to find any significant difference between patients who improved and patients who did not improve in psychotherapy on the amount of hair drawn on the figure or on excessive detailing of the hair. De Martino (25) found no significant differences between homosexual and nonhomosexual mentally retarded males in hair treatment.

The nose. The nose is considered by Machover (55, p. 54) to be a sexual symbol. She suggests that patients having sexual difficulties or feeling sexual immaturity, inferiority, impotence, or other sexual insufficiency are inclined to emphasize the nose by either reinforcing it, making it larger, erasing, or shading, or other emphasized treatment of this sort. She suggests that impotence in the older male, for example, is often symbolically indicated in the drawing by an excessively long nose. On the other hand, it is suggested that the shaded or cut off nose is primarily related to castration fears, particularly castration fears stemming from autoerotic indulgence. She suggests that if nostrils are indicated with any degree of emphasis they are regarded as a specific accent on aggression.

Holzberg and Wexler (44) found no significant differences between normals and schizophrenics of any type in any aspect of the nose including size, shading, and shape. De Martino (25) found no significant difference between homosexual and nonhomosexual mentally retarded males in the treatment of the nose. Goldworth (32) found no significant differences between normals, neurotics, schizophrenics, and brain-damaged patients in drawing the nose. However, he did find that schizophrenic and normal men apparently tend to draw conflict indicators on the male nose more often than schizophrenic or normal women.

Contact features

Contact features are the legs and feet and the arms and hands. Machover feels (55, pp. 59–60) that children and young adults will show more movement in their drawings than will older people because they are physically more active. As individuals grow older,

Machover feels that the representation of movement in the drawings tends to decrease just as the physical activity of people tends to decrease with age. In people in whom effective contact with the outside world has been weakened, such as in neurotic or psychotic patients, the contact features will be weakened. The figures may have stiff arms and legs, or weak, poorly developed arms and legs in which the arms are held stiffly at the sides rather than extending out toward the environment.

Arms and hands. The arms and hands are felt to be "weighted with psychological meanings referring primarily to ego development and social adaptation" (55, p. 60). It is with the arms and hands that the individual feeds and dresses himself, either caresses or hurts other people, and maintains contact with the environment. Arms extending out to the environment in a warm, accepting fashion indicate good relationships with the environment. Machover feels that the direction of the arm placement is important in determining the contact of the individual with the environment. She feels that "in general, the direction and fluency of the arm lines relate to the degree and spontaneity of extension into the environment." She feels that omission of the arms should never be considered an oversight. Schizophrenics or extremely depressed subjects may omit the arms as an indication of withdrawal from the environment. She notes that sometimes the arms of the female may be omitted by males, in which case it suggests that the male has been rejected by his mother, and has felt unaccepted by contemporary females. She notes that the hand is the most frequently omitted feature in the drawing and the implication of missing hands or hands that are vague or dimmed out suggests the lack of confidence in social contacts or in productivity or both.

Holzberg and Wexler (44) found that normal women significantly more often have the hands and arms present in the drawing than schizophrenic women, more frequently had the arms placed behind the back, more frequently had line emphasis on the outline of the arms, more frequently had the arms bent at the elbows, and more frequently shaded the arms. This, of course, suggests more conflict indicators were present in normal women than in schizophrenic women. However, the authors point out that their normal group was made up of girls who probably still had not completely resolved their adolescent conflicts related to contact with other people. Probably this difference is more a reflection of the fact that schizophrenics' drawings tend to be empty and lacking in detail, whereas the drawings of normals contain more detail and therefore would probably contain more conflict indicators.

Goldworth (32) found statistically significant differences between normals, neurotics, psychotics, and brain-damaged Ss in the drawing of the arms and hands. He found that normal Ss predominantly drew arms on their figures that were scored "accurate." The normals drew arms that were correctly proportioned. Normals usually drew their arms in motion or in a natural pose. Normal men tended to redraw the arms of the female figure, making changes in the size of the arms. Normal women tended to do much erasing on the arms of the female figure. Normal Ss rarely omitted the arms from the female figure or drew reinforced lines in the arms of the female figure. Normals also rarely omitted the arms on the male figure, but they drew more reinforced lines and did more erasing on the arms of the male figure than did any other group.

Goldworth found that the neurotics also tended to draw arms that were scored "accurate" but not quite as frequently as did the normals. Neurotics rarely drew arms that were disproportionate. Neurotics drew arms that were

rigid, or dangling, more frequently than did normals, and drew fewer arms that were in motion or in a natural pose than the normal Ss did. Neurotics rarely omitted or reinforced the arms, and shaded or erased the arms *less* frequently than any of the other groups.

Schizophrenics drew arms that were scored as "accurate" less frequently than the normals and neurotics. One-fifth of the schizophrenics drew arms scored "distorted." They drew disproportionate arms more frequently than the normals and neurotics. They drew arms that were rigid and lacking in muscle tone more frequently than any of the other groups. Schizophrenics omitted the arms and reinforced the lines in the arms more frequently than any of the other groups.

Brain-damaged Ss rarely drew arms that were scored "accurate." They drew well-proportioned arms less frequently than any other group. Their arms were drawn dangling more frequently than those of any other group. They tended to draw many size changes on the female arms, and tended to draw somewhat fewer reinforced lines, erasures, and shading on the arms of the female figure than did the other groups.

Normal Ss rarely drew distorted hands, but one-third of them attempted to hide the hands. Normals drew well-proportioned hands more frequently than any of the other groups. The normals had more shading and erasures in the hands than any of the other groups.

The neurotic Ss drew more distorted hands than the normals, and did not hide the hands as frequently as the normals. They tended to draw well-proportioned hands, but not as frequently as did the normals. The neurotics did less shading and erasing than did the normals, but they made more changes in the size of the hands than the normals did.

Schizophrenics drew hands scored as "accurate" about as frequently as the neurotics, and omitted the hands no more frequently than the neurotics did. They drew fewer well-proportioned hands than the normals. The schizophrenics erased less and drew less shading in the hands than the normals, but they redrew the hands, changing the size, more often than the normals.

Brain-damaged Ss rarely drew hands that had good accuracy and they rarely evaded drawing the hands. They drew fewer well-proportioned hands than any of the other groups. The brain-damaged tended to change the size of the hands more frequently than did the normals.

Woods and Cook (85) noted that there was an r of .43 (significant at the .01 level) between drawing proficiency and the tendency of eighth-grade students to draw the hands behind the back. Woods and Cook interpret this as indicating that as a student gets more proficient at drawing he becomes aware that drawing the hands is difficult and thus has a tendency to avoid drawing them. This suggests that a tendency to hide hands goes with normality and increased maturity. This seems to agree with the findings of Goldworth which are mentioned above.

On the negative side, Holzberg and Wexler (44) found no significant difference between normals and schizophrenics in poor proportion of arms (which does not agree with Goldworth), the drawing of very short arms, the drawing of very long arms, arms held at a distance from the body, arms held over the head, arms held in front of the body, arms perpendicular to the body, and arms misplaced in relation to the shoulders. They also found no significant difference in the drawings of muscular arms or in the hiding of hands or in the drawing of distorted hands or line emphasis or shading in the hands. De Martino (25) found no significant differences between homosexual and nonhomosexual mentally retarded males in the drawing of the arms or the hands. Gutman (40) found no significant differences between patients who improved and patients who did not improve in therapy in the drawing of arms or hands. Royal (67) found no significant difference between normals and neurotics in drawing figures with missing or hidden hands, or in the relation of the man's arms to the body or of the woman's arms to the body. As noted earlier Prater (66) found no significant differences between hemiplegics and normals in the drawing of the arms.

The fingers. According to Machover (55, p. 63), the fingers are extremely important in the experiential pattern of the person since they are the real contact points between the individual and the environment. Also they are important as the parts of the body that involve manipulation. Therefore she feels that grape-like fingers, though common in children, are generally indicative of either poor manual skill or infantility when found in adults. And she feels that shaded fingers or reinforced fingers are generally indicative of guilt. Speared or talon-like fingers indicate aggression and are considered to be paranoid features. She feels that the clutched fist, when held away from the body, indicates aggressive behavior which is fairly close to being acted out. When the clutched fist is held close to the body, it indicates inner repressed rebellion that is probably expressed in symptoms rather than in overt behavior. The mitten type of hand is also associated with repressed aggression, but is more evasive and noncommittal, generally being manifested by occasional outbursts of aggression rather than by symptoms. Abnormally long fingers in a drawing that is generally regressed suggest people who have "shallow, flat, and simple types of personality development." Hands that are drawn with more than five fingers on them suggest that the drawer is an aggressive, ambitious individual. Fingers that have the joints and nails carefully indicated suggest obsessive control of aggression. This is also true of drawings in which the fingers are formed like a claw or a mechanical tool.

There are few data relative to these hypotheses. Holzberg and Wexler (44) found that hebephrenic schizophrenic women had significantly fewer poorly proportioned fingers than normal women. Gutman (40) found that there were no significant differences between the patients who improved in therapy and patients who did not improve in therapy in the drawing of useless or confused fingers. Fisher and Fisher (28) found that speared fingers were not present in a majority of paranoid patients' drawings. De Martino (25) found no significant difference between homosexual and nonhomosexual mentally retarded males in the drawing of the fingers.

The legs and feet. The legs and feet are not only contact features, but also bear the responsibility of supporting and balancing the body and of moving the body about. Therefore, Machover feels (55, p. 65) that drawings showing nonexistent or weak legs and feet indicate an individual either unable to get about or having an uncertain footing or foundation. The legs of the female figure have sexual significance. If they receive conflict treatment in the form of reinforcement, erasures, or changes it suggests conflict in the sexual area. The foot may be a phallic symbol. An individual who draws a foot that looks like a phallus may be sexually inadequate and/or sexually preoccupied. Conflict treatment of the foot, such as erasures, lengthening, shortening, changing the line, or shading, suggest conflict in the sexual area. The foot may have aggressive implications, since it is an organ for propelling the body forward as well as an instrument for attack.

Goldworth (32) found that there were significant differences among his groups, in the accuracy with which they drew the legs. Four-fifths of the drawings of legs by normals were well proportioned. Normals were more accurate, particularly in the drawing of the female leg. There were a few distorted legs among the figures drawn by neurotics. Schizophrenics' drawings, he found, were much like those of the neurotics both in the accuracy of the legs and the proportion of the legs, but he did note that schizophrenics somewhat more frequently drew distorted legs than neurotics did. The brain-damaged group drew the greatest number of distorted legs, and rarely drew accurate legs. He found that there was a slight tendency for normal men to be less accurate than women in drawing the feet. Therefore, he made comparisons only between the drawings of men. He found that there were significant differences (.09 level of confidence) among the four groups in the drawing of the male feet and a significant difference (.02 level of confidence) in the drawings of the female feet. He noted that normals omit the feet as they did the hands more frequently than any of the other groups. Neurotics' drawings of the female figure are very similar to those of normals, but neurotic men do not omit the feet on the male figure as often as normal men do. This is because neurotic men tend to draw smaller male figures, and thus have enough room at the bottom of the sheet of paper for drawing the feet, whereas the normal men often draw a large male figure and do not have enough room at the bottom of the sheet of paper to get the feet on. Schizophrenics did not differ noticeably from neurotics. The brain-damaged drew the highest proportion of distorted feet. He found no significant differences among the four groups in the proportionate size of the feet. He found that there were significant sex differences in the female figure; he noted that schizophrenic women rarely drew conflict indicators on the feet, while schizophrenic men did a great deal of shading, erasing, and reinforcing compared to the women. Schizophrenic men more frequently reinforced, erased, or shaded the feet of the female figure than men in other groups. There were no significant differences between the groups in shading, reinforcing, or re-drawing the feet on the male figure.

Holzberg and Wexler (44) found that normal women significantly more often drew both legs and feet on their drawings than schizophrenic women, which is contrary to Goldworth's find-ings. Their normal women significantly more often drew very small, pointed feet on the drawings than schizophrenic women. The normals significantly more often than the hebephrenic schizo-phrenics drew the legs, drew a knee joint, and drew very small pointed feet. However, when the normal women were compared with the paranoid schizophrenics, it was found that the only significant difference was that the normals significantly more often used line emphasis on the outline of the legs. There were no significant differences between the groups in legs drawn off the bottom of the page, locked or closed legs, poorly shaped and dispro-portionate legs, stick legs, excessively short legs, or excessively long legs, shading the legs, naked feet, delinea-tion of toenails, poorly formed feet, ex-cessively large feet, penis-like feet, single-dimensioned feet, shading the legs and feet, or line emphasis in the outline of the feet or shoes.

Toes. According to Machover (55, p. 67), when toes are indicated in a figure that is not intended to be a nude they are regarded as an accent on aggressiveness that "is almost patho-logical in nature." Holzberg and Wex-ler (44) found no significant differences between normals and schizophrenics in drawing naked feet with the toes indi-cated, or in drawing feet with the toe-nails delineated.

Miscellaneous Body Features

The trunk. Machover states (55, p. 68) that the trunk is often limited to a simple oblong, a square box, or a cir-cular unit. She suggests that round figures are drawn by individuals who are passive and have feminine char-acteristics, whereas square trunks are drawn by masculine persons. The bot-tom of the trunk is left open in some drawings. Machover suggests that this indicates sexual preoccupation. Draw-ing an especially thin trunk on the figure of the same sex as the S is suggested as indicating that the subject is discon-tented with his body type. In the case of a thin individual, the thin trunk is a direct representation of body weak-ness, and in a heavy individual the thin trunk suggests "compensation for unwelcome rotundity."

Goldworth (32) found that normal men drew the trunk with greater ac-curacy significantly more often than normal women. He also found that there were significant differences be-tween normal men, neurotic men, psy-chotic men, and brain-damaged men. He observed that practically all normals drew trunks that scored at the "excellent" or "adequate" accuracy level. No normals scored at the "primitive" or "distorted" level. Neurotics drew few extremely good trunks and several drew distorted trunks, but no neurotics drew primitive trunks. Schizo-phrenics drew trunks that resembled those drawn by neurotics, but the schizophrenics drew primitive and dis-torted trunks more frequently than neurotics. The brain-damaged drew "primitive" trunks more frequently than the other three groups. Goldworth found that there were no sig-nificant differences between his four groups in the proportions of the male trunks they drew. There were sig-nificant differences between the four groups in proportions of the female trunks they drew. Normals drew female trunks that were correctly proportioned. Most of the grossly disproportioned female trunks were drawn by schizophrenics and brain-damaged patients.

Holzberg and Wexler (44) found the only difference between normal women and schizophrenic women was that the normal women significantly more often drew shading in the chest and waist areas of their figures. There were no significant differences between normals and hebephrenic schizophrenic women in any of the body characteristics, but normal women significantly more often shaded the chest than the paranoid schizophrenic women.

Royal (67) found in comparing his neurotics with normals that the neurotics tended to draw the head and trunk in a rectangular or circular shape significantly more frequently than normals. There was no significant difference between the two groups on the shading of the body.

Breasts. According to Machover (55, p. 69), the most consistent emphasis on breasts is noted in the drawings of the emotionally and psychosexually immature male. This sort of emphasis is generally found to consist of erasures, shading, or the addition of lines. Machover feels that it is important whether the breasts on the figure are the low, pendant sort of breasts typical of a mother-figure, or the high, firm breasts of the youthful female figure. She notes that the female who draws large breasts and a well-developed pelvis on her female figure is strongly "identified with a productive and dominant mother-image. . . ."

Holzberg and Wexler (44) found that normal women significantly more often than schizophrenic women delineated the breasts and shaded the chest. When the subgroups were compared no significant differences between normal women and hebephrenic schizophrenic women were found, but the normal women significantly more often delineated the breasts than the paranoid

schizophrenic women. There were no significant differences between the normals and the schizophrenics in drawing a very narrow chest, drawing a nude breast or breasts, in the line emphasis on the outline of the chest, or delineating the nipples on the breast.

Goldworth (32) found that breast emphasis was found primarily in the drawings of neurotic subjects.

Shoulders. According to Machover (55, p. 71), the width and massiveness of the shoulders are the most common graphic expression of physical power and perfection of physique. In drawings by males massive shoulders emphasized at the expense of other parts of the figure are generally drawn by adolescents and sexually ambivalent individuals as an overcompensation for feelings of body inadequacy. A female S who draws massive shoulders on the female figure may be suspected of having some degree of masculine protest. Massive shoulders on the figure of the same sex as the S indicate that the S feels physically inadequate.

Holzberg and Wexler (44) found that normal women significantly more often had shoulders present on their drawings than did schizophrenics. When the schizophrenic group was split into paranoid and hebephrenic subgroups and compared with the normal group, it was found that normals significantly more often drew broad shoulders, had shoulders present in the drawings, and emphasized the lines of the outlines of the shoulders than did hebephrenic schizophrenics. Normals significantly more often drew broad shoulders than did the paranoid schizophrenics. Kotkov and Goodman (47) found that obese females drew square shoulders more often than normal weight females. Goldworth (32) found there were no significant differences among his groups of male Ss in drawing the shoulders. However, he found that there were significant differences among his female groups. The normal women made many more erasures than did any of the other groups, and showed far fewer instances of omission, shading, or changing the size of the shoulders. He found that neurotics occupied a score position intermediate between the normals on one hand and the schizophrenic and brain-damaged on the other hand. The schizophrenic and brain-damaged women tended to have few erasures but had many omissions, and much shading or size changes on the shoulders of the female figure.

These studies provide no clear-cut test of Machover's hypotheses, but they suggest that the shoulders may have more significance for female Ss than for male Ss.

Hips and buttocks. According to Machover (55, p. 72), emphasis on the hips and buttocks is characteristic of homosexually inclined or homosexually conflicted males. This may be indicated by confusion, a break or change in the line, a particular widening or other conspicuous treatment of the buttocks. In female figures drawn by females exaggerated hips indicate that the woman is aware of the power that relates to the "functional potentialities of ample pelvic development."

Goldworth (32) found no significant differences between males and females in treatment of the buttocks; however, he did find significant differences between normals, neurotics, psychotics, and brain-damaged people. He found that normal individuals had the fewest conflict indicators in the drawings of male hips, while the brain-damaged showed the greatest number of conflict indicators on both the male and female hips. The neurotic drawings tended to fall midway between the drawings of normals and the drawings of the brain-damaged in the number of conflict indicators found in the hips.

No studies report a comparison of the drawings of hips by homosexual males with drawings of hips by non-homosexual males. This seems rather strange since this hypothesis would seem to be a fairly clear-cut and easy one to test.

Waistline. The waistline serves to separate the "above" part of the body from the "below" part of the body (55, p. 72). In the man the "above" part is the chest area which embraces the primary body features of physical strength. The "below" part refers to the area of sexual functioning. In the female the "above" part refers primarily to the breasts and nutritional factors, whereas the "below" part in the female refers to the sexual and reproductive functions. The legs of the female also are related to the sexual allure of the girl; therefore, adolescent girls "being at the threshold of adult sexuality," show the greatest amount of leg conflict. Machover feels that conflict in the waistline may be expressed by a delay in drawing the waistline, by a reinforced waistline, by a broken line at the waistline, by an elaborate belt drawn at the waistline, or by an excessively tightened waistline.

Holzberg and Wexler (44) found that normal women significantly more often than schizophrenic women shaded the waist area. When comparing the schizophrenic subgroups with normal women, they found no significant differences between normal women and hebephrenic schizophrenic women, but found that normal women did shade the waist area significantly more often than paranoid schizophrenic women; and also that normal women had an "absence of straight vertical lines for the waist" significantly more often than paranoid schizophrenic women. However, there were no significant differences between normal women and schizophrenic women in line emphasis on the outline of the waist.

De Martino (25) found no significant difference between homosexual mentally retarded males and nonhomosexual mentally retarded males on shading of the waist.

Anatomy indications. According to

Machover (55, p. 74), internal organs are not drawn in the DAP except by schizophrenics or actively manic patients. However, Holzberg and Wexler (44) found no significant difference between normal and schizophrenic women in the representation of internal organs. Few Ss in either group drew internal organs on their figures.

Machover feels that the inclusion of sexual organs in a drawing is not generally found except in the drawings of professional artists, people who are under psychoanalysis, and schizophrenics. But in this regard, too, Holzberg and Wexler (44) found no significant difference between normal women and schizophrenic women in any representation of the genitals, or in line emphasis or shading in the genitals.

Joints. Machover states that the drawing (55, p. 75) of joints suggests a faulty and uncertain sense of body integrity. She feels that this sign is found chiefly in schizoid and schizophrenic individuals.

Holzberg and Wexler (44) found that normal women showed the knee joints significantly more often than hebephrenic schizophrenic women. There were no significant differences between the normal and schizophrenic women in the representation of knuckles. These results are a direct contradiction of Machover's hypothesis.

Clothing

Machover feels (55, p. 75) that "it is generally accepted that clothes always have some libidinal significance." She feels that clothing is essentially a compromise between modesty and body display, and that most subjects tend to draw a vague indication of clothing. She feels that a person who asks whether or not he should draw a figure with clothes on it may be assumed to be troubled by a strong body self-consciousness. Often the identity of the drawn figure can be inferred from the clothes.

For example, a male drawing a figure with clothes appropriate for the 1920's suggests that the S identified with his father. She also states that a small proportion of Ss tend to underclothe or overclothe their drawings. The overclothed figure is drawn by a "clothes-narcissist." The clothes-narcissist is a superficially quite sociable and extroverted individual, but this sociability is motivated primarily by a desire for social approval and dominance rather than by an interest in people. Those who underclothe the figure are called by Machover "body-narcissists." Body-narcissists tend to display muscle power and tend to be schizoid and introverted.

Holzberg and Wexler (44) noted that normal women had a significantly greater tendency to draw clothing on their figures than did schizophrenic women. When the schizophrenics were broken down into subgroups, they noted that normal women significantly more often than both the hebephrenic and paranoid schizophrenic women drew figures in which there were clothes. Paradoxically, Holzberg and Wexler also report that normal women drew figures which were nude significantly more often than the paranoid women. There were no significant differences between the normal women and the schizophrenic women in the drawing of minimal clothing, in having inadequate clothing represented, or in having a special emphasis on more-or-less unusual clothing items such as jewelry. Normal women significantly more often than schizophrenic women drew a figure with a wide skirt. There were no significant differences between the two groups in the drawing of shoelaces, high heels, gloves, or overcoats.

Structural and Formal Aspects

Action or movement. Machover states that action is more commonly found in the drawings of males than in the drawings of females (55, p. 85).

Drawings obtained from psychiatric hospital patients tend to be static. A figure which conveys an impulse to movement that is blocked is most often drawn by schizophrenics who have strivings toward actions that are blocked.

Holzberg and Wexler (44) found no significant differences between normals and schizophrenics in action portrayed in drawings. There were no significant differences between the groups on figures running, figures sitting, figures kneeling, or bending. Royal (67) found no significant differences between normals and neurotics in movement portrayed by the figure.

Goldworth (32) found that normals drew the arms in motion more frequently than his other groups. Neurotics drew substantially fewer figures with the arms in a natural motion than did the normals. Schizophrenics had drawings that were similar to those of the neurotics, with the exception that the schizophrenics more frequently drew "floating figures." (This refers to figures who do not "have their feet on the ground.")

Succession. Most normal people draw a figure with some sort of systematic succession. It is suggested (55, p. 86) that people suffering from an impulse disorder, such as manic excitement or schizophrenic thinking, work in confusion, scattering all over the drawing without any particular plan. On the other hand, the compulsive individual will tend to develop each area quite carefully and in detail bilaterally. Holzberg and Wexler (44) found no significant differences between normals and schizophrenics in a tendency to begin a drawing on one part of the page and then start someplace else on another part of the page, turning the page over, etc.

Mid-line. Mid-line emphasis may be indicated either by a line down the middle of the body or by an elaborate treatment of the Adam's apple, tie, buttons, buckle, or the fly on the trousers. Machover feels (55, p. 89) that such emphasis indicates somatic preoccupation, feelings of body inferiority, emotional immaturity, and mother-dependence.

Holzberg and Wexler (44) found that their normal women significantly more frequently than schizophrenic women emphasized the mid-lines of their drawings. When the normals were compared with the hebephrenic schizophrenic subgroup, it was found that the normal women significantly more often than the hebephrenic women emphasized the mid-lines. However, no significant difference was found between the normal women and the paranoid schizophrenic subgroup.

Size and placement. It is felt (55, p. 89) that a figure that is placed on the right side of the page indicates a subject who is environment-oriented, while a figure placed on the left side of the page suggests a subject who is self-oriented. A figure placed high on a page suggests optimism, while a figure placed low on a page suggests pessimism. Large figures suggest high self-esteem and high energy level, whereas small figures suggest low self-esteem and a low energy level; or, as Machover states in the case of regressed schizophrenics, a small figure is an expression of "a low energy level and a shrunken ego." Grandiose paranoid individuals tend to draw large figures which suggest high self-esteem. Individuals suffering paranoid conditions associated with alcoholism or senility, in which the self-esteem is low, may draw a figure which is small in size but high up on the page, the position of the figure on the page suggesting the optimism characteristic of these individuals. Large figures may also be drawn by the aggressive psychopath. However, Machover feels that the psychopath will draw his large figure on the left side of the page, which indicates that he not only has high self-esteem, but also suggests the inadequacy he feels.

Cramer-Azima (22), in her study of the drawings of a man under ACTH treatment for beryllium-dust poisoning, noted that when the patient was meek and depressed, at the beginning of treatment, he drew a figure that was about 3¼ inches high. After twenty-one days of treatment the patient was showing signs of euphoria and later became grandiose. At this time, his figure was 8½ inches tall. After the discontinuation of treatment, when the patient's behavior became less euphoric and expansive, he drew a figure 6½ inches tall. In this case, the size of the figure seemed to increase as the subject became more euphoric, and the figure became smaller as he became less euphoric. Gutman (40) noted that patients who improved in therapy tended to draw figures that were more than four inches tall. Patients who did not improve in psychotherapy tended to draw figures that were less than four inches tall. Lehner and Gunderson (50) found that men tend to draw larger figures the older they get, until they get to 30 years of age. Beyond 30 years of age, men tend to draw figures smaller and smaller. Women tend to draw larger figures, the older they get, until they reach age 40. Beyond age 40, women tend to draw gradually smaller figures. This could be interpreted as a reflection of the self-evaluation of the individuals; that is, as a man grows older and more capable, he tends to draw larger figures, but as he passes the "prime of life" and begins getting older and less able, his figures become smaller. Kotkov and Goodman (47) found that obese women tended to draw figures that covered more horizontal area on the page than did normal weight women.

On the other hand, Goodman and Kotkov (35), in their study of obese women, did not find any significant relationship between insecurity and a tendency to place the figure on the upper left-hand side of the page. Fisher and Fisher (28), in their study of signs on the DAP which differentiate between paranoids and normals, used as one of the signs of paranoid schizophrenia the size of the drawing. In their study they were unable to significantly differentiate between normals and paranoid schizophrenics using this sign. Gutman (40) found no significant difference between patients who improved in psychotherapy and those who did not improve in psychotherapy in the tendency to draw their figures on the left side of the page. Holzberg and Wexler (44) found that normal women tended to draw figures that were small or constricted in size significantly more often than schizophrenic women. They found that normal women tended to draw small figures significantly more often than the hebephrenic subgroup, but that they did not draw small figures significantly more frequently than the paranoid schizophrenic subgroup. There were no significant differences between the normals and schizophrenics in a tendency to draw very large figures or in the placement of the figures on the page. The evidence presented here is conflicting. A carefully controlled definitive study of these hypotheses should clear up some of the conflict.

Stance. The stance in drawings (55, p. 92) is regarded as meaning the same thing as the stance of a real person. A figure in which the legs float off into space may be drawn by an individual with precarious stability. This kind of figure is supposed to be drawn, for example, by older chronic alcoholics. A stance in which the legs are closely pressed together suggests a tense, self-conscious, and repressed individual. In a female figure this is suggested as "a fear (or repressed wish?) of sexual attack." It is suggested that when this is seen in the female figure drawn by a male subject, he anticipates resistance to sexual advances.

Goldworth (32), found significant differences between his groups in the stance of their figures. He found that normals usually drew figures which had a "normal" stance. No normal subjects drew figures that lacked equilibrium or were floating. The neurotics tended to draw fewer figures in a natural motion or pose than did normal Ss. Several of the figures drawn by neurotics lacked equilibrium. However, floating figures were rarely drawn by the neurotics. Schizophrenics' drawings tended to be quite similar to the drawings of neurotics with one major exception: there were a substantial number of floating figures drawn by schizophrenics. The brain-damaged subjects drew the least number of figures which had a definite equilibrium, and the largest number of figures which were floating or lacked equilibrium. Over one-third of the drawings by the brain-damaged group were either floating or lacked equilibrium.

Gutman (40) found no significant difference between the DAP's of those who improved in therapy and those who did not improve in therapy when compared for stance. However, when stance was combined with a tendency to draw the same sex larger, it was found that those patients who improved in therapy tended to draw figures with a firm, assertive stance and drew the same-sex figure larger than the opposite-sex figure significantly more often than did the group of patients who did not improve in therapy. When stance was combined with the position of the legs as a sign, it was found that patients who improved in therapy tended to draw figures with a firm, assertive stance, and with the legs side by side, in parallel, significantly more frequently than patients who did not improve in therapy. However, an assertive stance when combined with pressure of the lines of the drawing did not differentiate significantly between patients who improved and patients who did not improve.

Fisher and Fisher (28) were unable to differentiate significantly between normal women and paranoid schizophrenic women using rigid stance as a sign of paranoid schizophrenia. Royal (67) found no significant difference between normals and neurotics in the inclination of the figures from the vertical axis.

Perspective. It is felt (55, p. 93) that drawing the figure in profile indicates evasiveness. But drawing a figure from the front view does not necessarily indicate accessibility or frankness. Machover states that boys and men draw a figure in profile more frequently than girls or women do. This suggests that females are more sociable and are more accessible to clinical contact than are men.

Cramer-Azima (22) noted that when her subject, being treated with ACTH for beryllium-dust poisoning, was behaving in a rather expansive and euphoric manner he drew his figures facing forward. In the other drawings, when he was inclined to be more depressed, tense, and anxious, he tended to draw the figures facing sideways. Royal (67) found no significant difference between anxiety neurotics and normals in the direction they drew the men's or women's heads facing. Holzberg and Wexler (44) found no significant difference between normal women and schizophrenic women in having one part of the body in profile and the other part of the body in front view.

Type of line. The line delineating the contour of the body is felt to be the wall between the body and the environment (55, p. 95). Machover feels that chronic schizoid alcoholics and others suffering from fears of depersonalization or from acute conflict over withdrawal trends may draw a heavy, thick line as a barrier between themselves and the environment. She feels that "the body wall is built as a substantial structure as though to ward off an attack of the environment and to guard securely the contents of the body." She feels that the apprehensive neurotic individual may also draw heavy lines for the same reason. In such a drawing, conflicts which are aroused by drawing special areas in the figure will be expressed by a sudden change in the line or a gap in the line. Dim lines are most frequently drawn by timid, self-effacing, and uncertain individuals. The dim line may be sketched or fragmented. Also, a body drawn with such a line may have uncertain contours and individual parts of the body may be blurred. Drawings in which the contour of the head is heavy and reinforced while the facial features are dimly sketched suggests that the drawer is an individual with a strong desire for social participation, but who is shy and timid and self-conscious in actual social expression. Lines which fade in and out with spotty reinforcement are suggested as being drawn by people given to hysterical reactions. In these cases, the head and facial features may be well delineated while the body is blurred, and the arms and legs fade away into random lines. The very faint, "ectoplasmic," line does not appear very often, and when it does it is generally drawn by withdrawn schizophrenics. Acutely excited schizophrenics generally draw very heavy lines. Broken or tremulous lines are generally drawn by the schizoid alcoholic, who is distinguished from the paranoid alcoholic who tends to draw the figure with a heavy line.

Gutman (40) found that patients who did not improve in psychotherapy tended to draw continuous and reinforced lines. Patients who did improve in psychotherapy tended to draw their figures with light or sketchy lines. Royal (67) found no significant difference between normals and anxiety neurotics on pencil pressure, continuity of lines, regularity of lines, single-line and multiple-line drawings. Holzberg and Wexler (44) found no significant difference between normal females and various kinds of schizophrenic females in the use of very light lines throughout the whole drawing, in the use of light lines in

parts of the drawing, in the use of fragmented or broken lines in all of the drawing, or in the use of broken lines in just parts of the drawing.

Conflict Indicators

Erasures. Erasures are a form of conflict treatment and are most apt to be noticed in the hands and feet, the shoulders, the arms, the nose, the ears, the crotch, and the hipline. Interpretation depends on the part of the body in which the erasure is found. This form of conflict treatment is felt by Machover (55, p. 98) to be seen primarily in neurotics, obsessive compulsive characters, and psychopaths with neurotic conflicts. Erasures are considered an expression of anxiety but differ from line reinforcement and shading in that they show overt dissatisfaction. She states that pubertal girls erase profusely.

Royal (67) found no significant difference between his normal men and his anxiety neurotic men in erasures. Holzberg and Wexler (44) found that normal women tended to erase significantly more often than paranoid schizophrenic women, but that there was no significant difference between normal women and hebephrenic schizophrenic women in this regard. Goldworth (32) found that, in general, normals drew more conflict indicators, both erasures and shading, than did other groups. He notes that, in the case of the hands, arms, ears, and hips, neurotics tended to show the least number of conflict indicators. In the case of the shoulders, the neurotics tended to show fewer erasures than the normals, but more erasures than the schizophrenic or brain-damaged patients. In the case of the nose, the neurotics show fewer erasures than either normal men or schizophrenic men.

These results appear to contradict Machover.

Shading. Shading as an indicator of conflict has already been partially considered in connection with the discussion of the particular parts of the body, but some of this discussion will be repeated here. According to Machover (55, p. 98) shading is an indication of anxiety. The particular area shaded suggests the source of the anxiety. Vigorous, aggressive scribbling to cover up something is considered to be a discharge of aggression and an expression of concealment. The most frequent kind of shading is done by using light, dim, and uncertain lines which accent particular parts of the figure. The most frequently shaded parts of the figure are the chest of the male figure, which Machover feels indicates sensitivity to physical inferiority, and the breasts of the female figure done by the male S, which suggest conflict concerning mother dependence. Female subjects may put a few subtle lines in the skirt in the area of the genitals suggesting "furtive and inhibited sexual concern."

Goldworth (32) summarized his findings on this topic by stating that the normals' drawings contained the least number of conflict indicators, including shading, of any group on only three scales: the male and female ears, and the male hips. On all the other parts of the body, he found that the normals showed proportionately the same amount of conflict indicators as other groups. He found the brain-damaged group consistently drew the largest number of conflict indicators.

Holzberg and Wexler's (44) findings regarding shading of particular parts of the body have already been presented in relationship to other parts of the body. Briefly these results will be repeated here. Normal women significantly more frequently than schizophrenic women tended to shade the following parts: mouth, arms, chest, and waist. Normal women did not shade any parts significantly more often than the hebephrenic schizophrenic subgroup. However, normal women did shade the following parts more frequently than

the paranoid schizophrenic subgroup: mouth, hands, chest, and waist.

Royal (67) found no significant differences between normal men and anxiety neurotic men in the shading of the hair or of the body and clothing. Gutman (40) found no significant difference between patients who improved in therapy and patients who did not improve in therapy in the amount of shading on the figure. De Martino (25) found no significant differences between male homosexual mental defectives and male nonhomosexual mental defectives in the shading of the waist, arms, legs, or other body parts. The results seem to indicate that normals show at least as much shading, on most body parts, as any group of abnormal Ss.

Differential treatment of male and female figures. Machover hypothesizes (55, p. 101) that the individual who is identified with his own sex will draw the self-sex figure first. She states that "some degree of sexual inversion was contained in records of all individuals who drew the opposite sex first. . . ." She also feels that Ss who scramble the sexual characteristics of the two figures they draw are suffering from sexual maladjustment. A pair of figures in which one figure is drawn disproportionately larger than the other suggests that the larger figure is viewed as the stronger, while the smaller figure would suggest that the figure drawn smaller is the weaker sex.

Barker, Mathis, and Powers (8) compared a group of 50 homosexual soldiers with a control group of 35 normal soldiers on the sex of the first drawn figure. They found no significant difference between the two groups. Hammer (41) found no significant difference between homosexual offenders in Sing Sing Prison and two groups of nonhomosexual offenders in the sex of the first drawn figure. Granick and Smith (37) found no relationship between the sex of the first drawn figure and scores on the masculinity-femininity subscale of the MMPI. De Koningh (24) found no significant relationship between sex of the first drawn person and sexual differentiation as measured by Swensen's (76) scale which is described below.

Swensen (76) developed a scale for rating sexual differentiation between the male and female figures on the DAP. Using this scale to measure sexual differentiation, he found that normals drew figures in which the differentiation between the male and female figures is significantly better than that of either neurotics or psychotics. Sipprelle and Swensen (70) used this scale and three other sexual indicators on the DAP in an effort to determine the relationship between the DAP and the S's sexual adjustment. They found no significant relationship. Cutter (23) used Swensen's scale to compare the sexual differentiation of normals, neurotics, and psychiatric patients suffering from severe personality disorganization (psychotics, alcoholics, etc.). He used as Ss 108 sexual psychopaths under observation at a state hospital, 59 sexual psychopaths committed to the hospital who were receiving psychotherapy, 22 psychiatric technician trainees who served as a control group, a group of 19 neurotics and a group of 17 suffering from "personality disorganization." The "personality disorganization" group was composed of "alcoholics, psychotics in remission, etc." He found that there were no significant differences between the different groups of sexual offenders, and that the sexual offenders did not differentiate between the sexes of the figures on the DAP any worse than the normals. However, he did find that the group of overt sexual offenders differentiated between the sexes on the DAP significantly better than the group of neurotics or the group suffering "personality disorganization."

Fisher and Fisher (29) related the femininity of the female figure drawn by 76 female psychiatric patients to the sexual adjustment of these patients. The femininity of the female figure was rated on a four-point scale. They rated the Ss on the following indices: general femininity, subjective satisfaction from sexual relations, range of past heterosexual experience, somatic sexual dysfunction, and bizarre sexual manifestations accompanying the onset of mental illness. Of 54 computed statistics, only 8 were significant at the .05 level. They reported that women who drew figures of low femininity tended to have had fewer heterosexual experiences than the other Ss, had more dysfunctions of the sexual organs, and had led constricted sex lives. Those who drew the most feminine figures tended to have had more promiscuous but unsatisfying sexual experiences. The Ss drawing figures of intermediate femininity reported more satisfaction from their sexual experiences.

Singer (69) attempted to test Machover's hypotheses relative to the projection of sexual conflict on the DAP. Singer hypothesized that in our culture pubescents should suffer more sexual conflict than prepubescents. He used a group of 18 pubescents matched with a group of 18 prepubescents for age, IQ, school grade, and socioeconomic status. He obtained DAP's from both groups and analyzed them by an "analytic" method using signs obtained from Machover, and also analyzed them by a "holistic" method in which he judged the drawings as a whole rather than by paying attention to specific parts of the drawings. His techniques did not significantly differentiate between the drawings of the pubescents and the drawings of the prepubescents.

None of the studies cited above provides evidence to support Machover's hypothesis concerning the significance of the sex of the first drawn person on the DAP. Only one of the studies cited suggests that particular sexual characteristics of drawings are related to the sexual adjustment of the Ss, and that one study (29) reports only 8 of 54 computed statistics significant at the .05 level. In view of the results reported by the other studies, it seems reasonable to suggest that the results reported by Fisher and Fisher (29) were due to chance.

Summary Table of Findings

For the purposes of illustration and discussion, the author prepared Table 5 to illustrate in a very rough way the conclusions the studies cited suggest concerning Machover's hypotheses about the significance of the content and structural and formal aspects of

tent and the structural and formal aspects of the DAP is that few of Machover's hypotheses have been explicitly tested by definitive studies. But those which have, such as her hypothesis concerning the sex of the first drawn figure, have not been supported by the experimental evidence.

Discussion and Conclusions

Evaluation of the DAP as a Clinical Tool

The evidence presented in this paper does not support Machover's hypotheses about the meaning of human figure

TABLE 5.   RESULTS OF COMPARISON OF EXPERIMENTAL RESULTS WITH MACHOVER'S HYPOTHESES CONCERNING BODY PARTS AND STRUCTURAL AND FORMAL ASPECTS OF THE DAP

Supported	Conflicting Evidence	Not Supported	Not Tested[a]
Neck	Facial Expression	Head	Chin
	Mouth	Ears	Eyebrow
	Lips	Nose	Trunk
	Eye	Legs and feet	Shoulders
	Hair	Fingers	Hips and buttocks
	Hands and arms	Toes	Clothing
	Waist	Anatomy	Pockets
	Buttons	Breasts	Tie
	Action	Joints	Shoe and hat
	Size	Succession	Theme
	Stance	Mid-line	Symmetry
	Perspective	Placement	
	Type of lines	Erasure	
		Shading	
		Sexual treatment	

a Items were included in this column if the reported research did not appear to test Machover's hypotheses, or if no research concerning them was reported in literature. Those for which no research is reported have been omitted from the previous discussion.

the DAP. It is not claimed that the table is entirely objective. If the reader prepared a table of his own it would probably come out slightly different from that presented here. But it does suggest that no considerable empirical support for Machover's hypotheses exists at the present time. Perhaps the most charitable thing that can be said for the hypotheses concerning the con-

drawings. More of the evidence directly contradicts her hypotheses than supports them. And, even in the studies where some support for her hypotheses can be found, many of the cases did not render the human figure drawings in the way that would be expected according to Machover. For example, Berman and Laffal's (10) study found a significant relationship between the body type of the S and the body type of the figure drawn by the S, but a majority of the Ss did not draw figures that were of the same body type as the S. Since in clinical work the reliable diagnosis of the individual case is of paramount importance, this lack of consistent evidence supporting Machover, on both the group level and the individual level suggests that the DAP is of doubtful value in clinical work.

On the other hand, many clinicians routinely use the DAP and feel that it is a valuable tool. Machover wrote her monograph on the basis of extensive clinical use of the DAP which convinced her that it was a valuable instrument. This "clinical evidence" needs to be considered.

The discrepancy between the results of research studies and the testimony of people with extensive clinical experience may stem from the fact that the two figure drawings obtained in the DAP, as it is usually administered, do not provide enough data for making a reliable assessment of personality dynamics in most cases. This conclusion is suggested by Caligor's study (18), in which he found that paranoid trends could be detected in only 25% of a group of paranoid schizophrenics when only one drawing was used but could be detected in 85% of the cases when a series of eight drawings was used. Although two drawings are not sufficient basis for the reliable diagnosis of most individuals, they can provide data that may be sufficient for the accurate diagnosis of some cases. Once in a while the clinician meets a client who draws figures that clearly illustrate his problem. For example, the Casper Milquetoast-type client who draws a small, weak-looking male figure, and a towering, overbearing, scowling female figure who bears a remarkable resemblance to the patient's wife. The clinician will probably remember this case long after he has forgotten twenty Casper Milquetoasts who

did not draw a weak-looking male figure and a powerful female figure. Since cases which do illustrate pretty clearly the dynamics of an individual case are more likely to stick in the memory of the clinician than cases which do not, this possibly explains why clinicians feel that the DAP is of value in clinical work, and also explains the sources of Machover's hypotheses.

But even though there is much evidence which does not support the use of the DAP in clinical work, there still may be a place for it. If, as has been suggested above, the nonsignificant results obtained in using human figure drawings are primarily because two drawings do not provide enough data for reliable diagnosis, figure drawings may still be of some value as one part of a diagnostic battery composed of several different kinds of test and behavioral data. And when it is used as a part of a diagnostic battery, it should be kept in mind by the clinician that the DAP, by itself, does not provide sufficient evidence for a diagnosis, but that the DAP must be considered in conjunction with other instruments. The DAP is easily and quickly administered, which is one advantage in using it as one type of data to be considered along with all of the other data obtained from the psychological test battery.

Another use for the DAP might be as a rough screening device, or as an indicator of "level of adjustment." That is, although it may not provide enough data for diagnosing the various factors or aspects of personality dynamics in the individual case, it may be useful as a device for screening large groups of people, or as a rough gauge of how well the individual patient is functioning. Several studies that have been previously cited (23, 32, 44, 78, 83) have reported significant differences between groups of normal Ss, neurotic Ss, psychotic Ss and brain-damaged Ss on many different aspects of the DAP. Margolis (58) and Cramer-Azima (22) have reported changes in the DAP which were concomitant with changes in the adjustment of the individual Ss. Also, Modell (62) studied the changes in the DAP's of 28 hospitalized regressed psychotics as they improved in adjustment. He gave the DAP to these patients serially during their course of treatment at the hospital. The DAP's of these patients were rated, using a scale devised by him, for "body image maturation" and "sexual maturation." On the "body image maturation" scale the immature body is represented by an oval. The mature body is a trunk or pelvis that resembles in shape that of a normal human being, with clothing and other pertinent details present. On the "sexual maturation" scale the drawing with immature sexual characteristics has few or no details which differentiate between the male and female figures. The drawing with mature sexual characteristics has male and female figures which can clearly be identified as male and female. In his study he found that as a patient recovered from regressed states, the "sexual maturation" and the "body image maturation" of their DAP's improved significantly. Albee and Hamlin (1, 2) obtained DAP's from 10 patients representing a wide range of emotional adjustment, and had 15 clinical psychologists rate the drawings, using the paired-comparisons technique. The judges judged which of the pair of DAP's was from the better adjusted S. By comparing each DAP with every other DAP they obtained a mean preference score for each DAP. The Ss were rated for emotional adjustment, the ratings based upon the patients' case histories. The rank-over correlation between the rating of the drawings and the rating of the case histories was .62, which is significant at the .05 level. Albee and Hamlin (2) then used the drawings mentioned in the previous study as a scale with which they rated the drawings produced by 21 out-

patients diagnosed as schizophrenics, 21 outpatient anxiety cases, and 30 dental patients. These cases were controlled for age, sex, education, and veteran status. It was found that the scale differentiated reliably between the normals (dental patients) and each of the outpatient groups, but did not differentiate between the schizophrenics and the neurotics.

But even though the evidence cited above suggests that the DAP might be used as a gross indicator of "level of adjustment," it still needs more precise evaluation for this purpose than any study has so far provided. As Meehl (61) has pointed out, it is possible for a test to significantly differentiate between two groups, and still be useless or worse than useless in making predictions in the individual case.

Suggested Approaches to Future Research

Research designed to systematically test the validity of a particular theoretical system is probably more likely to yield useful results than research randomly testing unrelated hypotheses. Since Machover's system of interpretation is probably going to continue to be used in figure-drawing analysis until a more valid system is proposed, future research is most apt to be fruitful if it is designed to test specific hypotheses of Machover's. It must have been evident to the reader, in the presentation of the studies reviewed in this paper, that few of the studies reported were designed to test specific hypotheses of Machover's.

Studies which attempt to evaluate the significance of patterns of signs on the DAP appear to be more promising than attempts to evaluate the significance of individual DAP signs. This is suggested by the results obtained by Goldworth (32) and Gutman (40). This, of course, has been pointed out by Machover (55, p. 21).

Studies are needed in which DAP's are taken, serially, from Ss while the Ss are undergoing treatment. Such studies, if they included adequate control groups, should throw some light on those aspects of the DAP which vary concomitantly with variations in the Ss' behavior.

Caligor's Eight-Card-Redrawing Technique (17, 18, 19) appears to be quite promising for research purposes. He developed this technique in an effort to get at factors that were buried too deeply in the unconscious to be revealed by the standard DAP method. In the Eight-Card-Redrawing Technique (usually shortened to 8 CRT) the S is given a pad with eight sheets of onion-skin paper in it. He is asked to draw a full-length picture of a person. After he has completed his first drawing the next sheet of onion skin is folded over the sheet upon which he has made his first drawing, and he is told to draw another picture of a person, making any changes he wishes to make. In this way he may see his first drawing through the transparent onion skin while he is drawing the second figure. When the second figure is completed a sheet of cardboard is put between the first drawing and the second drawing. A third sheet of onion skin is folded over the second sheet, and he is again asked to draw a new figure, making any changes he wishes to make from the second figure. This is repeated until the S has drawn eight figures. While he is drawing each figure, except the first, he is able to see the drawing he has just finished. If, as Caligor suggests, this technique taps more reliably various personality factors, it would appear to be worthwhile to use it to explore the significance of various gross and fine details of the DAP.

A series of carefully planned statistically sophisticated studies of the reliability of the various parts of the DAP are especially needed. Not only should the reliability of the individual parts and aspects be determined, but the reliability of patterns should also be studied. It would probably prove quite fruitful to factor-analyze the DAP in an effort to determine its basic dimensions.

Summary

1. Machover's hypotheses concerning the DAP have seldom been supported by the research reported in the literature in the past eight years.

2. It is suggested that the opinion of clinicians that the DAP is of value as a clinical instrument, despite the lack of experimental evidence to support this judgment, is due to the fact that the DAP, in a few cases which impress the individual clinician, does provide an indication of the nature of the individual client's problems.

3. Some evidence supports the use of the DAP as a rough screening device, and as a gross indicator of "level of adjustment."

4. Approaches to future research are suggested.

REFERENCES

1. ALBEE, G. W., & HAMLIN, R. M. An investigation of the reliability and validity of judgments inferred from drawings. *J. clin. Psychol.*, 1949, **5**, 389–392.
2. ALBEE, G. W., & HAMLIN, R. M. Judgment of adjustment from drawings; the applicability of rating scale methods. *J. clin. Psychol.*, 1950, 6, 363–365.
3. ANASTASI, ANNE, & FOLEY, J. P. A survey of the literature on artistic behavior in the abnormal: I. Historical and theoretical background. *J. gen. Psychol.*, 1941 **23**, 111–142.
4. ANASTASI, ANNE, & FOLEY, J. P. A

survey of the literature on artistic behavior in the abnormal: II. Approaches and interrelationships. *Ann. N. Y. Acad. Sci.*, 1941, **42**, 106.

5. ANASTASI, ANNE, & FOLEY, J. P. A survey of the literature on artistic behavior in the abnormal: III. Spontaneous productions. *Psychol. Monogr.*, 1942, **52**, No. 6.

6. ANASTASI, ANNE, & FOLEY, J. P. A survey of the literature on artistic behavior in the abnormal: IV. Experimental investigations. *J. gen. Psychol.*, 1941, **25**, 187–237.

7. ANASTASI, ANNE, & FOLEY, J. P. Psychiatric selection of flying personnel. V. The Human Figure Drawing Test as an objective psychiatric screening aid for pilots. *USAF, Sch. Aviat. Med. Proj. Rep.*, 1952, No. 21-37-002 (Rep. No. 5).

8. BARKER, A. J., MATHIS, J. K., & POWERS, CLAIR. Drawing characteristics of male homosexuals. *J. clin. Psychol.*, 1953, **9**, 185–188.

9. BERMAN, A. B., KLEIN, A. A., & LIPPMAN, A. Human figure drawings as a projective technique. *J. gen. Psychol.*, 1951, **45**, 57–70.

10. BERMAN, S., & LAFFAL, J. Body type and figure drawing. *J. clin. Psychol.*, 1953, **9**, 368–370.

11. BLUM, R. H. The validity of the Machover DAP technique. *J. clin. Psychol.*, 1954, **10**, 120–125.

12. BOUSSION-LEROY, A. Transparent drawings and level of development. *Psychol. Abstracts*, 1952, **26**, 178. (Abstract)

13. BRADSHAW, D. H. A study of group consistencis on the Draw-A-Person test in relation to personality projection. Unpublished master's thesis, Catholic Univer., 1952.

14. BRILL, M. The reliability of the Goodenough Draw-A-Man test and the validity and reliability of an abbreviated scoring method. *J. educ. Psychol.*, 1935, **26**, 701–708.

15. BROWN, F. House-Tree-Person and human figure drawings. In D. BROWER and L. E. ABT (Eds.), *Progress in clinical psychology*. New York: Grune and Stratton, 1952. Pp. 173–184.

16. BUHRER, LYDIA, DE NAVARO, R. S., & VALASCO, EMMA. A classification experiment of Goodenough's Draw-A-Man test. *Psychol. Abstracts*, 1952, **26**, 5603. (Abstract)

17. CALIGOR, L. The determination of the individual's unconscious conception of his masculinity-femininity identification. *J. proj. Tech.*, 1951, **15**, 494–509.

18. CALIGOR, L. The detection of paranoid trends by the eight card redrawing test (8 CRT). *J. clin. Psychol.*, 1952, **8**, 397–401.

19. CALIGOR, L. Quantification on the eight card redrawing test (8 CRT). *J. clin. Psychol.*, 1953, **9**, 356–361.

20. COHN, R. Role of the "body image concept" in pattern of ipsilateral clinical extinction. *A.M.A. Arch. Neurol. Psychiat.*, 1953, **70**, 503–509.

21. COOK, M. A preliminary study of the relationship of differential treatment of the male and female head size in figure drawing to the degree of attribution of the social functions of the female. *Psychol. Newsltr.*, 1951, **34**, 1–5.

22. CRAMER-AZIMA, FERN J. Personality changes and figure drawings: a case treated with ACTH. *J. clin. Psychol.*, 1956, **20**, 143–149.

23. CUTTER, F. Sexual differentiation in figure drawings and overt deviation. *J. clin. Psychol.*, 1956, **12**, 369–372.

24. DE KONINGH, H. L. Personal communication.

25. DE MARTINO, M. F. Human figure drawings by mentally retarded males. *J. clin. Psychol.*, 1954, **10**, 241–244.

26. FEATHER, D. B. An exploratory study in the use of figure drawings in a group situation. *J. soc. Psychol.*, 1953, **37**, 163–170.

27. FISHER, LILLIAN. An investigation of the effectiveness of the human figure drawing as a clinical instrument for evaluating personality. Unpublished Ph.D. thesis, New York Univer., 1952; Microfilm abstract, Ann Arbor, Mich.

28. FISHER, S., & FISHER, RHODA. Test of certain assumptions regarding fig-

ure drawing analysis. *J. abnorm. soc. Psychol.*, 1950, **45**, 727–732.

29. FISHER, S., & FISHER, RHODA. Style of sexual adjustment in disturbed women and its expression in figure drawings. *J. Psychol.*, 1952, **34**, 169–179.

30. GIEDT, F. H., & LEHNER, G. F. J. Assignment of ages on the draw-a-person test by male psychoneurotic patients. *J. Pers.*, 1951, **19**, 440–448.

31. GLUECK, B., GRANUS, J. D., & PANES, R. The use of serial testing in regressive shock treatment. In P. HOCH and J. ZUBIN (Eds.), *Relation of psychological tests to psychiatry.* New York: Grune and Stratton, 1952. Pp. 244–257.

32. GOLDWORTH, S. A comparative study of the drawings of a man and a woman done by normal, neurotic, schizophrenic and brain-damaged individuals. Unpublished Ph.D. thesis, Univer. of Pittsburgh, 1950.

33. GOODENOUGH, FLORENCE, & HARRIS, D. B. Studies in the psychology of children's drawings: II. 1928–1949. *Psychol. Bull.*, 1950, **47**, 369–433.

34. GOODENOUGH, FLORENCE. *The measurement of intelligence by drawings.* Yonkers, N. Y.: World Book, 1926.

35. GOODMAN, M., & KOTKOV, B. Predictions of trait ranks from Draw-A-Person measurements of obese and non-obese women. *J. clin. Psychol.*, 1953, **9**, 365–367.

36. GRAHAM, S. R. Relation between histamine tolerance, visual autokinesis, Rorschach human movement, and figure drawing. *J. clin. Psychol.*, 1955, **11**, 370–373.

37. GRANICK, S., & SMITH, L. J. Sex sequence in the Draw-A-Person test and its relation to the MMPI Masculinity-Femininity Scale. *J. consult. Psychol.*, 1953, **17**, 71–73.

38. GUNDERSON, E. K., & LEHNER, G. F. J. Reliability in a projective test (the Draw-A-Person). *Amer. Psychologist*, 1949, **4**, 387.

39. GUNDERSON, E. K., & LEHNER, G. F. J. Height of figure as a diagnostic variable in the Draw-A-Person test. *Amer. Psychologist*, 1950, **5**, 472. (Abstract)

40. GUTMAN, BRIGETTE. An investigation of the applicability of the human figure drawing in predicting improvement in therapy. Unpublished Ph.D. thesis, New York Univer., 1952.

41. HAMMER, E. F. Relationship between diagnosis of psychosexual pathology and the sex of the first drawn person. *J. clin. Psychol.*, 1954, **10**, 168–170.

42. HINRICHS, W. E. The Goodenough drawing in relation to delinquency and problem behavior. *Arch. Psychol.*, 1935, No. 175.

43. HOLTZMAN, W. H. The examiner as a variable in the Draw-A-Person test. *J. consult. Psychol.*, 1952, **16**, 145–148.

44. HOLZBERG, J. D., & WEXLER, M. The validity of human form drawings as a measure of personality deviation. *J. proj. Tech.*, 1950, **14**, 343–361.

45. JOLLES, I. A study of the validity of some hypotheses for the qualitative interpretation of the H-T-P for children of elementary school age: I. Sexual identification. *J. clin. Psychol.*, 1952, **8**, 113–118.

46. KING, J. W. The use of drawings of the human figure as adjunct in psychotherapy. *J. clin. Psychol.*, 1954, **10**, 65–69.

47. KOTKOV, B., & GOODMAN, M. The Draw-a-Person tests of obese women. *J. clin. Psychol.*, 1953, **9**, 362–364.

48. LEHNER, G. F. J., & SILVER, H. Age relationships on the Draw-a-Person test. *J. Pers.*, 1948, **17**, 199–209.

49. LEHNER, G. F. J., & GUNDERSON, E. K. Reliability of graphic indices in a projective test (Draw-a-Person). *J. clin. Psychol.*, 1952, **8**, 125–128.

50. LEHNER, G. F. J., & GUNDERSON, E. K. Height relationships on the Draw-a-Person test. *J. Pers.*, 1953, **21**, 392–399.

51. LEVY, S. Figure drawing as a projective technique. In L. E. ABT and L. BELLAK (Eds.), *Projective psychology.* New York: Knopf, 1950. Pp. 257–297.

52. MCCARTHY, D. A study of the reliability of the Goodenough Drawing

Test of Intelligence. *J. Psychol.*, 1944, **18**, 201–216.

53. McCurdy, H. G. Group and individual variability on the Goodenough Draw-a-Person test. *J. educ. Psychol.*, 1947, **38**, 428–436.

54. McHugh, G. Changes in Goodenough I. Q. at the public school kindergarten level. *J. educ. Psychol.*, 1945, **36**, 17–30.

55. Machover, Karen. *Personality projection in the drawing of the human figure.* Springfield, Ill.: Charles C. Thomas, 1949.

56. Machover, Karen. Human figure drawings of children. *J. proj. Tech.*, 1953, **17**, 85–91.

57. Mainord, Florence. A note on the use of figure drawings in the diagnosis of sexual inversion. *J. clin. Psychol.*, 1953, **9**, 188–189.

58. Margolis, Muriel. A comparative study of figure drawings at three points in therapy. *Rorschach Res. Exch.*, 1948, **12**, 94–105.

59. Meehl, P. E. *Clinical versus statistical prediction.* Minneapolis: Univer. of Minnesota Press, 1954.

60. Meehl, P. E., & Rosen, A. Antecedent probability and the efficiency of psychometric signs, patterns, or cutting scores. *Psychol. Bull.*, 1955, **52**, 194–216.

61. Meehl, P. E. Wanted—a good cookbook. *Amer. Psychologist*, 1956, **11**, 263–272.

62. Modell, A. H. Changes in human figure drawings by patients who recover from regressed states. *Amer. J. Orthopsychiat.*, 1951, **21**, 584–596.

63. Morris, W. W. Methodological and normative considerations in the use of drawings of human figures as a projective method. *Amer. Psychologist*, 1949, **4**, 267. (Abstract)

64. Morris, W. W. Ontogenetic changes in adolescence reflected by the drawing-human-figures techniques. *Amer. J. Orthopsychiat.*, 1955, **25**, 720–729.

65. Noller, P. A., & Weider, A. A normative study of human figure drawing for children. *Amer. Psychologist*, 1950, **5**, 319–320. (Abstract)

66. Prater, G. F. A comparison of the head and body size in the drawing of the human figure by hemiplegic and nonhemiplegic persons. Unpublished Master's thesis, Univer. of Kentucky, 1950.

67. Royal, R. E. Drawing characteristics of neurotic patients using a drawing-of-a-man-and-woman technique. *J. clin. Psychol.*, 1949, **5**, 392–395.

68. Schilder, P. *The image and appearance of the human body.* New York: International Universities Press, 1950.

69. Singer, H. Validity of the projection of sexuality in the drawing of the human figure. Unpublished Master's thesis, Western Reserve Univer., 1952.

70. Sipprelle, C. N., & Swensen, C. H. Relationship of sexual adjustment to certain sexual characteristics of human figure drawings. *J. consult. Psychol.*, 1956, **20**, 197–198.

71. Sloan, W. A critical review of H-T-P validation studies. *J. clin. Psychol.*, 1954, **10**, 143–148.

72. Smith, F. O. What the Goodenough Intelligence Test measures. *Psychol. Bull.*, 1937, **34**, 760–761. (Abstract)

73. Steinman, K. The validity of a projective technique in the determination of relative intensity in psychosis. Unpublished Ph.D. dissertation, New York Univer., 1952.

74. Stone, P. M. A study of objectively scored drawings of human figures in relation to the emotional adjustment of sixth grade pupils. Unpublished Ph.D. thesis, Yeshiva Univer., 1952.

75. Stonesifer, F. A. A Goodenough scale evaluation of human figures drawn by schizophrenic and nonpsychotic adults. *J. clin. Psychol.*, 1949, **5**, 396–398.

76. Swensen, C. H. Sexual differentiation on the Draw-a-Person Test. *J. clin. Psychol.*, 1955, **11**, 37–40.

77. Swensen, C. H., & Newton, K. R. Development of sexual differentiation on the Draw-a-Person test. *J. clin. Psychol.*, 1955, **11**, 417–419.

78. Swensen, C. H., & Sipprelle, C. N. Some relationships among sexual characteristics of human figure

drawings. *J. proj. Tech.*, 1956, **30**, 224–226.

79. WAGNER, M. E., & SCHUBERT, H. J. P. *D.A.P. quality scale for late adolescents and young adults.* Kenmore, N. Y.: Delaware Letter Shop, 1955.

80. WAXENBERG, S. E. Psychosomatic patients and other physically ill persons: a comparative study. *J. consult. Psychol.*, 1955, **19**, 163–169.

81. WEIDER, A., & NOLLER, P. A. Objective studies of children's drawings of human figures. I. Sex awareness and socioeconomic level *J. clin. Psychol.*, 1950, **6**, 319–325.

82. WEIDER, A., & NOLLER, P. A. Objective studies of children's drawings of human figures. II. Sex, age, intelligence. *J. clin. Psychol.*, 1953, **9**, 20–23.

83. WEXLER, M., & HOLZBERG, J. D. A further study of the validity of human form drawings in personality evaluation. *J. proj. Tech.*, 1952, **16**, 249–251.

84. WHITMYRE, J. W. The significance of artistic excellence in the judgment of adjustment inferred from human figure drawings. *J. consult. Psychol.*, 1953, **17**, 421–422.

85. WOODS, W. A., & COOK, W. E. Proficiency in drawing and placement of hands in drawings of the human figure. *J. consult. Psychol.*, 1954, **18**, 119–121.

86. YEPSIN, T. N. The reliability of the Goodenough Drawing Test with feeble-minded subjects. *J. educ. Psychol.*, 1929, **20**, 448–451.

87. ZIMMER, H. Predictions by means of two projective tests of personality evaluations made by peers. *J. clin. Psychol.*, 1955, **11**, 352–356.

Chapter 10

Validation of Apperceptive Techniques

■ Since Murray's pioneer work with the Thematic Apperception Test, a number of apperceptive techniques have appeared. Having the same basic assumptions in common, they differ primarily in the stimulus attributes of the cards. The characters portrayed range from dogs and bears through cartoon figures to children, adolescents, and adults of various races. In Shneidman's Make-A-Picture-Story Test (MAPS), the subject is free to select the characters for himself. Most of the techniques ask the subject to tell a story, although in the Rosenzweig Picture-Frustration Study he is required to indicate the verbal response of one cartoon character when insulted by another while in the Blacky Pictures a series of multiple choice questions about the stories is administered.

Despite these variations, the basic interpretive hypotheses about the techniques are quite similar. In essence, the needs indicated by the "hero" are generally assumed to be related to the needs of the story teller. The nature of the relation between these needs and overt behavior, however, is a matter of some controversy.

In the present chapter the primary emphasis is on the most widely used technique, the TAT. However, some data concerning the MAPS is also presented in one study, as are the results of experimentally modified cards in two others. Because of the underlying similarities, it is likely that the findings using one technique can be generalized to a certain extent to the other variations.

The chapter is divided into three parts. In the first part Gardner Lindzey reviews the evidence for ten basic assumptions of the TAT (and most other apperceptive devices). While there is not as much empirical evidence as might be desired regarding some of the assumptions, nevertheless, what data there are, are found to be generally consistent with the basic assumptions underlying the use of the test.

The second part consists of three studies of the clinical validity of the TAT and MAPS. In a study which parallels their work on the MMPI (Chapter 7), Little and Shneidman investigate the relation between clinicians' interpretations based on only the TAT and MAPS with the interpretations of other clinicians who have had access to the complete case record.

The next study, by Beverly Davenport, goes a step beyond the investigation of concurrent validity and asks how reliably judges can interpret a TAT protocol and how discriminable these interpretations are. The latter question gets at what Meehl has termed the "Barnum Effect" (see Chapter 13). "Barnum effect" statements are those which might apply to everyone in a given population. If we say that a psychiatric patient "manifests difficulties in interpersonal relationships" or that a couple's marital adjustment will improve "if each becomes more sensitive and responsive to his spouse's needs" we have written a statement which is probably quite accurate and valid but which is also trivial since it applies to almost everyone. Validity is important but so is discriminability, the extent to which the interpretation is a unique description of this unique personality. It is this dimension that Davenport focuses on in the second study of clinical validity.

The third study illustrates the importance of adequate normative data. In the course of clinical work with an instrument, certain patterns and signs come to be regarded as diagnostic of a given group. However, for a sign to be a valid diagnostic indicator, it not only has to be found frequently within a diagnostic group, but also not found in groups without this diagnosis. The presence of one nose and two eyes in the faces of most schizophrenics is not generally regarded as diagnostic of schizophrenia because observation indicates a relatively high frequency of this physiognomic pattern among non-schizophrenics as well.[1] But while clinicians have ample opportunity to observe the faces of normals, they have relatively little chance to examine their TAT protocols. Thus a pattern which is common to everyone in a culture may come to be regarded as characteristic only of the disturbed in the absence of normative studies. This is brought out by Leonard Eron's article in which he looks at the relative frequency of "schizophrenic TAT signs" among schizophrenics and normals.

The final section of the chapter is devoted to an exploration of how the relation between fantasy needs and overt behavior varies as a function of the stimuli, the setting, and the population being tested. Three studies, all dealing with the relation between Need Aggression and overt aggression, were chosen since the criterion of overt aggression is relatively clear-cut. They demonstrate how the relation between overt and fantasy aggression varies as a function of the socio-economic class of the subject (Mussen and Naylor), as a function of the mother's attitude toward aggression (Lesser) and as a function of how directly the stimulus card suggests a fighting theme (Kagan). One generalization which clearly emerges from the findings of these studies is that the relation between fantasy and overt behavior, as Rosenzweig pointed out, is complex and multiply determined.

The reader who wishes to read further on research using the TAT should consult Lindzey's article in Chapter 13 and Murstein's (1963) comprehensive review.

[1] If the APA had not done away with this classification, we might say that this pattern lacks "face validity."

REFERENCE

MURSTEIN, B. I. *Theory and Research in Projective Techniques* (*Emphasizing the TAT*). New York: John Wiley & Sons, 1963.

STUDIES OF BASIC ASSUMPTIONS

Thematic Apperception Test: Interpretive Assumptions and Related Empirical Evidence

Gardner Lindzey

The chief purpose of this article is to state the assumptions customarily involved in interpreting the Thematic Apperception Test,[1] and to examine the logical considerations and some of the empirical evidence that can be used to verify or reject each of these assumptions.

Aside from certain historical ties to psychoanalysis, the theoretical and empirical continuity between projective testing and the remainder of psychology

This paper is an outgrowth of a study of personality and the imaginative processes directed by Henry A. Murray and supported by grants from the Rockefeller Foundation and the Laboratory of Social Relations, Harvard University. I am deeply grateful to a number of colleagues for their generosity in reading and criticizing this manuscript. My greatest single debt is to Henry A. Murray whose constant stimulation and encouragement made this article possible.

Reprinted by permission of the American Psychological Association and the author from *Psychological Bulletin*, 1952, **49**, 1–25.

[1] These same assumptions are customarily employed in connection with other story-construction projective techniques, e.g., Make-A-Picture-Story Test, Four-Picture Test, Tri-Dimensionsal Apperception Test, etc.

has been a subject of little interest. This is true in spite of an increasingly large amount of research and formulation in other areas of psychology that is directly pertinent to the activities involved in projective testing. In particular, the research of the "new-look" perceptionists represents an important and fertile link between projective testing and more traditional domains of psychology. The initial outline of such a continuity has been traced by Blake and Wilson (7) in a study of the influence of depressive tendencies upon selectivity in Rorschach response, Bruner (9) in a discussion of the Rorschach test, Lawrence (39) in an investigation of temporal factors in perception, Siipola (75) in an examination of the effect of color upon Rorschach response and Stein (76) in an ingenious study employing tachistoscopic exposure of Rorschach stimulus material. All of these studies illustrate the feasibility and fruitfulness of relating perception findings to material elicited by Rorschach-like techniques. One of the aims of the present paper is to stress the desirability of relating such theory and research to the findings of investigators who employ the Thematic Apperception Test.

One may legitimately object to my proposal to appraise empirically statements that I am treating as given, or axiomatic. However, it is not clear that all psychologists would concur in giving axiomatic status to these statements. As is true of so much of psychological formulation, the distinction here between analytic and empirical is not clearly delineated—what is one person's empirical generalization is another's axiom. Further, I believe most psychologists agree with MacCorquodale and Meehl (44) in subscribing to a methodological position that emphasizes the use of *only* analytic constructs that interact smoothly with available empirical knowledge. Consequently, examination of these assumptions in the light of empirical evidence seems justified on the one hand by the questionable axiomatic status of the assumptions and on the other by the general acceptance of psychologists that axioms should not violate observational data.

The assumptions to follow vary greatly in their generality. In fact, they are logically related only by virtue of their frequent use in the interpretation of material secured from one particular type of projective technique. They do not represent all of the assumptions employed in making such interpretations. I have attempted to include only those that are not sufficiently general to be common among all psychologists and yet, within the prescribed situation, are sufficiently common so that almost any individual engaged in this activity would employ them. For the latter reason, I am not concerned here with the assumptions involved in "formal" or "sign" analysis of story projective material where the meaning, or the thematic qualities, of the material is minimized, e.g., Balken and Masserman (3) and Wyatt (84). Nor have I attempted to explore the assumptions involved in the

more recent "sequence analysis" (1) of projective responses.

The Assumptions and Related Evidence

The assumptions are divided into three crude groups. First, the most general assumption, fundamental to all projective testing. Second, those assumptions that are concerned with procedures employed in determining the diagnostically significant portions of the fantasy productions. Third, those assumptions involved in relating the significant portions of the protocols to other forms of behavior.

Primary Assumption: In completing or structuring an incomplete or unstructured situation, the individual may reveal his own strivings, dispositions, and conflicts.[2]

Assumptions Involved in Determining Revealing Portions of Stories:

1. In the process of creating a story the story-teller ordinarily identifies with one person[3] in the drama, and the wishes, strivings, and conflicts of this imaginary person may reflect those of the story-teller.

a. It is assumed further that the identification figure can be established through the application of a number of specific criteria; e.g., person appearing first in the story, person doing most of the behaving, person most similar to story-teller, etc.

b. It is also assumed that additional

---

[2] The terms "strivings, dispositions, and conflicts" are meant to designate all the attributes or aspects of the person that the clinician is interested in or wishes to measure. One could readily add to this list such terms as: personality organization, primitive fixations, complexes, needs and press, or any others that seemed necessary. to represent those aspects of the person that are being explored.

[3] Most investigators accept the possibility of multiple identifications. However, this necessitates the same assumption and only complicates somewhat the general problems of establishing interpretive rules.

figures in the stories such as father, mother, or brother often may be equated to the real-life counterparts of the storyteller and the behavior of the hero toward them used as indicative of the storyteller's reactions to these persons.

2. The story-teller's dispositions, strivings, and conflicts are sometimes represented indirectly or symbolically.

3. All of the stories that the subject creates are not of equal importance as diagnostic of his impulses and conflicts. Certain crucial stories may provide a very large amount of valid diagnostic material while others may supply little or none.

4. Themes or story-elements that appear to have arisen directly out of the stimulus material are less apt to be significant than those that do not appear to have been directly determined by the stimulus material.

5. Themes that are recurrent in a series of stories are particularly apt to mirror the impulses and conflicts of the story-teller.

Assumptions Involved in Deriving from Revealing Portions of Fantasy Material Inferences About Other Aspects of Behavior:

1. The stories may reflect not only the enduring dispositions and conflicts of the subject, but also conflicts and impulses that are momentarily aroused by some force in the immediate present.

a. The further assumption is frequently made that both the enduring and temporary processes are reflected in stories in the same manner.

2. The stories may reflect events from the past of the subject that he has not himself actively experienced, but rather has witnessed or observed, e.g., street scene, story, motion picture.

a. It is assumed further that, although the subject has not himself experienced these events, and is telling them as he observed them, the fact that he selects these events, rather than others, is in itself indicative of his own impulses and conflicts.

3. The stories may reflect group-membership or socio-cultural determinants in addition to individual or personal determinants.

4. The dispositions and conflicts that may be inferred from the story-teller's creations are not always reflected directly in overt behavior or consciousness.

I wish to emphasize that the research to be discussed in connection with the various assumptions can *not* serve as a validation of this kind of projective testing. At most, it can demonstrate that the very general assumptions lying behind this kind of activity are not in direct conflict with available empirical findings. This may increase the "plausibility" of projective interpretations, but the task of demonstrating the utility of specific rules of interpretation remains.

It is likewise important to realize that in this article I am omitting from consideration most of the pertinent empirical evidence resulting from clinical use of this technique. The omission of this idiographic research or observation is not the consequence of any feeling that such data are not of immense value. Rather, in an article emphasizing the relation of projective testing to the remainder of psychology, it seemed desirable to stress most heavily those kinds of research that came closest to meeting the experimenter's demand for empirical control and intersubjectivity of method. Thus, most of the evidence to be referred to has been secured with some attempt at maintaining adequate empirical controls.

Does the Individual Reveal His Own Dispositions and Conflicts in Completing an Unstructured Situation? This assumption is not limited to story-construction tests but lies at the heart of all projective testing. Fortunately, in view of its ubiquity, there is a host of very general experimental verification, some of it drawn from laboratory research.

One of the first investigators to point to the relationship between motivational factors and response in an unstructured situation was Sanford (71, 72). He demonstrated in a series of experiments that the food responses of subjects varied as a function of the amount of food deprivation they had undergone. The responses were given in the act of telling stories to ambiguous pictures, making word associations, and in other situations where the stimulus was sufficiently unstructured to permit either food or non-food responses. This same general function was later demonstrated under somewhat different conditions by Levine, Chein, and Murphy (40) and McClelland and Atkinson (48). The results of these three investigations do not agree in detail, but all were able to demonstrate some kind of variation in response to ambiguous stimulus situations as a function of food deprivation.

In an early study by Murray (55), it was shown that estimates of "maliciousness" of faces in photographs varied directly with an experimentally induced state of fear. After a fear-producing game children rated a series of photographed faces as significantly more malicious than they had rated the faces previous to the game. A recent study by Katz (34) has shown that the manner in which an individual completes an incompletely drawn face varies systematically with the kind of experience he has undergone previous to the activity. Thus, a group that had just failed on a test of reasoning ability differed significantly from a group that had just spent their time in a neutral activity. Presumably the manner in which the individual completed this unstructured situation was directly related to the motivational or emotional conditions aroused by the experimental treatment.

A series of investigations by Bruner and Postman (12) have demonstrated that when stimulus material is made ambiguous by very brief tachistoscopic exposure, the responses or "guesses" of the subjects vary systematically with motivational variables. These same investiga-

tors, as a result of their perception research, have come to occupy a much more extreme position than that implied by the above assumption. They suggest that:

Most experimenters who have worked with need and attitude factors in perception have assumed, sometimes quite explicitly, that only in highly equivocal stimulus situations can such "nonsensory" factors operate. . . . But all stimulus situations are potentially equivocal and cease to be so only to the extent that selection, accentuation, and fixation have taken place. Perception occurring without the contribution of such adaptive factors is as unthinkable as perception without the mediation of receptive nerve tissue (11, p. 301). . . . *Adaptive factors in perception are not limited to unstable stimulus situations* (11, p. 307).

In the light of this evidence, the assumption that motivational factors are revealed in completing unstructured situations seems clearly warranted.

Does the Subject Identify with Some Figure in the Stories He Tells and Can This Figure Be Established Reliably? There seem to be three modal positions that can be maintained in regard to identification in the story-telling process. First, we may make the assumption, indicated above, that there is *ordinarily* a single identification figure in each story. This assumption can be complicated greatly by a number of special conditions of the type already suggested by Murray (56). Second, we may assume a continuum of identification with those figures in the stories that are very similar to the story-teller possessing a maximum of the subject's attributes and those that are very dissimilar possessing a minimum. This is the assumption made by Sears (74), who, working primarily with doll techniques and heavily influenced by the notion of "stimulus generalization," has suggested specifiable dimensions along which the degree of identification can be expected to vary. Thus, in doll play figures resembling the subject in age and sex will show more characteristics of the subject than those figures that are dissimilar in age and sex. Third, we might, with Henry (31), Piotrowski (58), and others, make no attempt to locate the hero but simply look on all characters in the constructed stories as representative of aspects of the story-teller. This last alternative is perhaps the least happy, not only because a very large amount of diverse clinical experience militates against it, but also because it leads to certain drastic limitations upon the diagnostic use of the TAT. If we adopt this assumption, we are more or less forced to give up the attempt to appraise the subject's attitudes toward other persons. Thus, Piotrowski suggests that we eliminate the hero and assume "that every figure in the TAT stories expresses some aspect of the testee's personality" (58, p. 107), while somewhat later he suggests that many stories "reflect what the subject thinks and feels about persons represented by the TAT figures, i.e., about the old and the young, the male and the female" (58, p. 113). Thus, with no rules for differentiating, we are told that all figures represent characteristics of the hero, but also that the characteristics of some figures represent the story-teller's attitudes toward other persons. If we assume that all figures are equally representative of the story-teller's characteristics, either we must give up attempts to appraise the subject's attitudes toward other persons through this instrument or else engage in some kind of dialectic in the effort to defend such attempts.

There is, as yet, no unequivocal answer to the question of which of the above assumptions is most useful. In order to show that the assumption of a single identification figure is warranted, it is necessary to demonstrate relationships between the behavior of the subject and the imaginary behavior of the hero that do not exist between the behavior of the subject and the behavior of non-hero figures. If this difference is not shown, one can always suggest that the sensitivity of the test to aspects of the subject is a result not of any specific identification process, but rather of a generalized reflection of motivational state of the sort that Murray (55), Bruner and Postman (12), and others have reported. Thus, even if *all* figures in the stories represented aspects of the story-teller, we might arbitrarily decide to use only a certain percentage of these figures as diagnostic of the story-teller's attributes, i.e., employ the hero and non-hero distinction, and we would still expect the test to show some sensitivity to variations in story-teller behavior even though we were wasting much of its power. Just as the subject's motivational states are reflected in free association, or in the pre-solution hypotheses of tachistoscopic response, so also the verbal flow accompanying the story-telling process may mirror motivational states without any intervening identification with particular actors in the stories.

The distinction between "heroes" or identification figures on the one hand and "non-heroes" on the other is greatly complicated by the fact that the story-teller's orientation or attitudes toward other persons is intimately related to his own psychic makeup. Thus, we might mistakenly employ an identification figure as representative of the story-teller's attitudes toward other people and actually secure considerable information about the individual's external orientation because of the similarity between "self" and "perceived other." Or, conversely, we might take a figure intended by the story-teller as an "other" object and find mirrored in it much of real pertinence to the story-teller's own personality structure.

What is needed to answer the above question is a clear demonstration of more intimate relations between "hero" behavior or attributes and the story-teller than can be shown between "non-hero" behavior and the story-teller. Results such as Bellak's (5) showing that the frequency of aggressive words rises when the individual is frustrated do not demonstrate that the identification figure is necessarily displaying more aggressive behavior. Nor are studies satisfactory that simply demonstrate variations in "hero" activities or attributes that relate to behavior or attributes of the story-teller. Even if Bellak had shown that aggressive behavior on the part of heroes rose following frustration, this would still not provide the needed information. In this case it is quite possible that analysis of the behavior of the non-identification figures would reveal the same increase in aggressive behavior, indicating not identification, but simply an increase in verbal responses pertinent to the need or conflict in question.

Lindzey (43) has demonstrated that following a social frustration the incidence of aggressive acts in TAT stories carried out by heroes against others increased more than the incidence of aggressive acts carried out by "other" figures. If the incidence of the two kinds of acts is combined, the resulting shift is greater than the shift in either "self" or "other" figures alone. These findings are complicated by the fact that the frustration situation was of such a nature that both extra-punitive responses and a view of the environment as hostile and threatening would be expected to rise following the experimental treatment. Thus, the increase in aggressive responses on the part of non-hero figures might be considered a result of the increase in aggressive tendencies on the part of this story-teller or a reflection of the fact that the story-teller viewed the external world as a more hostile and threatening place. It is clear that what is needed is an experimental treatment where, given the subject's identification with a hero-figure, the predictions to be made for "hero" and "other" figures will either be opposed or widely different.

Accepting the desirability of locating identification figures, can these figures be specified precisely? Several studies (29, 79) in which relatively high-interscorer reliability coefficients were secured imply that it *is* possible to obtain reliable agreement among different scorers in establishing the identification figure. Presumably, a positive correlation for need and press ratings could be secured only if the different raters were treating the same figures as hero. In addition, Mayman and Kutner (45) report complete agreement in 89 per cent of the cases between two raters who independently determined the identification figure for a series of 91 stories.

In general, then, the feasibility of the identification assumption cannot be clearly demonstrated at present, although empirical evidence suggests that identification figures can be established with reasonable reliability.

Are Impulses and Conflicts of the Subject Sometimes Represented Symbolically? The clinical use of the concept of symbolism is intimately related to a number of psychological concepts employed by more rigorous and empirically oriented investigators. All behavior theorists have encounted the thorny problems posed by interchangeability or substitutability in behavior of stimuli and responses. These problems have led to the formulation of a number of psychological concepts including displacement, substitution, stimulus generalization, and vicarious mediation. Apparently most psychologists agree that when a response is interfered with either by internal or external barriers it will frequently become altered to another form or else be directed toward a new object. There is a large body of research, much of it carried out on animal subjects, demonstrating this relationship and exploring some of the conditions under which it operates (8, 15, 25, 31, 32, 38, 62, 63, 83). Of the animal investigations, perhaps the most pertinent to our discussion is Miller's (54) demonstration that a learned aggressive response can be generalized or displaced from an original stimulus object (another rat) to a substitute stimulus (doll) when the first stimulus is made unavailable. This process can be considered a rough paradigm of symbolic representation.

A special question of considerable importance to the projective tester is whether symbolic transformations can, and customarily do, take place without awareness of the subject. Most of the clinical studies discussed below deal with symbolic representations which the subject was not aware of initially and which he could become aware of only under special conditions, e.g., interpretation or therapeutic change. This capacity of the organism to engage in symbolic representation without awareness of the process has been demonstrated under better controlled circumstances by other investigators. Diven (17) and Haggard (27) have both shown that a word may become a substitute stimulus for an electric shock and evoke a galvanic skin response that differentiates it from "non-shock" words, even where the subject is unaware of the connection between the word and the electric shock. In similar fashion, McCleary and Lazarus (46) showed that words to which a galvanic skin response had been conditioned through the use of electric shock could elicit the galvanic skin response even when exposed tachistoscopically at such rapid speeds as to prevent conscious recognition.

Certainly since Freud, the clinical interpretation of diagnostic material, whether projective or not, has depended heavily upon the assumption of symbolic transformations. There is some clinical-experimental and a host of clinical-observational evidence to indicate that symbolic transformations are quite customary in human behavior, particularly where unacceptable or antisocial impulses are involved.

In case histories conversion symptoms and compulsions frequently present themselves dramatically as evidence of the fact that a given conflict or forbidden impulse may secure expression in a manner only indirectly related to the original impulse. Thus, it is generally accepted that hand-washing compulsions often represent symbolically the desire of the individual to cleanse himself of the consequences of masturbation. Likewise, in doll therapy there is excellent evidence that the child is able to discharge against surrogate objects the same impulses and feelings that he has developed toward persons in the real world. The extent to which this relationship between symbol and real-life counterpart is unequivocally demonstrated varies with the individual case. However, in many instances the relationship is effectively demonstrated as the symbolic behavior can be shown to vary directly with changes in the relationship between the subject and the referent of the symbol. Thus, the aggression directed against the father-doll may show a high inverse relationship to the extent to which the child is able to express such impulses against the original stimulus object— the father. Similarly, a symptom may disappear when the impulse or conflict that it is presumed to represent is dissolved by therapeutic procedure or through changes in the balance of environmental determinants. Levy (42) has described a number of clinical cases involving relatively convincing demonstration of symbolic representation of sibling rivalry, fear of castration, defecation, etc. Tomkins (80) reports the study of a single case under varying degrees of drunkenness. He found that in certain cases the hypothesized referent of the symbol was more and more directly represented as the amount of alcohol consumed increased.

Several investigators have attempted to combine the subject matter of clinical psychology with attempts at empirical control in the study of symbolic representation. An interesting study by Farber and Fisher (22) attempted to demonstrate the process of symbolic transformation by means of using hypnosis and asking subjects to create and interpret dreams. Although the study is not well controlled, if we accept the naivete of the subjects, the evidence is impressive, for some of the subjects, that not only is symbolic representation an observed form of behavior, but also that the process of assigning symbols in large part corresponds with the rules established by Freud from his examination of dream protocols. Consistently, Krout (38) in a better-controlled investigation studied interpretations based upon the assumption that individuals responded to line drawings, representative of basic experiences or objects, *as if* they were the symbol referent. She found that these interpretations could be verified through the inspection of independently collected validation data. In other words, the subjects did appear to respond to the line drawings in a manner consistent with the nature of the object that the Freudian would view as lying behind this symbol. Franck (23) and Franck and Rosen (24) have reported two studies in which there is some evidence that the response of the individual to male and female symbols varies with his sex and relative maturity. Klein (35) employing the method of hypnotically inducing dreams, was able to show that the dreamer characteristically transformed or disguised external stimuli that were incorporated into the dream.

In general, then, controlled empirical evidence supplements clinical observation to imply the existence of tendencies for human subjects to represent dispositions and conflicts symbolically. The rules for determining the symbol-referent relations are as yet imperfectly understood, although there is evidence indicating the Freudian view of the symbolic process possesses some utility.

Are the Stories that the Subject Creates of Unequal Importance as Diagnostic of His Impulses and Conflicts?
It is possible to assume that any behavioral information, no matter how scanty, contains in it the necessary elements to permit a complete understanding of the individual in question. This derivative of strict Freudian determinism is still defended by some investigators. It implies a theoretical model that is able to incorporate all possible empirical relationships and predict these relationships so precisely that once a single value has been inserted into the closed theoretical system, every other construct in the system can be assigned a value. In view of the present state of psychological theory, this assumption seems an exceedingly unwise one. Nor does it appear to guide the actual behavior of most clinicians. The tendency to view different stories as possessing different degrees of psychological significance is rather clearly revealed by the fact that not infrequently, even with twenty stories, the investigator will feel he has not sufficient material to make a diagnosis or come to any understanding of the dynamics of the individual in question. Apparently just as some sets of twenty stories are more difficult to interpret and are less revealing, so also some individual stories are less rewarding than others.

Although presumably implicitly present in the minds of most interpreters, the assumption is seldom mentioned and there has been little systematic attempt to state any criteria by means of which the more important stories are to be separated from the less important. Rapaport (61), who represents an exception to this generalization, has suggested that the more important stories may be distinguished in terms of certain "formal variables." He cites as illustration of these distinguishing characteristics: the consistency of the story with other stories of this individual, its consistency with stories told by other persons to this picture, the faithfulness with which the subject followed instructions in telling this story, and, finally, the extent to which the individual "has perceived and apperceived the picture adequately in all its parts."

Indirect evidence bearing on this question is provided by the common observation that stories derived from particular cards frequently have little information pertinent to given variables. Thus the individual interested in studying aggression may find that stories told to certain TAT cards will only rarely provide pertinent evidence. Not only do the stories told by the subject vary in significance but *for given purposes* the stories characteristically evoked by different cards vary in significance. Eron (20, 21) has shown that both incidence of themes and the emotional tone of stories differ significantly among the various TAT cards.

Although practical considerations and clinical experience indicate the necessity of an assumption of "crucial stories," there seems to be little empirical evidence that is directly pertinent.

Are Themes or Story Elements that Appear to Arise Directly out of the Stimulus Material Less Significant than Those that Are Not Directly Determined by the Stimulus Material? The extent to which this assumption is embraced by projective testers is made clear in the general emphasis upon the importance of bizarre responses, sex reversals, etc. Rotter (69) gives it explicit stress in his interpretative discussion of the importance of "unusualness" of response in the Thematic Apperception Test. In the scoring of sentence completion responses, Rotter (70) has reported finding special diagnostic significance associated with "twist" or "reversal" endings to incomplete sentences. Weisskopf (81) has emphasized the assumption heavily in her suggestion that one method of estimating the diagnostic efficiency of projective stimulus material is through the use of a "transcendence index." This index is derived from the

descriptive comments of the subject in responding to the stimulus material that go beyond "pure description."

The first difficulty we encouter in attempting to appraise this assumption is the question of how to go about measuring the degree to which a given response is determined by the stimulus material. This could be determined by estimating the structural similarities between the response and the stimulus. Or, one might develop empirical norms representing the common or usual response elements for each stimulus. Rosenzweig (67, 68) has chosen the second alternative in his attempt to establish "apperceptive norms." The function of these norms, in large part, is to enable the interpreter to differentiate that which derives naturally from the stimulus card from that which is projective or personally determined. The norms reported by Eron (20) could be used in similar fashion. Presumably most clinicians implicitly employ both of these approaches. On the one hand they note responses which are an obvious denial of the observable elements in the stimulus material, and on the other they build certain expectations in regard to what a "normal" story is to each stimulus and they tend to place special interpretive emphasis upon departures from these norms.

Some projective testers probably object to this assumption on the grounds that "any" response, no matter how normal or directly derived from the stimulus material, may have significance in projective protocols. They might point to this attribute as one of the chief differentiae between mental testing (normative) and projective testing (idiosyncratic). It is certainly true that the extent to which a response deviates from the norm is much less a matter of concern to the interpreter of projective protocols than it is to the "mental tester." However, the fact remains that if a particular response is given by one hundred per cent of the persons taking the test, this response cannot possess diagnostic significance unless it is combined with some other response element that is less frequently encountered. In the latter case it is clear that the second or less frequent response is determining the interpretation, not the "normal" response. Nevertheless, it must be remembered that even a response given by a very high percentage of the respondents may have broad significance as in the case of a yes-no response to a specific question. In the limiting case, a response may be given by ninety-nine per cent of the respondents and still be an important diagnostic sign, especially in those few cases where it is not encountered.

Limited empirical jusification for the view that significance and "stimulus-boundedness" are negatively related is provided in a study by McClelland, Burney, and Roby (49). They observed that *introduction* by the story-teller of an affiliated person into TAT stories where this person was not present in the picture was related to an experience the subjects had just undergone. A count of affiliated persons without consideration of whether or not they were in the picture did not reveal any relationship with the experimental treatment.

Supporting this assumption, we have the observation that most perception researchers accept the generalization that the more ambiguous the material, the easier it is to observe the operation of directive or motivational factors. Thus, they suggest that in those cases where the response bears relatively little relation to the stimulus material we are especially apt to observe dynamic or motivational factors. Closely related also is Bruner's (10) and Postman's (59) suggestion that the perceptual process may be represented as involving a relationship between the predetermining tendencies of the individual on the one hand, and information or stimulus constraints presented by the environment on the other. They imply that the

stronger the determining tendency, the less in the way of environmental supports are needed to produce a related percept and the more contradictory information will be needed to produce a percept in opposition to the predetermining tendency. The above assumption is quite similar to Bruner's and Postman's view, since it proposes that the stronger the stimulus constraints or supports, the less we know about the predetermining tendencies in the individual that have produced a response consistent with these constraints. However, if the stimulus material is not consistent with the report of the subject, presumably the predetermining tendency was sufficiently strong to produce an appropriate response, even though the stimulus did not call for it.

Thus, the assumption that stimulus-bound responses are less diagnostic than responses that do not depend so heavily upon stimulus constraints appears to fit well with available empirical data.

Are Recurrent Themes in a Series of Stories Particularly Likely to Mirror the Impulses and Conflicts of the Story-Teller? This is an assumption frequently stated but for which there is a minimum of pertinent empirical evidence. However, there are heavy rational considerations favoring such a view. The presence of the same theme even when the stimulus situation has been thoroughly altered implies strongly that there are impelling forces within the individual creating these themes rather than their being the inevitable outcome of stimulus constraints. The same theme following a change in stimulus material suggests that the response is not tied directly to, or produced by, a single specific stimulus. Thus, we may infer that the response tendency possesses generality and is more likely to be related to motivational factors than the response linked to a single stimulus. Even if we accept the view that in all instances the stimulus is evoking the response at question, we know that one measure of the strength of a drive is the extent to which stimulus generalization or displacement will occur. Thus, if the individual can equate a large number of stimuli in order to make this response, we may infer that the instigation lying behind the response is quite strong.

In addition, if interpretations are favored that incorporate a large amount of material, those based upon recurrent themes have a natural advantage in that the interpretation of one theme is automatically applicable to all of the other themes in the series. Finally, the presence of recurrent themes permits the investigator to sample or test the conditions under which these themes make their appearance.

In general, then, this assumption seems to have been accepted consistently by most projective testers although there is little or no direct evidence demonstrating its utility. However, there are a number of rational considerations that support such an assumption.

Do Stories Reflect not only Enduring Dispositions but also Momentary Impulses and Are These Both Reflected in the Same Manner? Most investigators are primarily interested in the Thematic Apperception Test as a means of measuring enduring dispositions, although occasionally, especially in research, the measurement of situational or temporary instigations to behavior may be crucial.

There have been numerous studies showing the sensitivity of the instrument to temporary or situational determinants. Bellak (5) showed that the number of aggressive words in TAT stories increased when the story-teller was rebuked for the low quality of the stories he told. Sanford (71, 72) and Atkinson and McClelland (2) have shown that TAT protocols vary with food deprivation, and McClelland, Clark, and Roby (50) have shown story variation as a result of exposure to failure in a test situation. Rodnick and

Klebanoff (66) have shown that TAT stories vary with relative success in a level of aspiration test. Lindzey (43) demonstrated that extrapunitive behavior on the part of the hero in TAT protocols increased significantly following failure in a social situation.

In similar fashion there are a number of studies that show the sensitivity of the stories to more enduring dispositions. It seems reasonable to accept individuals belonging to different psychiatric groups as differing in some enduring rather than situational attribute. Consequently, studies showing significant differences between groups separated on some diagnostic variable may be considered evidence of the test's sensitivity to enduring dispositions and conflicts. Balken and Masserman (3) observed significant differences in the TAT performance of patients categorized as conversion hysterics, anxiety hysterics, and obsessive compulsives. Renaud (64) was able with some difficulty to distinguish between psychoneurotics, traumatic brain disorder cases, and brain disease cases on the basis of TAT protocols. Cox and Sargent (16) found differentiating signs in the TAT performance of "stable" and "disturbed" school children. Working with mental hospital inmates Harrison (28) in approximately 77 percent of the cases was able to identify accurately on the basis of TAT stories the psychiatric category in which the patient had been placed. He reports (29) similar results when "blind analysis" was employed, that is, when the tests were administered by a different person than the interpreter.

Further evidence of the sensitivity of the test to non-situationally determined motivation is supplied by studies such as Murray and Stein's (57) where a relatively high positive relationship was found between leadership ratings of ROTC candidates based on TAT performance and leadership ratings independently executed by officers of the men in question. Likewise, Henry's (31) study of the Navaho and Hopi suggests the ability of the test to discriminate these two groups, and further to supply psychological information concerning them that is consistent with information secured from extended observation or through the use of independent instruments. White (82) showed that there was a significant relationship between TAT response and the dispositions leading to hypnotizability. Harrison (28) in those cases where he was able to match descriptive statements based upon TAT responses with independent information derived from mental hospital case histories was correct in 82.5 per cent of the instances.

The question of whether temporary and enduring tendencies are reflected in stories in exactly the same fashion is important for two reasons. First, the clinician is primarily concerned with the more enduring tendencies and, therefore, it is desirable that he have some means of differentiating between these two classes of determinants. Second, some research, especially McClelland's (2, 50), has implied that through studying the effect of situational factors upon TAT performance it is possible to arrive at means of interpreting TAT stories to reveal the operation of more enduring tendencies. If the reflection of these two kinds of motivational factors should prove to be very similar or the same process this would be unfortunate for the clinician, who would then be faced with the difficulty or impossibility of knowing whether a given tendency was temporarily instigated or whether this was a more permanent characteristic of the individual in question. On the other hand, such similarity in process would encourage experimental treatments as feasible means of approaching the task of specifying more exactly the means of inferring enduring tendencies.

McClelland (47) has supplied some evidence that the enduring and temporary processes are reflected in the same manner. He has demonstrated that the differences in subjects' TAT responses following experimental induction of a motivational state (threatening test situation) is related to other measures of the individuals' behavior, e.g., academic performance. This implies that the response of the subject to the immediate situation is related to his more permanent patterns of response.

McClelland and Liberman (51) derived a system for scoring need achievement in TAT responses that was based upon the differences produced in TAT protocols following experimentally induced failure in a situation related to achievement. In addition, they demonstrated that achievement as measured by this scoring technique was related to performance in an anagrams test and also related to the speed with which certain kinds of achievement related words could be recognized when exposed tachistoscopically. Thus, a measure of need achievement derived from a temporary instigation appeared to be related to other measures of achievement which were only distantly related to the initial instigating situation. While this evidence is not compelling, it does provide some support for the notion that temporary instigations affect TAT stories in a manner consistent with the way in which more enduring dispositions influence stories.

We appear to have excellent empirical evidence indicating that stories are responsive to both situational and enduring motivational factors. There is no conclusive evidence demonstrating the similarity or dissimilarity of the process whereby these two classes of determinants secure expression in the stories.

Do the Stories Reflect Events from the Past of the Subject That He Has Not Himself Actively Experienced? Are These Events Diagnostic of the Individual's Dispositions and Conflicts? Inquiry following the customary administration of the TAT has verified the hypothesis that individuals do incorporate material taken directly from scenes that they have witnessed or from movies or books they have been exposed to. Murray (56) has reported this. Further, any clinician who has worked at all extensively with the TAT has inevitably many cases in his own experience of stories drawn directly from the world of the novel or drama, frequently with accompanying remarks indicating explicitly that this was the case. This is directly consistent with Freud's (25) early dictum that each dream incorporates something from the events of the preceding day.

Given the influence of these non-participated events, the question then becomes one of whether motivational factors affect or are revealed in the recall of such experiences. The selective function of memory and the importance of motivational determinants in the memory process have been recognized for some time, certainly since the appearance of Bartlett's (4) treatise on memory. A number of studies have investigated, under reasonably well-controlled conditions, memory as a function of such motivational variables as political ideology, Edwards (19), Levine and Murphy(41); value as measured by the *Study of Values,* McGinnies and Bowles (52); sex membership, Clark (14); mental set, Carmichael, Hogan and Walter (13); attitude, Postman and Murphy (60); punishment, McGranahan (53). Although there are many other factors, e.g., primacy, recency, vividness, known to influence recall, it seems reasonably well established that motivational factors do serve as one important class of determinants of memory.

If we accept these studies as evidence of the extent to which memory is influenced by motivational factors, it seems reasonable that the individual, in the process of recalling past events or experiences, will reveal or expose important aspects of his own motivational state. Consequently, the assumption that

the particular events remembered by the subject are diagnostic of his dispositions and conflicts appears to be supported by available empirical data.

Do Stories Reflect Group-Membership, Cultural or Social Determinants as well as Personal or Individual Determinants? This assumption simply implies consistent differences between the fantasy productions of individuals who belong to, or have been socialized in, different social groups. Thus, a certain amount of the variation in any TAT production can be accounted for by the fact that the individual has grown up in a given milieu or social role. The importance of the assumption derives from the fact that overlooking this kind of variation introduces a serious source of error in the interpretation of imaginative protocols from members of more than one social group.

Although little effort has been made to explore the variations in fantasy productions between many of the important groups of our own society, it is quite widely accepted or expected that these differences exist. Even such an important cleavage as that between male and female has been little explored so far as TAT behavior is concerned, while such variables as socio-economic status, occupational role, and ethnic group-membership have also been of slight interest to most investigators. Rosenzweig and Fleming (68) have reported differences between a roughly equated group of men and women on a number of specific aspects of TAT response. An investigation by Riess, Schwartz, and Cottingham (65) designed as a critical appraisal of the Thompson (78) modification of the TAT led to the observation of certain relatively slight variations in story length as a function of geographic residence and Negro-white group-membership.

Henry (31) in his investigation of Navaho and Hopi children found that inferences based upon his adaptation of the TAT related to independently secured information concerning the children and also that there were systematic differences between the Navaho and Hopi fantasy productions. In addition, he reports differences between Navaho subjects who were members of different subgroups in this society.

Although there is a paucity of empirical evidence demonstrating differences in fantasy production between various socio-cultural groups, what evidence is available appears to support this assumption.

Are Impulses and Conflicts inferred from Stories Not Always Reflected Directly in Overt Behavior and Consciousness? Projective testers vary considerably in the manner in which they emphasize this assumption. Some see a very intimate relation between imaginative behavior and overt behavior. Thus, Piotrowski introduces nine rules designed to permit the translation of fantasied into overt with the following statement:

The rules proposed in this article are a new attempt to solve the problem of the relationship between the TAT and overt behavior. Since the TAT is mainly an exercise in creative imagination, it should reflect the patient's ideas and drives regardless of whether or not they find a direct expression in overt behavior. Thus, parts of the TAT always reflect the overt behavior of the subject while other parts reflect ideas which are not as directly manifested in overt actions. If this be so, we need a rule by means of which we could differentiate these two parts of the TAT. The rules presented below have been formulated largely for the purpose of meeting that need (58, p. 105).

Others are more cautious in stating their views of the relation between story-behavior and overt behavior. Murray, in his introduction to the TAT, suggests:

It may be stated, as a rough generalization, that the content of a set of TAT stories represents second level, covert . . . personality, not first level, overt or public . . . personality. There are plenty of ways of discovering the most typical trends; the

TAT is one of the few methods available today for the disclosure of covert tendencies. The best understanding of the total structure of personality is obtained when the psychologist considers the characteristics of manifest behavior in conjunction with the TAT findings . . . (56, p. 16).

In similar vein, Korner states:

. . . instead of deploring the fact that fantasy and reality behavior do not necessarily correspond, as we currently seem to be doing, we can use projective techniques as a shortcut to a person's fantasy and ideational life, which then can be compared and examined in the light of his present and past actual behavior patterns (37, p. 627).

Although the relationship between covert and overt is assessed differently by various investigators, all seem to agree that the relationship is not perfect —fantasy behavior does not exactly mirror overt behavior. This omnipresent assumption can serve one of two functions depending upon the orientation of the investigator. It *can* serve simply as a convenient means of avoiding the necessity of ever being wrong. Thus, whenever inferences based on story protocols fail to relate to appropriate, independent measures or observations, the clinician may simply point to the above assumption and add that only the naive would expect always to observe linear relationships between imaginal and overt or conscious behavior. On the other hand, the investigator can use this assumption as a signpost pointing to one of the most important and difficult empirical problems facing the projective tester. This problem is the determination of the conditions under which inferences based on projective material directly relate to overt behavior and the conditions for the reverse.

It is possible to defend the position that projective techniques should not be expected to provide statements concerning overt behavior. Such a view implies that the techniques will always be used only as an "imaginal supplement" to an otherwise adequate description of the individual. Thus, given a person who "behaves" in a particular way, examination of his fantasy productions may permit us to make consistent or to account for behavior that hitherto was unaccountable. Certainly this represents an important function of these techniques. Equally certain is the fact that this is not the only circumstance under which these instruments are used. They *are* used as means of inferring overt behavior tendencies and presumably with more adequate rules of transformation they would be so used much more widely.

Investigations by Sanford *et al.* (73) and Symonds (77), which unfortunately from the point of view of sampling were both based on adolescent populations, demonstrate clearly that in some cases instead of the impulses inferred from TAT records being reflected in behavior, their converse or opposite appear in behavior. This observation leads to the question of whether impulses that secure release in overt behavior may not need to be expressed in fantasy productions. However, the many positive relationships between imaginal impulses and overt behavior in these studies and others make it clear that it is not an either-or proposition and that the statement of the actual conditions under which the impulse is revealed or concealed must be complex.

Sanford *et al.* (73) studied the relationship in a group of school children between fantasy ratings derived from the TAT and overt behavior ratings provided by teachers who had observed the children. They found an average correlation of +.11 between the two sets of ratings indicating clearly that the fantasy ratings alone were not good predictors of overt behavior. However, there were striking differences between the different variables used in the extent to which fantasy and behavior corresponded. For some needs there was a relatively high positive relationship,

while for others there was a significant negative relationship between the overt and covert. In accounting for these findings, Sanford *et al.* suggested that those tendencies which were negatively sanctioned or prohibited would be high in fantasy and low in overt behavior, while those tendencies which were encouraged by society and for which the individual could secure complete overt expression would be high in behavior but low in fantasy. High ratings would be secured in both fantasy and overt behavior for those tendencies that society encouraged but did not permit complete freedom of expression in, e.g., achievement, dominance.

Murray (56) has suggested that tendencies not inhibited by cultural sanctions are apt to be highly correlated in their fantasy and overt expression. He reports a positive correlation of over .40 between fantasy and overt behavior for a group of college men on the following variables: abasement, creation, dominance, exposition, nurturance, passivity, rejection, and dejection. Negative correlations are reported between fantasy and overt for sex and no correlation between the two forms of expression for aggression and achievement. Korner (36) attempted to relate hostility as observed in a play situation with ratings of hostility in interpersonal relations with other children. She found no general relationship between the two sets of variables. Half of the children high on hostility in play situations were likewise high on hostility manifested in their dealings with other children. The remaining half who were high on hostility manifested in play situations were low on the second set of ratings. The investigator concluded that it was impossible to predict from the one situation to the other.

Symonds (77) related the fantasy themes of 40 adolescent boys and girls to adjustment ratings and teachers' ratings of behavioral characteristics. He concluded that the relationship between these two sets of variables was "insignificant and negligible."

Further evidence of the lack of a perfect relationship between fantasy and overt behavior is provided in those cases where an individual of known characteristics fails to reveal salient aspects of himself in his TAT constructions. Tomkins (80) reports the case of an individual who had a persistent spontaneous fantasy which included as an important theme a homosexual seduction. The TAT responses of this individual gave no sign of homosexual tendencies. In accounting for this and similar cases, Tomkins suggests that the important variables are the awareness of the subject of the impulse or tendency at question and the extent to which the tendency is condoned or accepted by society. If the impulse is known and unaccepted by society, the individual will prevent its appearance in the stories he tells. If he is unaware of the tendency, it will appear in his fantasy constructions even if it is negatively sanctioned by society. Bellak (6) reports several similar instances where TAT performance fails to reveal central aspects of the individual.

Relatively little has been done in the attempt to discover and formulate signs in the stories themselves that would provide evidence concerning the probability of overt expression. There is some evidence that, as Tomkins (79) proposes, the "psychological distance" maintained by the story-teller toward the impulse or disposition in question may be an important condition relating to the degrees of overt translation.

Available empirical evidence clearly indicates that the assumed imperfect correlation between fantasied and overt behavior is warranted. However, at present, we are far from an adequate formulation of the signs or cues that might permit specification from fantasy protocols alone of the behavioral tendencies that will secure overt expression as opposed to those that will not.

Research Implications

Almost all of these assumptions point to further research that would be useful in clarifying their status. Perhaps more important than research aimed at further demonstrating the warranty of these same assumptions is research that attempts to provide a more exact statement of the conditions under which the assumptions are applicable and the way in which they can be related to empirical data. For example: what are the means by which the important story in a series can be determined? How can we determine whether or not a given fantasy impulse will receive overt expression? In what way do we determine whether or not a given response has been determined by the stimulus material? What are the circumstances under which symbolic transformations must be engaged in? How do we determine the empirical referent of a given symbol? Answers to these and a host of related questions are necessary before we can hope to provide the TAT user with an explicit, repeatable set of operations for inferring motivational states.

In addition to problems connected with the interpretive assumptions and the more specific questions implied in the above paragraph, there is also the matter of formulating explicitly a method of scoring TAT protocols that is practical, intersubjective, and able to embrace a reasonable number of the behavioral variables in common use. To a large extent standardization and specific interpretive rules must wait until some agreement has been reached by most TAT users as to the major aspects of TAT response that will be focused upon in analysis.

Summary

This paper has stressed the continuity between projective testing and research and theory in other areas of psychology. In addition, it has presented ten assumptions commonly made in interpreting Thematic Apperception Test stories and has sampled briefly the empirical evidence that can be used to confirm or reject each of them.

REFERENCES

1. ARNOLD, MAGDA B. A demonstration analysis of the TAT in a clinical setting. *J. abnorm. soc. Psychol.*, 1949, **44**, 97–111.

2. ATKINSON, J. W., & McCLELLAND, D. C. The projective expression of needs: II. The effect of different intensities of the hunger drive on thematic apperception. *J. exp. Psychol.*, 1948, **38**, 643–658.

3. BALKEN, EVA R., & MASSERMAN, J. H. The language of fantasy: III. The language of the phantasies of patients with conversion hysteria, anxiety state, and obsessive-compulsive neuroses. *J. Psychol.*, 1940, **10**, 75–86.

4. BARTLETT, F. C. *Remembering.* London: Cambridge Univ. Press, 1932.

5. BELLAK, L. The concept of projection: an experimental investigation and study of the concept. *Psychiatry*, 1944, **7**, 353–370.

6. BELLAK, L. Thematic apperception: failures and the defenses. *Trans. N. Y. Acad. Sci.*, 1950, **12**, 122–126.

7. BLAKE, R. R., & WILSON, G. P. Perceptual selectivity in Rorschach determinants as a function of depressive tendencies. *J. abnorm. soc. Psychol.*, 1950, **45**, 459–472.

8. BROWN, J. S. The generalization of approach responses as a function of stimulus intensity and strength of motivation. *J. comp. Psychol.*, 1942, **33**, 209–226.

9. BRUNER, J. S. Perceptual theory and the Rorschach Test. *J. Personality*, 1948, **17**, 157–168.

10. BRUNER, J. S. Personality dynamics and the process of perceiving. In R. R. BLAKE & G. RAMSEY (Eds.), *Perception: an approach to personality.* New York: Ronald Press, 1951. Pp. 121–147.

11. BRUNER, J. S., & POSTMAN, L. Tension and tension release as organizing factors in perception. *J. Personality*, 1947, **15**, 300–308.

12. BRUNER, J. S., & POSTMAN, L. An approach to social perception. In W. DENNIS (Ed.), *Current trends in social psychology.* Pittsburgh, Pa.: Univ. Pittsburgh Press, 1948. Pp. 71–118.

13. CARMICHAEL, L., HOGAN, H. P., & WALTER, A. An experimental study of the effect of language on the reproduction of visually perceived form. *J. exp. Psychol.*, 1932, **15**, 73–86.

14. CLARK, K. B. Some factors influencing the remembering of prose materials. *Arch. Psychol.*, N. Y., 1940, No. 253.

15. COFER, C. N., & FOLEY, J. P., JR. Mediated generalizations and the interpretation of verbal behavior: I. Prolegomena. *Psychol. Rev.*, 1942, **49**, 513–540.

16. COX, BEVERLY, & SARGENT, HELEN. TAT responses of emotionally disturbed and emotionally stable children: clinical judgment versus normative data. *Rorschach Res. Exch.*, 1950, **14**, 61–74.

17. DIVEN, K. Certain determinants in the conditioning of anxiety reactions. *J. Psychol.*, 1937, **3**, 291–308.

18. DOUGLAS, ANNA G. A tachistoscopic study of the order of emergence in the process of perception. *Psychol. Monogr.*, 1947, **61** (6), Whole No. 287.

19. EDWARDS, A. L. Political frames of reference as a factor influencing recognition. *J. abnorm. soc. Psychol.*, 1941, **36**, 34–50.

20. ERON, L. D. A normative study of the Thematic Apperception Test. *Psychol. Monogr.*, 1950, **64** (9), Whole No. 315.

21. ERON, L. D., TERRY, DOROTHY, & CALLAHAN, R. The use of rating scales for emotional tone of TAT stories.

J. consult. Psychol., 1950, **14**, 473–478.

22. FARBER, L. H., & FISHER, C. An experimental approach to dream psychology through the use of hypnosis. *Psychoanal. Quart.*, 1943, **12**, 202–216.

23. FRANCK, KATE. Preferences for sex symbols and their personality corelates. *Genet. Psychol. Monogr.*, 1946, **33**, 73–123.

24. FRANCK, KATE, & ROSEN, E. A projective test of masculinity-femininity. *J. consult. Psychol.*, 1949, **13**, 247–256.

25. FREUD, S. The interpretation of dreams. In A. A. BRILL (Ed.), *The basic writings of Sigmund Freud.* New York: Modern Library, 1938. Pp. 181–552.

26. GRANDINE, LOIS, & HARLOW, H. F. Generalizations of the characteristics of a single learned stimulus by monkeys. *J. comp. physiol. Psychol.*, 1948, **41**, 327–338.

27. HAGGARD, E. A. Experimental studies in affective processes: I. Some effects of cognitive structure and active participation on certain autonomic reactions during and following experimentally induced stress. *J. exp. Psychol.*, 1943, **33**, 257–284.

28. HARRISON, R. Studies in the use and validity of the Thematic Apperception Test with mentally disordered patients: II. A quantitative validity study. *Character & Pers.*, 1940, **9**, 122–133.

29. HARRISON, R. Studies in the use and validity of the Thematic Apperception Test with mentally disordered patients: III. Validation by the method of "blind analysis." *Character & Pers.*, 1940, **9**, 134–138.

30. HARRISON, R., & ROTTER, J. B. A note on the reliability of the Thematic Apperception Test. *J. abnorm. soc. Psychol.*, 1945, **40**, 97–99.

31. HENRY, W. E. The Thematic Apperception Technique in the study of culture-personality relations. *Genet. Psychol. Monogr.*, 1947, **35**, 3–315.

32. HULL, C. L. *Principles of behavior: an introduction to behavior theory.* New York: Appleton-Century, 1943.

33. HULL, C. L. The problem of primary stimulus generalization. *Psychol. Rev.*, 1947, **54**, 120–134.

34. KATZ, I. Emotional expression in failure: A new hypothesis. *J. abnorm. soc. Psychol.*, 1950, **45**, 329–349.

35. KLEIN, D. B. The experimental production of dreams during hypnosis. *Univ. Texas Bull.*, 1930, No. 3009.

36. KORNER, ANNELIESE F. *Some aspects of hostility in young children.* New York: Grune & Stratton, 1949.

37. KORNER, ANNELIESE F. Theoretical considerations concerning the scope and limitations of projective techniques. *J. abnorm. soc. Psychol.*, 1950, **45**, 619–627.

38. KROUT, JOHANNA. Symbol elaboration test: The reliability and validity of a new projective technique. *Psychol. Monogr.*, 1950, **64** (4), Whole No. 310.

39. LASHLEY, K. S., & WADE, MARJORIE. The Pavlovian theory of generalization. *Psychol. Rev.*, 1946, **53**, 72–87.

40. LEVINE, R., CHEIN, I., & MURPHY, G. The relation of the intensity of a need to the amount of perceptual distortion: a preliminary report. *J. Psychol.*, 1942, **13**, 283–293.

41. LEVINE, J. M., & MURPHY, G. The learning and forgetting of controversial material. *J. abnorm. soc. Psychol.*, 1943, **38**, 507–517.

42. LEVY, D. M. Projective techniques in clinical practice. *Amer. J. Orthopsychiat.*, 1949, **19**, 140–144.

43. LINDZEY, G. An experimental examination of the scapegoat theory of prejudice. *J. abnorm. soc. Psychol.*, 1950, **45**, 296–309.

44. MacCORQUODALE, K., & MEEHL, P. E. On a distinction between hypothetical constructs and intervening variables. *Psychol. Rev.*, 1948, **55**, 95–107.

45. MAYMAN, M., & KUTNER, B. Reliability in analyzing Thematic Apperception Test stories. *J. abnorm. soc. Psychol.*, 1947, **42**, 365–368.

46. McCLEARY, R. A., & LAZARUS, R. S. Autonomic discrimination without awareness: an interim report. *J. Personality*, 1949, **18**, 171–179.

47. McCLELLAND, D. C. Measuring moti-

vation in phantasy: the achievement motive. In H. Guetzkow (Ed.), *Groups, leadership and men: Research in human relations.* Pittsburgh: Carnegie Press, 1951.

48. McClelland, D. C., & Atkinson, J. W. The projective expression of needs: I. The effect of different intensities of the hunger drive on perception. *J. Psychol.*, 1948, 25, 205–222.

49. McClelland, D. C., Birney, R. C., & Roby, T. B. The effect of anxiety on imagination. Paper read at Eastern Psychological Assn., 1950.

50. McClelland, D. C., Clark, R. A., Roby, T. B., & Atkinson, J. W. The projective expression of needs: IV. The effect of need for achievement on thematic apperception. *J. exp. Psychol.*, 1949, 39, 242–255.

51. McClelland, D. C., & Liberman, A. M. The effect of need for achievement on recognition of need-related words. *J. Personality*, 1949, 18, 236–251.

52. McGinnies, E., & Bowles, W. Personal values as determinants of perceptual fixation. *J. Personality*, 1949, 18, 224–235.

53. McGranahan, D. V. A critical and experimental study of repression. *J. abnorm. soc. Psychol.*, 1940, 35, 212–225.

54. Miller, N. E. Theory and experiment relating psychoanalytic displacement to stimulus-response generalization. *J. abnorm. soc. Psychol.*, 1948, 43, 155–178.

55. Murray, H. A. The effect of fear upon estimates of the maliciousness of other personalities. *J. soc. Psychol.*, 1933, 4, 310–329.

56. Murray, H. A. *Thematic Apperception Test manual.* Cambridge: Harvard Univ. Press, 1943.

57. Murray, H. A., & Stein, M. I. Note on the selection of combat officers. *Psychosom. Med.*, 1943, 5, 386–391.

58. Piotrowski, Z. A. A new evaluation of the Thematic Apperception Test. *Psychoanalyt. Rev.*, 1950, 37, 101–127.

59. Postman, L. Toward a general theory of cognition. In J. Rohrer & M. Sherif (Eds.), *Social psychology at the crossroads.* New York: Harpers, 1951.

60. Postman, L., & Murphy, G. The factor of attitude in associative memory. *J. exp. Psychol.*, 1943, 33, 228–238.

61. Rapaport, D. The clinical application of the Thematic Apperception Test. *Bull. Menninger Clin.*, 1943, 7, 106–113.

62. Razran, G. Stimulus generalization of conditioned responses. *Psychol. Bull.*, 1949, 46, 337–365.

63. Razran, G. Attitudinal determinants of conditioning and of generalization of conditioning. *J. exp. Psychol.*, 1949, 39, 820–829.

64. Renaud, H. Group differences in fantasies: head injuries, psychoneurotics, and brain diseases. *J. Psychol.*, 1946, 21, 327–346.

65. Riess, B. F., Schwartz, E. K., & Cottingham, Alice. An experimental critique of assumptions underlying the Negro version of the TAT. *J. abnorm. soc. Psychol.*, 1950, 45, 700–709.

66. Rodnick, E. H., & Klebanoff, S. G. Projective reactions to induced frustrations as a measure of social adjustment. *Psychol. Bull.*, 1942, 39, 489. (Abstract)

67. Rosenzweig, S. Apperceptive norms for the Thematic Apperception Test: I. The problem of norms in projective methods. *J. Personality*, 1949, 17, 475–482.

68. Rosenzweig, S., & Fleming, Edith. Apperceptive norms for the Thematic Apperception Test: II. An empirical investigation. *J. Personality*, 1949, 17, 483–503.

69. Rotter, J. B. Thematic apperception tests: suggestions for administration and interpretation. *J. Personality*, 1946, 15, 70–92.

70. Rotter, J. B., Rafferty, Janet E., & Schachtitz, Eva. Validation of the Rotter Incomplete Sentences Blank for college screening. *J. consult. psychol.*, 1949, 13, 348–355.

71. Sanford, R. N. The effects of abstinence from food upon imaginal processes: a preliminary experiment. *J. Psychol.*, 1936, 2, 129–136.

72. Sanford, R. N. The effects of abstin-

ence from food upon imaginal processes: a further experiment. *J. Psychol.*, 1937, **3**, 145–159.

73. SANFORD, R. N., ADKINS, MARGARET M., MILLER, R. B., et al. Physique, personality and scholarship: a co-operative study of school children. *Monogr. Soc. Res. Child Developm.*, 1943, **8**, No. 1.

74. SEARS, R. R. Effects of frustration and anxiety on fantasy aggression. *Am. J. Orthopsychiat.* (In press.)

75. SIIPOLA, ELSA M. The influence of color on reactions to ink blots. *J. Personality*, 1950, **18**, 358–382.

76. STEIN, M. I. Personality factors involved in the temporal development of Rorschach responses. *Rorschach Res. Exch.*, 1949, **13**, 355–414.

77. SYMONDS, P. M. *Adolescent fantasy: An investigation of the picture-story method of personality study.* New York: Columbia Univ. Press, 1949.

78. THOMPSON, C. E. The Thompson modification of the Thematic Apperception Test. *Rorschach Res. Exch.*, 1949, **13**, 469–478.

79. TOMKINS, S. S. *The Thematic Apperception Test.* New York: Grune & Stratton, 1947.

80. TOMKINS, S. S. The present status of the Thematic Apperception Test, *Am. J. Orthopsychiat.*, 1949, **19**, 358–362.

81. WEISSKOPF, EDITH A. A transcendence index as a proposed measure in the TAT. *J. Psychol.*, 1950, **29**, 379–390.

82. WHITE, R. W. Prediction of hypnotic susceptibility from a knowledge of subjects' attitudes. *J. Psychol.*, 1937, **3**, 265–277.

83. WICKENS, D. D. Stimulus identity as related to response specificity and response generalization. *J. exp. Psychol.*, 1948, **38**, 389–394.

84. WYATT, F. Formal aspects of the Thematic Apperception Test. *Psychol. Bull.*, 1946, **39**, 491. (Abstract)

STUDIES OF CLINICAL VALIDITY

The Validity of Thematic Projective Technique Interpretations

Kenneth B. Little and Edwin S. Shneidman

Several studies have been made in the attempt to establish a quantitative index of the validity, in clinical usage, of thematic projective techniques (1, 2, 3, 5, 6, 7). The major problem in

This investigation was supported by a research grant from the National Institute of Mental Health, of the National Institutes of Health, Public Health Service and was administered by the University of Southern California, Los Angeles.

Reprinted by permission of the publisher and authors from the *Journal of Personality*, 1955, **23**, 285–294.

such investigations is the difficulty of establishing a set of measurement dimensions which will cover all, or even most, of the information available in the responses of the subject. Until this can be done a projective technique cannot be considered a *test* in the usual psychometric sense, and no unique validity coefficient (or unique set of validity coefficients) can be determined. An alternative approach, however, is to consider the projective technique protocol merely as a sample of the subject's verbal behavior from which inferences of various sorts may be made by the interpreting clinician. These inferences can be compared with a criterion and an interpreter-protocol index of agreement obtained. The central tendency of such indices among competent interpreters working with a variety of protocols might legitimately be considered the "validity" of the projective technique itself.

The present paper is a report of an initial study of the range and magnitudes of interpreter-protocol validity coefficients using a number of interpreters and the thematic test protocols of a single subject.[1] In addition, the attempt was made to determine the types of inferences made from thematic protocols and the relation between the types of inferences made and their accuracy.

Procedure

Seventeen psychologists, all familiar with thematic projective technique interpretation (as indicated by their having published one or more books or articles on the subject), were presented with the Thematic Apperception Test (TAT) and the Make A Picture Story (MAPS) protocols of one subject who was identified to them as male, age 25, and single. Each of the judges wrote an essay-form personality description of this subject on the basis of his analysis of the protocols.[2] These reports were then separated, by the present investigators, into discrete statements about the subject. In all, 802 nonduplicated items were secured by this means. For each of the statements describing the subject another statement contradictory to the original was constructed. For example, the statement "He has a very high IQ" was paired with the statement "He is of average intelligence."

Of this total item population of 1604, 150 items were selected on a systematic sampling basis as representative of the personality attributes asserted, or implicitly denied, about the subject. These 150 items were returned to the original test interpreters, who sorted them into a forced quasi-normal distribution—a Q-sort (9)—on the basis of their truth or falsity for the subject. The resulting distributions of items were intercorrelated giving a 17-by-17 test-interpreter correlation matrix. The range of correlations was from .02 to .68, with a mean of .44.

The same 150 items were also submitted to 29 competent clinicians who independently performed Q-sorts of them on the basis of a complete clinical record (minus the test protocols and reports) of the subject. All of these criterion judges had had at least five years of professional experience, and three had had personal contact with the subject as therapists or consultants. They were of various doctrinaire hues—psychoanalytic, nondirective, neo-Freudian, eclectic, etc. The clinical record contained reports of medical examinations, social history, therapy-interview notes, laboratory data, reports of consultations, course-of-treatment notes, etc. The criterion-judge distributions of items were intercorrelated, giving a 29-by-29 criterion correlational matrix with a range from .04 to .76 and a mean of .52. In addition, each of the test-interpreter distributions was correlated with each of the criterion-judge distributions, giving a 17-by-29 test-interpreter versus criterion-judge correlation matrix. These correlations ranged from −.07 to .70, with a mean of .45.[3]

---

[1] A further study is currently being made using a variety of protocols, projective techniques, and interpreters to increase the representativeness of the results.

[2] The two test protocols and 17 interpretations—together with other test materials and case history data—are presented in *Thematic test analysis* (8).

[3] More detailed correlation tables of intercorrelation have been deposited as Document No. 4472 with the ADI Auxiliary Publication Project, Photoduplication Service, Library of Congress, Washington 25, D.C. A copy may be secured by citing the document no., and remitting $1.25 for photoprints or $1.25 for a 35 mm. microfilm. Make checks or money orders payable to Chief, Photoduplication Service, Library of Congress.

Results

Criterion Analysis

An initial attempt at a cluster analysis (10) of the correlations among the criterion judges indicated that all had very similar correlation profiles and could properly be considered members of a single cluster. A centroid factor analysis performed independently confirmed this in that there was a large general factor that could not be eliminated by any form of orthogonal rotation. None of the remaining four factors had loadings exceeding .38. It was decided, therefore, to use the first centroid factor as the best estimate of the criterion judge consensus inasmuch as it accounted for 90 per cent of the total communality among them. Table 1 gives the loading of each criterion judge on this factor.

To identify the criterion, factor scores were computed for each of the 150 items as the sum of the individual weighted scores assigned to it by the criterion judges. The appropriate weights were derived by the Gengerelli method (4). The factor scores of the items were then ranked in order of magnitude and

TABLE 1.   GENERAL FACTOR LOADINGS OF THE TWENTY-NINE CRITERION JUDGES

Judge	Factor Loading	Judge	Factor Loading
1	.744	16	.492
2	.740	17	.791
3	.710	18	.764
4	.800	19	.835
5	.754	20	.798
6	.777	21	.689
7	.610	22	.744
8	.833	23	.745
9	.884	24	.789
10	.833	25	.738
11	.772	26	.741
12	.696	27	.734
13	.209	28	.718
14	.803	29	.601
15	.725		

TABLE 2.   IDENTIFYING ITEMS OF THE CRITERION GENERAL FACTOR

Most True Items	Most False Items
1. He is in the early stages of paranoid schizophrenia.	1. He is not a particularly sick individual.
2. He has an enormous amount of hostility.	2. He has satisfactory interpersonal relationships.
3. His deep conflict in the sexual area is between sexual impulses and superego restraints.	3. His thought processes are orderly and well knit.
4. He has strong latent homosexual impulses.	4. He is not a schizoid individual.
5. He feels fearful.	5. He has very little guilt feelings concerning his aggressive impulses.
6. His aggressive impulses are both externally and internally directed.	6. He perceives the world as largely friendly.
7. He is concerned with "good" versus "bad."	7. He does not have much anxiety.
8. He identified more with his mother than with his father.	8. He does not show any evidence of hallucinatory behavior.
9. He lacks positive interpersonal relationships.	9. He seems little concerned with his bodily well being.
10. He feels depressed.	10. He is little concerned with physical violence.
11. He never adequately learned social skills.	11. There are no paranoid ideas of reference or malign influences.
12. He avoids social disapproval by engaging in solitary activity.	12. His superego is relatively mature.

TABLE 3.   ESTIMATED CORRELATIONS OF EACH TEST INERPRETER WITH EACH OF THE CLUSTER DOMAINS

Domain	\multicolumn{6}{c}{A}						\multicolumn{3}{c}{B}			\multicolumn{6}{c}{C}						\multicolumn{2}{c}{Resid.}	
	1	2	3	4	5	6	7	8	9	10	11	12	13	14	15	16	17
C_A	.83	.77	.74	.77	.78	.80	.52	.43	.39	.74	.75	.65	.64	.67	.71	.49	.57
C_B	.69	.52	.51	.54	.58	.49	.69	.65	.55	.40	.44	.21	.29	.26	.20	.16	.57
C_C	.76	.75	.66	.68	.74	.75	.29	.34	.13	.82	.82	.73	.77	.71	.75	.64	.48
h^2	.69	.59	.55	.59	.61	.64	.48	.42	.30	.67	.67	.53	.59	.50	.56	.41	.32

the upper and lower 8 per cent tabulated. Table 2 presents the 12 items with the highest ("most true") factor scores and the 12 items with the lowest ("most false") factor scores.

The items presented in Table 2 seem to be largely dynamic-descriptive but with a diagnostic flavor. There is little emphasis upon either etiology, or symptomatology but rather a cross-sectional picture of the subect's present psychological state.

Test Interpretation Analysis

The three groups of judges were isolated from a cluster analysis of the test-interpreter intercorrelations. These three clusters included 15 of the 17 judges; the remaining two (numbers 16 and 17) could not properly be placed in any single cluster and are classified as residuals. Table 3 gives the estimated correlations of each test judge with the cluster domains (analogous to factor loadings) and also an estimate of the communalities or extent to which each judge shares common sources of variance with the other judges. Table 4 presents the estimated correlations among the cluster domains.

A comparison was made between the theoretical correlations among the test judges (computed from the cluster loadings and the correlations among the cluster domains) and the empirical correlations. The distribution of differences between the theoretical correlations and their corresponding empirical correlations is not significantly different from the normal curve of error. Consequently, the hypothesis that the three clusters account for all the general sources of variance among the test judges cannot be rejected.

TABLE 4.   ESTIMATED CORRELATIONS AMONG THE CLUSTER DOMAINS

Cluster Domain	C_A	C_B	C_C
C_A	1.00	.71	.93
C_B	.71	1.00	.40
C_C	.93	.40	1.00

Identification of the clusters—the task of describing what the judges of one cluster have in common that sets them apart from the members of the other clusters—was made in the following fashion. The three estimated cluster scores of each of the 150 items were computed as the simple average of the scores assigned to it by the judges in each cluster. The items were then ranked in order of magnitude of their cluster scores for each of the three clusters, and the upper and lower 16 per cent of items examined. Considerable overlap was present, as would be expected from the magnitude of the correlations among the cluster domains. However, it was possible to isolate certain items that ranked high on one cluster and low, or moderately low, on the other two. Conversely, items were isolated that ranked low on one cluster and high or moderately high on the other two. These cluster-defining items are presented in Table 5.

The judges of cluster A are characterized by a preference for what is commonly called "dynamic" type items. These items are assertions about the nature of the intrapsychic conflicts, their genetic development, and the subject's affective response to them. A diagnosis for the subject appears only by implication. The judges of cluster C, on the other hand, show a preference for items describing the psychopathology presented by the subject with emphasis upon disorders of intellectual functioning. Cluster B is less clear-cut, possible because it was the smallest and least homogeneous of the three. However, in the formal characteristics of the defining items it resembles strongly cluster C. The difference between the judges of cluster B and those of cluster C seems to be one of diagnostic conclusion rather than of conceptual

TABLE 5.   IDENTIFYING ITEMS FOR THREE CLUSTERS OF
THEMATIC-TEST INTERPRETERS

Cluster A

Most true	Most false
He has incestuous desires that have precipitated intense conflict in him.	He has little conflict over his incestuous sexual impulses.
One of the main factors in his personality development was an extremely hostile, dominant mother.	He has satisfactory interpersonal relationships.
He lacks positive interpersonal relations.	He has resolved the conflict between his sexual needs and his interpretation of his mother's standards.
His deep conflict in the sexual area is between sexual impulses and superego restraints.	He shows little guilt over his incestuous sexual impulses.
He feels deprived of the oral gratifications of childhood.	
His aggression is aroused by illicit sexuality.	
Sexuality is strongly rejected by him.	
He suffers from feelings of rejection.	

Cluster B

Most true	Most false
His principal conflict is in the sexual area.	He displays certain catatonic features.
His reaction to sex is shame.	An acute break with reality has probably occurred.
He does not show any indication of hallucinatory behavior.	There are some indications that he has cosmic delusions.
He is probably not disoriented.	He is entirely out of contact with reality.
His thinking processes are well preserved.	He seldom uses self-punishment mechanisms.
He is not confused.	

Cluster C

Most true	Most false
An acute break with reality has probably occurred.	His thought processes are orderly and well knit.
His thinking is characterized by highly symbolic autistic processes.	He has the well preserved mind of a person who is not psychotic.
His verbal peculiarities are many and rather striking.	His thinking processes are well preserved.
There is some straining for effect in his use of language.	He is not confused.
He is in the early stages of paranoid schizophrenia.	There are no paranoid ideas of reference or malign influences.

framework with the latter asserting that the subject was psychotic and the former disagreeing.

Test Interpreter Versus Criterion Analysis

The general results of the comparison of the test interpreters with the criterion may be anticipated from an examination of the items defining each. However, a more precise estimate of the extent of the agreement of each test interpreter with the criterion was made by inserting his correlations with the criterion judges' into the criterion matrix as a thirtieth variable and computing his first centroid loading. These loadings, which may be considered as correlations with the criterion general factor, are presented in Table 6. They range from .215 to .755, with a mean of .605. The test judges of cluster A have an average of .688; the judges of cluster B, .310; and the judges of cluster C, .698. An analysis of variance of these coefficients indicates that there is no significant difference between the mean validity figures for clusters A and C but that the mean validity figure for cluster B is significantly lower than the other two. A further finding from the analysis was that there was no significant difference between the mean validity coefficients of clusters A and C and the average general factor loading of the criterion judges (Table 1).

Discussion

The results presented in the preceding section indicate that even among expert thematic projective-technique interpreters a wide range of validity coefficients may be obtained. The distribution, however, is skewed markedly towards the upper end. Two major categories of interpreters occur, those who show a slight preference for describing the subject in terms of "dynamic" characteristics and those who

TABLE 6. THEMATIC-TEST-INTERPRE-
TER LOADINGS ON THE CRITERION
GENERAL FACTOR

	Judge	Factor Loading
Cluster A	1	.710
	2	.738
	3	.662
	4	.650
	5	.660
	6	.705
Cluster B	7	.315
	8	.399
	9	.215
Cluster C	10	.755
	11	.694
	12	.716
	13	.654
	14	.682
	15	.697
Residuals	16	.533
	17	.465

show a slight preference for describing the subject in terms of standard psychopathology and diagnosis. The term "slight preference" is used advisedly here since the method of identifying the clusters is one that emphasizes differences rather than similarities. The rather strong agreement among the clusters is apparent from the size of the correlations among the cluster domains. The group of judges that show a slight preference for emphasis upon psychopathology can further be divided into two subgroups differing in the diagnostic conclusion they reached.

The rather peculiar finding that the two major clusters of test interpreters correlated with the criterion general factor as well as did the criterion judges themselves needs further study. The implication is that test interpreters working from a TAT and MAPS protocol can describe a person as accurately as can clinicians working from the elaborate data of a clinical folder. However ego-syntonic such a conclusion is, it must be viewed with considerable reservation. The present study indicates only the degree of agreement with a clinical criterion that *can* be achieved by competent thematic-test interpreters; it cannot be claimed that the same level of validity will occur with other cases. The subject selected for this study was chosen on the basis of the completeness of the clinical data available about him; there is no assurance that his thematic protocols were not unusually revealing. In addition, the areas of personality description included in the content of the Q-sort items were selected by the test interpreters themselves. In other areas, or on other levels of description, different results might occur.

A word should be said about the criterion at this point. In view of the range of theoretical orientations among the criterion judges, we had expected a diversity of opinion about the subject similar to that found among the test interpreters. The most feasible explanation of the marked agreement would seem to be the quasi-factual nature of many of the Q-sort items for the criterion judges. Practically all of the items required that the test interpreters make an extended series of deductions based upon clues in the protocols, their own previous experience, knowledge of personality theory, etc. For the criterion judges these same items would involve a much shorter chain of inferences. If, for example, the report of a psychiatric consultant in the clinical record contained the statement, "The patient is markedly disoriented for time and space," little disagreement would occur among the criterion judges as to the truth value of the Q-sort item, "The subject is or has been disoriented in the psychiatric sense."

The wide range of validity coefficients for the test interpreters who emphasized psychopathology (clusters B and C) is explicable on the above rationale. Items describing symptoms, diagnosis,

etc., would be the very ones the criterion judges would consider as having very high, or very low, truth values, thus the possibility of disagreement or of being "wrong" is magnified, as is the possibility of agreement or being "right."

As a final observation, the general results indicate the usefulness of Stephenson's Q-technique for dealing with some of the problems of the validation of projective techniques in that it allows the individual case to be described by the quantitative methods of nomothetic statistics.

Summary

The validity of inferences made from thematic projective techniques was tested using an interpreter population of 17 experts working with the TAT and MAPS protocols of one subject. The criterion was the consensus, in the form of a general factor, of 29 clinicians on the basis of a complete clinical record of the same subject. The results indicated that the test interpreters formed into clusters on the basis of their relative preference for "dynamic" type inferences or for inferences as to the psychopathology presented by the subject. The latter group of interpreters divides into two further groups on the basis of the diagnostic conclusion reached. Validity coefficients for these experts vary from .215 to .755, with a mean of .605. For the cluster of interpreters who made predominantly "dynamic" type inferences, and for the larger of the other two clusters, the mean validity coefficients were not significantly different from the average general factor loading of the criterion judges. The results were discussed and certain restrictions and limitations indicated.

REFERENCES

1. CALVIN, J. S. An attempted experimental validation of the TAT. *J. clin. Psychol.*, 1950, **6**, 377–381.

2. COMBS, A. W. The validity and reliability of interpretation from autobiography and the TAT. *J. clin. Psychol.*, 1946, **2**, 240–247.

3. DAVENPORT, BEVERLY F. The semantic validity of TAT interpretation. *J. consult. Psychol.*, 1952, **16**, 171–175.

4. GENGERELLI, J. A. A simplified method for approximate multiple regression coefficients. *Psychometrika*, 1948, **13**, 135–146.

5. HARRISON, R. Studies in the use and validity of the TAT with mentally disturbed patients. II. A quantitative validity study. III. Validation by the method of "blind analysis." *Charact. & Pers.*, 1940, **9**, 122–138.

6. HARTMANN, A. A. An experimental examination of the TAT in clinical diagnosis. *Psychol. Monogr.*, 1949, **63**, No. 8, p. 48.

7. SAXE, C. H. A quantitative comparison of psychodiagnostic formulations from the TAT and therapeutic contacts. *J. consult. Psychol.*, 1950, **14**, 116–127.

8. SHNEIDMAN, E. S. (Ed.). *Thematic test analysis.* New York: Grune and Stratton, 1951.

9. STEPHENSON, W. S. *The study of behavior.* Chicago: University of Chicago Press, 1953.

10. TRYON, R. C. *Cluster analysis.* Ann Arbor: Edwards Brothers, 1939.

The Semantic Validity of TAT Interpretations

Beverly Fest Davenport

Previous attempts to validate projective tests have been criticized for being either too atomistic or too holistic [1,

The material contained in this paper is abstracted from a Ph.D. thesis submitted to the Graduate Faculty of the University of Southern California. The paper is published with the permission of the Chief Medical Director, Department of Medicine and Surgery, Veterans Administration, who assumes no responsibility for the opinions expressed or the conclusions drawn by the author.

This study was conducted at the various facilities of the Veterans Administration Regional Office, Los Angeles, while the author was employed by them as a trainee in clinical psychology.

4, 5]. In the former case, elements of the raw data are counted and correlated with something, a process in which objectivity is retained, but the meaning and richness of the data are lost. The holistic methods, such as blind matching, indicate that there is something valid about the combination of projective test, interpretation, and clinician, [7]. They retain the richness of the raw data. However, nothing is learned from blind matching studies about the specific strengths and weaknesses of the interpretative process. Several authors have suggested that what needs to be studied, at present, are the separate interpretative statements which make up a full test interpretation [1, 3, 4, 5, 6]. This approach will have the shortcoming that the context will be lost, but it promises to be fruitful in providing clues as to how statements in test interpretations could be improved, in order to avoid semantic confusions. An interest in studying the separate interpretative statements was the starting point for this study.

The validity of projective test interpretations cannot be demonstrated unless there is a high degree of inter-interpreter reliability in the making of interpretations. The usual measure of inter-rater reliability involves the average per cent agreement or average intercorrelation between each possible pair of raters. These figures are ambiguous in their meaning and often do not lend themselves to tests of significance. They may be spuriously high due to a large number of test items which do not discriminate between the subjects or records being studied. When they are low, it is not known whether the test item was ambiguous, the process of interpretation invalid, or the clinicians unreliable. The discriminability of interpretative statements has never been investigated.

Day-to-day clinical experience in trying to understand test interpretations leads to the impression that different clinicians attach different meanings to the most common concepts, and that they are ambiguous.

In line with the problems discussed thus far, the concept of *reliable-discrimination* was developed. A *reliably-discriminating* statement is one which is used in the same manner by most clinicians, and which discriminates between data to which it applies and data to which it does not apply. Those statements which are reliably applied to all data or no data are excluded because they do not discriminate. Those statements applied by the same proportion of clinicians to all data, or which might be applied by some clinicians to any data, are also excluded for the same reason. What are left are *nonambiguous*

(operationally defined), *nonuniversal* statements. The major purpose of this study was to investigate reliable-discrimination. In addition, universality and ambiguity were studied.

Procedure

TAT records were obtained from a heterogeneous group of adult male veterans. Four were patients at the Veterans Administration Neuropsychiatric Hospital at Los Angeles. They included one patient diagnosed as psychotic ("dementia praecox, simple type, incompetent"), one character disorder ("passive-dependency reaction"), and two neurotics ("psychoneurosis with hypochondriacal features," and "obsessive-compulsive"). The remaining two subjects, considered normal, were successfully employed at white collar jobs, had no abnormally high MMPI scores, and had never been considered in need of psychiatric treatment. They suffered from none of the disorders often considered to be of psychosomatic origin, such as ulcers, hypertension, asthma, migraine, diabetes, spastic colitis, or glandular disorders.

The records from these subjects were interpreted by six clinical psychologists in training with the Veterans Administration Regional Office, Los Angeles. These were not the same persons who had administered the tests, since direct contact would have provided them with additional clues. The aim in selecting the person who were to do the interpretations was to obtain a representative sample of one class of "TAT users." We were not interested in studying the performance of a single interpreter, but rather in permitting a representative range of individual differences in language usage to enter.

The interpretations thus obtained were divided into separate statements. When a statement contained several ideas, it was separated into as many statements, and both the original complex statement and the separate parts were retained. Obvious duplications were removed. This process resulted in a sample of 207 interpretative statements.

The statements were studied to see that alternative and complementary statements were present, in relation to each topic covered. When such statements did not exist, the author invented a statement. Forty-three statements were thus added temporarily, but were eventually discarded for reasons to be explained later.

The statements were placed on separate cards. Once a week for six weeks, each of six experienced clinical psychologists saw one of the six original TAT records, and decided which of the interpretative statements applied to it, and which of them did not. A tally was made of the total number of times each statement was applied to each protocol. (Examples are shown in Table 1.) These tallies served as the basis for the evaluation of reliable-discrimination.

TABLE 1.   NUMBER OF TIMES A STATE-
MENT WAS APPLIED TO EACH RECORD,
AND TOTAL USE

State- ments	Patients						Total Use
	A	B	C	D	E	F	
1	6	0	2	3	2	4	17
2	0	0	0	1	1	1	3
3	6	6	6	5	5	5	33
4	3	4	5	4	3	2	21
5	3	3	3	3	3	3	18
Etc.							

It would have been desirable to rank all of the statements according to how well they discriminated between patients but no statistical methods have yet been devised for dealing with this type of problem.

It was possible, however, to group the statements into seven categories based on a continuum of reliable-discrimination, and to determine whether or not the data offered evidence of significant deviation from chance.[1] Reliable-discrimination was considered to be greatest when all six judges agreed that there was a difference in the applicability of a statement to at least two of the six records (Table 1, Statement 1). It was at a minimum when all of the records received the same number of applications of the statement. Seven categories of reliable-discrimination were based on the width of the *range* of numbers of applications to each record, for each statement. Each category was defined by a limiting pair of records. This can best be understood by reference to Table 2, which reveals the systematic basis for forming each category, and the number of statements which fell into it.

In addition to the above procedure, the 207 statements were rated on two six-point rating scales by twenty-six clinical psychologists not previously connected with the study. The scales dealt with ambiguity (statements with a vague or double meaning) and universality (statements applicable to any adult male). Mean ratings were obtained for purposes of ranking.

The total number of times each statement was applied by some rater was tallied, and statements ranked according to amount of use.

Statements were divided into two groups on the basis of their tendency to be ignored by all the raters (not applied to any record by more than three raters), or to be used readily (the balance). This frame of reference will be called *agreed-unused*.

Results

Reliable-discrimination. It will be noted in Table 2 that only 12 of the

[1] The equations for this problem were developed by Bernard Sherman, Ph.D., professor of mathematics at the University of Southern California.

TABLE 2.   DEFINITIONS OF CATEGORIES
OF   RELIABLE-DISCRIMINATION

Explanation	Limiting pairs	Range	Ob-ser. freq.
At least one record received six judgments of "applies" and at least one record received no judgments of "applies"	0–6	7	12
At least one record received five judgments of "applies" and at least one record received no judgments of "applies," or vice versa; or at least one record received six judgments of "applies" and at least one record received one judgment of "applies," or vice versa	0–5; 1–6	6	27
Et cetera	0–4; 1–5; 2–6	5	39
Et cetera	0–3; 1–4; 2–5; 3–6	4	72
Et cetera	0–2; 1–3; 2–4; 3–5; 4–6	3	34
Et cetera	0–1; 1–2; 2–3; 3–4; 4–5; 5–6	2	13
Et cetera	0–0; 1–1; 2–2; 3–3; 4–4; 5–5; 6–6	1	0

207 statements led to sets of judgments wherein a minimum of two of the six records had been discriminated with complete agreement among the six judges. An examination of the tallies for these 12 statements revealed that for 7 of them, only the two records had been thus discriminated; for 4 statements, three records; and for 1 statement, four records. In no instance was an interpretative statement applied to as many as five or six records in such a way that the judges divided the records into two groups, to one of which a statement would have applied, and to the other of which it would have been nonapplicable. In other words, either the statements were not used at all, or they were applied indiscriminately to everyone, or by the same proportion of raters to everyone, or they failed to discriminate between most of the patients.

In spite of the predominance of a lack of reliable-discrimination, it was possible to demonstrate (Table 3) that it exceeded chance expectancy. Chi square was 81.6. With four degrees of freedom, a chi square of 13.3 is significant at the .01 level. Table 3 also indicates that the only significant contribution to the chi square came from the upper ranges.

The statements from the upper ranges were compared by the author with those in the lower ranges to see if any

TABLE 3.　CHI SQUARE: OBTAINED VERSUS CHANCE FREQUENCIES IN FIVE CATEGORIES OF RELIABLE-DISCRIMINATION[*]

Ranges	Obtained	Expected	D^2/f_e
7,6	49	15.1	73.8
5	39	48.2	1.6
4	72	78.5	.5
3	34	53.4	5.5
2,1	13	11.2	.2
			$\chi^2 = 81.6$

$p = 13.3$ at .01 with 4 degrees of freedom.
[*] Yates's correction for continuity was made when obtained frequency was less than 50.

definable qualitative differences could be observed. None presented themselves. More specifically, it made no apparent difference whether the statements referred to symptoms, defenses, dynamics, family relationships, sexuality, ego strength, dominance-submission, or feelings.

No significant statistical relationships were found between reliable-discrimination, and universality or ambiguity.

Universality and use. The Pearson correlation between the mean ratings of universality and the total use of each statement was .43 ± .057, indicating that judges tended to prefer the use of universal statements and avoid the use of the more specific ones. If the more specific statements had been applied by many raters to only one patient, they would have fallen low on the use scale, adding to the above correlation, but this would have had quite a different interpretation than if each rater applied a statement once to a different patient.

Defining as *agreed-unused* those statements which had never been applied to any record more than three times, and the balance as *agreed-used,* the frequencies expected by chance of the 47 least universal, 49 most universal, and 111 of the middle group were obtained, and chi square computed. Table 4 shows the obtained and expected frequencies for the various categories. Chi square was 27.0. With two degrees of freedom, a chi square of 9.2 is significant at the .01 level.

Ambiguity. Ambiguity and use were not correlated. The Pearson coefficient was − .06 ± .069. The correlation between ambiguity and universality was negligible, being .12 ± .069.

The author examined the statements at both extremes of the ambiguity scale to see on what basis the raters had made their judgments. The most ambiguous statements were (*a*) heavily loaded with psychoanalytic terminology ("transfer his object," "introjection," "oral satisfaction," "persona," etc., as well as more generally used jargon such as "denial," "break with reality," "affectional needs," "schizoid tendency," "inadequate person," "over-ideational preschizophrenic," "superego"); (*b*) contained terminology which does not have a widely known or agreed upon meaning ("His concept of masculinity is to be assertive and not aggressive,"

TABLE 4.　OBTAINED AND EXPECTED FREQUENCIES FOR "AGREED-UNUSED" GROUPS AND UNIVERSALITY

Univer- sality	Amount of Use					
	Agreed-Used		Agreed-Unused		Totals	
	Obtained	Expected	Obtained	Expected	Obtained	Expected
Most	36	34.1	11	12.9	47	47.0
Middle	93	80.4	18	30.6	111	111.0
Least	21	35.5	28	13.5	49	49.0
Totals	150	150.0	57	57.0	207	207.0

"There are signs of severe sex shock"); or (c) were clumsily worded ("It may be postulated that the mother was moderately frustrating to the subject, yet had some inconsistency").

In contrast with the above, the least ambiguous statements contained no psychoanalytic terminology except for a few uses of words referring to mechanisms of defense ("projection," "intellectualization," "identify"). Otherwise it was difficult to define objective characteristics of a nonambiguous statement.

Author-originated statements. The six judges who studied the TAT's tended to avoid the use of the 43 complementary statements added by the author. Only 14 of them were applied by five judges to at least one record. Table 5 shows the obtained and expected frequencies of statements used less than three times, and the balance. Chi square was 8.48, significant beyond the .01 level. This seemed to offer evidence that the statements added by the author came from a different universe of interpretative statements than those obtained from the other clinical psychologists, so they were excluded from further statistical treatment.

TABLE 5. AUTHOR-ORIGINATED STATEMENTS USED LESS THAN THREE TIMES VERSUS THE BALANCE

	Obtained	Expected
Used less than three times	21	11.8
Balance	22	31.2

A systematic qualitative examination of the author-originated statements was attempted. It appeared possible that the judges were avoiding the use of statements referring to positive traits or assets of personality. Such avoidance did occur in spite of the fact that two of the TAT records were from normal subjects and should have provided an opportunity for the use of the statements. A related observation is that the original interpretations contained almost no references to positive traits or assets of personality.

Summary and Conclusions

Six clinical psychologists studied six TAT records taken from a heterogeneous group of subjects and decided whether or not each of 207 typical interpretative statements and 43 author-originated statements applied to each TAT, making possible an evaluation of reliable-discrimination.

In addition, the statements were rated by twenty-six other clinical psychologists according to degree of ambiguity, and later, according to degree of universality.

1. The most significant observation was the degree to which absence of reliable-discrimination predominated. It was significantly better than chance according to an unexacting criterion. However, in no case was an interpretative statement used with complete accord by six judges to discriminate among all six patients. A validation study would have been doomed to failure, and not necessarily because of faulty hypotheses.

2. Judges tended to apply statements rated as universal to any patient, and to "hedge" or avoid the use of more specific statements.

3. Qualitative examination suggested at least two factors worthy of further study: (a) the most ambiguous statements were heavily loaded with psychoanalytic terminology or other jargon, while the least ambiguous statements contained few of these references; (b) statements referring to positive traits or assets of personality were absent from the original sample of interpretative statements. When statements of this nature were added by the author, the raters avoided using them.

The main contribution of the experiment is to suggest a flexible methodology for the study of interpretative statements, and to call attention to the need for further research into the habits of projective test interpreters.

REFERENCES

1. CRONBACH, L. J. A validation design for qualitative studies of personality. *J. consult. Psychol.*, 1948, **12**, 365–374.
2. DAVENPORT, BEVERLY F. The semantic validity of TAT interpretations. Unpublished doctor's dissertation. Univer. Southern California, 1952.
3. DE GROOT, A. D. Some preliminary remarks to a methodology of psychological interpretation: On "falsification." *Acta psychol.*, 1950, 7, 196–224.
4. KRUGMAN, M. Review of Rorschach test. In O. K. BUROS (Ed.), *Third mental measurements yearbook*. New Brunswick, N. J.: Rutgers Univer. Press, 1949, pp. 132–133.
5. ROTTER, J. S. The present status of the Rorschach in clinical and experimental procedures. *J. Pers.*, 1948, **16**, 304–311.
6. ROTTER, J. S. Review of Thematic Apperception Test. In O. K. BUROS (Ed.), *Third mental measurements yearbook*. New Brunswick, N. J.: Rutgers Univ. Press, 1949, pp. 205–206.
7. SHNEIDMAN, EDWIN S., with WALTHER JOEL and KENNETH B. LITTLE. *Thematic Test Analysis*. New York: Grune and Stratton, 1951.

Frequencies of Themes and Identifications in the Stories of Schizophrenic Patients and Non-hospitalized College Students

Leonard D. Eron

Since the introduction of the TAT in 1935 [16], the technique has had a wide and varied application in clinical situations and in research. According to a recent survey it is one of the

Published with the permission of the chief medical director, Department of Medicine and Surgery, V.A., who assumes no responsibility for the opinions expressed or conclusions drawn by the author.

The author wishes to thank Dr. Ann Magaret for her considerable help in the execution of this research.

Reprinted by permission of the American Psychological Association and the author from the *Journal of Consulting Psychology*, 1948, **12**, 387–395.

two most widely used tests of personality [13] and an extensive body of literature concerned with it has accumulated. The validity and reliability of the test have been reasonably well established [4, 5, 6, 9, 11, 15, 21] and much has been written of its clinical applications [10, 12, 14, 18, 19]. However, one of the serious deficiencies in the literature is the lack of adequate normative data for the test. Many investigators state different characteristics as representative of the same clinical group and the same characteristics as representative of different clinical groups [10, 14, 18, 19, 20]. None of them, however, give frequencies substantiating these diagnostic cues. Rather, they seem to be the result of the total subjective impression left with the clinician after the examination of many patients with a given diagnosis. However valid these assumptions may be, they cannot be accepted by others without scientific verification based on actual numbers of patients of a given clinical group exhibiting these characteristics, the presence of which distinguishes them from other clinical groups and from normal individuals. The necessity for a clear-cut statistical treatment is obvious. This paper represents an attempt to secure some information about the actual themes made up in response to the test cards, and the identification of the characters in the pictures.

Subjects and Procedures

The 50 subjects used in this study were all male veterans of World War II. They comprised two groups of 25 each. Group I consisted of hospital patients with a final diagnosis of schizophrenia and Group II consisted of non-hospitalized college students. The two groups were distributed according to age, education, mental ability and marital status as shown in Table 1. Obviously they are very comparable in respect to these variables, with the ranges and means almost identical. No IQ scores were available for the college students, but it is assumed they are at least of average intelligence, and it has been reported in the literature [20] that after a normal intelligence level has been reached, there is no correla-

tion between quantity and quality of material and added increments of intelligence. Thus it is felt that this factor is also adequately controlled. All 20 cards recommended for adult males (Harvard University Clinic, 3rd edition) were administered to all subjects by the same examiner according to the standard directions of Murray [17] with one exception. All pictures were presented at one session with a 15 minute break between halves. This was necessitated by hospital procedure. However, control subjects were treated in the same manner.

After all the protocols had been collected, they were perused at least twice. The first time, each story was read through and the action taking place was summarized in a few words. After this was done for all the stories, the author, with the help of another psychologist, examined the summaries and identified three variables for later analysis—the theme, identification of central character, and level of interpretation. A check list of 98 themes was organized under the two general headings of disequilibrium and equilibrium, indicating the state of tension or adjustment displayed in the story. These two general groups were subdivided into interpersonal, intrapersonal, and impersonal classifications, depending upon the sphere to which the situation was referred. The interpersonal classification was further broken down into sections dealing with parent, partner, peer, and sibling. Each theme appearing in the classification was named and defined and examples of each given, so that the same list could be used in

TABLE 1. AGE, EDUCATION, MENTAL ABILITY, AND MARITAL STATUS OF SUBJECTS

Group	N	Age Range	Age Mean	Education Range	Education Mean	IQ Range	IQ Mean	Number Married
Schizophrenic	25	20–34	24.6	12–17	13.4	100–133	113	7
College Student	25	20–34	24.4	13–16	13.9			5

further research. The stories were then again examined in random order and the frequency of appearance of each theme on the check list was noted. Interpretation was kept to a minimum. Covert significance of the items was disregarded and only that actual behavior which occurred in the stories and was related by the narrator was used in the classification. There were no restrictions as to the number of themes per story and as each theme in the criterion list appeared it was tallied. For each story also, the identification of the characters was noted, and the level of interpretation, that is, whether the story was narrative, descriptive, symbolic, imaginary, etc. In collating and treating the results, an attempt was made to: (1) find any group differences between the schizophrenic subjects and the college students, and (2) determine differences in responses of the whole group to the individual test cards; that is, the problem of "picture pull."

Results

A total of 1,000 stories, containing 1,988 themes, was recorded for all the subjects. The outstanding feature in the comparison of the two groups of subjects is the striking similarity between them. Although the college students are more productive, the difference in the total number of themes produced by either group is not significant (total schizophrenic stories, 963; total student stories, 1,025). With rare exceptions there was no theme which appeared in one group and was absent from the other. In the few categories in which this did occur, the frequency in the single group reporting the theme was no more than one or two. Over 100 comparisons were made between the two groups and differences significant at or beyond the 5 per cent confidence level were found in 13 classifications. These appear in Table 2. It is interesting to note that

the difference showing the highest confidence level is one for themes of moral struggle in which the students have an excess over the schizophrenics. Yet this has been given as one of the diagnostic cues for schizophrenic stories [18]. If one accepts the concept of projection, some of the other differences can be explained in terms of the accepted dynamics of schizophrenia. Themes of curiosity and retirement are generally neutral in feeling tone and fit in with the picture of flattened affectivity. That these schizophrenes should have more themes of legal restriction is understandable since at the time of administration of the test they were patients in a mental hospital, many of them involuntarily so. Significantly fewer themes of aspiration and self-esteem on their part can be explained perhaps by feelings of inadequacy and loss of interest in the future; and of peer approbation, by their lack of concern over success in interpersonal relations. That college students should produce significantly more themes of moral struggle and illicit sex may be an indication of the preoccupation of college students with these matters; and that they show more themes of parental disequilibrium, feeling that they are a disappointment to their parents, may be due to the fact that as college students they are closer to the parental situation than these hospital patients.

Other differences which are not statistically significant according to our criterion of the 5 per cent confidence level but which may still show a trend and which are interesting in the light of some of the literature both on the TAT and schizophrenia in general are as follows. At the 10 per cent confidence level, college students contribute more themes of guilt and remorse and at the 20 per cent level more themes of pressure from parents, filial obligation, belongingness, and mental abnormality. Also the difference in the total number of themes of disequilibrium for the two

TABLE 2.   FREQUENCIES OF THEMES SHOWING DIFFER-
ENCES AT OR BEYOND THE 5 PER CENT LEVEL BETWEEN
SCHIZOPHRENIC PATIENTS AND NON-HOSPITALIZED
COLLEGE STUDENTS

Theme	Frequency College Student	Frequency Schizophrenic	χ^2	P
moral struggle	15	2	9.1912	.005
curiosity	10	27	7.3581	.01
self-esteem	18	5	6.7395	.01
parent disequilibrium	185	138	6.6942	.01
illicit sex	28	12	6.0062	.02
aspiration	63	38	5.9431	.02
death, illness of son	18	6	5.5104	.02
disappointment to parent	19	7	5.0865	.025
legal restriction	9	22	5.0403	.025
aggression from impersonal source	70	46	4.7067	.05
peer approbation	10	2	4.6875	.05
retirement	18	34	4.6202	.05
generalized restriction of environment	24	11	4.4643	.05

groups is significant at the 20 per cent confidence level with the students contributing more of these themes. Schizophrenes give more themes of religion, retribution, succorance from parents, pressure from heterosexual partner, and illness or death of heterosexual partner, all at the 20 per cent confidence level or better. The fact that schizophrenes do not produce as many themes of guilt or remorse does not fit in with the common picture of this type of personality disturbance, but when considered along with the excess of themes of retribution the possibility is suggested that they are concerned more with the payment of formal penalties for misdoings than with anxiety-laden feelings of guilt over them. Their comparative excess of themes of religion and lack of themes of belongingness would be expected and the fact that they show more themes of pressure from the partner and death of partner may be indicative of less satisfactory heterosexual adjustments. More themes of succorance from parents is perhaps a representation of the essential immaturity of schiz-

ophrenics, while less of other parental themes is in keeping with what has already been stated. Schizophrenics give more descriptions and less narratives for the pictures which might show a lack of emotional involvement and a tendency towards evasiveness. An unexpected finding is that the college students give more imaginary and symbolic stories than do the schizophrenics (at the 10 per cent and 20 per cent confidence levels respectively). From descriptions of schizophrenic behavior it would be expected that they would produce more of this type of story and this has indeed been listed by some investigators as a diagnostic cue [10, 18, 20].

While mentioning these differences between the two groups, it is important to bear in mind the even greater similarity between them and the large amount of overlap between their members in any given category. This corresponds to what has been found in an earlier investigation of the emotional tone and outcome of TAT stories in which this author participated [7].

There are no broad group differences. At least some of the schizophrenics fall into every one of the normal categories and only very few patients have exclusively "schizophrenic" characteristics. Responses on the TAT are determined more by the actual stimulus cards themselves, it would seem, than by the specific personality syndrome of the subject.

We come then to a consideration of neither case is this difference significant beyond the 10 per cent level. In making this analysis and also those to follow, schizophrenic and normal stories were pooled. This is justifiable because a picture-by-picture comparison between the two groups for differences in total number of themes of disequilibrium or equilibrium told by either group revealed only one significant difference at the 5 per cent level (college students

TABLE 3. MOST FREQUENT THEMES APPEARING IN 1000 TAT STORIES OF 25 MALE SCHIZOPHRENIC PATIENTS AND 25 NON-HOSPITALIZED MALE COLLEGE STUDENTS

| | Frequency* | | |
Theme	Entire Group	College Students	Schizo-phrenics
aggression, impersonal source	116	70	46
pressure from parents	106	61	45
aspiration	101	63	38
economic pressure	60	30	30
mental disturbance	59	36	
guilt-remorse	54	34	
vacillation	53		30
tranquility	53		32
retirement	52		34
illicit sex		28	
religion			27
curiosity			27
death or illness of partner			26
contentment with partner			25

* Included in frequency for entire group are only those themes which had a frequency of at least 50; and in frequency for the individual groups, only those with a frequency in that group of at least 25

the types of themes elicited by the different pictures. Table 3 contains a list of the themes appearing most frequently for the whole test, and it is apparent that there are certain themes which the TAT evokes rather consistently in both types of subjects. This table is self explanatory and no further comment need be made about it. As can be seen in Table 4, 16 of the 20 cards elicit significantly more themes of disequilibrium than equilibrium. Of the four remaining cards, only two, IX BM and X show an excess of themes of equilibrium, but in give more themes of equilibrium for picture number XVII BM than do the schizophrenics), and this is less than could be expected by chance. The two groups can thus be treated as comprising a homogeneous population insofar as this variable is concerned. It is obvious from Table 4 that themes of disequilibrium are the usual response in the TAT, at least for the cards here considered.

Much has been written of the confusion of sex of the characters depicted on the cards and its significance as an indication of a high feminine component in the male personality [10, 18, 20]. Instances of sex confusion, that is, interpretation of male character as female or indecision as to whether male or female, are tabulated in Table 5. There were confusions noted on eight different cards, and in all there were 47 instances of this phenomenon in the complete set of 1,000 stories. For one picture, III BM, 19 subjects were confused and

because in all of them a significantly greater number of subjects identify the character properly than err in identification. It is interesting to note that altogether the college students have more instances of sex confusion than do the schizophrenic patients, but a chi square of homogeneity shows that these two groups do not differ significantly in respect to this variable.

Finally the data have been examined

TABLE 4. FREQUENCY OF THEMES OF EQUILIBRIUM
AND DISEQUILIBRIUM FOR EACH PICTURE IN
STORIES TOLD BY ALL SUBJECTS

Picture	Disequi- librium	Equi- librium	χ^2	P
I	112	11	82.1158	.001
II	72	18	31.8027	.001
III BM	92	5	77.1365	.001
IV	116	22	68.8859	.001
V	59	12	30.4542	.001
VI BM	146	7	125.3742	.001
VII BM	80	2	71.3689	.001
VIII BM	73	3	63.5559	.001
IX BM	40	55	2.2132	
X	32	47	2.6614	
XI	69	4	56.9897	.001
XII M	91	23	39.9671	.001
XIII MF	134	1	130.0463	.001
XIV	79	28	28.8341	.001
XV	110	10	82.5021	.001
XVI	40	29	1.5978	
XVII BM	53	37	2.6694	
XVIII BM	119	3	109.3463	.001
XIX	32	15	5.7925	.025
XX	110	5	94.9587	.001

31 nonconfused. This difference is significant only at the 20 per cent confidence level, therefore it would seem difficult to say with assurance that misrecognition of the sex of this character is an indication of sex confusion, since significantly more males do not see it as a male than see it as a female. A possible interpretation of this finding might be that it is a function of the stimulus properties of the card more than a projection of the subject's female identification. The same cannot be said of the other cases of misrecognition, however,

to see if there are any differences in types of themes evoked by the first and last ten pictures. As shown in Table 6 there is little difference in the total number of themes elicited by either half of the test, and this applied to both themes of equilibrium and disequilibrium, although in the latter case the difference is somewhat larger, but significant only at the 20 per cent confidence level. The data show also that interpersonal themes predominate significantly in the first half of the test and intrapersonal and impersonal in the latter half of the test.

TABLE 5. NUMBER OF STORIES SHOW-
ING CONFUSION IN IDENTIFICATION OF
SEX OF CENTRAL CHARACTER

Picture	Non-confused	Con-fused*	χ^2	P
III BM	31	19	2.6450	.20
VIII	49	1	45.1250	.001
X	48	2	41.4050	.001
XII M	45	5	31.3050	.001
XIV	49	1	45.1250	.001
XV	45	2	38.4309	.001
XVI	40	4	28.6420	.001
XX	38	13	12.0050	.001

* Central character considered female, or story
teller is undecided as to whether male or female.

Also significantly more symbolic, descriptive, imaginary and fairy tale
themes are told for the second series of
pictures. These differences are no doubt
a function of the greater vagueness and
ambiguity of the last ten pictures and
also of the instructions after the tenth
card to make the stories as imaginative

as possible. These results are in line with
Murray's contention that stories composed in the first session are more closely
related to the outer layer of personality
(an individual's public behavior) than
those composed in the second session,
many of which express inner layer tendencies and complexes symbolically.

Conclusions

1. Results of this study indicate that
thematic material obtained on the TAT
is very much a function of the stimulus
properties of the cards themselves and
that the specific personality disturbance
of the subject is not nearly so important
in determining the type of theme that
individuals will produce. Every theme
appearing for normal subjects is also
related by at least some schizophrenics
and in over 100 comparisons made between the two groups there were differences found in only 13 categories which

TABLE 6. A COMPARISON OF THE RELATIVE
FREQUENCIES OF DIFFERENT CATEGORIES FOR
THE FIRST AND SECOND TEN PICTURES

Category	I-X	XI-XX	χ^2	P
Total number of themes	999	989	.0045	.95
Total dis-equilibrium	822	837	.1276	.80
Total equilibrium	177	152	1.8245	.20
Total parent	311	58	172.7812	.001
Total peer	60	117	18.0353	.001
Total partner	163	148	.6760	.50
Total sibling	10	5	1.3500	.30
Total interpersonal	544	328	53.5371	.001
Total intrapersonal	338	469	21.1032	.001
Total impersonal	117	192	17.9620	.001
Total number symbolic	5	26	13.5565	.001
Total number descriptive	2	13	7.3500	.01
Total number imaginary	7	26	10.3712	.01
Total number fairy tale	0	17	16.0147	.001

were significant at or beyond the 5 per cent level of confidence.

2. For 16 of the 20 cards under investigation in this study there is a wide and significant difference in the number of themes of equilibrium and disequilibrium, favoring the latter.

3. In one card, III BM, the number of subjects confused over the sex of the central character does not differ significantly from those not so confused.

4. The first ten cards produce significantly more interpersonal themes than the second ten, and the latter, significantly more intrapersonal and impersonal than the former. The second half also calls forth significantly more symbolic, imaginary, fairy tale, and descriptive stories than the first half.

5. In the light of these results it is felt that the individual examiner must be cautious in using the TAT as a diagnostic instrument and applying the cues reported in the literature by various investigators. In making a valid interpretation of any given protocol, due consideration must be given to the stimulus provided by the cards themselves which seem to be a more potent factor in determining the type of theme related than the psychiatric classification of the individual.

6. Table 7 shows the picture-by-picture tabulation of the most common themes appearing in the 1000 TAT stories of the combined group of 50 subjects.

TABLE 7. PICTURE-BY-PICTURE TABULATION OF THE MOST COMMON THEMES APPEARING IN 1000 TAT STORIES

Included in this table are responses of 25 hospitalized schizophrenics and 25 non-hospitalized college students. Both groups are comparable in terms of age, education, sex, IQ, veteran status, marital status. All are male veterans of ages 20 to 34 years, with 12 to 17 years education, and an IQ of at least 100. Twelve are married and thirty-eight single. All theme related by at least 10 subjects for each picture are included.

Theme	Definition	Frequency	Theme	Definition	Frequency
Picture I			economic pressure	compelled to or prohibited from, or limited in doing something because of lack of money	21
pressure from parents	parent figures are prohibitive, compelling, censuring, punishing, quarreling with child	26			
aspiration	dreaming of future, hoping for future, determination	26	*Picture III BM*		
vacillation	wasting time putting off a distasteful task, procrastination, loitering	12	pressure from parents	parent figures are prohibitive, compelling, censuring, punishing, quarreling with child	13
curiosity	wondering or inquiring about construction of object	11	suicide	attempted or completed, preoccupation with	12
inadequacy	realization, whether justified or not, of lack of success	10	generalized restriction	environment is generally frustrating	12
belongingness	desire expressed to be with or accepted by peers	10	*Picture IV*		
Picture II			pressure from partner	partner is prohibitive, compelling, censuring, punishing or quarreling, etc.	20
aspiration	dreaming of future, hoping for future, determination	26	partner comforts	a positive relationship, sets at ease, conciliates, regales	18

Table 7 (*Continued*)

Theme	Definition	Frequency
Picture V		
pressure from parents	parent is prohibitive, compelling, censuring, punishing, quarreling with child	20
curiosity	wondering about construction of object, contents of room, etc.	12
Picture VI BM		
pressure from parent	parent is prohibitive, compelling, censuring, punishing, quarreling with child	21
departure from parent	child is taking leave of parental home	18
filial obligation	child feels it his duty to remain with, comply with, or support parents	13
disappointment to parent	child does not live up to parent's expectations	13
concern of parent	parent is worried over physical or mental well-being of child	11
aggression toward environment	robbery, accident, murder (of unspecified individual)	10
Picture VII BM		
succorance from parents	child seeks or receives aid, advice, consolation, protection from parent	31
pressure from parents	parent is prohibitive, compelling, censuring, punishing, quarreling with child	11
Picture VIII BM		
aspiration	dreaming of future, hoping for future, determination	23
aggression from impersonal source	war, accident, nature, animal, disease	10
Picture IX BM		
retirement	central character asleep, resting, etc.	41
Picture X		
partner contentment	serenity in marital life, satisfaction with partner, marital bliss, heterosexual bliss	27

Theme	Definition	Frequency
Picture XI		
aggression from impersonal source	war, accident, nature, animal, disease	22
aggression towards peer	physical harm inflicted or intended for individual of same sex and approximately same age—physical violence between two animals	10
Picture XII M		
religion	prayer, seeking consolation from God, religious conflict, religious awakening	15
death or illness of son		14
Picture XIII MF		
guilt-remorse		22
death or illness of partner		18
illicit sex	extra or pre-marital heterosexual relation, non-incestuous	18
aggression towards partner	physical harm inflicted or intended for heterosexual partner	16
Picture XIV		
aspiration	dreaming of future, hope for future, determination	16
tranquility	peace of mind, content with environment and own accomplishments	15
Picture XV		
death or illness of partner		17
religion	prayer, seeking consolation from God, religious conflict, religious awakening	16
Picture XVI—Since there is no individual category of sufficient frequency, only more general categories can be included.		
intrapersonal disequilibrium		17
interpersonal equilibrium		15
impersonal disequilibrium		13

Table 7 (Continued)

Theme	Definition	Frequency
intrapersonal equilibrium		12
interpersonal disequilibrium		10
Picture XVII BM		
self esteem	egocentricity, self confidence, self respect, self approbation	14
Picture XVIII BM		
drunkenness		22
succorance from peer	seek or receive aid, advice, consolation, protection from peer	17
pressure from peer	friends are prohibitive, compelling, censuring, punishing, quarreling	15

Theme	Definition	Frequency
Picture XIX		
aggression from impersonal source	war, accident, nature, animal, disease	28
imaginary theme level		11
Picture XX		
vacillation	wasting time, putting off a distasteful task, procrastination, loitering	23
loneliness	central character misses someone, is an outcast, friendless, homeless	18

REFERENCES

1. BALKEN, E. R. A delineation of schizophrenic language and thought in a test of imagination. *J. Psychol.*, 1943, **16**, 239–273.

2. BALKEN, E. R. Thematic Apperception. *J. Psychol.*, 1945, **20**, 189–197.

3. BALKEN, E. R., & MASSERMAN, J. H. The language of phantasy. *J. Psychol.*, 1940, **10**, 75–86.

4. BELLAK, L. The concept of projection-experimental investigation and study of the concept. *Psychiatry*, 1944, **7**, 353–370.

5. COLEMAN, W. The Thematic Apperception Test. I. Effect of recent experience, II. Some quantitative observations. *J. clin. Psychol.*, 1946, **2**, 240–247.

6. COMBS, A. W. Validity and reliability of interpretation from autobiography and Thematic Apperception Test. *J. clin. Psychol.*, 1946, **2**, 240–247.

7. GARFIELD, S. L., & ERON, L. D. Interpreting mood and activity in Thematic Apperception Test stories. *J. abnorm. soc. Psychol.*, 1948, **43**, 338–345.

8. GRANT, D. A. Personal conversations with author.

9. HARRISON, R. Studies in the use and validity of the Thematic Apperception Test with mentally disordered patients. II. A quantitative validity study. III. Validation by the method of blind analysis. *Character & Pers.*, 1940, **9**, 122–138.

10. HARRISON, R. The Thematic Apperception and Rorschach methods of personality investigation in clinical practice. *J. Psychol.*, 1943, **15**, 49–74.

11. HARRISON, R., & ROTTER, J. B. Note on the reliability of the Thematic Apperception Test. *J. abnorm. soc. Psychol.*, 1945, **40**, 97–99.

12. KLEBANOFF, S. G. Personality factors in alcoholism as indicated by the Thematic Apperception Test. *J. consult. Psychol.*, 1947, **11**, 111–120.

13. LOUTTIT, C. M., & BROWNE, G. G. Psychometric instruments in psychological clinics. *J. consult. Psychol.*, 1947, **11**, 49–54.

14. MASSERMAN, J. H., & BALKEN, E. R. Clinical application of phantasy studies. *J. Psychol.*, 1938, **6**, 81–88.

15. MAYMAN, M., & KUTNER, B. Reliability in analyzing Thematic Apperception Test stories. *J. abnorm. soc. Psychol.*, 1947, **24**, 365–368.

16. MORGAN, C. D., & MURRAY, H. A. A method for investigating fantasies; the Thematic Apperception Test. *Arch. Neurol. Psychiat.*, 1935, **34**, 289–306.

17. Murray, H. A. *Manual for the Thematic Apperception Test.* Cambridge: Harvard Univ. Press, 1943.
18. Rapaport, D. *Diagnostic Psychological Testing.* Chicago: Year Book Publishers, 1946. Vol. II.
19. Renaud, H. Group differences in phantasies: head injuries, PN, and brain diseases. *J. Psychol.*, 1946, 21, 237–246.

20. Rotter, J. B. Thematic Apperception Test: Suggestions for administration and interpretation. *J. Pers.*, 1946, 15, 70–92.
21. Rotter, J. B. Studies in the use and validity of the Thematic Apperception Test with mentally disordered patients. I. Method of analysis and clinical problems. *Character & Pers.*, 1940, 9, 18–34.

THE RELATION BETWEEN OVERT AND FANTASY

BEHAVIOR AS A FUNCTION OF SYSTEMATIC

VARIATION OF STIMULUS AND SITUATION

The Relationships Between Overt and Fantasy Aggression

Paul H. Mussen and H. Kelly Naylor

Investigations of the relationship between fantasy and overt behavior have yielded varied results (5, 7, 8). Sanford *et al.* (7) found that ratings of some fantasy needs derived from the TAT were positively correlated with ratings of overt behavior manifesting these needs, while in other cases the strength of the needs expressed in fantasy was negatively correlated with the degree of overt expression. Correlations between TAT fantasy needs and final staff ratings on overt behavior ranged from +.41 to −.44, with an average of +.11. Murray (5) also found differences among the variables in the extent to which overt and fantasy expressions corresponded. In a group of college men, the two forms of expression were positively correlated on variables such as abasement, creation, dominance, exposition, nurtur-

Reprinted by permission of the American Psychological Association and the authors from *The Journal of Abnormal and Social Psychology*, 1954, **49**, 235–240.

ance, passivity, rejection, and dejection; but there was a negative correlation between fantasy and overt sex needs.

From these studies it may be concluded that some needs reflected in the TAT are also apparent in overt expression, while other needs which are revealed strongly in the TAT are seldom demonstrated in overt behavior. As Lindzey has pointed out, one of the major problems involved in interpreting the TAT is the "determination of the conditions under which inferences based on the projective material directly relate to overt behavior and the conditions for the reverse" (4, p. 18). With respect to aggression specifically, Murray (5) found no correlation between the intensity of the need in fantasy and its overt expression. On the other hand, Sanford *et al.* (7) found that aggressive needs were among those which occurred frequently in the TAT stories of adolescent subjects, but according to teachers' reports, were infrequently expressed in the overt behavior of this group. The correlation between ratings of the subjects' TAT aggressive needs and final staff ratings of the degree of their manifestation of this need was +.15

In explaining their findings, Sanford et al. (7) suggest that certain antisocial needs such as aggression may appear in the TAT stories but not overtly because cultural prohibition or internal conflict prevents the overt gratification of these needs and thereby increases their intensity in the individual's fantasies. According to these writers, needs which were frequently present in both fantasy and overt behavior were those which are encouraged by the culture, but, generally speaking, the individual does not have sufficient opportunity for their satisfaction.

In the middle class from which Sanford's and Murray's subject populations were drawn, there are strong punishments for the expression of aggression. However, in lower-class culture, aggressive behavior is not punished but is encouraged (1). Although the manifestation of aggressive needs is acceptable, different individuals within the group have, as a result of their particular backgrounds and experiences, different strengths of these needs. If Sanford's hypotheses are correct, it can be predicted that, in a lower-class population, those who have intense fantasy aggression needs will express these needs in their overt behavior.

The first hypothesis of the present study is based on Sanford's suggestions but is phrased in more quantitative terms. Specifically it states that, in a lower-class group, individuals who give evidence of a great deal of fantasy aggression will also manifest more overt aggression than those who show little aggression in their fantasies.

Sanford's statements about the withholding of the overt expression of aggressive impulses are consistent with the theories of Dollard et al. (2), the Yale frustration-aggression theorists, who maintain that "the strength of inhibition of any act of aggression varies positively with the amount of punishment anticipated to be a consequence of that act" (2, p. 33). Although, generally speaking, the inhibition of aggressive expression is not an important part of lower-class mores, many individuals of this class have experienced punishment following the expression of aggression and consequently have learned to withhold this expression. In short, although there is no cultural prohibition against the expression of aggression, some lower-class people have "internal conflict" about it, i.e., they anticipate punishment for aggressive behavior.

The second hypothesis of the present study, derived from the frustration-aggression hypothesis, states that individuals who have strong fears of punishment relative to their aggressive impulses will manifest less overt aggression than individuals whose fear of punishment, relative to their aggressive needs, is small. In testing this hypothesis, the amount of punishment anticipated and the strength of aggressive needs were expressed as a fraction referred to as the punishment-aggression (P/A) ratio. The second hypothesis, phrased in terms of this ratio, states that individuals with high P/A ratios will show less overt aggression than those having low P/A ratios.

If the first two hypotheses are supported or even partially supported, they may be combined into a third hypothesis which could also be systematically checked. If lower-class individuals with great fantasy aggressive needs express more overt aggression than those who have fewer fantasy aggressions (Hypothesis 1), and if individuals with low P/A ratios are more overtly aggressive than those with high P/A ratios (Hypothesis 2), then it follows that: among lower-class individuals, those who have high aggressive needs together with a low P/A ratio will manifest more overt aggressive behavior than those who have few fantasy aggressive needs together with a high P/A ratio (Hypothesis 3).

Method

Twenty lower-class white boys and nine lower-class Negro boys at the Bureau of Juvenile Research in Columbus, Ohio, served as subjects (Ss) in this study. Their ages ranged from 9–0 to 15–8, and almost all of them had been referred to the Bureau for behaviors which brought them into conflict with school and court authorities, i.e., truancy, stealing, disorderly behavior in school, running away, etc.

In order to check the three hypotheses, measures of fantasy aggression, fear of punishment, and aggressive behavior were required. The amounts of each S's fantasy aggression and anticipation of punishment were determined by analyzing his responses to TAT cards 1, 3BM, 4, 6BM, 7BM, 8BM, 12M, 13B, 14, and 18GF. These were administered in the standard way within two days after S arrived at the Bureau and before he joined the cottage group to which he was assigned for the remainder of his stay.

In the analysis of the stories, any act or thought of a hero of a TAT story which, implicitly or explicitly, had as its "goal response . . . injury to an organism (or organism surrogate)" (2, p. 11) was assumed to be a reflection of an aggressive need on the part of S. A fantasy aggression (FA) score was derived for each S by simply counting the number of times aggressive acts appeared in his 10 stories. The following were considered acts of aggression: fighting, killing, criminally asaulting; getting angry, hating, quarreling, cursing; criticizing, blaming, ridiculing; breaking and smashing objects; escaping restraint, running away, resisting coercion; being negativistic, resisting authority, lying, cheating, stealing, gambling;

forcing someone to change his behavior or ideas; domineering or restraining someone; rejecting, scorning, or repudiating someone; suicide, self-injury, self-depreciation. The occurrence of death, illness, or accident of the parents in a story was regarded as an indirect expression of hostility and hence scored as a fantasy aggression.

A measure of S's fear of punishment was derived in an analogous way. A punishment (P) score was obtained by cumulating the number of times the heroes of the stories were subjected to punishment press. As in the case of aggression, punishment was very broadly defined and any of the following was considered an instance of this press when it was directed toward the hero: punishment, assault, injury, killing; hate, threat, quarreling; deprivation of some privilege, object, or comfort; force, domination, restraint; physical handicap such as blindness, etc.; rejection, scorn, repudiation.

Suicide, self-depreciation, and death, illness, or accident of parents or other loved objects were scored as both fantasy aggressions and punishment press. The first two are obviously self-punitive; the last are included because a broad definition of punishment includes "injury to a loved object" (2, p. 34).

Observation of the overt aggressive behavior of S began the day he entered his cottage group and continued for two weeks. Five attendants and a handicraft teacher served as observers (Os) and recorded on two forms, a weekly rating scale and a daily behavior report that were designed to facilitate and objectify observations.

The daily behavior report, the first measure of aggressive behavior, consisted of a check list of twelve kinds of aggressive behavior: physical attack, bragging, threatening, teasing, saucy-impertinent, insulting namecalling, ridiculing, bullying, verbal castigation, malicious gossip, destructiveness, and temper tantrums. Each O filled out one of these reports each day for each of the Ss under his care, checking the appropriate space if that type of behavior occurred that day.

The total number of incidents of aggressive behavior as indicated by the total number of checks on the forms was tabulated for each child. Unfortunately, despite the original plans, not all Ss were observed for the same number of days or by the same number of Os; consequently, the number of reports submitted was not the same for all Ss. In order to get comparable measures of aggressive behavior, the total number of checks recorded for each S was divided by the number of reports submitted for him multiplied by 12, the number of aggressive behaviors listed on each report. This ratio, henceforth designated DBR, may be regarded as the proportion of the aggression observed to the total amount which theoretically could have been observed. These ratios ranged from .000 (least aggression) to .398 (most aggression), with a mean of .088 for the 29 Ss.

The second measure of aggression, the weeekly rating scales, consisted of five separate scales involving different aspects of aggression: uncooperative-cooperative, amiable-quarrelsome, aggressive-submissive, docile-rebellious, and antagonistic-friendly. These scales, which were designed to obtain an overall measure of aggressive behavior, were completed by each O for each S under his care at the end of the first week of observation and again at the end of the second. Each of the five aggression scales was divided into 11 equal units and scored according to the unit in which the rating check fell, 1 representing the minimum amount of aggression and 11 the maximum. The weekly rating-scale score for each S was the sum of the scores for the five scales. Since the number of reports submitted varied among Ss, average weekly rating (WRS) scores were used. For the 29 Ss, these scores ranged from 11.7

(lowest aggression) to 47.0 (highest aggression), with a mean of 29.38. The rank-order correlation between these two behavioral measures of aggression was .86.

Results

The two types of data obtained—scores for fantasy aggression and fear of punishment, and the objective aggressive behavior scores—were used in testing all three hypotheses. For this purpose, all distributions were dichotomized into high (median and above) and low (below median) groups.

If the first hypothesis is valid, there will be a positive relationship between FA score, derived from the TAT, and

TABLE 1. DISTRIBUTION OF AGGRESSIVE BEHAVIOR SCORES AMONG SUBJECTS HIGH AND LOW IN FANTASY AGGRESSION (FA)

Aggressive Behavior Scores	FA Scores	
	High	Low
High	12	3
Low	6	8

aggressive behavior scores on the weekly rating scales and the daily behavior reports. Table 1 shows the number of individuals with high and low FA scores who received high and low DBR ratios. The probability of obtaining this set of cell frequencies or all other possible sets which would be even more extreme (i.e., more favorable to our hypothesis) was calculated directly by the method suggested by Fisher (3, p. 101). The value obtained was $p = .046$.

The distribution of high and low FA scores was exactly the same in the case of the high-low dichotomy based on weekly behavior reports as it was in the case of the daily behavior reports; hence the same probability value was derived in testing the relationship between FA and the second measure of behavioral aggression.

As a further test of Hypothesis 1, the DBR ratios and WRS scores of the 10 Ss with the highest FA scores were compared with those of the 12 Ss with the lowest FA scores. Eight of the 10 highest FA scores also received high (median or above) WRS scores and high DBR ratios, while 9 of the 12 lowest FA scorers also received low (below median) scores on the two behaviorial measures of aggression. The direct calculation of the probability of obtaining this set of cell frequencies, or all other possible more extreme sets, yielded a p of .015. This finding also indicates a strong positive relationship between covert and overt aggression.

It may be concluded from these findings that the first hypothesis is strongly supported and that, among a group of lower-class children, those with a greater amount of fantasy aggression manifest more overt aggression than those with a smaller amount of fantasy aggression.

Hypothesis 2 was tested by making a specific prediction concerning the relationship between a measure of TAT punishment press relative to TAT aggressive needs (P scores divided by FA scores to yield a P/A ratio) and the amount of overt aggression expressed as measured in this study. It may be predicted from the hypothesis that Ss having high P/A ratios will have low overt aggression scores; Ss having low P/A ratios will have high overt aggression scores.

The number of individuals with high (median and above) P/A ratios and low (below median) P/A ratios in the high (median and above) and low (below median) categories of DBR and WRS is shown in Table 2. The distributions for the two measures of overt aggression were identical.

The probability of obtaining this set of cell frequencies or all other possible sets more favorable to the hypothesis was $p = .165$. Although there is not a statistically significant difference be-

TABLE 2.   DISTRIBUTION OF AGGRESSIVE BEHAVIOR SCORES AMONG SUBJECTS WITH HIGH AND LOW PUNISHMENT-AGGRESSION (P/A) RATIOS

Aggressive Behavior Scores	P/A Ratio	
	High	Low
Low	10	4
High	7	8

tween the proportion of Ss in the high and low P/A groups having high or low overt aggression scores, the difference is in the predicted direction and may therefore be considered a trend which is mildly supportive of the hypothesis.

Of the 10 Ss scoring highest in the P/A, seven received low DBR and WRS ratings, while of the 10 Ss having the lowest P/A ratios, only four received low overt aggression scores while six received high scores. The probability of obtaining this set of cell frequencies (or all other possible sets more favorable to the hypothesis) was calculated directly and the value yielded was $p = .153$. Again the finding may be regarded as favorable to the hypothesis since the direction of differences between the high and low P/A groups is as predicted.

It will be recalled that the third hypothesis was a synthesis of the first two. Translated into the measures used in this investigation, it states that individuals who have high FA scores together with low P/A ratios will have high scores on DBR and WRS, while individuals who have low FA scores and high P/A ratios will have low overt aggression scores. Among the 29 Ss, there were seven who had high (median and above) aggression needs together with low (below median) P/A scores and nine who had both low FA scores and high P/A scores. The number of individuals in each of these two groups in the high and low DBR categories is shown in Table 3, while the corresponding distribution in the high and low cate-

TABLE 3. DISTRIBUTION OF DAILY BE-
HAVIOR REPORT (DBR) RATIOS AMONG
SUBJECTS HIGH IN FANTASY AGGRESSION
(FA) BUT LOW IN PUNISHMENT-AGGRES-
SION (P/A) RATIOS AND SUBJECTS LOW IN
FANTASY AGGRESSION (FA) BUT HIGH IN
PUNISHMENT-AGGRESSION (P/A) RATIOS

DBR Ratios	FA-P/A	
	High FA-Low P/A	Low FA-High P/A
High	7	2
Low	0	7

gories of WRS scores is shown in Table
4. Direct calculation of the probabilities
of obtaining these sets of cell frequencies yielded the highly significant
values of $p = .003$ in the case of Table
3, involving the DBR, and $p = .020$ for
Table 4, involving WRS scores. These
findings are clearly supportive of Hy-

TABLE 4. DISTRIBUTION OF WEEKLY
RATING SCALE (WRS) SCORES AMONG
SUBJECTS HIGH IN FANTASY AGGRESSION
(FA) BUT LOW IN PUNISHMENT-AGGRES-
SION (P/A) RATIOS AND SUBJECTS LOW IN
FANTASY AGGRESSION (FA) BUT HIGH IN
PUNISHMENT-AGGRESSION (P/A) RATIOS

WRS Scores	FA-P/A	
	High FA-Low P/A	Low FA-High P/A
High	6	2
Low	1	7

pothesis 3. Among those who have high
fantasy aggression but relatively little
fear of punishment, there tends to be
a great deal of overt aggressive expression; among those who have few fantasy aggressive needs and relatively
great fear of punishment, there tends
to be little overt aggression.

Discussion

The results of this study support the
hypothesis that those lower-class Ss who
have a relatively high number of aggressive needs on the TAT show more overt
aggressive behavior than Ss having a
relatively low number of fantasy aggressive needs. It was also found that Ss
who scored high on punishment press
relative to aggressive needs in their
TAT stories tended to express less overt
aggression than Ss who scores low on
punishment press relative to their aggressive needs. However, this second
relationship was less marked than that
between TAT aggression and overt
aggression. When a high number of
aggressive needs on the TAT is accompanied by a low ratio of anticipation
of punishment to aggressive needs,
there is a very strong likelihood that
there will be a relatively great amount
of overt aggressive expression; where a
low number of aggressive needs on the
TAT is found with a high ratio of anticipation of punishment to aggressive
needs, there is little probability that a
a great amount of aggression will be
expressed overtly.

These findings help delineate the
conditions under which fantasy aggression may be used to predict overt aggressive expression, and consequently
may be very useful in the interpretation
of projective materials. For lower-class
boys, at least, the amount of aggressive
need shown by an individual in his TAT
stories is some indication of the amount
of aggression he will show in behavior.
However, before we make predictions
of overt behavior on the basis of the
amount of aggressive need appearing
in TAT stories, some attention should
also be paid to the amount of punishment press relative to the aggressive
need present. These conclusions should
not be overgeneralized since, as has
already been pointed out, earlier studies
have shown that in other social classes
and age groups the relationship between
covert and overt aggression may be
negligible or even negative. These
findings may not be at all applicable to
members of a social class which has

rather rigid taboos against the expression of aggression, or to older people whose internal controls of aggressive expression may be more firmly established.

It is probably impossible to make any overall statements about the validity of a projective test such as the TAT, which may be used to assess many different aspects of personality. As Tomkins (9) has pointed out, attention must be focused on whether or not specific inferences based on TAT protocols are valid. If effectiveness in predicting behavior in social situations is accepted as a criterion of validity, the findings of this study may be regarded as evidence for the validity of TAT inferences concerning broadly defined aggressive needs. Further research is necessary to elucidate the conditions under which other kinds of inferences from the TAT are valid.

Some of these data may be interpreted in terms of support of that aspect of the frustration-aggression hypothesis which states that inhibition of the expression of overt aggression will vary with the degree of fear of punishment. The second and third hypotheses of this investigation both concern the relationship of fear of punishment to the expression of aggression. The partial support for the second hypothesis, together with the strong support for the third, may be taken as evidence in favor of the validity of the hypothesis that the expression of overt aggression is inversely related to the amount of punishment expected.

Summary

The interrelationships among aggressive needs, anticipation of punishment, and overt aggressive behavior in 29 lower-class boys at the Bureau of Juvenile Research in Columbus, Ohio, were investigated in the present study. Analyses of Ss' TAT protocols yielded measures of strength of aggressive needs and fear of punishment, while ratings and behavior reports submitted by attendants provided indices of the amount of overt expression of aggression.

There was strong support for the first hypothesis of the study, which stated that among lower-class boys, those having a relatively great amount of fantasy aggressive needs indulge in more overt aggressive behavior than those who have relatively few fantasy aggressive needs.

As had been predicted from the second hypotheses, Ss whose TAT stories included a great deal of punishment press (i.e., fear of punishment) relative to the number of their aggressive needs demonstrated less overt aggression than Ss whose ratios of punishment press to aggressive needs were low. The relationship between the punishment press–aggressive needs (P/A) ratio and the behavioral aggression was not marked, but the findings may be regarded as mildly supportive of the hypothesis.

The third hypothesis, a synthesis of the first two, was strongly supported by the data. The hypothesis stated that Ss who have a great deal of fantasy aggression accompanied by a small degree of fear of punishment relative to their fantasy needs (low P/A ratio) show more aggression in their behavior than those who have a small amount of fantasy aggression accompanied by a high degree of fear of punishment relative to aggressive needs (high P/A ratio).

REFERENCES

1. Davis, A. Socialization and adolescent personality. *Adolescence, Forty-Third Yearbook*, Part I. National Society for Study of Education. Chicago: Univer. of Chicago Press, 1944.

2. Dollard, J., Doob, L. W., Miller,

N. E., Mowrer, O. H., & Sears, R. R. *Frustration and aggression.* New Haven: Yale Univer. Press, 1939.

3. Fisher, R. A. *Statistical methods for research workers.* (7th ed.) Edinburgh: Oliver & Boyd, 1938.

4. Lindzey, G. Thematic Apperception Test; interpretive assumptions and related empirical evidence. *Psychol. Bull.*, 1952, **49**, 1–25.

5. Murray, H. A. *Thematic Apperception Test manual.* Cambridge: Harvard Univer. Press, 1943.

6. Murray, H. A., & Stein, M. Note on

the selection of combat officers. *Psychosom. Med.*, 1943, **5**, 386–391.

7. Sanford, R. N., Adkins, M. M., Miller, R. B., Cobb, E. A., & others. Physique, personality and scholarship: a cooperative study of school children. *Monogr. Soc. Res. Child Develpm.*, 1943, **8**, No. 1.

8. Symonds, P. M. *Adolescent fantasy; an investigation of the picture story method of personality study.* New York: Columbia Univer. Press, 1949.

9. Tomkins, S. S. *The Thematic Apperception Test.* New York: Grune & Stratton, 1947.

The Relationship Between Overt and Fantasy Aggression as a Function of Maternal Response to Aggression

Gerald S. Lesser

In recent years, a voluminous literature has developed around the problem of establishing relationships between fantasy behavior and overt behavior. Different researchers have used different drive areas, different populations, different theoretical bases, and different methods of measurement. The most conspicuous conclusion is that the empirical findings are not in agreement.

The importance of this area of investigation for both clinical practice and personality theory has been elaborated by Lindzey (12). He concludes that one of the most important and difficult problems is the "determination of the conditions under which inferences based upon projective material directly relate to overt behavior and the conditions for the reverse" (12, p. 18). The present study concerns the differential condi-

Reprinted by permission of the American Psychological Association and the author from the *Journal of Abnormal and Social Psychology*, 1957, **55**, 218–221.

tions under which aggressive behavior is learned that may allow prediction of how aggressive expressions in fantasy are related to those in overt behavior.

Various studies (9, 13, 16, 18, 19) have demonstrated that the degree of correspondence between fantasy behavior and the associated overt behavior is greater for certain drives than for others. Significant positive correlations have been reported between TAT fantasy and overt behavior for variables such as abasement, achievement, creation, dependence, exposition, nurturance, etc. Significant negative correlations have been reported for sex, and inconclusive results have been obtained for a wide variety of other variables. For the variable of aggression, results include significant positive correlations between fantasy and overt expressions (8, 14), significant negative correlations (5, 16), and inconclusive findings (1, 2, 3, 4, 6, 10, 13, 15, 16, 18).

To resolve these inconsistent results,

it has been suggested (13, 14, 16, 19) that motives that are culturally encouraged are ". . . likely to be as strong in their overt as in their covert manifestations" (13, p. 16), while motives that are culturally discouraged are apt to show little or no relationship between the strength of fantasy and overt expressions.

Mussen and Naylor (14) have attempted to test the first segment of this formulation. They contended that lower-class culture encourages aggression, and predicted that ". . . in a lower-class group, individuals who give evidence of a great deal of fantasy aggression will also manifest more overt aggression than those who show little aggression in their fantasies" (p. 235). A mixed group of white and Negro boys, ". . . almost all of whom had been referred to the Bureau of Juvenile Research for behaviors which brought them into conflict with school and court authorities . . ." (p. 236), were used as subjects. The authors report a statistically significant but not especially strong positive relationship between ratings of overt aggression and number of aggressive TAT themes. Further investigation of Mussen and Naylor's hypothesis would profit from more precise measurement of parental response to aggression, control comparisons, and a more representative sample.

The present study seeks to examine the comparative consequences of both encouragement and discouragement of aggression through the hypothesis that under conditions of maternal encouragement of aggression a greater degree of correspondence exists between fantasy and overt aggression of children than under conditions of maternal discouragement of aggression.

Method

Subjects

The subjects (Ss) were 44 white boys (ages 10-0 to 13-2) and their mothers. The boys were drawn from one fifth grade and two sixth grades in two public schools. All of the boys and their mothers in these three classes participated except one mother who refused to be interviewed. The Kuhlmann-Anderson intelligence quotients of the boys ranged from 82 to 119, with a mean of 102. The two schools are in adjacent districts and the families constitute a relatively homogeneous upper lower-class group.

Maternal Attitudes and Practices

Only one aspect of the environmental conditions of learning of aggressive behavior was measured, i.e., the maternal attitudes and practices supporting or prohibiting aggression. A structured questionnaire-interview schedule was orally administered to the mothers in their homes by a male interviewer. Questions regarding the support or prohibition of aggression constituted only one segment of the total interview; the entire interview schedule is described in detail elsewhere (11). Pertinent to the present study were eight items concerning the mother's attitudes toward aggression in children, and thirteen items about the mother's practices in dealing with the aggressive behavior of her child. An illustrative item measuring maternal attitudes toward aggression is: "A child should be taught to stand up and fight for his rights in his contacts with other children." The four response alternatives of agree, mildly agree, mildly disagree, and disagree were allowed for this item. An example of an item measuring maternal practices concerning aggression is: "If your son comes to tell you that he is being picked on by a bully at the playground who is his own age and size, there would be a number of different things you might tell him. Would you tell him to ignore him and turn the other cheek?" Response alternatives for this item were yes and no. Items that did not involve judgments on a four-point scale were transformed to have approximately the same range of scores as the items that involved four alternatives.

A single score was obtained for each mother by combining all items, assigning plus scores to the responses indicating support of aggression and minus scores to responses indicating discouragement of aggression. The range of scores was from $+9$ to -7, with a median score of $+2$. The corrected odd-even reliability coefficient was .80.

The distribution of scores for maternal response to aggression was dichotomized to form one group of mothers (with scores above or at the median) whose attitudes and practices were more supportive of aggressive behavior than those of the other group (with scores below the median). The hypothesis demands that the correlation between fantasy and overt aggression for the children of the mothers in the former group be significantly more positive than the corresponding correlation for the children of the mothers in the latter group.

Fantasy Aggression

Fantasy aggression in the children was measured through an adaptation of the TAT procedure (13, pp. 3–5). A set of ten pictures was designed. In each picture two boys are interacting. The pictures differed from one another in the degree to which the instigation to aggression was apparent.

To insure complete and accurate transcription of the stories, tape recordings were taken. An introductory period preceding the fantasy task served both to establish rapport between the child and the male examiner and to familiarize the child with the recording device. Instructions were:

I'm going to show you some pictures. These are pictures of two boys doing different things. What I'd like you to do is make up a story to each of these pictures. You can make up any story you wish; there are no right or wrong stories. Say what the boys are thinking and feeling and how the story will turn out.

The ten pictures, in the order of presentation, were:

1. One boy is holding a basketball and the other boy is approaching him with arms outstretched.

2. One boy is stamping upon an ambiguous object and the other boy is reaching for the object.

3. One boy is sitting behind the other boy in a classroom and is leaning toward him.

4. One boy is walking down the street and the other boy, with fists clenched, is glaring at him.

5. One boy, with fists clenched, is staring at the other boy who is sitting, head bowed, on a box.

6. One boy is sawing a piece of wood and the other boy is leaning on a fence between them, talking to him.

7. The two boys, surrounded by a group of other boys, are approaching each other with arms upraised and fists clenched.

8. The two boys are making a fire. One boy is kneeling to arrange the wood and the other boy is approaching, ladened with wood for the fire.

9. One boy, who is looking back, is running down a street and the other boy is running behind him.

10. Two boys are standing in a field. One boy, with his hand on the other boy's shoulder, is pointing off in the distance.

A fantasy aggression score was obtained for each S by counting the number of times the following acts appeared in his stories: fighting, injuring, killing, attacking, assaulting, torturing, bullying, getting angry, hating, breaking, smashing, burning, destroying, scorning, expressing contempt, expressing disdain, cursing, swearing, threatening, insulting, belittling, repudiating, ridiculing.

Fantasy aggression scores ranged from 1 to 15, with a mean of 5.3. The corrected matched-half reliability coefficient was .86; the inter-judge scoring reliability coefficient was .92.

Overt Aggression

To measure overt aggression in the child, a modified sociometric device, the "Guess who" technique (7), was adopted. The Ss were presented with a booklet containing a series of written description of children, and asked to identify each of these descriptive characterizations by naming one or more classmates. Fifteen overt aggression items were used, such as "Here is someone who is always looking for a fight." A diversity of aggressive behaviors were included; items depicted verbal, unprovoked physical, provoked physical, outburst, and indirect forms of aggressive behavior.

An overt aggression score was obtained for each subject by counting the number of times he was named by his classmates. There were substantial differences among the three classes in the distributions of the overt aggression scores; in order to combine into one distribution the scores of children in different classes, overt aggression raw scores were transformed into standard scores.

The biserial correlation coefficient between the overt aggression measure derived from the children and teacher entries for the same "Guess who" aggression items was .76 ($p < .01$).

Results

Two Pearson product-moment correlation coefficients were obtained. For boys ($N = 23$) whose mothers are relatively encouraging or supportive of aggression, the correlation between fantasy aggression and overt aggression is $+ .43$ ($p < .05$, two-tailed test). For boys ($N = 21$) whose mothers are re-

latively discouraging of aggression, the corresponding correlation is $- .41$ ($p < .10$, two-tailed test). These coefficients are statistically different ($p = .006$, two-tailed test).

When the total sample is not separated into two groups on the basis of scores for maternal response to aggression, the overall Pearson product-moment correlation coefficient is $+ .07$. This coefficient is not significantly different from zero.

Discussion

Confirmation is found for the hypothesis that under conditions of relative maternal encouragement of aggression, a greater degree of correspondence exists between the fantasy and overt aggression of children than under conditions of relative maternal discouragement of aggression. Thus, the direction and extent of the relationship between fantasy and overt aggression in the child is apparently influenced by the maternal attitudes and practices surrounding the learning of aggressive behavior.

It has been predicted (13, 16) that those tendencies which are negatively sanctioned or prohibited will be high in fantasy expression and low in overt expression. This association is premised upon a compensatory or substitutive role of fantasy where overt expression is not allowed. A scatter plot of the fantasy and overt aggression scores for the children whose mothers discourage aggression (from which the $- .41$ coefficient is derived) reveals a considerable number of such high fantasy aggression, low overt aggression scores. However, children with low fantasy aggression and high overt aggression scores are as well represented in this scatter plot as those with high fantasy aggression, low overt aggression scores. Although mothers of children in this group were classified (relative to the others) as discouraging aggression, perhaps certain of them do so ineffectively, and thus allow the child sufficient release of aggressive feelings in overt behavior so that he may not need to express aggression in fantasy. An alternative speculation regarding the concurrence of low fantasy aggression and high overt aggression in the group exposed to maternal discouragement of aggression suggests that a child with strong aggressive needs whose mother prohibits aggression may assign this prohibitory attitude to the adult experimenter and suppress fantasy aggression expressions in the testing situation; yet this child may find avenues for overt expression of aggression among his peers.

In the present study, only one condition related to the learning of aggressive responses and controls was assessed, maternal attitudes and practices. Other possibly critical determinants that remain to be explored include fathers' behavior and teachers' attitudes and practices. This study has sampled a limited range of maternal attitudes and practices concerning aggression. Although there is no direct manner of determining the absolute degree of punitiveness of the most prohibitive mother in this sample, it appears unlikely that extremely severe and continuous maternal punitiveness is represented. Such severe condemnation of aggression might so limit or restrict both the fantasy aggression and overt aggression expressions of the child that no correlational analysis within such a group would be possible. Both the extremes of unimpeded permissiveness and severe condemnation warrant further investigation.

Summary

The relationship between fantasy and overt expressions of aggression was studied as a function of the maternal attitudes and practices toward aggression. Subjects were 44 boys and their mothers. The boys' fantasy aggression was assessed through a modified TAT approach, their overt aggression was measured through a modified sociometric technique, and maternal attitudes and practices toward aggression were measured by use of a questionnaire-interview device.

Support was found for the hypothesis that under conditions of maternal encouragement of aggression, a greater degree of correspondence exists between fantasy and overt aggression of children than under conditions of maternal discouragement of aggression.

REFERENCES

1. BACH, G. R. Young children's play fantasies. *Psychol. Monogr.*, 1945, **59**, No. 2 (Whole No. 272).
2. BIALICK, I. The relationship between reactions to authority figures on the TAT and overt behavior in an authority situation by hospital patients. Unpublished doctor's dissertation, Univer. of Pittsburgh, 1951.
3. CHILD, I. L., FRANK, KITTY F., & STORM, T. Self-ratings and TAT: Their relations to each other and to childhood background. *J. Pers.*, 1956, **25**, 98–114.
4. DAVIDS, A., HENRY, A. F., McARTHUR, C. C., & McNAMARA, L. F. Projection, self evaluation, and clinical evaluation of aggression. *J. consult. Psychol.*, 1955, **19**, 437–440.
5. FESHBACH, S. The drive-reducing function of fantasy behavior. *J. abnorm. soc. Psychol.*, 1955, **50**, 3–11.
6. GLUCK, M. R. The relationship between hostility in the TAT and behavioral hostility. *J. proj. Tech.*, 1955, **19**, 21–26.
7. HARTSHORNE, H., & MAY, M. A. *Studies in the nature of character.* II. *Studies in service and self-*

control. New York: Macmillan, 1929.

8. KAGAN, J. The measurement of overt aggression from fantasy. *J. abnorm. soc. Psychol.*, 1956, 52, 390–393.

9. KAGAN, J., & MUSSEN, P. H. Dependency themes on the TAT and group conformity. *J. consult. Psychol.*, 1956, 20, 29–33.

10. KORNER, ANNELIESE F. *Some aspects of hostility in young children*. New York: Grune & Stratton, 1949.

11. LESSER, G. S. Maternal attitudes and practices and the aggressive behavior of children. Unpublished doctor's dissertation, Yale Univer., 1952.

12. LINDZEY, G. Thematic Apperception Test: Interpretive assumptions and related empirical evidence. *Psychol. Bull.*, 1952, 49, 1–25.

13. MURRAY, H. A. *Thematic Apperception Test Manual*. Cambridge: Harvard Univer. Press, 1943.

14. MUSSEN, P. H., & NAYLOR, H. K. The relationships between overt and fantasy aggression. *J. abnorm. soc. Psychol.*, 1954, 49, 235–240.

15. PITTLUCK, PATRICIA. The relation between aggressive fantasy and overt behavior. Unpublished doctor's dissertation, Yale Univer., 1950.

16. SANFORD, R. N., ADKINS, MARGARET M., MILLER, R. B., COBB, E. A., et al. Physique, personality, and scholarship: A cooperative study of school children. *Monogr. Soc. Res. Child Developm.*, 1943, 8, No. 1.

17. SEARS, R. R. Relation of fantasy aggression to interpersonal aggression. *Child Developm.*, 1950, 21, 5–6.

18. SYMONDS, P. M. *Adolescent fantasy: An investigation of the picture story method of personality study*. New York: Columbia Univer. Press, 1949.

19. TOMKINS, S. S. *The Thematic Apperception Test*. New York: Grune & Stratton, 1947.

The Measurement of Overt Aggression from Fantasy

Jerome Kagan

Although the relation between overt and fantasy aggression has been the subject of much research, the results have been varied and sometimes contradictory. Korner (2), studying preschool children, found no relation between frequency of overt aggressive acts and occurrence of fantasy aggressive themes during doll-play sessions. However, separate studies by Bach (1)

The author wishes to thank Dr. Julian B. Rotter for his critical comments on the manuscript and Mr. W. Katkofsky and Mr. K. Anderson for assistance with the study.

Reprinted by permission of the American Psychological Association and the author from the *Journal of Abnormal and Social Psychology* 1956, 52, 390–393.

and Sears (7) indicate that children rated at both extremes on display of overt aggression, i.e., very aggressive or very nonaggressive, produced more doll-play themes of aggression than children who were rated as only moderately aggressive. Independent investigations by Murray (3), Pittluck (5), and Sanford et al. (6), on middle-class populations, all failed to find a significant relation between frequency of aggressive TAT themes and behavior ratings of overt aggression. Mussen and Naylor (4), however, did find a significant positive relation between ratings of overt aggression and number of TAT aggressive themes for a group of lower-class delinquent boys. The authors argued that overt aggression is subject to less punishment in lower-class families than in middle-class ones. Therefore, lower-class Ss should be less anxious over behaving aggressively and be less apt to inhibit overt behavior in response to aggressive motivation. Thus aggressive fantasy, which is a possible index of aggressive motivation, should be more predictive of overt aggression for lower- than for middle-class Ss.

The lack of agreement among existing findings might be due, in part, to a failure to consider two aspects of the fantasy material. The first concerns the ambiguity of the stimulus which elicits the fantasy. The major techniques for obtaining fantasy, i.e., TAT and doll play, confront the S with an ambiguous stimulus. It is assumed that interpretations of such stimuli are a measure of the individual's motives. Since aggressive activity is generally punished and prohibited, however, in order to predict the occurrence of overt aggression one must measure not only the strength of the individual's aggressive drive but also the amount of anxiety and inhibition associated with the overt expression of aggressive activity.

Stories told to stimuli that suggest aggressive content may provide a measure of an individual's anxiety over aggressive behavior. That is, if an individual does not report an aggressive theme to a stimulus which regularly elicits aggressive content one might assume that anxiety over aggression has led to inhibition of an aggressive interpretation. It is assumed that such an S is apt to inhibit overt aggressive acts in other interpersonal situations as well. Failure to produce aggressive themes to stimuli that do not regularly elicit aggressive content is probably a less sensitive index of the strength of these inhibitory responses. Such an approach is supported by Pittluck's (5) findings, which indicate the value of assessing the amount of anxiety associated with aggression in order to predict its oc-currence. Although she failed to find a relation between frequency of aggressive TAT themes and overt aggression, prediction of overt aggression improved significantly when statements suggesting anxiety over aggression (excusing, denial, or noncompletion of the aggressive theme) were taken into account.

Prediction may also be improved by narrowing the categories of overt and fantasy behavior that are correlated. In some studies the index of fantasy aggression includes a wide variety of behaviors (killing, fighting, suicide, anger, destruction, stealing, swearing, etc.) and there is often no differentiation with respect to the person toward whom the aggression is directed. This complex and undifferentiated index of aggressive fantasy is then correlated with categories of overt behavior that tend to be more restricted in goal object and mode of expression. Thus, although Bach (1) did not find a significant relation between overt aggression in a school situation and a complex index of doll-play aggression, he did find a direct relation between overt and doll-play aggression directed at the teacher. When the overt and fantasy behaviors were similar in goal object, a significant relationship emerged.

This study concerns the relation between frequency of fighting behavior among young boys and the stories told to a set of pictures that varied in ambiguity with respect to themes of fighting. On the basis of the previous discussion one might hypothesize that (a) frequency of fighting themes is more directly related than other types of fantasy aggression to overt fighting behavior and (b) pictures suggesting aggressive content are more predictive of overt aggression than more ambiguous pictures.

Procedure

The Ss were 118 boys drawn from seven classes (grades one through three) in a Columbus, Ohio, public school. Their ages ranged from 6-1 to 10-2 with a median age of 7-9. The school population was predominantly middle class, the majority of the fathers being skilled laborers and tradesmen. Before initiating individual interviews with each S the E spent several hours with each of the seven classes in order to become familiar with the children.

After some introductory games had served to establish rapport in the interview situation, the E introduced the fantasy task with the following communication:

Let's play a guessing game now. I have some pictures here and I want you to guess what's happening on the picture. You have to make up a story to tell what you think is going on in the picture.

Thirteen pictures were administered four of which depicted interactions between two or more boys. The pictures, in the order of their presentation, were as follows:

1. Four boys are in a circle around a baseball bat and, off to one side, a boy is tossing a closed penknife in the air.

2. A boy is sitting on a chair holding a broken shoe lace and a woman is standing in the background.

3. One boy is running behind a second boy in the street.

4. A crying boy is sitting on the floor and a woman, standing behind the boy, is looking down at him.

5. A boy with bowed head is standing near a bicycle which is turned over. A man is looking down at the boy.

6. A boy is stamping on an ambiguous object and a second boy is reaching toward the object.

7. A boy with bowed head is approaching a man sitting in a chair.

8. A boy with clenched fist is staring at a second boy who is sitting, head bowed, on a wooden box.

9. A boy is walking away from a woman who has her hands over her mouth.

10. A boy is holding his hand out to a man who is standing with one hand in his pocket.

11. A boy is crying and a woman is bending over the boy.

12. A boy with a cut on his arm is crying and a woman is standing in the background with her back to the boy.

13. A boy is crying and a man is standing in back of the boy looking down at him.

Each S was rated by one person, his teacher, on the following behaviors: (*a*) tendency to start fights at the slightest provocation and (*b*) tendency to hold in his anger and not to express it overtly. The ratings were made on a five point scale, the lowest rating defined to the teachers as, "A very low tendency to behave in this fashion. The child is hardly ever like this." The highest rating was defined as, "A very high tendency to behave in this fashion. The child is very often like this."

These two behaviors were selected in order to obtain a check on the consistency of the ratings. It was assumed that an S with a low rating on Variable *a*, i.e., never starts fights, would receive a high rating on Variable *b*, i.e., always holds in his anger. If the raters were consistent there should be a high negative correlation between the ratings on these two variables. The product-moment correlation was $-.94$.

On the basis of the ratings the sample of 118 was divided into five groups differing in degree of overt aggression. The three most aggressive and the three least aggressive Ss in each class were selected to make up two extreme groups of 21 boys each (Groups A and NA). The remaining Ss were divided into those rated frequently aggressive (Group FA), moderately aggressive (Group MA), and infrequently aggressive (Group IA).

The stories were scored for a variety of themes but those relevant for this paper are (a) fighting between boys, (b) destruction of property, (c) stealing, (d) swearing, and (e) physical aggression to an adult. The stories were scored independently by E and a graduate student in psychology without knowledge of the behavior ratings. Percentage of agreement was high for each type of theme and the over-all percentage of agreement was 98 per cent.

Results

The occurrence of themes involving fighting between boys (F themes) was almost exclusively restricted to the four pictures illustrating boy-boy interactions (pictures 1, 3, 6, and 8). Table 1 shows the percentage of Ss in each group who reported one or more F themes for the 13 pictures and the mean number of F themes for each group. The difference between Groups A and NA in regard to the percentage producing F themes was not statistically significant but was in the predicted direction ($.10 > p > .05$). All p values are for one tail. The mean number of F themes for Group A was greater than that of Group NA ($p < .01$), however, and the pooled

mean for Groups A and FA was larger than the pooled mean for Groups NA and IA ($p < .01$).

The remaining four categories of fantasy aggression were not produced as frequently as were themes of fighting. When stories containing destruction, stealing, swearing, and physical aggression to adults are pooled for all 13 pictures there are no significant differences among the groups in percentage producing any one of these content categories or in mean number of these themes produced. Thus, with this set of stimuli, only F themes were significantly related to ratings of fighting behavior.

Group A produced more of these nonfighting, aggressive themes, nevertheless, than did any of the remaining groups. Perhaps if some of the pictures had been more suggestive of stealing or swearing these fantasy categories might have differentiated between the aggressive and nonaggressive subjects.

The ambiguity of the pictures was determined by having graduate students judge the four pictures illustrating boy-boy interactions (1, 3, 6, and 8) with respect to the degree to which each suggested a fighting theme. Picture 1 was judged the least suggestive, Pic-

TABLE 1. FREQUENCY OF FIGHTING (F) THEMES
PRODUCED BY GROUPS RATED DIFFERENTLY ON
AGGRESSIVE BEHAVIOR

Group	N	Degrees of Aggression	Percentage of Group with One or More F Themes	Mean Number of F Themes per Group
A	21	Very aggressive	100.0	2.62
FA	17	Frequently aggressive	94.1	2.23
MA	34	Moderately aggressive	79.4	1.64
IA	25	Infrequently aggressive	96.0	1.76
NA	21	Very non-aggressive	81.0	1.52

TABLE 2.   FREQUENCY OF FIGHTING (F) THEMES IN RELATION TO STIMULUS
AMBIGUITY AND RATED BEHAVIORAL AGGRESSIVENESS

Pic-ture	Degree of Ambiguity	Percentage Producing F Themes					
		Group A	Group FA	Group MA	Group IA	Group NA	All Groups
1	Most ambiguous	28.6	35.3	44.1	32.0	23.8	32.8
3	Moderately ambiguous	66.7	41.2	32.4	16.0	28.6	37.0
6	Moderately ambiguous	42.9	47.1	35.3	40.0	42.9	41.6
8	Least ambiguous	95.2	88.2	52.9	80.0	57.1	74.7

ture 8 the most suggestive. Pictures 3 and 6 were judged moderately suggestive with the former slightly more ambiguous as regards aggressive content. Table 2 shows the proportion of each group producing F themes to each of the four pictures.

The data indicate a general increase in the occurrence of F themes with decreasing ambiguity of the pictures. However, more of the Ss in Group A, as compared with Group NA, produced F themes to the picture most suggestive of fighting ($p < .01$). There was no marked difference between Groups A and NA in proportion giving F themes to the picture least suggestive of aggression. Furthermore the difference between Groups A and NA on the most suggestive picture was larger than the difference between these two groups on the least suggestive picture ($p = .07$). The significance of this second order difference suggests that interpretations of stimuli suggestive of fighting may be more predictive of overt aggression than the interpretations of more ambiguous stimuli.

Discussion

The results tend to verify the hypothesis of a direct and positive relation between fighting behavior in fantasy and overt expression when the stimuli used to elicit the fantasy suggest aggressive content. If an individual responds with strong anxiety to aggressive thoughts, then a picture that suggests aggressive activity is apt to elicit sufficient anxiety to motivate responses that inhibit the reporting of aggressive stories. The S who associates less anxiety with aggression is more likely to report an aggressive theme when confronted with a picture that suggests this type of content. Thus, failure to tell aggressive stories to stimuli that regularly elicit such themes may be regarded as a measure of the amount of anxiety associated with the expression of aggressive thoughts. Prediction of overt aggression from fantasy themes is based on the assumption that an S who is anxious about telling aggressive stories to a psychologist will also be anxious over the expression of overt aggressive responses in other interpersonal contexts.

There is a limit to the amount of structure that should be imposed on a fantasy stimulus in order to measure an S's tendency to avoid aggressive interpretations. The nonpsychotic child strives to be accurate in his interpretation of external stimuli. A completely unambiguous stimulus, e.g., two boys actively fighting, would therefore not produce sufficient variability among the themes told by a group of nonpsychotic Ss. The pictures used in this study did not depict scenes of fighting and the child could tell nonaggressive stories without seriously distorting the stimulus.

These findings have some limited bearing on the problem of diagnosis and prediction in personality testing. Often the clinician is asked to predict the occurrence of behaviors that may elicit anxiety, e.g., aggressive, sexual, and overdependent behavior. It is suggested that storytelling techniques that include stimuli suggestive of these behaviors can provide the clinician with a measure of the amount of anxiety associated with these responses. Presumably, clinicians who use the Murray series of TAT cards interpret the lack of a sexual theme on picture 13 MF or of an aggressive theme on 18 GF as tentative signs of anxiety in relation to these behavior categories.

Summary

A direct and positive relationship between overt and fantasy aggression was predicted when (a) the fantasy stimulus suggests aggressive content and (b) the overt and fantasy behaviors are similar in mode of expression and goal object.

A set of specially devised pictures was individually administered to 118 boys aged 6-1 to 10-2 and the stories scored for five different categories of aggressive content. On the basis of teacher ratings of fighting behavior with age mates the sample was divided into five groups differing in degree of overt aggressivity.

The children who were rated as most likely to initiate fighting behavior produced significantly more fighting themes than those boys rated as extremely non-aggressive. Other categories of aggressive fantasy were not significantly related to the behavior ratings. In addition, more aggressive Ss than nonaggresive ones produced stories of fighting to the picture most suggestive of a fighting theme. Occurrence of fighting themes to the picture least suggestive of such content did not result in differences between the aggressive and non-aggressive boys. It was hypothesized that failure to give aggressive themes to pictures that suggest aggressive content may indicate anxiety over aggressive thoughts and behavior. This anxiety is likely to lead to the inhibition of aggressive fantasy and of overt aggressive activity.

REFERENCES

1. BACH, G. R. Young children's play fantasies. *Psychol. Monogr.*, 1945, **59**, No. 2 (Whole No. 272).
2. KORNER, A. F. *Some aspects of hostility in young children.* New York: Grune & Stratton, 1949.
3. MURRAY, H. A. *Thematic Apperception Test manual.* Cambridge: Harvard Univer. Press, 1943.
4. MUSSEN, P. H., & NAYLOR, H. K. The relationship between overt and fantasy aggression. *J. abnorm. soc. Psychol.*, 1954, **49**, 235–240.
5. PITTLUCK, PATRICIA. The relation between aggressive fantasy and overt behavior. Unpublished doctor's dissertation, Yale Univer., 1950.
6. SANFORD, R. N., ADKINS, MARGARET M., MILLER, R. B., COBB, E. A., & others. Physique, personality and scholarship: a cooperative study of school children. *Monogr. Soc. Res. Child Developm.*, 1943, **8**, No. 1.
7. SEARS, R. R. Relation of fantasy aggression to interpersonal aggression. *Child Developm.*, 1950, **21**, 5–6.

Chapter 11

Validation of Inkblot Techniques

■ Adolescent love affairs are not noted for their calmness or moderation. There is a tendency in such relationships to ascribe to the love object all the virtues that one can think of and fiercely to deny the existence of the tiniest imperfection. When reality intrudes to such an extent that the adolescent lover is no longer able to ignore some flaw in his inamorata, then he is apt to go to the other extreme and see her as totally without virtue or honor.

Many clinicians and personality researchers never advance beyond adolescence in their relationship with the Rorschach. The Rorschach, a experienced lady in her mid-40's, has long since lost her virginity and is today no paragon of virtue. Nevertheless, each succeeding generation of fledgling clinicians seems to see in the Rorschach a panacea for all their assessment worries. Many retain this attitude for life, blind to the evidence that indicates otherwise. Others become disillusioned and turn against the instrument, reviling it as worthless. Fortunately, after having gone through these emotional throes, many come to the next stage of maturity in which they are able to accept the lady for what she is, good for some things but not for others.

These emotional vicissitudes in the development of the clinician would not concern us if it were not for the fact that so many feel compelled to express themselves in writing while undergoing them. One result of this is that the Rorschach literature, numbering 3,030 titles in 1964 (Buros, 1965), is extraordinarily cluttered with poorly designed or irrevelant studies, so that it becomes increasingly difficult to locate the good ones among the poor. Since it is impossible for the Rorschach to live up to the claims of some of its more ardent admirers and since many of the better designed studies test (and disconfirm) irrelevant hypotheses, the net effect is to make the already imperfect Rorschach seem even worse than it really is (vide Ainsworth, 1954).

One of the goals of this chapter, and, indeed, this entire book, is to discourage people from asking such overly simple questions as, "Is the Rorschach valid?" and to ask instead, "Under what circumstances and for what purposes is the Rorschach valid?" Only thus can we develop a realistic understanding of the virtues and defects of this older lady who has known many lovers and learn to appreciate her for what she is rather than in terms of some adolescent idealized image of perfection.

In the first article in this chapter, Zubin, in a review of the Rorschach literature as of 1954, exemplifies this more realistic approach. Among the defects of the technique he lists the lack of reliability, the lack of an objective scoring system, the failure of specific Rorschach signs to relate to diagnosis and prognosis, the failure of the technique to better differentiate among normal samples, and the lack of evidence for many of the perceptual hypotheses. On the other hand, he concludes that the data indicate that clinicians using the Rorschach globally are often able to arrive at valid evaluations and that content analysis of the Rorschach is an apparent success.

The remaining articles in this chapter, all save one of which were published after Zubin's review, investigate specific aspects of the Rorschach technique.

First and foremost is the question of reliability.[1] A number of studies have been published of the split-half and test-retest reliability of various Rorschach scoring categories. Both of these traditional methods are, of course, questionable when applied to this instrument. The cards cannot be divided into equivalent halves and the test-retest method is confounded with the effects of memory and of changes in the client's mood or personality. In the next article, Datel and Gengerelli examine a more cogent form of reliability, the reliability of clinicians' Rorschach interpretations. The question here is not whether this set of blots consistently elicits the same response pattern from a subject, but whether a given set of protocols consistently elicit similar interpretations from clinicians and whether these interpretations can be effectively communicated in written reports.

The next two articles examine the validity of the Rorschach used fairly globally to predict (or post-dict) clinical criteria. Fisher, Gonda, and Little investigate the relation of the Rorschach to central nervous system pathology while Winslow and Rampersaud attempt to post-dict the outcome of shock therapy in schizophrenic patients.[2] In the former study several sets of "signs" of organicity are compared, most of which use a combination of perceptual determinants, such as Movement, and cognitive or verbal measures such as "impotence," while the latter study analyzes only the content.

The next four articles investigate the experimental and clinical validity of specific Rorschach variables. The attribution of movement or kinesthetic qualities to inkblots was first hypothesized to be a significant variable by Hermann Rorschach himself (Rorschach, 1942). Klopfer later distinguished human movement from animal or inanimate movement, and hypothesized that it was related to intelligence, introversive tendencies, imagination, the existence of a stable value system, and so forth (Klopfer et al., 1954). In the next article, Frank Barron investigates some of the correlates of move-

---

[1] For a review of the problems and findings in regard to Rorschach reliability, see Holzberg (1961).

[2] For a morale-boosting comparison of the relative validity of the Rorschach and various neurologic techniques on the prediction of brain pathology, see Fisher and Gonda (1955).

ment responses. This study is particularly noteworthy for its attempt to define the independent variable more adequately by the construction of a special series of blots whose capacity to elicit movement responses is known. This modified blot approach has been used most in the investigation of the role of color on inkblot responses (e.g., Siipola, 1950; Perlman, 1951) and has often been most helpful in investigating some of the links between inkblot and personality variables.

The use of color is another basic Rorschach variable; it is generally thought to be related to the subject's emotional responsiveness. Lacey, Bateman, and van Lehn investigate this, using as their criterion measure an index of autonomic reactivity under stress.

Rorschach originally was included to place more faith in the perceptual determinants than he was in the analysis of content. However, since Rorschach's time there has been an increasing emphasis on the use of content in the interpretation of inkblots. The use of content has taken two forms. The first, as Zubin pointed out in the first paper, is to use the Rorschach in the same manner one would use any other verbal production by patients and look for signs of thought disorder, concreteness, automatic phrases and the like. The second approach is to use the content symbolically as one might interpret a dream. This has been applied to individual percepts and in addition symbolic content-based scales of hostility, anxiety, and the like have been devised. Of the content scales that have been constructed, none is more intriguing than the "Barrier" scale of Fisher and Cleveland (1958) which is hypothesized to relate to the adequacy of the individual's perception of his body boundaries. This scale has been found to relate to a number of other measures and in the next article Seymour Fisher reviews some of the work that has been done using this content scale.

Perceptual determinants such as color and movement and content analysis as in the Br scale have often been studied in isolation as if the clinician had to use one or the other but not both. In practice, however, both types of variables are used in a configural approach. In the last of the articles testing the validity of various Rorschach measures, Robert and Dorothy Sommer demonstrate the integrated use of both content and perceptual variables in the prediction of assaultiveness.

This use of the configural approach points out a direction that future research should follow. As the relation between various individual Rorschach characteristics and certain behavioral parameters becomes known through studies such as those of Barron, Lacey *et al.*, and Fisher, the next step is to determine how the configuration or interaction of two or more such variables relates to the parameter. As studies such as these highlight the strengths and weaknesses of Rorschach, the next step is the modification of Rorschach procedures to maximize the desirable aspects while eliminating the pitfalls. Usually this consists of the clinician abandoning some interpretive hypotheses which appear to be invalid and substituting others for which better evidence has been found.

However, after four and a half decades of research with the Rorschach, some investigators feel that there is just so much tinkering that can be done with an instrument so psychometrically unsound and that it is time to trade in this 1921 vehicle on a new model without its basic defects. They feel that what is needed is a new set of blots designed to elicit adequate samples of the various determinants with a uniform administration and scoring procedure. One such investigator is Wayne Holtzman, who in collaboration with Joseph Thorpe, Jon Swartz, and Wayne Herron, has undertaken this Herculean task of constructing a psychometrically sound inkblot technique (Holtzman, Thorpe, Swartz, & Herron, 1961). In the concluding article, Holtzman describes this ambitious program of research and the inkblot test which has resulted.

For further material on the experimental and theoretical foundations of the Rorschach, the reader should consult Rickers-Ovsiankina (1960).

If the reader uses or plans to use the Rorschach for research or in practice, he should, if he has not already done so, read Hermann Rorschach's original monograph, *Psychodiagnostics* (Rorschach, 1942). This, the most quoted and least read book in the area of clinical assessment, is valuable not only for the understanding of the basic Rorschach hypotheses devoid of latter-day alterations, but also for an appreciation of the basic empiricism of Hermann Rorschach's approach. Although Rorschach's affair with the inkblots began while they were still virginal, few of their later lovers have been more realistic or mature in their attitude toward them.

REFERENCES

AINSWORTH, MARY D. Problems of validation. In KLOPFER, B., AINSWORTH, MARY D., KLOPFER, W. G., & HOLT, R. R. *Developments in the Rorschach Technique.* Vol. 1. New York: Harcourt, Brace & World, 1954.

BUROS, O. K. (Ed.) *The sixth mental measurements yearbook.* Highland Park, N.J.: The Gryphon Press, 1965.

FISHER, J., & GONDA, T. Neurologic techniques and the Rorschach test in detecting brain pathology: A study of comparative validities. *AMA Archives of Neurology and Psychiatry,* 1955, **74,** 117–124.

FISHER, S., & CLEVELAND, S. E. *Body Image and Personality.* Princeton, N.J.: D. Van Nostrand Company, 1958.

HOLZBERG, J. D. Reliability re-examined. In RICKERS-OVSIANKINA, MARIA A. (Ed.) *Rorschach Psychology.* New York: John Wiley & Sons, 1960. Pp. 361–379.

HOLTZMAN, W. H., THORPE, J. S., SWARTZ, J. D., & HERRON, E. W. *Inkblot Perception and Personality.* Austin: University of Texas Press, 1960.

KLOPFER, B., AINSWORTH, MARY D., KLOPFER, W. G., & HOLT, R. R. *Developments in the Rorschach Technique.* Vol. I. New York: Harcourt, Brace & World, 1954.

PERLMAN, JANET A. Color and the validity of the Rorschach 8–9–10 percent. *Journal of Consulting Psychology,* 1951, **15,** 122–126.

RICKERS-OVSIANKINA, MARIA A. (Ed.) *Rorschach Psychology.* New York: John Wiley & Sons, 1960.

RORSCHACH, H. (Trans. by P. Lemkau & B. Kronenburg) *Psychodiagnostics: A Diagnostic Test Based on Perception.* Berne: Huber, 1942. (First German ed., 1921; U. S. distributor, Grune & Stratton.)

SHPOLA, ELSA M. The influence of color on reactions to inkblots. *Journal of Personality,* 1950, **18,** 358–382.

Failures of the Rorschach Technique

Joseph Zubin

If Herman Rorschach had not been carried off by the infection following a minor operation, he would have celebrated his 68th birthday last November 8th. He would have looked approvingly on our efforts and would have helped make this symposium on failures a success by providing methods for their elimination in the future. For no one was more tentative in his conclusions, more demanding of continual self-survey and revision than the man who lent his name to the major projective technique. "The conclusions drawn," he says, "are to be regarded more as observations (remarks) than as theoretical deductions. The theoretical foundation for the experiment is, for the most part, still incomplete." He even went as far as hoping for ". . . control experiments taking up each symptom individually, and other psychological methods which might also be used in control research." (24).

It is both a brave and a wise move that the Society for Projective Techniques has undertaken in this symposium and it is to be congratulated on its maturity and integrity. Like the postmortem in surgery, failures in projec-

Reprinted by permission of the publisher and the author from the *Journal of Projective Techniques,* 1954, **18,** 303–315.

tive techniques ought to be far more revealing and instructive than the reports of successful cases. We stand to benefit from our mistakes, find out what changes need to be introduced, what hypotheses need to be altered and what expectations need to be amended. Following the custom of the surgeons, only the outstanding failures of the Rorschach technique will be discussed, the outstanding successes being omitted. A cataloguing of one's failures without scanning the successes is trying to even the most mature of souls, but since it is motivated by a search for improvement we can all bear up under it. After analyzing the failures, a hypothesis to explain them will be presented, which may perhaps repay, in part, for the masochistic trend a self-analysis may engender.

One outstanding Rorschach worker has made the following surmise about Rorschach's own reaction to the current scene: "Rorschach today would still recognize the cards. Brilliant though he was, I doubt if he could find time to read the voluminous literature which is well enroute to the thousand mark. I am certain that, if he could, he would be startled that from his little experiment following the 'scoring' of the responses, there emerge invaluable facts relating specifically to the way in which the patient sees his world, approaches and handles it, and of what this world consists. His anxieties and insecurities, his hurts and wishes, his fictions, his needs, his assets and liabilities, his likes and dislikes—all of these and more emerge to be viewed by the examiner. Moreover, the pattern reveals also the meaning of these things to him, the configuration of his personality which thus results, and the motivations of his behavior. It, furthermore, aids in differential diagnosis, particularly between the organic and functional types of illness, and among the affect and content disorders. The expert examiner can also obtain from the response record a practical estimation of such important personality features as intellectual efficiency, emotional maturity and balance, and degree and depth of reality acceptance. Finally, the procedure serves as a guide to therapy and an index of its success or failure." (19).

What validity do these claims have? Let us take a look at the record. The following questions need to be answered: (1) What reliability does the Rorschach technique possess? (2) What validity? (3) What relationship does it bear to the changes brought on by therapy, and (4) to the outcome of therapy, and (5) what light has recent research cast on these problems?

First, what about the reliability of scoring? This question has received but little attention and it is generally taken for granted that scoring has a high degree of reliability. Hertz, (18), however, has stated on the basis of her long experience that "scoring still remains a matter of skill—art, if you will." Though this statement was made 18 years ago, it still largely holds true today. Ramzy and Pickard (22) found that only after considerable discussion and arbitrary acceptance of certain conventions were they able to obtain consistency in their scoring. It is noteworthy that appeal to text-books only

increased their confusion. Even after this collusion, the degre of agreement was only 90% for the location category. Since Beck's location tabulations were followed, it is surprising that the degree of agreement was not perfect. For determinants of Form and the Movement variety, the agreement dropped to 83%, and for the Color and Shading determinants to 75%. As far as content was concerned, following Beck's classifications an agreement of 99% was obtained. Ames and her associates report their reliabilities in terms of product moment correlation coefficients: location categories, .92; form and movement categories, .90; color and shading, etc., .80; and content categories, .97 (1). These results are essentially in keeping with those reported by Ramzy and Pickard. Since according to Rorschach, "The actual content of the interpretations comes into consideration only secondarily" the determinants being of major importance, it is clear that the best estimate of agreement for the major scoring categories is only 80%. This is a far cry from the degree of agreement expected of an individual test. The lack of objectivity in scoring is further evidenced by Baughman's experiment (5) in which 15 Veterans Administration examiners disagreed significantly in scoring on 16 out of 22 scoring categories in records based on a random selection of cases culled from their files. It is clear that failure to provide an objective scoring system is our first failure.

The reliability of the test can not be judged by split-half methods because of the heterogeneity of the blots, nor can it be judged by test-retest because of the memory factor. Alternate forms are required for this purpose. Eichler (12) reports that he tried to obtain a reliability estimate by correlating the Behn-Rorschach with the Rorschach but obtained such low reliabilities that he concluded the two forms were similar but not parallel.

Thus, lack of reliability is the second failure.

The validity of the test will be analyzed from the following points of view: (1) subjective, (2) clinical, (3) statistical, and (4) experimental.

Subjective and Clinical

Subjective validation of the testimonial variety in which he who comes to scoff remains to pray, will not be commented on further. This type of evidence is so clearly discountable as utterly unscientific, that it is not even to be counted among our failures.

The clinical method sometimes consists of administering and scoring the test, collecting data on the subjects' subsequent behavior and then going back to the protocol, in which are "found" signs which "unmistakably" foretell such behavior. Unless a cross validation of these signs is undertaken in another study, it is fruitless to accept them as indicative of future behavior, because with sufficient imagination and exertion of effort through trial and error, pseudosignificant signs can be found in any test. Unfortunately, such cross validation is rarely encountered.

Blind analysis is one of the spectacular aspects of the Rorschach technique and has probably been the most important factor in the acceptance of the Rorschach. One would wish that this method could be made more explicit and more public, and that the enthusiastic proponents of this method were as ready to publish their failures as their successes. Until this method becomes more open to public scrutiny, it has to be placed in the doubtful category and counted neither as a success nor as a failure.

The matching technique is another way of demonstrating validity. Unfortunately, there are many inadvertant and tangential characteristics in this method, not germane to validity, which

may influence the outcome. Successful matching is frequently effected on the basis of minor details or coincidences, rather than essential equivalence. Heterogeneity of matches also makes the task too easy. Determination of the precise ground on which successful pairing is made is virtually impossible. Furthermore, most of the results indicate only that the matching is better than chance, an insufficient criterion for validity. Cronbach (9) has recently devised a trenchant methodology for freeing the matching methods from these defects, but it is quite intricate, and the one application which he made yielded no success in the matching process. Thus, the clinical evidence for validity cannot be accepted scientifically, even though it is impressive. Our failure to provide more cogent evidence for clinical validity must be regarded as our third failure.

Statistical Studies

In view of Rorschach's original purpose of devising a diagnostic test for mental disorders—especially for schizophrenia—we shall first review studies that deal with the diagnostic efficacy of the test. There are very few studies in which clinical scoring and interpretation disagree markedly with clinical diagnosis when the study is conducted in the same clinic and when the two diagnosticians have had considerable experience in working together. This is certainly highly in favor of the test, and the only question a carping critic might ask is: is there a tendency for collusion to occur in such cases, since only a few authors, such as Benjamin and Ebaugh (4), point out the care they took to avoid collusion. When we examine the relationship between the individual Rorschach scores and diagnosis, a totally different picture emerges. Guilford (16) found in 3 successive samples of about 50 neurotic patients, who were given the Rorschach in orthodox fashion, that no significant differences could be detected between their performance and that of a large normative group of cadets. Wittenborn and Holzberg (32) found zero correlation between Rorschach factors and diagnosis in 199 successive admissions. Cox (8) found only 5 scores out of a total of 43 scores differential between normal and neurotic children, and of these 5, 3 were in the content categories and only 2 in the determinant categories. These are only samples of the well-known failure of the individual Rorschach scoring categories to relate to diagnosis, which is in marked contrast to the success of the global evaluation claimed by clinical workers generally. This must be regarded as the fourth failure.

In prognosis too, the recent review by Windle (30) leaves one with very little faith in the efficacy of the prediction attributable to the Rorschach. The only successful prognostic elements seem to be based on content rather than formal factors as shown by McCall (21). This is the fifth failure.

Since Windle's article was published, two additional bits of evidence of failure of the Rorschach in the prognostic sphere have appeared. In Barron's study (2) in which the Rorschach, together with several other tests including the MMPI were given to both patients and therapists before the beginning of therapy, while the MMPI predicted outcome significantly, the Rorschach, despite all attempts ranging from the global to the atomic, failed to do so. Rogers, Knauss, and Hammond (23) report a similar experience. As long as other tests failed to predict outcome one might have attributed the failure to the heterogeneous nature of the patient group—to an admixture of early and chronic cases, for example. When other tests succeed where the Rorschach fails, one can either conclude that the Rorschach is unsuited to prediction, or that basic personality which

the Rorschach claims to measure is unrelated to the type of therapy involved.

The differentiation of organic from functional conditions has also had a checkered history of success and failure: success when viewed retrospectively but failure when the results of retrospective analysis were applied to a new sample. The latest in the series is the study by Dorken and Kral (11), who after demolishing the signs of previous workers propose a new set of their own, which will probably in turn be demolished by the next worker. The vitality of this search for signs despite so many failures can only command the awe and respect of the onlooker. Whether it will finally succeed only time can tell; meanwhile it must be placed in the doubtful category.

The success that clinicians have had in global evaluation of mental patients has not been duplicated in the global evaluations of normals. Here the series of failures is truly appalling. The story is too long to review. Some of the recent examples are Grant, Ives, and Ranzoni (15), who found zero correlation between Rorschach evaluations and case history evaluations of adjustments in 18-year-old normals. The more specific adjustment signs provided by Helen Davidson (10), fared a little better, yielding correlations from .23 to .56. The failure of the Rorschach to serve as a predictor of success in the screening programs of the armed forces, in the screening of clinical psychology students and students of psychiatry, is too well known to warrant further comment. I shall quote only from one of these:

"It was regarded as very important that the Rorschach test should be given full opportunity to show what it had to offer in a personnel-selection setting. It was recognized that neither time nor personnel requirements for the routine administration and use of this test were consistent with the mass testing required. . . . Yet the test was administered experimentally to several hundred students individually according to the prescribed procedures by members of the Rorschach Institute who were serving in one of the psychological units. Two methods of group administration were also tried, the Harrower-Erickson and our own version.

"The results were almost entirely negative. From the individual administration of the test, neither the 25 indicators taken separately or collectively nor the intuitive prediction of the examiner based upon the data he had from the administration of the test gave significant indications of validity against the pass-fail criterion. There were two samples, one of nearly 300 and the other of nearly 200. The Harrower-Erickson group-administration form also gave no evidence of being valid for pilot selection. The AAF group-administration form when scored for the number of most popular responses showed a coefficient of .24, based upon a sample of more than 600 students" (16). The inability to differentiate between normals is the sixth failure.

Special studies aimed at evaluating intelligence by means of the Rorschach also usually come a cropper. Wittenborn (33) compared the extreme groups selected on the basis of college-entrance examinations on 18 scores of the Rorschach and failed to find any significant relationship. (This is even worse than chance, because by chance you might have expected about one of these 18 scores to show significance on the .05 level.) The relationship of Movement to intelligence has been investigated by Tucker (28), in 100 neurotics, who found a very low correlation—.26. Wilson (31) made a more extensive study of a large college population and used Movement, Form level, Whole, Responses, Z (organization), diversity of content, and a new specially designed variable designated as

"specification"—and found zero correlation with intelligence.

The studies in creative ability conducted in our own laboratory on creative vs. non-creative writers, mathematical statisticians, and high school students have failed to reveal any differences on Rorschach performance and even tests especially designed to elicit Movement have failed (34). This is the seventh failure.

But the story of the use of the Rorschach with normals is not entirely a hopeless one. Sen (26), in England, one of Cyril Burt's students, applied the Rorschach to 100 Indian students who had lived together for at least two years. Scoring by means of Beck's scoring system, the correlations with personality evaluations by their colleagues were non-significant. However, when scored for content a la Burt, the correlations ranged from .57 to .66. When matching was resorted to, a global method, both scoring methods yielded a high degree of success: .85 for Beck's system, and even higher for Burt's system. Interestingly enough, however, when a factor analysis was performed on the Beck Scores and on the Burt Scores, the results of both analyses are equally trenchant in their relationship between the derived factor scores and personality. This is a general finding in the studies in which the raw Rorschach scores failed to relate to diagnosis or personality. When factor analysis is resorted to, a rotation of the factors usually permits certain striking correlations with behavior to emerge.

We might stop here a moment to differentiate between content analysis as used by Burt and in our own laboratory and the content category as used by Rorschach. In the Rorschach there are really 3 types of classifications: Location, Determinants and Content. The Location and Determinant categories are usually spoken of as the Formal Categories, and the Content

Categories are those which simply classify the percepts as animal, vegetable or mineral—so to speak—that is, the category of objects it belongs to. It might be better to contrast in the Rorschach the perceptual factors—or structural factors with the content categories. There are left reaction time, popular responses, and confabulations, contaminations, etc.—which are neither determinants nor locations and hence could be classified with content.[1] It is the non-perceptual part of the Rorschach performance—the thought content—which we designate as the content aspects of Rorschach performance.

Examples of the scales used for content analysis of the Rorschach protocols are: (1) Formal content a la Rorschach (2) Dynamic content—(a) degree of evaluation included in response as judged by qualifying adjectives, (b) degree of dehumanization, (c) ascendance-submission in concepts portrayed (slaves-versus-kings, for example), (d) definiteness of concept, (e) abstractness, (f) dynamic qualities—alive or dead, static or moving, (g) distance in time and space, (h) self-reference, (i) perseveration, (j) elaboration, (k) blot vs. concept dominance, (l) interpretive attitude, etc. (33). Further evidence for the success of this type of analysis is found in Elizur (13) and in Watkins and Stauffacher (29) in this country and Sandler (25) in England.

Elizur found that an analysis of content in relation to hostility yielded significant correlations with ratings of hostility. Sandler, working with Rorschach's content categories, (and not with the type of content analysis being discussed here) made a factor analysis of the content scores of 50 psychiatric patients at Maudsley Hospital, ranging over 8 types of mental disorder. He emerged with 4 factors and deter-

[1] Whether reaction time belongs here is debatable.

mined the psychological meaning of each factor by its correlation with the personality evaluation made by psychiatric interview and case history methods. These were drawn from three levels—previous personality, general background data, and present symptoms. The productivity factor, R, for example, was highly related to previous productivity in life, to chronicity of symptoms and to a schizo-affective picture at time of hospitalization. The Anatomy factor—internal anatomical objects vs. external objects as another example, was related to an insecure, withdrawn, "previous" personality picture, bad physical health and an emotional deluded state for the "present symptoms." The remaining factors were analyzed in similar fashion.

Watkins and Stauffacher (29) provided a series of indexes of "deviant verbalizations" based on the content of the protocols and found that such indicators had a reliability of .77 between two raters, and that these indexes distinguished normals from neurotics and the latter from psychotics.

Factor analysis, when applied to either the orthodox scoring categories or to the content scales emerges with factors like the following: fluency, generalizing ability, emotionality, imagination, extraversion-introversion, neurotic tendencies. Apparently, what the Rorschach expert does intuitively in evaluating the records of normals and neurotics can be obtained objectively by factor analysis. But it should be noted that direct statistical manipulation of the original Rorschach scoring categories does not lead to significant results unless they are distilled either through the mind of the expert or the hopper of factor analysis.

As for the relation of the Rorschach to changes accompanying psychotherapy, the results are in doubt. One study claims positive findings (21a) and three show negative results—Lord (20),

Carr (6), and Hamlin and Albee (17). The latter found that Muench's indicators of improvement did not hold up when groups exhibiting different levels of adjustment were compared; thus negating the one positive study mentioned.

Barry, Blyth, and Albrecht (3) compared test and retest data on the Rorschach with pooled judgment of patients at a Veterans Administration Mental Hygiene Clinic. Changes in ratings of adjustment level failed to correlate with changes on the Rorschach.

The recent topectomy study (7) offered an opportunity for testing what effect the lowering of anxiety induced by the operation might have on Rorschach performance. Neither orthodox scoring nor anxiety indicators (with the single exception of reaction time) succeeded in demonstrating any changes in the Rorschach performance of the patients, although other psychological tests showed such changes. Psychometric scaling, however, did reveal certain changes and also provided a prognostic indicator. Three pairs of patients were selected, each pair consisting of one individual who decreased in anxiety and one who increased in anxiety after operation. The judgment of loss and gain in anxiety was based on psychological interviewing by means of anchored scaling devices and on the judgment of the psychiatrist. Only those patients in whom the two criteria concurred were selected. The results indicated that perception of movement of whatever variety, regardless of whether it was accompanied by empathy, correlated positively with anxiety, rising when the anxiety level rose and dropping when the anxiety level fell. The degree of tentativeness or insecurity in giving responses also correlated positively with anxiety. The following variables showed only a unilateral relationship to anxiety levels, declining with a decline in anxiety but showing no corresponding rise with rise in anxiety

level: sensitivity to chiaroscuro, anatomical responses, perception of animate objects, perception of objects with texture, and degree of self-reference. The following variables also showed a unilateral but negative relationship with anxiety, showing increases as anxiety fell—accuracy of form perception and degree of congruity of the response. The statistical significance of these differences could be readily established since each patient could be analyzed as a separate sample and the significance of the difference for each patient determined. Only the variables that showed consistent changes from patient to patient were reported.

The fact that the classical Rorschach scoring is not sensitive to changes induced by somatotherapy is an old story. Lord (20) reports a similar finding in psychotherapy. Perhaps the Rorschach test reflects only basic personality structure. Someone has suggested that the goal of therapy is to arrest diseases into defects and then teach the patient to accept these defects. If therapy consists in nothing more than the acceptance of one's disabilities, no change in fundamental personality is to be expected.

Experimental Studies

Perhaps the most important question that the experimentalist would like to answer about the Rorschach technique is: what is the stimulus, what role does it play, and whether present scoring of stimulus qualities such as Color, Form, Shading and perhaps Movement have definite stimulus correlates. One way of answering this question is to alter the stimulus characteristic to see whether the responses will change correspondingly.

The most revealing study of the stimulus properties of the Rorschach is a still unpublished study by Baughman (5).[2] He set as his goal to differentiate as far as possible between that part of

[2] See this Journal, 1954, **18**, 151–164 (5a).

the response which inheres in the stimulus and that which inheres in the responder himself. Since the characteristics of the stimulus are more readily manipulated, he devised a series of modifications of the Rorschach plates so as to reveal the potency of a given part of the stimulus for evoking characteristic responses. He started off with the standard card and eliminated first the hue factor through photographing the standard series in black and white on panchromatic film, retaining all the nuances of the shading or differences in brightness and all the other characteristics of the blot. Then, he removed the shading by making line drawings of the more striking contours within the blot and the periphery. The third modification consisted of blotting out the inside details by making the entire inside of the blot black but leaving the islands of pure white, yielding a silhouette effect. The final modification consisted simply of the periphery or outline of the blot.

While it is difficult to draw up a correspondence between the altered appearance of the card and the specific Rorschach determinant which is most prominently present or absent, the following tentative suggestions can be made. The cards in which only the periphery was present would tend to accentuate whole responses and form responses. The cards with the inside details would tend to accentuate detail responses and perhaps organization (Beck's Z). The silhouette cards would tend to accentuate form responses and perhaps tend to suppress white space responses. The achromatic cards and the complete original set are too well known to require further discussion. The modified cards as well as the original set were administered to a group of 100 veterans, hospitalized for neuroses and character disorders. Each of the five series of blots was given to a group of 20 patients selected randomly which was equated with the other

groups on IQ and educational level. Beck's scoring system was employed.

When he compared the records of the various groups, which had been administered variants of the original stimulus cards, he found, instead of the theoretically expected changes, a considerable degree of constancy in the responses. Virtually all of the significant differences were attributable to differences in stimuli which were simply objectively necessary for the occurrence of a given category of responses. For example, Detail responses were found uniformly distributed in all the variant forms of the blots except for a drop in the case of the peripheral form series, when the stimulus for D is eliminated. Apparently color and shading are not important for the Detail category. Surprisingly, the M response occurred with significantly higher freguency in the silhouette version, indicating that perception of movement is independent of shading. Categories showing but slight differences from series to series were: R, W, Form level, P, T/R, A, FM, Total time, Diversity of content, and 8-9-10%. Baughman aptly summarizes these findings: "The severest assault upon the stimulus is necessary before significant changes in resulting performances are produced."

Another analysis of the data was made by submitting the protocols including the reaction time data and the responses to experienced Rorschach workers to see whether color and shading shock patterns occurred only in the appropriate series. As a result of this investigation, it is reported quite conclusively that the time latency and response patterns supposedly typical of color shock occur with the same frequency whether color is present or absent. The same was found to hold true of shading and shading shock. A very substantial question is thus raised as to the wisdom of continued use of the shock indicators. Further evidence against the concept of "color shock" is provided by Siipola (27). In a specially ingenious experiment, she concluded that the affinity that color bears to emotion is based on a misunderstanding. Color shock for example is not due to color itself, but to the incongruity between the color and contour of a given blot area. The conflict engendered in the observer will take different paths depending upon the personality of the subject. While Siipola's experiment is not itself conclusive, no statistical verification being given, her explanation of color shock is ingenious, to say the least.

Many of the moot questions in scoring could be answered by Baughman's research. Thus, "Bat" to Card I practically disappears as a response when "shading" and "black" are removed, while "Butterfly" occurs equally frequently in all the modified presentations. Similarly, "Map" occurs only when shading is present. Colored areas which yield anatomy responses practically cease to do so when color is eliminated. Color is of little importance in the response "Bat" to Card II-D32, in "Monkeys" in Card III-D3 and in "Bow-tie" and "Ribbon" to the same card. "Rejection" in this study was much more prominent when Color and Shading were absent, indicating that Form rather than Color or Shading is the primary source of rejection. This study needs to be repeated on groups other than the neurotic, with other scoring systems, and with other types of modification.

The second question deals with the effect of alteration of the state of the subject by means of drugs or hypnosis or shock. These experiments have not yielded very much because of the inexactness with which the psychological correlates of these induced states are known.

The third question deals with the effect of alteration of the circumstances surrounding the test. Prestige suggestions as to the importance of certain types of responses will alter the distribution of the responses in the direction of the prestige. Similarly, social situation, induced anxiety, etc.; have been tried out. Some of the changes expected by Rorschach workers were validated, others not. The important conclusion to be drawn is that standard conditions are required and that Rorschach performance is not as insensitive to external conditions as some workers have claimed.

To summarize our findings thus far, the following facts are seen to emerge from our survey:

(1) Rorschach scoring and sign evaluation has an *a priori* basis which is not always validated by experimentally contrived techniques such as alteration of stimulus, alteration of state of the organism, etc.

(2) Globally, the Rorschach is an apparent success when the Rorschach diagnostician and the clinical diagnostician work closely together.

(3) Atomistically it is an apparent failure.

(4) Content evalution whether done globally or atomistically is a success.

(5) Factor analysis of atomistic scores consisting of the usual combination of perceptual and content factors, or of content alone, correlate with personality.

What kind of a hypothesis, what kind of a model, could satisfy the above conditions? That is the scientific question before us. Before answering, let us examine Rorschach's technique as an experiment. Experiments must have as their minimal requirements—subject, experimenter, apparatus or stimulus of some kind, a well-defined task, directions for the task, acceptance by the subject of the task, a response made by the subject and recorded automatically or by the experimenter. But that is not all—the most important part is still missing—the hypothesis.

What is the hypothesis underlying the Rorschach experiment—Rorschach never stated it explicity, but it can be stated as follows:

(1) We perceive in the artificial Rorschach space in the same way we perceive in real space.

(2) The way we perceive in real space is determined by our personality.

Both of these assumptions are impossible to test at this time because we do not know how perception takes place in real space, nor how it takes place in Rorschach space. Gibson (14) has laid the foundations for the experimental determination of these two processes but we still have a long way to go before we can experiment with them. The relation between perception and personality must await the solution of the first two problems. What can be done meantime, and how can we explain the five facts which I have listed previously?

One hypothesis that suggests itself and which I humbly think merits consideration requires a shift of emphasis from the perceptual to the content aspects of the Rorschach. It is true that Rorschach veered away from the content analysis of ink-blots which was so popular with the psychologists of his day and espoused the formal aspects. He states "The content of the interpretations . . . offers little indication as to the content of the psyche." But he may have been wrong, or may have defined content too narrowly. If we define content as the essential elements of the protocol, and regard it as one would regard any other interview material, and analyze the content, the mystery is solved. Once the perceptual scoring is eliminated, and instead a content analysis of the verbal productions of the subjects is made according to such categories as: compulsive thinking, disorganized thinking, or creative thinking; poverty of ideas or fluency; confabulation or clarity; rigidity or flexiblity; contamination or its opposite; perplexity or straightforward-

ness; rejection or compliance, etc., etc., it will be discovered that such characteristics reveal themselves in the Rorschach the way they reveal themselves in the psychiatric interview. To be sure, the Rorschach interview is a standard interview and may lead to results which the free psychiatric interview can not lead to. But it is still an interview—an interview behind the veil of ink-blots.

This would explain why content of Rorschach protocols is related to personality, whether evaluated globally or in isolated scales, while formal Rorschach factors fail to relate to personality. This would also explain why factor analyses of both formal as well as content factors relate to personality. In the course of the analysis, the content factors affecting the formal scores are teased out—viz., the kind of mental content which serves to reduce R, disorganize F, disembody C or Sh, or prevent good M from arising in the mental patient and, mutatis mutandis, the kind of mental content which increases productivity and good responses in the normal, reveal themselves in the rotated factors. If this hypothesis be true, we should turn away from the indirect expression of mental content through determinants and location, and begin building scales for analyzing the content of the verbal productions directly. Such a beginning has been made by several workers and if we spend but ten per cent of the harnessed energy behind the Rorschach wheel to studying the interview basis of the Rorschach, we may bring nearer the day when the contradictions that now exist within the Rorschach field are resolved.

New developments in the interview itself are fast turning it into a scientific tool, and since the interview, in the last analysis, is the basis for personality evaluation, no test today can rise above it. If we obtain objective criteria via the interview for the classification and evaluation of personality, perhaps such criteria may serve as a basis for the validation of tests. But without an anchored interview, we float aimlessly in the sea of personality without compass or rudder.

Summary: This review of the failures of the Rorschach technique has found the following outstanding relationships:

(1) Global evaluations of the Rorschach seem to work when the Rorschach worker and the clinician work closely together.

(2) Atomistic evaluation, as well as global, of the content of the Rorschach protocols (as distinct from the perceptual scoring) seem to work.

(3) Atomistic analysis of the perceptual factors is a failure.

(4) Factor analysis of atomistic scores, of both the perceptual as well as the content variety, seem to work.

The best hypothesis to explain these four facts is that the Rorschach is an interview and that its correct evaluation, like the correct evaluation of any interview, is dependent upon its content. If we provide scales for analyzing its content, we shall be well on the way towards clarifying many of the present-day contradictions and obtain a better perspective on the evaluation of personality.

REFERENCES

1. AMES, L. B., LEARNED, J., METRAUX, R. W., and WALKER, R. N., *Child Rorschach Responses*, Paul B. Hoeber, 1952.

2. BARRON, F. X. Psychotherapy as a special case of personal interaction: Prediction of its course. (Doctoral Thesis, University of California, Berkeley, 1950) quoted in SANFORD, N. *Psychotherapy*, STONE, C. P. Editor, *Annual Review of Psychology*, Annual Reviews, Inc. Stanford, Calif., 1953, p. 338.

3. BARRY, J. R., BLYTH, D. D., and ALBRECHT, R. Relationship between Rorschach scores and adjustment level. *J. consult. Psychol.*, 1952, **16**, 30–36.

4. BENJAMIN, J. D., and EBAUGH, F. G. The diagnostic validity of the Rorschach test. *Amer. J. Psychiat.*, 1938, **94**, 1163–1178.

5. BAUGHMAN, E. E. Rorschach scores as a function of examiner difference. *J. proj. Tech.*, 1951, **15**, 243–249.

5a. BAUGHMAN, E. E. *A comparative study of Rorschach forms with altered stimulus characteristics*. Ph. D. Dissertation, Chicago, Illinois. March 1951.

6. CARR, A. C. Evaluation of nine psychotherapy cases by the Rorschach. *J. consult. Psychol.*, 1949, **13**, 196–205.

7. COLUMBIA GREYSTONE ASSOCIATES, F. A. METTLER, Editor. *Selective Partial Ablations of the Frontal Cortex*, Paul B. Hoeber, 1949.

8. COX, S. M. A factorial study of the Rorschach responses of normal and maladjusted boys. *J. genet. Psychol.*, 1951, **79**, 95–115.

9. CRONBACH, L. J. A validation design for qualitative studies of personality. *J. consult. Psychol.* 1948, **12**, 365–374.

10. DAVIDSON, H. *Personality and economic background: a study of highly intelligent children.* New York: Kings Crown Press, 1943.

11. DORKEN, H. J., and KRAL, A. The psychological differentiation of organic brain lesions and their localization by means of the Rorschach test. *Amer. J. Psychiat.* 1952, **108**, 764–770.

12. EICHLER, R. M. A comparison of the Rorschach and Behn-Rorschach ink blot tests. *J. consult. Psychol.* 1951, **15**, 185–189.

13. ELIZUR, A. Content analysis of the Rorschach with regard to anxiety and hostility, *Rorschach Res. Exch.*, 1949, **13**, 274–284.

14. GIBSON, J. J. *The perception of the visual world.* Boston: Houghton Mifflin, 1950.

15. GRANT, M. Q., IVES, V., and RANZONI,

J. H. Reliability and validity of judges' ratings of adjusting on the Rorschach. *Psychol. Monogr.*, 1952, **66**, 1–20.

16. GUILFORD, J. P. Some lessons from aviation psychology. *Amer. J. Psychol.* 1948, **3**, 3–11.

17. HAMLIN, R. M., and ALBEE, G. W. Muench's tests before and after nondirective therapy: a control group for his subjects. *J. consult. Psychol.* 1948, **12**, 412–416.

18. HERTZ, M. R. The Rorschach ink blot test: historical summary. *Psychol. Bull.*, 1935, **32**, 33–56.

19. KELLEY, D. M. Clinical reality and projective techniques. *Amer. J. Psychiat.*, 1951, **107**, 753–757.

20. LORD, E. Two sets of Rorschach records obtained before and after brief psychotherapy. *J. consult. Psychol.* 1950, **14**, 134–139.

21. McCALL, R. J. *Psychometric records in brain-operated patients.* Unpublished Ph.D. Dissertation. Columbia University, 1950.

21a. MUENCH, G. A. An evaluation of nondirective psychotherapy by means of the Rorschach and other tests. *Appl. Psychol. Monogr.*, 1947, No. 13.

22. RAMZY, I., and PICKARD, P. M. A study in the reliability of scoring the Rorschach ink blot test. *J. gen. Psychol.* 1949, **40**, 3–10.

23. ROGERS, L. S., KNAUSS, J., and HAMMOND, K. R. Predicting continuation in the therapy by means of the Rorschach test. *J. consult. Psychol.* 1951, **15**, 368–371.

24. RORSCHACH, H. *Psychodiagnostics* (translation by P. Lemkau and B. Kronenburg). Berne: Verlag Hans Huber, 1942.

25. SANDLER, J., and ACKNER, B. Rorschach content analysis: an experimental investigation. *Brit. J. med. Psychol.* 1951, **24**, 180–201.

26. SEN, A. A. A statistical study of the Rorschach test. *Brit. J. Psychol.* 1950, **3**, 21–39.

27. SITPOLA, E., KUHNS, F., and TAYLOR, V. Measurement of the individual's reactions to color in ink blots. *J. Pers.* 1950, **19**, 153–171.

28. TUCKER, J. E. Rorschach human movement and other movement responses in relation to intelligence. *J. consult. Psychol.* 1950, **14**, 283–286.

29. WATKINS, J. G., and STAUFFACHER, J. C. An index of pathological thinking in the Rorschach. *J. proj. Tech.* 1952, **16**, 276–286.

30. WINDLE, C. Psychological tests in psychopathological prognosis. *Psychol. Bull.*, 1952, **49**, 451–482.

31. WILSON, G. P. *Intellectual indicators in the Rorschach test.* Unpublished Ph.D. Dissertation, University of Texas, 1952.

32. WITTENBORN, J. R., and HOLZBERG, J. D. The Rorschach and descriptive diagnosis. *J. consult. Psychol.* 1951, **15**, 460–463.

33. WITTENBORN, J. R. Certain Rorschach response categories and mental abilities. *J. appl. Psychol.* 1949, **33**, 330–338.

34. ZUBIN, J. Experimental abnormal psychology. 1953 (mimeographed edition).

Reliability of Rorschach Interpretations

William E. Datel and J. A. Gengerelli

Problem

"The ultimate test (of the Rorschach) is, given a Rorschach record, will every examiner who scores and interprets it arrive at approximately the same conclusions? Further, will those conclusions coincide with other criteria, either clinical or experimental?" (8, p. 295). It is the answer to the first question, put into this form by Hertz and Rubenstein, which the present investigation seeks.

The experimental problem of the present work is whether or not, and to what extent, the language used in a written Rorschach interpretation can discriminate one patient from another. Or, similarly, can one psychologist read a "blind" Rorschach interpretation written by another psychologist and know which patient has been described? Further, does the level of interpretation used in the psychological report influence the exactness of patient description? Does the Rorschach protocol alone provide enough information to allow the psychologist to describe differently two very similar patients? Is the "Rorschach talent" of the particular clinical psychologist the most important variable underlying the communication or comprehension of a Rorschach interpretation?

It is felt that these questions are

The authors wish to give acknowledgment to those twenty-seven clinical psychologists who generously contributed an inordinate amount of time and services in acting as judges in the present investigation.

Reprinted by permission of the authors and publisher from *Journal of Projective Techniques*, 1955, **19**, 372–381.

relevant to the general topic of the reliability of Rorschach interpretations. This area has been the concern of previous investigators (3, 7, 8, 12, 14, 15) who have employed various experimental methods and whose results, in summary (4, p. 13), tend to support the notion that the Rorschach can be interpreted reliably, to one degree or another. However, these studies suggest the need for a more comprehensive evaluation of the reliability of Rorschach interpretations which would involve the cooperation of a large number of judges and which would take into account previously ignored variables. The present study attempts to meet this need.

Method

The *Matching Method*, as originally introduced to the area of personality evaluation by Vernon (16, 17) was the experimental method of choice. Notwithstanding its shortcomings, which Cronbach has emphasized (1, 2), the matching experiment permits a test of the reliability of clinical-type Rorschach interpretations. A desire to mimic, so far as possible, present-day clinical usage of the Rorschach dictated the experimental method and procedure used in the present investigation.

In general terms, the method consisted of having competent clinical psychologists score[1] and interpret "blind" Rorschach protocols and, later, having

[1] The study included an assessment of the inter-judge reliability of Rorschach determinant scores though these results are not included in this paper. For these findings the reader is referred to the dissertation (4).

these same psychologists attempt to match each others' written Rorschach interpretations against the original Rorschach protocols.

Sample of Judges

Twenty-seven clinical psychologists (22 males and five females) participated as judges in the study. While there was considerable range in the amount of clinical experience and "Rorschach prestige" within the group of judges, all 27 met the criteria demanded by Kelley (10) when he listed how much training is necessary before an individual may be considered competent to do good Rorschach work. Except for two[2] of the judges, all were currently, or had been previously students of Dr. Bruno Klopfer and were trained and experienced in the Klopfer method of Rorschach analysis (11). Table 1 gives a synopsis of the professional status and Rorschach experience of each of the 27 judges at the time the data were gathered.

Sample of Patients

The Rorschach protocols of 18 male hospitalized neuropsychiatric patients who ranged in age from 20 to 41 years provided the source for the judges' written Rorschach interpretations. These patients were divided into three groups of six patients each, termed, respectively, the *homogeneous, random,* and *heterogeneous* group. The *homogeneous* group was composed of six very bright, incipient paranoid schizophrenics, ranging in age from 25 to 41 years. Wechsler-Bellevue I.Q. scores were 130 or above. The *random* group was composed of six patients whose names were randomly chosen from the psychological test files at a neuropsychiatric hospital.

The age range was 24 to 36 years: I.Q. range, 96 to 130; diagnoses were somewhat varied. The *heterogeneous* group ranged in age from 20 to 41 years. Wechsler-Bellevue I.Q. scores ranged from 81 to 125, and the patients varied in the chronicity of their illness. The six patients in this group had different diagnoses: organic, acute schizophrenic, character disorder, hysteric, manic-depressive in depressed phase, and obsessive compulsive.

Rorshachs on each of the 18 patients had been administered by various examiners, all of whom were trained according to the Klopfer method of Rorschach administration. Diagnoses were on the basis of the psychological report accompanying the test records.

Procedure

Six Rorschach protocols were presented to each of the 27 judges, who scored each response for determinants and who wrote a "blind" Rorschach interpretation (psychological report) on each case. Data on each patient included the entire Rorschach protocol, the location scores with accompanying figure-location sheet, and the sex of the patient.

In writing their psychological reports on each case, the judges were instructed to keep their reports between 150 and 300 words in length. Also they were asked to describe the patient rather than the protocol so as to avoid direct references to the raw data of the protocol which might later be used as "give-away" cues in the matchings.[3] One-third of the judges were instructed to write reports strictly in terms of *diagnostic* language, one-third strictly in terms of *psychodynamic* language, and one-third in terms of a *combination* of

---

[2] In their clinical experience these two judges had become familiar with the Klopfer method through colleagues and through Dr. Douglas Kelley personally, but originally they received their Rorschach training from exponents of Beck's method.

[3] In spite of these instructions a few statements crept into the report which the authors felt would have provided direct cues when it came to matching report against protocol. Such statements were deleted from the report before incorporating it into the matching phase of the experiment.

Homogeneity-Heterogeneity Variable

	Language Level Variable		
	Diagnostic	Psychodynamic	Combination
Homogeneous Group	Judge M 1. VA Trainee 4. 0 2. No. 5. 150 3. 3 6. None	Judge V 1. VA Trainee 4. 0 2. No 5. 100 3. 2 6. 5	Judge D 1. VA Staff 4. 6 2. Yes 5. 500 3. 15 6. 1500
	Judge N 1. VA Trainee 4. 1 2. Yes 5. 150 3. 2½ 6. 50	Judge W 1. Univ. Staff 4. 1 2. Yes 5. 200 3. 6 6. 50	Judge E 1. State Hosp. Staff 4. 1 2. Yes 5. 125 3. 4½ 6. 15
	Judge O 1. VA Staff 4. 2½ 2. Yes 5. 150 3. 5 6. 50	Judge X 1. VA Staff 4. 3 2. Yes 5. 200 3. 5 6. 150	Judge F 1. VA Trainee 4. 0 2. No 5. 125 3. 3 6. Non
Random Group	Judge J 1. VA Trainee 4. 0 2. No 5. 100 3. 3 6. None	Judge A 1. VA Trainee 4. 0 2. No 5. 100 3. 4 6. None	Judge S 1. VA Staff 4. 4½ 2. Yes 5. 130 3. 6½ 6. 240
	Judge K 1. VA Staff 4. 3 2. Yes 5. 250 3. 9 6. 150	Judge B 1. VA Staff 4. 6 2. Yes 5. 400 3. 8 6. 1200	Judge T 1. State Hosp. Staff 4. 0 2. No 5. 175 3. 4½ 6. 15
	Judge L 1. Army Intern 4. 0 2. No 5. 100 3. 2 6. None	Judge C 1. VA Staff 4. ⅓ 2. Yes 5. 100 3. 3 6. 20	Judge U 1. VA Staff 4. 2 2. Yes 5. 200 3. 6 6. 60
Heterogeneous Group	Judge P 1. VA Staff 4. 6 2. Yes 5. 500 3. 9 6. 2500	Judge G 1. Univ. Staff 4. 1 2. Yes 5. 150 3. 4 6. 10	Judge A' 1. VA Staff 4. 2½ 2. Yes 5. 500 3. 6 6. 420
	Judge Q 1. VA Trainee 4. 0 2. No 5. 125 3. 4 6. None	Judge H 1. VA Trainee 4. 1 2. No 5. 150 3. 4 6. 20	Judge B' 1. Army Staff 4. 2 2. Yes 5. 200 3. 3 6. 100
	Judge R 1. Army Staff 4. 4 2. No 5. 1100 3. 6 6. 400	Judge I 1. VA Staff 4. 1½ 2. Yes 5. 100 3. 5 6. 50	Judge C' 1. State Hosp. Staff 4. ½ 2. Yes 5. 400 3. 6 6. 25

Legend:
1. Judge's professional position
2. Possesses Ph.D. degree in psychology?
3. Years of clinical experience with Rorschach
4. Years of Supervisory experience with Rorschach
5. Approximate no. of Rorschachs administered
6. Approximate no. of Rorschachs supervised

diagnostic and dynamic language.

After all of these data were gathered, each judge was contacted a second time for the purpose of performing the matchings. The judges' task in the matching phase of the experiment entailed an attempt to match two sets of six reports each, written by two other judges under the same set of experimental conditions, to the original six protocols which the judge himself had interpreted. To perform this task, each judge had at his disposal (a) the same six Rorschach protocols he had originally scored and interpreted, plus the corresponding psychological report which he had originally written to the case, (b) two sets of six psychological reports each, written by two other judges, and (c) any work notes which he may have made during the process of scoring and interpreting the protocols.

Experimental Design

A two-way factorial design determined the method by which the Rorschach data were originally distributed to the judges and also determined the method by which the matching phase of the experiment was executed. The two principal variables under consideration were (a) the level of interpretation made in the reports, classified according to *diagnostic, psychodynamic,* and *"combination"* interpretations, and (b) the variability of the patients within the group of Rorschach protocols interpreted, classified according to *homogeneous, random,* and *heterogeneous* groups of patients. The additional variable of "judge experience" was controlled as well as possible by the method of stratification.

Table 1 represents the design of the experiment. The two main variables are classified according to the three rows (homogeneity-heterogeneity variable) and the three columns (language level variable). There are nine cells in the design and three judges per cell,

which means that judges in groups of three performed identical tasks. For example, Judges M, N, and O each wrote diagnostic reports to the six Rorschach protocols on the homogeneous group of patients. And so on.

In the matching phase of the experiment, each judge matched the reports written by the two other judges in his cell to the Rorschach protocols. For example, Judge M matched the six reports written by Judge N to the six Rorschach protocols and he also matched the six reports written by Judge O to the six Rorschach protocols. Within the same cell, Judge N matched the six reports written by Judge M to the six Rorschach protocols and he also matched the six reports written by Judge O to the six Rorschach protocols. Likewise, Judge O matched the six reports written by Judge M to the six Rorschach protocols and he also matched the six reports written by Judge N to the six Rorschach protocols. And so on throughout the design.

The results were scored in terms of the number of correct matchings made on six events. Each of the 27 judges performed two sets of matchings (six events in each set) so that each judge received two scores. A total of 54 sets of matchings (or 324 discrete matchings) was made in all. The design allowed for the study of the following effects: (a) The statistical significance of the matching performances of individual judges; (b) The statistical significance of the matching performances of groups of judges; (c) The effect of language level upon number of correct matchings; (d) The effect of homogeneity-heterogeneity of patients within a group upon number of correct matchings; and (e) Individual differences among judges in their matching performances.

Results

Table 2 presents the results on all of the matchings. The results are presented

TABLE 2 RESULTS OF MATCHING AND CORRESPONDING PROBABILITY VALUES

	Language Level Variable		
Homogeneity–Heterogeneity Variable	**Diagnostic**	**Psychodynamic**	**Combination**

Homogeneous Group

Diagnostic

Judge	Matching	=	p	combined
Judge M:	N = D A B E C F	1	.632	.47
	A B C D E F	2	.265	
Judge N:	M = B F E D A C	1	.632	.20
	A B C D E F	3	.078	
Judge O:	M = B C E A D F	1	.632	.20 [>.20]
	N = A D C F E B	3	.078	

Psychodynamic

Judge	Matching	=	p	combined
Judge V:	W = D B C E A F	3	.078	.037
	X = F A E D C	3	.078	
Judge W:	V = D B C A E F	4	.022	.004
	X = E A C D F	4	.022	
Judge X:	V = C D B A E F	2	.265	.002 [<.001]
	W = A B C D E F	6	.001	

Combination

Judge	Matching	=	p	combined
Judge D:	E = F B D C A	1	.632	.47
	F = A C E B D	1	.265	
Judge E:	D = D A F C B	1	.632	.76
	F = D A B C	1	.632	
Judge F:	D = A D E F B	1	.632	.76 [>.80]
	E = C B A D E	1	.632	

Homogeneous Group summary (Combination): .01 > p > .001; mean = 2.2; median = 1.8; mode = 1

Random Group

Diagnostic

Judge	Matching	=	p	combined
Judge J:	K = 4 3 1 2 5 6	2	.265	.26
	L = 5 2 3 2 1 6	2	.265	
Judge K:	J = 4 6 5 3 2 1	0	1.000	.28
	L = 1 2 4 3 6 3	3	.078	
Judge L:	J = 5 3 2 4 6 1	2	.265	.47 [>.30]
	K = 4 2 5 6 1 3	1	.632	

Psychodynamic

Judge	Matching	=	p	combined
Judge A:	B = 2 3 6 5 1 4	0	1.000	.61
	C = 3 2 1 4 6 5	2	.265	
Judge B:	A = 1 6 4 5 2 1	1	.632	.76
	C = 2 6 3 5 3 1	1	.632	
Judge C:	A = 5 4 1 3 2 6	1	.632	.47 [>.80]
	B = 1 2 3 6 4 5	2	.265	

Combination

Judge	Matching	=	p	combined
Judge T:	S = 5 6 2 4 1 2	2	.265	.036
	U = 1 2 3 6 4	4	.022	
Judge S:	T = 2 3 1 5 2	1	.265	.002
	U = 1 2 3 4 6	6	.001	
Judge U:	S = 2 5 4 1 6	3	.078	.10 [<.001]
	T = 2 1 3 4 6	2	.265	

Random Group summary (Combination): .02 > p > .01; mean = 2.0; median = 1.9; mode = 2

Heterogeneous Group

Diagnostic

Judge	Matching	=	p	combined
Judge Q:	P = IV II III I V VI	4	.022	.004
	R = I III II IV V VI	4	.022	
Judge P:	V = I II III IV V VI	2	.265	.002
	R = I II III IV V VI	6	.001	
Judge R:	P = IV II I III IV V VI	2	.265	.002 [<.001]
	Q = I II III IV V VI	6	.001	

Psychodynamic

Judge	Matching	=	p	combined
Judge H:	G = IV II I V VI	4	.022	.004
	I = IV III III I V VI	4	.022	
Judge G:	H = I VI II III V VI	2	.265	.036
	I = I II III IV V VI	4	.022	
Judge I:	G = II I III IV V VI	6	.001	<.001 [<.001]
	H = III II III I V VI	4	.022	

Combination

Judge	Matching	=	p	combined
Judge B':	A' = IV II III I V VI	4	.022	<.001
	C' = I II III IV V VI	6	.001	
Judge A':	A' = VI III I II IV V VI	1	.632	.005
	C' = I II III IV V VI	6	.001	
Judge C':	A' = IV I III II V IV VI	3	.078	.013 [<.001]
	B' = II I III V IV VI	4	.022	

Heterogeneous Group summary (Combination): p < .001; mean = 4.0; median = 4.0; mode = 4

Column summaries:

Diagnostic	Psychodynamic	Combination
p < .001	p < .001	p < .001
mean = 2.5	mean = 2.9	mean = 2.8
median = 2.2	median = 3.0	median = 2.3
mode = 2	mode = 4	mode = 1

Grand totals: Grand p < .001; Grand mean = 2.7; Grand median = 2.4; Grand mode = 2 according to the pattern of the experimental design as previously set forth in Table 1. The contents within each of the 27 groupings indicate each individual judge's matching performances. The number of correct matchings with their corresponding probability values are listed for each judge and for groups of judges.

To illustrate the facts presented in Table 2, let us exemplify Judge M's results. First, let it be noted that Judge M wrote diagnostic reports to the protocols of a homogeneous group of patients, as did Judge N and Judge O. The series of letters A B C D E F, appearing in the center of Judge M's grouping, refer to the case numbers of the reports as written to the protocols by Judges N and O. The series of letters following N = and O = indicates the manner in which Judge M matched the reports written by Judge N and Judge O, respectively. Hence we see that Judge M matched the reports written by Judge N in the following manner: report on Case A was matched to Case D, report on Case B was matched to Case A, report on Case C was matched to Case B, D to E, E to C, and F to F. Judge M, therefore, matched one of Judge N's six reports correctly. This is so indicated by the number "1" which follows the presentation of how the reports were matched. One correct matching out of six events yields a probability value of .632 which is indicated after the number "1." Judge M matched the reports written by Judge O in the following manner: report on Case A was matched to Case A, report on Case B was matched to Case C, C to D, D to E, E to B, and F to F. This time judge M scored two correct matchings out of six and is credited with a probability figure of .265. The probability figure of .47, which appears between and slightly to the right of the two probability values for each matching performance considered singly, indicates the composite probability of the two matching performances (i.e., 1 out

of 6 and 2 out of 6) made by Judge M (9).

Each grouping in the design presents analogous information to the one just described. The judge who matched the two sets of reports is indicated, the manner in which he matched each set of reports written by the two other judges in his cell is presented, the number of correct matchings scored on each series of (6) matchings is given with the corresponding probability figure, and the composite probability value for each judge's two sets of matching performances is stated. Case designations vary depending upon the group of protocols interpreted. The boldface case designations indicate that a correct matching has occurred, while case designations in regular type indicate mismatchings.

The enclosed figure in the lower right hand corner of each cell gives the composite probability value of the performances of the three judges in that cell. For example, the figure > .20 is the probability value for M, N, and O's performances considered as a group (9).

Summary information on the performances occurring in each of the horizontal arrays is presented to the extreme right of the table and information on the performances occurring in each of the vertical arrays appears at the bottom of the table. The probability values listed here refer to the composite probability of the nine judges' performances in the corresponding array. The composite probability value for all 27 judges' performances is listed together with the grand mean, grand median, and grand mode in the lower right hand corner of the table.

Feller, in his Table 1 (5, p. 68) lists the probabilities of n correct guesses in calling a deck of N distinct cards. These probabilities were applied to the above data where N = 6 and were summed so that the probability values for a single set of matchings in our Table 2 denote the probability of getting n, or more, correct matchings out of six events. In

Table 2 it will be noted that three hits or better yield a probability of .078, while four hits or better yield a probability of .022. Thus a matching performance significant at the .05 level or better requires not less than four hits. The composite probability values were derived from Fisher's (6) method of transforming p values into chi squares in order to arrive at a composite p value. This method is discussed in detail by Jones and Fiske in a section of their paper entitled "The chi square model" (9, pp. 376–377).[4] The resulting composite p values in the above data denote the probability of the corresponding multiple performances, or better performances, having occurred if chance alone were operating.

Individual Results

Of the 54 sets of matchings performed, only seven were perfect matchings (that is, 6 for 6). Eleven more sets of matchings were 4 "hits" out of 6 events. The remainder, 36 sets of matchings, yielded scores of 3 hits or less. Thus, the results from two-thirds of all the sets of matchings performed were insufficient to be termed significantly different from chance expectation, provided the .05 level of confidence is taken as the cut-off point between statistical significance and statistical non-significance.

Employing the same criterion of statistical significance (i.e., the .05 level), it can be noted from the results in Table 2 that 14 of the 27 judges, or 52 per cent, did significantly better than chance in performing their two sets of matchings. Thirteen of the 27 judges matched the reports written by other psychologists no better than might be expected if chance alone were operating.

---

[4] The appropriateness of using this procedure for evaluating composite probabilities in the present material may well be questioned. A justification for its application is to be found in Datel (1. 8. pp. 65–68).

Group Results

The composite probability of the total number of matching performances is statistically very significant $(p < .001)$ for the entire group of 27 judges. However, the "average" number of hits for all the matchings is below 3: Grand mean = 2.7, grand median = 2.4, and grand mode = 2. Even if the largest of these three representative scores were to be considered as a typical matching result, it would not be considered as statistically significant.

Effects of Main Variables

Mood's distribution-free test (13, pp. 398–399) offered a method to ascertain if the number of correct matchings for a given array significantly exceeded those for another array. The results of the Mood analysis are presented in Table 3. The number of correct matchings on the heterogeneous group significantly exceeded those on the homogeneous and random groups. There were no significant differences among the arrays of the language level variable, even though Table 2 shows that the matchings dealing with psychodynamic interpretations have the highest mean, median, and modal scores.

In view of the fact that but one level of the systematic variables yielded a distinct effect, namely, the heterogeneous group, it is desirable to examine the overall results when the bottom horizontal array of Table 2 is eliminated. We then find that only two of the remaining six cells, and only five of the remaining eighteen judges, yield a composite probability of .05 or better. Indeed, of the 36 matchings which constitute the reduced table, only five give four hits or better and thus are significant at beyond the .05 level. The composite probability of these 36 matchings is one which is associated with a student's "t" of 3.63 at 72 degrees of freedom. While this value is less than

TABLE 3.   SIGNIFICANCE OF DIFFERENCES BETWEEN ARRAYS IN NUMBER
OF CORRECT MATCHINGS

Arrays	χ^2	df	p
Homogeneous-Random-Heterogeneous	11.777	2	< .01
Homogeneous-Heterogeneous	11.235	1	< .001
Random-Heterogeneous	10.802	1	< .01
Random-Homogeneous	2.160	1	> .10
Diagnostic-Dynamic-Combination	1.309	2	> .40
Diagnostic-Dynamic	1.080	1	> .20
Diagnostic-Combination	1.080	1	> .20
Dynamic-Combination	.432	1	> .50

.001, it is to be compared with the probability of a "t" of 8.38 at 108 degrees of freedom which results when the array dealing with the heterogeneous group is included. It is thus seen that much of the reliability of Rorschach interpretations achieved in this experiment is contributed by interpretations of the protocols of the heterogeneous group of subjects.

Individual Differences

Though the experiment was not specifically designed to investigate the matter of individual differences in "Rorschach talent" among judges (since in no instance did the same judge perform under different experimental conditions), it is interesting to compare the performances of judges P, B and D with the performances of the judges (other than P) who had been assigned to the heterogeneous group of subjects. These three judges, in the opinion of the authors, are the most pre-eminent in Rorschach prestige of the total group of 27 judges used, yet only one of them, Judge P,—who had been assigned to the heterogeneous group!—turned in a performance which was better than chance. Furthermore, every one of the judges who served in the heterogeneous group, "out-performed" the two prestigious judges who worked with the other groups of subjects. If there are individual differences in Rorschach talent among the judges, it is, in the present context, transcended overwhelmingly by the nature of the material.

Discussion

One of the prerequisites for establishing the reliability of Rorschach interpretations is that one psychologist be able to recognize the Rorschach interpretation communicated by another psychologist as belonging to a particular Rorschach protocol. In performing their matchings, have our judges demonstrated this ability? If so, under what conditions have they done so?

It is apparent from the composite probability value of < .001 that the overall matching results in Table 2 are not distributed according to chance. The number of hits is greater than would be achieved from randomly matching cards. This means that too many of the 54 matching performances were significantly better than chance (18 performances yielded four or more hits). Expressed differently, there were too many of the 27 judges whose performance was significantly better than chance (there were 14 such judges). Thus the variability in the performances obtained in this experiment cannot be attributed exclusively to accident. We are to conclude that the results of some of the Rorschach matchings must be attributed to *systematic factors*, i.e., some of the judges in some of the situations were not behaving as "automata."

It is noteworthy, however, that most of the successful matching performances occur when the heterogeneous group of subjects is involved. The 18 matching performances which constitute this array yield an average of four "hits" per performance. Of the 14 judges whose performances were significant at the .05 level, nine were individuals who had been assigned to the heterogeneous group: i.e., the composite performance of each of the judges assigned to this group was significantly better than chance. The other five are scattered throughout the table. Thus it would appear that our judges can reliably recognize each others' Rorschach interpretations as belonging to the "correct" protocol when the protocols come from a very heterogeneous group of patients. When the protocols of more homogeneous groups of patients are interpreted, inter-interpreter reliability drops rather markedly. This, of course, is a finding which can very well be expected with a wide variety of diagnostic instruments.

Leaving the context of the experimental design proper, it is important to ponder the implications of the overall results. A study of the matching data reveals the fact that the number of mismatchings is greater than the number of correct matchings. Of the total of 324 discrete matchings, 148 are hits and 176 are incorrect. What has gone awry in the numerous instances of mismatchings?

When one judge fails to match the interpretations written by another judge according to the actual protocol used by that judge, several reasons suggest themselves to help explain this occurrence: (a) The judge who matched the report "saw" the protocol differently than the judge who wrote the report; (b) the judge who matched the report would have written the report differently than the judge who did write the report; (c) the report which the judge tried to match failed to differentiate one patient from another within the set of cases interpreted.

In the event of (a) or (b), above, the mismatching may be attributed to the fact that judges do not derive common impressions or apperceptions about a patient from the patient's Rorschach protocol. To put it bluntly, the judges do not agree with one another. In terms of the problem of the present investigation, this would mean that "blind" interpretations stemming from a Rorschach protocol do not lend themselves to inter-interpreter reliability.

In the event of (c), above, additional factors come into play. For, under this circumstance, judges could very well be saying or thinking the same things about a patient from his Rorschach protocol, but unfortunately they say or think the same things about too many other patients within the set. This leaves the impression that the Rorschach simply does not provide enough information on a patient to allow the interpreter to describe that patient as different from other patients. Or could it be that clinical psychology, in general, does not yet have the necessary semantic equipment to set apart, in descriptive prose, one person from another?

An inspection of the content of the 162 written Rorschach interpretations (4, Appendix D) leaves the authors with the impression that much work needs to be done, not only with respect to increasing the reliability of Rorschach interpretations, but also with refining our techniques of verbal communication.

Summary

The study was concerned with an evaluation of the reliability of clinical-type Rorschach interpretations. "Blind" Rorschach interpretations were supplied by 27 clinical psychologists, competent with the Rorschach test, to the Rorschach protocols of 18 neuropsychiatric patients. The judges attempted to match each others' written Rorschach interpretations according to the pattern of a two-way factorial design, with one systematic variable being the level of interpretation made in the reports and the other the homogeneity-heterogeneity of the patients giving the protocols.

Fifty-two per cent of the judges performed matchings which were better than chance at the .05 level, while 48 per cent of the judges turned in matching results which were not credited as being statistically significant. Performing as a group, the 27 psychologists matched report against protocol at a high level of statistical significance ($p < .001$), though the average number of correct matchings for the 27 judges fell below the number of hits necessary for a single

matching result to be considered statistically significant.

The results of the matchings on a heterogeneous group of patients were significantly superior to the groups comprised of more similar patients. There was no evidence favoring one level of interpretation over another in the written reports as regards inter-interpreter reliability.

The fact that 13 of the 27 judges achieved no better than chance performances and that the composite performance of the group of 27 judges as a whole was satisfactory leads to the tentative conclusion that a substantial majority of Rorschach reports have very little communication value, but that there is a large minority which achieve significant inter-judge reliability.

REFERENCES

1. CRONBACH, L. J. A validation design for qualitative studies of personality. *J. consult. Psychol.*, 1948, **12**, 365–374.
2. CRONBACH, L. J. Statistical methods applied to Rorschach scores: a review. *Psychol. Bull.*, 1949, **46**, 393–430.
3. CUMMINGS, S. T. An investigation of the reliability and validity of judgments of adjustment inferred from the Rorschach test performance. Unpublished doctors' dissertation, Univer. of Pittsburgh, 1950.
4. DATEL, W. E. Reliability of interpretations and consistency of determinant scoring in the Rorschach. Unpublished doctors' dissertation, Univer. of California at Los Angeles, 1954.
5. FELLER, W. *An introduction to probability theory and its applications.* Vol. 1. New York: John Wiley and Sons, Inc., 1950.
6. FISHER, R. A. *Statistical methods for research workers.* (10th Ed.) London: Oliver and Boyd, 1946.
7. GRANT, MARGUERITE Q., IVES, VIRGINIA, and RANZONI, JANE H. Re-

liability and validity of judges' ratings of adjustment on the Rorschach. *Psychol. Monogr.*, 1952, **66**, No. 2.
8. HERTZ, M. R., and RUBENSTEIN, B. B. A comparison of three "blind" Rorschach analyses. *Amer. J. Orthopsychiat.*, 1939, **9**, 295–315.
9. JONES, L. V., and FISKE, D. W. Models for testing the significance of combined results. *Psychol. Bull.*, 1953, **50**, 375–382.
10. KELLEY, D. M. Requirements for Rorschach training. *Rorsch. Res. Exch.*, 1942, **6**, 74–77.
11. KLOPFER, B., and KELLEY, D. M. *The Rorschach technique.* New York: World Book Co., 1942.
12. KRUGMAN, JUDITH I. A clinical validation of the Rorschach with problem children. *Rorsch. Res. Exch.*, 1942, **6**, 61–70.
13. MOOD, A. McF. *Introduction to the theory of statistics.* New York: McGraw-Hill, 1950.
14. PALMER, J. O. A dual approach to Rorschach validation: a methodological study. *Psychol. Monogr.*, 1951, **65**, No. 8.

15. Ross, H. L. The sources and reliabilities of interpretations in Rorschach test analysis. Unpublished doctors' dissertation, Univer. of California, Los Angeles, 1953.

16. Vernon, P. E. The evaluation of the matching method. *J. educ. Psychol.,* 1936, **27**, 1–17.

17. Vernon, P. E. The matching method applied to investigations of personality. *Psychol. Bull.,* 1936, **33**, 149–177.

The Rorschach and Central Nervous System Pathology: A Cross-Validation Study

Jerome Fisher, Thomas A. Gonda, and Kenneth B. Little

In the everyday work of a hospital neurology ward varied diagnostic instruments and procedures are used. At this hospital techniques and methods of clinical psychology, including the Rorschach, are also employed. Over a period of years several investigators (3, 5, 7) have presented empirically derived sets of signs whose *presence* in a given Rorschach protocol indicates brain disease; and recently Dorken and Kral (2) presented a set of 7 Rorschach signs which, when *absent* to a stated degree, indicates organic impairment. In addition, Dorken and Kral found that, "Response to the Rorschach Test (varied) in accordance with the localization of brain lesion."

Despite some question about the utility of the Rorschach in neurologic diagnostic problems referrable to brain disease, we were impressed by our early successful application of the Dorken and Kral signs to cases with proven brain pathology: they were correctly identifying more than 90% of these cases. Moreover, scoring absence rather than presence of signs seemed more meaningful clinically since individuals with brain disease are unable to perform certain tasks as well as those without it. As a result we decided to conduct a comparative study of 4 commonly used sets of Rorschach "signs" for the diagnosis of brain disease: those of Dorken and Kral, Piotrowski (5), Hughes (3) and Ross and Ross (7).

Method and Materials

Since the purpose of this study was to cross-validate the Rorschach as a diagnostic procedure in cases with central nervous system pathology, a procedure was sought which would be as representative as possible of everyday diagnostic problems in hospital neurology. The procedure selected resembled one suggested by Piotrowski (6) who, about 13 years ago, stated:

The best control group for the cerebral group would seem to be one composed of patients who had been seriously considered to have cerebral lesions and in whom the possibility of cerebral lesions was excluded after a longer period of observation.

At the Veterans Administration Hospital, San Francisco, a general medical hospital, a sample of 118 patients who fulfilled the following requirements was selected: (1) admission to the neurology

Reprinted by permission of the publisher and the authors from *The American Journal of Psychiatry*, 1955, **111**, 487–492.

ward; (2) sufficient hospitalization for complete neurologic evaluation; (3) white, male veterans; (4) administration of Rorschach examination during hospitalization.

A brief description of the methods of admission and medical work-up is as follows: Cases are first "screened" by an admitting physician who decides whether or not hospitalization is indicated. If indicated or in question, the patients are referred to the admitting physician of the specialty involved, in this instance neurology. If admitted to the neurology ward the patients are given a complete medical work-up, including history, physical and neurologic examination, routine laboratory procedures (complete blood count, blood serology, urinalysis, and chest x-ray), and indicated consultations as well as special laboratory procedures. In addition, for over 6 years psychological diagnostic examinations have been requested for a substantial number of neurology patients as part of a continuous "baseline" study. These examinations include a personal and social history, Rorschach, Minnesota Multiphasic Personality Inventory, Wechsler-Bellevue Intelligence Scale, and others.

The completed hospital records of the 118 patients were presented to 2 attending neurologists who served as criterion judges.[1] Each judge reviewed the 118 records independently and separated the cases into 2 groups—those in which, in his judgment, central nervous system pathology was present *rostral to the foramen magnum,* and those in which

[1] The records included available follow-up clinic notes as special reports such as autopsy material and letters from other hospitals. All 118 cases had been seen in consultation during hospitalization by one or both of the judges. The authors are very grateful to Drs. Henry Newman and Lewis A. Roberts for their cooperation and assistance in serving as judges in this investigation. We wish also to thank Dr. Howard V. Petzold, former chief of the Neurology Section of this hospital, for his participation and help during the initial phase of the study.

no central nervous system pathology existed *rostral to the foramen magnum.*[2] In addition, a 3-point rating scale was provided on which each judge could indicate the degree of certainty with which he categorized each case, *viz.,* "3-most certain," "2-certain," "1-least certain." This rating scale was provided in order to approximate the manner in which clinical diagnoses are made, allowing for ambiguities and variations inherent in case material. The data obtained from the judges were tabulated as follows: If a case was categorized as having central nervous system pathology rostral to the foramen magnum, the judge's rating of certainty was given a plus value, *viz.,* $+1, +2, +3,$ from "least certain" to "most certain," respectively; if a case was categorized as having no central nervous system pathology rostral to the foramen magnum, the rating of certainty was given a minus value, *viz.,* $-1, -2, -3,$ from "least certain" to "most certain," respectively. The assigned plus and/or minus values for each case were added algebraically, yielding a spectrum from $+6$ to -6, thus reflecting the judgments of both neurologists.

The distribution of combined ratings was divided as follows: Cases whose combined rating was from $+1$ to $+6$ were specified as the criterion "organic" group and those with a combined rating from 0 to -6 as the criterion "nonorganic" group. The 2 groups included 84 "organic" and 34 control "nonorganic" cases. Using 118 cases rather than only those comprising the extremes of the distribution ($+5, +6$ and $-5, -6$) was decided upon because the use of the entire sample allows for greater approximation to problems imposed by the nature of clinical practice where di-

[2] We acknowledge that the foramen magnum is an arbitrary anatomical dividing line but in view of current limited knowledge of behavioral correlates of the central nervous system, such a point of demarcation is, in our opinion, a reasonable one.

agnostic judgments are in reality on a continuum from least to most certain.

How well do the neurologists agree between themselves? In 86% of the cases the judges agreed as to the presence or absence of central nervous system pathology above the foramen magnum. The coefficient of correlation (phi) is .64. When the degree of certainty is included in these ratings a correlation coefficient of .76 is obtained. The discrepancy between the 2 measures results from the fact that the latter correlation takes into account the high percentage of agreement of the judges in the extreme cases. The correlation coefficient of .76 between the two judges indicates substantial agreement in their classification of the 118 cases as "organic" or "nonorganic" but does not indicate how reliable or consistent these paired judgments are. However, since the best clinical criterion is the consensus of a large number of competent neurologists, an estimate of the validity of these paired judgments can be made from our data by using the Spearman-Brown formula (4, p. 195). This formula will give an estimate of the degree of agreement between the present 2 neurologists and a theoretical larger number of neurologists. Substituting the appropriate figures in the formula, the estimated reliability coefficient for the criterion was found to be .93, indicating that considerable confidence may be placed in these judgments.

Since one of the requirements of the experimental design was that the control "nonorganic" group have as intensive a neurologic investigation as the "organic" group, a comparison was made of the work-up of both groups. Table 1 shows that, with the exception of the pneumoencephalogram, equivalent procedures were performed on at least 75% of all control cases, and exclusion of the skull x-ray raises the minimum to 88%. It would seem, therefore, that this requirement has been met. No statistically significant difference was found between

the average age of the control "nonorganic" and the "organic" groups. For the "organic" group the range of ages is 21–60 with a mean age of 38 years. For the control "nonorganic" group the range of ages is 22–57 with a mean age of 33 years.[3]

Each of the 118 cases had been administered the Rorschach during hospitalization by one or another of 32 clinical psychologists. These workers varied

TABLE 1. PERCENTAGE OF CASES IN CRITERION GROUPS ON WHOM NEUROLOGIC PROCEDURES WERE PERFORMED

	Organics	Nonorganics
Complete history	100	100
Physical and neurologic examination	100	100
Neurologic consultation	100	100
Routine laboratory procedures	100	100
Electroencephalogram	98	94
Lumbar punctures	93	88
Skull x-rays	93	77
Pneumoencephalogram (ventriculogram and/or arteriogram)	63	21

considerably in experience, competence, and skill with the Rorschach. It may be argued that such diversity increases the variation of error within the Rorschach protocols to some undetermined degree. Yet, the number and differences in the background of these psychologists, including the error variations, provide for the kind of representativeness of design proposed by Brunswik (1), and approximate the situation in clinical practice today. All Rorschach protocols were reviewed and the scoring checked by one of us prior to the categorization of the cases by the judges. The "organic signs," as presented in the literature by Pio-

[3] The results of the analysis of other variables such as nature and duration of chief complaints and final diagnoses will be presented in a later paper since they are not directly relevant to the present one.

TABLE 2.   FREQUENCY DIAGRAMS AND PHI CORRELATION COEFFICIENTS OF THE RELA-
TIONSHIP BETWEEN 4 RORSCHACH SYSTEMS OF DETECTING BRAIN PATHOLOGY AND
THE CRITERION JUDGMENTS OF 2 NEUROLOGISTS

| | | Criterion | | | | | Criterion | |
		Nonorganic	Organic				Nonorganic	Organic
Piotrowski	Organic	2	32	34	Hughes	Organic	3	31	34
System	Nonorganic	32	52	84	System	Nonorganic	31	53	84
		34	84	118			34	84	118
			ϕ .32**					ϕ .28**

| | | Criterion | | | | | Criterion | |
		Nonorganic	Organic				Nonorganic	Organic
Dörken	Organic	26	73	99	Ross and	Organic	6	33	39
and Kral	Nonorganic	8	11	19	Ross	Nonorganic	28	51	79
System		34	84	118	System		34	84	118
			ϕ .13					ϕ .20*

* $.05 < P > .01$
** $.01 < P$

trowski, Hughes, Dorken and Kral, and
Ross and Ross, were tabulated for each
protocol. The cut-off scores recommended by these authors were then
used to categorize each case as "organic"
or "nonorganic."

For the purpose of analysis, 5 scores
were thus available for each of the 118
subjects. Four of the scores were the
"organic" indices derived from the Rorschach protocols of the subjects and the
fifth score was the sum of the 2 criterion
judges' certainty ratings as to the presence or absence of organic brain pathology.

Results

Table 2 presents the results[4] of the
comparison of each of the Rorschach
diagnostic systems of organic brain pathology with the criterion described
above. The entry in the upper left-hand
cell of each diagram indicates the number of cases identified by the Rorschach
system as "organic," but which were

[4] The authors are indebted to Professor
Robert C. Tryon of the University of California for his help in the analysis of the data.

"nonorganic" according to the criterion;
the entry in the upper right-hand cell
indicates the number of cases identified
as "organic" by the Rorschach system
and also by the criterion; the lower left-
hand cell contains the number of cases
identified as "nonorganic" by the Rorschach system as well as by the criterion;
and the lower right-hand cell contains
the number of cases indicated as "nonorganic" by the Rorschach system but
as "organic" by the criterion.

Under each table is given the correlation coefficient (phi) of the relationship
between the Rorschach system and the
criterion. Although these correlation coefficients may be interpreted in a number
of ways, we present them as a measure
of the degree of association (validity
coefficient) between the Rorschach indices of brain pathology and the criterion judgments of brain pathology.

With the exception of the coefficient
obtained for Dorken and Kral, all are
statistically significant, indicating that 3
of the 4 systems detect individuals with
brain pathology with better than chance
accuracy.

The data in Table 3 indicate that the

TABLE 3.   PERCENT OF SUCCESSES AND FAILURES OF 4 RORSCHACH
SYSTEMS FOR DIAGNOSING BRAIN PATHOLOGY

	System				
	Piotrow-ski %	Hughes %	Dörken and Kral %	Ross and Ross %	Expected by Chance %
Organic	94	91	74	85	71
Nonorganic	38	37	42	35	29
Organic cases not detected (false negatives)	62	63	13	61	29
Nonorganic cases not detected (false positives)	6	9	76	18	71

Piotrowski and the Hughes systems have a high level of accuracy in detecting "organics," i.e., when a person receives an "organic" score on either of these two systems, the chances are very good (over 90%) that the criterion will agree that such is the case. The Dorken and Kral system on the other hand, does only slightly better than chance and the Ross and Ross system is intermediate. However, this accuracy of the Piotrowski and Hughes systems is at the expense of missing a substantial number of the cases identified as "organic" by the judges, i.e., a "nonorganic" score is not conclusive.

The remainder of the information in Table 3 can be interpreted in a similar fashion. However, when the percentages of various kinds of "success" and "failure" of the several Rorschach systems are weighted and averaged, one again has the correlation coefficient (phi), the best single index of over-all predictive ability, or the validity.

For comparison purposes, the validity coefficients, in the form of a phi correlation, of the 4 systems were computed from previously published data. Those for the Piotrowski, Ross and Ross, and Dorken and Kral systems are based on data presented by Dorken and Kral in their initial article (2); the coefficient for the Hughes system is based upon

data presented by him (3). Table 4 gives the comparison between these coefficients and those obtained in the present investigation. With the exception of the Piotrowski system all show a marked and significant drop in validity in the cross-validation.

TABLE 4.   COMPARISON OF THE VALID-
ITY COEFFICIENTS OF THE 4 RORSCHACH
DIAGNOSTIC SYSTEMS OBTAINED IN PRE-
VIOUS STUDIES WITH THOSE OBTAINED
IN THE PRESENT ONE

System	Phi (Previous Studies)	Phi (Present Study)
Piotrowski	.31 (N 130)	.32 (N 118)
Hughes	.84 (N 218)	.28 (N 118)
Dörken and Kral	.77 (N 130)	.12 (N 118)
Ross and Ross	.55 (N 130)	.20 (N 118)

Discussion

The data presented in the Results section indicate that 3 of the 4 Rorschach diagnostic systems (Piotrowski, Hughes, Ross and Ross) do distinguish with better than chance success persons with brain pathology from those without in a representative neurology ward population. Two of the Rorschach diagnostic systems are *highly* accurate (over 90%) when they identify cases as "organics."[5] Compared with previous studies, all except the Piotrowski system show marked and significant drops in validity.

The decrease in the validity coefficient of the Dorken and Kral system is particularly striking. Examination of the frequency diagram (Table 2) and the data in Table 3, indicates that the errors of prediction of this system in our sample are primarily false positives. To determine this point more definitely a sample of patients admitted to the medical wards was taken. This group was screened by a neuropsychiatrist who eliminated all cases with the slightest suggestion of nervous system pathology, providing a sample of 50 cases to whom Rorschachs had been administered during hospitalization. Tabulation of the Rorschach scores of these 50 cases indicates that 31 of them (62%) are classified "organic" by the Dorken and Kral system despite the careful screening. This percentage was then compared with the percentage of false positives secured by the Dorken and Kral system on the neurology ward sample (76%) and found not to be significantly different. It seems reasonable to conclude, therefore, that the large number of false positives resulting when the Dorken and Kral system was applied to the neurology ward population was due to the fact that it categorizes about 3 out of 5 hospital patients as "organics."

Part of the drop in the validity coefficients for the Hughes, Ross and Ross, and Dorken and Kral systems may be accounted for on purely statistical grounds. That is, some shrinkage in correlation coefficients usually occurs in cross-validation since the original coefficients invariably capitalize on chance

---

[5] In fact the Piotrowski system compares favorably with standard neurological techniques, e.g., EEG, in predicting the criterion. The results of correlating Rorschach and standard neurological techniques with the criterion will be presented in another paper.

factors in the data. However, the decrease in correlations here observed is much too large to be based upon this factor alone. The more important determinant would seem to be the difference between the populations used in the previous studies and that used in our investigation. As far as can be determined, all 4 systems used an experimental group composed of cases in which the brain pathology was overtly and grossly manifest. For control subjects, Ross and Ross used psychoneurotics and normals and Hughes and Dorken and Kral used psychoneurotics, normals and psychotics. Predictive systems derived from the comparison of such extreme groups make at least 2 implicit assumptions: (1) those characteristics that distinguish between patients with gross brain pathology and persons with no suggestion of brain pathology will also distinguish between grossly manifest and "pseudo" cases of brain pathology, and (2) persons with moderate or slight brain pathology will show the same psychological deficits as the more gross forms, although perhaps to a lesser degree. These assumptions are plausible but, we suspect, specious. The evidence from the present study indicates that the Dorken and Kral system was skewered primarily on the first assumption resulting in a large number of false positives (76%), whereas the other 3 systems were impaled on the second assumption resulting in a large number of false negatives (61–63%). The slight superiority of the Piotrowski system is apparently due to the use of some "pseudo-organic" cases as controls in the derivation of the various signs. Thus a few of his control cases approximate ours, all of whom were admitted with primary complaints, signs, or symptoms referrable to the nervous system. Parenthetically, the fact that the Hughes and Ross and Ross systems reach a statistically significant level of validity in this study may be explained on the basis that both include a large number of the signs originally listed by Piotrowski. The major distinguishing feature between these two systems and Piotrowski's is that in the former the signs are variably weighted rather than simply counted.

The discussion above is not intended to minimize the value of the Rorschach investigation of personality patterns in patients with brain pathology as compared with other patient groups. Rather the intention is to point out that the major problem in differential diagnosis in neurologic practice is not in distinguishing between grossly "organic" patients and normals, psychoneurotics in general, and psychotics. The primary clinical problem in practice is to distinguish patients who present a number of neurologic signs and symptoms based on organic pathology from others, who, while presenting a very similar pattern of signs and symptoms, do not, in fact, have such pathology. Consequently, a Rorschach "organic" diagnostic system to be of any practical value must necessarily be derived from a sample having such characteristics. Otherwise predictive systems derived with great care and scientific rigor will fail to discriminate adequately in the workaday world of the clinician.

Summary

Four Rorschach systems for determining the presence or absence of brain pathology are compared using a sample of 118 patients. Representativeness of the sample was secured by selecting only patients admitted to a neurology ward with complaints, signs, and/or symptoms referrable to the nervous system. The sample was divided, on the basis of the combined judgments of 2 neurologists, into cases presumably having brain pathology above the foramen magnum (84 cases) and those presumably having no such pathology (34 cases). The patients in both groups had undergone thorough and equivalent neurologic investigation. Results of the comparison of the 4 Rorschach systems with this criterion indicate that 3 of the 4 systems can distinguish between persons with and those without brain pathology with better than chance accuracy. The Piotrowski and Hughes systems are highly accurate (94% and 91%, respectively) when they identify a case as "organic" (only 6% and 9% false positives). However, when these systems identify a case as "nonorganic" the finding is inconclusive in that they fail to identify 62% of the organic cases (false negatives). The Ross and Ross system is slightly less accurate. The Dorken and Kral system yields results that can be explained in terms of chance and shows a systematic tendency to identify too many cases as "organics," resulting in 76% false positives. Only 1 of the 4 systems, Piotrowski's, maintains a validity level comparable to that obtained in previous studies.

The results are discussed and recommendations for derivation of more efficient Rorschach diagnostic systems advanced.

BIBLIOGRAPHY

1. Brunswik, E. *Systematic and representative design of psychological experiments.* Univer. of Calif. Press, 1949, No. 304.
2. Dorken, H., Jr., & Kral, V. A. The psychological differentiation of organic brain lesions and their localization by means of the Rorschach test. *Amer. J. Psychiat.*, 1952, **108**, 764.
3. Hughes, R. M. Rorschach signs for the diagnosis of organic pathology. *Rorschach Res. Exch.*, 1948, **12**, 165.
4. Peters, C. C., and Van Voorhis, W. *Statistical Procedures and their Mathematical Bases.* New York: McGraw-Hill, 1940.
5. Piotrowski, Z. A. On the Rorschach

method and its application in organic disturbances of the central nervous system. *Rorsch. Research Exch.*, 1936, **1**, 23.

6. PIOTROWSKI, Z. A. Positive and negative

Rorschach organic reactions. *Rorschach Research Exch.*, 1940, **4**, 147.

7. Ross, W. D., & Ross, S. Some Rorschach ratings of clinical value. *Rorschach Research Exch.*, 1944, **8**, 1.

Postdiction of the Outcome of Somatic Therapy from the Rorschach Records of Schizophrenic Patients

Charles N. Winslow and Isaac Rampersaud

In surveying the evidence concerning the accuracy of clinical psychologists in predicting recovery from psychogenic psychoses, particularly shizophrenia, by means of the Rorschach Projective Technique, it is apparent that there is a considerable variability. It was conceived by the authors, therefore, that another procedure might be to examine the Rorschach protocols of schizophrenic patients after the success or lack of success in recovery was specifically known. In effect, it seemed possible that by the process of postdiction the diagnostic factors in the protocols which differentiate the patients who are capable of recovery from those who are incapable of it can be determined for use in prediction. In viewing the literature it was observed that two different types of analysis have been used in the methods of diagnosing mental illness, namely, the diagnostic-sign approach and the content-analysis approach. In many of the previous investigations the sign approach has been used exclusively, and only within recent years has the analysis of content been utilized to an appreciable extent. As early as 1943, however, a Rorschach

Reprinted by permission of the American Psychological Association and the authors from the *Journal of Consulting Psychology*, 1964, **28**, 243–247.

Content Analysis Test was devised by (Elizur, 1949). Among studies which have been reported concerning the efficacy of the sign approach are those of (Berkowitz & Levine, 1953; Filmer & Bennett, 1952; Reiman, 1953; Rogers & Hammond, 1953; Rogers, Knauss, & Hammond, 1951). All of these report relatively little predictive value from the sign approach. In comparing the diagnostic-sign and content-analysis approaches in their investigations (Grauer, 1953; Powers & Hamlin, 1955; Watkins & Stauffacher, 1952; Zubin, 1954), reported that the latter seems to be more reliable than the former as a procedure. A comparison by (Goldman, 1960), between the two approaches in evaluating the improvement to be expected from schizophrenic patients receiving therapy demonstrated that the content-analysis was more reliable than the diagnostic-sign approach.

Procedure

In view of the information obtained from previous investigations, it was decided to use predominantly the content-analysis approach, together with rating scales, in the procedure to detect the improvement of schizophrenic patients who receive somatic treatment while they are hospitalized. First, a design similar to that described by (Klopfer, 1957) in ascertaining the differentiation of cancer patients from the standpoint of the rate of growth of cancerous tissue by analyzing their Rorschach protocols was employed in a pilot study. In this three psychologists who had had 5 or more years of experience in using it as a diagnostic tool were given 10 protocols of schizophrenic patients together with specific identification of the five who were improved and the five who were not improved. Each psychologist was then asked to designate the concepts which he used in differentiating the improved from the unimproved. Although there were some differences in the terminology which they reported, a conference with them resulted in agreement upon four factors, namely: Conflict, Control, Flexibility, and Strength of Drive. In defining these factors the information supplied by Beck (1936), Rapaport (1945), and Piotrowski (1957), was consulted. The definitions of each of these four factors as decided by the authors were as follows:

A. *Conflict.* Struggle between opposing forces within the individual involving themes of being blown apart, and inability to give good responses to a card after having done so previously.

B. *Control.* Capability of individual to regulate behavior, as shown by awareness of problem of fit, or ability to delay responses to chromatic color.

C. *Flexibility.* Ability of individual to shift his mental set, indicated by the inclusion of a variety of location choices, determinants, and content variables.

D. *Strength of Drive.* The presence of energy, striving, and initiative in the response given, as revealed by the number of responses per card, and presence of inanimate and strong extensor movements.

Since some quantitative evaluation of the extent to which these four diagnostic factors are present in a Rorschach protocol would seem to be advisable, 5-point rating scales were constructed with each of the factors. These scales ranged from the lowest point of 1 to the highest point of 5. In their ratings it was agreed that the judges would use the cutting point between 2 and 3, that is, Points 1 and 2 for unimproved and Points 3, 4, and 5, for improved. The efficacy of rating scales was evaluated from the work of (Grauer, 1953; Powers & Hamlin, 1955; Watkins & Stauffacher, 1952).

The specific cues which were used in each of the 5-point ratings assigned to Conflict were as follows:

Rating

1. Evidence of archaic mechanisms in confronting conflict such as denial, regression, and withdrawal into fantasy, etc. Absolutely no recognition of conflict.

2. Indifferent attitude towards conflict; a feeble attempt toward its resolution.

3. Recognition of the presence of opposing forces, with some attempt toward equilibrium, which frequently fails.

4. Strong reaction to conflict, and the taking of active measures towards its solution, which in spite of effort may occasionally fail.

5. Very strong reactions to conflict with variety of approaches to solve it utilized, which may very seldom lead to failure. One example of a response rated as 5 on this scale was a response given to Card I: "Two women in the middle being pulled asunder by two witches. They certainly look determined to tear her apart."

The specific cues upon which each of the 5 points on the rating scale for Control were as follows:

Rating

1. Loose percepts, bizarre responses, loss of contact with reality with no attempt to recover.

2. Some, but fleeting, capacity for control.

3. Considerable capacity for control with episodic failure of reality testing; occasionally recovers.

4. Good control with some insight into discrepancy between percept and cards; usually recovers.

5. Very good control with high degree

of perceptual accuracy; always recovers. A response which illustrates the Point 5 rating on this scale was this one on Card VII: "Two delicately carved busts of women facing each other. They have head dresses on with a feather sticking up."

The specific cues which identified each of the 5 points on the rating scale for Flexibility were as follows:

Rating

1. Stereotype, perseveration, and an affective rigidity.

2. Some, but minor, indications of ideational and affective freedom.

3. An increased degree of ideational and affective movement.

4. Exercises high degree of adaptive reactions and does not rely on any one defense mechanism.

5. Very high degree of adaptability; employs a variety of defense mechanisms. The rating of five points on this scale, as mentioned previously, involved the presence of an extensive variety of location choices, of determinant factors, and a number of different objects in the content.

In rating the five points on the rating scale for Strength of Drive the specific cues were as follows:

Rating

1. Apathy, indifference, "burnt out-ness."

2. Minor indications of striving, generally passive, takes very little initiative.

3. Definitely takes some initiative, shows considerable indications of drive, but may be weakened under stress.

4. Strong fighting efforts, quite concerned over himself and his environment.

5. Very strong indications of striving, takes aggressive action. One criterion for assigning Point 5 on this scale was average or more than average the number of responses in the total protocol.

After standardization of the diagnostic factors and the characteristics to be used in assigning the points on the rating scales at which each of these factors was rated according to Rorschach records, 60 schizophrenic patients were selected from the hospital files. The criteria which were previously decided

upon as essential for the investigation were first, that a Rorschach had been administered to each patient upon admission and that the final diagnosis established by psychologists and psychiatrists in consultation was schizophrenia; second, that all patients had received somatic therapy, that is, electric or insulin shock, during their hospitalization; thirdly, that it was possible to secure information concerning the patients from relatives. Although very few of the patients had received the same number of shock treatments, the judgment of the attending psychiatrist concerning the number that would benefit each patient was accepted.

The 60 schizophrenic patients who were selected were all within the age range from 18 to 45 years, since after the age of 45 patients may have schizophrenic symptoms within the framework of a mental disorder associated with the aged, such as Alzheimer's disease or arteriosclerosis. The records were also checked to ascertain that no other major disability was diagnosed except schizophrenia. Care was taken not to include any patients who had mental deficiency, alcoholism, or some organic defect, for example.

The 60 schizophrenic patients who were selected included 30 who had shown noticeable improvement from somatic treatment and 30 who seemed to be unimproved. The criterion used in differentiating the improved from the unimproved patient was that he had remained in a state of uninterrupted remission for a period of at least a year following his discharge from the hospital. Specifically, these were the factors applied in identifying the unimproved: (a) Patient had been readmitted and received further somatic treatment within 1 year following his discharge from the hospital, or (b) had been transferred to a custodial treatment hospital. The names of the patients or any identifying data were omitted when the Rorschach records were presented to the three psychologists, and no statement regarding the status of the patients as to who had improved or who had not.

Prior to considering the results of the investigation, it is informative to demonstrate the extent of interjudge agreement in rating the 60 patients on the four scales, specifically Conflict, Control, Flexibility, and Strength of Drive. In Table 1 are presented the coefficients of

rated, therefore, by Points 3, 4, and 5 on the scales, and unimprovement by Ratings 1 and 2.

For the purpose of determining statistically the degree of accuracy of the three judges in rating the four factors with respect to the differentiation of the improved from the unimproved patients, chi-squares were computed and are presented in Table 2. It will be observed

TABLE 1. CORRELATION COEFFICIENTS OF INTERJUDGE RELIABILITY ON THE FOUR SCALES OF CONFLICT, CONTROL, FLEXIBILITY, AND STRENGTH OF DRIVE

Conflict ratings	Judge 1 and 2	.71
	Judge 1 and 3	.65
	Judge 2 and 3	.48
Control ratings	Judge 1 and 2	.66
	Judge 1 and 3	.64
	Judge 2 and 3	.40
Flexibility ratings	Judge 1 and 2	.52
	Judge 1 and 3	.69
	Judge 2 and 3	.49
Strength of drive ratings	Judge 1 and 2	.65
	Judge 1 and 3	.64
	Judge 2 and 3	.53

TABLE 2. CHI-SQUARE VALUES FOR EACH OF THE THREE JUDGES ON EACH OF THE FOUR VARIABLES WITH ONE DEGREE OF FREEDOM

Variables	Chi-Square Values			
	Judge 1	Judge 2	Judge 3	p
Conflict	13.44	12.13	9.89	$< .01$
Control	22.22	10.55	9.87	$< .01$
Flexibility	12.12	7.33	16.15	$< .01$
Strength of drive	8.33	11.09	13.20	$< .01$

Note—A 2×2 was utilized by combining Ratings 1 and 2 in one cell and Ratings 3, 4, and 5 in the other cell. The Yates correction for continuity was applied since there was only one degree of freedom.

correlation of the judges with each other on the scales. From this Table it is evident that the amount of interjudge agreement ranged from a correlation of .40 between Judges 2 and 3 on rating "Control" to .71 between Judges 1 and 2 in rating "Conflict." Considering the number of patients involved, all of the coefficients are significantly high.

Results and Discussion

In respect to the five points included on the four rating scales, it was decided, as stated previously, that the cutting point between the improved and unimproved would be between Ratings 2 and 3. This was in accordance with the statistical procedure used by Powers and Hamlin (1955). Improvement was

that all of the chi-square values for all of the four variables rated by each of the three judges is significant beyond the .01 level of confidence.

For the purpose of determining the extent of the agreement of the three judges with the classification which had previously been made by the hospital, biserial correlation coefficients for each of the four factors rated were computed. The results are presented in Table 3. Since the standard error of the biserial correlation varies with the size of the coefficient, the size of the sample, and the proportion of cases falling into each dichotomy, this was computed in order to determine the significance of each coefficient. Because biserial correlation coefficients are assumed to be normally distributed, coefficients greater than .258 times the standard error are significant at the .01 level of confidence. It is found from observing Table 3 that all of the coefficients meet this criterion, and range from a low of .48 for Judge 2 in rating "Flexibility" to .81 for Judge 1 in rating "Control." Of the three judges, Judge 1 had consistently the highest biserial correlations between his ratings and the hospital classification, and Judge 2 consistently the lowest.

TABLE 3. BISERIAL CORRELATION BE-
TWEEN JUDGES' RATINGS AND KNOWN
GROUP CLASSIFICATION OF EACH OF
THE FOUR SCALES

Scales	Judges	r_b	SE
Conflict	Judge 1	.75	.154
	Judge 2	.58	.187
	Judge 3	.66	.155
Control	Judge 1	.81	.153
	Judge 2	.57	.157
	Judge 3	.63	.154
Flexibility	Judge 1	.72	.154
	Judge 2	.48	.159
	Judge 3	.60	.155
Strength of drive	Judge 1	.65	.156
	Judge 2	.57	.157
	Judge 3	.66	.155

From the statistical evidence that is presented in the previous section of this report, it is evident that clinical psychologists who are experienced with the Rorschach technique are rather accurate in their postdiction of the outcome of somatic therapy administered to schizophrenic patients. It is recognized that the number of psychologists utilized is relatively small, however, and that they were presented with diagnostic factors which had been predetermined. It is also possible that there was some transfer effect occurring with each judge as he rated each of the four factors.

Inspection of the specific ratings of the judges on the four factors Conflict, Control, Flexibility, and Strength of Drive reveals that the ratings for the improved patients were skewed to the left on each factor with the exception

of Judge 3 on Control and Judges 2 and 3 on Flexibility. It also shows that the ratings on each factor were skewed to the right in the case of all three judges when rating the unimproved patients on all four factors. From this it is apparent that the judges were fairly consistent in their ratings of the four factors. One question which is not answered, however, is whether the four factors actually constituted independent dimensions in the diagnosis of the degree of impairment in schizophrenic patients. A second limitation of the investigation is that there was no attempt to differentiate the particular type of schizophrenia which the patients had. A third limitation is that only two dichotomies were provided for the judges, namely, improved or unimproved, and that the rating scales were rather narrow. Further research would be likely to determine the reliability of the results if these limitations were excluded or minimized. It is conceivable, however, that since this technique of diagnosing by postdiction of the severity of schizophrenia was fairly accurate, it might also be used in the prognosis of recovery from this type of mental illness.

Summary

The Rorschach protocols of 60 schizophrenic patients previously hospitalized were presented to 3 psychologists with the instructions to differentiate the 30 patients who had improved from the 30 who had not. The 4 factors of Conflict, Control, Flexibility, and Strength of Drive were selected and defined by the investigators together with the psychologists. Each patient was rated on a 5-point scale with the content analysis approach used primarily. The accuracy of all 3 psychologists in differentiating between the 2 groups of patients on all 4 of the factors was found to be significant beyond the .01% level of confidence according to the chi-square values obtained.

REFERENCES

AULD, F., & ERON, L. D. Use of Rorschach scores to predict whether patients will continue psychotherapy. *J. consult. Psychol.*, 1953, **17**, 104–109.

BECK, S. J. *Rorschach's test.* Vol. 2. New York: Grune & Stratton, 1946.

BERKOWITZ, M., & LEVINE, J. Rorschach scoring categories as diagnostic "signs." *J. consult. Psychol.*, 1953, **17**, 110–112.

BIALICK, I., & HAMLIN, R. M. The clinician as judge: Details of procedure in judging projective material. *J. consult. Psychol.*, 1954, **18**, 239–244.

CUMMINGS, T. S. The clinician as judge: Judgments of adjustments from Rorschach single card performance. *J. consult. Psychol.*, 1954, **18**, 243–247.

ELIZUR, A. Content analysis of the Rorschach with regard to anxiety and hostility. *J. proj. Tech.*, 1949, **13**, 247–284.

FILMER-BENNETT, G. T. Prognostic indices in the Rorschach records of hospitalized patients. *J. abnorm. soc. Psychol.*, 1952, **47**, 502–506.

GIBLEY, R. G., STOTSKY, B. A., MILLER, E. W., & MILLER, D. R. Validation of Rorschach criteria for prediction of therapy. *J. consult. Psychol.*, 1954, **18**, 185–191.

GOLDMAN, ROSALINE. Changes in Rorschach performance and clinical improvement in schizophrenia. *J. consult. Psychol.*, 1960, **24**, 403–407.

GRAUER, D. Prognosis in paranoid schizophrenia on the basis of the Rorschach. *J. consult. Psychol.*, 1953, **17**, 199–205.

HAMLIN, R. M. The clinician as judge: Implications of a series of studies. *J. consult. Psychol.*, 1954, **18**, 233–238.

KLOPFER, B. Psychological variables in human cancer. *J. proj. Tech.*, 1957, **21**, 331–340.

KURTZ, A. K. A research test of the Rorschach test. *Personnel Psychol.*, 1948, **1**, 41–51.

PIOTROWSKI, Z. A. *Perceptanalysis.* New York: Macmillan, 1957.

POWERS, W. T., & HAMLIN, R. M. Relationship between diagnostic category and deviant verbalizations on the Rorschach. *J. consult. Psychol.*, 1955, **19**, 120–124.

RAPAPORT, D. *Diagnostic psychological testing.* Vol. 2. Chicago: Year Book Publisher, 1945.

REIMAN, G. W. The effectiveness of Rorschach elements in the discrimination between neurotics and ambulatory schizophrenic subjects. *J. consult. Psychol.*, 1953, **17**, 25–31.

ROGERS, L. S., KNAUSS, JOANNE, & HAMMOND, K. R. Prediction continuation in therapy by means of the Rorschach test. *J. consult. Psychol.*, 1951, **15**, 368–371.

ROGERS, L. S., & HAMMOND, K. R. Prediction of the results of therapy by means of the Rorschach test. *J. consult. Psychol.*, 1953, **17**, 8–15.

STORMENT, C. T., & FINNEY, B. C. Projection and behavior: A Rorschach study of assaultive mental patients. *J. proj. Tech.*, 1953, **17**, 349–360.

WATKINS, J. C., & STAUFFACHER, J. C. An index of pathological thinking in the Rorschach. *J. proj. Tech.*, 1952, **16**, 276–286.

ZUBIN, J. Failures of the Rorschach Technique. *J. proj. Tech.*, 1954, **18**, 303–315.

Threshold for the Perception of Human Movement in Inkblots

Frank Barron

One of the variables conceptualized and scored as part of the Rorschach Psychodiagnostic (7) is the tendency of the subject to perceive human beings, or human-like animals, engaged in characteristically human activity in the blots (the *M* response). This response tendency is said to go along with a bent toward introversion rather than extraversion. Introversion has been variously defined; in general, it may be conceived of as a tendency to take thought rather than action, to experience vicariously and in fantasy rather than in real life and directly, and to create through the arrangement of symbols rather than through the arrangement of objects which stand for nothing but themselves.

The aim of the present investigation was to study the personality correlates of the human movement response tendency in a research situation which would

This research is supported in part by the United States Air Force under Contract No. AF 18 (600)-8, monitored by Technical Director, Detachment No. 7 (Officer Education Research Laboratory), Air Force Personnel and Training Research Center, Maxwell Air Force Base, Alabama. Permission is granted for reproduction, translation, publication, use, and disposal in whole and in part by or for the United States Government. Personal views or opinions expressed or implied in this publication are not to be construed as necessarily carrying the official sanction of the Department of the Air Force or of the Air Research and Development Command.

Reprinted by permission of the American Psychological Association and the author from *Journal of Consulting Psychology*, 1955, **19**, 33–38.

make it possible to obtain independent evidence concerning the personalities of the subjects. Such a situation is provided by the living-in assessment method, with its emphasis upon observation of the subjects through several days of informal social interaction, lifelike situational tests, group discussions, improvisations, group games, and the like. This makes it possible to discover how persons who have much or little readiness to perceive human movement in inkblots are described by skilled psychological observers who become acquainted with them but not with their test scores.

The measure of readiness to perceive human movement in inkblots was especially constructed for this study, and represents an attempt to supplement the Rorschach test itself as an instrument of observation when Rorschach theory is in question. As users of the test know, the Psychodiagnostic is very complex, both stimulus-wise and in its scoring scheme, and it does not lend itself well to any attempt to isolate variables and to separate out their correlational components. While this complexity is important to the test as a vehicle for clinical observation, it contributes to certain psychometric shortcomings and unnecessary difficulties when the verification of theory is the chief concern.

One important difficulty with the scoring scheme is that the number of responses varies widely for different subjects. Productivity is itself an important variable, of course, but the present method of obtaining a measure of it tends to confound the evaluation of other measures which may be equally important. Subjects now cannot be compared in terms of absolute incidence of a given type of response, since this is partly a function of total number of responses. Furthermore, subjects cannot be compared in terms of *relative* incidence, for relative incidence of response in a given category varies in some nonlinear and as yet undetermined fashion with total number of responses. This in turn is dependent to some extent on stimulus properties of the blots; there is clearly a limitation to the number of responses which can be given in any single category, and after a certain point in the production of responses the more limited categories begin to suffer relative to the others.

What is needed, then, is a method of keeping the number of responses more or less constant for all subjects, while yet providing considerable opportunity for the subject's response tendencies to emerge. At the same time, stimulus strength should be weighted properly in evaluating response strength; one difficulty with the Rorschach measure of M tendency is that it is a simple count of the number of human movement percepts which are verbalized by the subject, without regard for the power of the stimulus to evoke a human movement response in the average person.

Some of the difficulties may be met if these prescriptions are followed: (a) increase the number of blots; (b) score only one response, the first, to each blot; (c) take systematic account of the relationship between stimulus strength and response tendency by employing the conventional experimental index of this relationship, response threshold; (d) isolate the main Rorschach variables and study them one at a time before attempting to study them all together.

The rationale of these prescriptions is simple and clear. An increase in the number of blots should achieve more representativeness on the stimulus side and more total-score reliability (since reliability may be increased, up to a point, by increasing test length). Scoring of only one response to each blot makes the absolute number of responses in each scoring category comparable from subject to subject, and makes feasible the use of some sort of standard score, such as Z scores, so that the individual subject's performance may be immediately referred to that

of the general population.[1] The weighting of stimulus strength in evaluating response strength is essentially a more differentiated way of scoring, comparable to the use of refined rather than crude weights in prediction; the addition of the concept of threshold makes the human movement phenomenon more assimilable to established knowledge and methods in experimental psychology, which is all to the good so far as Rorschach theory is concerned. Finally, the study of variables in isolation, however unholistic it may seem, may really be the best possible foundation for the understanding of variables in interaction.

In the present study, then, the variable under consideration is threshold for perception of human movement in inkblots; the aim of the study is to construct a measure of threshold and to ascertain its personality correlates; the general method of personality research employed is the living-in assessment method.

Construction of the Measure of Threshold

The model for the construction of a measure of threshold for perception of human movement is the conventional stimulus series used to determine response thresholds in such sense modalities as the auditory, olfactory, tactile, and the like. Although stimulus strength or intensity is not determinable from physical properties of the stimulus in the case of inkblots, this is no great loss so long as relative frequencies of response can be established in large samples and with some stability. By arranging inkblots of known relative frequency in a

[1] It might be pointed out incidentally that Rorschach ratios, such as M: Sum C, may be much more meaningful if they are ratios of Z scores rather than absolute scores; Z ratios would be free of the often unrecognized and cumbersome assumption underlying absolute score ratios, viz., that the blots themselves present precisely equal opportunity for the two contrasting experience-types, introversive and extratensive, to manifest themselves.

regularly graduated series, with p values ranging from .00 to 1.00, a measure analogous to the usual perceptual stimulus series is constructed. The subject's threshold for human movement is then the ordinal position of that blot in the series at which he first gives a human movement response.

This ideal design was not carried out exactly as projected in the present study, largely because of time pressures in the scheduling of the assessments. One hundred and fifty achromatic inkblots had been constructed, using 4- by 6-inch sheets of white paper, which were then mounted on stiff cardboard of the same dimensions. The plan had been to select 26 blots from the 150, on the basis of observed frequencies, in such a manner as to make a series with graduations of approximately .04. It became necessary, however, to select the blots on the basis of observations in a small preliminary sample, and to order them initially in terms of observed frequencies in that sample. For this reason, the threshold score finally assigned to the assessed subjects was based on the relative frequency of M response to each blot *in the assessed sample itself*. This design is somewhat inferior to what was first intended, but it still fills the prescriptions specified for construction of a measure which would overcome some of the difficulties inherent in the Rorschach measure of M tendency.

As it turned out, the preliminary standardization yielded a fairly stable stimulus series. The rank-difference correlation between the order of presentation based on frequencies in the preliminary standardization group and the final ordering of the blots in terms of frequencies observed in the assessed sample is .85. The stability of the final ordering of the blots in the rather homogeneous Air Force officer sample is indicated by the rank-difference correlation between a rank order based on observed frequencies in the first 50 cases and a rank order based on observed

frequencies in the final 50 cases: rho is .99. For this homogeneous sample, the M-evocative power of inkblots is remarkably stable.

The possible range of scores for individual subjects is, of course, from 1 to 27 (the score of 27 being assigned to subjects who do not see M in any one of the 26 blots). The expected range, considering the method of construction of the measure, is from 2 (since no subject should see M on the first blot) to 26. The actual observed range was from 2 to 25, with the mean at 13. The form of the distribution was approximately rectangular.

The Sample and the Method of Study

The subjects in this study were 100 captains in the U. S. Air Force. As a group they were above average in intelligence, in education, in physical health, and in personal stability. The age range was from 27 to 50, with a mean age of 33. All of the subjects were men. All but three were married, and most of them had at least two children. In pre-army socioeconomic background they tended to be lower middle class. The majority of these officers were combat veterans, and many of them had been decorated for valor in World War II. In most ability measures they scored well above average, and were less variable than men-in-general.

The subjects were seen in groups of ten for three full days at the Institute house. The method of study placed considerable emphasis upon observation of the subjects in informal social interaction. The assessment staff psychologists sat down to meals with the subjects, took part in a social hour before dinner, and in general were participant observers throughout the three days of living-in assessment. Situational tests, interviews, group discussions, improvisations, charades, and the like were included in the assessment program, so that the social characteristics of the subjects had much opportunity to manifest themselves, and the raters were in a position to observe significant behavior.

Observations made by staff members during the three days of study were condensed and rendered easily susceptible of statistical analysis chiefly through two techniques: a set of 76 statements descriptive of personal functioning and permitting the expression of clinical inferences, and an adjective check list (3) consisting of common, personally descriptive adjectives. Both techniques were used by staff members at the conclusion of the three days of assessment to sum up their impressions of each subject.

The 76 statements were sorted on a 9-point scale (a so-called *Q* sort), the frequencies at each point being such as to make the final distribution conform closely to the normal curve. The 300 adjectives were checked simply as characteristic or not characteristic of the given subject. The *Q*-sort composite was obtained by averaging the placements of the items by four staff members, and then redistributing these averaged values on a normal curve. The adjective composite consisted of all adjectives which had been checked as characteristic of a subject by three or more raters.

These descriptions and ratings were of course given without knowledge of the objective test performances of the subjects. No rater knew the *M* threshold of any of the subjects at the time the ratings were made.

In addition to these descriptions based on social observation of the subjects, information is available concerning life-history factors. Each subject was interviewed for two hours by a psychiatrist or clinical psychologist (who did not otherwise participate in the assessment), and again a check-list method was used to summarize impressions from the interview. The life-history check list contained sections having to do with the subject's recollection of himself as a child, his imagery of his parents, his favorite games, his playmates, and so on.

Finally, certain objective test measures were obtained on all subjects. These included measures of general intelligence,

of originality, of personal stability, and of social attitudes. Scores from all of them were available for correlation with *M* threshold.

Correlates of M Threshold

It should be remembered, of course, that high scorers on the threshold measure are those with less readiness to perceive human movement; lower threshold means greater disposition to give an *M* response.

The observer adjective descriptions which are significantly (.05 level) related to threshold for *M* when the first quartile of the distribution (threshold scores from 2 to 8) is compared with the fourth quartile (threshold scores from 18 to 25) are as follows:

Early M *response (low threshold)*
    intelligent
    fair-minded
    mild
    anxious
    mannerly
    inventive
    interests wide

Late M *response (high threshold)*
    practical
    stubborn
    simple
    masculine
    arrogant

The composite *Q*-sort descriptions yielded the following items with significant (.05 level) differences between the groups:

Early M *response (low threshold)*
1. Highly cathects intellectual activity; values cognitive pursuits.
2. Gets along well in the world as it is; is socially appropriate in his behavior.
3. Is introspective; concerned with his self as object; frequently self-aware.
4. Has high degree of intellectual ability.

Late M *response (high threshold)*
1. Has narrow range of interests.
2. Allows personal bias, spite, or dogma-

tism to enter into his judgment of issues.
3. Prefers action to contemplation.
4. Is rigid; inflexible in thought and action.

At this point, an important discrepancy between observers' descriptions and actual test measures should be noted. Although subjects with greater M tendency were described as inventive, intelligent, and broader in their interests, correlations between M threshold and actual measures of intelligence, general information, and originality in problem solving were all in the neighborhood of zero. The aptitude tests used included the Terman Concept Mastery Test,[2] the Wesman Personnel Classification Test (9), the Arthur Stencil Design Test (1), the Idea Classification Test,[3] and the Test of Mechanical Comprehension (2). A 180-item General Information survey constructed by Gough (4) was also employed. Several tests from the Guilford Creativity battery (6), including the Unusual Uses, Plot Titles, Consequences, Match Problems, Gestalt Transformation, and Controlled Association tests, were used; none showed a significant relationship to M threshold. The failure to find such relationships occurred both when M threshold was correlated with these measures for the entire 100 cases, and also when the first quartile on M was compared with the fourth quartile.

What these facts plainly say is that subjects with greater readiness to perceive M appear to psychological observers to be more intelligent, more inventive, and broader in their interests in social situations, but that in controlled testing situations, when problem-solving activity is called for, M threshold is unrelated to test scores. If we assume the

[2] For a general description of the form of this test, which is as yet unpublished, see Terman and Oden (8). The test was made available through the generosity of Dr. Terman.
[3] Acknowledgment is made to Educational Testing Service for making this test available prior to its publication.

validity of the test measures, the most direct explanation of the discrepant adjective and Q-sort descriptions would seem to be that psychologists falsely attribute greater intelligence to persons who manifest more tendency to introspect, to take thought rather than to take action. A check on this hypothesis seems to support it: the Q-sort item "Has a high degree of intellectual ability" correlates .45 with the item "is introspective; concerned with his self as object; frequently self-aware." The latter item, however, correlates only .11 with the Arthur Stencil Design Test, .02 with the Idea Classification Test, .26 with the Wesman Personnel Classification Test, and .27 with the Terman Concept Mastery Test. Introspection thus appears to be weighted unduly by the psychological staff in judging intelligence. Perhaps, after all, the more "thoughtful" person is not always the more intelligent person, thoughtfulness being an intellectual disposition rather than an intellectual ability.

Some evidence concerning developmental factors related to M tendency is furnished by the life-history interview material. The subjects with low thresholds for M described themselves significantly (.05 level) more often as quiet and self-conscious during their childhoods. They were also less interested in sports, and took less part in rough-and-tumble play, than high-threshold subjects; the latter more often described themselves as having been active, and characterized their childhood as happy.

There are some possible related differences between the two groups of subjects in their descriptions of their mothers: the adjectives showing differences significant at the .05 level are nervous, protective, conservative, punishing, and worrying, all of them being more characteristic of the mothers of low-threshold subjects. The general picture we get from the life-history interview material is that the person who in adulthood has more disposition to see human movement in the inkblots was in childhood somewhat shy, sensitive, and overprotected, or even maternally dominated. In relation to this, it is of interest that the Femininity key of the California Psychological Inventory (5) correlates —.26 with *M* threshold (the more *M*-disposed subjects obtaining higher femininity scores).

In brief, readiness to see human movement in the inkblots seems to go along with *introspectiveness, thoughtfulness, fair-mindedness* (suggesting ethical discrimination based on cognitive principles), and a *high valuation of the intellectual processes,* based perhaps upon a certain inhibition of activity and greater recourse to fantasy in childhood. Such persons are seen in adulthood as relatively *mild, mannerly,* and even *anxious* as compared with the *practical, masculine,* and *simple* individuals who have less tendency to see movement in the blots. It appears too that an extreme lack of *M* tendency may at times be nonadaptive: the Q-sort items "is rigid; inflexible in thought and action," and "allows personal bias, spite, or dogmatism to enter into his judgment of issues" point clearly to the kinds of liabilities which accompany the static perceptual attitude. This is seen as issuing on occasion in *stubbornness* and *arrogance.*

Discussion

Rorschach's claim that movement responses are produced most abundantly by persons who "function more in the intellectual sphere, whose interests gravitate more towards their intrapsychic living rather than towards the world outside themselves" (7, p. 64), seems in general to be supported by these findings. In a sense, the fact that *M* threshold is unrelated to measured intelligence strengthens rather than weakens this conclusion. If two groups of subjects are equal in intelligence, but one group is characteristically described as more intelligent, more introspective, more concerned with intellectual activity, and more given to contemplation than to

action, then it seems fair to say that these latter individuals "function *more*" (not necessarily better) in the "intellectual sphere."

Rorschach himself, of course, thought of this tendency as "a component of intelligence" (7, p. 63). The production of many movement responses is, he claims, one of the characteristics of "intelligent subjects." Since this observation was based upon his own estimates of his subjects' intelligence, it may be that he was misled by the same occupational prejudice displayed by the psychologists of the staff of this Institute. (Rorschach was not above injecting his own biases rather freely into his experimental observations, as witness his entertaining preoccupation with "pedants" and "grumblers," two diagnostic categories which appear more frequently in the Psychodiagnostic than would seem warranted by ordinary nosological usage.)

In some ways, it seems preferable, from a psychological assessment standpoint, to have a well-defined and measurable variable which is entirely stylistic in character and free of correlation with measures of general ability. Where style is important in effectiveness of performance, such variables may add more to a prediction equation than do variables which are loaded with intelligence factors. This is especially true where personal interaction is concerned, and where certain combinations of styles of performance work better than others. Two-person situations with subjects selected especially for similarities or differences of style offer interesting possibilities for tests of hypotheses concerning the conditions which make for constructive and empathic interaction versus those which make for destructive, stultifying relationships. Rorschach suggests, for example, that a person with strong introversive tendencies can hardly be understood at all by a person whose bent is strongly extratensive; with adequate measures of such tendencies in perception, experimental verification of such a hypothesis would not be difficult.

The present measure of M threshold is as yet in a preliminary stage of development. It is evident that Guttman scale analysis is made to order for the psychometric goal of accurate placement of an individual in relation to others on such a dimension as M tendency. It seems quite possible that other Rorschach factors could be equally well measured, and that a series of separate tests could be produced which would be much better, from the point of view of perception theory and research, than the instrument with which Rorschach made his initial observations. He himself, of course, was quite open to such innovations, and indeed suggested a number of interesting possibilities in his classical monograph.

Summary

A measure of threshold for the human movement response was constructed by arranging inkblots of known M-evocative power in a regularly graduated series. The final series consisted of 26 blots, selected from a group of 150 blots for which the relative frequency of M response was known. The subject's threshold score, based on the final arrangement of the 26 blots, was given by the ordinal position of that blot in the series at which he first verbalized a human movement response.

The correlates of M threshold were studied in a sample of 100 military officers who took part in three days of living-in assessment, and who had been described by staff psychologists through the use of Q-sort and adjective checklist techniques. The psychologists did not, of course, know the M threshold scores of the subjects. It was found that M threshold was uncorrelated with measures of intelligence, originality, and associational fluency, but that subjects who displayed considerable readiness to give human movement responses were considered by staff psychologists to be more intelligent, inventive, introspective, contemplative, and the like. The conclusion was that the human movement tendency is a stylistic variable, and that it does indeed relate, as Rorschach thought it did, to a preference for "intrapsychic living" as opposed to interest in action, practical affairs, and "the world outside."

REFERENCES

1. ARTHUR, G. *A point scale of performance tests.* New York: Psychological Corp., 1947.
2. BENNETT, G. K., & FRY, D. E. *Test of mechanical comprehension.* New York: Psychological Corp., 1947.
3. GOUGH, H. G. *Predicting success in graduate training.* Berkeley: Univer. of California, Institute of Personality Assessment and Research, 1950.
4. GOUGH, H. G. *The General Information Survey.* Berkeley: Univer. of California, Institute of Personality Assessment and Research, 1953.
5. GOUGH, H. G. *A preliminary guide for the use and interpretation of the California Psychological Inventory.* Berkeley: Univer. of California, Institute of Personality Assessment and Research, 1954.
6. GUILFORD, J. P., WILSON, R. C., CHRISTENSEN, P. R., & LEWIS, D. J. A factor-analytic study of creative thinking: I. Hypotheses and descriptions of tests. *Rep. Psychol. Lab., Univer. Southern Calif.,* 1951, No. 3.
7. RORSCHACH, H. *Psychodiagnostics.* Bern: Huber, 1942.
8. TERMAN, L. M., & ODEN, M. H. *The gifted child grows up.* Palo Alto: Stanford Univer. Press, 1947.
9. WESMAN, A. G. *Personnel classification test.* New York: Psychological Corp., 1947.

Autonomic Response Specificity and Rorschach Color Responses

John I. Lacey, Dorothy E. Bateman, and Ruth Van Lehn

The purpose of this report is two-fold: (a) to present some data concerning intraindividual differences in the degree of activation of different physiological functions in response to stress; and (b) to illustrate the significance of such patterning of response for researches that seek to establish relationships between autonomic reactions and personality. In this paper the relationship studied is between physiological response to stress and an index of "emotionality" derived from the Rorschach Inkblot Test.

Cannon's researches (2, 3) have resulted in two assumptions that are implicit in many psychophysiological investigations. They are that only the sympathetic branch of the autonomic nervous system responds to unpleasant stress, and that all sympathetically innervated structures show equal increments or decrements of activity.

Recent studies, however, demonstrate that the autonomic nervous system does not respond as a whole in "normal" individuals. For one physiological measure an individual may be over-reactive, for another markedly under-reactive (4, 5). Malmo and his collaborators have shown similar results with psychosomatic patients (6, 7). Their work has led them to formulate a principle of symptom specificity. "This principle states that in psychiatric patients presenting a somatic complaint, the particular physiological mechanism of that complaint is

Reprinted with the permission of the authors and publisher from *Psychosomatic Medicine*, 14:256, 1952.

specifically susceptible to activation by stressful experience" (7).

It is not known whether this principle applies only to those who have already developed a psychosomatic disorder. The present study was undertaken to examine the question of response specificity in the "normal" case. We choose the term "response specificity" rather than "symptom specificity" to avoid the premature implication that the pattern of response secured in an individual not suffering from a psychosomatic complaint is predictive of the area of symptom production if psychosomatic neurosis develops. The specific hypothesis tested may be called *relative* response specificity: for a given set of autonomic measurements, individuals tend to respond with maximal activation in the same physiological function in a variety of stress situations.

First Experiment

Method

Eighty-five male college students, aged 19 to 22, were subjected to four stresses in sequence: mental arithmetic, hyperventilation, difficult word association, and the cold pressor test. The first stress was administered after fifteen minutes of relaxation. The subsequent stresses were administered after recovery from the preceding stress. Heart rate, beat-to-beat variability of heart rate, and palmar conductance (indicating sweat gland activity) were continuously recorded. Details of the procedure will be presented in a later and more com-

plete report of the physiological results.

The measure of reaction used in this
study was independent of the physiological level at which the stress was
imposed. The details and justification
for the mathematical procedure employed will be presented in a separate
report. In statistical terms, the regression of stress level upon base level was
removed. The end result of the procedure is a set of so-called T-scores, with
a mean of 50 and a standard deviation
of 10. Suppose an individual has a
T-score of 40 for palmar conductance
reaction. This means that the maximum
level of palmar conductance which he
reached during stress is one standard
deviation below the average *for individuals with his base level*. These measures
of Autonomic Lability, as we call them,
are highly correlated with absolute and
percentage changes. They have the important attribute, however, that their
correlations with base level are zero.
This is not true of either absolute or
percentage changes.

In this study, four degrees of relative response specificity may appear.
(1) "Maximum" response specificity,
within the limits of the experiment, is
shown by a subject who exhibits his
maximum T-score in the same physiological variable in all four stresses. (2)
"High" specificity is shown by a subject
who exhibits peak response in one variable three times, and in another variable
the fourth time. (3) "Low" specificity is
shown by a subject who yields his peak
response in one variable for two of the
four stresses, and in another physiological variable for the other two
stresses. (4) "Minimum" specificity is
shown by the subject who exhibits peak
response in all three variables over the
four stresses.

Results

Figure 1 shows the observed number
of cases demonstrating each of these
four degrees of response specificity, in
comparison with the frequencies expected on the hypothesis of independent
and equally likely events. These chance
expectancies are easily calculated using
the additive and multiplicative theorems
of the probability calculus.

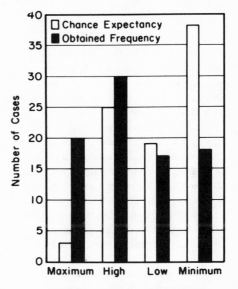

Figure 1

It can be seen in Figure 1 that there
is a marked excess of obtained frequency
over expected frequency in the category
"maximum degree of response specificity." There is a slight excess for the
"high" specificity category, a slight deficiency in the "low" specificity group,
and a marked deficiency in the "minimum" specificity group. For purposes of
testing the significance of these observed deviations from the theoretical distribution the data were recom-
bined into two classes, as shown in
Table 1.

This brings the theoretical frequency
in each cell above 10, and a chi-square
test may be employed legitimately. The
obtained χ^2 is 25.777. Reference to the
normal curve tabulation, entered with χ
as a normal deviate, gives a confidence

TABLE 1. FIRST EXPERIMENT: RESULTS

Degree of Response Specificity	Expected Frequency	Obtained Frequency	Discrepancy
Maximum and high	28	50	+ 22
Low and minimum	57	35	− 22

level of .0000006 The hypothesis certainly must be rejected that there is independence from stress to stress of the physiological function in which an individual exhibits his maximum reaction. The observed frequency distribution implies that we are dealing with a group of individuals some of whom have developed fixed patterning of the three physiological variables, in which one of the functions is maximally activated by any stress whatsoever; some of whom have developed modal patterns from which they depart only occasionally; and some of whom are random with respect to pattern of autonomic arousal.

These results call into serious question the typical design of many psychophysiological investigations that seek to establish covariation between physiological response to stress and various aspects of "emotionality." From the mistaken assumptions that the sympathetic nervous system alone is responsible for response to stress, and that this branch tends to respond as a whole, has come the practice of utilizing either a single measure of reaction as an index of *the* reactivity of the autonomic nervous system, or of utilizing a series of measures but treating them one at a time. It is clear, however, that individuals do not exhibit quantitatively equal response in all measures of autonomic function, and that this is due in part to relatively constant intraindividual differences in the degree of activation of different somatic functions.

Can a concept of general autonomic reactivity be rescued? In many instances

we do want to categorize individuals with respect to ease and amount of autonomic arousal. There are several possibilities. The one used in this paper assays the autonomic reactivity of each individual by using his maximal T-score, no matter in what variable that maximum is exhibited. If Case A has a maximum T-score of 68 in heart rate, and Case B has a maximum T-score of 68 in palmar conductance, we can say that the *maximal reaction* of these two individuals is the same, within the limits of the experiment.

Using such a measure as an index of general autonomic reactivity has no physiological rationale at the present time. Support for its use must be sought in the answers to two questions. First, does such a measure reliably discriminate between individuals; and second, does the measure relate to personality criteria more highly or more meaningfully than do single measures of reaction? The data of the following experiment were secured in a first approach to the latter question.

Second Experiment

Method

Twenty-six of the subjects of this study were given a Rorschach Inkblot Test by the senior author, who was ignorant of the autonomic findings until after the Rorschachs were scored. Scoring was in accordance with Beck's system. For 19 subjects, the Rorschach was given within one week after the autonomic measurements were made. For the other 7 subjects, the days elapsed before the Rorschach was given ranged from 8 to 26.

We were specifically interested in the relationship of autonomic reactivity to the use of color on the Rorschach, which is an alleged indicator of "emotionality." Rorschach scoring discriminates three types of color response. In the FC response, the form of the stimulus is the dominant determinant of the percept, and its color is a secondary determinant. This is spoken of as a controlled color response. In the CF response, color is more important than form as a determinant, and in the pure C response only color is a determinant. The CF and C responses are taken to represent uncontrolled use of color. In Rorschach doctrine, those who use color in uncontrolled ways are affectively immature, capable of violent explosive outbursts of affect. These points are in general accepted in clinical practice but lack experimental verification.

The Form-Color Index is: 0.5 times the number of FC responses minus 1.0 times the number of CF responses minus 1.5 times the number of C responses. These weights are the usual ones given to the responses in evaluating the affective status of the individual. A positive Index means that the individual used controlled color more than uncontrolled color; a negative Index means the reverse. The hypothesis to be tested is that the more negative the Index the greater the autonomic reactivity to stress.

The hypothesis was tested by computing rank difference correlations between the Index and measures of autonomic reaction. For 26 cases a correlation of 0.41 is required for significance at the 4% level, and of 0.46 for significance at the 2% level (8).

Results

We first computed correlations between the Form-Color Index and each of the measures of autonomic reaction separately. The correlations are shown in Table 2.

These correlations vary from −.07 to +.43. Only the correlation between the Form-Color Index and palmar conductance reaction to the cold pressor test (*Stress IV*) is significant. The median value of the 12 correlations is .23, an insignificant value.

TABLE 2. FORM-COLOR INDEX AND MEASURES OF AUTONOMIC REACTION: CORRELATIONS

	Stress I	Stress II	Stress III	Stress IV
Palmar conductance	.07	.27	.29	.43
Heart rate	−.07	.36	.32	.21
Heart rate variability	−.01	−.11	.20	.25

We next correlated the Index with maximum T-score in each of the four stresses. For the four stresses, the correlations were .09, .33, .30, and .34. All correlations are now positive, although none reaches acceptable significance levels. The median value is .315. This is .09 points greater than the median value of the correlations between the Form-Color Index and each of the autonomic measures tested one at a time.

The final step was correlating the Form-Color Index with the maximum reaction shown in all 12 measures. This correlation was 0.47, significant at the 2% level. A further increment of .15 points in the correlations was thus obtained.

One aspect of this correlation is shown in Fig. 2. The 26 cases were divided into approximately quartile groups with respect to their Form-Color Index, and the median value of the maximum T-scores for each of these quartile groups was determined. It can be seen that for the 6 cases showing Form-Color Indices between +2.5 and 0.0 the average value of the maximum T-scores was 60.5. The average increases progressively to 63, 66, and 71 as the Form-Color Index becomes increasingly negative.

A final point must be made in evaluating these results. An individual is free to give as many responses as he wishes to the Rorschach inkblots. A subject who is expansive and productive in general produces more of everything on his record. It is always necessary to

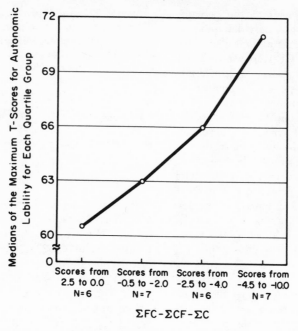

Figure 2

show in validating any Rorschach index that the results are specific to the index itself, and do not derive indirectly from the productivity of the subject. In our sample the rank difference correlations of the Form-Color Index with various aspects of productivity on the Rorschach are: (1) With total number of responses, .15; (2) With number of responses on the five colored cards, .01; (3) With number of responses on the three most highly colored cards (cards VIII, IX and X), .10; (4) With percentage of responses given to the five colored cards, .05; (5) With percentage of responses given cards VIII, IX and X, .06.

None of these correlations even approaches significance. The relation of the Form-Color Index to maximal autonomic reaction, therefore, is specific and does not depend upon differences in the productivity of the subjects.

Summary and Conclusions

Eighty-five male college students, between the ages of 19 and 22, were sub-jected to four different stresses. The stresses were mental arithmetic, hyperventilation, difficult word association, and the cold pressor test. Palmar conductance, heart rate, and heart rate variability were continuously and simultaneously recorded. Twenty-six of the subjects were later given the Rorschach Inkblot Test, which was scored for the use of form and color as determinants. The results may be summarized briefly.

(1) The principle of relative response specificity is strongly supported. For a given set of autonomic measurements, normal subjects tend to respond with maximal activation in the same physiological function in a variety of stress situations. The results suggest that we are dealing with a group of individuals, some of whom have developed fixed patterning of the physiological variables studied, in which one of the functions is maximally activated by any stress whatsoever. Some of them have developed modal patterns from which they depart only occasionally, and some are

random with respect to pattern of autonomic arousal.

(2) It is suggested that such response specificity must be taken into account in studying psychophysiological relationships. The phenomenon of patterned autonomic arousal suggests that success in demonstrating covariation between autonomic response and personality variables may be achieved only if the reactivity of the autonomic nervous system is assayed in terms of *maximal* reactivity, no matter in what stress or in what physiological function this maximal reaction is exhibited.

(3) This was shown to be true in a second study in which an attempt was made to validate the Rorschach Form-Color Index of "emotionality" against the criterion of autonomic response to experimentally induced stress. No convincing validity was found when the autonomic responses were correlated one at a time against the Form-Color Index. As response specificity and the sampling nature of measures of autonomic response were taken into account the correlations rose to a final value of .47, significant at the 2% level.

REFERENCES

1. BECK, S. J. *Rorschach's Test.* 1. *Basic processes.* New York: Grune and Stratton, 1950.

2. CANNON, W. B. *Bodily Changes in Pain, Hunger, Fear and Rage.* New York: Appleton, 1929.

3. CANNON, W. B. *The Wisdom of the Body.* New York: Norton, 1939.

4. LACEY, J. I. Individual differences in somatic response patterns. *J. Comp. & Physiol. Psychol.* 43:338, 1950.

5. LACEY, J. I. Differential emphasis in somatic response to stress: An experimental study. *Psychosom. Med.* 14:71, 1952.

6. MALMO, R. B., and SHAGASS, C. Physiologic study of symptom mechanisms in psychiatric patients under stress. *Psychosom. Med.* 11:25, 1949.

7. MALMO, R. B.; SHAGASS, C.; and DAVIS, F. H. Symptom specificity and bodily reactions during psychiatric interview. *Psychosom. Med.* 12:362, 1950.

8. OLDS, E. G. Distributions of sums of squares of rank differences for small numbers of individuals. *Ann. Math. Stat.* 9:133, 1938.

A Further Appraisal of the Body Boundary Concept

Seymour Fisher

It is known that one assigns qualities (e.g., size, attractiveness) to one's body in terms of personalized standards which bear little relationship to actual body

characteristics (Cleveland, Fisher, Reitman, & Rothaus, 1962; Fisher & Cleveland, 1958b; Lhermitte, 1935; Secord,

This review was partially supported by United States Public Health Service Grant M-5761.

Reprinted by permission of the American Psychological Association and the author from the *Journal of Consulting Psychology,* 1963, **27,** 62–74.

1953; Witkin, Lewis, Hertzman, Machover, Meissner, & Wapner, 1954). When an individual perceives his own body he seems to become uniquely ego involved (Beloff & Beloff, 1957; Wolff, 1943) and he introduces systematic biases which may reveal a good deal about him. The term "body image" has been adopted to designate the attitudinal framework which defines the individual's long-term concept of his body and also influences his perception of it. Investigators have explored many body image dimensions with the intent of predicting from them to other behavioral variables.

Fisher and Cleveland (1958b) proposed that a fundamental aspect of the body image has to do with the manner in which an individual perceives his body boundaries. It was suggested that there is variation in how definite or firm one perceives one's body boundaries to be. Thus, the individual may view his body as clearly and sharply bounded, with a high degree of differentiation from non-self objects. But contrastingly, he may regard his body as lacking demarcation from what is "out there." The view was taken that the process of learning to separate one's body from its environs is fundamental in the establishment of identity and that therefore the character of the body image boundary should provide important information about adjustment strategies. In translating the concept of body image boundaries into operational terms, Fisher and Cleveland developed a method which involves scoring the properties of the boundary regions of percepts elicited by ink blot stimuli. Boundary definiteness was found to be equivalent to the degree to which definite structure, substance, and surface qualities were assigned to the periphery of ink blot images. Responses such as the following were considered to represent an expression of definite boundaries: cave with rocky walls, man in armor, animal with striped skin, turtle with shell, mummy

wrapped up, woman in fancy costume. These percepts in which the boundary is positively highlighted in some way are labeled "barrier responses." A second boundary index was also formulated which concerns ink blot percepts emphasizing the weakness, lack of substance, and penetrability of persons and objects. The term "penetration response" is applied to them, and some examples follow: mashed bug, person bleeding, broken body, torn coat, body seen through a fluoroscope. The barrier and penetration scores are both significantly correlated with the total number of responses given by the subject to a set of ink blot stimuli (e.g., Rorschach or Holtzman blots). Therefore, it is necessary to request that the subjects produce a uniform number of responses for each blot. The interscorer reliability for evaluating barrier and penetration varies from .82 to .97, with most values clustering in the high .80s and low .90s (Fisher & Cleveland, 1958b; Holtzman, Thorpe, Swartz, & Herron, 1961; Mausner, 1961;[1] Ramer, 1961).

In a book entitled *Body Image and Personality* Fisher and Cleveland demonstrated that the body image boundary scores could predict a variety of behaviors. Rather surprisingly, these scores proved to be significantly linked with such a range of phenomena as patterning of body sensations; differences in body exterior versus interior physiological reactivity; psychopathology; and conduct in small group situations. Since 1958 when *Body Image and Personality* was first published many studies have been undertaken by the original authors and also others to crossvalidate and extend the findings that were obtained. The present paper seeks to summarize and integrate these studies. A series of circumscribed topical areas will be presented. Past findings pertinent to each

[1] B. Mausner, unpublished progress report entitled "Experimental Studies of Social Interaction," 1961, National Institute of Mental Health, Grant No. M-2836.

will be described and followed by accounts of more recent work.

Psychophysiological Patterns

Particular physiological patterns were among the first correlates of boundary definiteness to be observed. It had been initially noted that patients with rheumatoid arthritis, neurodermatitis, and conversion symptoms involving the musculature were characterized by higher barrier and lower penetration scores than patients with stomach ulcers or spastic colitis. From such findings the notion evolved that persons with definite boundaries who develop psychosomatic symptoms under stress tend to do so in the exterior body layers (viz., skin and muscle); whereas persons with indefinite boundaries manifest such symptoms in the interior body regions (viz., stomach, gut, and other internal organs). This exterior-interior model was later extended to persons in the normal range by findings which indicated that normal subjects with definite boundaries manifest relatively high reactivity in the muscles and skin (e.g., in terms of GSR and EMG) and low reactivity at interior sites (exemplified by heart rate); but with just the obverse pattern appearing for those with indefinite boundaries.

Since the first presentation of these formulations a variety of studies has been undertaken to evaluate them further. Cleveland and Fisher (1960) and Fisher and Cleveland (1960) reported a replication of the original differences they observed in barrier and penetration scores between patients with rheumatoid arthritis and patients with stomach ulcers. Arthritics ($N = 26$) exceeded patients with stomach ulcers ($N = 34$) in barrier responses (.001 level) and in turn were exceeded by them in penetration responses (.10–.05 level). It was also found that the arthritics were characterized by a significantly lower heart rate (interior reactivity) and

higher number of GSR responses (exterior reactivity) than the ulcer patients under stress conditions (both at .001 level).

Williams (1962) evaluated arthritic ($N = 20$) and ulcer patients ($N = 20$) and reaffirmed that the former had higher barrier (.10–.05 level) and lower penetration (.001 level) scores than the latter. In addition, he found significant trends for heart rate to be higher, and muscle potential lower, in ulcer as compared to arthritic patients under certain conditions. However, predicted differences in GSR were not observed.

Fitzgerald (1961) investigated children with Legg-Calve-Perthes (LCP) disease. This "disease," whose cause is unknown, results in damage to the hip joint which is perhaps analogous to some phenomena encountered in rheumatoid arthritis. Fitzgerald examined LCP from the perspective of the body image boundary theory. He compared 20 children with LCP to 15 controls. As hypothesized, the LCP children proved to have significantly higher boundary definiteness than the controls. Also, the LCP subjects as compared to the control subjects were significantly more motorically expressive and displayed relatively greater skill in performance than verbal tests (WISC).

Eigenbrode and Shipman (1960) are the only investigators to date who have failed completely to replicate the boundary distinction between psychosomatic patients with interior as opposed to exterior symptoms. They extracted from their clinical files the Rorschach protocols of 54 patients with "psychosomatic skin disorders" (exterior) and 29 patients with internal disorders (eg., stomach ulcer, genitourinary disease). Their scorings for the barrier and penetration variables revealed only chance differences between the two groups.

Malev (1961) extended the exploration of the exterior-interior hypothesis to normal children. His design involved 30 male 6-year-old and 30 male 8-year-old subjects. The subjects' mothers were interviewed to ascertain the frequency with which each subject had been characterized by exterior versus interior symptoms. In addition, GSR, heart rate, and blood pressure were recorded from the subjects under conditions of rest and stress. The data indicated that at both ages 6 and 8 the greater the boundary definiteness of the subjects the more likely they were to manifest a significant predominance of exterior over interior symptoms. Analysis of the physiological data demonstrated that in the 6-year-old group heart rate was significantly negatively related to boundary definiteness, but GSR bore only a chance relationship to it. In the 8-year-old group, all the physiological measures proved to be positively correlated with boundary definiteness. This pattern differs from that characterizing adults; and it led Malev to question whether the physiological correlates of boundary definiteness may not systematically differ at certain age levels from those found in adults. However, he did point out further that the symptom patterns reported by mothers in both 6- and 8-year-olds are correlated with the barrier and penetration scores in the same directions as they have been found to be in adults. He speculated on this basis that symptom reports by mothers about their children may be better indicators of long-term autonomic patterning than brief samples of physiological reactivity obtained in artificial laboratory situations.

Brown (1959) applied the barrier and penetration indices to the discrimination of 20 college students with contact dermatitis from 20 controls. He found a borderline tendency (.20–.10 level) for the dermatitis cases to have higher barrier and lower penetration scores than the controls. He noted that the experimental and control groups were "impure" insofar as the former probably contained people "exposed to powerful allergies" and the latter "young

adults who may yet develop contact dermatitis."

Cleveland and Johnson (in press) compared the boundary attributes of 25 young men with coronary disease with a matched group of 25 men awaiting surgery. They discerned no differences in barrier scores between the groups. However, penetration responses were signficantly higher in the coronary than in the presurgical patients.

Davis (1960) investigated reactivity in 25 men with unusually high barrier scores and 25 men with unusually low scores. He obtained electromyograph, skin resistance, blood pressure, and ballistocardiograph measures under rest and stress conditions. There were four differences during rest which were in the predicted direction but only two (EMG, stroke volume) were statistically significant. An analysis of changes in responsivity from rest to stress indicated that, as predicted, EMG was significantly greater in the high than the low barrier group and conversely that heart rate, stroke volume, and total cardiac output were of larger magnitude among low than high barrier subjects. A borderline tendency (.06 level) appeared for total peripheral resistance to be greater in high than low barrier subjects. Although no predictions had been made about blood pressure, it was found that during both rest and stress mean systolic blood pressure was more elevated in the low than high barrier groups. Davis considered his results to be supportive of the hypothesis that high and low barrier persons react differentially at exterior and interior body sites.

Fisher (1959b) sought to replicate Davis' findings in a population which was quite different in sex, age, and barrier score selectivity. Thirty girls with a median age of 14 were studied whose barrier scores were distributed over the entire range rather than representing extremes. GSR was taken as an exterior response index and heart rate as an interior index. Recordings were secured during both rest and stress. The barrier score proved to be significantly positively correlated with GSR frequency and negatively correlated with heart rate during stress. Under rest conditions only a borderline positive correlation (.10–.05 level) between the barrier score and GSR frequency appeared.

It is appropriate at this point to refer to Lacey's formulation (in Rubinstein & Parloff, 1959)

that skin conductance increase is excitatory, whereas increase of cardiac rate is inhibitory of . . . transaction of the organism with the environment. The pattern of response obtained when recording skin resistance and heart rate may reveal occasions when the individual is "open" to his environment and ready to react to it, or conversely, when the individual is not "open" and indeed, instrumentally "rejects" the environment (p. 205).

Lacey suggested on the basis of a review of experiments by Darrow (1929), Davis (1957) and Lacey (in Rubinstein & Parloff, 1959) that an attitude of being open and receptive to the world is accompanied by increased skin conductance and deceleration in heart rate, with the converse pattern typical of a closed unreceptive orientation. This formulation is obviously analogous to the inside-outside model which proposes contrasting levels of skin conductance and heart rate as boundary definiteness varies. Indeed, the analogy becomes even more precise if one considers that the definite boundary person (characterized by tendencies to high skin conductance and low heart rate) has been found to be more "open" and less defensive in dealing with the environment than the indefinite boundary person (Fisher & Cleveland, 1958b).

The tenor of the material presented in this section has been supportive of the boundary concept of exterior versus interior reactivity. Only one (Eigenbrode & Shipman, 1960) of numerous studies contradicted this model. Heart rate and muscle potential have fared best as measures, respectively, of interior and exterior reactivity. GSR and skin resistance have been inconsistent as indices of exterior reactivity and need to be evaluated further. Also, in two exploratory studies blood pressure has proved to be significantly but variably linked with boundary definiteness (viz., positively in children and negatively in adults).

Response to Stress

The possession of definite boundaries was shown in *Body Image and Personality* (Fisher & Cleveland, 1958b) to permit the individual to deal relatively efficiently with stress. There was particular evidence that reaction to the stress of body disablement was likely to be less severe in the definite than indefinite bounded individual. For example, adequacy of adjustment to polio disablement and also amputation were positively correlated with the barrier score. Landau (1960) has provided support for these findings. She studied 40 paraplegic men with spinal cord injuries. Their adjustment to their disablement was evaluated by observational ratings and by means of a sentence completion test. It was found that the higher a patient's barrier score the better was his adjustment as defined by behavioral ratings (.01 level) and sentence completion responses (.01 level). The penetration score had only a chance relationship to the criteria. Landau noted that the barrier score was not related to the duration of time the patient had been disabled. This is congruent with earlier studies (Fisher & Cleveland, 1958b; Ware, Fisher, & Cleveland, 1957) in which the barrier score seemed not to be influenced either by the amount or duration of damage sustained by the body. Indeed, more recently Fisher (1959a) found that the decline in physique accompanying advanced aging does not result in a decrease in barrier responses.

McConnell and Daston (1961) considered the responses of 28 women to the stress occasioned by their own pregnancies. Subjects were seen pre- and postdelivery. Initially, each was given the Rorschach; the Osgood Semantic Differential to be applied to her own body; and a structured interview. Postdelivery, only the Rorschach and the Osgood Semantic Differential were repeated. The favorableness with which the subjects viewed their pregnancies turned out to be positively linked with their barrier scores. It was also established that while the barrier score did not shift from the first to the second testing, the penetration score declined significantly during the same interval.[2] The decline in the penetration score was interpreted as indicating that women feel considerable anxiety about the vulnerability of their bodies while they are pregnant, but that such anxiety declines

once the delivery has been achieved. The fact that the barrier score did not change was considered by Daston and McConnell to be congruent with past findings that it is relatively independent of actual alterations in the body itself. No correlations were found between the body boundary scores and the Osgood scores (Evaluative, Potency, and Activity factors).[3]

In early studies the barrier score had also demonstrated itself to be positively correlated with the ability of the subjects to tolerate stress such as is produced by a mirror drawing task under frustrating conditions. More recently, Brodie (1959) evaluated the barrier score, among other measures, as a predictor of response to stress situations (e.g., delayed auditory feedback). The response to stress was examined in terms of the following dimensions: self-blame versus blame of other for failure; emotional expressivity; aggressiveness versus passivity; and tenacity in persevering at task goals. Thirty men and 30 women were studied. The barrier score proved to be significantly linked with a number of the criteria measures, but the relationships were inconsistent. It was negatively correlated (.05 level in men and .07 level in total group) with emotional expressivity under stress. High barrier subjects clustered at the end of the expressive continuum defined as "controlled" and "guarded"; whereas low barrier subjects were at the other extreme depicted as "impulsive" or "uninhibited." In relation to a second dimension, high barrier subjects were depicted as "unhappy," with low barrier subjects portrayed as "angry" and "assertive" (.02 level in men and .01 level in total group). High barrier women tended to be more tenacious in completing a hand steadiness task than low barrier women (.08 level). High barrier subjects rated the stress situations

[2] Previous to undertaking this study Daston and McConnell (1962) had evaluated the test-retest reliability of the barrier and penetration scores by obtaining test-retest Rorschach protocols (with an intervening 2-month period) from 20 male Veterans Administration patients hospitalized with long-term physical disorders. The reliability of the barrier score was about .89 and that for the penetration score .80. From such data it was concluded that both of the scores were sufficiently stable over time to be employed in test-retest designs.

Holtzman *et al.* (1961) have obtained lower levels of retest reliability when using equivalent forms of his ink blot test repeated after intervals ranging from 3 weeks to 1 year. The reliability coefficients under these conditions cluster in the .40s. However, the use of approximately equivalent forms rather than the repetition of the same test makes these findings not directly comparable to those of Daston and McConnell. Holtzman found too that in normal adult groups the odd-even reliabilities of barrier cluster around .70 and of penetration around .65–.70. Interestingly, in schizophrenic groups the corresponding reliabilities were in the .70s and low .80s. Cleveland (1960) noted after an analysis of Rorschach test-retest protocols (5 days intervening) collected by Rhoda Fisher (1958) on 50 schizophrenic women that the reliability for penetration was .89 and for barrier .65.

[3] Barts (1959) too has failed to find meaningful relationships between the boundary indices and Semantic Differential scores.

as more stressful than did the low barrier subjects (.05 level), but also evidenced a greater decline in anxiety during the course of the experiment (.05 level). One cannot readily integrate these findings. On the one hand, high barrier subjects appear as more "unhappy" and more concerned about the stress than the low barrier subjects; but on the other hand they manifest a greater decline in anxiety during the total session; and in the female group they tend to stick more tenaciously to the assigned task. Finally, it is difficult to know where to classify the fact that the high barrier subjects were more guarded than the low barrier subjects. Obviously, the barrier score was related to several aspects of the subject's stress behavior. However, it is at the same time unclear what the data signify with respect to the stress tolerance of well and poorly bounded individuals. They are more descriptive of modes of emotional expression than of effectiveness of response in relationship to task goals.

The results reported add confirmation to the proposition that ability to adjust to the stress of body disablement is positively correlated with boundary definiteness. However, little has been added in the way of clarifying previous findings about adjustment to stresses not related to body disablement.

Small Group Behavior

The manner in which the individual feels his body to be differentiated from its environs seems to play a role in his style of interaction in small groups. In four previous studies (Fisher & Cleveland, 1958b) the barrier score proved to be positively related to the following variables in group situations: spontaneous expressiveness,[4] independence,

[4] Pertinently, but yet somewhat tangential to "expressiveness" as it is here used, it should be mentioned that Fisher and Cleveland (1958a) found that high barrier subjects exceeded low barrier subjects in indices of sexual expressiveness.

promoting group goals, warmth and friendliness, willingness to face up to hostility. A picture emerged from this work of the high barrier person as more open and direct in his group dealings with others than the low barrier person, but simultaneously striving harder to achieve group cohesiveness.

Cleveland and Morton (1962) sought to cross-validate these findings by evaluating 70 psychiatric patients in a group oriented therapy program. In the final week of a 4-week period the subjects were asked to fill out a sociometric questionnaire[5] requesting nominations of group members who had been characterized by specific behaviors (e.g., putting group goals above individual goals or helping the group to be warm and friendly). When the sociometric nominations received by group members were related to their barrier responses, the results were supportive of previous findings in that 9 of 13 predictions were borne out. High barrier subjects significantly exceeded low barrier subjects in nominations for ability to influence the opinions of others, degree of acceptance by the group at large, ability to operate effectively without direction, setting group above individual goals, helping to resolve group differences, keeping the group "on the ball," and being preferred as a recipient of discussion. Cleveland and Morton (1962) summarized these results as follows:

High Barrier subjects receive the greater number of nominations for being the most influential group members, doing more to keep the group active and goal directed and operating without external support and guidance in the form of a leader. For the low Barrier members the results are not as clear . . . (p. 6).

Another provocative aspect of this project related the barrier score to how well an individual maintains his own

[5] This sociometric questionnaire was a shortened version of one which had been used in a previous study (Fisher & Cleveland, 1958b) of boundary and group behavior.

views when opposed by group pressures. In previous work (Fisher & Cleveland, 1958b) suggestibility appeared to be inversely related to boundary definiteness. As part of their study, Cleveland and Morton asked the subjects to view a movie in which the action focused on how a jury, in a murder trial beginning with one vote for acquittal and the remainder for conviction, shifted eventually to a unanimous decision of "not guilty." Subjects saw the film up to the point where the second ballot of the jury started. When the film was stopped, they were told that by the end of the story the jury would have changed its vote to acquittal. They were asked to list in rank order the sequence in which they felt the various jurors would shift their vote. Then, they formed into small groups that were instructed to arrive at unanimous group decisions with regard to the same ranking procedure. Finally, when the group decision had been registered, they were requested again to make their own second individual rankings. Degree of suggestibility was determined in terms of how much each subject had been influenced by the group discussion to alter his second ranking in comparison with the first. Suggestibility proved to be inversely related to the barrier score (.01 level).

Mausner[6] constructed a situation in which the subjects judged the numbers of briefly exposed dots. As they rendered their judgments, they were receiving reports of the same phenomena from a partner. Although the partner's statements seemed to emanate directly from him, they were actually manipulated by the experimenter so as to contradict the subject's reports. Each subject's responses to the contradictions were evaluated. It was found that the higher the barrier score the greater the likelihood that the subject would consider his own judgments,

rather than his partner's, to be correct. Also, the barrier score was positively linked with the degree that the subject felt satisfied with his own performance and negatively related to his level of anxiety. Incidentally, the barrier score was significantly and negatively related to the *L* (Lie) score on the MMPI. This suggested that the individual with definite boundaries has less need to present an exaggerated favorable picture of himself than does one who is vaguely bounded. There was no relation between the barrier score and degree of yielding behavior. Mausner[7] concluded: "To summarize, this preliminary analysis tends to confi.m the generalized personality description derived from the original Fisher and Cleveland work" (p. 124).

Ramer (1961) hypothesized that the high barrier person would exceed the low barrier person:

1. In initiating interpersonal communications.
2. In communicating committal, directive, and disagreeing statements rather than self-depreciating ones.

He studied 96 female subjects (in groups of four) in a setting in which each was isolated from the others. Instructions were given to write a story about several pictures and then to communicate with a fictitious partner about the story by writing messages which would presumably be delivered by the experimenter. One-third of the subjects were given no responses to the messages they sent; another third were given unfriendly replies from the fictitious partner; and the remaining third were given friendly replies. In this setting high barrier subjects sent more messages (.01 level) and more units of communication (.05 level) than the low barrier subjects. A significant difference in the same direction occurred with respect to number of committal messages as opposed to those asking for orientation.

[6] *Op. cit.*

[7] *Ibid.*

There were nonsignificant but consistent tendencies for the barrier score to be negatively related to such variables as number of self-depreciating or passive accepting messages but positively with the number of direction giving messages. Borderline evidence was obtained that the "barrier style of behavior" was most evident under threat conditions. Ramer considered most of his hypotheses to have been confirmed or at least supported by the results.

Differences in degree of communicative expression in group situations between high and low barrier subjects has been observed by Hornstra and McPartland[8] to hold true also in a schizophrenic population. They report that there are significant distinctions in the ward behavior of schizophrenic patients with relatively high and low barrier scores. Patients with relatively high scores are rated by ward personnel as displaying behavior which is restless, acting out, and initiatory of interaction. This is in contrast to patients with lower barrier scores who are depicted as showing "retarded and withdrawn behavior."

The studies just summarized affirm that boundary characteristics play a meaningful part in an individual's group behavior. The more clearly articulated an individual's boundaries the greater the probability that he will seek to communicate with other group members and also that his communications will be direct and active rather than passive or self-depreciatory. With regard to the matter of suggestibility, it should be noted that the Cleveland and Morton results were supportive, and those of Mausner not supportive, of previous findings. Whether this difference is a function of the unlike methods used to measure suggestibility remains to be seen.

[8] R. K. Hornstra and T. S. McPartland, unpublished progress report entitled "The Relation of Behavioral Constellations to Drug Use," 1961, National Institute of Mental Health, Grant No. MY 3308.

Psychopathology

The barrier and penetration scores were earlier found to discriminate schizophrenic from nonschizophrenic subjects. They did not distinguish between normals and neurotics, but roughly separated normals and neurotics (high barrier, low penetration) from schizophrenics (low barrier, high penetration) (Fisher & Cleveland, 1958b). Of course, the association of vague body boundaries with schizophrenia had for some time been remarked upon by clinical observers (e.g., Schilder, 1935).

Holtzman (Holtzman et al., 1961) applied his ink blot series to normal and pathological groups and observed that the barrier score was higher and the penetration score lower in normals than in chronic schizophrenics. However, only in the case of penetration was the difference significant (.01 level). In addition, he factor analyzed the intercorrelations of 23 indices (including barrier and penetration) derived from his ink blot test in 16 different samples of subjects. He discovered that the barrier score consistently loaded high on a factor which he associates with "well-organized, ideational activity, awareness of conventional concepts" (p. 171). The penetration score loaded high on several factors related to disturbance. It was particularly identified with indicators of immaturity, bodily preoccupation, and psychopathology. These factor analytic results tie the barrier score to ego integration and the penetration score to maladjustment.

Cleveland (1960) inquired whether there would be changes in the boundary scores as schizophrenics recovered from the acute phase of their disorganization. Twenty-five male schizophrenics were evaluated upon first entering the hospital with the Lorr Multidimensional Scale for Rating Psychiatric Patients. They were evaluated again after 5 and 13 weeks of treatment involving tranquilizers. Another criterion of the patient's response to treatment was whether he attained sufficient recovery to leave the hospital. Holtzman Ink Blots were administered predrug, and 5 and 13 weeks after treatment had begun. A significant rho of .60 was found between decrement in penetration scores and decrement in the Lorr morbidity rating during the period from the onset of treatment to the fifth week. The rho for the same relationship from treatment onset to the thirteenth week was .61. There was also a significant trend (.05–.02) level for patients judged capable of leaving the hospital to have declined in penetration. This contrasted with nondischarged patients who tended to increase their penetration scores. The barrier score failed to be related to any of the criteria of patient change.

A second phase of this study concerned 45 schizophrenics who had been administered the Rorschach on admission and again upon leaving the hospital. Each patient was psychiatrically rated upon admission and again at time of discharge. It was established that patients rated as improved or markedly improved showed a significant decline in penetration (.01 level). For barrier the only significant change was an increase from first to second testing in the markedly improved group. Cleveland (1960) considered that his results demonstrated in the recovering schizophrenic patient a "dramatic firming up and defining of the body image boundary" (pp. 259–260).

Pankow (in Burton, 1961) observed in her psychotherapeutic work with schizophrenics that their art productions are characterized by disrupted boundaries. She specifically compared this phenomenon to the boundary indefiniteness depicted by low barrier and high penetration responses characteristic of schizophrenic populations.

Reitman (1962) studied the body image changes in neurotics and schizophrenics following sensory isolation.

Twenty neurotics and 20 schizophrenics were exposed to sensory isolation conditions. Holtzman Ink Blot Tests, measures of tactile sensitivity, and estimates of body size were obtained before and after isolation. A control group received the pre- and postbattery of tests, but with isolation not intervening. No changes occurred in the scores of this group from pre- to postevaluation. However, there were significant changes in the experimental groups. The neurotics manifested decreased barrier and increased penetration scores following isolation.[9] The schizophrenics, contrastingly, obtained higher barrier and lower penetration scores. It was speculated that sensory isolation by minimizing stimulating input has a disruptive effect upon nonpsychotics which decreases boundary definiteness. But in the case of schizophrenics the sensory isolation seemed not to be disruptive. It seemed to provide a nonthreatening pattern of stimuli which fostered reorganization and more realistic body boundaries. This latter finding was in keeping with earlier reports (Azima & Cramer, 1956; Gibby, Adams, & Carrera, 1960) concerning the therapeutic effects of isolation on schizophrenic symptomatology. It is important to note that the results from the tactile threshold and body size estimate tasks were similarly reversed for the two experimental groups and in a direction congruent with the concept that isolation produces boundary alteration. Thus, the schizophrenics showed increased tactile sensitivity and a decreased concept of body size following isolation; but the nonpsychotics showed no change in tactile sensitivity and an increased concept of body size. There are previous studies by Wapner (1958) which sug-

[9] Using an entirely different methodology, Cambareri (1958) found that nonpsychotic subjects exposed to sensory isolation in a swimming tank made references to loss of body boundaries (e.g., "I had a difficult time after awhile in the tank distinguishing where I left off and the surrounding water began").

gest that the pattern of changes with regard to body size estimates in the schizophrenic group are related to increased awareness of the body periphery and those in the nonpsychotic group with lessened awareness of the periphery. It should be added that in estimating the sizes of non-self objects (e.g., baseball) the two groups did not shift their judgments from test to retest. Only judgments with regard to one's own body were sensitive to the sensory isolation effects.

In the area of psychopathology the boundary scores seem to distinguish grossly between schizophrenics and non-schizophrenics.[10] Furthermore, there is evidence that as an individual reorganizes following schizophrenic breakdown his penetration score declines. The barrier score is less successful in this respect. Cleveland reported that it increased as recovery proceeded in one category of patients, but that it otherwise failed to correlate with the reorganization process. Within the context of the changes produced by sensory isolation one finds that the barrier and penetration scores vary in opposite directions in schizophrenics and nonschizophrenics. Schizophrenics react to isolation with an increase in barrier and a decrease in penetration scores, with the converse holding true for the neurotics. In the first instance isolation seems to decrease definiteness of body image boundaries and in the second

it apparently helps to re-establish them.

Developmental Aspects

There have been scattered indications that aspects of the developmental process (Fisher & Cleveland, 1958b; Malev, 1961) might be related to boundary attributes.

Fish (1960) scanned the boundary correlates of several developmental parameters in children. She applied a multiple-choice version[11] of the usual Rorschach technique to measure barrier and penetration responses in boys at ages 7 ($N = 21$), 9 ($N = 25$), and 11 ($N = 25$). She also secured measures tapping such diverse variables as concept of time, resistance to perceiving aniseikonic induced distortions in one's mirror image, concept of one's height, and ability to define the adult role. As in a previous study (Fisher & Cleveland, 1958b), there were no indications of progressive change in boundary scores with age. It was ascertained, though, that the barrier score was positively (.05 level) correlated with ability to represent adult qualities in figure drawings at age 7. Also, the barrier score was positively correlated in 7- (.01 level) and 9-year-olds (.09 level) with a more "mature" mode of time perspective that involves the perception of future adult events as distant from, rather than close to, the present. The barrier score was not related to judgments of one's own height or to degree of distortion in self-image induced by aniseikonic lenses. In general, it is interesting that despite the use of an untried method of barrier measurement, the significant results which were obtained in relation to the barrier score linked it positively with

---

[10] The potential of the boundary scores for measuring other kinds of maladjustment aside from that in the category of psychosis is pointed up by Miner and De Vos (1960) finding that urban Arabs who are conflicted about their identity produce significantly higher penetration scores (.05 level) than oasis Arabs who have not yet been exposed to such extreme identity conflict. This, by the way, is confirmatory of previous data (Fisher & Cleveland, 1958b) which demonstrated that Japanese-American men who were struggling to adapt to United States life had less definite boundaries than native Japanese not beset by such identity problems.

[11] There was no attempt to determine the comparability of the multiple-choice method to the spontaneous response procedure usually used to obtain barrier and penetration scores.

certain indices of developmental maturity.

Discussion of Empirical Findings

The studies published since 1958 with regard to the boundary scores point up their versatility. There has been moderately good substantiation of the fact that boundary variations are accompanied by certain patterns of physiological reactivity. Both in terms of psychosomatic symptoms and measures of autonomic response the bulk of the newly reported data indicate that the higher the degree of boundary definiteness the greater the tendency to channel excitation to skin and muscle and the less the tendency to do so at interior sites like the stomach and heart. These findings have appeared in both adults and children and also in studies utilizing different designs and instrumentation. It is true that certain inconsistencies remain to be explained. For example, why does GSR sometimes correlate with barrier and sometimes not? Also, why do given autonomic measures (e.g., GSR and blood pressure) differ in the direction of their correlation with the barrier score in adults as opposed to children? Of course, the even larger task remains of clarifying the mechanisms whereby body attitudes and body reactivity patterns become linked with each other. However, what is of particular importance is that patterns of autonomic responsivity have been demonstrated which are meaningful within a body image framework but have no apparent ties with the conventional autonomic categories (e.g., sympathetic and parasympathetic). Lacey (in Rubenstein & Parloff, 1959) has already referred to the inadequacy of the conventional categories for dealing with the observed complexity of autonomic response patterns.

The boundary studies dealing with stress tolerance and psychopathology combine to reaffirm that with increasing boundary definiteness there is a diminished likelihood of psychosis and an enhanced ability to deal effectively with difficult, disturbing experiences (especially those involving body disablement). Even the findings about small group behavior have similar connotations with regard to adjustment effectiveness; for they portray the high barrier person as coping with group interrelationships in a more independent, realistic, and yet group integrative fashion than does one who is low barrier. In addition, of course, the results from the group studies point up that the way in which an individual delineates his body limits in relation to others plays a noteworthy role in his group conduct. It is still an unsettled matter as to which aspects of group interaction are most directly related to the boundary parameter. However, the trends cited suggest that high and low barrier subjects are best distinguished in their group behavior with respect to how much each tries to communicate with others for mutual facilitation and stimulation rather than for self-centered purposes.

An unexpected fact that has emerged from the newer studies is that the boundary scores are indicators of certain kinds of change in the individual. Cleveland (1960) detected shifts in the penetration score as schizophrenics recovered from disorganization. McConnell and Daston (1961) recorded meaningful changes in the penetration scores of pregnant women from pre- to postdelivery period. Reitman (1962) discovered the exciting fact that both barrier and penetration scores are altered in neurotics and schizophrenics during sensory isolation. Furthermore, these alterations are accompanied by equivalent changes in light touch threshold and concept of one's body size. Here one sees boundary score changes correlated with such widely different phenomena as personality reorganization, the completion of pregnancy, and the impact of decreased sensory experience. Apparently, fluctuations in boundary attributes do offer some promise as indicators of certain modifications of the individual. At this point one can only conjecture whether boundary fluctations represent initiating forces in change processes or whether they are subsidiary effects.

It should be specified that the penetration score has been the index primarily correlated with change phenomena. The barrier score was consistently related only to changes produced by sensory isolation. This tends to be congruent with results from earlier studies (Fisher, 1959a; Fisher & Cleveland, 1958b) which indicated that the barrier score was largely a measure of persisting attitudes rather than of short-term variations in state. The penetration score, by contrast, seems to be more sensitive to immediate situational conditions.[12] However, this differentiation can only be considered to be a tentative one which waits further confirmation.

Actually, the relationships of the barrier and penetration scores still remain to be worked out in detail. These relationships fluctuate in different populations (although often low and tending in a negative direction). The relative usefulness of the two scores is an open question and admittedly has been neglected as a matter of inquiry. Beginning attempts to combine them into one index of boundary definiteness have been made with fair success (e.g., Fitzgerald, 1961; Malev, 1961).

In general, one seems justified in saying that the studies which are reviewed are supportive of the major past findings

concerning body image boundary definiteness which have been reported.

Interpretation of Boundary Scores

It would be well in closing this overview to consider a general question which has been raised concerning the interpretation of the boundary scores. Wylie (1961), Mednick (1959) and others have criticized the assumption that barrier and penetration scores represent measures of body image, as such. They are inclined to view these scores as more indicative of cognitive or perceptual operations than of anything derived from body experience. They imply that the observed network of empirical relations between the boundary scores and other phenomena could just as well be explained within a perceptual framework as via body image constructs. Basically, they question whether there is adequate support for assuming that the properties assigned to the periphery of ink blot percepts reflect how the body boundary is experienced. Such criticisms cannot be easily dismissed. The complete absence of previous empirical work with regard to body boundary feelings has made it difficult to find adequate body image criteria against which to validate the boundary properties assumed to characterize barrier and penetration responses. There are, however, certain lines of evidence which have encourage the writer (and Sidney Cleveland) to persist in a body image conceptualization of the data which have accumulated:

1. Primary among these is the fact that the boundary scores are correlated with body phenomena to a degree unequaled by previous measures.[13] They

---

[12] The sensitive response of the penetration score to variations in state is further exemplified in a report by Herron (1962). He found that when the Holtzman blots were administered under neutral conditions and under conditions designed to arouse achievement-motivation, the penetration score was the most reflective, among a variety of other indices, of the achievement condition. It was significantly lower in the achievement oriented than in the neutral state.

[13] In a just completed and unpublished study the writer (and Rhoda Fisher) have found a significant relationship between the barrier score and the body associations given by normal subjects. High barrier subjects gave associations which indicated that they

predict various levels of body behavior in the way that a body image measure would be expected to do. They have shown themselves to be meaningfully related to ability to cope with disablement of one's body; to patterns of phantom sensation triggered by amputation; to experienced changes in body size and also light touch threshold following sensory isolation; to differential size judgments assigned to the right and left sides of the body; to concern about the vulnerability of the skin; and to degree of anxious concern about the body (Fisher, 1960; Fisher & Cleveland, 1958b). Incidentally, the last of these cited relationships is particularly pertinent because the boundary scores do not correlate with indices of general anxiety which are not specifically phrased in body terms.

It is further striking that the boundary scores predict patterns of body reactivity which involve a differentiation between the boundary and nonboundary regions of the body. Whether one assumes that the scores are reflections of differential levels of activation at such body sites (inside versus outside) or actually play a role in instigating the activation differences, the fact remains that a solid correlation exists. There is force in this congruence between boundary properties assigned to the ink blot periphery and the reactivity characteristics of the body periphery versus body interior. One cannot dismiss it as mere coincidence if one considers the fact that the existence of an exterior-interior activation pattern in normal subjects was specifically deduced from the model provided by the body image boundary concept. There are few, if any, non-body-image concepts which would

lend themselves to such a prediction phrased in terms of body "geography."

2. No dependable relationships have been found between the boundary scores and indices which might be considered to have cognitive or "perceptual style" connotations. The boundary scores are not consistently related to such variables as intelligence, verbal productivity, the Barron simplicity-complexity dimension, Gottschaldt figure judgments, conventional individual Rorschach determinants, speed of figure-ground alternation, rigidity, or authoritarianism.

It is recognized that more work needs to be done to establish the body image rationale which has been advanced for the boundary scores. As a matter of fact, the author has several studies under way which seek to demonstrate that an individual's introspective reports of body experience in various situations (e.g., under stress, in response to drugs, in response to placebo) conform to the particular ratio of exterior versus interior sensations that would be predicted from his barrier and penetration scores.

As a final word, it may be added that not the least of the attractions of a body image interpretation of the boundary scores is the fact that it has led to the successful testing of a variety of novel hypotheses. Is this not a major consideration in any research strategy?

Summary

A series of studies were reviewed which cross-validated and extended previous findings concerning the relationship of two measures of body image boundary definiteness (barrier and penetration scores) to various levels of behavior. Support was found for the view that the more definite an individual's boundaries the more likely he is to manifest relatively higher physiological reactivity in body exterior as contrasted to body interior sectors. There was substantial evidence too that with increasing boundary definiteness there is

exceeded low barrier subjects (.02 level) in the degree to which their awareness of the body boundary region (skin and muscle) exceeded their awareness of the body interior (stomach and heart). This study represents the most direct and convincing demonstration of the body image foundation of the barrier score to date.

greater ability to adjust adequately to disablement of one's body, to maintain normal ego integration, and to be effectively communicative in small group settings. Finally, the rationale was discussed for interpreting the barrier and penetration scores within a body image framework.

REFERENCES

AZIMA, D., & CRAMER, F. J. Effects of the decrease in sensory variability on body scheme. *Canad. J. Psychiat.*, 1956, 1, 59–72.

BARTS, G. J. The perception of body boundaries. Unpublished master's thesis, Ohio State University, 1959.

BELOFF, J., & BELOFF, H. Perception of self and others using a stereoscope. *J. abnorm. soc. Psychol.*, 1957, 56, 87–92.

BRODIE, C. W. The prediction of qualitative characteristics of behavior in stress situations, using test-assessed personality constructs. Unpublished doctoral dissertation, University of Illinois, 1959.

BROWN, D. G. Psychosomatic correlates in contact dermatitis: A pilot study. *J. psychosom. Res.*, 1959, 4, 132–139.

BURTON, A. *Psychotherapy of the psychoses*. New York: Basic Books, 1961.

CAMBARERI, J. D. The effects of sensory isolation on suggestible and nonsuggestible psychology graduate students. Unpublished doctoral dissertation, University of Utah, 1958.

CLEVELAND, S. E. Body image changes associated with personality reorganization. *J. consult. Psychol.*, 1960, 24, 256–261.

CLEVELAND, S. E., & FISHER, S. A comparison of psychological characteristics and physiological reactivity in ulcer and rheumatoid arthritis groups: I. Psychological measures. *Psychosom. Med.*, 1960, 22, 283–289.

CLEVELAND, S. E., FISHER, S., REITMAN, E. E., & ROTHAUS, P. Perception of body size in schizophrenia. *Arch. gen. Psychiat.*, 1962, 7, 277–285.

CLEVELAND, S. E., & JOHNSON, D. C. Personality patterns in young males with coronary diseases. *Psychosom. Med.*, in press.

CLEVELAND, S. E., & MORTON, R. B. Group behavior and body image: A follow-up study. *Hum. Relat.*, 1962, 15, 77–85.

DARROW, C. W. Differences in the physiological reactions to sensory and ideational stimuli. *Psychol. Bull.*, 1929, 26, 185–201.

DASTON, P. G., & McCONNELL, O. L. Stability of Rorschach penetration and barrier scores over time. *J. consult. Psychol.*, 1962, 26, 104.

DAVIS, A. D. Some physiological correlates of Rorschach body-image productions. *J. abnorm. soc. Psychol.*, 1960, 60, 432–436.

DAVIS, R. C. Response patterns. *Trans. N. Y. Acad. Sci. Ser. 2*, 1957, 19, 731–739.

EIGENBRODE, C. R., & SHIPMAN, W. G. The body image barrier concept. *J. abnorm. soc. Psychol.*, 1960, 60, 450–452.

FISH, J. E. An exploration of developmental aspects of body scheme and of ideas about adulthood in grade school children. Unpublished doctoral dissertation, University of Kansas, 1960.

FISHER, RHODA L. The effect of a disturbing situation upon the stability of various projective tests. *Psychol. Monogr.*, 1958, 72, (14, Whole No. 467).

FISHER, S. Body image boundaries in the aged. *J. Psychol.*, 1959, 48, 315–318. (a)

FISHER, S. Prediction of body exterior vs. body interior reactivity from a body image scheme. *J. Pers.*, 1959, 27, 56–62. (b)

FISHER, S. Right-left gradients in body image, body reactivity, and perception. *Genet. Psychol. Monogr.*, 1960, 61, 197–228.

FISHER, S., & CLEVELAND, S. E. Body image boundaries and sexual behavior. *J. Psychol.*, 1958, 45, 207–211. (a)

FISHER, S., & CLEVELAND, S. E. *Body image and personality*. Princeton: Van Nostrand, 1958. (b)

FISHER, S., & CLEVELAND, S. E. A comparison of psychological characteristics and physiological reactivity in ulcer and rheumatoid arthritis groups: II. Differences in physiological reactivity. *J. psychosom. Med.*, 1960, **22**, 290–293.

FITZGERALD, W. E. A psychological factor in Legg-Calve-Perthes disease. Unpublished doctoral dissertation, Harvard University, 1961.

GIBBY, R. G., ADAMS, H. B., & CARRERA, R. N. Therapeutic changes in psychiatric patients following partial sensory deprivation. *Arch. gen. Psychiat.*, 1960, **3**, 33–42.

HERRON, E. W. Intellectual achievement-motivation: A study in construct clarification. Unpublished doctoral dissertation, University of Texas, 1962.

HOLTZMAN, W. H., THORPE, J. S., SWARTZ, J. D., & HERRON, E. W. *Inkblot perception and personality.* Austin: Univer. Texas Press, 1961.

LANDAU, M. F. Body image in paraplegia as a variable in adjustment to physical handicap. Unpublished doctoral dissertation, Columbia University, 1960.

LHERMITTE, J. *L'image de notre corps.* Paris: Editions, de la Nouvelle Revue Critique, 1935.

McCONNELL, O. L., & DASTON, P. G. Body image changes in pregnancy. *J. proj. Tech.*, 1961, **25**, 451–456.

MALEV, J. S. Body image and physiological reactivity in children. Unpublished master's thesis, Baylor University, 1961.

MEDNICK, S. The body's barriers go Rorschach. *Contemp. Psychol.*, 1959, **4**, 276–277.

MINER, H. M., & DE VOS, G. *Oasis and Casbah: Algerian culture and personality in change.* Ann Arbor: Univer. Michigan Press, 1960.

RAMER, J. C. The Rorschach barrier score and social behavior. Unpublished doctoral dissertation, University of Washington, 1961.

REITMAN, E. E. Changes in body image following sensory deprivation in schizophrenic and control groups. Unpublished doctoral dissertation, University of Houston, 1962.

RUBINSTEIN, E. A., & PARLOFF, M. B. *Research in psychotherapy.* Washington, D. C.: American Psychological Association, 1959.

SCHILDER, P. *The image and appearance of the human body.* London: Kegan Paul, Trench & Trubner, 1935.

SECORD, P. F. Objectification of word association procedures by the use of homonyms: A measure of body cathexis. *J. Pers.*, 1953, **21**, 479–495.

WAPNER, S., WERNER, H., & COMALLI, P. E. Effect of enhancement of head boundary on head size and shape. *Percept. mot. Skills*, 1958, **8**, 319–325.

WARE, K. S., FISHER, S., & CLEVELAND, S. E. Body image boundaries and adjustment to poliomyelitis. *J. abnorm. soc. Psychol.*, 1957, **55**, 88–93.

WILLIAMS, R. L. The relationship of body image to some physiological reactivity patterns in psychosomatic patients. Unpublished doctoral dissertation, Washington University, 1962.

WITKIN, H. A., LEWIS, H. B., HERTZMAN, M., MACHOVER, K., MEISSNER, P. B., & WAPNER, S. *Personality through perception.* New York: Harper, 1954.

WOLFF, W. *The expression of personality.* New York: Harper, 1943.

WYLIE, R. C. *The self concept.* Lincoln: Univer. Nebraska Press, 1961.

Assaultiveness and Two Types of Rorschach Color Responses

Robert Sommer and Dorothy Twente Sommer

Much of the thinking about the relationship between Rorschach responses and other behaviors is based on the concept that the formal aspects of the responses (determinants) should have correlates in other behaviors of the person (introversion, anxiety, etc.). However, present-day thinking tends to regard information as to structural aspects of personality alone (e.g.., defense mechanisms) as insufficient for understanding the behavior of the individual. Past thinking was considered unsatisfactory in that it looked for relationships between energy, affects, or need and overt behavior without taking into account the channels the organism had developed for handling this energy. It was also felt that information as to these structures alone left one with a bare shell and still unable to predict the actual behavior of the person. What was needed was information regarding both the contents of fantasy *and* the person's techniques for handling his affects.

At least two approaches to Rorschach research are unsatisfactory: (a) to relate determinant scores to behavior

The study was supported by a grant from the State of Louisiana hospital research fund. Without the active cooperation of the staffs of Gulfport VA Hospital (especially Herdis A. Deabler) and of Southeast Louisiana Hospital (especially Joseph G. Dawson), the study could not have been undertaken.

Reprinted with the permission of the American Psychological Association and the authors from *Journal of Consulting Psychology*, 1958, **22**, 57–62.

without regard to the content of the responses;[1] (b) to relate content categories (e.g., destructive, oral expulsive, etc.) to behavior without regard to the formal aspects of the response (determinant score).

An attempt is made in the present study to base predictions on a combination of formal and content elements. The type of behavior selected for study is assaultive or explosive behavior where the Rorschach literature is both considerable (3, 4, 6, 7) and often contradictory. There have been several attempts to design experiments that would assess the merits of the hypotheses proposed, but the results are not easy to understand. With regard to structural correlates of explosive behavior, there are those who believe that either very many color responses or no color responses are indicative of it. With regard to the content of the responses, predictions can be both very specific ("tomahawk" to the white space on Card VII indicates aggressive acting out) or very general (many animal responses indicates stereotyped thinking). In the prediction of aggressive behavior from the Rorschach, there are two distinct groups of clinicians: (*a*) Some believe aggressive contents indicate that the person is able to express

[1] With some determinants there is a confounding of content and structure, as in *M* where the use of a human figure is usually required. Since this is a common but not necessary condition for *M*, it makes the meaning of any correlation between *M* and other factors quite ambiguous.

his hostile impulses in a socially acceptable way and hence has no need to act out. Phillips and Smith (5), for example, speak of blood responses as contraindicative of destructive acting out. (*b*) Others believe that the use of hostile content indicates a preoccupation with such thoughts. Depending upon the individual's impulse-control system, such behavior should be expected if the sample of the individual's life-history is adequate. Few tests have been based on the first approach except that of Stone (7) which met with essentially negative results. Those of Pitluck (6) and Finney (1) may be taken to support the latter view, although in the former case the results were not clear-cut.

The present problem is to determine the relationship between explosive behavior and two types of Rorschach color responses: (*a*) aggressive and explosive responses (volcano, fire, blood from a wound, etc.); (*b*) nonaggressive responses (bouquet, ice-cream, orchid, etc.). One essential condition is that the two groups should not differ in *Sum C;* the only difference should be in the content of the color responses. Our prediction, based on the work of Stone, Pitluck, and Finney, is that the "aggressive content" group will show more explosive and assaultive behavior than the "nonaggressive content" group. It was also decided to distinguish between physical explosiveness and assaultiveness (defined as explosive physical attacks on persons, objects, or animals in the environment) and verbal explosiveness and assaultiveness (explosive episodes where torrents of abuse are directed toward the outside world). Both definitions stipulate that the behaviors be characterized by an explosive quality in addition to being assaults upon the environment.

An ancillary hypothesis was that "aggressive movement responses" (e.g., fighting, kicking, etc.), when accompanying aggressive color responses,

would improve the prediction of aggressive acting-out behavior. However, the chief emphasis of the study was on the differences in behavior between Ss who gave "aggressive color responses" and those who gave "nonaggressive color responses."

Procedure

Our preference for criteria of assaultiveness was for meaningful acts by the individual in his own particular world. This type of material is most easily found by interviewing or in good case histories if they happen to be available. Yet if these are gathered for purposes other than for one's experiment (e.g., hospital records), one must always be aware that the interviewer may not have been interested in the behavior that one is studying. If the behavior studied is of considerable importance in the individual's relations with others, as is the case with assaultive behavior, the chances of the interviewer's overlooking it are minimal, although the possibility must still be considered.

Hence, our criteria of assaultiveness are incidents of such behavior in case histories gathered routinely by the social service department of a VA hospital. The procedure limited our sample to male psychiatric patients which is regrettable in terms of generalizing from the results but advantageous if aggressive acting-out is more prevalent in such a group.

Essentially, the method embodied an *ex post facto* design in which two investigators worked independently. The senior author spent several weeks going through the files of the psychology department of this hospital and looked over approximately 200 protocols (none of which he had seen before). He wrote down the names of those patients who had given explosive color responses (objectively defined as responses of volcanoes, explosions, fire, etc.) and those who had given exclusively nonaggressive color responses (orchids, bouquets, sherbert, etc.) and also whether or not the *M* responses could be classified as aggressive or not (objectively defined as actions of fighting, kicking, etc, in a way similar to Finney's category of "active destruction" in his Palo Alto scale). If a person with aggressive color responses also had several nonaggressive color responses, he was still included in the aggressive color category. If a subject had even six or seven nonaggressive color responses and one that was partially aggressive, he was *not* included in the nonaggressive color group.

The list of approximately 65 names, arranged in alphabetical order and with all other information removed, was given to the second investigator who was instructed to inspect the case history of the patient and rate the pre-hospital behavior along a seven-point scale for (*a*) physical assaultiveness and (*b*) verbal assaultiveness. If there was insufficient information for rating along a dimension, a zero could be used. Some attrition was expected in our sample as a few case histories had been sent to other installations or could not otherwise be located.

Results

The final data consisted of the ratings of the case histories of 26 aggressive color Ss and 31 nonaggressive color Ss. The ratings on both physical and verbal assaultiveness ranged over the full scale (from 1, very low, to 7, very high). The mean rating of physical assaultiveness for the total population was 2.98 while for verbal assaultiveness it was 3.39. The mean *Sum C* for the aggressive color group was 3.83, while for the nonaggressive color group it was 3.60. Neither of these differences are significant.

The data which test the hypothesis that aggressive color Ss exceed the non-aggressive color Ss in ratings on assaultiveness are presented in Table 1.

For physical assaultiveness, the aggressive color Ss significantly exceed the nonaggressive color Ss. The results on verbal assaultiveness are suggestive but fall slightly short of significance. If the ratings for the two types of assaultiveness are pooled to form a rating on general assaultiveness, the difference between the groups is significant at the .05 level. The biserial correlation between the type of color response given by the S and the pooled ratings of aggressiveness is .35 ($p < .01$).

Table 2 presents the percentage of correct and incorrect predictions when the assaultiveness ratings are divided at the median. It shows that although the results are in the expected direction, it would be hazardous to depend on

TABLE 1.   RATINGS ON EXPLOSIVENESS AND ASSAULTIVENESS

Measure and Group	N^a	Mean	S^2	t	p
A. Physical explosiveness					
Aggressive color Ss	22	3.41	3.14	1.69	.05
Nonaggressive color Ss	26	2.54	2.93		
B. Verbal explosiveness					
Aggressive color Ss	23	3.78	2.45	1.61	N.S.
Nonaggressive color Ss	28	3.07	2.22		
C. Physical and verbal explosiveness					
Aggressive color Ss	22	7.14	10.79	1.67	.05
Nonaggressive color Ss	25	5.52	10.33		

[a] The case histories of some Ss did not contain sufficient information for rating along all dimensions. Hence, the figure in the cells may vary slightly depending on the dimension compared.

TABLE 2. PERCENTAGE
OF CASES PREDICTED

Assaultiveness Rating	Rorschach Rating	
	Aggressive Color Ss	Non-aggressive Color Ss
Above median	59	40
Below median	41	60

this variable alone in making predictions about the potentiality for assaultive behavior in individual cases.

Some interesting results appear when the protocols are divided on the basis of Ss who gave aggressive, nonaggressive, and no movement responses. An overall rating of the movement responses had been made by the senior author at the time of classification of color responses. If there was doubt as to whether the tone was aggressive or nonaggressive, the cases were placed in a separate category and not included in the comparisons in Table 3.

Although the number of cases is necessarily smaller than in the preceding table, the differences are even more marked when based on type of C response *and* type of M response. In terms of the predictive value of a combination of movements to color responses, the biserial r for a comparison of the "aggressive color and aggressive or no movement Ss" with the "nonaggressive color and nonaggressive or no movement Ss" for their hostility ratings in .55 ($p < .01$). There are not enough cases where aggressive color Ss gave clearly aggressive M responses to use either of these categories in the comparisons.

Although the two groups of Ss had approximately the same *Sum C* and M totals, the *Sum C* of the aggressive color Ss contained more pure C responses than that of the nonaggressive color group, which in turn exceeded the former group in number of FC responses. The CF responses were approximately the same for the two groups. This result was hardly unexpected as most of the aggressive color responses could be scored C or CF,

TABLE 3. RATINGS ON EXPLOSIVENESS AND ASSAULTIVENESS
WITH Ss CLASSIFIED BY TYPE OF C AND M RESPONSES

Measure and Group	N	Mean	t	p
A. Physical explosiveness				
Aggressive C + Aggressive M	8	4.00	1.80	.05
Nonaggressive C + Nonaggressive M	12	2.67		
Aggressive C with no M	6	4.00	1.38	N.S.
Nonaggressive C + Nonaggressive M	12	2.67		
Aggressive C + Aggressive M	8	4.00	3.33	.01
Nonaggressive C with no M	8	1.75		
Aggressive C with no M	6	4.00	2.46	.05
Nonaggressive C with no M	8	1.75		
B. Verbal explosiveness				
Aggressive C + Aggressive M	8	4.13	1.44	N.S.
Nonaggressive C + Nonaggressive M	13	3.31		
Aggressive C with no M	6	4.17	.86	N.S.
Nonaggressive C with Nonaggressive M	13	3.31		
Aggressive C + Aggressive M	8	4.13	3.57	.01
Nonaggressive C with no M	9	2.22		
Aggressive C with no M	6	4.17	1.99	.05
Nonaggressive C with no M	9	2.22		

while "flowers" or "grasshoppers" generally rate scores of *FC* or at most, *CF*. It seemed in order to see if a division by determinant alone (*FC* versus *CF* + *C*) would prove to be of more predictive utility with the ratings on assaultiveness than the use of content regardless of form-color balance. Finney found that his groups of aggressive and nonaggressive *Ss* differed with regard to their *CF* + *C:FC* ratios.

Of our sample, 39 *Ss* had *CF* + *C* exceeding *FC*, while 11 had *FC* equalling or greater than *CF* + *C*. Analysis of these data showed that there was not a significant difference between the two groups on either physical or verbal assaultiveness.

Discussion

There were two theories about aggressive Rorschach color responses outlined at the beginning of this paper. The first was that such responses constituted a draining off of hostile impulses and we should find less acting-out in such *Ss*. This would postulate a concept of a level of unreality where the person can solve his problems without fear of retribution from a hostile environment. If he is able to do this, he will have no need to act-out in a socially unacceptable fashion. There is an implicit assumption here of a specific amount of psychic energy that the person can release either on a fantasy level or on a behavioral level or on both.

Two groups of empirical studies support this view. The first would be instances where tension released in overt behavior reduces the tension in the fantasy level. A case in point would be the Zeigarnik effect experiments where the act of completing certain tasks will reduce the psychic tension as measured by memorial effects. There are also the studies carried out at Clark University where physical restraint increased the number of *M* responses given on the Rorschach.

Conversely, there are those who believe that the use of a content area indicates a concern or even preoccupation with a given topic. Hence, we should certainly expect behavioral correlates if we look hard enough. This view implies that the Rorschach gives a sample of behavior in a particular situation (involving an interpersonal relationship, a cognitive task, and a subjective experience on the patient's part of being evaluated). We should logically expect to find other behavioral correlates of Rorschach behavior. Loose or uncontrolled responses to (hypothesized) affect-arousing stimuli should parallel analogous behaviors in similar situations. The patient who "explodes" during the Rorschach (or phrased less strongly, the patient who loses the ability to control his response to color) would be the person we might expect to "explode" in other situations.

Our results support this second view. Aggressive responses on the Rorschach are *not* negatively correlated with aggressive acting-out, they tend to be positively correlated with it. This has implications both for making predictions of such behavior from the Rorschach and for our understanding of the relationship between fantasy[2] and behavior. The "catharsis" view of test responses is not uncommon among clinicians, especially in the matter of blatant sex responses. The idea is often proposed that the person who reports several penises and vaginas will be a mature person who is capable of expressing his impulses in an appropriate manner and hence less likely to indulge in antisocial sexual behavior. Our hypothesis would be that this is an incorrect supposition. Research should show that individuals committing rape or indulging in self-destructive promiscuous behaviors will

[2] "Fantasy" as used here refers to an unknowable construct, literally "the person's inner world," the contents of which can only be inferred from verbalizations, parapraxes, etc.

produce significantly more blatant sex responses than patients hospitalized for other reasons. The hypothesis should hold even for veiled or suggestive test responses. One can recall the Levine, Chein, and Murphy (2) study in which responses of objects instrumental in eating (in addition to actual food responses) increased with food deprivation. Our hypothesis would be that except for rare instances, such as the autism of the schizophrenic, can fantasy serve as a *contraindication* of analogous overt behavior. Even the schizophrenic girl preoccupied with sexual fantasies will display seductive and exhibitionistic behaviors on many occasions. It is our view that evidence for the "catharsis theory of test responses" is based largely on inadequate samples of the person's behavior. It may be true that the girl with very strong sex fantasies will act prim and prudish when we interview her. Yet examine her behavior over the past year, or five years, or when she "let herself" have a few drinks, then we will find marked resemblances between fantasy life and other behaviors. Fortunately, in using case histories, we were able to view a sizable portion of the individual's life. In studies involving artificial stimulus situations or small isolated samples of behavior, we should not expect to find high correlations between fantasy contents and behavior.

Summary

The present study aimed at assessing the relationship between assaultive behavior and two types of color responses, aggressive and nonaggressive. The prediction was made that Ss giving aggressive color responses should show more assaultive behavior than the nonaggressive color Ss.

One investigator looked through approximately 200 Rorschach protocols of male patients in a VA hospital and listed the names of Ss giving aggressive color responses and those giving nonaggressive color responses. The second investigator was given the list (without any information as to the category of the S) and was asked to rate the case history of the S as to incidents of verbal and physical assaultiveness. The hypothesis was confirmed. The trends were especially clear in cases where S had given both aggressive color *and* aggressive movement responses.

Although the results were of theoretical relevance in assessing the relationship between fantasy and overt behavior, the correlations were not of sufficient magnitude to permit their use in individual prediction of assaultive behavior.

REFERENCES

1. FINNEY, B. Rorschach test correlates of assaultive behavior. *J. proj. Tech.*, 1955, 19, 6–17.
2. LEVINE, R., CHEIN, I., & MURPHY, G. The relation of the intensity of a need to the amount of perceptual distortion: A preliminary report. *J. Psychol.*, 1942, 13, 283–293.
3. LINDNER, R. M. The Rorschach test and the diagnosis of psychopathic personality. *J. crim. Psychopath.*, 1943, 5, 69–93.
4. LUBAR, G. H. Rorschach content analysis. *J. clin. Psychopath.*, 1948, 9, 146–152.
5. PHILLIPS, L., & SMITH, J. G. *Rorschach interpretation: Advanced technique.* New York: Grune & Stratton, 1953.
6. PITLUCK, PATRICIA. The relation between aggressive phantasy and overt behavior. Unpublished doctoral dissertation, Yale Univer., 1950.
7. STONE, H. The relationship of hostile-aggressive behavior to aggressive content on the Rorschach and Thematic Apperception Test. Unpublished doctoral dissertation, U.C.L.A., 1953.

Inkblot Perception and Personality: The Meaning of Inkblot Variables

Wayne H. Holtzman

Using "meaningless" inkblots to excite the imagination has been a fascinating pastime for centuries. Only in recent times, however, has serious attention been given to the study of personality by means of inkblots and associations to them. At the turn of the century, the famous French psychologist, Alfred Binet, employed inkblots as one of many devices for studying individual differences in intelligence. If a person could see a large number and variety of figures in an inkblot, it was interpreted as a sign he had a "lively visual imagination." While many of Binet's tentative ideas failed to materialize, the stage was set for Hermann Rorschach's famous experiments and the posthumous publication in 1921 of the method of psychodiagnosis bearing his name.

During the past 25 years, Rorschach's test has been more widely used, acclaimed, abused, and attacked than any other method ever developed for personality assessment. Thousands of scholarly articles have been written on the Rorschach, and in many circles the method has almost become a household word. It is a tribute to Rorschach's genius that the broad outlines of his

This paper is based upon an address given at the Menninger Foundation, Topeka, Kansas, September 12, 1962, in honor of Helen D. Sargent, whose untimely death on December 25, 1959, was an incalculable loss, both personally and professionally, to her many friends and colleagues. A slightly different version of this paper appeared in the *Bulletin of the Menninger Clinic*, 1963, **27**, 84–95, and the present paper is printed with the permission of the publishers and author.

system of analysis still stand today. He stressed the importance of analyzing a person's mode of perception—whether the inkblot was interpreted as a whole or in part; whether the form, color, or shading of the inkblot was primarily responsible for evoking the response; or whether the person reported a static, lifeless percept, or one imbued with life and action. He reported considerable success in the blind diagnosis of mental patients, a feat that was impressive to many at the time.

In the years after Rorschach's untimely death, competing systems of scoring and analysis flourished. Active proponents of the Rorschach method gradually attracted a large following of psychiatrists and clinical psychologists who were concerned mainly with the psychodiagnosis of abnormal personality. Outside the mainstream of academic psychology, the Rorschach movement often took on a cultist character lacking in scientific discipline. The great surge of psychological testing during and immediately after World War II, and the resulting fusion of academic and clinical psychology, produced a flood of critical scientific investigations that revealed major defects in the Rorschach while verifying its underlying premises.

In the standard Rorschach, the subject is encouraged to give as many or as few responses as he wishes to each of only ten inkblots. After the subject completes his associations to the ten inkblots, the examiner goes over them once again, asking questions to learn what determinants led to each response and to obtain any additional responses given spontaneously by the subject. The actual number of responses may vary from less than ten to over a hundred. The subject may give a fairly uniform number of responses to each card, or he may give no response to one card and half a dozen to another. Because the inquiry is always a highly individual matter, tailored to the particular subject and his responses, the interactive influence of the examiner upon the subject and vice versa is very high. Given such freedom of response, performance variation due to examiner, and the scoring difficulties which follow, it is small wonder that quantitative studies of Rorschach scores have run head-on into almost insurmountable obstacles. The great variation in number of responses, coupled by the fact that most Rorschach scores are related in a complex manner to quantity of output, makes it impossible to establish a firm normative basis for interpretation of Rorschach scores. The small number and variety of inkblots often results in a sparse record of questionable reliability. However, once one abandons the basic idea of using only ten inkblots, of permitting the subject as few or as many responses as he cares to give, and of conducting a highly variable inquiry for purposes of illuminating the scoring categories, most of the weaknesses inherent in the standard Rorschach can be overcome.

The Holtzman Inkblot Technique

An extensive program of research was begun in 1954 at the University of Texas to overcome psychometric limitations in the Rorschach by constructing completely new sets of inkblots. Our objective was to develop an inkblot test comprised of two alternate, interchangeable forms, each of which would contain many more inkblots than the Rorschach.

A professional artist helped to construct thousands of inkblots varying in symmetry, form, color, and shading. Experimental test forms were assembled and standardized responses to 135 of the more promising blots were obtained from both psychotic patients in mental hospitals and normal adults. Unlike the Rorschach where a person is free to give as few or as many responses to each inkblot as he wishes, our instructions encouraged the subject to give only one response to each card, thereby reducing variation in number of responses to a minimum. The subject was asked to look at each inkblot and tell what it might look like, what it might represent, or what it could be. After three years of developmental research, the final forms of the Holtzman Inkblot Technique were constructed by taking the best inkblots and arranging them in two sets, each containing 45 blots. The resulting Form A and Form B are strikingly similar, assuring their interchangeability as parallel forms of the same test.[1]

Major efforts were devoted to developing a new system of scoring and analysis which would take advantage of the recognized features of the Rorschach while overcoming most of the defects in previous systems. The much greater number and richer variety of inkblots in the new technique, the simpler instructions requiring only one response per blot, and the availability of a high speed electronic computer in the new Computation Center at the University played crucial roles in the successful outcome of our work.

Standardized inkblot records were obtained for over fourteen hundred cases in populations ranging from five-year-

[1] Largely supported by Grant M-3223 from the U.S. Public Health Service, this program of research is described in the monograph by Holtzman, W. H., Joseph S. Thorpe, Jon D. Swartz, and E. Wayne Herron, *Inkblot Perception and Personality*, University of Texas Press, 1961. The inkblot materials, record forms, and scoring guide may be obtained from the Psychological Corporation, 304 East 45th Street, New York 17, New York.

old normal children to superior adults, from mentally retarded individuals to chronic schizophrenic patients. Psychologists in universities and hospitals throughout the United States participated in the project by collecting test records and other relevant information from carefully defined populations of individuals. In one instance, for example, psychologists in eleven different Veterans Administration Hospitals cooperated in providing test data from depressed mental patients.

The samples employed are outlined in Table 1. In the case of four samples— Austin Elementary, 11th Graders, UT College, and Austin College—it was possible to administer the technique twice, using the alternate form for the second administration. The time between test and retest sessions varied from one week to one year for the different samples, permitting rather broad generalizations about the equivalence of the two forms and the stability of inkblot scores over time.

Analysis of an individual inkblot record is usually done in two ways: (1) by comparing the person's scores with normative distributions for various populations, such as schizophrenic patients,

depressed patients or normal adults; and (2) by studying the content of the responses as well as individual scores. The first approach has been greatly facilitated by special diagnostic reference tables and high speed computers for rapid preliminary diagnosis. The second approach requires usage by a trained and experienced person such as a clinical psychologist because of the reliance upon intuitive skills as well as objective material.

Pathognomic Verbalization is an example of a subtle, though very important, variable in inkblot responses that can be scored only by the trained psychologist who is familiar with the deviant, autistic thought process characteristic of the schizophrenic mind. The fundamental distinction between a pathological and a normal response has been sharpened considerably in the Holtzman Inkblot Technique by provision of a detailed scoring manual containing many examples of the different kinds of pathognomic verbalization.

One common type of deviant response is called autistic logic. The main characteristic of such responses is the presence of faulty, fantastic reasoning given by the subject as justification for his response. The autistic reasoning is given with an air of certainty in spite of the fact that it bears little or no relationship to reality or conventional forms of logic. In mild form such faulty reasoning is often subtle and difficult to detect. In severe form it is obviously autistic even to the ears of an untrained observer. For example, when asked what there was about a particular inkblot which made it look like "A heart bleeding bile," a subject replied, "because it's broken and bitter." Although the fantasy of "a heart bleeding bile" is bizarre even when considered alone, additional pathology is present in the reason given for the response. The subject's autistic logic reveals a pathological fusion of the more acceptable concepts, broken heart and the bitterness of bile or ill-humor.

TABLE 1. SUMMARY OF SAMPLES IN
THE STANDARDIZATION STUDY

Sample	Number of Individuals
5-Year-Old	122
Austin Elementary	60
4th-Graders	72
7th-Graders	197
11th-Graders	72
Austin Firemen	80
Housewives	100
UT College	143
UT Superior	92
Austin College	66
Waco Schizophrenic	99
Montrose Schizophrenic	41
Woodward Retarded	50
Austin Retarded	50
VA Depressed	90
Total	1334

Occasionally a normal person will give such deviant responses, assuming a certain amount of artistic license in giving his imagination free rein. For the most part, however, the person giving the test has no difficulty in distinguishing such behavior from the schizophrenic's response.

Standardized Inkblot Variables

The scoring system developed for the Holtzman Inkblot Technique includes twenty-two different variables that cover many aspects of an individual's response to an inkblot. The more important systems for scoring the Rorschach were carefully taken into account in defining these variables so that most Rorschach scores could be easily derived from the basic elements in them. Several criteria played a prominent role in the formulation of variables for the scoring system. First, the variable had to be one which could be scored for any legitimate response, making it at least theoretically possible for a score to range from zero to 45 when given unitary weight. Second, the variable had to be sufficiently objective to permit high scoring agreement among trained individuals. Third, the variable had to show some *a priori* promise of being pertinent to the study of personality through perception. And fourth, each variable had to be logically independent of the others wherever possible in order to code the maximum amount of information in the most flexible, efficient manner.

The name, abbreviation, brief definition, and scoring weights for each of the 22 variables when applied to a single response are given below.

Reaction Time (RT). The time, in seconds, from the presentation of the inkblot to the beginning of the primary response.

Rejection (R). Score 1 when S returns inkblot to E without giving scorable response; otherwise score 0.

Location (L). Tendency to break down blot into smaller fragments. Score 0 for use of whole blot, 1 for large area, and 2 for smaller area.

Space (S). Score 1 for true figure-ground reversals; otherwise score 0.

Form Definiteness (FD). The definiteness of the form of the concept reported, regardless of the goodness of fit to the inkblot. A five-point scale with 0 for very vague and 4 for highly specific.

Form Appropriateness (FA). The goodness of fit of the form of the percept to the form of the inkblot. Score 0 for poor, 1 for fair, and 2 for good.

Color (C). The apparent primacy of color (including black, gray or white) as a response-determinant. Score 0 for no use of color, 1 for use secondary to form (like Rorschach FC), 2 when used as primary determinant but some form present (like CF), and 3 when used as a primary determinant with no form present (like C).

Shading (Sh). The apparent primacy of shading as a response-determinant (texture, depth, or vista). Score 0 for no use of shading, 1 when used in secondary manner, and 2 when used as primary determinant with little or no form present.

Movement (M). The energy level of movement or potential movement ascribed to the percept, regardless of content. Score 0 for none, 1 for static potential, 2 for casual, 3 for dynamic, and 4 for violent movement.

Pathognomic Verbalization (V). Degree of autistic, bizarre thinking evident in the response as rated on a five-point scale. Score 0 when no pathology is present. The nine categories of V and the range of scoring weights for each is as follows:

Fabulation	1
Fabulized Combination	2,3,4
Queer Response	1,2,3
Incoherence	4
Autistic Logic	1,2,3,4

Contamination	2,3,4
Self Reference	2,3,4
Deterioration Color	2,3,4
Absurd Response	3

Integration (I). Score 1 for the organization of two or more *adequately* perceived blot elements into a larger whole; otherwise score 0.

Human (H). Degree of human quality in the content of response. Score 0 for none; 1 for parts of humans, distortions, cartoons; and 2 for whole human beings or elaborated human faces.

Animal (A). Degree of animal quality in the content. Score 0 for none (including animal objects and microscopic life); 1 for animal parts, bugs or insects; and 2 for whole animals.

Anatomy (At). Degree of "gutlike" quality in the content. Score 0 for none; 1 for bones, x-rays, or medical drawings; and 2 for visceral and crude anatomy.

Sex (Sx). Degree of sexual quality in the content. Score 0 for no sexual reference; 1 for socially accepted sexual activity or expressions (buttocks, bust, kissing); and 2 for blatant sexual content (penis, vagina).

Abstract (Ab). Degree of abstract quality in the content. Score 0 for none; 1 for abstract elements along with other elements having form; and 2 for purely abstract content ("bright colors remind me of gaiety").

Anxiety (Ax). Signs of anxiety in the fantasy content as indicated by emotions and attitudes, expressive behavior, symbolism, or cultural stereotypes of fear. Score 0 for none; 1 for questionable or indirect signs; and 2 for overt or clearcut evidence.

Hostility (Hs). Signs of hostility in the fantasy content. Scored on a fourpoint scale ranging from 0 for none to 3 for direct, violent, interpersonal destruction.

Barrier (Br). Score 1 for reference to any protective covering, membrane, shell, or skin that might be symbolically related to the perception of body-image boundaries; otherwise score 0 [from Fisher & Cleveland (1)].

Penetration (Pn). Score 1 for concepts which might be symbolic of an individual's feeling that his body exterior is of little protective value and can be easily penetrated; otherwise score 0 [Fisher & Cleveland (1)].

Balance (B). Score 1 where there is overt concern for the symmetry-asymmetry feature of the inkblot; otherwise score 0.

Popular (P). Each form contains 25 inkblots in which one or more popular percepts occur. To be classified as popular in the standardization studies, a percept had to occur at least 14% of the time among normal subjects. Score 1 for popular core concepts (or their precision alternatives) as listed in the scoring manual; otherwise score 0.

In addition to the 22 scores obtained by simple summation across the 45 cards, other scores can be derived by configural scoring of two or more variables at a time. For example, a human movement score can be obtained by linking M 1 or more with H 1 or 2.

In all of our work with the Holtzman Inkblot Technique, scores on the 22 variables are punched on IBM cards for analysis, one card per response or a total of 45 cards per protocol. Special computing routines have been developed for rapid data analysis using high speed electronic computers. For a given sample of protocols, split-half reliability coefficients, means, standard deviations, intercorrelations and factor analysis are routinely obtained. In addition, special programs for configural scoring have been developed, making it possible to generate any number of new scores from the basic elements coded and punched for each response. Given the extensive nature of the 22 variables in the test and the flexible, high speed procedures for generating new scores and analyzing them it is possible to examine a large number of hypotheses about inkblot perception and personality.

A number of studies which have been completed demonstrate the reliability and objectivity of these inkblot scores, as well as their validity in signifying certain important facets of an individual's personality, his thought processes, and his way of perceiving the world around him. Illustrative statistics bearing upon three different kinds of reliability are presented in Table 2 for eighteen of the twenty-two variables routinely scored.

Form Definiteness have uniformly high reliability. The reliability of measurement within the abnormal populations is likewise high for Form Appropriateness, Color, Shading, Movement, Pathognomic Verbalization, Human, and Animal. Only seven variables—Space, Sex, Abstract, Balance, Anxiety, Penetration, and Popular—yield estimates of reliability that are generally low. In most cases these latter variables are too skewed and truncated in distribution to permit adequate estimates.

The third kind of reliability estimate routinely obtained is the test-retest sta-

TABLE 2.   INTER-SCORER CONSISTENCY, SPLIT-HALF RELIABILITY, AND TEST-RETEST STABILITY OF INKBLOT VARIABLES[*]

Inkblot variable	r between 2 highly trained scorers (40 schizophrenics)	Split-half r's for 15 samples Range Median		Test-retest r with interval of 1 week (139 college students)
Reaction Time	%	.95 − .98	.97	.77
Rejection	%	.79 − .98	.93	.76
Location	.993	.86 − .94	.91	.82
Form Definiteness	.995	.81 − .96	.88	.68
Form Appropriateness	.98	.44 − .91	.85	.55
Color	.96	.70 − .94	.88	.59
Shading	.97	.62 − .94	.78	.70
Movement	.98	.71 − .93	.81	.70
Pathognomic Verbalization	.96	.49 − .96	.87	.68
Integration	.89	.59 − .84	.79	.70
Human	.995	.66 − .93	.79	.67
Animal	.994	.53 − .95	.70	.38
Anatomy	.98	.54 − .94	.71	.53
Anxiety	.993	.31 − .91	.66	.54
Hostility	.96	.54 − .89	.71	.61
Barrier	.95	.47 − .85	.70	.45
Penetration	.92	.41 − .92	.62	.54
Popular	%	.00 − .77	.51	.39

* No reliability coefficients are reported for Space, Sex, Abstract, or Balance because of the highly skewed nature of these variables.

% Inter-scorer consistency was not computed for Reaction Time or Rejection since these variables have little or no inter-scorer variance; it was also omitted for Popular since this variable was derived after all other variables were scored.

Inter-scorer consistency for highly trained scorers is usually high, demonstrating the objectivity of most inkblot variables when carefully scored. The best estimates of reliability in the traditional sense of internal consistency are those based on the split-half method. Regardless of population studied, Reaction Time, Rejection, Location, and

bility of scores over a specified period of time, using alternate forms of the inkblot technique for the two sessions. Most of the correlations for an interval of one week are moderately high. Similar results were obtained in other samples with intervals up to one year between testing sessions, indicating sufficient stability through time for most of the inkblot variables to justify their use in prediction studies.

The existence of two equivalent forms of the test makes it an unusually well-suited projective technique for the study of change in an individual through time. Form A can be given prior to some kind of treatment which is being evaluated, followed by Form B after termination of the treatment program. A number of such studies now under way in North America and Europe will evaluate the change in personality that can be attributed to drugs, psychotherapy, or other forms of treatment.

The Question of Validity

What can be said about the psychological meaning of inkblot variables, granted that they can be reliably measured? Three general methods have been employed in our research thus far to make a start in providing an answer to this fundamental question. First, inter-correlations have been computed among the 22 inkblot variables and factor analyses have been carried out independently for each of the 15 standardization samples to determine the common dimensions underlying inkblot perception and how they may differ in patterning from one population to the next. Second, some of the external correlates of inkblot variables have been determined and used as a basis for testing earlier hypotheses taken from the Rorschach, as well as for providing new empirical data bearing upon interpretation of personality. And third, numerous significant differences among well defined samples have been discovered which shed further light on the meaning of inkblot variables while also providing a basis for psychodiagnosis of the individual. Only the highlights of this work can be described in this brief review.

Almost invariably, six factors are necessary to explain the interrelationships among the 22 inkblot variables.

The first three are the most important and emerge repeatedly, regardless of the population studied. Defined primarily by Movement, Integration, Human, Barrier, and Popular, Factor I usually accounts for more variance than any other. Consistent with earlier studies on the Rorschach, a high amount of this factor would be indicative of well organized ideational activity, good imaginative capacity, well differentiated ego boundaries, and awareness of conventional concepts. The key variables in Factor II are Color and Shading, with Form Definiteness (reversed) also frequently present as a defining variable. This bipolar factor involves sensitivity or responsiveness to the stimulus qualities of the inkblots, including concern for the symmetry-asymmetry features (Balance) in some populations. Factor III is determined primarily by Pathognomic Verbalization, with Anxiety, Hostility, and Movement usually present. A high amount of this factor would be indicative of disordered thought processes coupled with an active, though disturbed, fantasy life. Although the pattern varies for the remaining three factors, the most common configuration involves Form Appropriateness and Location in Factor IV; Reaction Time, Rejection, and Animal (reversed) in Factor V; and Penetration, Anatomy, and Sex in Factor VI.

Results of inter-group comparisons and the study of external correlates bear out the general interpretation of high scores on Factor I variables as measures of developmental maturity and psychological integration. Mean scores on Integration, Movement, Human, and Popular increase markedly with developmental level, moving from young children to superior adults. Psychotics and mentally retarded individuals generally obtain much lower scores on the Factor I variables. Among schizophrenics, however, a moderate amount of "integrated ideation" may occur largely because the individual is overresponsive, circumstantial, and talkative, thereby getting a few of the easy popular human percepts (2).

The variables in Factor I are only slightly related to verbal intelligence, Integration, Movement, and Human typically correlating about .20 with tests of vocabulary or information. As would be expected, the Factor I variables are directly related to educational and occupational level among both normal adults and mental patients, again underscoring their value as indicators of developmental maturity.

The meaning of the Factor II variables, Color, Shading, and Form Definiteness, in the assessment of personality is not entirely clear as yet. Color, the best single measure of Factor II, is high in very young children, decreasing noticeably with age until adulthood when it is again high. Although there is no difference in mean scores between normals and schizophrenics, the standard deviation is much greater in schizophrenics, largely due to fewer form-controlled color responses. The schizophrenic tends to ignore the color or else to give undifferentiated color responses of a somewhat primitive nature. In a study of chronic paranoid schizophrenic patients, Color proved inversely related to length of illness, complete absence of color responses being more characteristic of long-standing schizophrenia. Related to this finding is the recent observation by Moseley, Duffy, and Sherman (5), that Color increased significantly more in repeated testing of depressed patients given drug treatment than of similar patients given a placebo. When taken together with earlier studies on the Rorschach, these findings suggest that lack of sensitivity to the qualities of an inkblot other than its form may be a sign of poor prognosis among certain psychotic patients.

Pathognomic Verbalization, the main variable defining Factor III, is clearly indicative of disordered thought processes and disturbing fantasies. Scores of 20 or above, for example, rarely occur among normal individuals except in very young children, although they are quite common among schizophrenics and, to a lesser extent, among mentally retarded persons. Most normal subjects show little or no Pathognomic Verbalization, although they may get moderately high scores on Anxiety or Hostility, the other two defining variables for Factor III. Incidentally, high scores on Anxiety or Hostility are not necessarily indicative of manifest anxiety or hostility in social interaction with others; rather, they are measures of the amount of anxious or hostile content in the fantasy life of the individual. Consequently, there is little or no correlation between Anxiety or Hostility from inkblot perception and manifest anxiety or hostility from self-ratings or sociometric data.

The study by Moseley *et al.* extended the construct validity of the Holtzman Inkblot Technique by correlating inkblot scores with scores on the Inpatient Multidimensional Psychiatric Rating Scale (IMPS) and the Minnesota Multiphasic Personality Inventory (MMPI) for 82 depressed patients studied before and after experimental drug treatment. The relationship of inkblot scores to the IMPS is of particular interest because the ratings on the ten psychotic syndromes comprising the IMPS are based upon psychiatric interviews with the patients. Several factors were obtained involving both sets of variables to a substantial degree. Two psychotic syndromes, Disorientation and Grandiose Expansiveness, joined with Sex, Pathognomic Verbalization, and Form Appropriateness (reversed) in defining a major factor tentatively labelled withdrawal and disorientation. Paranoid Projection and Perceptual Distortion (mostly hallucinations) were significantly loaded on the familiar Factor II from the inkblot variables. The reason for this particular configuration is not clear, although a certain amount of uncontrolled responsiveness to the environment is a common ingredient. A third factor involving Sex and ratings of Motor Disturbance (tension and grimacing) is also of some interest although it may be less stable than the others. The last factor containing both inkblot and external variables was concerned with disturbed bodily preoccupations as defined by Anatomy, Pathognomic Verbalization, and Form Appropriateness (reversed) from inkblots and Guilt from the MMPI.

Further insight into the meaning of inkblot variables can be obtained by careful study of inter-group differences. Means, standard deviations, and percentile norms for eight different populations have been published (3). Ranging from five-year-olds to college students among normal individuals and including chronic schizophrenics, mentally retarded persons, and depressed patients, these norms can be utilized both for testing hypotheses about inkblot variables and for developing multivariate classification models as aids in psychodiagnosis. Only examples of this approach to validation can be presented here; a more complete discussion is given in our book, *Inkblot Perception and Personality.*

As mentioned earlier, inter-group differences among the normal populations reveal striking developmental correlates of Factor I variables, substantiating the hypothesis that Integration, Human, Movement, and Popular provide measures of ego development and a form of intellectual organization untouched by the usual measures of verbal intelligence. Inferences about other inkblot variables can also be drawn from developmental group differences. Abstract responses occur fairly often among college students but are practically never given by young children or mentally retarded adults, suggesting that Abstract provides a measure of superior intellectual ability. When Location, Form Appropriateness, and Form Definiteness are considered together, one finds a progression from whole responses having

poor form definiteness or appropriateness in young children, through detail responses having good form definiteness and appropriateness in older children, to form-definite, form-appropriate whole percepts in adults. This developmental progression was well established by Phillips and his colleagues (6) for the Rorschach and has been more precisely verified with the Holtzman Inkblot Technique by Thorpe and Swartz (7).

One inter-group difference of particular interest among normal populations is the marked discrepancy in Reaction Time for pre-school children and those in the elementary grades or beyond. The mean Reaction Time for the sample of five-year-olds was only six seconds per inkblot, while that for children in grades two through six was seventeen seconds, almost as long as for adults. This finding plus earlier work with the Rorschach strongly suggests that Reaction Time is largely a measure of impulse-control, an hypothesis that is being checked more rigorously by followup studies of the five-year-olds. Consistent with this hypothesis is the fact that depressed patients as a group obtained significantly higher scores on Reaction Time than any other population studied in the standardization program.

More relevant to the problems of psychodiagnosis are the inter-group differences among the abnormal populations or between them and the normal groups. Although the number of such reference groups in our standardization program is severely limited, the populations sampled have been well defined and serve to illustrate the possibilities for differential diagnosis based upon inkblot scores, particularly when combined with other pertinent test data and information.

Five of the samples employed in the standardization program were selected by Moseley (4) for the construction of criterion groups to test out several alternative models for psychiatric classification. The major problem was to determine the most efficient method of classifying an individual into one of two or three categories, normal, schizophrenic, or depressed, solely on the basis of inkblot scores. The simplest approach would be to consider one inkblot variable at a time, selecting cutting points which would minimize the error of classification. For example, in differentiating between chronic schizophrenics and average adults of comparable education and social class background, a score of 12 or higher on Pathognomic Verbalization as a basis for calling a person schizophrenic would misclassify only five percent of the normals while catching nearly half of the chronic schizophrenics. Or one could be more cautious by saying that a person is schizophrenic when his score on Pathognomic Verbalization is 20 or higher, leaving all individuals with scores less than 20 in a doubtful category to be examined on other inkblot variables. This procedure would miss only two percent of the normals, an error rate well within acceptable limits, considering the fact that a small number of individuals in the general population from which the average adults were drawn may indeed be schizophrenic. But such a procedure is extremely inefficient and subject to the vagaries of chance unless very large samples are employed.

A more promising method is to consider simultaneously a number of variables, determining the optimal weights for each on the basis of the linear discriminant function. Moseley compared a variety of decision models for classifying individuals as either normal or schizophrenic on the basis of inkblot variables and found that the most powerful method was the discriminant function applied to all 22 inkblot variables in their raw score form, in spite of the fact that assumptions of the normality of the distributions of scores were grossly violated by the skewed, truncated nature of some inkblot variables. Using 100 schizophrenic patients and 100 adults for deriving the weights and cutting point for optimal classification, he was able to classify individuals correctly 90 percent of the time. When cross-validated on fresh samples of schizophrenic and normal subjects, the accuracy of diagnosis remained high. The results of his analysis are presented in Table 3.

A Look to the Future

Most of our efforts thus far have been devoted to the development and standardization of a new inkblot technique having adequate psychometric characteristics while still preserving the projective nature of the Rorschach and its rich qualitative properties. Only a beginning has been made on the all important problem of validity or psychological meaning of the resulting inkblot vari-

TABLE 3. EFFICIENCY OF THE LINEAR DISCRIMINANT FUNCTION FOR CLASSIFICATION OF AN INDIVIDUAL AS NORMAL OR SCHIZOPHRENIC USING ALL TWENTY-TWO INKBLOT VARIABLES IN RAW SCORE FORM (FROM MOSELEY, 4)

Assigned Classification	Actual Criterion Classification			
	Original		Cross-Validation	
	Normal	Schizophrenic	Normal	Schizophrenic
Normal	90	10	66	7
Schizophrenic	10	90	6	31
Total Cases	100	100	72	38
Percentage Misclassified	10	10	8	18

ables with reference to important aspects of personality. While most of the investigations dealing with this problem must of necessity be done by others in a variety of contexts, we are continuing our own studies along several lines.

Largely because of the extensive data already at hand and our unusual facilities for high speed analysis, we plan to extend our psychometric and statistical studies, employing configural scoring procedures and testing out new decision models for differential diagnosis. One analysis of particular interest is the breakdown of Pathognomic Verbalization into the nine, qualitatively different, scoring categories currently combined into one variable. Although the normative samples of five-year-olds, mental retardates and schizophrenics all have high scores on Pathognomic Verbalization relative to the samples of older children and adults, it is reasonable to expect that the more bizarre forms of Fabulized Combination, Queer Response, Incoherence and Self Reference should be more characteristic of schizophrenics than young children or mental retardates. Similarly it can be hypothesized that Absurd Response will occur more frequently among mentally retarded persons than others. With the large numbers of protocols already scored for these particular samples, it is a simple matter to carry out the additional analysis needed.

Some of the most striking inter-group differences in the standardization study were found among the samples of normal individuals when arranged on a developmental continuum. While these results demonstrate the validity of certain inkblot variables as measures of developmental maturity, the precise nature of the developmental aspects of perceptual-cognitive functioning can be determined satisfactorily only by the longitudinal study of large, representative samples with equal-interval, repeated measurement for which the Holtzman Inkblot Technique with its parallel forms is

uniquely suited. Such a study is now under way in the public schools of Austin, Texas. Over four hundred boys and girls have been selected from three different grade levels, three years apart, beginning with the first grade. Repeated measurements will be made each year for six consecutive years. A short battery of selected cognitive, perceptual, and personality tests will also be given each year, although the specific content of this battery will vary from one year to the next with only a small core repeated regularly. This design makes it possible to study a twelve-year developmental span in only six calendar years.

Related to this longitudinal study of children are several small investigations currently in progress. Of the 122 preschool children tested in 1960 as part of the standardization program, the majority have remained in Austin. Efforts have been made to obtain retest protocols on as many as possible of these children two years after the initial session. Because of the striking differences between the sample of five-year-olds and the samples of elementary school children in the normative studies—differences that are highly consistent with expectations from current theory and intriguing in their implications—it is of special importance to retest the five-year-olds after they have adapted to the conformity pressures and challenges of a classroom environment but before they have acquired the perceptual and cognitive skills typical of the third or fourth grader.

The second related study deals with children in Lois Murphy's Coping Project at the Menninger Foundation. Now ranging in age from 10 to 13 years, these children have been studied intensively from infancy to the present time. The sample of 32 children in the Coping Project has been augmented by a similar group in an extended investigation using Riley Gardner's cognitive control tests, the Rorschach, and the Holtzman Inkblot Technique. In this exploratory study, it will be possible to relate inkblot variables to cognitive control scores of scanning, field articulation, leveling-sharpening, equivalence range, tolerance for unrealistic experiences, and constricted-flexible control, as well as intelligence subtest scores and selected behavioral ratings. From preliminary results in this study, key measures of cognitive control have been selected for inclusion in the long-range longitudinal study of Austin children.

These several studies serve only to illustrate the many kinds of research needed to gain a full understanding of the value and limitations of approaches to personality through inkblot perception. The availability for the first time of a large number of standardized inkblots opens a whole new field of research in this important area. As with any new technique for the assessment of personality, the final verdict of its utility can be reached only after much investigation in a wide variety of situations, both experimental and clinical.

REFERENCES

1. FISHER, S., and CLEVELAND, S. E. *Body image and personality*. Princeton, N.J.: Van Nostrand Co., Inc., 1958.
2. HOLTZMAN, W. H., GORHAM, D. R., and MORAN, L. J. A factor-analytic study of schizophrenic thought processes. *J. abnorm. soc. Psychol.*, 1964, **69**, 355–364.
3. HOLTZMAN, W. H., THORPE, J. S., SWARTZ, J. D., and HERRON, E. W. *Inkblot Perception and Personality*, Austin, Texas: University of Texas Press, 1961.
4. MOSELEY, E. C. *Psychodiagnosis based on multivariate analysis of the Holtzman Inkblot Technique*. Unpublished doctoral dissertation, University of Texas, Austin, 1962.
5. MOSELEY, E. C., DUFFY, R. F., and SHERMAN, L. J. An extension of the construct validity of the Holtzman Inkblot Technique. *J. clin. Psychol.*, 1963, **19**, 188–192.
6. PHILLIPS, L., KADEN, S., and WALDMAN, M. Rorschach indices of developmental level. *J. Genet. Psychol.*, 1959, **94**, 267–285.
7. THORPE, J. S., and SWARTZ, J. D. Level of perceptual development as reflected in responses to the Holtzman Inkblot Test. *J. proj. Tech. pers. Assessment*, 1965, **29**, 380–386.

PART III

The Integration of

Clinical Data

in Assessment

Chapter 12

Validity of Clinical Assessment
Using Multiple Sources of Data

■ This chapter introduces Part III, which is devoted to the integration of clinical data in assessment. Our survey of the literature on the validation of individual instruments has shown that most are useful for some diagnostic tasks but not for others. Clinical assessment, however, is not based on any single source of data. In the typical assessment situation, the psychologist blends data from the case history, medical reports, observations of the client's behavior, interviews with the client, and, often, his relatives, physician, clergyman or probation officer, and, last but not least, the client's performance on psychological tests. The time has now come to ask how valid is this final assessment based on a number of sources of information.

In the ideal study of clinical assessment, each client would be examined in a uniform manner by several clinicians, each of whom was free to conduct the assessment exactly as he wished. This client would not be influenced by any of these evaluations and would thus remain constant for all clinicians. Each clinician would be free to integrate the data as he saw fit and write a report in his usual manner; despite this each clinician's report would be reliable and contain information on the same variables. These uniform yet unique reports would then be correlated with a perfectly valid criterion measure to determine their accuracy. In this best of all possible worlds, these reports would no doubt be found to be perfectly valid and the clinicians and researchers would then live happily ever after.

Unfortunately, the real world is not like this. No way has yet been found for us simultaneously to have perfect experimental rigor and completely natural or representative assessment situations. In practice, some form of compromise has to be reached which leaves both the clinician and researcher less than completely satisfied.

In the typical clinical situation, each clinician has direct personal contact with each client. During this time he is free to ask whatever questions he desires and to observe not only the client's verbal responses but also his dress, speech, tics, tremors, mannerisms, weeping, hesitations, and so on. He also has a chance to monitor his own emotional responses and thus perceive the client's effect on another person. Ideally, all these sources of data should also be available to the clinician in an empirical study of assessment. On the other hand, it is also desirable to obtain several evaluations of each client to determine the reliability of assessment. Since it is impossible to allow each clinician individual contact with a client who remans uninfluenced throughout (except possibly with a Korsakoff psychotic), some compromise must be reached. Either we must have a client who is to be subjected to a series of repeated interviews and test sessions, or we must deprive the clinicians of this personal contact and instead supply them with uniform data in the form of transcripts of test sessions or interviews conducted by someone else. The latter course is that usually followed.[1]

In almost all research studies the clinician is free to integrate the data provided as he sees fit and in this aspect they duplicate the clinical situation. However, constraints are placed upon the way he must communicate the resulting personality appraisal. Ideally he would be free to communicate his findings as he saw fit. However, if some variable such as aggressiveness or latent homosexual tendencies was not mentioned in his report, it would be impossible to know whether the examiner found no signs of such tendencies or merely did not choose to emphasize them. Thus several reports about a person might be quite different, as different examiners emphasized different aspects of the clinical picture; yet all might be quite accurate in what they did describe. The only way to avoid this is to require that each clinical assessment as well as the criterion assessment be on some form of uniform report such as a Q sort or a check list of personality statements. However, this uniform response measure obviously distorts the clinical task and forces the clinician into making decisions with which he is uncomfortable and which he would not make in a non-research situation. A Rogerian clinician, for instance, might find himself forced to decide to what degree an adolescent manifested signs of "superego lacunae."

Finally the criterion measures should be reliable, valid, and concern variables which the clinician can reasonably be expected to assess validly. In their search for reliable, valid criteria, researchers have all too often selected such variables as grade point averages or success in industrial training programs. Such criteria are not relevant to *clinical* assessment. On the other hand, clinical criteria, such as personality descriptions or psychiatric diagnoses, are themselves of dubious reliability and validity.

One research strategy is to compare an appraisal based on complete knowledge with one based on incomplete knowledge. The findings of these studies, however, are, strictly speaking, generalizable only to the validity of incomplete assessments. While most of us do incomplete assessments in clinical practice, none of us are about to admit this, which allows us to attack the relevance of such investigations.

The five studies in this chapter are ones which, in the editor's opinion,

---

[1] Perhaps a better compromise would be in the form of sound motion pictures of the testing session rather than written records, but to the editor's knowledge this has not yet been attempted.

strike a reasonable bargain between the dictates of research and the need to represent fairly the clinical situation.[2] A variety of dependent variables are used but all are ones which clinicians should be able to assess.

The studies are organized in terms of Meehl's criteria for the usefulness of an assessment technique presented in Chapter 1. It will be recalled that the minimal requirement of a technique is that it provide us with valid, semantically clear statements. This is the standard that Holsopple and Phelan, and Little and Shneidman employ.

The second level of usefulness is when the assessment provides data which are not only valid but also are not readily available from another source. Both Golden and Kostlan[3] attack this problem directly. They not only correlate the clinical reports with the criterion measures, but also compare the results with the predictions which could have been made on the basis of identifying data alone. Golden also poses the question of whether or not assessment improves as tests are added to a battery, while Kostlan seeks to determine which combination of tests is most useful in clinical assessment.

The ultimate level of usefulness is reached when a procedure provides unique, accurate data, earlier in time so that it can make a difference in the way a subject is to be treated or handled. Holtzman and Sells pose this type of test when they ask their clinicians to predict which flight candidates will fail because of personality disorders.

The results of these studies do not offer a great deal of comfort to clinicians. They indicate that some clinicians can make inferences at better than a chance level, sometimes and under some conditions. Psychological tests generally result in somewhat more accurate inferences than does minimal identifying information, but the increment is much less than we would like. Test data appear to be considerably inferior to case history data, and projective tests fare somewhat less well than structured tests.

One difficulty that is common to several of the studies is the amount of pathology clinicians find in well-functioning people. Harrower (1954), in commenting about the Holtzman and Sells study in which she took part, points out that those who succeeded in flight training exhibited much more pathology than she would have thought possible in a successful candidate. While she points to the problem of inference in an unfamiliar setting with an unfamiliar population, it could be that this is but one aspect of the clinician being overly sensitive to pathology at the expense of signs of health. Dealing exclusively with malfunctioning people it is easy to lose sight of how "sick" people can be and still function effectively. Thus in the Little and Shneidman study, members of the normal group were frequently judged as being quite maladjusted. One is reminded of Taft's (1955) findings that physical scientists and experimental psychologists are frequently better able to judge nor-

---

[2] Another such study which could not be included is that of Horowitz (1962).

[3] For a critique of Kostlan's study and a reply, see Patterson (1955) and Kostlan (1955).

mal people than are clinical psychologists, apparently because they use normal rather than pathological stereotypes.

It would appear from these findings that more research needs to be done on the proper weighting of signs of pathology, and that more clinical training should be devoted to building up stable internal norms of the personality patterns to be found among well-functioning people if the accuracy of personality assessment is to be improved.

REFERENCES

HARROWER, MOLLY. Clinical aspects of failures in the projective techniques. *Journal of Projective Techniques*, 1954, **18**, 294–302.
HOROWITZ, MIRIAM J. A study of clinicians' judgements from projective test protocols. *Journal of Consulting Psychology*, 1962, **26**, 251–256.
KOSTLAN, A. A reply to Patterson. *Journal of Consulting Psychology*, 1955, **19**, 486.
PATTERSON, C. H. Diagnostic accuracy or diagnostic stereotype? *Journal of Consulting Psychology*, 1955, **19**, 483–485.
TAFT, R. The ability to judge people. *Psychological Bulletin*, 1955, **62**, 1–23.

The Skills of Clinicians in Analysis of Projective Tests

James Q. Holsopple and Joseph G. Phelan

Introduction

With the recent sudden increase in the number of psychologists engaged in clinical practice, there has arisen an interest in the selection of persons to be trained for this work and to that end an interest in the development of reliable measures of diagnostic skill. Challman[7] and Kelly[12, 13] report on attempts to determine who may best be trained to formulate diagnoses. The University of Michigan group[13] was interested in the possibility of "demonstrating the relative and cumulative effectiveness of all available techniques as predictive of future professional suc-

Reprinted by permission of the publisher and the authors from the *Journal of Clinical Psychology*, 1954, **10**, 307–320.

cess" in this highly individualized specialty. In addition to paper and pencil tests of intelligence, achievement, personality, attitudes and temperament, and interviews, this group used individual and pooled ratings based on situational and real life procedures designed to reveal "aptitude for effective interpersonal relationships." Candidates for clinical training were asked to perform in a variety of situational tests and were rated by staff members. Staff members first made independent judgments which were later pooled in staff team predictions. Predictions, in the form of ratings, were made on 15 tentatively defined criterion attributes (e.g., skill in psychometry, skill in diagnostic interviewing, etc.), and on 23 tentatively defined personality traits, deemed to be predictive of one or more dimensions of successful clinical performance. This research showed that the conference method fails to enable judges to predict who may best be trained as diagnosticians, as do unstructured interviews, objective and projective tests and clinician-technique combinations of various sorts.

Estes[10] found, when psychiatric social workers were asked to make judgments about personality characteristics, that some social workers could demonstrate much greater ability to make use of cues than others. Existence or degree of this skill seemed not related to age, length of service, sibling status or to whether or not the judge had been analyzed. Horn,[11] working with Murray,[15] used an analysis of variance technique to compare the relative importance for successful diagnosis of the ability of the judge and the aspect of personality measured. His judges differed greatly in ability even though similarly trained. Horn felt that in presentation of data and in teaching of the clinical process it is important to single out or emphasize those aspects of personality which make for difficulty in diagnosis and to recognize the relative importance and weight to be attached to various kinds of clinical evidence.

The studies here reviewed dealing with the process of diagnosis, stress the finding that among clinicians with roughly equivalent training, some seem able to perform at an easily demonstrable higher level of efficiency than others similarly trained and experienced. It would be desirable to try to isolate those clinicians who possess the skill in order to study the individuals and the process, and ultimately to devise a method of selecting those who may best be trained.

Such a plan for isolating this diagnostic skill might borrow from the operational methods used in other disciplines, using a matching technique requiring the identification of a variety of data as belonging to one and the same individual. This seems preferable to the method used by Horn[11] and Estes[10] where the data were identified as belonging to the unique individual by requiring that the judge assign trait names or rate observed behavior on a list of traits and express their judgments in a series of ratings of abstract personality variables, on the meaning and value of which there could not be general agreement.

Problem

It is proposed to develop a practical test to isolate the excellent judges of personality patterns, and to discriminate the cues upon which their judgments are based. If such a test can clearly distinguish those who have such ability, it might be adapted for use to select those who have such ability at an early stage in their development. A test requiring that clinicians match projective protocols and identify them as products of the unique individual might throw some light on the mechanics of the diagnostic skill. The clinician could demonstrate ability by the frequency and consistency with which he recognizes productions and by the reasons he gives for choices and classifications. This procedure might contribute knowledge of the diagnostic process, and perhaps convert "private correlations" presently in use, informal and unverbalized, into mathematical statements into which the values of the individual on each of the factors could be fitted. After matching, clinicians would be required to indicate subjective certainty in matching. It would be possible in this case to compare accuracy with subjective certainty, and then to compare our findings with those of the earlier investigators and re-evaluate the relationships between subjective certainty and success in matching projective materials.

The aims of this experiment are as follows:

a. To devise a "test" which would enable the individual clinician to demonstrate skill in utilizing projective techniques.
b. To indicate statistical significance of the matching performance of the judges as a group.
c. To study the relationship between expressed subjective certainty and accuracy of judgment for experienced clinicians.

The Matching Method

Since the core of this problem lies in the determination of a practical technique for estimating presence and degree of diagnostic skill, the test performance should involve identification of a global array of records as having been produced by the same person by some type of matching technique. A survey of the literature shows that matching techniques have been widely used for the estimation of the validity of projective materials. Cronbach[9] asserts the primacy of this method in a discussion of statistical studies of Rorschach validity:

A Rorschach record is interpreted qualitatively and in a complex manner when the test is given in a clinic. A favorite technique for evaluating Rorschach results is matching . . . which permits a study of the case as a whole. When a set of Rorschach records, interpreted or not, and another set of data are available, one may request the judges to match the two sets in pairs. . . . Because of the peculiar character of clinical tests and the limitation of the conventional and mathematically sound procedures, and because statistical methods for such tests have not been fully developed . . . matching procedures in which a clinical synthesis of each Rorschach record is compared with a criterion are especially appropriate. . . . A portrait based on the Rorschach may be nearly right, yet be mismatched because of minor false elements.

Cronbach emphasizes that the limitations of the matching method are not statistical in nature but lie in the human limitations of the judges.

Horn,[11] presented experienced clinicians with a variety of biographical and projective materials serially. Judges were asked to check a list of personality trait names which seemed applicable for various subjects. His judges found that the biographical data contributed more to an understanding of the person, enabled them to predict behavior with greater accuracy than did other instruments.

Troop's study[17] required that judges match two Rorschach records for each person. 114 matches were correct out of a possible 120. Judges considered 5 pairs of records at a time; contingency coefficient 0.88. A coefficient of 0.40 was obtained when judges attempted to match the records of each case.

Krugman[14] validated Rorschach methods by proving that different evaluations of the same Rorschach protocol could be matched; that interpretations could be matched to the raw record and to criteria based on a case study. She found no differences in ability to match among her judges. In her work seven judges matched several series of Rorschach records with Rorschach interpretations. 25 Rorschach personality interpretations were matched with clinical case study abstracts in matching groups of 5 pairs. Krugman's results, reported in terms of Vernon's[19] contingency coefficient values, indicate high validity in all matching experiments.

Vernon[21] reported little success after extensive investigation of estimation of personality characteristics by the matching method. "We are hardly justified in talking of a general matching ability," he says. In his work, average intercorrelations between eight tests was only 0.085, giving a corrected consistence of -0.43. Even within a single type of material, as with 20 sets of photographs and vocations, or 35 sets of drawings of houses and men, the corrected reliability of the judges' rating was only 0.055 and -0.57.

Valentine[18] found intuitive judgments of personality unreliable. He required that judges (men and women students preparing to be teachers) rate selected personality traits of children and youths. Matching scores of judges, based on the criterion of ratings of trait-names, are no greater than chance expectation. Valentine also investigated the relationship between the degree of accuracy which his student-teacher judges expressed in their intuitive judgments when matching for personality characteristics and the accuracy of their judgments. Those judgments "which the student marked as having been given with special confidence proved often more inaccurate than other judgments." Polansky[16] obtained a correlation of 0.008 between the accuracy of predictions derived from case histories and the indications of judges as to "how well they thought they knew" the subjects of the histories. Wallin[22] in discussing such findings, concluded that some judges tend to "project," to mis-read the attitudes or motivations of others because they naively inject their personal feelings into observations of other people's behavior. This kind of judge, the projector, is likely to be wrong while absolutely certain he is right.

Vernon[19, 20, 21] advocates the matching method for reliability and validity studies of psychograms and other measures, pointing out extraneous factors which may be controlled in matching experiments if relationships between matched series of data are to be valid.

1. It is conceivable in matching that some of the judgments might reduce themselves to a process of elimination rather than genuine judging. We propose to control this by requiring that our judges match unequal elements. This provides a fairly direct control over the difficulty of the experiment.

2. Extraneous elements in the materials can afford peripheral clues to correct matching. An effort should be made to exclude characteristic turns of speech or other accidental clues.

3. The validity of the matching result is not affected statistically by the number of elements matched at a time. In spite of statistical equivalency, the results of experiments with different numbers of things matched must differ subjectively. Vernon[21] found that the number of things to be optimally matched must vary for each type of material depending on the number of impressions the average judge can keep clear in his mind.

The Method

A matching task of 16 documents was presented to 20 trained and experienced clinical psychologists, all of whom were Doctors of Philosophy and had at least two years of clinical experience. The documents were presented in four arrays with unequal matching; in each array the four tests given were representative of the same six individuals, as follows:

Array A.   4 standardized dictated autobiographies culled at random from 6 individual biographies.[1]

Array B.   4 complete T.A.T. protocols selected from the T.A.T. protocols of the identical 6.

Array C.   4 complete Rorschach results (with scoring and location charts) and Sentence Completion responses selected from records of the same group of 6 individuals.[2]

Array D.   4 sets of responses to standardized tests—Thurstone Primary Mental Abilities Test; Kuder Preference Record; and Guilford-Zimmerman Temperament Tests selected from the same 6.

Subjects differed widely in diagnosis, age, and socio-cultural background. Vernon[21] stresses the effect of homogeneity on the validity of matching and

[1] The "Form for Autobiography" prepared by H. A. Murray at The Harvard Psychological Clinic was used.[15]

[2] The Sentence Completion Test employed was the Holsopple-Miale Test.

suggests the use of as wide a diversity of materials as is practical. The subjects were:

(A) 34-year-old male, convict, college graduate, convicted on several charges of molesting young girls; diagnosed by prison psychiatrist as psychopath-sexual deviate, though Rorschach and T.A.T. record showed many signs and indications of schizophrenia.

(B) 23-year-old male, mental clinic out-patient, unmarried, with apparently no hetero-or-homosexual experience; diagnosis: anxiety state.

(C) 28-year-old married female, research scientist, living successfully in community, no need for treatment.

(D) 18-year-old high-school student, male, under psychiatric treatment, anxiety, homosexual panic.

(E) 36-year-old female, probationer, prostitute; no diagnosis, bland, immature, without foresight or concern.

(F) 36-year-old male, business executive; no diagnosis, apparently not in need of treatment.

All materials were edited with a view to eliminating extrinsic clues which might make matching possible without an evaluation of data. Where possible topical references, turns of speech or mannerisms were excised from proto-cols. Unequal matching was utilized. This procedure maximized the difficulty of the matching task and kept the num-ber of units to be matched within prac-ticable limits. Gaps occurred in the matching scheme as illustrated in Table 1 which shows the pattern of presenta-tion of the arrays of tests A, B, C and D. Each array consisted of four documents selected from the materials from the six subjects.

The described matching task was pre-sented to the judges in mimeographed form. There was no limit to the amount of time they could spend on it or the number of times they could re-read it. It was accompanied by the following instructions:

Appended hereto are 16 documents which are the results of standardized autobio-graphical interviews, objective tests and projective techniques administered to six individuals. You are asked to indicate to which of the six individuals any two or more of these documents could be attrib-uted, so that the documents which you assign to one person could only have been produced by one person. Each protocol has identifying call letters. Indicate on the attached form your matching of two, three or four documents as belonging to one person, indicate whether you feel quite sure, comparatively sure, or unsure of your choice by checking the appro-priate space. Each of the documents is identified by a pair of letters. This pair is the designation to be used in describing the matching judgment; for example, in filling out the accompanying form one might write: Documents AB (biographical sketch), CD (Rorschach—Sentence Com-pletion), EF (Thematic Apperception Test) seem to belong together, etc.

TABLE 1.   THE SCHEME OF PRESENTATION OF THE TASK (IN EACH ARRAY, FOUR UNITS, REPRESENTATIVE OF THE SIX SUBJECTS)

Arrays of Tests	Subjects					
	Convict (Male)	Mental O.P.D. Clinic (Male)	Research Scientist (Female)	High School Student (Male)	Proba-tioner (Female)	Business Executive (Male)
A. Autobiography	×	×	×		×	
B. T.A.T.		×	×	×		×
C. Rorschach-Sentence Completion	×	×		×	×	
D. Objective Battery (PMA, Kuder STDCR)	×	×		·	×	×

The primary aim of this task was to provide a vehicle by means of which judges could demonstrate skill in identifying and in relating inferred personality characteristics. It was necessary to devise a matching situation of sufficient difficulty to constitute a challenge and at the same time one which could yield valid results for experienced clinical psychologists. Because of the number of variables to be kept in mind simultaneously, the number of units of material which could be presented at once had to be limited. Vernon[21] points out that we have no clear idea of the point at which a given task becomes so difficult that the average judge cannot perform. "The point varied with the type of materials used and the optimum level of difficulty would vary with the experience, training and intelligence of the judges participating in the task."

The judges could attain a score of 36 points if all tests were correctly matched. If Judge A matched the Biography with T.A.T. for the Mental Clinic Patient he was credited with 1 point; Biography with Rorschach, 1 point; Biography with Objective Tests, 1 point; also 1 point for T.A.T.—Rorschach match; 1 point for T.A.T.—Objective Test match and 1 point for Rorschach—Objective Test match: a total of 6 points for all correct matches for each of six subjects. The judge received 1 point, naturally, in every case where he correctly located gaps in the data, as for example, when he judged that none of the given T.A.T. protocols went with the Biography of the Male Convict. The judges indicated that they had followed the suggestions in the instructions.

Results

Performance of Judges. Following Vernon[21] and Chapman[5] on the statistics of the matching method, it was possible to calculate the frequency with which a given number of correct matches could be expected to occur

when the judge was required to arrange six arrays of data, with six units in each array, against every other array. See appendix for formulae and calculations.

The performance of the judges, individually and as a group, is compared with chance expectancy in Table 2. Seven judges (A, E, H, I, M, N, R) performed better than chance at the .01 level of confidence. Three other judges (C, F, K) performed at the .05 level, making ten judges working at a level that such performance could be expected to occur by chance 5 times out of one hundred ($p < .05$). The remaining ten judges (B, D, G, J, L, O, P, Q, S, T) functioned within chance expectation ($p > .05$). Thus, differences between workers with similar training and experience in working with projective materials exist and are demonstrable. Some analyze and utilize these materials in an immediately relevant way and consistently. That they do so is shown in their success in recognition and identification of the individual person through a variety of expressive instruments.

In order to evaluate the performance of the judges as a group for significance, we need only consider performance of judges who complete the entire task, and score the task such that the greatest number of correct arrangements of data can equal 18, (one correct credit for each document successfully matched against Biography). In this situation, $x^2 = 5.26$, $p < .05$. Chance alone could not have operated in this circumstance; the performance of judges as a group exceeds chance expectation. (See appendix for x^2 computation.)

Qualitative differences in matching performance with various materials. It is important to compare the ways in which judges go about their task, how they work with different kinds of materials. Some judges might perceive the inter-relationships of material derived from two documents, such as Rorschach and Biography, and at the same time

TABLE 2. SIGNIFICANCE OF MATCHING JUDGMENTS FOR INDIVIDUAL JUDGES. TOTAL NUMBER OF JUDGES = 20. 14 JUDGES COMPLETED TASK. TOTAL NUMBER OF POSSIBLE CORRECT JUDGMENTS FOR EACH JUDGE = 36, OR 6 IN EACH CATEGORY

Judge	Number Correct						Total Correct	Total Incorrect	P Value
	Biog. T.A.T.	Biog. Ror.	Biog. Obj.	T.A.T. Ror.	T.A.T. Obj.	Ror. Obj.			
A	4	3	2	1	3	3	16	20	.0006
B	1	2	2	1	2	2	10	26	.0862
C	2	4	1	2	1	1	11	25	.0443
D	2	2	1	0	1	2	8	28	.2583
E	4	1	3	1	4	1	14	22	.0040
F	4	2	2	2	1	1	12	24	.0211
G	1	2	2	0	3	1	9	27	.1547
H	4	4	3	4	4	2	21	15	<.0001
I	4	2	2	1	3	1	13	23	.0094
J	2	1	2	1	2	1	9	27	.1547
K	1	3	2	0	0	6	12	24	.0211
L	0	2	1	1	1	3	8	28	.2583
M	1	4	3	1	1	3	13	23	.0094
N	3	3	0	4	3	3	16	20	.0006
O	0	1	1	2	1	1	6	18	Inc.
P	1	1	1	1	2	1	7	17	Inc.
Q	1	0	0	0	0	0	1	3	Inc.
R	2	3	2	4	4	1	16	8	Inc.
S	3	4	0	3	0	0	10	2	Inc.
T	3	2	0	1	0	0	6	10	Inc.
Total	43	46	30	30	36	33	218	390	

Significance of group of judges (N = 14) $\chi^2 = 5.26$ $p < .05$
Performance of 6 individual judges $p < .01$
Performance of 9 individual judges $p < .05$

TABLE 3.   RESULTS OF MATCHING TASK. PERFORMANCE OF BEST AND POOREST
MATCHERS IN COMPARISON OF BIOGRAPHICAL DATA AND PROJECTIVE MATERIALS
(NUMBER OF JUDGMENTS EACH CATEGORY = 6)

| | Clinicians who made 11 or more correct choices ($p<.05$) | | | | Clinicians with fewer than 11 correct choices ($p>.05$) | | |
Judge	Biog. vs T.A.T.	Biog. vs Rorschach	T.A.T. vs Rorschach	Judge	Biog. vs T.A.T.	Biog. vs Rorschach	T.A.T. vs Rorschach
A	4	3	1	B	1	2	1
C	2	4	2	D	2	2	0
E	4	1	1	G	1	2	0
F	4	2	2	J	4	2	1
H	4	4	4	L	0	2	1
I	4	2	1	O	0	1	2
K	1	3	0	P	1	1	1
M	1	4	1	Q	1	0	0
N	3	3	4	S	3	4	3
R	2	3	4	T	3	2	1
Total	29	29	20	Total	16	18	10

seem unaware of implications of other materials such as the T.A.T. (cf. Table 3—Judges C, K, M and L). Similarly, judges may do well with one subject with a particular kind of dynamics but be unable to empathize with or appreciate the implications of the problem of some other individual. Other judges may be able to perform significantly above chance with every kind of material and all subjects (cf. Judge H).

Table 3 brings out some of the results of the exceptionally good and the poor judges in their handling of the various projective documents and the biographical data. Good judges exceed poor judges in a two to one ratio in comparing Rorschach with T.A.T. protocol, the ratio closely approaches two to one when they matched Biography and T.A.T., and is about three to two in matching Biography and Rorschach. Both good and poor judges do much better when matching all projective materials with Biography than when matching Rorschach with T.A.T. or objective and projective tests.

Certainly an observation which bears further investigation is the possibility that the Biography covers a wider range of attitudinal material and thus over-

laps to a significant degree both Rorschach and T.A.T., whereas the Rorschach and T.A.T. are more specific, more limited in range, with less overlap, thus presenting greater difficulty for matching. Both the Rorschach and T.A.T. are considered by clinicians to deal with quite distinct "layers" of personality.

Validity of Tests Used. Some evidence concerning the validity of projective devices may be elicited from this experiment. It is necessary:

(1) To consider only the performance of those clinicians (14 judges, judges A–N) who completed the task.

(2) Vernon's statistic[21] for matching, the contingency coefficient and its probable error, cannot be utilized because of our employment of unequal matching series. In our situation, in which four units in each array are given and two withheld, the two absent units must be considered interchangeable; therefore Vernon's formula is inapplicable. The χ^2 statistic can be employed, the value which various tests have for clinicians can be measured by successes in matching compared with chance expectancy.

(3) The performance of judges as a group

TABLE 4. CALCULATION OF THEORETICAL
DISTRIBUTION

Number of pairs correctly matched	Number of judges to be expected to achieve such score
0	3.0632
1	4.9588
2	3.7184
3	1.4588
4	0.728
5	0.728

Theoretical number of judges	Less than 2 correct matchings	2 or more correct matchings	Sum
1 degree of freedom	8.022	5.978	14.0000

can be evaluated on the materials of the various orders by considering the matching of each array against every other array as a separate matching experiment. The theoretical distribution to be expected when 14 judges arrange one array of six documents against each other array is given in Table 4 (cf. appendix for calculation of these values). A measure of the deviation of our sample from this hypothetical population ratio can be obtained, and a means of judging whether or not our measure could be expected in sampling by use of the x^2.

From Table 5, it is seen that the judges were able to match Rorschach results with Biography with the highest excess of obtained over expected frequencies. The matchings of Biography $vs.$ T.A.T., Biography $vs.$ Objective Test, and Rorschach $vs.$ Objective Tests were next in efficiency. The type of matching in which the judges were least competent involved T.A.T. $vs.$ Rorschach comparisions and T.A.T. $vs.$ Objective Tests.

Judges in our experiment were less successful in matching than Krugman's judges. Her judges were presented with a much less challenging task, having fewer complex variables to keep in mind simultaneously.

The consistency of high level performance on the part of some judges in our experiment and the wide differences in performance between judges seem to indicate that an ability to match

TABLE 5. x^2 VALUES OBTAINED FROM COMPARING THE ARRAYS OF 4 UNITS REPRESENTATIVE OF THE SIX SUBJECTS WITH THE OTHER ARRAYS OF DIFFERENT MATERIALS. THE THEORETICAL EXPECTATION OF THE NUMBER OF JUDGES CORRECTLY MATCHING LESS THAN 2 IS 8, AND THE EXPECTED NUMBER OF JUDGES MATCHING 2 OR MORE IS 6

Matching Comparison	Obtained Frequencies Less than 2	2 or More	x^2	Level of Confidence
Biography vs. T.A.T.	5	9	3.15	$p<.10$
Biography vs. Rorschach	2	12	12.6	$p<.001$
Biography vs. Objective Tests	5	9	3.15	$p<.10$
T.A.T. vs. Rorschach	10	4	1.4	$p<.30$
T.A.T. vs. Objective Tests	6	8	1.4	$p<.30$
Rorschach vs. Objective tests	5	9	3.15	$p<.10$

materials of this type does exist, can be isolated, demonstrated and subjected to further study.

Methods Used by Judges. The number of judges in the group who were able to utilize the "series of tests" approach can be observed by inspection. Table 6 indicates the method and extent to which judges are able to recognize the subject by identifying most or all of his tests as being his as a matter of fact.

TABLE 6. RECORD OF 14 JUDGES (WHO COMPLETED THE TASK) IN CORRECTLY MATCHING RECORDS PRODUCED BY THE SIX SUBJECTS IN SERIES, WHEN TESTS WERE MATCHED AGAINST BIOGRAPHY AS A CRITERION

Judge	Number of tests correctly matched against biography		
A	9	1	2
B	4		
C	7	1	
D	5		
E	8	4	
F	5	1	
G	5	1	
H	11	2	2
I	8	3	
J	4	1	
K	6	1	
L	3		
M	9	3	
N	6	2	

In general, judges who match pairs of tests also excel in matching tests against biography in series. Judges A, C, E, H, I, and M, high scorers in paired matchings, seem able to follow the procedure of visualizing the individual, matching all his tests in series. Judges were able, not only to identify any two tests as belonging together, but also to identify tests in series as "going with" a given biography. In this case judges seem able to recognize the individual through several of his productions, rather than merely to match two tests.

Significance of Types of Errors. Vernon[21] asserts that the most important

of all the extraneous factors which influence the matching experiment is the homogeneity or diversity of the materials. Homogeneity is dependent on the distinctiveness or range of unlikeness among the subjects whose modes of expression and reflections of personality characteristics made up the data.

Randomness is usually examined by means of the standard deviation of subjects' scores, but in matching, the difference between the subjects in any one set of materials is qualitative so that no measure comparable to the standard deviation is available. A study can be made of the second choices and the "good" errors (those made by many judges, where similar aspects of two subjects are more pronounced than their differences). A study of these errors affords insight into the ways in which test results of seemingly widely different persons can seem similar to the analyzing judge.

Reasons given by the clinicians for mismatches tend to shed some light on method of analysis:

1. Convict (educated chemical engineer) was confused with female scientist because:
   a. Methodist religion   5
   b. T.A.T. expression of dissatisfaction over inability to compete with males, sexual inadequacy, being taunted about something small.   7
   c. Reaction to strict father, rigidity of attitude at home, social pressure.   4
   d. Extensive vocabulary, reference to schools and education.   7
   e. Early sex prohibition, concern with sex play, exhibitionism, discussion of homosexuality in both records.   9
2. Reasons for confusion of mental clinic outpatient (male age 23) with female probationer:
   a. Vocabulary limited, low educational level, vulgarisms, narrow range of interests   5
   b. Immaturity, childishness, lack of planning or foresight, irresponsi-

TABLE 7. ANALYSIS OF MISMATCHES MADE BY 20 JUDGES

Type of Mismatch	Number	Per Cent
Biography of convict matched with T.A.T. of female scientist	12	60
Biography of clinic outpatient subject matched with T.A.T. of female probationer	8	40
Biography of convict with Rorschach of Clinic Patient	8	40
Rorschach of high school student with T.A.T. of clinic outpatient	5	25
Rorschach of convict with biography of clinic outpatient	5	25
Rorschach of clinic outpatient with biography of female probationer	4	20

bility, living for moment, repressing guilt.   7

   c. Reference to movies and dancing.   3

   d. Attitudes typically female.   3

3. Reasons for confusion of convict with mental clinic outpatient:

   a. Rorschach obviously psychotic, must belong to patient under treatment.   5

   b. Impulsiveness in Rorschach and in biography.   3

   c. Avoidance of women, sexual confusion, difficulties with women.   3

   d. Rorschach mention of golf course, biography hit in eye with golf club.   2

   e. Obsessive-compulsive.   2

4. Reasons for confusion of high-school student (male, age 16) with mental clinic outpatient (male age 23—high school education):

   a. Impulsiveness, immaturity.   3

   b. Naivete, fear and avoidance of women.   2

   c. Expression of being threatened by strict, unreasonable, overwhelming demanding father figure.   2

   d. Fears of being criticized or disliked by age-mates (males).   2

In this experiment an attempt was made to select subjects who were heterogeneous as to personality characteristics and as to sociocultural status. A consideration of the mismatches indicates that the subjects frequently have characteristics in common when the data are closely analyzed that were not immediately apparent on first inspection; i.e., similarities in viewpoint,

attitude, mood and in dynamics.

In work with these subjects, judges frequently misidentified because of similarities between subjects which appeared to outweigh differences:

1. The female probationer and the mental hygiene clinic outpatient have a similar intellectual level, their cultural level is similar, many of their references are to movies and periodicals from which they borrow their limited stock of ideas. Both are described as immature, repressing guilt, impulsive, not looking ahead, living for the moment, nonintrospective.

2. The female scientist and the college educated convict are both well read and well spoken. Both have had scientific training. Expression of their reactions to early religious training is similar, as is reaction to both parents. Although they are of opposite sex, both make direct and indirect references to striving toward symbolic masculinity. Sex identification is similar as is reaction to marriage partner.

3. In biography one subject was identified as an outpatient of a mental hygiene clinic. Rorschach of the convict was obviously that of a disturbed person though the biography did not mention a diagnosis. Many matched the biography which mentioned treatment with the most disturbed projective test available. To do so was to give these materials only superficial analysis.

"Good errors" occur when similarities between subjects outweight differences so that the test results for the similar subject is very frequently misidentified with the right case.

Analysis of good errors constitutes a non-statistical method of evaluating randomness. Such errors are not numerous in this experiment, do not occur so often as to invalidate the experiment. The original materials contributed by subjects can be regarded as adequately heterogeneous.

Subjective Certainty of Judgments. The task of reporting degrees of certainty about judgments was optional in this experiment, and not all of our judges commented about their feelings of certainty. In only 24, or 6% of 378 judgments, did judges feel free to state that they were very sure of their judgments. This is in contrast to Valentine's results, where his untrained judges declared themselves absolutely sure in more than 50% of judgments. In our experiment when judges were very sure, they were wrong more often than right (wrong in 75% of cases) but not wrong a significantly greater percentage of time than were the general population of judges (wrong in 67% of judgments).

Experienced judges tended to be very conservative. With the exception of Judge G who declared himself very sure in almost every case, they did not know the tendency indicated by Valentine and Polansky and discussed by Wallin, to be most confident of correctness of judgment when most wrong in judging.

The tendency to "project," that is, to misread motivation, to think of others' actions in terms of one's own motivations, did not seem to govern the decisions of the trained judges.

In 29% of the judgments, clinicians felt "relatively sure" of the correctness of the judgment; in 13% of cases, they indicated that they were not at all sure. In both instances, though more often wrong than right, they were right more often (41% of the time), but not significantly more often than the general population of cases (right 32% of the time). Judges who indicated they were relatively sure or not sure, were explicit but conservative. They were right more often (41% of the time), but not significantly more often than those who did not feel free to comment or who did not bother to comment about feelings of subjective certainty (these were right 27% of the time.) Generally, those judges who were most often right described themselves as relatively sure or as not at all all sure of the correctness of their judgments. Table 8 shows the frequencies of judgments concerning which a degree of subjective certainty was expressed analysed according to actual correctness or incorrectness.

Summary

The purpose of this study concerns the clinical psychologist's ability to ar-

TABLE 8. NUMBER AND PERCENTAGE OF JUDGMENTS CONCERNING WHICH A DEGREE OF SUBJECTIVE CERTAINTY WAS EXPRESSED (NUMBER OF JUDGES 20)

Judgments		Degree of Certainty				
		Very Sure	Relatively Sure	Not Sure	No Comment	Total
Correct	No.	6	45	21	52	124
	%	25	40	42	27.1	32.9
Incorrect	No.	18	67	29	140	254
	%	78	59.9	58	72.9	67.1
Total	No.	24	112	50	192	378
	%	6.4	29.4	13.2	51.0	100

rive at an accurate diagnosis. In diagnosis, the data obtained from psychological examinations are interpreted by the examiner in such a way that these data become meaningful in terms of the particular individual examined. The one fact which all the data obtained from a single person have in common is the fact of their production by that individual, hence diagnostic skill can be determined through the identification of data as having been produced by that individual. The purposes of this experiment were:

(a) To construct a matching task to enable the clinician to demonstrate diagnostic skill in a direct fashion,
(b) to evaluate said instrument as a selection device for those to be trained as clinical psychologists,
(c) to evaluate judges' matching performance in terms of significance, individually and as a group,
(d) to shed light on the validity of tests used in the battery,
(e) to study the correspondence of subjective certainty in matching and the accuracy of judgments.

A matching task of sixteen documents, four autobiographies representative of six people, four Thematic Apperception Test protocols representative of the same six people, four Rorschach and Sentence Completion protocols and four Objective-type batteries (Thurstone Primary Mental Abilities, Kuder Preference Record and Guilford STDCR) was presented to twenty clinicians for matching. Judges were asked to match all documents in unequal series, to indicate degrees of subjective certainty, and to give reasons for matching.

Judges as a group performed at a higher level than could have been expected by chance. Individual judges performed considerably above chance. Performance of judges was differential, that is, judges who were superior in matching with one test were superior in most. A skill in the analysis of such materials exists.

The material in the biography, Rorschach and Thematic Apperception Test overlaps or corresponds to the extent that it may be matched with higher than chance expectancy, therefore these tests can be considered valid. Judges were able to identify tests correctly in series as belonging with a given biography. Without having been so instructed judges used the biography as the criterion. It was also possible to recognize subjects in terms of identifying tests as belonging to distinct persons when the biography or some other unit was not given. In expression of subjective certainty it was found that judges who were most often correct were unwilling to express confidence in their judgments.

The importance of the ability of the judge in matching materials of this type is indicated. It can be inferred that there exists a diagnostic skill, that some judges with roughly equivalent experience possess it and can demonstrate it in greater degree. The matching technique seems utilizable to isolate those with such skill and to select people with demonstrable diagnostic ability from among those entering the field.

BIBLIOGRAPHY

1. ALLPORT, G. W. *Personality, a psychological interpretation.* New York: Henry Holt and Co., 1937.
2. ALLPORT, G. W. *The use of personal documents in psychological science.* Soc. Science Research Council, N.Y., 1942. Bullet. 49, p. 1–210.
3. ALLPORT, G. W., & VERNON, P. E. *Studies in expressive movement.* New York: Macmillan, 1933, p. 1–269.
4. CHAPMAN, D. W. The generalized problem of matchings. *Ann. Math. Statistics.* 1935, **6**, 85–95.

5. CHAPMAN, D. W. The scoring of matching tests with unequal series. *Jour. Educ. Psychol.*, 1936, **27**, 368–370.

6. CHAPMAN, D. W. The statistics of the method of correct matchings. *Amer. Jour. Psychol.*, 1934, **46**, 287–298.

7. CHALLMAN, R. C. The clinical psychology program at Winter V. A. Hospital. *Jour. Clinical Psychol.*, 1947, 3, 28–31.

8. COMBS, A. A method of analysis for the Thematic Apperception Test and autobiography. *Jour. Clinical Psychol.*, 1946, **2**, 167–174.

9. CRONBACH, L. J. Statistical methods applied to Rorschach scores. *Psychol. Bullet.*, 1949, **46**, 393–429.

10. ESTES, S. G. Judging personality from expressive behavior. *Jour. Abnorm. Soc. Psychol.*, 1949, **44**, 329–344.

11. HORN, D. *An experimental study of the diagnostic process in the clinical investigation of personality.* Unpublished Ph.D. Thesis, Harvard Univ., 1943, pp. 1–75.

12. KELLY, E. L. Research on evaluation of clinical psychologists. *Jour. Consulting Psychol.*, 1949, **13**, 34–38.

13. KELLY, E. L., & FISKE, D. W. *The Prediction of Performance in Clinical Psychology.* Ann Arbor, Mich.: University of Michigan Press, 1951.

14. KRUGMAN, J. L. A clinical evaluation of the Rorschach with problem children. *Rorschach Research Exchange*, 1943, **6**, 61–70.

15. MURRAY, H. A. *Explorations in Personality.* New York: Oxford Univ. Press, 1938, pp. 245–248.

16. POLANSKY, N. A. How shall a life history be written? *Charact. and Personality*, 1941, **9**, 188–207.

17. TROOP, H. A comparative study by means of the Rorschach method of personality development in 20 pairs of identical twins. *Genet. Monog.*, 1938, **20**, 461–536.

18. VALENTINE, C. W. The relative reliability of men and women in intuitive judgments of character. *Brit. Jour. Psychol.*, 1929, **19**, 213–328.

19. VERNON, P. E. Evaluation of the matching test. *Jour. Educ. Psychol.*, 1936, **27**, 1–17.

20. VERNON, P. E. Some characteristics of the good judge of personality. *Jour. Soc. Psychol.*, 1933, **4**, 57.

21. VERNON, P. E. The matching method applied to investigations of personality. *Psychol. Bullet.*, 1933, **33**, 149–177.

22. WALLIN, P. The prediction of individual behavior from case studies, from HORST, P., *The Prediction of personal adjustment.* Social Science Research Council, Bullet. No. 48, 1943, pp. 1–445.

23. WOLF, R., & MURRAY, J. A. An experiment in judging personality. *Jour. Psychol.*, 1936, 3, 345–365.

24. WOLF, R., & MURRAY, H. A. Judgments of personality, from MURRAY, H. A. *Explorations in Personality.* New York: Oxford Univ. Press, 1938, pp. 243–281.

APPENDIX*

I. Method of computing probabilities that a given number of arrangements could occur by chance when an array (made up of 6 units) is matched against one or more other similar arrays.

Chance probabilities when one person arranges an array comprising six units against one other similar array:

$(m + t:t = 1 \times 6:6)$

Formulae:

1) $n (n - 1) (n - 2) \dots\dots\dots 1 = n$: the number of different arrangements of n things that can occur.

* Notation: hereafter 'm' shall represent the number of arrays or sets of material presented; 't' the number of things to be matched in any one array. For example (m × t : t = 4 × 6 : 6) shall mean that judges were required to match 4 arrays of material, each array comprising six units.

$$2)\ \frac{n!}{s!(n-s)\ !} = C\ \frac{s}{n} = \frac{n\,(n-1)\,(n-2)\,\ldots\ldots\,1}{s\,(s-1\,(s-2)\,\ldots.\,1\,(n-s)\,(n-s-1)\,\ 1}$$

the number of different ways that it is possible to take s things out of n things.

II. Chance expectancy when six things are arranged against another array of six things:

Number of Arrange-ments	2	3	4	5	6	% Frequency	Cumulative % Frequency
0	1	2	9	44	265	.3680	1.0000
1	0	$1C_{n}^{s}=3$	$2C_{4}^{3}=9$	$9C_{5}^{4}=45$	$44C_{6}^{5}=264$	.3665	.6320
2	1	0	$1C_{4}^{2}=6$	$2C_{5}^{3}=20$	$9C_{6}^{4}=135$	.1875	.2655
3		1	0	$1C_{5}^{2}=10$	$2C_{6}^{3}=40$	.0555	.0750
4			1	0	$1C_{6}^{2}=15$	.0208	.0222
5				1	0	.0000	.0014
6					1	.0014	.0014
Total	2! = 2;	3! = 6;	4! = 24;	5! = 120;	6! = 720		

III. Chance frequencies computed by entering the frequency distribution where one array is matched against one other array and against these same frequencies (representative of the consideration of a third array):

Number of Arrangements	% Frequency (one array against another)					
6	.0014					
5	.0000					
4	.0208	etc.				
3	.0555	etc.				
2	.1875	.0690	.0687	.0353		
1	.3665	.1349	.1343	.0687		
0	.3680	.1354	.1349	.0690	etc.	etc.
% frequency	.3680	.3665	.1975	.0555	.0208	.00	.0014
Number of arrangements	0	1	2	3	4	5	6

IV. It is mathematically possible to consider the probabilities that a given number of successful matchings could occur by chance alone when one array is arranged against three other sets of data. (In our experiment, judge X is asked to arrange one set of materials (6 T.A.T.'s representative of 6 persons) and a second set of materials (6 Rorschachs similarly matched) and a third (6 P.M.A.'s) against a criterion set (6 biographies).

Probabilities are arrived at by considering frequencies when two sets of material are arranged against a third, and entering the frequencies for another arrangement.

Number of Correct Matchings	% Frequency						
12							
11	.0000						
10	.0000						
9	.0009						
8	.0002						
7	.0033						
6	.0120						
5	.0360	etc					
4	.0911	.03353	.03339	.01708			
3	.1782	.06558	.06531	.03342			
2	.2723	.10021	.09798	.05106			
1	.2679	.09925	.09885	.05057			
0	.1354	.04983	.04962	.02539	etc.		
% frequency	.036800	.3665	.1875	.0555	.0280	.000	.0014
No. of arrangements	0	1	2	3	4	5	6

V. It is possible to compute probabilities that a given number of correct matchings could occur when judge X arranges 6 sets of materials, each set made up of 6 units, against criteria:

Number of Correct Matchings	% Frequency	Cumulative % Frequency
19	.00002	.00002
18	.00006	.00008
17	.00015	.00023
16	.00039	.00062
15	.00099	.00161
14	.00237	.00398
13	.00539	.00937
12	.01168	.02105
11	.02325	.04430
10	.04192	.08622
9	.06852	.15474
8	.10355	.25829
7	.13738	.39567
6	.16028	.55595
5	.16033	.71628
4	.13264	.84892
3	.08912	.93804
2	.04454	.98258
1	.01484	.99742
0	.00248	.99990

Median number of matchings which could be expected to occur by chance: 6.387.

VI. In order to test whether the obtained distribution of scores (number of correct matchings) could have arisen on the basis of a random sampling from a computed theoretical distribution, is it necessary to:

a) Consider only those 14 judges who completed the task (Judges A–N)

b) Work out the statement of χ^2 when the greatest number of correct arrangements can equal 18 (three arrays of data—Rorschach, T.A.T. and objective set) are considered to be matched against the criterion array (biographical material). (m × t:t = 3 × 6:6)

COMPARISON OF THEORETICAL AND OBTAINED
MATCHINGS FOR THE GROUP

Incidence	Scores		Sum
	0–3	4–18	
Theoretical	5.11	8.89	14.0
Obtained	1.0	13.0	14.0

$$\chi^2 = 5.26 \qquad p < .05$$

Congruencies Among Interpretations of Psychological Test and Anamnestic Data

Kenneth B. Little and Edwin S. Shneidman

In a clinical situation, when one uses diagnostic tools such as interview techniques or psychological tests the ultimate goal is usually to present a description of an individual in such a fashion as to facilitate accurate predictions of the tested S's future behavior. This description may be limited to a single statement (such as a diagnostic label) or may be in the form of an elaborate and detailed evaluation of the S's psychological status, including the genesis of his major personality characteristics and some specific recommendations for the modification of those attributes or for the development of new ones. In either case, the procedure is characterized by the intervention of an interpreter (the psychiatrist, psychologist, psychiatric social worker, or whoever) between the behavior of the S and the

This investigation was supported by a research grant from the National Institute of Mental Health, Public Health Service, under the sponsorship of the University of Southern California.

Reprinted by permission of the American Psychological Association and the authors from *Psychological Monographs*, 1959, **73**, (No. 6, Whole No. 476).

descriptive statements. Although, as Meehl (1954) has indicated, it may be possible to avoid the interpreting middle man, in current clinical practice this is rarely done. Instead, the final product of a diagnostic interview or psychological test examination consists of a series of statements based upon quasi-empirical norms, the personal experiences of the interpreter, deductions from a hypothesized personality structure, and just plain guesses. Consequently the effective validity and the effective reliability of the diagnostic tools are functions of both the instruments and of the users.

The primary purpose of the present study was to investigate the congruencies among personality descriptions made by clinicians when such descriptions are based on different sources of information (instruments). In particular, the study was designed to investigate congruencies (*a*) for several kinds of Ss —psychotics, neurotics, psychosomatic reactions, and psychiatrically normal; (*b*) for several *instruments*—the Rorschach technique, the Thematic Apperception Test, the Make A Picture Story test, the Minnesota Multiphasic Personality Inventory, and a psychiatric anamnesis; and (c) for several kinds of *interpretive tasks*—true–false factual items, true-false inferential items, Q-sort items, diagnostic labels, and ratings of adjustment.

Previous investigations of the congruencies[1] of the instruments considered here have usually been of two major kinds. In the first, every attempt was made to minimize the influence of the interpreter through the use of objective scoring systems (even though the clinicians occasionally crept in through the back door by means of rating scales). These studies have the advantage of presenting precise quantitative results amenable to statistical manipulations, but they have been subject to the criticism that they distort the way in which the test instruments are actually used in the clinical situation. The second type of study has treated the interpreter as a relevant part of the situation and has made comparisons of the similarities and the differences of molar descriptions based on different diagnostic techniques. These latter investigations are unable to measure with any assurance the degree of correspondence of one interpretation with another, based as they are on global matching procedures. The present study attempts to combine the advantages and to circumvent some of the shortcomings of both types of study mentioned above in an investigation of the effects of the psychological test used, the clinician who interprets the test results, and the S who is tested.[2]

Subjects and Procedure

Test Subjects

Twelve test subjects (Test Ss) were used, all hospitalized at the time of testing. Three of the Ss were categorized

[1] At this point, some concern with the definition of such concepts as "reliability" and "validity" might have been appropriate,

as "normal" or nonpsychiatric (Test S 1, 2, and 3), three as neurotic (Test S 4, 5, and 6), three as psychophysiological disorders (Test S 7, 8, and 9), and three as psychotic (Test S 10, 11, and 12). Selection of the Ss was based upon an initial screening of records of consecutive new admissions into two Veterans Administration hospitals: a general medical hospital and a neuropsychiatric hospital. Formal requirements in the inital screening were that all Ss be Caucasian, male, Protestants, native-born veterans of World War II, with an education no less than the 10th or more than the 12th grade, and between 20 and 35 years old. In addition, for the neurotics and psychotics it was required that they had not received shock treatment, that the entrance diagnosis be unequivocally psychotic or neurotic, and that they be in sufficient contact for psychological testing. For the non-psychiatric (normal) Ss it was required that they have no record of any previous psychiatric disorder and that the hospital diagnosis be a straightforward medical one with no functional aspects. For the Ss in the psychophysiological category, in addition to the lack of recorded previous emotional disorder, it was required that the hospital diagnosis be that of a psychophysiological disorder generally considered to be of functional origin.

After the initial screening, the pros-

but the authors have advertently chosen to place the discussion of these terms after the description of the procedure and the presentation of the results.

[2] There is also a fourth possible source of variance: the different test administrators. In the present study, this aspect was held constant in that all the tests administered to all the Ss were given by one test administrator. Also, it can be mentioned at this juncture that all the case histories were obtained by one interviewer. This opportunity is taken to extend our appreciation to Phillip A. Goodwin, and Seymour Pollack, who administered all the psychological tests and obtained all the case history data, respectively, for this study.

pective Test Ss were administered the Cornell Selectee Index, certain subtests from the Form I Wechsler-Bellevue Intelligence Scale (Digit Span, Block Design, and Similarities), and were interviewed by a clinical psychologist. All Ss with prorated IQ's less than 90 or greater than 115 were eliminated. Prospective nonpsychiatric Ss who answered items on the Selectee Index which indicated previous emotional disorders or who were, in the judgment of the psychologist, emotionally disturbed were also eliminated. All remaining Ss were then interviewed by a psychiatrist. In the case of the nonpsychiatric Ss, the psychiatrist's judgment had to concur with that of the psychologist as to lack of any emotional disturbance before the S was retained; if not, the S was dropped. For the neurotics, the decision was required that the disorder be definitely nonpsychotic and reasonable representative of one of the classical neurotic categories. For the psychotics, the decision was required that the disorder be definitely nonneurotic and representative of a functional psychosis.

All Test Ss were administered the Rorschach (Ror), the Thematic Apperception Test (TAT), the Make A Picture Story test (MAPS), and the group form of the Minnesota Multiphasic Personality Inventory (MMPI). All the protocols (other than the MMPI) were recorded on tape and transcribed verbatim. All the testing was done by one clinical psychologist, who had had seven years of clinical and testing experience.

In addition to the test materials, a comprehensive psychiatric case history was obtained from each of the 12 Ss. All the histories were obtained by one psychiatrist. Four to eight interviews of 1–3 hr. duration were held with the Ss to obtain the case histories. These histories ranged from 16 to 60 double-spaced typewritten pages and included such materials as presenting problem, developmental history, physical and laboratory findings, description of the

family life, etc. The age, marital status, occupation, hospital diagnosis, etc. for each of the twelve Test Ss are given in Table 1.[3]

Test Judges

Forty-eight clinical psychologists served as test judges (TJ) for the study. Twelve TJ's were selected to interpret the Rorschach (R1-R12), 12 to interpret the TAT (T1-T12), 12 to interpret the MAPS test (M1-M12), and 12 to interpret the MMPI (I 1-I 12). Selection of the MMPI judges was from lists of clinical psychologists provided by Robert E. Harris and Starke R. Hathaway; MAPS test judges were selected from a list provided by Edwin S. Shneidman; Rorschach and TAT judges were selected from lists drawn up by the authors in consultation with the editors of the *Journal of Projective Techniques*. The forty-eight TJ's constituted, therefore, a sample of skilled interpreters, rather than a random sample of clinical psychologists in general.

Anamnesis Judges

Twenty-three psychiatrists and one psychologist served as evaluators of the anamnestic materials. Eleven were practicing psychoanalysts, members of the American Psychoanalytic Association, one was a Diplomate in Clinical Psychology (A1-A12), and 12 were, by their own evaluation, nonanalytically oriented members of the American Psychiatric Association (P1-P12). Selections were from lists prepared in consultation with the officers of the local association.[4]

[3] Editor's Note: The original monograph contained an appendix which gave an abbreviated case summary for each S. Space limitations prevented the reprinting of this material. A complete case history for Test S 10 is presented as "A Case History of Paranoid Schizophrenia" in Burton and Harris (1956).

[4] Editor's Note: A complete list of the anamnestic and test judges was presented as Appendix B of the original monograph.

TABLE 1.   TEST SUBJECTS[a]

S	Age	Extraction	Marital Status	Occupation	Hospital Diagnosis
1	25	English-Swedish	Div.	Postal clerk, salesman, policeman	Fractures, left elbow, left tibia, left fibula. No psychiatric disorder.
2	23	Irish	Sgl.	Student at agriculture school	Fractures, right elbow, right hip, right ankle, pneumothorax. No psychiatric disorder.
3	23	Dutch	Sgl.	IBM repairman	Herniorrhaphy. No psychiatric disorder.
4	27	English-Dutch	Mar.	Store salesman	Chronic anxiety reaction, with hysterical conversion neurosis and depression.
5	29	Scotch-Dutch	Mar.	Mechanic	Anxiety reaction, a motor tension state, with symptomatic alcoholism.
6	33	Swedish	Mar.	Store salesman	Mixed psychoneurosis with obsessive-compulsive trends, with phobic reactions.
7	31	English-Dutch	Mar.	Waiter, aspiring composer	Gastro-intestinal irritable colon syndrome.
8	29	English-Irish	Sgl.	Carpenter	Psychophysiologic gastro-intestinal reaction with peptic ulcer syndrome.
9	26	French-English	Sgl.	Machinist	Psychophysiologic skin reaction manifested by atopic dermatitis.
10	22	Dutch-English	Sgl.	Student	Schizophrenic reaction, paranoid type.
11	29	English	Sgl.	Unskilled labor	Schizophrenic reaction, chronic, undifferentiated type.
12	26	Danish	Sgl.	Unemployed	Schizophrenic reaction, primarily catatonic in type.

[a] All Ss are male, Caucasian, Protestant, native born, 10th-12th grade education, 90–115 IQ, and between the ages of 22 and 33.

In the selection of both TJ's and AJ's an initial number somewhat larger than the final group was contacted and asked to participate. The study was described briefly and it was indicated that an honorarium of fifty dollars would be paid for participation. The final 72 judges were selected at random from those accepting.

Design and Procedure

Each TJ evaluated the test protocols of four Test Ss, one from each of the four subject categories. The only information provided the judges in addition to the protocols was that the Ss were Caucasian, male, veteran, Protestant, with high school education, and between 22 and 33 years of age.[5] The order in which any four protocols were

[5] It may be appropriate to indicate at this point that every effort was made to give no extraneous clues to the judges; e.g., the authors—who were then in a VA neuropsychiatric hospital setting—conducted their correspondence with the TJ's and AJ's on university stationery and with a university mailing address.

evaluated was a random one with the restriction that each protocol be once the first one evaluated, once the second, etc. Since there were 12 judges for each test type, four judges evaluated Ss T1, 4, 7, 10 (Set I), four evaluated Ss T2, 5, 8, 11 (Set II), and four T3, 6, 9, 12 (Set III). These same sets were used for all test types.

Ten days after all the conclusion of the evaluation of the four protocols, each TJ repeated the analysis of the first record of the four protocols he had seen, and, as another task, made an evaluation of an hypothetical individual (a "normal," a psychophysiological reaction, a neurotic, or a psychotic stereotype) corresponding to one of the four Test S categories. (The stereotype evaluations were for another study and are not considered further in this monograph.)

The AJ's evaluated two Ss on the basis of the anamnestic materials. They also performed a stereotype evaluation but did not, however, do a repeat analysis.

Interpretive Task

In order that comparisons might be made among the various TJ's and AJ's, the evaluation of the Test S on the basis of the materials was structured in the form of five tasks for the judges:

1. Answer the question, "How would you label this person diagnostically?"

2. Indicate on a line scale the degree of maladjustment of the S.

3. Complete a Q sort of 76 items describing behavioral reactions to social stimuli and general adjustive patterns.

4. Answer 117 true and false items representing the type of statements made in psychological test reports and also indicate the level of confidence in each answer.

5. Answer 100 true and false items of a more or less factual nature about the S's past and present life and also indicate the level of confidence in each answer.

The items of Tasks 2, 3, 4, and 5 are presented in Appendix I.[6]

The 76 items of the Q sort consisted of 48 items describing positive, negative, or neutral reactions to positive or negative stimuli from either other persons or the environment in general. The remaining 28 items were equally divided among statements of satisfactory general adjustment reactions and unsatisfactory adjustment reactions.

The 117 psychological report type items were selected from a population of 1706 such items, derived primarily by abstracting approximately 80 test reports on patients in neuropsychiatric and general medical hospitals and mental hygiene clinics. Inasmuch as these items were predominantly about negative personality characteristics, an equal group of statements was constructed, asserting a logical contradictory of each of the original items.[7] From this combined group of items a random sample of 500 items was selected and assigned, by one of the authors, into one of 18 psychological test report categories. These 18 categories are presented in Appendix II.[8]

A recategorization of the 500 items by the other author resulted in disagreement on only 16 items, and these 16 were then eliminated. From the remaining 484 items the final sample of 117 was selected by proportional sampling among the categories, following the percentages of items in each category indicated in a previous study.[9]

The 100 true-false, more or less factual items were a sample from an

---

[6] Editor's Note: Designated Appendix C in the original version of this monograph.

[7] The two logical contradictories should be mutually exclusive. For example, a logical contradictory of the statement "He hates his mother" is the statement "He has no strong feelings toward his mother."

[8] Editor's Note: Designated Appendix D in the original version of this monograph.

[9] These 18 categories, and the proportion of items in each category, came from Shneidman, Walther, and Little (1951), in which

initial list of 223 statements which could be asserted to be factually either true or false about each S on the basis of the anamnestic and hospital record data —e.g., "He was an only child"—and which were presumably relevant to personality description or development.

Results

The results of this study will be discussed under the following six general headings: Diagnostic Statements, Degree of Maladjustment, Q Sorts, True-False Personality Items, True-False Factual Items, and Reliability. In each of these sections the results will be described and the conclusions from, and implications of, these results will be discussed.

Diagnostic Statements

The first task of each TJ and each AJ was to indicate the diagnostic label he would assign to the Test S whose material he was evaluating. These diagnostic statements made by the judges are presented, verbatim, in Table 2. Although a complete statistical interpretation of this table cannot be given, some comments about its qualitative features can be made. The outstanding impression (a disappointing one) is that diagnostic labels given by the TJ's from the psychological tests were remarkably varied and inaccurate—if

one takes seriously psychiatric diagnosis and the authors' categorization of the patient. The second outstanding feature is that this inaccuracy is particularly noticeable in the case of the nonpsychiatric Ss.

These data have some interesting implications and lead to several speculations. One such speculation is that the training of clinical people tends to emphasize the pathological. (Only recently has there been any real attention to assets and to "ego strengths."). It is an unhappy fact that very few clinicians ever work with "normal" subjects and that clinicians as a group have no population of normals to use as an internalized reference from which to draw inferences. It is also relevant to indicate that inaccuracy of diagnostic labeling does not necessarily imply inaccuracy in describing psychodynamics, personality traits, etc. A psychological defense may have positive as well as negative value; a coping mechanism is not necessarily a deformity. There is an important difference between stating, on the one hand, "An individual has obsessive features," and, on the other hand, "An individual is an obsessive neurotic." The TJ's apparently made errors of confusing these two.

Certainly the data indicated in Table 2 give everyone interested in the use of psychological techniques some pause for thoughtful reflection.[10]

---

the authors developed this category set based on 21 test reports which had been analyzed into 1210 discrete items of personality description. It should be mentioned at this point that the present study (involving 12 Ss of four different categories) is a direct outgrowth of this former study which involved only one S, and thus raised many questions which could be approached only by multiplying the types of Ss and by having more than one S in each type. Two studies, one on the validity of MMPI interpretations (Little & Shneidman, 1956) and one on the validity of thematic interpretations (Little & Shneidman, 1955) based on the one case (and evaluated by several judges) have already been published.

[10] The findings presented in Table 2 raise the question—as in the case of the Holtzman and Sells (1954) study where projective techniques were not particularly successful in making predictions of flying success— that it may well be that the psychological tests were used either inappropriately or in a way in which clinicians ordinarily do not use tests. It is felt that to ask clinicians to make diagnoses, ratings of adjustment, to do Q sorts, and to complete T-F questionnaires are not especially inappropriate tasks for clinicians, but the present study does raise the entire issue of the role of the "blind diagnoses." This is cited, not to give any opinion on one side or another, but simply to indicate that the topic is most relevant to an understanding of the present data.

TABLE 2. DIAGNOSTIC LABELS ASSIGNED TO 12 TEST Ss BY 48 TJ'S AND 24 AJ'S

Test S 1 (Nonpsychiatric)

Judge

ROR
1. Passive dependent personality
2. Anxiety neurosis
3. Hysterical personality; passive aggressive
4. Schizophrenic with homosexual tendencies

TAT
1. Psychopath—immaturity reaction
2. Schizophrenic; hebephrenic and paranoid features
3. Aggressive reaction
4. Simple schizophrenia or alcoholic

MAPS
1. Schizoid character
2. Schizoid personality; organic brain damage?
3. Schizophrenic, chronic
4. Psychopathic personality with some schizoid trends

MMPI
1. Character neurosis
2. Chronic sub-optimum adjustment level
3. Hysteria
4. An extremely defensive normal

Anamnesis
1. No psychotic disease or disorder
2. Neurotic personality, mild
3. Character disorder, mild
4. Phallic-narcissistic character disorder

Test S 2 (Nonpsychiatric)

ROR
1. Schizoid character—depressive trends
2. Compulsive character
3. Passive aggressive personality disorder
4. Conversion reaction

TAT
1. Psychoneurosis, mixed, homosexuality
2. Anxiety neurosis
3. Neurotic, obsessive-compulsive
4. Character neurosis

MAPS
1. Passive aggressive (dependent) personality
2. Neurotic reactive depression
3. Neurotic (hysteric)
4. Anxiety reaction with compulsive features

Test S 2 (Continued)

MMPI
1. Normal
2. Hysterical character
3. Without personality disorder
4. Psychoneurosis, conversion hysteria reaction

Anamnesis
1. Within normal range—no psychiatric disorder
2. No psychiatric disease
3. No psychiatric disorder present
4. No psychiatric illness

Test S 3 (Nonpsychiatric)

ROR
1. Incipient schizophrenic
2. Schizophrenic, probably paranoid type
3. Paranoid schizophrenia
4. Schizoid personality, paranoid and homosexual trends

TAT
1. Schizophrenic
2. Anxiety neurosis with hysterical features
3. Character neurosis
4. Passive-aggressive reaction with schizophrenic episodes—emotional instability

MAPS
1. "Normal" with mild obsessive and compulsive trends
2. Schizophrenic, mixed type, chronic, severe
3. Schizophrenic reaction, catatonic features
4. Character disorder with hysterical and homosexual trends

MMPI
1. Passive-aggressive personality (asocial psychopath)
2. Hysterical personality
3. Simple adult maladjustment
4. Simple adult maladjustment, emotional instability

Anamnesis
1. Character neurosis, passive-aggressive type
2. Character within normal limits
3. Normal
4. Normal

Test S 4 (Neurotic)

ROR
1. Mixed neurosis with obsessive features
2. Obsessive compulsive, possibly with schizoid trends
3. Character disorder with anxiety hysterical features
4. Neurotic—obsessive compulsive, anxiety and depression conspicuous

TABLE 2. (*Continued*)

Test S 4 (Continued)

TAT 1. Normal adult with character defenses of an obsessive-compulsive nature
2. Character disorder, passive dependent features
3. Passive aggressive reaction with hysterical features
4. Psychotic features in a passive-feminine character

MAPS 1. Immaturity reaction
2. Obsessive compulsive homosexual
3. Obsessive compulsive
4. Hysteric phobic reaction with obsessive trends

MMPI 1. Normal
2. Essentially normal individual, mild obsessional reactions plus homoeroticism problem
3. Normal
4. Mild obsessive with some somatization

Anamnesis 1. Dissociative reaction (hysterical)
2. Anxiety reaction with depersonalization episodes
3. Psychoneurosis, severe, hysterical type
4. Personality trait disturbance with neurotic reaction

Test S 5 (Neurotic)

ROR 1. Paranoid schizophrenic in remission
2. Mixed pre-genital character, passive-aggressive personality, passive-aggressive type
3. Obsessive compulsive reaction
4. Schizophrenic reaction, paranoid type

TAT 1. Schizophrenia, paranoid trends
2. Paranoid schizophrenia in remission or partial remission, with possible acting out aggressive psychopath character structure
3. Schizophrenic reaction
4. Obsessive neurotic with depression

MAPS 1. Schizo-affective psychosis
2. Latent (incipient) schizophrenic reaction
3. Paranoid schizophrenic
4. Schizoid personality with alcoholism (possibly psychotic episodes)

Test S 5 (Continued)

MMPI 1. Simulated or acute psychosis in a basically psychopathic personality
2. Psychopathic personality
3. Manic depressive reaction, manic type
4. Psychosis, manic with paranoid features

Anamnesis 1. Passive-aggressive personality, aggressive type
2. Anxiety state, with alcoholism and paranoid trends
3. Latent schizophrenia
4. Anxiety reaction

Test S 6 (Neurotic)

ROR 1. Anxiety state, moderately severe
2. Anxiety and depression in a compulsive personality
3. Anxiety state (hysterical?)
4. Neurotic personality, hysterical defense mechanisms

TAT 1. Depressive or schizo-affective
2. Obsessive-compulsive neurosis, paranoid trends
3. Normal
4. Passive-dependency reaction with reactive alcoholism—psychoneurosis

MAPS 1. Anxiety reaction, mild, with obsessive compulsive features
2. Hysterical character
3. Could be a normal
4. Normal adult with mild homosexual conflict

MMPI 1. Anxiety neurosis superimposed on a latent paranoid schizophrenia
2. Mild neurotic depression
3. Psychoneurosis, mixed with depression, anxiety, and somatic complaints
4. Anxiety neurosis

Anamnesis 1. Psychoneurosis, obsessional, in a schizoid character
2. Severe obsessive compulsive neurosis with depressive trends
3. Mild, chronic, progressive schizophrenia, simple type
4. Mixed psychoneurosis, or schizophrenic reaction, acute, early type, undifferentiated

TABLE 2. (*Continued*)

Test S 7 (Psychophysiological)

ROR 1. A somewhat shy and inhibited normal
2. Obsessive compulsive character
3. Oral character disorder with ego restriction
4. Schizoid, inadequate personality

TAT 1. Immaturity reaction
2. Character disorder, passive-dependent, possibly alcoholic
3. Adjusted normal
4. Neurotic depression, anxiety state in a passive inhibited compulsive character

MAPS 1. Obsessive-compulsive
2. Paranoid schizophrenia
3. Anxiety reaction, possibly latent schizophrenia
4. Schizophrenic reaction, catatonic type

MMPI 1. Psychoneurosis mixed—somatic complaints
2. Psychoneurotic reaction in an immature and self-centered person
3. Hypochondriasis
4. Somatization reaction, probably stomach ulcer

Anamnesis 1. Somatization reaction, character problem
2. Anxiety reaction with gastro-intestinal somatization
3. Passive-aggressive personality with somatization of anxiety
4. Psychogenic gastro-intestinal conversion syndrome (non-psychotic)

Test S 8 (Psychophysiological)

ROR 1. Immature character, inadequate
2. Masochistic character
3. Personality trait disturbance, passive aggressive personality
4. Anxiety reaction

TAT 1. Schizophrenia mixed or catatonia. Possibly organic factors
2. Anxiety reaction in an inadequate personality
3. Passive dependency reaction
4. Neurosis with marked overt anxiety: phobias? obsessiveness? possible epileptic

MAPS 1. Chronic brain syndrome with psychosis
2. Psychogenic gastro-intestinal reaction

Test S 8 (Continued)

3. Borderline schizophrenia
4. Anxiety reaction with somatic complaints

MMPI 1. Depressive reaction in a chronically anxious and tense person
2. Depressive reaction
3. Reactive or neurotic depression
4. Anxiety neurosis

Anamnesis 1. Psychophysiologic gastro-intestinal reaction with peptic ulcer
2. Psychophysiologic gastro-intestinal reaction with peptic ulcer
3. Psychosomatic gastro-intestinal disturbance, ulcer
4. Anxiety, gastro-intestinal reaction

Test S 9 (Psychophysiological)

ROR 1. Psychoneurosis, mixed type —has some compulsive and hysterical trends
2. Mixed neurosis, hysterical-phobic and anxiety features predominating
3. Psychoneurosis, mixed, with anxiety and depression
4. Anxiety hysteria

TAT 1. Compulsive neurosis, or psychopathic
2. Character neurosis
3. Anxiety reaction, precariously maintained
4. Character disorder with narcissistic and psychopathic features

MAPS 1. "Normal" but with some obsessive features
2. Schizophrenia, mild, chronic, ambulatory
3. Essentially normal with some immaturity that may be largely a function of age
4. Obsessive character disorder, with much tension and anxiety

MMPI 1. Passive-dependent personality
2. Hysterical personality
3. Adult situational reaction
4. Normal personality

Anamnesis 1. Passive dependent with somatization (skin)
2. Passive dependent character disorder with severe inhibitions

TABLE 2. (*Continued*)

Test S 9 (Continued)

3. Psychophysiologic skin reaction, passive dependent character
4. Passive aggressive personality

Test S 10 (Psychotic)

ROR 1. Ambulatory schizophrenic
2. Compulsive character
3. Obsessive-compulsive personality breaking down
4. Inadequate character

TAT 1. Impulse neurotic, immaturity reaction
2. Character disorder, depressive features
3. Immaturity reaction and behavior disorder, "punishment seeker"
4. Neurosis: some depressive features and probably considerable anxiety

MAPS 1. Anxiety neurosis
2. Neurotic depression
3. Character disorder, psychopathic personality
4. Depressive reaction

MMPI 1. Paranoid schizophrenic
2. Acute agitated psychotic or severely disturbed neurotic
3. Paranoid schizophrenic episode with acute anxiety
4. Paranoid schizophrenic episode with marked anxiety

Anamnesis 1. Schizophrenic reaction, paranoid type
2. Schizophrenic, mixed type, paranoid defenses prominent
3. Schizophrenic, paranoid
4. Paranoid schizophrenia

Test S 11 (Psychotic)

ROR 1. Simple schizophrenic
2. Schizophrenic reaction in partial remission, chronic
3. Psychotic disorder, schizophrenic reaction
4. Schizophrenic reaction, paranoid type

TAT 1. Conversion hysteria
2. Schizophrenic in partial remission, paranoid features
3. Immaturity reaction; impulse neurosis
4. Schizophrenia

MAPS 1. Schizophrenic reaction
2. Normal
3. Simple schizophrenic or schizophrenic character disorder

Test S 11 (Continued)

4. Schizophrenic chronic with paranoid trends.

MMPI 1. Psychosis in a schizoid personality
2. Schizo-affective
3. Acute anxiety state
4. Manic depressive psychosis with paranoid features

Anamnesis 1. Schizophrenic episodes in a poorly organized personality
2. Schizophrenic reaction, chronic, severe, undifferentiated
3. Schizophrenic reaction, type undifferentiated
4. Schizophrenic reaction, undifferentiated

Test S 12 (Psychotic)

ROR 1. Passive aggressive character, passive dependent type
2. Neurasthenic with paranoid trends
3. Organic or simple schizophrenic
4. Schizophrenia, paranoid features

TAT 1. Psychosis, probably schizophrenic type
2. Anxiety neurosis
3. Highly schizoid but still obsessive personality
4. Schizophrenic process with decompensating obsessive compulsive defenses

MAPS 1. Schizoid personality
2. Schizoid character with moderate depressive and obsessive features
3. Schizoid personality
4. Passive dependent character disorder with borderline psychotic trends

MMPI 1. Reactive depression in a latent paranoid schizophrenic
2. Passive dependent personality
3. Psychoneurosis, obsessive compulsive type with depressive features
4. Paranoid schizophrenic, probably in partial remission

Anamnesis 1. Catatonic schizophrenic
2. Schizophrenic reaction, catatonic type
3. Schizophrenic reaction, catatonic type
4. Schizophrenic reaction, catatonic type

Although a complete statistical evaluation of the material in Table 2 was not undertaken, an estimate of the consistencies of the diagnoses for any given Test S, where diagnoses were based upon the same protocol or anamnestic material, was obtained in the following fashion:

1. Each diagnosis for each S based upon the same information source (i.e., the Rorschach, the TAT, etc.) was paired with every other diagnosis based upon that same source of information, e.g., the diagnosis of Judge R1 for Test S 1 was paired with each of the other Rorschach judges' diagnostic statements for S 1. Six paired comparisons were thus obtained. A similar procedure was used for the TAT, MAPS, MMPI, and AJ's. For each S, then, 30 pairs of diagnostic statements were available.

2. As a chance probability baseline, 23 sets of four diagnoses were selected at random from the 240 listed in Table 2. For each set, all possible pairings of the four diagnoses were made giving 138 chance combinations in all.

3. The total of 498 pairs of diagnoses were typed and distributed to four competent psychodiagnosticians with instructions to rate each pair on a six-point scale of similarity. The instructions to the raters and the defining points of the scale are given in Appendix III.[11] Since six possible scores (0–5) were available for each pair of diagnoses, product moment correlations were computed among all raters. The average correlation among the four psychodiagnosticians was .73 indicating a moderate degree of agreement among them. The chief source of disagreement appeared to be over the use of similarity of dynamics versus similarity of symptoms.

4. For each pair of diagnoses, the sum of the four ratings assigned by the judges was used as the index of

[11] Editor's Note: Designated Appendix E in the original version of this monograph.

similarity of the pair. These ranged from 0 to 20 where 0 indicated unanimous agreement on the part of the raters that the two diagnoses were utterly different and 20 indicated unanimous agreement that they were identical. The six figures thus obtained for the paired combinations of diagnoses for any one S based upon a single information source were in turn summed to give an index of similarity for each Test-S, information-source cell.

Table 3 gives the mean similarity indices (transformed back to a 0–5 scale) for TJ's and Test Ss. The fifth column presents the same figures for the AJ's.

The first analysis of these data was a two-way analysis of variance of the first four columns of Table 3 with test types as columns and S category as the rows. None of the possible effects were significant, i.e., similarity of diagnosis did not differ as a function of either test type or S category.

For the second analysis, simple t tests of the differences between the means for the TJ's and that for the AJ's were computed. The mean value for the AJ's was significantly higher (beyond the .05 level) in every case.

As a final analysis, each of the mean values for the four tests and for the AJ's were compared against the mean of the randomly selected sets of four diagnoses ($N = 23$). The mean of this distribution was 1.94 and the S was 1.34. The mean values for the Rorschach, MMPI, and the AJ's exceeded this chance value beyond the .05 level; the TAT and MAPS did not.

The results relative to agreement among diagnoses obtained from the above analyses may be summarized as follows:

1. Agreement among diagnoses where the diagnoses are based upon either the Rorschach, the MMPI, or anamnestic material, tend to be greater than chance.

TABLE 3.   MEAN DIAGNOSIS SIMILARITY INDICES AMONG
FOUR JUDGES GROUPED ACCORDING TO INFORMATION
SOURCE AND S TYPE

Ss		Ror.	TAT	MAPS	MMPI	Anam.
Nonpsychiatric	1	1.5	1.7	2.1	2.4	2.7
	2	1.9	2.6	2.5	2.0	4.9
	3	2.9	1.8	1.2	2.2	3.2
Neurotic	4	2.8	1.8	2.4	3.6	3.0
	5	2.0	2.7	2.6	2.1	2.3
	6	3.3	1.2	2.5	3.1	2.2
Psychophysi-	7	2.0	1.5	1.8	2.7	3.3
ological	8	2.4	1.4	1.4	3.8	4.5
disorder	9	3.8	2.2	1.7	2.2	3.2
Psychotic	12	1.8	2.1	3.4	2.0	5.0
	10	2.3	2.7	2.3	3.7	4.6
	11	3.2	1.4	1.6	1.9	3.9
Mean		2.50	1.76	2.12	2.64	3.57

2. Agreement among diagnoses based upon the MAPS or the TAT do not exceed chance agreement.

3. Agreement among diagnoses based upon anamnestic material is significantly greater than that based upon any other source of information.

4. Agreement among diagnoses based upon any of the sources considered do not appear to be affected by the type of S evaluated.

As a testament to the efficacy of psychodiagnostic instruments, these results leave something to be desired. Inspection of Table 2 has suggested that diagnostic labels based upon blind analyses of protocols may be quite wide of the mark and the present analysis indicates that the judges may not be even shooting at the same target.

How can one account for such disappointing results? Within the structure of the investigation there are certain factors that tend to influence the agreement index: extra weight was given to a single deviant diagnosis, agreement among the judges of similarity was by no means perfect, and the pool of diagnoses from which the chance index was

derived was of restricted range. The first two factors tend to lower the similarity index and increase its standard error while the latter raises the mean chance similarity index. However, even under these conditions, the finding that AJ's did significantly better than TJ's indicates that a higher degree of agreement is possible. Parenthetically, we might add that this higher degree of agreement of diagnoses based on anamnestic data as compared to test data is undoubtedly related to the derivation of our diagnostic labels themselves. They are based upon "the facts" of a man's life, e.g., a schizophrenic is not defined as a person with pure C on the Rorschach or a high Sc score on the MMPI, but rather as a man who hallucinates, is delusional, manifests autistic thinking, etc.—the very "facts" which are presented in a well-taken anamnesis.

The major implication of the present results is that the blind diagnosis of psychological test protocols for clinical purposes is of dubious value. It is possible that combinations of instruments may produce better agreement, but when tests are used singly, agreement on diagnoses among test interpreters is not to be expected.

Degree of Maladjustment

Each TJ and each AJ was asked to rate each S he evaluated on a maladjustment scale. Nine different scores, ranging from 0 through 8, were possible on the maladjustment scale. Four such scores were obtained for each Test S.

TABLE 4. ANALYSIS OF VARIANCE OF MALADJUSTMENT RATINGS FOR THREE SETS OF TEST Ss

Source	df	Variance Set I	Set II	Set III
TJ's	12	3.0	2.4	4.6
Tests	3	2.7	6.5	1.7
S type	3	14.4*	40.6*	17.8*
Test × S	9	8.4*	5.3*	6.0*
Remainder	36	2.6	1.8	2.0
Total	63			

* Significant at .01 level.

S. These scores were assembled into three sets corresponding to the three sets of Test Ss, i.e., Ss 1, 4, 7, 10; Ss 2, 5, 8, 11; and Ss 3, 6, 9, 12, and investigated by means of a three-way analysis of variance (McNemar, 1955, Model XVII). In each analysis, TJ's

formed the rows, type of S the columns, and tests the blocks. Results of the analyses are given in Table 4. Table 5 gives the mean maladjustment ratings of four judges for each S based upon the several information sources including the anamnestic data.

In each of the three analyses, differences among tests were not significant but differences among S types were. In addition, the interaction between test type and S type was also significant in each analysis. Differences among S types were to be expected but not in exactly the form obtained. In S Set I, the psychotic was judged most sick, the nonpsychiatric S and the psychophysiologic S next, and the neurotic as the least ill. In S Set II, the order was psychotic, neurotic, psychophysiologic, and nonpsychiatric; and in S Set III, psychotic, nonpsychiatric, neurotic, and psychophysiologic. These results may be compared with those of the AJ's who ranked the S types the same in all three sets.

The observation that information-source, S-type interaction was significant in all three analyses indicates, of course, variation in the order of ranking depending upon information source, i.e., profile differences. For example, in S Set I, the TAT judges considered the nonpsychiatric S most maladjusted,

TABLE 5. AVERAGE MALADJUSTMENT RATINGS FOR EACH S BY TJ'S AND AJ'S

Ss		Ror.	TAT	MAPS	MMPI	Anam.
Nonpsychiatric	1	4.0	6.5	5.0	3.5	1.8
	2	3.5	2.8	3.5	3.0	1.0
	3	6.0	5.0	5.8	3.5	2.0
Neurotic	4	3.5	3.8	4.2	2.0	6.5
	5	4.0	6.0	7.5	6.8	7.0
	6	4.8	3.8	2.2	6.5	6.8
Psychophysi-	7	4.0	3.0	6.2	5.0	3.5
ological	8	3.0	5.8	6.8	4.5	4.5
disorder	9	3.8	4.5	3.2	3.5	3.5
Psychotic	10	5.0	4.8	5.0	8.0	7.0
	11	7.0	7.2	5.8	7.5	7.0
	12	6.0	6.8	6.2	5.8	8.2

whereas the MAPS judges considered the psychophysiologic S most maladjusted and the neurotic S as the least. To test whether such patterns were stable ones, a fourth analysis was made using the data in the first four columns of Table 5 with S sets as rows, S type as columns, and tests as blocks. The results of this analysis are presented in Table 6. As would be expected from the preceding analyses, differences among S types were significant (in that

TABLE 6. ANALYSIS OF VARIANCE OF THE MEAN MALADJUSTMENT RATINGS OF EACH TEST S BY FOUR TJ'S

Source	Sum of squares	df	Variance
Sets	102.9	8	12.8
Test type	22.0	3	7.3
S type	350.8	3	116.9*
Test × S	62.7	9	7.0
Remainder	577.1	24	24.0
Total	1115.5	47	

* Significant at .01 level.

the psychotics were consistently considered most ill) and there were no significant differences in mean judgments among test types after the combination of the S sets. The interaction, moreover, was also nonsignificant, indicating that the apparent test by S-type effects observed previously were a function of the particular four Test Ss used in each of the three sets.

Finally, a two-way analysis of variance (McNemar, 1955, Case VIII) was made of the data in Table 5 for each of the four Test S types separately in order to compare the average ratings of the AJ's with that of the TJ's. Table 7 gives the results of these analyses.

Only in the case of the nonpsychiatric S are the mean maladjustment ratings of the TJ's significantly different from those of the AJ's. Judges for all test types tended to rate the nonpsychiatric Ss as significantly more maladjusted than the AJ's.

The results of ratings of maladjustment may be summarized as follows:

1. Psychotics as a group are rated as most maladjusted on the basis of all of the tests used.

2. No significant differences occur among over-all mean ratings of maladjustment for nonpsychiatric, psychophysiologic, or neurotic Ss.

3. No individual test elicits a significantly greater or lesser maladjustment index than any other test.

4. For nonpsychotic Ss, maladjustment ratings based on test protocols are significantly higher than those based on anamnestic material.

5. For other than nonpsychiatric Ss, maladjustment ratings based upon test protocols are not significantly different from those based on anamnestic material.

As a first observation, it is apparent

TABLE 7. ANALYSES OF VARIANCE OF MEAN MALADJUSTMENT RATINGS OF FOUR TYPES OF Ss BY TJ'S AND AJ'S

Source	df	Variance Non-psychiatric	Neurotic	Psycho-physiological	Psychotic
Ss	2	438.6*	654.4	186.2	115.2
Information source	4	556.2**	321.7	145.1	162.6
Interaction	8	63.8	248.9	125.4	92.1

* Significant at .05 level.
** Significant at .01 level.

that the maladjustment rating data reflect the same situation observed in relation to diagnoses. Nonpsychiatric Ss are tarred with the pathologic brush. One is reminded of Ernest Jones' response to the question as to the characteristics of a normal person—that he didn't know; he had never met one.

The present data do point up a phenomenon not tested in the analysis of the diagnoses; psychotics are distinguished from the other three classes of Ss. It seems probable, therefore, that although agreement among diagnoses is no greater for psychotics than for any other Ss, the diagnoses used are of a more pathologic nature.

Q Sorts

The first question asked in analyzing the Q-sort results was similar to that raised in connection with the diagnostic statements, i.e., Do judges working with different test types differ in the amount of agreement among themselves about the test subjects? The form of analysis used was the pseudo three-way analysis of variance with S sets forming the rows, tests the columns, and S types the blocks. Entries in the cells were the average coefficients for the six correlations among the four judges interpreting any particular protocol. None of the possible effects was significant, i.e., there were no differences among over-all average intercorrelations for the different tests nor for

the different S types. The interaction effect was also nonsignificant.

Table 8 gives the analysis of variance data and Table 9 the average intercorrelations among the Q sorts arranged by tests and by Test Ss. For comparison, over-all averages for tests, S types, and the average intercorrelations among the AJ's are also given.

The second question asked was whether the TJ's working with a specific test agreed among themselves to a greater extent than between tests. The following method of analysis was used to secure an answer to this question: For each Test S the six intercorrelations among the four TJ's working with a specific test were added to the six intercorrelations among the four TJ's working with another test and the average secured. This average was paired with the mean of the 16 correlations *between* the two sets of four judges and the difference obtained. For each pair of tests, 12 such differences were available, one for each Test S. A simple *t* test of the mean difference of these 12 correlated differences was then computed.

Table 10 gives the mean differences obtained by the above method. In all cases there was slightly greater agreement within tests than between, but only in the case of the MMPI paired with each of the other tests were the differences significant, i.e., agreement between MMPI judges and the other TJ's was significantly lower than the

TABLE 8.   ANALYSIS OF VARIANCE DATA OF THE
AVERAGE INTERCORRELATIONS
AMONG TJS' *Q* SORTS

Source	Sum of Squares	df	Variance
S sets	11574.3	8	1446.8
S types	1878.7	3	626.2
Tests	3635.2	3	1211.4
S type × Test	2986.1	9	331.8
Remainder	17411.0	24	725.4
Total	37485.3	47	

TABLE 9.   AVERAGE Q-SORT CORRELATIONS AMONG FOUR TJ'S USING
DIFFERENT INFORMATION SOURCES FOR EACH TEST S

Test	1	2	3	4	5	6	7	8	9	10	11	12	Average
Rorschach	56	44	−13	09	36	−06	45	58	−12	−03	64	61	31
TAT	46	14	−02	17	24	−09	51	41	16	23	19	67	27
MAPS	45	28	14	45	22	38	50	56	05	25	07	71	35
MMPI	28	44	23	59	52	39	04	49	21	70	45	08	39
Average	44	33	06	34	34	16	39	52	08	32	36	55	33
Anamnesis	54	72	54	23	60	59	12	42	66	72	40	44	52

agreement among judges working within a test type. Among the projective technique judges, however, agreement within tests was not, on the average, significantly higher than across tests.

TABLE 10.   MEAN DIFFERENCES IN AVERAGE INTERCORRELATIONS BETWEEN TWO TESTS COMBINED AND THEIR CROSS CORRELATIONS FOR 12 Ss

Test	Ror.	TAT	MAPS
TAT	.012		
MAPS	.027	.037	
MMPI	.087*	.176*	.187*

* Significant at .02 level.

The third question raised was the amount of agreement between the TJ's and the AJ's. This is, of course, the question of validity where psychiatric judgments are used as the criterion. To answer the question, the four correlations of each TJ with the four AJ's were transformed into z's and averaged. The average correlations (after back transformation) are given in Table 11. Those significantly different from zero at the .01 level ($\sigma_{av} z = .058$) are marked with an asterisk. Examining these values in conjunction with the average intercorrelation among the AJ's themselves (Table 9), it is apparent that part of the low agreement can be

accounted for on the basis of disagreement among criterion judges. The values are, however, rather distressingly low in spite of this mitigating factor.

To test differences among tests in correlation with the AJ's, three pseudo three-way analyses of variance were made, one for each S set. Table 12 gives the results of these analyses. In each, TJ's formed the rows, S types the columns, and test types the blocks. In all, differences among S types were significant, but in none were differences among tests significant. For Set I, the interaction between test and S type reached the 5% level of significance, but since the effect did not appear in the other two analyses it must be considered an artifact of the particular group of Ss in that set.

Although differences among S types were significant in each S set, the specific type with the highest mean correlation with the AJ's was different from set to set. In order to determine over-all effects, a fourth analysis was made using test types as rows, S types as columns, and S sets as blocks. Entries in the cells were the average correlations of four TJ's with four AJ's for one S. Table 13 gives the results of this analysis. As would be expected, the Test S × S set interaction was significant, i.e., in different S sets differing S types elicited the highest agreement

TABLE 11.   AVERAGE CORRELATION OF FOUR TJ'S WITH
FOUR AJ'S ON Q SORT

S		Ror.	TAT	MAPS	MMPI
Nonpsychiatric	1	−10	−38°	−39°	24°
	2	25°	−14	−17°	54°
	3	−05	−07	−11	11
Neurotic	4	13	17°	23°	18°
	5	41°	34°	39°	54°
	6	22°	00	−01	26°
Psychophysiologic disorder	7	02	09	02	03
	8	47°	38°	46°	41°
	9	08	05	11	09
Psychotic	10	07	−07	21°	38°
	11	32°	24°	30°	32°
	12	20°	53°	53°	16°

* Significant at .01 level.

with the AJ's. Block effects were also significant indicating differences in the over-all agreement between TJ's and AJ's for the different S sets. Highest agreement, for example, occurred between TJ's and AJ's for the Ss of Set II. Finally, over-all column effects were significant. Testing the differences among the means indicated that this effect was determined by the remarkably low agreement between TJ's and AJ's on the nonpsychiatric Ss. Differences among means for the other three S types were not significant.

A fourth question of interest is the amount of stereotypy in the TJ's evaluation of the S protocols. Since each

TJ made a Q sort for four different Test Ss, stereotypy may be defined as the difference between the average correlation among the judge's Q sorts and some index of the "true" similarity among the four Ss. The difficulty, of course, lies in securing an index of "true" similarity. For our analysis, we selected the mean of patterned samples of correlations between Test Ss within an S set but across judges within one test type. For example, on Set I, all possible correlations among the Q sorts of TJ's R-1 for TS-1, R-2 for TS-4, R-3 for TS-7, and R-4 for TS-10 were computed. To these were added the intercorrelations among the Q sorts of R-1

TABLE 12.   ANALYSES OF VARIANCE DATA FOR
MEAN Q-SORT CORRELATIONS OF TJ'S WITH FOUR AJ'S

Source	df	Variance		
		Set I	Set II	Set III
Judges	12	1049.8	647.8	540.7
Tests	3	1596.1	1711.0	47.5
S type	3	2728.5°°	1949.9°	4298.5°
Test × S type	9	841.6°	657.5	47.3
Remainder	36	350.7	453.6	1451.6
Total	63			

* Significant at .05 level.
** Significant at .01 level.

TABLE 13. ANALYSIS OF VARIANCE OF THE AVERAGE Q-SORT CORRELATIONS OF FOUR TJ'S WITH FOUR AJ'S

Source	df	Variance
Tests	9	4472.6
S sets	2	51551.3**
S type	3	23597.1**
S set × S type	6	6150.0*
Remainder	27	2061.9
Total	47	

* Significant at .05 level.
** Significant at .01 level.

for TS-4, R-2 for TS-7, R-3 for TS-10, and R-4 for TS-1; and R-1 for TS-10, R-2 for TS-1, R-3 for TS-4, and R-4 for TS-7. The average of these 24 correlations formed the baseline estimate of the "true" similarity among the four Test Ss for the Rorschach judges of Set I. Similar indices were computed for other TJ's and for other S sets. Since this baseline estimate might still include a specific bias due to test type, an initial two-way analysis of variance

was made of the baseline average correlations using S sets as rows and tests as columns. There were no significant differences among tests or among S sets.

A generalized bias resulting from a tendency of all clinical psychologists to say similar things about different Ss may still exist in the baseline estimates. However, no method of analysis eliminating this bias was available.

Table 14 presents the average correlations among Q sorts for four Ss for each TJ arranged by S set and test type. In the fifth row for each set is given the average of the mean values for each of the four judges in a given S set-test cell and in the sixth row, in italicized figures, the mean inter-S interjudge correlation used as a baseline. A two-way analysis of variance of the differences between the values in the fifth rows and sixth rows was made. Table 15 presents the results. Test type effects were not significant, i.e., there was no greater tendency for one test

TABLE 14. AVERAGE CORRELATIONS AMONG FOUR Q SORTS FOR FOUR DIFFERENT Ss BY EACH TJ

	Ror.	TAT	MAPS	MMPI
S Set I	−04	−06	22	−07
	26	−05	36	03
	41	−10	18	07
	28	22	26	−01
Mean baseline	228	000	255	005
	211	*−036*	*228*	*−012*
S Set II	35	38	16	00
	36	10	08	−09
	21	02	24	06
	08	24	18	−02
Mean baseline	250	185	165	−012
	193	*095*	*181*	*−065*
S Set III	25	15	28	56
	31	−10	48	38
	34	−07	10	09
	30	03	04	26
Mean baseline	300	002	225	322
	041	*000*	*135*	*145*

to elicit stereotyped *Q* sorts than any other. Subject set effects, however, were significant, suggesting that one group of *S* protocols (Set III) tended to elicit more stereotypic evaluations than the other two. Since TJ's and Test Ss were assigned at random to the three sets, no immediate explanation for this phenomenon occurs to us.

TABLE 15. ANALYSIS OF VARIANCE OF THE DIFFERENCES BETWEEN MEAN WITHIN-JUDGE *Q*-SORT CORRELATIONS AND MEAN ACROSS-JUDGE *Q*-SORT CORRELATIONS FOR FOUR DIFFERENT Ss

Source	*df*	Variance
S sets	2	2598.5*
Tests	3	362.3
S set × Test type	6	88.5
Total	11	

* Significant at .01 level.

As a last point, a simple test of the deviation of the mean of the difference correlations from zero for all tests and S sets combined was significant, i.e., a statistically significant degree of stereotypy exists among the TJ's. The absolute magnitude, of course, is quite small although examination of Table 14 indicates that certain judges have quite high intercorrelations among their four *Q* sorts.

The results of the analyses of the *Q*-sort data may be summarized as follows:

1. Agreement among judges interpreting the same protocol is not significantly affected by the tests.

2. Agreement among judges interpreting the same protocol is not significantly affected by the nosological category of the S.

3. Among projective tests, the degree of agreement among judges interpreting the same protocol is not significantly higher than the agreement with judges

interpreting a different projective technique protocol for the same S.

4. Agreement between interpretations of MMPI protocols and projective technique protocols for the same S is significantly lower than agreement among judges interpreting the same protocol.

5. The amount of agreement between test interpretations and judgments of psychiatrists is not significantly different for the four tests used in this study.

6. The amount of agreement between test interpretations for nonpsychiatric Ss and psychiatric judgments is significantly lower than that for neurotics, psychophysiological disorders, and psychotics.

7. Test interpreters tend to make their interpretations in a stereotyped manner independent of the S.

8. Nosological category of the Test S does not significantly affect the degree to which stereotyped interpretations of test protocols are made.

The fact that the degree of agreement among the judges interpreting specific projective technique protocols is no higher than their agreement with judges interpreting different projective test protocols for the same Ss probably implies a common psychodynamic approach to the interpretation of projective test protocols. This common approach seems to pervade interpretation to such an extent that unique contributions of the tests may be masked. The fact that the interpretations of MMPI protocols tend to be more in agreement among themselves than with the interpretations of projective techniques may well be a function of the following characteristics of the MMPI: that the data presented in the MMPI protocols have a fairly high degree of specificity; that there is less variability as to what MMPI (as compared with projective test) TJ's use for cues; that MMPI TJ's have fewer cues than the projective test TJ's; that conclusions drawn from MMPI data are less inferential and more close to the phenomenologically given (in that the MMPI is more similar to the anamnesis); and that, whereas the projective techniques obtain their intellectual permissiveness from psychoanalytic theory, the MMPI, on the other hand, operates within an empirical tradition and deals largely with more denotable aspects of behavior. Little wonder then that the "vision" of the clinicians who deal with questionnaire techniques (like the MMPI) is less blurred than that of the clinicians who must infer from projective techniques. However, it should be pointed out that the amount of agreement between test interpretations, on the one hand, and judgments from the anamneses, on the other hand, was not significantly different for *any* of the four tests used in this study.

It should be stated that the findings and implications of the Q sorts (and T-F items) should be clearly differentiated in the reader's mind from the findings and interpretations of the diagnoses and degree of maladjustment. That is to say, the rather disappointing findings that the tests do not do well in obtaining either inter-judge agreement or agreement between test judges and psychiatric judgments in terms of diagnostic labels does not necessarily mean that the tests do not retain a useful and important function in delineating psychodynamics and characteristics of personality as evidenced in Q-sort items and T-F items.

True-False Personality Items

Every TJ and AJ had (in addition to the diagnoses, estimates of maladjustment, and Q sorts), indicated whether he considered each of 117 psychological report type items true or false for each S. The analysis of these

data was limited to comparisons between the judgments of the TJ's based upon test protocols and those of the AJ's based upon the anamnestic materials.

The initial step in the analysis was to tabulate the judgments of the four AJ's on the 117 items for each Test S and to select those items in which 3 of the 4, or 4 of 4 AJ's agreed. Table 16 gives the number and percentage of the 117 items for each S on which 3 out of 4 or 4 out of 4 agreements occurred. A modal list was then constructed using

TABLE 16.   NUMBER AND PERCENTAGE OF 117 ITEMS MARKED THE SAME BY 3 OUT OF 4 OR 4 OUT OF 4 PSYCHIATRISTS

S	No.	%
1	87	74
2	111	95
3	94	80
4	85	73
5	101	86
6	99	85
7	84	72
8	99	85
9	105	90
10	105	90
11	102	87
12	99	85

the decision of the AJ's for the selected items as the criterion judgment. (Items were not included when the AJ's were evenly split on their truth or falsity.)

Tetrachoric correlations were used as the index of agreement between each TJ and the criterion. Four such indices were available for each TJ, one for each S evaluated.

As with the Q-sort material, three pseudo three-way analyses of variance were made of the present material, one for each S set. In each, TJ's formed the rows, S types the columns, and tests the blocks. Table 17 gives the analysis of variance data for the three analyses of variance.

The results varied from set to set. In

TABLE 17.   ANALYSIS OF VARIANCE DATA FOR
THE TETRACHORIC CORRELATIONS OF TJ'S WITH
THE MODAL JUDGMENT OF THE AJ'S ON REPORT
TYPE ITEMS

Source	df	Set I	Variance Set II	Set III
TJ's	12	1325.7	875.3	557.8
Tests	3	718.2	1073.3	2025.7*
S type	3	2567.0	10786.6**	16487.4**
Test × S type	9	2894.7*	23875.8*	3118.4
Remainder	36	1095.6	1022.3	1607.2
Total	63			

* Significant at .05 level.
** Significant at .01 level.

Set I only the interaction approached significance, the main effects did not. In Sets II and III there was a significant S-type effect, an interaction effect in Set II and a test effect in Set III. It is rather difficult to draw conclusions from such data, so the independent scores from the separate judges were averaged for a composite "validity" index. Table 18 gives these mean correlations with the criterion, of the four TJ's working with each S-test combination.

A fourth pseudo three-way analysis of variance was made of the data in Table 18 using Test Ss as rows, tests as columns, and S types as blocks. The results of this analysis, presented in Table 19, indicate significant differences in agreement with the psychiatrists for different S types and a significant interaction effect of the Tests × S type. The differences among S types is largely accounted for by the extremely low amount of agreement between the TJ's impressions of the nonpsychiatric Ss and the psychiatrists' impressions of these same individuals.

Only one definite conclusion can be drawn from these data: TJ's have a significantly lower correlation with AJ's

TABLE 18.   AVERAGE TETRACHORIC CORRELATIONS
OF FOUR TJ'S WITH THE MODAL JUDGMENT OF FOUR
AJ'S ON REPORT TYPE ITEMS

Ss		Ror.	TAT	MAPS	MMPI
Nonpsychiatric	1	−20	04	17	59
	2	−10	−20	12	47
	3	−31	−32	−19	38
Neurotic	4	34	36	39	−02
	5	74	42	64	22
	6	67	44	04	79
Psychophysiologic disorder	7	38	42	45	14
	8	72	75	65	55
	9	58	18	44	22
Psychotic	10	40	26	28	81
	11	65	37	32	80
	12	62	85	67	44

TABLE 19. ANALYSIS OF VARIANCE OF THE AVERAGE TETRACHORIC CORRELATIONS OF TJ'S WITH ANAMNESTIC MODAL JUDGMENT OF REPORT TYPE ITEMS

Source	df	Variance
Test Ss	8	793.0
S types	3	5956.5**
Tests	3	512.9
S × Test type	9	1070.7*
Remainder	24	389.8
Total	47	

* Significant at .05 level.
** Significant at .01 level.

on nonpsychiatric Ss than they do on the other three nosological categories. However, inspection of the average correlations in Table 18 in light of the significant interaction effect reported for Table 19 indicates varying degrees of efficiency of the four tests for different S categories. Specifically, the Rorschach seemed about equally efficient for the three S categories of neurotic, psychophysiological reaction, and psychotic, and markedly inefficient for the nonpsychiatric Ss; the TAT showed its optimum efficiency with the psychotic and psychophysiological Ss; the MAPS test indicated a pattern similar to that of the TAT, and the MMPI gave its best performance for the normal and psychotic Ss.

It is interesting that in the Q sorts there was a significantly higher degree of agreement between TJ's and AJ's for the psychotics than for any other nosological category, whereas with the True-False items there was a significantly lower degree of agreement of the TJ's with the AJ's for the nonpsychiatric Ss. In other words, there were no differences in the amount of agreement between test results and anamnestic results as far as the Q-sort data were concerned among the nonpsychiatric, neurotic, and psychophysiologic disorders, whereas for the True-False data there is no discrimination among the neurotic, psycho-

physiologic disorder, and psychotic Test S data. It would almost appear that the True-False personality items function to discriminate between normal on the one hand and all other ("sick") individuals on the other hand. In relation to the findings for the specific psychological tests, one comment can be made about the MMPI: specifically, that inasmuch as it apparently does differentiate the two extreme groups, its routine inclusion in a battery of tests is probably advisable, not so much to pick out the extremely aberrant individual, but more importantly to focus on the relatively well-adjusted (normal) S. Among the projective techniques, the present data would suggest that the Rorschach would be first choice for an additional test in the armamentarium of the clinician—as indeed the surveys of use of tests in clinics demonstrate.

True-False Factual Items

A series of analyses similar to that described for the personality type True-False items was made for the 100 True-False factual items which the TJ's had marked as True or False for each S. Criterion keys were established by examining the case histories of each S for positive evidence of the truth or falsity of each statement. When no evidence either way was available the item was eliminated. As a result, the total number of items considered varied somewhat from S to S, ranging from 89 to 100.

Each TJ's marks of true or false for the items from one S were matched against the key and the tetrachoric correlation between the two determined. Three pseudo three-way analyses of variance were made of the results, one for each S set. Table 20 presents the results of these analyses.

In all, differences among S types were significant, although the type of S most accurately described varied

TABLE 20.   ANALYSIS OF VARIANCE DATA FOR TETRACHORIC CORRE-
LATIONS OF TJ'S WITH CASE HISTORY KEY FOR FACTUAL ITEMS

| Source | df | Variances | | |
		Set I	Set II	Set III
TJ's	12	546.3	265.1	469.1
Tests	3	5815.8**	1255.7*	76.9
S type	3	3089.5**	2781.7**	3387.8**
Test type × S type	9	942.0	1150.2**	705.4*
Remainder	36	521.4	235.7	321.1
Total	63			

* Significant at .05 level.
** Significant at .01 level.

from set to set. In Set I, the psycho-physiological S was judged most correctly; in Set II, the neurotic; and in Set III, the psychotic. In all three sets the nonpsychiatric Ss were least correctly described.

In two of the sets (I and II) differences among test types were significant with the MMPI being superior as compared to the projective tests. In Set III, this difference did not occur. Also in two sets (II and III) the interaction of test by S type was significant.

A final analysis of the combined sets was also made. Table 21 gives the average correlations that constituted the data for the pseudo three-way analysis.

As in the case of the report type True-False items, Test Ss formed the rows, tests the columns, and S types the blocks. Table 22 gives the results of this analysis. None of the possible effects was significant, i.e., there was no difference among mean values for tests, S types, or interaction. The apparent superiority of the MMPI disappeared in the combined data.

It is apparent that the results of the analysis of the factual True-False items were inconclusive. One might question at this point whether psychological tests can, or ought, to correlate well with factual case history data. The whole issue of the postdictive function

TABLE 21.   AVERAGE TETRACHORIC CORRELATIONS OF FOUR TJ'S
WITH CASE HISTORY CRITERION FOR FACTUAL ITEMS

Ss		No. of Items	Ror.	TAT	MAPS	MMPI
Nonpsychiatric	1	96	−12	07	−22	42
	2	99	16	22	27	51
	3	98	−05	02	−20	10
Neurotic	4	98	12	12	09	53
	5	98	42	−10	50	41
	6	97	16	34	37	13
Psychophysiologic disorder	7	95	11	59	45	35
	8	98	−05	10	02	06
	9	99	15	−10	25	06
Psychotic	10	96	14	21	04	56
	11	94	32	04	06	13
	12	88	32	29	29	22

TABLE 22.   ANALYSIS OF VARIANCE OF
AVERAGE CORRELATIONS OF FOUR TJ'S
WITH CASE HISTORY CRITERION

Source	Sum of Squares	df	Variance
Test Ss	5596.0	8	724.5
S type	1709.5	3	569.8
Tests	1788.0	3	596.0
S type × Test type	2999.2	9	333.2
Remainder	6919.3	24	288.3
Total	19012.0	47	

of psychological tests is a debatable one. If one wants to know if an individual was an only child or came from a broken home, etc., a psychological test is not the optimal technique for ascertaining this type of information.

Reliability

The results reported in this section are comparisons of the interpretations made on the first protocol evaluated by the TJ's and interpretations made when the same protocol was re-presented approximately 10 days later (cf. Procedure). The data are in the form of coefficients of agreement between first and second evaluations.

Table 23 gives the two *diagnoses* of each TJ for the Test Ss classified by test and by S type. These 48 pairs of diagnoses were presented to four competent psychodiagnosticians who rated each pair on a 0–5 scale with 5 representing maximum similarity. The average correlation among the four raters for the 48 pairs was .83, indicating a good degree of agreement as to the similarity of the diagnostic pairs. The index of similarity for any specific pair of diagnoses was the mean of the ratings of the four judges. Table 24 gives the indices for each test type. A two-way analysis of variance of the data of Table 24 was made, using S type as rows and test type as columns. None of the possible effects was sig-

nificant, i.e., there were no significant differences among test types in amount of agreement between repeat diagnoses, nor among S types.

Ratings of the *degree of maladjustment* of the S were made on second evaluation in the same fashion as on the first. Disagreement between first and second ratings for each judge is indicated in Table 25 in the form of discrepancy scores. A negative number indicates that the judge changed his rating in the direction of increased maladjustment; a positive number indicates the converse, and a zero indicates no change. The changes range from zero to one-half the scale length (8 units). An analysis of variance, however, indicated no significant differences among tests in absolute amount of change of ratings.

Table 26 gives the correlations between Q sorts of first and second evaluations of the same protocol by each judge and the average for each test. Table 27 gives the analysis of variance data for Table 26. Differences among test types are significant in that the TAT judges have a significantly ($P = .01$) lower mean reliability coefficient than that for judges of the other tests.

Table 28 gives the tetrachoric correlations between first and second evaluations of the 117 *True-False report-type items* and Table 29 the analysis of variance data. As in the Q-sort results, the average reliability figure for the TAT judges is significantly lower ($P = .01$) than that of the judges for the other three tests.

Table 30 presents the tetrachoric correlations between the answers given to the 100 *True-False factual items* in the first and second evaluations. The analysis of variance data (Table 31) indicates that the situation is exactly the same as for Q sorts and report type items, i.e., that TAT judges have a significantly lower ($P = .05$) reliability figure than judges of other tests.

S	Rorschach	TAT	MAPS	MMPI
	Nonpsychiatric			
1	(a) Passive dependent personality [initial diagnosis]	(a) Psychopath—immaturity reaction	(a) Schizoid character	(a) Character neurosis
	(b) Inadequate personality, passive—dependency reaction [repeat diagnosis]	(b) Schizophrenic, probably catatonic; psychopath	(b) Schizoid character	(b) Neurotic reaction, very defensive
2	(a) Schizoid character—depressive trends	(a) Psychoneurosis—mixed—homosexuality	(a) Passive aggressive (dependent) personality	(a) Normal
	(b) Schizoid character—depressive trends	(b) Psychoneurosis, mixed, or psychosis, schizophenia, in remission	(b) Passive—dependent personality	(b) Essentially normal—basically a hysteroid personality
3	(a) Schizoid personality, paranoid and homosexual trends	(a) Passive-aggressive reaction with schizophrenic episodes—emotional instability	(a) Character disorder with hysterical and homosexual trends	(a) Simple adult maladjustment, emotional instability
	(b) Schizoid personality with decompensating features—although some ego is intact	(b) Mixed psychoneurosis, severe, with depressive, phobic, hysterical and passive aggressive features	(b) Passive dependent character neurosis	(b) Emotional instability
	Neurotic			
4	(a) Obsessive compulsive possibly with schizoid features	(a) Character disorder—passive dependent features	(a) Obsessive compulsive homosexual	(a) Essentially normal individual, mild obsessional reactions plus homo-eroticism problem
	(b) Obsessive compulsive	(b) Character disorder—hysterical and depressive features	(b) Obsessive compulsive	(b) Anxious, uncertain individual with probably homo-erotic problems

598

TABLE 23. (*Continued*)

S	Rorschach	TAT	MAPS	MMPI
5	(a) Mixed pre-genital character, passive-aggressive personality, passive-aggressive type	(a) Paranoid schizophrenia in remission or partial remission, with possible acting out aggressive psychopath character structure	(a) Latent (incipient) schizophrenic reaction	(a) Psychopathic personality
	(b) Anal character with obsessive compulsive and masochistic trends	(b) Depressive reaction in obsessive personality	(b) Schizophrenia (incipient)	(b) Psychopathic personality
6	(a) Anxiety and depression in a compulsive personality	(a) Obsessive-compulsive neurosis, paranoid trends	(a) Hysterical character	(a) Mild neurotic depression
	(b) Severe anxiety neurosis in an immature character. Intellectual and compulsive obsessive defenses too weak to protect him from anxiety	(b) Hysterical character, paranoid trends	(b) Hysterical character	(b) Hysterical personality with mild neurotic depression

Psychophysiologic Disorder

S	Rorschach	TAT	MAPS	MMPI
7	(a) Oral character disorder with ego restriction	(a) Adjusted normal	(a) Anxiety reaction, possibly latent schizophrenia	(a) Hypochondriasis
	(b) Passive dependency reaction with hysterical features	(b) Fairly well adjusted normal	(b) Schizophrenia	(b) Hypochondriasis (severe psychoneurosis with anxiety and hypochondriacal features predominating)
8	(a) Anxiety reaction	(a) Neurosis with marked overt anxiety: phobias? obsessiveness? possible epileptic	(a) Anxiety reaction with somatic complaints	(a) Anxiety neurosis

TABLE 23. (*Continued*)

S	Rorschach	TAT	MAPS	MMPI
	(b) Conversion reaction	(b) Not psychotic. Severe neurosis or character disorder with antisocial behavior	(b) Anxiety reaction with somatic complaints; immaturity personality	(b) Anxiety neurosis
9	(a) Psychoneurosis, mixed, with anxiety and depression	(a) Anxiety reaction, precariously maintained	(a) Essentially normal with some immaturity that may be largely a function of age	(a) Adult situational reaction
	(b) Neurotic or schizoid personality	(b) Character neurosis	(b) Normal, if age is in lower range	(b) Psychoneurosis, anxiety reaction, mild
		Psychotic		
10	(a) Inadequate character	(a) Neurosis; some depressive features and probably considerable anxiety	(a) Depressive reaction	(a) Paranoid schizophrenia episode with marked anxiety
	(b) Obsessive-compulsive neurotic with strong homosexual conflicts	(b) Passive-feminine character disorder with some depressive and some borderline schizophrenic trends	(b) Phobic reaction with depression	(b) Schizophrenia, paranoid type, acute
11	(a) Psychotic disorder; schizophrenic reaction	(a) Immaturity reaction; impulse neurosis	(a) Simple schizophrenia or schizophrenic character disorder	(a) Acute anxiety state
	(b) Psychotic disorder, probably a schizophrenic reaction	(b) Passive dependency reaction (immaturity reaction)	(b) Anxiety hysteria	(b) Psychotic reaction: schizophrenia
12	(a) Passive aggressive character, passive dependent type	(a) Psychosis— probably schizophrenic type	(a) Schizoid personality	(a) Reactive depression in a latent paranoid schizophrenic
	(b) Passive-dependent character—possibly alcoholic	(b) Schizophrenia	(b) Schizoid personality with a strong suspicion of organicity	(b) Reactive depression (and/or conversion?) with latent paranoid schizophrenic reaction

TABLE 24.   MEAN SIMILARITY INDICES BETWEEN FIRST AND
SECOND DIAGNOSES BASED UPON THE SAME TEST PROTOCOLS

Ss		Ror.	TAT	MAPS	MMPI
Nonpsychiatric	1	4.8	1.8	5.0	3.5
	2	5.0	2.5	5.0	4.5
	3	3.8	1.8	3.5	4.5
Neurotic	4	4.2	3.5	4.0	4.5
	5	2.5	.2	5.0	5.0
	6	3.5	1.8	5.0	3.8
Psychophysiologic disorder	7	3.0	5.0	2.2	4.5
	8	2.2	2.2	4.2	5.0
	9	2.5	2.2	5.0	2.5
Psychotic	10	1.5	2.0	3.0	4.8
	11	5.0	3.8	.2	1.0
	12	4.5	5.0	3.5	4.2
Mean		3.7	2.6	3.8	4.0

These reliability data may be summarized as follows:

1. Diagnoses based upon repeat evaluations of the same protocol vary from identical to markedly dissimilar.

2. Maladjustment ratings under the same conditions vary in a similar fashion with a mean absolute change of approximately 12% and a range from zero to 50%.

3. Q-sort reliability figures vary from − .07 to + .94 with an over-all mean of about .55 for all TJ's combined.

4. TAT judges make significantly less reliable Q sorts than judges of the Rorschach, MAPS, and MMPI.

5. Report type True-False item reliability figures vary from zero to + .96 with an over-all mean for all TJ's combined of about .73.

6. TAT judges have a significantly lower mean personality type True-False item reliability figure than do judges of the other tests.

7. Factual True-False items reliability figures vary from .33 to .94 with

TABLE 25.   CHANGES IN MALADJUSTMENT RATINGS FROM
FIRST TO SECOND OBSERVATION

Ss		Ror.	TAT	MAPS	MMPI
Nonpsychiatric	1	0	−1	0	0
	2	−2	−1	0	0
	3	−1	1	0	1
Neurotic	4	1	−3	0	0
	5	0	1	1	−1
	6	0	−2	1	0
Psychophysiological disorder	7	1	0	0	−1
	8	0	−2	−2	1
	9	2	1	0	0
Psychotic	10	0	−2	4	2
	11	1	0	2	0
	12	−4	0	0	1
Mean		1.00	1.17	.83	.58

TABLE 26.   Q-SORT RELIABILITY FIGURES
(PRODUCT MOMENT CORRELATION)
FOR THE 48 TJ'S

Ss		Ror.	TAT	MAPS	MMPI
Nonpsychiatric	1	66	61	94	62
	2	76	45	52	73
	3	70	17	19	51
Neurotic	4	67	58	76	59
	5	36	−01	80	88
	6	26	−07	50	79
Psychophysiological disorder	7	70	78	47	58
	8	51	32	69	84
	9	69	17	74	66
Psychotic	10	52	19	45	56
	11	68	24	54	12
	12	81	82	64	63
Mean		.610	.354	.603	.626

an over-all mean for all TJ's of about .72.

8. TAT judges have significantly lower reliability figures for factual True-False items than do judges of the other three tests.

The outstanding general finding from the reliability data is that the reliabilities of the interpretations made from psychological tests vary considerably except for the individuals interpreting

TABLE 27.   ANALYSIS OF VARIANCE OF Q-SORT RELIABILITY COEFFICIENTS

Source	Sum of Squares	df	Variance
S type	640.5	3	213.5
Tests	6064.2	3	2021.4*
Tests × S type	4272.7	9	474.7
Within cells	16177.3	32	505.4
Total	27154.7	47	

* Significant at .05 level.

TABLE 28.   REPORT TYPE ITEM RELIABILITY COEFFICIENTS
(TETRACHORIC CORRELATIONS) FOR THE 48 TJ'S

Ss		Ror.	TAT	MAPS	MMPI
Nonpsychiatric	1	72	67	80	91
	2	30	50	48	82
	3	73	59	93	73
Neurotic	4	92	79	88	93
	5	89	64	87	82
	6	85	52	92	83
Psychophysiological disorder	7	71	96	79	94
	8	74	58	94	90
	9	85	25	84	96
Psychotic	10	74	37	52	83
	11	90	00	59	61
	12	93	80	68	87
Mean		.773	.556	.770	.846

TABLE 29.   ANALYSIS OF VARIANCE OF
REPORT-TYPE ITEM RELIABILITY
COEFFICIENTS

Source	Sum of Squares	df	Variance
Tests	2383.6	3	794.5
S type	5648.8	3	1882.9*
Tests × S type	2484.1	9	276.0
Within cell	9766.7	32	305.2
Total	20283.2	47	

* Significant at .01 level.

Discussion

Rather than recapitulate the results and the comments given in the preceding pages, the present section is limited to some final thoughts and opinions on the over-all implications of the study.

One of the authors has reported a survey on the status of studies concerning the validities of projective techniques (Little, 1957) which indicates

TABLE 30.   FACTUAL ITEM RELIABILITY COEFFICIENTS
(TETRACHORIC CORRELATIONS) FOR THE 48 TJ'S

Ss		Ror.	TAT	MAPS	MMPI
Nonpsychiatric	1	70	86	88	83
	2	47	56	38	89
	3	75	60	60	60
Neurotic	4	87	67	75	73
	5	50	33	91	90
	6	86	66	83	81
Psychophysiological disorder	7	68	93	46	88
	8	83	47	89	84
	9	69	41	89	88
Psychotic	10	86	49	84	80
	11	77	47	89	48
	12	94	63	88	82
Mean		.743	.590	.767	.788

TAT materials (who were conspicuously low in their reliabilities). This variation of reliability cuts across the test used and the type of S for whom the protocol was interpreted. The most general implication of these findings has to do with the notion of the validity of the psychological tests, inasmuch as there are inextricable relationships between validity as defined and reliability of interpretation. Thus it would appear that efforts to establish the "validity" of our current psychological techniques —whether in terms of status validity, content validity, or congruent validity, etc.—are premature until adequate interpreter reliability has been established.

that these studies, taken as a group, are contradictory or equivocal and in genral do not give strong support to the contention that test procedures have clearly demonstrated validity. The gen-

TABLE 31.   ANALYSIS OF VARIANCE OF
FACTUAL ITEM RELIABILITY
COEFFICIENTS

Source	Sum of Squares	df	Variance
Tests	333.1	3	110.4
S type	2912.9	3	971.0*
Tests × S type	2281.2	9	253.5
Within cell	8652.7	32	270.4
Total	14177.9	47	

* Significant at .05 level.

eral over-all results of the present study do not reverse this state of affairs. With a variety of types of Ss, with more than one S in each category, with experienced judges doing blind interpretations in response to the same questions, the results of the analyses for four frequently used psychological tests did not yield the kind of positive correlations that would gladden the hearts of psychological test proponents.

The results are even somewhat more distressing when one considers the magnitude of correlations obtained even when they were significant. A small decrease in chance variation is a legitimate goal for screening instruments but relatively useless for tools such as projective techniques where individual prognosis is desired.

There are several legitimate objections to citing the results of the present study as indicating the level of clinical validity or reliability of the instruments used. "Validity" is a complicated and ambiguous term at best and the use of psychiatric consensus as a criterion does not improve it noticeably. The lack of agreement among the AJ's was quite clear for a number of the Test Ss. Moreover, one may argue reasonably enough that judgments such as required by the tasks in this study cannot be made from a single information source and that validity can be determined only on batteries of tests as actually used in clinical situations. This assumption of a summative effect and/or an interactive effect of various instruments is a testable hypothesis, although it was not tested in the present study. An objec-

tion similar to this last one may be raised to citing the relatively low agreements among judges as evidence of unreliability of the instrument or the judge. Again the effect of combined information sources on inter-judge agreement is testable, but was not within the scope of this study.

In a certain sense, the study may have imposed on the TJ's a "naive clinical" requirement, to use Holt's (1958) schema. Blind analyses prevent the clinically desirable progressive checking and modification of hypotheses against other sources presumed to be more valid. However, such control was an essential element of the design of the study inasmuch as it was the *individual* instruments that were being assessed.

Recognizing these restrictions on the simple application of the results to tests as used in clinical settings, the results still indicate room for considerable improvement in test interpretation. For the tests used, agreement on diagnoses will be only slightly better than chance, judgments of maladjustment will be skewed toward the pathological, agreement with psychiatrists as to personality dynamics will be modest, and the clinician's reliability in all these areas will leave much to be desired. Since there were marked differences in the correlations among the different judges, perhaps each individual clinical psychologist and psychiatrist should make it part of his business to ascertain his own personal validity and reliability coefficient with various categories of patients, as measured against various criteria.

REFERENCES

BURTON, A., & HARRIS, R. E. (Eds.). *Case histories in clinical and abnormal psychology.* Vol. 2. New York: Harper, 1956.

FRIEDMAN, I. Characteristics of the TAT heroes of normal, psychoneurotic and paranoid schizophrenic subjects. *J. proj. Tech.,* 1957, **21,** 372–376.

HOLT, R. R. Clinical and statistical prediction: A reformulation and some new data. *J. abnorm. soc. Psychol.,* 1958, **56,** 1–12.

HOLTZMAN, W. H., & SELLS, S. B. Prediction of flying success by clinical analysis of test protocols. *J. abnorm. soc. Psychol.*, 1954, 49, 485–498.

LITTLE, K. B. Whither projective techniques: Paper read at California State Psychol. Ass., Los Angeles, March 1957. *J. proj. Tech.*, in press.

LITTLE, K. B., & SHNEIDMAN, E. S. The validity of thematic projective technique interpretations. *J. Pers.*, 1955, 23, 286–294.

LITTLE, K. B., & SHNEIDMAN, E. S. The validity of MMPI interpretations. *J.* consult. *Psychol.*, 1954, 18, 425–428. Also in G. S. WELSH & W. GRANT DAHLSTROM (Eds.), *Basic readings on the MMPI in psychology and medicine.* Minneapolis: Univer. of Minnesota Press, 1956.

McNEMAR, Q. *Psychological statistics.* (2nd ed.) New York: Wiley, 1955.

MEEHL, P. E. *Clinical versus statistical prediction.* Minneapolis: Univer. of Minnesota Press, 1954.

SHNEIDMAN, E. S., WALTHER, J., & LITTLE, K. B. *Thematic test analysis.* New York: Grune & Stratton, 1951.

APPENDIX I

Items of Tasks 2–5

SCALE OF ADJUSTMENT

Instructions: Indicate where you believe this subject fits on the scale below by putting an "X" at the appropriate place on the vertical line.

Score[a]

0	Making a good or adequate adjustment.
1	
2	Functioning adequately, but at considerable psychological cost.
3	
4	Making a marginal or precarious adjustment.
5	
6	Poor adjustment; should have psychiatric care or be in a hospital.
7	
8	Is a custodial case; cannot survive without care.

[a] This column was not present on the rating scale. It is presented here to indicate how scores were assigned to equal divisions of the vertical line.

REPORT-TYPE TRUE-FALSE ITEMS

Instructions: Items 1–118 are statements (or inferences) about the subject's personality. On the basis of your contact with the subject, answer each item by circling T (True), F (False), or ? (Cannot say) on the Answer Sheet. Use ? (Cannot say) as infrequently as possible.

1. Lack of emotional security is his major problem.
2. Rarely expresses any strong emotion.
3. Is in poor contact with reality.
4. Feels that he is not worthy of the love of others.

5. Has at least bright normal intelligence.
6. Indulges in counterphobic masculine activity.
7. His fear of retaliation blocks any overt expression of his hostility.
8. Possesses much drive and ambition.
9. Few things seem to worry him much.
10. Is a fast thinker.
11. Feels, unrealistically, that he is under the influence of others.
12. He feels, deep down, that he is a no good, not worth while person.
   (This item was inadvertently omitted from the judges' lists.)
13. Considers sex a rather shameful thing.
14. His thinking and ideas tend to be clear-cut.
15. His sexual needs are only moderate.
16. Has marked independence strivings.
17. Has a great need to be loved.
18. Is extremely self-conscious.
19. Is often hostile without being aware of it.
20. Generally turns to alcohol for release when he is tense or anxious.
21. Is quite mature intellectually.
22. Shows strong tendency to intellectualization.
23. Is a calm person.
24. Heterosexual relations frighten him.
25. Is extremely competitive.
26. Needs affection but in a mature relationship.
27. Shows relatively few objective signs of anxiety.
28. Has considerable hostility toward authority figures.
29. Gets along better with men than women.
30. Generally develops some physical symptom when tense or anxious.
31. Is demanding and self-centered.
32. Becomes depressed very easily.
33. Is sensitive and introspective.
34. Shows no great fear of rejection.
35. His intellectual approach to problems is logical and orderly.
36. Tends to blame his mistakes upon others.
37. His behavior is somewhat effeminate.
38. Is neat and orderly.
39. Is frustrated by his inability to live up to his own high standards.
40. Has little need for affection.
41. Gets angry usually only when appropriate.

42. Is quite hostile towards women.
43. Some of his complaints resemble bodily delusions.
44. Sees most of his peer group as competitors.
45. Has episodes of marked emotionality.
46. Seems to accept his hostile impulses without great conflict.
47. Has considerable fear of getting emotionally involved.
48. Is a dominating individual.
49. Is fairly rigid and inflexible.
50. Is somewhat overly logical and precise.
51. His thinking is quite unrealistic.
52. Considers himself inferior to others in most respects.
53. Has a number of rather rigidly moralistic attitudes.
54. Is a mild and self-effacing person.
55. Has a definite homosexual conflict.
56. Is below average in intelligence.
57. Considers most people he knows as inferior to himself.
58. Has a reasonable amount of confidence in his own ability.
59. Plans things fairly effectively.
60. Seldom feels depressed.
61. His strong aggressive impulses are a source of marked conflict for him.
62. Has an infantile need for affection.
63. Is a restless and impatient person.
64. Has a strong desire to rebel against authority figures.
65. Has achieved a comfortable separation from his parents.
66. Is a cold and unresponsive person.
67. Feels adequate to handle most problems he meets.
68. His thought processes are confused.
69. Is rather unimaginative.
70. Has considerable anxiety over unacceptable sexual impulses.
71. Seems unable to concentrate.
72. Is a friendly and outgoing person.
73. Has a strong need for nurturance and passivity.
74. His hostile impulses are markedly inhibited by his fear of rejection.
75. Is a direct and resourceful person.
76. Has relatively poor intellectual control.
77. His homosexual trends are not a source of great conflict.
78. Feels pretty much on a par with his peer group.

79. Is an asocial person.
80. Has marked conflict between his heterosexual urges and his fear of women.
81. Has a strong heterosexual drive.
82. Is attracted to, yet afraid of his mother.
83. Is markedly depressed by adverse criticism.
84. Is eager for social approval.
85. Feels guilty over his hostile impulses.
86. Sees women as superior and threatening.
87. Shows many objective signs of anxiety.
88. Is a very quiet person.
89. Perceives masculine sexuality as involving hostile behavior.
90. Has a strong fear of aggression.
91. Does not seem to be particularly afraid of anything.
92. Hostility directed toward him does not seem to disturb him very much.
93. Has strong dependency needs.
94. Intellectually he is quite resourceful.
95. Always seems to distrust his own ability.
96. Shows agitated depression.
97. Is easily aroused emotionally.
98. Shows "resigned depression."
99. His sexual needs are intense.

100. Resents the restrictions and dominance of others.
101. Is impulsive.
102. Seldom feels guilty.
103. Sees himself as a rather ineffective person.
104. Admires his father.
105. Indulges in an unusual amount of fantasy.
106. Masturbation is not a problem for him at present.
107. Has an even temperament.
108. Is a fairly optimistic person.
109. Uses fantasy as his major outlet for hostile feelings.
110. Is an energetic person.
111. His range of expression of feelings is fairly wide.
112. In interpersonal conflict, he blames himself very readily.
113. Has strong feelings of guilt over his sexual impulses.
114. Considers women ineffectual and helpless.
115. Always has excuses for his behavior.
116. In interpersonal conflict, he tends to blame the other person.
117. Is conscientious and painstaking.
118. Justifies his feelings by attributing them to others also.

FACTUAL TRUE-FALSE ITEMS

121. His first 3 years were relatively untraumatic.
122. Was raised in foster home or orphanage.
123. Was an only child.
124. Was youngest child in the family.
125. Was oldest child in his family.
126. Has had severe blow on the head.
127. Had a sheltered childhood.
128. Had childhood hobbies.
129. As a child had some limiting disease or disorder.
130. As a child his family moved often.
131. As a child was closer to his father than to mother.
132. His father was a fairly stable, unexcitable person.
133. His mother was a fairly stable, unexcitable person.
134. His father was strict.
135. His mother was strict.
136. Was overprotected by his father.
137. Was overprotected by his mother.
138. Was rejected by his father.

139. Was rejected by his mother.
140. Had an ineffectual father.
141. Had an ineffectual mother.
142. As a child his home was maternally dominated.
143. Relied on his father for guidance.
144. Relied on his mother for guidance.
145. Was given intense corporal punishment by a parent.
146. Felt he did not have the love of one or both parents.
147. Had little contact with his father or mother.
148. His father spent little time with him.
149. His father was not regularly in the home.
150. His father was unemployed for long periods.
151. His father was alcoholic.
152. His mother prejudiced him against his father.
153. As a child felt free to communicate in his home.

154. As a child had enuresis, temper tantrums, nail biting, etc.
155. As a child was rejected by his peers.
156. Had a sibling or friend who was close to him.
157. As a child had an unfavorable social environment.
158. Has been on his own from a fairly early age.
159. As a child was hyperactive.
160. As a child was shy and withdrawn.
161. Ran away from home.
162. As a child had difficulties with other children.
163. As a child got into fights.
164. As a child was member of Boy Scouts, clubs, etc.
165. Had difficulties in school.
166. Made generally poor marks in school.
167. Was generally disinterested in school.
168. Had reading difficulties in school.
169. Was truant from school.
170. Dated girls when he was in high school.
171. Through high school was in relatively few social activities.
172. Participated on school teams.
173. Skipped grades in school.
174. Was given sex information by one of his parents.
175. Had early heterosexual play with peer.
176. Suffered early seduction or early sex trauma.
177. Had first sexual intercourse before puberty.
178. Was the aggressor in his first sexual relationship.
179. Had no sexual relations until after he was 21.
180. Has had intercourse with many women.
181. Has had intercourse with prostitutes.
182. Has suffered from guilt over masturbation.
183. Is married.
184. Has been married more than once.
185. Is living with his parents at present.

186. Is fairly religious.
187. Is excessively religious.
188. Is confused in his religious beliefs.
189. Drinks quite a bit.
190. Has strong ethnic prejudices.
191. Gambles quite a bit.
192. Is a non-conformist in much of his behavior.
193. Is extremely conforming in much of his behavior.
194. Is an overt homosexual.
195. Has had homosexual experiences.
196. Has anxiety attacks.
197. Is easily upset or easily tired.
198. Has nightmares.
199. Has fears or phobias.
200. Has obsessive thoughts or compulsions.
201. Has psychosomatic symptoms.
202. Is very seclusive.
203. Is very suspicious.
204. Hallucinates.
205. Is delusional.
206. Is depressed.
207. Has been in trouble with the law.
208. As an adult has been in fights or brawls.
209. As an adult has no interests or hobbies.
210. Has a definitely established gainful occupation.
211. Worked with father or in father's line of work.
212. Had had several jobs in last few years.
213. Had had to stop work because of psychological symptoms.
214. Was in the Service.
215. Happiest time of his life was while in the Service.
216. Suffered severe combat stress during Service.
217. Was court-martialled while in Service.
218. Had several promotions in the Service.
219. Volunteered for dangerous missions in the Service.
220. Suffered nervous breakdown under Service conditions.

Q-SORT ITEMS

1. He likes and seeks the companionship of women.
2. He usually withdraws in social situations.
3. He is obviously uncomfortable in his contacts with authority.
4. He gives in immediately when attacked.
5. He seems to adapt to his environment quite well.
6. Nearly all of his interpersonal relationships are superficial.

7. He meets aggression from others with counter aggression.
8. He has very few friends.
9. He blames himself when criticized.
10. He has difficulty in relating to people.
11. His contacts with authority are marked by strife.
12. He draws into himself in interpersonal situations.
13. He has quite a few relatively warm interpersonal relationships.
14. He does not invest affect in his interpersonal relationships.
15. He is constantly fighting his environment.
16. He is rather cold and impersonal in his interactions with women.
17. He goes out of his way to please people.
18. He accepts rather passively any impositions made upon him.
19. His social adjustment seems satisfactory.
20. He tends to retreat from the stress and strain of everyday living.
21. He meets the demands of his environment in a rather reasonable fashion.
22. He escapes into fantasy when threatened.
23. He tries to manipulate those around him to serve his own ends.
24. He is uneasy and uncomfortable around other men.
25. He becomes quite aggressive in most social situations.
26. He generally feels accepted by others.
27. He behaves rather passively in most situations.
28. He responds well to most of his environmental demands.
29. He reacts in a hostile and aggressive fashion in his interpersonal contacts.
30. He is unable to recognize affection when it is offered to him.
31. He retreats when people become aggressive toward him.
32. He competes very strongly with father figures.
33. He gets along quite well with his superiors.
34. He withdraws immediately at the slightest hint of rejection.
35. He becomes actively hostile when he is criticized.
36. He is only mildly responsive to friendly approaches from others.

37. He is generally composed and at ease with authority figures.
38. He is quite responsive when people show an interest in his welfare.
39. He faces unpleasant situations in a direct manner.
40. His immediate response when threatened is to fight back.
41. He gets along well with most people.
42. He responds gratefully to positive gestures from others.
43. He is quite passive in most of his interpersonal contacts.
44. He adapts easily to social situations.
45. His friendships seem rather stable and have relatively few conflicts.
46. His relations with mother figures are fairly happy.
47. He yields meekly to the demands of others.
48. He responds immediately to any show of tenderness or affection.
49. Rejection from others only makes him more aggressive.
50. He is tactful and considerate with other people.
51. He runs away from hostility in others.
52. He seems to handle criticism quite well.
53. Friendly gestures from others arouse his suspicion and hostility.
54. He is quite responsive to social stimuli.
55. He rarely responds to positive gestures from others.
56. He runs away from any show of tenderness or affection.
57. When others show an interest in him he immediately becomes aggressive and demanding.
58. He has little difficulty in dealing with other people.
59. He is responsive to the needs and wishes of others.
60. He likes to have people show an interest in him.
61. He avoids any display of friendliness on the part of others.
62. He responds in a realistic fashion to hostility from others.
63. He responds passively to any positive gestures made toward him.
64. He actively seeks social contacts.
65. Even the mere presence of other people produces immediate withdrawal in him.

66. He tries to dominate other people.
67. He gets along quite well with other men.
68. He actively rejects affection from others.
69. Almost any social situation arouses aggressive behavior on his part.
70. He seems quite meek in most of his interactions with others.

71. He shows decreasing involvement in social contacts.
72. He adapts fairly easily to authority demands.
73. He becomes negativistic when people show a friendly interest in him.
74. He is rather neutral towards others.
75. He is rather reserved in most situations.
76. He accepts affection passively.

APPENDIX II

Categories of Report-Type Items

1. Pressures; forces; press
2. Motivations; goals; drives
3. Outlooks; attitudes; beliefs
4. Frustrations; conflicts; fears
5. Affects; feelings; emotions
6. Sexual thought and behavior
7. Psychosexual level and development
8. Super-ego; values; ego ideals
9. Self control; ego strength; ego capacity
10. Self concept; insight into self
11. Personality defenses and personality mechanisms
12. Reality contact; orientation
13. Interpersonal and object relations
14. Quality of perception, fantasy, language, and thought
15. Intellect and abilities
16. Symptoms; diagnoses; etiology
17. Prognoses; predictions
18. Postdictions

APPENDIX III

Similarity Rating Scale

INSTRUCTIONS

On the following pages are a number of *pairs* of diagnostic statements. Your task is to judge the *similarity* of the two statements within each pair and to indicate your judgment by writing *one* of the six numbers following each pair of statements. In general, your judgment should reflect the extent to which you would consider both diagnoses reasonable and acceptable for one patient when made by two equally competent diagnosticians from the same thorough examination.

The scale is defined as follows:

5—Identical; perhaps minor differences in wording but no question but that the two statements in the pair mean the same thing.

4—Markedly similar; slight variations in minor symptomatology which would ordinarily be considered unimportant.

3—Similar; same general category but definite differences in implied or stated significant characteristics.

2—Different; diagnoses from different but adjoining broad categories; would require resolution of the discrepancies.

1—Markedly different; very rarely would one expect to see two such diagnoses on the same person; both cannot be accepted.

0—Utterly different; improbable that two competent diagnosticians could arrive at such opposite conclusions.

You will notice that some diagnoses are repeated but are paired with different diagnoses. Occasionally even a pair may be repeated. In such cases, you may feel free to refer back to your previous judgment. Do not linger too long on any one pair; it is your general clinical judgment that is desired.

Some Effects of Combining Psychological
Tests on Clinical Inferences

Mark Golden

A widely held belief among clinical psychologists is that the use of a battery of tests is a more valid assessment procedure than the use of individual tests, but there is little empirical evidence to support this view. In discussing the results of a study on the congruencies among personality descriptions based on four frequently used psychological tests and anamnestic data, Little and Shneidman (1959) attributed the low reliabilities and validities obtained to the fact that judges were asked to interpret the tests individually rather than in batteries as they are actually used in clinical practice, and hypothesized that by combining tests higher reliabilities and validities would be obtained. The present study was designed to determine whether the reliability and validity of clinical inferences based on three frequently used psychological tests —the Rorschach, TAT, and MMPI— increased as a function of increasing amounts of test data.

This article is based upon a dissertation submitted in partial fulfillment of the requirements for the degree of Doctor of Philosophy in the Department of Psychology at the University of California at Los Angeles in June 1960.

Reprinted with the permission of the American Psychological Association and the author from the *Journal of Consulting Psychology*, 1964, **28**, 440–446.

There are few studies reported in the literature which deal specifically with the problem at hand, but two studies, one by Kostlan (1954) and one by Sines (1959), are particularly relevant. Kostlan's study was designed to determine which three-source combination of four frequently used sources of information about psychiatric patients— the Rorschach, MMPI, Sentence Completion Test, and Case History—yielded the most valid inferences. Kostlan found that without the Case History no combination of sources yielded better results than Identifying Data alone, such as age, sex, etc., which allowed inferences significantly better than chance. However, Kostlan's design did not provide for comparisons between Identifying Data against each of the sources alone, the latter against various pairs of tests, and so forth, which the present study was designed to do. As the Kelly and Fiske (1951) study indicates, the relationship between amount of information and predictability is probably not linear. In Sines' study clinicians were asked to perform Q sorts sequentially, given increasing amounts of information about the *same* patients. The data evaluated by the clinicians consisted of a four page Biographical Data Sheet, MMPI, Rorschach, and a Diagnostic Interview conducted by the judge with the patients he was asked to assess. The

Biographical Data Sheet was always the first source evaluated, while the other sources were presented in different sequences. Sines found that: (a) The Diagnostic Interview consistently increased accuracy of judgements based on Q sorts of previous data, whereas, in general, the MMPI and Rorschach did not. (b) While the relationship between amount of data and accuracy was complex, there was a slight, though not significant trend in the direction of greater accuracy with increasing amounts of information. However, Sines also found that clinicians' inferences tended to crystalize early in the sequence, and seemed unwilling to change their descriptions as more data were made available to them. The operation of such a set would, of course, tend to reduce the chances of obtaining greater agreement with increasing amounts of data, a factor which was controlled for in the present study by having clinicians make judgements on the basis of increasing amounts of test data about different subjects.

Method[1]

Thirty experienced clinical psychologists were asked to complete a personality questionnaire describing five heterogeneous Subjects on the basis of Identifying Data alone, each of the three tests individually, in pairs involving all possible permutations, and all three tests combined.

Subjects

The 5 Ss used in the present study were selected from a larger pool of 12

[1] Using the Criterion Judgments and test protocols obtained in the Little and Shneidman study, where clinicians were asked to interpret the tests individually, the present writer submitted the same test protocols in various combinations to a different group of clinicians. The author wishes to express his appreciation to those authors who generously made available the data obtained in their study.

Ss used in the Little and Shneidman study. Of the 5 Ss used in the present study, all of them patients at a local Veteran's Administration hospital, one was a nonpsychiatric patient, two were diagnosed as neurotic, and one psychotic, and one psychophysiological reaction. The number of Ss selected, 5, was determined by the requirements of the experimental design and seemed adequate for the purpose of the study. The basis for selection of these particular Ss was twofold: (a) the writer wished to have as representative and heterogeneous (in terms of diagnostic category) a sample of Ss as possible; and (b) the Ss selected in each category were those for whom the Criterion Judges achieved the highest percentage of agreement. For a description of the manner in which the original 12 Ss were selected, the reader is referred to the Little-Shneidman monograph.

Test Judges

Thirty experienced clinical psychologists served as Test Judges. Twenty-five were PhDs with a range of 3 months to 13 years and an average of 4.6 years of clinical experience beyond the doctoral level. Several of them were Diplomates in Clinical Psychology. Five of the Judges were advanced clinical psychology trainees with a range of 2 to 12 years and an average of 4.8 years of clinical experience.

In regard to experience with the tests employed, the Judges were asked to indicate approximately how many MMPIs, Rorschachs, and TATs they had interpreted in their professional careers. The approximate number of MMPIs ranged from 40 to 2500, with a median of 200. The approximate number of Rorschach's ranged from 75 to 2000, with a median of 250. The approximate number of TATs ranged from 50 to 2000, with a median of 200. Some of the Judges were acknowledged experts with one or another of the tests used.

Criterion Judges and Validity Criterion

The Criterion Judges were 24 highly experienced psychotherapists, 23 psychiatrists, and 1 clinical psychologist. Eleven of the psychiatrists were practicing psychoanalysts, and members of the American Psychoanalytic Association. The other 12 psychiatrists were, by their own description, nonanalytically oriented members of the American Psychiatric Association. The psychologist was a psychoanalytically oriented Diplomate in Clinical Psychology.

The Criterion Judges were asked to complete a 117-item true-and-false personality questionnaire describing the 12 Ss on the basis of extensive Case History material. Each Criterion Judge made judgments about 2 Ss, and each S was judged by four Criterion Judges. Their pooled judgments on 5 of the 12 Ss served as the validity criterion in the present study.

Considering the fact that two groups of psychotherapists, differing widely in their theoretical orientations, served as Criterion Judges, the level of agreement (defined as percentage of items answered the same way for each S by at least 3 out of 4 Judges) was fairly high, ranging from 72% to 95%, with an average of 83.5% agreement. The level of agreement for the 5 Ss used in the present study was somewhat higher, ranging from 85% to 95%, with an average of 88% agreement.

Personality Questionnaire

The questionnaire used in the present study was developed by Little and Shneidman (1959) and consists of approximately 100 true-and-false items, covering a wide range of personality

functioning. The items were selected from a larger pool of such statements extracted from 80 psychological test reports. The areas covered include such categories as "Interpersonal and object relations"; "Quality of perception, fantasy, language, and thought"; "Personality defenses and mechanisms," and so forth. The specific items include such statements as "Is somewhat overly logical and precise," "Has a strong desire to rebel against authority figures," and so forth. The reader is referred to the Little-Shneidman monograph for a more complete description of the way in which the items were derived, as well as a list of the categories of functioning covered and the questionnaire items.

While the Little-Shneidman questionnaire yielded a rather high level of agreement among the Criterion Judges, the authors did not determine how much of this agreement may have been due to the presence of "universally valid" (Forer, 1949) items—i.e., statements which are true (or false) about most people. A large number of such items would, of course, spuriously raise the level of agreement. Those items which were ascribed as true (or false) by the pooled Criterion judgments for at least 10 out of the 12 Ss were designated as "universally valid" by the present writer and excluded from the questionnaire. Only 13 out of 117 items were excluded on this basis, indicating that the questionnaire not only permits judgments of fairly high reliability, but that the items comprising it are capable of discriminating among a relatively heterogeneous group of individuals.

Just as predictive accuracy may be spuriously high if a large proportion of universally valid statements are used, it may be spuriously low if items are ambiguous or difficult to answer on the basis of the information provided. Therefore, those items on which the Criterion Judges could not agree (i.e., where less than 3 out of 4 judges answered an item in the same way) were also excluded from the questionnaire. The number of items and the particular items excluded on this basis varied from subject to subject, so that the questionnaires submitted to the Test Judges were "tailor-made," so to speak, for each subject. After both types of items were excluded, the personality questionnaires used to describe the 5 Ss in the present study varied from 86 to 98 items.

Experimental Design and Procedure

The ideal experimental procedure would have been to ask the Test Judges to complete personality questionnaires about the Ss on the basis of: (a) Identifying Data alone; (b) each of the three tests individually; (c) all possible combinations of two tests; and (d) all three tests combined. However, this would have entailed asking Test Judges to complete personality questionnaires under 8 different experimental conditions, which may have made an excessive demand on Judge's time. Given too many protocols to interpret, they might have performed the tasks in a perfunctory manner, a serious possible source of invalidity.

The writer, therefore, decided to reduce the number of tasks required of each Test Judge to a bare minimum, but in a manner which would allow him to make the most important comparisons on the same Test Judges. This was achieved by reducing the original design to three sub-experiments, each employing a five by five replicated Graeco-Latin square which could be analyzed separately.

Ten Test Judges, five in each replication, were assigned to each of the following experimental groups:

Group 1 was given: (a) Identifying Data alone; (b) MMPI; (c) Rorschach; (d) MMPI and Rorschach; and (e) MMPI, Rorschach, and TAT.

Group II was given: (a) Identifying Data; (b) MMPI; (c) TAT; (d) MMPI and TAT; and (e) MMPI), TAT, and Rorschach.

Group III was given: (a) Identifying Data; (b) Rorschach, (c) TAT; (d) Rorschach and TAT; and (e) Rorschach, TAT, and MMPI.

Judges in each experimental group were asked to make interpretations about every S and under every experimental condition, but no S or experimental condition was repeated for any Test Judge. Moreover, Test Judges were asked to complete these tasks a week apart, in different random sequences. Condition a was included to serve as a base line against which to compare the various combinations of tests. Judges were also given Identifying Data under conditions b through e.

Validity was measured by percentage of agreement between the Criterion Judges, describing the 5 Ss on the personality questionnaire on the basis of extensive Case History material, and the Test Judges, performing the same task, given various combinations of psychological tests. It should be emphasized that validity, as measured in the present study, pertains to *concurrent validity*, the degree of agreement between two groups of judges using different kinds of data about individuals, and *not* to predictability or accuracy of inferences derived from psychological tests. Reliability was measured by percentage of agreement between Test Judges, within experimental groups, given identical sets of test protocols. The percentages were transformed into arcsines, and analyses of variance were computed on the transformed scores. The reasons and procedure for transforming percent scores into arcsines are described in Snedecor (1956).

Results

The results of this study will be presented under two general headings:

(a) Validity Data and (b) Reliability Data.

Validity Data

Three separate analyses of variance were computed for each subexperiment.[2] The F for Sources of Information in Experiment I was 5.71, which is significant at the .01 level for 4 and 20 degrees of freedom. The F for Sources in Experiment II was 2.55, which falls short of the .05 level. The F for Sources in Experiment III was 3.08, significant at the .05 level.

Since the Fs for *Sources* were significant in Experiments I and III, orthogonal comparisons were made among Sources in each subexperiment. The procedure for making these comparisons is described in Walker and Lev (1954). With 4 degrees of freedom associated with the sums of squares for Sources, it was possible to make 4 orthogonal comparisons in each experiment, each with 1 degree of freedom.

In all three Experiments only when Identifying Data were compared to all combinations of tests were the Fs significant: in Experiment I, F was 20.30, which is significant at the .001 level; in Experiments II and III, the Fs were 8.65 and 12.24, respectively, both significant at the .01 level. An examination of the sums of squares for the Sources of Information in each Experiment showed that *most* of the variance for Sources was accounted for by the difference in level of agreement between Identifying Data and any combination of tests. For example, in Experiment III the total sum of squares for Sources was 1032. The sum of squares for the orthogonal

comparison between Identifying Data and the various test combinations was 1026.82; so that the variance due to differences in percent of agreement among the various test combinations was only 5.89. Although the magnitudes differed, the same general pattern held for the other two Experiments.

The Mean percentages of agreement with the criterion obtained for the various test combinations in all three Experiments ranged from 66.3 to 73.7%, with a Mean of 68.5% The probability that these percentages exceeded the level of agreement that would be expected on the basis of chance, on the assumption that 50% represents chance probability, exceeded the .001 level of significance.[3] The Mean percents obtained for Identifying Data in the three Experiments ranged from 46.7 to 58.0%, with a Mean of 51.3%. None of these percentages differed significantly from chance. The Mean percentages of agreement between Test Judges and Criterion Judges for sources of information and Subjects, as well as the probabilities associated with them based on Critical Ratios, appear in Table 1.

Reliability Data

Three separate analyses of variance were computed for each of the three Experiments. The results of these analyses can be summarized briefly: None of the Fs for Sources of Information, or any of the other Sources of Variance, in the three Experiments were significant.

The Mean percents of interjudge agreement obtained for the various test combinations in all three Experiments

---

[2] Analysis of variance tables for each subexperiment for the validity and reliability data have been deposited with the American Documentation Institute. Order Document No. 8021 from ADI Auxiliary Publications Project, Photoduplication Service, Library of Congress, Washington, D.C. 20540. Remit $1.25 for 35-mm microfilm or $1.25 for 6 x 8 inch photo-copies.

[3] These figures represent the probabilities for CRs (critical ratios) based on an N of 86, and a p of ½, the null hypothesis being 50%. Since it was not feasible to compute probabilities for *average* percentages, based on 10 scores, probabilities were computed for the percentages of *individual* Judges based on an N of 86 corresponding to the various average percentages, so that the probabilities only represent approximations.

ranged from 56.1 to 72.9%, with a Mean of 64.9%. Two of these percentages— 58.1% for the TAT and 56.1% for three tests combined (both in Experiment III)—do not represent significantly better than chance agreement. The probabilities associated with the rest ranged from .01 to beyond the .001 level of significance. The Mean percentages obtained for Identifying Data in the three Experiments ranged from 54.0 to 69.7%, with a Mean of 64.3%. The 54.0% obtained in Experiment III does not represent better than chance agreement. The probabilities associated with the other two percentages for Experiments I and II exceeded the .001 significance level.

Discussion

The results of the present study *do not* support the view that clinical inferences based on a battery of tests are more reliable and valid than those based on individual tests. With a variety of types of Ss, with experienced clinicians interpreting different combinations of three frequently used psychological tests —the Rorschach, TAT, and MMPI— reliability and validity did not increase as a function of increasing amounts of test data, nor were there any differences in this respect among individual tests or pairs of tests.

The Test Judges agreed significantly more with the Criterion Judges when they were given any individual test or combination of tests than on the basis of Identifying Data alone. The average percentages of agreement with the criterion based on all combinations of tests, though not especially high, were highly significant, whereas this was not the case for Identifying Data. These findings differ from those of Kostlan (1959), where interpretations made on the basis of a test battery without the Case History were not more valid than those based on Identifying Data, which allowed inferences significantly greater than chance. Although these differences may, in part, be attributed to the fact that a different criterion was used in the two studies, another important difference is that Kostlan included in his Identifying Data the information that the Ss were psychiatric patients, a powerful source of inference about individuals, whereas this information was not provided in the present study.

The most striking finding in regard to

TABLE 1. MEAN PERCENT OF AGREEMENT BETWEEN TEST JUDGES AND CRITERION JUDGES FOR SOURCES AND SUBJECTS

Subjects	ID	MMPI	ROR	TAT	MMPI ROR	MMPI TAT	ROR TAT	MMP ROR TAT
1. Nonpsychiatric	61.0*	60.2*	59.4*	66.6***	49.5	67.3***	45.9	59.3*
2. Neurotic	36.0**	72.8***	74.7***	70.2***	69.1***	83.7***	77.5***	72.8***
3. Neurotic	54.8	58.1	73.5***	62.2**	75.0***	64.0***	75.6***	73.3***
4. Psychophysiologic disorder	58.3	66.6**	66.9***	61.9**	66.9***	75.0***	72.7***	74.2***
5. Psychotic	47.2	81.1***	56.6	75.0***	70.2***	70.2***	58.5*	65.2***

* p ≤ .05.
** p ≤ .01.
*** p ≤ .001.

the reliability data was the fact that experienced clinical psychologists did not agree more among themselves in their personality descriptions of a heterogeneous group of Ss on the basis of any combination of tests than they did on the basis of Identifying Data, which only included information about a person's age, sex, race, religion, education and service status. Most of the average percents of agreement for the various sources of information, although relatively low, were also highly significant.

The major difference between the reliability and validity data appears to be that the reliability of the clinical judgments for Identifying Data was as high as that for psychological tests, whereas the validity of these judgments was significantly lower than was obtained on the basis of tests. These seemingly paradoxical findings suggest that, while the absolute level of agreement remained the same, when Test Judges were given any combination of tests, they may have agreed on different items, which enabled them to predict the criterion better. There is reason to believe that, given only minimal information about Ss, Test Judges tended to use a stereotype—that of the "normal" person in our culture—to describe Ss. Such a stereotype would, of course, permit relatively fair agreement among Test Judges, but since the three psychiatric patients used as Ss in the study did not "fit" the stereotype, the level of agreement with the Criterion Judges was relatively poor. On the other hand, Test Judges may have been able to predict the criterion better on the basis of tests merely by shifting to another stereotype, a "pathological" one. This hypothesis finds some support in the fact that, in general, while the level of agreement with the criterion was higher for the "normal" S on the basis of Identifying Data, the reverse was true on the basis of test data. The average percentage of agreement on the basis of Identifying

Data for the "normal" S was 61.0%, whereas the percent of agreement for the three psychiatric patients ranged from 36.0% to 54.8%. On the other hand, the percent of agreement for the "normal" S on the basis of Test Data was 58.3%, whereas the percentages of agreement for the three psychiatric Ss ranged from 68.1% to 74.4%. Little and Shneidman found that the Test Judges in their study tended to perceive a great deal of psychopathology in all Ss, regardless of nosological category.

While the reliabilities and validities obtained were, in general, highly significant, the results of the present study should not be an occasion for rejoicing among psychological test proponents. Two aspects of the study, which may be open to serious criticism, should be discussed: (a) the interpretive task required of the Test Judges—describing individuals on a true-and-false personality questionnaire, and (b) the validity criterion employed—psychiatrists' judgments on the basis of extensive Case History material.

In regard to the interpretive task, a legitimate objection can be made that the use of a true-and-false questionnaire is not an optimal procedure for describing the complexity and particularly the structure and organization of an individual's personality, and it is not what clinicians do when asked to interpret psychological tests. In a study on the reliability of Rorschach interpretations, Datel and Gengerelli (1955) asked their Judges to write brief personality descriptions of Ss on the basis of Rorschach protocols. The Judges then had to match the test reports written by different clinicians about the same Ss. The level of agreement among the personality descriptions of the same Ss was generally quite low, despite the fact that the interpretive task more closely approximated the procedure used by psychologists in most clinical settings. Whatever obvious shortcomings the interpretive task employed in the present study may have, it allowed for a fairly high level of agreement among the Criterion Judges, permitting them to discriminate among a relatively heterogeneous group of individuals, despite the fact that two groups of psychiatrists, differing widely in theoretical orientation, served as Criterion Judges, and that the items in the questionnaire, selected from psychological test reports, should have favored the Test Judges.

In regard to the validity criterion, the choice of a criterion in such a study is, in a sense, arbitrary. Psychiatrists' descriptions of individuals based on case history material merely represent the judgments of another group of clinicians using another source of information. Perhaps it would be more accurate to describe the results of the present study in terms of correlations among personality descriptions on the basis of different kinds of data about individuals, and conclude that the correlations based on case history material and psychological tests, while statistically significant, were of a low order of magnitude. Nevertheless, a major cause of the low correlations or validities obtained must be attributed to the unreliability among the Test Judges and this would have been the case regardless of the criterion employed. The average validity score— the percent of agreement with the criterion for all conditions in which test data was available—was approximately 68%. The average reliability score—the percentage of agreement among Test Judges given identical sets of protocols to interpret—was approximately 64%. When scores are dichotomous, such as in the true-and-false personality questionnaire used in the present study, instead of obtaining percent of agreement, it is possible to compute a *fourfold point* or *phi coefficient*, which is a product moment correlation for a 2 x 2 table (Edwards, 1950, p. 88). The *phi coefficients* associated with 68% and 64%

are approximately .39 and .30, respectively.[4] Since *phi* is a product moment correlation, it is possible to apply a *correction for attenuation,* which provides an estimate of what the validity coefficient would have been if the Test Judges agreed perfectly among themselves (Nunnally, 1959, p. 102). The corrected correlation was .71, a difference of 32 points. However, because of the manner in which the *phi coefficients* for the validity and reliability data were derived, the estimate of the effect of the unreliability among the Test Judges on the validity scores can only be considered a crude approximation.

There is evidence that, in addition to such factors as individual differences among clinicians, the reliability of clinical judgments tends to diminish when clinicians are given large masses of data to process (Borke & Fiske, 1957; Cutler, Bordin, Williams, & Rigler, 1958; Forer, 1961; King, Ehrmann, & Johnson, 1952; Kostlan, 1954). Given perhaps too great an amount of data to evaluate, different clinicians may focus on different aspects of the data, resulting in different judgments about the same individuals, thus lowering reliability. While the reliability among the Test Judges in the present study did not seem to be affected by the number of tests used, one cannot conclude that the reliability of clinical judgments is unrelated to quantity of information. A psychological test protocol does not constitute a single unit of information, but rather a complex, inter-

[4] Since it was not feasible to compute an average *phi coefficient* for a number of scores with different Ns, an estimation of the *phi coefficient* associated with 68% was obtained by computing separate *phi*'s for three Test Judges obtaining validity scores of 68% based on an N of 86 items. The *phi*'s obtained were .38, .39, and .40; thus .39 was designated as the *phi coefficient* associated with the mean validity score of 68%. The same procedure was used to obtain an estimate of the *phi coefficient* associated with the mean reliability score of 64%.

related network of cues. It is conceivable that a less "global" approach, in which smaller bits of information were combined, might show that increasing amounts of data resulted in greater reliability up to a certain point, perhaps diminishing as more and more information was added, and finally stabilizing at a uniformly low level of agreement. The reliability among the Test Judges in the present study may not have changed as a function of the number of tests used because the amount of information contained in a single test protocol already exceeds the quantity at which reliability has stablized. The reader is referred to a paper by Mahrer and Young (1961) which describes a more "molecular," perhaps potentially more fruitful approach to the study of how psychodiagnostic cues are combined, reinforce, and modify each other.

A major shortcoming of the present and similar studies is that, while they show that the reliability and validity of clinical judgments based on psychological tests, though perhaps statistically significant, are generally low, they tell us nothing about the inferential process. What is needed in future research is a shift away from a concern only with the correlations among the end products of the judgemental process—the statements generated about individuals on the basis of psychological tests or interviews—to an examination of the inferential process itself and, in particular, the cognitive activity of the clinician (Arnhoff, 1960; Meehl, 1960; Tagiuri, 1958).

Summary

The study was designed to determine whether the reliability and validity of interpretations based on 3 frequently used psychological tests—Rorschach, TAT, MMPI—increased as a function of number of tests employed. 30 clinical psychologists completed personality questionnaires describing 5 Ss on the basis of identifying data alone, each test individually, pairs of tests, and all 3 combined. Reliability and validity did not increase as a function of number of tests, nor were there any differences between tests or pairs of tests. The validity scores for test data ranged from 66% to 73%, with a Mean of 68%. The reliability scores ranged from 56% to 72%, with a Mean of 64%.

REFERENCES

ARNHOFF, F. N. Some aspects of clinical judgment. *J. clin. Psychol.*, 1960, **16**, 123–128.

BORKE, H., & FISKE, D. W. Factors influencing the prediction of behavior from a diagnostic interview. *J. consult. Psychol.*, 1957, **21**, 78–80.

CUTLER, R. L., BORDIN, E. S., WILLIAM, J., & RIGLER, D. Psychoanalysts as expert observers of the therapy process. *J. consult. Psychol.*, 1958, **22**, 335–340.

DATEL, W. E., & GENGERELLI, J. A. Reliability of Rorschach interpretations. *J. proj. Tech.*, 1955, **19**, 372–381.

EDWARDS, A. L. *Experimental design in psychological research*. New York: Rinehart, 1950.

FORER, B. R. The fallacy of personal validation: A classroom demonstration of gullibility. *J. abnorm. soc. Psychol.*, 1949, **44**, 118–123.

FORER, B. R., FARBEROW, N. L., FEIFEL, H., MAYER, M. M., SUMMERS, V. S., & TOLMAN, R. S. Clinical perception of the therapeutic transaction. *J. consult. Psychol.*, 1961, **25**, 93–101.

KELLY, E. L., & FISKE, D. W. *The prediction of performance in clinical psychology*. Ann Arbor: Univer. Michigan Press, 1951.

KING, G. F., EHRMANN, J. C., & JOHNSON, D. M. Experimental analysis of the reliability of observations of social behavior. *J. soc. Psychol.*, 1952, **35**, 151–160.

KOSTLAN, A. A method for the empirical study of psychodiagnosis. *J. consult. Psychol.*, 1954, **18**, 83–88.

LITTLE, K. B., & SHNEIDMAN, E. S. Congruencies among interpretations of psychological test and anamnestic data. *Psychol. Monogr.*, 1959, **73**, (6, Whole No. 476).

MAHRER, A. R., & YOUNG, H. H. The combination of psychodiagnostic cues. *J. Pers.*, 1961, **29**, 428–448.

MEEHL, P. E. The cognitive activity of the clinician. *Amer. Psychol.*, 1960, **15**, 19–27.

NUNNALLY, J. C. *Tests and measurements.* New York: McGraw-Hill, 1959.

SINES, L. K. The relative contribution of four kinds of data to accuracy in personality assessment. *J. consult. Psychol.*, 1959, **23**, 483–495.

SNEDECOR, G. W. *Statistical methods.* Ames, Iowa: Iowa State College Press, 1956.

TAGIURI, R. Introduction. In R. TAGIURI and L. PETRULLO (Eds.), *Person perception and interpersonal behavior.* Stanford: Stanford Univer. Press, 1958.

WALKER, H. M., & LEV, J. *Statistical inference.* New York: Holt, 1954.

A Method for the Empirical Study of Psychodiagnosis

Albert Kostlan

The scientific study of psychodiagnosis requires that the clinician-subject should operate in a context which resembles the actual conditions of his service function. To accomplish this with any degree of rigor without first reducing the process to useless oversimplicity raises many

The statements and conclusions published by the author are the result of his own study and do not necessarily reflect the opinion or policy of the Veterans Administration.

This article is based upon a dissertation submitted by the writer in partial fulfillment of the requirements for the Ph.D. degree, University of California (Berkeley), 1952.

The author wishes to thank Dr. Theodore R. Sarbin, Department of Psychology, University of California, Berkeley, and Dr. Robert E. Harris of the Langley Porter Clinic, San Francisco, California, for their critical reading of this paper.

Reprinted by permission of the American Psychological Association and the author from the *Journal of Consulting Psychology*, 1954, **18**, 83–88.

problems. While making a diagnostic study the clinician typically uses first-hand observations, a battery of tests, and usually some kind of case history material, in combination. The clinician manipulates cues obtained from various sources and arrives at inferences for the purpose of making clinical predictions, descriptions (i.e., diagnosis), or making decisions about a person. He may make accurate inferences, but often cannot communicate to others the process underlying the inferential product. He may be unaware of the existence, value, or source of the cues he uses.

This complex process must be studied by isolating meaningful problems. One aid in doing so is to conceptualize psychodiagnosis as an inferential process regardless of how subjective or intuitive it may appear to be [4]. Relationships may be determined and measured between the cues presented on the one hand and the verbalized inferences on the other—with the clinician, with whatever processes he uses, considered as an intervening variable.

With this point of view, one aspect can be isolated for empirical study, the sources of cues. It may be approached by modifying research designs in other fields of psychological study. The "fractional omission" design introduced by Brunswik [1] as a model for research in perceptual constancy lends itself to the study of sources of cues in an inferential context. The present experiment demonstrates the application of the fractional omission method to the following problem: Which of several sources of cues permits the clinician to make the most valid inferences when he uses them in certain combinations? The larger study [3] of which this is a part tested several specific hypotheses; but for the purpose of illustrating the method, only the stated problem will be considered.

Procedure

Four sources of information, typical of a battery a clinician might use, were systematically eliminated one at a time, allowing the others to operate in a representative manner. The clinical judgments made from the altered batteries were measured and compared. It was necessary to use a small number of tests so that the absence of one would have a reasonable chance to produce a measurable difference. In attempting to duplicate, as far as practicable, the actual clinical situation, three tests and a social case history were chosen as the sources of information to be studied: a projective test, the Rorschach examination; an objective personality test, the Minnesota Multiphasic Personality Inventory (MMPI); a "semistructured" projective test, the Stein Sentence Completion Test [6]; and a Standard Social Case History. The last named is routinely gathered from every patient

at the Oakland (California) Veterans Administration Mental Hygiene Clinic where the test data were obtained. The Social Case Histories comprised reports of intake interviews by social workers, and briefly covered such information as identifying data, family background, work history, military history, present social status, and presenting complaints. They were edited only to delete directly identifying information. The five histories varied in length from one-half to two pages of single-spaced typewritten script. The social workers who reported the interviews were not aware that their reports were to be used in any research study. These reports were used for sources of social data because they are typical in every sense, and thus are representative of the kinds of data available to the psychodiagnosticians at the clinic, and because it can be assumed that they reflect no systematic bias as far as this experiment is concerned. The tests and histories were obtained from five male outpatients, each of whom was in individual psychotherapy.

The problem of establishing suitably valid criteria was approached in two ways. One was to establish "internal" validity, or the consensus of opinion of expert judges who had all four sources of information on the patients. The other validity criterion was an "external" one, the progress reports written by the patients' therapists. In order to establish the internal criterion, the test results and case histories were reproduced on standard forms and presented to eight criterion judges. The selection of criterion judges was based upon the following qualifications: (a) a Ph.D. in clinical psychology, (b) a minimum of three years' experience in psychodiagnosis, (c) familiarity with the tests used and with psychiatric patients who were World War II veterans. The criterion judges were asked to study all the information available to them and then make "true-false" judgments on an empirically derived check list verbalized in psychologists' language.

This check list was compiled as follows: Sentences were copied from various psychological reports and reduced to grammatically simple sentences. Half of them were rewritten in the logical or psychological opposite so there would be roughly an even number of possible "true" and "false" answers regardless of how ill the patient might be. Without this precaution, the more ill a patient is, the greater would be the number of "true" answers since psychologists' reports usually contain a predominance of statements of pathology. A population of 1,000 such statements was thus gathered. From this, a sample of 400 items was obtained by means of a table of random numbers. Duplicate or near-duplicate items were removed, resulting in the final check list of 283 items. The choices of the criterion judges were item-analyzed for each patient. Any item upon which at least six judges (75 per cent) agreed was accepted as being "internally valid." Between 55 and 60 per cent of the items survived this consensual criterion.

A second group of statements was compiled from the progress notes kept by the patients' therapists. These items were termed "externally" validated. Only behavior that could be observed directly by the therapist or that was reported by the patient was considered. This precaution was taken to minimize confounding the therapist with the patient—which would have been the case if the therapists were allowed to make inferences about the patients. Thus, for each patient two independent sets of items were prepared. These were combined into a single check list for presentation to the subjects, but were later analyzed separately.

In addition to the systematic elimination of the four sources of information, a fifth experimental condition was devised. There was an expectation that clinicians can make inferences which

are more accurate than chance simply by knowing that a person is a psychiatric patient. For this reason, in one of the experimental conditions the subjects were furnished with only the kind of information that would be available on a face sheet. This consisted of age, marital status, occupation, education, and source of referral to the clinic. The subjects were told that all the patients were white, male, veterans of World War II, and patients at the clinic. Thus there were five experimental conditions presented to each subject:

  I. The MMPI, Sentence Completion Test, Social Case History; *but minus the Rorschach.*
 II. The Rorschach, Sentence Completion Test, Social Case History; *but minus the MMPI.*
III. The Rorschach, MMPI, Social Case History; *but minus the Sentence Completion Test.*
 IV. The Rorschach, MMPI, Sentence Completion Test; *but minus the Social Case History.*
  V. Minimal (face-sheet) data only.

Twenty clinical psychologists, each of whom had had at least two years of psychodiagnostic experience, and who were familiar with veteran-patients and with the tests used in this study, were the subjects of the experiment, hereinafter referred to as *judges*. They were divided into four groups of five each. Every experimental condition for every patient could not be given to every judge since the judges would remember characteristics of a given patient from one experimental condition to the next and thus be contaminated. It was necessary to restrict the patient-condition combinations so that each judge had every patient and every experimental condition, but neither a patient nor a condition was repeated for any judge. The design was accomplished by making a five x five table, assigning experimental conditions to the columns, judges to the rows, and patients to the cells by restricted randomization from a table of random numbers. It can be seen that such an arrangement fulfills the conditions of a latin square [2]. Four such random squares were separately drawn so that in a sense there were four replications of the experiment—each with five different judges. The data were combined for the final statistical analysis.

The judges were instructed to study the information available, just as they would in a typical diagnostic study. They were then told to answer the items on each patient's check list. The judges were permitted to refer to the materials as often as they wished. For the condition of minimal data they were told to read what was available and then fill out the check list in the regular way, and to try to get as many "hits" as possible.

Since the patients were identified to the judges only by numbers (one through five), it is likely that the judges would have begun their evaluations with patient 1 and gone through to patient 5. This may have resulted in a systematic bias since inferences made on the patients evaluated first could influence the judgments made on the last few patients. To avoid such bias due to order of presentation, the judges were required to follow a specified order which was randomized for each judge.

The check lists returned by the judges were scored for number of dis-

agreements with the "internally valid" or "externally valid" statements. These were considered to be errors. Errors were transformed into percentages of errors since there were slight variations of possible correct answers for each patient. To allow the assumption of homogeneity of variance to be made, the percentages were then transformed into angles equal to the arc sine of the square root of the percentage [5]. The results presented in Tables 2, 3, and 4 are in terms of these angles, which closely approximate percentage errors. The "internally" validated and "externally" validated items were scored and analyzed separately.

Results

The subjects were able to make inferences which were more accurate (as defined by this experiment) than chance expectancy under each of the five experimental conditions. Table 1 presents the results of chi-square tests on the "internal" and "external" items for condition V, minimal data, the condition under which the greatest number of errors were made. Chance expectancy was taken as 50 per cent. The chi square for both sets of items is significant beyond a p of .01.

The variance was analyzed for the four replications combined for each of the two sets of items. The experimental

TABLE 1. CHI-SQUARE TESTS BETWEEN PROPORTION OF ERRORS MADE UNDER CONDITION V (MINIMAL DATA) AND CHANCE

Frequencies	Incorrect	Correct	Chi Square
	Internal Items		
Expected	50	50	
Observed	23	77	15.726**
	External Items		
Expected	50	50	
Observed	32	68	6.696*

* p equals .01.
** p equals .001.

TABLE 2.   SUMMARY OF ANALYSIS OF VARIANCE OF THE POOLED DATA

		Internal Items Mean Square	F	External Items Mean Square	F
Source	df				
Conditions (columns)	4	66.86	3.56°	143.52	7.01°°°
Patients (cells)	4	134.89	7.18°°°	112.72	5.50°°°
Subjects (rows)	19	49.19	2.62°°	60.52	2.96°°
Squares × patients	12	21.09	1.12	30.10	1.47
Residual (error)	60	18.78	—	20.48	—
Total	99				

 * p equals .05.
 ** p equals .01.
 *** p equals .001.

design allows application of the latin-square analysis of variance. These data are summarized in Table 2. Variance contributed by patients, conditions, and by judges is significant.

The means derived from the experimental conditions for the two sets of items are presented in Table 3. According to the size of the means yielded, the experimental conditions follow about the same order for the two sets of items. More "errors" were made on the "external" items. Significance of the differences between these

TABLE 3.   MEAN ARC SINE PERCENTAGE ERRORS FOR THE EXPERIMENTAL CONDITIONS

Conditions	Internal Items	External Items
I Battery minus the Rorschach	25.50	31.65
II Battery minus the MMPI	28.15	34.40
III Battery minus the Sentence Completion Test	27.45	31.65
IV Battery minus the Social History	29.65	36.30
V Minimal data only	30.05	37.35

means was tested by means of t tests, using the standard error of the mean differences (to account for correlational term). Twenty such tests were possible and were made. These are presented in Table 4. There is a similarity of results obtained on the two independent sets of items which adds confidence to the interpretation that they represent actual differences.

On the "internal" items, i.e., those psychological statements which were validated by consensus of the criterion judges, the only batteries which differed significantly from the performance made on the basis of minimal data (condition V) are those minus the Rorschach (I) and those minus the Sentence Completion Test (III). One thing these conditions (I and III) have in common is the *presence* of both the MMPI and the Social Case History. That is, fewer errors were made by batteries which contained both the Social Case History and the MMPI. On the "external" items, i.e., those statements taken from the therapists' progress notes, these same differences appeared, plus two others: The batteries which contained the MMPI and the Social Case History (I and III)

TABLE 4. SUMMARY OF THE t TESTS FOR THE DIFFERENCES
BETWEEN MEANS OF THE EXPERIMENTAL CONDITIONS

Compared Conditions	Internal Items Mean Diff.	t	External Items Mean Diff.	t
I-II	−2.65	1.78	−2.75	1.66
I-III	−1.95	1.30	0.00	0.00
I-IV	−4.15	2.03	−4.65	3.69**
I-V	−4.55	3.05*	−5.70	3.37**
II-III	0.70	0.54	2.75	1.36
II-IV	−1.50	0.80	−1.90	1.12
II-V	−1.90	1.46	−2.95	1.86
III-IV	−2.20	1.12	−4.65	2.77*
III-V	−2.60	2.17*	−5.70	2.82*
IV-V	−0.40	0.24	−1.05	0.76

Note.—Experimental conditions are: I battery minus Rorschach; II battery minus MMPI; III battery minus Sentence Completion; IV battery minus Social History; V "minimal" information only.
* p equals .05.
** p equals .01.

also resulted in fewer errors than the batteries that contained all the tests, but which were without Social Case Histories (IV).

Several conclusions can be made on the basis of these results:

a. "Minimal" data allow inferences to be made which are more accurate than those expected on the basis of chance alone. Hence, it follows that all the batteries allow inferences to be made more accurately than on the basis of chance alone, because the most errors were made under the condition of "minimal" data.

b. On the basis of three tests, but without the Social Case History, clinicians can make no more accurate inferences than they can make on the basis of only "minimal" information.

c. The most efficacious batteries are those which included both the MMPI and the Social Case History.

d. Patients differ with respect to the accuracy with which they can be diagnosed.

e. Clinicians differ with regard to diagnostic skills.

It is not possible to draw conclusions as to which is the best *single* source of information, for this was not tested by the experiment. The answer must be found by future experimentation.

Discussion

The procedure of the present experiment is representative of the clinical situation in the following important ways: It permits use of several sources of information in combination. Tests are not interpreted "blindly," but with a background of a social case history except where its elimination is a condition of the experiment. It allows the clinician to use whatever approach he chooses, to be as subjective and intuitive as he wishes, in arriving at his formulations. Finally, the inferences are verbalized in language typical of that used by clinical psychologists in their diagnostic reports, except those taken from the therapists' notes. These latter, however, may also be said to be verbalized in psychological language.

The chief difference between the conditions of this experiment and a normal clinical situation is that the clinicians were required to make a dichotomous (true-false) choice on a series of inferences which had been taken out of context. In the clinical situation the clinician integrates his inferences in the matrix of a psychological report where one statement logically precedes another until they form a cohesive description of the patient. Taking statements out of context may have had a vitiating effect upon the judgments. Other conditions differed, too. The judges were all busy, unpaid volunteers, and it is not inconceivable that they placed more emphasis on the MMPI and Social History, which take comparatively little time to interpret, than they did on the Rorschach which presumably requires hours of careful study. These differences between the experimental procedures and the clinical situation must be kept in mind when considering the conclusions drawn from this study.

There seems to be a superiority of the Social Case History both as a source of cues and especially as the background against which the tests were interpreted. This should not be surprising. The case history method has behind it a long tradition of purposefully gathering information which is pertinent to diagnosis. Social workers are especially trained to provide this valuable adjunct to the clinicians' skills. "Blind" diagnosis made from test results without regard for the patients' background seems to be ineffective. The results of this study also suggest that perhaps it might be profitable for clinical psychologists to withdraw some of the energy and interest now invested in the study of projective techniques and study ways and means by which the Social Case History may be made into an even better instrument than it now seems to be.

Summary

A method was described which permitted comparison of the relative validity of several sources of psychodiagnostic information used in combination, under conditions somewhat representative of the actual clinical situation. An experiment was reported to illustrate the application of this "fractional omission" method using a Social Case History, an MMPI, a Stein Sentence Completion Test, and a Rorschach examination, which were gathered from five Veterans Administration Mental Hygiene Clinic outpatients. These were presented to eight expert criterion judges who made *true-false* judgments on an empirically derived list of psychological inferences. Items upon which at least six criterion judges agreed were considered to be "internally" validated. Other items, taken from the patients' therapy progress notes, were considered to be "externally" validated. The two sets of items were combined for presentation to the subjects, but were later analyzed separately.

The judges (subjects) were twenty clinical psychologists, each of whom was randomly deprived of a different source of information for each of four patients, and given only "minimal" data for a fifth patient (i.e., age, occupation, education, marital status, and source of referral to the clinic). Judges answered the items on the basis of the information available to them. The experimental conditions were: (I) Rorschach missing, (II) MMPI missing, (III) Sentence Completion Test missing, (IV) Social Case History missing, and (V) "minimal data" only. Errors were compared between experimental conditions by latin-square analysis of variance of the pooled data, and by *t* tests.

Results were highly similar for both sets of items, and permitted the following conclusions: (*a*) "Minimal data" permitted inferences which were better than chance. (*b*) Without Social Case Histories, inferences were no more accurate than on the basis of "minimal data." (*c*) The superior batteries were those which included both the MMPI and the Social Case History. (*d*) Patients differ with regard to the accuracy with which they can be diagnosed. (*e*) Clinicians differ with regard to diagnostic skills.

REFERENCES

1. Brunswik, E. *Systematic and representative design of psychological experiments.* Berkeley & Los Angeles: Univer. of California Press, 1949.
2. Grant, D. A. The latin-square principle in the design and analysis of psychological experiments. *Psychol. Bull.*, 1948, 45, 427–442.
3. Kostlan, A. A representative approach to the empirical study of psychological inference. Unpublished doctor's dissertation, Univer. of California,

Berkeley, 1952.
4. Sarbin, T. R., & Taft, R. *An essay on inference in the psychological sciences.* Berkeley: Garden Library Press, 1952.
5. Snedecor, G. W. *Statistical methods.* (4th Ed.) Ames, Iowa: State College Press, 1946.
6. Stein, M. I. The use of a sentence completion test for the diagnosis of personality. *J. clin. Psychol.*, 1947, 3, 46–56.

Prediction of Flying Success by Clinical Analysis of Test Protocols

Wayne H. Holtzman and Saul B. Sells

In relation to the problem of developing a battery of personality and motivational measures to predict adjustment to military and combat flying, the following questions were considered: (a) Can a group of expert clinical psychologists, given a description of the problem and a definition of the criterion, predict this criterion on the basis of a battery of personality tests? (b) If such predictions can be made successfully, what are the effective predictor signs which the clinicians use, and how do they integrate these signs to obtain successful predictions? The experiment reported below was undertaken primarily for the purpose of developing hypotheses for the systematic, quantitative scoring of a group of experimental psychiatric screening tests for flying personnel.

The six tests in this study were part of one experimental battery of group tests similar to those used by psychologists in clinical practice. These tests are: (a) Background Information, a biographical history inventory; (b) Ink-Blot Test, a group adaptation of the Rorschach test; (c) Feeling and Doing, a psychosomatic inventory reporting both symptoms experienced and what the subject did about them; (d) What

The research reported here was conducted under terms of Contract No. AF 33(038)-13887 between the U. S. Air Force and The University of Texas in coordination with the Department of Clinical Psychology, USAF School of Aviation Medicine, Randolph Field, Texas. This research was discussed at a symposium entitled "Clinical Prediction of Flying Success," American Psychological Association, Washington, D.C., September, 1952.

Reprinted by permission of the American Psychological Association and the authors from the *Journal of Abnormal and Social Psychology*, 1954, 49, 485–490.

Is He Saying?—a sentence completion test designed for Air Force use; (e) L-D Test, a group test booklet of the Szondi test; and (f) Drawing Test, a group version of the Draw-A-Person test. These tests have been described in detail by Sells and others in a series of Air Force publications (1, 2, 4, 6, 7).

A major problem in adapting these clinical testing procedures to selection use is that of developing adequate formal, quantitative scoring techniques that meet the requirements of psychometric standards and at the same time incorporate the interpretive schemes of the clinical method. This problem was attacked in a number of ways, for the most part by empirical analyses in which empirical scoring keys were developed by painstaking and systematic comparison of the responses of discrete bipolar criterion groups and cross-validated on independent samples.[1] The present experiment was undertaken as one part of the coordinated attack on this problem.

Method

After careful consideration of the test and criterion data, the probable availability of skilled clinicians to evaluate the test protocols, and the objectives of the research program, an experimental design for the clinician study was developed. From a total of 1,504 test subjects (Ss) for whom complete criterion data were available, 100 aviation cadets

[1] Of the six tests used in this study, empirical studies have thus far developed valid scoring keys for three. Reports on the Rorschach (6) and Sentence Completion Test (7) have been published. Unpublished results on the Background Information inventory are reported in a general discussion of the psychiatric selection research program by Sells and Barry (5). Two studies of the Draw-A-Person test, one by Anastasi and Foley (1) and an unpublished study by Nurse and Barry, a series of analyses of the Szondi test by Ellis and Sells, and an extensive study of the Feeling and Doing test by Barry and Cobb have all yielded negative findings on cross-validation of experimental keys.

were selected for the present study. Fifty of them had made a highly successful adjustment to the stress of flight training, and 50 had been eliminated from the program because they developed overt personality disturbances and were unable to complete the training course. The nature of the overt personality disturbances varied, but in every case the disturbance was sufficiently severe to be called to the attention of the flight surgeon, psychiatrist, and psychologist. The criteria used for selection of the 100 cadets are:

Successful Group

1. Passed the flight training course
2. Pilot aptitude of Stanine 6 or higher
3. No evidence of personality or disciplinary difficulty
4. Leadership rating above the 75th percentile as judged by fellow cadets
5. Satisfactory ratings by four independent instructors on over-all suitability for role of Air Force pilot and officer

Unsuccessful Group

1. Elimination from the flight training program for reasons other than physical disability
2. Pilot aptitude of Stanine 6 or higher
3. Evidence of overt personality disturbance contributory to elimination

Since the number of cadets meeting these criteria was more than 50 in each group, 50 successful and 50 unsuccessful cadets were selected at random from the available cases. Code numbers were assigned to these 100 individuals, and five independent sets of 20 cadets each were drawn up randomly. In this manner, the a priori probability that a given cadet passed or failed was fixed at .50, with the number of successful cadets in a given set of 20 varying randomly about an expected value of 10. Consequently, the success of a given clinician could be evaluated directly by use of the binomial distribution.

Each test protocol was photographed, and sufficient photostatic copies were made to provide each participating psychologist with a complete set of test materials for his particular group of 20 cadets.

Meanwhile a select list of psychologists, many of whom had served as military psychologists during World War II, was compiled; it consisted chiefly of recognized authorities in clinical procedures as applied to test interpretation and psychodiagnosis. As partial remuneration for the time-consuming clinical evaluation of 20 cadets, a small honorarium of $100 was offered each collaborator for his participation. The 19 psychologists who accepted this invitation are:

Lawrence Abt	James Layman
Arthur Benton	Ivan Mensh
Sidney Bijou	Daniel Miller
Gerald Blum	Z. A. Piotrowski
Charles Cofer	Victor Raimy
Molly Harrower	Thomas Richards
Max Hutt	William Schofield
Seymour Klebanoff	Meyer Williams
Bruno Klopfer	Lee Winder
Samuel Kutash	

TABLE 1.   EXPERIMENTAL DESIGN

Group	No. of Clinicians	No. of Cadets	No. of Cadets Who Passed
1	3	20	9
2	3	20	8
3	3	20	12
4	3	20	12
5	7	20	9
Total	19	100	50

To provide uniform background information concerning the nature of the criterion and the flight-training program, three chapters from Sells' (4) comprehensive outline of the research program which described the population and the case histories of unsuccessful cadets and outlined the critical requirements for success were included with the test materials. Detailed instructions for making and recording judgments, a brief summary of the over-all experimental design, and a short description of each test were also enclosed.

Two forms of recording sheet were used, one for recording judgments based on only one test at a time and one for recording global evaluations based on consideration of all or part of the available data for a given individual. Although each psychologist was encouraged to use first the single-test approach and then the global approach, the single-test analysis was made entirely optional. In addition to judging pass-fail for each cadet, each psychologist was asked to state, where possible, the cues which formed the basis for his evaluation. A three-point "confidence" scale was also provided so that each clinician could state the degree of confidence he had in the validity of each judgment he made. A confidence rating of "A" was to be given when the clinician felt quite sure of his judgment; a rating of "B" was to be used when he felt his judgment was questionable; and a rating of "C" denoted no confidence whatsoever in the judgment.

Table 1 summarizes the essential features of the experimental design. Four of the five sets of test protocols were each judged independently by three different psychologists; the fifth set was evaluated by seven psychologists. Replication through judges made possible a study of the clinician as a variable and permitted the use of pooled judgments for a single case. The additional replication in the fifth group was designed to provide a more accurate estimate of inter-clinician variability than was possible with only three clinicians per cadet.

The experimental design used in the present study permits several different approaches to testing the general hypothesis that adjustment to the training program could be predicted significantly better than chance by skilled clinicians from an examination of individual test protocols. Two sets of predictions were made by most of the psychologists. Every psychologist made a prediction of success or failure for each individual in his group of 20 cadets. One class of predictions consists of these over-all or global evaluations. In addition to using the global approach, 12 psychologists made predictions for each cadet based upon consideration of only one test at a time. A second class of predictions consists of these single-test evaluations. In either case, the data may be examined for one psychologist independently of the others, or combined predictions can be obtained by pooling the judgments of individual psychologists for each cadet.

Results

Let us first examine the validity results of the global judgments. The number of correct judgments among the 19 psychologists ranged from 4 to 14 with a mean of 10.2. Since 20 cadets were judged by each psychologist, and since the a priori probability that a single prediction is correct by chance alone is .50, the expected chance number of correct predictions for a single clinician is 10. The results of this analysis are presented in Table 2. If we disregard confidence ratings, none of the psychologists was able to predict adjustment to training significantly better than chance with the global approach to test evaluation.[2]

A similar analysis was made using only the predictions with confidence ratings of A, which signified that the clinician was quite sure of his judgment. The number of over-all predictions that were rated A by a single psychologist varied from 0 to 12. The a priori chance expectation for number correct is one-half the total number of cadets assigned

[2] One psychologist (R) did make predictions which, when considered alone, were significantly *worse* than chance.

TABLE 2. SUCCESS OF OVER-ALL (GLOBAL) EVALUATIONS FOR INDIVIDUAL CLINICIANS[*]

Group	Clinician Code No.[†]	Correct Predictions
1	C	11
	A	10
	B	9
2	R	4
	O	11
	M	8
3	L	14
	S	14
	J	13
4	G	12
	Q	13
	F	12
5	I	8
	D	8
	E	10
	K	9
	P	12
	H	10
	N	6

[*] Chance expectation is 10 correct out of 20. Mean number of correct predictions per clinician is 10.2.
[†] The code numbers have no relation to the order of listing of the clinicians' names.

an A confidence rating in each case. Only two psychologists (L and S) were able to predict the actual adjustment of the cadets better than chance at the 5 per cent level of significance. These results, however, must be interpreted with great caution since seven of the psychologists had *fewer* correct predictions rated A than would be expected by chance alone.

Similarly, when the results obtained for the B and C confidence ratings are considered alone, none of the predictions rises significantly above chance expectation.

Since it seems quite reasonable that greater stability of predictions can be obtained by pooling judgments, the global evaluations made by each psychologist for a given cadet were combined. Two different methods of pooling judgments were used. In one case, whatever was predicted by a simple majority (2 out of 3, or 4 out of 7) of psychologists was accepted as the pooled judgment. A more severe criterion of agreement was obtained by considering only those cadets for whom there was unanimous agreement in Groups 1–4 and a majority agreement of 5 out of 7 psychologists in Group 5. On an a priori basis, the expected number of correct predictions by chance alone is one-half the total number of cadets for whom predictions are available. Inspection of Table 3 clearly reveals that there is little relationship between actual adjustment and predictions obtained by pooling global judgments.

When judgments based upon the single-test approach are examined, the results are essentially the same. Twelve of the clinicians made judgments using the single-test approach as well as the global approach. When confidence ratings are disregarded, only 3 of 68 different sets of predictions were sufficiently accurate to prove significant at the 5 per cent level. When only those predictions which the clinician rated A, indicating that he was quite sure of his judgment, are considered, the results are essentially the same. Only one set of predictions, that made by psychologist B using Background Information, is significant at the 5 per cent level. Since a total of 68 significance tests was implicitly made, one for each set of predictions, the ap-

parent success of psychologist B may well be considered a chance fluctuation.[3]

As in the case of the global evaluations, an analysis was made of the results obtained for each separate test, using majority agreement of individual clinicians as a basis for prediction. The number of correct predictions did not differ significantly from chance expectation for any of the six tests. Clearly, there is little relationship between actual adjustment and predictions based upon an analysis of one test at a time.

Discussion

In the present study there is little doubt that the clinical assessments of beginning aviation cadets have no relationship to a criterion of adjustment in the basic flight-training program. The objective findings can hardly be ignored, and it is of utmost importance to con-

[3] A partial test of this hypothesis was made for psychologist C who did about as well as B on Background Information. C offered to make predictions for two additional groups of 20 cadets each (Groups 2 and 5), using only cues provided by Background Information. To aid him in improving his subsequent judgments he was given the criterion data for his original set of protocols (Group 1). C first made predictions for the 40 cadets without specific knowledge of his earlier successes and failures. Twenty-five of the 40 predictions later proved to be correct. Then C re-evaluated the 40 test records after examination of the earlier data, and changed several predictions. Twenty-two of the 40 predictions were correct. Since in both cases chance expectation was 20 correct, the null hypothesis could not be rejected.

TABLE 3.   SUCCESS OF POOLED GLOBAL EVALUATIONS

Condition	Number of Correct Predictions	Chance Expectation of Correct Predictions
Majority agreement	54 out of 100	50
Majority agreement (A ratings only)	17 out of 35	17.5
Unanimous agreement	28 out of 50	25

sider the possible explanations of these results in order to appreciate fully their significance.

1. *Are the criterion data faulty?* A major factor in the success or failure of any prediction experiment is the validity of the criterion measure. This immediately raises the question "Validity for what?" The present study is concerned with predictions of the adjustment to the stresses of flight training of two groups of aviation cadets carefully selected to reflect highly effective and highly inadequate patterns of behavior. The clinician is called upon to predict (in retrospect) the *future* behavior of each cadet on the basis of test performance obtained when he first entered training. In this sense, the evaluations called for are prognostic of later adjustment rather than diagnostic of present behavior.

The likelihood that our criterion groups of successful and unsuccessful cadets are in error is small. Few, if any, experimental investigations of adjustment to stress have been based upon criteria as objective and manifold as those used in the present study. Although it is true that some members of the successful group may later experience breakdown under high situational stress and may manifest behavior indicative of poor adjustment, the anxiety, functional disorders, and overt personality disturbance which played a prominent role in the failure of each cadet in the unsuccessful group are outright evidence of maladjustment and preclude consideration of these cadets in any other category.

One explanation of the inability of the psychologists to predict the criterion may be the relatively restricted range of adjustment. Since each cadet entering flight training had successfully passed a number of hurdles prior to admission, the likelihood of an individual with severe neurotic or psychotic manifestations being included in the test population is extremely small. This objection has been partially overcome by selecting a small experimental sample of 100 cases from a much larger group in such a way as to reflect only the extremes. This was deliberately done to maximize the likelihood of obtaining significant predictions.

2. *Is it possible that test evaluations were valid with respect to adjustment at the time the test data were gathered, and that later adjustment has little relationship to assessment of initial personality status?* Because of the exhaustive mental, physical, and educational requirements for aviation cadets, an overtly neurotic or disturbed candidate is rare. However, the problem of prediction is to discover latent or subclinical characteristics which constitute predisposition to later manifestation of excessive stress reaction when the actual stresses of military flying are experienced. Hence, if the clinical assessments were concerned with manifest indications of disturbance at the time the tests were administered, it might be expected that they would be unrelated to later adjustment, unless a very disturbed applicant were found. It is possible that this task is unfair to the clinicians before more detailed empirical research data are available on the signs indicative of predisposition. However, at the time the research was undertaken it was hoped that the insights of the clinicians might facilitate the prosecution of the empirical studies. The results of the empirical studies which have been completed, such as those with the Rorschach, sentence completion, and other tests, confirm the conclusion that the items found most discriminating are frequently not those which were expected on a priori grounds.

3. *Were the judges sufficiently familiar with the prediction problem to evaluate the test protocols in a proper context?* The psychologists who participated in this study represented a wide variety of interest and background. Several, while recognized as highly skilled

clinicians, had had little or no contact with military populations. The majority, however, had served during the past war as military psychologists, and a few were thoroughly familiar with the problem, having either gone through a flight-training program themselves or worked as psychologists on similar problems for the Air Force. In addition, to ensure some familiarity with the problem, an extensive discussion of the training situation and the types of stress present, together with several representative case reports of cadets who failed to adjust, was forwarded to each participant. The *uniformly* negative results strongly suggest that lack of familiarity with the training situation and the types of adjustment which characterized the criterion groups is not a deciding factor.

4. *Did the judges have sufficient previous experience with the types of test materials to interpret them properly?* Inexperience with the tests used in the Randolph Field battery may have contributed appreciably to the lack of positive findings. To make feasible their administration to large groups, each of the six tests had been adapted from more familiar individual testing procedures. The Ink-Blot Test was a mixture of the commonly accepted individual and group Rorschach tests with one or two minor innovations. The L-D Test was a group form of the Szondi with only one trial rather than several spread over different days as is standard practice when individually administered in a clinical setting. Though similar in structure to other such tests, the SAM Sentence Completion Test (What Is He Saying?) was devised especially for use with student pilots. A large number of the test items, however, were identical to those used in earlier, well-known tests of this type. Except for the lack of an "inquiry," the group form of the Draw-A-Person test was essentially similar to the standard individual procedure. Similarly, the general type of response given in Feeling and Doing and in Back-ground Information was familiar to most clinicians, although the context in which the responses were made was different from the usual clinical setting.

Several participating psychologists have expressed the belief that these modifications of standard procedures in order to make group administration feasible may have changed the meaning of test responses as commonly interpreted in clinical practice. Others have argued that the basic response patterns should remain relatively constant, although less information may be available in the group tests. Whatever the case may be, it is worth noting that many of the psychologists felt they were making meaningful interpretations of the data.

5. *Is it possible that the personality evaluations were largely correct, but the criterion predictions failed due to inadequate integration of the various personality characteristics observed?* The judgment process consists of at least two phases: (a) the description of the individual's personality, and (b) the weighing of assets and liabilities noted in the individual and the prediction of adjustment to the training program. Since none of the predictions exceeded chance expectations, it is impossible to tell from the predictions alone whether the personality descriptions are invalid or whether they have been used inappropriately in arriving at predictions. In all likelihood both phases of judging have suffered from faulty inferences. Because at least three different psychologists evaluated each cadet, the variation in personality descriptions from one clinician to the next in the kind and degree of personality descriptions written makes a thorough, systematic analysis of this type impossible. Even when only those cases on which there is unanimous agreement as to predicted outcome are considered, there is little congruence of terminology, each clinician favoring concepts related to his own frame of reference. A major problem in further analysis of data of this kind is

finding an adequate system for classifying descriptive terms to make comparisons among clinicians.

In spite of such variability, there are underlying consistencies among clinicians which cannot be ascribed to chance alone. The a priori probability that three judges will unanimously agree in their predictions for a single cadet is .25. For the global approach the amount of agreement among the psychologists was significantly better than chance. There was a low but statistically significant agreement in predictions based upon Background Information, Feeling and Doing, and the Drawing Test, when considered individually. Less reliability was present in predictions based upon the Ink-Blot Test and the SAM Sentence Completion Test. No agreement among clinicians was observed for the L-D Test. Although none of the psychologists was able to predict beyond chance expectation the actual adjustment of the cadets, they did tend to use the test battery as a whole, and to some extent the individual tests, with some degree of consistency.

To see what cues formed the basis for judgments, the evaluations of cadets upon whom there was unanimous agreement were examined. A rating of failure seemed to depend frequently upon the presence of signs of low motivation for flying, immaturity, strong dependency needs, anxiety, and sexual conflict. Ratings of success were less consistent and often based upon conflicting cues. In general, too few clinicians listed cues in sufficient numbers to permit any systematic analysis. Further development and standardization of terms for the description of personality must take place before any appreciable understanding of the process of judging will be possible.

In view of the results of the present study, several questions immediately arise. What are the implications of these findings with respect to the problem of predicting individual adjustment to other life stress situations? Can these results be accepted as reliable evidence of the general invalidity of clinical assessment procedures as presently constituted for coping with prediction problems of this nature? How do the results of this study fit in with the general picture as it is gradually unfolding in somewhat similar studies such as the Michigan VA clinical trainee assessment program?

In the opinion of the writers, the improvement of clinical judgments based on psychological tests and other clinical evidence will depend upon the completion of adequate quantitative, controlled empirical research relating standardized measurement instruments to specific criterion situations. Such situations include diagnostic groups, job criterion groups, and various other life situations. In this respect, the present results are closely related to those of the Michigan program.

REFERENCES

1. ANASTASI, ANNE, & FOLEY, J. P., JR. A research program on the psychiatric selection of flying personnel: V. The Human-Figure Drawing Test as an objective psychiatric screening aid for student pilots. *USAF, Sch. Aviat. Med., Proj. Rep.*, 1952, No. 21-37-002, Rep. No. 5.

2. BARRY, J. R., & RAYNOR, G. H. A research program on the psychiatric selection of flying personnel. Research on the Cornell Index. *USAF, Sch. Aviat. Med., Proj. Rep.*, 1953, No. 21-0202-0007, Rep. No. 2.

3. KELLY, E. L., & FISKE, D. W. *The prediction of performance in clinical psychology.* Ann Arbor: Univer. of Michigan Press, 1951.

4. SELLS, S. B. A research program on the psychiatric selection of flying personnel: I. Methodological introduction and experimental design. *USAF, Sch.*

Aviat. Med., Proj. Rep., 1951, No. 21-37-002, Rep. No. 1.

5. SELLS, S. B., & BARRY, J. R. A research program to develop psychiatric selection of flying personnel: I. Theoretical approach and research design; II. Research progress. *J. aviat. Med.,* 1953, **24,** 29–47.

6. SELLS, S. B., FRESE, F. J., JR., & LANCASTER, W. H. Research on the psychiatric selection of flying personnel: II. Progress report on development of SAM Group Ink-Blot Test. *USAF, Sch. Aviat. Med., Proj. Rep.,* 1952, No. 21-37-002, Rep. No. 2.

7. TRITES, D. K., HOLTZMAN, W. H., TEMPLETON, R. C., & SELLS, S. B. Psychiatric screening of flying personnel: research on the SAM Sentence Completion Test. *USAF, Sch. Aviat. Med., Proj. Rep.,* 1953, No. 21-0202-0007, Rep. No. 3.

Chapter 13

The Clinical Psychologist: Betty Crocker or Escoffier—Mechanical or Creative Combination of Clinical Data?

■ Psychologists surveying studies such as those in Chapter 12 occasionally ask whether there might not be a better way to integrate clinical data than via the oft-fallible brain cells of the clinician. Rather than wasting our energies training clinical students to a modicum of ability, why not program computers to excellence and turn our attention from assessment to therapy or research? Instead of a "every man a king," the slogan would be "every machine a Klopfer."

Until recently this question was quite academic. To be sure Meehl had published a book (Meehl, 1954) in which clinicians were pitted against actuarial tables in a number of studies;[1] like the cat in the animated cartoons the wily clinician with his tests and degrees made a brave show at the start but was inevitably defeated by the humble clerk in the outer office armed with nothing more than an actuarial table. While this was upsetting, no agencies were reported to have fired their clinicians any more than the neighborhood grocer got rid of his cat after seeing cats outwitted in cartoon after cartoon. The reason was the same in each case: there was no practical substitute for either cat or clinician.

But times are changing for clinicians if not for cats. Not only are computers getting larger and faster, but also actuarial procedures are becoming more sophisticated. It is now possible to have a clerk administer an MMPI and feed the results to machines which will score the protocol and pass the scales on to a computer which will analyze them and write a personality description. The psychologist who insists on interpreting MMPIs on his own is now open to a charge of featherbedding and the spectre of technological unemployment is upon us. No wonder formerly respectable clinicians surreptitiously enter other fields such as the editing of books.

The basic goal for both the clinician and the actuary is the best possible assessment with the least expenditure of time, effort, and money. In order to justify the use of expensive clinical talent either in collecting data or in integrating them, it must be empirically demonstrated that the clinical data

[1] For another good review of the history of the clinical and actuarial prediction problem see Gough (1963).

and/or the clinical integration of the data result in a better job of assessment. In other words, for both Escoffier and Betty Crocker, the proof of the pudding is in the eating. And thus far, Betty's puddings have been as good or better than Escoffier's.

There are, however, a number of clinicians who feel that Escoffier came off second best because Betty seduced him into cooking in her kitchen. Given only a pantry full of packaged mixes and an opportunity to cook nothing but pudding, Escoffier didn't get a chance to show his true talents. Not only was he limited in his ingredients and in his range of dishes, but moreover Betty had been spending years perfecting this one recipe while it was Escoffier's first attempt. In short, instead of a contest it was more like an ambush. Perhaps in his own kitchen with a multitude of richer ingredients and time for trial and error, Escoffier could not only make a better pudding but also have the flexibility to create a whole host of new dishes designed to suit any possible occasion.

There was only one difficulty for this defense and that was the lack of evidence for it. Studies accumulated in which Betty ventured to try not only the bland pudding of predicting grade point averages but also to attempt some of Escoffier's clinical dishes such as psychiatric diagnosis. In a study by Meehl (1959), Betty and her cookbook recipes proved superior to a bevy of cordon bleu clinicians in discriminating psychotic from neurotic MMPI profiles, although it must be pointed out that the Escoffiers might have done better with richer ingredients.[2]

In the present chapter, Meehl acts as the somewhat reluctant spokesman for the Betty Crocker approach, while Robert Holt defends Escoffier and adduces some evidence designed to show that given equal time to perfect a recipe Escoffier can do better than Betty. It remains for Gardner Lindzey to demonstrate the clear superiority of the Escoffier approach in a novel situation, however. Using the very rich and actuarially rather indigestible ingredients of the TAT, he demonstrates how the Escoffier approach can lead to a good discrimination of homosexuals in a college sample. Betty Crocker is able to copy the recipe well enough to achieve reasonable success. However, when confronted with a distinctly different sample, Betty's recipes are failures while the Escoffiers are able to adapt and once more produce valid discriminations. Meehl (1965) has described this study as the first good example of the clinical approach's superiority. However, lest the clinicians rejoice too soon, it should be noted that Betty Crocker is probably busy working on a new recipe for this special situation and unless the clinical approach proves superior to this modified recipe, economics will argue in favor of using her recipe, for cookbooks are cheap and plentiful while Escoffiers are rare and expensive.

[2] In his article, Meehl (1959) also delineated several situations in which the clinical approach should be superior to the actuarial.

This of course points to one possible integration of the two approaches in the future. Perhaps it is a waste of talent for Escoffiers, who are able to create a variety of wondrous dishes, to spend their time cooking meals which will soon be consumed and forgotten. Perhaps instead they should try to preserve their talents for posterity by trying to specify how they do it . . . in short by writing better and more complex cookbooks than are currently available.

In the concluding article in this chapter, Wayne Holtzman examines the question of whether or not Betty can ever build or program a computer that will replace Escoffier. He examines the relative abilities of both computers and clinicians in an effort to determine how they can perhaps achieve a mutually rewarding peaceful coexistence with each performing the tasks they are best suited for.

Until this optimal modus vivendi is reached, however, we can expect Betty Crocker to be busy turning out more and better cookbook recipes, while Escoffier endeavors to train more creative clinicians in his image. If both succeed, the body of knowledge regarding clinical assessment can only gain weight and become more solidly based.

REFERENCES

GOUGH, H. G. Clinical versus statistical prediction in psychology. In POSTMAN, L. (Ed.) *Psychology in the Making*. New York: Alfred A. Knopf, 1963.

MEEHL, P. E. *Clinical Versus Statistical Prediction*. Minneapolis: University of Minnesota Press, 1954.

MEEHL, P. E. A comparison of clinicians with five statistical methods of identifying psychotic MMPI scores. *Journal of Consulting Psychology*, 1959, 6, 102–109.

MEEHL, P. E. Seer over sign: The first good example. *Journal of Experimental Research in Personality*, 1965, 1, 27–32.

Wanted—a Good Cookbook

Paul E. Meehl

Once upon a time there was a young fellow who, as we say, was "vocationally maladjusted." He wasn't sure just what the trouble was, but he knew that he wasn't happy in his work. So, being a

Presidential Address, Midwestern Psychological Association, Chicago, April 29, 1955.

denizen of an urban, sophisticated, psychologically oriented culture, he concluded that what he needed was some

Reprinted by permission of the American Psychological Association and the author from *The American Psychologist*, 1956, 11, 263–272.

professional guidance. He went to the counseling bureau of a large midwestern university (according to some versions of the tale, it was located on the banks of a great river), and there he was interviewed by a world-famous vocational psychologist. When the psychologist explained that it would first be necessary to take a 14-hour battery of tests, the young man hesitated a little; after all, he was still employed at his job and 14 hours seemed like quite a lot of time. "Oh, well," said the great psychologist reassuringly, "don't worry about *that*. If you're too busy, you can arrange to have my assistant take these tests *for* you. I don't care who takes them, just so long as they come out in quantitative form."

Lest I, a Minnesotan, do too great violence to your expectations by telling this story on the dustbowl empiricism with which we Minnesotans are traditionally associated, let me now tell you a true story having the opposite animus. Back in the days when we were teaching assistants, my colleague MacCorquodale was grading a young lady's elementary laboratory report on an experiment which involved a correlation problem. At the end of an otherwise flawless report, this particular bobby-soxer had written, "The correlation was seventy-five, with a standard error of ten, which is significant. However, I do not think these variables are related." MacCorquodale wrote a large red "FAIL" and added a note: "Dear Miss Fisbee: The correlation coefficient was devised expressly to relieve you of all responsibility for deciding whether these two variables are related."

If you find one of these anecdotes quite funny, and the other one rather stupid (I don't care which), you are probably suffering from a slight case of bias. Although I have not done a factor analysis with these two stories in the matrix, my clinical judgment tells me that a person's spontaneous reactions to them reflect his position in the perennial conflict between the tough-minded and the tender-minded, between those for whom the proper prefix to the word "analysis" is "factor" and those for whom it is "psycho," between the groups that Lord Russell once characterized as the "simple-minded" and the "muddle-headed." In a recent book (10), I have explored one major facet of this conflict, namely the controversy over the relative merits of clinical and statistical methods of *prediction*. Theoretical considerations, together with introspections as to my own mental activities as a psychotherapist, led me to conclude that the clinician has certain unique, practically unduplicable powers by virtue of being himself an organism like his client; but that the domain of straight *prediction* would not be a favorable locus for displaying these powers. Survey of a score of empirical investigations in which the actual predictive efficiency of the two methods could be compared, gave strong confirmation to this latter theoretical expectation. After reading these studies, it almost looks as if the first rule to follow in trying to predict the subsequent course of a student's or patient's behavior is carefully to avoid talking to him, and that the second rule is to avoid thinking about him!

Statisticians (and rat men) with castrative intent toward clinicians should beware of any temptation to overextend these findings to a generalization that "clinicians don't actually add anything." Apart from the clinician's therapeutic efforts—the power of which is a separate issue and also a matter of current dispute—a glance at a sample of clinical diagnostic documents, such as routine psychological reports submitted in a VA installation, shows that a kind of mixed predictive-descriptive statement predominates which is different from the type of gross prediction considered in the aforementioned survey. (I hesitate to propose a basic distinction here, having learned that proposing a distinction between two classes of concepts is a sure road to infamy.) Nevertheless, I suggest that we distinguish between: (a) the clinician's predictions of such gross, outcome-type, "administrative" dimensions as recovery from psychosis, survival in a training program, persistence in therapy, and the like; and (b) a rather more detailed and ambitious enterprise roughly characterizable as "describing the person." It might be thought that a always presupposes b, but a moment's reflection shows this to be false; since there are empirical prediction systems in which the sole property ascribed to the person *is* the disposition to a predicted gross outcome. A very considerable fraction of the typical clinical psychologist's time seems to be spent in giving tests or semitests, the intention being to come out with some kind of characterization of the individual. In part this characterization is "phenotypic," attributing such behavior-dispositions as "hostile," "relates poorly," "loss in efficiency," "manifest anxiety," or "depression"; in part it is "genotypic," inferring as the causes of the phenotype certain inner events, states, or structures, e.g., "latent n aggression," "oral-dependent attitudes," "severe castration anxiety," and the like. While the phenotypic-genotypic question is itself deserving of careful methodological analysis, in what follows I shall use the term "personality description" to cover both phenotypic and genotypic inferences, i.e., statements of all degrees of internality or theoreticalness. I shall also assume, while recognizing that at least one group of psychologists has made an impressive case to the contrary, that the description of a person is a worthwhile stage in the total clinical process. Granted, then, that we wish to use tests as a means to securing a description of the person, how shall we go about it? Here we sit, with our Rorschach and Multiphasic results spread out before us. From this mess of data we have to emerge with a characterization of the person from whose behavior these profiles are a highly abstracted, much-reduced distillation. How to proceed?

Some of you are no doubt wondering, "What is the fellow talking about? You look at the profiles, you call to mind what the various test dimensions mean for dynamics, you reflect on other patients you have seen with similar patterns, you think of the research literature; then you combine these considerations to make inferences. Where's the problem?" The problem is, *whether or not this is the most efficient way to do it.* We ordinarily do it this way; in fact, the practice is so universal that most clinicians find it shocking, if not somehow sinful, to imagine any other. We feed in the test data and let that rusty digital computer in our heads go to work until a paragraph of personality description emerges. It requires no systematic study, although some quantitative data have begun to appear in the literature (2, 3, 6, 7, 8, 9), to realize that there is a considerable element of vagueness, hit-or-miss, and personal judgment involved in this approach. Because explicit rules are largely lacking, and hence the clinician's personal experience, skill, and creative artistry play so great a role, I shall refer to this time-honored procedure for generating personality descriptions from tests as the *rule-of-thumb* method.

I wish now to contrast this rule-of-thumb method with what I shall call the *cookbook method.* In the cookbook method, any given configuration (holists please note—I said "configuration," not "sum"!) of psychometric data is associated with each facet (or configuration) of a personality description, and the closeness of this association is explicitly indicated by a number. This number need not be a correlation coefficient—its form will depend upon what is most appropriate to the circumstances. It may be a correlation, or merely an ordinary probability of attribution, or (as in the empirical study I shall report upon later) an average Q-sort placement. Whatever its form, the essential point is that the transition from psychometric pattern to personality description is an automatic, mechanical, "clerical" kind of task, proceeding by the use of explicit rules set forth in the cookbook. I am quite aware that the mere prospect of such a method will horrify some of you; in my weaker moments it horrifies me. All I can say is that many clinicians are also horrified by the cookbook method as appplied in the crude prediction situation; whereas the studies reported to date indicate this horror to be quite groundless (10, chap. 8). As Fred Skinner once said, some men are less curious about nature than about the accuracy of their guesses (15, p. 44). Our responsibility to our patients and to the taxpayer obliges us to decide between the rule-of-thumb and the cookbook methods on the basis of their empirically demonstrated efficiency, rather than upon which one is more exciting, more "dynamic," more like what psychiatrists do, or more harmonious with the clinical psychologist's self concept.

Let us sneak up the clinician's avoidance gradient gradually to prevent the negative therapeutic reaction. Consider a particular complex attribute, say, "strong dependency with reaction-formation." Under what conditions should we take time to give a test of moderate validity as a basis for inferring the presence or absence of this complex attribute? Putting it negatively, it appears to me pretty obvious that there are two circumstances under which we should *not* spend much skilled time on testing even with a moderately valid test, because we stand to lose if we let the test finding influence our judgments. First, when the attribute is found in almost all our patients; and second, when it is found in almost none of our patients. (A third situation, which I shall not consider here, is one in which the attribute makes no practical difference anyhow.) A disturbingly large fraction of the as-

sertions made in routine psychometric reports or uttered by psychologists in staff conferences fall in one of these classes.

It is not difficult to show that when a given personality attribute is almost always or almost never present in a specified clinical population, rather severe demands are made upon the test's validity if it is to contribute in a practical way to our clinical decision-making. A few simple manipulations of Bayes' Rule for calculating inverse probability lead to rather surprising, and depressing, results. Let me run through some of these briefly. In what follows,

P = Incidence of a certain personality characteristic in a specified clinical population. $(Q = 1 - P, P > Q)$

p_1 = Proportion of "valid positives," i.e., incidence of positive test finding among cases who actually have the characteristic. $(q_1 = 1 - p_1)$

p_2 = Proportion of "false positives," i.e., incidence of positive test findings among cases who actually lack the characteristic. $(q_2 = 1 - p_2)$

1. When is a positive assertion (attribution of the characteristic) on the basis of a positive test finding more likely to be correct than incorrect?

$$\frac{P}{Q} > \frac{p_2}{p_1}$$

Example: A test correctly identifies 80 per cent of brain-damaged patients at the expense of only 15 per cent false positives, in a neuropsychiatric population where one-tenth of all patients are damaged. The decision "brain damage present" on the basis of a positive test finding is more likely to be false than true, since the inequality is unsatisfied.

2. When does the use of a test improve over-all decision making?

$$P < \frac{q_2}{q_1 + q_2}$$

If $P < Q$ this has the form

$$Q < \frac{p_1}{p_1 + p_2}$$

Example: A test sign identifies 85 per cent of "psychotics" at the expense of only 15 per cent of false positives among the "nonpsychotic." It is desired to make a decision on each case, and both kinds of errors are serious.[1] Only 10 per cent of the population seen in the given setting are psychotic. Hence, the use of the test yields more erroneous classifications than would proceeding without the test.

3. When does improving a sign, strengthening a scale, or shifting a cut improve decision making?

$$\frac{\Delta p_1}{\Delta p_2} > \frac{Q}{P}$$

Example: We improve the intrinsic validity of a "schizophrenic index" so that it now detects 20 per cent more schizophrenics than it formerly did, at the expense of only a 5 per cent rise in the false positive rate. This surely looks encouraging. However, we work with an outpatient clientele only one-tenth of whom are actually schizophrenic. Since these values violate the inequality, "improvement" of the index will result in an increase in the proportion of erroneous diagnoses. N.B.—*Sampling errors are not involved in the above.* The values are assumed to be parameter values, and the test sign is valid (i.e., $p_1 > p_2$ in the population).

Further inequalities and a more detailed drawing out of their pragmatic implications can be found in a recent paper by Albert Rosen and myself (12). The moral to be drawn from these considerations, which even we clinicians can follow because they involve only

[1] Inequalities (2) and (3) are conditions for improvement if there is no reason to see one kind of error as worse than the other. In trait attribution this is usually true; in prognostic and diagnostic decisions it may or may not be. If one is willing to say how many errors of one kind he is prepared to tolerate in order to avoid one of the other kind, these inequalities can be readily corrected by inserting this ratio. A more general development can be found in an unpublished paper by Ward Edwards.

high-school algebra, is that a great deal of skilled psychological effort is probably being wasted in going through complex, skill-demanding, time-consuming test procedures of moderate or low validity, in order to arrive at conclusions about the patient which could often be made with high confidence without the test, and which in other cases ought not to be made (because they still tend to be wrong) even with the test indications positive. Probably most surprising is the finding that there are certain quantitative relations between the base rates and test validity parameters such that the use of a "valid" test will produce a net rise in the frequency of clinical mistakes. The first task of a good clinical cookbook would be to make explicit quantitative use of the inverse probability formulas in constructing efficient "rules of attribution" when test data are to be used in describing the personalities of patients found in various clinical populations. For example, I know of an outpatient clinic which has treated, by a variety of psychotherapies, in the course of the past eight years, approximately 5000 patients, not one of whom has committed suicide. If the clinical psychologists in this clinic have been spending much of their time scoring suicide keys on the Multiphasic or counting suicide indicators in Rorschach content, either these test indicators are close to infallible (which is absurd), or else the base rate is so close to zero that the expenditure of skilled time is of doubtful value. Suicide is an extreme case, of course (14); but the point so dramatically reflected there is valid, with suitable quantitative modifications, over a wider range of base rates. To take some examples from the high end of the base-rate continuum, it is not very illuminating to say of a known psychiatric patient that he has difficulty in accepting his drives, experiences some trouble in relating emotionally to others, and may have problems with his sexuality! Many psychometric reports bear a disconcerting resemblance to what my colleague Donald G. Paterson calls "personality description after the manner of P. T. Barnum" (13). I suggest—and I am quite serious—that we adopt the phrase *Barnum effect* to stigmatize those pseudo-successful clinical procedures in which personality descriptions from tests are made to fit the patient largely or wholly by virtue of their triviality; and in which any nontrivial, but perhaps erroneous, inferences are hidden in a context of assertions or denials which carry high confidence simply because of the population base rates, regardless of the test's validity. I think this fallacy is at least as important and frequent as others for which we have familiar labels (halo effect, leniency error, contamination, etc.). One of the best ways to increase the general sensitivity to such fallacies is to give them a name. We ought to make our clinical students as acutely aware of the Barnum effect as they are of the dangers of countertransference or the standard error of r.

The preceding mathematical considerations, while they should serve as a check upon some widespread contemporary forms of tea-leaf reading, are unfortunately not very "positive" by way of writing a good cookbook. "Almost anything needs a little salt for flavor" or "It is rarely appropriate to put ketchup on the dessert" would be sound advice but largely negative and not very helpful to an average cook. I wish now to describe briefly a piece of empirical research, reported in a thesis just completed at Minnesota by Charles C. Halbower, which takes the cookbook method 100 per cent seriously; and which seems to show, at least in one clinical context, what can be done in a more constructive way by means of a cookbook of even moderate trustworthiness.[2] By some geographical co-

incidence, the psychometric device used in this research was a structured test consisting of a set of 550 items, commonly known as MMPI. Let me emphasize that the MMPI is not here being compared with anything else, and that the research does not aim to investigate Multiphasic validity (although the general order of magnitude of the obtained correlations does give some incidental information in that respect). What Dr. Halbower asked was this: given a Multiphasic profile, how does one arrive at a personality description from it? Using the rule-of-thumb method, a clinician familiar with MMPI interpretation looks at the profile, thinks awhile, and proceeds to describe the patient he imagines would have produced such a pattern. Using the cookbook method, we don't need a clinician; instead, a $230-per-month clerk-typist in the outer office simply reads the numbers on the profile, enters the cookbook, locates the page on which is found some kind of "modal description" for patients with such a profile, and this description is then taken as the best available approximation to the patient. We know, of course, that every patient is unique—absolutely, unqualifiedly unique. Therefore, the application of a cookbook description will inevitably make errors, some of them perhaps serious ones. If we knew *which* facets of the cookbook sketch needed modification as applied to the present unique patient, we would, of course, depart from the cookbook at these points; but we don't know this. If we start monkeying with the cookbook recipe in the hope of avoiding or reducing these errors, we will in all likelihood improve on the cookbook in some respects but, unfortunately, will worsen our approximation in others. Given a finite body of information, such as the 13 two-digit numbers of a Multiphasic profile, there is obviously *in fact* (whether we have yet succeeded in *finding* it or not) a "most probable" value for any personality facet, and also

---

[2] I am indebted to Dr. Halbower for permission to present this summary of his thesis data in advance of his own more complete publication.

for any configuration of facets, however complex or "patterned" (10, pp. 131–134). It is easy to prove that a method of characterization which departs from consistent adherence to this "best guess" stands to lose. Keep in mind, then, that the raw data from which a personality description was to be inferred consisted of an MMPI profile. In other words, the Halbower study was essentially a comparison of the rule-of-thumb versus the cookbook method where each method was, however, functioning upon the same information—an MMPI. We are in effect contrasting the validity of two methods of "reading" Multiphasics.

In order to standarize the domain to be covered, and to yield a reasonably sensitive quantification of the goodness of description, Dr. Halbower utilized Q sorts. From a variety of sources he constructed a Q pool of 154 items, the majority being phenotypic or intermediate and a minority being genotypic. Since these items were intended for clinically expert sorters employing an "external" frame of reference, many of them were in technical language. Some sample items from his pool are: "Reacts against his dependency needs with hostility"; "manifests reality distortions"; "takes a dominant, ascendant role in interactions with others"; "is rebellious toward authority figures, rules, and other constraints"; "is counteractive in the face of frustration"; "gets appreciable secondary gain from his symptoms"; "is experiencing pain"; "is naive"; "is impunitive"; "utilizes intellectualization as a defense mechanism"; "shows evidence of latent hostility"; "manifests inappropriate affect." The first step was to construct a cookbook based upon these 154 times as the ingredients; the recipes were to be in the form of directions as to the optimal Q-sort placement of each item.

How many distinguishable recipes will the cookbook contain? If we had infallible criterion Q sorts on millions of cases, there would be as many recipes

as there are possible MMPI profiles. Since we don't have this ideal situation, and never will, we have to compromise by introducing coarser grouping. Fortunately, we know that the validity of our test is poor enough so that this coarseness will not result in the sacrifice of much, if any, information. How coarsely we group, i.e., how different two Multiphasic curves have to be before we refuse to call them "similar" enough to be coordinated with the same recipe, is a very complicated matter involving both theoretical and practical considerations. Operating within the limits of a doctoral dissertation, Halbower confined his study to four profile "types." These curve types were specified by the first two digits of the Hathaway code plus certain additional requirements based upon clinical experience. The four MMPI codes used were those beginning 123', 13', 27', and 87' (5). The first three of these codes are the most frequently occurring in the Minneapolis VA Mental Hygiene Clinic population, and the fourth code, which is actually fifth in frequency of occurrence, was chosen in order to have a quasi-psychotic type in the study. It is worth noting that these four codes constitute 58 per cent of all MMPI curves seen in the given population; so that Halbower's gross recipe categories already cover the majority of such outpatients. The nature of the further stipulations, refining the curve criteria within each two-digit code class, is illustrated by the following specifications for code 13', the "hysteroid valley" or "conversion V" type:

1. Hs and $Hy \geqq 70$.
2. $D < (Hs$ and $Hy)$ by at least one sigma.
3. K or $L > ?$ and F.
4. $F \leqq 65$.
5. Scales 4, 5, 6, 7, 8, 9, 0 all $\leqq 70$.

For each of these MMPI curve types, the names of nine patients were then randomly chosen from the list of those meeting the curve specifications. If the patient was still in therapy, his therapist was asked to do a Q sort (11 steps, normal distribution) on him. The MMPI had been withheld from these therapists. If the patient had been terminated, a clinician (other than Halbower) did a Q sort based upon study of the case folder, including therapist's notes and any available psychometrics (except, of course, the Multiphasic). This yields Q sorts for nine patients of a given curve type. These nine sorts were then pairwise intercorrelated, and by inspection of the resulting 36 coefficients, a subset of five patients was chosen as most representative of the curve type. The Q sorts on these five "representative" patients were then averaged, and this average Q sort was taken as the cookbook recipe to be used in describing future cases having the given MMPI curve. Thus, this modal, crystallized, "distilled-essence" personality description was obtained by eliminating patients with atypical sortings and pooling sortings on the more typical, hoping to reduce both errors of patient sampling and of clinical judgment. This rather complicated sequence of procedures may be summarized thus:

Deriving cookbook recipe for a specified curve type, such as the "conversion V" above:

1. Sample of $N =$ nine patients currently or recently in therapy and meeting the MMPI specifications for conversion V curve.
2. 154-item Q sort done on each patient by therapist or from therapist notes and case folder. (These sorts MMPI-uncontaminated.)
3. Pairwise Q correlations of these nine patients yields 36 intercorrelations.
4. Selection of subset $N' =$ five "modal" patients from this matrix by inspectional cluster method.
5. Mean of Q sorts on these five "core" patients is the cookbook recipe for the MMPI curve type in question.

Having constructed one recipe, he started all over again with a random sample of nine patients whose Multiphasics met the second curve-type specifications, and carried out these cluster-and-pooling processes upon them. This was done for each of the four curve types which were to compose the cookbook. If you have reservations about any of the steps in constructing this miniature cookbook, let me remind you that this is all preliminary, i.e., *it is the means of arriving at the cookbook recipe.* The proof of the pudding will be in the eating, and any poor choices of tactics or patients up to this point should merely make the cookbook less trustworthy than it would otherwise be.

Having thus written a miniature cookbook consisting of only four recipes, Halbower then proceeded to cook some dishes to see how they would taste. For cross validation he chose at random four new Mental Hygiene Clinic patients meeting the four curve specifications and who had been seen in therapy for a minimum of ten hours. With an eye to validity generalization to a somewhat different clinical population with different base rates, he also chose four patients who were being seen as inpatients at the Minneapolis VA Hospital. None of the therapists involved had knowledge of the patients' Multiphasics. For purposes of his study, Halbower took the therapist's Q sort, based upon all of the case folder data (minus MMPI) plus his therapeutic contacts, as the best available criterion; although this "criterion" is acceptable only in the sense of construct validity (1). An estimate of its absolute level of trustworthiness is not important since it is being used as the common reference basis for a comparison of two methods of test reading.

Given the eight criterion therapist Q sorts (2 patients for each MMPI curve type), the task of the cookbook is to predict these descriptions. Thus, for each of the two patients having MMPI code 123', we simply assign the Q-sort recipe found in the cookbook as the best available description. How accurate this description is can be estimated (in the sense of construct validity) by Q correlating it with the criterion therapist's description. These eight "validity" coefficients varied from .36 to .88 with a median of .69. As would be expected, the hospital inpatients yielded the lower correlations. The Mental Hygiene Clinic cases, for whom the cookbook was really intended, gave validities of .68, .69, .84, and .88 (see Table 1).

How does the rule-of-thumb method show up in competition with the cookbook? Here we run into the problem of

differences in clinical skill, so Halbower had each MMPI profile read blind by more than one clinician. The task was to interpret the profile by doing a Q sort. From two to five clinicians thus "read" each of the eight individual profiles, and the resulting 25 sorts were Q correlated with the appropriate therapist criterion sorts. These validity coefficients run from .29 to .63 with a median of .46. The clinicians were all Minnesota trained and varied in their experience with MMPI from less than a year (first-year VA trainees) through all training levels to PhD staff psycholo-

TABLE 1.   VALIDATION OF THE FOUR COOKBOOK DESCRIPTIONS ON NEW CASES, AND COMPARATIVE VALIDITIES OF THE COOKBOOK MMPI READINGS AND RULE-OF-THUMB READINGS BY CLINICIANS

1. Four patients currently in therapy Q-described by the therapist (10 hours or more therapy plus case folder minus MMPI). This is taken as best available criterion description of each patient.
2. MMPI cookbook recipe Q-correlated with this criterion description.
3. For each patient, 4 or 5 clinicians "read" his MMPI in usual rule-of-thumb way, doing Q-sorts.
4. These rule-of-thumb Q-sorts also Q-correlated with criterion description.
5. Cross-validation results in outpatient sample.

| Validities | MMPI Curve Type | | | |
	Code 123'	Code 27'	Code 13'	Code 87'
Cookbook	.88	.69	.84	.68
Rule-of-thumb (mean)	.75	.50	.50	.58

Range (4–5 readers) .55 to .63 .29 to .54 .37 to .52 .34 to .58
Mean of 4 cookbook validities, through $z_r = .78$
Mean of 17 rule-of-thumb validities, through $z_r = .48$
Cookbook's superiority in validly predicted variance = 38%

6. Validity generalization to inpatient (psychiatric hospital) sample with different base rates; hence, an "unfair" test of cookbook.

| Validities | MMPI Curve Type | | | |
	Code 123'	Code 27'	Code 13'	Code 87'
Cookbook	.63	.64	.36	.70
Rule-of-thumb (2 readers)	.37, .49	.29, .42	.30, .30	.50, .50

Mean of 4 cookbook validities, through $z_r = .60$
Mean of 8 rule-of-thumb validities, through $z_r = .41$
Cookbook's superiority in validly predicted variance = 19%

gists with six years' experience. The more experienced clinicians had probably seen over two thousand MMPI profiles in relation to varying amounts of other clinical data, including intensive psychotherapy. Yet not one of the 25 rule-of-thumb readings was as valid as the cookbook reading. Of the 25 comparisons which can be made between the validity of a single clinician's rule-of-thumb reading and that of the corresponding cookbook reading of the same patient's profile, 18 are significant in favor of the cookbook at the .01 level of confidence and 4 at the .05 level. The remaining 3 are also in favor of the cookbook but not significantly so.

Confining our attention to the more appropriate outpatient population, for (and upon) which the cookbook was developed, the mean r (estimated through z transformation) is .78 for the cookbook method, as contrasted with a mean (for 17 rule-of-thumb descriptions) of only .48, a difference of 30 points of correlation, which in this region amounts to a difference of 38 per cent in the validly predicted variance! The cookbook seems to be superior to the rule-of-thumb not merely in the sense of statistical significance but by an amount which is of very practical importance. It is also remarkable that even when the cookbook recipes are applied to patients from a quite different kind of population, their validity still excels that of rule-of-thumb MMPI readers who are in daily clinical contact with that other population. The improvement in valid variance in the hospital sample averages 19 per cent (see item 6 in Table 1).

A shrewd critic may be thinking, "Perhaps this is because all kinds of psychiatric patients are more or less alike, and the cookbook has simply taken advantage of this rather trivial fact." In answer to this objection, let me say first that to the extent the cookbook's superiority did arise from its actuarially determined tendency to "follow the base

rates," that would be a perfectly sound application of the inverse probability considerations I at first advanced. For example, most psychiatric patients are in some degree depressed. Let us suppose the mean Q-sort placement given by therapists to the item "depressed" is seven. "Hysteroid" patients, who characteristically exhibit the so-called "conversion V" on their MMPI profiles (Halbower's cookbook code 13), are less depressed than most neurotics. The clinician, seeing such a conversion valley on the Multiphasic, takes this relation into account by attributing "lack of depression" to the patient. But maybe he over-interprets, giving undue weight to the psychometric finding and understressing the base rate. So his rule-of-thumb placement is far down at the nondepressed end, say at position three. The cookbook, on the other hand, "knows" (actuarially) that the mean Q placement for the item "depressed" is at five in patients with such profiles—lower than the over-all mean seven but not displaced as much in the conversion subgroup as the clinician thinks. If patients are so homogeneous with respect to a certain characteristic that the psychometrics ought not to influence greatly our attribution or placement in defiance of the over-all actuarial trend, then the clinician's tendency to be unduly influenced is a source of erroneous clinical decisions and a valid argument in favor of the cookbook.

However, if this were the chief explanation of Halbower's findings, the obvious conclusion would be merely that MMPI was not differentiating, since any test-induced departure from a description of the "average patient" would tend to be more wrong than right. Our original question would then be rephrased, "What is the comparative efficiency of the cookbook and the the the rule-of-thumb method *when each is applied to psychometric information having some degree of intrinsic validity?*" Time permits me only brief mention of the several lines of evidence in Halbower's study which eliminate the Barnum effect as an explanation. First of all, Halbower had selected his 154 items from a much larger initial Q pool by a preliminary study of therapist sortings on a heterogeneous sample of patients in which items were eliminated if they showed low interpatient dispersal. Second, study of the placements given an item over the four cookbook recipes reveals little similarity (e.g., only two items recur in the top quartile of all four recipes; 60 per cent of the items occur in the top quartile of only one recipe). Third, several additional correlational findings combine to show that the cookbook was not succeeding merely by describing an "average patient" four times over. For example, the clinicians' Q description of their conception of the "average patient" gave very low validity for three of the four codes, and a "mean average patient" description constructed by pooling these clinicians' stereotypes was not much better (see Table 2). For Code 123' (interestingly enough, the commonest code among therapy cases in this clinic) the pooled stereotype was actually more valid than rule-of-thumb Multiphasic readings. (This is Bayes' Theorem with a vengeance!) Nevertheless, I am happy to report that this "average patient" description was still inferior to the Multiphasic cookbook (significant at the .001 level).

In the little time remaining, let me ruminate about the implications of this study, supposing it should prove to be essentially generalizable to other populations and to other psychometric instruments. From a theoretical point of view, the trend is hardly surprising. It amounts to the obvious fact that the human brain is an inefficient recording and computing device. The cookbook method has an advantage over the rule-of-thumb method because it (a) samples more representatively, (b) records and stores information better, and (c) computes statistical weights which are closer to the optimal. We can perhaps learn more by putting the theoretical question negatively: when should we *expect* the cookbook to be inferior to the brain? The answer to this question presumably lies in the highly technical field of computing machine theory, which I am not competent to discuss. As I understand it, the use of these machines requires that certain rules of data combination be fed initially into the machine, followed by the insertion of suitably selected and coded information. Putting it crudely, the machine can "remember" and can "think routinely," but it cannot "spontaneously notice what is relevant" nor can it "think" in the more high-powered, creative sense (e.g., it cannot invent theories). To be sure, noticing what is relevant must involve the exemplification of some rule, perhaps of a very complex form. But it is a truism

TABLE 2. VALIDITIES OF FOUR CLINICIANS' DESCRIPTION OF "AVERAGE PATIENT," OF THE MEAN OF THESE STEREOTYPES, AND OF THE COOKBOOK RECIPE (OUTPATIENT CASES ONLY)

MMPI Curve Type	Validities of "Average Patient" Descriptions by 4 Clinicians	Validity of Mean of These 4 "Average Patient" Stereotypes	Validity of Cookbook Recipe
Code 123'	.63 to .69	.74	.88
Code 27'	−.03 to .20	.09	.69
Code 13'	.25 to .37	.32	.84
Code 87'	.25 to .35	.31	.68

of behavior science that organisms can *exemplify* rules without *formulating* them. To take a noncontroversial example outside the clinical field, no one today knows how to state fully the rules of "similarity" or "stimulus equivalence" for patterned visual perception or verbal generalization; but of course we all exemplify daily these undiscovered rules. This suggests that as long as psychology cannot give a complete, explicit, quantitative account of the "dimensions of relevance" in behavior connections, the cookbook will not completely duplicate the clinician (11). The clinician *here* acts as an inefficient computer, but that is better than a computer with certain major rules completely left out (because we can't build them in until we have learned how to formulate them). The use of the therapist's own unconscious in perceiving verbal and imaginal relations during dream interpretation is, I think, the clearest example of this. But I believe the exemplification of currently unformulable rules is a widespread phenomenon in most clinical inference. However, you will note that these considerations apply chiefly (if not wholly) to matters of *content*, in which a rich, highly varied, hard-to-classify content (such as free associations) is the input information. The problem of "stimulus equivalence" or "noticing the relevant" does not arise when the input data are in the form of preclassified responses, such as a Multiphasic profile or a Rorschach psychogram. I have elsewhere (10, pp. 110–111) suggested that even in the case of such prequantified patterns there arises the possibility of causal-theory-mediated idiographic extrapolations into regions of the profile space in which we lack adequate statistical experience; but I am now inclined to view that suggestion as a mistake. The underlying theory must itself involve some hypothesized function, however crudely quantified; otherwise, how is the alleged "extrapolation" possible? I can think of no reason

why the estimation of the parameters in this underlying theoretical function should constitute an exception to the cookbook's superiority. If I am right in this, my "extrapolation" argument applies strictly only when a clinician literally *invents new theoretical relations or variables* in thinking about the individual patient. In spite of some clinicians' claims along this line, I must say I think it very rarely happens in daily clinical practice. Furthermore, even when it does happen, Bayes' Rule still applies. The *joint* probability of the theory's correctness, and of the attribute's presence (granting the theory but remembering nuisance variables) must be high enough to satisfy the inequalities I have presented, otherwise use of the theory will not pay off.

What are the pragmatic implications of the preceding analysis? Putting it bluntly, it suggests that for a rather wide range of clinical problems involving personality description from tests, the clinical interpreter is a costly middleman who might better be eliminated. An initial layout of research time could result in a cookbook whose recipes would encompass the great majority of psychometric configurations seen in daily work. I am fully aware that the prospect of a "clinical clerk" simply looking up Rorschach pattern number 73 J 10–5 or Multiphasic curve "Halbower Verzeichnis 626" seems very odd and even dangerous. I reassure myself by recalling that the number of phenotypic and genotypic attributes is, after all, finite; and that the number which are ordinarily found attributed or denied even in an extensive sample of psychological reports on patients is actually very limited. A best estimate of a Q-sort placement is surely more informative than a crude "Yes-or-No" decision of low objective confidence. I honestly cannot see, in the case of a *determinate trait domain* and a *specified clinicial population*, that there is a serious intellectual problem underlying one's uneasiness. I invite you to consider the possibility that the emotional block we all experience in connection with the cookbook approach could be dissolved simply by trying it out until our daily successes finally get us accustomed to the idea.

Admittedly this would take some of the "fun" out of psychodiagnostic activity. But I suspect that most of the clinicians who put a high value on this kind of fun would have even more fun doing intensive psychotherapy. The great personnel needs today, and for the next generation or more, are for psychotherapists and researchers. (If you don't believe much in the efficacy of therapy, this is the more reason for research.) If all the thousands of clinical hours currently being expended in concocting clever and flowery personality sketches from test data could be devoted instead to scientific investigation (assuming we are still selecting and training clinicians to be scientists), it would probably mean a marked improvement in our net social contribution. If a reasonably good cookbook could help bring about this result, the achievement would repay tenfold the expensive and tedious effort required in its construction.

REFERENCES

1. CRONBACH, L. J., & MEEHL, P. E. Construct validity in psychological tests. *Psychol. Bull.*, 1955, **52**, 281–302.

2. DAILEY, C. A. The practical utility of the clinical report. *J. consult. Psychol.*, 1953, **17**, 297–302.

3. DAVENPORT, BEVERLY F. The semantic validity of TAT interpretations. *J. consult. Psychol.*, 1952, **16**, 171–175.

4. HALBOWER, C. C. A comparison of actuarial versus clinical prediction to classes discriminated by MMPI. Unpublished doctor's dissertation, Univer. of Minn., 1955.

5. HATHAWAY, S. R. A coding system for MMPI profiles. *J. consult. Psychol.*, 1947, **11**, 334–337.

6. HOLSOPPLE, J. Q., & PHELAN, J. G. The skills of clinicians in analysis of projective tests. *J. clin. Psychol.*, 1954, **10**, 307–320.

7. KOSTLAN, A. A method for the empirical study of psychodiagnosis. *J. consult. Psychol.*, 1954, **18**, 83–88.

8. LITTLE, K. B., & SHNEIDMAN, E. S. The validity of MMPI interpretations. *J. consult. Psychol.*, 1954, **18**, 425–428.

9. LITTLE, K. B., & SHNEIDMAN, E. S. The validity of thematic projective technique interpretations. *J. Pers.*, 1955, **23**, 285–294.

10. MEEHL, P. E. *Clinical versus statistical prediction.* Minneapolis: Univer. of Minn. Press, 1954.

11. MEEHL, P. E. "Comment" on McArthur, C. Analyzing the clinical process. *J. counsel. Psychol.*, 1954, **1**, 203–208.

12. MEEHL, P. E., & ROSEN, A. Antecedent probability and the efficiency of psychometric signs, patterns, or cutting scores. *Psychol. Bull.*, 1955, **52**, 194–216.

13. PATERSON, D. G. Character reading at sight of Mr. X according to the system of Mr. P. T. Barnum. (Mimeographed, unpublished.)

14. ROSEN, A. Detection of suicidal patients: an example of some limitations in the prediction of infrequent events. *J. consult. Psychol.*, 1954, **18**, 397–403.

15. SKINNER, B. F. *The behavior of organisms.* New York: Appleton-Century-Crofts, 1938.

When Shall We Use Our Heads Instead of the Formula?

Paul E. Meehl

My title question, "When should we use our heads instead of the formula?" is not rhetorical. I am sincerely asking what I see as an important question. I find the two extreme answers to this question, namely, "Always" and "Never," equally unacceptable. But to formulate a satisfactory answer upon the present evidence seems extraordinarily difficult.

I put the question in the practical clinical context. This is where Sarbin put it in his pioneering study 14 years ago, and this is where it belongs. Some critics of my book (5) have repudiated the whole question by saying that, always and necessarily, we use both our heads and the formula. No, we do not. In research, we use both; the best clinical research involves a shuttling back and forth between clever, creative speculation and subsequent statistical testing of empirical derivations therefrom. So far as I am aware, nobody has ever denied this. Even the arch-actuary George Lundberg approved of the clinician as hypothesis-maker. In research one cannot design experiments or concoct theories without using his head, and he cannot test them rigorously without using a formula. This is so obvious that I am surprised to find that people will waste time in discussing it. The clinical-statistical issue can hardly be stated so as to make sense in the re-

Presented at the 1956 Convention of the American Psychological Association, Chicago.

Reprinted by permission of the American Psychological Association and the author from the *Journal of Counseling Psychology*, 1957, **4**, 268–273.

search context, and I should have thought it clear that a meaningful issue can be raised only in the context of daily clinical activity.

In the clinical context, on the other hand, the question is sensible and of great practical importance. Here we have the working clinician or administrator, faced with the necessity to make a decision at *this* moment in time, regarding *this* particular patient. He knows that his evidence is inadequate. He can think of several research projects which, *had* they been done already, would be helpful to him in deciding the present case. If he is research-oriented he may even make a note of these research ideas and later carry them out or persuade someone else to do so. But none of that helps him *now*. He is in a sort of Kierkegaardian existential predicament, because he has to act. As Joe Zubin kept repeating when I last tangled with him on this subject, "Every clinical decision is a *Willensakt*." And so it is; but the question remains, how do we make our *Willensakts* as rational as possible upon limited information? *What clinician X knows today* and *what he could find out by research in ten years* are two very different things.

The question, "When shall we use our heads instead of the formula?" presupposes that we are about to make a clinical decision at a given point in time, and must base it upon what is known to us at that moment. In that context, the question makes perfectly good sense. It is silly to answer it by saying amicably, "We use both methods, they go hand in hand." If the formula and your head invariably yield the same predictions about individuals, you should quit using the more costly one because it is not adding anything. If they don't always yield the same prediction—and they clearly don't, as a matter of empirical fact—then you obviously can't "use both," because you cannot predict in opposite ways for the same case. If one says then, "Well, by 'using both,' I mean that we follow the formula except on special occasions," the problem becomes how to identify the proper subset of occasions. And this of course amounts to the very question I am putting. For example, does the formula tell us "Here, use your heads," or do we rely on our heads to tell us this, thus countermanding the formula?

The Pragmatic Decision Problem Stated

Most decisions in current practice do not pose this problem because no formula exists. Sometimes there is no formula because the prediction problem is too open-ended, as in dream analysis; sometimes the very categorizing of the raw observations involves Gestalted stimulus equivalences for which the laws are unknown, and hence cannot be mathematically formulated (although the clinician himself exemplifies these laws and can therefore "utilize" them); in still other cases there is no formula because nobody has bothered to make one. In any of these three circumstances, we use our heads because there isn't anything else to use. This presumably will be true of many special prediction situations for years to come. The logical analysis of the first two situations— open-endedness and unknown psychological laws—is a fascinating subject in its own right, especially in relation to psychotherapy. But since our original question implies that a formula does exist, we will say no more about that subject here.

Suppose then that we have a predic-

tion equation (or an actuarial table) which has been satisfactorily cross-validated. Let us say that it predicts with some accuracy which patients will respond well to intensive outpatient therapy in our VA clinic. We are forced to make such predictions because our staff-patient ratio physically precludes offering intensive treatment to all cases; also we know that a minority, such as certain latent schizophrenias, react adversely and even dangerously. The equation uses both psychometric and nonpsychometric data. It may include what the Cornell workers called "Stop" items —items given such a huge weight that when present they override any combination of the remaining factors. It may be highly patterned, taking account of verified interaction effects.

So here is veteran Jones, whose case is under consideration at therapy staff. The equation takes such facts as his Rorschach $F+$, his Multiphasic code, his divorce, his age, his 40 per cent service-connection, and grinds out a probability of .75 of "good response to therapy." (The logicians and theoretical statisticians are still arguing over the precise meaning of this number as applied to Jones. But we are safe in saying, "If you accept patients from this population who have this score, you will be right 3 times in 4.") Here is Jones. We want to do what is best for him. We don't *know for sure*, and we can't by any method, actuarial or otherwise. We act on the probabilities, as everyone does who chooses a career, takes a wife, bets on a horse, or brings a lawsuit. (If you object, as some of the more cloud-headed clinikers do, to acting on "mere probabilities," you will have to shut up shop, because probabilities are all you'll ever get.)

But now the social worker tells us that Jones, age 40, said at intake that his mother sent him in. The psychology trainee describes blocking and a bad $F-$ on Rorschach VII; the psychiatrist adds his comments, and pretty soon we are concluding that Jones has a very severe problem with mother-figures. Since our only available therapist is Frau Dr. Schleswig-Holstein, who would traumatize anybody even without a mother-problem, we begin to vacillate. The formula gives us odds of 3 to 1 on Jones; these further facts, not in the equation, raise doubts in our minds. What shall we do?

Importance of "Special Cases"

In my little book on this subject, I gave an example which makes it too easy (5, p. 24). If a sociologist were predicting whether Professor X would go to the movies on a certain night, he might have an equation involving age, academic speciality, and introversion score. The equation might yield a probability of .90 that Professor X goes to the movie tonight. But if the family doctor announced that Professor X had just broken his leg, no sensible sociologist would stick with the equation. Why didn't the factor of "broken leg" appear in the formula? Because broken legs are very rare, and in the sociologist's entire sample of 500 criterion cases plus 250 cross-validiating cases, he did not come upon a single instance of it. He uses the broken leg datum confidently, because "broken leg" is a subclass of a larger class we may crudely denote as "relatively immobilizing illness or injury," and movie-attending is a subclass of a larger class of "actions requiring moderate mobility." There is a universally recognized "subjective experience table" which cuts across sociological and theatrical categories, and the probabilities are so close to zero that not even a sociologist feels an urge to tabulate them! (That this is the correct analysis of matters can be easily seen if we ask what our sociologist would do if he were in a strange culture and had seen *even a few* legs in casts at the movies?)

I suppose only the most anal of actu-aries would be reluctant to abandon the equation in the broken leg case, on the ground that we were unable to cite actual statistical support for the generalization: "People with broken legs don't attend movies." But clinicians should beware of overdoing the broken leg analogy. There are at least four aspects of the broken leg case which are very different from the usual "psychodynamic" reversal of an actuarial prediction. First, a broken leg is a pretty objective fact, determinable with high accuracy, if you care to take the trouble; secondly, its correlation with relative immobilization is near-perfect, based on a huge N, and attested by all sane men regardless of race, creed, color, or what school granted them the doctorate; thirdly, interaction effects are conspicuously lacking—the immobilization phenomenon cuts neatly across the other categories under study; fourthly, the prediction is mediated without use of any doubtful theory, being either purely taxonomic or based upon such low-level theory as can be provided by skeletal mechanics and common sense. The same cannot be said of such an inference as "Patient Jones has an unconscious problem with mother-figures, and male patients with such problems will not react well in intensive therapy with Frau Dr. Schleswig-Holstein."

Theoretical Derivation of Novel Patterns

When the physicists exploded the first atomic bomb, they had predicted a novel occurence by theoretical methods. No actuarial table, based upon thousands of combinations of chemicals, would have led to this prediction. But these kinds of theoretical derivations in the developed sciences involve combining rigorously formulated theories with exact knowledge of the state of the particular system, neither of which we have in clinical psychology. Yet we must do justice to the basic *logical* claim of our clinician. I want to stress that he is not in the untenable position of denying the actuarial data. He freely admits that 75 per cent of patients having Jones' formula score are good bets for therapy. But he says that Jones belongs to the other 25 per cent, and therefore thinks we can avoid one of our formula's mispredictions by countermanding the formula in this case. There is nothing intrinsically wrong with this suggestion. Perhaps the clinician *can* identify a subclass of patients within the class having Jones' actuarial attributes, for which the success rate is less than .5. This would be perfectly compatible with the over-all actuarial data, provided the clinician doesn't claim it too often.

At this point the actuary, a straightforward fellow, proposes that we tabulate the new signs mentioned in staff conference as indicating this subclass before proceeding further. Here we again reduce our clinician to a hypothesis-suggestor, and seem to put the current prediction problem back on an actuarial bases. But wait. Are we really prepared to detail someone to do such "case-oriented" research every time a clinical prediction is made? Actually it is impossible. It would require a superfile of punch-cards of colossal N to be available in each clinic, and several major staff doing nothing but running case-oriented minor studies while clinical conferences went into recess pending the outcomes.

However, this is a "practical" objection. Suppose we circumvent it somehow, so that when a sign or pattern is used clinically to support a counter-actuarial prediction, we can proceed immediately to subject the sign to actuarial test on our clinic files. There are serious difficulties even so. Unless the several staff who produced these records had in mind all of the signs that anybody subsequently brings up, we have no assurance that they were looked for or noted. Anyone who has done file research knows the frustration of having

no basis for deciding when the lack of mention of a symptom indicates its absence. But even ignoring this factor, what if we find only 3 cases in the files who show the pattern? *Any split* among these 3 cases as to therapy outcome is statistically compatible with a wide range of parameter values. We can neither confirm nor refute, at any respectable confidence level, our clinician's claim that this pattern brings the success-probability from .75 to some value under .5 (he doesn't say how far under).

Here the statistician throws up his hands in despair. What, he asks, can you do with a clinician who wants to countermand a known probability of .75 by claiming a subclass probability which we cannot estimate reliably? And, of course, one wonders how many thousands of patients the clinician has seen, to have accumulated a larger sample of the rare configuration. He also is subject to sampling errors, isn't he?

Non-frequentist Probability and Rational Action

This brings us to the crux of the matter. Does the clinician need to have seen *any* cases of "mother-sent-me-in" and Card VII blockage who were treated by female therapists? Here we run into a philosophical issue about the nature of probability. Many logicians (including notably Carnap, Kneale, Sellars, and most of the British school) reject the view (widely held among applied statisticians) that *probability* is always *frequency*. Carnap speaks of "inductive probability," by which he means the logical support given to a hypothesis by evidence. We use this kind of probability constantly, both in science and in daily life. No one knows how to compute it exactly, except for very simple worlds described by artifiical languages. Even so, we cannot get along without it. So our clinician believes that he has inductive evidence from many different sources, on different populations, partly actuarial, partly experimental, partly anecdotal, that there is such a psychological structure as a "mother-surrogate problem." He adduces indirect evidence for the construct validity (1) of Rorschach Card VII reactions. I am not here considering the actual scientific merits of such claims in the clinical field, on which dispute still continues. But I think it important for us to understand the methodological character of the clinician's rebuttal. If Carnap and some of his fellow logicians are right, the idea that *relative frequency* and *probability* are synonymous is a philosophical mistake.

Of course there is an implicit future reference to frequency even in this kind of inductive argument. Carnap identifies inductive probability with the betting odds which a reasonable man should accept. I take this to mean that if the clinician decided repeatedly on the basis of what he thought were high inductive probabilities, and we found him to be wrong most of the time, then he was presumably making erroneous estimates of his inductive probabilities. The claim of a high inductive probability implies an expectation of being right; in the long run, he who (correctly) bets odds of 7:3 will be able to point to a hit-rate of 70 per cent. But this *future* reference to success-frequency is not the same as the *present evidence for* a hypothesis. This seems a difficult point for people to see. As a member of a jury, you might be willing to bet 9 to 1 odds on the prisoner's guilt, and this might be rational of you; yet no calculation of frequencies constituted your inductive support in the present instance. The class of hypotheses where you have assigned an inductive probability of .9 should "pan out" 90 per cent of the time. But the assignment of that inductive probability to each hypothesis need not itself have been

done by frequency methods. If we run a long series on Sherlock Holmes, and find that 95 per cent of his "reconstructions" of crimes turn out to be valid, our confidence in his guesses is good *in part just because they are his.* Yet do we wish to maintain that a rational man, ignorant of these statistics, could form no "probable opinion" about a *particular* Holmesian hypothesis based on the evidence available? I cannot think anyone wants to maintain this.

The philosophical recognition of a nonfrequency inductive probability does not help much to solve our practical problem. No one has quantified this kind of probability (which is one reason why Fisher rejected it as useless for scientific purposes). Many logicians doubt that it can be quantified, even in principle. What then are we to say? The clincian thinks he has "high" (How high? Who knows?) inductive support for his particular theory about Jones. He thinks it is so high that we are rationally justified in assigning Jones to the 25 per cent class permitted by the formula. The actuary doubts this, and the data do not allow a sufficiently senstive statistical test. Whom do we follow?

Monitoring the Clinician

Well, the actuary is not quite done yet. He has been surreptitiously spying upon the clinician for, lo, these many years. The mean old scoundrel has kept a record of the clinician's predictions. What does he find, when he treats the clinician as an empty decision-maker, ignoring the inductive logic going on inside him? Let me bring you up to date on the empirical evidence. As of today, there are 27 empirical studies in the literature which make some meaningful comparison between the predictive success of the clinician and the statistician. The predictive domains include: success in academic or military training, recidivism and parole violation, recovery from psychosis, (concurrent) personality description, and outcome of psychotherapy. Of these 27 studies, 17 show a definite superiority for the statistical method; 10 show the methods to be of about equal efficiency; none of them show the clinician predicting better. I have reservations about some of these studies; I do not believe they are optimally designed to exhibit the clinician at his best; but I submit that it is high time that those who are so sure that the "right kind of study" will exhibit the clinician's prowess, should *do* this right kind of study and back up their claim with evidence. Futhermore, *a good deal of routine clinical prediction is going on all over the country in which the data available, and the intensity of clinical contact, are not materially different from that in the published comparisons.* It is highly probable that current predictive methods are costly to taxpayers and harmful to the welfare of patients.

Lacking quantification of inductive probability, we have no choice but to examine the clinician's success-rate. One would hope that the rule-of-thumb assessment of inductive probability is not utterly unreliable. The indicated research step is therefore obvious: We persuade the clinician to state the odds, or somehow rate his "confidence," in his day-to-day decisions. Even if he tends over-all to be wrong when countermanding the actuary, he may still tend to be systematically right for a high-confidence sub-set of his predictions. Once having proved this, we could thereafter countermand the formula in cases where the clinician expresses high confidence in his head. It is likely that studies in a great diversity of domains will be required before useful generalizations can be made.

In the meantime, we are all continuing to make predictions. I think it is safe to say, on the present evidence, that we are not as good as we thought we were. The development of powerful actuarial methods could today proceed more rapidly than ever before. Both theoretical and empirical considerations suggest that we would be well advised to concentrate effort on improving our actuarial techniques rather than on the calibration of each clinician for each of a large number of different prediction problems. How should we meanwhile be making our decisions? Shall we use our heads, or shall we follow the formula? Mostly we will use our heads, because there just isn't any formula, but suppose we have a formula, and a case comes along in which it disagrees with our heads? Shall we then use our heads? I would say, yes—provided the psychological situation is as clear as a broken leg; otherwise, very *very* seldom.

REFERENCES

1. CRONBACH, L. J., & MEEHL, P. E. Construct validity in psychological tests. *Psychol. Bull.,* 1955, **52,** 281–302.
2. HUMPHREYS, L. G., McARTHUR, C. C., MEEHL, P. E., SANFORD, N., & ZUBIN, J. Clinical versus actuarial prediction. *Proceedings of the 1955 Invitational Conference on Testing Problems,* pp. 91–141.
3. McARTHUR, C. C. Analyzing the clinical process. *J. counsel. Psychol.,* 1954, **1,** 203–207.
4. McARTHUR, C. C., MEEHL, P. E., & TIEDEMAN, D. V. Symposium on clinical and statistical prediction. *J. counsel Psychol.,* 1956, **3,** 163–173.
5. MEEHL, P. E. *Clinical versus statistical prediction; a theoretical analysis and a review of the evidence.* Minneapolis: Univer. of Minn. Press, 1954.
6. MEEHL, P. E. Comment on Analyzing the Clinical process. *J. counsel. Psychol.,* 1954, **1,** 207–208.
7. MEEHL, P. E. Wanted—a good cook-

book. *Amer. Psychologist*, 1956, 11, 263–272.

8. MEEHL, P. E., & ROSEN, A. Antecedent probability and the efficiency of psy-chometric signs, patterns, or cutting scores. *Psychol. Bull.*, 1955, 52, 194–216.

Clinical *and* Statistical Prediction: A Reformulation and Some New Data

Robert R. Holt

The controversial discussions started a few years ago by Meehl's tightly packed little book *Clinicial vs. Statistical Prediction* (10) still continue—especially among graduate students in psychology, most of whom have to read it. Clinical students in particular complain of a vague feeling that a fast one has been put over on them, that under a great show of objectivity, or at least bipartisanship, Professor Meehl has actually sold the clinical approach up the river. The specific complaints they lodge against the book are, in my opinion, mostly based on misinterpretations, wishful thinking, or other errors, yet I have felt for some time that there was something valid in the irrational reaction without knowing why.

What I propose to show here is that clinicians do have a kind of justified grievance against Meehl, growing out of his formulation of the issues rather than his arguments, which are sound. Finally, I want to offer a slightly different approach to the underlying problems, illustrated by some data. It may not quite make the lion lie down with the lamb, but I hope that it will help us all get on with our business, which is the making of a good science and profession.

The Issues Restated

Meehl's book contains a review of the controversy, a logical analysis of the nature of clinical judgment, a survey of empirical studies, and some conclusions. I am not going to go into his treatment of the logical issues and his psychological reconstruction of clinical thinking; for the most part, I agree with this part of the book and consider it a useful contribution to methodolgy. I want to focus rather on his conception of what the issues are in the controversy, on his treatment of the evidence, and on some of his conclusions.

Many issues make better reading when formulated as battles, and the field of the assessment and prediction of human behavior has not lacked for controversy-loving gauntlet-flingers. The sane and thoughtful voices of Horst and his collaborators, urging compromise and collaboration (5), have been shouted

The research reported in this paper was supported by the Veterans' Administration, the New York Foundation, and the Menninger Foundation, and was carried out jointly by Dr. Lester Luborsky and the author, with the collaboration of Drs. Wm. R. Morrow, David Rapaport, and S. K. Escalona.

Reprinted by permission of the American Psychological Association and the author from the *Journal of Abnormal and Social Psychology*, 1958, **56**, 1–12.

down by the warcries of such partisans as Sarbin (14) on the actuarial side and Murray (12) on the clinical or (as he put it) organismic. Meehl approached the problem with a full awareness of the feelings on both sides, and apparently with the hope that the therapeutic ploy of bringing them all out into the open at the beginning would enable him to discuss the issues objectively.

In a recent discussion of the stir his book has raised, Meehl has expressed surprise and dismay (11) that his effort to take a balanced and qualified position has led so many people to misunderstand him as claiming that clinical prediction has been proved worthless. Yet he is not blameless; by posing the question of clinical *vs.* statistical prediction, he has encouraged two warring camps to form. This in turn makes it appear all the more compellingly that there *are* two clear-cut types of prediction to be compared.

The root difficulty, I believe, lies in Meehl's acceptance of *clinical* and *actuarial* as concepts that can without further analysis be meaningfully applied to a variety of predictive endeavors of an experimental or practical sort. Accepting them as valid types, he can hardly do anything other than pit one against the other and try to decide what is the proper sphere of exercise for each. But the terms in this antithesis mean many things; they are constellations of parts that are not perfectly correlated and can be separated.

The issue cannot therefore be sharply drawn so long as we speak about anything as complex as "clinical prediction" or "the clinical method." Rather, I think the central issue is the *role of clinical judgment in predicting human behavior.* By clinical judgment here, I mean nothing more complicated than the problem-solving or decision-reaching behavior of a person who tries to reach conclusions on the basis of facts and theories already available to him by thinking them over.

Let us make a fresh start, therefore, by examining the logical structure of the predictive process with an eye to locating the points where clinical judgment may enter. The following five-step process is idealized, and in practice some of the steps are more or less elided, but that does not hurt this analysis.

First, if we are to predict some kind of behavior, it is presupposed that we acquaint ourselves with what we are trying to predict. This may be called job analysis or the study of the criterion. Perhaps those terms sound a little fancy when their referent is something that seems so obvious to common sense. Nevertheless, it is surprising how often people expend a great deal of time and effort trying to predict a kind of behavior about which they know very little and apparently without even thinking that it might help if they could find out more. Consider the job of predicting outcome of flight training, for example. Many attempts to predict passing or washing out have been made by clinicians without any direct experience in learning to fly, without any study of flight trainees to see what they have to *do* in order to learn how to fly a plane, or of the ways they can fail to make the grade (cf. 4).

There is a hidden trick in predicting something like success in flight training, because that is not itself a form of behavior. It is an outcome, a judgment passed by someone on a great deal of concrete behavior. The same is true for grades in college, success in any type of treatment, and a host of other criteria that are the targets in most predictive studies. Because it is hidden by the label, there is a temptation to forget that the behavior you should be trying to predict exists and must be studied if it is to be rationally forecast. In the highly effective pilot selection work carried out by psychologists during the war, careful job analyses were an important step in the total predictive process and undoubtedly contributed a good deal to the over-all success.

This first stage is hardly a good point at which to try to rely on clinical judgment. The result is most likely to be that guesses, easy and arbitrary assumptions, and speculative extrapolations will attempt to substitute for real information. And no matter how remarkable clinical judgment may sometimes be, it can never create information where there is none.

The *second* logical step is to decide what intervening variables need to be considered if the behavior is to be predicted. As soon as we get away from the simplest kind of prediction—that someone will continue to act the way he has been acting, or that test behavior A will continue to correlate (for an unknown reason) with criterion behavior B—we have to deal with the inner constructs that mediate behavior and the determining situational variables as well. You cannot make a rational choice of the kind of information you will need to have about a person to make predictions without some intervening variables, though they may remain entirely implicit. At this point, judgment enters—always, I think, though it may be assisted by empirical study. The best practice seems to be to give explicit consideration to this step, and to supply judgment with as many relevant facts as possible. This means studying known instances, comparing people who showed the behavior in question with others who in the same situation failed to.

All too often, when the problem of intervening variables is considered at all, it is handled by unaided clinical judgment. For example, in the Michigan project on the selection of clinical psychologists (7), a good many personality variables were rated, but there was no previous work highlighting the ones that might be related to success as a clinical psychologist. It was left up to each judge to form his own conception (from ex-

perience, theory, and guess) about what qualities mattered most. Again, this puts a greater burden on clinical judgment than it should reasonably be asked to bear. Yet some clinicians seem to have the mistaken notion that they are being false to their professional ideals if they stir from their armchairs at this point; nothing could be further from the best in clinical tradition, which is unashamedly empirical.

Third, it is necessary to find out what types of data afford measures or indications of the intervening variables, and can thus be used to predict the criterion behavior. If a good job has been done of the preceding step, it may be possible to rely entirely on judgment to make the preliminary selection of appropriate means of gathering predictive data. For example, if a job analysis and study of persons who have done well at the performance in question both suggest that verbal intelligence and information of a certain type are the main requisites, it would be easy to make good guesses about appropriate instruments to provide the predictive data. I use the word "guesses" deliberately, however, to emphasize the fact that judgment can do no more than supply hypotheses; it cannot substitute for an empirical trial to see whether in fact and under the conditions of this particular study the likely-looking instruments do yield data that predict the criterion.

Notice that almost any actuarial predictive system presupposes carrying through this step. If there is to be an actuarial table, one has to collect great numbers of cases to determine the success frequencies for each cell in the table; if a regression equation is to be used, there must be a preliminary study to fix the beta weights. Unfortunately, it is possible to work clinically *without* first getting an empirical check on one's hypotheses about likely-seeming instruments. At the risk of boring you, I repeat: there simply is no substitute for empirical study of the actual association between a type of predictive data and the criterion. Just as judgment is indispensable in forming hypotheses, it cannot be used to test them.

Perhaps this caution seems misplaced. Do I seem to be urging that you should first *do* a predictive study before embarking on one? I am. That is exactly what happens in actuarial prediction: the formula or table being pitted against judgmental prediction is typically being *cross*-validated, while in none of the studies Meehl cites were the clinical predictions under test being cross-validated. This alone is a major reason to expect superior performance from the actuarial predictions, and again it is a disadvantage under which the clinician by no means has to labor.

The next step, the *fourth* one, is to gather and process the data to give measures of the intervening variables. Meehl clearly recognizes that at this point clinical judgment either may play a large role or may be minimized. At one extreme, the data-yielding instrument may be a machine, a gadget like a complex coordination tester, which automatically counts errors and successes and makes a cumulative record of them. The resulting numbers may be directly usable in a regression equation without the intervention of anyone more skilled than a clerk. At an intermediate level, scoring most psychological tests requires a modicum of clinical judgment, though a high degree of reliability may be attained. At the other extreme is the interview; a great deal of clinical judgment is needed to convert the raw data into indices of the constructs the interviewer wants to assess.

It is easily overlooked that judgment needs the help of empirical study in this phase of the work too. The clinician's training supplies this empirical base in large part, but when he is using a familiar instrument to measure unusual intervening variables, or when he is working with an unfamiliar instrument,

judgment grows fallible, and it is no more than prudent to piece it out by careful study of the same kind of predictive data on known subjects on whom the intervening variables have been well assessed independently.

The *fifth* and final step is the crucial one: at last the processed predictive data are *combined* so as to yield definite predictions in each case. The job can be done by clinical judgment, or it can be done by following a fixed rule (an actuarial table or regression equation) in a mechanical way. That much is clear; indeed, this is the locus of Meehl's main interest. I am taking it as granted that a clinician often integrates data in a different way than a statistician—as Meehl says, by performing a creative act, constructing a model of the person from the given facts put together with his theoretical understanding and thus generating perhaps a new type of prediction from a pattern he has never encountered before. We are all curious to know how well good clinicians can do it, and wonder if actuarial combination of data can do as well or better.

But it now seems plain that Meehl has been *too much* interested in this last stage, and as a result has neglected to pay enough attention to the way the earlier aspects of the predictive process were handled in the studies he has reviewed. Here I want to state my main critical point: *If two attempts to predict the same behavior differ significantly in the role played by clinical judgment as against actual study of the facts in one or more of the four earlier parts of the predictive process, a comparison of the successes of the two attempts can tell us nothing definite about the effectiveness of clinical judgment at the final, crucial stage.* For this reason, in none of the 20 studies Meehl cites were the comparisons pertinent to the point. Particularly at the vital third step, the predicting statisticians have had the advantage of having previously studied the way their predictive data are related to the criterion; the clinicians have not.

If your reaction is, "So much the worse for the clinicians; nobody stopped them," I am afraid you are thinking about a different question from the one Meehl has raised. If the issue were whether some clinicians have made themselves look foolish by claiming too much, then I should agree: these studies show that they have, and unhappily, they have brought discredit on clinical methods generally. But the studies cited by Meehl and more recently by Cronbach in the *Annual Review of Psychology* (2) unfortunately have too many flaws at other points to tell us what clinical judgment can or cannot do as a way of combining data to make predictions. It is as if two riflemen were having a target match, but one took a wrong turn on the way to the shoot, never showed up, and lost by default. He demonstrated himself to be a poor driver, perhaps, but we never found out how well he could shoot, which is what we really wanted to know.

The other point I want to make in connection with the five-step analysis of the predictive process is this: Since there are so many ways in which clinical judgment can enter, for better or for worse, it makes little sense to classify every attempt to predict behavior on one side or the other of a simple dichotomy, clinical vs. statistical. There can be many types of clinical and actuarial combinations, and many are in fact found in Meehl's mixed bag.

For purposes of exposition, I should like to suggest an only slightly extended typology. Extracting from the best actuarial studies those parts of their procedure during the first four steps that are simply the application of common sense and the scientific method, I propose that we make it quite plain that these can be separated from actuarial prediction at the final step by creating a third type. Thus we should have:

Type I. *Pure actuarial:* Only objective data are used to predict a clear-cut crite-rion by means of statistical processes. The role of judgment is held to a minimum, and maximal use is made of a sequence of steps exemplified in the most successful Air Force studies in selecting air crew personnel (job analysis, item analysis, cross-validation, etc.).

Type II. *Naive clinical:* The data used are primarily qualitative with no attempt at objectification; their processing is entirely a clinical and intuitive matter, and there is no prior study of the criterion or of the possible relation of the predictive data to it. Clinical judgment is at every step relied on not only as a way of integrating data to produce predictions, but also as an alternative to acquaintance with the facts.

Type III. *Sophisticated clinical:* Qualitative data from such sources as interviews, life histories, and projective techniques are used as well as objective facts and scores, but as much as possible of objectivity, organization, and scientific method are introduced into the planning, the gathering of the data, and their analysis. All the refinements of design that the actuarial tradition has furnished are employed, including job analysis, pilot studies, item analysis, and successive cross-validations. Quantification and statistics are used wherever helpful, but the clinician himself is retained as one of the prime instruments, with an effort to make him as reliable and valid a data-processor as possible; and he makes the final organization of the data to yield a set of predictions tailored to each individual case.

If we now re-examined the studies cited by Meehl and Cronbach, we see that most of them have pitted approximations to Type I actuarial predictive designs against essentially Type II naive clinical approaches. It seems hardly remarkable that Type I has generally given better results than Type II; indeed, the wonder should be that the naive clinical predictions have done as well as they have, in a number of instances aproaching the predictive efficiency of actuarial systems.

Other studies cited have come closer to comparing Type II with Type III— naive vs. sophisticated clinical prediction instead of clinical vs. statistical. For example, the prognostic studies by Wittman (16) compared predictions of reaction to shock treatment made in a global way at staff conference with a system she devised. But her system used highly judgmental predictive variables, as Meehl himself points out (ranging from *duration of psychosis to anal erotic vs. oral erotic*), and they were combined using a set of weights assigned on judgmental, not statistical grounds.[1] What she showed was that a systematic and comprehensive evaluation of the thirty items in her scale (all based on previous empirical work) made better predictions of the outcome of shock treatment than global clinical judgments not so organized and guided. A study of movement in family case work by Blenkner came to a very similar conclusion with somewhat different subject matter (1). When social workers rated an initial interview according to their general impressions, they were unable to predict the outcome of the case, whereas when their judgments were organized and guided by means of an outline calling for appraisals of five factors which had been shown in previous studies to be *meaningfully*, not statistically related to the criterion, then these judgmentally derived predictive variables, combined (like Wittman's) in an a priori formula, predicted the criterion quite well. Yet both studies are tallied as proving actuarial predictions superior to clinical.

Meehl's conclusion from his review of this "evidence" is that clinical prediction is an expensive and inefficient substitute for the actuarial method, and one that keeps clinicians from using their talents more constructively in psychotherapy or exploratory research.

The evidence available tells us hardly anything about the relative efficacy of clinical judgment in making predictions. The weight of numbers should not impress us; as long as the studies don't really bear on the issue, no matter how many are marshalled, they still have no weight. Remember the *Literary Digest* poll: many times more straw votes than Gallup used, but a faulty sampling principle, so that piling up numbers made the conclusion less valid as it got more reliable. Moreover, the studies tallied are so different in method, involving varying amounts of clinical judgment at different points (in the "actuarial" instances as well as the "clinical" ones), that they cannot sensibly be added together.

What is fair to conclude, I think, is that many clinicians are wasting their time when they try to fall back on their clinical judgment in place of knowing what they are talking about. They have been guilty of over-extending themselves, trying to predict things they know nothing about, and learning nothing in the process of taking part in what Cronbach calls "horserace experimental designs," in which clinicians and statisticians merely try to outsmart each other. A multiplication of such studies will not advance clinical psychology.

One kind of comparative study might teach us something even though it would be hard to do properly: simultaneous attempts to predict the same criterion from the same data by clinicians and statisticians *who have gone through the same preliminary steps.* As the statistician studies the original group to determine the critical scores for his multiple cutting point formula (or whatever), the clinician will study the configurations of these scores in individuals of known performance. Then we will see how their respective predictive techniques work.

Does it really make sense, however, for both to use the same data and predict the same criterion? A second possibility would be for two otherwise equally sophisticated methods to predict the same criterion, each using the kind

---

[1] It is true that the weights were applied in the same way for all cases; in this respect, the system deviates from the ideal Type III.

of data most appropriate to it. Or, third, the more clinical and the more statistical methods would not predict the same criterion, but each would undertake to predict the kind of behavior it is best suited to, using the most appropriate kind of data.

Doesn't this third proposal abandon experimental controls necessary for intelligible results? To some extent, yes; but one may have to give up some control to avoid absurdity. As long as clinician and statistician are trying to predict the same criterion, the clinician is likely to be working under a severe, though concealed, handicap. The study will usually have been designed by the statistician; that is his business. He will naturally choose the kind of criterion for which his methods seem best adapted; indeed, the nature of his method makes it impossible for him to choose the kind of predictive task that would be most congenial to the clinician, such as drawing a multidimensional diagnostic picture of a total personality, or predicting what a patient will do next in psychotherapy. Thus, the statistician takes advantage of the foolish boast of the clinician, "Anything you can do, I can do better," and plans the contest on his own grounds. The clinician ends up trying to predict grade-point average in the freshman year by a "clinical synthesis" of high school grades and an intelligence test. This is a manifest absurdity; under the circumstances, how could the clinician do other than operate like a second-rate Hollerith machine? If clinical judgment is really to be tested, it must operate on data that are capable of yielding insights. Moreover, it makes hardly any more sense to expect it to grind out numerical averages of course grades than to expect an actuarial table to interpret dreams.

For reasons of this kind, McArthur (9) recently called for studies of the third type just listed, and maintained that there have as yet been no studies in which the clinician has been given a chance to show what he can do on his own terms. I want therefore to present briefly some results from one such attempt: a study in which clinicians tried to predict criteria of their own choosing, using clinical types of data—interviews and psychological tests (mainly projective techniques).[2] Since some preliminary reports of this work have already been quoted as showing the ineffectiveness of clinical predictions (cf. 2), I have a special desire to set the record straight.

Validating Naive and Sophisticated Clinical Predictions: Some New Data

The project was an effort to improve the methods by which medical men were selected for specialty training in the Menninger School of Psychiatry. It was begun by Dr. David Rapaport, together with Drs. Karl A. Menninger, Robert P. Knight, and other psychiatrists at the Menninger Foundation at the time the Menninger School of Psychiatry was founded 11 years ago. In the late summer of 1947, Dr. Lester Luborsky and I began work on it, and since then we have jointly carried major responsibility for the project although quite a number of other people have made important contributions.

Our work consisted of two predictive studies. Following the terminology suggested above, one used a naive clinical method, while the other was an attempt at a more sophisticated clinical method. The naive clinical design was simple: Psychiatrists and psychologists used their favorite means of assessing personality to forecast the level of future performance of psychiatric residents at the time when they applied to the School. The applicant came to Topeka after some preliminary correspondence, having survived a rough screening of credentials and application forms. He was seen by three psychiatrists, each of

[2] This study is presented at length in a forthcoming book (3).

whom interviewed him for about an hour, rated his probable success as a resident on a 10-point scale, and made a recommendation: Take, Reject, or Doubtful. The psychologist made similar ratings and recommendations after analyzing results of a Wechsler-Bellevue, Rorschach, and Work Association test. In addition, both psychologists and psychiatrists submitted brief qualitative reports of their appraisals of the man's positive and negative potentialities. All of the data and predictions were turned over to the Admissions Committee, which made the final decision to accept or reject each man.

During the years of the project, from 1946 through 1952, six successive classes of residents were chosen. The first 456 applicants who went through this procedure formed our experimental population (excluding small numbers of Negroes, women, and persons from Latin-American and non-European cultures, since these minorities offered special problems of assessment). A little over 62 per cent of these applicants were accepted by the Committee, but only 238 actually entered the School; 46 changed their minds and went elsewhere. Nevertheless, we kept in touch with them and the 172 rejectees by a mail follow-up questionnaire for several years, so that we have data on certain aspects of their subsequent careers.

The clinicians making the predictions had in some cases had considerable experience in training psychiatric residents, but there was no explicit job analysis or preliminary study of criterion groups. They simply fell to and made their predictions and their decisions.

To test the validity of these clinical decisions, let us use as a criterion, first, whether or not a man passed the certifying examination of the American Board of Psychiatry and Neurology—the criterion set up by the specialty itself. We have this information on all subjects from the lists published by the Board. The Admissions Committee's decisions had a good deal of validity as predictors of this criterion: 71 per cent of the men they voted to accept had passed the Board examination in psychiatry by the end of 1956, while only 36 per cent of the rejected candidates had done so. This difference is significant at better than the .001 point. The recommendations made by interviewers (taking them all as a group) and the recommendations of the psychological testers to accept or reject likewise were highly valid predictors of this criterion, significances in both cases also being beyond .001.

It is interesting that the Committee decisions were slightly *better* at predicting both staying in psychiatry and passing the certification examination of the American Board of Psychiatry and Neurology—better than either the psychiatric interviewers or the psychological testers. It is possible, however, that much or all of this apparent superiority is due to the fact that rejection by the Committee did discourage a few applicants from seeking training elsewhere.

Data of this kind are encouraging to the people trying to run a school of psychiatry but hard to interpret in a larger context. Who knows but that an actuarial table based on objectively ascertainable facts like grades in medical school, marital status, age, etc. might not have done just as well? We never took such a possibility very seriously, but we did try out a few such objective predictors in our spare time, just out of curiosity. None of them showed any particular promise as a predictor of any criterion taken alone, though it is possible that patterns of them such as an actuarial table uses might have operated a little better than chance.

The criteria on which we spent most time and labor were measures of competence in psychiatric work during the last two years of the three-year residency. Whenever a resident completed a period of time on a particular service, we would interview the staff men, consultants, and others who had directly supervised his clinical work, and get them to rate it quantitatively. The resulting criterion measure had a coefficient of internal consistency above .9[3] (for the last few classes), and we have every reason to think it has a great deal of intrinsic validity. We also got the residents to rate each other's work. The reliability of their pooled ratings of over-all competence is also .9, and this criterion (which we call "Peers' Evaluations") correlates from .66 to .78 with Supervisors' Evaluations.

These criterion judgments enable us to test the validity of the predictive *ratings*. The validity correlations are not exciting, though for the entire group of residents in the Menninger School of Psychiatry they are all significantly better than zero at the one percent point. Taking the *mean* of the ratings given by the psychiatrists who interviewed an applicant, this predictor correlates .24 with Supervisors' Evaluations. The predictions of the psychological testers were not significantly better: the validity coefficient is .27. There was some fluctuation from class to class, the interviewers' validities varying from exactly .00 to .52, the tester's validities from .12 to .47. Likewise, the validities of ratings made by individual clinicians vary over the same range: psychiatric interviewers from .01 to .27 $(N = 93)$ or .47 (significant at only the 5 per cent point because the N was only 13), and psychologists from .20 to .41 $(N = 40)$. At the same time, those individual clinicians all did much better in making the basic discrimination: recommending acceptance of men who actually became psychiatrists.

These correlations are nothing to get excited about, and nothing to be ashamed of either, particularly in view of the restriction of range in this se-

[3] Correlations in bold type are significant at the one per cent point, those in italics, at the five per cent point. One-tailed tests are used throughout to test the null hypothesis that the predictor does not correlate *positively* with the criterion.

lected, accepted sample. They show that the naive clinical method depends a good deal on the ability of the particular clinician doing the predicting, and that—at least in this study—a pooling of judgment helped make up for the deficiencies of individuals.

Let us turn now to the second experimental design, which I have called a *sophisticated clinical* type of prediction. I shall have to skip lightly over many complicated details, and make things look a little more orderly than they actually were. The design included a job analysis of the work done by psychiatric residents, which was broken down into a few major functions (such as diagnosis, psychotherapy, administration of wards) and 14 more specific aspects of work. Then we attempted to specify attributes of personality that would facilitate or hinder a man in carrying out such work, first by collecting the opinions of persons who had had long experience in training psychiatrists, psychotherapists, or psychoanalysts. The second way we went about it was to make an intensive study of a dozen excellent residents and a dozen who were rated at the bottom by their supervisors. We went over all the original assessment data on them, interviewed them and tested them extensively, trying out many novel approaches and then seeing what discriminated these known extreme groups. Thus, we learned what personological constructs differentiated good from poor residents, and what tests and test indicators gave evidence of these constructs. Hoping to guide clinical judgment in the use of interviews and projective tests, we used the data from these small samples of extremes to help us write detailed manuals on the use of the interview, TAT, Rorschach, and other techniques in the selection of psychiatric residents. The manuals listed discriminating cues, both positive and negative, which were to be summed algebraically. We then made preliminary cross-validations of these manuals (as many as we could) with encouraging results (cf. 8) and revised them after studying predictive successes and failures.

As a last step, we set up another predictive study to submit our manuals to a final cross-validation on a group of 64 subjects and to accomplish several other purposes at the same time. Four psychologists served as judges; each of them scored tests or interviews according to our manuals and also made free clinical judgments based on increasing amounts of data. Two of the judges made such predictive ratings after going through an entire file of assessment data: credentials, intellectual and projective tests, and a recorded and transcribed interview.

How did we make out? Considering first the manuals, only indifferently well. Of the six, two proved worthless (TAT Content and a special projective test); the other four all showed more or less promise, but there was none that yielded consistently significant validities regardless of who used it. Reliability, in terms of scorer agreement, was on the whole not very good, for a good deal of clinical judgment was still demanded. Consider, for example, one TAT cue that worked well for one judge (validity of .26 against Supervisor's Evaluations of Overall Competence). This cue called for judgments of the *originality* of each TAT story, obviously a matter on which psychologists might fairly easily disagree: scores by Judges I and II correlated −.04. The validities attained by the manuals for the Interview, Rorschach, Formal Aspects of the TAT, and Self-Interpretation of the TAT were on about the same general level as those from our first, naive clinical design— mostly in the .20's.

Now for the free clinical predictive ratings. When the judge had only one test or an interview to go on he usually added little by going beyond the manual and drawing on his general experience and intuition. Some judges did slightly

better with free ratings than with manual scores, some a little worse. At this point, you may wonder at all this exposition for so small a result: barely significant validity coefficients, about the same size as those from a naive clinical approach, despite the attempt to create a sophisticated clinical predictive system that involved many actuarial elements. I believe that the lesson of our findings up to this point is simple: *With an inadequate sample of information about a person, no matter how sophisticated the technique of prediction, there is a low ceiling on the predictive validity that can be attained.* In our experience, even a battery of two or three tests (if exclusively projective), or an interview and a couple of projective techniques, does not give an adequate informational sample to enable clinicians to make very accurate predictions of complex behavioral outcomes over a period of three years.

Look next at the results when experimental judges made their predictions from as complete a body of information about a man as could be assembled at the time he applied. The hard-headed statistical expectation *should* be that validities would at best remain at the same level, and more likely would decline. The widely read preliminary report of the Michigan project on the selection of clinical psychologists (6) reported declining validities as increasing amounts of information were made available to judges (in a design which, for all its complexity, was essentially a naive clinical one). Not so many people have read the full final report (7), where this issue is not discussed; it is necessary to pore over many tables and tally numbers of significant correlations at various stages to find out for oneself that with the final criteria there was a slight *rising* trend in validities of clinical predictions as the amount of information available to the predicting judge was increased.

The same thing is true of our results,

TABLE 1. SOME VALIDITIES FROM SYSTEMATIC CLINICAL ASSESSMENT OF APPLICANTS FOR RESIDENCIES IN THE MENNINGER SCHOOL OF PSYCHIATRY

| | Validities of Predictors Against Criterion Evaluations of: | | | | | | | | | |
| Predictors: | Overall Competence | | Competence in Psychotherapy | | Competence in Diagnosis | | Competence in Management | | Competence in Administration | |
	Sup.[a]	Peer[a]	Sup.	Peer	Sup.	Peer	Sup.	Peer	Sup.	Peer
Predictive Ratings										
Judge I: PRT[b]	.26	.23	.12	.26	.13	.21	.31	.00	.20	.10
Judge II: TAT	−.10	−.02	−.16	−.01	−.05	.20	−.08	.01	.04	.11
Judge I: All data	.57	.52	.48	.55	.58	.42	.52	.36	.55	.42
Judge II: All data	.22	.48	.15	.36	.24	.42	.13	.24	.24	.27
Liking Ratings										
Judge I: PRT	.29	.34	.16	.35	.24	.36	.15	.17	.19	.16
Judge II: TAT	−.02	.13	−.08	.15	.00	.30	−.17	−.02	−.14	.10
Judge I: All data	.58	.64	.45	.58	.51	.52	.52	.52	.50	.46
Judge II: All data	.25	.49	.20	.47	.21	.56	.10	.30	.18	.30

a Sup. = Supervisors' Evaluation; Peer = Peers' (Sociometric) Evaluations.
b PRT = Picture Reaction Test, a specially devised projective test similar to TAT.
Numbers of cases: For Judge I—Supervisors' Evaluations, PRT: 63, all data: 87
                   Peers' Evaluations, PRT: 45, all data: 30
For Judge II—Supervisors' Evaluations, TAT: 63, all data: 64
                   Peers' Evaluations, TAT: 45, all data: 46

but in a dramatic and unmistakable way (see Table 1). Considering only the two judges who went through the entire mass of material, their final free clinical ratings of Over-all Competence correlated **.57** and *.22* with Supervisors' Evaluations and **.52** and **.48** with the sociometric Peers' Evaluations. In considering these correlations, remember that they are attenuated by a significant restriction of range, since all subjects had successfully passed through an Admissions Committee screening which had considerable validity. They have not been corrected for less than perfect reliabilities, either.

An incidental finding is even more remarkable. The predictive analysis was made approximately a year after the assessment data had been gathered. The judges went right through the entire series of cases, making their ratings in a *blind* analysis; names and other identifying data were concealed, and there was no direct contact with the subjects. Nevertheless, judges formed rather vivid impressions from the material, including a feeling of how well they would like each candidate personally. For control purposes, they were required to rate this feeling of *liking*. When we undertook to correlate the liking rating with predictors and criteria so as to partial out this possible source of error, we found that it was the best predictor we had! These ratings of liking by Judges I and II correlated highly with their predictive ratings, but even more highly with Supervisors' Evaluations (**.58** and *.25*) and especially with Peers' Evaluations (**.64** and **.49**).[4] A study of these

liking ratings suggests to us as the most plausible explanation that they differed from our intentional clinical predictions in being somewhat more irrational, affective—perhaps intuitive—reactions to the same data.

In all of the correlations I have been citing, you will perhaps have noticed that one judge consistently did slightly better than the other. This is certainly to be expected. When clinical judgment is the main technique of processing data, there are bound to be differences due to the skill of clinicians in doing this particular job.

Are we justified in citing these few high validities as evidence of what the sophisticated clinical method can do in a study where it is given a chance to prove itself on grounds of its own choosing? I believe that we are. The psychologists who were our Judges I and II were considered to be good but not extraordinary clinicians, certainly no better than the best of the psychologists and psychiatrists who made the "naive clinical" predictions. They differed principally in that they had an adequate sample of data and had been through

---

[4] One consequence of the delay between the gathering of the data and their analysis was that some of the Ss who entered the Menninger School of Psychiatry became known to the predictive judges, raising the possibility of contamination of their predictions by criterion-relevant knowledge. Despite the fact that the analysis of the assessment material was done "blind," identifying data having been removed or concealed, Judge I fairly often recognized the identity of Ss at the final stage of analysis. He therefore did

not make predictive ratings, which is why his Ns are so low for this stage. There were a few borderline instances of partial or questionable recognition, however, in which Judge I (four cases) or II (two cases) had some information or misinformation about the subject. If these cases are eliminated, Judge II's validities go up more often than they go down, the range being from a decrease of .16 to an increase of .15. Judge I's validities against Supervisor's Evaluations are negligibly affected, the range of effects extending from a loss of .08 to a gain of .20. Most of his validities against Peers' Evaluations were more seriously affected, however, especially at the final (all-data) stage of analysis, where losses of up to 28 correlation points occurred. On the whole, however, even a very conservative handling of the problem of possibly contaminated cases does not change the essential import of the results: It was still possible for Judge I to obtain four validities of **.50** or higher, and for Judge II to obtain two validities of **.36** or higher. (For a fuller discussion of the problem of contamination in these results, see [3].)

all the preliminary stages of studying the criterion in relation to the predictors in earlier groups of subjects. Moreover, they used systematic methods of analyzing the data, attempting to record all inferences and working with a set of intervening variables—personality constructs which were directly inferred from the test and interview data, and from which in turn the behavioral predictions were made. In a true sense, their clinical ratings were not naively based on unguided and uncontrolled judgment; they constituted a cross-validation of a whole structure of hypotheses about the determinants of psychiatric performance based on intensive prior study. Even so, our study left a great deal to be desired as a model of the sophisticated clinical approach— particularly on the scores of (a) a better job analysis, (b) a more broadly based, configurational approach to the design of manuals, and (c) a better stabilized criterion (see 3).

By way of contrast, a few more data before a final summing up. You remember that the battery of tests used in the first naive clinical predictive design consisted of the Wechsler-Bellevue, Rorschach, and Word Association tests. (The Szondi was also given, but was usually ignored; and the Strong Vocational Interest Blank was also routinely given, but was never scored in time to be used in the actual assessment for the Admissions Committee.) The Rorschachs we gave were of course scored in the conventional way as well as by our special manual, and we thought it might be fun to see how some of the usual Rorschach scores would be related to the criterion. So we tried 14 scores and simple indices (like A%) with one class, and were surprised to find some rather high correlations. We decided therefore to see how a straight statistical-actuarial method of using the Rorschach would perform. Scrutinizing the table of intercorrelations between the Rorschach scores, we chose five of them that prom-

ised the greatest chances of success: DR%, number of good M, new F+%, F% and Stereotype% (scored after Rapaport, 13)—the last two because they looked as if they might be good "suppressor variables." A multiple regression equation was worked out to give the best linear combination of these variables to predict Over-all Competence; R for this Class was .43 ($N = 64$). We noticed, however, that in the regression equation only the first two scores seemed to be playing any appreciable part, and in fact the multiple correlation using only per cent of rare details and number of good M was also .43. The other three were dropped from the formula, which was then tested on the Rorschach scores and criterion ratings of the first three classes. As expected, the correlation dropped out of sight on being cross-validated; with the new group of 116 subjects, it was .04.

The Strong Vocational Interest Blank, which (with an intelligence test) gave the best validities in the Kelly-Fiske study, likewise failed to yield any good predictor of competence in psychiatry. Even the special key ("Psychiatrist A") produced by Strong from a statistical analysis of thousands of blanks filled out by diplomates in psychiatry (15) failed to predict any of our criteria at a statistically significant level—no r's as high as .2. This last finding deserves emphasis, because Strong's key was the product of a highly developed statistical technology, had an adequate numerical base, and had every opportunity to show what a pure actuarial method could achieve.

We made a further attempt to combine the best-predicting scores from the tests used in the standard battery into a regression equation. The R between Verbal IQ (Wechsler-Bellevue), Lawyer key (Strong VIB), DR% and No. Good M (Rorschach), and Overall Competence was .56 on the original group of 64; cross-validated on 100 cases, it dropped to .13.

Some Practical Implications

If we had concentrated on an actuarial rather than a clinical approach and had come up with a simple, objective procedure that had a high and stable level of validity in predicting psychiatric performance, it could have been misused. It might have tempted many psychiatric training centers to adopt a single mold from which would have been cast a generation of psychiatrists who would have had to meet the problems of the future with a standard set of resources derived from the past. The more successful we are in finding objective, impersonal, and statistical methods of selecting members of a profession in the image of its past leaders, the more rigid will be the pattern into which it is frozen.

For a concrete example, consider Strong's Psychiatrist A key again for a moment. It expresses the pattern of interests held in common by men who were diplomates in psychiatry at the end of the war, most of whom must have trained fifteen to twenty years ago. It should hardly be surprising that residents whose interests most closely approached this pattern tended to have skills as administrators and diagnosticians rather than as psychotherapists. If they had happened to achieve a high correlation with our over-all criterion, it might have helped populate American psychiatry of the 1960's and 1970's with near-replicas of the old state hospital superintendent.

It might be argued, however, that a similar result could have been expected if we had succeeded in providing explicit methods of clinically analyzing other types of data to select psychiatric residents. They too would have been based on a study of men who were successful at one time in history, and would have suffered the same danger of getting out of date. The answer is that even sophisticated clinical prediction never gets quite that rigid. Changes creep in; the result may be that validities gradually regress, or the drift may be determined by valid appraisals of newly important variables. Clinical methods are more flexible than their actuarial counterparts; they *can* be more readily modified by new studies based on observations of developing trends in the criterion. Moreover, valid clinical impressions can be obtained from an intensive study of a few known cases, while it takes large samples to set up or revise an actuarial system. There can be no guarantee that clinical methods *will* be kept up to date, of course, nor that the attempt to do so will not spoil their validities. Any predictive system needs constant overhaul and revalidation.

By sticking with the only capriciously accurate, sporadically reliable, and eminently flexible method of clinical judgment in selecting trainees, psychiatry will at least be able to keep in touch with developments in a growing and changing profession. Moreover, it will be able to maintain a healthy diversity within its ranks. There are many jobs to be done in psychiatry, requiring quite different kinds of men. There must be thoughtful men who like to sit in deep chairs and analyze patients all day long. There must be activists to organize new institutions and give inspirational leadership to groups of colleagues. Psychiatry needs many more men than it has whose main interest is in research and teaching, others to work with broad preventive programs in public health, group therapists, specialists in somatic treatments, and many more varieties of the general species. If the pure actuarial approach were to be seriously applied to psychiatry, it would be necessary to develop a formula for each of many different types of practice and to revise it constantly as new developments created needs for new types of practitioners. To do so would be impossibly expensive and laborious. Psychiatry is well-off, therefore, sticking with a basically clinical approach to assessment and prediction in selecting its members, but trying constantly to make it more scientific.

The important issue, however, is not what method of selecting its members is best for any particular profession, but the relative inertia of actuarial predictive systems and the maneuverability introduced when the generating of predictions is done by clinical judgment. This freedom is a source of weakness as well as strength; it enables the clinician to fall into errors of many kinds (to which statistical predictions are less subject) and also to adapt himself sensitively to all kinds of changing circumstances. When clinical methods are given a chance—when skilled clinicians use methods with which they are familiar, predicting a performance about which they know something—and especially when the clinician has a rich body of data and has made the fullest use of the systematic procedures developed by actuarial workers, including a prior study of the bearing of the predictive data on the criterion performance, then sophisticated clinical prediction can achieve quite respectable successes. I hope that clinicians will take some heart from our results, but I urge them to refine their procedures by learning as much as possible about statistical prediction and adapting it to their own ends.

To summarize: Meehl failed in his aim to mediate the statistical-clinical quarrel because he defined the issues in a way that perpetuates competition and controversy. The real issue is not to find the proper sphere of activity for clinical predictive methods and for statistical ones, conceived in ideal-type terms as antithetical. Rather, we should try to find the optimal combination of actuarially controlled methods and sensitive clinical judgment for any particular predictive enterprise. To do so, we must strike the right balance between freedom and constraint, a balance which may shift a good deal in one direction or the other depending on the nature of the behavior being predicted. But we can find such balances only if clinically and statistically oriented workers give up contentious, competitive attitudes and seek to learn from each other.

REFERENCES

1. BLENKNER, M. Predictive factors in the initial interview in family casework. *Soc. Serv. Rev.*, 1954, 28, 65–73.
2. CRONBACH, L. J. Assessment of individual differences. In P. FARNSWORTH & Q. McNEMAR (Eds.), *Annual review of psychology*, Vol. VII. Stanford, Calif.: Annual Reviews, 1956, pp. 173–196.
3. HOLT, R. R., & LUBORSKY, L. *Personality patterns of psychiatrists*, Vols. I & II. New York: Basic Books, 1958.
4. HOLTZMAN, W. H., & SELLS, S. B. Prediction of flying success by clinical analysis of test protocols. *J. abnorm. soc. Psychol.*, 1954, 49, 485–490.
5. HORST, P., *et al. The prediction of personal adjustment.* New York: Soc.

Sci. Res. Council Bull. 48, 1941.
6. KELLY, E. L., & FISKE, D. W. The prediction of success in the VA training program in clinical psychology. *Amer. Psychologist*, 1950, 5, 395–406.
7. KELLY, E. L., & FISKE, D. W. *The prediction of performance in clinical psychology.* Ann Arbor, Mich.: Univer. of Michigan Press, 1951.
8. LUBORSKY, L. L., HOLT, R. R., & MORROW, W. R. Interim report of the research project on the selection of medical men for psychiatric training. *Bull. Menninger Clinic*, 1950, 14, 92–101.
9. McARTHUR, C. Clinical versus actuarial prediction. In *Proceedings, 1955 invitational conference on test-*

ing problems. Princeton, N. J.: Educational Testing Service, 1956. Pp. 99–106.

10. MEEHL, P. E. *Clinical vs. statistical prediction.* Minneapolis: Univer. of Minnesota Press, 1954.

11. MEEHL, P. E. Clinical versus acturial prediction. In *Proceedings, 1955 invitational conference on testing problems.* Princeton, N. J.; Educational Testing Service, 1956. Pp. 136–141.

12. OSS ASSESSMENT Staff. *Assessment of men.* New York: Rinehart, 1948.

13. RAPAPORT, D., GILL, M. M., & SHAFER,

R. *Diagnostic psychological testing.* Vol. II. Chicago: Yearbook Publishers, 1946.

14. SARBIN, T. R. A contribution to the study of actuarial and statistical methods of prediction. *Amer. J. Sociol.,* 1943, **48,** 593–603.

15. STRONG, E. K., JR., & TUCKER, A. J. The use of vocational interest scores in planning a medical career. *Psychol. Monogr.,* 1952, **66** (9), No. 341.

16. WITTMAN, M. P. A scale for measuring prognosis in schizophrenic patients. *Elgin Papers,* 1941, **4,** 20–33.

Seer Versus Sign

Gardner Lindzey

The task of the investigator is inextricably linked to the individual observer, and nowhere is this more frustratingly evident than in the study of personality. Although the efforts of psychologists to dehumanize—more positively, to "objectify"—the process of data collection have been many and ingenious, it remains true that behind

This research was supported by a grant from the Ford Foundation and research grant M-1949 from the National Institute of Mental Health. The paper was written while the author was in residence at the Center for Advanced Study in the Behavioral Sciences. Final preparation of the manuscript was facilitated by sage comments from Lee J. Cronbach, Anthony Davids, Edward E. Jones, and David T. Lykken. I received valuable assistance in the collection and analysis of data from Jean Bradford, James Kincannon, and Harvey D. Winston. The late Ephraim Rosen generously served as one of the judges in the second study.

Reprinted by permission of the Academic Press and the author from the *Journal of Experimental Research in Personality,* 1965, **1,** 17–26.

every validity coefficient or network of justifying concepts and operations there lurks, at some point, an observer, hopefully a sensitive and unbiased observer. Few psychologists have accepted this fact more gracefully than Henry A. Murray and none has labored more diligently and imaginatively to maximize the contribution of the observer and to provide him with a respected position within the field of psychology.

The present investigations may be viewed as minor attempts to assess the relative merits of the trained human observer in a particular setting. More specifically, they compare the judgment of one or more unaided clinicians with objective and actuarial methods of prediction under conditions where the special strengths of the clinician are given a reasonable opportunity to manifest themselves. As such they belong to a growing body of investigations concerned with the relative merits of mechanical, objective, and (typically) quantitative methods of prediction as opposed to the relatively subjective and qualitative predictions of the clinician. Such studies have been summarized ably by Meehl (1954), Cronbach (1956), and Gough (1962) among others, and the area of investigation owes much to the earlier writing of Allport (1937, 1942), Sarbin (1941, 1942), and Murray (1938, 1948).

It is worth noting that this issue possesses certain significant links to the idiographic-nomothetic question, and like the latter controversy it has proved sturdily resistant to the frequent suggestion (for example, Holt, 1958; Zubin, 1956) that sophisticated examination of the problem reveals little or no real basis for maintaining such a distinction or issue. Just as species survival may be considered the ultimate test of "fitness," so too the persistence of a conceptual distinction or empirical issue over many years in the face of repeated efforts to obliterate or dissolve it may be considered evidence of theoretical-empirical fitness or significance.

Study I

In this study, which already has been reported in part (Lindzey, Tejessy, and Zamansky, 1958), it was possible to compare the predictive (literally, postdictive) effectiveness of a number of objective TAT indices of homosexuality (individually and in combination) with the comparable effectiveness of clinical predictions by an experienced interpreter of the TAT.

Method

Subjects. The Ss consisted of 20 undergraduate male students who had acknowledged overt homosexual acts and a group of 20 undergraduates comparable in sex, age, and educational level but with no known history of homosexuality. They were volunteers and received no pay for their participation.

Procedure. Five TAT cards (4,

6BM, 7BM, 10, 18BM) were administered individually by an experienced male administrator. The resultant protocols with all identification of individual Ss removed were then scored for 20 different variables or indices that were believed on the basis of prior research or formulation to be indicative of homosexual tendencies (Lindzey, Bradford, Tejessy, and Davids, 1959). The variables, scoring procedures, and reliabilities are described in greater detail in an earlier publication (Lindzey *et al.*, 1958), and they are briefly identified in Table 1.

The TAT protocols were also sorted blindly by an experienced interpreter of the TAT who was generally familiar with all the objective indices used in the study but was permitted to make his classification without justification or specification of the basis for his decision. He also divided the predictions into those of which he was confident and those of which he was uncertain.

Results

The results summarized in Table 1 indicate clearly that the objective indices functioned very well in comparison with similar indices derived from TAT protocols that have been examined in previous studies (Lindzey and Newburg, 1954; Lindzey and Tejessy, 1956). However, it is equally clear that none of the indices serves by itself as a powerful basis for discrimination between the homosexual and normal groups. Indeed, when compared with the judgments of an experienced clinician they fare very poorly. The judge was able to sort the protocols with 95% accuracy—classifying incorrectly one S from each group. Moreover, of the 29 judgments which he considered "confident," there were no incorrect classifications.

The question remains whether it is possible to combine after the fact the information contained in the 20 objective indices and produce findings that

TABLE 1. DIMENSIONAL TAT COMPARISON OF COLLEGE STUDENTS

Variable	Normal (N = 20)		Homosexual (N = 20)		p^a
	M	Freq.	M	Freq.	
1 Misrecognition of sex		3		3	—
2 18BM: Attack from the rear		4		9	<.10
3 Feminine identification	1.05		1.55		<.005
4 Attitude toward marriage	−.32		.48		<.005
5 Man killing woman		0		5	<.02
6 Sexual references	.55		1.25		NS
7 Unstable identification	1.65		2.25		<.005
8 Feminine feelings, emotions	2.10		2.05		NS
9 Shallow heterosexual relations	.90		1.75		<.005
10 Male embrace		0		1	—
11 Attitude toward opposite sex	−.32		.18		NS
12 Tragic heterosexual relations		2		7	.06
13 Attachment to mother		2		4	NS
14 18BM: Symbolism or allegory		0		6	.01
15 Attachment to father		5		1	.18
16 Derogatory sexual terms applied to women		0		7	.004
17 Homosexual content		0		6	.01
18 Incest		0		1	—
19 10BM: No elderly couple		16		11	NS
20 18BM: Positive introduction of female		5		0	.02

a Values of *p* for differences between means are based on *t* tests. Those for variables 2 and 19 are based on χ^2, and the remainder, on Fisher's Exact Test. Only the variables on which the difference was not in the predicted direction (8, 15, 19) were assigned to a two-tailed test of significance.

parallel, or closely resemble, those produced by qualitative, clinical judgments. The first step in answering this question was simply to arrange all indices (no matter what the prediction or expectation had been) so that a high score was typical of the homosexual group and a low score of the normal group. This involved reversing two variables (15 and 19). We then cumulated raw scores across all variables for each S, ignoring the different ranges of scores permitted by the various scoring procedures. The resultant distribution of scores for the two groups are reported in Fig. 1. Next we divided the scores for each

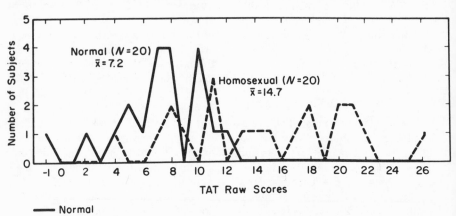

Figure 1. Comparison of normal and homosexual college students on total TAT scores.

variable as close to the median as possible so that we had a high and low group. Then for each S we simply counted the number of variables in which his score placed him in the high group, and the results for the two groups are summarized in Fig. 2. Both of these procedures functioned effectively; indeed, if we permit ourselves the luxury of maximizing diagnostic accuracy by identifying a cutting point after the fact,

while for the pattern low, low, low for variables 14, 16, and 17 there were 7 homosexual Ss and 20 normal Ss, leading to the prediction of normality. It is also possible to provide a "validity coefficient" for each pattern which is based upon the number of cases in the original group displaying the pattern and the amount of difference between criterion groups in frequency for this pattern.

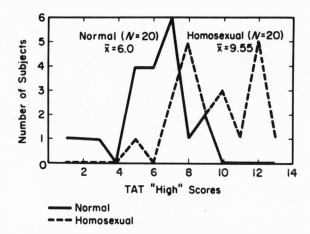

Figure 2. Comparison of normal and homosexual college subjects on total TAT "high" scores.

we are able to identify such a score for each distribution that will correctly classify 34 of the 40 Ss.

A third objective approach used in the attempt to extract the diagnostic information potentially available in these indices emphasized pattern or configural analysis. We employed an ingenious technique devised by Lykken [(1956); Lykken and Rose (1963)] that utilizes dichotomous predictor variables to make up actuarial tables for the various patterns of scores. Each table represents the observed frequency from each criterion group for one particular pattern; for example, for the pattern low, high, high for variables 14, 16, and 17 there were 5 homosexual Ss and 0 normal Ss, thus leading to the prediction of homosexuality from this pattern,

In the present study we used five actuarial tables, consisting of three variables each, which included most of the individual indices that seemed to function effectively. The variable groups employed were 14-16-17, 12-19-20, 2-12-16, 6-2-11, and 3-4-15. With this method it proved possible to predict correctly (after the fact) 34 out of the 40 cases when the prediction for each case was that indicated by three or more of the five tables. This performance could be increased slightly (36 correct identifications) if the prediction was based upon the difference for each S between the summed validity coefficients for the homosexual predictions as opposed to the normal predictions.

In summary, we find that the informed but unfettered and nonquantified clinician functioned slightly better than any of the actuarial combinations of objective scores. The relative similarity in performance of the two approaches must be evaluated against the background of a deliberate maximizing after-the-fact of the information contained in the objective indices, even when this meant reversing the intended direction of scoring. Thus, the clinician made his predictions before the fact while the objective procedure was adjusted to maximize its sensitivity after the fact. Under these circumstances one may naturally expect a great deal of shrinkage when the actuarial procedure is applied to an independent sample of observations. Study II was intended to permit an estimate of just how effectively the two systems would function when applied to a new source of data.

Study II

In this study we compared clinical judgment with our actuarial procedures when applied to two groups of Ss that were distinguished from each other in terms of overt homosexual acts but otherwise were quite different from the Ss of the previous study. We were interested in further evaluating the two different methods of prediction and also in examining the situational generality of findings concerned with the relation between a particular TAT sign or index and an underlying disposition or personal attribute.

Method

Subjects. The Ss consisted of 30 male prisoners in a state maximum security prison. The group was divided into 14 who were known to have been overtly homosexual prior to imprisonment (11 were convicted of sodomy charges) and 16 who provided no evidence of homosexuality prior to imprisonment or during incarceration. The

groups were matched in terms of age, education, intelligence, period of imprisonment, and place of residence. The normal group was selected in such a manner as to exclude persons convicted of crimes of violence, and consequently it included predominantly persons convicted of charges related to crimes against property. The Ss were paid for their participation in the study and all knew that they were participating in a study that involved, among other things, an interest in homosexuality.

Procedure. The TAT was administered individually (Cards 2, 3BM, 6BM, 9BM, 10, 12, 13MF, 18BM) by two male administrators who were unaware of the group to which any S belonged. Each examiner tested an equal number of normal and homosexual Ss.

The stories were scored for 20 variables according to the procedures developed in the earlier studies by two raters who were unaware of the group to which any S belonged. Discrepancies between the two sets of scores were eliminated by discussion between the two raters so that the final score represented a composite rating. The scoring was the same as in the previous study except that the larger number of cards increased in range of scores for a number of variables, and for two variables (4, 11) the numerical score assigned for the five categories was changed from (-2 to $+2$) to (0 to $+4$).

The Ss were classified by two judges independently as being homosexual or nonhomosexual on the basis of the TAT stories and knowledge of the true distribution of cases in the two categories. One judge (A) was unfamiliar with the objective indices and the findings of the previous studies, but the other judge (B) was intimately familiar with these findings although he did not make any systematic effort to use this information. Judge B was the same judge who had made the comparable ratings in the first study. Each judge divided his predictions into those of which he was confident and those of which he was uncertain.

Results

Examination of the findings summarized in Table 2 indicates a consistent failure of the objective indices to differentiate between normal and homosexual Ss in a manner comparable to that revealed in the first study. Of 20 comparisons only one achieved conventional significance in the predicted direction; there were four reversals in the expected direction of the difference, and most of the 10 group differences in the predicted direction were minute. It seems clear that these indices, even though "validated" in several previous studies (Davids, Joelson, and McArthur, 1956; Lindzey *et al.*, 1958), have little merit when applied under the conditions of the present study.

Not surprisingly, in view of the results for the individual variables, the application of the actuarial procedures used in the previous study to combine these indices were highly ineffective. Whether we use raw scores cumulated (Fig. 3), number of high scores (Fig. 4), or the configural scoring method,

TABLE 2. DIMENSIONAL TAT
COMPARISON OF PRISONERS

Variable	Normal (N = 16)		Homosexual (N = 14)	
	M	Freq.	M	Freq.
1	2.31		1.86	
2		2		4
3	3.50		3.79	
4	15.75		15.00	
5		4		4
6	1.75		1.93	
7	1.44		1.43	
8	1.94		1.79	
9	.56		.64	
10		0		0
11	15.94		15.86	
12		5		5
13		3		8
14		1		1
15		0		0
16		4		4
17		0		0
18		0		2
19		6		6
20		14		12

we arrive at the same "hit rate" of 17 out of 30, or 57%. Even an additional, and more complicated application of Lykken's technique failed to improve upon the 57% figure. In this method each S was compared with all 40 of Ss in the previous study, and for each pair-comparison a deviation score was com-

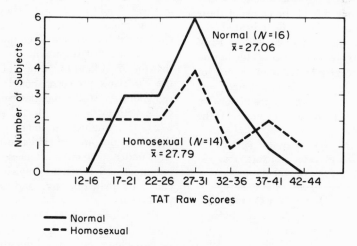

Figure 3. Comparison of normal and homosexual prisoners on total TAT scores.

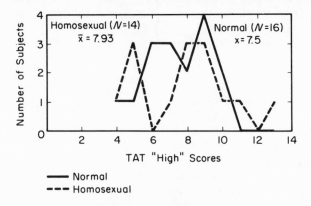

Figure 4. Comparison of normal and homosexual
prisoners on total TAT "high" scores.

puted that represented the number of times the two Ss were discrepant on a variable (one high and the other low). Then those Ss in the comparison group who had deviation scores of six or less were identified, and a prediction was made based upon whether the majority of these similar patterns had been drawn from homosexual or normal Ss.

In contrast, the judges' performance (Table 3), although variable, appears distinctly better. The most efficient of the judges was able to identify group membership with 80% success. While the less successful judge was able to identify correctly only 60% of the cases, of those 14 judgments in which he indicated confidence he was correct in 86% or 12 of the cases. Thus Judge A was able to predict significantly better than chance for all Ss, and Judge B functioned well above chance for those predictions of which he was confident; none of the

actuarial methods proved able to function above the level of chance.

Discussion

Clinical Versus Actuarial Prediction. The studies we have just discussed may be viewed as a direct, although modest, response to a challenge issued by Paul Meehl following a comprehensive review of the clinical-statistical research literature. His survey failed to reveal any clear evidence for the superiority of the clinical method, and he concluded, "I have reservations about some of these studies; I do not believe they are optimally designed to exhibit the clinician at his best; but I submit that it is high time that those who are so sure that the 'right kind of study' will exhibit the clinician's prowess, should *do* this right kind of study and back up their claim with evidence" (Meehl, 1957, p. 272). Our findings, although far from definitive, do provide evidence that, at least under some circumstances, clinical judgment may function somewhat more efficiently than objective and actuarial prediction.

For such findings to be of more than glancing importance, however, it must be possible to state something about the conditions that have played a role in producing these discrepant results. In

TABLE 3. ACCURACY OF JUDGES'
PREDICTIONS FOR NORMAL AND
HOMOSEXUAL PRISONERS

Predictions	N	Per Cent Correct Judge A	Judge B
Over-all	30	80	60
Confident	14	71	86
Uncertain	16	88	38

the present study it seems to us the events predisposing in favor of the sensitive and informed clinician relate to the psychometric intractability of the TAT. In brief, we have here an instrument that elicits a large amount of complex response data and which is accompanied by very little in the way of rules for effectively transforming or encapsulating these responses within a finite number of scores, variables, or indicants. Thus, although there have been many attempts to establish dimensions or categories for analyzing TAT responses (cf. Lindzey *et al.*, 1959), none of them has met with spectacular success. It appears that the massive and unwieldy qualitative data of the TAT continue to provide predictive cues for the skilled clinician that are not represented adequately in the objective indices upon which actuarial prediction must rest. To generalize, it seems reasonable to expect that, under circumstances where there is little available in the way of sensitive and objective guidelines, the experienced clinician is likely to function relatively better than in a psychometrically highly developed terrain.

It may appear that I am suggesting that clinical predictions function better only in very primitive areas of psychological measurement. Indeed, overlooking the role of the clinician as a source of ideas or hypotheses that may lead to further objectivity and specification, this is precisely what is implied. Insofar as the objective basis for clinical prediction's operating better than chance can be made explicit and verbalized, it will usually prove possible to devise substitutive methods that are freer of error than the human mind. On the other hand, there is little doubt that much of psychological measurement, defined broadly, is still in a very primitive state and, consequently, it may be no trivial accomplishment to function relatively well under conditions such as those that prevailed in this study.

It is clear, in addition, that conditions in the present study come closer than most studies in this area to meeting the demands that the criterion to be predicted is at least as familiar to the clinician as to the psychometrician. Comparison of the two methods of prediction in connection with academic achievement, or some comparable outcome variable, favors the actuarial method both because this area of behavior is more often studied by psychometrist than clinician and also because the objective indices for predicting such behavior are relatively efficient and readily susceptible to quantitative analysis. McArthur (1956), Meehl (1956), and Cronbach (1960) have pointed to the importance of studying clinical predictions on their home terrain, and all have suggested that here the performance of the clinician may be relatively more encouraging, as indeed it appears to be.

It is worth emphasis that, contrary to a frequent misunderstanding, Meehl has always believed in the probable superiority of the clinician over the actuary under certain circumstances. Indeed, in a recent paper (Meehl, 1959) he has identified six factors that should favor the clinician. The first is *open-endedness*, where the event to be predicted cannot be represented by means of a single dimension or a small number of categories but where the predictor himself is determining the terms or content of the prediction. Second is *unanalyzed stimulus-equivalences*, where the rules for analyzing or classifying the relevant data are not objectively specifiable. Third is the existence of *empty cells*, where particular events or combinations of events have not been observed in the past and consequently have not yet gained a place in the actuarial tables. Fourth is the possible role of *theory-mediation*, where there is an active process of theoretical reasoning and hypothesis formation intervening between the observational data and the particular prediction to be made. Fifth is the situation which offers *insufficient* time for the application of actual methods simply because an immediate decision must be made. Sixth is the case where there is a *nonlinear* and particularly a *configural* or pattern association between the predictor variables and the criterion. The performance of the clinicians in the present studies is presumably consistent with the implications of Meehl's statements in regard to "unanalyzed stimulus equivalences" and "empty cells" as factors favoring the effectiveness of clinical prediction. That is, the clinicians responded to stimuli that had not yet been objectively identified and classified, and among these cues there may even have been some that had not been encountered in previous studies and consequently could not have been used by the actuarial methods. It is impossible to completely rule out the role of theory-mediated hypotheses, but the subjective report of the judges and the state of theory in this area make such a contingency most unlikely.

Our findings are only obliquely related to Holt's (1958) distinctions between pure actuarial, naive clinical, and sophisticated clinical prediction. However, insofar as the distinction between naive clinical and sophisticated clinical can be mapped into this study, we would have to place Judge A in the naive category and Judge B in the sophisticated class, on the basis of the fact that Judge B had made comparable predictions from a similar data base before and was intimately familiar with objective findings in this area. Our evidence suggests that the native clinical judge did at least as well as the sophisticated clinical judge, contrary to Holt's expectation, although one would not like to generalize far from only two judges.

If we recklessly accept the difference between Judge A and Judge B as a real and stable difference, we are faced with the mild embarrassment of increased experience and sophistication appearing to diminish accuracy or sensitivity. Obviously this is not necessarily the case. Judge A may simply have been a better diagnostician, and with increased experience his advantage might have been even greater than it was. However, it is at least possible that experience with predicting this variable under conditions of the first study, and a thorough knowledge of the TAT literature on homosexuality, might make a negative contribution to prediction in the second study. Remembering how poorly the objective indices functioned in the second study, it seems altogether conceivable that if Judge B was deriving many of his diagnostic cues from these indices he might have operated at a disadvantage.

Utility of Projective Technique "Signs" or Objective Indices. In view of the fact that the indices and related variables studied in the present investigations comprise one of the most successful sets of "signs" in the history of TAT research, their almost total collapse upon further cross-validation might be considered a serious indictment of this entire approach to measurement. On the other hand, such a finding should scarcely come as a surprise in view of the many investigations (for example, Kenny, 1954, 1961; Lindzey and Silverman, 1959; Masling, 1960) and formulations (Lindzey, 1952, 1961; Gleser, 1963) that have made clear the extent to which these instruments are responsive to a wide array of diverse determinants. Given this multiplicity of conditions that determine projective technique response, only a small proportion of which are related to personality variables or dispositions, it is inevitable that strictly empirical findings secured in one situation will not be likely to generalize effectively if we change a great many of the situational factors as well as nonpersonality attributes of the Ss.

Let us consider some of the respects in which the Ss and conditions of test administration differed between our first and second studies. The Ss of the second study were much more heterogeneous than Ss of the first study in age, socioeconomic status, education, intelligence, employment history, indeed on almost any other variable one might care to mention other than criminality. Not only was the second group more variable on these attributes but also there were sizeable differences in the group average for most variables, including verbal facility, intelligence, and socioeconomic status. The differences in situational determinants of test performance were at least as striking as the differences in demographic and personal attributes. To mention only the most salient of these differences, one group of tests was given in a maximum security prison and another in an institution of higher learning; one group of Ss was paid for participation and the other was not; one group of homosexual Ss knew the examiner was aware of their homosexual behavior while the other group did not; one group of homosexual Ss included a large number who had been harshly punished by society for homosexual acts while the comparable group in the other study included no such Ss. A large number of studies have been conducted that demonstrate projective technique responses to vary with conditions such as those just described. Many of these investigations are described or referred to in recent publications by Masling (1960) and Lindzey (1961).

Generalizations of the sort dealt with in this study must be accompanied by a statement of the parametric limits within which they operate, and among the group differences mentioned above there are undoubtedly many such parameters that must be attended to in order to permit effective generalization of findings. To cite only a single illustration, a great deal of the research and clinical literature on projective techniques has tended to ignore the difference between the situation in which the S sees the ex-

aminer as sympathetically involved in a cooperative and supportive enterprise and the situation in which the S, accurately or not, perceives the examiner as hostile, as a barrier to some desired goal, or as the potential revealer of some deeply defended aspect of the S's inner world. There seems little doubt that one of the reasons for the failure of the second study to even approach a replication of the findings of the first study concerns just this difference. Indeed, when reporting the initial results of the first study we indicated that ". . . most of the indices of homosexuality that functioned successfully tended to be relatively directly related to homosexuality and thus might be expected to be readily subject to censoring or inhibition" (Lindzey et al., 1958, p. 74). Given this observation it is altogether predictable that, with less cooperative Ss, the TAT indices would fare more poorly.

What has just been said concerning the parametric limits within which one may expect a given relation between projective technique sign and personality disposition to be maintained might be considered banal if it were not for the fact that the majority of studies concerned with such diagnostic relationships fail even to mention the importance of such parameters. Thus, much of the existing interpretative lore, both that based upon controlled research and that derived from clinical observation, is certain to be misleading because there has been no attempt to state the reasonable bounds within which the interpretation or relationship is likely to be sustained.

The sensitivity of the TAT to situational variation is obviously a serious problem for the person interested in enduring and personological traits, albeit the problem is equally perplexing with structured tests and other techniques for assessing personality. Until and unless we are able to identify objective cues that prove to be linked with personality traits in an invariant manner over many different situations, the clinician or investigator must be exceedingly cautious in attempting to make personality inferences concerning respondents who are examined in a novel setting.

Summary

Thematic Apperception Test (TAT) protocols from homosexual and normal college Ss and homosexual and normal prisoners were employed in two consecutive studies concerned with clinical and actuarial prediction. In the first study a clinician blindly predicted the criterion from TAT protocols with 95% accuracy. Twenty objective TAT indices, when combined after the fact using actuarial methods, functioned nearly as well as the clinician. When applied to the prison population, the actuarial methods were totally ineffective, while two clinicians were more successful in predicting the criterion. The findings are discussed in terms of their implications for the clinical-actuarial prediction controversy as well as the probable utility of objective "signs" derived from projective technique protocols.

REFERENCES

ALLPORT, G. W. *Personality: a psychological interpretation.* New York: Holt, 1937.

ALLPORT, G. W. *The use of personal documents in psychological science.* Social Science Research Council Bull. No. 42, 1942.

CRONBACH, L. J. Assessment of individual difference. In P. R. FARNSWORTH and Q. McNEMAR (Eds.), *Annual review of psychology,* Vol. 7. Palo Alto, Calif.: Annual Reviews, 1956, pp. 173–196.

CRONBACH, L. J. *Essentials of psychological testing.* New York: Harper, 1960.

DAVIDS, A., JOELSON, M., and McARTHUR, C. Rorschach and TAT indices of homosexuality in overt homosexuals, neurotics, and normal males. *Journal of Abnormal and Social Psychology,* 1956, 53, 161–172.

GLESER, GOLDINE C. Projective methodologies. In P. R. FARNSWORTH (Ed.), *Annual review of psychology.* Vol. 14. Palo Alto, Calif.: Annual Reviews, 1963, pp. 391–422.

GOUGH, H. G. Clinical versus statistical prediction in psychology. In L. POSTMAN (Ed.), *Psychology in the making.* New York: Knopf, 1962, pp. 526–584.

HOLT, R. R. Clinical *and* statistical prediction: A reformulation and some new data. *Journal of Abnormal and Social Psychology,* 1958, 56, 1–12.

KENNY, D. T. Transcendence indices, extent of personality factors in fantasy responses, and the ambiguity of TAT cards. *Journal of Consulting Psychology,* 1954, 18, 345–348.

KENNY, D. T. A theoretical and research reappraisal of stimulus factors in the TAT. In J. KAGAN and G. LESSER (Eds.), *Contemporary issues in thematic apperceptive methods.* Springfield, Ill.: Thomas, 1961, pp. 288–310.

LINDZEY, G. Thematic Apperception Test: Interpretive assumptions and related empirical evidence. *Psychological Bulletin,* 1952, 49, 1–25.

LINDZEY, G. *Projective techniques and cross-cultural research,* New York: Appleton-Century-Crofts, 1961.

LINDZEY, G., and NEWBURG, A. S. Thematic Apperception Test: A tentative appraisal of some "signs" of anxiety. *Journal of Consulting Psychology,* 1954, 18, 389–395.

LINDZEY, G., and SILVERMAN, M. Thematic Apperception Test: Techniques of group administration, sex differences and the role of verbal productivity. *Journal of Personality,* 1959, 27, 311–323.

LINDZEY, G., and TEJESSY, CHARLOTTE. Thematic Apperception Test: Indices of aggression in relation to measures of overt and covert behavior. *American Journal of Orthopsychiatry,* 1956, 26, 567–576.

LINDZEY, G., TEJESSY, C., and ZEMANSKY, H. Thematic Apperception Test: An empirical examination of some indices of homosexuality. *Journal of Abnormal and Social Psychology*, 1958, **57**, 67–75.

LINDZEY, G., BRADFORD, JEAN, TEJESSY, CHARLOTTE, and DAVIDS, A. *Thematic Apperception Test: An interpretive lexicon for clinician and investigator. Journal of Clinical Psychology, Monograph Supplement*, 1959, No. 12.

LYKKEN, D. T. A method of actuarial pattern analysis. *Psychological Bulletin*, 1956, **53**, 102–107.

LYKKEN, D.T., and ROSE, R. Psychological prediction from actuarial tables. *Journal of Clinical Psychology*, 1963, **19**, 139–151.

McARTHUR, C. Clinical versus actuarial prediction. In *Proceedings of the 1955 invitational conference on testing problems*. Princeton, N. J.: Educational Testing Service, 1956, pp. 99–106.

MASLING, J. The influence of situational and interpersonal variables in projective testing. *Psychological Bulletin*, 1960, **57**, 65–85.

MEEHL, P. E. *Clinical versus statistical prediction*. Minneapolis: Univer. of Minnesota Press, 1954.

MEEHL, P. E. Clinical versus actuarial prediction. In *Proceedings of the 1955 invitational conference on testing problems*. Princeton, N.J.: Educational Testing Service, 1956, pp. 136–141.

MEEHL, P. E. When shall we use our heads instead of the formula? *Journal of Counseling Psychology*, 1957, **4**, 268–273.

MEEHL, P. E. A comparison of clinicians with five statistical methods of identifying psychotic MMPI profiles. *Journal of Counseling Psychology*, 1959, **6**, 102–109.

MURRAY, H. A. *Explorations in personality*. New York: Oxford Univer. Press, 1938.

MURRAY, H. A., *et al. Assessment of man*. New York: Rinehart, 1948.

SARBIN, T. Clinical psychology—art or science? *Psychometrika*, 1941, **6**, 391–400.

SARBIN, T. A contribution to the study of actuarial and individual methods of prediction. *American Journal of Sociology*, 1942, **48**, 593–602.

ZUBIN, V. Clinical versus actuarial prediction. In *Proceedings of the 1955 invitational conference on testing problems*. Princeton, N.J.: Educational Testing Service, 1956, pp. 107–128.

Can the Computer Supplant the Clinician?

Wayne H. Holtzman

Twenty years ago, much of what is commonplace today in the computer world would have been laughed off as science fiction, surely beyond attainment within the foreseeable future. And yet today we have a number of commercially available computers which can operate at such amazing speeds that a symmetric, 80-by-80 matrix can be in-

Reprinted by the permission of the publisher and the author from the *Journal of Clinical Psychology*, 1960, **16**, 119–122.

verted in 75 seconds, a tedious task of almost impossible magnitude before the advent of high-speed computers. Of course, most such computers are too busy for routine application in psychology, but the opportunity is there for those with initiative, a little imagination, and money.

The psychologist who reads about these fantastic machines cannot help but wonder how they will affect his own activities. Is it conceivable that hardware advances in computers and new schemes for programming the machines will produce some kind of super-robot which has the capacity to solve problems, to invent new ideas, to replace the human brain in many operations? Admittedly, a machine can greatly surpass the human being right now in arithmetic computations, and even in certain logical operations. But surely the area of creative thinking is sacrosanct to man, at least in the eyes of individuals not intimately acquainted with recent advances in this rapidly growing field. No one is foolhardy enough to claim that existing machines can seriously compete with the human brain in most perceptual and cognitive activities. It has been said, for example, that even such a simple task as looking up a number in a phone book would require the equivalent of nine, high speed, IBM 704 computers to do the job in the short time that it takes a human being (7). Nevertheless, recent work in the machine simulation of human problem solving, notably that of Newell, Shaw, and Simon (5, 6) has already made some significant progress in the construction of machines that can think.

What are the immediate implications of these recent advances for the clinician? Is it likely that the computer will supplant the clinician in certain activities? In searching for an answer to this question, let us first examine in detail what a clinical psychologist does, both in his everyday, practical activities and in his role as research scientist.

Whether in a research or service setting, the unique quality that the clinician has to offer is himself. Trained to focus upon the steady stream of interaction between himself and the person with whom he is working, the clinician constantly revises his image of the individual's personality, adapting his behavior to that of his client, reasoning intuitively without full awareness of his own thought processes, gradually sharpening his concept of the person with whom he is interacting—in short, using himself as the primary instrument for collecting, processing, and interpreting information about his client. This intuitive, interactive process is the method *par excellence* of the skilled clinician, whether he is engaged in psychotherapy or is concerned with the evaluation of personality for some other purpose. It is difficult to imagine how a machine could replace a clinician in his primary role of a person interacting with another person. Surely in this respect the clinician is safe from any job displacement by machines.

Granted that the unique quality of the clinician is his face-to-face role interacting with the client, what are some of the other functions performed daily by the clinician where the introduction of a machine might supplant certain activities? Aside from counseling or psychotherapy, the main role of a clinician is diagnosis and evaluation of the individual and his personality. As a diagnostician, the clinical psychologist's activity can be separated into three different phases: (a) the collection of information about the person; (b) the preparation and translation of this information for analysis; and (c) the interpretation of this information. All three phases occur simultaneously when the clinician is using himself as an instrument in face-to-face contact with the client. In most settings, however, the clinician spends a major portion of his time and energy focusing upon one of these three phases at a time.

Let us examine each of these three aspects of the diagnostic process one at a time with respect to three questions: What is the nature of the clinical activity? Is it theoretically feasible for a machine to take over all or part of the clinician's function? If theoretically feasible, how practical is the machine in economic competition with the human being?

Clinician Versus Machine as a Collector

The collection of information in clinical diagnosis runs all the way from self-report forms and tests that can be given by a clerk, to depth interviews and projective techniques that require the clinician-subject interaction. While it is conceivable that such routine information as simple biographical items or responses to objective-type tests such as the MMPI could be obtained by completely automatic methods once the subject is introduced to the machine, it will probably remain impractical from an economic standpoint for some time to come. Clerks and low-level technicians are easy to come by.

As one moves through the range of possibilities to the interview and projective techniques, the machine is not only impractical from an economic point of view, but it is also theoretically unfeasible because of the interpersonal nature of the interview or testing situations. While there are many ways in which the clinician can utilize clerks and technicians to assist him in his role as a collector of information, it is highly unlikely that machines will play an important part in this initial phase of the diagnostic process.

Clinician Versus Machine as a Processor

A good deal of the clinician's time is spent in the scoring, coding, and analysis of information to prepare it for interpretation and evaluation. This processing of information ranges from the routine counting and scoring of items in a test to the more intuitive analysis of interview and projective materials. From the clinician's point of view, the diagnosis of personality calls for an intensive qualitative analysis of many subtleties within test protocols, as well as the compiling of more objective scores and signs from the available information. If the clinician is viewed as a free-floating processer with no hard and fast rules,

if he typically generates his categories of description and analysis on an *ad hoc* basis as he builds his picture of the unique personality before him, and if he is generally unaware of his own thought processes during the analysis, then no machine can conceivably take over this function as a processor of information.

But even granting the clinician his right to use the information of his choice and to make the analysis of his choice, the high speed computer can still be a useful servant in processing some of the information for the clinician. I daresay that every psychodiagnostician spends considerably more time than he cares to admit, in processing his raw data by means that are really better adapted for a machine than for the human brain. To illustrate my point, let me cite some uses to which we have put computers in the processing of information in the responses to a new inkblot test developed in our laboratories.

The Holtzman Inkblot Test consists of two parallel forms, each containing 45 inkblots to which the subject is asked to give only one response (2). These two major changes in the Rorschach procedure, lengthening the test and instructing the subject to give only one response per card, make it possible to process the data along psychometric lines without sacrificing the rich, projective quality of the testing procedure. At present 22 variables are scored for each of the 45 cards in the test. These variables cover a wide range of concepts varying from Location, Form Appropriateness, Color, and Movement, to such content variables as Anxiety, Hostility, and Anatomy. As in many other clinical tests, the scoring of the verbal record is the first step in processing the data. While it may be theoretically possible for a large computer to score most of the raw data, the cost would be completely prohibitive. At this first stage in analysis, the clinician or, better still, his trained assistant can run rings around the best computers. But once this primary codifying is completed, the situation is reversed.

The scores are entered as digits in boxes following each response on the printed test booklet. The scored protocol is given to a key-punch operator who punches one IBM card for each response, yielding a total of 45 cards. The cards are fed to an IBM tabulator which punches out a summary card containing total scores for the 22 variables as well as miscellaneous identifying information. Of course this particular job could be done faster by an electronic computer, but at this stage in processing, the cheaper, more accessible tabulator is highly satisfactory. If a simple summation of the individual scores completed the information-processing phase of the analysis, the machine would have only a slight edge on the human being, and then in terms of speed and accuracy. Certainly the machine would be impractical for everyday use.

But suppose after several years of research, a great deal is learned about the test that has diagnostic value. And suppose further that this acquired information deals with many complex configurations of scoring elements, as well as their simple summation into single, isolated scores. Isn't this focus upon multiple signs and complex configurations precisely the approach that most clinicians believe constitutes one of their important, unique contributions as processors?

Once the basic scoring elements are punched on cards, any conceivable configuration of the scores can be computed by machine with perfect accuracy and high speed. A large number of such response patterns can be scored simultaneously and either stored in the computer's memory for further analysis or printed out for use by the interpreter. If enough research has been completed on the test to indicate what kinds of configural scores are diagnostically significant, the computer can go one step further. Prior to running the response data through the computer, a diagnostic reference table containing all the significant information from available research is stored in the computer's memory. As the basic scoring elements are fed to the computer, it generates signs and configural scores, scans its memory for relevant information in the diagnostic reference table, assigns appropriate weights to the significant scores, and prints out a summary for further interpretation by the clinician.

Granted that it is theoretically feasible for the computer to handle this important kind of problem, how efficiently can the task be done by machine as compared to the human brain? Once the psychologist has specified the nature of the desired signs and configural scores so that an adequate computer program can be written, the machine should easily outstrip the human brain in both speed and accuracy. Recently, my assistants, Edward Moseley and Gary McCollough, wrote a 650 general purpose program for configural scoring. Any conceivable pattern involving any number of variables up to a total of 22 can be recognized and counted. Fifty patterns can be scored simultaneously in one sweep of the cards through the 650 computer. At present the method is unduly slow because of its general nature and lack of optimal programming, taking several seconds to process one card. With a little more work, it should be possible to reduce the time for configural analysis to the read-in time of the data cards, about three responses a second. Can you imagine yourself as a clinician counting simultaneously fifty complex patterns involving a number of variables in each of 45 responses to an inkblot test? Obviously the machine has a great advantage over the human being for this type of information-processing.

Clinician Versus Machine as an Interpreter

Closely following on the heels of information-processing is the problem of interpretation. This third and final phase of the psychodiagnostic process consists of one or more of the following—description and classification; prediction of future behavior in either a general or specific sense; and post-diction of past behavior or events. The interpretation may be in a simple form such as, "He is a schizophrenic individual." Or it may consist of highly complex, contingent predictions such as, "His severe anxieties will diminish if he consults a female psychotherapist, if his wife doesn't leave him, and if he continues to hold his job." The nature of the interpretations may range from an actuarially based decision to an extensive clinical evaluation. Obviously for some kinds of interpretation the machine is completely out of place. For others, however, it may prove a highly useful adjunct to the clinician.

Most of you are aware of the debate that has been raging the past several years over the relative merits of actuarial methods versus clinical methods in psychodiagnosis or the prediction of behavior. Somewhat the same kinds of arguments can be applied in considering the clinician and the computer. If you side with Paul Meehl (4) regarding the value of a cook-book method as opposed to rule of thumb, then obviously the computer has an important future in the interpretation as well as the processing of information. Base rate information can be stored in memory for various reference groups of diagnostic interest, together with probability values and cutting points for making a decision. If you side with Holt (2) or McArthur (4), the machine will serve only a minor role, if any, as an interpreter, since the clinician is completely free to over-rule any of the evidence in favor of his own judgment. In either case, as yet the

computer has not proven economically practical as an interpreter.

But there is no reason why it cannot be made highly practical in the future, even with existing computer hardware, if anyone cares to work out the necessary programs for this purpose. The truth of the matter is that there are mighty few psychodiagnostic situations in which enough is known of the factors influencing the outcome to provide the parameters necessary in the computer's memory to make intelligent interpretations. The same problem of validity plagues the clinician, but at least he can lean back on his subjective experiences and intuition, both of which are conspicuously lacking the computer except in a trivial sense.

Let us return to our original question. Can the computer supplant the clinician? When one reviews the many functions of a clinical psychologist in his role as psychodiagnostician, it is obvious that the answer is, "Yes, but only in part." As a collector of information, the computer has little to offer that cannot be done better by the clinician or his assistant. As a processor of information, machines can greatly surpass the human brain once the primary coding of information has been done by the clinician or his assistant. As an interpreter of information, once again the clinician has a definite edge over the computer, at least until much more research has been undertaken which gives us the rules of interpretation and the essential parameters for a valid decision. As Meehl has said (4, p. 271), "The clinician . . . acts as an inefficient computer, but that is better than a computer with certain major rules completely left out (simply) because we can't build them in until we have learned how to formulate them."

REFERENCES

1. HOLT, R. R. Clinical and statistical predictions: A reformulation and some new data. *J. abnorm. soc. Psychol.*, 1958, **56**, 1–12.
2. HOLTZMAN, W. H. Objective scoring of projective tests. In BASS, I., & BERG, B. M. (eds.) *Objective approaches to personality assessment.* Princeton, N.J.: Van Nostrand Company, 1959. Pp. 119–145.
3. McARTHUR, C. Clinical versus actuarial prediction. In *Proceedings, 1955 invitational conference on testing problems.* Princeton, N.J.: Educational Testing Service, 1956. Pp. 99–106.
4. MEEHL, P. E. Wanted—a good cook- book. *Amer. Psychol.*, 1956, **11**, 263–272.
5. NEWELL, A., SHAW, J. C., and SIMON, H. A. Elements of a theory of human problem solving *Psychol. Rev.*, 1958, **65**, 151–166.
6. NEWELL, A., SHAW, J. C., and SIMON, H. A. *The processes of creative thinking.* Santa Monica, California: The Rand Corporation. Revised January 28, 1959.
7. UHR. L. Latest method for the conception and education of intelligent machines. *Behav. Sci.*, 1959, **4**, 248–251.

*Page numbers of articles by person listed
are given in italics.*